The Greenwood
Encyclopedia of Daily Life
in America

2

THE CIVIL WAR, RECONSTRUCTION, AND INDUSTRIALIZATION OF AMERICA, 1861–1900

The Greenwood Encyclopedia of Daily Life in America

James M. Volo and Dorothy Denneen Volo
VOLUME EDITORS

Randall M. Miller
GENERAL EDITOR

The Greenwood Press "Daily Life Through History" Series

GREENWOOD PRESS
Westport, Connecticut • London

Library of Congress Cataloging-in-Publication Data

The Greenwood encyclopedia of daily life in America / Randall M. Miller, general editor.
    p. cm.—(The Greenwood Press daily life through history series, ISSN 1080–4749)
    Includes bibliographical references and index.
    ISBN 978–0–313–33699–7 (set)
    ISBN 978–0–313–33703–1 (v. 1)
    ISBN 978–0–313–33704–8 (v. 2)
    ISBN 978–0–313–33705–5 (v. 3)
    ISBN 978–0–313–33706–2 (v. 4)
    1. United States—Civilization—Encyclopedias.   2. United States—Social life and customs—Encyclopedias. 3. United States—Social conditions—Encyclopedias. I. Miller, Randall M.
E169.1.G7553   2009
973.03—dc22   2007042828

British Library Cataloguing in Publication Data is available.

Library of Congress Catalog Card Number: 2007042828
ISBN: 978–0–313–33699–7 (set)
      978–0–313–33703–1 (vol. 1)
      978–0–313–33704–8 (vol. 2)
      978–0–313–33705–5 (vol. 3)
      978–0–313–33706–2 (vol. 4)
ISSN: 1080–4749

First published in 2009

Greenwood Press, 88 Post Road West, Westport, CT 06881
An imprint of Greenwood Publishing Group, Inc.
www.greenwood.com

Printed in the United States of America

The paper used in this book complies with the
Permanent Paper Standard issued by the National
Information Standards Organization (Z39.48–1984).

10 9 8 7 6 5 4 3 2 1

Every reasonable effort has been made to trace the owners of copyright materials in this book, but
in some instances this has proven impossible. The editors and publisher will be glad to receive
information leading to more complete acknowledgments in subsequent printings of the book and in
the meantime extend their apologies for any omissions.

The publisher has done its best to make sure the instructions and/or recipes in this book are correct.
However, users should apply judgment and experience when preparing recipes, especially parents and
teachers working with young people. The publisher accepts no responsibility for the outcome of any
recipe included in this volume.

CONTENTS

Contents

TOUR GUIDE:
A PREFACE FOR
USERS

During the time of the American Revolution, the writer Hector St. Jean de Crevecouer asked the fundamental question that has dogged Americans thereafter: "What then is this new man, this American." Countless students of American history have searched every aspect of political, economic, social, and cultural history to discover "this American." In doing so, they have often focused on the great ideas that inspired a "free people" and defined public interest since the inception of the United States; the great events that marked American history; and the great changes wrought by democratic, industrial, communications, and other revolutions shaping American life, work, and identities. And they have been right to do so. But more recently other students of history have insisted that finding the *real* American requires looking at the details of everyday life. Therein, they argue, Americans practiced what mattered most to them and gave meaning to larger concepts of *freedom* and to the great events swirling about them. The ways Americans at home and at work ordered their daily life have become the subject of numerous community studies and biographies of the so-called common man or woman that were created by combing through all manner of personal accounts in diaries, letters, memoirs, business papers, birth and death records, census data, material culture, popular song, verse, artistic expression, and, indeed, virtually any source about or by common folk.

But making sense of so much individual study and providing a clear path through the history of Americans in their daily life has waited on a work that brings together the many and diverse ways Americans ordered their individual worlds at home and at work. *The Greenwood Encyclopedia of Daily Life in America* promises such a synthesis; it also promises to find "this American" in what Americans ate, who they courted and married, how they raised their children, what they did at work, where they traveled, how they played, and virtually every aspect of social life that Americans made for themselves. As such, it brings to life "this American" on his or her own terms. It also suggests that by discovering the ordinary it becomes possible to understand that extraordinary phenomenon of the American.

Features and Uses

The Greenwood Encyclopedia of Daily Life in America is a reference work and guide that provides up-to-date, authoritative, and readable entries on the many experiences and varieties of daily life of Americans from the dawn of the republic through the first years of the twenty-first century. In spanning the roughly 250 years from the mid-eighteenth century to the new millennium, the four volumes of *The Greenwood Encyclopedia of Daily Life in America* employ both a chronological and a topical, or thematic, approach. Doing so invites many uses for the volumes as reference guides; as touchstones for inquiries to a host of questions about the social, cultural, economic, and political history of Americans and the nation; and, taken together, as a broad view of daily life in the United States.

Users can read the articles separately or as a running narrative, depending on interest and need. The organization of the work collectively according to time period and within each volume according to time period, geography, daily activity, and group allows readers to explore a topic in depth, in comparative perspective, and over time. Also, because each section of each volume opens with a synthetic overview for purposes of historical context, the material in each section becomes more readily linked to larger patterns of American social, cultural, economic, and political developments. By structuring the volumes in this manner, it becomes possible to integrate and apply the encyclopedia within modern and flexible pedagogical frameworks in the classroom, in the library, and in home-schooling settings.

Cross-referencing within the articles and the cumulative subject index to the encyclopedia found at the back of each volume together expand the reach of individual topics across time and in different places. Thus, for example, the discussion of marital patterns and habits in the antebellum period of the nineteenth century, which includes mentions of courtship patterns, marriage rites, family formation, parenting, and even divorce, easily bridges to treatments of the same topics in other periods. Likewise, a reader wanting to compare foodways as they developed over time might move easily from representations of the early American "down-home" cooking of a largely agricultural society, through the increased portability and packaging of foods demanded by an urbanizing society during the nineteenth century, to the recent preference for such paradoxes in food choices as fresh foods, exotic foods, and fast food in the post-industrial United States.

Readers might go backward as well as forward, or even sideways, in following their interests, looking for the roots and then growth and development of habits and practices that defined and ordered the daily lives of Americans. In doing so, they might discover that each successive modern society has had its own search for the simpler life by trying to recover and reproduce parts of a supposedly more settled and serene past. They also will discover not only the changes wrought by ever more modern means of production, transportation, communication, and social and economic organization but also some striking continuities. Old ways often continue in new days. Americans have been a people on the go from the beginning of the nation and have become more so over time. As such, staying in touch with family and friends has ever been central to Americans' sense of place and purpose in organizing their lives. Whether carrying a daguerreotype image while heading west or to war in the nineteenth century, shooting photos with a Kodak camera from the late nineteenth century well into the twentieth century, or taking pictures with a video camera, a digital camera, or even with a cell-phone in the twenty-first century, Americans sought ways to keep visual images of the people, animals, possessions, and places that mattered to them. Letter writing also has become no less important a means of communication when the words move electronically via e-mail than when they were scratched out with a quill pen on paper. The encyclopedia provides a ready way to measure and map such social and cultural patterns and developments.

In its organization and with its reference supports, the encyclopedia encourages such topical excursions across time. Thus, the encyclopedia promises ways to an integrated analysis of daily life and of the core values, interests, and identities of Americans at any one time and over time.

Sidebars (found in volumes 3 and 4, and called Snapshots), chronologies, illustrations, and excerpts from documents further enrich each volume with specific examples of daily life from primary sources. They add not only "color" but also significant content by capturing the sense of a particular people or place in song, verse, speech, letters, and image and by giving voice to the people themselves. Readers thus engage Americans in their daily life directly.

The life and use of the encyclopedia extends beyond the physical volumes themselves. Because the encyclopedia derives much of its material from the vast resources of the Greenwood Publishing Group archive of works in ongoing series, such as the *Greenwood Press Daily Life Through History* Series and the *Daily Life in the United States* Series, to name the two most prominent, and on the many encyclopedias, reference works, and scholarly monographs making up its list, and on the many document-based works in its collection, the encyclopedia includes up-to-date and reliably vetted material. It also plugs into the *Greenwood Daily Life Online* database, which ensures a continuous expansion, enhancement, and refinement of content and easy searching capabilities. In that sense, *The Greenwood Encyclopedia of Daily Life in America,* like the American people, literally exists in a constant state of renewal to live beyond its original creation.

Organization and Coverage

The Greenwood Encyclopedia of Daily Life in America has a wide sweep in terms of time, topics, and themes related to the ordering of the daily lives of Americans. It also includes the many and diverse Americans, understanding that no one experience or people spoke or speaks for the variety of daily lives in the United States or explains even the unity of common experiences many different Americans have had and sought. That said, the encyclopedia is not a simple fact-by-fact description of every group or daily activity conducted in the United States. The encyclopedia is consciously selective in topics and coverage, with an eye always to relating the most significant and representative examples of the daily lives of different Americans.

The coverage of particular people and topics varies due to the availability of sources by and about them. Thus, for example, such peoples as the Iroquois, Cherokee, and Lakota Sioux get more explicit notice than, say, the Shoshone, simply because they left a fuller record of their lives and were observed and written about, or painted or photographed, in their daily lives more fully than were some other Native peoples. Then, too, the daily life of immigrant peoples receives extensive coverage throughout the volumes, but the extent and depth of coverage varies due to the size of the group and, more important, due to the available source material about any particular group. Thus, for example, when combined, the several major governmental and foundation studies of eastern and southern European immigrant groups in industrial America in the late nineteenth and early twentieth centuries, the rich tradition of publishing ethnic newspapers, the relating of personal lives in memoirs and oral histories, and a conscious effort to recover an immigrant past by the children and grandchildren of the first generation all explain the wider focus on such groups as representative types for their day. We simply know much about such people at work and at home. Such coverage of some people more fully than others does not mean any one experience counts more than others. It is, rather, mainly a matter of the critical mass of information at hand.

The encyclopedia includes all age groups in its coverage, but, again, the documentary record is richer for people coming of age through their adult lives into retirement than it is for the very young or the very old. Then, too, more is known about the daily lives of the upper classes than the lower classes, the privileged than the underprivileged, and the free than the unfree. The encyclopedia boasts significant inclusion of the many diverse American people, irrespective of wealth, circumstance, race or ethnicity, religion, or any other marker, and, indeed, it makes special effort to embrace the fullest range and diversity of experiences of daily life from birth to death.

The four volumes, each of which was edited by a prominent specialist or specialists in the field, are arranged by time periods as follows.

- Volume 1: The War of Independence and Antebellum Expansion and Reform, 1763–1861; edited by Theodore J. Zeman
- Volume 2: *The Civil War, Reconstruction, and Industrialization of America, 1861–1900*; edited by James M. Volo and Dorothy Denneen Volo
- Volume 3: *The Emergence of Modern America, World War I, and the Great Depression, 1900–1940*; edited by Francis J. Sicius
- Volume 4: *Wartime, Postwar, and Contemporary America, 1940–Present*; edited by Jolyon P. Girard

Each volume follows a similar format in that it organizes the material into seven principal topics, which are then generally divided into the following subtopics.

Those subtopics are sometimes arranged in a different order within the volumes due to emphasis, but they remain continuous throughout the encyclopedia.

1. *Domestic Life:* Covering such subtopics as Men, Women, Children, Pets, Marriage, and so on.
2. *Economic Life:* Covering such subtopics as Work, Trade, Class and Caste, Urban and Rural Experience, and so on.
3. *Intellectual Life:* Covering such subtopics as Science, Education, Literature, Communication, Health and Medicine, and so on.
4. *Material Life:* Covering such subtopics as Food, Drink, Housing, Clothing, Transportation, Technology, and so on.
5. *Political Life:* Covering such subtopics as Government, Law, Reform, War, and so on.
6. *Recreational Life:* Covering such subtopics as Sports, Music, Games, Entertainment, Holidays and Celebrations, and so on.
7. *Religious Life:* Covering such subtopics as Religion, Spirituality, Ritual, Rites of Passage, and so on.

Users are guided through this enormous amount of material not just by running heads on every page but also by *concept compasses* that appear in the margins at the start of main topical sections. These compasses are adapted from *concept mapping*, a technique borrowed from online research methods and used in *The Greenwood Encyclopedia of Daily Life*. The concept compasses will help orient readers in the particular volume they are using and allow them to draw connections among related topics across time periods. Following is an example of a concept compass:

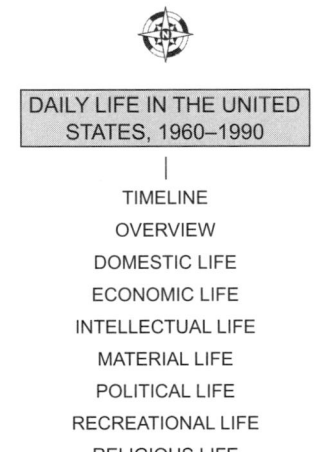

DAILY LIFE IN THE UNITED STATES, 1960–1990

TIMELINE
OVERVIEW
DOMESTIC LIFE
ECONOMIC LIFE
INTELLECTUAL LIFE
MATERIAL LIFE
POLITICAL LIFE
RECREATIONAL LIFE
RELIGIOUS LIFE

The individual volumes also have several variations in their internal arrangements and coverage of topics that speak to the particular chronological period under review. Volume 1, for example, does not begin at a fixed date, as do the other volumes, and it covers a longer time period than any of the other volumes. Its primary focus is on the period from the American Revolution through the Civil War, but it also looks back in time in its descriptions of many elements of daily life that continued from the preindustrial colonial period through the first rumblings of the so-called market revolution of the early nineteenth century. It does so to provide not only an understanding of the continuities in many aspects of life—from the ways people raised crops and livestock, manufactured and sold goods, organized family life, worshipped, and practiced the rituals of birth, marriage, and death, to name several—but also to mark the changes wrought by the age of revolutions that came with new understandings of political, economic, social, cultural, and even parental authority following the American Revolution. In the subsequent volumes, there is some overlap in terms of beginnings and endings for the chronological periods because social history does not have neat markers as does American political history with its election cycles. Each of the final three volumes covers roughly a half-century of time, reflecting the growing complexity of life in the modern era.

The encyclopedia covers the whole of the United States. The geography of the United States has expanded mightily over time, but the importance of geographical identity within the United States has varied at different times and more recently has declined. The first three volumes recognize the salience of regional variations in defining daily life and break the material, in varying degrees, into regions within the United States (e.g., Northeast, South, Midwest, Pacific West). But the fourth volume, covering the last half of the twentieth century—by which time a national market, telecommunications, and popular culture had done much to break down regional identities and create a national culture—discounts the importance of region in many areas of daily life. To be sure, as Volume 4 reveals, regional identities still persisted, even pridefully so, in "the South" and "the West" especially, but throughout the United States the rhythms of life moved in strikingly similar ways in a nation increasingly knit together by interstate highways, television, and, more recently, by the Internet and by a mass consumption economy and culture. Class, race, and occupation, more than regional cultures, now count more in defining daily life and social ties. Religion, too, matters much in ordering individual lives and distinguishing groups from one another in the United States, easily the most "churched" nation in the industrial world. In some cases, particular subtopics disappear from successive volumes because Americans at different times gave up particular ways of working and living or because the representative ways of working and living changed, from those of an agricultural world to those of an industrial and urban one and then to a postindustrial suburban one, for example.

Throughout the encyclopedia the most basic ways people arranged their daily life make up the principal content of the volumes. But the coverage of any topic is not constant. Take time, for example. It is useful to note that historically over time, *time* literally has been speeding up for Americans. Americans who lived by Nature's times of season and sunrise and sunset occupied a different world than people who have made time a commodity to be metered out in nanoseconds for purposes of productivity and even pleasure. The multiplicity of clocks and watches made possible by the industrial revolution, the imposition of factory time in the workplace, the dividing of the nation into time zones demanded by the railroads, the breakdown of time ordered by the moving assembly line, the collapse of time realized by telecommunications and then the radio, and the more current compression of time by microchips in all manner of computers, cell phones, and gadgetry that seemingly now run daily life and work—all this change in understanding and managing time transformed not only the pace but also the direction of life. Each volume marks the changing of time, the ways people used their time, and the times. Thereby, the attention to matters of time becomes a topic of growing importance with each successive volume of the encyclopedia.

Finally, in terms of coverage and content, the encyclopedia combines a *macro* with the *micro* view of daily life. External factors such as wars, natural disasters (e.g., fires, floods, hurricanes and tornados, ice storms, and droughts), epidemic diseases, environmental transformation, economic and political change, and population movements profoundly affected how, where, and why people lived as they did and, indeed, even which people lived at all. The Revolutionary War and the Civil War, for example, uprooted countless people from their homes as armies tramped about, armies that also liberated enslaved people who then used the upheavals to run to freedom or to fight for it. Daily life for refugees, for the "freedpeople," for the losers of political power and economic advantage was altered to its core by war. Dealing with the loss of loved ones in the Civil War changed the ways many Americans approached the meaning and management of death—in embalming, in funerary practices, in memorializing the dead, in shifting family responsibilities in the wake of a parent's death. The total mobilization of World War II touched every American household, and the G.I. Bill that came with it opened up opportunities for education, home ownership, and medical benefits that helped make possible a middle-class life for many Americans. So, too, massive floods, such as the 1927 flooding of the Mississippi River basin, swept away people, possessions, and patterns of living across a wide swath. Government actions also influenced, even determined, people's daily life. The many New Deal programs that insured bank accounts; underwrote home mortgage loans; brought electricity to rural America; built dams for hydroelectric power and economic development; constructed roads, bridges, airports, and public buildings; encouraged the arts, music, and literature, and so much more left a physical, social, and cultural imprint that still matters in Americans' daily living. Thus, relating the *macrohistory* of larger historical events and developments to the ways such factors informed and influenced the *microhistory* of individual daily life is essential to understanding the dynamics and consequence of changes and continuities in the daily life of Americans. The panoramic perspective plots the landscape of social history, while the microscopic examination observes its many forms. All that said, the primary focus of this encyclopedia remains on what students of social and cultural history term "the infinite details" of Americans' social and material arrangements in their daily life. The title tells the tale.

The Greenwood Encyclopedia of Daily Life in America, in the end, still makes no claim to comprehensiveness in trying to bring in all Americans and all manner of life. No reference work dare do so. Recognizing such a limitation rather than retreating from it, this encyclopedia serves not only as an introduction to the varied and complex American peoples in their daily lives but also as an invitation to bring other peoples into view, which responsibility, one hopes, the students and teachers using this encyclopedia will assume.

A Note on the Conception and Creation of the Encyclopedia

The encyclopedia is the product of many hands. It is both a collective work and, in its separate volumes, also very much an individual one. The encyclopedia was developed collectively by editors at Greenwood Press, who originally sought to provide a companion encyclopedia to the very successful six-volume *Greenwood Encyclopedia of Daily Life*, which covered the world from prehistory to the end of the twentieth century. The editors at Greenwood also sought to capitalize on the many reference works and individual volumes Greenwood Press has published on various aspects of daily life in the United States. At Greenwood, Michael Herman conceived of the idea for such an encyclopedia and drafted the broad design for it. John Wagner then stepped in and in many essential ways translated idea into product. He helped recruit volume editors, managed relations with the editors by means of correspondence and providing sample materials and other forms of guidance, read the individual volumes for content and fit regarding the collective set, and managed the details of moving manuscripts to production.

Each author/editor assumed the primary, almost complete, responsibility for his or her individual volume. Early in the planning process, several author/editors gathered by correspondence and even in person to discuss the scope of the work, to mark off the time boundaries of the individual volumes, to agree on essential topics, and more. The general editor coordinated such discussions; guided the works in progress; read the individual volumes for content, coverage, and fit with the other volumes and overall purpose and design of the encyclopedia; and in other ways moved production along. It is important to note that each author/editor has assumed principal responsibility for the content of his or her volume, from selecting, arranging, and editing the articles, to getting permission to use materials, to providing the context for the articles, to fact-checking and proofreading the volume, to ensuring the highest quality in content and presentation. The general editor thus disclaims any responsibility for the specific content of or in any volume. The individual author/editor's name on the title page of each volume places the responsibility where it deservedly should rest, with the true creators. It also is important to note that in creating each volume, the author/editor did much more than compile, collate, and arrange materials derived from other sources. Each author/editor wrote the introductions to the respective volumes, the introductions to the subsections of each volume, the transitions within each article excerpting materials from other sources, the headnotes in each volume, and some of the text in each volume. Because of the uneven, or even nonexistent, source material on daily life for the two volumes treating the twentieth century, both Francis Sicius and Jolyon Girard wrote much original material. This was so much so in Girard's case that he became more author than editor of Volume 4.

In sum, then, the creation of this encyclopedia mirrors the American experience. It was, and is, an example of the nation's guiding principle of continuous creation as a people—e pluribus unum. It also is a recognition that people make history. We hope that by discovering the American people in their day-to-day lives and the life they have sought to create and live, readers will find that elusive "new man, this American" and themselves.

—Randall M. Miller

CHRONOLOGY: 1860–1900

1860	November: Republican Abraham Lincoln is elected president in a four-man contest over Stephen Douglas (Democrat), John Bell (Constitutional Union), and John C. Breckinridge (Southern Democrat).
	December: South Carolina secedes from the Union.
1861	January: Kansas is admitted to the Union.
	January: Mississippi, Florida, Alabama, Georgia, and Louisiana secede from the Union.
	February: Seceded states form the Confederate States of America in Montgomery, Alabama, and Jefferson Davis of Mississippi is elected president of the Confederacy.
	March: Texas secedes from the Union.
	April: Virginia, Arkansas, North Carolina, and Tennessee secede from the Union following the Confederate bombardment of Fort Sumter in Charleston Harbor.
	July: First Battle of Bull Run, a Confederate victory, is fought in Virginia.
1861–1865	American Civil War is fought.
1862	August: Second Battle of Bull Run, another Confederate victory, is fought in Virginia.
	September: Battle of Antietam, a Union victory, is fought in Maryland.
1863	January: President Abraham Lincoln issues the Emancipation Proclamation freeing all slaves in territory controlled by the Confederacy; Homestead Act becomes law, allowing settlers to claim land (160 acres) after they have lived on it for five years.
	June: The unionist western portion of the seceded state of Virginia is split off from Virginia and admitted to the Union as the state of West Virginia.
	July: Battle of Gettysburg, a Union victory, is fought in Pennsylvania.
	November: President Abraham Lincoln delivers the Gettysburg Address while dedicating the Union Cemetery at the site of the July battle.

1864	September: Union General William T. Sherman captures Atlanta.
	October: Nevada is admitted to the Union.
	November: Republican President Abraham Lincoln is reelected, defeating Democrat George B. McClellan.
1865	April: Fall of Richmond, Virginia, the Confederate capital.
	April: Civil War ends with the surrender of Confederate General Robert E. Lee to Union General Ulysses S. Grant at Appomattox Court House, Virginia.
	April: President Abraham Lincoln is assassinated in Washington, D.C., by John Wilkes Booth and is succeeded by Vice President Andrew Johnson.
	December: The 13th Amendment to the Constitution is ratified prohibiting slavery in the United States.
1866	Ku Klux Klan is founded in Tennessee by Confederate Army veterans.
1867	March: Nebraska is admitted to the Union.
	March: Congress passes the First and Second Reconstruction Acts.
	March: United States purchases Alaska from Russia for $7.2 million.
	July: Congress passes the Third Reconstruction Act.
	August: United States annexes Midway Island.
1868	An eight-hour workday is instituted for federal employees.
	February: President Andrew Johnson is impeached by the House of Representatives.
	March: Congress passes the Fourth Reconstruction Act.
	May: President Johnson is acquitted by one vote in trial in the Senate.
	July: The 14th Amendment to the Constitution is ratified defining citizenship.
	November: Republican Ulysses S. Grant is elected president, defeating Democrat Horatio Seymour.
1869	May: Union Pacific Railroad meets the Central Pacific at Promontory, Utah, thereby completing the first transcontinental line.
1870	February: The 15th Amendment to the Constitution is ratified giving blacks the right to vote.
1871	October: Chicago fire kills 300 and leaves 90,000 people homeless.
1872	September: Crédit Mobilier scandal, involving several members of Congress, becomes public.
	November: Republican President Ulysses S. Grant is reelected, defeating Democratic/Liberal Republican candidate Horace Greeley.
1876	February: Baseball's National League is founded.
	March: Alexander Graham Bell patents the telephone.
	June: Lt. Col. George A. Custer's regiment is wiped out by Sioux Indians under Sitting Bull at the Little Big Horn River in Montana.
	August: Colorado is admitted to the Union.
	November: A disputed presidential election is decided (in February 1877) in favor of Republican Rutherford B. Hayes, who, despite receiving fewer

	popular votes than Democrat Samuel J. Tilden, is awarded one more electoral vote.
1877	First telephone line is built from Boston to Somerville, Massachusetts.
	President Hayes returns federal troops to their barracks in the southern states, thus ending Reconstruction.
1878	President Rutherford B. Hayes has the first telephone installed in the White House.
	United States-Samoa Treaty makes Pago Pago in the South Pacific a U.S. Navy coaling station.
1879	Women lawyers are permitted to argue cases before the U.S. Supreme Court.
	Thomas Edison invents the incandescent light.
1880	November: Republican James A. Garfield is elected president, defeating Democrat Winfield Scott Hancock; both candidates were Union generals during the Civil War.
1881	July: President James A. Garfield is shot by Charles Guiteau in Washington, D.C.; the president dies from complications resulting from his wounds in September and is succeeded by Vice President Chester A. Arthur.
1882	November: United States adopts standard time.
1883	January: Civil Service is established with passage by Congress of the Pendleton Civil Service Reform Act.
1884	May: Congress organizes the Alaska Territory.
	November: Democrat Grover Cleveland is elected president, defeating Republican James G. Blaine.
1886	May: Haymarket Square labor riot in Chicago results in the deaths of 11 people.
	October: Statue of Liberty is dedicated.
1888	George Eastman's Kodak camera initiates amateur photography.
	November: Despite receiving fewer popular votes than his opponent, Republican Benjamin Harrison is elected president, defeating incumbent Democratic President Grover Cleveland.
1889	November: North Dakota, South Dakota, Montana, and Washington are admitted to the Union.
	April: Oklahoma Territory is opened to settlers.
1890	Samuel Gompers founds the American Federation of Labor (AFL).
	Congress organizes the Oklahoma Territory.
	National American Woman Suffrage Association (NAWSA) is founded with Elizabeth Cady Stanton as president.
	In reporting the results of the 1890 census, the Census Bureau announces that the frontier line has closed.
	July: Congress passes the Sherman Antitrust Act, thereby prohibiting combinations in restraint of trade.

	July: Idaho and Wyoming are admitted to the Union.
	December: Last major "battle" of the Indian Wars occurs at Wounded Knee, South Dakota.
1892	Strike at Carnegie Steel results in the deaths of 10 people.
	January: Ellis Island in New York Harbor becomes the chief immigration station of the United States.
	November: Reversing the outcome of the 1888 campaign, Democrat Grover Cleveland, the former president, defeats incumbent Republican President Benjamin Harrison.
1896	January: Utah is admitted to the Union.
	May: In its landmark *Plessy v. Ferguson* decision, the U.S. Supreme Court holds that racial segregation is constitutional, thus paving the way for the passage of repressive Jim Crow laws in the South.
	November: Republican William McKinley is elected president, defeating Democrat William Jennings Bryan.
1898	February: U.S. battleship *Maine* blows up in Havana Harbor, initiating an outcry for war against Spain.
	April: United States declares war on Spain.
	July: United States annexes Hawaii.
	December: Treaty of Paris ends the Spanish-American War; Spain gives up Cuba, which becomes an independent republic, and cedes Puerto Rico, Guam, and (for $20 million) the Philippines to the United States.
1899	Following the Spanish-American War, the United States annexes Guam, the Philippines, and Puerto Rico.
1900	United States annexes American Samoa.
	November: Republican President William McKinley is reelected, defeating his 1896 opponent, Democrat William Jennings Bryan.
1901	September: President William McKinley is assassinated by an anarchist.

HISTORICAL OVERVIEW

Remembering the "Good Olde Days"
—First used in 1844 by Philip Hone,
Mayor of New York

A Century of "-isms"

The forces of industrialization, reform, expansion, religion, politics, and warfare walked hand-in-hand during the nineteenth century. Often they passed along singly, providing a glimpse at some discrete facet of American life. At other times they crashed together simultaneously like ocean waves, devastating all that had been there and leaving behind almost unrecognizable consequences. Driven by these forces the United States went through a period of national maturation during the antebellum years, came apart during the Civil War, reconstituted itself in the postwar era, and emerged as a world industrial power. The process involved changes in governance, justice, economics, finances, industry, manufacturing, communications, travel, agriculture, social structure, and family order, among others.

Contemporary observers of the latter half of the nineteenth century noted the prevalence in American speech, writing, and publications of a wide variety of "isms." Modernism seems to be the catchall term used by historians today when referring to the period, but urbanism, abolitionism, feminism (women's rights), humanitarianism, reformism, commercialism, and others filled the consciousness of the nineteenth-century public. The ideals of traditionalism, Americanism, and nativism seem to have come to loggerheads with the shifting patterns of political republicanism and social pluralism in mid-century over the prospect of increasing immigration and the expansion of slavery. With the Civil War prominent among the pivotal historical

Alcoholism, sexual deviancy, poverty, unemployment, immigration, and economic and political disputes are all lampooned in this political cartoon from the pre–Civil War period. Courtesy Library of Congress.

events of the century, abolitionism, sectionalism, racism, secessionism, and radicalism are commonly thought to have prevailed; but nationalism, militarism, and expansionism, in many fields—geographical, social, political, scientific, and economic—were equally influential in forming the character of the period.

It seems certain that different individuals and groups manipulated these "isms" for a variety of reasons, but the fact that large segments of the nineteenth-century population believed in them and chose to follow through on them suggests that the "isms" had real meaning. Dedication for or against certain reform "isms" such as those attached to slavery, voting rights, public education, alcohol consumption, or women's issues tended to polarize the population of the nation and strike metaphorical sparks; while others like territorial expansion, industrialization, the application of military power, or the adoption of technology for farming were greeted with a more general acceptance or were viewed in the light of inevitability.

Cultural and social changes were sweeping the cities of America during the nineteenth century. Over the course of the century the process of economic transformation that accompanied American industrialization proceeded at different rates in different parts of the country. Industrialization began much earlier, for example, in New England and the Mid-Atlantic regions, than in North Central and Southern regions. By 1870, close to 35 percent of the population in Massachusetts and New York lived in places with populations greater than 25,000, more than three times the national average of 11 percent. Similarly, while manufacturing accounted for only 7 percent of employment nationally, more than 20 percent of the population of Massachusetts and Rhode Island was employed in manufacturing. Industrialization and urbanization were also closely linked to high rates of immigration, although many of the foreign born could also be found in more agricultural regions.

Industry and urbanization had moved the North toward a more modern society with an unprecedented set of novel cultural values, while the South had essentially lagged behind in the traditions of the past. Historians have noted that the differences between the folk culture of the South and the modern culture of the North fueled many of the broad-based reform movements of mid-century and also may have ignited the turmoil over state sovereignty and slavery in a form of a culture war. The debate surrounding these questions, driven by an intensely partisan press, "not only aroused feelings of jealousy, honor, and regional pride, but raised fundamental questions about the future direction of the American society" (Sewell 1988, xi).

Domestic Life

Families can take on many functional and acceptable forms, and a wide diversity of kinship systems could be found in nineteenth-century America. While each family has discrete characteristics, in general they can be condensed into a handful of archetypes with real families falling into a gray region between any of the discrete sets of characteristics associated with particular types. Of all the general forms of family structure social historians normally include these four among those found in America: *nuclear families, extended families, stem-nuclear families,* and *clan-like families.*

Each of these familial structures has its own peculiar characteristics, but modeling like this, based largely on statistical data, provides only a snapshot of family living without duration. It is precisely the correlation of *individual time* (birth, childhood, youth, adulthood, and old age) with *family time* (courtship, marriage, the birth of the first and the last child, the empty nest, the death of a spouse) that can provide a more meaningful framework for the study of family. Certain concepts concerning time can also be shaped into a descriptive model known as a *temporal orientation,* which can be separated into two types: *reckoned time,* as in determining the duration of a period or a place in time as in a specific date, and *social time,* the purposeful scheduling of both optional and obligatory community activities.

In simple societies the demands of time were usually well articulated with one another, and individuals were rarely torn by mutually exclusive temporal commitments. On the other hand, reckoned time, generally unimportant to the functioning of day-to-day life in the antebellum period, quickly became the driving force of both social and economic as schedules, appointments, and timekeeping became pivotal to the functioning of American industry.

The nuclear family had been the predominant form in Europe for almost 300 years. The true *nuclear family* was composed of a married couple living with their children under the same roof and apart from all other relatives. Some researchers considered the tendency of nineteenth-century Americans to form and maintain simple patriarchal nuclear families to be overwhelming. Post-adolescent sons were clearly expected to move out of the home, while daughters generally remained until they married, on average at age 20.7 years. Only in the 1890s did the median age of women at first marriage increase to 24.4 years. In the next decade it returned to its former historical level, and the reasons for the anomaly remain a matter of conjecture (Wells 1979, 523). Moreover, solitary residence among unmarried men—single living in a distinctly separate dwelling, not boarding or lodging—was practically unknown in the nineteenth century except on the most isolated fringes of civilization as among some prospectors, mountain men, missionaries, or soldiers (Hareven and Vinovskis 1978, 15).

A *stem-nuclear family* occurred when a child married, moved with his bride (or vice versa) into their parents' home, and raised the next generation there creating a three-generation homestead. The absence in the nineteenth-century data of married or unmarried white children in their parents' homes over 20 years of age is pronounced, signaling perhaps the rarity of this form (Hareven and Vinovskis 1978, 38). The stem-nuclear form sometimes found among black families was often matriarchal and imposed upon them by the conditions of slavery or the exigencies of extreme poverty and intense racism.

An *extended family* structure, much like the nuclear one for individual parents and minor children, was a matter of living arrangement. In the nineteenth century, to the extent that nonnuclear adults were present in individual households, they were most likely to be limited to a single nonrelated farm worker or domestic servant, or a female relative such as a widowed mother or unmarried sister living under the protection of close and loving relations. Data from the period suggest that the presence of nonrelated persons vastly outnumbered those cases of nonnuclear blood relations of this sort (Hareven and Vinovskis 1978, 17).

Daughters who remained unmarried into their adult years were often given the social position of companion to their parents or aunts if they were widowed (Hareven and Vinovskis 1978, 34). Although the incidence of never married, foreign-born white women remained remarkably high (approximately 27%) throughout the second half of the century, the number of native-born white women who remained unmarried increased from 1850 (15%) to 1890 (22%), and then declined sharply until 1920 (11%) (Uhlenberg 1978, 511).

In the *clan-like family* structure, the basic unit of habitation was clearly nuclear, but the members of each clan claimed a common ancestry, usually carried a common name, and, most importantly, recognized a common identity beyond the bounds of the nuclear family that was largely unaffected by any daily living arrangement. It was the acknowledged continuity and maintenance of ancestry that defined the clan. This was usually patrilineal, but matrilineal family relationships were never abandoned. The clan-like family was extremely rare in the North and Midwest during the period under consideration, but Southern and frontier families often continued to evince this structural pattern even in the post–Civil War years.

The Southern planter aristocracy was very clan-like in its structure. Led by a privileged planter class whose elite lifestyle was maintained at the expense of the rest of society, the planter aristocracy relied on its kinship network and social status as a means to personal success. Southern culture and institutions were seen by outsiders as backward, inefficient, and harmful to the American nation as a whole. Nonetheless, the Southern elite voluntarily assumed the role of benefactor and knight errant to all other levels of their society. Like cavaliers on a quest, Southern men felt obliged to counsel and defend not only their own families, but also all females and minor children placed under their protection. This obligation was extended to their slaves in an ambiguous, but serious, way. Many Southerners were genuinely concerned for the physical and moral welfare of their slaves, but only in terms of continued racial separation and subjugation.

A Place in Society

The keeping of good company—be they friends and associates of a brother, a sister, or a spouse—was thought to be very important in the nineteenth century especially among the middle and upper class. Appropriate acquaintances were intelligent and well-bred persons, whose language was chaste and whose sentiments were both pure and edifying. Proper deportment was expected among any circle of friends, and their conduct was to be directed by the highest of moral precepts. Young women were particularly enjoined to "hold a steady moral sway" over the male associates of their brothers and husbands, "so strong as to prevent them from becoming . . . lawless rowdies" (Haines and Yaggy 1876, 78).

Yet the necessity of selecting proper female associates for young women was not considered a point of so great an interest. There was an expectation among all but the lowest ranks of society that young women of good breeding, while under the protection and control of their parents, would avoid many of the promiscuous associations that threatened their more independently minded brothers. Nevertheless, both men and women needed to take great care in avoiding pernicious influences in the selection of their company, and each needed to develop a degree of elegance and manner that would be pleasing in any social circle, whether at home or abroad (Haines and Yaggy 1876, 111). Sarah Bennett editor of the *Advocate and Family Guardian,* a New York publication of the American Female Guardian Society, warned, "If yon beautiful belle of eighteen has no reverence for the Sabbath, no love for the house or worship of God, but only as connected with her own personal display; then is her loveliness perfect deformity, more loathsome than the decay of the carnal house. . . . Remember that piety is a greater beautifier than cosmetics" (Bennett 1865, 27).

A family's circle of adult friends and acquaintances reflected its place in society. This circle was much wider for men with their business and work connections than for women who were thought to spend their lives in the domestic shelter of the family, with their girlhood friends, or among the matrons of their own class in the wider community. Women were generally not permitted to freely correspond with men who were not blood relations or who had not been formally introduced to them through their parents or other close relation or friend. Many young women had little knowledge of men until after their marriage. A brother and his friends were often a young woman's only exposure to the ways of men. After marriage their social relationships with males were further limited to the friends and acquaintances of their husbands. Great importance was attached to the prudent selection of these associates, and it was important for a young wife to direct her husband's associations as well as she could.

Courtship and Marriage

The continuation of the family name and fortune through marriage was of great importance, and the rules, customs, and traditions that surrounded courtship and marriage were well established. The obvious objectives of marriage were to provide an acceptable outlet for sexual activity, to recognize the legitimate children of a union, and to assure the continuity of the family fortune through the instrument of inheritance. Since colonial times the instrument of inheritance—usually limited to the handing down of farmland—had been very important. In the nineteenth century the bestowing of the family fortune, home, business, and social standing on one's children overtook the need to pass on property or partition farmland. Moreover, in a period when family name and influence were very important to future success, clearly illegitimate children were often denied access to certain professions, schools, and possible marriage partners. It was very difficult for such persons to go through life expecting to be ashamed of something over which they had no control and could not change. Illegitimate children took great pains to hide their infirmity, and the legitimate children of some men often went to great lengths to undo those parts of their father's will favorable to their illegitimate siblings. The courts rarely upheld a will favorable to children from the wrong side of the blanket in the face of a concerted effort by their rightful relations, especially if they were the elder sons.

Marriage within one's class was the cement of the American social structure. Yet a middle- or upper-class man could not hope to prosecute a courtship successfully before he had established himself in a profession or come into his inheritance. Courtship could be protracted if the suitor's financial expectations took some period to come to fruition. This fact tended to drive up the age of eligible suitors or increase the disparity in years between a well-established husband and young wife still in her childbearing years. Nonetheless, in the North the difference in age between man and wife during the antebellum period averaged a mere two years, while Southern couples were separated by an average of six years due mainly to earlier marriages among Southern females. All young, respectable women were expected to begin seeking out a marriage partner appropriate to their social position as soon as they left adolescence. Period advice authors T. L. Haines and Levi Yaggy warned, "It is of vital interest to every young female, how careful she should be in taking to her bosom for life a companion [husband] of dissolute habits and morals. Such an act might destroy all the domestic felicity she might have hoped to enjoy" (Haines and Yaggy 1876, 111).

For daughters of the planter class, romance was not to be found among the requirements for a marriage partner. This is ironic in a period and section of the country known for its romantic trappings. Romantic entanglements were greatly feared by parents because even the hint of inappropriate behavior could create a sexual scandal that would leave a daughter unmarriageable.

Wealth, rather than love, was the primary factor in arranging a marriage or choosing a husband, and maintenance of one's social position was a close second. Intermarriage between cousins, far enough removed to dispel charges of consanguinity, was common among the planter aristocracy but almost unheard of in the North. Women in the South married at a younger age—almost four years younger on average—than their Northern counterparts. This may be because many Southern parents expected their daughters to begin the formal courtship process as soon as they entered puberty. Northern parents, more open to the idea that their daughters might become working women for some time before entering a marriage, did not press them as vigorously.

The oppressive control of parents in this regard would not be tolerated by most women today, nor would the absolute domination of fathers or husbands be sustained in most modern households. Yet in actual practice middle-class American women were better treated than their European sisters in this regard. In 1876 an observer noted that "the Englishman respects his lady; the Frenchman esteems his companion; the Italian adores his mistress; [but] the American loves his wife" (Haines and Yaggy 1876, 25). American women generally enjoyed higher social status, greater responsibility, and greater freedom at a younger age. By comparison to their British counterparts, young American women were thought to enjoy great liberty until they married, after which "they buried themselves in their families and appeared to live only for them." As wives they were generally faithful and thrifty and, although their social lives were often "joyless and monotonous," they exhibited few of the vices commonly associated with their Victorian Era husbands (Hunt 1914/1993, 31). As the nineteenth century proceeded, a major cultural change took place as women gradually gained a modicum of control over themselves and the property that they brought to a marriage. These generally paralleled similar developments in Britain (Nye 1960, 143).

Women who remained unmarried often lived with other relatives where they hoped to be "regarded and guarded as a daughter" (Unidentified author, "The Needs of Working Women," 1871, 53–54). They often relied on these relatives during financial emergencies. Many young women looked especially to their maternal aunts and uncles in this regard for support, guidance, and companionship. In the absence of a father or uncle, a young woman might depend on her own brother for a roof over her head. Few men could shirk their responsibilities to a female relative without a loss of reputation and community standing. This was especially true in the South where the role of benefactor was an essential characteristic of the plantation aristocracy. Nonetheless, an unmarried adult woman was often awkwardly placed in the kinship scheme of a nuclear family, and many found little consolation while living in the household of another woman. For this reason they were often found in the home of a widowed father or brother where they could still be mistress of the household. Often they took on a position as a domestic, a private teacher, or a governess with an unrelated family where their place in the household was a contractual one and their interactions those of an employee with an employer.

Only for a brief period—usually between puberty and marriage—did women have any real control over their fate. Yet this control was very limited, residing solely in their ability to choose a husband from among a set of suitors acceptable to her family. "Women," according to one contemporary observer, "were beautiful until they were twenty-five years old, when their forms changed, and by the time they were thirty their charms had disappeared" (Hunt 1914/1993, 31). A particularly attractive or well-heeled woman might have groups of suitors vying for her attentions. Such groups, calling together upon a young woman at her home, were not discouraged by her parents as the practice prevented unwanted gossip. Under such circumstances young men had little opportunity for measuring the woman's attitude toward their individual suit. Most gentlemen resorted, therefore, to a go-between in the early stages of any serious courting to gauge whether or not their more formal attentions would be rebuffed. The woman's brothers or male cousins often served in this capacity.

It was in the area of women's rights that many of the most significant changes in social mores took place during the last half of the nineteenth century. More than 90 percent of American-born white women could read. They began to move forcefully into higher education and into the day-to-day workplace especially as office and factory workers, store clerks, and teachers. They thereby came into more casual contact with men than had previously been the case. It was at this point that dating and going out became fashionable. Nonetheless, all but the most eligible men met with a series of mild rebuffs as young woman were discouraged by their parents from taking too many prospective fiancés into their social circle before selecting one from a small group of two or three as a husband.

Unmarried couples—even those who were formally engaged—might easily offend the community if their behavior was perceived to be sexual in any context. The betrothed might never have touched, and certainly should never have shared a romantic kiss. A contemporary self-help advisor warned young persons, "During the period that intervenes between forming an engagement and consummating the connection, let your deportment toward the individual to whom you have given your affections be marked by modesty and dignity, respect and kindness" (Haines and Yaggy 1876, 442). Overt sexuality at any stage in a woman's life before marriage would certainly meet with social ostracism and might actually result in criminal indictment for fornication in some jurisdictions.

Upon their marriage young women passed from the domination of their fathers to the equally powerful authority of their husbands. In many Northern homes, the focus of the family increasingly came to rest on the wife and children as fathers spent most of their waking hours away from home at work or in the social company of men. Increasingly, the whole machinery of the day-to-day operation of the household, "domestic economy and rule, all authority and discipline and influence, devolve[d] upon the wife, who in her own appointed sphere [had] quite enough to do." In response to the increased importance of female domesticity, there evolved a growing formalism and rigid authoritarianism that husbands demanded of their families and households when they were present. Many contemporary observers decried the "neglect" of home that some nineteenth century men excused as "the inexorable will of business." These observers questioned what business was so important that it had the right to contravene the traditional organization of the home with the father as the head of household (Ware 1864, 38).

In many jurisdictions in the nineteenth century, husband and wife were considered one person in law, and the very existence of the woman was often incorporated and consolidated into that of their husband. Until late in the period, married women had little or no legal standing in the courts, could not sign enforceable contracts, and held no tangible assets in their own name in most states. The property brought to a marriage by the wife legally became that of her husband. Many widows disdained remarriage having in their bereavement finally found relief from the overbearing power of even the best of husbands and fathers. Nonetheless, in some states widows might lose their property rights to their adult sons, if not otherwise provided for by the will of their spouse. A widower with young children was expected to remarry for the sake of his motherless offspring if no appropriate female relation, such as an unmarried sister or aunt, was available to care for them.

Using Census Data

Researchers generally have demographic data for families during the nineteenth century, but the statistics are neither as complete nor as articulate as modern researchers would like. Although the first official census of the United States was taken in 1790, the early federal government was principally interested in sampling the growth, structure, and redistribution of the population. The census of 1890, 100 years later, reported that the unsettled areas of the country from the previous decades had been so broken into isolated bodies of settlement that a line for the frontier could no longer be traced on a map. That line had been drawn and redrawn repeatedly from the founding of Jamestown on, and it had finally disappeared into a jumble of small overlapping and ever-diminishing circles (Davidson 1951, 292).

The collection of vital data (birth, death, marriage statistics) was generally left to state and local agencies. Infant mortality and life expectancy figures were not kept by the federal government until 1850. Although some large cities had registered similar data in the previous decade, Massachusetts, in 1842, was the first state to initiate the continuous recording of births, deaths, and marriages. As late as 1865 the New York State Census was limited to obtaining "data for determining the natural increase of the population in this state among the various classes" (Bash 1979, 435).

Almost all statistics in this period reflected institutionalized racism and were kept in terms of whites, colored, and slave. For whites there are compilations of data concerning absolute birth rates, fertility, infant mortality, and life expectancy for the entire century and beyond. The same data does not begin for blacks until 1850, and much of it is averaged or otherwise questionable. Not until 1933 were the vital statistics for the entire nation recorded with any precision.

If the year 1850 is taken as a threshold date for the period under consideration, some of the limitations of the census data become obvious. In the 1850 census, all individuals were assigned to families that were defined solely by their joint occupation of a dwelling place. The nineteenth-century definition of a family dwelling was clearly broader than the current meaning of the term, literally including every structure from a teepee to a penitentiary. The term family could thereby denote a single person living in a tent or cabin, several persons living together in a more conventional home, or even several dozen unrelated persons living in a boarding house, hotel, military barracks, or hospital.

Over 10 percent of the total population counted in 1850 resided in multifamily dwellings that were counted as single units in the sample. This high frequency of group living, when compared to the eighteenth century, demonstrates the increased use of tenements, boarding houses, hotels, and other large institutional domiciles with which the government researchers were simply not ready to deal. British author Rudyard Kipling described the city tenements in Chicago, "I went out into the streets, which are long and flat and without end.... I looked down interminable vistas flanked with nine, ten, fifteen-storied houses, and crowded with men and women, and the show impressed me with great horror. Except in London ... I had never seen so many white people together, and never such a collection of miserables ... to huddle men together in fifteen layers, one atop of the other" (Kipling 1891).

The chief liability of the census techniques used in 1850 was that in sampling by dwelling the number of individual family observations was greatly reduced, and the resulting data may have become clustered for low-income groups more than for upper-income ones. Moreover, data for colored, or black families were usually more under registered than for whites. This may also be true to a lesser extent for immigrants as opposed to native-born families (Hareven and Vinovskis 1978, 11). Perhaps households should have been distinguished by some other characteristic such as a common source of support; a blood relationship; or even by separate cooking facilities, sleeping quarters, or entrances.

Recent historical research, however, has begun to sift through the data to present a more dynamic and precise picture of family structure. An analysis of common surnames allows researchers to discriminate among blood kin and disaggregate the statistics, thereby relieving the limitations somewhat; but these methods do not answer the questions concerning family structure that census takers do today. For instance, the disappearance of maiden names through marriage (especially where marriage records are unavailable) renders extensive kinship reconstruction almost impossible when the census is used as a sole source of data. Moreover, there were many unsettled people in nineteenth-century America. It has not yet been determined whether these constituted a propertyless, floating population of those who moved about constantly, a series of successive waves of emigrant families moving onto the frontiers, or an occupationally mobile core of persisters who generally returned to their home communities after completing a task elsewhere. Nonetheless, with these limitations in mind, some generalizations can be made about the nineteenth-century family, and secondary sources of family and population study can be tapped to provide both a qualitative and quantitative analysis (Glasco 1978, 155).

Vital Statistics

The range of change among data in the second half of the nineteenth century is remarkable. As an example, average white life expectancy at birth in 1850 sat at a remarkably low 39 years, and white infant mortality rates for the same year sat at 217 per 1,000. The former numbers were significantly higher than those of 1900 with a life expectancy of 52 years and an infant mortality rate of 111 per 1,000. In all the decades under consideration between 1850 and 1890 the probability of women dying between the ages of 25 and 45 was higher than that of men in the same age bracket, indicating perhaps the continued influence of death due to childbirth. Data from Massachusetts in 1867 attribute fully 10 percent of female deaths to childbirth (Uhlenberg 1978, 510).

There are no reliable data for black life expectancy or infant mortality until the early twentieth century, but in 1850 black life expectancy was estimated at a mind-boggling low of 23 years. By 1900 this had improved but was recorded at a mere 42 years. The 1850 number must be viewed with suspicion because it may include a very high proportion of infant deaths estimated at an incredible 340 per 1,000. In 1900, black infant mortality stood at 170 per 1,000, one-half that estimated 50 years earlier.

White, immigrant women generally had higher fertility rates than their native-born counterparts, and second-generation immigrants usually evinced an intermediate level of fertility between that of their parents and that of the native population. This may have been due to an Americanization effect, yet many contemporary researches tended to write of "the Irish" or "the Italians" or "the Jews" as if they were homogeneous subgroups lacking variations among themselves. This was certainly not the case, and further study has found significant variations among identical ethnic groups living in different parts of the same city.

Recent research suggests that the decline in white reproduction from 1850 to 1900 may have been affected by the growing women's rights movement with women taking greater control over their reproductive lives—a luxury not afforded to black women of child-bearing years who were either enslaved or newly freed during much of the period. Some researchers have also suggested that declining birth rates may be related to land availability, increasing industrialization, the education of women, or the pressure of elderly dependents in the home (Easterlin et al. 1978, 65–73).

Most women were exposed to the rigors of almost continuous pregnancy, interrupted only by a painful and dangerous labor, and months of nursing. So frequent were these bouts with nature that many women, conceiving again before fully recovered from a previous pregnancy, gave birth to underweight or physically weakened children who were prime candidates for an early death. Even in a society where large families were the norm and were valued and wanted, at least some women must have dreaded the prospect. Childlessness, according to the data, was so low as to be implausible for most married women, and the positioning of nonnuclear adopted children or stepchildren as actual offspring of a mother may be a reflection of a bias in the sampling techniques toward nuclear families.

Total fertility and birth rates started very high in the nineteenth century and declined as the century progressed. In 1830 the average white woman living in the Northeast had 3.3 live births in her childbearing years. In 1890, this number had fallen to 2.4 live births. Foreign-born data for the same period shows significantly higher but also declining numbers, 5.7 and 3.5, respectively. These figures were followed by a lagging and uncertain decline in the infant mortality rate and total life expectancy—both of which reversed more than once between 1850 and 1890. These data combined both rural and urban samples.

The Fragility of Life

A high rate of infant mortality and a low life expectancy in the general population may have reflected exposure to a number of infectious diseases easily spread in an urbanized environment including tuberculosis, cholera, typhoid, smallpox, and diphtheria. Nineteenth-century cities were particularly unhealthy places, and not until the 1890s did city managers begin to complete major public works sanitation projects such as piped water, sewer systems, water filtration, and trash collection. On the other hand, frontier and farm living were also dangerous. Starvation, exposure, snakebite, farming and hunting accidents, lack of medical attention, bad water, severe weather, and Indian attack added to the list of common dangers and afflictions that made life tenuous.

Great care was needed when children were about, but even the most vigilant parents sometimes failed to protect the young. Schoolteacher John Roberts sadly reported, "Yesterday one of my smallest pupils was severely hurt by falling from a teeter or plank put across the fence, on which two of them were riding seesaw fashion. I must put a stop to this sport as it is dangerous" (England 1996, 174). Accidents and common childhood diseases claimed nearly half of all children before the age of five. In Henniker, New Hampshire, seven children were scalded to death and two others died after falling into a fireplace. Toddlers aged two and three were both scalded by the falling of a kettle of boiling soap from the fireplace crane. Both children died the next day and were buried in the same coffin.

City children plummeted to their death from the windows of multistoried houses. The *New York Herald* editorialized, "We hope this notice will prove a caution to parents, who carelessly allow their children to swing themselves at a window without protection." The newspapers noted that a mother, who was "subject to fits of derangement," slit the throats of three of her children, then her own throat. "The father, on his return from labor to his house, found his family in this deplorable condition." A sample of the weekly death reports in Brooklyn was recorded in the May 15, 1850, issue of the *New York Herald* as two drowned, six dead from consumption, one from "abortion," and 32 others, including 22 children.

For women, childbirth remained the greatest danger to their lives; the second leading cause of death among women remained death from fire. Open flames and hot stovetops were everywhere. Long skirts made of flammable materials and children's clothing of cotton or linen were easy targets for accidental injury and death. More people lost their lives to fire rather than to Indian attacks on the frontier. Moreover, with buildings made largely of wood, town fires were almost inevitable. Fire destroyed dozens of buildings annually even in small towns, and a single devastating incident could destroy whole communities. Virtually the entire town of Tombstone, Arizona, burned three times in as many decades. The most famous fire of the period was the Chicago City Fire, which consumed 1,700 acres of the city in 1871. This was followed in 1872 by a huge conflagration in Boston that caused city fathers to rethink this aspect of urban and town safety. New building codes and stricter enforcement, architectural designs that included fire exits and escapes, and the development of professional firefighting forces and equipment began to lessen this danger in the final quarter of the century.

Improvements in diet, clothing, and shelter over the two decades beginning in 1870 also contributed to a declining death rate and an increased life expectancy. Ironically, much of this was due to the experience gained by doctors in the battlefield surgeries and convalescent hospitals of the Civil War where medical skills were honed and surgical risks taken that would not have been possible in peacetime. The advance of life expectancy from the turn of the century onward was remarkable. In 1890, the newborn grandchild of a Civil War veteran could expect only 46 years of life, yet most lived longer than the statistics predicted. In 1920, the newborn child's own children could expect 57 years of life; and 50 years later, in 1940, the average life expectancy of the original child's own grandchildren had risen to an amazing 65 years, while they themselves had lived two decades longer than originally predicted. These children, "Baby Boomers" born in the wake of another war (World War II) are just now at the threshold of Social Security retirement with a statistical life expectancy of 75+ years and the probability of living to twice the age of their great grandparents.

With all of these statistical and health considerations taken into account, it seems safe to conclude from the remaining data that the average white family in 1850 had between four and five children over one year of age from a common mother, while blacks families had between five and six offspring from a common mother. Data concerning the age of the mother at first marriage shows that young women were delaying marriage from a mean age of 20.7 years in the eighteenth century to a mean age of 24.4 at the end of the nineteenth century. Also, the mother's age at the birth of her last child suggests a modal shift from between 40–44 in the eighteenth century to between 35–39 during the nineteenth century. This indicator suggests that deliberate family limitation was an ongoing process that increased in scope and magnitude through the early nineteenth century (Osterud and Fulton 1979, 408–9).

The estimates of the total number of births per dwelling in a single year are extraordinary, nonetheless. For states and territories with data available—approximately half of them in 1850—between 13 percent (South Carolina) and 21 percent (Missouri) of all dwelling places experienced a birth annually. For many of the most populous states with large immigrant communities like New York, Massachusetts, and Pennsylvania, complete data in this regard are simply not available (Volo and Volo 2007, 34).

Nuclear families were also the basic social element in the frontier states of the Great Lakes region. Households in Indiana from 1820 to 1830 featured about 2.2 births per family during the decade. The median range of the number of children over one year old was between four and five per household. As the frontier moved through and beyond the state boundaries to the west in the next 10 years, the

10-year number of births fell to 1.8 per family. Pennsylvania and Ohio experienced similar rates and changes during the same phase of their development (Modell 1979, 420). A sample of family size and birth data taken in central New York in 1865 showed completed families of four to five children among rural farming households. These data were isolated for 4,300 white women who had been married only once, and omitting any plural marriages or stepchildren for either spouse. Family size and birth rate, in the New York study, were lowest in densely populated areas. In fact, population density was found to be the most important single factor in predicting the birth rate and family size for this sample population. The highest birth rates were found among the isolated but well-established families in mountainous and hilly sections of New York. With a high death rate among women of child-bearing years and a great deal of speedy remarriage by widowers, it has been estimated that white families there hovered around five children per household (Bash 1979, 438–39).

The Cost and Standard of Living

As people learned to live in a mass society, they progressively spent more for goods and services that they had previously not needed or were able to meet without monetary expenditure. The enduring effects of industrialization, urbanization, and invention can be gleaned from many working-class family budgets. Streetcar fares, gas or kerosene lighting, and the cost of heating fuel can be taken as examples of the financial stress placed on families by the modern standard of living in most urban areas.

In a rural and largely agricultural nation, daily transportation expenses were all but unnecessary as a budgetary item. People walked or rode their own animals from place to place, if they traveled any distance at all. Time was on their side, and they could afford to spend an entire day going to market in the town or visiting friends and relatives. The introduction of the factory system and the work-for-wage economy made time more dear than money, however, and a man gladly spent a few cents each day to be at work on time rather than to jeopardize his employment.

Artificial lighting had been provided by candles, grease lamps, or floating tapers since colonial times, and in many rural areas they continued to be popular because of their low cost. Most of these were produced at home from the rendering of waste animal fat into tallow or oils, or by actively gathering beeswax or bayberries. Whale oil was a significant exception to this rule because it had to be bought at the general store and burned in a peculiar double-wicked lamp. Rural and urban families generally continued to use these means of lighting until mid-century. Slowly new lighting devices made their way onto the American scene, and as with most technological advances, they appeared first in the cities. The most significant new means of lighting was the natural gas light, which by 1855 was appearing on both the main and secondary streets of even moderately sized cities and towns. Manufactured gas, acetylene, had been invented as early as 1816, but it was the natural gas pipelines placed under the streets of American cities that fed into even moderately priced homes that defined the Gaslight Era. More significant for most Americans, especially those in rural regions, was the development of kerosene lamps. These came into wide use after the development of the petroleum industry in Titusville, Pennsylvania. In 1859, Col. Edwin Drake brought in his first oil well with the specific intent of using the oily kerosene liquid as a lighting fuel. Although its adoption was initially hampered by the Civil War, the kerosene lamp became a ubiquitous device in most homes immediately thereafter. Even with the invention of the electric light in 1879 and its application to street lighting, kerosene remained the main source of artificial lighting in many farming and frontier communities into the twentieth century. In 1900 only eight percent of the homes nationwide were wired for electricity, and most of these were upper-class dwellings, which had their gas fixtures converted to electric lights. Plug-in lamps, while available, were not common before the turn of the century.

In the same vein, farmers and frontiersmen commonly took their fuel for heating and cooking from their own woodlots or from mesquite bushes, corncobs, or dried manure (so-called buffalo chips). These were provided by the application of one's own time, labor, and sweat rather than by the expenditure of cash. Despite the availability of many kinds of patented iron woodstoves, most Americans experienced cold mornings and chilly nights from November to April. The use of kerosene stoves (or heaters) in many homes became popular after the Civil War, and several kerosene-fueled devices were patented for warming irons for pressing clothes. Like the lamps and stoves that used the same volatile liquid fuel, these devices were particularly dangerous if upset while lit. Many cities banned the use of kerosene heaters in multifamily dwellings as fire hazards. For many city dwellers, firewood, charcoal, or hard coal needed to be purchased with cash from dealers who carted these items into the city centers. By the latter half of the nineteenth century hard coal had become the fuel of choice in city tenements for heating when used in fireplace gratings, cast-iron stoves, or tenement furnaces; but charcoal or firewood remained the choice for cooking purposes until they were replaced by gas. In 1870 more than 15 million tons of hard coal were mined in the United States and by the end of the period this had increased fivefold.

Family Wealth

The federal censuses of 1850, 1860, and 1870 gathered information regarding income and property ownership. The 1850 census collected data only on real property, while the subsequent censuses sampled both real and personal property. The data can be disaggregated by race, residence, occupation, place of birth, and age and can be used to provide a look at the economic health of the family during the late nineteenth century. The 1870 census sampled more than 7.5 million families with an average wealth of almost $3,000, much of the total held by a small minority of very wealthy families. Sixty-nine percent of American families had property valued at more than $100. This included real property (land and houses) and personal property (cash or items of value). Given that the $100 threshold for inclusion masks some details regarding the poorest third of the population, it is still clear that wealth among the majority of families in this mid-nineteenth-century sample lacked any equality in how it was distributed.

No one should be surprised that economic inequality was greater among blacks than among whites, especially in the South where wealth was most unequally distributed across all subgroups. Researchers using random samples from the census taken in these periods, however, found "that property was nearly as unequally distributed in some parts of the Northeast, and in the Pacific and Mountain regions." Moreover, property inequality was also higher in urban rather than rural areas, it was higher in industrial rather than agricultural areas (the plantation South excepted), and it was higher among sales occupations rather than among wage earners. Differences in skilled versus unskilled pay rates—a proxy for income inequality—were greatest in areas in the earliest stages of industrialization. Wealth was more equally distributed among farmers, professionals, and clerical or office workers. What is remarkable is that by 1870, at least, there was little inequality based on ethnicity in terms of being native- or foreign-born. Inequalities also varied with age. Not surprisingly, young adults had the smallest portion of income. Older persons within every category of occupation or residence were much closer to one another than the young in terms of wealth distribution (Rosenbloom and Stutes 2005, 4–5).

The average wealth of households headed by older, foreign-born, white males was higher than that of the general population if they were employed in manufacturing. Among these, regional and urban-rural distributions were quite similar as a whole. About 11 percent of all households were headed by native-born, rural females, made heads of households largely because they were widowed. Two-thirds of these female heads-of-household were black. With their limited economic prospects and an average age five years older than their male counterparts, it is not surprising that black women reported less property or no property more often than other group of persons.

State and regional differences in wealth were pronounced ranging from an average high of almost $5,000 per family in the Pacific region to an average low of just under $1,000 in the Mountain states. Wealth in the Northern states was two to three times greater than in the Southern states, but in the border states of Maryland, West Virginia, and Kentucky it was higher than in the Deep South of Georgia, Mississippi, or Alabama. Among the northern states, the New England manufacturing centers of Connecticut, Rhode Island, and Massachusetts had much higher levels than the more rural states of Vermont, New Hampshire, and Maine. In New England the value of real property (57%) accounted for a smaller portion of wealth than elsewhere (70%). Property ownership also varied across the region with the North Central states (80%) leading, and the Northeast (70%) and the Southern states (50%) lagging behind (Rosenbloom and Stutes 2005, 8).

In terms of wealth nationwide, 27 percent of real property and 38 percent of personal property was owned by the top one percent of the population. Wealth was most concentrated among a few families in South Carolina, Louisiana, California, and the New England manufacturing states. The recently settled western states reported little wealth of any kind, and the agricultural states of New York, Pennsylvania, and the North Central region had a generally equitable distribution of wealth in terms of farm land. Real property inequity was greatest in the South, and personal property inequity greatest in New England and the Mid-Atlantic states. Black families were about 30 percent less likely to report owning any property, and those that did have property valued it at little more than half that of comparable white families. There was no significant difference between native-born and foreign-born real property owners, but immigrants reported about 20 percent less personal property. Literacy and advancing age increased the likelihood of property ownership, but wealth peaked at age 55 to 60. Women, as a subgroup, were less likely to own any reportable property and had less of it than men of the same class when they did. Modest city dwellers were less likely to own property of any kind, and the odds of ownership fell with the increasing size of the city. This may have been due to a great number of renters. Those urban families with wealth, however, were generally better off if they lived in a large city rather than a small city (Rosenbloom and Stutes 2005, 13).

There were marked differences in wealth distribution across occupational groups. General laborers and domestics, as expected, were the least likely to own property of any kind, but farmers, because of their land, were the most likely to report real property ownership. In terms of wealth, professionals and managers were among the wealthiest occupations, but farmers also placed very high along the wealth spectrum. Craftsmen and machine operators came next with salesmen and clerks being last in wealth among persons with specific occupations reported in the census data (Rosenbloom and Stutes 2005, 28).

Farm Unrest

American farmers, as a group, have often expressed dissatisfaction with their economic lot, but in the post–Civil War years they were extraordinarily united in their discontent. The second half of the nineteenth century was one of persistent and vocal dissent with the way farmers viewed they were being treated by the rest of society. Increasing complexity in the emerging national and international marketplaces overwhelmed many farmers. Their frustration was largely fueled by declining prices, increasing costs, and lackluster profits. In 1873, and for five years thereafter, the Upper Midwest farming region was plagued by grasshoppers and several states were grievously affected.

From the 1860s to 1900, farmers formed cooperatives, interest groups, and associations to voice their complaints. They even went so far as to support significant third party candidates to defend their interests in the national political arena. Among these were the National Grange of the Order of Patrons of Husbandry founded in the 1860s; the Greenback Party significant in the 1870s; the Farmer's

Alliance of the 1880s; and the People's or Populist Party of the 1890s. A series of weather-related hardships drove the agitation in the Plains, and competition from abroad generally drove that in the Midwest. A major complaint was the treatment they received from the railroads and the high freight rates the railroads imposed. Southern farmers were more muted in their complaints largely because they were not so hard pressed by extremes of weather and could fall back on river transport to move their produce to market. The groups formed around generally monolithic racial and ethnic groups, and black, Native American, and mixed-race farmers were generally excluded.

The complaints of farmers throughout the period were well-articulated and can be easily summarized. Their foremost complaint was that farm prices were falling along with their incomes. Had this not been the case little would have been said. Farmers were practical, rather than ideological, in their discontent. They alleged that monopolistic railroads and grain elevators charged unfair prices for their services, and they perceived a lack of credit, a shortage in the money supply, and an unfair level of interest charged by banks. Falling prices during periods of deflation forced the farmers to repay debts in dollars that were worth significantly more than those they had borrowed. Yet their basic complaint concerned the undue influence over policy making and government held by railroads, financial institutions, and industrialists. It is evident that the farmers were reacting against the loss of influence traditionally held by the agriculturist in American society.

Currency Reform

In 1862, the Lincoln Administration began to issue paper currency as a wartime economic measure. Called *greenbacks*, more than $450 million (1860 dollars) in engraved paper bills were issued. Ever since the days of the Federalists, paper currency had been issued by the government, but it had always been backed by specie (gold) held in government vaults. Lincoln's greenbacks were based only on the good credit of the United States Government. During the war, the greenbacks generally fell in value when compared to gold and silver coins, but they remained legal tender and held most of their face value as long as specie circulated freely. Had the coins begun disappearing from circulation, as they did in the Confederacy, the value of the greenbacks would most certainly have fallen further.

As it was, at the end of the war, U.S. paper currency was valued at a discount large enough to attract banks and financial organization to buy them up cheap and present them to the federal government at face value. These interests demanded that the bills be treated like government bonds that were paid in gold for both the principle and the interest. The enabling legislation of 1862 had specifically prohibited this. A few soft-money politicians and greenbackers opposed the gold payments, but the hard-money Democrats were in complete accord with the idea. The argument seems frivolous to present-day Americans who are used to unsupported paper currency, valued only on the full faith and credit of the U.S. Treasury. Yet the greenback issue was actually a battle drawn between substantial economic interests, and it remained a foundational political issue throughout the remainder of the century.

Big business and banking had found the fixed gold standard most favorable for their operations and a hedge against economic downturns, but farmers and laborers bore the brunt of the financial loss caused by a gold standard in each successive depression or panic. The most recent of these in the postwar period was the Panic of 1873, but significant downturns had occurred in 1837, 1854, and 1858. After each panic the nation slowly recovered, regaining much of its prosperity and expanding under the influence of the giant gold strikes in California and the mountain West. Large silver reserves discovered in the Washoe area of the Sierra Nevadas in 1859 (known as the Comstock Lode or Nevada Bonanza) also relieved the distress somewhat.

With gold and silver flooding the market, their monetary values diminished with gold being the more stable monetary metal and silver varying as a commodity metal. For the remainder of the century, therefore, general price levels were in a deflationary downturn. Eastern financial interests were trading on the international markets in an increasingly gold-based world economy, and they wanted standardized gold money that increased in intrinsic value during periods of deflation. Farmers and other interior interests, who borrowed money, found that deflation had the effect of increasing the real value of interest paid on loans. Many populist, labor, and radical organizations favored soft monetary policies (particularly paper currency) that were inflationary on the grounds that farmers, wage earners, and small businesses could pay off their debts with cheaper, and more readily available, dollars. Creditors would then bear the burden of depreciating currency values.

In 1878, the soft money forces passed the Bland-Allison Act, which required the Treasury to redeem at least $2 million in paper (bonds and bills) each month through the use of silver bullion at one dollar per troy ounce. Most Greenbackers joined the soft money forces in backing the compromise that kept most greenbacks in circulation and helped to maintain their face value. Thereafter they were known as Free Silverites. After a long fight in Congress and the courts, specie payments in gold were resumed in 1879. In 1896 William Jennings Bryan, the Democratic candidate, adopted the Populist opposition to the gold standard as a policy position, and he hoped to attract farmers and other soft money interests to the voting booth. Many Populist sentiments can be found in his famous Cross of Gold speech.

Immigration

Throughout the second half of the nineteenth century there was a strong cultural undercurrent of discrimination based on race, ethnicity, religion, or class. The existence of race-based slavery allowed discrimination to be broad-based, systemic, open to public scrutiny, and acceptable to a very large segment of the American population. Besides blacks, the targets of discrimination were often the recent immigrants to this country. These came in successive waves depending largely on economic conditions elsewhere in the world. Those immigrant groups that became targets of bigotry included the Irish, Germans, Chinese, Italians, and Eastern Europeans.

There were a number of factors that drove immigration to the United States. These can be categorized as *push* and *pull* factors carrying people from Europe, or Asia, to the United States. The same pull factors generally applied to all of the countries of origin. These included jobs with relatively high wages, free or inexpensive land, ease of travel in the form of steamships, ease of migration in the form of railroads, and (after the Civil War) a seeming political stability. These were all attractive incentives for families willing to settle permanently in the United States.

The push factors were generally specific to the environment of the immigrants' home nation. Most were economic in nature revolving around the growth of European population and the resultant shortage of land and jobs. A trend toward the large-scale commercialization of agriculture in Europe had pushed many peasants and renters off the land. Some emigrants left their home to avoid religious persecution. Jewish emigrants from Eastern Europe, Russian Mennonites, Danish Mormons, and German Baptists all suffered some form of religious oppression in their countries of origin (Husband and O'Loughlin 2004, 7). Others left to avoid the horrors of constant European warfare, conscription, and political instability.

Intellectual Life

American literary independence was not achieved simultaneously with its political separation from Britain. The development of a cadre of American authors, nationalistic themes, and an independent writing style could not be realized until the instruments of culture were sufficient to produce trained writers, sensitive critics, and receptive readers. Schools and colleges, libraries, and publishing houses needed time to evolve and establish themselves. There were great controversies regarding schooling with Prussian-style pedagogical principles in ascendancy during much of the period. There were also disputes over tax-supported schools, religious schools, and curriculum development. Two of the premiere universities in America, Harvard and Yale, fell into an interminable dispute over the essentials of a college education. In the 1880s, Harvard introduced elective courses and a voluntary system of recitations approximating the European style of university education. Yale continued to represent itself as a place of general training—in moral as well as intellectual pursuits—where the professors stood *in loco parentis* providing not only the means of instruction, but also its direction and enforcement. Harvard seemed to have been aiming at the student taking as much or as little of what was being offered at his own discretion. The student was seemingly free to follow a course of study that omitted essential and fundamental branches of knowledge. The one positive of the elective system was that it increased the general interest of students and teachers alike to partake of the system. The negatives were that it seemingly required no specific studies, regimen, attendance, or rules; and it took no responsibility for the moral or intellectual improvement of the student (Hofstadter and Smith 1968, 732).

It has been observed that six of America's greatest authors were born within 16 years of one another during the first decades of the nineteenth century: Ralph Waldo Emerson (1803), Nathaniel Hawthorne (1804), Edgar Allan Poe (1809), Henry David Thoreau (1817), Herman Melville (1819), and Walt Whitman (1819). Certainly the list could be lengthened to include the authors, male and female, who produced the bulk of the printed work enjoyed by the common population of American readers; but it does indicate that America was not ready to produce its own literature until its spirit of democracy and nationalism had had time to coalesce and take root. Prior to the beginning of the antebellum period, American writers tended to imitate European styles even when they were working on nationalistic topics. "As a turning point, one might well designate the years 1819 to 1821, when Washington Irving published his *Sketchbook* of essays and stories, when William Cullen Bryant's first collection of poems appeared, and when James Fenimore Cooper, after one false start, won acclaim for *The Spy*, a novel set in the Revolutionary period" (Fehrenbacher 1969, 118–19).

Prior to 1820 more fashionable and less expensive English texts had almost closed the literary market to American authors and publishers. In that year, Sidney Smith, an eccentric clergyman, wrote in the *Edinburgh Review*: "In the four quarters of the globe, who reads an American book? or goes to an American Play?" (Lupiano and Sayers 1994, 60). In 1834, as our authors grew to manhood fewer than 500 American titles were published in the United States. However, by 1862, as the country and its writers grew to maturity, this number had grown to 4,000 (Fite 1976, 256). The literary pendulum in authorship and publishing had begun to swing from the theoretical, intellectual, and theological writing that had dominated the Revolutionary and Federalist periods to the more emotional, physically stirring, and mystical writing of novelists, romantics, and the socially conscientious (Volo and Volo 2004, 203–4).

In the second half of the nineteenth century, the majority of native-born Americans were literate with literacy rates of 93 percent for men and 91 percent for women in the 1860s. Illiteracy was highest among destitute whites, poor blacks and recently freed slaves, and non-English speaking immigrants (who may have been literate in their own language). Reading played a prominent role in the lives of many Americans. Before the explosion of entertainment media in the second half of the twentieth century, reading materials such as books, magazines, tracts, and newspapers were the only mass media for diversion; and reading was considered a vital leisure activity. Moreover, in a largely Protestant society Bible reading was an essential religious obligation. Indeed, for the middle class, familiarity with scripture and the "right" literature became a mark of class distinction, producing a common experience, language, and values among the better sort. Reading was, nonetheless, an important activity for virtually all Americans (Shrock 2004, 151).

There was also a much wider selection and availability of reading materials in nineteenth century America than at any previous time in its history. This was largely due to technological advances in the printing and publishing industries and the expansion of transportation facilities that allowed printed materials to be shipped at a reasonable cost to the consumer. The annual rate of production of newly published hardcover books increased by 300 percent from 1800 to 1900. There was a corresponding increase in the growth of newspapers. Although tremendously popular at mid-century, the newspaper industry experienced a 700 percent increase in circulation from 1870 to 1900. Magazine circulation, especially that of illustrated magazines, journals, and gazettes, grew dramatically and stood at 65 million in 1900, which meant that there were up to three magazines for every four people in the American population (Shrock 2004, 151).

Henry Seidel Canby, editor of the *Saturday Review*, noted in his memoirs of the last quarter of the nineteenth century, *The Age of Confidence* (1934), "My reading memories are of absorption in a book, earless, eyeless, motionless hours, a life between covers more real than outer experience.... It was an extension without break or casualty of our own lives, and flowed back freely to become part of our mentality." Reading the properly chosen materials illustrated the gentility and refinement of the reader, serving as a class marker that differentiated the respectable folk from the rough. Such activities fostered self-improvement and created a common literary heritage that united the classes (Shrock 2004, 157).

Chief among the genre that played a role in life were the advice books written by authors whose authoritative position had come through academic and professional credentials rather than social and familial connections. These authors suggested histories, biographies, geographies, and works on natural science and travel literature that they considered the best path to self-improvement. However, it was the novel that was in the highest demand during the period dominating both sales and library borrowing. British authors like Charlotte Brontë, Walter Scott, William Thackeray, Dinah Mulock, George Eliot, and Anthony Trollope were highly recommended. However, American authorship, especially that of professional writers, increased tremendously in the period. Louisa May Alcott, Nathaniel Hawthorne, Harriet Beecher Stowe, Mark Twain, William Dean Howells, Henry James, Francis Parkman, Frank Norris, and Stephen Crane stand out as examples.

Mass literacy also made it possible for new forms of reading material to reach the public. Among these were dime novels, story papers, and other products of what came to be known as the cheap press. There is strong evidence that native- and Irish-born working-class families spent a substantial fraction of their income on newspapers, magazines, and books. Indeed, though children and young adults read story papers (comic book-length pamphlets) and dime novels, they were not the only or even primary audience of the publishers. The cheap press did very well during the Civil War with soldiers, but few admitted to reading it in their letters and diaries. After the conflict, it established a following among young, working-class men.

Western tales, detective stories, crime periodicals like the *National Police Gazette*, and other forms of sensational material also had an undeniable appeal. Indian massacres, gruesome crimes, and love entanglements filled these works. Love crimes, ghastly murders, gothic tales of terror, lynching, seductions, urban vice, and women posing as men were all topics covered with some regularity. These were often accompanied by graphic illustrations of the scene. Scantily clad women often appeared in the illustrations, but so did strong women doing things ordinarily reserved for men often in settings like saloons, hotels, and sporting events. Weekly circulations of over 100,000 copies were not unusual (Shrock 2004, 175).

Although authorship by women was generally frowned upon before 1850, female writers like Mary Wollstoncraft Shelley (*Frankenstein, or the Modern Prometheus*) had gained a grudging acceptance in Britain that helped American women to enter the field as amateurs. Shelley's novel was made available when she was just 21 years old, but the first edition (1818) was widely accepted as the work of her husband, Percy Shelley.

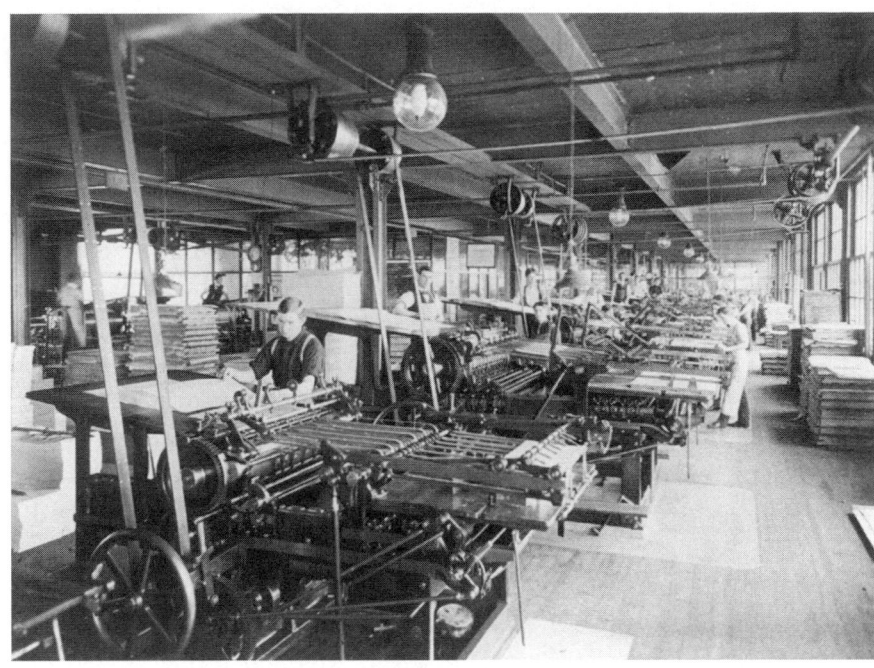

The nineteenth-century printing office had changed from the small two- to three-man shop with a hand-operated press, to a multiemployee modern version of a publishing house resembling other industries that had turned to mass production and steam presses. Courtesy Library of Congress.

Many readers could not accept that a young woman could write such a shockingly repellent tale. Mary Shelley clearly acknowledged her authorship in 1821, and she is known, along with the American author Ann Radcliffe, for giving form to the Gothic horror genre. Lydia Child, a prominent self-help and advice author from this period, decried such "profligate and strongly exciting works," and she found the "necessity of fierce excitement in reading...a sort of intellectual in temperance producing a weakness and delirium in women and young girls." Nonetheless, the genre grew and women authors became even more successful as the century advanced (Volo and Volo 2004, 210).

The development of the juvenile literature genre illustrates the growth of a consumer ethic and a distinctively youthful culture. Although there were genteel values shared by all youthful readers, the standard Victorian way of thinking about the genders was well-entrenched, and this affected the content of the material that each was expected to read. For boys, characters with manly attributes like courage, physical power, and aggressiveness were favored. For girls, the domestic world—less rugged, more emotional, and certainly more mannerly and pious—was portrayed. Female characters were presented as polite, reserved, and respectful; males as honest, heroic, and even aggressive. Young people had a serious impact on reading material and they made their voice heard regarding the storylines and authors that they liked. Close attention was paid to these youthful readers, and while Victorian attitudes remained dominant, the desires of young readers created a distinctive space in the publishing world (Shrock 2004, 168).

Militarism

Militarism rather than diplomacy was to prove the most efficient tool for achieving the nation's manifest destiny during the nineteenth century. In 1790, the entire United States Army numbered just 80 men. During the Civil War there would be more than two million men under arms. Statesmen of that latter day seemed willing to accept the scourge of war to shape American society. Moreover, the American public from New York to New Orleans and from Charleston to Chicago generally supported these military efforts and followed their development—and the war news in particular—with rapt attention. The shifting tides of battle were often viewed like a sporting event (Millis 1956, 13).

The military system of mid-century had become so specialized that it needed to be described on a series of schematic diagrams, yet the old tradition of cavalier gallantry—drinking, carousing, and fighting—remained alive permeating the ranks of both the army and the navy. The military was seen as an acceptable professional career for many men and formal education in the concepts of warfare were not generally looked down upon as they are in some circles today. A contemporary observer expressed the absolute faith that nineteenth century Americans had in their military, "It is our army that unites the chasm between the culture of civilization in the aspect of science, art, and social refinement, and the powerful simplicity of nature" (Marcy 1993/1859, xi).

Although the American Civil War stands out as the major conflict during this period—some say the formative experience in the history of the nation—from 1785 to 1898 the country was involved in several other conflicts that helped to formulate its character. About once a decade, fathers, sons, and brothers were called forth in defense of their homes and country. They were also called upon to advance the frontiers of the nation, to underpin the emerging industrial complex by attacking strikers, to control slaves and freedmen, and to expel or exterminate the aboriginal owners of the land. The so-called Indian Wars of the second half-century stand out in this respect. Americans also fought a series of conflicts and policing actions along the Mexican-American and Canadian-American borders as well as an extended war with Spain in the Philippines and Cuba.

Summary

The Civil War involved the entire population in a way unparalleled by any conflict since the American Revolution. An incalculable number of civilian lives were permanently disrupted in its wake. Before a single man had been killed in battle, the absence of men from the countinghouse, factory, plantation, or farm had had an immediate effect on their families as well as their communities. The military mobilization of close to four million men in as many years—the largest attempted in

American history to that time—generally affected their ability to properly support their families in ways that few had envisioned.

So common were the battlefield deaths on both sides—some 620,000 men in four years—that whole communities were in simultaneous mourning. The absence of a so-called bread winner or other male source of income most stressed middle- and lower-class families who had few financial resources or reserves. Many upper-class women had servants, hired help, or slaves on which to rely in the absence of their men, but they found their situations strained nonetheless. After watching her brothers depart for the war, Kate Stone correctly speculated that they who stayed home might find it harder than those who left (Browne and Kreiser 2003, 11).

The post–Civil War period of American history known as Reconstruction (1865–1877) did little to buttress any of the political, economic, or social objectives gained on the battlefield. For many ex-Confederates Reconstruction was relatively brief. It was long enough, however, to foster a lasting bitterness between traditional and progressive Southern whites, but not long enough to sustain the nascent black political power that was kindled at the end of the war or to engender genuine economic independence among former black slaves.

During the second half of the nineteenth century, America emerged as a world power both economically and militarily. Some historians consider the Gadsden Purchase of 1853 the end of the era of expansion. Others understand that such events also shape the future, and their inevitable consequences lend a radically different perspective to all that preceded it. The era of expansion marked by wagon trains and railways simply gave way to an equally vibrant era of exploitation. Nor does the end of expansion in mid-century explain the purchase of Alaska in 1867, the annexation of Hawaii in 1898, the diplomatic involvement in China, or the submission of Cuba, Puerto Rico, and the Philippines at the end of the Spanish American War 50 years later.

According to the perceptions of a number of nineteenth century observers, "acquisitiveness," if not greed or avarice, took a hold on the minds of many men in the Industrial Age, at the end of the century, and they became focused on being more than merely comfortable in their homes and communities. They seemed in a great haste to become conspicuously wealthy. The rising middle class also aspired to an idyllic life filled with pastimes, diversions, and attempts at personal improvement without recognizing many of the underlying fundamentals of the economy or the national psyche.

The history of finance and industry in the Industrial Age is the story of a handful of businessmen who became superrich in the second half of the nineteenth century by applying innovative methods to the processes of mass industrialization. Many of the features that distinguish our present machine-based industrial economy were developed during this period. At no time since humans first learned to control fire had society been so profoundly modified by technology.

Such matters have sent historians delving into the depths of old newspaper columns, official records, letters, diaries, photographic files, and memoirs to unearth the details of constitutional pressures, agricultural and industrial production, battlefield strategies, and political evolutions. Many of these have been recorded in this volume.

FOR MORE INFORMATION

Barney, William L., ed. *A Companion to 19th-Century America*. Malden, MA: Blackwell Publishing, 2006.

Bash, Wendell H. "Differential Fertility in Madison County New York, 1865." In *Studies in American Historical Demography*, ed. Maris A. Vinovskis. New York: Academic Press, 1979.

Bennett, Sarah. "Words to a Woman." *Advocate and Family Guardian* 31, no. 3 (February 1, 1865).

Browne, Ray B., and Lawrence A. Kreiser Jr. *The Civil War and Reconstruction*. Westport, CT: Greenwood Press, 2003.

Cary, John H., and Julius Weinberg, eds. *The Social Fabric: American Life from the Civil War to the Present*. Boston, MA: Little, Brown and Company, 1975.

Davidson, Marshall B. *Life in America*. Boston, MA: Houghton Mifflin Company, 1951.

Easterlin, Richard A., George Alter, and Gretchen A. Condran. "Farms and Farm Families in Old and New Areas: The Northern States in 1860." In *Family and Population in Nineteenth Century America* by Tamara K. Hareven and Maris A. Vinovskis. Princeton, NJ: Princeton University Press, 1978.

England, J. Merton, ed. *Buckeye Schoolmaster: A Chronicle of Midwestern Rural Life 1853–1865*. Bowling Green, OH: State University Popular Press, 1996.

Fehrenbacher, Don E. *The Era of Expansion, 1800–1848*. New York: John Wiley and Sons, 1969.

Fite, Emerson David. *Social and Industrial Conditions in the North During the Civil War*. Williamstown, MA: Corner House, 1976.

Frank, Stephen M. *Life with Father: Parenthood and Masculinity in the Nineteenth-Century American North*. Baltimore, MD: Johns Hopkins University Press, 1998.

Glasco, Lawrence. "Migration and Adjustment in the Nineteenth-Century City: Occupation, Property, and Household Structure of Native-Born Whites, Buffalo, New York, 1855." In *Family and Population in Nineteenth Century America* by Tamara K. Hareven and Maris A. Vinovskis. Princeton, NJ: Princeton University Press, 1978.

Haines, T. L., and Levi W. Yaggy. *The Royal Path of Life: Or Aims and Aids to Success and Happiness*. Chicago, IL: Western Publishing House, 1876.

Hareven, Tamara K., and Maris A. Vinovskis. *Family and Population in Nineteenth-Century America*. Princeton, NJ: Princeton University Press, 1978.

Hofstadter, Richard, and Wilson Smith. *American Higher Education: A Documentary History*. Chicago, IL: University of Chicago Press, 1961.

Hunt, Gaillard. *As We Were, Life in America, 1814*. Stockbridge, MA: Berkshire House Publishers, 1914. Reprinted in 1993.

Husband, Julie, and Jim O'Loughlin. *Daily Life in the Industrial United States, 1870–1900*. Westport, CT: Greenwood Press, 2004.

Kipling, Rudyard. *American Notes*. 1891. URL: http://www.chicagohs.org/fire/queen/pic0521.html (accessed July 2007).

Lupiano, Vincent DePaul, and Ken W. Sayers. *It Was a Very Good Year: A Cultural History of the United States from 1776 to the Present*. Holbrook, MA: Bob Adams, 1994.

Marcy, Randolph B. *The Prairie Traveler, A Hand-book for Overland Expeditions*. Bedford, MA: Applewood Books, 1993. Reprint of the 1859 edition.

McIntosh, Elaine N. *American Food Habits in Historical Perspective*. Westport, CT: Greenwood/Praeger Press, 1995.

Millis, Walter. *Arms and Men, A Study of American Military History*. New York: A Mentor Book, 1956.

Modell, John. "Family and Fertility on the Indiana Frontier, 1820." In *Studies in American Historical Demography*, ed. Maris A. Vinovskis. New York: Academic Press, 1979.

Nye, Russel B. *The Cultural Life of the New Nation, 1776–1830*. New York: Harper & Row, 1960.

Osterud, Nancy, and John Fulton. "Family Limitation and Age at Marriage." In *Studies in American Historical Demography*, ed. Maris A. Vinovskis. New York: Academic Press, 1979.

Quay, Sara E. *Westward Expansion*. Westport, CT: Greenwood Press, 2002.

Rosenbloom, Joshua L., and Gregory W. Stutes. *Reexamining the Distribution of Wealth in 1870*. Cambridge, MA: National Bureau of Economic Research, 2005.

Sewell, Richard H. *A House Divided: Sectionalism and the Civil War, 1848–1865*. Baltimore, MD: Johns Hopkins University Press, 1988.

Shrock, Joel. *The Gilded Age*. Westport, CT: Greenwood Press, 2004.

Timmons, Todd. *Science and Technology in Nineteenth-Century America*. Westport, CT: Greenwood Press, 2005.

Uhlenberg, Peter R. "A Study of Cohort Life Cycles." In *Family and Population in Nineteenth Century America* by Tamara K. Hareven and Maris A. Vinovskis. Princeton, NJ: Princeton University Press, 1978.

Unidentified author. "The Needs of Working Women: Homes for Working-Girls." *Arthur's Lady's Home Magazine* 37, no. 1 (January 1871).

Volo, Dorothy Denneen, and James M. Volo. *The Antebellum Period*. Westport, CT: Greenwood Press, 2004.

———. *Family Life in Nineteenth-Century America*. Westport, CT: Greenwood Press, 2007.

Ware, John F. W. *Home Life: What It Is, and What It Needs*. Boston, MA: Wm. V. Spencer, 1864.

Wells, Robert V. "Demographic Change and the Life Cycle of American Families." In *Studies in American Historical Demography*, ed. Maris A. Vinovskis. New York: Academic Press, 1979.

Williams, Susan. *Food in the United States, 1820s–1890*. Westport, CT: Greenwood Press, 2006.

2

THE CIVIL WAR

Overview

THE IRREPRESSIBLE CONFLICT

In 1860 the federal capital at Washington was highly valued as a symbol by nineteenth-century Americans. Carefully laid out in a district allocated from within the boundaries of Maryland to salve the pride of the South, the nation's capital city had been under construction since the turn of the century. Americans pointed proudly to the imposing structure of the Capitol building, as well as the General Post Office, the Bureau of the Treasury, the Smithsonian Institution, and the Executive Mansion, as representative of a vigorous young nation preparing to take its place among the leading countries of the world.

Unfortunately, Washington was also symbolic of other things. The plans for the city, like the basic founding concepts of the nation itself, were as pretentious as they were visionary, and in 1860 both lay unfulfilled and disordered. Sprawling along the banks of the Potomac with the "Old City" of Alexandria, Virginia, across the water, the great buildings of the new capital remained incomplete even after the expenditure of vast sums of money and six decades of effort. The Capitol building lay unfinished with its original dome removed—a scaffolding and a towering crane representative of restructuring and rethinking. The wings of the building were stretched bare and unfinished, devoid even of steps. The imposing obelisk of the Washington Monument lay as a mere foundation. Blocks of marble, lumber, cast-iron plates, and the tools of workmen strewn about the district gave quiet testimony to the fact that the plan for the nation's first city, like the social and political plan for the American nation itself, was incomplete and open to revision (Leech 1941, 5–6).

At the head of the James River, 100 miles south of Washington and in sharp contrast to it, was Richmond, Virginia. As the third largest city in the South, Richmond had proven an elegant state capital with fine buildings and traditional architecture. Although the city was cultivated and cosmopolitan, it was also the center of Virginia's economy, with mills, railways, and trading establishments. In 1861, Richmond was the finest city in the South and one of the better places in which to live in the entire country. Within a few months of secession, though, Richmond had been made the capital of the new Confederate nation, and its tenor changed dramatically. On the eve of war the city teemed with soldiers, wagons, and government officials. Defenses in the form of artillery emplacements, trenches, and earthworks rimmed its suburbs. The South's only major foundry, the Tredegar Iron Works, turned out cannon, rails, and plates for gunboats. But in a mere four years the once stately city would be a ruin comparable to the broken hulk of Berlin at the end of World War II. Its people would be described as looking "hungry, gaunt, ghastly, and yellow." Even the young were so pale and thin that it was "pitiful to see" (Croushore 1949, 35).

The War of Southern Secession, a civil war, had come to America. It would be one of the most tragic events in the nation's history, resulting from a dispute among its citizens over just what the new country should look like. For four years the country passed through a traumatic military and social upheaval that touched the lives of its people in many ways.

At the outbreak of the war, all but the most astute observers thought that the question of national unity would be settled in a single afternoon of combat. Yet in the first great battle of the war (Bull Run, or First Manassas), the intrinsic drama of Americans locked in mortal combat diverted everyone's attention from the fact that indecisiveness had crept into warfare over the centuries. From 1861 to 1865 Yankees were bushwhacked in western Virginia and Rebels sniped at near Washington. Federal "Red Legs" and Confederate "Partisans" mauled one another across the plains of Kansas and Missouri and were held in contempt by the politicians on both sides.

Simultaneously, giant armies trudged across northern Virginia, Louisiana, and middle Tennessee in efforts to either defend or dismantle the Old South and its characteristic lifestyle. The war policies of both governments so extended into the lives of the local populations that people came to look seriously upon the result as the hard hand of war. Meanwhile, the terrible cost of war, measured in tens of thousands of lives, afflicted the North with such a palpable weariness that Abraham Lincoln despaired of winning reelection in 1864. He began to lay plans for turning the federal government over to a successor who would end the war by simply declaring it finished. The timely taking of Atlanta probably saved the election for Lincoln.

The 1863 Battle of Gettysburg, the bloodiest and largest ever fought on the North American continent, has long been a focal point of Civil War historians. Taken with the simultaneous fall of Vicksburg—the Confederate stronghold on the Mississippi—the federal victory at Gettysburg should have been one of the most decisive military actions in history. Yet the internecine struggle continued, seemingly powered by the undiminished will of the Southern people to prevail. "We shall not give up the contest," said one Confederate officer after the fall of the Southern stronghold at Port Hudson, "and I think we shall tire you out at last." From the rousing partisan raids of cavalier clad horsemen in Tennessee to the dreary siege warfare of the Petersburg trenches, the obstinate refusal of the ragged troops to be forced from a thousand battlefields left the issue of what constituted the American nation undecided for four long years (Volo and Volo 1998, xi–xiii).

In just 1,500 days of armed conflict more than 600,000 soldiers died from wounds and disease, and an incalculable number of civilian lives were lost or permanently disrupted by war. Such matters have sent historians delving in the depths of old newspaper columns, official records, letters, memoirs, diaries, and other sources to unearth the details of constitutional pressures, agricultural and industrial production, social development, and political evolution, thereby producing over the intervening decades an enormous and ever-growing body of printed work. More than 100,000 volumes have been written about the American Civil War.

No event in American history has had so much written about it, but much of the research has dealt with battles, operations, commanders, and military personalities. When a nation is at war, it is not just the soldiers whose lives are changed. The lives of the civilians who remain behind, whether they are joined to the battle by the ties of love or not, are altered just as irrevocably.

Immediately after the war, the public was swamped with war stories, journals, memoirs, and battle descriptions. Former army commanders renewed wartime arguments about tactics and strategies in print—the pen and the printing press their only weapons. Battlefield opponents, and sometimes former comrades, aired the dirty laundry of their respective commands before an awaiting public. Southern apologists, particularly, tried to rationalize their lost cause by finding unexploited opportunities, scapegoats, excuses, and martyrs. For quite some time—in fact for almost as long as the veterans of the war lived—this was the stuff of Civil War history.

However, in the 1940s and 1950s historians became mesmerized by the idea of identifying the reasons for the conflict, setting off a new wave of printing. Yet the causes proved so lost in a maze of interrelated factors and so obscured by the hidden agendas of those who wrote, or rewrote, history that there was no possibility of identifying all of them. Historians found that more than two years before the outbreak of hostilities, Americans had already identified, to their satisfaction at least, a very powerful cause for the bloody struggle that loomed between the increasingly antagonistic sections of their country. "It is an irrepressible conflict between opposing and enduring forces," declared William H. Seward in 1858. Some modern historians still agree with this outspoken antislavery Republican, but others disagree, believing the war could have been avoided by compromise. Nonetheless, it seems certain, from the distance of generations, that some form of civil upheaval was inevitable (Donald 1961, 124).

A more meaningful debate has centered in recent years around the people who found themselves caught in undercurrents of history so strong and compelling that they were unable to avoid conflict. This discussion has sparked several interesting lines of research into the nature of American society before and during the conflict, and historians have studied constitutional theory, politics, economics, geography, and society in an attempt to understand the wartime generation. Research in these areas has been particularly helpful in producing a mass of documentary evidence concerning the lives of the people of the Civil War era (Volo and Volo 1998, 3–4).

—*James M. Volo*

FOR MORE INFORMATION

Browne, Ray B., and Lawrence A. Kreiser Jr. *The Civil War and Reconstruction.* Westport, CT: Greenwood Press, 2003.

Croushore, James H., ed. *A Volunteer's Adventure, by Captain John W. De Forest.* New Haven, CT: Yale University Press, 1949.

Donald, David H. *The Civil War and Reconstruction.* Boston, MA: Heath, 1961.

Leech, Margaret. *Reveille in Washington.* New York: Harper & Brothers, 1941.

Stewart, James Brewer. *Holy Warriors: The Abolitionists and American Slavery.* New York: Hill and Wang, 1976.

Volo, Dorothy Denneen, and James M. Volo. *Daily Life in Civil War America.* Westport, CT: Greenwood Press, 1998.

Domestic Life

THE HARD HAND OF WAR

The visions of a nation wrenched apart by civil war and of soldiers battling on many fronts are often used to capture the emotion and turmoil of the period. While the physical debris of war was obvious, the full extent of the tragedy was somewhat obscured. The broken implements of battle, the uneven lines of shallow graves, the torn earth upturned by shot and shell rather than by the plow were all visible evidence of the tragedy that had been visited upon the nation. Yet the same imagery proved equally valid when applied to families and civilians during those troubled times.

The war placed the institution of the family under a siege equally as violent as any that occurred on the field of battle. Loved ones were wrenched apart as men and boys marched off to fight, many never to return—sometimes not even in death. It has been estimated that up to 200,000 Southerners, mostly refugees, were on the move during the war years. White refugees often took their slaves with them to keep them from the hands of the Federals. The states of the trans-Mississippi west like Texas and Arkansas seemed the safest, but riding herd on dozens of slaves through unfamiliar territory was difficult with a federal army on your heels offering immediate freedom to your bondsmen. Economic shortages, strained agricultural productivity, and social upheaval beset civilians, North and South, in various forms. Like brave soldiers themselves, many civilians managed to stand apart from the war and cope with its vagaries while trying to preserve some semblance of their social order, standard of living, and values. Thus, even though the war might rage at their very doorsteps, the civilians lived through it and in spite of it.

The vast majority of Southern and Midwestern citizens were small farmers who planned their lives around rural activities and seasonal chores such as barn raising, quilting bees, planting, haying, and harvesting. Their concept of time was based on sunrise, noon, spring, or summer, and they set their appointments or ended the workday by this standard. Free white laborers and artisans were paid at the completion of a task, and rarely by the clock or calendar. The system provided continuity in the work relationship between employer and employee, and it was not unusual for one family to be employed by another in the same capacity for several generations. Family members usually cooperated in completing chores. This togetherness was thought to foster feelings of kinship and traditional family values. Fathers and mothers worked beside their children and grandchildren in an idyllic, if not a mechanically efficient, simplicity. While many Northerners were still farmers, a growing segment of the population was becoming tied to the cities and factories. This trend would continue throughout the century. Middle-class men who had grown up in the first half of the century could remember a childhood spent living in a family working environment, either on the farm, in a cottage at the mill, or in a room behind the family shop. But as the century progressed, men's work increasingly took place in the special atmosphere of business premises such as the factory or office. Fathers commonly left the home to work for 10 to 14 hours, and their children rarely saw them during daylight hours. A father's work and workplace became foreign to his children. This tendency to go to work, rather than to work at home, led to the virtual removal of men from the home environment, leaving it the province of the female. The modern nineteenth-century home increasingly came to focus almost solely on the wife and children. The evolution to a female-dominated household may help to explain the growing formalism and rigid authoritarianism that Victorian fathers demanded when they were present.

Nonetheless, family structures were often more flexible than they are sometimes presented. Any imbalance created in the nuclear family living in an industrialized and urbanized environment may have "resulted from the breakup of the family as an economic partnership, a fragmentation caused by separation of place of work from place of residence and by the spread of a wage and money economy" (Chudacoff 1999, 204–5). The husband's added importance as a wage earner may also have prompted wives, particularly newlywed ones, to form extended ties of their own (especially with their mothers and maternal aunts) as a counterforce to men's increased power prerogatives.

—*James M. Volo*

KINSHIP TIES

The overwhelming pervasiveness of nuclear families in America did not mean that they were isolated. Kinship ties persisted outside the nuclear household, and they were of prime importance in determining a family strategy for its interactions with, and within, the institutions of the larger community. The carryover of kinship ties from the rural and agrarian settings of the eighteenth century to the urban and industrialized settings of large American communities in the nineteenth century served most families well. Kin acted as immigration agents, labor recruiters, and social supports for working-class persons moving from Europe to America, from the farm to industry, or from one industrial town to another. They offered the members of their group basic protections and economic support while on the move to the frontier or while establishing themselves in a new factory, a new business, or a new home.

Family was the most inviolable of upper-class institutions. Many of the best American families had resided in the same section of the country for hundreds of years. By the time of the Civil War, there was hardly a family of note that did not occupy at least the same social position that it had at the time of the founding of the colonies. Periodically, the family would gather, and cousins, aunts, and grandparents would trace the family tree from long before the Revolution. To maintain their high social position and authority, it was important for socially elite families to have a strong sense of obligation to their blood relatives.

In this regard, maternal uncles and aunts played an essential role of great trust. "A mother's trust that her [own] brothers and sisters would take care of the children in case of her death gave special significance to the role of the uncle and aunt." While uncles and aunts could be relied upon for monetary assistance, guidance, or support, their nieces or nephews need not be orphaned to call upon them. The extension of business and social influence to nephews was particularly evident at this time, but extenuating circumstances of many kinds could and did bring the influence of these relatives into play in terms of a tightly knit kinship network (Clinton 1982, 52–53).

Intermarriage between second and third cousins was common in the South because it perpetuated the family name, fortune, and bloodline. As women were not permitted to freely correspond with men except in the most formal of circumstances, it was possible for a susceptible young woman to trade the benevolence of a strict father for the exploitive control and abuse of a less forgiving husband. For this reason, many women favored cousin marriages where they were at least familiar with the personality of their prospective partner. However, the practice, though more common in Britain, was almost unheard of among Northern families. In a historical study of Southern and Northern families numbering 100 each, 12 percent of Southern marriages were between cousins while not a single case was found in the Northern sample. While such findings could be laid at the door of Southern clannishness, it should be remembered that many more Northern young people lived in cities and towns where they had opportunities to meet prospective mates unrelated to them by blood. Southern youth were largely isolated on widely scattered farms and plantations (Clinton 1982, 178).

With kinship came advantage and obligation. Birth into one of America's leading families was essential to making a political career almost everywhere. Social prominence, business and political influence, and the presumption of ability—whether it was present or not in an individual—were inherited from one's father or grandfather in much the same way that businesses, land, or slaves were inherited. Fathers expected their first-born male heirs to follow in their footsteps, and they were protective of their daughters providing their sons-in-law with influence, if not money. Granddaughters in similar circumstances were treated in much the same way, especially in the absence of a living father. Men were similarly solicitous of their nieces, daughters-in-law, and all their children. So pervasive was the assumption that kinship ruled that men were given positions as sheriffs, justices of the peace, militia captains, or county lieutenants by influential relatives without the slightest charge of favoritism being made by anyone in the system (Volo and Volo 2000, 157–58).

FAMILY LIFE

Household Structure

A husband and wife were considered one person in law in most states, and the very existence of the woman was often incorporated and consolidated into that of her husband. Until late in the nineteenth century, married women had little or no legal standing in the courts, could not sign enforceable contracts, and held no tangible assets in their own name in most states. The property brought to a marriage by the wife legally became that of her husband. Many widows disdained remarriage having in their bereavement finally found relief from the overbearing power of even the best of husbands and fathers. Nonetheless. in some states widows might lose their property rights to their adult sons, if not otherwise provided for by the will of their spouse. A widower with young children was expected to remarry for the sake of his motherless offspring if no appropriate female relation, such as an unmarried sister or aunt, was available to care for them.

Most nineteenth-century American households were clearly nuclear in structure and remarkably similar in size. Although this pattern varied slightly across urban, rural, and ethnic lines, the variations were minimal. Moreover, the household structure of many urban immigrants from Europe was also clearly nuclear, but they tended to show a greater extension in urban environments than in rural ones.

The family expanded and contracted at different stages of its life cycle, and the members of the household responded and reacted when the web-like strands of their individual life changes pulled at each other. As the years passed and the family life cycle lengthened, these familial ties tended to weaken or adjust. Within these variations, it is safe to say that 75 to 80 percent of households were clearly nuclear within the urban environment. A young married couple might live with their parents for a brief time until they found separate quarters but rarely would the arrangement continue beyond the birth of their first child. Once established in their own residence, these households rarely changed in composition. Among those newlyweds yet without children about one in five took in a relative or a boarder. Yet with the arrival of their first child, about half the households with relatives as lodgers expelled them. Ironically, the vast majority of such households did not expel their boarders (Glasco 1978, 178).

Native-born migrants, newly arrived in a city or frontier community, initially settled themselves as heads of nuclear households, or boarded temporarily in the homes of strangers. Research indicates that approximately 44 percent of newcomers to cities set up their own households directly upon arrival, and as few as 12 percent lived with blood relations. This leaves a sizeable group (also 44%) that needed to make other living arrangements in boarding houses, rooming houses, or commercial hotels. Many of these were single men or young women in the transitional stage between their parents' household and their own (Glasco 1978, 164–65).

Siblings in most households were treated in a hierarchical manner with all the male offspring being given a superior position over their sisters—a circumstance sometimes supported by state law. Nonetheless, sisters might exert great influence over their brothers, and a fluid and cooperative interaction between the children formed an important element of a happy household. A boisterous or selfish boy might try to dominate a weaker or more dependent girl, but "generally the latter exerted a softening, sweetening charm. The brother animated and heartened, the sister mollified, tamed, refined." Sisters were like the polished cornerstones of a temple, brothers the rough-hewn foundation stones (Haines and Yaggy 1876, 91).

It was noted that many men "passed unharmed through the temptations of youth, [owing] their escape from many dangers to the intimate companionship of affectionate and pure-minded sisters." A true gentlemen's character was formed to a great extent by the ladies with whom he associated before entering the adult world of business and society. Young men were more likely to refrain from mixing with the corrupting influences of unrefined friends and low society when they had sisters at home (Haines and Yaggy 1876, 70).

The inferior position of sisters among siblings implied an obligation that was placed upon brothers to defend their honor. This obligation was often extended to brotherless female cousins. Because young women were often thought of as "silly, senseless, thoughtless, giddy, vain, proud, frivolous, selfish, low and mean" and apt to make "an exhibition of [themselves]," a brother could intervene in the affairs of his sisters and their circle of friends with or without their permission (Haines and Yaggy 1876, 83). At times these brothers could take on a very combative stance, especially when dealing with a sister's reputation, and her outbreaks of passion and his unbridled impetuosity sometimes made their companionship uncongenial and drove them apart. Yet it was believed that the compensating power of a true friendship would ultimately draw them back together (Haines and Yaggy 1876, 78).

—*James M. Volo*

Vital Statistics

Some historians attribute the dominance of the nuclear family during this period to the consequences of industrialization or a trend toward female domesticity. Yet it has been established that this household structure had dominated not only in America, but in the Western world for more than 300 years.

Generally, in the decade of the 1860s the typical white, native-born women had seven or eight pregnancies during her childbearing years, and raised five or six children. Fully 95 percent of women were unmarried at age 20. This age seems to have been a temporal interface in women's lives. Almost 31 percent of all females born in 1830, 1850, 1870, respectively, failed to live to age 20. This proportion decreased for those born in the 1890s to approximately 26 percent. The majority of the survivors, where data is available, seem to have married at an average age of 20 years and given birth to their first child within one or two years. Nationally, about 10 to 12 percent of all women aged 20 to 24 were pregnant at any one time. In the 1860s, the median period of childbearing was about 10 years, and in the 1890s this had lengthened to somewhat longer than 11 years. All of these data remained remarkably stable throughout the second half of the nineteenth century (Wells 1979, 524).

White, immigrant women generally had higher fertility rates than their native-born counterparts, and second-generation immigrants usually evinced an intermediate level of fertility between that of their parents and that of the native population. It may also be assumed that birth rates everywhere were somewhat depressed by the interposition of the Civil War as they most surely were in New England between 1861 and 1865 (Bash 1979, 439).

Average white life expectancy at birth in 1850 sat at a remarkably low 39 years, and white infant mortality rates for 1850 at 217 per 1,000 were significantly worse than those of 1900. There are significant improvements seen when these data are compared to a decade later. Average white life expectancy at birth in 1860 sat at a still remarkably low 44 years, and white infant mortality rates for 1860 at 181 per 1,000. There is no reliable data for infant mortality or life expectancy for blacks until the early twentieth century, and most of the analysis of black birth rates in the previous century was focused on the question of deliberate slave breeding by white plantation owners rather than on the intentions of the black slave women who bore the children. Among slaves there were seemingly no income restraints to impinge upon a women becoming pregnant as the costs of care and maintenance of the expectant mother, and later the child, as well as health care and food for the family were generally assumed by the slave owners.

Blacks (from data beginning in 1850) sustained decreasing, but still higher, fertility and birth rates (eight or nine pregnancies and seven to eight children) than their white counterparts throughout the remainder of the nineteenth century. Enslaved women were generally shown some indulgence for three or four weeks previous to childbirth, and they were generally allowed four weeks after the birth of a child, before they were compelled to go into the field. Thereafter, they generally took their children with them while working. Most black slaves nursed for three years to naturally limit their fertility during the period of lactation. White women generally nursed for only two years.

—*James M. Volo*

Men

Throughout the nineteenth century men were the unequivocal masters of their households, but proper family men were expected to exhibit several personal qualities that would lead to a happy and well-ordered home. Among these were *competency*, *character*, *identity*, and *industry*. These traits were common benchmarks throughout the nineteenth century.

When a man took a wife, he was expected to provide for her (and their children) during the rest of his life in a manner similar to that in which he found her in her family home. Moreover, a man's economic endeavors, whether they be in the form of wages, investments, or business enterprises, had to be adequate enough to provide some ease and affluence in his old age or for his widow, if the occasion arose. Men looked for work that would provide their families with a comfortable subsistence and a maintenance of their social standing. Beyond this minimum level was an income that was often termed a certain competency of means that allowed for comfort and security if not wealth.

The 1850 census collected data only on real property, not income or wages. Detailing the actual dollar amounts considered an average competency in the decade before the war is therefore difficult. Yet it seems safe to say that in the 1850s men meant much the same by *competency* as their colonial forbearers—an income or degree of wealth sufficient to keep his family in a fashion equivalent to that of his neighbors during his life and off the public dole in the case of his demise. In August 1861, the federal government instituted an income tax law that provided additional information. The 1860 census and income tax figures (1861–1865) yield an average per capita income of $140 after base exemptions ($800 per family) and a progressive rate scale (5–10%) were taken into consideration (Randall and Donald 1961, 340). However, in this period men shared with women and children the task of producing the necessities of family life in this period, and what proportion of the family income was required of a father to prove his competency is unknown.

By *character* the nineteenth-century man meant his good reputation in terms of meeting his family, social, and business obligations. Many men's character and courage were sorely tested during the experiences of Civil War battle. A man's character, measured largely by his integrity, was thought to command the respect of all who knew him, or knew of him. While lesser men might succumb to evil appetites, men of character would triumph over difficulties and sail through perils. Circumstances like these tended to raise questions among more sober minds about the character and integrity of their fellows. The more philosophical among contemporary observers recoiled at such unfettered ambition and superficial rewards. "The men of our time seek too much for immediate results. They are too impatient for applause, honor and wealth.... They seek advancement through letters of recommendation and the influence of friends." Men of real merit and dignity, those who had a good heart and who loved virtuous action because it was right, were considered to have developed "the highest excellence" of character and integrity. Richard Henry Dana considered such a man a virtual paragon, "pure-minded, elevated, intellectual, religious, literary, accomplished in manners, just, humane, kind, polite, with a high degree of pride and reserves, yet truly modest" (Smith 1981, 783).

A cynical Timothy Titcomb, writing in 1861, believed that absolute integrity was a rarity among nineteenth-century Americans. "There are men in all communities who are believed to be honest, yet whose word is never taken as authority upon any subject." There was some "flaw or warp" in the perceptions of such men, "which prevents them from receiving truthful impressions. Everything comes to them distorted. [T]he moment their personality, or their personal interest, is involved, the fact[s] assume false proportions and false colors" (Titcomb 1861, 73–74).

All truth for Titcomb was tainted by the medium through which it passed, and that medium in the nineteenth century was self-interest, the personal vices of greed and alcoholism, and the scourges of sectionalism, slavery, and partisan politics. "It is possible for no man who owns a slave and finds profit in such ownership, to receive the truth touching the right of man to himself, and the moral wrong of slavery. . . . It is impossible for a people who have allowed pecuniary interest to deprave their moral sense to this extent, to perceive and receive any sound political truth, or to apprehend the spirit and temper of those who are opposed to them" (Titcomb 1861, 75).

Personal and public *identity* were an important part of nineteenth-century life. A man's identity—who he was in his own mind and the place that he occupied in the ultimate scheme of the world around him—was composed partly from his social position, partly from his religious affiliation, and partly from his chosen vocation. During the war the idea of public identity was quickly transferred to a man's position in the military infrastructure. Gentlemen were expected to serve as officers, and officers were always expected to behave as gentlemen. Men in the cavalry walked with a decided swagger; those in the artillery exuded an exacting confidence; and the infantry exhibited both the best and worst of the characteristics of a band of brothers. Each identified with his unit and was conscious of its reputation, battle honors, and his place within its corporate identify.

Finally, men were expected to possess the quality of *industry*, the mental and physical energy needed to meet the difficulties of a busy life and overcome them. This was often measured by his perseverance. Such industry gave men the impulse to accomplish every action or effort. A man possessing these qualities in the proper proportions was considered meritorious and worthy of the respect and esteem of his family and community (Haines and Yaggy 1876, 65–66).

The war adversely affected the ability of men to support their families, especially in the manpower-hungry South. Louisa Walton reported that her South Carolina had been thinned out of men by 1862, and Margaret Junkin Preston described Virginia as "a world of femininity" with a line of boys and octogenarians. In Shelby County, Alabama, 1,600 of the 1,800 male residents were in the army. Even before a single man had been killed, their absence had an effect on their families and the community at large. Many women were trying to do a man's business, managing businesses and farms, and working for wages for the first time. In some cases they seemed to have usurped their husbands' place. This situation created a gender crisis that transformed the roles of men and women during the war and may have had a destabilizing effect in its aftermath. With their means of making a living gone and their place in the community ripped asunder, Southern men were left with little more than their personal honor and unblemished character after the war. Unlike most Southern men, many Northerners avoided this confrontation, and came home with the sustaining knowledge of having fought the good fight and of having won the war.

A man was supposed to be masculine in his manner, his clothing, his interests, and his sentiments. Such traits were part of his true identity. Contemporary advisors produced a long list of personal attributes that were thought to be appropriate for the middle classes, but as the century wore on respectable persons increasingly valued those qualities that separated them further from the working classes. Among these were gender-neutral qualities such as obedience, virtue, thrift, or loyalty. However, some traits were thought to have a specific masculine or feminine quality: patience, kindness, affection, or sentimentality for women; honesty, industry, courage, and dedication to duty for men. As the business world expanded its sphere of influence, thrift, punctuality, attention to detail, cleverness, and a reserved manner became highly regarded as workplace attributes (Volo and Volo 2007, 47–53).

WOMEN

Civil War Wives

The wave of romanticism that swept the nation in the nineteenth century left its mark on more than literature and art. It raised love to an important, if not the most important, reason for selecting a mate. Certainly, some couples entered into marriage primarily for economic considerations or to please their parents, but increasingly, couples were drawn to make the commitment out of love. European visitors to the United States were struck by how different marriages were in America to those in Europe. Harriet Martineau, during her visit to the United States, observed that if there was any country on earth where the course of true love might be expected to run smoothly, it was America. It was a country where the troubles arising from conventional considerations of rank and connection were entirely absent.

American girls had greater liberty in the selection of a mate than their European counterparts. Certainly, some parents made strong attempts to influence a child's choice but advice manuals warned against it. Counseling mothers with regard to matrimonial speculations for their daughters, Lydia Marie Child bid them to leave the affections to nature and to truth, and all will end well. Young, single women were given far more latitude in their social interactions as well. European diarists were disconcerted by what they observed. While young women may have invited whom they wanted into their homes and couples were given privacy in the parlor or on the porch, there was generally someone within earshot.

The price of premarital sexual conduct among the upper classes—should it be detected—was just too great in terms of the social consequences that it engendered. Couples from the lower classes were less restricted in their romancing, and they were given greater freedom away from watchful eyes and ears.

While the chastity of the bride was always presumed, this was less likely to be the actual case outside the socially elite classes. Records often show significant numbers of early births and wedding night conceptions to couples that were married less than a year. These, of course, were mostly a convenient fiction. One Southern doctor—more frank than his colleagues—professed that, in his locale, illegitimate births among the poorer classes were as common as those born in wedlock.

Courtship and marriage were undergoing a number of changes during this time. Women were always expected to wait for the man's profession of love before she gave voice to her own. Convention prescribed that a young man first speak to the father of the young woman whom he desired to make his wife; but the reality, even among the upper classes, was that most couples had made their plans prior to the future groom's petition.

On this issue a period advice book for young women counseled that, when addressed by a gentleman on the subject of marriage, it was proper to give his proposal immediate and serious consideration. It was unnecessary to ask advice of anyone. Parents should be consulted out of filial respect, but it was she who was the one to decide. It was further advised that the young woman be sure that she was satisfied with the character of the man, and the degree of affection she had for him.

Once accepted, the marriage proposal was more binding on the man than on the woman. Social—and in some cases legal—consequences were imposed upon men who repudiated an engagement, yet it was acceptable for a woman to call it off. As a law student, George Cutler ruminated about a bride-to-be in his diary, noting that she had the liberty of violating her engagement in lieu of her power of choice, because the contract is so much more important in its consequences to females than to males. Women, he noted, subject themselves to the husband's authority. They depend upon their husband for their society, their happiness, the enjoyment of their lives, more than the man does upon the wife.

The proposal. Courtship in the 19th century was rather formal, and the steps taken in finding a spouse were not taken lightly. An engagement had the force of a legal contract between two people broken only by mutual consent only under the most pressing of circumstances. These included infidelity, adultery, dishonor, and failing economic circumstances. Courtesy Library of Congress.

As the century progressed, the general trend in weddings was toward larger and more elaborate ceremonies with greater focus on the couple than their parents. Beginning in the 1830s brides began wearing white gowns and veils made specifically for their wedding day. Prior to this women were usually married in their best dress, and many young women continued that practice for decades. Those fortunate enough to be able to afford such a specialized garment tended to wear dresses that might be considered plain by ballroom standards. Expense was more likely to be put into the fabric rather than the trim. Wedding dresses were essentially day dresses with jewel necklines and long sleeves. Headdresses and veils tended to lie flat on the head. Coronets of real or artificial flowers were arranged so that they framed the face.

Wedding ceremonies became more elaborate during this period particularly in cities and for those who could afford

A sample of high fashion to the ladies of New Orleans. Cartoon concerning Benjamin Butler's so-called "Woman Order," as military governor of New Orleans, to prevent local women from insulting U.S. soldiers, 1862. Courtesy Library of Congress.

the expense. By the second quarter of the century bridal parties were expanded to include multiple bridesmaids. The typical wedding party had one or two bridesmaids and groomsmen. During the first decade of the century, weddings were commonly held on Tuesday, Wednesday, or Thursday to accommodate the minister's busy Sabbath schedule. It had also been the custom for weddings to take place in the family parlor, but by the 1860s more couples were choosing to be married in a church that could accommodate a larger number of guests.

Elaborate wedding dinners and dancing usually followed the ceremony. These events were generally held at a hotel or at the bride's parents' house. From the 1830s on, middle-class couples sent out printed invitations to scores of guests, a custom that had been embraced by the upper class during the previous decade.

Wedding cake became the featured food item at these celebrations instead of the meats and pies served in previous times. The wedding cakes of the nineteenth century were usually rich fruitcakes similar to modern holiday cakes of the same name, and for many decades—even into the twentieth century—the topmost layer of wedding cake remained a fruitcake so that it could be saved for the couple's first anniversary. The groomsmen cut the cake, and the bridesmaids handed it around. In some places, the served pieces of cake were passed around the company in attendance three times for good luck.

Beginning in the 1840s, it became fashionable for both the man and the woman to wear engagement rings, and rings specifically designated as wedding rings began to be mentioned at about the same time. An etiquette book from 1846 counseled the bridegroom to procure a plain gold ring prior to the ceremony.

Wedding nomenclature also changed during this period. In the past, betrothals were announced in church—usually by the minister at some point during the Sabbath service. By the 1860s, however, couples began announcing their engagement themselves through letters to friends or in the local newspapers. Nonetheless, several religious groups—particularly the Roman Catholics—continued to post the traditional bans of marriage into the twentieth century. Newlywed couples no longer traveled with friends and relatives on their wedding tour, but went instead on a honeymoon. Honeymoons, thereafter, became a more private period for the couple than was previously the case. An etiquette book of the period advised that, following the ceremony, the couple should enjoy a honeymoon of repose, exempted from the claims of society. Popular honeymoon destinations included New York City, Niagara Falls, the Green Mountains of Vermont, Montmorenci Falls in Canada, and—in the Midwest—the city of Cincinnati (a new metropolis considered worthy of a visit).

Marriage was a far more crucial decision for a woman than for a man because she often had her own identity legally incorporated into that of her husband. Husbands were increasingly described as providers, and wives and minor children were identified as dependents. This dependency—whether real or imagined—had unfortunate consequences. The *Baltimore American and Commercial Daily Adviser* charged wives never to forget that a wife owes all her importance to that of her husband. Even familial nomenclature changed. Instead of calling the wife "Mistress," a title used to describe the woman's responsibility over servants, apprentices, and journeymen, she was now referred to as "Mrs." with her husband's name fully appended. Her given name was not used in the address. The wife's identity was totally absorbed by the husband. Many women authors even published as "Mrs. _____" without mention of her given name. Newspaper accounts would identify a woman as "Mrs. _____, wife of _____."

The event of marriage marked an important era in the life of a young female. One advice book warned that it devolved upon her a set of cares, duties, and responsibilities to which she has hitherto been unaccustomed. Many felt that the carefree and frivolous life that middle-class and affluent young women were allowed to enjoy in the nineteenth century ill-prepared them for the serious duties of being wives and mothers. Lydia Marie Child asserted that the bride was awakened from her delightful dream in which carpets, vases, white gloves, and pearl earrings are oddly jumbled up with her lover's looks and promises by the unpleasant conviction that cares devolve upon her.

So-called coveture laws in many states deprived married women of their legal rights. Married women did not have the right to acquire any property solely in their own name during marriage. They could not make contracts, transfer property, or bring a lawsuit. Their legal persona was totally overshadowed by that of their husbands. The 1848 women's property rights acts passed in New York State were a bellwether development in this regard, and they were amended in 1860 to provide even more rights for New York women. Late in the nineteenth century, women's rights to control their property were extended even further, but they did not reach full equality until the second half of the twentieth century. Ironically, women's property rights were often more closely protected in the Southern states where the maintenance of property and wealth within the family was considered of primary importance even in the face of the death or divorce of a spouse.

A wife had three major areas of responsibility. She was expected to obey and satisfy her husband; she was charged with keeping the children physically and morally healthy; and finally, she was accountable of the maintenance of the household. In an editorial entitled, "Advice to the Bride," Sarah Josepha Hale reminded the newlywed that her duty was submission to her husband who is, by the laws of God and of man, her superior and never to give him cause to remind her of it. Continuing her counsel, she advised the married woman to let her entire enjoyment center in her home and let her home occupy the first place in her thoughts for that is the only source of happiness.

In the nineteenth century, the home was the center of both family and society; and while the husband was the head of the household, the wife was the heart of the home. She was the essence of domesticity, a font of virtue and the quintessence of nature. The *American Woman's Home* (Beecher and Beecher Stowe, 2002) declared that the family state was the aptest earthly illustration of the heavenly kingdom, with women as its chief ministers. Newspaperman Wilber Fisk wrote that women carried civilization in their hearts and men who lived in the privileges of female society became more refined. Women were considered central to good social order. A Connecticut soldier wrote of military life during the Civil War that there was no society in the camps because there was nothing but men.

This divergence of male and female obligations in a marriage was a major change from previous centuries when home and work were less distinct. Men and women in colonial times spent most of their time living and working side-by-side. It was common for the wife of a shopkeeper or tradesman to work with her spouse in the retail establishment. The wife of a weaver might wind the quills for him. A farmer's wife would help at critical times such as planting or harvest. The daily routines and tasks of a husband and a wife might have been very distinct, but they worked toward a common goal, the well-being of the family. She could cross over into her husband's world without staking claim to it. In the nineteenth century this relationship changed drastically. Only on the farm did it retain much of its traditional form. Industrialization increasingly drew husbands away from the home to work in towns and cities. The nature and manner of their work became foreign to their wives, who remained at home isolated from the immediate pressures of the business world. In fact, wives were cautioned never to be curious and pry into their husband's concerns.

This physical separation of the household and workplace helped to bring about a new concept of the family and family roles. Men went to work, and women stayed at home. The midday meal—where the entire family had taken a respite from their duties to gather together in the shop or in the fields—was replaced by an evening meal consumed in increasing formality. Even farm families adopted a more distinct gender division of labor. Jobs that farm wives would have done in prior centuries were being done by hired hands.

Free of many of the time-consuming drudgeries of home production, middle-class women began to define their roles in terms of nurturing and childrearing. The average home no longer housed a productive economic unit and subset of a larger community, which provided the physical needs of its residents. It now served as the base for the intellectual and emotional needs of the family, and became a sanctuary and refuge from the community. Such levels of privacy were particularly important to middle-class families whose level of wealth failed to insulate them from the seamier realities of urban life.

The public sphere was thought to be too harsh for a woman. It was full of temptations, violence, and distress. A woman's place was thought to be in the private sphere of the home where she could be protected from the harsh realities of the world. Women's magazines, religious tracts, advice books, and novels all described this new ideal of womanhood and the home. Referred to as the *Cult of Domesticity*, this ideology redefined a woman's duty and prescribed a set of virtues that all proper women should cultivate. Nineteenth-century women were expected to uphold values of stability, morality, and republican order by making the home a safe haven from an immoral world. Women were expected to be pure, pious, submissive, and domestic. Feminine purity was highly revered, and any mention of female sexuality became taboo.

Religion was seen as a remedy for the potentially restless feminine spirit. It would guide women to accept their role as handmaidens of the Lord, who would help to bring the world out of sin. This new role for woman was largely a response to the Second Great Awakening, a religious movement that swept the nation during the early nineteenth century. The clergy promoted women by praising their moral virtue. Soon the press took up the cry, anointing women as the moral guardians of society. The proliferation of newspapers, magazines, and books that characterized the period abound with moralistic stories and editorials that reinforced women's role as society's moral compass.

Mothers, pastors, and advice books advised acquiescence to a husband. She should try to learn her husband's feelings and view of things and endeavor to conform to them. She should make him her counselor on all occasions and her confident. An advice book proffered that the one quality on which woman's value and influence depended was the renunciation of self. Rev. Daniel C. Eddy in his 1859 work, *The Young Woman's Friend; or the Duties, Trials, Lives and Hopes of Woman*, was more specific, saying that a wife's pleasures will all bend to her husband's business. Women were counseled to give their husbands what they wanted and to make as few demands as possible upon them.

Family developed very differently for the urban working class, and the concept of cooperative family work from prior centuries persisted for them even as that of the social elites evolved. Very few families were able to achieve the middle-class ideal of the husband as sole breadwinner and provider. Older children were expected to remain at home longer and to contribute to the household income. Wives took on additional domestic burdens such as sewing, doing laundry, or taking in boarders to earn money. Increasing financial pressures took their toll. Husbands often worked hours that prohibited them from eating at the same time as their children. Mothers were sometimes forced to send the children out to play in the streets so that their fathers could rest in the cramped quarters of their apartment. Some men left home for extended periods of time working at higher-paying jobs that were far away.

While unmarried American women enjoyed a greater freedom of social interaction than their European counterparts, once they entered into marriage, they were subject to strict rules of deportment, manners, and dress. More restraint was imposed upon married women. Rarely were the matrons foremost in the community events. They attended, as observant and influencing members of society, but not as the principal actors. Married women were so totally sheltered from public life that in the previous half century they were often absent from holiday festivities such as the Fourth of July when military musters and all male parades were the hallmark of annual communal celebration. By mid-century, women could be seen on porches, balconies, or on special stands waving and cheering, but they were not included in the parade even though young unmarried women could be seen on the floats. New holidays like Thanksgiving and a more secularized Christmas that centered on the home began to become popular.

One activity outside the home open to women of the upper classes was visiting (calling). In addition to its recreational value, calling was a required social function that was strictly governed by convention. Visiting not only upheld a woman's social position, it enhanced that of her husband. Ceremonial calls were to be kept brief. Half an hour amply sufficed for a visit of ceremony. Upon exiting, the caller would leave a card, which would be placed in a cardholder kept in the front hall for that purpose. The distribution of cards allowed a woman to keep up a ceremonious acquaintance within a social circle too large for friendly visiting as that consumed far more time than could be given to the number of persons with which she had to be acquainted.

Socially conscious women kept a list of family members and business acquaintances that formed a basic calling circle. It would be expected that persons on this list would be visited at least twice a year. Failure to reciprocate would be considered a grievous slight. Brides were kept particularly busy making rounds as they introduced themselves in their new social position. Women were reminded that it was the custom for a wife to take her husband's cards with her, and to leave one or two with her own.

Another acceptable activity outside the home was philanthropy and social activism. Women, who were financially able to free themselves from household toil through the use of domestic servants, often dedicated time to organizations that helped the old, the poor, or those considered socially distressed. Even less affluent women visited invalids and tended to the sick. Prior to the Civil War, charitable endeavors were usually limited to neighbors within a community, but during the war there was a great movement to reach out to those in need.

Women collected clothing and sewed for the urban poor and western Indians. Some women ventured into urban ghettos to personally help in the missions. Others, less comfortable outside the home, raised money to hire workers who would carry out these good works. Louisa May Alcott worked in such a capacity at a Boston mission collecting clothing, teaching sewing, distributing food to immigrants, and conducting a school for black children. A group of free black women advertised in 1847 that they were giving a fair for benevolent purposes. They gave notice that all the delicacies of the season will be served up in the most palatable style including ice creams, cakes, lemonades, jellies, fruits, nuts, and such.

Some women became involved in social reform movements such as temperance, women's rights, abolition, prison reform, and child protection. Women conducted prayer meetings in front of bordellos. They marched in the streets advocating temperance, even occasionally breaking up saloons. After a young man was killed in a bar in Ohio, a large number of respectable ladies of the town, accompanied by the bereaved mother, proceeded to the saloon and with axes and other weapons knocked in the heads of barrels and casks, and demolished bottles and fixtures.

The abolition movement received tremendous financial support from money raised by women at antislavery fairs. Women made scarves, doilies, and needlework bags with antislavery messages such as, "May the points of our needles prick the slaveholders' consciences." They sold pen wipers exhorting "Wipe out the blot of slavery." Lydia Child made a cradle quilt embroidered with the words "Think of the Negro mother when her child was torn away" (Volo and Volo 2007, 222).

Involvement in reform causes permitted women to have a social standing outside of the home. These reform activities were socially acceptable because, in essence, they were an extension of a woman's nurturing role. The Beecher sisters (Catharine and Harriet) explained that woman's great mission was self-denial and self-sacrificing labors for the ignorant and weak: if not her own children, then the neglected children of her Father in heaven. They urged women to help the orphan, the sick, the homeless, and the sinful, and by motherly devotion train them to follow Christ, in educating his earthly children for true happiness in this life and for his eternal home. A period advice book for young women encouraged such involvement, saying that women would fulfill their own high and lofty mission precisely because the manifestation of such a spirit was the one thing needful for the regeneration of society. It was from her being the depository and disseminator of such a spirit, that woman's influence was principally derived. Involvement strengthened the bond of womanhood among the matrons of the community, served as an example for unwed females, and breached the isolation of the home. These activities gave women the strength to organize and to exert their influence. Ultimately, the church groups, aid societies, charitable leagues, and antislavery and temperance organizations laid the foundation for women to make the move into public life and careers in the following century (Volo and Volo 2007, 223).

Women's Response to War

When the Civil War began, Northern and Southern women had similar responses to the call to arms. They attended meetings to proclaim their allegiance (to the Union or the Confederacy), pledged to roll bandages, and made clothing and flags for the soldiers. The Northern women's efforts soon mushroomed into a national organization called the United States Sanitary Commission, which played a major role in providing food and medical supplies to the federal troops. Alfred Bloor of the Sanitary Commission credited women saying that almost all the supplies amassed by the organization were collected, assorted, and dispatched, and re-collected, re-assorted, and re-dispatched to the battlefield by women representing every level of society in the Republic.

This cover from *Harper's Weekly* from June 29, 1861, depicts one of the many roles played by women during the Civil War. Courtesy Library of Congress.

Women's groups raised money not only for soldiers but also for their orphans and widows. One method of raising money was the charity cookbook in which women compiled favorite recipes into books and published them. The first such books appeared in the Civil War. Bearing such lengthy and intriguing titles as, *The Massachusetts Woman's Temperance Union Cuisine* and *The Parish Cookery Book of the Ladies Aid Society of Saint Peter's Church*. Charity or community cookbooks continued in the postwar years as popular fundraisers to support causes that were religious, political, or local.

The Civil War placed the institution of the family under siege. Economic shortages, strained agricultural productivity, and social upheaval beset civilians in various forms. Many women managed to stand apart from the war and cope with its vagaries while trying to preserve some semblance of their social order, standard of living, and values. Thus, even though the war might rage at their very doorsteps, the women lived through it and many in spite of it (Volo and Volo 1998, 189).

Women on the homefront sewed socks, pants, and shirts for needy soldiers. At way stations and refreshment saloons, civilians distributed food and clothing to soldiers traveling toward the front lines. More than 3,000 women served as nurses in army hospitals, an otherwise traditional male occupation. Female nurses won praise from their soldier patients, despite enduring criticism from many doctors jealous of their professional territory (Browne and Kreiser 2003, 11).

The U.S. Sanitary Commission donated $15 million worth of various supplies to comfort soldiers ranging from medicine and clothing to writing paper and stamps. Kitchens staffed with dietary nurses were established by the Sanitary Commission in 1862 largely as a result of the efforts of Annie Wittenmyer. She worked very hard to see that a system was developed to feed wounded soldiers in field hospitals. Women volunteers had been scrounging milk, eggs, and vegetables for the wounded who were too ill to eat the standard pork and beans field ration. Wittenmyer's system established the means for providing appropriate meals for the men (Volo and Volo 1998, 235). Similar efforts in Southern communities were unable to match the organization and productivity of the North. Southerners were equally sympathetic to the plight of their soldiers, but the South lacked the efficient transportation and resources necessary for mounting matching endeavors (Browne and Kreiser 2003, 11). Much of the care for convalescing Confederates was given at home by their female relations. Those too badly wounded to make the journey were left to the charitable care of local women who volunteered their parlors, hallways, and barns as makeshift hospitals.

The blockade and the resulting interruptions in trade caused great hardships for many Southern women who had once been the most fashionable element of the population. Inflation was rampant. Nonetheless, by drawing upon their resourcefulness and creativity, Southern women managed to rework prewar finery and make use of natural materials. Some Southern ladies continued to dress and to dance in whatever prewar style they could manage as a means of keeping up their courage. With Yankee gunboats anchored off Baton Rouge and Union troops occupying the city, Sarah Morgan rationalized that if Southern women each took a fancy to consider themselves the most miserable of mortals, and acted accordingly, going about with their eyes streaming, groaning over their troubles, and never ceasing to mourn, the world would be an even worse place. Better days were coming, she asserted, even if most of her female friends didn't really believe it (Volo and Volo 1998, 241–42).

Receipt books and newspapers carried suggestions for dealing with the food shortages. When successful replacements were discovered, the revelation was readily disclosed to the public in print and by word of mouth. Coffee was a popular beverage, and the blockade made it very difficult to procure. Parthenia Hague wrote that one of their most difficult tasks was to find a good substitute for coffee. Coffee quickly rose to $30 per pound; from that it went to $60 and then to $70 per pound. Good workmen received $30 per day; so it took two days' hard labor to buy one pound of coffee, and scarcely any could be had at that fabulous price.

Northern and Southern women attempted to adjust as best as possible to the extended absences of husbands and fathers. The task was more difficult in the Confederacy. Southern women had to cope with the threat of slave insurrection and northern invasion, all while raising their children and running their households. After watching her brothers depart for the war, Kate Stone speculated that those who stayed home would find it harder than those who left (Browne and Kreiser 2003, 11).

Additional hardships were caused by raids of Northern troops upon individual homes. Mary S. Mallard remembered hearing the clash of arms and noise of horsemen late one afternoon. By the time she and her mother got downstairs, they saw 40 or 50 men in the pantry, flying hither and thither, ripping open the cheese and pie safe with their swords and breaking open the crockery cupboards. Fearing they might not have a chance to cook, her mother had some chickens and ducks roasted and put aside for the family. The men seized them whole, tearing them to pieces with their teeth like ravenous beasts. They clamored for whiskey, and ordered the older woman to open her locked pantry, whereby they took every particle of meal and flour they had. The men threw the sacks across their horses. The older woman remonstrated and pointed to her helpless family but their only reply was: "We'll take it!" (Volo and Volo 1998, 231).

Many Confederate women rallied enthusiastically behind the war effort, withstanding ever-present daily hardships and worry over the fate of their loved ones in uniform. Yet many other women questioned the need for continued self-sacrifice, especially as the Confederacy lurched closer and closer toward an obvious military defeat. After Union forces captured Atlanta during the fall of 1864, Gertrude Thomas asked herself if she was willing to give her husband to regain the Georgia city for the Confederacy. Her answer was a resounding, "No, No, No, a thousand times No!" Another woman felt compelled to express her displeasure directly to Confederate President Jefferson Davis after her second son entered the military. She declared her devotion to her country; acknowledged the sacrifices she had already made; and pledged to make more if necessary. But she pleaded that her eldest boy might find it harder to be left behind than those who went to fight. A North Carolina mother wrote no less passionately to her son during the last winter of the war begging him to tell them all to stop fighting and come home to live. "I want you all to come home," she pleaded (Browne and Kreiser 2003, 11–12).

—Dorothy Denneen Volo

CHILDREN

Children: 1855–1865

Throughout much of the nineteenth century, children were viewed as guileless creatures with a propensity to mischief. Parents were told that with discipline, reason, and love they could produce a child of good character. They were encouraged to toilet train their children early, for if children learned control of their bodies, they would achieve discipline of mind and spirit. Parenting became a very conscious process. Self-discipline was an important characteristic at this time, and children were expected to develop an active conscience and a propensity for introspection.

Childhood was seen as a period of guardianship—free from the harsh realities of the world and increasingly devoted to training, schooling, and preparation for life. Children were protected from the adult worlds of death, profanity, and sexuality. This attitude grew out of evangelical changes that called upon parents to take the innocent souls of their children and turn them toward God. It was further enhanced by a growing spirit of romanticism, which viewed children as symbols of purity and innocence. They were seen as fonts of spontaneity, expressiveness and intuition. This idealization of childhood could be seen in John Greenleaf Whittier's nostalgic poem, "The Barefoot Boy" (1855).

The bond between siblings was idealized as well. This relationship was seen as the most innocent and longest lasting of all social relationships. With birthrates declining among the middle and upper classes, children were closer in age, and they remained home longer, thus giving sibling relationships time to develop more intensely than in the previous century. Same-sex siblings commonly slept in the same room and frequently in the same bed. Parents encouraged strong sibling bonds instilling in their children the belief that they had an obligation to look out for their brothers and sisters. Children were encouraged to play with their siblings or with their cousins.

During the first half of the century, middle-class childhood had come to be recognized as its own separate stage of life with clothing, furniture, literature, and social activities developed specifically for children. Small children were placed in specially designed high chairs that could be brought to the table so that they might comfortably dine with the rest of the family. Urban middle-class mothers began to assume the exclusive responsibility for raising their children as fathers spent a large portion of the day away from the home while at work. It was up to her to provide the proper environment during the child's early years. The family circle provided children with the nurturing and protection they required. Children were often affectionately referred to in such endearingly innocent terms as "kitten," "lamb," or "pet." Baby talk—frowned upon in former times as damaging to proper child development—not only became acceptable, it was thought to be endearing.

By comparison to former times, childhood dependency became prolonged, and children often remained in the parental home until their twenties. Childrearing became a more conscious and intensive activity. Instructional books such as Lydia Marie Child's *The Mother's Book* (1831) became popular guides for mothers who wanted to do the best job of raising her children. In 1860 the first outpatient clinic for children was established. Doctors began to specialize in the care of children. Dr. Abraham Jacobi, considered the father of pediatrics in America, was the first physician in the United States to devote his practice solely to the care of children. He performed emergency surgery on more than 2,500 children dying of a blocked windpipe, a complication of diphtheria.

Despite the indulgences some parents may have bestowed upon their progeny, children were always expected to exhibit good behavior, to display profound respect for their parents, and to respond with prompt obedience. A writer in an 1865 newspaper was even stronger with his advice that first and most important of all lessons to be taught was obedience. He opined that the success in inculcating this lesson depends upon the future character of the child and without obedience to authority no moral virtue could be secured.

From a very young age children were encouraged to participate in the popular social causes of the period. Children's books contained messages suggesting that money, which they spent for useless toys, might be given to the poor and that many a tear would be dried up for it. Children were involved in helping the poor, and during the Civil War they were encouraged to bring comfort to the soldiers. They collected books for soldiers and raised money for soldier's homes and hospitals. Girls knitted mittens, rolled bandages, and scraped away at the linen to make fluffy piles of the soft lint that was used to pack the soldiers' wounds. Children also executed fairs for good causes. They would make bookmarks, pen wipers, thimble boxes, pincushions, and other small items, which were sold at church fairs. These items were also supplemented by the sale of apples and candy. Funds raised from the sale of these items would be used for orphans or the needy.

Reform newspapers like the *Advocate and Family Guardian* carried letters from children who donated money to a children's home. Two children sent the money they were awarded by their foster parents for going without butter for 100 days. Another sent a dollar explaining that he did not wish to spend it for candy or playthings when there are so many little children who have no food to eat or clothes to wear. Some of the donations came as commodities. One pair of siblings had been given a corner of their father's garden to tend over the summer. At their mother's suggestion they sent the fruits of their harvest, dried corn, popcorn, and beans, to the Children's Home.

Parents wanted to protect their children from the temptations and contaminations of the outside world. They wanted to provide their children with a safe, pure, and nurturing environment in which to grow. Families who could afford it had a nursery for the children. The dedication of a room or rooms for children reflected the importance placed upon childhood. The nursery provided a retreat where children could be protected and where they would receive a controlled exposure to the world. It could limit and direct the stimulations a child received and might hopefully protect him or her from the accidents and disease that claimed so many children. Modest households had a single nursery room often found on the third floor of the home. Although children of the same sex often shared a bedroom in their early years, the plan book ideal was that, if possible, each child should have a separate room. Affluent households could afford both day nurseries for play and night nurseries for slumber. Furniture, painted in pastels and decorated with baby animals and characters from nursery rhymes, was produced in child-sized proportions.

Day nurseries were playrooms that also often doubled as schoolrooms for those children who were taught by the governess. In such cases, they would also contain globes, maps, and perhaps a blackboard as needed for instruction. These rooms were designed to withstand the abuse that children can sometimes inflict on furnishings. Walls were often whitewashed. Curtains were simple. There would be a table with several chairs. These might be simple pine furniture bought for the purpose or cast-off furniture from other rooms. There were shelves and cupboards for books and toys and perhaps an armchair or two. The children of more affluent families enjoyed a greater degree of privacy in the home than their farming or working-class counterparts. They spent most of their time in their nursery away from their parents but kept safe by their isolation. Poorer children, on the other hand, enjoyed more parental supervision and interaction inside the home, but they also had a great deal more autonomy outside where much of their play took place.

Once lessons were done and chores completed, children's remaining hours were free to be devoted to play and exploration of the world around them. Once seen as a youthful manifestation of innate wickedness, vigorous play was now viewed as a natural part of childhood and a vehicle to help children develop skills and to teach them usefulness and virtue. Writing about creating a happy home for children, C. C. North advised that little children cease to be troublesome when amply supplied with toys, pictures, drawing-books, slates, hobby-horses, and such for indoors; and hoops, jumping-ropes, swings, and such for outdoors. For the country, he suggested little spades, hoes, barrows, and rakes.

The availability of playthings varied widely with social class. Manufacturing increased the number of store-bought toys and board games that were available to those who could afford them. Working-class and farm children played with simple, homemade toys—usually whatever a loving father might carve from a piece of wood by a winter's fire or what a mother might fashion from her bag of material scraps. Children, too, were resourceful. Jacks might be made from corn kernels, dolls from cornhusks, a tea set from discarded pieces of crockery. Even lower-class children had some exposure to simple commercially produced toys. Dolls with papier-mâché heads or those made from fabric were affordable for even poorer children.

The Civil War involved the entire population in a way paralleled by no other conflict since the Revolution. Photographs of war dead and almost instantaneous reports from the front by telegraph made the war years difficult for both parents and children. In imitation of the news headlines, children played at soldiers and held mock parades, drills, and skirmishes. Margaret Junkin Preston, a Virginia mother, wrote that her children's entire sets of plays were referenced to a state of war. She reported that her five-year-old, George, got sticks and hobbled about, saying that he lost a leg at the second battle of Manassas and told stories of how he cut off Yankees' heads and bayoneted them. Future president Theodore Roosevelt, who had two uncles who fought for the Confederacy, enjoyed playing "Running the Blockade" when he was seven. Lilly Martin Spencer's painting, *War Spirit at Home*, shows three children marching about

War Spirit at Home by Lilly Martin Spencer (1822–1902). The Newark Museum/Art Resource, NY.

while beating a pot and blowing a horn as their mother reads to them the newspaper account of the battle of Vicksburg (Lothrop 1968, 51).

Play was forbidden between Sabbath service and Sunday school almost everywhere and especially in New England. The day was particularly rigorous for children. Emily Wilson recalled that Sunday was not like any other day. Long church services with Sunday school in between were inevitable. The children did not play games nor read the same books. They did not take long walks nor use the family horse and carriage except to visit the graveyard, or occasionally to attend a prayer meeting.

Children were only allowed to read or to listen to the Bible or other religious literature on the Sabbath. All toys were put away except those that were considered of a religious or moral nature, and these were called Sabbath toys. One such plaything was a Noah's Ark. Sets varied, but they all contained a boat, Noah and his wife, an assortment of pairs of animals, and a dove. More extensive sets included Ham, Shem, Japheth, and their wives. Some had scores of animal pairs numbering as many as 100. Noah's Ark toys date back to the late seventeenth century but reached a peak during the Victorian era. Bible stories inspired other toys as well. Jacob's Ladder, made of six thin wooden rectangles connected by a cloth tape, was roughly reminiscent of a ladder. When held vertically and released, it created the illusion of tumbling blocks. The blocks were often covered with biblical scenes. The Wolf in Sheep's Clothing was a small wooden wolf hidden within a removable fleece. The Pillars of Solomon had two pillars connected with a string, which when cut, maintained the illusion that the pillars were still attached. Some doll play was permitted. Termed "church dolls," these figures could be assembled as a congregation to whom the child delivered a sermon. Some came with tiny carved coffins in which the corpse could be placed. Puzzle maps of Palestine (the Holy Land) were also considered appropriate (Volo and Volo 2007, 269).

The growing consumerism and mass production made middle-class children, in particular, the direct beneficiaries of their family's more privileged social position, and they were the first generation outside the social elite to enjoy mass-produced toys and games. Unlike children from earlier times, they were largely protected from the outside world and kept secure in a home where childhood was celebrated as a stage of life full of innocence and purity. In these homes, children's labor was not a necessity. Although they were expected to be of assistance to their family, the purpose of their household chores was to instill good habits and to teach lessons of personal responsibility. Girls were expected to sew and mend for practical purposes, but they were also expected to practice embroidery and other decorative needle arts.

For farming and working-class families, however, the situation regarding child labor was very different. The growing market economy put tremendous stress on both groups. Farmers—fathers, mothers, and children—worked together through necessity, and most boys from mining, lumbering, and seafaring communities followed their fathers into the mines, the forests, or aboard ship. They had done so for generations. What was new was that many children from manufacturing regions now entered the impersonal environment of the factory rather than an apprenticeship with a local master. The factory, unlike the shop, left the child with no skill, no trade, no place in the community—only the memory of mind numbing hours of repetitive drudgery. Yet by comparison the factory or mill paid well for youthful labor, and the value of the income of even young children (8-, 10-, or 12-year-old boys and girls) was often an essential part of a family's economic health. Children's earnings often amounted to 20 percent of the family's total income, and it was not unusual for teenage boys to earn more than their fathers.

Children who grew up on farms had always been expected to contribute to the family's productivity. A children's story about a 10-year-old farm girl had her beating up the beds and making tidy the upper rooms, scouring the knives, darning great holes in stockings, digging for parsnips, sewing, learning to milk cows, feeding chickens, and doing things that were disagreeable to an older person. Small children helped with simple, unskilled tasks, and their work increased in difficulty as they grew in size and skill. Ellen Chapman Rollins remembered that in mid-century New England, the driving of cows to pasture passed by rotation from one child to another and that both boys and girls worked among the sheaves in the field.

Girls were often employed in tasks related to the production and mending of clothing. They were taught the carding and spinning of wool at a young age and took up knitting as soon as they could hold and manipulate the needles. Children as young as four could knit stockings. By age six girls, and some boys as well, were making important contributions to the family's supply of stockings and mittens. Girls also helped to process food for either immediate consumption or preservation. Even very young children could snap the ends off beans or husk corn. Churning butter was another task that could be performed by children. The process was boring but uncomplicated.

Boys were never without work due to the endless need for firewood and water, and they were expected to give regular care to the livestock. Many of their duties were out-of-doors. Help was needed with farm chores in any season. Work continued throughout the cold weeks of winter with the gathering of logs for firewood and fencing materials. Feeding and watering the animals generally fell to the boys of the household. They were also expected to guard the livestock in the pasture. They helped with preparing the fields for planting and sewing the seeds in the furrows. At harvest they helped gather in the crops. Boys hunted and fished; and, while this may have some recreational value for them, the food these activities provided was a welcome and, sometimes, necessary addition to the table or the larder.

Maple sugaring heralded the arrival of spring, and all hands were needed to execute this great labor. Boys joined adult males as they spent several nights in the sugar camp set up in the woods among the last of the winter snows. Surely this must have been an exciting time for the boys with the teams dragging the sugar sledge from tree to tree and the maple-scented smoke of the fires filling the forests. The boys collected sap buckets and helped to process the tremendous volume of wood needed to maintain the fires under the huge sugar pots as they boiled off the syrup.

All farm children were engaged in harvesting and weeding the household or kitchen garden, gathering nuts, collecting eggs, and picking berries. Even the very young were given pails or baskets and were taken by older siblings to gather berries. Some entrepreneurial youngsters would gather wild cherries, known as choke cherries, and sell them. These were used for making cherry rum or cherry bounce.

A good size tree would yield approximately six bushels. Young boys often used spare time, particularly in winter to make birch splinter brooms, which could be sold to storekeepers. Older children would lend a hand in making hay—gathering and collecting the bundles of sweet smelling grass into stacks or driving the hay wagon from field to barn.

Employing children in laborious tasks was a necessity in a time when farm families had to compete in an increasingly industrialized economy. After her father died, Lucy Larcom's mother decided to move to the city and set up a boarding house. Lucy wrote that the change involved a great deal of work. Boarders signified a large house, with many beds. Piles of sewing accumulated and even the child had to take their part. Larcom recalled that the seams of those sheets did look to her as if they were miles long! Describing a New Hampshire farm family, Louisa May Alcott wrote that there were no servants, the little daughters were the only maids, and the stout boys helped their father, all working happily together with no wages but love, learning in the best manner the use of the heads and hands with which they were to make their own way in the world. Many rural parents believed that it was these life skills, which their children would need to maintain their own families, that were more important than reading and writing. Rural children attended school for shorter periods of time during the year and for fewer years than urban children.

The loss of male family members and farm workers to the Civil War increased the burdens already sustained by the farming families. The Confederacy was the first to initiate a mandatory draft that removed many poor white farmer workers from the soil, but exempted many of the trades and slave owners with more than 20 slaves. The federal government followed with its own draft that also exempted tradesmen and mechanics, which made conscription more likely for the unemployed immigrant populations of the cities. This left lower-class farm families at a distinct manpower disadvantage, and brought forth in many quarters accusations of "Rich man's war, Poor man's fight!" Children were forced to fill the need for labor. At age 12 Marion Drury had to assume the work and responsibilities of a man because most of the farmhands had gone into the army. Anna Shaw was only 14 when she took on her father and brothers' jobs, clearing fields and teaching school in addition to her sewing, cleaning, and tending boarders. At 15 Helen Brock was branding calves and erecting fences, and Fannie Eisele began to plow the family fields when she was only 10 years old (Volo and Volo 2007, 319).

Newspapers offered employment to many city boys. Newsboys were first employed in 1833 to hawk the penny paper dailies, whose low price made selling them through traditional adult conduits financially unfeasible. Newsboys bought papers at a small discount early in the morning and were unable to return unsold copies. Johnny Morrow's memoirs give insight to the finances of the trade. He had 56 papers for his morning's stock, for which he paid 84 cents. If sales totaled $1.12, leaving him a profit of 28 cents, 9 cents were spent for breakfast, and he had 19 cents to spare. As profits accrued only after they had covered their initial investment, successful newsboys turned into clever businessmen who assessed the weather and the events of the day prior to purchasing their day's stock. The *First Annual Report of the Children's Aid Society* in 1860 called them the "shrewdest and sharpest" of street children. The headline cries of the newspaper boys soon became an integral part of the sounds of the city.

While some of these street-wise entrepreneurs had families, many newsboys were orphans, actually or in effect, having been abandoned by their parents. Those who had no homes found shelter in the alleys and back streets, fighting for warm spots around grated vent-holes that let out the heat and steam from the underground pressrooms. Others went to live in one of a number of Newsboys' Lodging Houses that were set up in several cities to provide shelter and safety for the lads. Additionally, they offered the lads classes in reading and writing. The path to refinement was likely to have been a difficult one. The *Second Annual Report on the Children's Aid Society* (1884) reported that the newsboys were then apparently the most wild and vicious set of lads in New York City. Their money, which was easily earned, was more quickly spent in gambling, theaters, and low pleasures, for which, though children, they had a man's aptitude. The superintendent of the Newsboys' Lodging House in New York acknowledged that although its arrangements were popular with the boys, the temptations of a street life to such boys, and its excitements were so strong, that it was exceedingly difficult to get them in and induce them to stay. The boys were free to come and go in the lodging houses as long as they behaved. It was like a hotel and, as such, the boys were asked to pay a small amount for their bed and their meals (Volo and Volo 2007, 327).

—*Dorothy Denneen Volo*

Soldiers' Orphans

The death of over 600,000 men in the Civil War left many children fatherless, and the high incidence of death among young women of childbearing years made many so-called full orphans having no living parent whatsoever. Other parentless children—half orphans—had mothers (or fathers) who simply could not afford to work while paying for someone to watch over the children and still put food on the table. Many orphaned children found homes with relatives; others relied on community aid; and still others had to fend for themselves on the streets.

It is estimated that up to 2,700 children were orphaned by the Civil War in Pennsylvania alone, and Ohio had 2,300 more made orphans by the war. Orphanage records are often incomplete or missing, but there may have been 20,000 to 30,000 soldiers' orphans nationwide. The breadth of the problem can be estimated by the reaction to it, which seemingly peaked in July 1863 after the Battle of Gettysburg.

Many states dealt with the orphan crisis by erecting new institutions, or enlisting existing orphanages, asylums, and elder care institutions to look after the children of fallen soldiers. Nine northern states—Ohio, New Jersey, Pennsylvania, Illinois, Indiana, Iowa, Kansas, Wisconsin, and Minnesota—founded state-run soldiers' orphans homes. Other states relied on a large number of preexisting and privately funded institutions. In all, Americans built as many orphanages—both public and private—in the 1860s as the nation had founded in the two decades prior to the war. In addition many older institutions were pressed into service to meet the need. These were essentially the only recourse for orphans in the former Confederate states because Southern communities were largely destitute of money and materials for such humanitarian endeavors. The total number of soldiers' orphans in the former Confederate states can only be surmised when compared to the less than complete records found in the North. It is certain that the war created thousands of full- and half-orphans in the South who were suddenly thrust upon a society ill-equipped to care for them. Many of these orphaned and displaced children were forced to find refuge in poorhouses, reformatories, and prisons (Reef 2005, 76).

War widows with children often tried to cope with the situation faced by their fatherless brood, and the federal government began to award pensions to the widows of federal soldiers and sailors as early as July 1862. Yet the wife of a private soldier received only $8 per month without regard to the number of her children. This was the same pension given to wounded men disabled in the war, but it was simply not enough. Many single parents were forced to place some or all of their children into institutional care. In 1866, Congress increased the monthly payment by adding $2 for each child under the age of 16. This left a gap in the federal safety net for those orphans who had no parent to make or receive the claim. Two years later Congress extended the $2 monthly payment directly to children under 16. Southern widows and orphans, lacking any government intervention, relied on family or local care and generosity (Reef 2005, 65–66).

Among the orphaned children of the Northeast region were a large number of Irish, indirect causalities of the brave stands made by the poor immigrant Irish who had joined the Union army. The 63rd and 69th New York (Fighting Irish), the 9th and 28th Massachusetts, and the 116th Pennsylvania Infantry made up the so-called Irish Brigade. A Second Irish Brigade (155th, 164th, 170th, and 180th New York Infantry) was formed by war's end. Of the roughly 140,000 immigrant Irish in the Union army, one third came from eastern cities (chiefly Boston, Philadelphia, and Pittsburgh), one third came from New York City alone, and the remainder served in scattered units raised in the Midwest and Western theaters of the war. Most Irish immigrants had only a skeletal kinship network to fall back upon in America and were exceedingly poor when they entered service.

One of the earliest solutions to the orphan problem was taken by the Catholic Church in New York. In 1863, the Catholic Protectory for Homeless and Wayward Children in New York City opened its doors to soldiers' orphans in response to the loss of their fathers in the crucial battles of 1862 in the Eastern theater of the war: the Peninsular Campaign (June and July), Antietam (September), and Fredericksburg (December). By the end of the year, the Catholic Protectory was caring for more than 1,000 city youngsters, many of whom lost parents at the battles of Chancellorsville (May 1863) or Gettysburg (July 1863).

May 1864 was the bloodiest month of the Civil War with more than 100,000 total casualties in the East alone. General Ulysses S. Grant was called a butcher, but he continued to fight through the Wilderness and Spotsylvania Campaigns ending up in front of Petersburg in July 1864. In response, the Pennsylvania Soldiers' Orphan Schools Association was established. In one of the most comprehensive soldiers' orphans responses, the state provided educational instruction for the children as well as food, clothing, furnishings, and care until age 16. There were 46 individual member sites in Pennsylvania including those sponsored and staffed by Protestant and Catholic churches. As of 1887, the number of children who had received care through the Pennsylvania system numbered more than 14,000.

In his second inaugural address (March 4, 1865), Abraham Lincoln had pledged "to care for him who shall have borne the battle and for his widow and his orphans." Less than six weeks later Lincoln was dead, felled by an assassin's bullet. Andrew Johnson, now president, took up the call, and in June 1866 Congress passed an act forming the National Soldiers' and Sailors' Orphans Home in Washington, D.C. In 1869, the Grand Army of the Republic (GAR)—a society of Union Civil War veterans—founded the Ohio Soldiers' and Sailors' Orphans Home on 100 acres of land donated by the people of Xenia, Ohio. The home had beds for only 75 children, but over 900 children were housed in the institution through 1900.

One dead Union soldier found on the Gettysburg battlefield presented a sad puzzle with regard to his children. The man's body was unidentified except for a photograph of three children that were presumed to be his. In October 1863, the *Philadelphia Enquirer* ran a story that described the children in detail in an effort to discover their identity. Newspapers at that time did not have the technical ability to reproduce photographs in print. Other newspapers reprinted the story. Philinda Humiston of Portville, New York, read the article in the *American Presbyterian* a month later, and strongly suspected that the description fit a photograph sent to her husband Amos some months before the battle. She was able to confirm that the children Frank, Alice, and Fred were in fact the children in the picture. Amos Humiston had been a sergeant in the 154th New York Volunteer Infantry. The incident led to the founding of the National Homestead at Gettysburg in October 1866 with funds coming in from businessman Jay Gould. The three Humiston children became residents there when their mother was given a position helping to run the home.

In the 1870s and 1880s, a number of Soldiers' Orphans homes closed due to the fact that the children had grown to adulthood. The Wisconsin Soldiers' Orphans Home closed in 1874, after the trustees found foster care for the children remaining there. The National Homestead at Gettysburg was closed in 1879 after several scandals involving physical abuse and mismanagement of funds. Other institutions continued to serve the orphans of U.S. servicemen killed in action in other conflicts.

—James M. Volo

SERVANTS AND SLAVES

Although the views of some contemporary writers suggest a different conclusion, many Southerners often wrote of being dishonored in the eyes of their revolutionary ancestors should they fail to defend their families or the Southern cause and lifestyle against Northern aggression. Northerners retaliated by pointing out the tendency of Southern aristocracy to build great mansions and populate them with scores of servants and black slaves. "[F]ine palaces make us despise the poor and poverty; [and] a great number of domestics flatter human pride, which uses them like slaves; valor oftentimes turns brutal and unjust; and a high pedigree makes a man take up with the virtues of his ancestors, without endeavoring to acquire any himself" (Haines and Yaggy 1876, 492).

The family was an important social institution among blacks. That it was an incredibly unstable institution was due significantly to the influence of whites. A former slave noted, "There were on this plantation about seventy slaves, male and female: some were married, and others lived together as man and wife, without even a mock ceremony.... The slaves, however, think much of being married by a clergyman." Since marriage was considered a legal medium by which property was handed down, and the slave had no property, the law saw no reason to recognize the union of slaves as binding. Some morally scrupulous planters encouraged formal slave marriage but such arrangements lacked the force of law to protect them.

Investigators in New Orleans during the federal occupation recorded more than 500 marriages that had taken place while the couples involved had been slaves. Of these, fewer than 100 had remained unbroken. While some unions lasted from 20 to 40 years, the average length of a slave marriage as recorded in the Louisiana sample was a mere 5.6 years. Records indicate that 70 percent of these marriages ended due to death or personal choice, and only 30 percent of the slave unions were broken up by the planters. Many planters professed an aversion to breaking up slave families because the practice increased unrest among the blacks; but the extravagant lifestyle of the planters, coupled with the regularity of foreclosures on mortgages and demands for the repayment of loans, caused many slaves to see the auction block at least once in their lives. Slaves could be bought or sold, rented out, gambled away, or left in a will as an inheritance to almost anyone; and the law did not provide for the continuity of the slave family as a unit.

In law, slave children did not belong to their parents but generally were considered the property of the mother's master. The father and the father's master, should he be a different person, were denied any standing in regard to the offspring of slave unions. The offspring of a free man with a slave woman was thereby a slave; yet the offspring of a slave with a free woman was considered to be freeborn even if the woman were black. Even the children of a white master by a slave mother were born slaves. In the case of a dispute in this regard, with very few exceptions, whenever a slave's human rights came into conflict with a master's property rights, the courts invariably decided in favor of the master. The first activity of many refugee slaves during the war was to begin a search for their missing mates or children (Volo and Volo 1998, 74–75).

PETS

Both rural and urban residents lived in close contact with livestock as well as cats and dogs. Pigs and poultry alike roamed the streets of even the largest cities until the middle of the century. Many of these animals worked for their keep. Cats were expected to control the rodent population. Dogs served as guards for both homes and businesses and worked in other roles as well. They assisted with hunting and herding in country settings. In cities, some were used to pull small carts used by ragmen and newsboys. Dogs were even used to run treadmills that powered butter churns and grinders.

By mid-century an increasing number of animals were kept more as companions and playmates. Pets became a symbol of contented family life. They were a sign of social status and leisure for the new middle class. Pet owners became indulgent of their pets. Pets were included in family celebrations. Some pets received presents for Christmas and on other special occasions. Pet lovers were often photographed with their favorite pet. Some even had their pets photographed posthumously, a practice also done for small children. Many beloved pets were given solemn burials at home.

The newly emerging middle class played a key role in altering society's attitudes toward pets and reassessing man's relationship with animals. Kindness to animals was viewed as a building block of good character. It was closely associated with good citizenship. Advice books for parents, Sunday school books, and children's stories reinforced the importance of protecting and caring for animals. It was believed that caring for animals in childhood would lay the foundation for the responsibility, later in life, of caring for dependents in society such as children, the sick, the aged, and the poor. Cruelty to any creature was thought surely to lead to violence in the future. It became a sign of good parenting to provide their children with a pet for which to care. By the 1860s, rabbits, white mice, and guinea pigs were often given to city children. They were small, gentle, and did not require specialized care. Squirrels were also popular. Captured from the wild, they were sold in pet stores throughout the century. Many children, even city dwellers, had chickens as pets. In addition to caring for them, children could be taught the rudiments of business by selling eggs and extra chicks to neighbors and relatives. In rural locals, children were given charge of small livestock. These creatures lived on the cusp of pet and product, and many children suffered when it came time for the animal to make the transition to market or table. Lithographs depicted children and domestic animals as playmates. Children's books abounded with stories featuring pets as protagonists. Advertisements and trade cards displayed charming images of animals, many in anthropomorphic positions.

Pet interest expanded to include more than the family cat or dog. From colonial times, settlers kept native songbirds they had trapped or purchased. Keeping birds crossed lines of class, ethnicity, and race and may have been the most favored indoor pet. The perceived devoted parenting of birds made them models for the middle class and living examples for children. The canary, which had been introduced from Germany in the 1820s, became extremely popular. Soon they were being raised for sale domestically. The first pet stores, which began in Eastern cities around 1840, were called bird stores and sold both caged indigenous birds as well as canaries. Shop owners also mixed and sold seeds, medicines, tonics, and ointments for the caged birds.

Fish also became popular. Keeping a goldfish in a small globe became another favored parlor ornament in the city residence. The price of goldfish remained so high until the 1880s that people would only purchase a single fish. Aquariums were invented mid-century and native freshwater fish caught in local ponds and streams populated most. Enthusiasts used the Balanced Aquarium approach. This consisted of a tank in which the air surface of the water, aided by plants, would supply sufficient oxygen and the plants and scavengers consumed most of the waste from the catch fish. Aquarium owners fashioned underwater landscapes complete with mermaids, sea monsters, and underwater cities.

Interest in purebred dogs and selective breeding began in the 1840s. By the 1860s dogs were being shown competitively at bench shows, where dogs compete against their breed ideal. Some livestock shows included dogs during the 1860s. An international dog show was held in Washington, D.C., in 1863 as a charity event for the U.S. Sanitary Commission. P. T. Barnum also hosted some dog shows, but, unlike modern events, these shows only judged beauty among particular species. Until the American Kennel Club was founded in 1884, there were no written breed standards or registry books in the United States. The average family dog was, however, not a purebred but rather some kind of mix, although one recognizable as a specific breed.

Pets commonly shared the diets of their owners. Cooks made dog stews by combining cornmeal, rice, and potatoes along with meat and vegetable scraps. A company called Spratt's invented dry dog food in the 1860s, but acceptance of the product came slowly.

Southerners developed a profound fondness for hunting and love of their hunting dogs that had its roots in the eighteenth century. Plantation owners ran their dogs alone or with their neighboring planters. They hosted organized hunts running deer, bear, bobcats, and feral cattle as well as foxes. The hunting dogs were usually a compilation of purebreds and mixed breeds. Slaves handled the dogs and cared for the horses and people as well. With the outbreak of civil war, the pageantry that often accompanied these events declined but Southerners continued to use their dogs to hunt.

Dog ownership and the passion for hunting in the South crossed both class and racial boundaries. Dogs were key to helping slaves and poor whites put meat on the table. Most Southern states had restrictions on dog ownership by slaves but many slave owners continued to permit their slaves to run them. While wealthy planters boasted of their purebreds, most Southerners kept mongrels.

Some Southerners trained their dogs to hunt for more than game. Dogs were specifically trained to hunt runaway slaves. Some pursued game as well, but most who were trained to do this were specialists. These dogs were permitted to see blacks only when being trained to chase them. Slaves were made to run from the dogs that chased them until they climbed a tree. The dogs were then rewarded with meat. Slave hunters advertised their services in local newspapers, boasting of their dogs' success. General William Tecumseh Sherman ordered Union troops to kill the bloodhounds and other slave-hunting dogs they came across on their march through Georgia in 1864.

Civil War units sometimes adopted a troop pet. Focusing attention and affection on these animals provided release of tension and served as a reminder of home. While many such relationships developed, several pets achieved notoriety. Old Abe the War Eagle was a bald eagle carried by Company C of the 8th Wisconsin Regiment and was wounded twice during the conflict. After the war ended, Abe toured the country. Sallie Ann Jarrett was a female bull terrier that was presented to the captain of the 11th Pennsylvania volunteers while training near West Chester, Pennsylvania. She tended daily drills and guarded the bodies of wounded and dead members of the unit. Sally was killed alongside her soldiers at Hatcher's Run near Petersburg, Virginia, in 1865. A life-sized statue at Gettysburg commemorates her devotion and demonstrates the love of her regiment (Grier 2006, 221).

—*Dorothy Denneen Volo*

FOR MORE INFORMATION

Bash, Wendell H. "Differential Fertility in Madison County New York, 1865." In *Studies in American Historical Demography*, ed. Maris A. Vinovskis. New York: Academic Press, 1979.

Browne, Ray B., and Lawrence A. Kreiser Jr. *The Civil War and Reconstruction*. Westport, CT: Greenwood Press, 2003.

Campbell, Edward D. C., Jr., and Kym S. Rice, eds. *A Woman's War: Southern Women, Civil War and the Confederate Legacy*. Charlottesville: University Press of Virginia, 1996.

Chudacoff, Howard P. "Newlyweds and Family Extension." In *Family and Population in Nineteenth-Century America*, by Tamara K. Hareven and Maris A. Vinovskis. Princeton, NJ: Princeton University Press, 1978.

Clinton, Catherine. *The Plantation Mistress: Woman's World in the Old South*. New York: Pantheon Books, 1982.

Deer, Mark. *A Dog's History of America: How Our Best Friend Explored, Conquered, and Settled a Continent*. New York: North Point Press, 2004.

East, Charles, ed. *Sarah Morgan: The Civil War Diary of a Southern Woman*. New York: Touchstone, 1991.

Faust, Drew Gilpin. *Mothers of Invention: Women of the Slaveholding South in the American Civil War*. Chapel Hill: University of North Carolina Press, 1996.

Frank, Stephen M. *Life with Father: Parenthood and Masculinity in the Nineteenth-Century American North*. Baltimore, MD: Johns Hopkins University Press, 1998.

Glasco, Lawrence. "Migration and Adjustment in the Nineteenth-Century City: Occupation, Property, and Household Structure of Native-Born Whites, Buffalo, New York, 1855." In *Family and Population in Nineteenth Century America*, by Tamara K. Hareven and Maris A. Vinovskis. Princeton, NJ: Princeton University Press, 1978.

Green, Harvey. *The Light of the Home*. New York: Pantheon Books, 1983.

Grier, Katherine C. *Pets in America: A History*. Chapel Hill: University of North Carolina Press, 2006.

Gwin, Minrose C., ed. *Cornelia Peake McDonald: A Woman's Civil War. A Diary with Reminiscences of the War from March 1862*. Madison: University of Wisconsin Press, 1992.

Hague, Parthenia Antoinette. *A Blockaded Family: Life in Southern Alabama during the Civil War*. Reprint. Bedford, TX: Applewood Books, 1995.

Haines, T. L., and Levi W. Yaggy. *The Royal Path of Life: Or Aims and Aids to Success and Happiness*. Chicago, IL: Western Publishing House, 1876.

Haskell, E. F. *Civil War Cooking: The Housekeeper's Encyclopedia*. Mendocino, CA: R.L. Shep, 1992.

Larcom, Lucy. *A New England Girlhood*. Boston, MA: Northeastern University Press, 1986.

Livermore, Mary A. *My Story of the War: A Woman's Narrative of Four Years' Personal Experience*. New York: Da Capo Press, 1995.

Lothrop, Margaret M. *The Wayside: Home of Authors*. New York: American Book Company, 1968.

Lunt, Dolly Sumner. *A Woman's Wartime Journal*. Atlanta, GA: Cherokee, 1994.

Marten, James. *The Children's Civil War*. Chapel Hill: University of North Carolina Press, 1998.

Massey, Mary Elizabeth. *Women in the Civil War*. Lincoln: University of Nebraska Press, 1966.

McGuire, Judith W. *Diary of a Southern Refugee during the War by a Lady of Virginia*. Lincoln: University of Nebraska Press, 1995.

Moskow, Shirley Blotnick. *Emma's World: An Intimate Look at Lives Touched by the Civil War Era*. Far Hills, NJ: New Horizon Press, 1990.

Paul, James Laughery. *Pennsylvania's Soldiers' Orphan Schools*. Harrisburg, PA: Lane S. Hart Publisher, 1876.

Reef, Catherine. *Alone in the World: Orphans and Orphanages in America*. New York: Clarion Books, 2005.

Sanchez-Eppler, Karen. *Dependent States: The Child's Part in Nineteenth-Century American Culture*. Chicago, IL: University of Chicago Press, 2005.

Smith, Page. *The Nation Comes of Age: A People's History*. 4 vols. New York: McGraw-Hill Book Company, 1981.

Sullivan, Walter. *The War the Women Lived: Female Voices from the Confederate South*. Nashville, TN: J.S. Sanders, 1995.

Titcomb, Timothy. *Lessons in Life, A Series of Familiar Essays*. New York: Charles Scribner & Co., 1861.

Volo, Dorothy Denneen, and James M. Volo. *Daily Life in Civil War America*. Westport, CT: Greenwood Press, 1998.

———. *Encyclopedia of the Antebellum South*. Westport, CT: Greenwood Press, 2000.

———. *Family Life in Nineteenth-Century America*. Westport, CT: Greenwood Press, 2007.

Wells, Robert V. "Demographic Change and the Life Cycle of American Families." In *Studies in American Historical Demography*, ed. Maris A. Vinovskis. New York: Academic Press, 1979

Woodward, C. Vann, ed. *Mary Chesnut's Civil War*. New Haven, CT: Yale University Press, 1981.

Economic Life

THE VALUE OF A DOLLAR

To set a standard for the study of economics in the later half of the nineteenth century, it is important to evaluate the worth of a U.S. dollar. Oddly the value of a dollar was exactly the same in 1860 as it was in 1900. There had been inflation during the Civil War, and it took $1.96 to equal an 1860 dollar in purchasing power in 1865. However, the monetary history of the U.S. dollar during the rest of the century was one of deflation from this high. It is safe to assume that an 1860 U.S. dollar (USD) was equivalent to approximately $18 in 2008 U.S. currency. Oddly, the intrinsic worth of the present dollar is less stable because it is unsupported by precious metals (gold or silver) as was the 1860 dollar.

The average family income in the United States from 1860 to 1900 in modern dollars (2008) was a remarkably low $7,000, or just under $400 in 1860 money. A generally rising standard of living in the United States raised hourly wages, while the incorporation of labor-saving devices limited the average number of hours worked. Yet this kept the annual wage approximately equal through four decades. Service wages (maids, cooks, footman, for instance) tended to rise as the century wore on due to increased demand. A maid in 1860 might be hired for an annual wage of as little as $70 ($1,300 in 2008), while in 1900 she could demand and receive $240 ($4,000 in 2008), more than three times as much. Nonetheless, people generally worked for less than might be thought, and a family with an average income of $2,500 in 1860 dollars could afford to hire a cook, a housemaid, and a nurse for the children. Doctors, lawyers, and civil servants—considered the middle of the middle class—made between $1,500 and $2,500 annually depending on whether they practiced in rural or urban areas of the country, respectively. A nineteenth-century millionaire could expect almost $30,000 (equivalent to a half million dollars in 2008) income simply from his investments in three percent bonds (Schollander and Schollander 2002, 217).

When comparing international monetary values during the later half of the nineteenth century, the normal exchange rate of $5 per British pound sterling (£1) was commonly used. The difference between the two was a function of their value in gold rather than the unsupported strength of the currency as it is today. Dollars were simply smaller units of value than pounds.

—James M. Volo

WORK

King Cotton

Cotton saved the plantation system and breathed new life into slavery. By midcentury cotton accounted for two-thirds of the exports of the United States and created an unprecedented demand for agricultural laborers. In 1790, annual cotton production had amounted to only 3,000 bales, but it rose to 178,000 bales in just 20 years. This increase is generally attributed to the introduction of the cotton gin in 1793. The widespread adoption of the cotton gin, which economically removed the seeds from desirable long staple varieties of cotton, resurrected the plantations of the Deep South in the antebellum period. A slave, who could process 100 pounds of cotton per day without the cotton gin, could produce 1,000 pounds of fiber in the same time with the cotton gin. In terms of dollars, the antebellum period witnessed cotton becoming the King of domestic exports.

The Civil War disrupted cotton production. Southern strategy during the Civil War continued to emphasize a total defense of Confederate territory against Yankee aggression. Southern leaders were particularly worried about losing control of areas where Unionists might free the slaves and thereby instigate widespread slave insurrections. The country was organized into an array of impracticably large departments and districts based on state lines and geographical imperatives that were not always adapted to the prosecution of the war. They also feared the vast economic cost represented by seized cotton, destroyed manors, burned fields, and wrecked fences. This defensive outlook caused the Confederates to disperse their forces widely and to expose much of the South to destruction.

Working for a Living

In the nineteenth century every man worked for his living, but not all men worked in the same way. Almost everyone below the uppermost classes of society needed to make a living through the application of their own physical labor. Workers at this time could be divided into several categories, among them laborers, farmers, clerks, craftsmen, machine operators, shopkeepers, metalworkers, and mariners. There were also those who dealt in the extraction trades like mining, timbering, or fishing. Before the Civil War clerks and machine operators represented a numerous, but decided minority of city workers. In some urban areas unskilled laborers made up to 40 percent of all workers. Craftsmen and shopkeepers have often been considered a privileged class somewhat akin to small businessmen, but many of the persons involved in crafts or shopkeeping were actually women, not the middle-class employers of apprentices and journeymen, but petty proprietors with just enough income and business acumen to rest on the lower rung of middle-class status.

Employment opportunities were not equally available to all classes and levels of society. Young men of the upper class preparing for life in a profession—physician, engineer, or lawyer—expected to be able to maintain a standard of living and social status commensurate with their services to the community. Churchmen and teachers expected a salary that reflected their educational qualifications and a respectful place in the scheme of social hierarchy. Those born to wealth might lead an indulgent life or work as managers of the family business or plantation without regard to the willingness of their neighbors to provide them an income. They formed the highest rungs of the economic ladder because of their birth or family connection. Industrialization brought a new category of worker into the mix. This was the factory manager, or overseer, who directed the labor of others in the mills and manufactories (Volo and Volo 2007, 73–74).

The Extent of Industry

Although the nineteenth century is often thought of as a period of industrial growth, the vast majority of the nation still made its living in agriculture. New York, the most populous state in 1850 with a population of just over three million residents, had only 6.5 percent of its workers involved in manufacturing. This data suggests that the state was still remarkably rural in character, as was the entire nation. Massachusetts, Rhode Island, and Connecticut were the most industrialized states in the Union, each with double-digit percentages of persons employed in manufacturing, but none of these even closely approached a majority. Massachusetts, with a population of 986,000, was the most industrialized state in the nation with 17.0 percent manufacturing workers. Rhode Island (15%) and Connecticut (13%) ranked second and third nationally. Of the six New England states only Vermont (2.7%) had a manufacturing base smaller than 5.0 percent in terms of employment. By way of contrast Pennsylvania and Ohio, among the top three states in population with more than 2.2 million and 2.0 million respectively, had 6.5 percent and 3.0 percent working in manufacturing in 1850. Virginia, with nearly a million residents had a mere 3.0 percent involved in industry, and fifth place Illinois, with 800,000 people, was still remarkably rural with only 1.4 percent of its population working in factories or mills. Only 10 states had greater than 5.0 percent of their population involved in manufactures in 1850. Of these only Maryland and Delaware bestrode the Mason-Dixon Line, and none of them would enter the Southern Confederacy.

For this reason it is commonly thought that the economy of the American South was deficient when compared to that of the North in many critical areas of industry including manufacturing, transportation, and communications. Certainly the North, all the states that fought the Civil War treated as a separate nation, was one of the giants of industrial production on the world stage ranking just behind Great Britain in the value of its manufacturing output. However, the Southern Confederacy, also taken as an independent nation, would have ranked fourth richest among all the economies of the world in 1860 having more wealth than many industrial countries such as France, Prussia, or Denmark. Admittedly, Southern economic strength lay largely in its agricultural production, but its manufacturing base was better developed than many other nations at the time that were considered to have entered the industrial age.

Much of the South's fortune and capital continued to be tied up in land and in slaves leaving little for other investment. With increasing wealth in the North built upon shipbuilding, whaling, shopkeeping, iron production, and textile production, there was no similar lack of uncommitted capital. The growth of the factory-owning middle class in the North during the first decades of the antebellum period was rapid and remarkable. New factories and machinery absorbed more than $50 million of Northern investment capital in the decades of the 1820s and 1830s alone. Some Northern money went to fund canals and other long-term projects. In the 1840s and 1850s, capital was diverted toward the construction of railroads, but only a small portion of Northern wealth found its way into Southern industrial development.

Oddly, reliable statistics concerning Southern industry, transportation, and manufacturing are rare and difficult to assess from the distance of more than a century. Some historians have noted that the generally accepted view of the industrial capacity of the South in the antebellum period may need revision, and some limits may need to be put to the present generalizations made by the economic historians of the past. One linchpin of this thinking is the idea that by the very act of secession, the industrial capability of the Southern states "was brought to a pinnacle of development" only to perish in the war that followed. The demands of a wartime economy and the destruction wrought upon it may have blurred a true measure of the extent of the South's prewar industrial system, while immediate postwar analyses by Northern observers may have been prejudiced against any positive findings (Wilson 2002, ix).

Southern apologists and other contemporary spokespersons pointed out the strength of the Southern economy before the war intervened. Although some of their positive comments concerning Southern industrial capacity can be classed as propaganda, much of the data they cited could not be denied. Senator Andrew Johnson of Tennessee, later vice president and president of the United States, noted in 1860 that the copper mines of his state kept seven smelting furnaces in constant operation annually and that the number of residents engaged in manufacturing was virtually the same as that in Illinois. Moreover, Tennessee produced more woolen textiles, more corn, more wheat, and 150 times more pig iron than New Hampshire, and it was building 1,100 miles of railway annually while New Hampshire was laying down only 200 miles.

Representative Alexander Stephens of Georgia, later vice president of the Confederacy, made similar, if less accurate, statistical comparisons between his state and Ohio, then one of the most prosperous states in the Union. Stephens noted that with half the population, Georgia produced more agricultural products than Ohio (even if cotton were excluded), as well as more beef, pork, and wool. Georgia had 38 state-of-the-art cotton and woolen mills, 1,000 more miles of railroad than Ohio, and twice the annual capital investment in new manufacturing ventures. Some of Stephens' remarks were disingenuous and did not take into account the fact that much of the investment in Ohio predated that in Georgia, leaving Ohio's present annual rate of investment lower although the absolute dollar amount was higher.

Thomas J. Kettell, contemporary author, economist, and Southern apologist, made a number of interesting comparisons between the Southern states and the nations of Europe. He pointed out that the South as a whole in 1860 had approximately 9,000 miles of railway as compared to 6,000 in England and Wales, 4,000 in France, and a little over 2,000 in Prussia. There were 31 major southern canals, 2 of the 10 largest ocean harbors in the world (both serving New Orleans), and 2 major inland ports (Louisville, Kentucky, and St. Louis, Missouri). In the United States, one third of all the telegraph lines (15,000 miles of it) were in the Southern states, more than in all of continental Europe at the time.

Joseph Kennedy, superintendent of the federal census in 1860, noted the South's 52 paper mills producing 12 million pounds of paper annually, its 1,300 leather shops and tanneries, its three major iron works capable of making locomotives and steam engines, its more than 100 smaller iron furnaces, foundries, and rolling mills, and its 115 precision machine shops. Southern shoemakers produced 65,000 pairs of work boots annually, and Southern workers provided the entire nation, North and South, with most of the hides and most of the tree bark needed for tanning them into leather. Kennedy also noted the establishment in the South of 250 cotton mills, 153 woolen mills, and almost 500 carding and fullering mills. There were 45 woolen mills and 63 carding mills in Virginia alone that produced over one million yards of fabric annually, enough to make 200,000 suits of clothing. Based on findings like these, modern researchers have begun to reevaluate historic judgments about the extent of the technological inferiority of the Southern states before the war and to reshape the picture of Southern industry commonly advanced during the century thereafter (Volo and Volo 2007, 74–76).

The Work of War

The work of war is soldiering, but the vast majority of the men who served in the Civil War were neither professional soldiers nor draftees. The largest percentage were farmers before the war. The available data make no distinction between the plantation owner, the small farm owner or his children, and the paid agricultural worker. The data also ignore all those who were too young to have an occupation when they enlisted, such as teenagers and students. Many of these were listed as unskilled workers.

Skilled laborers made up the second largest group of men to serve in either army. These skilled laborers included carpenters and furniture makers, masons, machinists, wheelwrights and cartwrights, barrel makers and coopers, shoemakers and leather workers, smiths of many kinds, and other skilled tradesmen. The particular trade by which an artisan made his living rarely prepared him for military service. Exceptions to this may have been made for artisans like butchers, blacksmiths, and farriers, who were organized within the service to practice their trades for the army.

Professional and white-collar occupations made up the largest portion of those who served as Union officers, while planters made up a significant number of Confederate officers. Professional men included lawyers, physicians, clergymen, engineers, professors, and army and navy officers. The white-collar category is somewhat obscured, as it is distinguished from the professional class more by degree than by any other characteristic, and many men often crossed the line between the two. These included bankers, merchants, manufacturers, journalists, clerks, bookkeepers, and schoolteachers.

In the South a man could have an exemption from the military draft based on a war-related occupation considered more critical to the cause than his service at the front. Among those exempt from the draft were iron founders, machinists, miners, and railroad workers; ferrymen, pilots, and steamboat workers; government officials, clerks, and telegraphers; ministers, professors, teachers of the handicapped, and private teachers with more than 20 pupils. Slave owners, or slave overseers who had more than 20 slaves under their care, could be exempt—one from each plantation. There were protests over the exemptions; but the only outcome of a public outcry was an extension of the exemption to physicians, leather workers, blacksmiths, millers, munitions workers, shipyard workers, salt makers, charcoal burners, some stockmen, some printers, and one editor for each paper.

The protests over exemptions were generally not fueled by antiwar sentiment— quite the reverse. Until 1864 when the rising tide of federal victory became obvious, the war was very popular, almost disturbingly so even in the South. Those exempt were thought to be neglecting their obligation to defend their country or to do battle against slavery or federalism, depending on the side on which they served. Many men who warranted an exemption refused it. Although there were charges of rich man's war and poor man's fight, many slave owners and their sons voluntarily served in the army, very often as highly placed officers and leaders of local partisan groups. Among many examples was Wade Hampton, a leading slave owner—considered to be the richest man in the South—who served with great distinction throughout the war and was wounded several times. Both his brother and his son lost their lives in battle. On the federal side, there was Robert Gould Shaw—son and grandson of a wealthy Massachusetts family. A dedicated abolitionist, the 26-year-old Shaw served as colonel of the 54th Massachusetts Infantry, a black regiment, dying with many of his men in the attack on Battery Wagner in South Carolina in 1863.

Notwithstanding their civilian occupations, each man who served on the battlefield came with a set of values that mirrored the home and community he left behind. The majority of the recruits in the first year of the war were volunteers, and they pledged themselves to serve for three months, expecting that the first major battle would decide the issue of secession (Volo and Volo 1998, 100–101).

FINANCE: COTTON BONDS

The dedication to states right by its several member governments made a wide-ranging system of centralized revenue measures difficult for the Confederacy. The governments of several Confederate states railed at any policy that came out of Richmond smelling of centralizing power. The three principal methods used to finance the Southern war effort were direct taxation, bonds and loans, and treasury notes. The Confederate government in Richmond was reluctant to rely on the first of these because it might greatly stress the loyalty of the Southern people who were paying the cost of its defense with their economic lifeblood or the actual lives of their sons and fathers. This was especially true in large areas of the South like Tennessee and Louisiana that were being overrun by Northern armies early in the war. The federal armies, and particularly its blockading navy, kept import and export duties from bringing in much revenue. A direct tax on real estate, slaves, and other luxury property was enacted, but off-setting exemptions were allowed for funds paid to the individual states in both Confederate currency and specie. Less than $18 million was realized from direct taxation.

The Confederacy imposed an excise and license tax similar to that of the North in 1863, but it included taxes on additional items important to the Southern economy like naval stores, turpentine, sugar, molasses, and salt. Southern salt works were a priority target for the invading Federals. Only five months into the war the Southern papers began to fret over a shortage of salt, which was worth its weight in gold.

The same legislation created an income tax of 1 percent on the first $1,500 over a base exemption of $1,000 to 15 percent on all incomes over $10,000. No tax was levied on land or slaves, but after reserving certain amounts for their own use, all farmers and planters were required to pay to the central government one-tenth of their wheat, corn, oats, rye, buckwheat, rice, sweet and Irish potatoes, cured hay and fodder, sugar, molasses, cotton, wool, tobacco, beans, peas, and bacon. The legislation was expanded in 1864. This tax-in-kind means of financing and supplying the troops was very unpopular in some states and was tolerated in others. North Carolina and Georgia complained bitterly that their produce and materials should be used only for their own state troops. A final tax of 25 percent was levied on all coins, bullion, and foreign moneys exchanged in the Confederate states in February 1865. This came much too late to reenergize lagging Southern revenues. Since so much of the levy was paid in kind, it is difficult to attach a dollar amount to the revenue generated by these taxes. Nonetheless, it has been estimated that the Confederacy raised about one percent of its income from these sources (Randall and Donald 1961, 258).

The South was more successful in borrowing money secured by its paper pledges known as *Cotton Bonds*. The Confederacy imported a remarkable amount of military supplies through the federal blockade. More than 400,000 rifles, 3 million pounds of lead, and 2 million pounds of saltpeter for gunpowder production, as well as food, clothing, shoes, accouterments, medicines, and paper, were brought through the blockade. To pay for these supplies, more than 500,000 bales of cotton were shipped out of the South during the war, and cotton bonds for additional bales worth millions of Confederate dollars were issued to creditors mostly located in England and France.

Alexander H. Stephens, Confederate vice president, proposed the sale of cotton as a way of financing the war. His initial plan entailed taking two million bales of cotton from the 1861 crop, paying $100 million for them in eight percent bonds issued to the growers, adding to them two million more bales purchased at the prewar market price, and shipping the whole four million bales to Europe. Here the cotton would be stored until shortages at the textile mills in England and France caused by the expected federal blockage increased the market price to a staggering $1 billion. This would net the Confederacy a neat $800 million in a single operation. The operation was hopelessly optimistic, but it might have been feasible if the four million bales and the ships to move them had been available and left unmolested by the federal navy.

The South was much more successful in carrying out its cotton financing schemes on paper. Its first loan, based on cotton bonds, was for $15 million in 1861, and it was taken up domestically by the South's own loyal citizens. The residents of New Orleans picked up two-fifths of the issue. A $100 million loan was taken later the same year, this was taken up by the planters themselves and was paid in paper currency and produce, especially raw cotton. The most famous of these loans was arranged in 1863 by a French financier named Erlanger, who sold Confederate bonds backed by cotton futures in the European financial markets for a sizeable profit. The bonds had a purchase price of $90 (CSA), and Erlanger undertook them at a $13 discount. They rose to $91.75 in May 1863 and never saw such a level again. The value of the bonds fluctuated widely following the fortunes of Confederate armies in the field. In December 1863 after the effects of Gettysburg and the fall of Vicksburg had set in, they bottomed at $35.50, rebounded somewhat in 1864 when Confederate forces threatened Washington, D.C., and settled thereafter at near half their issue price until spring 1865. They then quickly plummeted to single digits, and at the final surrender of Confederate forces in May 1865 were worth only $8.

—*James M. Volo*

COST OF LIVING

Wealth

Wealth had always conferred a certain level of social acceptability in American society. Antebellum planters ruled from plantations that sat like isolated city-states throughout the South claiming social privileges and sustaining an elite lifestyle at the expense of the rest of society. Few in the Southern planter class actually had aristocratic roots that would have legitimatized the role they assumed as community leaders during the colonial or postrevolutionary period. This greatly intensified the need of the social structure and the hierarchy of the South to define itself in historically acceptable terms. The planters, therefore, invented a social mythology in which the blood of their class was deemed noble or at least blue by incorrectly tracing their family origins to European royalty, past kings, or Celtic chieftains. There were enough Southern families with legitimate connections to maintain the truth of the fiction.

Rich Southerners maintained their planter aristocracy in the face of northern criticism through the Revolution and into the antebellum period. As the decades of the century worn on toward secession, George Fitzhugh found some necessity to explain the structure of Southern aristocratic life. In Cannibals All, or Slaves without Masters (1857), he wrote, "Pride of pedigree...Ancestral position...[and] respectable connexion [sic]...will, ere long, cease to be under the ban of public opinion....What vile hypocrisy, what malicious envy and jealousy, to censure and vilify in others, that which every man of us is trying with might and main to attain...[the] desire to found a family and make aristocrats of their posterity" (Volo and Volo 2004, 9).

The planter aristocracy was sorely tested during the Civil War, and in many cases their social and financial prominence did not meet the test. Economic security, once the hallmark of the great plantation and the foundation stone of social prominence, gradually became eroded and less certain. Although wealth and social position maintained their hold on the structure of Southern society, many aristocratic families lost scions to the fates of battle, and industry displaced family ties as a new means of attaining social status. Fitzhugh had seen this coming: "Every man in America desires to be an aristocrat, for every man desires wealth, and wealth confers power and distinction, and makes its owner an unmistakable aristocrat." Nonetheless, in the 1850s "new money" acquired through trade and industrialism still required the seasoning of a generation to be considered legitimate (Volo and Volo 2004, 9).

Southern Shortages

Southern nationalism, and the traditional "Old South," died as surely in the city streets, farmyards, and banking institutions as it did on the battlefields. The price of consumer goods in the South was most directly affected by the federal blockade. From 1860 to 1863 the monthly cost of feeding a small family was reported to have gone from $6.55 to $68.25.

A severe food shortage led to the Bread Riots in several urban areas of the South in the latter part of March 1863. Initially a group of women in Salisbury, North

Carolina, demanded that store owners charge them no more than the fixed price the government would ordinarily pay for foodstuffs and goods. Some of the merchants obliged the ladies by lowering their prices. There were several such episodes in the South at the same time. The most significant took place in the capital city of Richmond, where Mary Jackson promoted a concerted action by the women of that city to influence the price of goods and foodstuffs.

Beginning at the Belvidere Hill Baptist Church, the women, armed with persuaders such as pistols, knives, and hatchets, and led by Mary Jackson, marched on Capitol Square in protest. Here the governor of Virginia, John Letcher, spoke to the crowd and expressed his sympathy, but he offered no concrete solution to their problem. As the crowd disgorged from the square, the gathering of women clearly became a mob and began to loot the stores and take the goods of the merchants. Seemingly no attempt was made to buy articles at any price, including prices fixed by the government. A number of merchants simply tried to close their doors, and at least one, a Mr. Knott, tried to appease the women by handing out packages of sewing needles—considered a luxury item at the time.

This episode was widely reported in the antigovernment papers and the Northern press as a bread riot. Although there is no indication that any bread was taken or asked for, some foodstuffs, including bread, meat, and rice, were distributed to the needy by the Young Men's Christian Association. "Boots are not bread, brooms are not bread, men's hats are not bread, and I have never heard of anybody's eating them," retorted a government clerk to the reports (Tice 1974, 14; Volo and Volo 1998, 58–59).

Standard of Living

Family income was the measure by which sociologists and social reformers in both Britain and the United States differentiated between the poor and the very poor. In the nineteenth century it was clear that there was a difference between the poor, who had small incomes, and those known as paupers, who were on the public dole. Acting out of concern for an understanding of the working-class unrest that gripped Europe in 1848, statisticians and sociologists began about 1850 to take data and to conduct studies of family income and expenditures to shed light on any differences. Sociologists formulated the novel idea of poverty studies in which family income was compared to family expenditure as a measure of a *standard of living*. They attempted to show that poverty was not simply a matter of low income.

To facilitate his research, B. Seebohm Rowntree developed the idea of a family *budget* composed of three factors: Food, Rent, and Household Sundries (clothing, lighting, fuel, etc.). He also calculated different minimum incomes for families of various sizes that defined a *poverty line*. This concept thereafter became the common measure by which the standard of living was measured. For a family of four (two parents and two children) the poverty line in 1850 amounted to $238 annually, and for a family of five $274.

The 1850 census suggested that the average annual income for male workers was $300. The *New York Times* reported in 1853 that an average family of four living in the city with a minimum of medical expenses required $600. When corrected for inflation this figure was 28 percent higher than the minimum needed by a rural family of five in the previous decade, which may put its accuracy in question. Yet it seems certain that city families required more than an average single income simply to survive. A clear sign of this was the fact that one-third of the manufacturing work force in the city was composed of women. The demand market for female labor set the residents of New York City apart somewhat from the experience of the rest of America (Volo and Volo 2007, 54–55).

URBAN-RURAL ECONOMY: YEOMEN FARMERS AND POOR WHITES

On the surface at least, the Southern section of the country was doing well in 1850. The Old South's importance as a comprehensive producer of agricultural products was waning in the prewar period, however, being replaced by the produce of farms in Michigan, Iowa, Kansas, and Missouri. Tobacco remained an important crop in North Carolina and Kentucky, but the tobacco plantations of Virginia and Maryland were feeling the effects of depressed prices and depleted soils. Cotton was the South's principal cash crop, but the largest Southern crop was corn, which was consumed locally by man and beast. Rice was an important export item, and the rice of plantations of South Carolina and Georgia were still prosperous on the eve of the Civil War.

Southern cotton production had originated along the tidewater coast and had moved into the backcountry of South Carolina and Georgia by the end of the eighteenth century, but it quickly spread into all the states that would make up the Confederacy. The significance of cotton in the money-conscious nineteenth century resulted primarily from the fact that it was a cash crop. By mid-century more than five million bales were being produced annually, causing cotton to be termed the king of agricultural exports. The Southern cities, particularly New Orleans, Mobile, Savannah, and Charleston, continued to flourish because of their dedication to the export of cotton. Seventy-five percent of all cotton came from plantations, as did almost all of the rice, sugar, and tobacco. The success of the plantation economy, and of the cotton plantations in particular, was vital to the continuation of the genteel Southern lifestyle. This was an unmodernized lifestyle led by the planter elite, and it was maintained at the expense of African and poor white labor.

The vast majority of Southern citizens were farmers like their Northern counterparts. These small farmers (so-called yeomen farmers) owned no slaves, although they may have harbored a desire to do so. Absent the growing manufacturing base of the North, they farmed for a living—usually a little above the subsistence level. This allowed them to purchase few luxuries in a lifetime of hard work.

Whites in the South were anxious to maintain their status as freemen, even if it required that they be very poor freemen. They supported the plantation owners with regard to slavery for that purpose. At all levels of Southern society individual liberty, manliness, and respect for authority and position were held in such high esteem that

Small farmers, North and South, planned their lives around rural activities and seasonal chores such as barn raising, quilting bees, planting, haying, and harvesting. Family members usually cooperated in completing chores. This togetherness was thought to foster feelings of kinship and traditional family values. Father and mother worked beside their children and grandchildren in an idyllic, if not mechanically efficient, simplicity. Courtesy Currier and Ives.

one put his life and personal honor on the line to protect them.

The lower classes of the Northern cities were exceedingly poor and were composed largely of immigrants. Many of the poorest immigrants were Irish Catholics. The Irish were the first truly urban group in America, living in crowded slums rife with crime and disease, and experiencing severe religious prejudice at the hands of the Protestant majority. Help wanted advertisements often stated, "Irish need not apply." One of the ironic characteristics of the new modernism in Northern society was the simultaneous existence of antislavery sentiment and severe ethnic prejudice among upper-class Protestants. This is especially surprising in view of the prominence of social reform movements in the North.

Many established Americans in the North viewed immigration as a social problem and viewed the immigrants only in prejudicial terms. They blamed the slum-like conditions on the immigrants themselves, ignoring the bigotry of employers and the cupidity of landlords. In addition to being the victims of social prejudice, the immigrant population was also accused of selling their votes to unscrupulous politicians, of voting illegally, and of engendering crime and violence. Immigrants from Britain, most being Protestant, quickly became a part of American society, and many of the Germans separated themselves from the cities to move to the rural areas of Pennsylvania or the Midwest. They were thereby able to avoid a great deal of bias, and they formed a greater social solidarity than any other immigrant group (Volo and Volo 1998, 8–11, 37–38).

FARMING/HUSBANDRY

Cotton and Grain

At the commencement of the war, almost all of the South's capital and most of its fertile land was devoted to agriculture—much of it in cotton. Estimates show that by 1860 there were more than 3.6 million black slaves in the states that were to form the Confederacy. These represented hundreds of millions of dollars. Profits from cotton in the Carolinas and from sugar in Louisiana provided a financial bulwark for slavery in the Deep South. The profitability of cotton increased both the number and the value of slaves as plantation owners put more and more acreage under cultivation and attempted to spread the practice of slavery to new territories. The plantation system would have faded into obscurity were it not for the ability of slavery to provide the labor needed to produce these crops. Virginia, noted for its production of tobacco rather than as a cotton producer, became a major supplier of slaves to other areas of the South. In 1860 the estimated value of all the slave property in the Old Dominion alone was more than $300 million.

The North, which relied so much on manufacturing for its economic domination, might thereby have been at a disadvantage with regard to food, but the reverse was true because a great portion of the Northern population was composed of wheat and corn farmers. Preconceived notions of a rising wartime demand for food caused Northern farmers to overplant in 1860. Wheat and corn production soared. An additional boon came in the form of good weather, an event not shared by Europe, which experienced crop shortages during this period. The North was able to sell surplus wheat and flour to Europe, thus gaining additional funds that could be invested in the war.

The war actually provided an impetus to the development of farming in the North as underdeveloped land was put into production to support the war effort. The departure of men to service in the army raised the wages of agricultural laborers, and the demand for foodstuffs generated a significant involvement of small farmers in a commercial market that they had often ignored in the prewar years. The Homestead Act was quickly passed in 1862 granting free land to anyone willing to plant it. This virgin soil produced impressive yields, unlike the over-farmed Southern soil. Northern industry developed and produced machinery, which could additionally improve productivity. In 1861, McCormick's reaper was offered for sale to Northern farmers at $150 but required only a $30 down payment. The balance was to be paid in six months if the harvest was good, or longer if it was poor. At war's end farm families found themselves tied to the commercial economy more closely than ever before (Faust 1996, 11).

Although the plantation South was heavily agricultural, the North was not so heavily disadvantaged as may commonly be thought. Agriculture employed 70 percent of the North's five million workers in 1860. Using the various information sources available from the period and modern estimates, the following represents a

Produce and Grain Production, 1860 Estimates

	North	South	Border
Corn (bushels)	396	280	156
Wheat (bushels)	114	31	18
Oats (bushels)	138	20	12
Cotton (bales)	0	5	.004
Tobacco (pounds)	58	199	171
Rice (pounds)	0	187	.05

Source: Bruce Catton, ed. *American Heritage Picture History of the Civil War.* New York: Viking, 1996.

rough assessment of the produce and grain available in 1860 in the Northern, Southern, and Border states with units in millions.

Southern communities were never able to organize anything that approached the organization and productivity of the North, and the war brought about many shortages. On Southern plantations in areas controlled by the Federals the situation was temporarily acute as slaves with their new-won freedom abandoned the fields and streamed north across the Union lines. Plantation families that had lived in an atmosphere of wealth and refinement all their lives were often reduced to abject poverty because of the lack of labor.

As the war progressed and was continually fought on Southern soil, federal troops destroyed even the modest plantings in the gardens of Southern families. Cornelia Peake McDonald described a visit by the blue-coated soldiers. They "began to pull up the potatoes…[and] did not stop after getting enough for dinner, but continued amid roars of laughter and defiant looks at me to pull them till all were lying on the ground…to wither in the sun. The [potatoes] were no larger than peas, and the destruction seemed so wanton that I was provoked beyond enduring" (Gwin 1992, 58).

The blockade of Southern ports caused great hardship, and a poor system of transportation prevented the Confederacy's small resources from being effectively distributed throughout the South. Children were often recruited to solicit funds door-to-door and to collect nonperishable groceries such as jellies or crackers from merchants to be sent to soldiers at the front. In some farming communities, families set aside portions of their land to the production of easily stored crops, such as potatoes, onions, and turnips. Schools held "onion" or "potato" days to collect produce, which was later delivered to the troops.

The war ended without any cogent plan for bringing Southern agriculture back into production at prewar levels. There was no plan to deal with the seceded states and their people, nor was there any idea of what to do with millions of freed slaves. Accustomed to being told what do to, many freedmen did not know how to proceed in the uncertain times. Others misinterpreted freedom as meaning that they would be fed and sheltered without having to work as their white masters had seemingly done. Most freed people sought land and a way to work for themselves. The white yeoman farmer and the former black slave both faced ruined homes, desolate fields, no hope of income, and seemingly no way to improve the situation (Volo and Volo 2007, 187–88, 192).

Livestock

The production of large herds of cattle, horses, and mules was much more labor-intensive than tending hogs, sheep, fowl, or milk cows. Many farms combined open-range cattle raising with winter feeding in pastures or barn lots. These cattle were often branded or earmarked and left to forage on the forest margins and hillsides. To keep them near home farmers often put out salt licks near water sources. Farmers in the Appalachian foothills moved their stock to higher or lower pastures as the season dictated. Their agricultural activities were not characteristic of the Southern plantations that focused on exporting cotton, tobacco, sugar, and rice. They produced livestock and poultry (geese and turkeys) for export. Poultry exports were not enumerated in the census data, and chickens were generally raised for domestic consumption and for their eggs. In 1860, the southern Appalachians exported a good deal of livestock "on the hoof" to the rest of the South. These included annually one million hogs, a half-million cattle, and more than 90,000 horses and mules. These and their byproducts like hams and slab bacon were much more profitable for small Appalachian farmers than crop cultivation (Dunaway accessed 2007, 1).

There were without doubt endless arguments about the comparative qualities of mules and oxen as draft animals for everyday farm use. In 1843 Peter H. Burnett, an oxen fancier, wrote, "The ox is a most noble animal, patient, thrifty, durable, gentle, and easily driven." Burnett, later governor of California, found oxen "greatly superior to mules." In 1849, James Stewart, a mule proponent, expressed the following sentiment on the subject, "It is a noble sight to see those small, tough, earnest, honest Spanish mules, every nerve strained to the utmost, examples of obedience, and of duty performed under trying circumstances." A period price list from 1850 shows a pair of oxen for $50, while a single mule cost $75—an extravagance when compared to their bovine counterparts, but a great deal less expensive than they were to be found 15 years later. In 1865, some mule teams cost $700 a pair (Volo and Volo 2000, 173).

Riding horses and harness mules were not really interchangeable. Large wagons required a minimum four-mule team, while lighter ones could be pulled with two horses or two mules. A very light buggy could manage with one of either. In any case both mules and horses were more fleet of foot than the slow plodding but powerful oxen.

Using the various information sources available from the period and modern estimates, the following represents a rough assessment of the livestock (poultry not included) available in the Northern, Southern, and Border states in millions of head in 1860.

Livestock Resources in 1860

	North	South	Border
Beef Cattle	5.4	7.0	1.2
Dairy Cattle	5.0	2.7	0.7
Pigs/Hogs	11.5	15.5	3.0
Sheep	14.0	5.0	2.0
Horses	3.4	1.7	0.8
Mules	0.1	0.8	0.2

Source: Bruce Catton, ed. *American Heritage Picture History of the Civil War.* New York: Viking, 1996.

When fresh meat was not available, the enlisted men were provided with a basic preserved meat ration of pork—boiled ham, salt pork, or bacon being most common. Bacon, a common foodstuff reminiscent of home cooking, proved highly acceptable to the tastes of most soldiers. Bacon was made from the sides or flanks of the hog, kept in a slab, soaked in brine, and smoked. This operation cured the meat and so retarded the growth of bacteria that bacon could be kept for long periods of time. Thick slices could be cut from a single slab for several days with no noticeable deterioration of the remainder, and several rations of bacon could be carried in a haversack, wrapped in an oilcloth, without spoiling for some time.

The North and Midwest seemingly went through a huge expansion of the meat-packing industry during the war. Under the pressure of war, the packing plants in Chicago, Cleveland, and Cincinnati were transformed forever. The South quickly realized that it would experience a wartime meat shortage, and Richmond established an extensive government pork-packing program in close proximity to the rail and river transportation of Tennessee. These plants and their associated salt works were constantly in danger of capture or destruction by federal forces.

Federal forces also relied heavily on preserved pork. Pork production for commercial use in the North in 1865 was twice that of 1860. Pork's prominence as a foodstuff, when compared to preserved beef, did not lie in any intrinsic nutritional value, although the high fat content provided an excellent source of caloric intake. It was simply easier to preserve than beef and tasted better than pickled beef, which was so poor and unpalatable that the soldiers called it "salt horse." No effort was made to comply with dietary restrictions due to individual medical or religious preferences.

In camp boiled ham was often pulled from a barrel into which it had been packed for some months in a thick covering of grease that came from the boiling. The meat came out in long, unappetizing strips, and when brought to the surface the sound of the suction was like the noise made when one pulled his feet out of mud. The grease was scraped off and saved by many soldiers to be used as an ingredient in other recipes. The meat could be fried, roasted, or eaten sliced between two pieces of soft bread or with hardtack.

Salt pork was easy to make and had been used since colonial times as a mainstay of the diet for soldiers and sailors. Salt pork was a favorite among veteran soldiers, who sometimes declined fresh beef for a good piece of salt pork, but recruits had to learn to ignore its overwhelmingly salty flavor and to appreciate its nutritional qualities. The amount of salt used in its processing was staggering, but salt pork could last, unspoiled, for a long time in a sealed barrel. However, once a barrel was opened, the meat had to be used quickly or it would spoil. One reason for the spoiling of salted meats in transit was the lack of good barrels, which sometimes opened between the staves. Southern armies suffered severely from increasing numbers of poorly made barrels as experienced coopers, white and black, were drafted to fill the ranks on the firing lines or streamed north to freedom. So great was the domestic war demand that there developed a worldwide shortage of quality American barrel staves.

From the start, the Southern cavalry was more effective than that of the North. This was largely because it was better organized and better mounted. Southern recruits brought their own horses and horse accoutrements with them. The federal army could not meet the initial demand for artillery and cavalry horses. The horses that it acquired were often as untrained as their riders. Both required long periods of familiarization with the exigencies of cavalry operations before they could take the field with any hope of matching the Southern cavalry. Robert E. Lee often expressed worry over the large number of cavalrymen who had become dismounted, and the number of horses that had become worn down through long service.

Meanwhile, the federal riders were gaining in experience and confidence supplied with horses through a system of remount stations. All federal cavalry regiments were required to hold monthly inspections of the mounts and send the reports to Washington on the mileage traveled, the treatment and shoeing of animals, and any deficiencies of forage. The demand for fit horses was greatest during the third year of the war.

—James M. Volo

INTERNATIONAL TRADE: THE CONFEDERATE COMMERCE RAIDERS

The damages due to the attacks of Confederate commerce raiders on the Northern merchant marine during the American Civil War have continued to serve as the keystone of the traditional explanation for the years between 1866 and 1890 being called "The Dark Ages of American Oceanic Enterprise."

On November 6, 1865, the CSS *Shenandoah* ended her journey of destruction in Great Britain having captured or destroyed 38 vessels. The *Shenandoah*, powered by sail with auxiliary steam, was the last of approximately 18 commerce raiders commissioned by the Confederate government. Of these, only eight achieved any substantial results, four of these: *Shenandoah, Tallahassee, Florida*, and *Alabama*, being credited with the lion's share of the damage. The raiders captured or destroyed a total of 239 vessels, or 105 thousand tons, causing a direct loss to Northern shipping interests of between twenty and twenty-five million dollars. Remarkably, not a single American merchant sailor was killed during these operations.

It was the purpose of the Confederacy to damage Northern trade by driving up the cost of maritime insurance without which no major shipowner could afford to operate. War risk rates were supplemental premiums set beyond the cost of ordinary marine insurance for which the fees were considerably lower. In the case of loss due to natural disaster or act of war, the insurance covered the financial damage to the owners up to, but not beyond, the value of the vessel and cargo. At the time of the War of 1812, rates ranged from 40 percent to 75 percent on runs to the Far East, and insurance at any cost for an American vessel was unavailable to Europe, the Mediterranean, and the West Indies (Albion 1968, 63, 70).

War risk rates were set by taking into consideration the route of the vessel, its type and cargo, and the ability of its navy to protect it. Used in this manner war risk rates are a significant indicator of the control of the seas in a conflict. Since the Southern naval forces in the American Civil War were never comparable to those of the

North, it may be concluded that the higher rates reflected a panic in Northern shipping circles that did more damage than the actual ravages of the raiders. This panic may have been rooted in America's own experience with commerce raiding during the American Revolution (Albion 1968, 169).

During the Civil War period, the premiums for war risks on Northern shipping ranged from 1 to 3 percent in 1861, to 10 percent in 1863 at the height of Confederate raiding activity. As early as 1863 the *New York Times* (August 4, 1863, 1:1) reported that British opinion was of the mind that "American shipping had almost become valueless in consequence of the seizures made by the Confederate cruisers." Nonetheless, insurance premiums of 10 percent or less were small when compared with historically high rates for war risk in other periods. Moreover, the highest war risk rates in the Civil War period reflected insurance only to the more distant runs in the East Indies and the Pacific. War rates on Northern vessels to Europe, the West Indies, and along the Atlantic coast remained remarkably low, ranging from as little as 0.5 percent to 3.5 percent throughout the period (G. W. Dalzell 1940, 239–40; Albion 1968, 169–70). As the war progressed strategic commercial intersections such as the English Channel, Gibraltar, Capetown, and Bahia in the South Atlantic proved to be patrolled by an ever increasing number of federal cruisers purposely detached from the blockading squadrons to these locations in an attempt to stop the raiders (West 1957, 277).

The depredations of the Confederate raiders did little to depress the domestic coasting trade, and coasters found the nearby Atlantic waters generally safe throughout the war. Although their loss was to produce the greatest panic, as few as 50 coasting vessels, exclusive of other types of craft, fell prey to the Confederates. There were calls for harbor protection and coastal convoys as fear spread from port to port. Fortunately such coastal forays were relatively rare events, and the raiders had to hit and run as word of their presence spread by telegraph to Union bases. Ironically the reports of the raiders proceeding along the coasts probably did more damage than the actual captures (Volo and Volo 2001, 287–88).

In October 1864, however, two Confederate raiders escaped from the federal forces blockading Wilmington and burned several coasting vessels, ships, and a pilot boat off the New Jersey coast, Sandy Hook, and Block Island causing a financial panic in the New York markets. Although the Confederates destroyed 20 vessels, they proved to be of little monetary value. Even so, the presence of these raiders did cause considerable local panic, and the psychological impact of the depredations on the Northern public was enormous.

Commerce destruction was considered a secondary objective of the Confederate naval effort when compared to the primary goal of drawing Union blockading vessels away from the Atlantic and Gulf coasts. In this they failed, and the 1864 exploits of the Confederate navy were considered by some contemporaries to be counterproductive. No blockading vessels were dispatched north to intercept the raiders. Instead, the very success of the raiders resulted in a tightening of the blockade, which denied the South badly needed supplies when they were needed the most (Volo and Volo 2001, 291–92).

As a single identifiable class, the whalers were the most preyed upon of U.S. flag vessels during the conflict. Almost 15 percent of the U.S. whaling fleet was destroyed or otherwise removed from operation during the war years. Yet the demise of U.S. whaling was symptomatic of deep weaknesses in the industry that included overharvesting and depressed market prices. The fleet, in fact, saw a brief increase in the whaling tonnage in 1866, but statistics indicate that the whaling underwent a sudden collapse in 1867, which is generally attributed to the introduction of cheap petroleum fuels and lubricants. These products had begun to gain a market share as early as 1859. Whale oil as a lighting fuel was driven from the marketplace by 1873 to be replaced by kerosene, and only less profitable whale byproducts retained any market. Consequently, the whaling fleet gradually shrank as vessels became worn out. The process was enhanced by the twin disasters of 1871 and 1876 in which 41 whaling vessels were crushed in the encroaching polar ice (Clark 1949, 125).

The decline of the U.S. foreign carrying trade in the final quarter of the nineteenth century, especially the profitable transatlantic trade, seems to be best understood in terms removed from a continued emphasis on the activities of the Confederate raiders and the permanence of their consequences (Simons 1983, 161). The failure to modernize the foreign carrying fleet, at a point in time when America's standing in world commerce was already under attack, serves as a more rationale mechanism for the enduring nature of the decline. As one historian has noted: "The elements contributing to the decline of the merchant marine were already apparent before the Civil War, and the results would have been the same if the conflict had not occurred" (Bauer 1989, 241; Volo and Volo 2001, 292–94).

FOR MORE INFORMATION

Albion, Robert G., and Jennie B. Pope. *Sealanes in Wartime*. Portland, ME: Archon Books, 1968.

Bauer, K. Jack. *A Maritime History of the United States: The Role of America's Seas and Waterways*. Columbia: University of South Carolina Press, 1989.

Clark, Victor S. *History of Manufactures in the United States*. 3 vols. New York: Peter Smith Publishers, 1949.

Dalzell, G. W. *The Flight from the Flag: The Continuing Effect of the Civil War upon the American Carrying Trade*. Chapel Hill: University of North Carolina Press, 1940.

Dunaway, Wilma A. "Slavery and Emancipation in the Mountain South: Sources, Evidence and Methods," Virginia Tech, Online Archives. http://scholar.lib.vt.edu/faculty_archives/mountain_slavery/cival war.htm (accessed July 2007).

Faust, Drew Gilpin. "The Civil War Homefront." http://www.cr.nps.gov/history/online_books/rthg/chap6.htm

Gwin, Minrose C. *A Woman's Civil War*. Madison: University of Wisconsin Press, 1992.

Heidler, David S. and Jeanne T. Heidler, eds. *Daily Life of Civilians in Wartime Early America, From the Colonial Era to the Civil War*. Westport, CT: Greenwood Press, 2007.

McGuire, Judith W. *Diary of a Southern Refugee during the War by a Lady of Virginia*. Lincoln: University of Nebraska Press, 1995.

Miers, Earl Schenck, ed. *A Rebel War Clerk's Diary, by John B. Jones, 1861–1865*. New York: Sagamore Press, 1958.

Pollard, Edward A. *Southern History of the War*. New York: Fairfax Press, 1990. Reprint of the 1866 edition.

Randall, J. G., and David Donald. *The Civil War and Reconstruction*. Boston, MA: D.C. Heath and Company, 1961.

Scharf, J. Thomas. *History of the Confederate States Navy*. New York: Fairfax Press, 1887.

Schollander, Wendell, and Wes Schollander. *Forgotten Elegance, The Art, Artifacts, and Peculiar History of Victorian and Edwardian Entertaining in America*. Westport, CT: Greenwood Press, 2002.

Simons, Gerald, ed. *The Blockade: Runners and Raiders*. Alexandria, VA: Time-Life Books, 1983.

Tice, Douglas O. "Bread or Blood: The Richmond Bread Riot." *Civil War Times Illustrated*, February 1974.

Volo, Dorothy Denneen, and James M. Volo. *The Antebellum Period*. Westport, CT: Greenwood Press, 2004.

———. *Daily Life in Civil War America*. Westport, CT: Greenwood Press, 1998.

———. *Daily Life in the Age of Sail*. Westport, CT: Greenwood Press, 2001.

———. *Encyclopedia of the Antebellum South*. Westport, CT: Greenwood Press, 2000.

———. *Family Life in 19th-Century America*. Westport, CT: Greenwood Press, 2007.

West, Richard S., Jr. *Mr. Lincoln's Navy*. New York: Longmans, Green and Co., 1957.

Whitehurst, Clinton H. *The U.S. Shipbuilding Industry: Past, Present, and Future*. Annapolis, MD: Naval Institute Press, 1986.

Wilson, Harold S. *Confederate Industry, Manufactures and Quartermasters in the Civil War*. Jackson: University Press of Mississippi, 2002.

Wise, Stephen R. *Lifeline of the Confederacy: Blockade Running during the Civil War*. Columbia: University of South Carolina Press, 1988.

Intellectual Life

THE EMERGENCE OF AMERICA

The British author Charles Dickens visited America in 1842, and thousands of Americans citizens turned out to greet him in New York City, Boston, Philadelphia, Cleveland, St. Louis, and Richmond. Dickens came to see an America he believed was the hope and promise of the world, but he found its cities filthy and unsophisticated. In his *American Notes*, written upon his return to England in 1842, he described New York as crude, violent, and lacking in the basic manners expected for the English middle class. He was greatly aghast at the conditions he found in America. He considered the tenements hideous, the prisons loathsome, and the taverns low and squalid; and he expressed a strong aversion for the American press and its politicians, calling them a "foul growth" upon America's utilitarian society. Dickens also toured the West, or what was then considered the West. He disliked

Cleveland, Ohio and reported that the Indians, who were so highly esteemed by the authors of romantic literature, were actually wretched creatures (Volo and Volo 2004, 220–21).

Notwithstanding Dickens' opinion of American society, never in history had mankind experienced such revolutionary changes in everyday life as was experienced in the nineteenth century. In 1800, horses were the fastest mode of both transportation and communications; in 1900, railroads and steamships traveled at speeds unimagined a century earlier, and communications were made all but instantaneous with the telegraph and the telephone. At the beginning of the century, farmers had worked their small fields with implements very similar to those used by their ancestors, and farm wives made the family clothing and preserved almost the entire stock of winter food in their homes. Most Americans in 1900 lived a life so fundamentally different that it would not have been recognized only a few generations earlier. These fundamental changes in everyday life shaped the growth of American intellectual life (Timmons 2005, 1).

Most American intellectuals of the prewar period were widely read in the literature of European romanticism, and they used romantic allusions in their prose and poetry. A romantic movement that emphasized feeling, imagination, and nature swept the nation in the decades before 1860. It embraced the past, drawing strongly on the styles and ways of ancient civilizations and medieval times. Romanticism could also be found in architecture, painting and decoration, and even in the institutions of government. The number of those that tried to cultivate a sense of letters, the sciences, and the arts was immense.

Literary pursuits were deemed a gentleman's avocation in the decades prior to the Civil War though by the 1840s, if not earlier, women writers produced an increasingly large output of novels, stories, verse, and advice books for the market. American gentlemen loved their books and often acquired a polished literary style, but they seldom ventured into print. To write a treatise on surveying, mining, or husbandry and share it among one's social equals was one thing, but to publish them for the common people to read often offended their sense of propriety. Their style was utilitarian and conversational, and it seemingly excluded the stiffly artificial, indirect, and abstract forms of classical Europeans for a style that more closely resembled modern American prose.

—*James M. Volo*

SCIENCE

The American System

One of the problems inherent in an attempt to address the development of science and technology in the nineteenth century is that—unlike the twentieth century—there was no well-established basis for connecting technology to science. The United States in this period, even more than in European countries, was a society steeped in a pronounced affection for the utilitarian. The United States was a land of mechanics. There was often a marked disconnect between theoretical concepts (generally left to Europeans) and the practical considerations faced by American inventors. Alexis de Tocqueville observed when he visited America that in democracies those who studied science were always afraid of getting lost in utopias. He even offered a reason for this peculiarity of Americans for the utilitarian and practical. Everyone in America seems to be on the move, in quest of power or of other gain—be it financial or personal. The endless chase after wealth left little time for the pursuit of the intellectual (Timmons 2005, 2).

Perhaps the most important development in the century was the emergence of an entirely new system of manufacturing, a system uniquely American that became the envy of the rest of the world. The term "American System," coined at midcentury, referred to the perception of many Americans that their country needed an industrial identity different than—and superior to—the European system that had been in place since the previous century. In fact, the term itself was first used by a British commission created to investigate the success of American inventions and technology—in particular the Colt Revolver and the McCormick Reaper—at the famous Crystal Palace Exhibition in London in 1851. Driven almost to a patriotic frenzy by Henry Clay and other orators, promoters of this new system pointed to every conceivable segment of the manufacturing industries, from its workforce to its manufacturing methods (Timmons 2005, 4).

Celebrations marking the completion of any major technological project involved everyone from local dignitaries to the workers responsible for the labor to the citizenry affected by its implementation. In 1825, the parade marking the opening of the Erie Canal included firemen, carpenters, millwrights, merchants, militiamen, cabinetmakers, and many other workers. A similar celebration in 1828 for the opening of the Baltimore and Ohio Railroad included more than 5,000 persons, and the meeting of the transcontinental railways at Promontory, Utah, was accompanied by blaring bands, the driving of a golden spike, and a well-known and oft-reproduced photograph (Timmons 2005, 6).

SCIENCE GOES TO WAR

Science and technology took on their most gruesome aspects during the Civil War. With the exception of the cavalry, who were provided with a wide assortment of firearms including pistols and rapid-fire repeaters, both armies issued muzzle-loading rifled muskets with percussion cap ignition to the infantry. This replaced the flintlock ignition of earlier days with a fulminate of mercury ignition cap. Most commonly the muskets were American made .58 caliber Springfields or British .577 caliber Enfields. The soldiers found Enfields more accurate than Springfields. Troops would trade their weapon for an Enfield on the battlefield if the opportunity presented itself, and whole companies were sometimes rearmed in such a manner after a major engagement.

The similarity in musket calibers proved a great advantage in distributing supplies and was a godsend to the Confederacy, which could use captured federal ammunition. The ammunition for Springfields and Enfields was interchangeable for all practical purposes, but cavalry ammunition was generally made in a smaller caliber, .52 caliber being a popular size, to relieve some of the recoil experienced with lighter weapons. The most common pistol calibers were .36, .44, and .45, but almost any size bullet might be fired from the hundreds of private weapons carried to the battlefield by recruits. Thousands of metal cartridge pistols, sometimes advertised as "lifesavers," were returned to families in the North by Federals who found them useless encumbrances once they had become veterans.

With the minié ball, a conical bullet with a hollowed base developed by Captain Claude Minié, the rifled musket was capable of hitting a man-sized target at 800 yards and had plain sights that were adjustable to that range. Effectively, a target the size of a man could barely be seen at 800 yards. However, used in a volley—hundreds of muskets firing simultaneously—the musket could be deadly over open ground. Even at long ranges the soldiers were rather afraid of them. The need to ram down the charge before firing slowed the sustained rate of fire of most troops to about three aimed shots per minute.

Sharpshooting, the use of carefully aimed shots by individuals designated to pick off officers, artillerymen, or other conspicuous persons, was a peculiar characteristic of the Civil War battlefield that hearkened back to the activities of the fringe-shirted riflemen of the Revolution. Generally, no special weapon was used for this purpose, though many sharpshooters were equipped for the first time with long telescopic sights.

Breechloaders like the Sharps or Smith carbines could fire 9 rounds a minute, and the fully self-contained brass cartridge of the Spencer repeating rifle allowed for 20 rounds a minute. There was a genuine concern among military experts—lasting through World War I and diminishing only after World War II—that the soldiers would quickly expend all of their available ammunition with repeating weapons. Nonetheless, breech-loading designs and revolvers were widely issued to the cavalry and other specialty troops.

Breech-loading also made rifled artillery more effective and quicker to fire. Explosive shells that flung large metal fragments around the battlefield had been used for many decades, but a new type of shell filled with hundreds of musket balls was developed by Henry Shrapnel after the revolution as an antipersonnel weapon. Shells with large balls were used against horses and artillery. Both the torpedo (water mine) and the land mine were used during the war; and warships—both steam and sail—were fitted with rifled ordnance, revolving turrets, and iron cladding (Volo and Volo 1998, 141–42).

EDUCATION

In this period schooling had a regional flavor. In the North and Midwest, schools were community or common schools. These schools would be open to all children from the community. The South was far behind in providing any form of education for the masses. In the South's defense, its sparse white population density and large number of black slaves made common or community schools impractical. Private tutors for one or two children, or private teachers of small groups were more often found than community educational systems.

Conditions in common schools varied tremendously not only from North to South but from community to community. School revenue was directly tied to the success or failure of local commerce. In an 1861 report, numerous county superintendents in Pennsylvania reported frosts in June and early July. The resulting loss of the wheat crop caused more than ordinary pecuniary embarrassment, in addition, teaching time was shortened, and in some communities, the wages of the teachers were reduced. More than one superintendent lamented a false system of economy that reduced teachers' wages so much that some of the best teachers left the county or became engaged in other pursuits. Some districts chose to suspend school for the entire year. Nonetheless, remaining teachers were applauded for their self-denial and the manner in which they bore up during a difficult time. In the same year, where lumbering districts were favored by high water, there was increased prosperity.

School buildings were constructed in a number of ways and might be of brick, frame, log, or stone. In the 1861 state report, 58 percent of the Pennsylvania superintendents who responded used negative terms to describe their schools. It was not unusual to see claims that the schools were "less fit for the purpose of schooling, than would be many modern out houses for sheltering cattle." One schoolhouse was described as "a crumbling, dilapidated, damp, unwholesome stone building with a ceiling eight feet high, room about twenty-six by thirty feet into which one hundred and seventeen are crowded, and placed at long, old fashioned desks, with permanent seats, without backs." One superintendent reported finding "the teacher and pupils huddled together, shivering with cold, and striving to warm themselves by the little heat generated from a quantity of green wood in the stove." Additional complaints included a lack of outhouses and other appliances necessary for comfort and convenience. Concern was expressed over the fact that schoolhouses were placed far off the road and buried in the wilderness forest. Schools were often crowded. Henry Hobart, a teacher in Copper County, Michigan, reported that he had 130 scholars in a schoolroom large enough to accommodate 75 (Volo and Volo 1998, 272–73).

Hobart concluded that people were very indifferent to the education of their children. He reported that most of the schoolhouses were fitted to torture the children rather than add to the comfort and ease. Under such circumstances, he observed, many children disliked going to school because they were so uncomfortable that they could not learn (Volo and Volo 2007, 284).

Yet a number of new schools were described in more favorable terms. One report described a tasteful brick building 30 by 45 furnished with first-class iron frame furniture for 62 pupils. Other new buildings were of wood, and one was 24 by 36 with four tiers of seats for two pupils each accommodating 64 pupils. Another superintendent boasted that all the rooms were warmed by coal stoves, most of them had ceilings of proper height, windows adapted to ventilation; plenty of blackboard surface; and they were tolerably well seated. A new schoolhouse was proudly described as having an anteroom, closets, and a platform and was superior to most of the other houses in every respect.

The schools in most states were supervised by a group of designated citizens who oversaw operations. Their duties included the levying of tax, the location of schoolhouses, the purchase and sale of school property, the appointment and dismissal of teachers, and the selection of studies and textbooks. The dedication and expertise of these directors was, however, often called into question.

Rural districts were often unsuccessful in obtaining a normal school graduate and had to settle for whatever reasonably well-educated person they could find. Although both men and women taught, male teachers were preferred. As the Civil War progressed, many young men left the schoolroom to serve in the army or to fill better-paying jobs. This dearth of males opened the doors for women in education. A county superintendent of schools wrote that the employment of female teachers caused some dissatisfaction, as they were believed inadequate to the task of controlling a winter school. But superior cleanliness and arrangement of their rooms, the effect of their natural gentleness and goodness on the scholars amply compensated for their want of physical force. These qualities were appreciated even more when it was found that the generally younger women could be paid lower salaries than the male teachers. The average salary reported in 1861 for a male teacher was $24.20 per month. Women were paid $18.11.

One superintendent expressed concern that the majority of teachers were between 18 and 25, and some of the teachers were little more than children themselves. Another superintendent complained that parents would urge their sons and daughters to seek to become teachers at so early an age and in great error school directors, as a general rule, employ them. He noted that the same men engage persons of mature age and experience on the farm, in the shop or store, in the kitchen or dairy room, but they hire girls or boys of 15 or 16 to train up and educate their offspring (Volo and Volo 1998, 272–73).

School districts began to establish examinations to certify that teachers were competent to assume their duties. Most exams were a combination of written and oral questions. Some were held publicly, and attended by numbers of citizens, who had a desire to see and hear for themselves. Emma Sargent Barbour's sister, Maria, wrote about the examination process in Washington. She was to be examined, when her companion remarked that she had a good mind to try the exam herself, just for fun. She went in and passed an excellent examination and the following Monday took a position at Maria's school. Not all examinations were quite as simple as Maria implies. Many superintendents in Pennsylvania reported having to turn away applicants who had failed, while others indicated that, considering the rural nature of their district, they were lucky to find teachers at all. Many parents preferred to have their children work in the mines or learn a trade, and thus but few become qualified to teach school.

Institutes were held periodically to help teachers to improve their skills. Some met only once a year, while others were held semimonthly on alternate Saturdays. Naturally, not all teachers performed to the satisfaction of the districts. A Wayne County,

Pennsylvania, superintendent wrote that two of his teachers in winter school had the reputation of having intemperate habits, and others were rough and rowdy in their manner (Volo and Volo 2007, 286–87).

About 50 percent of children outside the South attended school with some regularity. Some areas of the Midwest and New England had enrollments as high as 90 percent. Attendance in rural areas still suffered from the fact that many parents kept their children at home to help with farm labor, and it was not until such seasonal tasks were finished would they be allowed to start school. Not everyone was convinced that public education was beneficial, but public sentiment was gradually becoming more favorable to the system (Volo and Volo 2007, 297).

Most Southerners were opposed to tax-supported education. The school reformers and educational advocates of the 1840s were mostly Northerners. This contributed to a certain skepticism on the part of Southerners, who felt that the school systems were at least partially responsible for Northern attitudes in the decade preceding the war. Most Southerners preferred to send their children to private institutions. By 1860 only four Southern states and a few isolated communities had common school systems.

Popular instructional materials included *McGuffey's Eclectic Reader*, *Ray's Arithmetic*, and Webster's "blue back" *Speller*. Spelling was just becoming standardized. *Leach's Complete Spelling Book* of 1859 contained a "Collection of Words of Various Orthography," which included words of "common use, which are spelled differently by the three most eminent Lexicographers...Webster, Worcester and Smart." Students were graded by the reader from which they read. Many schools suffered from a lack of uniform class sets of texts and used old books, some of which, carefully preserved, had descended from grandfathers, although the adoption of uniform texts was frequently a goal.

In many schools sufficient blackboards were also wanting. Blackboards were made by taking smooth boards—painted black—and covering them with a chalk dust, which provided the erasable surface. Well-supported schools not only had blackboards but also outline maps, spelling and reading cards, charts, and globes. The average school had only one or two of these instructional materials. Paper was scarce in rural schools. Students commonly wrote on wood frame slates, although these were initially confined to those who had made advancement in arithmetic, but in time, even the smallest scholars were writing with slates.

Furniture was, at best, sparse in most classrooms. One superintendent lamented that it was useless to complain of school furniture because it seemed that people would sooner see their children have spinal or pulmonary affliction, than furnish the schoolroom with proper desks and seats. A York County, Pennsylvania, superintendent reported witnessing a great deal of uneasiness, even intense suffering, among the small children who were seated too high. In some instances, the desks were attached to the wall, the scholars with their backs to the teacher.

There were few, if any, educational standards at this time. The length of the school day and year varied as the individual community saw fit. The average length of the school term in 1860 was five months and five and one-half days. A typical school day ran from nine to four with an hour for recess and dinner at noon. The day often commenced with a Scripture reading followed by a patriotic song. Emma Sargent Barbour received a letter from her sister, Maria, describing her teaching day. She reported that she rose at seven, had breakfast at half past, practiced her little singing lesson and was ready to start for school at half past eight. She would direct the students how to behave and hear their lessons until twelve, then from twenty minutes to a half an hour, she would hear missed lessons and eat lunch, chat with the boys until one o'clock, then proceed as before until three.

Most learning was done via rote memorization and recitation. To motivate the students, less interesting material, such as geographic facts, was sung to popular tunes. Multiplication tables were often taught in verse; for example, "Twice 11 are 22. Mister can you mend my shoe?" or "9 times 12 are 108. See what I've drawn upon my slate." Hobart complained that he found very few scholars who could give a proper explanation of the various principles that are brought out in the various steps in arithmetic or in fact any study. He observed that most students went over the pages of the book and yet knew very little of what they read. Mental arithmetic was still an innovative technique in 1860, but it was all the rage in educational journals. More than one district reveled in the fact that it was taught in their schools. One boasted that mental arithmetic had been extensively introduced over the previous two years and predicted that it would soon be considered an indispensable item even in the primary schools.

In Connecticut, towns with 80 families were required to have a single school for young children that taught English grammar, reading, writing, geography, and arithmetic. Towns with 500 families added a school for older students that offered algebra, American history, geometry, and surveying. Places with larger populations offered study of the physical sciences—sometimes referred to as natural or revealed philosophy—and Greek and Latin. The subjects taught depended on the competency of the teacher and varied greatly from school to school. In the annual report of Armstrong County, Pennsylvania, the superintendent boasted that the number of schools in which geography and grammar were not taught was steadily diminishing. There was a considerable increase in the number in which mental arithmetic was taught. Algebra was taught in 11 schools; history in 4; natural philosophy in 2; Latin in 1; composition in 5, and in several there were exercises in declamation and vocal music.

In the same report, Beaver County noted that the Bible was read in 140 of the 147 schools. The report hoped that teachers would become so deeply impressed with a sense of their duty in the moral education of their pupils that they would soon be able to report that the Bible was read in every school. In addition to the three R's, schools were expected to infuse a strong moral sense, foster polite behavior, and inspire good character. Another instructional objective, presented in a reading text, was "a desire to improve the literary taste of the learner, to impress correct moral principles, and augment his fund of knowledge." An introductory geography book contained the following extraordinary attestation in its preface: "The introduction of moral and religious sentiments into books designed for the instruction of young persons, is calculated to improve the heart, and elevate and expand the youthful mind; accordingly, whenever the subject has admitted of it, such observations have been made as tend to illustrate the excellence of Christian religion, the advantages of correct moral principles, and the superiority of enlightened institutions."

Readers contained lessons entitled "The First Falsehood," "Effects of Evil Company," "Contrast between Industry and Idleness," and "Dialogue between Mr. Punctual and Mr. Tardy." Stories, poems, and essays used in instruction drilled the message that good triumphed over evil, frugality surpassed extravagance, obedience superseded willfulness, and family always came first. This can be seen even in brief multiplication rhymes—"5 times 10 are 50. My Rose is very thrifty" or "4 times 10 are 40. Those boys are very naughty." The last was inscribed beneath a picture of two boys fighting.

Some texts published in the North during the war contained distinctly pro-Union sentiments. *Hillard's Fifth Reader*, printed in 1863, contained such readings as "Liberty and Union" and "The Religious Character of President Lincoln," as well as "Song of the Union," the poem " Barbara Frietchie," and an essay on the "Duty of American Citizens" among many similar patriotic themes. Caroline Cowles Richards noted in her 1861 diary that at school she recited "Scott and the Veteran," while others recited "To Drum Beat and Heart Beat a Soldier Marches By" and "The Virginia Mother." She observed that "everyone learns war poems now-a-days."

Rural schools were often ungraded and had no standard final examinations or report cards. Scholastic success was still given a showcase via exhibition bees and quizzes held for parents. Students demonstrated their expertise in spelling, arithmetic, geography, and history. In addition to praise, winners were given certificates and prizes such as books or prints. Gifted students could pass through the entire local system of schools by age 14 or 15, but only the most affluent could move on to college or university. A foreign visitor to New England found that most men had a basic education that stressed reading and writing, but that few exhibited the fine formal education available in Europe.

Southern teachers were even more challenged by the need for educational materials than their Northern counterparts. The South had depended on the North and Europe for texts prior to the war. Once the war began, Northern publications were held in contempt and the blockade curtailed European imports. A movement commenced in the South to produce its own texts, but shortages of materials and the destruction of printing equipment impeded implementation of the plan. What texts were published tended to be extremely propagandistic and of low quality. Marinda Branson Moore of North Carolina was probably the most audacious of Southern authors in this regard. She published *Dixie Primer for Little Folks* (1864) and *Dixie Speller* (1864), which was revised from Webster and adapted for Southern schools leaving out all Yankee phrases and allusions. Her geography addressed the issues of slavery and secession and laid blame for the war on the North.

Southerners regretted having allowed Northerners to teach their children prior to the war. Teaching was a respectable vocation, but women who taught in the South were often pitied for their obvious dire financial situation. With the outbreak of hostilities, the distaste for Northern teachers spread rapidly. Advertisements for teachers soon came to request that applicants be natives of Dixie or from Europe. Wartime dangers eventually suspended many Southern schools, and the task of educating youngsters fell to the mothers.

While common schools were well established by this time, and enrollments grew throughout the war in Northern cities, the development of high schools, slow before the war, faced even more obstacles. The lure of the military, or opportunities made available by army enlistments, siphoned off many would-be students. High schools were essentially an urban institution, founded with the intention of providing opportunity for boys who wished to become merchants or mechanics. Such an education was seen as terminal. Boston, a leader in educational matters, did not open a high school for girls until 1855. Although some Northern areas required larger cities to establish high schools, most people felt that this was a form of higher education and should not be part of the legal public school system. By 1860 there were 300 high schools in the United States, 100 of which were in Massachusetts.

College enrollments also suffered as idealistic young men rushed to join the forces of their cause. Caroline Cowles Richards listed in her diary a number of young men who talked of leaving college and going to war. She described a rally at the Canandaigua Academy in New York and detailed how the captain drilled the Academy boys in military tactics on the campus every day. She also noted that men were constantly enlisting. Southern colleges had the additional complications of the loss of funding, physical destruction from battle, and conversion to hospitals, barracks, and headquarters.

College studies were heavily classical. Students read Latin and Greek from Livy, Cicero, Homer, Plato, and others. As in primary school, recitation was the most common form of instruction. Work in the sciences, which covered physics and astronomy, with some chemistry and geology, consisted mostly of lectures along with occasional laboratory demonstrations. Mathematics explored geometry, trigonometry, and calculus and encompassed memorization of rules with some effort to apply them to problems. Rhetoric students studied composition as well as speaking. Other studies included philosophy and logic.

The year 1862 was an important one for education. The Morrill Act passed through the U. S. Congress, establishing the land grant colleges. It was also the year in which Washington, D.C., made the first provisions for so-called Negro schooling. While the effects of both of these events may have been felt more after the war, they nonetheless show an extremely positive federal attitude toward education, even amid the turmoil of war.

It has been estimated that at the outbreak of the war only five percent of slaves could read. As federal troops occupied an area and set the slaves free, many former slaves established schools to help others prepare for freedom. Often Union commanders occupying an area mandated the creation of such schools or allowed their creation by Northern missionaries. These practices led to the creation of the Freedmen's Bureau in 1865, through which the federal government took a formal stance toward the education of former slaves. Northern teachers who traveled to the South during the war suffered tremendous hardships. They were deeply resented by Southerners, who commonly refused them any accommodations, and overworked by the

Northern agencies that sent them. What passed for schoolrooms were often worse than the most desolate of Northern facilities.

While the North provided for the education of some free blacks, the idea of racially integrated schools was vehemently opposed. When before the war Prudence Crandall attempted to integrate her fashionable Connecticut school for girls, the white students were quickly withdrawn by outraged parents. Crandall herself was insulted, threatened, and stoned. In the interest of the safety of her students, she was forced to acquiesce. Some common school systems established schools for minority groups such as Amerindians and free blacks. Considering the inadequate support many regular schools were given, one can imagine the facilities that would have been provided when a separate school was established for a minority group. An observer of a Colored School remarked that although the black pupils were progressing, if the same facilities be afforded to them, which are given to the children in other schools in the borough, they would soon compare favorably with them, not only in the lower levels, but also in the more advanced departments (Volo and Volo 1998, 275–80).

—*Dorothy Denneen Volo*

LITERATURE

Literacy

Literacy was quite high in America. In the South at least 70 percent of the white male population could read, and in the North the ability to read may have run as high as 90 percent. What people read during the war was dependent on what was available. In the Northern urban centers there was an almost unlimited amount and variety of reading material, but Southern civilians had their literary choices disrupted not only by the vagaries of the war, but also by the blockade. Newspapers printed what was available. Confederate battlefield heroes and other men of prominence were given front-page treatment. The boredom of battle reports, advertisements, and political tracts was broken, for example, when the personal letters of General George A. Custer to a young woman were captured. The Richmond papers printed them and provided some spicy reading for the ladies.

Books were read, reread, and loaned among friends and acquaintances. Many women and men turned to instructive reading, spending time with books on history, geography, painting, foreign languages, surveying, and needlework. A number of books were available on etiquette, manners, propriety, the rearing of children, husbandry, and oratory. There was a renewed interest in the Bible and religious tracts, the plays of Shakespeare, and the novels of Charles Dickens, Walter Scott, and James Fenimore Cooper.

Prior to 1820, English texts, less expensive and more fashionable, had almost closed the literary market to American authors. The emergence of a new popularity of reading and writing among the middle class underpinned a new national interest in publishing and professional authorship. This circumstance was further fostered by the need to while away long hours of boredom created by the lack of normal social activities brought on by the war. Four types of reading material have been identified as popular with Civil War era readers: religious reading, purposeful (or instructive) reading, newspaper and magazine reading, and reading for escape. These categories, while somewhat arbitrary, can serve to describe the majority of the printed materials sought by nineteenth-century readers (Kaser 1984, 3).

Northern tastes in literature dominated the American publishing industry, and only a few Southern writers like Paul Hamilton Hayne and Henry Timrod could boast a national following. Much of Southern writing was dedicated to pro-South apologies or tales featuring local color that did not tempt readers from other regions. Moreover, the majority of publishing houses, type manufactories, paper mills, and book binderies in the country were located in the North.

—*James M. Volo*

The Novel

Beginning in the second decade of the nineteenth century, the novel, the most popular form of escapism, was found to have a growing acceptance and appeal among the general reading public. Middle- and upper-class women have long been recognized as the chief consumers of this literary form. Fictional characters possessed a remarkable ability to influence nineteenth-century readers. Uncle Tom, Topsy, Ivanhoe, Hawkeye, Hester Prynne, and Ebenezer Scrooge were deeply familiar characters to a society that read as much as nineteenth-century Americans did. These characters often seemed to become nearly as real and as influential to the reader as actual friends and relations.

So great was the popularity of the novel that it drew criticism. As late as 1856 the state of New York recognized the necessity of excluding from all libraries "novels, romances and other fictitious creations of the imagination," including a large proportion of the lighter literature of the day. "The propriety of a peremptory and uncompromising exclusion of those catch-penny, but revolting publications which cultivate the taste for the marvelous, the tragic, the horrible and the supernatural...[is without] the slightest argument." Librarians and school officials expressed an obvious disgust for works dealing with "pirates, banditti and desperadoes of every description." The novels of Camden Pelham, Augusta Jane Evans, Edward Maturin, Matthew G. Lewis, and Ann Radcliffe were all identified as having "an unhealthy influence upon the soul" that should be avoided (Volo and Volo 1998, 205).

The "Pelham novels" were the works of Camden Pelham, who wrote *The Chronicles of Crime* (1841), a series of memoirs and anecdotes about British criminals. They were illustrated by H. K. Browne, the famous illustrator of Dickens' works who went by the pseudonym "Phiz." The historical novels of Irish American author Edward Maturin were particularly steeped in the romantic. They included *Montezuma, the Last of the Aztecs* (1845), a brilliant, if overly impassioned, history; *Benjamin, the Jew of Granada* (1847), set in fifteenth-century Moslem Spain; and *Eva, or the Isles of Life and Death* (1848), a romance of twelfth-century England. One of his more fiery books was *Bianca* (1852), a story of a passionate love between a woman from Italy and a man from Ireland (Volo and Volo 1998, 205).

Many novels were written by women in this early period. Women who practiced the profession of letters seem to have been viewed with less disapprobation than those who became teachers, nurses, or lawyers. Several women were acclaimed in the Southern press for their published work. The great sensation of the Southern literary world during the war was a novel by Augusta Jane Evans, published in 1864 and entitled *Macaria, or Altars of Sacrifice*. The author dedicated this novel, about a pair of heroines sacrificing their romantic love for dedication to the cause, to the Confederate forces.

The works of the English novelist and social commentator Charles Dickens were widely read in America. In Dickens's very popular works both sections of the country found some character, situation, or condition that seemed to bolster the very different views of modern society Americans held. Many social reformers, like Dickens himself, championed the cause of the poor. Nonetheless, Dickens was generally unconcerned with the economic aspects of social reform, choosing rather to deal with an increased appreciation of the value of the human being. Ignorance, for him, was the great cause of human misery. In 1843 he gave a speech in the city of Manchester in which he pleaded for an end to the ragged schools that had been set up by well-meaning but untrained volunteer teachers to give England's poor children the rudiments of an education. Dickens proposed that the surest improvement in the nation's future was tied to a public investment in education sponsored by the government.

Dickens's stories emphasized the need to change traditional ways of thinking. But many in the South misread Dickens's message and saw the misfortune, destitution, and disease that fills his works as characteristic of all urban life. Modern urban life was the great evil haunting the romantic domains of the Southern imagination. Dickens's novels, Southerners argued, mirrored the inevitable bleak future of America if Northern concepts of social progress continued to be implemented as English ones had for decades without noticeably improving society.

Southerners despised such ambiguous social remedies as the poorhouses and the workhouses that filled Dickens's pages. The debtors' prison of *Little Dorrit* (1857) and the orphanage of *Oliver Twist* (1838) were obviously not sufficient to solve the social ills of an urban society. Southerners were left with a portrait of cities, like those of the North, veritably teeming with the exploited masses from which they chose to be separated. Apologists for the Southern way of life proclaimed that Scrooge's treatment of Bob Cratchit in *A Christmas Carol* (1858) emphasized the abuses possible in an age governed by the "work for wage" system that so lacked a sense of personal involvement and family dedication. By their own reckoning the personal responsibility many Southerners felt toward their neighbors, their workers, and even their slaves seemed noble in contrast to the socially anonymous caretaking for the unfortunates found in Dickens's works.

The most popular book of the war period was by Victor Hugo titled *Les Miserables* in 1862. This was closely followed by Alfred Lord Tennyson's 1864 narrative poem *Enoch Arden,* in which a shipwrecked sailor returns home to find that his wife, thinking him dead, has remarried. Sir Walter Scott's *Waverley* novels were immensely popular. Their theme of the Scottish struggle to throw off the dominance and oppression of the English served as an analogy for the position in which the South saw itself with respect to the North. Scott's use of romantic characters, lords and ladies, knights in armor, and grand estates was particularly resonant with the Southern image of itself. So familiar was Scott's work to Southerners that in later years Mark Twain only half-jokingly blamed Scott for causing the Civil War.

Second only to Scott's in popularity were the American adventure novels of James Fenimore Cooper. Although his first novel was poorly accepted by American readers, largely because it imitated the British form, Cooper's second work, *The Spy*, published in 1822, was an outstanding success. Cooper's subsequent novels emphasized American manners and scenes as interesting and important. Still, many Americans considered novels to be "trivial, feminine, and vaguely dishonorable" because they appealed to the emotions and aroused the imagination. Nonetheless, Cooper found that there was a great demand for adventure tales derived from the Revolution, and his writing was sufficiently manly and moral to find acceptance by a wide audience (Volo and Volo 1998, 208).

Like Scott, Cooper promoted a social vision of a stable and genteel society governed by its natural aristocracy, "perpetuating property, order, and liberty" as represented by a reunited American gentry. That this view resonated with the Southern image of itself would have upset Cooper, with his very Northern attitudes. *The Pioneers* (1823), Cooper's third book, was dedicated to the proposition that the American republic, poised on the verge of "demagoguery, deceit, hypocrisy, and turmoil," could be transformed into a stable, prosperous, and just society. Although the theme of "reconciliation...on conservative terms" was almost three decades old, Cooper's novels were very popular with the soldiers, mainly because of their masculine adventure themes, and were often found among their most prized possessions. Dog-eared copies circulated through the camps and were often read aloud around the campfire to eager audiences (Volo and Volo 1998, 208).

Numerous American authors followed the success of Scott and Cooper, though not with equal fame at the time. These included James Kirk Paulding, John Pendleton Kennedy, William Gilmore Simms, and others. Nathaniel Hawthorne, convinced that most American literature ran too close to the British style, devoted himself to a uniquely symbolic and allegorical form. *The Scarlet Letter*, published in 1850, was certainly familiar to American readers, and its author was considered a literary giant. But Hawthorne's persistent dark emphasis on guilt and sorrow ran counter to the popular tastes and religious sentiment of Americans at mid-century. In 1851 and 1852, respectively, he published *The House of the Seven Gables* and *The Blithedale Romance*. This last was a study of failed utopian efforts to improve society.

Although soldiers were quick to write home about finishing *Nicholas Nickleby* (1839), *The Pickwick Papers* (1836), *The Deerslayer* (1841), *Ivanhoe* (1820), or other works of obvious quality, they also read a great deal of low-quality material. Many of these works have been identified. They include such masculine titles as *Con Cregan, Gold Friend, The Quadroon of Louisiana, Son of the Wilderness, Scar Chief the Wild*

Halfbreed, Wild West Scenes, and *Our Own Heroes,* but also more popular and seemingly unmanly romances such as *Lady Audley's Secret, The Mystery, Macaria,* and *Louisa Elton.* This fact helps to point out the potential influence that literature of all kinds had on the population.

Soldiers, "burdened by huge blocks of time during which they have nothing to do but wait," were suddenly possessed of an abundant amount of time to read, which "had previously been in short supply to American men." Of the five most common leisure-time camp activities—individual foraging, gambling, sleeping, talking, and reading—only reading was seen to be "a positive force" for the improvement of the troops (Kaser 1984, 18, 36).

American books, as opposed to British ones, were also in large supply for the first time during the war. In 1834 fewer than 500 titles were published in the United States. By 1862 this number had grown to almost 4,000. By coincidence the first dime novels were published in June 1860. These were inexpensive paperbound adventure stories. The first title, *Malaeska, the Indian Wife of the White Hunter,* by Ann Stephens, makes it abundantly clear that this was escapist literature of the lowest class. Publisher Irwin P. Beadle's dime novels and their many imitators initiated a whole era of cheap publishing just eight months prior to the war.

At the time there were also a number of distinguished American authors of an age to serve in the field and provide a firsthand professional description of the face of war. Theodore Winthrop had written a number of successful books prior to the war, and he volunteered to serve. Unfortunately, Winthrop was killed in one of the first engagements of the war at Great Bethel in June 1861.

Another young author distinguished before the outbreak of hostilities was John W. De Forest. From 1851 through 1859 De Forest wrote several books, including the *History of the Indians of Connecticut* and the novels *Witching Times, Oriental Acquaintance, European Acquaintance,* and *Seacliff.* De Forest went to war as a captain with the 12th Connecticut Volunteers. He worked simultaneously as a war correspondent, and many of his battlefield reports were printed by *Harper's Monthly.* In these De Forest shared the simple truth of life in the army and on the battlefield. In 1864 he published *Miss Ravenel's Conversion from Secession to Loyalty,* a novel of the effect of occupation on the South.

The enormous hunger for reading material in the camps was supplied to some extent by social and religious agencies, which recognized the need. In part the soldiers and their comrades found their own supply of reading material, but both armies were largely at the mercy of outside sources for their books and newspapers. Much of the work involved in providing books to the troops was done by the U.S. Christian Commission, which supplied both religious and secular reading material. Almost one million Bibles were distributed to the troops, and more than 30,000 other volumes were circulated through a system of almost 300 portable libraries. Each contained from 70 to 125 volumes that were transported and stored in wooden, shelved boxes about three feet square. Many of the books were printed in smaller than standard size and included classical titles as well as history, poetry, science, philosophy, and religion. The Confederate Bible Society and the South Carolina Tract Society provided religious works for the Southern troops, but the South had no system of portable libraries (Volo and Volo 1998, 211).

Juvenile Literature

From the first landings of English settlers in America, youngsters were expected to read the Bible, do their lessons from their schoolbooks (if there were any), and read little less in the way of entertaining literature. Had they chosen to read for diversion, there was little else available in any case. Nonetheless, several publications surfaced during the century to attempt to fill the gap between dry religious tracts and scandalous romance novels. The Rev. Joel Hawes, like Lydia Child, advised the young to avoid novels, but he went even further suggesting that a young person's character could be "ruined by reading a single ill-advised volume." This, of course, was blatant hyperbole, but Hawes confessed that one book, "wisely selected and properly studied" could "do more to improve the mind, and enrich the understanding, than skimming over the surface of an entire library" (Volo and Volo 2004, 216).

As early as 1827, a weekly literary magazine was founded in Boston with the purpose of providing what was deemed appropriate reading material for children. Known as *The Youth's Companion,* the magazine remained in publication for more than a century and received contributions from many famous American and European authors including Alfred Lord Tennyson, Thomas Hardy, Rudyard Kipling, Louisa May Alcott, John Greenleaf Whittier, Robert Louis Stevenson, and Jules Verne. In 1830, Sarah Josepha Hale published a similar work, *Poems for Our Children,* that included classics such as "Mary Had a Little Lamb." In 1853 and 1854 respectively, Nathaniel Hawthorne published his tales for children: *A Wonder Book* and *The Tanglewood Tales*.

School readers made their first appearance in the classroom during this period. The *Peerless Pioneer Readers* containing stories of interest to children, were first introduced in 1826 by William Holmes McGuffey, and the first of a long list of McGuffey's *Eclectic Readers* was published in 1836. Six readers in this series appeared between 1836 and 1857 with their sales reaching a peak during the Civil War. In 1846, Epes Sargent's *School Reader* made its appearance. Elijah Kellogg's blank verse *Spartacus to His Gladiators* appeared in Sargent's first edition and became a standard exercise in classroom declamation for young students for decades. Literally millions of copies of these readers found their way into schoolrooms and children's nurseries during the remainder of the century (Volo and Volo 2004, 216–17).

—*James M. Volo*

Periodicals

The main means of communicating with the public was the newspaper. New York publisher Frank Leslie produced amazingly moving woodcut illustrations for his *Illustrated Newspaper*. His use of graphics to interpret ongoing news events was a new concept in the American newspaper business that was quickly adopted by other news agencies.

Frank Leslie, whose true name was Henry Carter, had emigrated from Britain in 1848. There he had worked as an engraver for the *Illustrated London News*, which was the first newspaper to employ graphics. In London, Leslie learned the processes for turning pencil sketches into woodcut engravings that could be transferred to newsprint. In 1852 P. T. Barnum, the famed American showman, developed a process by which the sketch was divided into several pieces to be engraved on as many blocks by individual engravers, then carefully assembled into a single printing surface. This speeded processing. Leslie was hired by Barnum as a supervising engraver for the short-lived *Illustrated News*. Leaving Barnum, by 1854 he had set up his own organization and published the first issue of *Frank Leslie's Ladies' Gazette of Paris, London, and New York*, one of the first illustrated fashion magazines in America. This was quickly followed by the *Illustrated Newspaper* in 1855. Leslie employed more than 130 engraving and print artists as well as a substantial number of roving sketch artists.

Frank Leslie introduced a number of illustrated newspapers to American readers: the *Illustrated Zeitung*, a German-language edition aimed at the German immigrant population of the North; the *Budget of Fun*, a whimsical publication featuring cheap fiction; the *Ten Cent Monthly*; the *Lady's Illustrated Almanac*; and the *Lady's Magazine and Gazette of Fashion*. All of these bore his name: Frank Leslie's.

Within four years two independent graphic news weeklies were launched in competition with Leslie's newspaper empire: *Harper's Weekly* and the *New York Illustrated News*. Fletcher Harper, the well-financed publisher from Harper and Brothers, actively tried to recruit *Leslie's* artists and engravers, and aggressively tried to exceed *Leslie's* circulation. Leslie provided poor and erratic pay for his artists, many of whom he lost to competitors. By the opening of the war the circulation of the two newspapers were within 10,000 copies of one another, with the *New York Illustrated News* a distant third.

Much of the success of illustrated newspapers and magazines was due to the artistry of just a few brave men who went into the field of battle armed only with a pencil and a sketchpad. Two of the best sketch artists of the period were the brothers William and Alfred Waud. William worked for *Leslie's* and Alfred for *Harper's*. William proved particularly adept at ingratiating himself with the social elite of South Carolina during the secession crisis. Because of the paper's uncommitted stance, wherever Waud traveled he found individuals to be cooperative and helpful. Leslie instructed him to use the utmost care in making his sketches and to avoid giving any indication of political sympathies toward one side or the other. Nonetheless, Waud left *Leslie's* in 1863 to work at *Harper's* with brother Alfred and another fine artist, Theodore Davis.

William Waud's genius and discretion were matched by an army of artists who continued to be employed by *Leslie's*, including Eugene Benson, a young artist who eagerly went to the front to record the visual images of battle; Arthur Lumley, who was hired to follow the Army of the Potomac full time; Henry Lovie, who found his fame in continually sketching George B. McClellan; C. S. Hall and F. H Schell, who recorded the war in northern Virginia; F. B. Schell, who covered the Vicksburg campaign; and Edwin Forbes, who stayed with the Army of the Potomac until 1864 and became *Leslie's* most prolific artist. This 22-year-old artist followed the federal army from 1862. Forbes was not interested in the great generals and battles of the war, but rather in the day-to-day activities and lifestyle of the soldiers. So well drawn were Forbes's sketches that readers often scanned the drawings for familiar faces.

Reporting from the battlefield was exacting and dangerous work. Many artists fell ill with the same maladies that afflicted the troops. Two of *Leslie's* artists were captured and released by Robert E. Lee, and one part-time artist, James O'Neill, was killed during combat. C.E.F. Hillen was badly wounded in the Atlanta campaign. Largely because of the danger, *Leslie's* failed to have a correspondent with Sherman on his campaign to the sea, while *Harper's* artists accompanied the general. Consequently, by 1864 *Harper's* and other Northern journals had surged ahead of *Leslie's* in circulation.

The artists often found it difficult to get their sketches from the battlefield to the engravers, and they sent many that were incomplete when they had the chance. Unfinished sketches of prominent figures in the scene with backgrounds and lines of soldiers roughed in and labeled as "trees here" or "artillery battery here" were often sent off to the engravers to be filled by hands whose eyes had never seen battle. The quality of the sketches was not always reproduced faithfully by the engravers, and in viewing these graphic scenes great care must be taken. What the artist drew was not so much reproduced as copied. In many cases this made the scene more one created by imagination than reality. The results were sometimes unfortunate with details of weapons, uniforms, and topography being incorrect. As a consequence the errors were clearly visible when compared to the photographs coming from the battlefront. Yet the technology for turning photographs directly into newspaper illustrations would not be accomplished during the war, and they too needed to be copied by the same process.

The South had been generally dependent on Northern publishers to print its books and newspapers. In the entire South there was only one newspaper type factory, no facilities for printing maps, and an entire inability to make inexpensive wood-pulp paper. In 1860 a well-illustrated magazine such as *Harper's* or *Leslie's* could not be published in the South. *The Southern Illustrated News* and other papers were often limited to a single sheet of newsprint folded once to create just four pages. These publications made an attempt to mimic *Harper's* and *Leslie's* with crude engravings but were obviously not comparable to the Northern news outlets.

Moreover, the Confederate mails were two to three times more expensive than those in the North, severely limiting circulation. Even soldiers at the front had to pay to have newspapers and mail brought to them, and by 1864 the Confederate postal system had so completely broken down that thousands of personal letters remained undelivered. The inability of the Confederacy to establish and maintain an information system based on the printed word rather than hearsay and word of mouth had no little effect on the deterioration of Southern morale. Nonetheless, patriotic Southerners bombarded their newspapers with so much unsolicited poetry on national themes that some publications began charging to print it. Newspapers like the *Montgomery Daily Advertiser* were particularly successful in creating a wide public identification with the stirring events of the winter and spring of 1861 (Volo and Volo 2004, 240–46).

Poetry

A contemporary observer of the antebellum American scene noted that "we have no national school of poetry.... We've neither a legendary past nor a poetic present." This observation may help to explain America's fascination with stories of the Revolution like Cooper's, with tales of medieval times like Scott's, or even with whimsical anecdotes of the New York Dutch like Washington Irving's. Yet George Templeton Strong, the upper-class New York City sophisticate who wrote the comment, was clearly mistaken. The antebellum period began a golden age of American poets, which, though interrupted by war, continued throughout the nineteenth century. An anthology of American poets published in 1842 sold over 300,000 copies at $3 a copy. It has been pointed out that each great American poet was also a hyphenated something else. William Cullen Bryant was the period's newspaper editor-poet, John Greenleaf Whittier its abolitionist-poet, Oliver Wendell Holmes its doctor-poet, James Russell Lowell its gentlemen-poet, and Henry Wadsworth Longfellow its professor-poet. Each was important in his own area of expertise, but Longfellow would become the great popular poet of the century (Smith 1981, 972).

William Cullen Bryant began life as a lawyer, but in 1814 he published "The Yellow Violet," which combined a praise of nature with a moral principle thereby setting the mode of American poetry for the century. One year later he wrote "Thanatopis" and "To a Waterfowl." He started his life as an aggressive Federalist, became the editor of the *New York Evening Post*, turned Democrat, and ended as an antislavery Republican. Much of Bryant's work exhibited strains of the traditional Puritan ethic: propriety in one's private life, devotion to the task at hand, a deep interest in public affairs, and a faith in the American citizen. Many of his poems engaged the concept of unmourned death, a nineteenth-century preoccupation. Both the devoted Christian and the transcendentalist could read his work with pleasure.

Of all the literary figures of the time, John Greenleaf Whittier, the son of Quaker parents, was the one most closely identified with antislavery. Even William Lloyd Garrison, premiere antislavery activist and newspaper editor, took note of him in *The Liberator*. In the late 1820s, Whittier worked feverishly for several abolitionist newspapers, finally becoming editor of the prestigious *New England Weekly Review*. His early works—*New England Legends in Prose and Verse* and *Justice and Expedience*—urged immediate emancipation for all blacks. In 1846 Whittier published *Voices of Freedom*, a book of antislavery poems. He served as a speaker and lecturer for the cause, and supported the rising Republican Party in the 1850s. His work praised nature and looked to the pleasure of common things. A contemporary, Carl Schurz, described him as "a breath of air from a world of purity and beneficence." Although many of his verses have become mere historic curiosities with the passing of slavery, his rhymes caught the manners and morals of the common people. His famous poem "Barbara Frietchie" was written during the war (Smith 1981, 977).

The works of Oliver Wendell Holmes and James Russell Lowell were almost indistinguishable to the casual reader. Both were Harvard graduates, but it was Lowell who became the leader of their literary circle called the Fireside or Schoolroom Poets. This group included Whittier, Holmes, Longfellow, and sometimes Ralph Waldo Emerson. Lowell's work was blatantly moralistic, making him seem conservative by modern standards, but he was hardly considered so in his own time being an ardent abolitionist and temperance advocate. His poem, "The Present Crisis," was written in 1844, and it made a deep impression on Northern audiences. Four years later, Lowell published four volumes: *Poems, Fable for Critics, The Biglow Papers,* and the *Vision of Sir Launfal.* Of these, only the *Biglow Papers* was political. *Sir Launfal* with its emphasis on the value of heartfelt charity was America's contribution to the Arthurian Holy Grail legend. In 1857, Lowell became editor of the *Atlantic Monthly* magazine, and during the war he helped edit the *North American Review.*

Holmes left Boston after Harvard to study medicine in Paris, and he returned to find that the aging frigate *Constitution* was rotting in its mooring. Energized by a report that the heroic ship from the War of 1812 was to be demolished, he penned the immortal poem "Old Ironsides" that appeared in the *Boston Daily Advertiser* in 1830. The poem helped to save the vessel from destruction and prompted its preservation. It quickly became the subject of classroom recitation everywhere. One of Holmes' most famous poems was "The Chambered Nautilus," which drew an analogy between the ever expanding shell of the creature and the need for constant spiritual growth. His work in the decades after the Civil War made his reputation as a poet extraordinary.

Henry Wadsworth Longfellow was a born storyteller producing romantic tales of far away and long ago much like the other successful authors of the period. He was perfectly democratic in his poetry, and his work needed little scrutiny to make its point. Longfellow held the chair of literature at Harvard. His most popular poems among those available during the period were "The Village Blacksmith," "The Song of Hiawatha," "The Wreck of the Hesperus," and "The Courtship of Miles Standish." When published in 1855, "The Song of Hiawatha" sold 50,000 copies in five months at one dollar a copy. "The Landlord's Tale: Paul Revere's Ride," appeared in Longfellow's *Tales of a Wayside Inn* (1863). Written in 1860, this largely inaccurate and romanticized version of Revolutionary history became popular during the Civil War, but it ignored many of the facts of the encounter at Lexington in 1775 including the capture of Revere and the contributions of other alarm riders. The poem became the subject of classroom recitations and American history lessons into the twentieth century. For generations of Americans, Longfellow was their poet, and he lived for three-quarters of a century thereby fixing his place above all the others in the minds of most Americans.

Ironically, though little poetry of value was produced below the Mason-Dixon Line at this time, Southern life served as the inspiration for some of the most original and endearing of American lyrics. Frances Scott Key's "The Star Spangled Banner" is undoubtedly the most famous. The earliest Southern poet considered to be of any merit is William Crafts who celebrated the sporting passion of his native Charleston in "The Raciad" and later penned "Sullivan's Island." William Grayson authored several volumes of poetry, but only "The Hireling and the Slave" (1856) gained any notice because it purported to show the superior condition of the unpaid Southern slave to the paid Northern hireling.

While Southern women were frequent writers of letters and diaries, writing as a profession was not one to which the Southern woman aspired. Few periodicals of the day contained few female contributions even in the area of poetry. One notable exception was Caroline Howard Gilman. Although born in Boston, Gilman spent her adult life in Charleston where she wrote a number of stories, poems, and novels. Her 1837 *Recollections of a Southern Matron*, like other women's writing in the North, was highly sentimental. It told the story of a plantation girl as she grows into womanhood, and was noteworthy as the first Southern work on that theme. Additionally, Gilman founded a children's magazine, *Rose Bud* in 1832.

The literary product of female writers in the prewar period was largely written in private documents that were never intended to be made public In recent years several diaries and journals have been rescued from oblivion. The quality of the writing, the insight provided, and the dedication of the authors comes through to the modern readers (Volo and Volo 2004, 232–34, 250–51).

Regional Literature: The Abolition Press

No discussion of Civil War era literature is complete without mention of the abolitionist press and slave narratives. *Uncle Tom's Cabin* was first released in America and Britain as a newspaper serialization like many other works of the period. When Harriet Beecher Stowe published *Uncle Tom's Cabin* in 1852, the book sold 300,000 copies in America and Britain in one year. Stowe's work was one of fiction; it stressed the evils of slavery and presented a picture of the humanity of the slave and the brutality of slavery. Lincoln supposedly praised it as the "little book that caused a big war." Mrs. Stowe had little personal knowledge of slavery. The factual basis for the story was in part Theodore D. Weld's abolitionist tract entitled *Slavery as It Is: The Testimony of a Thousand Witnesses*, which was published in 1839. *Uncle Tom's Cabin* was immensely more effective in preaching the antislavery message in the form of a novel than the earlier tract had ever dreamed of being.

The South considered Stowe's work a slander and regarded it as abolitionist propaganda. A Southern woman, familiar with slavery and slaves, wrote that she could not read a book so filled with distortions as it was "too sickening" to think that any man would send "his little son to beat a human being tied to a tree." The same woman goes on to suggest, using other literary references, that Stowe's work portrays as much fiction as Squeers beating Smike in Dickens's *Nicholas Nickleby* or the gouging of Gloucester's eyes in Shakespeare's *King Lear*. "How delightfully pharisaic a feeling it must be, to rise up superior and fancy [to] we [who] are so degraded as to defend and like to live with such degraded creatures around us...as Legree" (Volo and Volo 1998, 210).

Nonetheless, many Northerners found the passages describing the murderous brutality of Simon Legree indicative of the typical behavior of Southern slave owners. The significance of the story, as of many of the attacks on the institution of slavery, lay in its ability to dramatize and emotionalize the issue of slavery. Writing and speech making on the subject of slavery in particular—and of the Southern culture in general—were becoming increasingly stereotypical, and the stereotypes, even when presented in novels, were taking on a reality in the minds of the people.

The first examples of writing in the formal genres by blacks was seen in the 1820s. Some marginal works appeared as poetry, as did several slave narratives, but the slave narratives that began to be published in the 1830s had the greatest effect and popularity. While the influence of antislavery editors was clearly visible in some narratives, others were clearly the work of the avowed author. Frederick Douglass's 1845 *Narrative* has garnered the most lasting fame. Other significant works were penned by William Wells Brown—America's first black novelist—Josiah Henson, and Henry "Box" Brown. Slave narratives sold very well in the North and abroad supplying sensationalism and sentimentality to an audience who relished both.

From 1845 to 1860, Frederick Douglass was the most prominent black abolitionist. Douglass's *Narrative of the Life of Frederick Douglass, an American Slave, Written by Himself* was filled with noble thoughts and thrilling reflections. Douglass was a slave in Baltimore for more than 20 years; and his book, published by the American Antislavery Society, was replete with the physical abuses of slavery including whippings, rape, unwarranted punishments, and cold-blooded murder, but its emphasis was on Douglass's self-education and liberation as a man. The work appealed to a wider audience of reformers than just those who favored emancipation. Proponents of women's rights, temperance, public education, and immigration reform all found something to stir them in Douglass's work.

Southern readers pointed with incredulity to many of Douglass's childhood memories of the whipping and murder of his fellow slaves and dismissed his work as patently false. Nevertheless, between 1845 and 1850 the book sold more than 30,000 copies, and was regarded by many in the North as a true picture of slavery in Maryland. The reviewer of the *New York Tribune*, himself an abolitionist, praised the book upon its publication for its simplicity, truth, coherence, and warmth.

Emancipation advocates declared that only the great weight of slavery had deteriorated the natural goodness and intelligence that the Negro had brought from Africa. "It has a natural, an inevitable tendency to brutalize every noble faculty of man." Frederick Douglass served as a favorite symbol of the ideally regenerated freeman, and was portrayed as a victim of slavery with a "godlike nature" and "richly endowed" intellect. Douglass was showcased as a naturally eloquent "prodigy—in soul manifestly created but a little lower than the angels" (Douglass 1845, vi). He was a favorite speaker on the antislavery lecture circuit, and hundreds of people flocked to his addresses.

However, Douglass was not satisfied with the limits of such audiences. He reached out to the black community of the North to support their brethren in bondage. One of the more effective means that he used in the 1850s was *Frederick Douglass' Paper*, later called *Douglass' Monthly Magazine*. Unlike the other black papers that were locally popular and short lived, Douglass's work was circulated through 18 states and 2 foreign countries. It had more than 4,000 subscribers and survived for more than 13 years.

Once the war commenced, Douglass argued not only for ending slavery but also for having blacks accepted in white society as equals in law and rights. He agitated constantly for the establishment of black regiments of federal soldiers feeling (optimistically in light of future events) that those who fought to save the Union would find an equal place in it after the war. At first he and other advocates met with stubborn resistance, but finally Union needs led to creating all-black infantry units from among slaves and free-black volunteers. Two of Douglass's sons volunteered for this duty and served with distinction. Ultimately, black troops were placed in combat roles where their performance proved laudable and, at times, heroic.

Born in Kentucky, William Wells Brown was taken by his owner to Missouri in 1816 where he remained a slave under three successive masters. On the first day of 1834 Brown slipped away from a river steamer that was docked at Cincinnati, and, fearing discovery every step of the way, made his way to Cleveland and freedom. Brown thereafter worked in the print shop of Elijah Lovejoy, who was to become the first abolitionist martyr, and eventually turned to the study of medicine. His intellectual development, and literary and oratorical skills, however, made him a stellar candidate for the antislavery lecture circuit. Here he distinguished himself, and was later equally eloquent for temperance movement.

In 1847, the *Narrative of William Wells Brown, Fugitive Slave, Written by Himself* was published. His book was one of the most widely circulated and acclaimed of all the many slave narratives that appeared in this period. This work was followed by *The Anti-Slavery Harp: A Collection of Songs for Antislavery Meetings* (1848). Brown's play *The Escape: Or, A Leap for Freedom* (1858) is acknowledged as the first by a black American writer. His most noteworthy literary effort may well be *Clotel* (1853), the first complete novel published by a black American. There are four editions, and several spellings, of *Clotel*. It was first published while Brown was living in London where he sought safety from the fugitive slave laws. While each of the four versions differs in details, they essentially tell the same melodramatic tale of a beautiful female slave. Even though it contains a scathing rebuke of Southern racial attitudes, the novel endorses integration rather than separatism. Brown was a diverse writer who also produced a collection of letters from his European travels and four notable works on black history. Ultimately, Brown returned to America and was able to practice as a physician. He spent most of the last quarter century of his life practicing medicine in Boston (Volo and Volo 2004, 249–50).

COMMUNICATIONS

Telegraphy

A fundamental revolution in communications was begun in 1844 when Samuel F. B. Morse sent the first telegraph message from Baltimore to Washington. The development of long-distance telegraphy was more important to the history of communications in the nineteenth century than that of the telephone because into the middle of the next century few people in rural areas had telephones in their towns much less their homes. Moreover, many of the advances in science that allowed telegraphy to develop were also crucial to telephony almost a half-century later.

The essential technological advance that allowed Morse to create electric telegraphy was the ability to draw out copper wire at an economical price developed by the British metallurgical industry a decade earlier. Up to that point, electric communication over long distances was simply not feasible, even if the technological challenges of telegraphy had been surmounted earlier. Morse's ability to send a message by electric current over wires many miles apart was done over a decade of research and was built upon the development of the wet cell battery by Italian Alessandro Volta in 1800 and upon the electromagnetic studies of the American scientist Joseph Henry at Princeton in 1836.

Volta had used the natural characteristic of two different metals and an acid to build a voltaic cell or battery. By the time of the Civil War a practical battery made from two different compounds of lead and sulfuric acid was available. A group of these batteries hooked in series allowed the U.S. Military Telegraph, a branch of the federal army, to send a message over 10 miles of wire without repetition from a single wagon fitted with telegraphic equipment.

Joseph Henry—working part time—had increased the size and power of the battery and had invented the first electromagnet, the first electric motor, and the first electromagnetic telegraph—sending a faint signal through a mile-long wire maze arrayed around his laboratory. While neither his motor nor his telegraph were more than laboratory toys, Henry had also devised a system of relays by which a current, made faint by traveling through a long length of wire, might be increased and exactly repeated. This was a pivotal discovery shared by Henry during his meetings with Morse in 1835 and utilized by Morse to make long-distance transmission possible. Henry also suggested in 1843 that Morse's wire could be insulated by stringing it high above the ground from glass knobs fixed to wooden poles. In the same year Morse ran an underwater wire, insulated in a natural material similar to rubber known as gutta-percha, 13 miles from Martha's Vineyard to Nantucket.

The telegraph key used to send the sets of dots and dashes was designed by a partner of Morse named Alfred Vail. It was a simple strip of spring steel that could be pressed against a metal contact to send letters and numerals via a predetermined code. Later models of the transmitting key and the signal receiver were developed about a pivoting lever action that allowed the gap to be more easily adjusted for rapid transmission. Also significant was Morse's consultations with another partner, Leonard Gale, a professor at New York University, regarding electrochemistry. Armed with the discoveries of Volta, Henry, Vail, and Gale, and his own innovations, Morse produced a telegraph that was an immediate success. The 1844 patent application for the telegraph also included an automatic method for recording the dots and dashes on paper. This and the code itself were the only parts of the invention solely attributable to Morse.

Within 10 years of the first telegraphic message, more than 23,000 miles of telegraph wire crisscrossed the country. Newspapers quickly began using the wires to collect news, and the Associated Press and other news agencies set up their own wire services. By 1848 even small communities were reading dispatches from the Mexican War. However, there was no traffic control system for the various independent telegraph companies or even for individual operators within the same company. Several operators might obliterate any meaning among the hundreds of dots and dashes by trying to use the same line at the same time. In 1856, Hiram Sibley founded Western Union, which eventually bought up all the patents for competing telegraphy systems and combined the best features of each into one dependable system.

In 1858, after two attempts, Cyrus W. Field was able to lay a continuous transatlantic telegraphic cable from Newfoundland to Ireland. It worked for some time, and the public reacted with jubilation. However, mishandling of the insulation during the cable's deployment caused the underwater line to fail. Nonetheless, the cause of fault was known and could be addressed, but not before the war intervened.

On the eve of the Civil War telegraph wires connected most Eastern cities, a transcontinental telegraph connected New York to California, and a transatlantic telegraphic cable—although presently silent—stretched from Canada to Europe. The telegraph profoundly affected Americans. It helped develop the American West, made railroad travel safer, allowed businesses to communicate more efficiently, and spread political speeches and ideas across the country in a single day. Yet not everyone was pleased with these advances. When informed of the success of the transatlantic telegraphic cable, Sam Dodd, a lawyer in Franklin, Pennsylvania, stated bitterly, "Life's already too harried. It won't be worth living unless we stop making inventions to annihilate time and space. Why do we have to tie continents together with electric bands?" (Dolson 1959, 59).

Morse was plagued by lawsuits regarding his telegraphic patents. This was a common circumstance among inventors during the period as they sought to claim sole credit for complex inventions. Although Henry consistently backed Morse and frequently appeared in his defense in court, Morse became embittered toward him. This may have been due to the scientific community's recognition of Henry as the first builder of an electromagnetic telegraph. This generally ended the controversy, and Henry went forward to help found the National Academy of Sciences and the American Association for the Advancement of Science. During the Civil War, Joseph Henry served as a science advisor to President Lincoln (Volo and Volo 2004, 52).

Military Signals

Communications were particularly important to the management of a battle when separate parts of the army were spread across miles of war zone. At the outbreak of hostilities both armies lacked a military telegraph system. The Confederate army utilized the existing civilian telegraphic system of the South to issue orders between regional commanders and to communicate with the government in Richmond, and

Abraham Lincoln was known to spend long hours contemplating the war reports in the Western Union office in Washington. However, telegraphy also brought the horrors of battle and long lists of casualties from the front lines of the war almost instantaneously to the parlors of America.

While the Confederacy continued to rely almost solely on flags and civilian telegraph lines for battlefield communications, the Federals established a military telegraph to supplement the older system. The Signal Corps advocated the use of flying telegraphic teams organized around light electric battery wagons that would move with the army, erect telegraph lines, and gain tactical control on the battle-field with the use of dial-type message encoding equipment. The rival U.S. Military Telegraph Service obtained its equipment and personnel from the existing civilian companies and relied on the more common Morse type telegraphic equipment.

The use of flag bearers and drummers remained essential for the maintenance of alignment and the transmission of orders on the company and regimental level; but across greater distances a more effective method of managing the army was needed. During the 1850s the U.S. Army had adopted a wig wag flag system for field com-munications. This flag system remained the principal means of passing orders and intelligence for the Federals and Confederates throughout the war.

—*James M. Volo*

HEALTH AND MEDICINE: BATTLEFIELD DOCTORING AND NURSING

When the Civil War began the medical services of the armed forces were almost nonexistent. The federal government began the war with fewer than 130 surgeons and assistant surgeons scattered among its many forts and military posts. Medical officers and their assistants were commonly assigned to individual regiments, and musicians served as stretcher-bearers and orderlies. The ships of the navy each had a surgeon, but the smaller vessels often had only medical orderlies assigned to their complement.

Some of the medical personnel working for the federal government were dismissed for suspected disloyalty in 1860, and many of them served with the Confederate forces. The federal army in January 1861 counted only 98 surgeons and the Confed-erates a mere 24. With time the lack of physicians corrected itself somewhat as medi-cal men volunteered or contracted for service. A total of 17,000 doctors served on the battlefields and in the hospitals of the Civil War from 1861 through 1865. Only 4,000 of these served the South. At the Battle of Gettysburg, the Army of the Po-tomac had 650 doctors attached to it to serve over 90,000 men. The 14,000 Union wounded had a mere 105 doctors to care for them once the bulk of the Northern Army—and 85 percent of its doctors—moved on. The Army of Northern Virginia had a less determinate, but certainly smaller, number of physicians to deal with the seriously wounded left behind in its retreat (Patterson 1997, 45). It was not un-usual after a battle to find a mingling of medical personnel—friend and foe, blue and gray—busily tending the wounded men of both sides "engaged in the common work of helping the suffering" (Patterson 1997, 86).

When compared to what is known today, medicine was mired in an intellectual wasteland in the nineteenth century. A form of vaccination against smallpox (known as variolation) had been pioneered by Edward Jenner in the eighteenth century and used by the army of the American Revolution, but the true causes of epidemic disease, general infections, and gangrene (putrefaction) were largely unknown. These were the great killers of the Civil War, and the last was particularly deadly among the wounded.

Germ theory had been proposed in France by Louis Pasteur as early as 1856, but it was generally ridiculed by the medical and scientific establishment as unproven and speculative. With sober sincerity, many doctors assigned the cause of infection and epidemic disease to bad odors and miasmic mists. It would take additional research by men like Pasteur and British surgeon Joseph Lister for these theories to be accepted. At the time of America's Civil War, battlefield surgeons often worked under appalling conditions, wore previously bloodstained garments while operating, and failed to wash their hands or instruments between procedures. They often amputated limbs that appeared susceptible to putrefaction even before the infection had appeared as a prophylactic procedure. Postoperative patients often rested in beds with dirty linens that were not changed between occupants, or they were deposited in the fields surrounding the aid stations along with the rows of dead and piles of severed limbs.

Private Rice C. Bull, 123rd New York Volunteers, recorded his experience on the battlefield after being wounded in action. "When I reached the stream the banks were already lined with many dead and wounded. Some had been carried there, others had dragged themselves to the place to die. Many were needlessly bleeding to death [for lack of a personal first-aid kit or tourniquet]. Many died who would have lived if only the simplest treatment had been in the hands of the men themselves. My mind was clear…I knew I could not get to the rear without help, so made no further attempt. Fortunately my canteen had been filled; my thirst had become great and I had some water to wash the blood from my face. During this time the battle on our front continued with unlessening fury….Looking back I saw a scattered line of the enemy coming toward us on the double quick….They had to cross around or over the wounded and were cautioned by their officers to be careful not to disturb them more than was necessary. They passed over us carefully, without any unkind actions or words. With us for a time all was quiet. There was nothing to disturb us but the occasional cries and groans of the wounded; not a word of complaint was heard….Nearly all knew we were not only wounded but were now prisoners….The enemy's surgeons went among our wounded looking for those that required amputation….The arms and legs were thrown on the ground, only a few feet from the wounded who lay nearby. As each amputation was completed the wounded man was carried to an old house and laid on the floor. They said they could do nothing at that time for those others less critically wounded….The condition of most of these was deplorable" (Bauer 1977, 58–60).

There were a large number of so-called contract surgeons serving with the federal army. These doctors had been recommended by the Sanitary Commission and served in military facilities during the emergency. These private physicians were a "spoiled lot with little tolerance for personal discomfort and a distaste for sustained labor in the field." The regular army doctors quickly tired of the complaints, and found that private physicians were of little benefit. For their part, the private physicians tended to look down upon the military doctors as second-class practitioners incapable of sustaining themselves in general practice (Patterson 1997, 99). Nonetheless, most of the physicians who volunteered or enlisted in the army (or navy) during the war had little or no surgical expertise. In the antebellum period, surgery was often dangerous or ineffective. Few practic-

The surgeon of the Army of the Potomac and other medical personnel treating wounded soldiers, 1862. Courtesy Library of Congress.

ing physicians attempted surgical procedures except for the most minor ailments. Medical colleges offered two-year programs leading to a medical degree, but there were few, if any, organizations overseeing the medical practice. The American Medical Association—the first of its kind to monitor its members—would not be founded for a decade.

A number of surgical manuals were produced through the auspices of the federal government as a temporary solution to this lack of surgical knowledge. Among these were three by Dr. Frank H. Hamilton, professor of military surgery at Bellevue Hospital Medical Center (New York): *A Practical Treatise on Fractures and Dislocations* (1860); *Practical Treatise on Military Surgery* (1861); and *Amputations in Gunshot Fractures of the Femur* (1863). In addition Dr. Samuel D. Gross (Jefferson Medical College of Philadelphia) wrote *A Manual of Military Surgery* (1861); Dr. Joseph Javier Woodward wrote the *Hospital Steward's Manual* (1862) adopted by the army for its hospitals; and Dr. Stephen Smith authored *Gray's Anatomy, Descriptive and Surgical* (1862). Many other works were available, but all these titles were available in the Surgeon General's Office throughout the war.

The period from 1830 to 1870 was the heyday of American-made surgical instrumentation. Before this period, and after 1900, most of the highest quality medical instruments available were made in Europe and imported into the United States. During the Civil War, a committee of doctors on the staff of the U.S. Army Hospital Department (including Hamilton and Smith) were assigned the responsibility of selecting the instruments to be placed in federal surgical sets. It was distressing but practical that the field case contained a larger assortment of bullet probes, forceps, and bone saws than the other sets. Confederate surgeons generally used those instruments they had acquired in private prewar practice or those taken or captured from the federal forces.

Prior to the Civil War the U.S. Army had not provided ambulances for the wounded and sick. In 1859 experimental carts were tested on the Western plains and a less than satisfactory two-wheel version was adopted. Not until 1863 did the federal army organize and outfit a formal ambulance corps for the Army of the Potomac. Under General Order No. 85 only four-wheel, two-horse wagons would be used as ambulances. Each ambulance had five men assigned as stretcher-bearers and drivers. Three ambulances were permanently allocated to each infantry regiment, two to each cavalry regiment, and one to each artillery battery. Moreover, two army wagons were designated to carry only medical supplies for each corps, and two more were placed at the division level. Several canvass stretchers with four short legs were provided to each ambulance. This organization was sorely needed, but it fell far short of the real need, as three ambulances and a dozen stretchers were hardly adequate to support a regiment of 1,000 men of whom 100 might become casualties in the first hour of battle.

The use of inhalation anesthesia (either sulfuric ether or chloroform) had been added to the repertoire of military and civilian medicine in 1846 and 1847, respectively. Its introduction had coincided with the advent of the Mexican-American War of 1846–1848, and ether at least had been used under combat conditions in limited cases to relieve the torture of extended surgery. By 1849, ether (compound spirits of sulfuric ether or spirits of nitric ether) was officially issued to U.S. Army medical staff. Chloroform came later, but it was the anesthesia of choice on the Civil War battlefield for surgeons on both sides—Federal and Confederate. Liquid morphine (16 grains per fluid ounce), opium pills (powder of ipecac, or camphor, and opium in five gram pills), and laudanum (tincture of opium in ethyl alcohol) were all supplied in the Civil War surgeon's pannier in moderate amounts—the liquids in 4 to 24 ounce bottles, and the pills in boxes from 20 dozen to 60 dozen.

The overwhelmingly successful application of chloroform during the Crimean War (1854) by French and British military doctors helped to establish it as part of the surgical protocol, and the authors of military surgical manuals written in the 1860s generally endorsed the use of some form of anesthesia. Nonetheless, not all medical professionals agreed. Samuel Gross believed that anesthesia should be withheld from wounded men too bewildered by shock because they felt very little pain in any case. A number of physicians, who had learned their trade in the preanesthesia era, moralized on the duty and privilege accorded to suffering warriors, and they characterized the painful cries of the wounded as music to the ear. Infrequently, a patient died immediately after the administration of anesthesia, and these occurrences were often well publicized in the press. Consequently, a number of patients, including wounded soldiers, refused the use of anesthesia, choosing instead to endure surgery while awake or under the inebriating effects of rum, whiskey, or other liquors (Echols 2007, 5).

Once off the battlefield, the plight of the wounded was complicated by limited medical knowledge, malnutrition, and disease. While American military hospitals were better than those in Europe, they were nonetheless inadequate. Civilian corpsmen, hired by the army at $20.50 per month to staff army hospitals, often proved unreliable. A nursing service, directed by Dorothea Dix and staffed by women, had been established to care for the wounded and sick in the numerous soldiers' rests and regimental hospitals; but the recruitment of nurses was hobbled by the strict moral requirements Dix placed on potential candidates. Women were required to be of high moral character, no less than 30 years of age, plain looking, and unadorned. There was no requirement that they be efficient or capable.

In March 1863, Secretary of War Edwin M. Stanton established a Corps of Invalids from among the walking wounded and convalescent soldiers of the army to serve as nurses and medical aides. More than 60,000 men ultimately served in the invalid corps. These were scattered randomly among the regiments of the army and wore pale blue coats so that they would not become targets for the enemy. Although only 42 members of the corps were killed in action, more than 1,600 died of the diseases to which they were exposed in the sick wards. The invalid corps concept received little support from the army hierarchy, and General Grant opposed all plans for retaining it as a part of the postwar army.

Thousands of Catholic nuns served as nurses in the military hospitals of Boston, New York, Philadelphia, Baltimore, Washington, and other cities. Sisters of Charity, Sisters of Mercy, and Sisters of Saint Vincent de Paul were all conspicuous in their unique religious habits. The nuns volunteered to serve without pay even though they were often abused by anti-Catholic hospital personnel and patients. Their patience, skill, and persistence won over a good number of bigots. "My mind was filled with prejudice," wrote one soldier. "I did not believe that anything good could come from the Sisters. But now I see my mistake all too clearly" (Volo and Volo 1998, 168).

Catholic sisters were "conspicuously neutral" in their attitude toward the war. Confederate hospitals in Richmond, Charleston, Nashville, and New Orleans were also staffed with at least some Catholic nuns. The sisters consistently failed to leave their work when the vagaries of war changed the nature of the occupying force from South to North, and in Vicksburg they suffered the siege, the ensuing bombardment, and the near starvation with the beleaguered of the city. The sisters proved to be expert medical and surgical nurses, as they had experienced service in asylums and civilian hospitals during their long novitiates. A Southern woman noted that the work of the sisters made "all the difference in the world" in the Confederate hospitals of Richmond (Volo and Volo 1998, 168).

A number of civilian organizations helped to fill the need for additional medical care. The Women's American Association for Relief was closely associated with a number of eminent doctors in New York and furnished medical supplies to the army. Beyond this the U.S. Sanitary Commission made provisions for the relief of the sick, provided ambulances, and cared for the wounded and the dead. Commission representatives oversaw the diet and personal cleanliness of the soldiers in camp, provided housing for white refugee families, and raised money to expand their work. A single Sanitary Commission fundraiser in New York City raised over $1 million. A woman wrote, "The amount realized will no doubt do much toward relieving the poor wounded and suffering soldiers than all the surgeons do. No one can know how much good is done by the Sanitary Commission who is not in the Army" (Volo and Volo 1998, 169).

The South mounted a less formal assault on the medical chaos that plagued the Confederate forces. Fewer than 30 surgeons and surgeon's assistants from the old army chose to serve with the Confederacy, and wounded or sick men were often left to the tender care of their mates or the local populace. The military hospitals of the South were overwhelmed by the task before them, and wounded men were often shipped home to recuperate under the care of their families. Those who were capable, but still considered invalids, were formed into local militias and railroad guards, rather than hospital orderlies, by the manpower-hungry state governments.

Southern ambulances and stretchers were provided by subscription. A newly painted Confederate ambulance, apparently donated by a well-meaning supporter from Fairfax, was among the early acquisitions of federal pickets in northern Virginia. "This capture was an object of much curiosity around the federal camp near Alexandria. Soldiers stood off and stared at it in awe...an omen of what might lie in store for them, this wagon designed for toting the wounded or the dead" (Volo and Volo 1998, 169).

FOR MORE INFORMATION

Albin, Maurice S. "The Use of Anesthetics during the Civil War, 1861–1865." *Pharmacy in History* 42, nos. 3–4 (2000): 99–114.

Bauer, K. Jack, ed. *Soldiering: The Civil War Diary of Rice C. Bull.* Novato, CA: Presidio, 1977.

Browne, Ray B., and Lawrence A. Kreiser Jr. *The Civil War and Reconstruction.* Westport, CT: Greenwood Press, 2003.

Casper, Scott E, Joan Chaison, and Jeffery D. Groves, eds. *Perspectives on American Book History: Artifacts and Commentary.* Amherst: University of Massachusetts Press, 2002.

Dolson, Hildegarde. *The Great Oildorado, The Gaudy and Turbulent Years of the First Oil Rush: Pennsylvania, 1859–1880.* New York: Random House, 1959.

Douglass, Frederick. *Narrative of the Life of Frederick Douglass, an American Slave, Written by Himself.* 1845. Reprint, New York: Penguin, 1968.

Echols, Michael. "American Civil War Surgical Antiques: The Private Collection of Dr. Michael Echols." http://www.braceface.com/medical/index.html (accessed October 2007).

Freemon, Frank R. *Gangrene and Glory: Medical Care during the American Civil War.* Urbana: University of Illinois Press, 2001.

Hofstadter, Richard, and Wilson Smith, eds. *American Higher Education, A Documentary History.* Chicago: University of Chicago Press, 1968.

Johnson, Clifton. *Old-Time Schools and School-books.* New York: Dover Publications, 1963.

Kaser, David. *Books and Libraries in Camp and Battle: The Civil War Experience.* Westport, CT: Greenwood Press, 1984.

Kelley, R. Gordon, ed. *Children's Periodicals of the United States.* Westport, CT: Greenwood Press, 1984.

Mason, Philip P., ed. *Copper County Journal: The Diary of Schoolmaster Henry Hobart, 1863–1864.* Detroit, MI: Wayne State University Press, 1991.

Mondale, Sarah, and Sarah B. Patton, eds. *School: The Story of American Public Education.* Boston, MA: Beacon Press, 2001.

Mott, Frank Luther. *A History of American Magazines.* 5 vols. Cambridge, MA: Harvard University Press, 1930–1968.

Patterson, Gerard A. *Debris of Battle, The Wounded of Gettysburg*. Mechanicsburg, PA: Stackpole Books, 1997.

Rutkow, Ira M. *Bleeding Blue and Gray: Civil War Surgery and the Evolution of American Medicine*. New York: Random House, 2005.

Smith, Page. *The Nation Comes of Age: A People's History of the Antebellum Years*. New York: McGraw-Hill Book Company, 1981.

Taylor, Alan. "Fenimore Cooper's America." *History Today* 46, no. 2 (February 1996): 21–27.

Tebbel, John, and Mary Ellen Zuckerman. *The Magazine in America, 1741–1990*. New York: Oxford University Press, 1991.

Timmons, Todd. *Science and Technology in Nineteenth-Century America*. Westport, CT: Greenwood Press, 2005.

Volo, Dorothy Denneen, and James M. Volo. *The Antebellum Period*. Westport, CT: Greenwood Press, 2004.

———. *Daily Life in Civil War America*. Westport, CT: Greenwood Press, 1998.

———. *Encyclopedia of the Antebellum South*. Westport, CT: Greenwood Press, 2000.

———. *Family Life in Nineteenth-Century America*. Westport, CT: Greenwood Press, 2007.

Material Life

HOME, SWEET HOME

The nineteenth century was one of tremendous evolution in the material life of the family. The century opened much like the previous one, where the home was a self-contained unit and the homemaker was responsible for virtually all the needs of her family. A wife's domain consisted of her home and the yards surrounding it. The specifics varied—as did a family's economic situation and, to some extent, whether the location was rural or urban. It was the woman's responsibility to manage and direct the economic productivity of her household. This included caring for the children and overseeing the servants. Certainly the scope and nature of the duties of a plantation mistress or the lady of a town mansion differed from those of the frontier woman or a poor farmer's wife, but no matter what her social status, the comfort of a family was directly linked to a woman's skill in the ways of homemaking.

As the century progressed, however, the effects of industrialization brought dramatic changes to the ways of home management. One of the first domains of the housewife to experience change was food production. Prior to industrialization, farm families bartered some portion of their excess food production with tradesmen and others in exchange for services, finished goods, luxury items, and cash. As the nineteenth century unfolded, however, it became increasingly common for a woman to purchase food commodities rather than make them herself, and a cash economy came to dominance in many places. Husbands left the home to earn money that would allow families to purchase what they would have produced themselves. Urban living and industrialization removed people from their food sources transforming many of the former food producers into food consumers.

The nineteenth century path to significant material success lay not in the workshop or on the farm, but in the emerging industries and enterprises of consumer capitalism. Nineteenth-century men looked less to the quality of a man's labor as an indicator of his respectability and more to the nonreligious implications of his financial success. Between 1820 and 1840 wealth made a remarkable statistical redistribution to the top of the social ladder largely due to the crushing effects of overwhelming numbers of poor rural immigrants pouring into the country at the same time that its commercial economy was undergoing a phenomenal rate of expansion.

In some men the drive toward wealth could become excessive or even destructive. The sharing of a man's income, in the form of money or wages, among his children or with his spouse quickly formed a more significant source of men's authority than in former times. Acquisitiveness—in the form of material possessions, fine clothing, a more than modest house, and servants—came to dominate the desires and goals of many American families.

FOOD AND DRINK

Food Technology

The Civil War brought developments that for many would alter the patterns of eating from home cooking to professional cooking, and from country cooking to city cooking. The seeds of these changes had already been sown as the war approached, but the dynamics of the conflict acted to speed their growth during the remainder of the century. The war may have retarded the growth of conveniences for civilians, but when it came to providing food for the armies, war drove the implementation of technological advances. Specifically, three major agents of change were at work: improvement in refrigeration, increased speed of transportation, and industrialization of food processing. These served to vastly increase the variety of foods available to Americans (Volo and Volo 1998, 225).

STORAGE

Food storage in the mid-nineteenth century was a problem for everyone, no matter what their economic status. In addition to recipes for preparing food and suggestions on maintaining the household, receipt books like *Miss Beecher's Domestic Receipt Book* customarily contained suggestions on topics such as how to restore the flavor of rancid butter. (Miss Beecher advised using chloride of lime.)

Heat is a great villain when it comes to spoiling food. In the absence of practical mechanical systems for making things cold—which did not arrive until the 1870s—the easiest way to keep food from spoiling during warm weather was to use ice. Freshwater ice was cut from frozen ponds in large blocks and kept in structures called icehouses, which were constructed partially below ground. The temperature a few feet below ground rarely rises above 45° Fahrenheit. The ice was then covered in sawdust to help insulate it. Ice would be gathered when it was thickest, generally late January. Shielded from the heat, ice could theoretically last forever, but practically it could be expected to last through October if conditions were favorable. By the Civil War, the icehouse had become an indispensable component of the farm. Meat, poultry, and perishable fruit could be kept in good condition much longer in the cool temperatures of icehouses or iceboxes.

The icebox also gave individual city homes a means of keeping food fresh. In 1850 *Godey's Lady's Book* called the icebox a "necessity of life." First patented by Thomas Moore in 1803, it consisted of one wooden box inside another, insulated by charcoal or ashes, with a tin container at the top of the interior box for the ice. In 1825, Frederick Tudor and Nathaniel Wyeth solved the problem of preserving ice for long periods and made ice a commercial interest. Just prior to the war, Boston families could obtain 15 pounds of ice a day from an iceman for two dollars a month. Ice was harvested from New England ponds and shipped to the South or even to the West Indies. New Orleans increased its demand for ice 70-fold between the 1820s and the beginning of the Civil War. Once the war commenced, the South could no longer depend on this improved source of food preservation (Volo and Volo 1998, 225–26).

MODERN ADVANCEMENT

By mid-century the railroads had become the prime cause of the increasing diversity of food for the American table. Perishables such as milk, oysters, and lobsters were transported by rail to large cities in insulated ice cars or packed in barrels of ice. The speed of the railroads not only augmented the diet, it served to improve the quality of the food. Beef was more tender, more tasty, and less expensive, because the cattle no longer were driven to market on the hoof, and hence they developed less muscle. The cattle were fed on grain shipped via the railroad, thus improving the flavor of the meat. Finally, meat cost less because less weight was lost between pasture and market. A similar situation arose with pork. Before the railroads were built, long legs were a desirable breeding factor in pigs, as the hog was expected to walk to market. With the advent of rail shipping, breeders began to focus on tastier meats and fatter hogs.

The railroads continued to supply the North and Northern troops with fresh meat during the war. Chicago opened its first stockyard in 1865, and its rail connections facilitated the shipment of fresh meat to the entire country. By 1870 meat on the table had taken on many of the characteristics of a epicurean fad or culinary craze even among the middle classes.

The processing and preservation of food had always been a domestic activity until vacuum-packed, hermetically sealed jars were invented by a Frenchman named

Nicholas Appert early in the nineteenth century. In 1825 the first American patent for tin cans was filed. By 1849 a machine was developed that limited the amount of hand labor needed to produce tin cans, further stimulating commercial food processing. The first salmon cannery in the United States was opened in Washington, California in 1864. Salmon and lobster were the first foods to be commercially canned, rapidly followed by corn, tomatoes, peas, and additional varieties of fish. By 1860, five million cans a year were being produced.

In 1863, the fledgling Great Atlantic Tea Company—destined to become the A&P grocery store chain (Great Atlantic and Pacific Tea Company)—began to sell a line of canned groceries to supplement its tea business. Two famous brand names emerged from the war—Borden and Van Camp. Gail Borden's first efforts at canned foods met with little success, but his canned condensed milk was extremely popular. In 1856, Borden patented a method for making condensed milk by heating it in a partial vacuum. This not only removed much of the water so the milk could be stored in a smaller volume, but it also protected the milk from germs in the air. Borden opened a condensed milk plant and cannery in Wassaic, New York, in 1861. His condensed milk was used by Union troops and its popularity spread. Gilbert Van Camp's pork and beans quickly became a best seller, and he was given an army contract to supply the Union troops.

Federal soldiers returning from the war had become so accustomed to canned foods that many insisted that canned foods be served at home so that they could continue to eat out-of-season products with consistent quality. Americans living in isolated western territories particularly welcomed the profusion of canned foods; prices ranged from $1.00 to $2.25 per can by the mid-1860s. A line from the song, "My Darling Clementine" describes Clementine's footwear as "herring boxes without topses," referring to the oval-shaped fish tins plentiful in mining towns.

Despite these movements toward modern food packaging, the single most important controlling factor of the Civil War era diet remained availability. Those who could afford to pay had wider choices, but even these were limited. For most people, the majority of fresh food choices continued to be governed by region and season (Volo and Volo 1998, 226–28).

FOOD ATTITUDES

Issues of vitamins, salt, fiber, and fat content were virtually nonexistent for most people during the 1860s. *Peterson's Magazine* contained advice from a Dr. Radcliffe who recommended that the mouth be kept shut, and the eyes should be kept open. He explained by that he meant that corpulent persons should eat little food, and that the quantity of sleep should be diminished. Most meals at this time contained meat, which was likely to be high in fat content, and bread in one form or another. Frances Trollope, a visitor to the United States in the 1830s, remarked on the extraordinary amount of bacon eaten in American homes noting that ham and beef steaks appeared on tables morning, noon, and night. Equally astonishing to her was the way eggs and oysters, ham and applesauce, beefsteak and stewed peaches, salt fish and onion were eaten together.

In the early part of the nineteenth century there emerged a number of movements that advocated lifestyle changes such as regular exercise, daily bathing, and proper nutrition. In 1829 in pursuit of the healthful diet, Rev. Sylvester Graham invented a cracker made of unsifted and coarsely ground wheat flour. Graham was an avid vegetarian, who promoted the use of his so-called graham flour for its high fiber content. Dr. James Caleb Jackson created the first breakfast cereal, which he called Granula, and patented it in 1865. Jackson baked thin sheets of dough formed of graham flour, broke them up, and baked the pieces a second time. The resulting cereal was far from convenient. It had to be soaked overnight in milk before it was even possible to chew the dense, bran-heavy nuggets. It was a financial failure embraced only by radical health advocates (Volo and Volo 1998, 228).

DINING HABITS

Middle-class women served as the arbiters of good manners and taste in the dinning room, as well as elsewhere in he household. As the nation shifted from an agrarian to a cosmopolitan urban economy and culture, women's importance as domestic producers in the family economy declined. No longer required to spin and weave, to make butter and cheese, many American women moved into a new sphere, one charged with the maintenance of the moral character of the family. Their new worth as homemakers and domestic engineers, was expressed in terms of their ability to create household environments that would inculcate their children and households with the Protestant values of thriftiness, industry, and sobriety.

Dinner had a tremendous cultural power, shaping not only individuals but also the nation at large. Within the realm of the dining room, middle-class women aspired to nurture gentility, to counter the deleterious effects of the outside world, and to educate family members in the arts of gracious living, self-restraint, and refined behavior. The rules of etiquette played a key role in this process. Eliza Leslie, in her book, *The Ladies Guide to True Politeness and Perfect Manners*, offered advice on a variety of social activities including conversation, manners, dress, introductions, and shopping. She discussed situations at the table, either at home, in company, or at hotels.

Efforts to enforce new standards of gentility and self-restraint at the table extended beyond polite consumption of food into the realm of conversation. Leslie instructed diners to avoid discussions of sickness, sores, surgical operations, dreadful accidents, shocking cruelties, or horrible punishments. Writing in 1864 and sensitive to the issues of the day, she added political and sectarian controversies to her list of topics to shun (Williams 2006, 155–57).

In the midst of such turmoil, ordinary routines helped preserve some measure of normalcy, at least for those on the home front. Every day, families reinforced their ties by breaking bread together, sharing their triumphs and difficulties, and partaking of the basic rituals of family life. These rituals divided their days into predictable segments, at home and at work. Breakfast began the day, with various members departing for scattered destinations, some carrying lunch or dinner pails to school or work, some eating their midday meal out, and some engaging in morning marketing or social calls before returning for luncheon. Family dinner in the middle of the day, once the norm for most American families, was quickly becoming a thing of the past, especially, for those families living in towns and cities. End-of-the-day meals were defined by class. Working-class Americans, especially those of Northern European origin, came home to tea, a meal of tea with milk and sugar plus cold meat, bread or whatever other leftovers or simple dishes might be available. A more hearty working-class meal, called supper, could have included soup, stew, or any of a wide variety of made dishes. For the middle class, dinner had shifted from its traditional midday place to evening. Geography also factored into the mealtime and meal type. Rural families continued to follow eighteenth-century meal schedules long after urbanites had shifted to a more modern system (Williams 2006, 161–62).

COMMON FOODS

Pork was the most common kind of meat, particularly in the Southern diet. Pigs were relatively easy to maintain. They required little space and tolerated a wide variety of foodstuffs, including leavings from food preparation. Pigs did not have to be put to pasture and consumed less feed than cattle to add the same amount of weight. Pork could be easily preserved in a number of ways, including pickling, salting, and smoking, without becoming offensive in taste or texture.

Chicken was important in the South, too. Chickens required little space and turned available reserves of corn and meal into meat; but chicken meat was both difficult to preserve and prone to spoil. Like other domesticated fowl, chickens were generally eaten fresh. They had the additional appeal of being egg producers while they lived.

Lamb, or mutton, was not a popular meat in America. Sheep were kept almost exclusively for their wool, and their value as wool producers far outweighed any worth they had as food. Certainly mutton would be eaten in place of other meats in times of scarcity if it was available, but it was not easily preserved. Moreover, the meat of mature sheep had a strong taste that had to be masked by careful preparation.

Supplements to the diet were often regional. In rural areas, hunters would supplement the family larder by bringing home such victuals as geese, rabbits, squirrels, wild turkeys, partridges, pheasants, deer, and reed birds. Contrary to popular belief, Southerners had no particular predisposition for the taste of opossums, snakes, or woodchucks in their diet. Fish and other forms of marine seafood including clams, oysters, mussels, and eels were eaten in shore communities. Freshwater fish included bass, sturgeon, pickerel, perch, pike, whitefish, and catfish. Fish could be salted or smoked, but much of it was eaten fresh. Oysters were extremely popular. They were eaten fresh but were also pickled, smoked, and canned.

Eggs were another good source of protein. Miss (Catharine) Beecher advised homemakers to preserve eggs by packing them in fine salt, small end down, or by packing them small end down and then pouring a mixture of four quarts of cold water, four quarts of unslacked lime, two ounces of salt, and two ounces of cream of tartar on them. Hard-boiled eggs were sometimes pickled in vinegar.

Vegetables were eaten fresh in season. Only in the very Deep South were they available during the winter. Small amounts of vegetables could be grown in hot frames, which utilized the heat of manure to keep temperatures warm enough to produce year round as far north as Virginia. Vegetables such as beets, cabbage, carrots, cauliflower, onions, parsnips, potatoes, radishes, rutabagas, sweet potatoes, turnips, and winter squash were stored in root cellars where the climate allowed. In other areas they were packed in straw and stored in barrels. The straw acted as a barrier to prevent the spread of spoilage to the entire barrel. Carrots were often buried in sawdust boxes. Other vegetables such as corn, beans, and peas were dried and used in cooking. Green corn was preserved by turning back the husk, leaving only the last, very thin layer, and then hanging it in the sun or in a warm room to dry. When it was needed for cooking, it was parboiled and cut from the cob. Sweet corn was parboiled, cut from the cob, dried in the sun, and stored in a bag that was kept in a cool, dry place. Sweet corn was also dried in the husk and then buried in salt. String beans, squash, pumpkin, and, in the South, okra were strung on thread and hung up to dry. String beans were strung whole, while other produce was sliced thinly and dried in strips.

Vegetables could also be preserved by making them into catsups and relishes. Mushroom and tomato catsups were popular. Catsup was the general name given to sauces made from vegetables and fruits. Cabbage was made into sauerkraut. In 1858 John Mason patented the Mason jar with which we are familiar today. These threaded glass jars had zinc lids with threaded ring sealers. They were a welcome improvement for both city and rural homemakers, although many still relied on older methods of sealing jars such as pouring a seal made from molten wax, or tying on leather tops with string (Volo and Volo 1998, 228–29).

FOOD PRICES

Food was still accepted in certain areas of the country as payment in kind. An account book from a doctor in Butler, Illinois, showed that accounts for medical service during the war were paid by a variety of items other than cash. The doctor kept specific records of the amount and price of each item and providing some insight into prices outside of the South. Accounts were settled by "4 3/4 lbs. of pork—.20; 16 bushels of corn—8.00; 7 1/2 lbs. meat—10 cts. per—.75; one bushel of apples—.40; 10 lbs. of beef 4 1/2 cts.—.45; 13 lbs. of honey 15 cts. per lb.—1.95; 50 lbs. flour 4 cts. lb.—2.00; 1/2 bushel potatoes—.75; 350 pickles—2.10" (Volo and Volo 1998, 229–30).

The Effect of War

At the commencement of the war, virtually all of the South's most fertile land was devoted to agriculture. As the war progressed and was continually fought on Southern soil, Southern crops were destroyed. Cornelia Peake McDonald described a visit by federal troops. She reported that they pulled up the potatoes and did not stop after getting enough for dinner, but continued, amid roars of laughter and defiant looks, at her to pull them till all were lying on the ground to wither in the sun. The destruction of the spuds, which were no larger than peas, seemed so wanton that she was provoked beyond enduring.

The war actually provided an impetus to the development of farming in the North. Wheat and corn production soared to meet wartime demand. Pork preservation for commercial use in 1865 was twice that of 1860. An additional boon came in the form of good weather, an event not shared by Europe, which experienced crop shortages during this period. The North was able to sell surplus wheat and flour to Europe, thus earning additional funds that could be invested in the war and contesting with "King Cotton" for diplomatic advantage (Volo and Volo 1998, 230).

Shortages

The war brought about many shortages in the South. A poor system of transportation prevented the Confederacy's small resources from being effectively distributed throughout the South. Furthermore, the blockade of Southern ports caused great hardship. Blockade-runners took tremendous risks and expected tremendous profits. To make the risk worthwhile, they tended to carry luxury items for those who could afford to pay, rather than the staples of daily life for everyone. Prices soared in proportion. In November 1862 Judith McGuire wrote that coffee was $4 per pound, and good tea from $18 to $20; butter ranged from $1.50 to $2 per pound; lard 50 cents; corn $15 per barrel; and wheat $4.50 per bushel. In an April 1863 message to Southerners, President Jefferson Davis urged people to give priority to food crops over cotton and tobacco and to plant corn, peas, and beans. Additional hardships were caused by raids of Northern troops upon individual homes.

Receipt books and newspapers carried suggestions for dealing with the food shortages. When successful replacements were discovered, the revelation was readily disclosed to the public in print and by word of mouth. A handwritten receipt book contained a recipe for rice bread, which McGuire dubbed "Southern Bread," as a way of dealing with the unavailability of flour. It began with one gill of rice boiled very soft. When it was cold, 3/4 lbs. of wheat, one teacup of yeast, one teacup

In the absence of refrigeration, nineteenth-century homemakers utilized a great variety of practical devices to preserve or store their food. Many had so-called root cellars dug into the ground or basements where temperatures remained relatively cool. One of the many safes used by housewives was the cheese safe pictured here. The doors were lined with fine screens to keep out flies and other vermin while allowing air flow so the cheese wheels could dry. Safes were also used to hold cooked meats and pies. Courtesy James Volo.

of milk were mixed in and salt was added to taste. After three hours, it was kneaded in enough flour to render the outside hard enough for the oven and baked.

Coffee was a popular beverage, and the blockade of the South made it very difficult to procure. There are reports of Southern soldiers trading with their Northern counterparts for coffee across the lines during times of truce. Parthenia Hague wrote that one of the most difficult tasks was to find a good substitute for coffee. She reported that coffee rose to $30 per pound and from that it went to $60 and then to $70 per pound. Good workmen received $30 per day, so it took two days' hard labor to buy one pound of coffee and scarcely any could be had at that fabulous price.

The best substitute for coffee was said by some to be okra seeds. This was unfortunate because okra became increasingly difficult to acquire as the war progressed and agricultural output diminished. Other alternatives included yams and carrots, either of which would be peeled, sliced, dried, parched, and ground. Acorns, wheat berries, corn, peanuts, sugar cane seed, chicory, beets, dandelion root, cotton seed, and English peas were also used in various conditions of having been browned, parched, burned, and ground. By 1862 Confederate troops had even embraced peanuts as a coffee substitute. The *Confederate Receipt Book*, which was published in 1863 and is believed to be the only cookbook published in the South during the war, contained a recipe for a substitute for coffee that used roasted ripe acorns with a little bacon fat, which was touted as a splendid cup of coffee.

Tea was also a scarce item, but there have always been many satisfactory herbal substitutes for this mainstay. Tea can be made from a wide variety of leaves, roots, and berries. Some favorites included sassafras root, raspberry, huckleberry, and blackberry. Hague wrote in her memoirs of the war that they had several substitutes for tea. Prominent among these substitutes were raspberry leaves. During the blockade, many people planted and cultivated raspberry vines all around their gardens as much for tea as the berries for jams or pies. The leaves were considered the best substitutes for tea. The leaves of the holly tree, when dried in the shade, also made a palatable tea.

Butter was also difficult to obtain because it was largely imported from the North. Many Southern dairy cows had been slaughtered for their meat by invading and local armies and even by some civilians. Judith McGuire wrote in March 1863 that butter was $3.50 per pound in market and other things in proportion. She was resolved to the situation noting that there must be scarcity, particularly of such things as butter, because the cattle had gone to feed the army. Sunflower seed oil was often used as a replacement for butter.

A related casualty in this regard was the want of milk and cream. Judith McGuire wrote milk was so very scarce and high that they only had it once for many months. The *Confederate Receipt Book* gave this solution for the undersupply of cream: "Beat the white of an egg to a froth, put to it a very small lump of butter, and mix well, then turn the coffee to it gradually, so that it may not curdle. If perfectly done it will be an excellent substitute for cream. For tea omit the butter, using only the egg."

Flour, too, was scarce. Prices continued to escalate throughout the war. It was reported that in Richmond a barrel of flour sold for $250 during the closing months of the war. Sarah Morgan wrote in 1862, if anyone had told her she could have lived off corn bread, a few months ago, she would have been incredulous but she had come to the point where she returned an inward grace for the blessing, at every mouthful. She resigned herself to the fact that she would not have a piece of wheat bread until the war was over. Parthenia Hague recalled that bolted meal, when obtainable, made a good substitute for flour, though millers said it injured their bolting cloth to sift the corn meal through it. She reported that nearly every household that sent its grist to be ground would order a portion of the meal to be bolted for use as flour. Such bolted meal when it was sifted through a thin muslin cloth mixed up with scalding water became more viscid and adhesive, and was as easily molded into pie crust with the aid of the rolling pin as the pure flour. She was pleased with the nice muffins and waffles that could be made of bolted meal, and also of a very nice cake made with homemade brown sugar.

Perhaps the distress over the lack of flour is somehow tied to the American housewife's extreme pride in her bread making. Miss Beecher devoted an entire chapter to bread making. She counseled: "A woman should be ashamed to have poor bread, far more so, than to speak bad grammar, or to have a dress out of fashion.... When it is very frequently the case that a housekeeper has poor bread, she may set herself down as a slack baker and negligent housekeeper." Commercially produced bread was one area in which modern convenience was strongly resisted until the early years of the following century.

Households that did not produce corn, which could be ground into meal, were often at the mercy of the war economy. Judith McGuire lamented that meal had been bought up by speculators and was selling at $16 per bushel. She prayed that what she called "those hard-hearted creatures" could be made to suffer. Mary A. H. Gray's diary records the lengths to which people would go to obtain, or in this case reclaim, corn. She reported that they spent the day in picking out grains of corn from cracks and crevices in bureau drawers, and other improvised troughs for federal horses, as well as gathering up what was on the ground. In all they gathered about a half bushel.

Salt became a highly prized commodity. Dolly Sumner Lunt Burge describes disguising a barrel of salt, which had cost her $200, as a leaching tub to conceal it from marauders. In 1862, Union forces destroyed a large saltworks on Chesapeake Bay, causing difficulty for individuals and salt pork producers alike.

Burge wrote: "The obtaining of salt became extremely difficult when the war had cut off our supply. This was true especially in regions remote from the sea-coast and border States, such as the interior of Alabama and Georgia. Here again we were obliged to have recourse to whatever expedient ingenuity suggested. All the brine left in troughs and barrels, where pork had been salted down, were carefully dipped up, boiled down, and converted into salt again. In some cases the salty soil under old smokehouses was dug up and placed in hoppers, which resembled backwoods ash-hoppers, made for leaching ashes in the process of soap-manufacture. Water was then poured upon the soil, the brine of which percolated through the hopper was boiled down to the proper point, poured into vessels, and set in the sun, which by evaporation completed the rude process. Though never of immaculate whiteness, the salt that resulted from these methods served well enough for all our purposes, and we accepted it without complaining."

Resourceful people living near the shore could obtain salt by evaporating ocean water. Sometimes coltsfoot, a wild plant that gave a salt-like flavor to foods, was used in cooking. But lack of salt posed problems other than taste preference. Salt was used extensively as a meat preservative. Parching fish and meat Indian style was only a stopgap expedient. Meat could also be cured in a brine using a lesser amount of salt than other methods. Even the availability of meat to preserve was a problem. Once Vicksburg fell in 1863, Union forces had control of the Mississippi, virtually cutting off the supply of western beef to the Confederacy.

Soda, or baking soda, used as a leavening agent, was also a victim of the blockade. Parthenia Hague wrote that it was discovered that the ashes of corncobs possessed the alkaline property essential for raising dough. She noted that it was best to select all the red cobs as they were thought to contain more carbonate of soda than the white cobs.

Sugar, too, was difficult to acquire. Even though the South possessed its own sugar plantations, most were in federally occupied Louisiana for most of the war. Honey, molasses, and sorghum were used in its stead. Parthenia Hague told the story of a woman who even used a surplus of watermelon to make sugar and syrup. The deficit of sugar also inhibited the making of jellies, jams, and preserves. Red corncobs were again found to be useful. The cobs were boiled, and the juice was thickened into syrup. The *Confederate Receipt Book* gave this recipe for cider jelly: "Boil cider to the consistency of syrup, and let it cool, and you have a nice jelly." When apples to make vinegar were in too short supply, Southerners turned to molasses, honey, beets, figs, persimmons, and sorghum. The *Confederate Receipt Book* even had a recipe for "Apple Pie Without Apples" that was made with one small bowl of crackers, soaked until no hard parts remain, one teaspoon of tartaric acid, some butter, a little nutmeg and sweetening to taste.

Apparently not all Southerners were subject to deprivations. Mary Boykin Chesnut recorded the menu of a luncheon to ladies given by Mrs. Jefferson Davis in January 1864. It included gumbo, ducks and olives, supreme de volaille, chickens in jelly, oysters, lettuce salad, chocolate jelly cake, and claret soup champagne.

The U.S. Sanitary Commission was a Northern civilian organization that coordinated widespread war relief. Funds were raised through "Sanitary Fairs," which sold homemade pies and jellies and held raffles for quilts and other homemade crafts, and from direct solicitation. Children were recruited to solicit funds door-to-door and to collect nonperishable groceries such as jellies or crackers from merchants to be sent to soldiers at the front. In some farming communities, families set aside portions of their land for the production of easily stored crops, such as potatoes, which were delivered to the Sanitary Commission. Schools held "onion" or "potato" days to collect produce.

Dietary kitchens staffed with dietary nurses were established by the Sanitary Commission in 1862 as a result of the efforts of Annie Wittenmyer. She worked very hard to see that a system was developed to feed wounded soldiers. Women volunteers had been scrounging milk, eggs, and vegetables for wounded soldiers in field hospitals who were too ill to eat the standard pork-and-beans field ration. Wittenmyer's system established the means for providing appropriate meals for the men.

Similar efforts in Southern communities were unable to match the organization and productivity of the North. Southerners were equally sympathetic to the plight of their soldiers, but the South lacked the efficient transportation and resources necessary for mounting such endeavors (Volo and Volo 1998, 230–35).

Feeding the Troops

Hundreds of officers and men were engaged in the day-to-day duty of providing food for the troops. The overall responsibility fell to the Subsistence Department in Washington, headed by a commissary general who contracted for the various types of rations with private manufacturers or packers. The foodstuffs were then apportioned to the respective army commissaries, and by them, in turn, to the corps, brigade, and regimental commissaries. They were then distributed to the troops. Washington continued, from the beginning of the war until its end, to let contracts to private suppliers for all of its rations in this manner.

The government rations distributed to the troops varied slightly with the season and the availability of local supply. Nonetheless, a complete list of all the possibilities is short. These included hardtack, coffee, sugar, soft bread, flour, rice, cornmeal, dried peas, dried beans, desiccated vegetables or dried fruits, fresh or dried potatoes (called chips), salt pork, bacon or ham, pickled beef (called salt horse), fresh meat, and occasionally onions, molasses, salt, pepper, and vinegar.

With only a rudimentary understanding of balanced nutrition, it is a wonder that any soldier survived the war on such a diet. However, the standard ration provided a daily average of over 3,000 calories, heavy in carbohydrates and fats, but providing few vitamins or complete proteins.

The vitamin deficiencies and the lack of protein could have been devastating. An unrelieved diet of cornmeal and salt pork, while sufficient in calories, would ultimately produce such diseases as scurvy and pellagra. Fresh meats will provide protein but cannot afford sufficient protein to make up the deficit alone. Both beans and cornmeal are high protein sources but are individually incomplete in amino acids; yet, in combination they are complementary and provide all the essentials needed to sustain health. Rice and peas are another complementary pair with similar characteristics. In offering these pairs among a small variety of foodstuffs, the government unwittingly supplied a nearly complete diet to its soldiers, yet the unresolved question of a lack of essential vitamins had serious health consequences that cost many lives.

The lack of variety in the soldiers' diet resulted from the need to keep the rations from spoiling while they were being shipped and stored for use. In the absence of refrigeration, meats, if not freshly slaughtered, had to be salted or pickled; and breads, vegetables, and fruits, if not for immediate consumption, had to be dried. Salting and drying retarded the growth of bacteria, as did pickling, smoking, and sugar curing. With the exception of meals aboard naval vessels, there is an amazing absence from the records of cheese being issued as a regular part of the ration.

There were two standard rations in the federal army. One was the *camp ration*, and the other was the *campaign* or *marching ration*. The *camp ration* tended to be more diverse, and for one soldier in the federal army consisted of meat (1 1/4 lbs. of salted or fresh beef, or 3/4 lb. of pork or bacon); and bread (1 lb., 6 oz. of soft bread or flour, or 1 lb. of hardtack, or 1 1/4 lbs. of cornmeal). He also received approximately 1 1/2 ounces of dried vegetables, rice, dried potatoes, peas, or beans. Fresh potatoes were to be had, but fresh vegetables were rare and allotted in only very small quantities. Salt and pepper were allowed in minuscule quantities. About 1/2 ounce of vinegar was provided for each man daily to help prevent scurvy. About the same amount of molasses was allowed when available. The *marching ration* consisted of 1 lb., or 8 crackers, of hard bread; 3/4 lb. of salt pork, or 1 1/4 lbs. of fresh meat; sugar, coffee, and salt. The beans, rice, and so on, were not issued to the soldier when on the march, as he could not carry them.

When fresh meat was not available the enlisted men were provided with a basic preserved meat ration of pork—boiled ham, salt pork, or bacon being most common. The South quickly realized that it would experience a meat shortage, and Richmond established an extensive government pork-packing program in close proximity to the rail and river transportation of Tennessee. These plants and their associated salt works were constantly in danger of capture or destruction by federal forces.

Federal forces also relied heavily on preserved pork. Pork's prominence as a foodstuff, when compared to preserved beef, did not lie in any intrinsic nutritional value, although the high fat content provided an excellent source of caloric intake. It was simply easier to preserve than beef and tasted better than pickled beef, which was so poor and unpalatable that the soldiers called it salt horse. No effort was made to comply with dietary restrictions due to individual medical or religious preferences.

In camp boiled ham was often pulled from a barrel into which it had been packed for some months in a thick covering of grease that came from the boiling. The meat came out in long, unappetizing strips, and when brought to the surface the sound of the suction was like the noise made when one pulled his feet out of Virginia mud. The grease was scraped off and saved by many soldiers to be used as an ingredient in other recipes. The meat could be fried, roasted, or eaten sliced between two pieces of soft bread or with hardtack.

Salt pork was easy to make and had been used since colonial times as a mainstay of the diet for soldiers and sailors. Salt pork was a favorite among veteran soldiers, who sometimes declined fresh beef for a good piece of salt pork, but recruits had to learn to ignore its overwhelmingly salty flavor and to appreciate its nutritional qualities. The amount of salt used in its processing was staggering, but salt pork could last, unspoiled, for a long time in a sealed barrel. However, once a barrel was opened, the meat had to be used quickly or it would spoil.

HARDTACK

The staple ration of the federal army was a square cracker, 3 1/8 by 2 7/8 inches, with small holes in its top, known as hardtack. Referred to as both army bread and biscuit, it was a very dry, incredibly hard product without leavening, and bore little resemblance to either. The army was not being purposely cruel to its soldiers by giving them hardtack to eat. Hardtack was not a new product. It was used as ship's bread for centuries. The dryness and hardness were functional characteristics. It was dry when packaged to keep the cracker from spoiling, and hard so it could be carried in the soldier's haversack without crumbling. Southern soldiers relied on cornbread, but they ate hardtack when it was captured from the enemy.

COFFEE

The importance of coffee to the Civil War soldier cannot be underestimated. Their diaries and letters are full of reverent references to the hot brown liquid. Coffee was included in the official federal ration, as was sugar to sweeten it. Condensed milk of two brands, Lewis's and Borden's, and a dry powder called the Essence of Coffee were available through the sutlers.

Federal soldiers rarely had trouble getting their regular daily ration of 1 1/2 ounces of coffee beans. Confederate soldiers showed an equally intense liking for coffee, but due to the effectiveness of the blockade, they often had to do without coffee or find a coffee bean substitute. Soldiers resorted to the same substitute materials available to civilians to make coffee or to stretch a limited supply. The quality of this substitute coffee was questionable, and Confederates would take great risks to trade scarce Southern tobacco for good Union coffee by trading with the enemy pickets across the lines.

The Army of the Potomac used 80 tons of coffee and sugar every week. Nonetheless, federal soldiers were very concerned lest they somehow be deprived of even the smallest part of this coffee and sugar allowance, and steps were taken to ensure that favoritism in apportioning the ration was thwarted. The appropriate amount having been issued on a company level, the orderly sergeant would place a gum blanket on the ground and make as many piles of coffee beans and sugar as there were men to receive the ration. Great care was taken to ensure that the piles were uniform. To prevent any charge of unfairness, the sergeant would turn his back, and an assistant would point to a pile randomly. The sergeant would call out the company roll by name, and the named man would retrieve his allowance. The veteran soon learned to place both the sugar and the coffee together in a cloth bag and scoop out the two together without ceremony, but some men preferred to keep them separate and use each in proportion to their taste.

Coffee was furnished to the soldier as green beans from the sack. Roasting was done in a camp kettle, which often meant the beans were burned rather than roasted. To grind the beans the soldier seized his musket by the barrel and used the butt as a tamper. The ground coffee more properly should have been called cracked coffee, as many of the grains were halved, more quartered, and the rest of a very coarse texture.

The army recognized the stimulant value of coffee, and each soldier was issued a tin dipper in which to boil his portion. This was a large metal cup holding between a pint and a quart of liquid. The ground coffee was placed directly into the water without a filter of any sort. Such utensils soon disappeared, to be replaced by a tin can with an improvised wire handle. Astonished recruits were amazed to see veteran soldiers holding this improvisation on the end of a stick, boiling their coffee at the campfire in happy security. For those who recoiled at resorting to cast-off tin cans, sutlers offered an improved device for boiling coffee with a hinged lid and a stout wire handle by which it might be hung over the fire. The price of such an article could strain the financial resources of a single soldier, but several men might pool their money to purchase one and take turns carrying it.

The Civil War soldier would not be denied his coffee. If an early morning march was intended, and fires were permitted, the march was preceded by a pot of coffee. If a halt was ordered in mid-afternoon, coffee was made. Coffee-making equipment was generally carried strapped to the outside of the kit where it was easily accessible. The movement of an army could be heard from far off by the resultant rattling of countless coffee boilers and tin cups. So significant was this noise that special orders were frequently issued prior to stealthy movements of the army to place these items inside the haversack or otherwise muffle them. At the end of each day's march, as soon as the army began to bivouac, small groups of men would invariably make the preparation of coffee their first task. A supper of hardtack and coffee followed, and then each man would roll up in his blankets for the night.

In camp, company cooks were issued large coffeepots holding several gallons. Coffee was available at meals and between meals; and men going on guard and coming off guard drank it at all hours of the night. The U.S. Christian Commission made the rounds of the camps with coffee wagons made from old artillery limbers nicknamed by the troops "the Christian Light Artillery." The coffee wagon was provided with compartments for ingredients and three large coffee boilers that could produce 90 gallons of coffee every hour. Whatever grumbling there may have been about the quality of the other rations, the opinion concerning the coffee was one of unqualified approval.

COOKWARE

Initially the government in Richmond ignored the need for the wide-scale provision of camp equipment, and little beyond firearms, bayonets, and canteens was issued to Confederate troops. On the other hand, the federal authorities encumbered their troops with several standard items of camp equipment, including kettles, mess pans, and coffeepots. A set of metal crutches with a sturdy crossbar served to hang the pots over the fire. The kettles were made of tinned sheet iron in sizes that allowed them to be nested within each other for ease of transportation. Large iron mess pans were used to serve the food. The company mess kettles were provided to make coffee, soups, and stews, but in typical soldierly fashion, they proved excellent for washing clothes. The mess pans were made to fry pork and bacon, yet they also served as washbasins. Such double duty was less than polite society would have tolerated, but for the soldiers any other course was considered impractical.

Each company was initially issued a mule upon which the company cookware was to be carried on the march. Camp cooking equipment was cumbersome and took up much of the limited space assigned to each company in the regimental baggage train. As the mules required careful attention, they quickly disappeared from the line of march; and the company cooking gear, whether through design or by accident, frequently deteriorated or was purposely abandoned. The concept of company cooking quickly disappeared under all but the most favorable of circumstances.

In this manner both Johnny Reb and Billy Yank found themselves in surprisingly similar situations. Each soldier was obliged to use only the limited array of cookware that he could carry. A coffee boiler of some sort was considered a necessity, and any utensil that could serve as a frying pan became indispensable. Small groups of men would pool their money to purchase a coffee boiler or a real frying pan from the sutler, and each would take turns carrying it on the march. The person so designated often was entitled to the utensil's first use when camp was made. If one of the owners was wounded, killed, or otherwise removed from the companionship of his fellow investors, his share could be sold to an outsider.

As with the soldiers of most wars, Civil War soldiers quickly adopted any serviceable device that proved light to carry and easy to replace. A particularly common cookware solution was to unsolder the seam between the two halves of an extra canteen acquired from the battlefield. Each half served as a tolerable lightweight frying pan or plate and could be carried strapped over the canteen. The sure sign of a veteran was the simplicity of his cooking utensils, and many wide-eyed raw recruits—weighed down with government-issued pots, pans, and knapsacks—marveled at the war-weary, blanket-wrapped soldiers sitting by a fire calmly heating their coffee in a discarded tin can with a wire bail handle (Volo and Volo 1998, 116–31).

HOUSING

There was no single characteristic American house style during the Civil War period, but the elegant plantation homes built in the South, with their central entrances, balconies, columns, and formal ballrooms, came closest to representing a discrete architectural style for the antebellum period. The focus on Southern architectural characteristics somewhat distorts the character of home building in the period. Actually the majority of homes built from 1820 to 1860 were Greek Revival, Classical Revival, and Federalist style structures or some adaptation thereof. Many more Americans lived in Georgian-style houses that reflected building in the earlier Federalist period than those who lived in plantation mansions. Moreover, surviving examples of stately Northern mansions and palatial Southern plantation houses reflect only the power, idealism, and tastes of the wealthiest Americans. Unlike the homes of the wealthy, most of the functional and sturdy structures belonging to average Americans no longer exist in an unmodified form, having undergone numerous renovations in the twentieth century. Their original contours and characteristics were seldom recorded except by accident in a photograph, painting, or sketch.

Although home ownership served as an ideal during the period, many families, especially in the cities, had to settle for apartments, boarding houses, and tenements.

Even among individual home owners, there was a wide diversity of residences including mansions, villas, multi-story houses, cottages, cabins, and so-called shanties. The Irish immigrants were noted by observers at the time for building shanties—structures that were virtual shacks.

The majority of homes built during the period were simple frame farmhouses. Many were characteristic of the half-house, a two-story center hall colonial floor plan with one wing eliminated. This left a diminished center hall including the staircase to the second floor, two first-floor rooms (usually a parlor and dining room), and two second-story bedchambers above them. The kitchen was often a shed lean-to either separate from, or attached, at the back of the building. An outhouse served everyone's needs in the family. In the largely rural areas of a young America, a husband and wife might sit down, pencil and paper in hand, with thoughts focused on corn fields or pumpkin patches rather than on cornices or pilasters. These amateur architects tended to design plans for a practical house, a functional barn, a predator-proof chicken coop, or a well-drained pig pen. Fenced farm fields and properly planted orchards were far more important to the common farm family than symmetrical facades or grand staircases. Many of these plans were piecemeal and disordered, and few such original drawings survived.

Yet in an odd custom among rural societies in nineteenth-century America, some of the best plans were rescued from obscurity. Prizes were sometimes offered to amateur planners for successful farmhouse designs by a number of agricultural improvement societies. Many of the most functional plans were submitted and displayed at county fairs or published in farm journals. Ordinary periodicals often carried house plans, and few illustrated magazines failed to carry a floor or building plan of the month. Evidence gleaned from sources like these has allowed historians to construct a good picture of the average farm home.

In addition a number of architectural pattern books were published during the period that contained a variety of house plans of different sizes and prices. Among these was *Rural Residences* first published in 1837 by Alexander Jackson Davis. This particular architectural pattern book was thought to have introduced the Gothic Revival style to North America. In a similar manner *Victorian Cottage Residences* and *The Architecture of Country Homes* were published by Andrew Jackson Downing in 1842 and 1850, respectively. Both books emphasized the Carpenter Gothic style. Digests and catalogs of some of the most popular and original designs available were gathered from a variety of sources and were published by George E. Woodward throughout the second half of the century. These included plans and details drawn to a working scale with a full set of specifications and estimates of their cost (Volo and Volo 2004, 115–17).

CLOTHING

Women's Fashion Fundamentals

Nineteenth-century fashion was revolutionized and democratized by several innovations. The first practical sewing machine, using dual threads and an under-thread shuttle, was developed by Elias Howe in 1845 and patented in the following year. The sewing machine was advertised as being 10 times faster than the human hand and hailed by many as a great labor-saving device. The widespread acceptance of the sewing machine allowed the fashion industry to expand quickly. Sewing machines had been available for decades but sales skyrocketed after the 1860s, which certainly was a major factor in the explosion of the sewing pattern industry. The sewing machine led the way in revolutionizing American clothing. All kinds of new undergarments were developed, and clothing details became increasingly complex. Hemmers, binders, tuckers, rufflers, puffers, braiders, and other machine attachments were invented to satisfy the desire for new styles.

The popularity of the sewing machine was a major factor in the explosion of the pattern industry, creating a thriving market by the 1860s. The patterns, which were printed in graduated sizes and included explicit sewing instructions by Ebenezer Butterick and James McCall, provided women with the ability to recreate complicated, fashionable styles. Together, the sewing machine and the paper pattern industry made fashionable dress accessible to households of only modest means (Browne and Kreiser 2003, 65–66).

Overall, one of the greatest influences on American women's fashion during the nineteenth century was *Godey's Lady's Book*, a magazine founded by Louis B. Godey in July 1830. In addition to serials, essays, poems, and craft projects, it featured engraved fashion plates. Each month the magazine depicted morning dresses, walking dresses, seaside costumes, riding habits, dinner dresses, and ball gowns. Such wardrobe depth was seldom needed for the vast majority of the magazine's readers, whose clothes could generally be divided into public or social and domestic or work, with a few seasonal additions for summer and winter. As time passed, *Godey's* began to show fashions better suited to the lifestyle of the American woman. By the 1860s *Godey's* had become a fashion institution, setting the standard for fashion savvy. A woman living in the blockaded South bemoaned the fact that in her secluded settlement women wore the same style the whole four years of the war, because not a fashion plate or ladies magazine was seen during that entire period. Other magazines such as *Peterson's*, *Arthur's*, *Graham's*, *Leslie's*, and *Harper's* began to follow suit or grew in popularity.

Whether a woman could afford the extravagances touted by the fashion plates of the day or not, the look she was hoping to attain was the same. Women of the Civil War period wanted to create the appearance of a narrow waist. Virtually all lines of garments emphasized the smallness of the waist by creating the illusion of width at the shoulders and hips. This was further accentuated by foundation garments that altered the body's physical appearance.

The dress bodices during this period can be classified by three basic styles. There was the "O" bodice, the "V" bodice and the "Y" bodice. Regardless of style, bodices ended at the natural waistline. The bodice portion of the dress fastened at the center front by hooks and eyes, while the skirt portion had a side-front closure. This created an awkward opening that extended vertically from the neck, then horizontally along the waist, and then vertically again down a few inches along the left front skirt seam. The armscye, or armhole, was almost always diagonal or horizontal to give the shoulders a sloping and wider appearance. Sleeves were very full, particularly at the elbow, again imparting the illusion of the slender waist. Often sleeves had sleeve caps. These were ornamental pieces of fabric that covered the top few inches of the sleeve, supporting the image of the wide, sloping shoulder. Short cap sleeves that revealed a woman's arm could only be found on ball gowns.

The necklines of day dresses usually came to the base of the neck. Collars were basted inside to protect the garment from wear and soiling. They could easily be removed for frequent launderings from which the entire garment could be saved. Sometimes these collars had matching sets of cuffs that were similarly attached and served the same purpose.

Many of the fabrics and dyes used at this time did not hold up to frequent laundering. Garments were often taken apart and re-sewn when cleaned. The *Housekeeper's Encyclopedia* (Haskell, 1992) provided nine pages of instructions for washing various fabrics, which included rice-water, bran, ox-gall, salt, elixir of vitriol, and egg yolk. Most women's dresses were never totally laundered but rather spot cleaned as needed.

Skirts were long but seldom touched the ground. An exception was the elliptical skirt popular during the late-war period. These skirts were shorter in the front but lengthened in the back to a point where some actually dragged on the ground. Hem tapes were common on skirts. The tapes or trims were wrapped around the finished hem and could be removed for cleaning or replacement. Skirts were very full and were either fully gathered or pleated at the waistline. No effort was made to make the stomach area appear flatter because, once again, the fuller an area away from the waist seemed, the narrower the waist appeared.

Fabrics used for dresses and skirts included silk, linen, wool, and cotton. These were available in an almost infinite variety of weights and weaves, some of which are no longer available today. By far cotton and linen were the most common choices for everyday wear. Silk was expensive. If the average woman owned a silk dress, it would be saved for very special occasions. Linen, because of its extreme durability and ability to be produced at home, was considered frontier or laborer clothing. This was particularly true in the South, where it was in common use among the slave population. Wool continued to have its place because of its warmth and especially because of its fire-retardant qualities. Cotton, a status symbol earlier in the century, had become readily available and affordable for even modest households by the 1830s, thanks to the tremendous development of the textile industry after the invention of the cotton gin. From time to time, there were movements in the North among abolitionist women to avoid the use of cotton due to their belief that it was produced largely as a result of slave activity, but this tended to be confined to relatively small groups.

The blockade and the resulting interruptions in trade caused great hardships for Southern woman who had once been the most fashionable element of the population. One Southern woman described every household as a miniature factory in itself, with its cotton, cards, spinning-wheels, warping-frames, and looms. Some Southern ladies continued to dress and to dance in whatever prewar style they could manage as a means of keeping up their courage. Drawing upon their resourcefulness and creativity, Southern women managed to rework prewar finery and to use natural materials. Prices soared. By 1864 one Southern woman recorded prices that would give a purchaser pause today including $110 for ladies' Morocco boots; $22 per yard for linen; $5 apiece for spools of cotton, and $5 for a paper of pins. Women needing funds to keep their households together often reworked old finery to create collars, undersleeves, neckties, and other items that brought handsome prices in the inflated Confederate currency.

The color palette available at this time was basically that which could be achieved by natural dyes. While Southern women tended to wear lighter hues, popular colors included browns, soft blues, greens, lavenders, and grays. Yellows and deep berry-toned reds were also in use. Black was a common color for trim and detailing. Even though chemical dyes had been introduced by the end of the 1850s, these colors were mostly found in decorative fabrics for the home. Although some showy young women in the North did wear them, proper ladies did not.

By the 1860s white wedding dresses had come into fashion. However, many women still followed older traditions and were married in their best dress. Those fortunate enough to be able to afford such a specialized garment tended to choose dresses that might be considered plain by ballroom standards. Expense was more likely to be put into the fabric rather than trim. Generally, weddings were held during the day. Wedding dresses were therefore day dresses with jewel necklines and long sleeves. In keeping with the look of the day, headdresses and veils tended to lie flat on the head to avoid adding height. Coronets of real or artificial flowers were arranged so that they framed the face and added width.

Quite possibly, undergarments reached the highest level of complexity in fashion history during this period. Undergarments served to protect the outer garment from body soiling, molded the body to create the ideal look, and served to distribute the weight of the extremely full skirts. Like the previously discussed collars and cuffs, undergarments were constructed of serviceable fabrics that could be laundered. They were usually white.

The garment worn closest to the skin was the chemise—a knee-length, loose-fitting shift. A number of garments were worn with the chemise. Drawers, known as pantalettes, were worn beneath the chemise. They were constructed of two independent legs attached to a waistband and extended to just below the knee. Sometimes they were decorated with tucks, fancy stitching, or eyelet.

The corset was worn on top of the chemise. The purpose of this garment was to make the waist look small compared to other parts of the body and to shape the upper portion of the body upward and outward from the waist to the bust. Corsets were lightly boned and usually had steel clasps at the front and lacing up the back to allow for adjustment. Some had laces in the front with a busk inserted for rigidity. Light corsets were introduced to girls around age 12 and certainly by the age of puberty. Over the corset was worn a corset cover or camisole.

The next layer of undergarment is perhaps the single garment most associated with women's clothing during the Civil War, the crinoline or hoop. Crinolines were worn beneath petticoats to make the skirt appear more full. They also helped in the practical task of distributing the weight of the skirt, which could become quite oppressive depending on the type and amount of fabric used. Generally, crinolines for day dresses were somewhat smaller than those for evening wear. Atop the crinoline were placed one or more petticoats for added fullness and to soften the ridges that could be created by the hoops. Skirts tended to be so much greater in circumference than the crinolines that they tended to drape over this support in folds.

Even a small sampling of period photographs would indicate that few women actually wore hoops with the extreme proportions depicted in fashion plates of the day. Normally, the diameter of the hoop was approximately 50 to 70 percent of the wearer's height. Women engaged in vigorous work would decline to wear them. Hoops did wear out, posing a great problem for women in the blockaded South. The hoop was often made of a long, thin strip of whalebone, called baleen, turned back on itself in a circle. Baleen was also used to make buggy whips, and since it was generally acquired from New England, it was largely unavailable during the war.

When it came to outerwear, women had a wide variety of options, including capes, cloaks, shawls, jackets, and coats. Capes varied in length from just below the hip to just above the ankle. Consistent with the fashion ideal of sloping shoulders, they fit the top portion of the torso closely. Some capes had arm slits for ease of movement. Cloaks were extremely full to accommodate the full sleeves and skirts. Jackets and coats naturally followed dress lines, making them many times wider at the hem than at the shoulder.

Shawls were very popular. They were oversized and extended well down the back of the skirt. Commonly, two-yard squares were folded into a triangle. Double square shawls could be 64 inches by 128 inches or more. Some shawls were knitted or crocheted. Others were made from wool or lace. Many were decorated with fringe, ruffles, or lace. Paisley shawls were particularly popular.

The bonnet style specific to the 1860s was the spoon bonnet, so named because the brim curved high over the forehead, causing the wearer's face to look as though it was cradled in a large spoon. Bonnets were one item of apparel women could constantly update by reworking the trim or decorations to meet the current vogue. Favored decorative features included ribbon, lace, and clusters of silk flowers or berries. These were used on the outside of the bonnet as well as inside the brim to frame the face. Huge ribbons several inches wide were tied in large bows beneath the chin. The outsides of bonnets were covered in silk or, more commonly, polished cotton, which was then pleated, ruched, piped, or quilted. A gathered flounce or skirt was often found attached to the base of the bonnet at the nape of the neck. For summer wear, bonnets were often made of straw.

For country wear, there was the flat-crowned, wide-brimmed picture hat made from felt or straw. This often had a lace edging that hung down, almost like a veil. These hats were decorated with materials similar to those used on bonnets, but less elaborately. As the decade progressed, the brim shrank and curved slightly over the eyes, the lace was removed, and the crown became more rounded. Hats continued to shrink as the decade progressed. A popular style was the so-called pork pie, which resembled a turban in shape with very little space between the brim and the crown. Another type of walking hat had a round crown and a small, rolling brim often decorated by a drooping ostrich feather.

When serious protection from the sun was needed, the slatted bonnet came to the rescue. These work garments were made of cotton or linen and bore neither decorations nor trim. They had long back pieces that extended over the shoulders, and the front could be folded back or fully extended to shade the entire face. During the first federal occupation of Winchester, Virginia, it was reported that the Master Provost opposed the wearing of sunbonnets by women on the street, claiming that the so-called secession bonnets were worn for their cheapness and for their defense against staring soldiers and that they were intended as an insult by intimating that the women did not care how they dressed while the Northern troops were there.

Indoors, women frequently wore morning caps. These were dainty caps made of muslin, lace tulle, and ribbon. They would never be worn outdoors. Crocheted nets were also worn, but they were generally not considered suitable for dress occasions. Some conservative older women wore more substantial caps, often with lappets, which fully covered the head and were reminiscent of the caps worn during the previous century.

Aprons were an important item in a nineteenth-century wardrobe. Household aprons were extremely large, enveloping almost the entire skirt from front to back and extending down to within a few inches of the hem. Often they had rectangular tops, known as pinners because they were held in place by pins rather than a neck strap as was the norm in the twentieth century. Aprons would often be made from fabrics with small plaids or checks to help hide stains. While they could be solid, they were seldom white. Aprons were made from linen, flannel, wool, or cotton. Wool was greatly preferred for safety around fires. It does not burn as quickly as linen, and its odor when burning gives fair warning. Burns were the second leading cause of death for women at this time, surpassed only by death during childbirth. Smaller aprons would be worn for mealtimes unless servants served the meals. Separate aprons were kept for particularly dirty household chores.

As with other fashion items, hairstyles wanted to emphasize a broad upper body. To that end, the center part is almost universal in period photographs. This allows for a wide, bare forehead, making the face appear broad while adding no height on top. To continue this illusion, the fullest part of the hairstyle was at or below the ears. Some teens wore their hair cut blunt just below the earlobes. Most women, however, had long hair that they wore rolled, braided, or otherwise confined and pulled toward the back of the head. If the hair was not confined, it was generally fixed in long finger curls and pulled to the side of the face. The variety of curls and hair rolls was as rich as the ingenuity of the women who styled them. As the war drew to a close, hairstyles were beginning to change to include tendrils and greater height. Ladies' magazines of the period offered many suggestions for elaborate hair dressing for evening wear and suggested incorporating such items as flower blossoms, pins, combs, chains, feathers, and false curls.

Men's Fashion Fundamentals

Like women's clothing, men's clothing in practical application tended to fall into formal and informal, summer and winter. New clothes would be considered best dress until they became worn, and they would then be relegated to work status.

A shirt, vest, and trousers would be the very least in which a man would allow himself to be seen. A man appearing with anything less was considered to be in a state of undress. Even laborers and farmers would not allow themselves to go with less. It was the basest menial or workman who would not be so attired, such as the blacksmith, who would wear a heavy leather apron, which covered him above the waist.

Dress shirts were made of white cotton. Longer than the modern shirt, they were pullovers that buttoned from the mid-chest to the neck. Small vertical tucks commonly decorated either side of the buttons, but this became less favored as the 1860s progressed. Shirts had neck bands and detachable collars. For formal day wear, the collar was upright with a gap between the points, which just touched the jaw, allowing for freer movement of the head and neck than had been the style earlier in the century. For informal occasions, men wore either a shallow single collar with sloping points meeting at the center and forming a small inverted "V" opening, or a shallow double collar similar to the modern collar. Work shirts were made in a variety of colors and checks and could be made from cotton or linen.

Cravats, which more closely resemble the earlier neck stock than the modern tie, were worn around the neck. The term necktie was just coming into use. The cravat might have been tied in a flat, broad bow with the ends extending across the top of the waistcoat or secured with a pin. Basically, however, it was a band of fabric passed around the neck and tied in either a bow or a knot with hanging ends. Silk was the fabric of choice, and it was one area where a man might be able to display his good taste even if his purse prohibited further extravagances. The decade began with a preference for light-colored cravats, occasionally decorated with embroidery or other fancy work. As the war progressed, however, darker colors became more prominent. Striped, plaid, and dotted cravats were also worn, but with less regularity. Even laborers would simulate the look, although they may only have been able to knot a cotton kerchief around their neck.

Vests or waistcoats could be made of the same fabric as the suit, or they could be of much finer, dressier fabrics such as silk taffetas, embossed silks, or brocades. Patterns ranged from tone-on-tone to stripes, checks, and paisleys. Watch pockets became common. Suits were either loose-fitting, almost baggy, or very formal with knee-length frock coats. The fuller suit seems to have been favored by the average man, perhaps because it was more comfortable or needed less skilled tailoring. The formal suit appears to have been the look to which men of power aspired. Work trousers had buttoned, full fall fronts, while dress trousers had French flys, which concealed the buttons.

Wool was the fabric of choice for these items, with linen being popular during the summer, especially in the South. Farmers seemed to favor tweeds and more sturdy woolens. Generally, solids dominated, with browns and grays most common. Black was the choice of professionals, who also preferred fine woolen broadcloth, serge, and twill. These fabrics often had a certain amount of silk woven in to give them a finer finish and lighter weight.

Hat styles varied. The stovepipe hat favored by Abraham Lincoln also came in a shorter version. Many Southern gentlemen favored what has come to be called the plantation hat. This is a low-crowned, stylish hat with a substantial, but not overstated, brim. Another hat commonly found had a round crown with a medium brim. Flat-topped straw hats were in summer. Rural men often wore wide-brimmed, high-crowned hats, which offered less in fashion but more in protection from the elements.

When it came to lounging in the privacy of one's home, gentlemen had several specialized items of attire. Lounging or smoking caps were elaborate items made of rich fabrics and adorned with embroidery, beadwork, or braid. They generally came in three basic styles: the round pillbox style, the fitted six-panel cap, and the teardrop-shaped Scotch style. The first two styles ended with a tassel on top. The last was finished with a narrow ribbon at the back of the cap at the point. Ladies' magazines also carried patterns for making and decorating these caps. In addition to slippers, which greatly resembled the woman's slipper for relaxed footwear at home, a man might have preferred the dressing, or lounging, boot.

Men wore their hair parted to the side. Facial hair was very stylish. Men sported beards of all styles, lengths, and degrees. Mustaches were equally in favor. Period photographs show a tremendous variety of styles. The names of most of these have become meaningless to modern observers. The term sideburns, however, can be traced to General Ambrose Burnside, who sported distinctively bushy whiskers. The size and style of sideburns and beards varied greatly between individuals and over time.

Children's Fashion Fundamentals

Children's clothing rivaled women's fashions both in complexity and ornateness. Some middle- and upper-class children were dressed in layers of clothing often constructed of impractical fabrics. Gauze, silk, wool, and taffeta were common fabric suggestions for children's dress in ladies' magazines. Print fabrics tended to be small geometric or abstract designs. These designs allowed for the economical use of material since it was easier to match such prints, and there was less waste. Braid or ribbon were popular trims even for children.

In rural areas, children's clothing was considerably more practical, much the same as their parents'. Muslin and cotton were the fabrics of choice for country and poorer folk. To allow for growth, it was common for seams at the shoulders and under the arms to be folded in an inch each, so that they could be let out as the child grew. Sometimes a waistband was added as the child grew to lengthen skirts and trousers. Several tucks, of an inch or so, were often made near the hems of skirts and trousers. These created an attractive detail and could later be let down to accommodate growth.

Little girls were dressed very much as were their mothers. *Godey's Lady's Book* even contained an illustration for a corset for a little girl that laced down the back only. This was not encouraged by everyone, however, as the "Editor's Table" in *Peterson's* questioned the physical effects on organs and bones not fully formed.

The main difference between a woman's attire and a girl's attire was that girls' skirts were considerably shorter, ending about mid-calf. Pantalettes hung just below the edge of the dress. These would be plain for everyday wear and would be adorned with lace or eyelet for dressier occasions. These pantalettes differed from women's in that the crotches were sewn and they buttoned at the sides. Like her mother, a little girl wore a chemise as the basic undergarment. By age seven a girl would have begun to wear a hoop, although it would likely have only one hoop ring at this time. Once again, like an adult woman, she would wear under and over petticoats.

Fancy aprons were popular. They tied around the waist and covered almost the entire skirt portion of a dress. The top covered only part of the dress front and crossed over both shoulders on top. They were commonly decorated with flounces, bows, and other decorative details. Pinafores, which covered almost the entire dress, were more practical and much more common across all economic lines. They were constructed in such fabrics as muslin, calico, or linen. The pinafore fit closely to the chest and hung down loosely to the hem. Another layered style for young girls was the white dress covered by another jumper-like dress.

Boys wore a series of different types of outfits, each befitting a certain age group. Very young boys often had shirts that buttoned to the waistband of their pants and provided a neater look. From ages one to four, boys wore a nankeen suit. This was a dress-like costume worn over white underdrawers not unlike a girl's pantalettes, although likely to be less fancy. The top portion of the suit was a blousy sack, often with a large sash or a cord tied around the waist.

Between the ages of four and seven, there was the French blouse. Essentially, it was a loose, dress-like tunic secured at the waist by a belt and large buckle or sash. This would have been worn over loose knee pants, although it was also worn over a skirt by very young boys. Boys may also have been attired in a loose jacket and waistcoat, once again with loose knee pants. Boys may also have been clad in a suit-like outfit with a slightly cut-away jacket, gently rounded in front, and very loose trousers that extended to about mid-calf.

From 7 to 12 a boy may have worn what would be thought of as a suit-like outfit comprised of loose, ankle-length trousers and waist-length sack coat with a ribbon tie fashioned into a bow. The pants might have box plaits. Suspenders could be introduced at this point. Some boys in certain areas did not wear long pants until 14 or 15 years of age.

It is no wonder that older boys who were as yet considered too young for trousers welcomed the Knickerbocker suit. These suits consisted of a button-faced jacket fastened merely with a hook and eye at the top; a ten-button waistcoat with small slits at the sides to allow for ease of movement and better fit; and knickerbockers, loose-fitting pants that came tight against the leg just below the knee.

As older teens, boys dressed much as adult men did. They wore pants, vests, and jackets. Jacket types included sack, frock, and a short, military style. Boys' undergarments included an undershirt and drawers that reached down to the knee. When boys graduated into longer pants, they wore longer, ankle-length drawers that fit the leg more closely.

Girls wore their hair in a short, ear-length blunt cut that was pushed behind the ears. Some wore their hair in long finger curls. The latter style seems to have been more popular among girls of higher economic status. Occasionally ribbons were used to keep the long hair out of the face. Girls of about eight or nine began to wear their hair in hair nets. Sarah Morgan, aged 19, wrote in her diary that she had gathered her hair in a net because it fell and swept down half way between her knees and ankles in one stream. Like their mothers', girls' hair was center parted. Boys parted their hair to the side. The sides and back were usually short. Because fashions for young children were not strongly differentiated by sex, when looking at photographs, the part is often the only clue to the sex of the child.

Infants wore long gowns that were often twice the length of the child. This was done to keep the child warm. Long gowns could not be cast off as loose blankets could. The gowns were generally white to withstand the frequent washings infant clothing required and were made of a soft material, entirely free from starch. For the first few weeks after birth, infants wore long, narrow strips of fabric known as belly bands. These were several yards long and were designed to protect the navel. In addition to diapers, or napkins, as they were called, infants wore a shirt, a pinner that contained their lower limbs, a skirt or skirts, and a dress. Babies also wore caps, for which women's magazines frequently carried patterns.

Slave Clothing

The clothing of slaves varied with the economic status of the slaveholder and with the tasks the slave was required to do. Slaves who worked in the household, often well dressed in suits, dresses, or traditional colonial outfits, were seen by visitors to the home, and therefore their appearance would have been a reflection on the slaveholder. Slaves who worked in the fields needed serviceable clothing that would survive the rigors of the work being done. Any benefit that the slave gained in the way of clothing was an accidental advantage of the owner's desire to run an efficient plantation and a model household.

A daughter of a Mississippi plantation owner who held 150 slaves described the semiannual process of getting clothes ready for the slaves as "no light work." When the time would come to have everything cut out, a room would be cleared out and the great bolts of white woolen jeans, Osnabergs, with bolt after bolt of red flannel for the little ones, would be rolled in and the women with great shears would commence their work. There were several sets of patterns with individual ones for the very tall and the very fat, but there was not much attention paid to the fit.

Male slaves were furnished with only two or three suits a year. Women were supplied with a calico or linsey dress, head handkerchiefs, and gingham aprons for Christmas. The fabric was sturdy and became as soft as flannel as it was washed. The slaves often dyed the white suits tan or gray with willow bark or sweet gum.

The quality and quantity of clothing for slaves during the war varied greatly, and generally both suffered as the war continued. These garments often represented white folks' hand-me-downs, remnants, and discards. Slaves, especially those in urban areas, could often be seen in slightly unfashionable, but serviceable, suits of clothing and dresses of cotton and wool. As whites felt the pinch of the blockade, hand-me-downs and discards took on a new value in their eyes and were rarely passed on to slaves. In this manner the slaves were made to bear the worst effects of the shortages.

Plantation slaves were often clothed in coarse but durable Negro cloth, which was produced from linen in the mills of New England, or in coarse woolen broadcloth. Prior to the opening of hostilities, plantation owners commonly purchased cloth by the yard and allowed the slaves to fashion the clothing on the plantation. This cloth took the form of trousers and shirts for the men and boys, while slave women wore woolen dresses with cotton aprons. The wool helped to prevent the skirts from catching fire and was favored by women, both black and white, who worked near open hearths. Both sexes used straw hats and handkerchiefs in a variety of ways, but generally they were tied to form head coverings or neck cloths.

Shoes were a difficult item to provide for the slave at a reasonable cost, and most ex-slaves complained of rarely having owned shoes that fit well. One diarist described the shoes as about as pliable as wood. It took many greasings before the wearer could comfortably bend their feet. Unless they owned a slave that was trained in shoemaking from raw leather, plantation owners resorted to buying shoes in bulk. There existed an entire trade in New England dedicated to the manufacture of cheap shoes for slaves. These shoes rarely gave long use without the services of a cobbler. Wooden clogs, a type of sandal with a large wooden sole, often served in place of shoes. Slaves generally preferred to go barefoot in the fields, as did their white farmer counterparts, because shoes do not hold up well in plowed fields. Contemporary illustrations from *Harper's* and *Leslie's* almost always show slaves to be shod. Slaves who were forced to go barefoot in winter greased their feet with tallow to protect the skin, but this circumstance seems to have been rare except in the Deep South. Slaves rarely went unshod in town or in the Northern border states as such a thing would have been impractical for the slaves and embarrassing for their owners.

Mourning Clothes

Mourning dress was one of the first areas where mass-produced clothing gained acceptance. The need for the proper attire to conform to the rigid rules regarding dress often came unexpectedly. There were many people who felt that it was unlucky to keep black crepe in the home between deaths. Surviving items from previous losses were often discarded when no longer required. Providing mourning attire and accessories became a worthwhile commercial endeavor. Some retailers, such as J. S. Chase and Company of Boston, dealt exclusively in mourning goods. There was a great demand for black crepe for veils, collars, cuffs, skirt trim, and armbands. Other needed items included black hatpins, straight pins, and buttons. Millinery and jewelry that met the expectations of society were equally in demand. Mourning caps were such a common item, with virtually no design differences for age or demand for customization, that milliners commonly made them when they had nothing else to do. Those in mourning also required stationery and calling cards bordered in black. Many companies made fortunes on mourning clothing and related ancillary materials.

Widows were expected to remain in mourning for two and a half years. This time was divided into three segments. During heavy mourning the widow wore only black, with collars and cuffs of folded untrimmed black crepe. No other trim was used. She might wear a simple bonnet but never a hat. Her face would be covered entirely in a long, heavy black crepe veil whenever she left home. Silk fabrics used for dresses, bonnets, or capes had to have matte finishes. Not even ribbons were allowed to have a gloss. Kid gloves were not permitted. Gloves had to be made from cotton or silk, or crocheted or knit from thread. Handkerchiefs were made of the sheerest white linen with a broad, deep border. Jewelry was restricted to black jet—usually unpolished—and even that would not be worn during the initial months. Dark furs were permitted in cold weather. Throughout the entire mourning period a widow's hair had to be worn simply.

This period was followed by full mourning, which still required the wearing of black, but permitted black lace collars and cuffs. Veils were permitted to be shortened and could be made of net or tulle. Lighter veils were also allowed. Handkerchiefs needed only to have a narrow black band border. Polished jet jewelry was allowed as well as some gold or glass beads.

Half mourning was the final stage. During this period, print and solid-colored dresses of gray or lavender were permitted. Some women, of course, chose to remain in mourning for longer periods, even the rest of their lives. For a woman who wanted to remarry in a period of less than two and a half years, an accommodation was made. She was permitted to be married in a conservative gray dress. However, she was expected to complete the period of mourning following the new union out of respect for the first husband. If a woman married a widower, she was expected to dress in half mourning for the remainder of her husband's mourning period.

Not so surprisingly, men were not as restricted as women. Their period of mourning lasted as little as three months to a year. Fashion required them to wear a plain white shirt with black clothes, shoes, gloves, and hat. This differed little from what the properly dressed businessman would wear in any case. Some men followed this with a period of gray. The only distinguishing additions would be a black crepe band on their hat or black-bordered cuffs. Widowers were encouraged to remarry following a respectable period, particularly if they had young children. Mourning attire was suspended for the wedding day but reestablished immediately thereafter.

Children were not sheltered from death and mourning. In *The Mother's Book* (1831), Lydia Child advises mothers not to allow their children to be frightened by death. She encourages them to share the beautiful imagery of returning to heaven to be with the angels with even very young children. Older children wore black and crepe upon the death of a parent for six months, followed by three months each of full and half mourning with lessening degrees of black. Children in mourning under the age of 12 wore white in the summer and gray in the winter. Suits were trimmed with black buttons, belts, and ribbons. Even infant robes were trimmed in black. Often, out of practicality, children's regular clothing was dyed for mourning rather than purchased new.

A woman mourning the death of her father, mother, or child wore black for a period of one year. For grandparents, siblings, or someone having left the mourner an inheritance, the proper period was six months. The obligation for an aunt, uncle, niece, or nephew extended for only three months, and white trim was allowed throughout this time.

—Dorothy Denneen Volo

TECHNOLOGY: STEAM

The steam engine was the prime mover of greatest importance to the nineteenth century. Yet the technologies needed for steam driven mills, steam propulsion for vessels, and steam engines for railroad locomotives developed separately. Simple steam systems were advanced enough to be applied to small boats and factory machinery. The giant stationary steam engines with their thick leather drive belts was a common sight in most mills. In America, especially after the Civil War, the leather was often provided through the use of buffalo skins taken from the herds that roamed the Great Plains. Powerful steam locomotives and ocean-going steamships were not developed until improved steam boiler and multiple expansion engine technologies were adopted. Thereafter, the railroads flourished even though American steam shipping failed to keep pace with British ocean navigation.

Steam engine technology often outpaced thermodynamic theory in the early part of the century. Steam technology for water propulsion was generally regarded as superior to that used for locomotion because engines carried aboard vessels could be made larger than those used on early locomotives. Nonetheless, steam power in any form was wasteful of fuel when compared to the free use of wind power on the oceans, and even river steamers were seen to regularly stop along the river banks to take on loads of firewood stacked by local landowners expressly for this purpose. Woodcutter's huts—sometimes manned by a slave or youngster—could be seen along the banks of most rivers. The humble woodcutter played an essential role in the steamboat industry, and the landowner could realize a tidy annual sum by contracting with the operators of the lines. Similar arrangements were often made along the railroad right-of-way. Before the end of the Civil War Southern locomotives relied entirely on wood as fuel, while many Northern lines had switched to coal.

The publication of William Rankine's *The Steam Engine and Other Prime Movers* in Great Britain in 1848 was a major step forward for the application of steam technology to transportation. Rankine was the professor of steam engineering at the University of Glascow in Scotland, one of the first schools to establish such a formal program. His book soon became the standard text for steam-engineering students and practitioners across the world. Engineers using Rankine's principles were able to make steam locomotives and steamboats much more efficient and powerful by utilizing double- and triple-expansion engine designs that made use of the pressure of the steam several times before exhausting it to the atmosphere.

Nonetheless, it was the development of superior boilers that most affected the technology. Prior to 1825, steam boilers were made in a box shape by riveting iron and steel plates together along their edges. This design proved particularly prone to fatal boiler explosions and other structural failures because the pressures built up at the corners and edges of the boiler rather than on the face of the plates. Consequently, most applications of steam for propulsion were limited to low-pressure engine types. The earliest boilers were based on the English designs of Bolton and Watt and had gauge pressures between 10 and 12 pounds per square inch, but with time, a high-pressure boiler, invented by Oliver Evans of Philadelphia, with 30 to 40 pounds of pressure became the standard.

Boiler explosions on steamboats averaged about 10 per year, killing more than 200 persons annually in the United States. Alarmed by the persistence of the problem, the federal government stepped in with the establishment of several safety regulations embodied in the Steamboat Act of 1852. Thereafter, with the widespread adoption of the cylindrical fire-tube boiler design, which made high-pressure steam (up to 150 pounds per square inch) safer and more efficient, the incidence of boiler explosions decreased to an average of only four per year with a national death toll of less than 50 (Volo and Volo 2004, 322–23).

Table of Steam Engines Operating in the United States 1825 to 1838

Year	Stationary		Steamboat		Locomotive	
	Number	Aver. HP	Number	Aver. HP	Number	Aver. HP
1825	23	27	13	50	0	0
1829	88	29	36	58	0	0
1834	407	16	120	52	42	16
1838	578	17	332	63	219	21

Source: Louis C. Hunter. *A History of Industrial Power in the United States, 1780–1930.* Charlottesville: University Press of Virginia, 1979, 230.

TRANSPORTATION

The Horsecars

The average physical size of American cities increased from less than a one-mile radius to that of four or five miles during the nineteenth century. The development of public horse-drawn trams, known as *horsecars,* made daily commuting from such a distance possible, but most Northern men were willing to make the half-hour walk from their homes to their place of work to save the fare. Southerners did not share this characteristic of Northern males choosing instead to ride astride their horse for even short distances.

Before the widespread development of steam railways in the Northern states, horse-drawn omnibuses crossed through many major cities. In 1826 a horse drawn railroad paralleled the Main Line from Philadelphia to Columbia on the Susquehanna River. In 1828, Quincy, Massachusetts, had the first horse-drawn line of the Old Colony System, and Rochester, New York, established a two-mile-long line that ran to Lake Ontario from the Erie Canal in 1831. New York City opened a horse-drawn service in 1832 from Prince Street to 14th Street, and it was still adding to the extent of track with a line in East Harlem in 1853. Two of the more extensive systems, the Metropolitan Horse Railroad in Boston (1856) and the Baltimore City Railroad (1859) served their cities with well-appointed, horse-drawn cars and miles of interconnecting track right through the Civil War. Travel on the horse-drawn railroad was often accompanied by a thundering noise caused by the combination of iron wheels on iron rails and street stones that was almost deafening.

—*James M. Volo*

Railroads

The abominable condition of Southern roads during the rainy season and in the winter added to the importance of its railways. Although the South controlled only one-third the railway mileage of the North before the Civil War, the Southern railways were strategically located within the theater of operations and were used with great tactical skill by Confederate commanders. Virginia was crossed by several important railways that could be used with great effect to move supplies and manpower throughout the Eastern theater. At First Bull Run, Confederate reinforcements were brought to the field by rail in time to turn the tide of battle and rout the Federals.

Much of the Northern rail mileage was used for the distribution of manufactures in the Northeast. The most prominent railways—the Pennsylvania, the Erie, and the New York Central—were outside the war zone. Those in New England were almost entirely shut off from army transport. However, the north-south lines—the Illinois Central and the Cleveland, Columbus, and Cincinnati—prospered on army business.

The Baltimore and Ohio, with a right-of-way in the war zone, was strategically important as a line of communications between Washington and Ohio. In May 1861, General Thomas J. "Stonewall" Jackson was able to steal 300 railroad cars and 56 locomotives from the B & O in a single operation attesting to the vast size of the railroad operation. Much of this rolling stock was horse-drawn down the Shenandoah Valley Pike from Winchester to Strasburg to be used on the Southern railways. At a later date, when loss of the line to federal forces seemed imminent, Jackson was given the task of destroying the 400 mile railway. He burned the bridges, derailed the freight cars, and burned more than 40 engines. The Federals learned to repair the damage quickly, but raids along the B & O were a constant source of trouble to federal commanders.

The railways of the Western theater, which had been built in the 1850s, far in advance of any immediate need, proved very important to the war effort. The line between Louisville, Kentucky, and Nashville, Tennessee, provided a vital link for the invading

The second half of the nineteenth century was noted for the development of railroads. Transportation of passengers, produce, and freight was greatly enhanced by the expansion of railway mileage and the development of more powerful locomotives. A distinct American type of engine with a so-called balloon smokestack was developed that weighed an average 20 tons and could travel safely at 25 miles per hour with a load of 120 tons. In its day this was considered high-speed when compared to other forms of transportation. Courtesy Currier and Ives.

Federals. Yet no further strategic railways were built, and no thought was given to the development of the principles of military operations and maintenance of railways during the war years. In no direction could cars run long distances without changes and delays. Freight, as well as passengers and their luggage, often had to detrain and cross town from one line to another either by wagon or on foot. The construction of five short connections between competing lines, for a total of 140 miles, would have provided the Federals with an uninterrupted railway from Washington to the entire North.

An obstacle to rail transport in all parts of the country was the different gauges, or track widths, used on different lines. In New York and New England a gauge of 4 feet 8 1/2 inches was used. In Ohio, and to the west and south of Philadelphia, the gauge was 4 feet 10 inches. Some rails were placed as much as 6 feet apart in special cases. Many ingenious expedients were used to overcome this problem. These included third rails, wide wheels that would accommodate both narrow and wide track, and adjustable train axles. The longest single gauge track of the war belonged to the Atlantic and Great Western line, which connected New York with St. Louis more than 1,000 miles away.

There was an attempt by the Confederate government in Richmond to adopt a standard gauge of five feet throughout the Southern nation, but a national dedication to the ideal of states' rights generally got in the way of any standardization. The length of Southern railway mileage, the tonnage of rolling stock and engines, and the number of interconnecting systems were severely limited throughout the war. Nonetheless, there were more than 1,000 miles of strategically important track in Tennessee alone with connections passing to the southeast. The heart of this rail network lay in Corinth, Mississippi. The line connecting Cairo, Illinois, with Corinth drove directly south and continued on to New Orleans, creating a network that pumped vital supplies from the Gulf north to Tennessee and east to Virginia. The Confederates were therefore theoretically able to use their railways to bring troops from the Deep South into Virginia or the Western theater. In 1862 more than 2,500 men and their equipment were brought to Nashville from Louisiana in just two weeks—a remarkable feat given the dilapidated state of the railways and the fact that the troops had to wait for available cars or march between unconnected lines.

A major limitation on the use of Southern railways for military purposes remained a lack of maintenance. In April 1863, Robert E. Lee wrote to the War Office that unless the railroads were repaired, to permit speedier transportation of supplies, he could not maintain his position in the field. Yet damaged cars and worn-out engines increasingly became the victims of the South's limited industrial technology. A damaged locomotive boiler might take more than a thousand man-hours to repair if the boilerplate were found to do the job. Tracks and especially wooden ties were simply unable to withstand the wear and tear of wartime demand. The wooden ties were rotted, the machinery was almost exhausted, the rails were worn out, and the speed and capacity of the trains were greatly reduced. An engine could be required to lug a supply train weighing up to 120 tons (Volo and Volo 1998, 155–58).

Roads

If railroads were the arteries of the nation, then the roads were its veins. A long march on dirt roads was almost inevitable for the soldiers of both armies in the Civil War. The very poor condition of Southern roads and turnpikes was one of the few circumstances for which the federal army did not provide in its initial offensive planning. The Confederates understood the defensive qualities of many of the roads in northern Virginia, which were very narrow—mere ditches—surrounded by dense forests of second growth pine or virgin oak that would snarl the movement of an invading army with its wagons and artillery. With high humidity and abundant vegetation, the rain-soaked road surfaces of Virginia remained wet and were churned into a sticky morass that was barely passable by thousands of feet and hundreds of wagon wheels.

Northern commanders greatly anticipated the improvement of the roads when the mud froze as it did in the North during November and December, providing a supportive surface on which to march troops, haul supplies, or move artillery. However, increased daytime temperatures prevented the freezing of the roadways until much later in the season than Northerners expected. federal operations in the early winter of 1863 therefore encountered an unforeseen obstacle. The armies spent considerable time and effort building corduroy roads by laying bundles of saplings and small tree trunks across the muddiest parts of the road surface. Although uneven and bumpy, they allowed the wheeled vehicles to pass without sinking into the mud. Corduroy was very hard on the foot soldier and almost impossible for the cavalry, who often opted to ride across the open fields. Plank roads, as the name suggests, were municipal roads built with several layers of wooden planking covered with dirt. The Orange Plank Road and the Orange Turnpike, connecting Fredericksburg and Chancellorsville with the valley of western Virginia, were two of the good roads that proved critical to the strategy of the opposing forces.

The Columbia Pike south out of Nashville was a well-maintained road of macadam—a type of compressed broken stone. The Valley Pike, the main road that ran down the center of the Shenandoah Valley, was also of macadam and proved a veritable highway for the South. Flanked by the North Branch of the Shenandoah River and the western part of the Manassas Gap Railroad, the advantages of such a surface to the movement of military forces were obvious. The Valley Pike played a prominent role in Jackson's Valley campaign of 1862; and in subsequent years it figured prominently in the operations of Confederate General Jubal Early no less than it did in the operations of Federal Generals Franz Sigel, David Hunter, and Philip Sheridan. The battles at Cross Keys, Port Republic, New Market, Front Royal, Cedar Creek, and Kernstown were overshadowed only by the more than a dozen seesaw occupations of the city of Winchester, which straddled the pike (Volo and Volo 1998, 158–60).

Steamboats

In 1807, Robert Fulton was the first to operate a steamboat as a commercial success on the Hudson River. *The Clermont* went from New York to Albany (150 miles)

The opening of the Mississippi marked by the arrival of the steamer *Imperial* at New Orleans from St. Louis, 1863. Courtesy Library of Congress.

in about 32 hours. The superiority of steam-powered vessels over flatboats, keelboats, and rafts on the nation's rivers and lakes quickly demonstrated itself, especially on the upriver leg on any journey. The number of steamboats on America's rivers and in its ports rapidly increased. Moreover, there were significant developments in the use of steam on the Great Lakes, in the Lake Champlain-Lake George corridor, and on the Finger Lakes in central New York State. It was on the lakes that American steamers proved the feasibility of operating steam vessels with metal hulls in the swell of open waters, but it was not until the post–Civil War years that meaningful advances were made in transoceanic propulsion.

Although it would have been possible to build a continuous canal-lake-river system of powered water transportation, the cost of such a project would have been prohibitive. Oddly, steam-powered canal boats were technologically possible—and several were tried on canals in Connecticut—but the churning water wreaked havoc on the banks of most canals that had not been steeled with a protective coating of stone. The Great Lakes route, when combined with the Erie Canal and Ohio Canal, caused marine traffic to grow steadily, nonetheless. Steamboats transported agricultural produce and livestock, and all types of industrial supplies, manufactured goods, and metallic ores. In the Northeast, coal—used to heat the tenements of cities and process the iron and steel of numerous mills—was one of the most common cargoes of waterborne commerce.

Steamboat capacity on the Mississippi River system alone grew to more than 120,000 tons by 1850, greater than the entire steam-powered tonnage of the British Royal Navy at the time. In that year, the 25-day trip on the Mississippi of 1816 had dwindled to only four and a half days. Multi-decked, multi-purpose steamers had become common, and those that carried passengers grew larger and more luxurious with the passing years. Riverboats were just as romantic to the passengers that rode them and the onlookers on the banks as they are to us today. The 1850s proved to be the golden age of river steamers, with their cabins splendidly appointed with carved woodwork and gold-leafed furniture, crystal chandeliers, carpeting, and mirrors. Some steamboats were fitted with a steam calliope, on which popular tunes were played when approaching a city.

Steamboats joined the river cities of Pittsburgh, Cincinnati, Memphis, Natchez, Lexington, and Louisville and the farmlands of the central part of the country to the markets of the world through the gateway ports of New Orleans, Mobile, and Galveston. Steamboat lines sprang up to fill the gaps between Eastern railroads and the incomplete Western rail lines. Westward expansion along the growing system of canals and the successful navigation of the Western rivers by steamboats, made a number of inland ports equally important. St. Louis, in particular, served as a central hub for river traffic. Located on the Mississippi River near the junction of the Ohio and the Missouri, St. Louis benefited from its connections with both the states of the Midwest and the Western territories of the Great Plains and Rocky Mountains. In 1857, with many of the rail lines connected, the connecting steamboat lines began to fail economically (Volo and Volo 2004, 321–25).

FOR MORE INFORMATION

Browne, Ray B., and Lawrence A. Kreiser Jr. *The Civil War and Reconstruction*. Westport, CT: Greenwood Press, 2003.

Hague, Parthenia Antoinette. *A Blockaded Family: Life in Southern Alabama during the Civil War*. Reprint. Bedford, TX: Applewood Books, 1995.

Haskell, E. F. *Civil War Cooking: The Housekeeper's Encyclopedia*. Mendocino, CA: R. L. Shep, 1992.

Hunter, Louis C. *A History of Industrial Power in the United States, 1780–1930*. Charlottesville: University Press of Virginia, 1979.

Lord, Francis A. "The United States Military Railroad Service: Vehicle to Victory." *Civil War Times Illustrated*, October 1964.

McIntosh, Elaine N. *American Food Habits in Historical Perspective*. Westport, CT: Greenwood/Praeger Press, 1995.

Mitchell, Patricia B. *Cooking for the Cause*. Chatham, VA: Sims-Mitchell House, 1988.

Root, Waverly, and Richard de Rouchemont. *Eating in America*. New York: William Morrow, 1976.

Rowland, K. T. *Steam at Sea: The History of Steam Navigation*. New York: Praeger Publishing, 1970.

Spaulding, Lily May, and John Spaulding, eds. *Civil War Recipes: Recipes from the Pages of Godey's Lady's Book*. Lexington: University Press of Kentucky, 1999.

Swartwelder, A. C. "This Invaluable Beverage: The Recollections of Dr. A. C. Swartwelder." *Civil War Times Illustrated*, October 1975, 10–11.

Timmons, Todd. *Science and Technology in Nineteenth-Century America*. Westport, CT: Greenwood Press, 2005.

Trager, James. *The Food Chronology*. New York: Henry Holt, 1995.

Volo, Dorothy Denneen, and James M. Volo. *The Antebellum Period*. Westport, CT: Greenwood Press, 2004.

———. *Daily Life in Civil War America*. Westport, CT: Greenwood Press, 1998.

———. *Family Life in Nineteenth-Century America*. Westport, CT: Greenwood Press, 2007.

Williams, Susan. *Food in the United States, 1820s–1890*. Westport, CT: Greenwood Press, 2006.

Woodward, George E. *Victorian City and Country Houses: Plans and Designs*. New York: Dover Publications, 1996.

———. *Woodward's Architecture and Rural Art*. New York: Privately printed, 1868.

———. *Woodward's National Architect*. New York: Da Capo Press, 1975.

Zanger, Mark H. *The American History Cookbook*. Westport, CT: Greenwood Press, 2003.

Political Life

A SIGNAL FOR SECESSION

In the election of 1856, the northern and southern wings of the Democratic Party split over the passage of the Kansas-Nebraska Act of 1854. With the Democrats' former political hegemony in pieces, the newly formed Republicans ran an attractive candidate (their first) for president. This was the explorer, soldier, and abolitionist senator from California, John C. Frémont. He lost to James Buchanan, a prosouthern unionist Democrat from Pennsylvania because of the inclusion of a weak Nativist candidate in the person of former president Millard Fillmore. Any mandate that Buchanan may have enjoyed after his minority win was marred by intraparty wrangling and an uncooperative cabinet. He was the last president to serve before the outbreak of Civil War.

During the Senate campaign debates with Stephen A. Douglas in 1858, Abraham Lincoln had expressed both support for black colonization and a belief in an inherent social inequality among the races, but he also insisted on the moral wrong of slavery and the equality of blacks to the right to be free to earn their own living. In 1860, the Republican Party ran Abraham Lincoln for president. Unlike the unsuccessful Liberty Party, which had a single issue—immediate abolition—with which to attract voters, the Republicans inserted other important economic and sectional issues into their rhetoric along with a strong moral agitation against slavery. This attracted a wider range of potential supporters than simple antislavery sentiments. Nonetheless, the Republican Party was so closely associated with abolition that Lincoln's minority election in the popular vote (under 40%) in a four-way race caused the almost immediate secession of several Southern states.

The election of Lincoln was the signal for secession, and the South lost no time in forming a national government of its own in early 1861. The new Confederate Constitution was closer to the U.S. Constitution than it was to a revolutionary document. With the exception of a few omissions and changes in phraseology, and with the important explicit endorsement of slavery in its structure and purpose the two documents were similar. The purpose of disunion was to establish a government that would preserve Southern culture and society as it was. The act of secession was the end product of a conservative political uprising, and the Confederate Constitution has been described as "a theoretical time capsule that embodies the distinctive principles of Republican government." These principles tended to focus on the anti-Federalist view of the government that had been obscured by the development and implementation of Federalist political theory since 1789. Confederate President Jefferson Davis wrote, "We have changed our constituent parts, but not the system of our government." This statement exemplifies the true nature of the Confederacy as the Southerners saw it. The new government was to be a continuation of those ideals fostered in the first American Revolution and that Southerners thought had been continually altered by a "fanatical and immoral" North (Volo and Volo 1998, 54–55).

However, as champions of a new conservative revolution and defenders of the Southern nation, the Confederates gave up much of what they held dear. The South embraced a centralized wartime government fully as determined to control the reins of government as that in Washington. The concept of states' rights was sacrificed—not without the determined resistance of some state governments—for the defense of the country as a whole. Southern cities swelled in size, urbanization increased, factories and manufacturing took on a new importance, and men and women went to work much like the wage earners of the North. Ultimately even slavery changed as the Confederate Congress provided for the enlistment of black soldiers in the last months of the war and dallied with bartering black emancipation for foreign recognition by Britain in the name of its own independence.

The Southern planter aristocracy was sorely tested during the Civil War, and in many cases their social and financial prominence did not meet the test. Although wealth and social position maintained their hold on the structure of Southern society, service in the military created new avenues to prominence. Many aristocratic families lost scions to the fates of battle, while many of the masters of plantations proved unfortunate choices as military leaders.

The infant Confederate government brought prominence and power to many of those who had been outside the upper classes of society before the war. Alexander Stephens, who was from a poor Georgia family, nonetheless became the vice president of the new country. Judah Benjamin, of Jewish ancestry, rose to be one of the most capable members of the Confederate cabinet and a respected and loyal friend of President Jefferson Davis. The greatest hero in the South during the war was an orphan and an impoverished college professor who raised himself to the rank of lieutenant general—Thomas J. "Stonewall" Jackson.

It is an often overlooked fact that the importation of slaves into the United States was outlawed in 1808, and the U.S. Navy attempted to curtail the ocean transportation of slaves from Africa. Yet the ownership and selling of slaves within the confines of the country continued, and slavery spread westward.

In early 1861, federal forces coming upon the first trickle of escaped slaves returned them to Confederate lines in obedience to the Fugitive Slave Act of 1850, but General Benjamin F. Butler, a swashbuckling pro-war Democrat from Massachusetts, sidestepped the law by declaring the blacks "contraband of war" and open to seizure. Lincoln reluctantly approved the ruling, and blacks thereafter abandoned the plantations in the hundreds or thousands whenever federal forces were nearby. At first it seemed that the slaves had traded one master for another, but Congress passed a series of laws that further refined their status in 1861 and 1862. The term "freedman" was adopted in official correspondence after the publication of the Emancipation Proclamation in January 1863, but to the soldiers in the field escaped slaves remained known as "contrabands." After 1863, black men were also free to enter the armed service of the United States. The First South Carolina Volunteers was the first (organized in 1862) Northern regiment composed entirely of escaped slaves and black refugees.

A growing Southern nationalism accompanied the development of the Confederate States of America. Nationalism was on the rise throughout Europe in the nineteenth century, and Confederates were quick to draw parallels between their struggle to found a Southern nation with those of the Dutch Republic and the Portuguese against Spain; the Italian revolutions in Sicily and Naples led by Garibaldi; the Polish rebellion against the power of Russian imperialism; and the ongoing Piedmontese struggle against Austria. Confederate diplomats held forth these examples to the world in the hope of gaining international support and recognition for their fledgling country.

The North had similar nationalistic views, but they were more capitalistic and utopian than those of its Southern counterpart. The Northern nation was dedicated to physical liberty, freeing the slave from his bonds, separating the poor from their circumstances, and relieving the alcoholic from his dependence on liquor. By contrast the Southern nation was more dedicated to an abstract liberty defined by traditional political ideology and personal freedom of action unrestricted by governmental intervention and the belief that black slavery ensured white liberty. As the two cultures diverged during the first half of the nineteenth century, their separate concepts of which social, political, and cultural characteristics should be indicative of America's ideal national identity diverged also.

—James M. Volo

GOVERNMENT

The Wartime Federal Government

Abraham Lincoln probably would not have won the presidency in 1860 had the election not become a four-way race. The Democratic Party split between two candidates: pro-slavery John C. Breckinridge, a former vice president of the United States; and Stephen A. Douglas, a moderate, but also a vigorous advocate of expansion. The fourth candidate, on the ticket of the new Constitutional Union Party, composed of former Whigs and nativists, was John Bell of Tennessee. Tariffs, homesteads, railroads, immigrants, and political corruption all figured in the campaign, but slavery and the fear of disunion remained the pivotal questions. When it became obvious to the candidates based on the results of gubernatorial elections in Pennsylvania and Indiana that Lincoln was going to win, Breckinridge proclaimed dedication to immediate disunion but Douglas, to his credit, disavowed any ideas of contesting the election, saying, "If Lincoln is elected, he must be inaugurated" (Sewell 1988, 76).

Lincoln won the election with just under 40 percent of the popular vote and 59 percent of the electoral votes. He carried 18 states; yet, with the exception of coastal California, not one of them was below the Mason-Dixon Line. This result reinforced his position as a sectional leader rather than a national one. Significantly, Douglas, who beat both Breckinridge and Bell with 30 percent of the popular vote, represented the views of at least some of the electorate in all parts of the country but he received a mere four percent of the electoral votes. Breckinridge, with 18 percent of the popular vote, carried every state that would come to be in the Confederacy except Mississippi and Virginia. The former vice president also carried the border states of Maryland and Delaware. Bell captured the states of Kentucky, Tennessee, and Virginia and received 13 percent of the popular vote. Notwithstanding this result, 70 percent of the voters had shown support for at least a moderate stand against slavery, but they almost all resided in the North.

A group of moderate Virginia residents declared that "the election of a sectional president even with odious and dangerous sentiment" would not of itself be sufficient cause for secession. Yet they saw the election result as an alarming indication of the ripening schemes of abolitionists to plunder and outrage the Southern way of life with their growing fanaticism. The abolitionists exacerbated the seriousness of the situation by taunting Virginia as a "Plunderer of Cradles—she who has grown fat by selling her own children in the slave shambles: Virginia! Butcher—Pirate—Kidnapper—Slavocrat—the murderer of John Brown and his gallant band—at last, will meet her just doom" (Jordan 1995, 16). Secessionists warned that Virginia could soon expect an invasion of armed abolitionists and would become, as it subsequently did, the primary theater of the military campaign to eradicate slavery.

The Lincoln administration was immediately faced with the greatest threat ever to face the United States, and he had no time to finesse a highly articulated response to secession. Moreover, many of Lincoln's cabinet members were much better educated than he, and no doubt some, or maybe all, felt that they could do a better job as president. However, it is a tribute to Lincoln's management style that he was able to keep the cabinet moving in the right direction, despite the efforts of some of its members to derail his policies.

—*James M. Volo*

The Wartime Confederate Government

Jefferson Davis expected to be offered the post of secretary of war in the new Confederate government because he had held the post in the administration of Franklin Pierce. He was somewhat disappointed at being chosen president of the Confederacy. According to his own account, *The Rise and Fall of the Confederate Government* (1881), Davis had found his term as secretary of war the most satisfying and happy time of his political career. Nonetheless, Davis was wholeheartedly devoted to the Confederacy rather than to Mississippi—something that could not be said with confidence of all central government officials in the South, many of whom put the welfare of their home state before that of the Confederacy. Davis embraced the theory of centralized control, and thereby sacrificed some of the jealously guarded individual sovereignty of seceded states.

The Davis administration was the only national government the Confederacy would ever have, and it mirrored that of the federal government in most of its aspects with the exception of the term of its president, which was set at six years, rather than four. Davis, therefore, did not have to deal with a reelection campaign in the mist of a changing series of wartime successes and failures as did Lincoln. Nonetheless, the Confederate cabinet was in constant turmoil even during the earliest and most successful years of the war for the South.

The details surrounding the Davis administration have attracted a good deal of second thinking concerning his abilities as a political leader and the government's ideological roots. The Confederate government lasted somewhat less than the six years its constitution had envisioned for the presidency making scholarly arguments concerning the lack of a two-party system, a single-term presidency, and the effects of state's rights on a centralized system of governance somewhat superfluous.

—James M. Volo

Third Parties

In the decade before the Civil War, third parties became an important part of national politics for the first time. Federalists and anti-Federalists (aka Jeffersonian Republicans, Democratic-Republicans) had faced off during the early years of the Republic, and the Whigs had emerged in the 1830s as the leading second party opposing the Democrats, when the Federalists had collapsed after the War of 1812. It seemed for the first seven decades that two and only two parties could compete for national recognition at a time. Many of the older issues that had driven the two-party system had been resolved by 1848. The tariff, the National Bank, and the regulation of internal commerce rank high among these. At mid-century, both the Whigs and Democrats were searching for new issues that would mobilize the voters behind the old party structure. This attempt to underscore the meaning of the old parties was to have far-reaching consequences as political and social agendas began driving forward proposals that required strong federal action. One unforeseen consequence of trying to bolster the old parties was that, ironically, it eventually led to the virtual dissolution of both.

A political realignment of the old two-party system composed of Whigs and Democrats can be seen in the reaction to the passage of the Kansas-Nebraska Act in 1854. A product of the optimism of the Northern Democrats and Stephen Douglas, the Kansas-Nebraska Act seemingly sabotaged the political compromises over slavery that had characterized the previous decades of American politics. The measure was popular among Northern Democrats, and the Southern Democrats gave it support, but its passage ultimately caused a split in the party. Moderates in the North felt betrayed. Outraged by the act, Northern voters began to speak of the existence of a slave power conspiracy. In response, moderates in the South began to harden their position and seriously consider disunion.

While the Northern Democrats were hurt by the response to the act, the Whigs were devastated by it. The Southern wing of the Whig Party, sympathetic to compromise on the slavery issue, bolted, thereafter aligning themselves with the Southern Democrats; and the Whig Party, already weak after years of deterioration, was left in disarray and all but destroyed. A serious misreading of the temper of the voters had taken place, and they were left simmering in anger at the old parties. Significantly, this political upheaval came at a time when the old party system was already suffering from weakening voter support and poor party discipline. Yet in the wake of the disaster that followed the Kansas-Nebraska Act, interest in politics and political discussions increased, and several new parties moved in to fill the void.

Among these, two major new parties stood out, the Nativists and the Republicans. The Nativist (or American) Party rose very rapidly in popularity but failed in carrying its agenda to the national scene. The Republicans, after a strong showing in

1856, managed to win the White House in 1860, a victory that brought secession and then civil war.

The 1856 election proved to be the death knell of the old two-party system of Democrats and Whigs. In the presidential race the Republicans championed the slogan "Free Speech, Free Press, Free Soil, Free Men, Fremont and Victory." John C. Frémont may have been made a national hero for his role in mapping and exploring the West, but he was an unacceptable presidential candidate in the South. Governor John Wise warned that if Frémont won the 1856 election, Virginia would secede. Consequently, the Democrats, fearing to incur the wrath of the Northern voter by nominating Stephen A. Douglas, the author of the Kansas-Nebraska Act, decided to run James Buchanan of Pennsylvania. Buchanan won the election against Frémont due to the entry into the race of a weak candidate from the American Party, a coalition of Nativists and Know-Nothings. This third party candidate was former president Millard Fillmore. Buchanan received only a minority of the popular votes for president, yet he handily won the electoral college.

The Republican Party benefited from the collapse of the Nativists; developing more slowly, it avoided a similar meteoric rise and fall. Even early Republicans were astute politicians. The party agenda called for no further extension of slavery into the territories—the common interest that bought together the former Whigs, anti-Nebraska Democrats, Free Soilers, Nativists, and others into the party. The positions also taken on abolition, education, internal improvements, and free labor were all carefully crafted to foster a positive public impression of the party (Volo and Volo 1998, 16–18).

LAW, CRIME, AND PUNISHMENT

Crime and Criminals

Crime took on new definitions in the nineteenth century as the nature and style of crimes changed with massive immigration, the emergence of a mass urban society, and the ready availability of firearms. In addition, corporations and government entities used injunctions to halt the power of labor unions, and this strategy was upheld in 1895 by the Supreme Court. The Comstock Law represented Victorian efforts to criminalize the growing sex industry by attacking pornographic and obscene materials (including birth control information) sent through the mail. Many states built modern penitentiaries and cities further professionalized their police forces. In 1880, census data indicates the United States had 13,700 police officers serving in varying capacities. The white elite criminalized many behaviors in an attempt to suppress vice, to contain the militancy of organized labor, and to control immigrant populations and newly freed African Americans (Shrock 2004, 11).

Youth and Street Gangs

The seeming lawlessness of the nineteenth century often stemmed from violence and criminal behavior of young men. Ironically, even as middle-class thinkers were reconstructing upper-class children into innocents, who should be allowed to play and display their creativity, they increasingly came to fear the violence and crime of working-class youth, who seemed to have no controls placed on them. Shocking crimes were common on the streets of most cities, and the newspapers fed on the media frenzy surrounding any youthful killer, printing sometimes wild speculations concerning how a boy could commit malicious acts of violence. A *New York Times* editorial (July 26, 1874) clearly illustrated American's fascination and fear of a boy "who kills other boys and girls for no other reason than the love of inflicting torture and death, and a curiosity to see how they will act while he cuts their throats and stabs them" (Shrock 2004, 37).

Shocking crimes were part of the perceived overall lawlessness in the great cities of the United States, which was brazenly exhibited by street-corner gangs. Reformer Jacob Riis reported on the prevalence and misdeeds of these gangs in *How the Other Half Lives* (1890). "Every corner has its gangs," claims Riis, and they were made up of "the American-born sons of English, Irish, and German parents." The Alley Gang, Rag Gang, Wyho Gang, Rock Gang, Dead Rabbits, Paradise Park Gang, Stable Gang, Short Tail Gang, Gophers, Dutch Mob, Battle Row Gang, Gas House Gang, and many others populated the street corners of New York's neighborhoods and other cities had their counterparts. Gang members sported distinctive hats, shirts, and pants (Shrock 2004, 37).

Urban neighborhoods were sometimes referred to by descriptive sobriquets such as Hell's Kitchen, the Back Bay, China Town, or Germantown among many others. Some of these names continue in use today. One of the worst and most crime ridden ethnic neighborhoods was Five Points in New York City, named for the conjunction of streets at its center. Philip Hone, mayor of the city, noted that gangs of young men were often seen stalking the streets in the Bowery, on Canal Street, and near the infamous Five Points. In one case several houses and a church were destroyed, and it took 3,000 militia to quell the disturbances (Volo and Volo 2007, 15).

Juvenile crime, in particular, increased at a frightful rate, and even the interposition of the Children's Aid Society and similar philanthropic organizations failed to stem its growth. The perpetuation of such social ills was ascribed at the time to a lack of public will in implementing the appropriate cures, which the reformers thought they had clearly identified. Yet the dire predictions were borne out by the subsequent decades of urban poverty even in the face of best efforts by governmental and private agencies. A number of distinctive American characters appeared on the stage at this time including the tough-fisted, tenement-dwelling Bowery B'hoy. However, there was little for the average law-abiding citizen to like about the gangs or their members, and some critics found the character vulgar, coarse, and in bad taste (Volo and Volo 2007, 12).

The gangs of young ruffians thrived on bravado, impressing their peers with stunning escapades and surviving on robbery and petty theft. Members commonly abused the use of alcohol as well as drugs like morphine, the opiate laudanum, and cocaine—all of which were legally available at the time. The Hudson Dusters were notorious for their cocaine use, and they were feared for their violence when under the influence of the drug. Riis reported that in New York City over one-eighth of those arrested were under the age of 20. The casual violence of these gangs was well known and frightening. Within 30 minutes of a visit to the infamous Montgomery Guards, Riis found two gang members in police custody accused of robbing a peddler and of trying to cut off his head for the fun of it (Shrock 2004, 37).

—*James M. Volo*

INTERNATIONAL DIPLOMACY

Suppression of the Atlantic Slave Trade

The role of the U.S. Navy during our nation's first tottering steps toward the abolition of race-based slavery is often overlooked. Slavery within the United States was not totally abolished when Abraham Lincoln signed the Emancipation Proclamation of 1863. That would have to wait for a constitutional amendment. Nonetheless, President Thomas Jefferson had made the international trade and transportation of slaves illegal a half-century earlier in 1808 by signing the U.S. Slave Trade Act.

From the start, the act proved unenforceable largely because of Jefferson's opposition to an advanced program of naval shipbuilding. The lack of ships denied the U.S. government any power to halt the slave trade where it was weakest—in the Middle Passage at sea. At the same time, rising cotton production in the South was expanding the demand for slave labor, and slave ships continued to take blacks from West Africa and the Caribbean and secretly bring them in to American ports for black-market sale and trade. Perhaps as many as 50,000 slaves came in that way. Estimates show that by 1860 there were more than 3.6 million black slaves in the states that were to form the Confederacy, and almost all were American born.

The efforts of the U.S. Navy to suppress the international slave trade through cooperation with the British Royal Navy were initially hindered due to the antagonism left over from the Revolution, and all efforts were suspended during the War of 1812. Under several treaties between 1817 and 1830, the Spanish and Portuguese also made the slave trade illegal. The plantation South despised the agreements, but the U.S. Navy was, nonetheless, required to help enforce them. It was common for abolitionist forces in America to complain that the navy was not taking the law seriously. They pointed out that while the British Royal Navy went out of its way to actively patrol the West coast of Africa and the Caribbean for slavers, the Americans only seemed to enforce the restrictions when it was convenient. Nonetheless, Sir George Collier, commander of the British antislavery squadron, reported that the American navy on all occasions acted with the greatest zeal and the most perfect unanimity with His Majesty's forces with respect to stopping the slavers.

Slaves huddled on the deck of a slave ship. Courtesy Library of Congress.

In May 1820, Congress passed a new bill, which allowed severe punishment for violation of the Slave Trade Act. Slaving at sea was thereafter considered an act of piracy and any American caught could be punished with death. The navy was empowered to seize slave ships wherever they were found. President James Monroe allocated $100,000 to enforce the act immediately sending a flotilla of warships to the African coast. This was the first occasion on which the United States acted against slavery as an international partner with Britain.

In 1843, a permanent African Squadron under Matthew C. Perry was sent to patrol all known slave harbors, but he was called away to serve with the Gulf Squadron during the Mexican War in 1846. The African Squadron continued but remained undermanned until the Civil War.

—*James M. Volo*

The Trent Affair

In March 1861, the Confederate secretary of state dispatched several diplomats to Europe. Among these were William L. Yancey, Pierre Rost, and A. Dudley Mann. Each carried letters from the Confederate government promising advantageous treatment with regard to Southern cotton. The price was recognition of the Confederate States of America. These men were received cordially but coolly in Britain and France. In May, Queen Victoria extended so-called belligerent rights to Confederate vessels and neutral shipping carrying military supplies and raw materials to the South. The federal government was furious at this development, but nothing else seemed likely to happen on the diplomatic front.

In November 1861, James M. Mason and John Slidell sailed from Havana, Cuba on the British ship *Trent*. The next day, while in international waters, the United States warship *San Jacinto* overtook the *Trent*, and a boarding party removed Mason and Slidell. Charles Wilkes, the federal captain, brought the two men under arrest to Boston. The British were incensed and threatened war. U.S. Ambassador Charles Francis Adams did all he could to calm the situation suggesting strongly that Wilkes had acted without orders, and promising the Mason and Slidell would be released. By the time the two Southern diplomats reached London and Paris, respectively, the furor had died. Neither man was greatly effective in their diplomatic role.

—*James M. Volo*

The Southern Quest for Recognition

The Southern war effort was supplemented by the efforts of Confederate agents in Europe, such as Mason and Slidell. Although foreign recognition escaped them, several Confederate agents were successful in other ways. James D. Bullock was responsible for building and arming a number of Confederate vessels in Britain. Bullock has been characterized as "worth far more to the Confederacy than most of its best-known generals" (Stern 1962, 34). Edwin De Leon, former U.S. Consul to Egypt, resigned his federal post and sailed to Europe to oversee Southern propaganda efforts in Britain and France. He was quite critical of the efforts of his colleagues, however. His candid visit with the British Prime Minister Palmerston in July 1862 convinced De Leon that recognition by Britain was a virtual impossibility as long as the South supported slavery. He left his interview with Napoleon III of France, however, with greater expectations suggesting that the Confederates promise to initiate gradual emancipation of slaves and to give France a monopoly on Southern cotton production in return for diplomatic recognition. But Union victories and effective diplomacy countered such measures. No nation recognized the Confederacy's independence.

DISCRIMINATION: NATIVISM

Nativism appeared intermittently throughout the century and under the guises of several All American movements that targeted immigrants, the best known being the Know-Nothing Party. The Nativist movement was truly reactionary and discriminatory in its nature. During the second half of the nineteenth century, Nativist propaganda was widely promulgated throughout the nation, and even those who disagreed with Nativist positions were well aware of them. Immigrants of all types were the targets of the Nativists. Between 1820 and 1860 the three major sources of origin of immigrants in the order of their numerical importance were Ireland, Germany, and Great Britain. These three countries supplied 85 percent of all immigrants to the United States in the antebellum period (Volo and Volo 2007, 13).

By mid-century more than half of the residents of New York and Boston were foreign born. In Philadelphia 30 percent of the population were immigrants, and major concentrations of Irish and Germans could be found in all three cities. San Francisco, Cincinnati, St. Louis, and Milwaukee also had large groups of foreign-born residents. Moreover, several Southern cities including Charleston, Mobile, Richmond, Memphis, and New Orleans supported a large proportion of free white immigrants mostly Irish and Germans, as laborers or skilled help (Volo and Volo 1998, 63).

Germans settled in Eastern cities outside New England. Others tended to separate themselves from traditional America by moving away from the cities into more rural agricultural areas in Pennsylvania and the upper Midwest. Immigrants from Britain continued to come to the United States in large numbers, but they were easily assimilated into the English-speaking, Protestant background of America, They were also the most likely to return to their home countries utilizing inexpensive steamships that encouraged frequent crossings (Husband and O'Loughlin 2004, 7).

Many of the immigrants to America were highly sectarian in their religious beliefs. Irish immigrants, in particular, introduced an ever increasing Roman Catholic presence into a largely Protestant urban population that was ill-disposed to accept them. Nativists were solidly Protestant and radically anti-Catholic in their rhetoric. For support they tapped into the growing fear and resentment that paralleled the rapid changes taking place in American society. Irish Catholics had an unfortunate history of poor relations with their Protestant cousins in Great Britain that followed them to the New World. They were considered the greatest threat to American unity before the war. Nativist rhetoric portrayed Catholics, and especially the Catholic immigrants, as crime-ridden and intemperate, a drag on the economy, and a danger to the fabric of society that might rise up on orders from the Pope to overthrow American culture (Volo and Volo 2007, 13).

The Irish were the first truly urban group in America. Poverty forced many into crowded slums rife with crime, drunkenness, and disease. They came in large numbers, generally during the Irish Potato Famine of 1845–1849. They were also the only immigrant group in which females outnumbered males. With men leaving the rural regions of Ireland to find work in the cities, Irish women had less of an opportunity to marry, which encouraged them to emigrate as well (Volo and Volo 2007, 13).

The Irish in America often considered themselves exiles, forced by poverty, famine, and British policy, to flee to Ireland. Poverty kept them in the United States. Their rate of return was so low that those who stayed behind in Ireland often held American wakes for those who were departing and for whom they never expected to return. This is borne out by the census statistics. The number of first generation Irish-Americans overtook the number of first-generation British-Americans in the 1870s even though twice as many Britons than Irish had arrived in America by that decade (Husband and O'Loughlin 2004, 8).

Many established Americans saw these developments only in prejudicial terms and blamed the slum-like conditions in which the Irish lived on the Irish themselves, ignoring the anti-Irish bigotry of employers and landlords. In addition to being the victims of social prejudice, the Irish were also accused of voting illegally, of selling their votes to unscrupulous politicians, and of engendering crime and immorality. Advertisements for help were often followed by signs stating "Irish Need Not Apply."

Among the Nativist texts circulating through the bookstores and publishing houses of America were a number of anti-Catholic works including escaped nun publications. The ostensible theme of this genre was the immorality of the Catholic Church and its institutions. While in the guise of being uplifting and informative, these stories actually served as a sort of pornographic literature. The most successful of the escaped nun stories was Maria Monk's *Awful Discourses of the Hotel Dieu Nunnery of Montreal* that was first published in 1834. Herein Maria detailed her stay in the Ursuline convent and charged that she saw holy sisters killed for failing to surrender their bodies to the lusts of the priests. Having been ravished in this manner herself, she claimed to be pregnant. Maria also detailed the hiding places of the bodies of the babies born to the inmates of the convent and killed to keep the awful secret of Catholic lust and degeneration. The book, conveniently interspersed with the intimate details of this sexual activity, claimed that the Roman Church actively promoted the "prostitution of female virtue and liberty under the garb of holy religion" (Wish 1950, 319).

Of course, Maria Monk's tale was as false as the author herself. She was almost immediately unmasked as a prostitute of long standing who had never seen the inside of a convent. Unscrupulous publicists and radical crusaders continued to use the work with reckless abandon, however. A mob of about 50 workmen, incensed in part by the book, took it upon themselves to burn the Mount Benedict Ursuline Convent-School in Charlestown near Boston in 1834. Irish Catholic homes were burned, and a number of Irish men were attacked in the streets. In 1844 a similar incident took place in Philadelphia where two Catholic churches and 30 homes were burned. Protestant crusaders clashed with Irish Catholic bands, leaving more than a dozen dead and scores injured. *Awful Discourses*, more popular than most slave narratives and antislavery tracts of the period, sold more than 300,000 copies before the Civil War, a volume of sales rivaled at the time only by Harriet Beecher Stowe's *Uncle Tom's Cabin*. Stories of the Maria Monk genre were trotted out again by anti-Catholic forces in 1928 when Alfred E. Smith, a Catholic, ran for president of the United States, but they were too blatantly obvious to impact a more sophisticated electorate in 1960 when John F. Kennedy, also a Catholic, ran for office (Wish 1950, 319).

As late as 1869, a Protestant minister lashed out against the Catholics from his own pulpit, "Only by fusing all foreign elements into our common nationality and making our entire population in spirit and intent Americans, shall we preserve our unity and concord as a nation" (Sutherland 2000, 234). The Catholic archbishop of New York, John Hughes, took an unquestionably militant stand in defense of his church. He rallied the largely Irish Catholic population of the city in defense of Catholic institutions, and surrounded churches, convents, and schools with armed guards after his house was attacked by anti-Catholic, anti-Irish rioters. Hughes also fought to have anti-Catholic books banned from the public schools. Hughes also undertook a series of lectures in which he predicted the inevitable victory of Catholicism over the Protestant heresy.

Unable to remove Protestantism from the public schools, Hughes set up his own system of Catholic education, as did bishops elsewhere. Sectarian control over education in Virginia, Maryland, and Massachusetts in operation since colonial times had gradually declined. However, the development of free public schools under state control caused a continuing controversy over questions of state aid for religious programs that were a common feature of nineteenth-century education.

In October 1841, Hughes made an inflammatory speech supporting the alteration of school funding to inhibit the commingling of religious and public monies, and attempting, according the New York's Mayor Phillip Hone, "to mix up religion with politics—an unpalatable dish." Hone was in New York in 1841 when Governor William Seward authorized the use of state money "for the establishment of separate schools for the children of foreigners, and their instruction by teachers of their own faith and language." The public outcry that followed this pro-Catholic decision was as immediate as it was massive. Seward was faced with the partisan charge of trying to curry favor with the Irish Catholics, and it was alleged that he was in a conspiracy with Hughes. The final result of the New York controversy was the elimination of all Bibles and Bible reading from the tax-supported schools. Hone observed, "Bishop Hughes…deserves a cardinal's hat at least for what he has done in placing Irish Catholics upon the necks of native New Yorkers" (Nevins 1927, 570).

Ironically, this very early separation of church and state crusade, led by a priest, clearly sharpened the dispute and helped to swell the ranks of the Nativists in the political campaigns of the 1840s and 1850s, which used anti-Catholicism and the evils of Popery as foundation stones of their all-American rhetoric.

Nativists tapped into these widely held feelings appealing for a wide-ranging all-Americanism in their political platform, and they pointed to the acceptance of Catholics by the Northern wing of the Democratic Party as proof that the old political system would fail to support traditional American values. By tapping into a growing sense of resentment of politics as usual, out of touch with the pulse of the people and dedicated only to entrenched interests, the Nativists found an agenda designed to ensure the defeat of the old parties.

The Nativists were deeply immersed in the evangelical movement, and they were strongly supported by some of the finest established families of the North. Politically, they made some gains at the state level, especially in Massachusetts, only to have the party collapse after a few years because it came apart over the slavery question and failed to reform governments when it did win elections locally. Nativists were particularly embarrassed by their inability to bring about the passage of more stringent immigration laws. They did poorly with Southerners, who were more accepting of immigrants and more tolerant of Catholicism than many in the North. More generally, the Nativists failed because of their lack of political experience, their association with several prominent old party Whigs, and their violent anti-Catholic rhetoric, which bothered many politically active Protestants (Volo and Volo 2000, 200–201).

—*James M. Volo*

REFORM: FROM SLAVERY TO CONTRABAND

Reforming the system of slavery into one that recognized freedmen as equals was no simple task. No one knew what to do with the flood of escaped or newly freed blacks that came streaming into the federal lines at the beginning of the war. Such a volume of displaced persons, especially women and children, had not been anticipated. In spring 1861 the first of this wave of escaped slaves to appear were those that came to Fortress Monroe, an old federal installation near Norfolk, on the southeastern tip of Virginia. They had been working on nearby Confederate fortifications, and took advantage of the proximity of Union lines to flee. By July 1861, at least 900 slaves had gained their freedom at Fortress Monroe, but while they had been given food and shelter, they had also been put to work on the federal entrenchments.

Over the next four years, tens of thousands of African Americans changed their status from slaves to contrabands by fleeing to Union army posts and occupied territory. Many of these were house servants and skilled craftsmen from local plantations who thought they had the most to gain through freedom and the best chance to integrate into the black community in the North. Most escaped to northern and southeastern Virginia, the Sea Islands off South Carolina, parts of Tennessee, and other places taken over by Union forces early in the war. Thousands fled south. At least 50,000 crowded into enclaves along the Mississippi River, from Cairo, Illinois, all the way south to New Orleans, Louisiana, one of the first cities to have fallen to federal forces (April 1862).

Some of the temporary contraband camps grew into functioning villages, with schools, churches, and shops. Freedman's Village, built along the Potomac River on the site of Robert E. Lee's property in Arlington, Virginia (and now occupied by Arlington National Cemetery), was created to relieve the severe crowding among 10,000 or so black refugees living in the District of Columbia. The government built whitewashed duplexes for the refugees in the village, employed them in workshops and on government farms, and provided a school, chapel, and hospital. Another model contraband camp grew near Corinth, Mississippi, where slaves from northern Mississippi and Alabama and southern Tennessee began arriving after the federal victory at nearby Shiloh (April 1862). The contrabands built themselves log cabins along the streets laid out and numbered by the army engineers. The little town was even divided into wards. Like Freedman's Village, the camp at Corinth soon had a school, hospital, stores, an administrative office, and a church. Within a few months, some of the African American men had been organized into a kind of militia, relieving white troops of the necessity of guarding the camp. A number of American Missionary Association workers came to Corinth to teach and to preach, and by the summer of 1863 there were nearly 400 pupils attending school. The Union Christian Church of Corinth, as the missionaries called their little chapel, regularly attracted hundreds of worshipers to services that sometimes featured the preaching of four black ministers recently escaped from slavery. More than 300 children attended Sunday School classes. Families were also encouraged to grow their own food in individual gardens; a little cotton field and a large field of vegetables for the hospital were also maintained. The Corinth camp, by the summer of 1863, had become a fully functioning little town.

However, most contrabands did not experience such well-organized and improving conditions. In some places, freed slaves had to live in old packing crates, tobacco barns, sod huts, and, if they were lucky, abandoned houses. Single rooms sometimes housed six families. The supplies that were supposed to be distributed to the contrabands were sometimes sold on the black market by army officers or other officials, and the medical care in the camps (usually provided by army surgeons) was unreliable. Many camps offered material deprivations to the escaped slaves rivaling if not exceeding those of the plantations from which they had escaped.

A Northern woman working at a hospital for freedmen in the middle of a muddy field near Washington began her description by writing, "If I were to describe this hospital it would not be believed." In this place "are gathered all the colored people who have been made free by the progress of our Army." The overburdened hospital cared for "all cripples, diseased, aged, wounded, inform, from whatsoever cause." Their patients included black army teamsters beaten nearly to death by white soldiers and desperate mothers carrying dying children into camp. Up to 50 sick, injured, or simply exhausted men, women, and children arrived each day. At least one baby was born daily, but nurses "have no baby clothes except as we wrap them up in an old piece of muslin. . . . This hospital consists of all the lame, halt, and blind escaped from slavery" (Heidler and Heidler 2007, 174).

Conditions in some makeshift camps were even worse. An agent for the Cincinnati Contraband Relief Commission revealed the horror of some contrabands' lives when he described a temporary shelter near Davis Bend, Mississippi. In an open cattle shed lived 35 "poor wretched helpless Negroes." The band consisted of a nearly blind man, 5 women, and 29 children all under the age of 12 years.

Not surprisingly, the death rates in the teeming camps soared, especially among the children. Out of the 4,000 black refugees living in Helena, Arkansas, in 1863–1864, about 1,100 died. In Memphis, 1,200 out of 4,000 contrabands died in only three months, while the camp at Natchez suffered a nearly 50 percent mortality rate in 1863. To make matters worse, Confederate guerrillas frequently attacked defenseless contraband settlements, sometimes kidnapping and selling men, women, and children—each of whom brought as much as $100 in federal money on the slave market.

The blacks living in government camps—men, women, and children—rarely received food and shelter free of charge. Contraband of all ages had to work in return for the security, rations, and housing the army provided. By the age of 10 or 12, as they had as slaves, freed children took their places in the fields alongside older African Americans.

Yet many of these newly freed children—not to mention adult contrabands—also had access to schools. After living their entire lives in a society that actually made it illegal for them to learn to read or write, the contrabands eagerly crowded into schools of all sizes and in all conditions almost as soon as they reached federal lines. An escaped slave opened one of the first schools for black students in Norfolk in the fall of 1861; two years later there were 21 teachers in 11 schools with 3,000 day and night students of all ages. Scores of individuals, missionary associations, and even the army sponsored or staffed schools throughout the occupied South; over 1,400 men and women were teaching in 975 schools for blacks in the year after the war ended. These schools ranged in size from a few girls being taught by a lone teacher (sometimes the young daughters of Union army officers) to the 1,422 in public schools run by the military in New Orleans and more than 14,000 in schools operated in rural parishes in southern Louisiana.

A number of the teachers in contraband schools were African American—some escaped slaves themselves. In fact, the American Missionary Association's first school in Norfolk opened under the leadership of Mary Smith Peake, the free daughter of a white man and a mulatto woman. The school would later become Hampton Institute, alma mater of Booker T. Washington and other notable black leaders. Some teachers, such as "Uncle" Cyrus White, who taught school in Beaufort for several months in 1863; William D. Harris, a plasterer, and his assistant, Amos Wilson, who taught at Grosport, North Carolina were former slaves. But most black teachers came from the North in the employ of the American Missionary Association (AMA). Edmonia Highgate of Syracuse, New York, had lectured and raised money for the AMA before the war and had taught in the Binghamton public schools; she became a teacher and a principal in Norfolk before the war. Her colleague, Sara G. Stanley, came from Cleveland via Oberlin College. A teacher at the AMA school at Camp Baker in Washington, Stanley was a former slave, but she had been an educator and writer in Brooklyn for 20 years before joining the AMA. Northern publications produced flash cards and textbooks for contraband schools. The American

Tract Society even published a monthly magazine, *The Freedman,* to be distributed to black soldiers and to be used in contraband schools (Heidler and Heidler 2007, 173–75).

FOR MORE INFORMATION

Broder, Sherri. *Tramps, Unfit Mothers, and Neglected Children: Negotiating the Family in Nineteenth-Century Philadelphia.* Philadelphia: University of Pennsylvania Press, 2002.

Cook, Fred J. "The Slave Ship Rebellion." *American Heritage,* Feb. 1957, 60–64, 104–15.

Davis, William C., ed., *Secret History of Confederate Diplomacy: Edwin De Leon, Late Confidential Agent of the Confederate Department of State in Europe.* Lawrence: University Press of Kansas, 2005.

Heidler, David S., and Jeanne T. Heidler, eds. *Daily Life of Civilians in Wartime Early America, From the Colonial Era to the Civil War.* Westport, CT: Greenwood Press, 2007.

Husband, Julie, and Jim O'Loughlin. *Daily Life in the Industrial United States, 1870–1900.* Westport, CT: Greenwood Press, 2004.

Jones, Howard. *Mutiny on the Amistad.* New York: Oxford University Press, 1987.

Nevins, Allan, ed. *The Diary of Philip Home, 1828–1851.* New York: Dodd, Mead and Company, 1927.

Perkins, Robert. "Diplomacy and Intrigue, Confederate Relations with the Republic of Mexico, 1861–1862." http://members.tripod.com/~azrebel/page11.html (accessed August 2007).

Shrock, Joel. *The Gilded Age.* Westport, CT: Greenwood Press, 2004.

Stern, Philip Van Doren. *The Confederate Navy: A Pictorial History.* Garden City, NY: Doubleday, 1962.

Stewart, James Brewer. *Holy Warriors, The Abolitionists and American Slavery.* New York: Hill and Wang, 1976.

Sutherland, Daniel E. *The Expansion of Everyday Life, 1860–1876.* Fayetteville: University of Arkansas Press, 2000.

Volo, Dorothy Denneen, and James M. Volo. *The Antebellum Period.* Westport, CT: Greenwood Press, 2004.

———. *Daily Life in Civil War America.* Westport, CT: Greenwood Press, 1998.

———. *Encyclopedia of the Antebellum South.* Westport, CT: Greenwood Press, 2000.

———. *Family Life in Nineteenth-Century America.* Westport, CT: Greenwood Press, 2007.

Wish, Harvey. *Society and Thought in Early America, A Social and Intellectual History of the American People through 1865.* New York: Longmans, Green and Co., 1950.

Recreational Life

DIVERSIONS IN THE CAMPS

The daily regime of life in the camps allowed little in the way of free time for the soldiers. Drill, fatigue duty, cutting trees and brush, collecting firewood, digging entrenchments, foraging, and service in the outposts consumed most of the soldiers' day when he was not marching or fighting. Just keeping warm and supplied with dry cloths required a great deal of time. After a hard day most soldiers were happy to cook and eat a meal, down a cup of hot coffee, and roll up in their blankets to catch some much-needed sleep.

Nonetheless, individuals and groups did find some time for entertainment. Writing letters and journals, reading, whittling, and drawing were common activities. Simple musical instruments—notably the banjo and harmonica—were played in camp, and singing was a great pastime. Games such as checkers, chess, and dice were popular, as were a number of card games. Common civilian board games were often crudely reproduced on a piece of canvas or the inside of the ubiquitous gum blanket (raincoat), and played with stones, bones, or corncobs as game pieces. Gambling was strictly forbidden by the Article of War, but the prohibition was almost impossible to enforce. Nonetheless, in many instances, soldiers feared being found dead on the battlefield with gambling implements like cards or dice in their possession because they might disappoint their parents or loved ones.

—James M. Volo

SPORTS AND GAMES

Games have always been popular in America, and in the nineteenth century, indoor board games were just coming into their own. Many games dated from the eighteenth century, and they served as inspiration for a host of nineteenth-century imitators. American board makers copied other games as well, especially those that were newly popular in Britain. Americans were a sporting people seemingly in love with the out-of-doors lifestyle in the nineteenth century, but they were also individualistic, gravitating toward solitary activities like hunting and fishing. Both soldiers and civilians attempted to entertain themselves during the Civil War years through the use of sports, games, reading, the playing of music, and attendance at lectures, the theater, or the opera.

Upper-class families throughout the nation frequently tried to absent themselves from the cities during the fever seasons that came with the intolerably hot and humid weather of summer. In the antebellum years, upper-class fami-

This grouping illustrates an American family of the "better sort" with its playthings, including balls, hoops, teeter-totters, and a cricket bat. It is hard to imagine children recreating themselves in the clothing they are wearing. Courtesy Library of Congress.

lies throughout the nation frequently took long vacations in the mountains or at the seashore. Much of this activity was curtailed during the war, and American families soon resorted to a variety of optical toys, board games, and crafts that could be practiced in their drawing rooms and parlors. Many of these were closely associated with the war effort as with the making of flags, the rolling of bandages, or the writing of war poems. Outside the home civilians attended lectures given by politicians, abolitionists, reformers, preachers, or war heroes. The war created great difficulties with regard to recreation—more in the South than in the North.

Team sports did not gain popularity until the 1840s. English-style cricket was played in America. There were, for instance, organized clubs and cricket pitches in Staten Island, New York, but the breadth of the sport's popularity is open to question. Nonetheless, period illustrations sometimes show cricket bats among children's toys, but these may have been based on British rather than American concepts of sport. There was a rudimentary form of football popular among the college set that was remarkably similar to English rugby and adapted to any terrain or number of players. These early football games were "splendidly unorganized and offered a fine spectacle of players scrimmaging in stovepipe hats" (Bishop 1969, 58).

Although the first recorded intercollegiate athletic contest was a boat race held between the rowing clubs of Harvard and Yale in 1852 on Lake Winnipesaukee in New Hampshire, the first truly organized team sport in America was probably baseball, which may trace its origins in America back to 1825.

Baseball

In 1825 a local newspaper editor, Thurlow Weed, organized a baseball team in Rochester, New York, at Mumford's Meadow. Nonetheless, Abner Doubleday is generally credited with beginning the sport at Cooperstown, New York in 1839. However, Doubleday was in attendance at West Point Military Academy in 1839 making it highly unlikely that he would have time to organize the sport (Andrews 2002, 23). By the 1840s baseball had evolved into a recognizable sport with teams and rules resembling those of modern times. Some obvious differences between the modern and early forms of the game are the lack of baseball gloves, catcher's masks, and other protective equipment. Of course, the ball itself was not as hard and did not carry as far as modern ones.

Although some form of baseball was played by the soldiers in the camps during the Civil War, which may have led to its association with General Doubleday, there is no dependable description of the game extant from that time. A National League with uniform rules governing the game was not adopted until after the conflict was over. The National Association of Base Ball Players, an organization of amateur clubs, adopted the first set of official rules at a convention in 1866.

Professional baseball was particularly popular near the end of the century, and baseball parks were opened to accommodate crowds that sometimes numbered 20,000. The simple wooden structures that served as seats for the spectators were a hazard. In the 1890s there were at least two dozen major ballpark fires, and in several cases the stands simply collapsed under the weight of the fans. At the turn of the century baseball parks began to be built of strong, fireproof steel and reinforced concrete. By the 1910s baseball was being heralded as the national sport.

Softball was not invented until 1887. George W. Hancock organized the first game indoors using boxing gloves and a broom. Although the equipment became more baseball-like in the interim, the game did not move outdoors until 1895. The sport was very popular with groups of adults and students at school during the depression of the 1930s. From its inception, softball has been known by several names including Depression Ball, Diamond Ball, Kitten Ball, Fast Ball, Recreation Ball, and, of course, Playground Ball.

—*James M. Volo*

FENCING AND SWORDSMANSHIP

Nowhere in America, and possibly in the Western world, was dueling so universally practiced as in the South in the antebellum years. It was in New Orleans that the practice reached its zenith from 1830 to 1860. This period is often called the Golden Age of Dueling. The specter of becoming involved in an affair of honor shadowed every public social and political events, and there were few men of prominence that had not issued or accepted a challenge. A nineteenth-century commentator, Major Ben C. Truman, noted that the purpose of the duel was to resolve a point of honor, not simply to kill an opponent. For this reason swords or rapiers were considered the proper weapons for a duel. Those who lost sight of this were often looked upon as murderers by purists, who saw the process as an exercise in character. Although seen as uniquely Southern, dueling actually had a long history throughout America. Aaron Burr had killed Alexander Hamilton in a pistol duel in New Jersey (Volo and Volo 2000, 83).

Swordsmanship in the eighteenth century had been taught largely by dancing masters; but as the activity became more popular, these masters abandoned their dance students to teach the finer points of fence, lunge, and parry. The basics of the fence were essentially established at Domenico Angelo's fencing school in England, and these fundamentals of posture, footwork, attack, and defense remain largely unchanged even today. These students were intended to prepare for real combat, and while padded jackets were common, no masks were used.

Well-known duelists occupied much the same position in society that sports figures hold today. They were followed through the streets, given the best tables in restaurants and the finest seats in theaters, and their mannerisms and fighting styles were copied by young men. It was, nonetheless, against the law to duel, and for this reason no attempt was made to keep a record of the number of encounters or of the butcher list that proceeded from them. Estimates put the number of duels between 1830 and 1860 in the thousands, and the fatalities in the hundreds.

The violence of the Civil War seemingly quenched the thirst of most duelists for killing, but the popularity of swordsmanship as a physical activity remained. The need to train swordsmen for combat in a nonlethal manner at military schools and academies led the activity to have a sporting component from its beginnings. Cadets practiced with the spadroon (a light straight-bladed military sword of the cut and thrust type), the rapier (a straight cutting and thrusting weapon popular in dueling), and the heavy cavalry sabre with its curved blade. These addressed the combat needs of infantry and cavalry officers, but in the postwar years their use fell into disfavor rapidly due to the widespread availability of revolvers as battlefield sidearms. Bayonet fencing experienced a somewhat slower decline and was still being pursued at a few schools in the 1940s and 1950s.

Many schools and colleges adopted fencing as a physical activity in the second half of the nineteenth century where the instruction was intended for competition rather than bloodletting. The purposes of sport fencing were far removed from their martial roots, and fencing was largely followed to train competing athletes in the most effective tactics to use within the rules of the sport. Academic fencing eschewed sharp blades and utilized padding and masks to prevent unwanted injuries.

The Amateur Fencers League of America was founded in 1891, and collegiate competitions were held under the auspices of the National Collegiate Athletic Association (NCAA). Fencing competitions were recognized by the Olympics in 1896. Most of the conventions and vocabulary used in American fencing were established in the late nineteenth and early twentieth centuries by European sword masters especially those from Italy and Hungary. Perhaps the most notable of these was Italo Santelli, who was active from the 1880s until the 1940s. It would be an error to underestimate the influences of Prussian swordsmen in the development of the sport. Prussian educational theories concerning academics, discipline, and, particularly, physical education were very popular among American educators. The types of sporting fence were organized around the foil, épée, and sabre and were recognized in competition. While competition points could be scored only with the points of the foil or épée, they could be scored with the blade, flat, and point of the sabre.

—*James M. Volo*

MUSIC

Before the Civil War, the most common means of distributing a song was by word of mouth. Though formal printed sheet music scores were popular with the musically trained and the upper classes, most Americans lacked the ability to read music and were more likely to learn songs by simple imitation. Thus, the most common means of song distribution were song sheets and songsters. Unlike sheet music, which contained the full musical score, song sheets were single printed sheets with lyrics but no musical notation except, perhaps, the name of the tune to which the lyrics were to be sung. Some of America's favorite songs, including "The Star-Spangled Banner" and "The Battle Hymn of the Republic," were originally distributed as song sheets. Although song sheets had been printed in the British Isles as early as the sixteenth century, their popularity in the United States reached its peak during the Civil War. Song sheets often fit new lyrics to familiar tunes, "Yankee Doodle" and "Just Before the Battle, Mother" being especially vulnerable to adaptation and parody. "The Last Rose of Summer" was parodied as "The Last Potato," a comical ode to the tuber. Other song sheets offered lyrics of newly written popular songs, and as such they provide a glimpse of the topics that dominated Civil War popular culture: the evils of alcohol, slavery, the grief of mourning, and the extremes of fashion were all popular subjects in song. Song sheets reflected civilian attitudes toward the war ranging from unbridled patriotism to hesitancy about the continuation of the conflict to even occasional war resistance. Many of the Civil War songs, like "Mother Kissed Me in My Dream," "The Children of the Battlefield," and "Lorena," were mawkishly sentimental.

The song sheets' counterpart was the songster or songbook. Like the song sheets, they contained only lyrics, but these inexpensive bound books, sometimes selling for just a few cents, usually contained from 60 to 100 selections gleaned from folksongs, ballads, popular songs, and minstrelsy. They usually indicated the tune to which the song was to be sung, in lieu of a printed score. By 1860, these small songbooks were published in America by the hundreds, but they became even more popular during the war, as soldiers carried the slim volumes in their packs. Songs were also published in newspapers and magazines, especially in the South. In taverns, in town squares, and in houses, songs were often accompanied by stringed instruments (and after the war by the piano). The banjo was generally the folk instrument of choice, and it was the predominant instrument in minstrelsy and vaudeville.

Many Victorians believed that song could enhance and stimulate intellectual activity and instill correct moral values. Music could make for a happier and more useful life on earth and even carry on toward heaven. One of the leading proponents of this philosophy, William B. Bradbury (1816–1868), published 921 of his own hymns, more than three million copies of which had been sold by the end of the nineteenth century. His best known was *Esther, the Beautiful Queen* (1856), a long musical drama based on the biblical Book of Esther. By the end of the war, 255,000 copies of *Esther* were in circulation.

During the war years and the sentimental decades that followed, popular music served as a cohesive force in American society. Songs often served as a form of self-entertainment or accompanied tedious labor such as railroad construction, dock work, or field work. Some workers accumulated large repertoires, taking solace from hard labor in their singing. Everywhere the beneficial and useful influence exerted by music on the individual, and on society in general, was recognized. Song energized an increasingly politicized and partisan population. The editor of *Songs of the People: The Union Republican Campaign Glee Book* (1868) stated unequivocally that the party that sang the loudest, longest, and oftenest was always sure to win the election. What was sound judgment for political campaigning was equally valid for boosting general spirits and morale.

Classical music during this period was largely reserved for the upper classes and therefore had limited distribution. Symphony orchestras, where they existed at all, were likely to be temporary organizations convened for a season with whatever freelance musicians might be available. In the larger cities, the new Italian operas of Giuseppe Verdi and the English operettas of Gilbert and Sullivan were special favorites, but in general, classical music failed to attract much of a following outside the metropolitan areas, the proliferation of small town opera houses (which were more likely to host melodramas and burlesque than opera) notwithstanding.

A few individuals sought to direct and cultivate the general public's musical taste, however. George Templeton Strong, a New York lawyer whose passion was the music of Beethoven, recognized the urgency of accommodating the growing middle class. After a night at the Academy of Music in New York, he wrote that nine-tenths of the assemblage cared nothing for Beethoven's music and had chattered and looked about and wished it was over. He felt that the beneficial value of such music lay in bringing masses of people into contact with it.

Of all the popular composers of the period immediately preceding the Civil War, the favorite was Stephen Collins Foster (1826–1864). Because his music fit the sentiment of the period, it was popular during the war and into the period of Reconstruction.

Foster was born near Pittsburgh and was a musical prodigy. He learned to play the guitar and flageolet (a kind of flute) and wrote high-quality ballads and songs that drew heavily on black and white folk traditions. Foster soon discovered that he could earn a living composing songs for minstrel shows, a popular form of entertainment in which white performers darkened their faces with burnt cork and performed in stereo-typical "Negroid" fashion. After the success of his "Old Uncle Ned" and "Oh Susannah," Foster composed mainly for E. P. Christy's Minstrels, one of the most important blackface troupes of the period. Foster eventually wrote some 400 songs, usually favoring themes common to everyday life in both the North and the South during the period—such as love, beauty, and contentment—although many of his characters had black faces. Many of Foster's greatest minstrel-show hits, such as "Old Folks at Home" (often incorrectly called "Way Down Upon the Suwannee River") (1852), "My Old Kentucky Home" (1853), "Old Black Joe" (1860), "Camp Town Races" (1852), and "Massa's in de Cold, Cold Ground" (1850) depict the South as a land of sunshine, nostalgia, contented whites and loyal, happy-go-lucky slaves—the common themes of many minstrel-show songs. In fact, Foster knew very little about the South from personal experience. Foster's sentimental songs, such as "Jeanie with the Light Brown Hair," "Come Where My Love Lies Dreaming," "Beautiful Dreamer," "Gentle Annie," and "Our Bright Summer Days Have Gone" successfully exploited the sentimentality of the era. Despite his successes, Foster died in the New York Bowery an impoverished alcoholic, with three pennies, 35 cents worth of script, and the words "Dear Friends and Gentle Hearts"—perhaps the title of a new song—in his pocket.

The early 1850s saw the flowering of brass band music in America. The all-brass band was predominant in America during that decade, but European immigrants, who introduced woodwinds to the ensembles, were slowly influencing instrumentation. The New York Seventh Regiment Band introduced flutes, piccolos, and reed instruments as early as 1852. When Patrick S. Gilmore, the most popular and influential bandmaster of the Civil War era, introduced reed instruments into his brass band in 1859, it signaled the decline of the all-brass band.

The military used music to provide signals, sustain morale among the troops and lend an air of formality to ceremonial occasions. Military music consisted of two distinct types: field music and band music. Field musicians, including company drummers, fifers, and buglers, signaled troops in daily routine as well as in battle. Company musicians were often too young to enlist as regular soldiers. Drummer boys as young as 12 or 13 were celebrated in such popular songs as Will Hays's "The Drummer Boy of Shiloh" (1863), the poignant story of a youngster not old enough to shave but old enough to beat the drum and stop a bullet.

Military bands generally were brass and percussion ensembles originally ranging from 8 to 24 members and were usually attached to a regiment or brigade. Among the many unusual bands that entered military service was Frank Rauscher's cornet band from Germantown, Pennsylvania, composed of colorfully uniformed Zouaves from General Charles Collies's brigade. Collies had the good fortune to be associated with Captain F. A. Elliot, a wool merchant, who kept the troops supplied with fresh, Turkish-style uniforms and he donated money for their purchase of instruments. An unexpected glut of Union volunteer bands such as Rauscher's during the first year of the conflict caused the U.S. War Department to limit the number of ensembles, and the Confederacy soon imposed a similar limit. Congress passed a bill on July 17, 1862 that ordered the mustering out of regimental bands in October of the same year, and the War Department forbade the further enlistment of regimental bandsmen. With 10 companies to a regiment and 2 musicians generally allowed to each company, a regiment could assemble at most an ensemble of 20 men.

The musician's meager pay was usually supplemented by contributions from the unit's officers. The bandsmen also performed nonmusical, noncombat duties, often carrying stretchers and assisting in field hospitals. Gilmore's 24th Massachusetts Volunteer Infantry was required not only to play in camp, but also to follow the regiment into the field where the musicians were put to work as hospital corpsman. One member of the band appears to have been lost in action.

A full military brass band most often consisted of two or more E-flat cornets or saxhorns, two or more B-flat cornets or saxhorns, two alto horns, two tenor horns, one baritone horn, one brass horn and one percussion section of snare drum, brass drum, and cymbals. A few bands included woodwind instruments. The most common brass instruments in the bands of both sides were saxhorns, a valve-actuated bugle with a backward-pointing bell that directed the music to the troops parading behind the band. It was this last characteristic of the saxhorn that made it so noticeable among the bandsmen. Levels of skill varied widely among military musicians. While some musicians had learned to play only after enlisting, others, like the members of the band of the 25th South Carolina Infantry regiment, had been professional musicians before the war.

Away from the front, military bands supplied music for ceremonies and special events. Their repertoire ran the gamut from marches, patriotic songs, and dance tunes to hymns, funeral dirges, and special arrangements of overtures and other symphonic pieces.

The Confederacy did not have many professional composers, so it had to rely more on semiprofessional pieces, folk songs, and ballads. A Confederate favorite was "The Bonnie Blue Flag." First published by A. E. Blackmer & Brother in New Orleans, its origins are uncertain. Early editions state the tune was "composed, arranged and sung by Harry Macarthy, the Arkansas Comedian." Other sources credit the lyrics to Annie Chambers Ketchum and the melody to a derivation of an old Irish tune called "The Jaunting Car." The song so fired up the Confederates that it became anathema to Yankees. After the fall of New Orleans, General Benjamin Butler (dubbed "The Beast of New Orleans" by the Confederates) reportedly fined its publisher $500 and anybody caught singing the song had to cough up $25.

Another of the Confederacy's favorite songs, "The Homespun Dress," was a sentimental ode to the privations Southern women had to endure for the sake of their cause. A Lieutenant Harrington, who rode into Lexington, Kentucky, with Morgan's cavalry and was impressed by the quality and beauty of the ladies' homespun gowns, supposedly wrote this song. His song became popular, appealing to sentiment and promoting self-sacrifice, and was printed in numerous Civil War songbooks.

The most popular Confederate rallying song of the conflict, however, was "Dixie." Daniel D. Emmett composed the song in 1859 for Dan Bryant's minstrel show adaptation of the comedy *Pocahontas*. Emmett was Ohio born and one of the first white entertainers to perform in blackface. As a Northerner who opposed the war, he bitterly resented the way the Confederates appropriated his song for their own purposes but was never able to suppress their misuse of his piece. Originally titled, "I wish I was in Dixie's Land," it made its debut at Mechanics Hall, New York, on April 4, 1859. There is circumstantial evidence that Emmett first heard the tune in Ohio from two African American musicians, Ben and Lou Snowden.

With its lively tune and sentimental words and the walk around at the closing number, when the entire cast paraded across the stage, "Dixie" immediately became popular in all sections of the country. When it reached New Orleans in 1860, it became a favorite song onstage and off, and it grew to become the unofficial Confederate national anthem. Its seeming sympathy with Southern sentiment gave it appeal throughout the South and Southerners did everything possible to make "Dixie" their own song. Confederate citizens rewrote "Dixie" in at least 210 variations. Many were couched in terms of fire and valor. One popular Southern version was written by Confederate General Albert Pike: "Southrons, hear your country call you! / Up, lest worse than death befall you! / To Arms! To Arms! In Dixie Land!"

Emmett's original version of "Dixie" was played at the inauguration of Jefferson Davis in Montgomery, Alabama, in February 1861. Ironically, the song was also a favorite of Abraham Lincoln's. As the war drew to its conclusion in April 1865, Lincoln visited the Union camps below Richmond aboard the paddle wheeler, *River Queen*, accompanied by a young French count who said that he did not know "Dixie." When a band came aboard, Lincoln asked them to play the song, saying to the Frenchman: "The tune is now federal property, and its good to show the Rebels that with us in power, they will be free to hear it again. It has always been a favorite of mine, and since we've captured it, we have a perfect right to enjoy it." A week later, Lincoln ordered "Dixie" played as a peace offering upon Robert E. Lee's surrender at Appomattox.

In the North, the heat of war generated numerous songs. Julia Ward Howe recast an old and popular hymn, "Say, Brother, Will You Meet Us?" into the firebrand "Battle Hymn of the Republic." With its powerful patriotic and religious undertones, Howe's piece, like "Dixie," occasionally underwent transformation. "John Brown's Body" was widely parodied in such songs as "Hang Abe Lincoln on a Sour Apple Tree," or, depending on the singer's point of view, "Hang Jeff Davis on a Sour Apple Tree."

"When Johnny Comes Marching Home" (1863), based on an Irish tune, has occasionally been revived in wartime. With its rollicking march tempo, the tune was adapted for numerous Civil War parodies. George F. Root's "Tramp, Tramp, Tramp, the Boys Are Marching" (1864) captured the foot soldier's spirit, as did Henry Clay Work's "Marching Through Georgia," one of the North's favorites.

On the home front, music was used to recruit volunteers, foster patriotism, and create public support for the war effort. Recruiting rallies relied on brass bands to attract crowds. Sheet music of the Civil War period often glorified the soldier's life or related sentimental tales of fallen heroes and broken homes. Other popular songs, like "Kingdom Coming" (Henry Clay Work, 1862) and "Sixty-Three Is the Jubilee" (J. L. Greene and D. A. French, 1863), celebrated the advent of emancipation and showed the musical influences of blackface minstrel songs. Battles and leaders were commemorated in elaborate piano pieces, such as "General Bragg's Grand March" (Rivinac, 1861) and "Beauregard Bull Run Quickstep" (J. A. Rosenberger, 1862). More elaborate still was the "battle-piece," an extended and often quite bombastic orchestral depiction of a specific engagement.

Lamentations over the deaths and the sadness caused by the Civil War were numerous and heartrending. Generally they bemoaned the absence of a family member who was away at war, leaving his loved ones heartbroken and sometimes financially destitute. One song flowing with tears over separation and death was "We Shall Meet But We Shall Miss Him" (words by George Frederick Root, music by H. S. Washburn, 1861). The subject is the man who has gone off to war, for whom "there will be one vacant chair" reserved for his spiritual presence at all future meetings of the family: "We shall meet but we shall miss him / There will be one vacant chair / We will linger to caress him / As we breathe our evening prayer." There was a national outpouring of grief following Abraham Lincoln's death, much of it expressed in such songs as "Farewell, Father, Friend and Guardian" and "Live But One Moment," the latter based on the words spoken by Mary Todd Lincoln as her husband lay dying. The president's death left a lingering impression on songwriters, who continued to pen memorial songs well into the 1870s and beyond.

One of the most popular sentimental songs of the Civil War was "Lorena." Written in 1857, the song remained largely unknown until the war years, when it became a favorite in both the North and the South and was frequently parodied. Sometimes called "Lorena and Paul Vane," its lyrics were attributed to H.D.L. Webster and set to music by J. P. Webster, of no relation.

During the Civil War, both presidents (Lincoln and Davis) were lampooned in song. Often these songs carried double messages and were filled with innuendoes and symbols. Confederate Jefferson Davis was the subject of the vitriolic "Jeff in Petticoats," which sprang from reports that he had fled Richmond disguised as a woman, ahead of advancing Union troops. During this period, hardly any insult could be greater than accusing a man of disguising himself in women's clothes. Such insults, then as now, could be created merely on rumor, and the facts in this case have long since become muddled.

Abraham Lincoln also appeared as the subject of countless song parodies set to folk melodies and minstrel-show tunes. One election-year parody of the song "Old

Dan Tucker" declared, "Old Abe is coming down to fight / And put the Democrats to flight." Another song, "Lincoln and Liberty too," was sung to the tune of "Rosin the Bow," an old melody popular in both the North and the South. "Old Abe Went to Washington" was set to the tune of "When Johnny Comes Marching Home," while "Brave Old Abe" used the Scottish tune, "Auld Lang Syne." Not all songs treated Lincoln approvingly. One that did not, sung to the tune of "Pop Goes the Weasel," claimed, "Old Abe is sick, old Abe is sick / Old Abe is sick in bed." Another called "Old Honest Abe" characterized Lincoln as "an arrant fool, a party tool / A traitor, and a Tory." "John Anderson, My Jo, John," an 1824 air often appropriated for political satires, turned up in "Old Abe, My Jolly Jo John," a Copperhead blast at the president in four stanzas. The English ballad, "Lord Lovell," was also widely adapted for vitriolic attacks on the president.

For many Southerners and their sympathizers, the differences between Lincoln and Davis were summarized in four short lines, apparently sung by folk on all social levels: "Jeff Davis rides a white horse. / Lincoln rides a mule. / Jeff Davis is a gentleman, / and Lincoln is a fool."

For African American slaves, singing was a way to ease their burdens, adapt and preserve some of their native musical traditions, and even communicate clandestinely. Sometimes slaves were forbidden to sing out of fear that the songs could contain hidden messages. In Savannah, a congregation of slaves attending a baptism one Sunday was arrested, imprisoned, and punished with 39 lashes each for singing a song. The situation was rarely so draconian, however. Slaves' singing more often served as a source of entertainment for the plantation owners as well as their guests. Former slave Frederick A. Douglass reported that slaves were generally expected to sing as well as do work and that a silent slave was not liked by masters nor overseers. It was to this attitude that he attributed the almost constant singing heard in the Southern states. Douglass pointed out the mistake of presuming that the slaves were happy because they were singing and noted that the songs represented sorrows rather than joys and that even in the most boisterous outbursts of rapturous sentiment there was ever a tinge of deep melancholy.

Slaves often adapted songs from those they heard at the master's houses or in other contacts with whites. The fusion of white material with such African elements as syncopation, chanting, call-and-response, hand clapping, and foot stomping was to have a profound influence on the development of American popular music, leading eventually to the development of such uniquely American musical styles as blues, ragtime, and jazz.

Since most slaves were illiterate and knew music only intuitively, many of their songs were lost. Others were only written down long after the war and were often heavily revised to appeal to the tastes of white audiences. A few are still extant. One, called simply, "Civil War Chant," lists all the materials that Lincoln possessed to whip the Confederacy, including clothes, powder, shot, and lead. Another popular slave song was "Old Jawbone," a ditty about eating and talking—and virtually anything else one wanted to do—that went on for as many stanzas as the singer had breath, always punctuated with the chorus: "Jawbone walk and jawbone talk / and Jawbone eat with knife and fork." White patrols who roamed the plantations and villages looking for absent or runaway slaves were the subject of much derisive humor, especially in songs like "Run, Nigger, Run," which outlined ways of escaping and the terrible punishment if caught (Browne & Kreiser 2003, 119–33).

LEISURE ACTIVITIES: VACATION HOTELS

The vacation hotel rose to prominence during the nineteenth century. Throughout the South it was the habit of the low-country plantation families to remove themselves inland to a seasonal cottage, a resort, or a city with a finer climate than that of the miasmic swamps of the tidewater or the streets of many cities in summer. It has been estimated that the gentry of South Carolina alone spent more than a half million dollars a year outside the state on such trips. Moreover, upper-class families throughout the nation frequently tried to absent themselves from the cities during the fever seasons that came with the intolerably hot and humid weather of summer.

These excursions were more than just leisurely flights of fancy. Cities were often plagued by diseases of epidemic proportions during the summer months. Philadelphia, for example, had experienced almost continuous outbreaks of yellow fever each summer during the decade of the 1790s, and New Orleans was often visited by nearly simultaneous plagues of cholera and yellow fever. In 1832 and 1853, for example, large fractions of the city's population died as the yellow fever raged for six weeks to be followed by an almost month-long epidemic of cholera. One observer noted that the dead were taken away in wagons and carts like cordwood. Getting away often meant getting away from illness or even death.

Cape May in New Jersey became the summer destination for a wide variety of upper- and middle-class families from both the North and the South because of its central location on the Atlantic coast at the entrance to Delaware Bay. Families from New York, Philadelphia, Washington, Baltimore, Wilmington, and Norfolk often made the Jersey shore their summer destination. John Hayward, contemporary author and gazetteer, wrote that Cape May, "situated at the mouth of Delaware Bay...[had] become an attractive watering-place, much frequented by the citizens of Philadelphia and other [cities]. During the summer season, a steamboat runs from the city to the cape, and affords a pleasant trip. The beach is unsurpassed as a bathing place" (*Gazetteer of the United States*, 1853, 667).

Abraham Lincoln vacationed in Cape May at the seaside Congress Hotel, which exhibited all the services of a world-class residence during the summer months. The Congress Hotel was a massive structure for a seaside building with its high exterior porticos and towering exterior pillars. The interior ceilings of the ground floor were high, the marble floors were pleasantly cool, and the double-hung windows were large and numerous. The interior appointments were appropriately ornate for a seaside establishment, and the layout of the building allowed for cross ventilation from almost every direction. The majority of the rooms had ocean views, and the seaside boardwalk was only a few yards from the front entrance. It was remarkable that a seasonal clientele could support such an enterprise, but they paid willingly because the sea breezes and salt air were thought to be therapeutic as well as invigorating.

While Southerners abandoned their own beaches as pestilential and unhealthy in summer, New England beaches—particularly those within easy access of large Northeastern cities—were considered a "delightful retreat in the summer months, for those who wish to enjoy the luxuries of sea air, bathing, fishing, fowling, etc." The "constant sea breeze and convenient sea bathing" were considered to "have a fine effect in restoring the exhausted energies of the human system." The coasts of Connecticut and the rocky islands and points of Maine were particularly popular; and the shoreline and island of Rhode Island's Narragansett Bay drew the wealthy to build palatial summer residences there. The island of Newport in the center of the bay became a Mecca for the wealthy after the Civil War (Haywood 1853, 655).

Good accommodations, hotels, and boarding houses of the first order could be found at most seaside resorts around New York City, and some places provided special services for invalids and the elderly. Rye Beach, Glen Island, Locust Grove, and Flushing Bay on Long Island Sound and Rockaway Beach and Coney Island on the Atlantic were all popular destinations for New York residents. Most could be reached by railroad or steamboat for a day trip or weekend outing.

Coney Island, "much resorted to by visitors for the sea air and bathing," was considered a convenient destination for New Yorkers even though they had to pay a toll to cross the bridge over the narrow channel that separated it from the mainland (Haywood 1853, 184). Rockaway Beach was 20 miles from the city, but it could be easily approached by railroad or by coach. The Marine Pavilion at Rockaway was "a splendid establishment erected in 1834 upon the beach," while a number of boarding houses offered "invigorating ocean breezes with less cost and display than at the hotels" (Haywood 1853, 667).

Locust Grove, an outdoor recreational facility in Nassau County, Long Island, New York, was the destination for the unfortunate excursion steamboat *General Slocum* on June 15, 1905. The boat was filled with 1,300 mostly German-American residents from a lower east side neighborhood in Manhattan known as Little Germany (Kleindeutschland). The neighborhood lived up to its name with German language clubs, theaters, bookshops, restaurants, and beer gardens. St. Mark's Lutheran Church commonly hired the steamboat to take groups for a day of picnicking, food, games, and swimming at Locust Grove. However, on this day a fire broke out aboard while the boat was still in the East River and more than 1,000 passengers died, mostly from drowning. The fire on the *General Slocum* was the most deadly peacetime maritime disaster in American history. The tight-knit community suffered greatly because almost everyone in the neighborhood knew, or was related to, one or more of the victims (Volo and Volo 2007, 340–41).

OPTICAL NOVELTIES

Americans seem to have enjoyed a variety of optical phenomena in their drawing rooms and parlors. Some photographs were stereotypes, two simultaneously recorded images set side-by-side, giving a three-dimensional view when seen through a viewer designed for the purpose, known as a stereoscope or stereopticon. Such devices go back to 1838, and stereotypes of period places, buildings, monuments, and naval vessels predominate. Very few stereotypes of battle dead survive, and no stereotypes of the poor or of the squalid condition of the nation's slums are known. Photographers understood that to sell their pictures they would have to appeal to well-heeled customers who did not wish to be reminded of the nation's failures.

Propelled by a fascination with photography, optical novelties were very much in vogue. The magic lantern had been around for over 200 years, used by showmen and hucksters to beguile audiences with mystical images. It consisted of a metal box into which an oil lamp was placed; a polished metal reflector, which focused the light on a painted slide; and a hole with a lens through which the light was projected. These lanterns were notably improved as a result of photographic discoveries, and their use became widespread. Lecturers used lanterns to enhance their presentations, and they also became very popular as a parlor toy to show comic pictures. A number of hand-colored glass slides of the war have recently been restored.

Another optical curiosity was the zoetrope. This consisted of a revolving drum with equally spaced slits around the sides. The interior of the drum contained a series of sequential pictures. The pictures were taken by a series of still cameras activated by trip wires. Walking men and running horses were prominent subjects of the zoetrope. When the drum was rotated, the pictures gave the impression that they were moving. Because many people could view it at one time, the zoetrope enjoyed popularity as a parlor amusement.

A similar device was the phantascope. This simple contrivance was comprised of a cardboard disc with a series of slits equally spaced around the center and a handle that acted as a pivot around which the phantascope was rotated. The reverse side contained a series of pictures set between the slits. When the operator held the device in front of a mirror and rotated the disc, the pictures appeared to be moving (Volo and Volo 1998, 218–19).

CULTURAL INSTITUTIONS

The decade beginning in 1860 spawned an abundance of cultural institutions in the North and West. War involvement and subsequent poverty retarded a similar movement in the South for almost 20 years. The interest in art, music, literature, and nature that permeated the parlor surged forth, creating museums, symphonies, libraries, and parks. These, in turn, engendered a host of ancillary institutions such as literary societies, study groups, and reading clubs.

These organizations were gender specific. Male organizations attracted businessmen and professionals. In addition to the obvious activities such organizations would conduct, they created a venue that was ripe for the founding of additional social projects. The distaff version of these clubs provided activities for middle- and upper-class women beyond domestic and church endeavors. The clubs furnished an arena for women to pursue their intellectual development. Study clubs met twice monthly for 10 months a year to discuss such topics as literature, history, and art. Meetings commonly were held in members' homes and consisted of conversation, presentation of papers, and subsequent discussions (Volo and Volo 1998, 219).

READING CLUBS

Many civilians, particularly the women who were doomed to sit out the war while their husbands and lovers fought, found reading one of the few sources of entertainment available to them. Like their loved ones in the army camps, many women read in groups and met regularly to do so. Books were frequently read aloud, making it possible to share the books and newspapers that were "all too scarce in the print-starved Confederacy." Even in the North, where books were widely available, oral presentation by an articulate reader often enhanced the literature and allowed the majority of the women to do other chores such as sewing and embroidery. Reading aloud became an activity with many of the characteristics of theater. Books provided women with an almost pure escape from the realities of war, suffering, and death. More important, oral presentation discouraged continual war gossip among the women, and the camaraderie of the group helped to alleviate depression and gloom among those who were without loved ones, displaced from their homes, and anxious about their own futures (Volo and Volo 1998, 219).

LECTURES

To some extent, literary society or study club meetings took the place of the public lectures that had enjoyed tremendous popularity from about 1840 forward. The war had interrupted many lecture series, which were curtailed, and in some cases suspended. Lectures had been particularly popular among ambitious young men, many of whom joined their cause on the battle line. Northerners often demanded that the remaining lecturers make their concern matters related to the conflict. Topics sought by lecture audiences included denunciations of the South, glorification of Union causes, and narrations detailing the reforms that would follow the Northern victory. Popular speakers included Senator Charles Sumner, Major General Cassius Clay, Theodore Tilton, and Wendell Phillips. Lectures featuring scientific and technological topics were also popular (Volo and Volo 1998, 219–20).

DIME MUSEUMS

Dime museums were another venue of entertainment for those with limited funds. The museums normally housed a motley assemblage of human and natural oddities, perhaps a few paintings, some scientific marvels, and a theater. They were also one of the first venues to attempt to attract respectable audiences, specifically, middle-class women. They did this by banning prostitutes, barring liquor and tobacco, and eliminating bawdy acts. Moses Kimball opened one of the first such museums, the Boston Museum in 1841, followed by P. T. Barnum's American Museum in New York in 1848, which burned down in 1865. Like Kimball, Barnum ran mainly reform melodramas like *The Drunkard: Or the Fallen Saved.* Barnum's museum theater was quite large, with seating for 3,000 people. Museum theaters sprang up in cities throughout the nation, and some hired resident acting companies that produced some of the finest actors in the nation.

The typical dime museum show consisted of a parade of scientific oddities like the bearded lady or the dog-faced boy and then an array of fairly standard performers. First came the quick crayon-sketch masters, magicians, illusionists, mind-readers, sword-swallowers, glass-chewers, fire-eaters, and contortionists followed by the comics, Irish tenors, banjo players, acrobats, dancers, and educated animal acts. New York City's Bowery, however, housed the cheaper museums that catered to a male audience seeking titillation, and they booked acts much like the concert saloons (Shrock 2004, 212–13).

GAMES

Games have always been popular in America. One popular game was solitaire (not the card game), played on a circular board containing 33 holes. Marbles or pegs were placed in all but the center hole. A peg was moved forward, backward, or sideways, but not diagonally, over an adjacent peg, which was then removed from the board. The game ended when the remaining pegs could not make a move. The object of the game was to have only a single peg remaining, preferably in the center hole.

Board games were just coming into their own during this time. Most board game publishers were located in the Northeast, particularly in Boston and New York. *The Mansion of Happiness, an Instructive Moral and Entertaining Amusement* is generally acknowledged as the first board game published in the United States. This 1843 game, produced by S. B. Ives, closely resembles the formerly imported *The Game of Goose*, a game that dates back to the eighteenth century, but had a distinctly moral message. The rules stated that whoever possesses piety, honesty, temperance, gratitude, prudence, truth, chastity, sincerity, humility, industry charity, humanity or generosity was entitled to advance toward the *Mansion of Happiness*. Players rolled the dice and advanced along the board, incurring a variety of changes in fortune involving penalties and bonuses. Players landing on squares marked "gratitude" or "honesty" advanced more rapidly toward their goal. The game served as inspiration for a host of imitators including Milton Bradley's *Checkered Game of Life* (1860).

American board makers copied other games as well. "The Game of Pope and Pagan, or the Siege of the Stronghold of Satan by the Christian Army" and "Mohamet and Saladin, or the Battle for Palestine" were both based on the centuries-old game "Fox and Geese." Other published games took the form of card games and included, "Dr. Busby," "Yankee Trader," "Uncle Tom's Cabin," "Heroes," "Master Redbury and His Pupils," and "Trades." The last of these consisted of lithographed cards; some depicted such tradesmen as shoemakers, farriers, and tax gatherers, and others showed the symbols of each trade. The object of the game was to collect tricks, which matched the tradesman and the symbol. It is thought that this game served as the inspiration for the very popular English game "Happy Families."

Other popular games included cribbage, checkers, tangrams, and lotto—a forerunner of bingo—which was played with cards of three horizontal and nine vertical rows. Five numbers from one to ninety appeared on the cards, with the remaining spaces blank. Children's versions of the game were developed to teach spelling, multiplication, botany, and history (Volo and Volo 1998, 220).

CROQUET

Croquet became popular among the British elite by the 1850s. The first record of a croquet court in the United States was at Nahant, Massachusetts, in 1859. The game was unique in that it is probably the first outdoor game played by both men and women in America. In 1864, James Redpath of Boston published *Croquet* by adventure author Captain Mayne Reid. That same year, the popular *Peterson's Magazine* described the game of Troco, or Lawn Billiards. The Park Place Croquet Club of Brooklyn organized with 25 members in 1864. By 1865 several croquet rulebooks were published in the United States. One of them was based on the version of croquet played at the exclusive resort in Newport, Rhode Island, and while admitting that croquet taxed mental capacities less than whist or chess, it touted the game as combining the delights of out-of-doors exercise and social enjoyment, fresh air and friendship—two things, it noted, most effective for promoting happiness. Lightweight backyard croquet kits were mass-produced by American industry, and the game spread into the backyards of the American middle class in the 1860s and 1870s. American artist Winslow Homer painted a series of canvases portraying croquet players in both 1865 and 1869.

—*Dorothy Denneen Volo*

LADIES' CRAFTS

Women engaged in a variety of needlework crafts including tatting, knitting, crocheting, and netting. Ladies' magazines carried a profusion of patterns for trims, fashion accessories, and small household items that could be made using these handicrafts. Patchwork quilts were another popular activity. Women worked on quilts alone for their families and in group quilting bees, as community activities. Prior to the war, groups of Northern women used their quilting talents to raise money for the cause of abolition. They renamed some traditional patchwork patterns to draw attention to the cause. "Job's Tears" became known as "Slave Chain." "Jacob's Ladder" became "Underground Railway." "North Star" was so named after the star that guided runaway slaves to freedom.

Once the war commenced, Northern women mobilized relief efforts and began to produce quilts to be sent to soldiers in need. Quilt making was undertaken by many women who viewed it almost as a patriotic responsibility. Many of the quilts were more utilitarian than those their makers had created in the past, but it is likely that they were made with no less love. To one quilt was pinned this note: "My son is in the army. Whoever is made warm by this quilt, which I have worked on for six days and most of six nights, let him remember his mother's love." Quilts were made approximately seven feet by four feet so as to fit a military cot and bedding pack. U.S. Sanitary Commission (the largest private agency channeling donated supplies to soldiers) records show that an estimated 250,000 quilts were distributed during the war. In Hartford, Connecticut alone, 5,459 quilts were collected during 1864. The U.S. Sanitary Commission also sponsored fairs to raise money for their relief efforts. These fairs became well-attended social events held in decorated halls in larger cities. Women, many of whom had turned away from their prewar fancywork, once again took their needles to create more elaborate, decorative pieces that would bring higher prices at the fairs. The U.S. Sanitary Commission raised $5 million for Northern war relief (Volo and Volo 1998, 221–22).

Confederate women also made quilts for soldiers. The Southern blockade, however, severely limited the availability of the requisite materials. Confederate quilts produced during the war were made from whatever makeshift materials were available, including old sheets stuffed with newspaper. The war also inspired a rash of flag bees where women worked to make flags for the South. A contest was held in 1861 to choose a flag to be used as the Confederate Flag (Volo and Volo 1998, 222).

The lack of available materials also created a revival of knitting among Southern women. As the century progressed knitting had shifted from economic necessary to creative craft. The blockade-created shortages forced many Southern women to turn to knitting to provide their families with necessities such as capes, gloves, socks, stockings, undergarments, and braces (suspenders). Even this, however, had its challenges as the necessary yarn and threads were also in short supply, leaving many women to manufacture their own. The homemade materials were often coarse and uneven. To hide these imperfections, women would add crocheted decorations to the knitted items to camouflage blemishes that would be obvious in plain work. Knitting and crochet can be done in limited light and were activities that women undertook after it was too dark to sew or spin. The women even carried their knitting with them when they visited to optimize the production of items for their families and for the soldiers. Once the war was over, knitting returned to its prewar pastime status.

—Dorothy Denneen Volo

THEATER

In the sociable and pleasure-seeking decades of the antebellum period, theater experienced a metamorphosis from a crude form of entertainment for the common folk to a spectacle at which the upper classes might show themselves. Prior to the Revolution, Anglo-Americans considered themselves more English than American, and colonial New Englanders, mirroring their Puritan heritage, generally scorned theatrical productions. Plays and theatricals of any nature were totally banned in New England and in many Middle colonies as well as in the entire British Isles during the Puritan-dominated Republican Period of English History (c. 1642–1660). As late as 1698, Jeremy Collier, a pastor and author (A Short View of the Immorality of the English Stage) decried the lewdness of theatricals and stage actors, and exposed the abuse hurled from the stage upon the clergy, government, and monarchy in the form of ridicule, satire, and caricature. Playwrights were persecuted, and actors and actresses were fined. In Boston, theaters were formally prohibited by law in 1750, and the prohibition was strictly enforced under the American Republic up to 1792 and not struck from the state statues until 1796.

In the American South, theater enjoyed a continued and uninterrupted prestige among the planter aristocracy similar to that bestowed upon it by their seventeenth-century Royalist counterparts. Theater had been popular during both the Elizabethan and Restoration periods that flanked the rise of Puritanism. During the early eighteenth century, performances became more characteristic of modern theater. Women appeared on stage, strict decorum on stage was abandoned, moral outcomes at the end of plays were no longer a forgone conclusion, and a new style of comedy was improvised that was generally considered superior to the bathroom humor and sexual innuendo of earlier periods.

As Southern cities grew, Alexandria, Charleston, Savannah, New Orleans, Mobile, and Richmond each established fine theaters, but the playhouses themselves were rudimentary, seating no more than a few hundred patrons. These were often subscribers to the theater rather than patrons buying individual seats at a box office. Due largely to the extremes of American weather, the theater season was modified from the English standard of summer and winter into spring and fall seasons. There were three distinct theater circuits followed by the repertoire companies. Ultimately New York and Boston, having overcome their outdated inhibitions, came to accept theater forming the principal northern circuit; Philadelphia, Baltimore, and Annapolis formed the center; and Charleston and New Orleans made up the southern circuit. The central circuit was the favorite of theater managers and foreign companies visiting from Britain.

By the 1850s most major cities had theaters and opera houses were just coming into vogue. Some of the largest establishments were in New York: the Bowery Theater (2,500 seats), Christy and Woods' Theater (2,000 seats), the Broadway Theater (2,000 seats), Niblo's Garden Theater (1,800 seats), Burton's Theater (1,700 seats), and the Academy of Music (1,500 seats) among the largest. At the same time, Chicago had at least three theaters, the newest, McVicker's, costing $85,000 to build.

Although American repertoire companies relied largely on English plays and classics like Shakespeare and Marlowe to firm up their offerings, by the outbreak of the Civil War at least 700 uniquely American plays had been written and produced. Many others were performed, but they may have escaped the keen research of historians simply because they were never formally published. The lack of enforceable copyright protection caused many authors to limit copies of their work to the needs of the cast.

Many newly written plays were available, and authors could expect a one-time payment of approximately $500 for a new work. Many writers adapted novels, poems, and classical works for the stage. These brought as little as $100. Several of James Fenimore Cooper's works were adapted for the stage, and Harriet Beecher Stowe's *Uncle Tom's Cabin* saw a number of adaptations—one produced by showman P. T. Barnum. Many distinctive American characters were introduced to the stage in this period such as the rural Yankee farmer, the noble savage, or the tough-fisted Bowery B'hoy.

The critics were not always impressed by the quality of this work. They found many of the plays vulgar, coarse, and in bad taste; and many of the performances of standard repertoire works were thought routine, tedious, or slipshod. The audiences—especially those composed in large part of middle- and lower-class patrons—were generally unrestrained, and they let their feelings about the quality of the show be known during the performance. This included calling out, throwing foodstuffs and other items at the actors, and mounting the stage itself to confront the actors directly. Near riots in the theaters were not uncommon (Volo and Volo 2004, 283–84, 287–88, 292–93).

HOLIDAYS AND CELEBRATIONS

Independence Day

Independence from Great Britain was the pivotal event in the brief catalog of United States history prior to the Civil War, and it was widely celebrated in all the states and territories of the nation. The processions of public dignitaries, the patriotic speeches, and the formal dinners that brought together entire communities on the Fourth of July in the first half of the nineteenth century quickly gave way to more lighthearted celebrations in the years leading up to the Civil War. This was especially true in the South where parallels were continually being drawn between the Revolution and the present circumstances of the Southern states with respect to the federal government. While small, rural towns continued traditional events like games, picnics, illuminations, and fireworks to mark the day, in larger cities lively parades were held and people enjoyed boating regattas, band concerts, and steamboat excursions.

Fire companies, tradesmen's guilds, and civic groups, most notably temperance organizations, joined the regular army, state militia, and volunteer units as they marched down city boulevards. Larger parades often included horse-drawn floats with patriotic themes. By 1860 the veterans of the War of 1812 and the Mexican War (1846) had replaced all of those from the Revolutionary War, but the forefathers were still honored by units of men costumed in replica Continental Army uniforms. Many of these garments have been wrongly identified as original to the Revolutionary period by well-meaning, but woefully inaccurate docents and antiquarians.

Parades in cities with large immigrant populations—like New York or Boston with their large Irish populations—included ethnic contingents from groups such as the Shamrock Benevolent Society, the Hibernian Universal Benevolent Society, and the Hibernian Benevolent Burial Society. On Independence Day, 1860, New Yorkers could view a military parade composed of 7,000 men, a regatta in the waters off Battery Park at the tip of Manhattan Island, and fireworks displays at 11 different sites around the city. They could also take one of the many steamboat trips to places outside the city (Appelbaum 1989, 79).

July 4, 1861, was the first Independence Day following secession. The first major battle of the Civil War with its significant and alarming numbers of killed and wounded—Bull Run, or First Manassas—would not be fought for almost three weeks (July 21, 1861). Southerners were divided on how Independence Day should be observed. Some believed withdrawal from the Union was no different than what the Founding Fathers had done in 1776 and celebrated the day as always with the exception that a cannon gave an 11-gun salute to represent the Confederate states instead of the national 34. Others, like a Wilmington, North Carolina, editor, believed that the day belonged to the history of a nation that no longer existed and should be passed unrecognized.

The states of the Confederacy did not celebrate the holiday for the remainder of the conflict. However, Southern newspapers ran editorials in respect of the first American Revolution and many drew parallels between the revolution of 1776 and that of 1861. In many Confederate cities stores continued to close, and the slaves on many plantations were given a holiday by their masters. Northerners continued to observe the day with military parades, fireworks, and excursions albeit within a somewhat restrained atmosphere brought on by lists of war dead and grim news from the battlefront. Speeches and editorials continued to memorialize the deeds of Washington and his army but included exhortations for increased enlistments (Appelbaum 1989, 91–92).

News from the almost simultaneous victories at Gettysburg and Vicksburg on July 3–4 generally came too late to effect the Fourth of July celebrations in 1863. While the North's Independence Day celebrations during the war became increasingly subdued, especially as the war dragged on, the Fourth of July 1865—the first since Lee's surrender at Appomattox Courthouse—was celebrated more enthusiastically than any holiday in living memory. Although the specter of a presidential assassination the previous April was generally acknowledged in speeches and newspaper editorials, businesses closed early on the third to give folks a head start on festivities for the following day. Parades were short on military units, especially since most of the volunteer units had disbanded, but there were plenty of marching bands, fire and police department contingents, civic groups, and school children. The cornerstone of the Soldier's Monument at Gettysburg was laid, beginning a six-decade-long tradition of dedicating war memorials on the Fourth of July. Supporters of the Confederacy had little to celebrate, but Southern blacks throughout the South rejoiced with public picnics, parades, and dances.

—*Dorothy Denneen Volo*

Thanksgiving

Thanksgiving celebrations were irregularly observed during the early nineteenth century with each state governor setting a date for the holiday to take place. As early as 1827, Sarah Josepha Hale, editor of *Godey's Lady's Book,* advocated a movement to establish Thanksgiving as a national holiday. She believed that Thanksgiving, like Independence Day, should be considered a national festival and observed in all the states and territories. In 1858, she petitioned President James Buchanan to declare it a national holiday. She saw the spiritual dimension of Thanksgiving as a means for preventing the looming Civil War. When her pleas were ignored by the men who ran the nation, she turned to her readers, the women of the country. After hostilities broke out between North and South, she bombarded both national and state officials with requests for the national holiday, hoping that Thanksgiving could bring the nation together once again.

In 1863, Abraham Lincoln proclaimed the last Thursday in November to be Thanksgiving Day to bolster the Unionist spirit. After the war, Congress established Thanksgiving as a national holiday. Widespread national observance, however, caught on only gradually as many Southerners viewed the new holiday as an attempt to impose Northern customs—especially those of New England—on the rest of the nation.

Thanksgiving's emphasis on home and family embodied two of the most popular social institutions of the time. Hale wrote that Thanksgiving was the exponent of family happiness and household piety, which women should always work to cultivate in their hearts and in their homes. By the last quarter of the nineteenth century women had come to embrace the holiday. Currier and Ives, the preeminent printmakers of the period, captured the essence of the holiday in sentimental tableaux of families in communal celebration and thereby further helped to fix its place in popular culture. For the millions of immigrants this truly American holiday was a way to affirm their new country. For many Americans the religious aspect of the day was observed with a church service in the morning followed by a large meal in the afternoon. The menu usually embraced Victorian interpretations of traditional New England dishes of turkey, cranberries, vegetables, and pumpkin pie. An important part of the holiday for many families was joining together to prepare Thanksgiving food baskets for less fortunate families.

—*Dorothy Denneen Volo*

Christmas

To the Puritans, Christmas was a purely religious event. They saw sin in the feasting and drinking that characterized the celebration of the season in England. From 1659 to 1681, the celebration of Christmas was actually outlawed in Boston. After the Revolution, some attitudes began to change, but it was not until 1856 that Christmas was recognized as a legal holiday in Massachusetts. This austere attitude was not embraced by all the colonies. The Dutch in New York and the Swedes in Delaware kept the Christmas traditions they brought from their homelands. In the South, Christmas was an important part of the social season and was celebrated with balls, hunts, and extended visits. The first three states to make Christmas a legal holiday were in the South: Alabama in 1836 and Louisiana and Arkansas in 1838. By 1865, 28 jurisdictions included Christmas Day as a legal holiday. During the second half of the nineteenth century, however, Americans reinvented Christmas, and changed it from a raucous holiday into a family-centered day.

Santa Claus is generally traced back to the Dutch veneration of St. Nicholas and the custom of Sinter Claas [sic] bringing gifts to children on December 6th, St. Nicholas' name day. While the Dutch may have brought their custom to America, it was contained within the small community and once the English assumed control of New York, little was made of the practice. In Washington Irving's 1809 *Diedrich Knickerbocker's History of New York,* a satire of contemporary life, St. Nicholas played a prominent part as patron saint of the city. In a new edition of the *History of New York,* Irving referred to St. Nicholas as riding over treetops in a wagon, bringing gifts to children. He described how the smoke from St. Nicholas's pipe spread like a cloud over his head and how he placed a finger to the side of his nose prior to making his exit. That same year William B. Gilley published a children's book that showed Santa Claus with his reindeer. The following year, Dr. Clement Clarke Moore, a teacher and scholar, is said to have composed the poem, "A Visit from St, Nicholas" for his children, while traveling to the city to purchase a turkey for Christmas dinner. On Christmas day he gathered his family around and read those now famous lines, "Twas the night before Christmas and all through the house...." A family friend later read the poem and sent it to the *Troy Sentinel,* a paper in upstate New York, which published it on December 23, 1823. It was reprinted numerous times over the years, and in 1844 Moore published it under his own name. By then, virtually every family was familiar with the poem.

Various illustrators created images of Santa Claus, who was commonly portrayed as a gaunt, somber man, but it was political cartoonist, Thomas Nast, who created the prototype of the endearing Santa that is known today. Santa was not the only image for which Nast is famous. He also invented the Tammany Tiger, the Democrat Donkey, and the Republican Elephant. Nast was an illustrator for *Harper's Weekly* covering the Union forces during the Civil War. His first published drawing of Santa Claus appeared in the January 3, 1863, issue of the magazine. Santa, wearing a fur-trimmed, star-spangled shirt and striped pants, was seated on a sleigh distributing packages to the soldiers. As the years passed Nast continued to work on his Santa, providing *Harper's* with a Christmas image, usually of Santa, every year until 1886.

Christmas trees had been a tradition in many German homes even in the eighteenth century. It wasn't until 1848, when a full-page illustration of Queen Victoria, her German husband, Prince Albert, and their children standing around their tree at Windsor Castle appeared in the *Illustrated London News* that the custom gained popularity. The picture epitomized family togetherness and happiness and captured the hearts and imagination of her subjects. The picture was accompanied by a description of the tree. Each of the six tiers of branches was illuminated by a dozen candles. Most of the other decorations were edible and an angel topped the tree. Victoria was very popular with her subjects, and what was done at court immediately became fashionable. Two years later the almost exact illustration appeared in *Godey's Lady's Book*, only the royal family had been transformed into an American one by the removal of Victoria's coronet and Albert's mustache and royal sash. Americans too embraced the image. The first retail tree lot was set up on a sidewalk in New York City in 1851 and sold out quickly. Christmas trees have been sold commercially ever since. Benjamin Harrison was the first president to have a Christmas tree in the White House.

The earliest trees were displayed on tables, but an 1860 issue of *Godey's Lady's Book* published the first account of a tree being placed on the floor. Dressing the tree usually took place on Christmas Eve and was done by parents and older children. Trees were decorated with ornaments made from paper, straw, lace, yarn, seedpods, pinecones, and scraps. Scraps were pieces of paper printed in color lithography. The pictures were pressed into cookies or pasted on cardboard and small boxes. Sometimes scrap faces were placed on cotton batting that had been formed to resemble angels, cherubs, and even Santa. Berries were strung onto cords and festooned around the tree boughs. In addition to ornaments, trees were also decorated with small toys and treats. Cornucopias fashioned from cardboard and paper were filled with candy and nuts. Larger gifts were often secured to the branches by a basketwork of ribbon. On Christmas morning, the children waited outside the room where the tree was displayed while parents lit the candles that were used to illuminate the tree. Candles were lit on Christmas morning and possibly again for special parties, but the threat of fire was great, and a bucket holding a wet sponge on a long stick was always nearby to extinguish any fire.

Children were encouraged to participate in making decorations for the tree, and ladies magazines provided instructions for them by the scores. Paper was used to make chains, flowers, and fans. Tinsel-wrapped wire was twisted into various shapes and placed around cardboard decorated with scrap. Prunes and nuts were wired into human forms, and eggs shells were used to make nests and other egg fancies.

—*Dorothy Denneen Volo*

Maple Sugaring

Maple sugaring-off parties were described by one period writer as one of the most pleasant of rural gatherings. The traditional party, usually in late February or early March, which brought together townspeople and farmers, men and women, young and old, celebrated the end of winter and welcomed spring. Sap was gathered from the sugar maple trees in sap buckets and brought to the sugarhouse, a rough, often temporary, structure built near a barn. There, the sap was boiled over an open fire all day and all night until it thickened into syrup, which was tested by dropping some hot syrup onto the cold snow. The syrup congealed into a taffy-like substance, called sugar-on-snow, which tradition dictated had to be eaten with plain cake doughnuts and pickles. When all the work was done, the effort was celebrated with an evening of bonfires, music, pancakes, and baked ham.

—*Dorothy Denneen Volo*

Emancipation Day

Emancipation Day was celebrated by freedmen in Southern states to commemorate their emancipation from slavery. The news and actual emancipation usually came with the arrival of the Union army in most states, so the dates of celebration varied from state to state. Sometimes the celebration was called Juneteenth, a corruption of "June" and "nineteenth," the day of the observance commemorating the announcement of the abolition of slavery in Texas. On June 19, 1865, Union General Gordon Granger and 2,000 federal troops arrived on Galveston Island to take possession of the state and enforce the emancipation of its slaves. Former slaves in Galveston rejoiced in the streets with jubilant celebrations. Juneteenth celebrations began in Texas the following year. They were local affairs with speeches, camaraderie, and food. Other Juneteenth events included a parade, music, and dancing or even contests of physical strength and intellect. Juneteenth was observed mainly in eastern Texas, Alabama, and Mississippi. Other locales celebrated the day as Emancipation Day.

—*Dorothy Denneen Volo*

FOR MORE INFORMATION

Appelbaum, Diana Karter. *Thanksgiving: An American Holiday, An American History*. New York: Facts on File, 1984.

———. *The Glorious Fourth: An American Holiday, An American History*. New York: Facts on File, 1989.

Bellinger, Martha Fletcher. *A Short History of the Theater*. New York: Henry Holt, 1927.

Bishop, Morris. "The Lower Depths of High Education." *American Heritage* XXII, no. 1 (December 1969).

Browne, Ray B., and Lawrence A. Kreiser Jr. *The Civil War and Reconstruction*. Westport, CT: Greenwood Press, 2003.

Cameron, Kenneth W. *The Massachusetts Lyceum During the American Renaissance*. Hartford, CT: Transcendental Books, 1969.

Carnegie Library of Pittsburgh. *Annotated Catalogue of Books Used in Home Libraries and Reading Clubs*. Pittsburgh, PA: Carnegie Library, 1905.

Castello, Julio Martinez. *Theory of Fencing: Foil, Sabre, Dueling Sword*. New York: St. Marks Printing Corporation, 1931.

Chudacoff, Howard P. *The Age of the Bachelor: Creating an American Subculture*. Princeton, NJ: Princeton University Press, 1999.

Clay, C. F., trans. *Secrets of the Sword by the Baron de Bazancourt*. Bangor, ME: Laureate Press, 1998.

Cohen, Hennig, and Tristram Potter Coffin, eds. *The Folklore of American Holidays*. Detroit, MI: Gale Research Company, 1987.

Crawford, Richard. *America's Musical Life: A History*. New York: W. W. Norton & Company, 2001.

Dahlhaus, Carl. *Nineteenth-Century Music*. Berkeley: University of California Press, 1989.

Elliott, Jock. *Inventing Christmas: How Our Holiday Came to Be*. New York: Abrams, 2002.

Finson, Jon. *Voices That Are Gone: Themes in Nineteenth-Century American Popular Song*. New York: Oxford University Press, 1994.

Glazer, Tom. *A Treasury of Civil War Songs*. Milwaukee, WI: Hal Leonard Corporation, 1996.

Grover, Kathlyn, ed. *Hard at Play: Leisure in America, 1840–1940*. Amherst: University of Massachusetts Press, 1992.

Hayward, John. *Gazetteer of the United States*. Hartford, CT: Case, Tiffant and Co., 1853.

Hewitt, Barnard. *Theater, USA: 1668 to 1957*. New York: McGraw-Hill Book Company, 1959.

Hutton, Alfred. *The Sword through the Centuries*. Mineola, NY: Dover Publications, 2002.

Jackson, Richard. *Popular Songs of Nineteenth-Century America: Complete Original Sheet Music for 64 Songs*. New York: Dover Press, 1976.

Jenkins, Susan, and Linda Seward. *The American Quilt Story: The How-to and Heritage of a Craft Tradition*. Emmaus, PA: Rodale Press, 1991.

Kaser, David. *Books and Libraries in Camp and Battle: The Civil War Experience*. Westport, CT: Greenwood Press, 1984.

Kelley, R. Gordon, ed. *Children's Periodicals of the United States*. Westport, CT: Greenwood Press, 1984.

Kingman, Daniel. *American Music: A Panorama*. New York: Schirmer Books, 1990.

Kiracofe, Roderick. *The American Quilt*. New York: Clarkson Porter, 1993.

LaRocca, Donald J. *The Academy of the Sword: Illustrated Fencing Books, 1500–1800*. New York: Metropolitan Museum of Art, 1998.

Louisiana State Museum. *Playthings of the Past: 19th and early 20th Century Toys*. New Orleans: Louisiana State Museum, 1969.

McAuley, James. *The New and Improved Broad Sword Exercise, As Recently Taught at the U.S. Military Academy, West Point, N.Y.* Columbia, SC: Printed at the Telescope office, 1838.

McNeil, Keith, and Rusty McNeil, *Civil War Songbook*. Riverside, CA: McNeil Music, Inc., 1999.

Monroe, Lewis B. *Public and Parlor Readings: Prose and Poetry*. Boston: Lee and Shepard, 1871.

Nicholls, David, ed. *The Cambridge History of American Music*. New York: Cambridge University Press, 1998.

Nye, Russell. *The Unembarrassed Muse: The Popular Arts in America*. New York: Dial Press, 1970.

O'Neil, Sunny. *The Gift of Christmas Past, A Return to Victorian Traditions*. Nashville, TN: The American Association for State and Local History, 1981.

Rader, Benjamin. *American Sports: From the Age of the Folk Games to the Age of the Spectators*. Englewood Cliffs, NJ: Prentice-Hall, 1983.

Shrock, Joel. *The Gilded Age*. Westport, CT: Greenwood Press, 2004.

Silber, Irwin. *Songs of the Civil War*. New York: Dover Publications, 1995.

Stirn, Carl P. *Turn-of-the-Century Dolls, Toys, and Games: The Complete Illustrated Carl P. Stirn Catalog from 1893*. New York: Dover Publications, 1990.

Time Life Books. *Time Life Book of Christmas*. New York: Prentice Hall, 1987.

Volo, Dorothy Denneen, and James M. Volo. *The Antebellum Period*. Westport, CT: Greenwood Press, 2004.

———. *Daily Life in Civil War America*. Westport, CT: Greenwood Press, 1998.

———. *Encyclopedia of the Antebellum South.* Westport, CT: Greenwood Press, 2000.

———. *Family Life in Nineteenth-Century America.* Westport, CT: Greenwood Press, 2007.

Wechsberg, Joseph. *The Lost World of the Great Spas.* New York: Harper & Row Publishers, 1979.

Weissman, Judith Reiter, and Wendy Lavitt. *Labors of Love: American Textiles and Needlework, 1650–1930.* New York: Alfred A. Knopf, 1987.

Religious Life

THE TIDE OF RELIGIOUS THOUGHT

The United States has been a predominantly religious country from its inception, and the nineteenth century was one of great religious revivals fueled largely by a Protestant crusade in the East, camp revivals in the settlements and on the frontiers, and a political backlash brought about by an immense influx of Irish Catholics into the cities of America. The religious character of the country was essentially rooted in the Protestantism of England, Scotland, and Wales, but many new sects and denominations had joined the list of traditional Christian religions popular before the American Revolution. The flow of religious thought between Europe and America, and vise versa, cannot be overemphasized.

Europe was swept by great religious wars and moral awakenings during the colonial period that resulted in waves of religious zealots and exiles crossing the Atlantic. Spanish and French Catholics, Protestant Walloons and Huguenots, Dutch Calvinists, English Puritans, Quakers, Scotch-Irish Presbyterians, German Lutherans, Baptists, Anabaptists, Moravians, and others were all moved by much the same religious spirit. Yet religious bigotry influenced many largely well-meaning clergymen—Catholic, Protestant, Pietist, non-conformist, and unconventional—and encouraged intolerance among those who chose to do God's work.

The First Great Awakening, a complex movement among a number of interrelated religious groups, had swept through colonial America in the eighteenth century. Begun in the 1720s by Rev. Theodore J. Frelinghuysen, a Dutch Reformed minister from New Jersey, this movement spread into New England to reach its peak in the 1740s under men like Jonathan Edwards. In the South it continued through the American Revolution in several distinct phases led respectively by Presbyterians, Baptists, and Methodists. The First Great Awakening stressed personal religion and multiplied the number and variety of churches and congregations everywhere. An estimate of the number of religious congregations in the former English colonies at the close of the colonial period gives a total of more than 3,100. While this number was almost equally divided among the three regions of New England, the Middle colonies, and the South, there was an unequal distribution among the different denominations giving each region a distinct religious character that carried through to the Civil War period and beyond. By the end of the nineteenth century, the number of congregations had multiplied 20-fold.

The Protestantism of the framers of the Constitution from New England had been essentially related to the Puritanism of the Congregational churches, while those from the South was generally Church of England (Anglican in the United Kingdom, Episcopalian in the United States). Quakers, considered dissenters and nonconformists since colonial times, congregated mainly in Pennsylvania, while pockets of English Catholicism could still be found in Maryland at the turn of the century. The country was also characterized by a wide variety of newcomers: Germans, Scandinavians, Swiss, Welsh, French Huguenots, and Jews. The Scotch-Irish immigrants added an element of Presbyterianism to American religious life, and later the Baptist church became popular among the Welsh and Germans. The Appalachian frontier and the Old Northwest Territory digested a wide variety of these immigrants, but most of them were within the same religious compass of essential Protestantism. Both the Presbyterians and the Baptists played a major role on the frontier. Lutherans—largely Germans and Scandinavians—were the first to introduce a new element to the religious mix. Nonetheless, their churches were essentially Protestant, and they had been assimilated with little fuss into the American social fabric.

Yet not all of the religions in America were considered legitimate by the society in general because many minor sects espoused doctrines that were on the fringe of traditional Christian belief. Although it was not the only new religion to originate in America, the Church of Jesus Christ of the Latter Day Saints, known as Mormons, was viewed with particular animosity and actively persecuted from its establishment in 1823 until recent times when adherents to its tenets, running for national political office, still need to address a lingering cloud of suspicion.

Some Christian evangelical revivals, particularly those headed by powerful preachers such as Rev. Charles G. Finney of western New York and Rev. Lyman Beecher of Boston, provoked less thoughtful followers of mainstream American Protestantism to take up the rhetoric of the anti-immigrant and anti-Catholic Nativists, who created and published salacious rumors and anecdotes that distorted the beliefs and activities of many of these minority religions.

A number of these minority religions can be considered Pietist in nature because they generally abandoned an ordained ministry, a strict church structure, and a national hierarchy. Shakers, Quakers, Moravians, Mennonites, Anabaptists, and other Pietist sects generally placed their emphasis upon inner spiritual life and a personal path to salvation, while denying the need for a more formal ecclesiastical organization.

Although Quakers and Moravians had been major components of American religious life since colonial times, they were essentially Pietist religions whose pacifist adherents were viewed with suspicion by many Americans during the Civil War. Moreover, the English-speaking Quakers and Shakers were largely distinct from the Mennonites, Amish Anabaptists, and Moravians that had their origins in Germany, Switzerland, and other parts of central Europe. The Germans penetrated into the far northwestern portion of New Jersey and west into the region of Reading, Lancaster, and Harrisburg in Pennsylvania. They tended to separate themselves from other groups, a process aided by their persistent use of the German language.

The abolitionist movement seriously affected the structure of many denominations. In the 1840s and 1850s, radical abolitionists disrupted religious services with uninvited lectures on antislavery at churches not dedicated to the immediate abolition, even if the doctrine of the church accepted slavery as an evil and believed in gradual emancipation or colonization of former slaves in Africa. Abolition leaders like Stephen S. Foster, Parker Pillsbury, and William Lloyd Garrison rose to denounce the clerical establishments as "thieves, blind guides, and reprobates" (Stewart 1976, 114). Others like Gerrit Smith and Lewis Tappan—the financier of immediate emancipation in New York State—withdrew from their own denominations and formed free churches of their own in which slave owning was considered a sin and any attitude other than that of immediatism was viewed with suspicion. Presbyterians, Baptists, and Congregationalists all experienced serious defections among their church membership in the East and Northeast, and Methodists experienced a formal division of their denomination into pro- and antislavery groups.

Repelled by the clergy's stubborn resistance to immediate abolition and the seeming hollowness of conventional worship, many abolitionists abandoned the formal organization of churches and sought out a personal religion. Theodore D. Weld, Angelina Grimké Weld, Lydia Marie Child, Elizur Wright, and other anticlerical abolitionists moved toward a diffuse and generally unorganized religion of humanity that discarded the formal precepts of Biblical doctrine for a purely humanitarian creed built on immediate emancipation. Viewed through this lens of Christian utopianism, all human agencies seemed retrograde and all institutional churches seemed weak, no matter how determined they were to see the ultimate end of slavery.

—James M. Volo

MORALITY

Sincere religious reflection was a hallmark of soldiers in both armies in the Civil War, and it was generally an authentic religiosity rather than a battlefield conversion to spirituality. This is not surprising as these characteristics were found in the general population. Americans, despite their politics, were a strongly religious and highly moral people. As the conflict wore on, the soldiers were exposed to a number of evils characteristic of camp life: gambling, swearing, fighting among themselves, and prostitution. A number of religious organizations were established to help maintain the high moral fiber of the troops. Bible societies, moral reform organizations, and social uplift associations of all kinds sent missionaries and representatives into the field in an attempt to improve the physical and moral environment of the troops.

Chief among these were the U.S. Sanitary Commission and the U.S. Christian Commission with offices located in Washington, D.C. There is some dispute over the exact role they played in the war, but the latter and its western affiliate were later in forming than the Sanitary Commission. The Christian Commission sprang from an association of the Young Men's Christian Association (YMCA), the American Bible Society, and the American Tract Society, and it was somewhat more evangelical in its agenda than the Sanitary Commission, which looked more to the physical environment of camp living. Most historians agree that both commissions provided quality reading materials for the troops and tried to establish a moral standard for the soldiers of the federal army. However, their agendas were essentially religious and evangelical in nature. Although there was some friction between the various organizing groups over the sectarian content of their message, no less than $500 million was raised for religious and philanthropic purposes during the war.

Most regiments North and South had resident chaplains to look to the spiritual needs of the soldiers, and many of the commanding officers were steadfastly religious and not hesitant in demanding a certain adherence to moral standards among their men. Catholic priests attended to the needs of some of the all-Irish regiments. Since whole regiments were often raised from a single community, the clergy were often well known among the men they served. One Confederate general, Leonidas Polk, was a consecrated bishop of the Episcopal Church, but many other officers were full- or part-time ministers in civilian life.

Although religious tracts and Bibles were circulated throughout the army camps and Sabbath services were held with regularity, Captain J. W. De Forest observed that "the men are not as good as they were once; they drink harder and swear more and gamble deeper." The same officer noted that "the swearing mania was irrepressible." Nonetheless, De Forest tolerated the use of inappropriate language in the heat of battle. "In the excitement of the charge it seemed as if every extremity of language was excusable, providing it would help toward victory" (Croushore 1949, 65, 80).

The most egregious violation of morality that went uncurbed was the flock of prostitutes who followed the armies wherever they went. It simply did not seem possible to keep the men away from these women even though the provost (military police) were given orders to discourage their trade in amorous economics. At one point in the war, the problem was so uncontrolled in the federal camps of the Army of the Potomac that the prostitutes were known as "General Hooker's girls," after the army commander Joseph Hooker. The name seems to have stuck with the term hooker becoming a synonym for prostitute.

Notwithstanding these limitations, public demonstrations of piety and religious worship, organized by ministers, priests, lay preachers, officers, and the men themselves, were common events in camp and were well attended by the troops. General Thomas "Stonewall" Jackson's fanatical Presbyterian evangelical devotion came to be almost stereotypical of Confederate religious sentiment, although there is little evidence to indicate that the majority of Confederate soldiers were any more dedicated to religion or immune from temptation than their counterparts in the federal forces. Stories of a higher moral tone among Confederate troops are largely a postwar product of the writers of *Lost Cause* literature. Nonetheless, when two dozen general officers of the Confederate army were seen at the same church service in 1864, it was suggested by a female worshipper frustrated by the Southern army's recent lack of success on the battlefield that "less piety and more drilling of commands would suit the times better" (Woodward 1981, 585).

—*James M. Volo*

RELIGION

The Religious Compass

To better understand the role of religion in nineteenth-century American life, it is important to provide a brief thumbnail sketch and history of the various religion sects prominent during the period especially those on the margins of Protestant orthodoxy. It is also important to discuss the effects of traditional Euro-American religious beliefs on the Africans and African Americans living in a white dominated society.

The dominant Protestant religions—Presbyterian, Congregational, Episcopalian, Baptist, and Methodist—were essentially from within the same religious compass, despite some doctrinal and organizational differences. With historical roots firmly established in the Puritan movement and adherence to the principles of the Church of England, Congregational and Episcopalian churches had initially dominated New England and the South, respectively. There were 668 Congregational denominations in the colonies in 1750, while the Episcopalians came in second with 289. By 1850, however, the largest number of congregations were Lutheran (16,400), closely followed by Methodists (13,200), and Baptists (9,400).

Sectional issues surrounding the Civil War like the continuation of slavery and secession affected each religious group as geography rather than doctrine dictated. The Presbyterians, Baptists, and Methodists each broke apart into pro-Northern and pro-Southern branches before the war, as issues of slavery and ways to read the Bible divided the denominations.

Religious diversity characterized America. A look at some of the variety of religious expressions and experiences suggests the range and diversity of religions interest.

Religious Denominations in America, 1650–1850

Affiliation	1650	1750	1820	1850
Congregational	62	668	1,096	1,706
Episcopal	31	289	600	1,459
Quaker	1	250	350	726
Presbyterian	6	233	1,411	4,824
Lutheran	4	138	800	16,403
Baptist	2	132	2,885	9,375
Dutch Reformed	0	90	389	2,754
Catholic	6	30	124	1,221
Methodist	0	0	2,700	13,280
Disciples of Christ	0	0	618	1,898
Unitarian/Universalist	0	0	0	891

(Volo and Volo 2007, 129).

Quakers

Quakerism, or the Society of Friends, was begun in seventeenth-century England by George Fox and Margaret Fell. The first adherents to the new sect—many of whom were of Welsh ancestry—were drawn largely from farmers who lived on the fringe of the cultural, economic, and social mainstream. Quakerism was a radical religion that attracted these generally independent people by preaching the virtues of the family as the basic disciplining and spiritualizing authority in society as opposed to that of magistrates and church prelates. Thanks, in part, to their devotion to the decentralization of authority, many Quakers devoted themselves to their religious duties by creating nearly autonomous personal households. Everything in the Quaker household—wives, children, and business—was subjected to a familial order rooted in morality. The burden of producing, sustaining, and incorporating morality, and civic and economic virtues, into the household was taken on by the entire family and supported by the community at large. Outside authorities such as an intolerant established priesthood, an authoritarian upper class, or even a pedantic university system were considered not only unnecessary but even pernicious.

Although sparsely settled throughout much of the country, Quakers maintained a political influence in Pennsylvania that well outweighed their number. Their neat, well-tended farms, and social solidarity were among the characteristics that made the state one of the most prosperous in America. Yet the unique form of the Quaker community and its pacifist sentiments left the Society of Friends distrusted by the wider community in general. In applying their principles Quakers relied heavily upon a religious and spiritual form of human relations. Although Protestant in their origin, they radically reorganized their church from one that required the performance of a series of external disciplines and the reception of a well-prepared sermon, as among the Episcopalians, into one in which the silent meeting and a personal conversion took precedence.

The Quaker community also gave unprecedented moral authority within the household and within the congregation to the women of their sect. They thereby radically changed the structure of the traditional household, especially in the areas of authority over childrearing, courtship, and marriage. Women were encouraged to discuss and legislate on women's matters in specially designed women's meetings set up for the primary purpose of controlling courtship and marriage within the community. This integrated well with wider movement toward advancing women's rights during the nineteenth century. Angelina and Sarah Grimké, for instance, were sisters born to a slave-owning family in South Carolina. Upon their father's death, the young sisters took up the twin crusades of abolition and women's rights. Originally members of the Episcopal Church, they were attracted to the Quaker sect by friends who lived in Philadelphia, but found that they lacked the Quaker self-restraint to curb their unequivocal hatred of slave owners. Sarah and Angelina began their careers by addressing small groups of women on both feminist and antislavery topics, and ultimately entered the reform lecture circuit.

The basic unit of Quaker settlement in America was the family farm of about 250 to 300 acres—an initial size to which much was added with time. The overwhelming majority of Quaker children in America married other Quakers locally and tended to stay within the meeting house discipline. They thereby quickly found themselves related to one another in their local communities, not only by religion, but also by shared genetics. This web of kinship was partly responsible for the strong ties exhibited by a community of people who were otherwise defiantly anti-institutional.

Moravians

The Moravians were among the least fanatical of the sects that came to America. With roots in the teachings of John Hus and John Wycliffe, the Moravians (*Fratres Unitas*) had become an important Protestant group in central Europe at the beginning of the seventeenth century. Although their influences were more important in colonial times than in the antebellum period, their religious beliefs strongly influenced John Wesley, a leader in the evangelical movement and the founder of Methodism. Nonetheless, because Moravians refused to take oaths or to bear arms in times of war, they were viewed with a good deal of suspicion by the majority of other Protestants. Only their very small numbers and general isolation from other communities kept them from being the targets of prejudice and repression.

Shakers

For some historians and social scientists, the Shakers serve as the epitome of the splinter religious sects during the nineteenth century with their material style and style of living being assigned to the classification of furniture, tools, and architecture. Founded in Britain in 1758 by Ann Lee, who styled herself the Mother of the community, Shakerism was a celibate religious movement rooted in Protestantism. The religion is noted for being founded by a woman, and there was a strand of early feminism that punctuated its doctrine and organization. Actually named the United Society of Believers in Christ's Second Coming, the religion took on the name of Shakerism because of the dancing and shaking that characterized some of those who attended its rituals and prayer meetings.

Shakerism was brought to America by Mother Ann Lee in 1774 and was most successful in New England. In the antebellum period it made great gains in membership in Ohio and Kentucky. Like many other groups that followed a social gospel or a utopian Christian doctrine, the Shakers believed in communal living, productive labor, and a closed self-sustaining economic unit. "Without Money, Without Price" was one of their mottos. Shakers came to be known for a distinctive craftsmanship and folk art characterized by its simplicity, and they printed, published, and distributed their own writings in the nineteenth century.

The religious doctrines of the community included a belief in the direct communication of some of its members, known as seekers, with other celestial realms inhabited by Most High God, Holy Mother Wisdom, Lord Jesus Christ, Mother Ann, and a cast of angles, patriarchs, prophets, apostles, and saints drawn from the Bible. Although families with existing children were welcomed as members, Shakers practiced absolute celibacy, and suffered from the need to attract new adherents to their communities as there was no natural increase due to birth. By the 1850s this aspect of the religion caused a good deal of concern as the number of young men entering the fold diminished to the point that many communities were entirely populated by females and had to hire nonadherent male workers to perform heavy tasks such as plowing and woodcutting.

Judaism

Jews made up only a small proportion of the American population before the late nineteenth century. However, Sephardic Jews, those whose ancestry lay in the Iberian Peninsula, had significant communities in New York, Philadelphia, Charleston, and Louisiana. The practice of Judaism in New York was almost as old as the colony itself, and at least one Jewish congregation was active in New Amsterdam under Dutch rule during the seventeenth century. In 1845, an economic depression caused many European Jews, especially those of German descent, to immigrate to America. They brought an early form of Reform Judaism with them. In their synagogues, they innovated the ritual, used German, English, and Hebrew in their services, and allowed men and women to be seated together. Nonetheless, most still observed the traditional laws in their homes, and read and spoke the Torah in Hebrew only. The lack of intermarriage between the German and Russian-speaking newcomers to America and the more established Sephardic Jews tended to keep the communities apart. Apparently, Jews in their insular communities experienced little overt anti-Semitism during the period, and several individuals played important roles in the coming war as commanders and in government.

Catholics

By the 1860s the Roman Catholic Church was possibly the only religion in America not divided over doctrine. The Roman Church was intolerant of criticism, unapologetically authoritarian, resolute, and unalterable in its structure. It was the oldest and best-organized religion in the western world, and it demanded the unquestioned obedience of its members to the will of the Pope. A "Protestant Crusade" to stem the growing influence of the Catholics began in the 1820s and increased in proportion to Catholic immigration, which grew most precipitously in the 1840s and 1850s with the flood of Irish immigration. The nativist movement, truly reactionary and discriminatory in its nature, was rooted in a traditional abhorrence of authoritarian Roman popes, and it focused largely on the mass of Irish Catholic immigrants who were filling the northern cities.

The Catholic archbishop of New York, John Hughes, took an unquestionably militant stand in defense of his church. He rallied the largely Irish Catholic population of the city in defense of Catholic institutions. This response clearly sharpened the dispute and helped to swell the ranks of the Nativist, or Know Nothing political party, which used anti-Catholicism and the evils of popery as foundation stones of their all-American rhetoric.

Fourierists

The followers of social architect Charles Fourier would be relatively unimportant except that they included a group of literary giants from New England known as Transcendentalists, who practiced a form of Christian humanitarianism at Brook Farm in Massachusetts. These literary giants included Ralph Waldo Emerson. Fourier's views were somewhat convoluted and difficult to grasp. The basic tenet of Fourierism was a crusade for social harmony. Fourier believed that the basic force that ruled all the aspects of social order, including passion, was attraction. Social harmony could be attained only by balancing all the possible attractions.

The religious aspects of Fourierism were essentially organized around the shared Protestant beliefs of its adherents, while the social aspects of the movement were dedicated to balancing individualism and ego with group membership and shared responsibility. Communal production was segregated into specific working groups with more than 40 discrete craft specializations that were ultimately assembled into a larger series of tasks. The final products were meant to sustain a small, self-contained community. The New England group at Brook Farm sought to propagate the movement by buying a weekly column in Horace Greeley's *Daily Tribune* and by publishing their own literary work in *The Dial*. Nonetheless, the movement was largely unsuccessful in sustaining itself, falling heavily in debt because of the lack of expertise exhibited by its adherents, who were much better at crafting essays and poems than furniture and textiles.

Mormons

Those who chose to follow the Mormon religion (Church of Jesus Christ of the Latter-day Saints) may have been the persons most vigorously persecuted for religious reasons in the nineteenth century. As possibly the most important fringe religion of the period, Mormonism was the great catch-all of the evangelical movements. Patriarchs, angels, and demons seemed to punctuate the semi-Biblical rituals of Mormon metaphysics. At one time or another, according to its critics, every Protestant heresy in America was championed by one or the other of the spokesmen for the Latter-Day Saints. Yet Mormons were generally courageous, dedicated, and hard working people unfairly targeted by the more established religions. Only by removing themselves to the remote desert southwest during the period of expansion did Mormons escape persecution. There they made the desert bloom through the creative use of irrigation and inventive farming practices. The community of saints was self-disciplined and, of necessity, hostile to outsiders. The Mormon religion is presently the fourth largest discrete religion in the United States.

African American Religion

The Africans, who were first brought to the Americas as slaves, came from diverse cultural and religious backgrounds. Upon arrival at a plantation, they found themselves intermingled with other blacks who held a wide range of beliefs and practiced a multiplicity of religious rites. The desire to hold true to ancestral customs was a strong one, and some slaves would periodically steal away to neighboring farms to join in worship with others from their same ethnic group. This diversity, however, produced an openness that transcended cultural differences with a common mystical relationship to the divine and the supernatural. African religious practices were marked by a communication with the natural world and exponential religion, which opened them to the practice of laying on of hands, spiritual possession, baptism in quaker and emotional expression—all of which would make evangelical Protestantism later appealing. Lacking an understanding of the African cultures and having no desire to cultivate one, slaveholders did their best to strip slaves of their native religious cultures. Effectively, however, these practices were merely driven underground to be practiced in secret.

By the close of the eighteenth century and as a outgrowth of the First Great Awakening, some whites felt it was their duty to bring Christianity to the slaves. Protestantism leveled all men as sinners before God, regardless of wealth or color, and an intense commitment by evangelists and revivalists to black conversion was focused largely on the slave communities. The success of the undertaking was facilitated by a number of factors. Generally, the slave community was open to this religious movement. Second-, third-, and even fourth-generation African Americans had fewer cultural and linguistic barriers to Christian instruction than their forbearers. The emotionalism, congregational response, and plain doctrine of revivalist preaching proved favorable to well disposed blacks, and it resonated somewhat with their religious heritage. Remnants of African dance and song found a home in the spirituals of evangelical Protestantism.

The egalitarian perspective of this religious movement opened the way for black converts to participate actively in churches as preachers and even as founders of their own congregations. Slaves had the freedom to attend church with their owners (although discretely seated in the rear or among the rafters), but in some instances, they were allowed to worship at independent black churches. Even so, the majority of slaves who had the opportunity to become church members in the first decades of the nineteenth century were household servants, artisans, and urban residents rather than field hands.

By the 1830s evangelical churchmen had become increasingly committed to the idea of an aggressive program of developing plantation missions to bring Christianity to rural slaves. Planters were generally amenable to the concept of slave conversion in a theological sense, although two slave conspiracies led by black preachers—Denmark Vesey and Nat Turner—found validation for their cause in Scripture. These events produced huge setbacks in any latitude afforded slaves regarding their traditional religions. Planters were expected to bring the Gospel to the slave quarter by joining missionary societies and supporting local churches with money for the plantation missionaries. Proponents of the cause adopted the techniques of Northern bible and temperance societies to raise Southern consciousness by printing sermons and essays, adopting resolutions, and devoting entire conferences to the topic. However, the distance between plantations made ordinary pastoral care almost impossible.

Southern slave owners began to see that Scripture could be used to sanction a kind of Christian social order based on mutual duty of slave to master and master to slave as found in Ephesians 6:5–9. The ideal of a Christian master-slave relationship fed the Southern myth of the benevolent planter-patriarch that oversaw the simple, helpless black. As the decades advanced, growing uneasiness toward Northern abolitionists created an ambivalence in Southerners regarding the instruction of slaves in Christianity. However, the criticism of Northern churchmen made Southerners more sensitive to their duty, and the supporters of plantation missions continued to remind slaveholders of their religious duties toward their blacks. Plantation mistresses in particular were urged to take an active role in slave instruction by reading sermons to them, including them in family prayers, and conducting Sabbath schools. Some household slaves were led in prayer each morning by the mistress.

By the eve of the Civil War it was not unusual for slaves to outnumber whites at racially mixed churches. This manifestation of the plantation missionaries' success was misleading, however, because it represented only one component of the slaves' religious experience. In the secrecy of their cabins and amid brush or hush arbors, slaves met free from the owner's gaze and practiced a religion that addressed many issues other than a slave's Biblical subservience to his master. Absolute freedom was often the subject of their prayer. Through prayer, song, and feeling the spirit slaves gained renewed strength through hope. These informal prayer meetings were filled with spirituals that perpetuated a continuity with African music and performance. The drums, which had once been a vital part of African spiritual expression, were replaced by rhythmic hand clapping and foot-stomping known as shouting. Rather than truly adopting Christianity, the slaves had adapted it to themselves.

Generally, slaves faced severe punishment if they were found attending nonsanctioned prayer meetings. Gathering in deep woods, gullies, and other secluded places, they created makeshift rooms of quilts and blankets that had been wetted down to inhibit the transmission of voices. A common practice was to place an iron pot or kettle turned upside down in the middle of the floor to catch the sound. The roots or symbolism of this belief have been lost. On occasion, rags would be stuffed into the mouth of an overzealous worshiper. Slave narratives repeatedly speak to the uplifting nature of these meetings.

An underground culture of voodoo, magic, and conjuring were practiced in areas where there were large numbers of slaves from the islands of the Caribbean or where African snake cults—which handled serpents as part of their ritual—had been imported and adapted. It would be a mistake to believe that the majority of slaves followed Voodoo. That was more characteristic of those from Haiti and other West Indian Islands. However, many slaves exhibited a respectful attitude toward occult practices in general. Newly imported slaves from Africa brought with them a periodic infusion of non-Christian religious practices and mystical beliefs that kept the echoes of an older naturalistic religions alive. Nonetheless, the power of the Voodoo priests and other conjurers never reached the level it had enjoyed in the islands or in Africa.

The Quaker religion openly welcomed black and native American worshipers. While the Catholics had a minority black representation in their churches in the

North, they were able to maintain their position in the South only by making seating concessions to the etiquette of white supremacy. Separate black congregations also grew in number among many Protestant sects because the white congregations of their several denominations did not welcome them. A growing army of black ministers was, thereby, able to found parishes among the freemen and slaves of the South. The African Methodist Episcopal (A.M.E.) Churches had some of the most prominent black ministers of the period.

—*James M. Volo*

FOR MORE INFORMATION

Beringer, Richard E. *The Elements of Confederate Defeat: Nationalism, War Aims, and Religion.* Athens: University of Georgia Press, 1988.

Croushore, James H., ed. *A Volunteer's Adventure, by Captain John W. De Forest.* New Haven, CT: Yale University Press, 1949.

Hankins, Barry. *The Second Great Awakening and the Transcendentalists.* Westport, CT: Greenwood Press, 2004.

Stewart, James Brewer. *Holy Warriors, The Abolitionists and American Slavery.* New York: Hill and Wang, 1976.

Sweet, Leonard I. *The Minister's Wife: Her Role in Nineteenth-Century American Evangelism.* Philadelphia, PA: Temple University Press, 1983.

Woodward, C. Vann, ed. *Mary Chesnut's Civil War.* New Haven, CT: Yale University Press, 1981.

3

RECONSTRUCTION

Overview

RADICALS, FREEDMEN, AND KLANSMEN

With the Confederate army defeated, the Southern government in flight or surrendered, and slavery legally abolished, the process called Reconstruction was an attempt to resolve many of the issues remaining after the Civil War that had not been addressed by the effusion of blood. If the Confederate experience did nothing else, it gave white Southerners of all classes a corporate identity for the first time. There had always been some black "Freemen" in the South, but now there was a mass of former slaves who were considered "Freedmen." The difference between the two was not lost on Southern whites or on the blacks themselves.

Running from the surrender of Confederate forces in 1865 to the end of the presidency of Ulysses Grant in 1877, the period of Reconstruction addressed the return to the Union of the secessionist Southern states, the status of the leaders of the Confederacy, and the constitutional rights and legal status of all blacks. Reconstruction came in three consecutive and largely mutually exclusive phases: Presidential Reconstruction and reunification along the lines that Abraham Lincoln had envisioned before his death; radical Reconstruction driven by a Congress dedicated to establishing a pro-union government in the South and bringing basic rights as citizens to all blacks; and redemption Reconstruction, which placed the fate of the former Confederate states and all blacks living in the South in largely white Southern hands.

In March 1865, the U.S. War Department established the Bureau of Refugees, Freedmen and Abandoned Lands, which was normally called just the Freedmen's Bureau. It supervised the relief efforts—shelter, rations, clothing, and medicine—relating to refugees and escaped slaves at the end of the war. During Reconstruction, the Bureau provided practical aid to more than four million newly emancipated blacks. It oversaw

The Freedmen's Bureau was often the only government agency that stood up for the rights of blacks in the former Confederate states. This powerful image from *Harper's Weekly* is symbolic of the isolation experienced by the officers of the agency when involved in disputes between black freedmen and white Southerners. Courtesy Library of Congress.

the building of hospitals, schools, and shelters, and the dispensing of rations, medical care, and justice to millions of black citizens in the face of sometimes cruel oppression and palpable terror perpetrated by their former masters.

Reconstruction had its darker side in the North also. The victory of federal arms and the occupation of the former Confederate states was seen as a golden opportunity to humiliate and eliminate the influence of the Southern aristocracy. Sometimes violent controversy erupted over how to tackle these issues, especially the reluctance of the South to accept defeat on the issue of black emancipation. Many Southerners refused to consider blacks as equal citizens and forced them into leasing their homes and sharecropping their fields at a great financial disadvantage to themselves. Only the great fear that Southern whites had for unrestricted blacks can explain the recklessness with which the South defied the North during Reconstruction. Nonetheless, all 11 former Confederate states had been readmitted to the Union by 1871.

Reconstruction came in three phases that were largely driven by momentous events. Presidential Reconstruction (1863–1866) was envisioned by Lincoln and followed by his successor Andrew Johnson, with the goal of quickly reuniting the country through moderate programs and policies. It was during this phase that the most determined of the Southern states passed their Black Codes in an attempt to retain white supremacy. Radical Reconstruction (1867–1873) was a program favored by certain factions of radical Republicans that gained political power after the elections of 1866. These emphasized the civil and voting rights of blacks, the establishment of Republican governments in the Southern states, and the eradication of the decades-old concept of States' Rights. The final stage of Reconstruction is sometimes called the Redemption (1874–1877). This was characterized by overt racism and the substitution of fear and violence for the rule of law in the form of organizations like the Ku Klux Klan.

Reconstruction spanned the presidencies of Abraham Lincoln, Andrew Johnson, and Ulysses Grant. Long before the end of Grant's second term the course of Reconstruction was presumed at an end. The final stage began with a strong showing by Democrats in the national bi-election of 1874. They won a majority of 70 seats in the House and almost took control of the Senate. Reconstruction ended in 1877 with the inauguration of Rutherford B. Hayes, who declared the policy of Southern reconstruction a failure and returned to a prewar pattern of cooperation between Southern Democrats and conservative Republicans in the Congress and white domination in the South. The new political alliance marked the end of force as an element in postwar politics and a return to the ways of reconciliation and compromise.

The period of Reconstruction was one of the most controversial in U.S. history. During 12 years (1865–1877) changes took place that fundamentally altered American society. It set the stage for many of the controversies that would populate the next century including civil rights, the supremacy of the federal government over the states, the growth of industrialization and urbanism at the expense of agriculture and rural living, and the rejection of caste and race as the basis for social order in favor of money and influence.

It must be remembered that the period of Reconstruction was abnormal, filled with ambiguities and contradictions. A president had been assassinated for the first time, and his successor had been impeached—also for the first time in U.S. history. Moreover, the policy of Reconstruction cannot be understood in simple terms of Constitutional legalities and precedents. The Constitution had not addressed the concept of secession and Civil War. Some historians have written of the period as an era of tragedy and an age of hate, and certainly bigotry, racism, and corruption marked its passing. During this period a coalition of freedmen, Carpetbaggers (Northern politicians), and Scalawags (Southern politicians) controlled most of the Southern states. The sometimes blatantly dishonest practices of these men caused an upsurge of reactionary groups. From 1873–1877, white supremacist Southerners known as Redeemers jockeyed for control of their state governments. They ultimately defeated the Republicans in their states and took control of each under the old political banner of Southern Democrats. The Redeemer movement also engendered the formation of the Ku Klux Klan and the White League.

Yet it should also be remembered that the South received the mildest punishment ever inflicted on the losing side in a civil war in all of recorded history to that time. Within a decade of the first shot fired at Fort Sumter, all of the states in the rebellion had been readmitted to the union with full constitutional rights and privileges. With the exception of Major Henry Wirz, commander of the notorious prison camp at Andersonville, no military or political leader of the Confederacy was executed, and the ex-president of the Southern states, Jefferson Davis, was released within two years of his capture.

—James M. Volo

FOR MORE INFORMATION

Foner, Eric. *Reconstruction: America's Unfinished Revolution, 1863–1877*. New York: Harper Collins Publishers, 2002.

Franklin, John Hope. *Reconstruction after the Civil War*. Chicago, IL: University of Chicago Press, 1961.

Stampp, Kenneth. *The Era of Reconstruction, 1865–1877*. New York: Knopf, 1965.

Sutherland, Daniel E. *The Expansion of Everyday Life, 1860–1876*. Fayetteville: University of Arkansas Press, 2000.

Domestic Life

KINSHIP SYSTEMS: REFUGEES

The hard hand of war drove many Southern families to flee from the federal armies as they occupied increasingly larger portions of the South. An editor in wartime Alabama estimated that 400,000 persons were refugees in the whole of the Confederacy, but modern estimates are about half that number. It is impossible to determine how many families were displaced voluntarily or involuntarily. Two-thirds of the population of Alexandria, Virginia, voluntarily left town out of fear of the uncertainties of military occupation in 1862, whereas in Atlanta in the fall of 1864, U.S. General William Tecumseh Sherman ordered all residents to leave the city or suffer the consequences. Dense crowds of people thronged the streets moving their meager belongings in carriages, carts, wheelbarrows, or piled high on the backs of slaves. Every sort of man, woman, or child made their way to the railway cars, or trudged down the dusty roads away from the advancing federal lines.

It is safe to say, nonetheless, that tens of thousands of Confederate families were displaced during the war. Many left their homes for brief periods of time or simply moved in with relatives in another county or state—others never returned to their original homes. Their general lack of preparation for an extended stay or means to finance one created great burdens on relatives, especially those who had their own financial problems caused by fathers and brothers away at war. A place on the farm or plantation of a friend or relation was best because a few more mouths were more easily tolerated. Yet economic security, once the hallmark of the plantations that stood like agricultural city-states amid their thousands of acres, was no longer a certainty. Cities offered employment, opportunities for socializing, a variety of alternative living arrangements, and the psychological security of being among a white majority rather than being a white minority among so many slaves. Soon even large communities became congested and rents rose to where decent lodgings could not be found.

Although Southerners of all classes became refugees, the quickest to flee tended mostly to be from among the planters and their families—men who feared being arrested because they were local political leaders—and families with property, including slaves, which they feared would be taken by invading Yankees. They crowded into supposedly safe places anywhere from Richmond to East Texas, looking for work and provisions. Middle-class refugees also suffered from their dislocation. Teachers found themselves looking for students, ministers for congregations, and tradesmen for customers with money and the livings that went with them. Unlike the poor, these rarely went hungry or jobless. They had no lack of influential friends and relations to find them something more than the bare necessities of life and an employment of sorts, even if it was not in their normal realm of work.

Small farmers—yeomen, sharecroppers, and tenants—tended to keep to their land until the pressure of an advancing enemy army forced them away. This pressure came in many forms. Both sides resorted to foraging for foodstuffs, and sent out groups of men, usually cavalry, to strip the countryside of provisions—a standard practice of armies since ancient times. There was also the threat of informal foraging by deserters, refugees, and escaped or recently freed slaves. Many farms were visited repeatedly and stripped bare by friend and foe alike.

The farms in middle Tennessee and the Shenandoah Valley had been the prime focus of army foragers time and again. The area around Winchester, Virginia, changing hands between the North and South more than a dozen times, was left sorely pressed and economically destitute by constant foraging. In 1863, the Southern government had begun impressing items of all kinds—horses, wagons, hogs, cattle, grain, potatoes—leaving the farmers only enough for their own subsistence. The incredibly large herds of army horses, requiring unending amounts of fodder, stripped the region of hay and grass and made husbandry over the winter and plowing in the spring barely possible. Even the hogs, which were generally allowed to roam the scrub and woodlots of most farms, seem to have become a favorite target of the foragers.

The economic pressures brought upon a sanctuary community by the influx of so many refugees, often changed attitudes of sympathy or pity into indifference and disgust as food, shelter, and employment became scarce for everyone. Those who had been landowners became tenants for the first time, enduring high rents, imperious landlords, frayed tempers, and a lack of privacy. Sometimes the tension between locals and refugees exploded into violence, especially among teens too young to enter service and men too old for the battlefield. Youngsters got into frequent scraps, older men often resorted to duels.

Local residents often viewed refugees with suspicion—especially rich refugees whose war seemed less demanding to less fortunate families. A contemporary observer, Kate Stone, herself a member of a displaced family from near Vicksburg, shared the contempt that the wealthy refugees often expressed about their new neighbors: "[T]he more we see of the people," she wrote shortly after moving in, "the less we like them, and every refugee we have seen feels the same way." She attributed the attitude of her Texas hosts to "envy, just pure envy. The refugees are a nicer and more refined people than most of those we meet, and they see and resent the difference." At a Texas barbecue, a refugee friend complained about their less-than-perfect surroundings and asked, "Why should we dine with plebeians?" After making an appearance and seeing "the animals feed," in the memorable words of Kate's mother, the Stones returned to their lodgings.

In the final stages of the war, it became obvious to many that the South would succumb to Northern might. Many Southern families sold their clothing, jewelry, silver plate, china, slaves, crops, land, houses, and other possessions. They then made arrangements to convert the Confederate dollars they received into Yankee paper or, preferably, silver and gold coin as quickly as possible to avoid the rampant depreciation. Many chose to move to Canada or Mexico after the war.

In the final year of the war federal troops systematically and vigorously searched even the poverty-stricken homes of Southern sympathizers to remove any provisions that could be of use to the Rebel army. In a conscious attempt to disable the Army of Northern Virginia the effort was carried out with ruthless efficiency. Provisions that could not be carried off were destroyed; livestock were slaughtered; freshwater wells were fouled; 2,000 barns were destroyed; and fields were burned. Although lacking in humanity, as a warlike measure this was very effective. Ultimately the farm family was left without any means of subsistence, and they too were added to the legions of homeless wanderers.

While the Confederacy was generally sympathetic to the plight of refugees, it was overwhelmed by the demands of the war on the battlefield and did little to ameliorate the wants of displaced families. Once the government had failed, there was nothing that the South could do and generally no one to do it. The U.S. Sanitary Commission, which made provisions for the relief of the sick, provided ambulances, and cared for the wounded and the dead during the war, also operated in the South and in the West, overseeing the diet and personal cleanliness of the soldiers in camp, provided housing for white refugee families, and raising money to expand their work. A single Sanitary Commission fundraiser in New York City at war's end raised over $1 million for the effort.

In the aftermath of the surrender at Appomattox, everyday inconveniences plagued the daily life of refugee families. Schooling was particularly bothersome. Many tutors and schoolmasters were with the army, and normal schooling was interrupted with every move the family made. A new community meant a new school, if there was one, and children were subject to taunts and teasing until they found their place in the new community of youngsters. Many children were sent away to schools in areas thought safe from the more gruesome after-effects of the war. Special occasions like birthdays and holidays were difficult when the family was not gathered around its own hearth. It was also difficult to send and receive mail with any confidence that it would be received or forwarded, and news of family members, especially soldiers missing on the battlefield or those in prison camps, was often misrouted or simply lost.

Moreover, the Confederate mails were two to three times more expensive than those in the North, and even soldiers at the front had to pay to have mail brought to them. By 1864 the Confederate postal system had so completely broken down that thousands of personal letters remained undelivered. The inability of the Confederacy to maintain the mails had no little effect on the deterioration of Southern morale.

The tribulations associated with displacement were not isolated to Southern families. Families sympathetic to the Union living in the South, and vice versa, were often forced from their homes by uncompromising neighbors. This was especially true in Tennessee where secessionist sentiment was somewhat split along geographical lines. Because large areas of the border states like Missouri and Kentucky were quickly brought under federal control, actual secession was impractical; nonetheless, when the new Confederate battle flag had been designed, it sported 13 stars, the last 2 representing the fiction that Missouri and Kentucky were willing but unable to join their sisters. The use of 13 stars was thought to reinforce the symbolic connections between the infant Confederacy and the American Revolution. Many people who had tried to maintain a cautious neutrality during the war found themselves caught in undercurrents of history so strong and compelling that they were unable to avoid further conflict without moving.

—James M. Volo

FAMILY LIFE

Household Structure

Generally, in the decade of the 1870s the typical white, native-born woman had seven or eight pregnancies during her childbearing years, and raised four or five children. Where data is available, women seem to have married at a median age of 20 years, and given birth to their first child within one or two years. In the 1870s, the median period of childbearing remained at about 10 years. Foreign-born women continued to have higher fertility rates than native-born women, and second generation foreign-born women were somewhere in between (Wells 1979, 524).

The absolute changes in black birth rates during Reconstruction are hard to determine as it is commonly agreed among researchers that blacks were undercounted in the 1870 and 1880 censuses. Blacks (from data beginning in 1850) sustained decreasing, but still higher, fertility and birth rates (eight or nine pregnancies and seven to eight children) than their white counterparts throughout the remainder of the nineteenth century. The end of slavery shifted the decision-making process concerning additional pregnancies to the black family along with all the economic, social, and legal arrangements under which children were conceived and raised. Yet, the initial response of former slaves to emancipation after 1865 seems to have been a continuation of the old fertility patterns of the plantation. Only with time did black fertility decrease markedly (Engerman 1978, 129–30).

Vital Statistics

Average white life expectancy at birth in 1860 was 44 years, and white infant mortality rates for 1860 at 181 per 1,000 were significantly worse than those in 1900. There were significant improvements when these data are compared to a decade later. Average white life expectancy at birth in 1870 remained low at 45 years, and white infant mortality rates for 1870 improved slightly at 176 per 1,000. There is no reliable data for infant mortality or life expectancy for blacks until the early twentieth century.

—James M. Volo

MEN

Early nineteenth-century social structure was based mostly on wealth and ancestry—an accident of birth, bloodline, and race that often put a man in his place and established his identity as he drew his first breath. Antebellum Northerners openly attacked this stratified order as antiquated and immoral especially in the South where social life was largely based on these principles; but Northerners substituted a new and equally unsound social order of their own upon the community—that of work. "The legitimacy of the North's political culture was based on the dignity it offered the common white laborer, on the sanctified importance of the hard, white working day for the economic and moral advancement of society. The legitimacy of the South's political culture was based on the dignity it offered the common white farmer, on the sanctified importance of black slavery as the guarantor of all that it meant to be white and free" (Berry 2006, 259).

Southern whites, reeling from the defeat of a generations-old cause rooted in the traditional inequality of the races, scrambled to maintain their identity during Reconstruction as the foundation of their social order collapsed under their feet. The members of the planter aristocracy—with its wealth largely dissipated, if not destroyed—fell back upon the laurels it had gained in warfare, retaining their military rank and referring to their peers as "Captain" or "Colonel" in an effort to bolster a fading identity. Yet this was an affectation available to only a few former Confederates. It was equally important for the mass of private soldiers who had fought for the South to emphasize that they remained free and white even after defeat. In no other matter were white men more equal than in their subjugation of other races. Unfortunately, the structure of the reconstructed South allowed most white men to be not only free, but poor. Their place in the structure of society was slowly becoming equivalent to that of freedmen. This aspect of Southern identity may help to explain the attraction poor whites had for race-based supremacy organizations like the Klan during the Reconstruction period where they found a new place and identity.

Amid the increasing urbanization, industrialization, and capitalism of the nineteenth century, it was a man's work, in particular, which gave him his place and identity in the North. A man was seen as a banker, a doctor, a teacher, a tradesman, or farmer before much else was known of his family background, character, or aspirations. His place in society was as firmly set by his vocation as it had been in former times by his bloodline. Profession or vocation, thereby, defined to a large degree one's public identity.

J. Clinton Ransom, writing from the perspective of the 1880s, believed that a man's natural attributes fitted him for his profession and for his place in society. He wrote, "We do not believe that all men, or any considerable number of men, could enter upon...totally different lines of action and succeed in all." A man who followed his vocation for a lifetime "with utter faithfulness" and "mastered the duties around him" could expect no surprises as he arrived at eminence and social respectability. "It is entirely natural that he should be there, and he is as much at home there and as little elated as when he was working patiently at the foot of the stairs. There are heights above him, and he remains humble and simple." A man who lost his place at business or failed in his profession also lost part of his identity (Ransom 1889, 435).

Most people believed that certain personality traits were attached to a man via his vocation and vise versa. A bookish youth might find teaching or law an appropriate profession; a dull child—manual labor or storekeeping; a clever lad—a trade or craft; an ingenious one—a career in engineering; an aggressive boy—a commission in the army or navy. Writing in 1876, Haines and Yaggy warned, "Be what nature intended you for, and you will succeed....The young man who leaves the farm-field for a merchant's desk, thinking to dignify or ennoble his toil, makes a sad mistake.... He barters a natural for an artificial pursuit.... The more artificial a man's pursuit, the more debasing it is, morally and physically.... Thousands who might have been happy at the plow, or opulent behind the counter; thousands dispirited and hopeless,... disgusted with their vocations, [are] getting their living by their weakness instead of by [the] strength of their natural character" (Haines and Yaggy 1876, 131).

It was well for young men to have a defined objective in the choice of their vocations. According to Haines and Yaggy, the decision to follow a particular vocation "once taken is taken forever, and a mistake at this point is a vital mistake from which it is impossible to recover.... To spend years at college, at the work-bench, or in the store, and then find the calling the wrong one, is disheartening to all but men of the toughest fiber." Once in the busy life that surrounded a chosen vocation, a man studied it with zeal and mastered it. Great men were thought to have a mission in this regard, which they followed through peril and difficulty to its full realization. This concept of an internal battle or quest fed upon the perception of the masculine gender role, and many men were thought to have led a life of failure solely due to the lack of a sufficiently noble professional objective (Haines and Yaggy 1876, 131).

A man was supposed to be masculine in his manner, his clothing, his interests, and his sentiments. Such traits were part of his identity, but many men sought to create a look that outwardly reinforced these qualities. Often they attempted to accomplish this by having their hair, beard, or moustache trimmed, set, or curled in the tonsorial parlor in forms that made them almost caricatures of themselves. The better classes never frequented barber shops—commonly reserved for the lower classes—and might threaten their employment if found doing so. In a time before the invention of the disposable safety razor, a daily or every other day professional shave was not uncommon.

Contemporary advisors produced long lists of personal attributes concerning clothing and accoutrements that were thought to be appropriate for those aspiring to rise from the middle classes, and as the century wore on respectable persons increasingly valued those qualities that separated them further from the working classes. Silk caveats and waistcoats, walking sticks, stickpins, gold pocket watches and chains, and top hats were suggested as items that reinforced an upper-class and successful look.

Among those qualities of character most highly valued were gender-neutral ones such as obedience, virtue, thrift, or loyalty. However, some traits were

A period illustration by Currier and Ives of the successful and honored man in the bosom of his family. Courtesy Currier and Ives.

thought to have a specific masculine or feminine quality: patience, kindness, affection, or sentimentality for women; honesty, industrious, courage, and dedication to duty for men. As the business world expanded its sphere of influence, thrift, punctuality, attention to detail, cleverness, and a reserved manner became highly regarded as workplace attributes (Volo and Volo 2007, 51–53).

WOMEN

Women as Housewives

By 1870 in the industrializing North, most production for the marketplace had moved out of the home, dramatically changing cultural understandings of women's roles and home life. Families made few of their own consumables and much production had shifted from artisan craft shops and farms to factories. The middle-class home was no longer understood to be an extension of the commercial and political world. Americans began to think of the home as a sanctuary from those competitive arenas. They idealized the home as a haven from a heartless world and a place where women were to nurture their harried husbands, educate their children, and compensate for a spiritually impoverished world outside of the home. With the rapid growth of a wage-dependent population and a shift toward a more market-oriented economy, Americans understanding of the roles of men and women underwent a dramatic shift.

Most American women were expected to live their lives in separate spheres. Men were expected to enter the competitive, impersonal marketplace and political arena. In this public sphere, Americans believed that a Darwinian logic ensured that only the strong and shrewd prospered. The resulting competition for survival was a positive force leading to human progress. It was the role of women, according to this line of thinking, to compensate and spiritually heal men brutalized by the public sphere. Women were expected to remain in the home, caring for children, cleaning cooking, washing, and overseeing the physical and spiritual health of the family. In this private sphere, an alternative ethic of cooperation and self-sacrifice was supposed to prevail. Through high praise for the angel in the home and condemnation of the so-called unnatural women who entered the public sphere, women were presumed to confine themselves to the household.

Middle- and upper-class women were increasingly valued for their spirituality, their beauty, and their remoteness from the everyday strife of the marketplace and political realm. Americans of this era expected women to be concerned with their children and husbands but not with larger political and economic issues. A typical statement of this ideology of separate spheres appeared in an 1869 article from the women's magazine, *The Household*. Entitled "Women's Relations to the State," the article claimed that women were the divinely commissioned teachers of their race charged with the sacred and crucial task of rearing and educating men who would "become citizens" and determine "the condition of the state." Women were uniquely equipped, moreover, to educate the future citizens of the nation precisely because women were excluded from the "strife" of the noisy world. Should women go about making public speeches, editing newspapers, or holding public office, they would be made unfit for their role as the spiritual leaders of their families.

Women's restricted status was somewhat elevated, however, by new beliefs about childhood, childrearing, and the development of domestic science. Because children were increasingly understood to respond better to loving influence than stern punishment, women raising young children were given greater esteem than childless or older females. The advent of the so-called domestic sciences also served to elevate women's sphere. Starting with the widely read 1869 volume, *The American Woman's Home*, advisors encouraged women to apply scientific methods and the latest technology to improve the health and happiness of their homes. Harriet Beecher Stowe, renowned author of *Uncle Tom's Cabin*, and her sister, Catharine Beecher, famous in her own right as an educator, penned *The American Woman's Home* to "elevate woman's true profession" and to "embody the latest results of science." The sisters began their chapter on "a healthful home" with a short anatomy lesson demonstrating the importance of pure air and a properly ventilated home to the heart and lungs.

The Beecher sisters and other domestic science writers and advisors advanced women's status, not by arguing for an enlarged role in the public spheres of life, but by attempting to professionalize the private spheres. They argued that women's domestic responsibilities were just as important as men's political and economic responsibilities, and that they consequently should have just as much formal preparation for their daunting labors.

The labor of women, whether working class or middle class, was daunting. In an era when public schools were still relatively rare in some sections of the country, women were responsible for educating their children. They also nursed family members through many common, contagious diseases, which often resulted in months of attention to invalids in bed. They cleaned the home without the aid of vacuum cleaners, washed clothes without the aid of motorized washers or dryers, cooked on wood or coal burning stoves that had to be refueled frequently, ironed using irons heated in the fire, sewed much of their family's clothing, and often carried fuel and water into the home.

Upper- and middle-class women may have had servants to help them with the multitude of chores, but such women often commented on the difficulty of managing the help. In addition, working-class women sometimes labored all day in factories or took in piecework, sewing, or laundry to help support their families. It is no wonder then that Lydia Maria Child, talking about the stresses of being a woman, commented in frustration to her brother Convers "that great labors strengthen the intellect of a well-balanced character, but the million Lilliputian cords of housewifery tied down the stoutest Gulliver that ever wrestled in their miserable entanglement."

While many women might have felt similarly overwhelmed by the volume and physical demands of housework, the ideology of separate spheres discouraged them from reconsidering the tasks that ought to comprise their duties. Domestic writers often portrayed housework as an expression of love rather than as labor. It was important that women did not think of themselves as workers because the home would then become an artisan's shop rather than a haven against a hostile, even, corrupt world.

The early nineteenth-century wife did strenuous work and was valued for her labor, but she rarely received any pay. As Americans increasingly entered a wage paying economy, society came to accept that money was a neutral index of economic value. Unpaid housework in the home ceased to be valued as real work. The angel in the home seemingly produced a clean house, a plentiful and tasty meal, and well-educated children through her virtuous nature rather than through strenuous exertion. While working-class women may have engaged in paid labor outside the home, they were still responsible for the women's work inside the home.

There were women who protested the restriction in women's roles. Elizabeth Cady Stanton and Susan B. Anthony continued in as advocates of a woman's right to vote and to participate more fully in public life. Anthony traveled extensively urging women's rights in many school districts and local governments across the country. In the postwar years, Frances Willard and the members of the Woman's Christian Temperance Union—founded in 1873—began to look beyond the issue of alcohol consumption and to frame their arguments in terms of women's maternal role. This gave their arguments a special perspective in politics. They asserted that women needed to be given the right to vote because they had the moral perception to clean up the increasingly corrupt world of male politics. Such arguments were often ridiculed in the popular press, and women could expect little support from the men in their families for their ambitions in the public realm.

In the South, even with the emancipation of slaves, the social system was based on a more rigid class hierarchy, a less fluid labor market, and a far less industrialized economy. A Southern model of family life placed less stress on the private, nuclear family and more on the extended family or clan. Even housing differed significantly in the warmer climate of the South. The kitchens in large homes were commonly detached from the main house to keep the home from becoming overheated in the summer. Consequently, Southern family life reflected different norms from those valued in the North (Husband and O'Loughlin 2004, 99–104).

From women's perspectives the most important invention of the nineteenth century was likely the sewing machine. It transformed both the work women did and that which they no longer had to do. Prior to the invention of the sewing machine, most women made all of their family's clothing by hand.

The first operational sewing machine was patented in 1846, and by 1860 companies such as Singer were selling more than 30,000 units per year. Nonetheless, the machines were expensive and remained out of reach for many. Improvements in manufacturing techniques and the expiration of expensive patents resulted in much more affordable sewing machines by the late 1870s. Most households, even poor ones, owned sewing machines by 1880 in part because they had become available and in part because they could be used to supplement a family's economy. With the invention of the sewing machine, people could sew much more rapidly and the cost of ready-made clothing declined significantly. Most women continued to make women's and babies' clothing in the home, but by the 1880s very affordable men's and boy's clothing could be purchased at department stores and through mail-order catalogs (Husband and O'Loughlin 2004, 106).

The cast-iron stove was widely purchased during the industrial era and made cooking a less arduous and safer task for women. Previously, women had cooked over open hearths, a method that required constant tending to keep it burning steadily and far more trips to the woodpile. It was difficult to control temperature on the open hearth, and the equipment was heavy and cumbersome. The kitchen fireplace was a constant hazard to young children who did not keep their distance and to women whose long skirts dragged close to the ground and where stray embers could drop.

The cast-iron stove with its vent and fuel efficiency reduced the amount of smoke in the home. The interior oven could also be heated to a hotter temperature. Because the fire was enclosed, it posed less of a risk to the family. Ornate stoves also provided a decorative addition to the kitchen, though some domestic advice columnists warned that they were difficult to keep clean (Husband and O'Loughlin 2004, 109).

Following the Civil War commercial cheese factories began to boom, removing a time-consuming task from the housework repertoire. By 1875 there were more than 500 cheese factories in New York State alone. In those days before refrigeration the factory had to be within a half-hour drive of the dairy because the milk had to be transported by wagon. In 1878, a German immigrant named Julius Wettstein started a cheese factory in Monroe, New York where he produced a fine line of German, French, and Swiss types that were traded over the entire length of the Erie Canal. He sold these quality cheeses at a high price, and also taught the cheese-making arts to locals for $3.00 per day. He returned to Germany a rich man after only a few years. Mrs. E. P. Allerton in her essay "Dairy Factory System—A Blessing to the Farmer's Wife" noted that in many farmhouses, the dairy work loomed up every year like a mountain that took all summer to scale. The cheese factory, she explained, had removed that mountain, and for that she exhorted, "Let us be thankful" (Volo and Volo 2007, 237).

Women's Responsibilities: A Typical Week

Most women took great personal pride in their household crafts. At a time when mass production increasingly robbed men of the satisfactions they once had in creating a unique finished product, women still designed elaborate clothing, specialty cakes, and decorations for the home. With the exceptions of domestic servants, women in the home also had more control over their work schedules than men who reported to supervisors. Their work more closely followed the natural rhythms of days and seasons than did factory or office work. Finally, much of that work took place in a social atmosphere. Women might take their sewing over to a neighbor's home for a sewing circle. Some cooked alongside other women in the home. If they hung laundry outside or gardened in a small, urban lot, they found occasions to socialize with their neighbors. Generally, they were surrounded by their young children, which, while it may have complicated their round of tasks, it also enlivened them.

The following schedule illustrates the tasks of women who did not work outside their own homes. For women who labored in the factories, these tasks would fall to another member of the family or would have to be abbreviated to fit into the little time a factory woman would have at home. For those in domestic service, only

Sundays and one evening per week would likely be available for time with their families. Consequently, few married women went into domestic service. Women fortunate enough to have older daughters in the home might share these tasks with them.

Washing a family's clothes and bed linen was a physically onerous task, and most women set aside one day a week just to do the laundry. Because people generally wore fresh, clean clothes on Sunday, Monday was typically the day for washing. Wood or coal had to be gathered for heating water, and in homes without indoor plumbing, water also had to be carried from outdoor wells. One family's laundry, using just one wash, one boiling, and one rinse required about 400 pounds of water, which usually had to be carried from outside in buckets each load weighing as much as 40 or 50 pounds. The bathtub or smaller tub would be set up in the kitchen, though some wealthy homes had a special room set aside for laundry. The laundry would be soaked in separate tubs, depending upon the color of the fabric and the amount of dirt. During the soaking, women used little if any soap. Most soaked clothes overnight; others started the soaking stage early in the morning. While the laundry soaked, a woman would tend to her other daily chores such as childcare, cooking, fueling fires, and the like. At the end of the soaking stage, women would add soap and wash each item by rubbing it across a washboard. After wringing out each item by hand or in a wringer, she would set it aside for the boiling stage. She might rub soap on persistent stains.

During the boiling stage, women would cut up bar soap and dissolve it in boiling water. One domestic advice book recommended adding concentrated ammonia and powdered borax to the boiling water, a mixture that would sting and severely dry women's hands. Women then transferred the heavy, damp cloths to the kettle of boiling water. After a quick boiling, during which they stirred the clothes with a heavy stick, they removed the clothes into a rinse of plain water. Some recommended a second rinse with bluing, a preparation meant to counteract the yellow stains on sweat-stained clothes, and another wringing.

Then the laundry had to be hung, generally, outside, even in winter weather. Pioneer Mary Dodge Woodward had a special room built for hanging laundry in the winter. She advocated that everyone in Dakota have such a place speculating that the cost of such a structure would be well outweighed by less wear and tear on the clothing and less stress on the health of the women who did the laundry. When weather was too inclement, women had to do the laundry indoors. The smell of boiling, soaking soiled clothing would fill the home. On laundry day, women had to stand next to the stove or outdoor fire for most of the day, heaving heavy, damp clothes between basins of water and hoisting them onto laundry lines to dry. It is no wonder that it was commonly referred to as the most dreaded of women's chores.

Laundry was one of the first tasks to be hired out when a family became more prosperous because it was so physically onerous, and it could be easily done outside of the individual house and yard. Even the working class commonly took men's collars and cuffs to individual laundry women or commercial laundries. Wealthier families might either drop off all of their wash or have a laundry woman come weekly to pick it up. For working-class women, laundry service provided a way for them to earn money while staying home. Toward the close of the century, commercial laundries, benefiting from large equipment and economies of scale, drove individual laundry women out of business.

Most clothing and table linens had to be pressed on the day after laundry day. To press clothes, women placed three to six flat irons on a cast-iron stove or on a hot piece of sheet iron set in the hearth. Before each use, each iron had to be wiped with beeswax to keep it from sticking to fabrics and then tested on a piece of scrap material to make sure it would not scorch the clothing. Women dipped cuffs, collars, and shirtfronts in starch. The rest they sprinkled with water. They used towels or put potholders to grasp the heavy iron and used it until it began to cool, when they exchanged the iron for another. It was heavy labor and a dangerous job during which many women were burned.

Bread required a full 24 hours to bake and was, consequently, one of the first prepared foods Americans purchased outside the home. Nonetheless, by 1900, 75 percent of women still baked their own bread because homemade bread was a source of pride for many women. On the day before baking white bread, women mixed up the flour, yeast, sugar, and water, and left the dough to rise. The next day they divided this into loaves, and left it to rise more. They might also chop fruits or mince meats for pies the night before baking. On baking day, they finally baked the white bread as well as brown bread, biscuits, cakes, and pastries for the next few days. Faster acting yeast, developed during the industrial era, ultimately made it possible to abbreviate the process of making white bread. Women generally baked on Saturdays in preparation for the Sabbath and one other day during the week, usually Tuesday or Thursday.

In general, the most time-consuming housework was cooking. In an era before most Americans could afford to purchase canned goods or prepared foods, and at a time when they expected to eat three large meals per day, preparing food consumed hours every day. Breakfast, for example likely consisted of bread, fried or baked potatoes, cooked or raw fruit, and beef, ham, or fish. Many women, however, found this work comparatively enjoyable since a good cook often received much appreciation from her family. Moreover, nutritious, tasty food was considered an expression of a woman's love for her family.

Tending to the fire was a central task for women. Both the cast-iron stove and open hearth had to be carefully fueled and the ashes removed regularly. In the winter, the kitchen might be the only heated room in the house. Consequently, the family gathered in the kitchen to conserve on fuel. Cooking could be a highly social activity for women and one that often involved all of the family's capable females.

Most foods were either grown on the property or bought in the marketplace unprepared. Even urban families commonly kept vegetable gardens to defray costs. Cooks ground their own spices, roasted and ground their own coffee, and sifted flour, which was purchased in an impure form. With refrigeration being relatively rare, urban families brought live chickens home from the market and then killed and plucked the chickens themselves.

The frequency of cleaning chores varied depending on the chore. Daily tasks included sweeping the kitchen, washing the dishes, making beds, and tending lamps. Washing dishes in houses without running water meant hauling a great deal of water by hand from an outdoor pump. Even making beds was a complex task. Feather beds had to be fluffed, adjusted, and frequently flipped to keep them from becoming uncomfortably lumpy.

Tending kerosene lamps could also be a time-consuming job. It meant wiping the top chimneys, replacing or trimming the wicks, and filling the lamp with oil. Despite the time it took to maintain kerosene lamps, they were a big improvement over candles. Kerosene lamps produced a brighter, steadier light than candles. Still, improperly tended, they presented some drawbacks. A dirty chimney would result in a dimmer light and sootier stains on the walls above the lamp.

The soot and grime produced by even well-tended lamps, along with that from the cast-iron stoves, mixed with the dust, mud, dirt, and horse manure brought in from the unpaved streets, meant that the well-kept home required daily, weekly, and seasonal cleaning routines. Rugs had to be pulled up, hung outside, and beaten to remove loose dirt. Each spring, women thoroughly cleaned their homes, beginning by taking up the heavy carpets and drapery and washing them, a physically arduous chore. They also washed windows and floors, polished their wood furniture, scrubbed walls, repainted the kitchen, cleaned the furnace if they had one, put away extra heating stoves, and replaced or refurbished the ticks or covers on beds. Women sometimes sewed new ticks or replaced the feather or hay stuffing inside the ticks. Blankets and comforters were also washed at this time (Husband and O'Loughlin 2004, 110–14).

Mary Mason's *The Young Housewife's Counselor and Friend: Containing Directions in Every Department of Housekeeping, Including the Duties of Wife and Mother* (1875) was written expressly for the benefit of residents of the Southern states. Mason advised homemakers to thoroughly clean their chambers every February. She also instructed that the walls be whitewashed, the floors scoured, the paint well washed with soap and water or soda and water. The bedsteads should be taken apart, and every portion wiped over with pure cold water, and when set up again, all the joints and cracks should be filled up with turpentine soap mixed with red pepper.

Two girls under big tree with mother, 1888. Courtesy Library of Congress.

It fell to women to care for the ill, who generally recuperated at home, rather than in hospitals. Whereas doctors administered medicines and specialized in treatments, protracted illnesses required more constant care and attention than a doctor could provide. In *The American Woman's Home*, Catharine Beecher described women as especially suited to nursing as an extension of their maternal natures.

According to Beecher, nursing a sick person, whether through cold-like symptoms, dyspepsia, or nervous ailments, required a well-run sickroom. She advised covering the patient for warmth and then opening all of the windows to ventilate the room twice a day. To remove impurities in the bedding, it too was to be aired and washed frequently and the patient was to be given periodic sponge baths.

Beecher stressed the calming effects of a neat and well-ordered sickroom, explaining that a sick person has nothing to do but look about the room and when everything is neat a feeling of comfort is induced. To relieve the discomfort of fever, she recommended cooling the pillows, sponging the hands with water, and swabbing the mouth with a clean linen rag on the end of a stick (Husband and O'Loughlin 2004, 115).

Mary Mason also provided instructions for nursing the sick. She instructed the caretaker to avoid creaking shoes, hasty, noisy movements, or impatience of any kind. In fact, she advised wearing slippers and to move slowly, quietly, carefully, and not clumsily because everything in the sickroom should project an air of cheerfulness, quietude, and comfort. There should be no loud talking or whispering, but the voice should be carefully attuned to a moderate and, if possible, in musical key.

—*Dorothy Denneen Volo*

CHILDREN

Children: 1865–1877

Childhood seemingly entered a Golden Age following the Civil War. The literary market was flooded with children's stories that were no longer moralistic tales veiled as entertainment, but were designed to excite a child's imagination and to provide them with fantasies of escape. These stories were devoured by middle-class children who lived in the highly protected world of the Victorian era. Mark Twain's *Tom Sawyer* and *The Adventures of Huckleberry Finn* provided heroes who were largely free to act outside parental control and who moved from one adventure to another confounding accepted standards of behavior, but coming ultimately to a just and moral end. Besides dealing with the effects of the war on average families, Louisa May Alcott's *Little Women* addressed many of the family issues and emotions that young middle-class girls were expected to suppress. In an age of childhood regimentation and control, novels such as these established a romantic picture of childhood and young adulthood as a time of adventure, exploration, and fulfillment.

A gender segmentation of the market that emerged mid-century generated adventure stories for boys that fostered manly independence like Richard Henry Dana's *Two Years Before the Mast* (1840). Putting a new twist on this theme in 1867, Horatio Alger created a different kind of boy's adventure story that centered on the upward struggle to economic success. *Ragged Dick: or Street Life in New York* commenced a series of rags-to-riches tales focusing on the rewards of hard work, perseverance, and concern for others. Stories targeting the female audience were mainly sentimental domestic stories and novels with a young female protagonist, usually orphaned, who had to make her way in an often unkind world. Among these were Sophie May's *Little Prudy* series (1863–1865), Martha Finley's 28-volume saga *Elsie Dinsmore* (1867), and Susan Warner's *The Wide, Wide World* (1850).

Manufacturing increased the number of store bought toys and board games that were available to those families who could afford them. By the 1870s middle-class children had many commercially produced toys. Board games, alphabet blocks, and jigsaw puzzles were colorfully adorned with stunning chromolithographic prints. Brightly painted cast metal soldiers allowed boys to replay real and imagined battles. Doll making achieved a high level of sophistication during this period. Dolls had quasi-realistic faces, hands, and feet made of porcelain. Some had glass eyes and real hair rather than yarn hair. Rocking horses, too, reached new heights of decoration and realism. Horses with finely carved heads, painted bodies, flowing manes, and tails also sported miniature saddles and bridles. They were often presented as galloping steeds with outstretched legs fixed upon turned rockers.

Many commercially produced toys were designed as educational aids, which would serve to amuse the children while helping them learn their alphabet or numbers. Of these, alphabet blocks were the most ubiquitous. Word making tiles contained letters that children could use to build words. Expensive sets were made from bone or ivory, but cardboard letters were available at the lower end of the market. Some alphabets were capable of being projected on the wall through a Magic Lantern and provided entertainment for the entire family. Numeracy aids included Domino-Spel [sic], a set of engraved cards with humorous scenes that incorporated spots as an aid to learning. Tangrams or Chinese Puzzles were sets of thin wooden triangles, squares, and rectangles that children were asked to arrange into various patterns contained on the accompanying cards. Board games commonly used teetotums, small multisided tops marked by a number or set of dots rather than dice. Dice had the negative association of being the devils bones and were not considered appropriate for children (Volo and Volo 2007, 270).

Employment for children and adult attitudes toward child labor ranged widely. Many children continued to work in traditional settings, as on family farms alongside their parents. Farm work was often regarded as wholesome or character building. Juvenile delinquents and orphaned or abandoned children, in fact, were frequently sent to the countryside as workers on family farms. Many children, however, experienced farm work far differently than those who extolled it imagined. Some children worked long hours as itinerant laborers, picking sugar beets or dragging heavy bags of cotton. Stooping for 12 hours a day under a hot sun could result in heat exhaustion or back injury.

Children who sold newspapers, matchbooks, and gum or who scavenged for junk comprised another class of child laborers, whose economic plight was often viewed romantically by writers and artists. These street merchants seemed to turn work into play, roaming the streets with familiarity an élan many adults admired. They frequented bars, gambling houses, and theaters. They gave some of their earnings to their parents, but often kept some for candy and other treats.

Nonetheless, the majority of these children were constantly living on the edge of economic disaster. Some street merchants, most notably the newspaper boys, lived on the streets rather than with their families. Some were orphans; others were abandoned by their parents or had fled overcrowded or abusive homes. By 1870, Newsboy's Lodging Houses had been well established and provided shelter and meals for them for a set fee.

Street peddlers who did live at home commonly played in the streets where, to middle-class observers, they appeared to be unsupervised. In fact, adults were often within close reach as mothers checked from tenement windows and shop owners looked on from their shops and carts (Husband and O'Loughlin 2004, 127–28).

With no other place to go, working-class children flocked to the streets and appropriated them as their own. Police officers often viewed the space quite differently. Children in New York and Chicago were arrested for so-called crimes as various as playing baseball on the street, shooting craps, throwing snowballs, and loafing on the docks. Children who were found gambling were likely to be sternly rebuked by police and have their change seized. Penalties for more serious offenses, however, differed dramatically for boys and girls.

A boy found sleeping out might be taken to one of the Newsboy's Lodging Houses, where his stay was voluntary. A girl accused of the same offense was viewed as a greater social threat, someone likely to become a prostitute. If she was under 16 and deemed vulnerable but not yet corrupted, she was likely to be sentenced in probate court to a reform school.

The first such state reform school for girls, the State Industrial School for Girls in Lancaster, Massachusetts, was opened in 1856 and became the model for wayward girls in cities across the country. Lancaster took in girls aged from 7 to 16 who had been sent by the state-appointed judge or commissioner as a result of being homeless or leading an idle, vagrant, and vicious life. About one-fifth of the girls sent to Lancaster were sent there for thievery; the rest were sent for behavioral, rather than property crimes. The institution primarily sought to save girls from promiscuity or prostitution; consequently homeless girls, girls exposed to sexually illicit behavior in the home, and stubborn girls were all eligible. The term stubborn was a catchall label applied to girls who frequented taverns or brothels, ran away from home, or befriended low men and women. Fifty-five percent of the girls admitted to Lancaster between 1856 and 1905 were labeled stubborn.

Initially, the institution offered a common school education as well as moral guidance from a male superintendent and female matron living in one of 30 cottages. The education and food offered was so valued by poor parents that some had their daughters designated as stubborn just to be relieved of the burden of feeding another mouth.

By 1870, however, the focus of Lancaster and similar institutions had shifted. Rapid industrialization, poverty, and the breakdown of more local forms of social welfare and discipline in cities resulted in a large population of girls considered delinquent. Lancaster increasingly paid little attention to the girl's schooling. By 1869 the girls were only encouraged to acquire only basic literacy and simple arithmetic (Husband and O'Loughlin 2004, 129–31).

—Dorothy Denneen Volo

Orphanages and Asylums for Black Children

Many black children were left orphans or displaced from their parents and relations by the Civil War. The eastern seaboard from Savannah to Boston teemed with abandoned and parentless black children. In the South before, during, and after

Reconstruction, these orphaned blacks were generally left to the good will of other blacks, and local Southern governments had little incentive to provide food, clothing, or homes for them. In Northern cities blacks were often among the poorest residents and occupied the least favored neighborhoods and housing.

There were many humanitarian groups that tried to aid the plight of these destitute black children, but most orphanages, homes, and institutions refused to mix blacks into their otherwise white population. Many of these poor children were sent to prisons and asylums where their minimum physical needs were addressed, but little else. Many were placed in so-called industrial schools where they were expected to work as laborers or learn the duties of servants. Their condition was only a little better than slavery. It was not considered necessary to provide black orphans with an education, and in some states they did not have to be taught reading and writing until attitudes toward black children changed in the last quarter of the century.

Those housed in prisons were often separated from the criminal population, and there was some attempt to treat orphans differently from youths assigned to prison because they had committed a crime. Physical barriers like walls and fences were often erected to separate blameless youths from criminal youths in work areas, dormitories, and exercise yards. Nonetheless, the line between the two quickly faded in the minds of the overtaxed institutional personnel. Moreover, many small children were locked up with older youths, who had repeatedly broken the law and served as a bad example to them.

In the 1870s, well-meaning humanitarians supported laws that banned keeping orphaned children in asylums or poorhouses unless they were unteachable, epileptic, or otherwise considered physically or mentally defective. Unfortunately, many black children seem to have been included under these exceptions, and they were often misplaced in institutions for lunatics or in asylums for the disabled where education was not a part of the service provided. Moreover, foster placement for black children was very difficult and little effort was made to place black orphans with families of their own race. Thousands of black orphans were still living in poorhouses and asylums into the 1880s, and many more remained on the streets.

Some informal adoption took place among the free African American community, and a large number of private persons opened orphanages specifically for black youth. One of the first of these was the Colored Orphan Asylum that had been founded by a Quaker group in Manhattan in 1836. The three-story brick structure was attacked and burned by the largely Irish immigrant mob during the violent New York Draft Riots of July 1863. The orphans, who were turned out into the streets by the enraged white rioters, found temporary refuge in a nearby local police station and an asylum for white children. The Colored Orphan Asylum was rebuilt in 1867 on 143rd Street near Harlem Heights north of present-day Central Park. This was considered part of the city suburbs at the time. It was later moved to the Westchester County line at Riverdale, in the Bronx. The Quakers also founded an asylum for orphan and destitute Native American children on the Seneca Indian Reservation in western New York State in 1855.

—*James M. Volo*

SERVANTS AND FREEMEN

The upper classes in America—as in all of Europe and many other places—had servants, among them both freemen and bondsmen, male and female. There were servants among the original colonists at Jamestown in 1607 and at Plymouth in 1623. The Hudson Valley Dutch in New York owned black slaves and established tenants on their lands who were little less than serfs. In colonial and revolutionary times indentured servants, apprentices, and slaves were available to do odious or heavy tasks around the house or shop.

However, beginning in the second decade of the nineteenth century, there was a sharp decline in the use of apprenticeships (a form of personal service), and many among the immigrants that came to America did not come as indentures but rather as redemptioners, who could buy off their passage with cash instead of time. As the decades passed, there grew among the class of immigrants those with a growing network of family and friends already established in America who were willing to aid those who wished to emigrate from their native lands. It is also generally true that decreases in the cost of passage across the Atlantic allowed many more immigrants to pay for their fares from their own resources without encumbering themselves as servants. By the 1830s indentured servitude among European immigrants to America had almost entirely ended. Yet personal service contracts could still be found among immigrants from Asia, largely confined to California and the West. In the South during this same period, the use of slaves increased manyfold as the number of white workers—both free and bound—decreased.

As indentured servitude grew more rare and the number of persons willing to work for a wage increased, the relative cost of employing indentures rose. This contributed to the end of the practice in the United States by about 1840. Many employers, however, continued to consider wage labor and abject servitude interchangeable—a development much despised by white workers living in the slave-owning South. The lack of indentures and the increased pool of young women willing to work for wages tended to augment the development of paid domestic service as an alternative to forced service. Yet, contemporary observers noted that "in the present state of prices [1869], the board of a domestic costs double her wages, and the waste she makes is a more serious matter still" (Beecher and Stowe 2002, 235).

The mistresses of households at the beginning of the century had often relied on temporary, short-term paid help from among the young women of the neighborhood. These were often the supernumerary daughters of local families from the middle range of the local social hierarchy. The vast majority of these part-time servants were single women between 15 and 25 years of age who fully expected to become mistresses of their own homes in the fullness of time. They often alternated work in their family home with that in the homes of their neighbors. They were usually of the same class as the mistress of the house and expected to work beside her in doing the normal tasks required of proper housewifery. "Such shuffling and reshuffling of workers was part of a larger system of neighborly exchange that sustained male as well as female economics in the period." In the nineteenth century this common feature of domestic service changed (Ulrich 1990, 82).

As a servant to a prominent New England family, Robert Roberts, a free black, wrote a guide for those who cared to enter domestic service. *The House Servant's Directory* (first published in 1827 and available throughout the nineteenth century) provides a number of insights into the social structure, hierarchy, and maintenance of a manor house. Roberts wrote: "Now, my friends, you must consider that to live in a gentlemen's family as a house servant is a station that will seem wholly different from any thing. I presume, that ever you have been acquainted with; this station of life comprises comforts, privileges, and pleasures, which are to be found in but few other stations in which you may enter; and on the other hand many difficulties, trials of temper, &c., more perhaps than in any other station in which you might enter, in a different state of life....When you hire yourself to a lady or gentlemen, your time or your ability is no longer your own, but your employers; therefore they have a claim on them whenever they choose to call for them: and my sincere advice to you is always to study to give general satisfaction to your employers, and by so doing you are sure to gain credit for yourself" (Roberts 2006, 12)

The treatment of black laborers in the North was often brutish, and blacks applying for positions in white households were often met with distain. Many whites—caught by the sudden explosion of a freed black population into a formerly white only world—expressed mixed feelings about the former slaves and blacks in general. Due to the recent emancipation of slaves in the South, the hiring of blacks to serve as domestics could prove an embarrassment even for white abolitionist families. Beecher and Stowe noted that "the condition of domestic service [in America]... still retain[ed] about it something from the influences of feudal times, and from the near presence of slavery" (Beecher and Stowe 2002, 235–37).

For example, George and Elizabeth Custer were usually accompanied by their cook, Eliza, a former slave who had served them since the second year of the Civil War. The Custers were postwar Democrats (and very political), and they had made many friends during their residence in the South who were cool to the idea of incorporating blacks into white society. George Custer, like many Midwestern whites, believed in emancipation but regarded the granting of suffrage to blacks as absurd, and he did not hesitate to say so publicly.

The Custers were very affectionate toward their black cook. On a trip through Louisiana after the war, the proprietor of a lunchroom tried to banish Eliza from the Custers' dining table because of her color; but the general insisted that she stay because "no other table had been provided for servants." At another time, General Custer succeeded in having Eliza wear a colorful turban when accompanying him in public. It was one of the fads of the day to have black servants dress in Turkish or Hindustani costume (Custer 1971, xiv).

Elizabeth, "Libbie," Custer had lost her mother as a child, and was the product of a women's boarding school education. In her diary she freely admitted a "deficiency in housekeeping skills, possibly because of the overindulgence of her stepmother." Her husband, too, did not highly value these skills in a wife, and because he was demanding of her time and attention in other areas, he saw no reason for her to do tasks that could be turned over to others. Consequently, in addition to Eliza, George Custer hired additional domestic help whenever possible. This freed Elizabeth to pursue a career as a writer and journalist. Ultimately, it was this aspect of Elizabeth's life that fueled the so-called Custer Myth after his death at Little Big Horn and kept Custer from becoming just another statistic in the Indian Wars (Custer 1971, xxiii).

Northerners were willing enough to hire black freemen to do manual labor, to tend the lawn, garden, or stables, or to serve as ornaments as coachmen or footmen; but they preferred white help in the confines of the family quarters. Not until the twentieth century did the hiring of black domestics become fashionable. In New York City at mid-century, Irish domestics composed the largest recognizable group of female workers, which suggests the extent of the demand for such workers and the Irish response to it. Moreover, domestic service in general was the leading occupation in the city employing 15 percent of the total male and female working population. The 1870 census—the first to break down occupation for women by age and race—determined that there was one female domestic for every 8.4 families. These were most prevalent in urban areas and in the South. Half of all working women were employed in private or public housekeeping in 1870. By 1890 this proportion had fallen to one third, and by 1920 to one sixth. Nonetheless, domestic service remained the largest occupation for women in every census until 1940 (Volo and Volo 2007, 351–52).

PETS: THE PROTECTION OF ANIMALS

Among the many reform movements begun in the nineteenth century were those that espoused animal rights for the first time in an organized fashion. Henry Bergh found a receptive audience when he called for the creation of an organization that would actively seek the protection of animals. Fortified by the support of wealthy contacts who signed his "Declaration of the Rights of Animals," Bergh proposed the creation of the Society for the Prevention of Cruelty to Animals (SPCA) to the New York State Legislature. On April 19, 1866, nine days after being granted a charter for the SPCA in New York, the legislature passed an anticruelty law and granted the society the right to enforce it. Bergh worked tirelessly to improve the conditions in which animals lived. He visited businesses and stables checking under collars and saddles for raw flesh, exposed dog pits, and lectured to children in public schools.

Animal welfare organizations spread. Many began to take over control of stray animals from communities and promoted animal adoption. The American Humane Education Association was one of several groups that pushed for organized classes for adults and children and promoted pet centered community events such as parades and shows. The New York Poultry Society expanded to include lop-eared rabbits, cats, and dogs in 1869.

Among the social reform movements that women joined during this period were animal protection societies. The Women's Branch of the Pennsylvania SPCA, based in Philadelphia, advocated for kinder, more rational methods of animal control and encouraged adoptions. They lobbied the mayor for control of the management of the pound. They built what they named a shelter for strays in 1870 and made sure that the animals were provided with proper water and food. The women were responsible for changing the methods for which stray dogs were cared. They opposed the annual roundup of dogs in summertime and instituted ongoing, routine control procedures where unwanted dogs could be relinquished. They also instituted painless killing of canines and cats at first by chloroform and later through a euthanasia chamber that used carbonous oxide gas (Grier 2006, 217).

Ironically, some very cruel practices survived. Even caring pet owners accepted the practice of drowning unwanted litters of kittens and puppies. Ambivalence to this action was so great that even animal advocates cited the practice as a kindness rather than let the innocents make their own way in the world.

—*Dorothy Denneen Volo*

FOR MORE INFORMATION

Aron, Cindy S. "The Evolution of the Middle Class." In *A Companion to 19th-Century America*, ed. William L. Barney. Malden, MA; Blackwell Publishing, 2006.

Beecher, Catharine E., and Harriet Beecher Stowe. *The American Woman's Home*. New Brunswick, NJ: Rutgers University Press, 2002.

Berry, Stephen W. "The South: From Old to New." In *A Companion to 19th-Century America*, ed. William L. Barney. Malden, MA; Blackwell Publishing, 2006.

Brewer, Priscilla J. *From Fireplace to Cookstove: Technology and the Domestic Ideal in America*. Syracuse, NY: Syracuse University Press, 2000.

Deer, Mark. *A Dog's History of America: How Our Best Friend Explored, Conquered, and Settled a Continent*. New York: North Point Press, 2004.

Engerman, Stanley L. "Changes in Black Fertility, 1880–1940." In *Family and Population in Nineteenth Century America*, by Tamara K. Hareven and Maris A. Vinovskis. Princeton, NJ: Princeton University Press, 1978.

Frank, Stephen M. *Life with Father: Parenthood and Masculinity in the Nineteenth-Century American North*. Baltimore: Johns Hopkins University Press, 1998.

Green, Harvey. *The Light of the Home*. New York: Pantheon Books, 1983.

Grier, Katherine C. *Pets in America: A History*. Chapel Hill: University of North Carolina Press, 2006.

Haines, T. L., and Levi W. Yaggy. *The Royal Path of Life: Or Aims and Aids to Success and Happiness*. Chicago, IL: Western Publishing House, 1876.

Heininger, Mary L. *A Century of Childhood, 1820–1920*. Rochester, NY: Margaret Woodbury Strong Museum, 1984.

Husband, Julie, and Jim O'Loughlin. *Daily Life in the Industrial United States, 1870–1900*. Westport, CT: Greenwood Press, 2004.

McClinton, Katherine Morrison. *Antiques of American Childhood*. New York: Bramhall House, 1970.

McGuire, Judith W. *Diary of a Southern Refugee during the War by a Lady of Virginia*. Lincoln: University of Nebraska Press, 1995.

Mintz, Steven. *Huck's Raft: A History of American Childhood*. Cambridge, MA: Harvard University Press, 2004.

Ransom, J. Clinton. *The Successful Man in His Manifold Relation with Life*. New York: J. A. Hill & Co., 1889.

Reef, Catherine. *Alone in the World: Orphans and Orphanages in America*. New York: Clarion Books, 2005.

Roberts, Robert. *The House Servant's Directory, An African American Butler's 1827 Guide.* Mineola, NY: Dover Publications, 2006.

Schenone, Laura. *A Thousand Years over a Hot Stove.* New York: W. W. Norton & Company, 2003.

Strasser, Susan. *Never Done: A History of American Housework.* New York: Henry Holt and Company, 1982.

Ulrich, Laurel Thatcher. *A Midwife's Tale: The Life of Martha Ballard, Based on Her Diary, 1785–1812.* New York: Vintage Books, 1990.

Volo, Dorothy Denneen, and James M. Volo. *Family Life in Nineteenth-Century America.* Westport, CT: Greenwood Press, 2007.

Wells, Robert V. "Demographic Change and the Life Cycle of American Families." In *Studies in American Historical Demography,* ed. Maris A. Vinovskis. New York: Academic Press, 1979.

Economic Life

WORK

A Laborious World

The nineteenth-century environment was a laborious world—one filled with work of all types. There was no place in a properly ordered society of this type for men who were indolent or lacking in energy. T. L. Haines and Levi W. Yaggy, in *The Royal Path of Life: or Aims and Aids to Success and Happiness,* wrote in 1876, "It is not study, not instruction, not careful moral training, not good parents, not good society that make men.... It is employment.... No man feels himself a man who is not doing a man's business. A man without employment is not a man. He cannot act a man's part.... Hence [the world] sets its boys to work; gives them trades, callings, professions; puts the instruments of man-making into their hands and tells then to work out their manhood" (Haines and Yaggy 1876, 131–32). If a man needed to work for a living, if he needed to pursue a vocation and hoped to attain a "high station" or anything that resembled success, he needed to invest either his "brow-sweat or brain-sweat" until he accomplished it. The same observer noted, "Working men walk worthy of your vocation!" (Haines and Yaggy 1876, 187).

A man could successfully grapple with resistance by applying mental as well as physical force, if he possessed the quality of industry. Possession of this quality enabled him to work his way through "irksome drudgery and dry detail." Haines and Yaggy observed, "What can be more beautiful than to see a man combating suffering with patience, triumphing in his integrity...and...pressing on with unconquerable zeal to the end?" (Haines and Yaggy 1876, 254–55). Honest success, based on merit and gained through the application of perseverance and industry, "should neither be despised or idolized." Moreover, it was thought that success "extends its bright and prophetic vision through...the distant time and bequeaths to remote generations the vindication of its honor and fame, and the clear comprehension of its truths" (Haines and Yaggy 1876, 269–70; Volo and Volo 2007, 53–54).

Men's Roles as Settlers

Although the farming frontier of the Great Plains may have fulfilled, for some, the dream of owning property, it was neither an adventure nor an idealized acting out of the Jeffersonian concept of the yeoman farmer. Although there were variations in both the scope and methods of farming—most notably the large-scale, nearly industrialized bonanza wheat farms of the Red River Valley or the irrigated farms around Salt Lake City—most farms on the Plains were small, labor-intensive operations in which men, women, and children struggled against nature to eke out a marginal existence. For most families, 160 acres was more than enough land to farm. Work could be brutal with little power other than human and few mechanical contrivances. A man often had to walk miles to borrow a neighbor's team of oxen to plow his fields; after an exhausting day he'd return the animals and face another long walk home. They'd cut grain with cradles, dig wells with broken-handled picks, hoe corn, and chop whatever wood was available with dull axes. A sense of the homesteader's hardships is reflected in Hamlin Garland's dedication to *Main-Traveled Roads* (1881): "To My Father and Mother Whose half-century pilgrimage on the main-traveled road of life has brought them only toil and deprivation, this book of stories is dedicated by a son to whom every day brings a deepening sense of his parents' silent heroism."

Work was hard, almost as inexorable as the cycle of seasons that it followed. All work tested animal and human endurance. One of the most difficult jobs was breaking the sod for the first time. The ordinary breaking plow turned a strip of sod 20 to 33 inches wide; to accomplish this, one needed a yoke of six oxen. (Most farmers preferred oxen to horses for their strength.) However, many farmers had no team at all, or only a couple of animals, so they either had to borrow a neighbor's team, hire the work done (which was rarely possible for cash-strapped newcomers), or do the work with what they had. Sometimes the first-year settlers only planted sod corn, gashing the sod with an ax and then dropping in seed corn. This was, however, only a temporary measure, postponing the almost epic struggle of man and beast against sod unbroken since prehistory. Hamlin Garland remembers a "giant" neighbor bracing himself for the shock of the plow, pulled by four straining horses; his father sat on the beam to add weight and keep the coulter in the ground. "These contests had the quality of a wrestling match, but the men always won" (Garland 1925, 104).

The work exacted its toll. Oscar Micheaux learned from experience that gummy soil was best tilled with plows that made a slanting cut; his made a square cut, causing roots and grass to collect on the plowshare, requiring frequent stops to clean it. He was not used to driving horses, nor could he keep the plow in the ground at first. He later wrote, "I hopped, skipped and jumped across the prairie, and that plow began hitting and missing, mostly missing. . . . I sat down and gave up to a fit of the blues; for it looked bad, mighty bad for me." Eventually he mastered the technique, and by the end of the summer he'd broken more than 120 acres. (Most homesteaders broke only a few acres at a time, planted them, and then tackled a few more. Micheaux, however, being the only black in his part of South Dakota, wanted to prove he was the equal of white farmers.) However, he paid for the accomplishment: "As it had taken a fourteen hundred mile walk to follow the plow in breaking the one hundred and twenty acres, I was about 'all in' physically when it was done" (Nelson 1986, 51–52). It was not for nothing that Willa Cather invested the plow with an almost epic significance in her novel of Nebraska, My Ántonia (1918).

Usually after the land was plowed, it had to be dragged or harrowed, breaking up clods and pulverizing the soil prior to planting. Garland remembers that "dragging is even more wearisome than plowing…for you have no handles to assist you and your heels sinking deep into the soft loam bring such unwonted strain upon the tendons of your legs that you can scarcely limp home to supper" (Garland 1925, 100). Once the crop was in, the war of weeds began. Howard Ruede describes day after day hoeing corn, his blue shirt bleaching to red across his back from sun and sweat (Garland 1925, 87, 106–7).

In the early years the harvesting of wheat, rye, and oats, as well as cutting hay, was done with a sickle. The harvester would grasp the stalks in his left hand and, with his right, draw the sickle close to where the bunched stalks were held. Consequently most harvesters bore one or more scars on their left hands from the sickle coming too close. Periodically the harvester would stop, hang the sickle on his belt, and bind the sheaves. Using such techniques, a man could harvest, on average, three-quarters of an acre a day. The work was easier and more efficient with a scythe or cradle, but it was not until the arrival of horse-drawn McCormick reapers, which could cut fifteen acres a day that the farmer was freed from back-breaking labor.

Generally neighbors would move from farm to farm (especially during harvesting and threshing seasons) helping each other and eliminating the need to hire help. In addition men would often exchange labor, using a monetary value to determine the length of services provided. For example, Howard Ruede cut wood for neighbors at the rate of $1 per cord; rather than paying him in cash, one neighbor planted potatoes for him and another agreed to break an acre of sod for every three cords of wood. On another occasion he worked at the sorghum mill at the rate of one gallon of molasses per day; he then made a deal with another neighbor to plant his wheat in exchange for molasses. Oftentimes no cash at all was involved in these transactions. People did whatever work was required. Ruede dug cellars, plowed, shelled corn, and stripped sorghum at the mill. With skills he thought he'd abandoned back in Pennsylvania, he set type for the town newspaper and, when the editor was gone, published it himself. For this he was sometimes paid in cash, though at no set rate (Ruede 1966, 66–67, 157, 40, 69).

Men with carpentry or painting skills could work in the burgeoning new towns; there too they could find jobs in livery stables, saloons, stores, or pool halls. Some families made a little money selling farm surplus in town. Many women made butter, kept chickens for eggs, spun flax or wool for sale. Keturah Penton Belknap recorded in her journal the prices she and her family received in Iowa in the 1840s: 12.5 cents a pound for butter, 6.5 cents a dozen for eggs, fresh pork for 5 cents a pound; corn at 12.5 cents a bushel unshucked, and, for their wheat, $3 a barrel after having had it ground, buying barrels, and hauling it sixty miles to Keokuk. At the end of one year, she noted rather proudly, they had $20 in silver to "put in the box" (Luchetti and Olwell 1982, 136; Jones 1998, 189–93).

Women's Roles as Settlers

It is clear that on the homesteader's frontier everyone worked and work was not gender-specific. Though milking cows was often considered women's work, men did that chore too; conversely, when more help was needed in the fields, women pitched in. Women, however, were generally in charge of the house and the children. They tended the garden, nursed the sick, taught the children before a school was organized, sewed and repaired the family's clothing, cooked and baked—often without benefit of a stove. Washday was often a nightmare. Before a good well was dug on the claim, women saved a little water every day for the week's washing. Miriam Davis Colt recalls going "to the spring five times today; three times is my usual number," making "five miles travel for me [on foot] to bring sixty quarts of water" (Colt 1862/1966, 106).

Many women also had to make their own soap. Priscilla Merriman Evans describes her technique: "[I] took an ox and a gunny sack and went out into the field where the dead cattle had been dragged [after the disastrous winter of 1885–86] and I broke up all the bones I could carry home. I boiled them in saleratus and lime, and it made a little jelly-like soap" (Luchetti and Olwell 1982, 167). Miriam Davis Colt wondered what her mother back east would think of her white clothes in this land of little soap or water. All she could say was that they were "clean for brown—but...awful dirty for white." She and her family stopped wearing nightclothes, she said, once they got to Kansas, "because I could not bear to have them take on the brown color" (Colt 1862/1966, 135–36).

When the first labor-saving devices—the sewing machine and the washing machine—became available, women who could afford them were ecstatic. The sewing machine was driven by human power, with the woman working a treadle with her feet. The washing machine was essentially a small tub with a hand-turned paddle for agitating the clothes; its primary advantage was that the children could be assigned the task of operating it, freeing their mother from the drudgery of scrubbing the clothes on a washboard.

Though some women took their unremitting labor in stride—Mollie Sanford said, "I can put my hand to almost anything" (Sanford 1959, 58)—some historians suggest that the hymns they sang may have reflected their hopelessness, their exhaustion, and their yearning for release as much as they did their religiosity.

Death, to some, might be preferable to unending labor. Hamlin Garland, remembering his mother, confirmed this: "I doubt if the women—any of them—got out into the fields or meadows long enough to enjoy the birds and the breezes. Even on Sunday as they rode away to church, they were too tired to react to the beauties of the landscape" (Garland 1925, 138–39; Jones 1998, 193–94).

Children's Roles as Settlers

Children, too, were expected to work. Garland remembers trying to be a "good little soldier" and live up to the expectations of his father, a Civil War veteran. Early on he and his brother had the responsibilities of grown men. They chopped and stacked wood, hunted cattle that had wandered off, and harrowed and cross-harrowed the fields until "tears of rebellious rage" creased the dust on their faces. At age 10 he had been taught to handle bundles of thoroughly dried barley shocks; at age 14 he was one of five men on a crew binding straw after the reaper had passed (Garland 1925, 149–51). Kept out of school during October and November, he first plowed and then husked corn. His father was not unkind, giving him the freedom to do what he wanted and go where he liked on Sunday as long as he was back in time for milking.

His experiences were not unique. Other children, some as young as age four to six, had chores: to carry in enough fuel—wood or cow chips—each night to last the next day, to bring in water from the barrel outside, to fill kerosene lamps.

For recreation, many children had to make do and use their imaginations because toys weren't available. Elinore Stewart remembers her daughter calling a block of wood her "dear baby," a spoke from a wagon wheel "little Margaret," and a barrel stave "bad little Johnny" (Stewart 1914, 13–14).

Sometimes children worked off their homestead. Parents controlled their children's labor, and a father could generally claim his son's wages until he was 21 years old (Schob 1975, 174). In 1858, 14-year-old Frank O'Brien was hired out to work on a farm seven miles away; having walked there, he found his quarters to be in the attic, which he shared with seed corn, dried pumpkins, and field mice. His work included washing dishes, helping with the threshing, churning butter, turning the grindstone as his employer sharpened tools, and cleaning the hay mow (Schob 1975, 189–90). Farmers, especially widowers, often advertised for hired girls; because of the disproportionate male-female ratio, many girls married early.

Children's work was not always voluntary. On at least one occasion a farmer, with too many mouths to feed, agreed to indenture two of his children to another man looking for "draft animals." The agreement was that the employer would buy them each a pair of shoes if they worked out. Their mother, who had not originally been consulted, so harassed her husband that a week later they rescued the children, sick, terrified, bewildered, and maltreated (Schlissel, Gibbons, and Hampsten 1989, 221–23).

Given the often brutal hardship of work on the frontier and given such treatment of children, it is not surprising that tired animals were also sometimes mistreated. Mollie Sanford told of one man, angered because his horse was balky, who after piling hay around him literally set a fire under the animal, then left him in agony until Mollie's father shot him (Sanford 1959, 66; Jones 1998, 194–95).

FINANCE: NORTHERN GREENBACKS AND BONDS

Owing to the initial expectation of a short war, the federal government raised its war chest chiefly by taking loans and issuing paper money and bonds. The government generally failed to raise enough funds through these methods, running in deficit throughout the conflict. Expenses ran eight times the revenue from taxes.

After encountering serious difficulties in marketing government bonds, Secretary Simon P. Chase authorized the firm of Jay Cooke and Company to be the sole subscription agent for the sale of federal bonds. Through his network of sub-agents, his many newspaper advertisements, and his vivid speeches appealing to workingmen to put their savings into the war effort, Cooke quickly marketed the bonds. He was thereafter known as "the financier of the Civil War." The failure of his firm in 1873, however, sparked a deep national recession.

Nonetheless, the money raised by selling bonds was inadequate. In August 1861, the federal government required each state in the Union to fill a revenue quota for the war based on population. How each state raised the money was left to its own devices. It was hoped that $20 million would be raised, but only $17 million was forthcoming.

Another source of war funding was found in the adoption of a personal income tax, the first tax of its kind ever levied by the United States government. As first envisioned, it fixed a 3 percent tax on family incomes over $800, but by June 1864 the exemption fell to $600 and the minimum rate rose to 5 percent on incomes up to $5,000. The rates increased progressively to 7.5 percent on incomes between $5,000 and $10,000, and 10 percent on those over $10,000. During the 3 war years 1863, 1864, and 1865, the income tax yielded only $55 million.

To raise additional funds, the federal government established an excise tax. This was an internal revenue tax that was added to the price of a broad range of items, and it served as the main source of federal financing for the war. Ostensibly the seller paid a tax on the sale price of the item, and the purchaser paid a personal property tax on its ownership. These taxes were applied to a list of commodities that included a three percent tax on malt liquor, spirits, tobacco, and stamps; manufactures of cotton, wool, flax, hemp, iron, steel, wood, and stone. Meats were taxed at 30 cents per butchered steer, 10 cents per hog, and 5 cents per sheep. Carriages, billiard tables, gold and silver plate, yachts, and other top-tier items were charged a luxury tax. Moreover, many professions and trades were forced to pay fees for licenses, and many forms of entertainment were required to collect taxes as part of their ticket price. Railroads, banks, insurance companies, and telegraph companies were required to pay at rates and in ways best fitted to their business operations. The law was so extensive and so minute in its detail that it required 240 pages and more than 20 thousand words to express its provisions. In 1864, and 1865, these excise taxes yielded close to $210 million (Randall and Donald 1961, 344–45).

Although buoyed by the influx of precious metals from California and the Mountain West, in 1862, the Lincoln administration began to issue paper currency as a wartime economic measure. Called greenbacks, more than $450 million in engraved paper bills were issued. Ever since the days of the Federalists, paper currency had been issued by the government, but it had always been backed at a specific rate ($20 per troy ounce) by specie (gold) held in government vaults. Lincoln's greenbacks were based only on the good credit of the United States government. Inevitably, in the midst of a war of disunion, a difference between gold value and paper currency value appeared on most commodities, and trading in currency became complex and volatile.

Gold being the universal liquidator of commerce, the first premium on gold coins and bullion was seen when importers of foreign goods were required by their suppliers overseas to pay in gold rather than paper. Domestic commodities and internal business exchanges were less affected than foreign ones. The premium set in motion a speculative trade in greenbacks and gold futures that caused the value of both to fluctuate. In January 1862, gold opened at a mere 1 1/2 cent premium, but it quickly increased. Exactly two years later, it was at 52 cents per dollar, and in June 1864, the gold premium stood at more than 95 cents. In other words, almost two paper dollars were needed to make the equivalent of one in gold. In July the premium reached its greatest excess at $2.85 of paper currency for $1 in gold money.

Finding their shops swamped with business customers trading in dollars and gold, Wall Street money brokers, who commonly dealt in foreign currency exchanges, moved into a suitable building that was dubbed the Gold Exchange. There were numerous reasons for the fluctuations in gold premium. Indeed, the whole gold market was as sensitized to the political and economic pulse of the country as was the stock market. Changing currents in fiscal policy, debates in Congress, international crises, battle results, changes in army or government personnel, rumors, and many other factors affected the price of gold and had the inverse effect on greenbacks. When the Confederate forces under General Jubal A. Early were loose in Maryland and threatening the federal capital on July 11, 1864, the paper price of gold reached $2.84 per $1.00 in gold money. Early was met by a hastily improvised force under Federal General Lew Wallace, and when he turned away from Washington, the premium price of gold fell, some say in proportion to Early's distance from the federal capital. Although the Gold Exchange was a wartime phenomenon, it remained in operation for 17 years. After a long fight in Congress and the courts over the conversion of greenbacks to gold, specie payments were resumed in 1879, and the price of gold was again fixed by the government.

—*James M. Volo*

COST AND STANDARD OF LIVING

Real and Personal Property

The 1850 census collected data only on real property, while the subsequent censuses sampled both real and personal property. The data can be disaggregated by race, residence, occupation, place of birth, and age and can be used to provide a look at the economic health of the family during the late nineteenth century. The 1870 census sampled more than 7.5 million families with an average wealth of almost $3,000, much of the total held by a small minority of very wealthy families. Sixty-nine percent of American families had property valued at more than $100. This included real property (land and houses) and personal property (cash or items of value). Given that the $100 threshold for inclusion masks some details regarding the poorest third of the population, it is still clear that wealth among the majority of families in this mid-nineteenth-century sample lacked any equality in how it was distributed.

No one should be surprised that the inequality was greater among blacks than among whites especially in the South where wealth was most unequally distributed across all sub-groups. Researchers using random samples from the censuses taken in these periods, however, found "that property was nearly as unequally distributed in some parts of the Northeast, and in the Pacific and Mountain regions." Moreover, property inequality was also higher in urban than rural areas, higher in industrial than agricultural areas (the plantation South excepted), and higher among sales occupations than among wage earners. Differences in skilled versus unskilled pay rates, a proxy for income inequality, were greatest in areas in the earliest stages of industrialization. Wealth was more equally distributed among farmers, professionals, and clerical or office workers. What is remarkable is that by 1870, at least, there was little inequality based on ethnicity in terms of being native- or foreign-born. Inequalities also varied with age. Not surprisingly, young adults had the smallest portion of income. Older persons within every category of occupation or residence were much closer to one another than the young in terms of wealth distribution (Rosenbloom and Stutes 2005, 4–5).

The average wealth of households headed by older, foreign-born, white males was higher than that of the general population if they were employed in manufacturing. Among these, regional and urban-rural distributions were quite similar as a whole. About 11 percent of all households were headed by native-born, rural females, made heads of households largely because they were widowed. Two-thirds of these female heads-of-household were black. With their limited economic prospects and an average age five years older than their male counterparts, it is not surprising that black women reported less property or no property more often than other groups of persons.

State and regional differences in wealth were pronounced ranging from an average high of almost $5,000 per family in the Pacific region to an average low of just under $1,000 in the Mountain states. Wealth in the Northern states was two to three times greater than in the South, but in the border states of Maryland, West Virginia, and Kentucky it was higher than in the Deep South of Georgia, Mississippi, or Alabama. Among the Northern states, the New England manufacturing centers of Connecticut, Rhode Island, and Massachusetts had much higher levels than the more rural states of Vermont, New Hampshire, and Maine. In New England the value of real property (57%) accounted for a smaller portion of wealth than elsewhere (70%). Property ownership also varied across the region with the North Central states (80%) leading, and the Northeast (70%) and the Southern states (50%) lagging behind (Rosenbloom and Stutes 2005, 8).

In terms of wealth nationwide, 27 percent of real property and 38 percent of personal property was owned by the top 1 percent of the population. Wealth was most concentrated among a few families in South Carolina, Louisiana, California, and the New England manufacturing states. The recently settled Western states reported little wealth of any kind, and the agricultural states of New York, Pennsylvania, and the North Central region had a generally equitable distribution of wealth in terms of farm land. Real property inequity was greatest in the South, and personal property inequity greatest in New England and the Mid-Atlantic states. Black families were about 30 percent less likely to report owning any property, and those that did have property valued it at little more than half that of comparable white families. There was no significant difference between native-born and foreign-born real property owners, but immigrants reported about 20 percent less personal property. Literacy and advancing age increased the likelihood of property ownership, but wealth peaked at age 55 to 60. Women, as a subgroup, were less likely to own any reportable property and had less of it than men of the same class when they did. Modest city dwellers were less likely to own property of any kind, and the odds of ownership fell with the increasing size of the city. This may have been due to a great number of renters. Those urban families with wealth, however, were generally better off if they lived in a large city than a small one (Rosenbloom and Stutes 2005, 13).

There were marked differences in wealth distribution across occupational groups. General laborers and domestics, as expected, were the least likely to own property of any kind, but farmers, because of their land, were the most likely to report real property ownership. In terms of wealth, professionals and managers were among the wealthiest occupations, but farmers also placed very high along the wealth spectrum. Craftsmen and machine operators came next with salesmen and clerks being last in wealth among persons with specific occupations (Rosenbloom and Stutes 2005, 28; Volo and Volo 2007, 61–63).

Standard of Living and Family Budget

A prominent American figure in the area of family income and budget was Carroll D. Wright, chief sociologist for the Massachusetts Bureau of Statistics of Labor from 1873 to 1888 and head of the U.S. Bureau of Labor from 1888 to 1905. Wright published one of the earliest studies of American family spending in 1875 in an attempt to understand the growing problems of labor unrest, poverty, and slums in Massachusetts. Wright's study included a sample of 397 working-class families and made it possible to calculate the annual surplus or deficit from income and to gauge the details of family expenditures using categories much like those developed by English researcher B. Seebohm Rowntree. Wright found that "if a man is earning only $2 or less a day, as is the case with thousands of men... with families, he must be very near the condition of poverty or want.... If he have no loss by sickness and permit himself no vacation $526 can be taken as a reasonable annual estimate for their poverty line" (Fisher 1993, 3–4).

The work of Wright, and that of Ernst Engle, came to the attention of James Cook, a Congregationalist minister and proponent of the social gospel then prevalent among some American Protestant reformers. In a series of talks (given in 1877 and 1878) known as the "Boston Monday Lectures," Cook proposed a distinction between *starvation wages* and *natural wages* (just wages). He concluded that a five-person middle-class family in which neither the wife nor the children worked for wages needed an annual income of about $850 (1874) if it was not to "inevitably graduate members unfit to become part of [the] popular sovereignty." He also concluded that a working-class family would need a minimum of between $520 and $624 a year "to live according to the standard of the workingmen of America." This agreed well with Wright's idea of a poverty line. In another lecture he made a distinction between *family wages* and *bachelor wages* that was very near to the tenets of Marxism noting that a married man might work for $1.50 per day at the same task as a bachelor who got $0.80 a day with equal justice (Fisher 1993, 5).

To control food costs, an American sociologist and nutritional scientist, Wilbur Atwater, proposed a minimum caloric diet that contained no fresh meat, although boiled bacon was included three times a week. Atwater also used his expertise to develop a series of ideas concerning poverty and family income. He argued that American workers were extravagant in their food-buying habits. The average annual expenditure for food for a workingman's family was calculated to be $422. Atwater said that if workers would use this amount to buy their food more efficiently, they would meet their dietary needs at a cost noticeably less than their current wasteful food expenditures. He held that the purchase of fresh fruits and vegetables and fresh meats was among the most wasteful and extravagant means for working families that needed more calories and protein. He recommended the use of grains, cereals, beans, and preserved meats such as bacon in their place. Of course, the vitamin value of fresh food items was not yet known, but Atwater should have realized the need of fresh foods in preventing diseases such as scurvy and pellagra even if he did not recognize the mechanism by which they were prevented (Fisher 1993, 5–6).

Atwater's argument that the poor were poor because they made wasteful and extravagant expenditures appealed to factory and business owners who were under siege by workers demanding higher wages. Likewise his scientific theories gave cultural backing to the growing middle-class attitude that poverty among the lower classes was somehow self-inflicted. Social reform movements fueled by true altruism had begun early in the century, but over time as the programs of reform failed to alleviate the problems of society, many persons decided that the poor and unemployed were at fault for their own condition. Nationwide studies done in the early twentieth century, however, showed that the idea that lower-class families spent their incomes inefficiently or wastefully was incorrect. Research has shown that nineteenth-century families repeatedly received more nutrients and a better balance of diet per dollar than higher-income families. The problem was that the dollars were too few to provide for appropriate nutrition after the cost of rent, transportation, and fuel were accounted (Fisher 1993, 6).

—*James M. Volo*

URBAN-RURAL ECONOMY

Life among the Farms

During Reconstruction there was a national slump in farm prices with wheat falling from 67 to 43 cents a bushel, corn from 75 cents to 38 cents, and cotton from 31 cents to 9 cents a pound. In the second half of the decade of the 1860s, a group of Midwestern farmers formed a secret society aimed at attacking the railroad monopolies and their high freight rates. These Grangers, Patrons of Husbandry, were among the largest fraternal orders during the postwar years, but they quickly turned political. Hard economic times suffered by farmers in the 1870s caused the Granger movement to rapidly gain membership. The organization recorded its highest membership numbers in the period in 1875, at 850,000 members.

Popular backing made the Granger movement the driving force in agricultural life. The Grangers established cooperatives and banks and pushed through legislation regarding railroads and grain elevators, among other notable economic and political accomplishments. Improving agricultural conditions and competition from similar organizations caused the political wing of the Granger movement to go into decline during the 1880s, but it maintained a diminished base involved in social activities and horticultural education (Browne and Kreiser 2003, 99).

Local Granger meetings became the focus of picnics, dances, and other social festivities. The highlights of the social season, however, occurred during separate celebrations for Harvest day, celebrating the end of the crop-growing season; Children's Day, praising the contribution made by youth to farming and agricultural life; Anniversary Day, commemorating the establishment of the Granger movement on December 4 of each year; and Independence Day, celebrating the nation's birthday. Food, games, signing, and the occasional parade characterized each of the four celebrations (Browne and Kreiser 2003, 99).

Life in the Towns

To those dwarfed by the immensity of the Plains, a trip to town—even if it was ostensibly to buy a sack of sugar and a pair of new boots, or to arrange for milling grain, or to meet a relative arriving by train to take up a homestead—was an opportunity for socialization. The general store, the barber shop, Main Street itself provided opportunities to exchange information on crops, catch up on news and gossip, quaff a beer, or attend a political rally. Just as in California those who had provided goods and services to the miners prospered more than the miners, so, also, to Plains towns gravitated the "butcher, baker, bootmaker, banker, merchant, saloonkeeper, doctor [and] barber. Inevitably their ranks also included desperadoes, shysters, prostitutes, and scalawags, but mostly they were serious men and women bound upon the honest mission of building a new society in the wilderness" (Wheeler 1975, 19–20). Though the Civil War slowed the town-building process, the Homestead Act spurred it, until by 1890 there were villages of "at least some pretension every ten miles or so across the central grasslands" (Wheeler 1975, 20).

The railroads were instrumental in establishing many towns. They had been granted up to 20 square miles of public land per mile of track as a subsidy to encourage construction. This land they could sell as they chose to finance laying the rails. Surveyors moved ahead of the tracks, selecting town sites every 6 to 10 miles. The "team haul" principle was consciously applied; town sites were placed at the distance farmers could travel to town by horse and wagon and return in the same day (Nelson 1986, 85; 192, n.5). Every 70 miles or so, transcontinental railroads established a main depot, or division point, where repair shops for rolling stock could be built.

Others also sought to establish towns. Through the Townsite Act of 1844, settlers and/or speculators could stake out 320 acres and take possession for $1.25 an acre. Usually such sites were divided into town lots of 125 feet by 25 feet (approximately 1/8 acre), with the profits from sales ranging from $50 to $1,000 per lot. At one point, what with surveyors working for the railroads and for others platting towns, a Missouri River steamboat captain observed he could make more money by "carrying survey stakes than by transporting passengers" (Wheeler 1975, 64).

Many towns were established by special interest groups. For example, Neosha, Kansas, was founded by a group of vegetarians; Amana, Iowa, by Mennonites; Cheever, Kansas, by prohibitionists; and many Kansas towns by the New England Emigrant Aid Society, whose members were ardent abolitionists. Nicodemas, Kansas, was founded by the colored people of Lexington, Kentucky, and Runnymede, Kansas, was established as a haven for dissipated young English aristocrats, who spent their time playing tennis and riding to the hounds—after coyotes, not foxes (Wheeler 1975, 66).

Most town plats were reasonably regular grids, drawn as T towns in which the railroad and Main Street formed a T. The railroad depot was usually at one end of Main Street; at the other end was a public building, such as a courthouse, with businesses lining the streets and banks being situated on prime corner locations (Nelson 1986, 85). Probably two of the most unusual town plats were the Octagon Plan of Neosha, Kansas, and one designed by Frederick Law Olmsted in which there were no straight lines and the blocks were shaped like melons, pears, and sweet potatoes.

Once the town was platted, boosters aggressively encouraged settlers. Newspapers, sometimes called mother's milk to an infant town, were at the outset vehicles for public relations and development rather than for newsgathering. The town promoters shipped such advertising pamphlets and propagandizing papers east to attract new settlers. It was observed that if a town had several papers, it must be desperately in need of promotion. An English visitor who asked how a young town could afford four newspapers was told that "it took four newspapers to keep up such a city" (Wheeler 1975, 65). Other methods were also tried to promote new towns. Some railroads ran free excursion trains from the East, putting up potential settlers in the local hotels, sometimes established just for this purpose. Other towns auctioned off prime lots or, as a gimmick, offered free lots to desirable professionals, to the first couple married in the town, or to the first baby born there. Clearly such towns intended to project an air of permanence.

However, some promotional brochures projected an image vastly different from reality. An 1858 brochure for Sumner, Kansas, showed steamboat docks, a waterfront business district, a mill, a machine shop, a factory, four churches, fine residences on tree-lined streets, and even a domed college. In reality, the town then consisted of a couple of general stores dotted along one graded street, and about two hundred houses, most of them shabbily constructed of wagon boxes and sod slabs and roofed in canvas or straw. Beautifully produced, the brochure was later condemned as a "chromatic triumph of lithographic mendacity" (Wheeler 1975, 54).

No matter how they were established, most towns that survived in their competition for railroad spurs, the right to be county seat, and settlers had certain common denominators: a blacksmith shop, a livery stable, a general store, one or more saloons, and a hotel. Conditions were often somewhat primitive. At one hotel a guest complained about the grimy condition of the roller towel; he was told that there'd been "26 men that went before you and you're the first one that complained" (Wheeler 1975, 27). Grace Fairchild tells of a Fort Pierre, South Dakota, hotel infested with lice (Wyman 1972, 39–40). Main Street was unpaved—usually dusty but a wallow of mud after rain.

Initially town businesses were constructed of any materials that were at hand and presented a hodgepodge of styles. However, when lumber became available an almost universal style appeared. The false-front building with its phony windows and massive cornice may have been unabashed braggadocio, an attempt to be imposing in an architectural manifestation of the town's boosterism. Some townsmen took advantage of prefabricated buildings brought from Midwestern lumberyards by freight wagons or boxcars.

The general store was stocked with staples—whiskey and Bibles and everything in between. One proprietor proudly announced that he carried "anything you might call for, from a $500 diamond ring to a pint of salt" (Wheeler 1975, 88). As a town became more established, other stores catered to more specialized needs: the meat market, combined drugstore and doctor's office, dry goods and clothing stores, and an emporium for boots and shoes. There were, in addition, offices for real estate/insurance/loan agents, dressmakers' shops, restaurants as well as saloons, and small establishments selling fruits and cold drinks. Aaron Montgomery Ward, a dry goods salesman who had traveled throughout the West and heard customers' complaints about prices, printed his first catalog of only 167 items in 1882. His goal: to sell directly to the consumers and thereby save them the middleman's markup. Naturally storekeepers objected, referring to the mail-order house derisively as "Monkey Ward," especially as the catalog swelled to 2,000 items by 1875 and to 75,000 before the end of the century (Wheeler 1975, 118).

For the farmer, the town provided an incredible gamut of entertainment ranging from brutal animal fights and boxing matches to lyceum lectures and Gilbert and Sullivan operettas. The offerings were kaleidoscopic: minstrel shows, brass bands, itinerant jugglers and magicians; prostitutes and taxi dancers—girls who were employed by saloonkeepers to dance with patrons for a fee of 25 cents a dance; freak shows, traveling zoos and stereoscope exhibits, which one proprietor called "choice works of art" but which the county judge deemed to be "obscene and lascivious pictures." Major actors played the West; Hamlin Garland remembers seeing Edwin Booth in *Hamlet*. The audiences, however, were not always sophisticated. During one performance of *Uncle Tom's Cabin*, just as the bloodhounds had almost caught up with the escaping Eliza, a drunken cowboy "came to her rescue" and shot the trained animals dead (Wheeler 1975, 178). During election years political rallies, speeches, and debates offered both entertainment and intellectual stimulation. Baseball was popular; in one nearly endless game the Blue Belts of Milford, Nebraska, beat the Seward team by a score of 97 to 25! But the favorite, for most people, was the circus.

In contrast to the democracy of the Plains where no one was looked down on for poverty or unfashionable clothes, some townsmen considered themselves to be superior to the hayseeds and clodhoppers who reveled in such entertainment. These townsmen inaugurated a new trend in the West—joining organizations, many of which had women's auxiliaries, for philanthropic or recreational purposes. At first many of these, such as the local militias or fire companies, had primarily civic functions to help build the community and maintain public order. But when one examines a list of organizations established in Colorado towns between 1882 and the turn of the century, one sees that the frontier, that "border between civilization and savagery," was indeed gone.

A whole range of specific denominations—Baptist, Methodist, Episcopal, Catholic, Congregational, African Methodist Episcopal, and Christian Science—established churches, a far cry from the comparative ecumenicism of earlier days. Some provided outlets for Civil War veterans of both sides: the Grand Army of the Republic, and the Sons of Civil War Veterans. Fraternal organizations proliferated—Masons, International Order of Odd Fellows (IOOF), Knights of Pythias, the independent Order of Good Templars—as did professional and trade organizations—the Western Colorado Stock Growers' Association, the Typographical Union, the International Brotherhood of Locomotive Engineers, the Real Estate Exchange, and the Mesa County Teachers Association. There were cultural organizations such as the Chatauqua Literary and Scientific Circle, the Shakespeare Club, or the Young Men's Cultural Club; and others celebrated hobbies and recreation—the Jockey Club, the Rifle Club, the Amateur Dramatic Club, and the Grand Junction Wheel [bicycling] Club.

In short, in contrast to the unending labor of early days on the homesteads, people in towns scattered liberally across the Plains now had leisure to spend on recreational activities. This, as much as the Bureau of the Census announcement in 1890 that there was no longer a frontier line, marked the end of the frontier. Only the paroxysms of the Indian wars needed to be experienced before the process of transforming the Great Plains was complete (Jones 1998, 205–10).

FARMING/HUSBANDRY: HARDSHIPS FOR THE SETTLERS

No matter how potential settlers acquired the land, and no matter how they got there—by steamboats, trains, farm wagons, stagecoaches, or on foot—many were in for a rude awakening. Though establishing a farm in the grasslands initially seemed easier than it had been in the woodland East where trees had to be girdled, cut, and burned and stumps grubbed out before land could be plowed, the environment of the Great Plains was far from hospitable. This was, after all, a region that George Catlin had pronounced "almost one entire plain of grass, which is and ever must be, useless to cultivating man" (Dick 1937, 164). Yet, Catlin was an artist who viewed the world through a painter's eyes. A farmer saw the treeless expanse as an agricultural wonderland with no stumps to plow around. A Michigan farmer noted, "You can behold the vast plain of twelve thousand acres, all waving in golden color, ripe for the...harvest" (Davidson 1951, 410–11).

The climate, however, was a trial. Howard Ruede remembered that August in Kansas produced temperatures of 108°F in the shade and 128°F in the sun (Ruede 1966, 140). Hamlin Garland recalled summer in Dakota Territory as "ominous":

The winds were hot and dry and the grass, baked on the stem, had become as inflammable as hay. The birds were silent. The sky, absolutely cloudless, began to scare us with its light. The sun rose through the dusty air, sinister with flare of horizontal heat. The little gardens... withered, and many of the women began to complain bitterly of the loneliness, and lack of shade. The tiny cabins were like ovens at mid-day. (Garland 1925, 308)

Winter was equally formidable. Garland observed, "No one knows what winter means until he has lived through one in a pine-board shanty on a Dakota plain with only buffalo bones for fuel" (Garland 1925, 309). Grace Fairchild remembered a cow breaking the ice and stepping into a water hole one winter; one back leg froze and "the next spring her leg dropped off." Her husband fashioned a wooden leg, but after the cow kicked out and the leg hit him in the head, they fattened her and butchered her in the fall. "We couldn't tell any difference between a three-legged cow and a four-legged one when the steaks were on the table" (Wyman 1972, 23). The winter of 1885–1886 was especially hard. According to a South Dakota folk saying, "It was so cold that when he died they just sharpened his feet and drove him into the ground" (Wyman 1972, 115). Elinore Stewart remembered such extremes in Wyoming: "They have just three seasons here, winter and July and August" (Wyman 1972, 6).

Though there were summer droughts, when the rains came they turned the soil to a thick, viscous gumbo. Many settlers recall it clinging to wagon wheels until it was 8 to 10 inches thick before it fell off of its own weight. Later, graded gravel roads made travel easier, but the soil was unchanged. As settlers said, "If you stick to this country when it's dry, it will stick to you when it is wet" (Nelson 1986, 40).

Across the open plains the wind was omnipresent and often nerve-wracking. Mary Clark wrote to her parents from her South Dakota claim:

The wind was too fierce. Really it was something awful and it hardly ever goes down. It actually blows the feathers off the chickens' backs....I can't put up many pictures and things for every time the door opens they all blow off the wall.....It's so funny—we noticed how terrible loud everyone talks out here and now we find ourselves just shouting away at the top of our voices. We discovered it must be the wind and unless you yell you can't be heard at all. (Nelson 1986, 37)

If a windstorm hit on washday, everyone rushed outside to get the clothes before they blew away. Buckets, pails, and lightweight tools might be blown for miles if they didn't first catch on fences. The same winds, blowing over sun-baked land, produced dust storms, clouds of soil hundreds of feet high that blotted out the sun, filled the house with dust, almost smothered cattle in the stable, exposed the roots of young wheat, causing it to wither and die, and sent homesteaders into "dull despairing rage" (Garland 1925, 128).

Bad as summer winds were, winter blizzards were worse. The Ammons sisters, returning from school, saw a blizzard coming "like white smoke," and before they got home they could not see their hands before their faces (Nelson 1986, 35). With the thermometer at –30°F and the snow blowing at 80 miles per hour, it seemed as if the sun had been "wholly blotted out and that the world would never again be warm" (Garland 1925, 110). Homesteaders rigged ropes between house and barn so they wouldn't get lost going to feed the animals. Dr. Bessie Rehwinkel, returning from a house call, was caught in a sudden Wyoming snowstorm. Driving blindly, her horses becoming more exhausted by the minute, she recalled, "My whole body was becoming numb, and I began to feel an almost irresistible drowsiness creeping upon me." Finally, miraculously, she saw a light through the gloom, and "covered from head to foot with an icy sheet of snow which had frozen into a crust so that I had become a human icicle," she was welcomed into that very house she had left three hours earlier (Rehwinkel 1963, 76–77). Another winter wanderer was not so lucky. Lost in a storm he killed his horse, ripped him open, and crawled into the body cavity to stay warm. He was found several days later, frozen into his equine tomb (Dick 1937, 222).

One of the most terrifying natural disasters was the prairie fire, which might be caused by a lightning strike, a spark from a train, or human carelessness. It was simultaneously horrifying and awesome. "The sky is pierced with tall pyramids of flame, or covered with writhing, leaping, lurid serpents, or transformed into a broad ocean lit up by a blazing sunset. Now a whole valance of fire slides off into the prairie, and then opening its great devouring jaws closes in upon the deadened grass" (Dick 1937, 216). Such a fire could roar across the plains destroying homes, barns, haystacks, even whole settlements in its path. It was the unwritten law that whenever a fire broke out, every able-bodied person must pitch in to fight it, plowing firebreaks, setting backfires, and slapping tongues of flame with wet rags. To be the cause of such a fire not only was embarrassing but also brought legal penalties. A settler convicted of carelessness with fire could receive six months in jail and a thousand-dollar fine (Nelson 1986, 38).

Settlers were also pestered by native critters. Mosquitoes were so bad during summer that some farmers would build a fire at the door and let the wind blow smoke into the house; eyes smarting from the smoke were, to most people, preferable to the welts raised by the voracious insects (Ruede 1966, 89). Flies mercilessly attacked cows in their stalls—and the women or children milking them. During August and September when men were in the field cutting oats or hay, crickets ate coats or hats left beside the haystack, gnawed pitchfork handles, and devoured any leather straps left lying about (Garland 1925, 209). On occasion cinch bugs, small, "evil-smelling" insects, devoured the wheat crops at harvest time, bringing financial disaster to farmers (Garland 1925, 215).

Another hazard, the rattlesnake, was mentioned so often by diarists as to be commonplace. Miriam Davis Colt remembered seeing rattlers crawling or hanging over sills near her front door. At night she'd hear peculiar noises under the floor, which at first she thought were rats. Instead they were snakes, and her husband kept a stout hickory stick near their bed to drive the snakes away (Colt 1966, 104). Mollie

Sanford, in her bare feet, heard the tell-tale sound, killed a snake, and hung its 11 rattles on a tree as a trophy. The snakes did not fear people but slithered into homes, barns, and cellars. Children playing in the yard were their most frequent victims, though adults and livestock also died of snakebite. Nearly everyone carried a hoe to kill any rattlers they might encounter. Sometimes they actually invaded the house. One young boy awoke in the night complaining that his brother, sleeping in the same bed, was pinching him; the parents quieted the boys, and in the morning one was dead—of snakebite.

It was no wonder, with all these natural disasters and herpetological and ento-mological plagues, that Grace Fairchild "questioned in my own mind how a sane man could [drag] his family into such a…country" (Wyman 1972, 13). Indeed, faced with such disasters some homesteaders who could afford it left the country, the sides of their wagons emblazoned with bleakly humorous slogans such as "From Sodom, where it rains grasshoppers, fire and destruction" (Dick 1937, 206; Jones 1998, 186–89).

THE CATTLE MARKET

In the 1850s, Texas ranchers had begun to market the Texas longhorn, a new breed descended from the Spanish criollo, to which had been introduced other genetic strains including the English shorthorn. The Civil War interrupted development of the Texas cattle industry. Not only did many of the ranch hands find themselves in the Army of the Confederacy, but the war made it difficult to get their cattle to market. Thus, by the end of the war a large number of longhorns—some estimate as many as five million—roamed free in Texas.

The longhorn is an extremely tough, resilient animal, able to travel great distances with little water; moreover, it can protect itself against predators with horns measuring up to five feet from tip to tip. However, it is not an ideal beef animal, reaching its full weight of 1,000 pounds only after 8 to 10 years. It has often been described as "eight pounds of hamburger on 800 pounds of bone and horn." At the end of the Civil War these longhorns were a glut on the Texas market, selling at only $3 to $6 a head. In contrast, a good-quality steer sold in New York for $80; in Illinois, for $40; and in Kansas, for $38 (Milner, O'Connor, and Sandweiss 1994, 255). Clearly it made good business sense to move Texas cattle north and east to more lucrative markets.

There was, however, one major—though tiny—problem. The Texas cattle carried a small tick that transmitted splenic fever, commonly known as Texas or Spanish fever, to which the longhorns were generally resistant. However, on the trail north the ticks dropped off and found new hosts, devastating dairy herds, breeding stock, and oxen that lacked resistance. Tick fever was the first cause of trouble between farmers and cowboys on the Plains. Because of the tick, Missouri had banned Texas cattle as early as 1851; in 1867 Kansas established a quarantine line east of which the cowboys could not drive their herds.

It was discovered, however, that cold Northern winters killed the tick. Thus, cattle could be driven north to fatten for a winter or two, after which they were ready for market—and tick-free, thus welcome in the eastern markets. Nearly simultaneous results of the tick problem and its solution were the creation of cattle towns and an infusion of entrepreneurial capital into the cattle business.

The first of the cow towns was Abilene, established in 1867 by Joseph McCoy at the juncture of the Kansas Pacific Railroad and the Chisholm Trail. In that year an estimated 35,000 cattle came up the Chisholm Trail; over 20 years, the number reached two million (Milner, O'Connor, and Sandweiss 1994, 255). Each summer the herds moved north to Abilene and other towns such as Wichita, Ellsworth, and Dodge City; the towns and the trails that fed them moved progressively west as farmers and their quarantines moved into the region.

The longhorn, however, still did not produce prime beef—and beef was what the American public now wanted. Pork had been supplanted as the meat of choice as cookbooks and magazines began to describe pork as "difficult to digest, unwholesome and unhealthy"; beef became a "health food" (Milner, O'Connor, and Sandweiss 1994, 256). But consumers wanted nicely marbled beef. Cattlemen thus began importing purebred Hereford and Shorthorn bulls to the Plains to improve the longhorn stock.

In 1871, Dr. Hiram Latham, a public relations man for the Union Pacific Railroad published a booster pamphlet entitled *Trans-Missouri Stock Raising* that unabashedly sought investors in the Western cattle business. He argued in part that if the United States was to be competitive in international markets, it must furnish its laborers with cheap food, including beef. Land in the West was cheap and animals fattened well there, Latham and other such boosters argued, guaranteeing immense profits. Newspaper stories promising 40 percent annual returns brought a flood of investors and the formation of new cattle companies on the northern plains. In 1883 alone, 20 new companies were organized with a capitalization of $12 million (White 1991, 223). Baron Walter von Richthofen, the uncle of the Red Baron of World War I fame, published *Cattle Raising on the Plains of North America* in which he projected that from an initial herd of 100 cows one could, in 10 years, have a herd of 2,856, assuming four out of five had calves every year and that heifers starting calving at two years of age (Forbis 1973, 62). Such optimism now sounds unbeliev-

The Chicago stockyards were immense as can be seen in this early twentieth-century photograph of the Union Yards. There were 250 miles of railroad track within the stockyards in the 1890s. They brought together about 10,000 head of cattle every day, and as many hogs, and half as many sheep—which meant some eight or ten million live creatures turned into food every year. Courtesy Library of Congress.

able. Nonetheless, Eastern investors included William Rockefeller; Marshall Field of Chicago; August Busch, the brewer; James Gordon Bennett, editor of the *New York Herald*; and Theodore Roosevelt.

To achieve great profits, production costs also had to be controlled. With the introduction of railroad refrigerator cars, pioneered by Gustavus Swift, shippers no longer had to pay freight on live animals; a dressed carcass cost half as much to ship as did a live animal. By the 1880s refrigerated beef was less expensive in the East than fresh beef; between 1883 and 1889 the price of prime cuts dropped 40 percent (Milner, O'Connor, and Sandweiss 1994, 256). Beef became mass produced, with a few packing houses such as Swift and Armour dominating the market.

There thus grew up a dichotomy between the cattleman—the investor, the entrepreneur, the businessman—and the cowboy, his employee. Though he was essential to the enterprise, the cowboy usually received from $25 to $40 a month plus room and board (Milner, O'Connor, and Sandweiss 1994, 261–62). Teddy Blue describes receiving 25 cents per head for running a herd of beef in the last open range in Montana during 1878; he notes that he made $125 a month, "big money for a boy in those days when the usual wages ran as low as ten dollars" (Abbott and Smith 1939, 34). A transplanted Englishman, Frank Collinson, recalled earning $14 a month on his first job in Medina County, Texas, in 1872 (Collinson 1963, 8). Charles A. Siringo noted that the greenhorn who wanted to be a cowboy might at first have to work only for his "chuck" (i.e., his board), but this was worth it to "acquire all the knowledge and information possible on the art of running cattle." Starting wages, he remembered, were from $15 to $40 a month, depending on latitude. On northern ranges the wages were higher, but so were expenses; cowboys needed warmer clothing and bedding during the long, severe winters. He continued: "After you have mastered the cow business thoroughly—that is, learned not to dread getting in mud up to your ears, jumping your horse into a swollen stream when the water is freezing, nor running your horse at full speed, trying to stop a stampeded herd, on a dark night, when your course has to be guided by the sound of the frightened steer's hoofs—you command good wages, which will be from $25 to $60 per month" (Siringo 1886, 340).

On the debit side, the cowboy's equipment required an initial outlay of funds that could range considerably. A fancy outfit might cost $500: saddle, $100; saddle blanket, $50; quirt and riata, $25; a pearl-handled Colt .45, $50; a Winchester rifle, $75; Angora goat chaps, $25; and a Spanish pony, $25. However, a serviceable outfit could be bought for $82: pony, $25; leggings, $5; saddle, $25; saddle blankets, $5; spurs, bridle, and stake rope, $5; and Colt .45, $12 (Sawey 1981, 28–29).

In the early Texas cattle industry, it was the custom for cowboys who assisted at branding to receive a portion of the cattle in return. Cowboys could also acquire mavericks (motherless calves whose owners could not be determined). Thus, some cowboys could take the first steps toward becoming cattlemen. However, on the northern plains the mavericks were declared the property of the stock raisers' associations and auctioned off. Thus "mavericking—a way to begin a career of enterprise—became rustling—a way to begin a career of crime" (Milner, O'Connor, and Sandweiss 1994, 265).

Often the cowboy was laid off during the winter months, for ranch owners could get by with a skeleton staff and did not want to pay idle hands. During this time, especially on the northern plains, cowboys would take odd jobs around saloons or livery stables, trap or hunt wolves, mine, or simply ride the chuck line—that is, ride from ranch to ranch, staying at each until their welcome wore out. But at roundup, ranches needed a full complement of help (Jones 1998, 165–67).

INTERNATIONAL TRADE: THE CHINA TRADE

In the first half of the nineteenth century American Clipper ships opened trade with China, the South Seas, and Japan; and in the second half-century the U.S. Merchant Marine entered its heyday under canvas only to be supplanted late in the century by British steam. Rare spices and unusual fragrances could be found in most up-scale markets, and many wealthy Americans had collections of Chinese porcelain, silks, lacquered ware, and various other Oriental items like rugs, draperies, and wallpaper arranged in special rooms *à la Chinoise*. The so-called China Trade was actually a misnomer involving about a half dozen major trading destinations other than China in the Far East. These included—besides mainland China and Formosa—India, the East Indies (Spice Islands), the Siamese and Malay peninsulas, Japan, and the Philippines. Traders visited hundreds of small ports and isolated islands in their quest to complete a cargo of rare goods (Gardner 1971, 47).

Asian produce like peppercorns, cinnamon, nutmegs, and cloves were the big four among the fragrant spices. So desirable were these spices that a pocketful of peppercorns, for instance, was valued the same as a nugget of gold. Many of the rarest spices originated in the islands of the Molucca Sea, near New Guinea, so that the group came to be known as the Spice Islands. Although steps were taken to isolate the source of the plants to these islands, ultimately plants and seeds were smuggled out to other areas in the tropics where they could be grown. By such means India ultimately became a source of pepper and ginger; the West Indies and Brazil sources of cloves; Zanzibar and Madagascar producers of black pepper; and Nigeria and Sierra Leone traders in ginger.

Chinese porcelain was particularly admired in America and Europe, and it was soon imitated, especially by European potters, who tried to duplicate the hard Chinese porcelain but could only copy shapes and patterns from China on tin-glazed earthenware. The result was a flourish of decorative potting technique in Europe. The imitative process produced a white opaque surface sometimes known as creamware, pearlware, or faïence in English, as Saint-Porchaine ware or faïence blanche in French, and as the familiar delft in Dutch. On these white glazed ceramics the potters used cobalt blue to imitate Chinese figure scenes, flowers, birds, and other common patterns from late Ming and Kangxi porcelains. None of these were comparable to actual Chinese porcelain. European copies did not have the resonance, hardness, translucence, or luster of the Chinese originals.

The desire for spices, authentic Chinese items, or other Oriental products drove the American China Trade, and New England skippers lined up to get command of trading vessels destined for the western and southern Pacific, the Indian Ocean, or the South China Sea. Sea captains made good use of the prevailing winds when making these voyages. In an era largely dependent on sail, the seasonal monsoons provided a reliable source of propulsion. Moreover, a good run to the east could be made in the westerly winds of the southern latitudes and a fair run to China could be enjoyed in the northeasterly trade winds (Morison 1953, 130).

A common gathering point for ocean traders was the port city of Malacca, an international port on the west coast of the Malay peninsula overlooking the strategically important strait that linked the South China Sea to the Indian Ocean. Over the centuries, Chinese, Islamic, and Malaysian traders had called there every year trading silk and porcelain from China; textiles from Gujarat and Coromandel in India; nutmeg, mace, and cloves from the Molucca Islands; gold and pepper from Sumatra; camphor from Borneo; sandalwood from Timor; and tin from western Malaya. It was said that whoever held Malacca "held the throat" of far eastern commerce with Europe.

In the nineteenth century, Malacca was a great anchorage for European and American trading vessels awaiting the monsoon winds. The harbor was filled with Chinese sampans and junks, Arab *fellucas* and dhows, and western brigs and schooners all waiting for the winds to India, Africa, or home. When Malacca became overcrowded, many skippers chose the alternate route through the Sunda Straits by way of the Java Sea. The Sunda Straits and a stretch off Borneo were dangerous waters, where the threat of Malay or Chinese pirates was added to natural perils. The route was infested with Atjeh and Rian buccaneers who had established pirate havens in southeastern Sumatra. Famous among these in the nineteenth century was Chui Apoo who made his headquarters at Bias Bay. Yet this was not the only pirate threat. The Malay and Dayak pirates had a base in Borneo from which they attacked ships moving to and from Singapore and Hong Kong, and the Balarini pirates based at Jolo generally preyed on ships going to and from the Philippines. There were many tight passages among the islands of Indonesia, and sailors were glad to get clear of the straits.

Initially, the island of Formosa (Taiwan) showed promise as a place where direct trade with the Chinese might be possible, but ultimately it was found that merchants in the Chinese port of Canton were almost always offering the best deals. The Chinese merchants advertised their wares in their shops with bright red characters as they had for hundreds of years. It is through these early interactions between Europeans and the Chinese that words like Cantonese, Cantonware, and their complements derived their common use in English.

Although tea accounted for most of the imports from China, the manifest for one ship's cargo illustrates the great variety of goods Yankee traders would bring back including fresh Bohea tea of the first quality; China in many varieties; clothe including satins, silks, and taffetas; satin shoe-patterns; pearl buttons fixed with gold figures and inlays; superfine lambskins, a type of clothe; ivory and lacquered ware; tea-caddies; lacquered tea-trays, waiters, mirror frames, and bottle-stands; silk handkerchiefs, hair ribbons; cinnamon, cinnamon buds, black pepper, and sugar.

The British-Chinese Treaty of Nanking that ended the Opium War of 1842 effectively overthrew the original Chinese mercantilist system by means of forcing open the ports of Canton, Amoy, Foochow, Ningpo, and Shanghai to British trading. Seeing that Britain could now easily eliminate foreign competition in China with its new privileges and considerable trading prowess, the Americans, who had stayed on the sidelines in the conflict, needed to establish formal diplomatic relations and a commercial equality in China. For almost six decades the Americans had been interacting with China merely through their business transactions, without government-to-government communication. The American decision to acquiesce was based on the twin assumptions of the futility of a direct and forceful confrontation with the Chinese, and the profitability of letting Britain do precisely that, while Americans posed as friends and allies.

The administration of President John Tyler sent Caleb Cushing to negotiate a treaty in 1844 that would give Americans the same privileges as Britain. The Sino-American Treaty of Wanghia not only achieved this goal but also won for the Americans the right of extraterritoriality, which meant that Americans accused of crimes in China were to be tried by American courts only. The treaty also included the right to buy land in five Chinese ports, the right to provide Christian missionaries to the Chinese people, and the right to learn the Chinese language. This treaty was monumental in that it laid the foundation for a more extensive and better regulated American trade with China. The opium trade was explicitly declared illegal, and the United States agreed to hand over any offenders against that law to Chinese officials. More importantly, these privileges were gained without war and without the recriminations that war often leaves.

The China trade facilitated a worldwide circulation of wealth. Practically every known port and trade route of the eighteenth and nineteenth centuries was utilized by the China traders. Americans reinvested the wealth that they accumulated in the China trade, not only in stateside ventures, but also in such Chinese enterprises as the Shanghai Steam Navigation Company. They also financed charitable projects in China on a scale comparable to stateside public endowments like the Canton Hospital. Native Chinese merchants also ventured their capital in worldwide investments that included American railroads and other projects.

—James M. Volo

FOR MORE INFORMATION

Abbott, E. C. ("Teddy Blue"), and Helena Huntington Smith. *We Pointed Them North: Recollections of a Cowpuncher*. New York: Farrar & Rinehart, 1939.

Bartlett, Richard A. *The New Country: A Social History of the American Frontier, 1776–1890*. New York: Oxford University Press, 1974.

Browne, Ray B., and Lawrence A. Kreiser Jr. *The Civil War and Reconstruction*. Westport, CT: Greenwood Press, 2003.

Burgess, William W. *The Voyages of Capt. W. W. Burgess, 1854–1885*. Plymouth, MA: Jones River Press, 2003.

Citro, Constance F., and Robert T. Michael, eds. *Measuring Poverty: A New Approach*. Washington, DC: National Academy Press, 1995.

Collinson, Frank. *Life in the Saddle*. Edited by Mary Whatley Clarke. Norman: University of Oklahoma Press, 1963.

Colt, Mrs. Miriam (Davis). *Went to Kansas*. Ann Arbor, MI: University Microfilms, 1862.

Davidson, Marshall B. *Life in America*. Boston, MA: Houghton Mifflin Company, 1951.

Dick, Everett. *The Sod-House Frontier, 1854–1890: A Social History of the Northern Plains from the Creation of Kansas & Nebraska to the Admission of the Dakotas*. New York: D. Appleton-Century Co., 1937.

Donald, David H., Jean H. Baker, and Michael F. Holt, *The Civil War and Reconstruction*. New York: W.W. Norton, 2001.

Dulles, Foster Rhea. *The Old China Trade*. New York: Houghton Mifflin Company, 1930.

Fisher, Gordon M. "From Hunter to Orshansky: An Overview of Unofficial Poverty Lines in the United States from 1904–1965." (A paper presented October 28, 1993 at the Fifteenth Annual Research Conference of the Association for Public Policy Analysis and Management in Washington, DC available from the Department of Health and Human Services.)

Forbis, William H. *The Old West: The Cowboys*. New York: Time-Life Books, 1973.

Gardner, Brian. *The East India Company*. New York: Dorset Press, 1971.

Garland, Hamlin. *Son of the Middle Border*. New York: Macmillan Co., 1925.

Goldstein, Jonathan. *Philadelphia and the China Trade 1682–1846*. University Park: Pennsylvania State University Press, 1978.

Haines, T. L., and Levi W. Yaggy. *The Royal Path of Life: Or Aims and Aids to Success and Happiness*. Chicago, IL: Western Publishing House, 1876.

Jones, Mary Ellen. *Daily Life in the Nineteenth-Century American Frontier*. Westport, CT: Greenwood Press, 1998.

Luchetti, Cathy. *Women of the West*. In collaboration with Carol Olwell. St. George, UT: Antelope Valley Press, 1982.

Lupiano, Vincent DePaul, and Ken W. Sayers. *It Was a Very Good Year: A Cultural History of the United States from 1776 to the Present*. Holbrook, MA: Bob Adams, 1994.

Milner, Clyde A., Carol A. O'Connor, and Martha A. Sandweiss. *The Oxford History of the American West*. New York: Oxford University Press, 1994.

Morison, Samuel Eliot. *By Land and By Sea*. New York: Alfred A. Knopf, 1953.

Nelson, Paula M. *After the West Was Won: Homesteaders and Town-Builders in Western South Dakota, 1900–1917*. Iowa City: University of Iowa Press, 1986.

Randall, J. G., and David Donald. *The Civil War and Reconstruction*. Boston, MA: D.C. Heath and Company, 1961.

Rehwinkel, Alfred M. *Dr. Bessie*. St. Louis, MO: Concordia Publishing House, 1963.

Rosenbloom, Joshua L., and Gregory W. Stutes, *Reexamining the Distribution of Wealth in 1870*. Cambridge, MA: National Bureau of Economic Research, 2005.

Ruede, Howard. *Sod-House Days: Letters from a Kansas Homesteader, 1877–78*. Edited by John Ise. New York: Cooper Square Publishers, 1966.

Sanford, Mollie Dorsey. *Mollie: The Journal of Mollie Dorsey Sanford in Nebraska and Colorado Territories, 1857–1866*. Lincoln: University of Nebraska Press, 1959.

Savage, William A., Jr. *The Cowboy Hero: His Image in American History and Culture*. Norman: University of Oklahoma Press, 1979.

———. *Cowboy Life: Reconstructing an American Myth*. Norman: University of Oklahoma Press, 1975.

Sawey, Orlan. *Charles A. Siringo*. Boston, MA: Twayne Publishers, 1981.

Schlissel, Lillian, Byrd Gibbons, and Elizabeth Hampsten. *Far from Home: Families of the Westward Journey*. New York: Schocken Books, 1989.

Schob, David E. *Hired Hands and Plowboys: Farm Labor in the Midwest, 1815–1860*. Urbana: University of Illinois Press, 1975.

Siringo, Charles A. *A Lone Star Cowboy*. Santa Fe, NM: n.p., 1919.

————. *A Texas Cow Boy, or Fifteen Years on the Hurricane Deck of a Spanish Pony*. Chicago: Siringo and Dobson, 1886.

Stewart, Elinore Pruitt. *Letters of a Woman Homesteader*. Boston, MA: Houghton Mifflin, 1914.

Sutherland, Daniel E. *The Expansion of Everyday Life, 1860–1876*. Fayetteville: University of Arkansas Press, 2000.

Van Dyke, Paul A. *The Canton Trade, Life and Enterprise on the China Coast, 1700–1845*. Hong Kong: Hong Kong University Press, 2005.

Volo, Dorothy Denneen, and James M. Volo. *Family Life in Nineteenth-Century America*. Westport, CT: Greenwood Press, 2007.

Wheeler, Keith. *The Townsmen*. New York: Time-Life Books, 1975.

White, Richard. *"It's Your Misfortune and None of My Own": A New History of the American West*. Norman: University of Oklahoma Press, 1991.

Wyman, Walker D. *Frontier Woman: The Life of a Woman Homesteader on the Dakota Frontier*. River Falls: University of Wisconsin–River Falls Press, 1972.

RECONSTRUCTION
|
OVERVIEW
DOMESTIC LIFE
ECONOMIC LIFE
INTELLECTUAL LIFE
MATERIAL LIFE
POLITICAL LIFE
RECREATIONAL LIFE
RELIGIOUS LIFE

Intellectual Life

SCIENCE: PHOTOGRAPHING AMERICA

The early history of photographic science in America transcends the nineteenth century. Daguerreotype, tintype, and wet-plate photographic portraiture were ill-suited to outdoor use, and the practical use of photography to record large-scale historical events was not attempted until the Crimean War of 1854. Moreover, there were no published manuals for photographers prior to that printed by George B. Coale in 1858, and it is doubtful that the pocket-sized booklet could be used to successfully teach the intricacies of the photographic art in the absence of face-to-face instruction. The domination of the complicated wet-glass plate colloid process from 1855 to 1888 helps to explain why outdoor photography remained in the hands of professionals.

Among the many brave photo- journalists who recorded the battle scenes and war dead of America's Civil War were Alexander Gardner, George N. Bernard, and Captain Andrew J. Russell among others. Although he limited most of his work to the studio, Matthew Brady is possibly the best-known photographer of the period, and people flocked to him to have photographic portraits and *cartes de visite* taken in their best clothes. Historians continue to dispute Brady's active participation on the battlefields of the Civil War, but there is no question that the Brady studios sponsored many of the most productive photographers of the period.

In this period individual images from negatives were almost exclusively made on chloride paper, and the technology of reproducing photographs for the printing press was almost nonexistent before the end of the century. The usual way of reproducing a photograph for a newspaper, magazine, or book was to have an artist redraw it and make a woodcut or engraving as with battlefield sketches. This process neutralized most of the advantages of photography for the print medium. Moreover, Americans seem to have favored the more romanticized full-page chromolithographs and engravings over the generally small black and white photographs made by contact printing.

Nonetheless, hundreds of photographs of battlefields and personalities

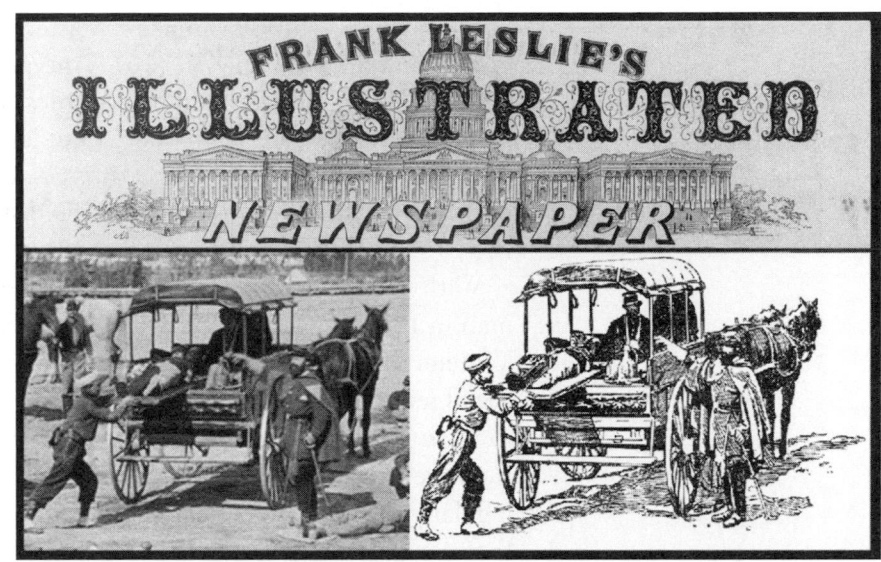

This composite showing wounded being loaded into an ambulance shows how Leslie's engravers turned a photograph (left) into a half-tone illustration (right) capable of being reproduced on newsprint. In many ways the illustration is superior in quality to the photo as it removes the fussy parts of the photograph caused by the motion of the subjects and redistributes or eliminates elements to emphasize the meaning of the scene. Courtesy Library of Congress. Leslie's by James Volo.

were shown in galleries in the major cities of the North during the Civil War years. The pictures, including some of the first to show war dead on the battlefield, were poignant and realistic, and may have helped to create an antiwar feeling in the North. Nonetheless, the photographic galleries in New York and Washington, in particular, were very popular and admission was expensive. The South also had its photographers. George S. Cook, J. D. Edwards, and A. D. Lytle, among others, were able photographers committed to the Southern cause, but their work was much more circumspect than that of their fellows from the North being generally limited to portraiture. The South's limited technical facilities forced the public to be content with rough woodcuts, engravings, and paintings.

It was through the older and simpler technology of the metal-plate process, however, that photography was introduced to the rural American public. All through the last half of the nineteenth century itinerant photographers traveled the fairs and road shows producing tintypes (sometimes called ferrotypes). Some tintypists traveled alone, riding a regional circuit of towns and seasonal stops, and returning to them at regular intervals to update the images of children and record the likenesses of newborns or recently married couples. Beginning with the presidential election of 1860, tintype campaign pins became the single most important electioneering apparel of the period with the exception of printed ribbons. All four major candidates for president that year had their slightly out-of-focus features photographically placed on dime-sized brass buttons. These tintype pins were considered invaluable as an electioneering tool, and they remained popular with the candidates until the 1880s. One inventive photographer took out a patent on "tombstone tintypes" made to fasten an image of the dearly departed to the grave marker (Holzer 1979, 316). Tintypes were less expensive than paper prints, but they were one of a kind works unless taken with multiple lens. There was no negative from which prints could be duplicated. The tin was itself the product of the exposure. Nonetheless, tintypes were long lasting and accurate in their portrayals. Tintype photographers could still be found working the county fairs in the 1920s.

With the development of faster acting dry-plate glass negatives by George East-man in 1888, photographers were better able to take their instruments out-of-doors. William Kurtz was the first to specialize in night photography using flash powder, and social reformer Jacob Riis used the dry-plate system to capture the misery of slum life in New York's tenements. A young politician (then police commissioner), Teddy Roosevelt, often took Riis with him when enforcing the city's health and safety regulations to make a permanent record of the violations. Also noted at the time for their images of street scenes and immigrants were Percy Byron and Lewis Hine (New York), Sigmund Krausz (Chicago), and Arnold Genthe (San Francisco). The new realism of such photographs became the vogue among Americans and generated a post–Civil War generation of documentary photographers (Volo and Volo 2007, 396–97).

EDUCATION

Enduring the ordeal of the Civil War changed the world of American youth. The very idea of adolescence was beginning to change during the 1860s and 1870s. Prior to the mid-nineteenth century, Americans generally referred to people in their late teens and early twenties when they talked about the passage from childhood to adulthood. With the faster pace of American life following the war, Americans turned their attention toward the maturation process among children in their pre- and early teens.

Going to school represented a milestone that children experienced in increasing numbers during the postwar era. Americans had placed high value upon the educational basics of reading, writing, and arithmetic since the late colonial era, at least for white children, but formal education for young people became the norm only during the late 1870s with the establishment of common schools in all states. Leading educational reformers believed that publicly supported schools would both foster social equality among students from diverse economic backgrounds and produce future workers and managers capable of sustaining economic growth. The push to extend educational opportunities to all white children caused the common school enrollment rates to skyrocket during the postwar era. By 1870, 60 percent of white Americans between the ages of 5 and 19 attended publicly supported schools, up from only 35 percent in 1830. Opportunities for higher education also increased with the passage of the Morrill Land Grant Act by Congress in 1862. The Morrill

Act gave individual states land to support colleges that taught both practical and academic subjects. With the passage of the act, agricultural colleges and institutes of technology joined universities in growing numbers across the nation. By 1870, the United States boasted 500 colleges and universities, more than all of Western Europe combined. These numbers must be read with some caution, however, because college students still formed a select breed in post–Civil War America. Only about 50,000 students attended college during the early 1870s, about one percent of the college age population.

Children who attended common schools during the late 1860s and early 1870s experienced an educational environment that their parents and grandparents would have found familiar in many ways. Most notably, educators continued to believe school an institution of moral uplift. William Holmes McGuffey, an Ohio college professor, authored a series of four elementary readers during 1836–1837 that taught reading skills and moral precepts to equal degree. The books became the most widely used school texts during the mid- and late-nineteenth century, selling more than 60 million copies by 1879. Stories, poems, and essays in McGuffey's readers offered children proof that virtue and faith went with God; and that thrift and industry went with success. McGuffey's *Second Reader* (1836), for example assured children "A little child who loves to pray, and reads his Bible, too, shall rise above the sky one day, and sing as angels do." A line from the *Fourth Reader* (1836) taught children that true happiness came from inside the person. "Wealth, rightly got and rightly used," McGuffey wrote, "Power fame, these are all worthy objects of ambition, but they are not the highest objects, and you may acquire them all without achieving true success."

Other elementary textbook authors followed McGuffey's lead, although never gaining the same level of distribution and sales. Salem Town, also the author of a reader, declared that his goal was to improve the literary taste of the learner, impress correct moral principles, and augment his fund of knowledge. S. Augustus Mitchell, the author of an elementary geography text, expressed a similar sentiment proffering that the introduction of moral and religious sentiments into books designed for the instruction of young persons was calculated to improve the heart, and elevate and expand the youthful mind and that observations had been made to illustrate the excellence of Christian religion, the advantages of correct moral principles, and the superiority of enlightened institutions.

In other ways, much had changed in common schools after the Civil War. Women increasingly replaced men as teachers, in part an attempt by educators to base classroom discipline and learning upon what they termed moral suasion rather than corporal punishment. Troublemakers, of course, still remained in the classroom. Boys in particular were into mischief, especially as they grew to be larger, lustier, and more masculine according to one Illinois school official. School officials increasingly drew a hard disciplinary line, however, expelling young rowdies into the work world rather than submitting to their antics. Women also became teachers in increasing numbers because, with few other employment alternatives, they were willing to work for lower wages than men. In Massachusetts, the state with among the most

In the second half of the nineteenth century public education became more common especially in the large urban areas. In this illustration a teacher instructs a class of girls in the sewing arts under the watchful eyes of visiting members of the Board of Education. Please note the formal lines of desks and chairs fastened to the floor, the common set of textbooks on the teacher's desk, and the large number (50+) of students. Courtesy Library of Congress.

complete educational records, female teachers earned less than one-half the pay of male teachers.

In addition to school officials hiring women teachers, they grouped students together by age. Prior to the mid-nineteenth century, educators made little distinction between learning needs among students of different ages. The result was that teachers instructed pupils who ranged in age and physical development from toddlers to young adults. George Moore, a teacher in Massachusetts, recorded that the 70 students he taught in 1828 ranged in age from a 4-year-old girl to a 20-year-old young man. With children entering common schools in increasing numbers following the end of the Civil War, however, educators concentrated students by what they termed "age grading." Children between 8 years and 13 years of age were grouped into intermediate schools. And teenagers between 14 and 19 were grouped into high schools. The age range of high school students in small rural towns and villages often was younger, generally between 11 and 17, to enable students to begin full-time work on family farms sooner. Age grading in intermediate schools and high schools also influenced the ages of students attending college. By the end of the nineteenth century, most college students ranged between 18 and 22 years of age, with much younger and older pupils as a rarity.

The increased emphasis upon public schooling in late-nineteenth-century America opened educational opportunities for both African American youth and young women. Blacks across the former Confederate states expressed an eagerness to learn, painfully aware that the denial of education had been a hallmark of the slave system. One Mississippi freedman promised that if he never did anything more worthwhile in his life, he would give his children the opportunity to go to school because education was the next best thing to liberty. Southern blacks worked with the federal government and various Northern-backed benevolent societies to establish schools of their own. By the 1870s, about one quarter of former slaves attended public school, while others received educational instruction at their church. Black schools often suffered from overcrowding and stingy state financial aid. To many African Americans, the advantages in educational opportunities seemed miraculous. Ambrose Headen recalled how difficult it was, when he was a slave in Alabama, to build a private academy for white boys when he had no right to educate his own sons. After the war, the building was purchased as a school for black children. When

Headen saw his own children coming from the same school, carrying their books under their arms, he remarked that he thought he must be dreaming.

Young women also made striking gains in education during the postwar era. The first public high school for girls had opened in Massachusetts in 1824. By the early 1870s, girls constituted the majority of high school graduates. Many female students attended coeducational public schools, a far less costly alternative to single-sex academies. Between 1850 and 1870, the number of public high schools attended by both boys and girls in the United States had more than doubled, from 80 schools to 170 schools. The expansion of women into secondary education fostered greater access to higher education. By 1870, nearly one-quarter of college students were women. Many women attended newly created women's colleges including Vassar, opened in 1865; and Wellesley and Smith both opened 10 years later. Other women attended previously all-male schools. Boston University and Cornell opened their doors to women during the postwar period, joining Oberlin, Antioch, and Swarthmore as coeducational institutions. Additionally, eight state universities opened under the Morrill Act admitted women. The number of coeducational colleges and universities continued to grow through the remainder of the century (Browne and Kreiser 2003, 27–30).

LITERATURE

Novels

Two genres of popular literature reemerged after the Civil War—the mystery tale and the historical romance novel. The historical romance was an old form that had been popular since the birth of storytelling. It abandoned reality for fantasy and told its stories in the realm of imagination where any kind of characters and actions could be presented. Women authors became very adept at historical romance. (Browne and Kreiser 2003, 111).

Although authorship by women was generally frowned upon before 1850, many novels were written by women in the period. The widespread popularity of sentimental and often formulaic domestic novels written in this period caused Nathaniel Hawthorne to complain that "America is now wholly given over to a damned mob of scribbling women" (Browne and Kreiser 2003, 110). Writing was an acceptable female hobby, but women who practiced the profession of letters seem to have been viewed with less disapprobation than those who became teachers, nurses, or lawyers. Several women were acclaimed in the Southern press for their published works in which heroines sacrificed their romantic love for dedication to the Southern cause and the Confederate forces remaining in the field (Volo and Volo 1998, 215–16).

The historical romance branched off into various forms, such as love stories, detective stories, westerns, and gothic tales. Edgar Allan Poe was especially good at the gothic and detective genres. He first Americanized the detective story in the 1840s with his tales of "ratiocination and detection," including "The Murder in the Rue Morgue" (1840), "The Mystery of Marie Roget" (1842–1843, based on the actual murder in New York City of Mary Celia Rogers), and "The Purloined Letter" (1845). Lesser known than Poe, Anna Katherine Green, the daughter of a well-known lawyer, challenged the earlier author's grip on the detective genre with her novel *The Leavenworth Case* (1878). Herein she introduced the fat and amiable character Ebenezer Gryce, who like her own lawyer father had an appearance and manner that belied his shrewd and unrelenting detective work (Browne and Kreiser 2003, 111).

Lew Wallace, a Civil War general who served as governor of New Mexico Territory, was also a novelist. He published a best-selling historical novel, *The Fair God,* in 1873, but his best-known work was *Ben Hur* written in 1880. Another late period author working in the genre was Francis Marion Crawford (nephew of poet Julia Ward Howe). Crawford wrote some 45 historical novels with Europe as the setting, particularly Italy where he was born and lived for many years. Crawford's first novel, *Mr. Isaac's* (1882) was an immediate success but his second, *Dr. Claudius* (1883) confirmed him as a major author. In defense of the novel Crawford wrote, "[It is] a marketable commodity…an intellectual artistic luxury…meant to amuse and please, not teach and preach." His third novel, *The Roman Singer,* was printed serially in the *Atlantic Monthly* and published in book form in 1884. Crawford continued writing into the twentieth century (Browne and Kreiser 2003, 111).

Juvenile Literature

Particularly important in the field of juvenile literature was *The Youth's Companion* founded in 1827 and growing to a behemoth circulation of 500,000 in 1900. It set the format for juvenile periodicals in the nineteenth century. Yet it was another publication, Scribner's *St. Nicholas Magazine,* begun in 1873, which is generally considered the best children's periodical of the era. *St. Nicholas* benefited from absorbing a number of short-lived children's magazines that came and went during the period. Among these were *Our Young Folks* and *The Children's Hour* in 1873 and *The Little Corporal* and *Schoolday Magazine* in 1875. Others like the *Riverside Magazine for Young People* (1867), *Wide Awake* (1875), and *Pansy* (1874) simply disappeared in the new, competitive market for children's literature. They may also have been affected by the continuing effect of the economic downturn known as the Panic of 1873 that simply sucked the life from all but the best-founded enterprises.

The editors and owners of these periodicals like G. P. Putnam, Charles Scribner, and James and John Harper consciously viewed themselves as "custodians of morals and culture" and sought to bring genteel values into their publications. *Our Young Folks,* absorbed by *St. Nicholas* in 1873, starkly illustrated the connection between the values of the creators of children's periodicals and those of their youthful audience. The editors invited their readers to write essays on a number of socially appropriate topics. The best of these appeared in subsequent issues. One such invitation issued in 1871 concerned the nature of a true gentlemen. Over 400 young people replied with a list of values that appeared in the very stories that the publishers had run in their periodical: integrity, modesty, manners, purity of heart, dedication to service, bravery, justice, generosity, temperance, self-control, and good taste. The editors had promoted these values in the articles and essays that they placed in their publications believing, as most of good society did, that they were vital for all youth. Spotless character, intellectual curiosity, moral refinement, and a dedication to public service were all considered essential ingredients in genteel children's literature (Shrock 2004, 166–67).

Periodicals

During the 1870s and 1880s, the South was winning in the pages of popular magazines and novels the culture war it had lost on the battlefield in the 1860s. It was a victory that was costly to Southerners in the long run because it blinded them to a good part of their own social history. During the 1880s a number of major magazines in the North began to feature articles steeped in the romance of an earlier and less menacing prewar period. The antebellum South conjured romantic images of oversized verandas, lazy rivers churned by the paddle wheels of luxurious steamboats, exaggerated hoopskirts, and trees hung with Spanish moss. The slower pace of this period seems to have rendered it an era untouched by time, and filled with an extravagant hospitality for all those who shared the Southern heritage. The reality, however, was exceedingly complex and replete with contradictions (Volo and Volo 2000, vii).

In Margaret Mitchell's novel, *Gone With the Wind,* written in 1936 and made into a significant and influential motion picture in the magical cinemagraphic year of 1939, the author described the loss of the Southern way of life in the winds of Civil War and the crusade of one young women, Scarlett O'Hara, to find her own redemption in the world of Southern Reconstruction. Mitchell's work was primarily romantic fiction, not meant to be a history or a social commentary on the South, but it has had a greater influence in forming the modern consciousness of the lifestyle it portrayed and the interpersonal relationships it presented than many formal studies. Moreover, it was—unknowingly perhaps—the culmination of an extended literary crusade to resurrect the image of the South after the war.

Once Reconstruction ended, the majority of white Southerners united in an attempt to remove blacks from local politics—by force if necessary. They pursued blacks with multifarious personal humiliations, lynch laws, and Jim Crow. Some claimed that these violations of human and civil rights were an explosion of pent-up frustrations over the loses of the Civil War long suppressed under the weight of federal occupation troops, few though they were. Regardless of its cause, the situation on the ground was often ugly and violent. In most Southern communities, it was the newly won set of black civil rights, rather than the antebellum white lifestyle, that was gone with the wind.

In the 1880s, *The Century,* a beautifully illustrated monthly magazine aimed at the genteel reader, began to run articles heavily favorable to things Southern. An abundance of articles appeared showcasing notable painters, Gothic architecture, and rambles through foreign and exotic lands. *The Century* also ran lengthy pieces on the "Battles and Leaders of the Civil War," in which equal time and equal editorial comment was given to Blue and Gray alike. *Harper's*, the *Atlantic*, and *Lippincott's*, among others, joined *The Century* in featuring Southern literature in which a familiar pattern began to appear. "Gentle and faithful old blacks would relate, with a comic mismanagement of the longer words, tales of how their cleverness or faithfulness had helped their beloved masters when the Yankees came" (Weisberger 1975, 108).

The story line usually involved a planter family, one or more high-spirited sons, and a beautiful and virtuous daughter in love with a Yankee from the North. The course of true love, thwarted by family feuds or the coming war, finally ran smooth in the postwar resurrection of the South. If the Yankee was a scoundrel, he was soon dismissed, but in most cases he was of a better sort that recognized the gallantry of Southern tradition. He, at least, had come to understand that it was only right that the South had been restored to proper white upper-class hands. He was usually rewarded for his epiphany, and the curtain fell on a scene of tender love and understanding with the old black family retainers peeping slyly from the shrubbery (Weisberger 1975, 108).

The story lines found in magazines like *The Century* gave the South an arm to lean on during the difficult postwar years, and the wave of moonlight-and-magnolia writing had a strong effect in putting to final rest many of the ideological ghosts of the Civil War. Southerners soon came to accept this fiction, relegating slavery to a tender and sentimental form of black welfare, and ennobling the sacrifices of their sons in gray. Reformers in the North, fighting battles between pure Republican government and the unwashed legions of city machine voters, were no longer focused on reforming the South. They lost their last vestiges of interest in the fate of Southern blacks in a sea of two-dollar-a-vote foreign immigrants. According to Edwin L. Godkin of *The Nation*, blacks would never be worked into the government that he and his fellow civil service reformers envisioned in any case. Richard W. Gilder, *The Century's* editor, observed that blacks constituted a peasantry wholly untrained in, and ignorant of, the concepts of constitutional liberty and social progress that were the birth-right of every white American (Weisberger 1975, 109).

Prominent in these stories was the stereotypical character of the female slave generally known as Mammy, who was so close to the family that she shared in its most personal secrets and aspirations. Besides being characterized as benign and maternal, Mammy exhibited wisdom and folksy common sense. She represents a social relationship between blacks and whites that transcends the auction block, fetters, injustices, and punishments of the overseer. Mammy interacts directly with the white slave owning family without offending the traditional hierarchy of a stratified and race-conscious society.

Plantation records from the antebellum period acknowledge the presence of female slaves who held a position equivalent to that of a head housekeeper or caregiver to their master's children. Yet their appearance in the historical record is incidental and outnumbered to a great degree by the employment of white governesses and nurses. The secure place of Mammy—or of a male Uncle Tom equivalent—in the mythology of Southern life was created by a combination of historic revisionism and romantic imagination that seems as first to have been a projection of the slave owner's own delusions about how their household slaves were devoted to them on a personal level—a repeated allusion found in contemporary Southern diaries, especially those of young women (Volo and Volo 2004, 66).

No historian or revisionist cemented the image of Mammy (or the loyal black family retainer) more firmly in this mythology than the actress Hattie McDaniel, who portrayed the character Mammy in the 1939 film version of *Gone With the Wind*. McDaniel's characterization exhibits all of the characteristics of "Mammy-ism" developed in the earlier nineteenth-century print media. She chides the debutante Scarlett in a motherly way, is concerned in family complications, weeps during its tragedy, is aware of its most personal feelings, and remains loyal to it during its reconstruction. While McDaniel's performance as Mammy provided moving, warm moments in the film (garnering her an Academy Award), there is no hard evidence that such persons existed as anything other than a balm for Southern consciences (Volo and Volo 2000, 180).

—*James M. Volo*

Poetry

During both the Civil War and Reconstruction, Americans read the classical poets—Shakespeare and Milton—and the antebellum American giants—Bryant, Whittier, Holmes, Lowell, and Longfellow. Yet there were also other forms of poetic materials that were widely appreciated: the instructive and everyday poetry by and for the people. In his *Library of Poetry and Song* (1872), William Cullen Bryant pointed out the values of both kinds of poetry. Some poems, he wrote, were "acknowledged to be great." Others, though less perfect in form, "have, by some power of touching the heart, gained and maintained a sure place in the popular esteem." Following the philosophy of the time, Bryant believed both forms were worthy art. Other poets and commentators on poetry preferred the popular form. Henry M. Coates's *Fireside Encyclopedia of Poetry* (1879) included only poems that "have touched the human heart" (Browne and Kreiser 2003, 112).

Henry Wadsworth Longfellow (1807–1882) wrote musically cadenced poems that were everywhere admired. His "Psalm of Life," with its uplifting and inspiring sentiment, was widely read and appreciated. The public took it to their hearts and gave it the ultimate compliment, setting it to song and parodying it in dozens of ways. Walt Whitman (1819–1892) is difficult to place in the popular poetry of the Civil War and Reconstruction eras. Though he lived during the period, his work transcended it. During the war, he was a hospital nurse caring for battlefield wounded in Washington, D.C., and once got to shake the hand of his hero, Abraham Lincoln. His *Democratic Vistas* (1870) outlined his vision of democracy in America.

The heat of war generated much popular poetry. A great deal of it took a predictably sentimental view of the tragedy of war and people's feeling in reaction to it. Many popular poems were set to music and sung straight or parodied. Perhaps the most sensationally popular poem of the war—at least with Northerners—was John Greenleaf Whittier's "Barbara Frietchie," published in the *Atlantic Monthly* in 1863. The poem was based on an apocryphal incident in Frederick, Maryland, that had been relayed to

Whittier by novelist Emma Southworth. It told of an aged woman's defiance of Confederate Lieutenant General Thomas "Stonewall" Jackson in flying a Union flag from her window. Whittier had his heroine utter the immortal line, "Shoot if you must this old gray head, but spare your country's flag." The incident was almost certainly a fabrication, but Whittier's poem captured the imagination of a nation hungry for heroes. It was widely reprinted throughout the North and even made into a popular song.

Also in the North, the Rev. Theodore Tilton wrote the hymn-like "God Save the Nation," Harvard University philosophy professor F. H. Hedge penned "Our Country Is Calling," and George H. Boker, a prominent playwright, wrote "March Along!" For the South, Albert Pike, a lawyer, editor, and poet-turned-Confederate-general, wrote "Southrons, Hear Your Country's Call." James Randall's "My Maryland" was sung straight as well as being parodied and twisted into dozens of different versions. In both parts of the nation, hundreds of poems with titles like "Following the Drum," "The Soldier's Mother," and "The Volunteer to His Wife," were written in reaction to the horrible sadness of parting, loneliness, and death.

The Northern longing for reconciliation predominated in the works of such poets as Edmund Clarence Stedman, Thomas Bailey Aldrich. Edward Roland Sill, Cincinnatus Heine, and Thomas Buchanan Read. Some of the poems were so passionate in their appeal to patriotism or reconciliation, or to human dignity and universal love of mankind and country that they appealed equally to both sides. Stedman's "Wanted—A Man" was such a poem. It so impressed President Lincoln that he reportedly read it to his cabinet in 1862, when it was clear that the president needed above all else a general of the army who could successfully lead his troops against the Army of Northern Virginia.

In Southern poetry, nostalgia and defiance were common themes. The Southern poet Henry Timrod, called upon to produce a Confederate anthem, initially refused; then in March 1862 penned "A Call to Arms," just one of many such calls to battle that would be produced by Southern writers during the course of the war. Paul Hamilton Hayne, known in his lifetime as the "Poet Laureate of the South," began writing verse while in law school, which he left to take over the *Literary Gazette*. Too frail for military service, he turned to writing patriotic and martial poems. Hayne's sentimental poems exalted the glories of antebellum life and were blamed for contributing to sectional divisiveness, although Hayne personally was said to be nonpartisan. After the war, his works were published widely in the *Atlantic Monthly*, *Scribner's Monthly*, and other respected magazines (Browne and Kreiser 2003, 111–13).

Regional Literature: The Lost Cause

Immediately after the Civil War, the public was swamped with war stories, journals, memoirs, and battle descriptions. Former army commanders renewed wartime arguments about tactics and strategies in print—the pen and the printing press now their only weapons. Battlefield opponents, and sometimes former comrades, aired the dirty laundry of their respective commands before an awaiting public. Southern apologists, particularly, tried to rationalize their loss by finding unexploited opportunities, scapegoats, excuses, and martyrs. Many pointed to the exhausted condition of the Southern manpower pool and its economic infrastructure as proximate causes for the South's surrender—not its defeat. For quite some time—in fact for almost as long as the veterans of the war lived to tell and retell their experiences—this was the stuff of Civil War history. Many of these authors drew sweeping conclusions from sometimes superficial and anecdotal evidence. In 1881, Francis M. Palfrey—a federal veteran and war historian embittered by the increasingly sympathetic light in which the Army of Northern Virginia was being portrayed—wrote, "A few more years, a few more books, and it will appear that Lee and Longstreet, and a one-armed orderly, and a casualty with a shotgun, fought all the battles of the rebellion and killed all the Union soldiers except those who ran away" (Newton 2000, 3).

The term "Lost Cause" first appeared in 1866 in the title of a book by historian Edward A. Pollard, *The Lost Cause: A New Southern History of the War of the Confederates*. Southern writers, like Pollard, made it clear that the arguments over states rights and secession, and not slavery, were the precipitating controversies of the war. As expressed by one abolitionist, the prominence of secession as a cause of the war becomes obvious: "Who cares now about slavery. Secession, and the Oligarchy built upon it, have crowded it out" (Lewis 1991, 163). Although antislavery was a prominent reform movement of the period, other causes, such as temperance, women's rights, religious revival, public education, concerns for the poor, and prison reform, were as zealously pursued by activists. Of these only slavery and states rights became politically charged issues in the antebellum period; and as the middle ground of compromise on such issues was eroded, only the extreme positions became viable, until disunion (secession) brought on armed conflict. Universal abolition, never an overall war aim of the North, was not even recognized by the Proclamation of Emancipation of 1863. Only in the afterglow of victory did the federal government dare to propose the universal abolition of slavery and full citizenship and voting rights for American blacks.

In 1865, Alexander H. Stephens was imprisoned for several months in Fort Warren in Boston Harbor. As former vice president of the Confederacy, Stephens had been a lackluster leader often at odds with the policies of President Jefferson Davis. Denied his seat in the 1866 U.S. Senate by the Republicans, Stephens undertook to write a book justifying the course of the South in the recent unpleasantness detailing the route from states rights to secession, war, and defeat. Like many Southern writers, he became immersed in the process of political rationalization that characterized the "Lost Cause."

A Constitutional View of the Late War between the States was a work in two volumes written by Stephens and published in 1868 and 1870, respectively. Stephens played down the slavery issue as a cause of the war and played up the controversy over states rights—the absolute ultimate sovereignty of the several states in the federal system. The book sold well and was widely read especially by Southerners. The case for states rights had flourished for more than seven decades before the war, and it would seem, from an unbiased reading of the record, that the secessionists had at least an arguable case for disunion on their side. By comparison, the case for a perpetual union and the supremacy of the federal government had been a recent product of the sectional conflict of the 1850s. Moreover, its fundamental legal principles, especially with regard to the 10th Amendment to the Constitution, were far from perfect, and the logic behind its arguments was fraught with ambiguity.

Stephens argued that the conflict from 1861–1865 had been no civil war, but a "war between the states." This position was a reaction to the Radical Republican demand that the unreconstructed states be treated as territories under the rule of federal political and military authorities. Southerners adopted the concept of a war between the states to reinforce their political position, and they insisted upon using the designation for the recent conflict, although the phrase had been seldom if ever used before Stephens proposed it in 1868.

Ultimately it was the series of articles written by former Lieutenant General Jubal A. Early for the Southern Historical Society in the 1870s that established the Lost Cause as a long-lasting and often-used literary phenomenon. Early claimed that his inspiration for the series came from Robert E. Lee, who wanted the world to understand the odds against which the Confederate Army (and the Army of Northern Virginia, in particular) had to contend. John Bell Hood, J.E.B. Stuart, and even Jefferson Davis were made scapegoats for the loss of Confederate independence, but the most powerful image used by Early was the failed attack on the third day of Gettysburg known as Pickett's Charge. He blamed the failure squarely on Lee's premiere subordinate, Lieutenant General James Longstreet, accusing him of failing to carry out his part in the attack. Longstreet was widely disparaged by Southern veterans during the postwar decades—not so much for his behavior during the war, which was laudable in most cases, but for his support of federal Reconstruction and his defection to the Republican Party. This made him the key villain in the Lost Cause mythology. Robert E. Lee, who had ordered the attack against an entrenched and numerically superior enemy, across open ground, free of protective cover, and obstructed by two substantial fence lines, received no scrutiny during his lifetime (and for some considerable time after his death). Lee's admitted tactical and strategic brilliance remained sacrosanct in the Lost Cause debate. He was viewed in the postwar period as the ideal Southern gentleman—sage, pious, unflappable, and honorable—who had selflessly sacrificed himself for the cause.

The fact was that the South had not merely lost the war. It had been beaten and beaten badly. Its economy, industry, agriculture, and population had been sorely pressed. The end of Reconstruction had restored the right of the South to be, once more, fully American. Yet Southern men and women were not willing to uproot their traditional way of life and replace it with machines, railroads, and factories. They clung to their un-machined ways and yielded only reluctantly to progress. Above all, white Southerners feared and resisted most of all changes of any kind that threatened their "biracial world, the fabric of white control of Southern life—a control which might be cruel or benevolent depending on time and place, but which in their view had to be unquestioned" (Weisberger 1975, 100).

—*James M. Volo*

COMMUNICATIONS: THE PONY EXPRESS

The Pony Express was founded as a subsidiary of the freight and stage company of Russell, Majors, and Waddell. The official company name was the Central

Overland California and Pike's Peak Express Company. Financially, the Pony Express was an abject failure. The owners invested $700,000 and left a $200,000 deficit when the company failed. The express mail service ran from April 3, 1860, through October 1861, being put out of business by the completion of the transcontinental telegraph and competition from the Overland Stage Lines. The company was sold at auction to Ben Holladay in March 1862. Four years later he sold out to Wells Fargo for $2,000,000. The Pony Express had proved that the central route to California was usable year round, and the Overland Mail Company, which held the mail contract, relocated from the southern/Butterfield route to the central route in 1861.

The idea of using a series of horses and riders to bind together the region between St. Joseph on the fringe of western settlement and the mining communities of California was challenging and bold, but it was not new. From ancient times, such post riders had served to bind together the provinces of monarchies, empires, and republics. The 1,966 mile route from St. Joseph, Missouri, to Sacramento, California, was a particularly difficult one, however, passing by ferry over the Missouri River and through the states (or territories) of Kansas, Nebraska, Colorado, Wyoming, Utah, Nevada, and California was done in approximately 10 days. The fastest trip was 7 days and 17 hours. These riders were carrying President Lincoln's first inaugural address. Keeping the lines of communication open and the mail flowing may have influenced California to remain in the Union.

There were between 80 and 100 riders working for the Pony Express at an average wage of $100 per month. The riders ranged in age from teens to men in their mid-forties. Each had to weigh less than 125 lbs. and be agile in the saddle. William "Buffalo Bill" Cody supposedly rode for the Pony Express. The youngest rider was 11-year-old Bronco Charlie Miller, but some of the first riders to attempt the express route are well known: Johnny Fry (St. Joseph), James Randall (San Francisco), and Billy Hamilton (Sacramento). The riders were changed every 75 to 100 miles depending on the geography, and the horses were changed every 10 to 15 miles galloping at approximately 10 miles per hour. The stations along the route—almost 200 of them—were supplied with 400 mustangs and Morgan horses. Mail cost $5 per 1/2 ounce at first, but the price fell to $1 per 1/2 ounce just before the company went under.

—James M. Volo

HEALTH AND MEDICINE

The General Practice

No medical instruments are so characteristic of the general practitioner in his office than the stethoscope and ophthalmoscope. Virtually every modern child's medical playset includes the double-tube stethoscope to place in their ears and the curved mirror with the hole in it (the ophthalmoscope) to wear on their forehead. Both of these important diagnostic instruments were introduced to medical science during the nineteenth century as medical screening devices.

The acoustic stethoscope was invented in France in 1816 by René Laennec. It consisted of a single (monaural), hollow wooden tube with a trumpet-like bell on one end that was almost indistinguishable from the common ear-trumpet used to aid the so-called hard-of-hearing for centuries. Laennec placed the bell of his microphone on the patient's chest and listened on the other end to the collected sounds of heartbeat or breathing. In 1851, Arthur Leared of Dublin invented the biaural (two tube) stethoscope with a small hollow cup replacing the bell, and in 1852 George Cammann of New York perfected the design that has become so familiar. This form—made possible largely by the development of thin rubber and metal tubing—was immediately put into commercial production, and was very popular with physicians. Cammann also wrote a treatise on the diagnostic used of his stethoscope. By 1873, there were proposals for a stereo stethoscope that absorbed sound from two locations at once, but the design was not widely adopted even though the concept was a good one.

Sound waves are composed of pressure differentiations that spread out from the source. Diagnostic stethoscopy (also called auscultation) used the sound waves produced in the body or on the skin surface by concentrating them and allowing them to travel up the tubing to the physician's ears. Used together with a light tapping on the chest or back quickly became a fundamental nonintrusive medical protocol. The qualities of the sounds emitted by the patient's body—especially the heart, lungs, blood vessels, and intestines—can denote the health or abnormality of the organs. Many diseases can be recognized, even in their early stages, by the skillful use of the stethoscope. The instrument was not without its flaws, however. One problem was that the sound emitted by the body was extremely faint. Moreover, the sources of the sound varied in their location, amplitude, and frequency. The hollow cup transmitted low frequency sounds better than high frequency ones. A diaphragm stethoscope, looking much like a metal disk rather than a cup, transmits higher frequencies better than the bell. In the twentieth century, physicians (Howard Rappaport and Maurice Sprauge) developed a two-sided chest piece that incorporated both chest pieces in a single instrument.

The ophthalmoscope is used to diagnose the eye. Initially invented as a freestanding table device by Charles Babbage in 1847, and independently by Hermann von Helmholtz in 1851, the instrument was not widely utilized until reinvented in a hand-held format by Andreas Anagnostakis, a Greek physician studying in France. It was presented at the first Ophthalmological Conference, which was held in Brussels in 1857. The concave mirror with a hole in it, allowed the physician the free use of one hand. It was later attached to a head strap that allowed both hands to be free. The mirror concentrated light on the eye and the ophthalmologist could examine the internal structures of the eye by viewing through the hole in the mirror and the eye's pupil. The entire retina can be examined and magnifying glasses and lens can be used by the physician to see even minute structures clearly. Its present form makes use of an incorporated source of light, but the nineteenth-century version is indistinguishable from many modern instruments.

The Discovery of Anesthesia

An advance in both general and surgical practice in both medicine and dentistry was the discovery of the anesthetic properties of ether, nitrous oxide, and chloroform. The discovery of general anesthetics and their subsequent applications to surgery revolutionized medicine in the United States and throughout the world. Before anesthesia, surgery was a frightening process for the patient and the surgeon alike. Once a patient had agreed to an operation, even an amputation, no further attention was paid to cries of protest and pain until the procedure was complete. This was found to be the only practicable method by which an operation could be performed under the gruesome conditions that prevailed before the advent of anesthesia. For obvious reasons, such surgeries were delayed until absolutely necessary: often until after it was too late to save the patient.

Although it is difficult to assign credit to one person as the discoverer of anesthetics, several Americans played a seminal role in their discovery and application. Scientists, most notably Sir Humphrey Davy, had experimented with nitrous oxide since the late-eighteenth century. The gas-induced antics of nitrous oxide users provided comical relief for various demonstrations given to the general public in the nineteenth century—hence the term laughing gas. In 1844, a Connecticut dentist named Horace Wells witnessed such a show and realized the possible uses for nitrous oxide in dentistry. Wells began administering it to his patients, providing pain-free tooth extractions. It's difficult to imagine modern dentistry without anesthesia. For instance, when American George Green patented the first electric dental drill in 1875, such a device would certainly have found limited use in the mouth of an unanesthetized patient. Wells's experiments came to a tragic end (at least for Wells himself), when he committed suicide in despondency over a failed demonstration of nitrous oxide to medical students at Massachusetts General Hospital.

Other Americans soon took up the experimental use of general anesthetics in various types of surgeries. Among these early pioneers were Wells's protégé, William Morton, who began using ether to induce sleep before dental procedures; Crawford Long, who had used ether in operations without publicizing the fact as early as 1842; Charles T. Jackson, who experimented with the use of several anesthetics on himself; and John C. Warren, who also experimented with the use of ether in surgery. Within a few years of the first demonstrations of the power of general anesthesia for surgery, the technique had spread across the country and to Europe, offering a mixed bag of results for physicians and their patients. Among these was an increase in the number of surgical interventions, and a decrease in the time lag that ensued between the onset of a problem and the decision to resort to surgery. Ironically, the larger number of surgeries increased the number of postoperative problems, including death, as the so-called hospital fevers—gangrene, erysipelas, septicemia, and so forth—rose in proportion due to the lack of an antiseptic environment. Nonetheless, through the use of anesthesia physicians were able for the first time to attempt a number of operations on the head, chest, and abdomen that were just too painful to imagine without it. Combined with a new understanding of germ theory and antiseptic practices, anesthesia ultimately made a significant difference in overall mortality rates (Timmons 2005, 147–49).

FOR MORE INFORMATION

Bradley, Glenn D. *The Story of the Pony Express: An Account of the Most Remarkable Mail Service Ever in Existence, and Its Place in History.* Chicago, IL: A. C. McClurg, 1913.

Browne, Francis F. *Bugle-echoes: Collection of Poetry of the Civil War Northern and Southern.* New York: White, Stokes & Allen, 1886.

Casper, Scott E., Joan Chaison, and Jeffery D. Groves, eds. *Perspectives on American Book History: Artifacts and Commentary.* Amherst: University of Massachusetts Press, 2002.

DiCerto, Joseph J. *The Pony Express: Hoofbeats in the Wilderness.* New York: F. Watts, 1989.

Duffy, John. "Science and Medicine." In *Science and Society in the United States,* eds. David D. Van Tassel and Michael G. Hall. Homewood, IL: Dorsey Press, 1966, 107–34.

Fahs, Alice. *The Imagined Civil War: Popular Literature of the North and South, 1861–1865.* Chapel Hill: University of North Carolina Press, 2001.

Glass, Andrew. *The Sweetwater Run: The Story of Buffalo Bill Cody and the Pony Express.* New York: Doubleday, 1996.

Hofstadter, Richard, and Wilson Smith, eds. *American Higher Education, A Documentary History.* Chicago, IL: University of Chicago Press, 1968.

Holzer, Harold. "Photographs on Tin: The Ferrotype Endures." *The Antique Trader Annual of Articles,* Volume X (September, 1979).

Johnson, Clifton. *Old-Time Schools and School-books.* New York: Dover Publications, 1963.

Kelley, R. Gordon, ed. *Children's Periodicals of the United States.* Westport, CT: Greenwood Press, 1984.

Lewis, Thomas A. *The Guns of Cedar Creek.* New York: Bantam, 1991.

Mason, Philip P., ed. *Copper Country Journal: The Diary of Schoolmaster Henry Hobart, 1863–1864.* Detroit, MI: Wayne State University Press, 1991.

Mautz, Carl. *Biographies of Western Photographers: A Reference Guide to Photographers Working in the 19th-Century American West.* Nevada City, CA: Carl Mautz Publishing, 1997.

Meredith, Roy. *Mathew Brady's Portrait of an Era.* New York: W.W. Norton & Company, 1982.

Mondale, Sarah, and Sarah B. Patton, eds. *School: The Story of American Public Education.* Boston, MA: Beacon Press, 2001.

Mott, Frank Luther. *A History of American Magazines.* 5 vols. Cambridge, MA: Harvard University Press, 1930–1968.

Newton, Steven H. *Lost for the Cause, The Confederate Army in 1864.* Mason City, IA: Savas Publishing Company, 2000.

Nye, Russel B. *The Unembarrassed Muse: The Popular Arts in America.* New York: Dial, 1970.

Shrock, Joel. *The Gilded Age.* Westport, CT: Greenwood Press, 2004.

Tebbel, John, and Mary Ellen Zuckerman. *The Magazine in America, 1741–1990.* New York: Oxford University Press, 1991.

Timmons, Todd. *Science and Technology in Nineteenth-Century America*. Westport, CT: Greenwood Press, 2005.

Volo, Dorothy Denneen, and James M. Volo. *The Antebellum Period*. Westport, CT: Greenwood Press, 2004.

———. *Daily Life in Civil War America*. Westport, CT: Greenwood Press, 1998.

———. *Encyclopedia of the Antebellum South*. Westport, CT: Greenwood Press, 2000.

———. *Family Life in Nineteenth-Century America*. Westport, CT: Greenwood Press, 2007.

Weisberger, Bernard A. *The LIFE History of the United States: Steel and Steam, Volume 7: 1877–1890*. New York: Time-Life Books, 1975.

Material Life

FOOD AND DRINK

Changes in Cooking

The Reconstruction period was a time of transition both in the methods of acquiring food and in the food itself. Thomas Defoe, a New York butcher and observer of the market scene, published a guide to the marketplace in 1867. He noticed significant changes in the manner in which New Yorkers acquired their food, particularly a loss of contact with purveyors of the foods that they were purchasing. He noted, "Some fifty years ago it was the common custom of the thrifty 'old New Yorker' when going to market, to start at the break of day, and carry along with them the large 'market basket,' then considered a very necessary appendage for this occasion. His early visit gave him the desired opportunity to select the cuts of meat wanted from the best animals, to meet the farmer's choice productions, either poultry, vegetables, or fruit and catch the lively jumping fish, which ten minutes before were swimming in the fish-cars." He lamented that by the era of Reconstruction, heads of families rarely visited public markets, doing all of their purchasing through agents from their shops—butchers, confectioners and others (Williams 2006, 13–14).

The food distribution network had become international in scope and was governed by an industrialist capitalist economy. Corn, oats, and barley, once traditional staples of the Anglo-American diet, were being supplemented by a massive wheat enterprise in the Midwest. Bread, once a homemade or locally baked commodity, poured out of commercial ovens. Housewives turned to making muffins, cakes, biscuits, and other baked goodies found in cookbooks (Williams 2006, 15).

With the rise of industrialism, there were astonishing changes in how some Americans ate. Railroad shipping, industrial food processing, and new nutritional ideas began to stimulate the culinary landscape. Class had a significant impact. Northern slum dwellers, Southern sharecroppers, small farmers on the Great Plains, and recently freed slaves were less affected by the innovations. This was partly due to the

The so-called modern kitchen of the nineteenth century had its cast-iron cook stove, running water, and convenient pantry. The cook stove was a particular improvement over open hearths that often sent cinders into the room or caught long skirts on fire. Yet accidents persisted as housewives made adjustments in their kitchen protocols. House fires decreased as the number of cook stoves increased, but the number of reported superficial burns, especially among small children making contact with hot metal, became greater. Courtesy Library of Congress.

fact that people with more money could afford to buy more food and food of a better quality, but the difference was not purely financial. Food was one way in which social classes distinguished themselves from each other (Husband and O'Loughlin 2004, 152–53).

By the 1870s women were cooking on cast-iron ranges and using so-called modern utensils. Cooking techniques became more scientific. Recipes no longer called for butter the size of an egg or a teacup of sugar. New standardized tools for measuring ingredients ensured that the final product would be generally replicable without previous training or experience. By mid-century, cookbooks, domestic advice manuals, and household management literature became widely available, and they continued to be published throughout the period. These texts offered their readers a window into cooking cultures that far exceeded the traditional bounds of place and family. New issues of economy, nutrition, fashion, and taste entered the American kitchen, reshaping daily menus and family diets (Williams 2006, 53).

By the period of Reconstruction stoves had evolved from relatively small boxes with a two-hole cooking surface, to massive ranges with between four and eight potholes, multiple ovens and large attached tanks for heating water. The stoves reflected the period craving for ornamentation and had relief-molded side panels and nickel-plated doors. "The Housekeeper," a high-end range produced by Philadelphia stove-maker Charles Noble & Co., was intended to be first class in every respect. It had nickel-plated knobs and ornaments, front illumination, a nickel-plated shifting guard-rail, a shaking and dumping clinker-less grate, ash fire, and hot-air arrangements to heat any number of rooms and many other desirable characteristics. This grandiose range, for which its manufacturer won a medal at the Philadelphia Centennial Exhibition in 1876, had six burners and two ovens and was embellished with cast-iron panels depicting standing stags, rabbits and lion's heads. Renaissance ornaments crowned the top. More furniture than appliance, it would have been just as suitable in a bedroom or parlor as in a kitchen.

One important outcome of the shift from fireplace hearth cooking to stove cooking was that on a stove, a woman could more easily cook multiple items at once. As a result, family menus became more complex, involving more courses and more complicated recipes. Women had to acquire new skills. Opening and closing dampers and flues could moderate temperatures, but it required great practice and familiarity with the range to master the individuality of each range (Williams 2006, 57).

Common Foods

In general, Americans ate as much meat as they could and at every meal, if they could afford it. Beef was the meat of choice, and as Americans became wealthier, they ate more beef. Pork, however, was the most consumed meat because it was less expensive. The distinction took on social dimensions as middle- and upper-class cooks looked down upon pork as a lesser or cruder meat (Husband and O'Loughlin 2004, 153).

Pork, sheep, and beef raised in the West and Midwest were transported to stockyards where they were slaughtered, packaged, and transported around the country. P. D. Armour opened the first meat-packing plant in Chicago in 1868, and the first refrigerated railroad cars left Chicago with a load of fresh meat in 1877. Thomas DeVoe noted that the producer was often hundreds of miles in one direction, while the consumer might be as many hundred in another from the mart at which the products were sold and purchased (Williams 2006, 15).

By the Civil War most families were purchasing factory-made cheese. DeVoe's *The Market Assistant* (1867) noted that the best cheeses in New York State came from Herkimer and Jefferson Counties and that a Colonel Meacham of Oswego, with a dairy herd of 154 cows, was able to produce 300 wheels of cheese weighing 125 pounds each (Williams 2006, 22–23). While cheddar had been the overwhelming favorite from early times, the arrival of new, non-English immigrant groups brought new cheese-making skills and tastes. In Wisconsin, German artisan cheese makers made that state a center of cheese production by the post–Civil War era. John Jossi, a native of Switzerland, living in Lebanon, Wisconsin, created American Brick cheese in 1877.

The growing affluence of the period also brought a taste for imported cheeses. European cheeses began to appear in marketplaces as well as in restaurant menus. The Parker House, one of Boston's finest restaurants, listed five different cheeses on its 1874 menu including Roquefort, Neufchatel, Gruyere, and two traditional American cheeses, American and Sage (Williams 2006, 24).

Vegetables, at the beginning of the Victorian era, consisted mainly of cabbages, corn, root vegetables, onion, squash, and potatoes. They were all relatively easy to grow, easy to keep, and easy to cook. By the later nineteenth century, American tastes for vegetables were expanding. This was due, in part, to the improving economic situation and the resulting demand for more status foods. The completion of the transcontinental railroad in 1869 permitted the shipping of more exotic vegetables from California and the South to the East and Midwest. DeVoe reported that the market gardeners of New Jersey, Connecticut, Long Island, and other New York suburbs could no longer meet the demand for produce. Requisitions, he noted, were being made to the Southern states and Bermuda Islands to send their early supplies to Northern markets prior to the production of the native supply. Tomatoes, potatoes, peas, cabbage, and onions were brought in twice a week from Charleston,

Norfolk, Savannah, and the Bermudas. Some of the items were brought in by hundreds of barrels at a time. DeVoe observed that many rare vegetables and other edibles were brought to Northern markets by the facilities afforded by railcars and steamboats, thus inducing, as it were, artificial seasons in those latitudes. DeVoe wrote his book to provide consumers with a sweeping view of what was available in the New York markets and included dozens of vegetables in his discussion. Luxury goods, such as asparagus, abounded in and out of season. He described the vegetable as one of the best and choicest luxuries of the vegetable kind and pronounced it as a wholesome, digestible, and light food. He wrote that potatoes were undoubtedly the most useful, wholesome, and nutritive of all roots in use at the time and speculated that scarcely a dinner was prepared without having them on the table. He also praised tomatoes for their health benefits and quoted Dr. Bennett who argued that the tomato was excellent for dyspepsia and indigestion and advised that it should be used daily either cooked, raw, or in the form of catsup (Williams 2006, 30–31). Vegetable varieties and vegetable preparation techniques continued to expand throughout the period. In 1872, chefs at the Palace Hotel in San Francisco invented Green Goddess salad dressing and Oysters Kirkpatrick and popularized a new vegetable—the artichoke.

From the beginning of the century cookery literature included recipes for piquant sauces, catsups, relishes, chutneys, and mustards, all of which added flavor and zest to foods. The use of these condiments was so popular that it became common for castor sets to adorn middle- and upper-class tables during the late-nineteenth century. Castor sets were metal, often silver plated, stands that held a number of glass bottles. Many were highly ornate. Sets contained as many as five or six bottles to hold such savory items as flavored vinegars, pepper sauces, Worcestershire sauce, red and black pepper, and mustard, or whatever condiments the family preferred. Marion Harland devoted an entire section to catsups and vinegars in her popular 1871 cookbook, *Common Sense in the Household: A Manual of Practical Housewifery*. She offered readers recipes for store sauces, to compete with the array of bottled sauces, largely imported from England, which were available in American markets. In 1869 Henry J. Heinz and L. Clarence Noble formed a company to manufacture Heinz's mother's pickled horseradish. They marketed it in clear glass bottles so that consumers could be assured of its purity. By 1876 the company was also producing ketchup, celery sauce, pickled cucumbers, sauerkraut, and vinegar. One of Harland's recipes, identified as "A Good Sauce," contained horseradish, allspice, nutmeg, pickled onions, whole black pepper, cayenne, salt, sugar, and vinegar. After it had rested for two weeks, she suggested that it was an excellent seasoning for any gravy, sauce, or stew. Harland also attempted to replicate the most famous of bought sauces, Worcestershire sauce. Her version had a walnut or tomato catsup base flavored with cayenne, shallots, anchovies, vinegar, and powdered clove (Williams 2006, 38).

As with vegetables, fruit options expanded during the Victorian era. In addition to apples, pears, peaches, cherries, raspberries, blueberries, cranberries, plums, and other fruits, improvements in communication and transportation brought pineapples, oranges, lemons, limes, bananas, and other tropical and warm weather fruits to markets in the North and Midwest.

Fruit formed the basis of many desserts in Victorian America, whether pastries, puddings, pies, or served alone. In 1871 Jane Cunningham Croly wrote that fruit alone made a very good dessert and when in season a plentiful and cheap one. Generally, though, the American sweet tooth preferred its fruit in combination with sugar, flour, and fat as suggested in cookery literature (Williams 2006, 40–41).

The title page of Eleanor Parkinson's *The Complete Confectioner* (1864) stated that the book would provide recipes for all sorts of preserves, sugar-boiling, comfit, lozenges, ornamental cakes, ices, liqueurs, water, gum-paste, ornaments, syrups, jellies, marmalades, compotes, fancy biscuits, cakes, rolls, muggings, tarts, and pies. All of these confections required some sort of sweetener, and by the nineteenth century, many choices were available. DeVoe listed sweeteners available in New York's urban markets as molasses, maple sugar, maple syrup, and honey. Molasses, a by-product of sugar production, became an alternative syrup for sweetening in the eighteenth century, but was typically used for cookies, puddings, cakes, and other cooked dishes, rather than as a table sweetener. Cane sugar became the primary sweetener for most people in the nineteenth century, as a result of improvements in sugar cultivation and processing, as well as transportation. As refining techniques improved, sugar became cheaper and whiter, which added to its status and appeal. Loaf sugar was preferred for its fineness and texture. By 1871, however, it was replaced by granulated sugar. Loaf sugar, sold in cone-shaped blocks, had to be cut into lumps or pounded into powder before use. Granulated sugar was loose and much more convenient to use (Williams 2006, 41–43).

A wide variety of sweets and desserts relied on the new abundance of sugar. Penny candies, sheathed in brightly colored wrappers, were widely available and affordable for most children by the 1860s. In 1871 German immigrant, F. W. Rueckhcim opened a popcorn stand in Chicago. He expanded his merchandise to include marshmallows, caramel candy, peanuts, and molasses taffy. Rueckheim noticed that his best sellers were peanuts, popcorn, and molasses taffy. Thinking that his customers would enjoy them all the more if they were mixed, he combined them into one product. He named his new product after the exclamation of a friend who shouted "Cracker Jack!" upon tasting it.

Early nineteenth-century cookbooks included soup recipes, but only in a limited way. Working-class families consumed much soup, which for those of lesser means was an important way of stretching meat with grains, legumes, root vegetables, and liquid. Wealthier families ate soup as well, but on their tables it followed European recipes for consommés, broths, and potages. By mid-century cookbooks were featuring more soup recipes. Eliza Leslie's soup offerings reflected a considerable degree of gentrification and included Fine Beef Soup, Rich Veal Soup, *Soupe à la Julienne*, Vermicelli Soup, Rich White Soup, Mock Turtle/Calf's Head Soup, Asparagus Soup, Mullagatawny (as made in India), and two dozen others. The most prevalent ingredient in the soups was veal, followed by beef, fowl, ham, oysters, and clams. They were seasoned with almonds, cayenne, cloves, onions, bacon, nutmeg, celery, sweet marjoram, coriander seeds, mint, and mace. The growing taste in Victorian America for diverse soups coincided with the rise of mechanized food processing, specifically canning. James H. Huckins began producing canned soup in Boston around the time of the Civil War and advertising his canned tomato soup in 1876 (Williams 2006, 26–27).

While coffee was available long before the Civil War, the high cost kept it off the table of most American families. Many young men went off to war never having even tasted coffee. Army rations in the North, however, included coffee, and it soon became a favorite beverage, which soldiers were not inclined to abandon. Following the war there was a rush of coffee importing, coffee wars, and the development of coffee-roasting devices. The Oriental Tea Company of Boston, Massachusetts, introduced "Male Berry Java," which they touted as the very best coffee in the world. They claimed that it had powerful strength, richness of aroma, and healthy drinking properties. While critics and competitors pointed out that if the berry had any gender at all, it would not be male, consumers embraced the coffee and sales were brisk despite the fact that it was the company's most expensive coffee. Other coffee companies offered premiums. Osborn's Celebrated Prepared Java Coffee proudly advertised that they offered no prize packages, no orders for spoons or dolls, just coffee worth the price.

At this time coffee was distributed in small paper bags, and coffee quickly went stale and rancid. Arbuckle's developed a process of coating, or glazing the beans to lengthen their shelf life. With the same goal in mind, Dillworth Bros. developed a steam polisher. To discredit Dilworth Bros., Arbuckle's circulated a woodcut handbill showing a roasting facility with barrels of dubious materials and people claiming to realize why they had been sick. The newspaper advertising campaigns that followed were bitter and anxiously followed by the public.

The coffee business was plagued by many unscrupulous roasters, wholesalers, and retailers who sold adulterated products at lower prices. The *Philadelphia Grocer* warned readers that the adulteration of coffee was very common and that all sorts of wasted grains, nuts, and shells were used. Charcoal, red slate, bark, and date stones were also employed. Chicory root was the most common adulteration, and adulterers went so far as to grind the root into a powder, mold it into the proper shape, and color it to resemble the coffee berry. Coffee extract was a popular patent compound that contained little if any coffee. Adulteration also occurred at the retail end. Cheap boarding houses often mixed it with real coffee (Johnson 1961, 74–77).

To avert the commercial adulterations, many people preferred to roast their coffee themselves. Some people used simple roasting pans, but a variety of small machines were developed and patented to fill the need. These devices tumbled small amounts of beans inside metal cylinders or globes that were placed over coals.

—*Dorothy Denneen Volo*

Beverages

Americans consumed a variety of beverages depending on the meal, the occasion, religious and political convictions, climate, and social status. While cookbooks from earlier in the century provided recipes for the home production of current wine, ginger beer, hop beer, lemon brandy, spruce beer, and medicinal drinks, people were increasingly turning to the commercial production of such beverages following the Civil War. Small beers, or low-alcohol beers carbonated by the action of yeasts, had been traditional and nutritious drinks for children, women, and men for centuries. When colonists arrived in North America, they found new varieties of spruce and birch for their beers, and discovered Native Americans using such novel flavorings as the roots of sarsaparilla and sassafras as well.

Root beer was a tonic health drink. *Dr. Chase's Recipes* from 1869 touted it as an alternative to medicine and suggested that families make it every spring, and drink freely of it for several weeks, and thereby saving, perhaps, several dollars in doctors' bills. In 1876, Charles E. Hires began marketing packets of the herbal ingredients necessary to make "the Greatest Health-Giving Beverage in the World" at the Centennial Exposition in Philadelphia advertising it as "the National Temperance Drink." This kit for making root beer was supposed to contain 16 roots, herbs, barks, and berries, including sassafras, the dominant flavoring, and required home fermentation with yeast. In 1884 Hires decided consumers would be more interested in an easier-to-use product and began selling a liquid concentrate and soda fountain syrup, as well as bottled root beer.

Chocolate had been a less stimulating alternative to coffee and tea since the sixteenth century. Typically consumed at breakfast, chocolate was associated with indulgence and torpor. In the nineteenth century, technology transformed it into a commodity that was widely available for all, especially children, to enjoy. The traditional drink was made by dissolving solid chocolate, made from cocoa beans, in hot water or milk, often adding such other flavorings as sugar, vanilla, nutmeg, or even wine. The rising demand for chocolate, however, made it a target, like coffee, for adulteration by unscrupulous producers and manufacturers. Chocolate was adulterated by a variety of starch-grain items including powdered dried peas, rice or lentil flour, and a particular favorite, potato starch. In 1872, "A Boston Lady" included a section on cacao in *The Dessert Book*. Her discussion of chocolate focuses mainly on it as a drink. She cautioned her readers about adulterated chocolate noting that people who believed that chocolate thickens when prepared were mistaken because the coagulation was indicative of the presence of farina (Coe and Coe 2007, 244–45).

Cider was a staple drink in colonial American homes and continued to be popular through the nineteenth century, especially in rural areas. Families that had large orchards had the option of pressing their own fruit at home with a portable press or having it processed at a local cider mill. Some people simply purchased cider from the mill. In addition to being consumed plain, cider was the basis for a number of other drinks. It could be mulled, mixed with beaten eggs, sugar, and spices. Cider could also be made into cider vinegar, an important component in the pickling process. It could also be fermented and turned into a potent alcoholic beverage, but with the rise of the temperance movement, it lost much of its following. Temperance reformers originally exempted beer, wine, and cider but by the 1870s zealous reformers rampaged through the countryside destroying acres of apple orchards (Williams 2006, 44–45).

In place of hard cider many families turned to softer drinks. The temperance and health reform movements made water a politically charged beverage. Bottled spring waters and manufactured soda water became fashionable. Soda fountains became very popular as an outgrowth of the temperance movement. Gustavus Dows invented, patented, and operated the first marble soda fountain in 1863, and in 1870, he patented a more advanced and modern form of the soda fountain. Solon Robinson, a writer, agriculturalist, and founder of the Lake County Temperance Society published a small volume in 1860 entitled *How to Live, or Domestic Economy Illustrated* where he mentioned that the previous summer he had gotten into the habit of taking tea iced, and really thought it better than when hot (Williams 2006, 45). By 1871 the new beverage competed with iced milk and iced water on hot summer days at fashionable hotels in New York. Shrubs, made from fruit-flavored sweet vinegar mixed with water, were also popular drinks on a hot day.

As wine became more fashionable among the middle class, cookbooks increased the number of recipes for making wine at home. Jane Cunningham Croly included directions for making currant champagne and wine from grapes as well as from currants, blackberries, elder flowers, rhubarb, gooseberries, and ginger. She described a grape syrup, which she recommended as a nonalcoholic wine. In addition to wines, she provided recipes for other beverages, alcoholic and not, which would be useful for entertaining such as blackberry and cherry brandies; hop; ginger; quick and spruce beers; mead; shrub and claret punch; May Drink (a German favorite); Oxford Swig (a potent mix of beer, sherry, sugar, and lemon); Sack Posset; lemonade; milk punch; and Christmas eggnog (Williams 2006, 46).

Beer, once brewed by housewives, became a consumer product in the nineteenth century. With the influx of German immigrants came a new kind of commercial beer production. The earliest brewers brewed top-fermented English style ales and stout, but in the 1840s and 1850s with the arrival of bottom-fermenting beer yeast, they began to make Bavarian-style lagers and pilsners. These new brews utterly transformed beer consumption in America, and they became popular with working-class, native-born Americans as well as immigrants. By 1873, there were 4,132 breweries in the United States, producing nine million barrels of beer annually.

—*Dorothy Denneen Volo*

Canned Foods

Commercially produced canned goods gained popularity throughout the period. By 1819 the William Underwood Company in Boston, was providing canned oysters, lobsters, fish, meat, soup, fruits, and even some vegetables, both for export and domestic consumption. At the same time, another canning pioneer, the New York City firm of Ezra Daggert and Thomas Kensett, also began packing salmon, oysters, and lobsters and in 1825 received a patent for a tin can. Packing in tin (actually tinned iron) had advantages over packing in glass, especially for shipping, but it was more costly and less safe for consumption because the iron often imparted an unwanted metallic flavor to the food. Glass bottling and tin canning continued to grow over the next three decades. Handmade tin cans became obsolete with the introduction of machines that made them automatically.

Tomatoes were one of the earliest canned foods to be widely accepted by the public. A cannery in Philadelphia was processing 18,000 baskets of tomatoes in 1855 and a New Jersey processing plant processed 150 bushels of tomatoes a day in 1864. By 1870 tomato canneries had sprung up in many places including Mystic, Connecticut (Williams 2006, 40). Underwood's line of highly seasoned or deviled canned meat sandwich spread became very popular. In 1867, their Red Devil logo became the first registered food trademark in the United States.

Despite the invention of the can opener by Ezra Warner in 1858, canned foods remained a luxury for most people until after the Civil War. Warner's device looked like a bayonet and was used by grocery clerks to open the cans before they left the store. The canning industry received a tremendous boost from the war. From 1860 to 1870 there was a sixfold increase in the number of canned goods sold nationwide from 5 million cans to 30 million. William Lyman invented the modern can opener, with a cutting wheel that rolls around the rim, in 1870.

While canned goods were a boon to settlers in the West and on the Plains, the situation in the East was different. The poor were unable to afford canned goods and the middle and upper classes were initially suspicious of canned goods ability to resist spoiling. For many housewives there was also the issue of pride in using only fresh ingredients in cooking. Additionally, after refrigerated cars were introduced in 1870, fresh produce became more available. Despite initial resistance, canned food became popular with most middle-class households.

—*Dorothy Denneen Volo*

Dining Habits

Ordinary family meals by the 1870s were normally divided into two or possibly three courses. Jane Cunningham Croly provided a set of menus to her readers for an entire year. Most of her normal dinners began with meat or fish, accompanied by vegetables and possibly a relish, and dessert. For February, she proposed a dinner of baked pork and beans, with boiled codfish, mashed potatoes, pickles, applesauce, and apple fritters for dessert. A "Sunday Dinner" involved a slightly elevated array, as in a menu she proposed for April of roast chicken, stewed tomatoes, new or a "Bermuda" potatoes, spinach, canned corn, and for dessert, lemon meringue pie. A "Company Dinner" listed for January was even more elaborate, beginning with vermicelli soup. This was followed by boiled turkey with oyster stuffing, as well as roast chicken, boiled ham, cranberry jelly, celery, fried potatoes, canned corn, tomatoes, stewed parsnips, cauliflower, macaroni, plum pudding, nuts, oranges, and raisins (Williams 2006, 162).

HOUSING: TENEMENTS, APARTMENTS, AND FLATS

During the nineteenth century America's fastest growing cities were often growing up as well as outward. The six-story Adelphi Hotel, built in New York in 1827, was the city's first skyscraper, and the Boston Exchange Hotel, built in 1830, sported eight floors. Two- and three-story structures with dressed stone, brick, or cast-iron facades became common sights in the older urban districts often replacing buildings of wood. Shops and workplaces were often located on the lower floors and residential quarters could be found in the back or on the upper floors. Often called apartment houses, or flats, these dwellings initially accommodated three or more sets of tenants, living and cooking independently from one another usually on different floors or in a basement apartment. Each apartment usually had its own toilet and bathing facilities.

Northern cities were generally characterized by a well-defined business district and a manufacturing area within easy access of the railroad tracks or other transportation hub such as a waterfront or canal. This area was usually surrounded by lower-class residences, the style of which often became characteristic of whole parts of the city known loosely as neighborhoods. A style of row housing (the brownstone dwellings of Manhattan's east side, for an example) was developed in most major cities so that many people (related by race, language, or ethnicity) lived near each other and near their work. These neighborhoods were sometimes referred to by descriptive sobriquets such as Hell's Kitchen, the Back Bay, China Town, Germantown, or Little Italy among many others. Some of these names continue to be in use today. One of the worst and most crime ridden ethnic neighborhoods was Five Points in New York City named for the conjunction of streets at its center.

Ethnic neighborhoods were often characterized by buildings known as tenements, which were usually viewed in a negative connotation by the upper classes of urban society. Before they decayed into slums and ghettos of the 1870s and 1880s, these buildings had accentuated the appearance of uniformity and equality among their mid-century residents, at least as viewed from the street. However, they were quickly abandoned by the better-heeled segments of the population for free-standing homes in the nineteenth-century equivalent of the suburbs. In Manhattan the 1850s boundary of the suburbs was at the present south end of what would become Central Park (approximately 59th Street and Columbus Circle).

Unscrupulous landlords often subdivided the living space in urban dwellings into separate living areas with little regard for space, light, or ventilation. Tenement residents, like apartment dwellers, had separate family quarters, but they often shared toilets and baths. Rents were determined by the size of the living space or their location in the building with lower amounts demanded for those on upper floors or in the rear. Monthly rates in New York City averaged between $5 and $6 for a single room with a cooking area, and so many living units were created that a landlord could realize a monthly income of $600 from some buildings.

Jacob A. Riis, who immigrated to New York from Denmark in the 1870s, became a newspaper reporter working for the *South Brooklyn News* and later for the *New York Tribune*. Aware of what it was to live in poor and overcrowded conditions (he was one of 15 children), he documented the life of tenement dwellers in New York City in several articles and pamphlets, but his major work was a study of tenement life called *How the Other Half Lives* (1890). Riis noted, "There had been tenant-houses before, but they were not built for the purpose. Nothing would probably have shocked their original owners more than the idea of harboring a promiscuous crowd; for they were the decorous homes of the Old Knickerbockers, the proud aristocracy of Manhattan in the early days....Neatness, order, cleanliness, were never dreamed of in connection with the tenant-house system, as it spread its localities from year to year; while redress, slovenliness, discontent, privation, and ignorance were left to work out their invariable results" (Riis 1890, 1).

The New York State Legislature commissioned a report on the city's tenements in 1857. The commissioners were alarmed. "In the beginning, the tenant-house became a real blessing to that class of industrious poor whose small earnings limited their expenses, and whose employment in workshops, stores, or about the warehouses and thoroughfares, render their near residence of much importance...[but] large rooms were partitioned into several smaller ones, without regard to light and ventilation, the rate of rent being lower in proportion to space or height from the street; and they soon became filled from cellar to garret with a class of tenantry living from hand to mouth, loose in morals, improvident in habits, degraded, and squalid as beggary itself" (Riis 1890, 1). In one of his articles, Riis described an "attic with sloping ceiling and a single window so far out on the roof that it seemed not to belong to the place at all. With scarcely room enough to turn around in [the residents] had been compelled to pay five dollars and a half a month in advance." There were four such rooms carved from a single small attic space (Riis 1890, 3).

The growing number of poor and uneducated persons in the cities soon turned the older tenements and apartment buildings from acceptable, if crowded, residences into ethnically segregated slums and ghettos. These were described as old buildings—crowded rear tenements in filthy yards, damp basements, leaking garrets, shops, outhouses, and stables converted into dwellings. This was largely an unfortunate consequence of social and ethnic prejudice combined with unchecked levels of immigration and population growth. In 1889 alone more than 350,000 persons entered New York City. More than 100,000 came from England, Scotland, and Ireland, 75,000 came from Germany, 31,000 from Poland and Russia, 29,000 from Italy, 16,000 from Hungary, and 5,400 from Bohemia (Volo and Volo 2007, 8–9).

CLOTHING

Women's Fashion

One of the biggest changes in women's fashion during the postwar period was the change in the silhouette. Hoopskirts had been decreasing in circumference since 1865. Skirts became more formfitting, with fullness below the knee and in the back and sporting tiny trains. The hoop was finally overtaken during the winter of 1869–1870 by the dress improver or bustle. Made either of horsehair with a series of ruffles in the back or of steel rods encased in fabric, the bustle moved the bulk of the skirt fabric to the back of the wearer, leaving the front of the skirt relatively flat. Bustles continued to grow throughout the 1870s reaching enormous proportions as equally absurd as some hoops from the previous decade. Waist and hips were closely fitted, and some of the smallest waists can be found during the first half of the decade.

Tunics or overdresses became ubiquitous. They were caught up at the sides and decorated with bows, rosettes, and other various trimmings. Dresses were very highly decorated. Bodices were cut high, and sashes to match the outfit were popular for evening as well as street wear. Sleeves came down to cover the hand. Dresses had long trains for dress occasions, but street attire ended just above the instep. Bonnets and hats were very small and flat. The popularity of croquet led to the creation of a new type of striped costume that showed high walking boots with a tassel in front.

Hair was braided and rolled at the nape of the neck. The front and side hair was made into finger puffs on the top of the head. Sometimes curls were formed into a soft cluster that hung over the braid. A favorite style was to let a single, long finger curl out from the braid hang out over the left shoulder. For dress occasions, artificial flowers were placed at intervals between finger curls.

—*Dorothy D. Volo*

Men's Fashion

The plain white shirt, the business uniform of the 1860s gave way in the 1870s to the colors and stripes, and neckwear became increasingly garish as the nineteenth century progressed. Top hats of silk, beaver, or other exotic materials remained popular with the professional classes, but new styles such as bowlers and derbies also met with increasing favor. Straw hats [so-called skimmers] were popular in summer. Facial hair, particularly moustaches and mutton-chop sideburns, were considered stylish, and in some quarters the clean-shaven face was considered effeminate. For the professional, a trip to the barbershop was a weekly ritual.

Laborers wore plain, rugged work clothes of canvas, denim and other coarse fabrics. Levi Strauss's copper-riveted denim trousers were the choice of miners and laborers. Originally offered only in brown, by 1870 they were dyed a deep indigo, the beginning of the uniquely American blue jean.

The urban footwear choice was the leather-soled high top shoe, fastened with either the traditional button or the newly introduced shoelace. Sports shoes with rubber soles and fabric tops were considered fashionable for lawn games, such as croquet or tennis. Laborers and farmers wore heavy-soled boots, sometimes studding the smooth soles with hobnails for better traction (Browne and Kreiser 2003, 67).

Children's Fashion

Children's clothing did not change appreciably from the Civil War period. However, in 1874, Britain's Prince Albert (Son of Victoria and Albert, and later Edward VII) had his own son photographed in sailor suits, and the publication of the images set off a clothing craze that affected two continents. Sailor suits were popular among upper-class parents for boys aged 7 to 14. There were many variations of this nautical theme—white blouses for summer and navy blue for winter. The open-necked shirts were equally comfortable in cotton or wool as the season demanded. On cold days a nautical reefer jacket could be worn on top. The sailor suit proved one of the most sensible of children's fashions and could be adapted for girls by replacing the trousers with a pleated or gathered skirt. The style was noted for its looseness and freedom of movement, and it was thought to be durable and protective, covering all the limbs.

The Aesthetic Movement that swept Britain also affected the United States in this period. It led illustrators to provide images of generally frivolous and impractical dress on the children that they drew. There was a particular emphasis on large frilled caps and bonnets, flounced tippets and fichus, high waists, and mittens for girls. The children looked pretty and picturesque in print, but unlike the practical and functional sailor suit, the clothing was largely unsuited to the needs and comforts of most active children. Possibly as a result of nostalgia for the older country-style, smocked dresses in cotton and linen remained fashionable. These were loosely modeled on the smocks worn by agricultural workers and craftspersons.

This sampling of children's clothing styles from newborn to youngster shows how prevalent the use of ruffles and bows had become in the nineteenth century. The clothing was artistic in its conception but wildly impractical and expensive. Courtesy Library of Congress.

Poor children wore simply cut clothing of cotton or linen much like what had been worn by their parents. Much of this was cast-off or was cut down from adult garments. Horatio Alger's poor boy character, Ragged Dick, was rather peculiar. "His pants were torn in several places, and had apparently belonged to a boy two sizes larger than himself. He wore a vest, all the buttons of which were gone except two, out of which peeped a shirt which looked as if it had been worn a month. To complete his costume he wore a coat too long for him, dating back, if one might judge from its general appearance, to remote antiquity" (Seelye 1985, 3).

—*James M. Volo*

TECHNOLOGY

The Hydraulic Turbine

Waterwheels were an ancient technology used to power mills and furnace bellows, lift water and drain land (as in Holland), and do other mechanical work. So-called over-shot, side-shot, and under-shot waterwheels were very common in colonial

America. A waterpower system turns the potential energy stored in water into kinetic energy of motion by redirecting its natural fall. Typically, water was channeled out of a river or pond at a certain height above its point of use by a power canal. This canal led to a point from which the water would fall to a lower level. During its fall, the water filled the buckets of a vertical waterwheel, and this weight moved the wheel around under the influence of gravity. Power was usually taken from a driveshaft attached to the wheel by a series of primitive gears.

In the nineteenth century, engineers designed a turbine that could replace the waterwheel. The turbine system, reconfigured and reengineered through many iterations over the years, was organized so that water entered the wheel at its center. The energy was directed outward by stationary vanes (stators) that turned a second set of moveable vanes (rotors) that were attached to a driveshaft. Power was taken off the shaft and transmitted through a series of shafts, countershafts, belts, and gears. The relatively compact turbine was intrinsically more efficient than the larger and more cumbersome waterwheel.

The turbine was developed largely as an outgrowth of intellectual curiosity in France in the 1820s and 1830s. The first successful turbine was invented by Benoit Fourneyron in France in 1827. It was an outward-flow (axial) device with curved vanes that was about 80 percent efficient. In the following year, Feu Jonval developed an axial-flow turbine that required a much smaller height of falling water (head) for operation. Samuel B. Howd of Geneva, New York advanced the technology in 1838 by inventing an inward-flow device that was somewhat smaller, and less expensive to build and maintain. The Howd design, improved by James B. Francis in 1849, ran at much higher speeds than earlier forms. "The [American] development [of the turbine] was almost totally pragmatic and empirical, largely ignorant of and indifferent to theoretical considerations" (Hunter 1979, 307). Turbines saw extensive use in the United States being introduced in the Mid-Atlantic states in the 1840s by Ellwood Morris and Emile Geyelin, and in New England by Francis, Uriah A. Boyden, and George Kilburn. The turbines designed by Boyden and installed at the mills at Lowell, Massachusetts, by Francis in 1858 generated between 35 and 650 horsepower.

—James M. Volo

The Philadelphia Water Works

The sounds of the waterworks could not be heard in any other locale in America during the 1820s: mechanical pumps moving frothing water into different ponds and through pipes. The futuristic scene attracted onlookers from around the world and clearly defined Philadelphia as one of the world's most advanced cities. But this was just the beginning. Upstream from the waterworks, the city had also set aside the land directly along some of the rivers that fed the city's water system. Converted into Fairmont Park, these open spaces offered some of the nation's first urban green spaces (Black 2006, 41).

Benjamin Henry Latrobe's plan to create the Philadelphia Water Works in 1798 was later extended into the Fairmont Park and Water Works. The initial works planned by Latrobe utilized two steam engines to lift water from the Schuylkill River, into two huge water tanks (three million gallons), and finally into the city through a series of wooden water mains under the influence of gravity. The ingenuity of the water pumps was matched only by the splendor of the classical architecture that surrounded them. This system, however, was plagued with problems, and if the engines failed, the water supply to the city was totally closed off. Consequently, the Committee of Health turned to John David and Frederick Graff to redesign the system and expand it to fill the needs of an increasing urban population. In 1822, a 1,600-foot-wide dam was built across the Schuylkill River to direct the flow of the river to three waterwheels that replaced the steam engines in lifting drinking water. Some time later Jonval turbines were installed to produce the lifting power.

The technology to supply and purify Philadelphia's water placed this city ahead of nearly every city in the nation. However, in prioritizing the symbolic value of this accomplishment—one of the first public works in American history—the technology was carefully wrapped in an aura of classical art. The wheels of the primary works, for instance, were contained in a building resembling a Greek temple. By veneering the cutting-edge technology, the works linked the classical styles with the modern age of technology. The works became a magnet for visitors including British author Charles Dickens, who praised it for its pleasant design and public usefulness.

The heavily designed buildings contrasted with the rustic, natural surroundings of the brown-gray fieldstones, trees, and river. Designers did not attempt to blend the works with their natural surroundings; the instruments were intended to stand as monuments of a new era. Even so, the open land around the waterworks still became part of Fairmont park, the nation's first planned recreational natural environment (Black 2006, 41–42, 55).

TRANSPORTATION: STREETCARS AND TROLLEYS

Mass transit played an important part in the development of cities and their extension into the nineteenth-century equivalent of suburbs. It should be noted that the suburban areas of many nineteenth-century cities are today found firmly rooted in what is considered the downtown area. As an example, the area north of Columbus Circle at the southern end of New York's Central Park was considered a suburb in the last quarter of the century, and Park Avenue East and Park Avenue West were lined with charming suburban homes rather than high-rise apartments overlooking the park.

Although railroad companies built steam rail connections from the suburbs into the city centers, including an elevated steam railway in New York City in 1876, the greater revolution in urban transportation in the nineteenth century came with the introduction of the mechanically powered (not horse-drawn) street cars. The cable car and the electric streetcar (or trolley) quickly displaced the horse-drawn cars that had served city dwellers for several decades. Streetcars remained in common service until displaced by the combustion engine bus in the 1950s in most cities, and today they would be roughly equivalent to light-rail service.

The first of these innovations, the cable car, was patented by Andrew Hallidie in 1871. Hallidie constructed a passenger cable car system in San Francisco in 1873 and forever changed the face of urban transportation. Hallidie's system included a moving cable buried beneath the ground, pulled though a continuous loop by a powerful stationary steam engine, and accessed through a slit in the roadbed. The cable car was outfitted with a device attached below street level that gripped the moving cable. The car traveled at the speed of the cable. By releasing the device (and applying a mechanical handbrake when necessary), the gripman controlled the overall movement and speed of the car. The cable car soon spread to other major U.S. cities, and for a few decades it was a predominant form of urban transportation.

The South adopted streetcars earlier than other areas of the country. Electric streetcars were built in New Orleans and Montgomery, Alabama, but the first commercially successful electric streetcars began service in Richmond, Virginia, in the 1880s. The basic idea for the electric streetcar had been around since the early 1800s. The first electric streetcar prototypes, unfortunately, ran on batteries—a power source then in its infancy that was much too bulky and inefficient to be practical.

Frank Sprague, a former assistant to Thomas Edison, contributed scores of electrical inventions to nineteenth-century America including electric locomotives, electric elevators, and other devices. He solved many of the problems associated with electric streetcars, including an improved direct current motor and a better way to mount it in the vehicle. Sprague's success led to a buy-out offer from Edison's General Electric Company, and by 1890 two hundred cities had built or were in the process of building electric streetcar systems with about 90 percent based on Sprague's patents.

Less than 20 years after the cable car appeared in San Francisco, the electric trolley threatened to displace it. Practicality dictated that electric streetcars receive their energy from a central generating source. The first of these streetcars were powered by two rails that were fed current of different polarities. The dangers of this system were evident as accidents regularly occurred when people or animals touched both rails simultaneously. The problem was rectified by the installation of overhead wires to which a troller (hence the word trolley) made contact from the top of the car. The rails served as a ground for the current, but the hot wires were safely suspended high in the air. Showers of yellow and white sparks cascaded from the troller as the cars passed. Similar systems are still used in bumper cars at amusement parks. It was relatively easy for a city with a horse-drawn system to string these overhead wires along the existing rail system and retire their animals to more remote routes. The number of electric trolleys went from 130 in 1888 to more than 8,000 in 1892, and by 1902 they registered 5.8 billion riders annually. Trolleys were also used to transport farm produce from outlying farms to the marketplace in the city center (Timmons 2005, 34–36).

FOR MORE INFORMATION

Black, Brian. *Nature and the Environment in Nineteenth-Century American Life*. Westport, CT: Greenwood Press, 2006.

Browne, Ray B., and Lawrence A. Kreiser Jr. *The Civil War and Reconstruction*. Westport, CT: Greenwood Press, 2003.

Coe, Sophie D., and Michael D. Coe. *The True History of Chocolate*. London: Thames & Hudson, 2007.

Elkort, Martin. *The Secret Life of Food*. Los Angeles, CA: Jeremy P. Tarcher, 1991.

Grover, Kathlyn, ed. *Dining in America: 1850–1900*. Amherst: University of Massachusetts Press, 1987.

Hooker, Richard J. *Food and Drink in America: A History*. New York: Bobbs-Merrill, 1981.

Hunter, Louis C. *A History of Industrial Power in the United States, 1780–1930*. Charlottesville: University Press of Virginia, 1979.

Husband, Julie, and Jim O'Loughlin. *Daily Life in the Industrial United States, 1870–1900*. Westport, CT: Greenwood Press, 2004.

Johnson, Laurence A. *Over the Counter and On the Shelf: Country Storekeeping in America 1620–1920*. Edited by Marcia Ray. Rutland, VT: Charles E. Tuttle Company Publishers, 1961.

Jones, Mary Ellen. *Daily Life on the Nineteenth-Century American Frontier*. Westport, CT: Greenwood Press, 1998.

Levenstein, Harvey Q. *Revolution at the Table: The Transformation of the American Diet*. New York: Oxford University Press, 1988.

McIntosh, Elaine N. *American Food Habits in Historical Perspective*. Westport, CT: Greenwood/Praeger Press, 1995.

Nelson, Paula M. *After the West Was Won: Homesteaders and Town-Builders in Western South Dakota, 1900–1917*. Iowa City: University of Iowa Press, 1986.

Nye, David E. *Electrifying America: The Social Meanings of New Technology, 1880–1940*. Cambridge, MA: The MIT Press, 1990.

Riis, Jacob A. *How the Other Half Lives, Studies among the Tenements of New York*. New York: Charles Scribner's Sons, 1890.

Seelye, John, ed. *Horatio Alger, Jr., Ragged Dick and Struggling Upward*. New York: Viking Penguin, Inc., 1985.

Smith, Merritt Roe, and Leo Marx, eds. *Does Technology Drive History? The Dilemma of Technological Determinism*. Cambridge, MA: MIT Press, 1994.

Timmons, Todd. *Science and Technology in Nineteenth-Century America*. Westport, CT: Greenwood Press, 2005.

Volo, Dorothy Denneen, and James M. Volo. *Family Life in Nineteenth-Century America*. Westport, CT: Greenwood Press, 2007.

Wheeler, Keith. *The Townsmen*. New York: Time-Life Books, 1975.

Williams, Susan. *Food in the United States, 1820s–1890*. Westport, CT: Greenwood Press, 2006.

Woodward, George E. *Victorian City and Country Houses: Plans and Designs*. New York: Dover Publications, 1996.

———. *Woodward's Architecture and Rural Art*. New York: Privately printed, 1868.

———. *Woodward's National Architect*. New York: Da Capo Press, 1975.

Wyman, Walker D. *Frontier Woman: The Life of a Woman Homesteader on the Dakota Frontier*. River Falls: University of Wisconsin–River Falls Press, 1972.

Zanger, Mark H. *The American History Cookbook*. Westport, CT: Greenwood Press, 2003.

Political Life

CARPETBAGGERS AND SCALAWAGS

For many ex-Confederate states the postwar period of Reconstruction was relatively brief. It was long enough, however, to foster a lasting bitterness between traditional and progressive Southern whites, but not long enough to sustain the nascent black political power that was kindled at the end of the war. Black Southerners and freedmen saw Reconstruction as their opportunity to enter the American political mainstream. The presence of federal troops and the support of the Freedmen's Bureau was strong enough to give Southern blacks a taste of the rights and privileges they were supposed to enjoy under emancipation. They were particularly buoyed by the presence of armed U.S. Colored Infantry on the streets and at the polling places. Nonetheless, the black soldiers serving as occupation troops were not numerous enough—nor were the white soldiers well-enough disposed toward Negroes—to garrison every Southern street corner, patrol every country crossroad, or defend every black family from violation.

Reconstruction brought many new groups into the Southern political process. Besides newly emancipated slaves, there were blacks who had been free before the war but unable to vote or run for office. Some of these had owned businesses, buildings, and shops. Free blacks were sometimes slave owners themselves holding their workers and even their relatives in legal bondage. This helped to stabilize their workforce and provided a modicum of legal protection for their families. Black slave owners had their few limited rights recognized in law in most Southern states. These men were highly educated, cultured, and sophisticated in their outlook, and at the beginning of the war some of them were openly supportive of the Confederacy (Volo and Volo 1998, 66).

White politicians from the North known as carpetbaggers, and Southern unionists known as scalawags also came to power. Southern mythology holds that both groups were conniving opportunists, and this may be true for a minority of them. Yet many Northerners saw the unreconstructed South as a land of opportunity for both honest enterprise and long-overdue reform. Many came south as missionaries of Yankee ideology with a real sense of spreading the gospel of Yankeeisms including black education, women's rights, and universal temperance. Resentment of Northern meddling in Southern affairs had been one of the factors in bringing about disunion. Most Southerners were not going to allow it simply because they had lost an encounter on the battlefield, but now Northern meddling served as a convenient excuse of overt racism, intimidation, and violence (Thomas 1973, 198–99).

The scalawags that took part in the reconstruction of Southern government were often portrayed as apostates and traitors because they jumped on the postwar Republican Party bandwagon, supported the black franchise, and combated racist organizations like the Ku Klux Klan. Some were former petty politicians seeking an advantage in the vacuum left behind by the collapse of the great families. They sought to trade their support for reforms in taxation, governmental structure, and social order for political access under the new state governments that had been denied to them in former years by the plantation owners.

This plantation aristocracy had successfully dominated Southern society for many years by applying their wealth and political influence to the wheels of government, yet their numbers were so small that no more than 50,000 persons—men, women, and children—in a population of several million qualified as part of this class. The war had decimated a generation of aristocratic Southern youth and economic security, once the hallmark of the plantations, was no longer a certainty. Moreover, the historic political power of the planter class had largely been conveyed to a new moneyed aristocracy in the North vested in industry, commerce, banking, and railroads.

Many poor whites in the South had only recently gained their own franchise from a generally unyielding plantation aristocracy that needed their support in the secession congresses and on the battlefield. In an effort to garner wider public support for their agendas, Southern patricians consciously moved the decision-making process from the gatherings of a few influential individuals into the open. Although the smoke-filled back room still played its role, the politicians recognized a need to develop a following in the electorate. Inevitably these tactics led to the benefits of an extended franchise and the removal of property qualifications for office holding. As the process expanded to include persons never before allowed to participate in politics, many were attracted to socially acceptable outlets for their newfound zeal. During Reconstruction the control of state politics gradually shifted away from its traditional base, and, in many cases, came to reside in unexpected hands.

Ironically, the poor white population also provided willing recruits for the violent racist organizations that wanted a return to Southern traditionalism through the mechanism of white superiority. Race-based slavery had promoted a type of equality among all white Southerners regardless of their social status. The lowliest white man could find comfort in the knowledge that he was the legal superior of even the wealthiest black freeman. Emancipation had changed all of this, and the amendments to the Constitution that guaranteed blacks full citizenship also made them the legal equals of all white men—a circumstance that many whites found abhorrent.

The sum total of all these elements in Southern Reconstruction—blacks, carpetbaggers, occupation forces, Freedmen's Bureau, scalawags, and poor whites—varied from state to state. Some states like South Carolina came to a semblance of bona fide republican governance. Others, like Virginia, reverted almost immediately to a form of Southern conservatism almost indistinguishable from the prewar form of governance; or they became so corrupt, like Louisiana, that they rivaled in infamy some of the most dishonest political machines to be found in the urban North.

—*James M. Volo*

"This is a white man's government. We regard the Reconstruction Acts (so called) of Congress as usurpations, and unconstitutional, revolutionary, and void."—Thomas Nast lampoons the Democratic platform and its unholy alliance of former confederates, Irish immigrants, and self-seeking Northern politicians. Courtesy Library of Congress.

GOVERNMENT

Presidential Reconstruction

On March 4, 1865, in his second inaugural address, Abraham Lincoln reiterated a policy of reconstruction that he had personally favored since the twin federal victories at Gettysburg and Vicksburg in July 1863. He reassured his listeners that his purpose on the occasion of his first inaugural had been to save the Union without war, but the Southern states had chosen to "make war rather than let the nation survive" while the remainder of the states would "accept war rather than let it perish." Now with the fall of Savannah in hand and the final campaigns in Tennessee and Virginia coming to a conclusion, Lincoln had consented to receive Southern representatives with talks of peace provided they renounce secession and accept the consequences of the war. In his address in 1865, he assumed an imminent end of the Civil War. "The progress of our arms...is, I trust, reasonably satisfactory and encouraging to all." He said of the North and the South, "Neither party expected for the war, the magnitude, or the duration, which its has already attained. Neither anticipated that the cause of the conflict [slavery] might cease with, or even before, the conflict itself should cease." Of course, the President was alluding to the Emancipation Proclamation (January 1863) that he had signed two years earlier that had effectively ended slavery. He ascribed this to the "true and righteous" judgments of the Lord (Current and Garraty 1965, 11–12).

Finally, Lincoln reached out to the disaffected sections of the country by proposing an evenhanded and fair policy for the postwar future. "With malice toward none; with charity for all; with firmness in the right, as God gives us to see the right, let us finish the work we are in; to bind up the nation's wounds; to care for him who shall have borne the battle, and for his widow, and his orphan—to do all which may achieve and cherish a just, and lasting peace, among ourselves, and with all nations." On collateral issues outside the immediate end of open hostility on the battlefield, Lincoln showed a substantial generosity, assuring Southerners that executive policy would be lenient and remarking that he was open to consideration of compensation to slave owners for emancipating their bondsmen, a position he changed soon enough where even union slaveholders refused to recognize slavery was dead. In six weeks Lincoln would be dead, killed by a Southern assassin's bullet. With him would die any hope of the just and unprejudiced period of national reconstruction that he envisioned (Current and Garraty 1965, 12).

Andrew Johnson, who succeeded as president, was put on the Republican ticket in 1864 because he was the most anti-Confederate Democrat with Southern roots that the Republican Party could find to strengthen Lincoln's chances for reelection. Johnson had told a street crowd that given the chance he would hang Jeff Davis and all of his crew in Richmond. This peeled off some of the prowar Democratic support from Lincoln's opponent, George B. McClellan, who was running on a platform that included ending the war at the earliest possible moment by declaring it finished regardless of the situation on the battlefield. The political pundits of the day had misjudged the temper of the public, and Lincoln won the popular vote by 400,000. The fact that almost 70 percent of the soldiers in the federal army voted for him shows how badly the antiwar sentiment in the country had been gauged.

Undoubtedly the Radical Republicans in the Congress believed that Johnson could be pushed gradually into their view that a social and political revolution was needed in the South even though most of the Northern electorate was looking for nothing more than the restoration of the Union and Southerners' acknowledgment of their defeat. In this Johnson would fail them, and they were outraged when the newly constituted Southern state assemblies adopted new sets of black codes under his program of presidential reconstruction. Even if Johnson had been more authoritarian, the Radicals would still have found the restoration of the South to a form of their liking filled with difficulty. The real temper of the people of the North was not reflected in the angry speeches they gave in the halls of Congress calling for recriminations and punishment, but rather in the demobilization of the armies and a return to the normalcy of growing their crops or earning their wages.

—*James M. Volo*

Radical Reconstruction

Radical Republicans were led in the Senate by Charles Sumner, who argued that secession had destroyed the status of the Confederate states as political entities and left the Constitutional authority of the federal government to rule and protect the individuals in those states as if they were residents of territories. Alexander H. Stephens, the ineffective former vice president of the Confederacy, led the opposing view that the Southern states retained their prewar political sovereignty and status as members of the Union. Stephens and other former Confederates were elected to the Congress by their respective states in 1865 under Johnson's program, but they were refused admission by the Republicans who controlled that body. Thaddeus Stevens, congressman from Pennsylvania and leader of the Radical Republicans in the House of Representatives, had no sympathy for any ex-Confederate. What was the use, he asked, of having fought and won a war at great expense in lives and money, if Jefferson Davis, Robert E. Lee, and the other enemies of the Union could march right back into the halls of government and take over the legislative branch or even the White House?

Radicals like Sumner and Stevens, who had fought the battle of ideas in the Congress with the Southern representatives of Slave Power before the war, wanted Reconstruction to completely change what the South had previously been. Stevens planned to carve up the rebel provinces and fill them with new white settlers and black farm families. The lands of the rebel leaders and plantation owners would be divided into 40 acre farms and sold to their former slaves at $10 per acre. But such a proposal went nowhere, for most Republicans respected property rights. There was no confiscation of land or redistribution of land after the war ended (Butterfield 1947, 186).

Since the war was over and reunion was important to the health of the nation, the Congress of 1866 decided to take control of the course of Reconstruction. It claimed the right, without supporting precedents, to dictate how government and republicanism [small "r"] would operate in each readmitted southern state. In 1867 the Congress passed two Reconstruction Acts that virtually wiped out most of what Johnson had pursued. Johnson's veto of the first of these, which excluded the electoral votes of the former Confederate states, was overridden, and Stevens declared, "I was a Conservative in the last session of Congress, but I mean to be a Radical Henceforth" (Randall and Donald 1961, 592).

The Republican program focused on establishing the basic civil rights of the black freedmen. The 13th Amendment ended slavery as a legal institution. Then came the black schools, the relief centers, and the special courts for blacks in the South. Black male suffrage was established under army protection and any offensive rules found in state black codes were abolished. The 14th Amendment gave full citizenship to blacks, and the 15th Amendment barred the states from interfering with their right to vote on the basis of their race, color or previous condition of servitude. These later amendments forced the South to yield on the subject of black freedmen, but it also forced Northern states like Michigan, Ohio, Kansas, and others to accept what they also had rejected immediately after the war—black enfranchisement.

Thus just five years after the Emancipation Proclamation, there was the potential that the newly freed blacks might be politically dominant in the South, and that they could thereby hold the balance of electoral power in the nation. In the 1868 presidential election Ulysses Grant ran as a Republican against Horatio Seymour, Democratic governor of New York. Grant's victory in the Electoral College was overwhelming: 214 to 80; and in the popular vote Grant posted 3,015,071 votes to Seymour's 2,709,613 votes. This was a less comfortable margin of victory. More importantly, however, contemporary election watchers noted that Grant's total included approximately 700,000 black votes without which he would have lost the popular vote to Seymour. This was a lesson concerning the power of the black vote that the politicians were not quick to forget. Lacking their own political leaders and largely uneducated, black freedmen in the South for a time fell under the influence of Northern carpetbaggers and Southern scalawags. Southern legislatures were often corrupt, but they were no more so than those in many Northern states (Butterfield 1947, 194).

—James M. Volo

Impeachment of President Johnson

Enacted in 1867, the Tenure of Office Act required the approval of the Senate for the removal of officers originally appointed by the president with senatorial consent. The act thus affected President Johnson's ability to dismiss, for instance, members of his cabinet. When Johnson, disregarding the act, dismissed Secretary of War Edwin M. Stanton in 1867, his action became one of the reasons for his subsequent impeachment by the House of Representatives. The trial of the president was held in the Senate before Chief Justice Salmon P. Chase in 1868. Senator Sumner, a leading Radical, declared Johnson "an impersonation of the tyrannical Slave Power," and voted him guilty of "high crimes and misdemeanors" as well as 10 other charges (Randall and Donald 1961, 614); however, the final Senate vote of 35 to 19 failed to reach the necessary two-thirds threshold for the president's removal. Although the impeachment was the high-water mark of Radical power, the acquittal of Johnson was made possible by the votes of seven Republican Senators, added to those of all the sitting Democrats. These defections prevented the president's removal from office. The constitutionality of the Tenure of Office act was never tested, but, in 1926, in regard to another statute, the U.S. Supreme court upheld the president's independent power of removal of executive branch personnel for any reason whatsoever without the consent of the Senate (Randall and Donald 1961, 614).

—James M. Volo

Redemption

The final stage in Reconstruction is sometimes called the Redemption. Conservative whites rejected Republican governments as illegitimate because they enfranchised blacks and recoganized their basic rights. The editor of the Tuscaloosa, Alabama *Independent Monitor* wrote of the "galling despotism that broods like a night-mare over these Southern States...a persistent prostitution of all government, all resources and all powers, to degrade the white man by the establishment of a negro supremacy" (Butterfield 1947, 190). James S. Pike, a Maine Republican, endorsed this view in his book *The Prostrate State: South Carolina under Negro Government* (1873). No other book of the period did so much to disillusion Northerners about Radical Reconstruction or to prepare them to accept a return to white supremacy. Pike, no adherent of race-based prejudice, was, nonetheless, a segregationist who believed that blacks should either be deported to Africa or confined on a vast reservation cut out from the conquered territory of the Confederacy, preferably in the West near those already set aside for the Indian nations. He like many other whites feared that the nation would otherwise become Africanized.

A friend of Horace Greeley, and a political enemy of Ulysses S. Grant, Pike made an inspection tour of South Carolina in the 1870s keeping notes in a private journal that he quickly published as a multichapter book. Herein he wrote an unflattering description of the corrupt Republican-controlled government of the state that formed an image of ex-slave-and-carpetbagger governments on all levels that poisoned the minds of Northern moderates against them and animated Southern bigots.

Albion W. Tourgee, a Union war veteran from Ohio and a Radical Republican politician in North Carolina, termed the policy of Reconstruction "a magnificent failure." An acquaintance and supporter of future president James A. Garfield, Tourgee wrote, "Reconstruction was a failure so far as it attempted to unify the nation, to make one people in fact of what had been one only in name before the convulsion of civil war. It was a failure, too, so far as it attempted to fix and secure the position and rights of the colored race. They were fixed, it is true, on paper, and security of a certain sort taken to prevent the abrogation of that formal declaration. No guaranty whatever was provided against their practical subversion, which was accomplished with an ease and impunity that amazed those who instituted the movement....The doctrine of 'State Rights' is altogether unimpaired and untouched by what has occurred except in one particular; to wit, the right of peaceable secession. The war settled that. The Nation asserted its rights to defend itself against disruption" (Current and Garraty 1965, 72).

Most Americans were unconcerned by the course of these events in the unreconstructed South. The old bitterness between North and South was largely forgotten amid the realities of everyday life and work, only to be trotted out at election time by fawning politicians waving the bloody shirt or rallying the veterans of the Grand Army of the Republic (GAR). Despite oratory about Negro Supremacy and Africanization, the South had remained under white leadership during all phases of Reconstruction even though black voters were a numerical majority. The problematic effect on Southerners was that the white leaders had been Republicans or transplanted Northerners. The few black politicians that had gained office during Reconstruction were intelligent and surprisingly conciliatory in their political views and activities. Ironically some of them had worked hand-in-hand with Democrats to restore white rule to the South (Butterfield 1947, 223).

The so-called Solid South, a political designation, was born in the compromise of 1877, and Republican President Rutherford B. Hayes was its godfather. After his inauguration Hayes declared Reconstruction a failure and immediately sent the federal troops in the Southern states back to their barracks. By April 24, 1878, only seven weeks into his administration, the last federal garrison in the South at New Orleans was recalled. With remarkable ease, the Southern states thereafter negated the 15th Amendment so far as black voting was concerned, and it became solidly Democratic for the next 75 years.

—James M. Volo

Third Parties

The Greenback Party was a political third party that was active between 1874 and 1884. The party was founded largely in response to the Panic of 1873. Also known as the Independent Party, the National Party, and the Greenback-Labor Party among the several state organizations, the Greenback Party opposed the shift from Civil War-era paper currency back to a specie-based monetary system. The party was most successful in the elections of 1878 when it helped to elect 21 independent members to the U.S. Congress. It ran James B. Weaver as a presidential candidate in 1880.

The name referred to the greenbacks on most paper bills. It was believed that the banks and corporations would amass gold and silver coins and bullion and thereby acquire the power to dictate the value of products, produce, and wages. Party supporters also thought that paper currency was more likely to remain in circulation, as it had during the Civil War, and help to free the money supply to aid farmers and small businessmen through higher prices and lower debts. In 1878, the soft money forces in Congress passed the Bland-Allison Act, which required the Treasury to redeem at least $2 million in paper each month through the use of silver bullion. Most Greenbackers joined the soft money forces in backing the compromise that kept most paper currency in circulation and at face value. Thereafter, they were known as Free Silverites. After a long fight in Congress and the courts, specie payments in gold were resumed in 1879. In 1880 the Greenback Party broadened its platform to support an income tax, an eight-hour work day, and women's suffrage. Its influence declined thereafter, and many party members switched their support to the Populist Party.

—*James M. Volo*

LAW, CRIME, AND PUNISHMENT

Law Enforcement: The Provost

In the face of the advancing Union armies, Confederate civil government crumbled, and the federal army became for a time, the sole source of law and order in occupied areas. Therefore the army had to improvise a system of law enforcement, and the method that most naturally developed was to extend the functions of the provost marshals (military police) from policing its own troops to policing the population of the occupied states. The provost marshals decided which Southern citizens should be taken into custody and which should remain free to follow their livelihoods and day-to-day tasks.

The provost marshals were given the task of policing the Southern population everywhere except in General William T. Sherman's department because he chose to continue the civil authority of the Southern governments. The provost elsewhere soon met challenges to their authority from a population accustomed only to their local officials. The provost developed a system of loyalty oaths as a means of testing the inclinations of Southern citizens and determining how much freedom and local control to allow them.

To make Presidential Reconstruction policies as coherent and as effective as possible, Andrew Johnson had pardoned most former Confederates upon their taking of a simple loyalty oath, allowing them to reestablish their civil governments under the watchful eye of the army of occupation. Johnson's program was so lenient that it encouraged Southern whites to return to political views and governmental protocols with respect to blacks that were hardly different from those they had held before the war. With Johnson's permission, the restored state governments reorganized their state militias with personnel drawn from the Confederate forces—many issued gray uniforms. The principal activities of these forces were to enforce the reissued Black Codes and to intimidate blacks at the polls.

—*James M. Volo*

Black Codes

Slave uprisings in the antebellum South had been perceived as a very real physical threat. There had been three important black insurrections in the South: the Gabriel Revolt in 1800, the Denmark Vesey Conspiracy in 1822, and the Nat Turner Revolt in 1831. Only the Turner Revolt had led to any deaths among white Americans, but these had numbered mostly women and children among the 60 or so killed. Coupled with the knowledge of major slave revolts and the mass murders elsewhere, such doings were taken seriously by slave owners.

During the decades before the Civil War, therefore, a number of restrictions on blacks—both slave and free—had been adopted, and most of the legal procedures and accepted protocols for controlling slaves were set down in the so-called slave codes. The prewar codes were fairly comprehensive. Unlike white employees, slaves in the pre-emancipation South were not free to change their condition should it become too burdensome. Slaves were defined principally as property rather than as people. They, their children, and their loved one could be bought, sold, or traded. Without the written permission of their owners they were restricted to their plantations. It was illegal to teach black children to read or write, although some adults were taught to do so as part of their work. Slaves could be physically chastised by their masters for many forms of disobedience, for insolence involving a white person, and for petty crimes. Within his own household and on his property the master ruled completely, in law. Incredibly, masters did not have unlimited legal power over their slaves if their slaves harmed other parties or brake the law. A slave accused of a felony—even murder—could not be purposely mutilated, maimed, or killed as a punishment without the intervention of a court. While slaves had no right to a trial by their peers, their masters could make a defense, call witnesses, and submit evidence. The jurisdiction of these courts varied from place to place, but they were almost always composed of white slave owners.

During the period of Reconstruction a new set of Black Codes were adopted in many states to regulate the newly freed black population. To summarize all the laws passed by the various Southern states is beyond the scope of this work, but a sampling of common principles reveals their basic thrust.

- Existing black marriages, regardless of their nature, were recognized, but future unions were required to be licensed and duly solemnized.
- Mixed race marriage was forbidden.
- Marriage by apprentices required permission.
- Abandonment of a spouse or minor child was made a misdemeanor.
- Parents were made responsible for all their children regardless of the circumstances of their birth.
- No black person could enter any employment other than agriculture or domestic service without a license from a judge.
- Compulsory apprenticeships for blacks entering the mechanical trades were instituted.
- Regulations for labor contracts and work schedules were specified.
- Servants could not leave the premises of their employers without permission.
- The eviction of hapless or elderly slaves from their plantation quarters was prohibited. Future occupancy was to be by lease.
- Unemployed or disorderly persons, peddlers, gamblers, those in disreputable occupations, unlicensed strolling players, and beggars were to be considered vagrants and made liable to fine, imprisonment, and/or hard labor.
- Blacks had access to the courts—the ability to plead, defend, sue, and testify in all cases—but they could not sue or testify against whites.

- Blacks could serve as witnesses, but could not sit on juries in most states.
- Segregation of blacks in schools and other public places was provided.
- Landowning by blacks was restricted to certain districts or types of real estate.
- Blacks were forbidden to carry arms (Randall and Donald 1961, 576–77).

South Carolina's acceptance of blacks in its legal system was remarkable in that it seemingly worked so well. The federal military government transferred the courts back to state's jurisdiction in October 1866. Thereafter, several whites were convicted of crimes based on black testimony, and several black defendants were acquitted based on the word of other black witnesses. However, after the occupation troops were withdrawn, Alabama added a restriction on the right of blacks to testify in court against whites, and Mississippi ultimately allowed so-called vagrants to be bound-out to work until they could pay their fines. Many Northerners viewed these restrictions as efforts to reestablish a form of slavery.

Moderate Republicans, unwilling to trust the Southern governments, joined with the Radicals to place the oversight of black rights under the Freedmen's Bureau, which had been created in March 1865 to feed and care for Southern refugees, black and white. The Bureau was now charged to protect the civil rights of blacks from discrimination in Southern communities and to counteract somewhat the effect of the most grievous of the black codes. The Bureau was most important in areas where blacks were being terrorized by local racist groups acting as Jayhawkers, Regulators, Black-Horse Cavalry, or other pseudonyms. It was said in some circles that the South hated the Freedmen's Bureau more than they detested the freedmen.

—James M. Volo

INTERNATIONAL DIPLOMACY

Trouble in Mexico

The Mexican Civil War that brought Benito Juarez to prominence ran from 1857 to 1861. It was a war of reform launched by the liberal forces in Mexico dissatisfied with the reigning conservative government with its strong ties to the Catholic Church. The so-called War of Reform ended in 1861 with the installation of Juarez as president in Mexico City and the development of a new constitution that reflected the principles of the Great Charter of 1857. This document called for general elections, the expansion of the franchise, and the establishment of federated states under a republican system of central governance.

The Juarez government abrogated many of the contracts and nullified the debts owed to Spanish, British, and French business interests, and the three European countries sent troops to Mexico to intervene over the objections of the United States. The Spanish and British quickly withdrew their forces, however, when it became apparent that the French planned to conquer Mexico. Although the French army suffered an initial defeat at Puebla on May 5, 1862 (the origin of the Cinco de Mayo holiday still celebrated by Mexicans today), they eventually defeated the Mexican republican forces. The members of the Juarez government were forced to retreat to Vera Cruz taking the government treasury with them. French troops entered the capital at Mexico City in June 1863, and a conservative junta of 35 persons was established to govern the country under French oversight.

Meanwhile, Napoleon III of France offered the so-called Mexican throne to Duke Maximilian of Austria. It is difficult to believe that the French would have so brazenly challenged the precepts of the Monroe Doctrine had the United States not been involved in a civil war of its own. A rightful member of the Habsburg line, Maximilian was enthroned as Emperor of Mexico, and he and his wife Carlotta arrived in Mexico City in May 1864. Maximilian was no dictator, and he believed in a limited form of monarchy tempered by an elected legislature. He also took steps to abolish child labor, to limit working hours, and to reform the system of land tenancy. He was quickly left with no support whatsoever. The conservatives who had initially cheered his acceptance of the throne were put off by his liberal ideas, and the republican Juaristas considered Maximilian an enemy simply because he existed. This circumstance also cooled Napoleon III's ardor somewhat, and left Maximilian with few friends and numerous enemies.

The United States had supported Juarez and his republican forces, but Lincoln (who viewed French intervention in Mexico disturbing) found that he was too busy with his own Civil War to intervene on the part of the Juarez government. The U.S. Congress passed a unanimous resolution opposing the establishment of any monarchy in Mexico. American diplomats demanded that the French withdraw their forces and that Austria recall Duke Maximilian, but nothing happened. Immediately after the end of the American Civil War, however, President Andrew Johnson took steps to visibly threaten the French by supplying arms to the Juarez government. General Phillip Sheridan was ordered to place 50,000 federal troops on the American-Mexican border along the Rio Grande, and the U.S. Navy set up a blockade of the Mexican coastline to prevent French reinforcements.

Napoleon III withdrew his support of Maximilian in 1867, and the Mexican emperor was forced to capitulate. The capture and execution of Maximilian (June 19, 1867) ended the crisis. Juarez restored order to the country and was reelected president. He died in 1872, and left Sabastián Tejada as president. During this period, the United States was attempting to suppress the Apache, who used the diplomatic uncertainties along the Mexican-American border to their advantage.

—*James M. Volo*

The Alabama Claims

Many of the most effective vessels of the Confederate Navy were built and armed in Britain. These included the CSS *Alabama*, *Tallahassee*, *Shenandoah*, and a half dozen other raiders. Since the Confederate raider *Alabama* made the largest share of the Civil War era seizures of United States shipping, the resulting litigation between the United States and Great Britain over damages and punitive payments came to be know as the Alabama Claims. The United States, in an arbitrated settlement in 1872, received over $15 million in reparations from the British for that nation's complicity in building, supplying, manning, and otherwise aiding the raiders. The two governments also agreed to arbitration of the northwest boundary with Canada (decided in favor of the United States) and a partial settlement of a Grand Banks fishing dispute (completed in 1877).

In laying the foundation of its case against the British in the Alabama claims, Charles Francis Adams, representing the U.S. government, also demanded payments for the virtual destruction of the maritime commerce of the United States during the war years. This demand amounted to an assertion that the raiders and, by extension, Great Britain were entirely responsible for the decline of the U.S. merchant marine during the Civil War period. These *indirect damages* were ultimately disallowed by the Geneva Arbitration Tribunal that oversaw the settlement of the case.

The rationale of the government's argument for indirect damages, which serves as a foundation for the Flight from the Flag theory, was rooted in the concept that the existence and reported success of the Confederate raiders had undermined American preeminence in the foreign carrying trade to the extent that British carriers were unfairly able to displace the Americans. By driving war risk insurance premiums higher than was warranted by the accomplishments of the raiders, Adams argued U.S. commerce was forced to suffer. American shippers were forced to seek neutral carriers, often British ones. Moreover, he charged that Lloyd's of London, which set the underwriter's standards for vessels and held the position as the largest marine insurer of the world's fleet, had given British vessels favorable treatment. Northern shippers, already working on small profit margins, had been forced to *sell foreign* (legally sell to foreign owners) in the face of the financial ruin brought on as port charges mounted on their unused vessels.

The terminology of *selling foreign* and that of *flying a flag of convenience* are often confused. Vessels that were sold foreign were considered to actually have been sold so that their former owners no longer held a financial stake in their operations. Flying a flag of convenience was a different matter. It amounted to a paper transaction, wherein the former owners still retained financial and practical control of the vessels, but had legally transferred their ownership to another national registry.

In the face of close scrutiny, therefore, the Confederate commerce raiders fade as a cause for the severe distress documented to have taken hold of the U.S. merchant marine trades; and the importance of the raiders' depredations in the patchwork of causes for the decline of the foreign carrying trade seems to be based more on anecdotal evidence provided by former Confederates and the owners of economically distressed shipyards rather than on documented statistics. While the wartime figures evidence a decline, they do not seem to support a general abandonment of the U.S. flag or an extinction of its commerce.

Rather than a general abandonment of U.S. registry, the facts seem to indicate that only a minority of owners, generally of large sailing vessels, deserted the flag. Moreover, the reliance on the psychological apprehension of loss and on the fear of high war risk rates as compelling mechanisms for owners to change registry fails to answer one salient question convincingly. Since the owners of vessels captured or destroyed by the Confederates were paid for their vessels and cargoes by the insurance or by the foreign purchasers in the case of sale, why were these vessels not replaced after the Civil War as the hundreds of captured and destroyed merchant vessels had been after the colonial and Revolutionary wars of the eighteenth century? Furthermore, the insurance rates returned to their prewar levels with the end of hostilities, but foreign carrying continued to decline even in the absence of the raiders. This was the central weakness in the argument of the continuing effect of the raiders, especially because it fails to suggest a mechanism by which the immediate effects of the raiders could prove so enduring (Volo and Volo 2001, 288–91).

DISCRIMINATION: THE WHITE SUPREMACY MOVEMENT

While on an intellectual level Southerners claimed racial superiority for the white race, they nonetheless depended on blacks to tend their animals, repair their vehicles, cook their food, and care for their children. White Southerners, more than those of the North, had been intimately involved with blacks almost all of their lives. In the isolation of the great plantations, it was possible that most of a white person's dealings, in human terms, were either with family members or blacks.

Race-based prejudice promoted a type of equality among all white Southerners regardless of their social status. The lowliest white man could find comfort in the knowledge that he was the superior of even the wealthiest black freeman. Although it is uncertain with how much respect these whites viewed the black freedmen, it would be common for them to have to deal with free blacks as laborers, tradesmen, servants, and artisans. The working white population in much of the South exhibited far less abhorrence of blacks than did many in the upper and middle classes in the North.

The treatment of blacks in Northern states was often brutish, and they were often despised and treated with contempt. In the decades after emancipation, towns and cities were flooded by thousands of freed blacks, some of whom had fought in the federal army and navy with distinction; and any plan for a general bestowing of legal equality had to deal with the touchy problem of free blacks living in a white-dominated, racist society. This led many sympathetic whites to fear for the ultimate welfare and safety of a black population suddenly foisted on an unfriendly America.

In the South a number of white vigilante groups evolved. The Ku Klux Klan was the best known of the underground organizations and secret societies prominent during the Redemption founded to restore white supremacy. One of its founders was Nathan Bedford Forrest. Widely regarded as one of the most brilliant generals on either side in the war, Forrest was said to have had 29 horses shot out from under him in battle and to have killed more men in single combat than any other general officer in the Civil War. Nonetheless, Forrest's reputation was tainted by his association with the massacre of black federal soldiers at Fort Pillow after they had surrendered.

The Klan was not a reaction to Northern radicalism, but rather an attempt to reinstate white supremacy. It was founded at Pulaski, Tennessee, in 1865 almost two years before congressional Reconstruction began. It utilized whippings, murders, terror, and crude warnings such as newspaper cartoons, handbills, and burning crosses to intimidate not only blacks but also Northern carpetbaggers and Southern scalawags. Of the former one Klan posting noted, "The genus carpet-bagger is a man [with the] habit of sneaking and dodging about in unknown places—habiting with negroes in dark dens and back streets—a look like a hound and the smell of a polecat." Of scalawags they wrote, "Our scalawag is the local leper of the community. Unlike the carpet-bagger, he is native, which is so much worse. Once he was respected in his circle; his head was level, and he would look his neighbor in the face. Now he is possessed of the itch for office and the salt rheum of Radicalism, he is a mangy dog, slinking through the alleys, haunting the Governor's office, defiling with tobacco juice the steps of the Capitol, stretching his lazy carcass in the sun on the Square, or the benches of the Mayor's Court...He hath bartered respectability; hath abandoned business, and ceased to labor with his hands...while discussing the question of office" (Butterfield 1947, 190).

The Klan was not alone in its brutality and terror-mongering, but it is possibly best known for its hoods, masks, and robes. Such regalia were common to the white supremacy movement, and as the concept expanded these organizations came out of the dark to parade openly in city streets and to endorse candidates for office. Other underground organizations of this ilk were the Knights of the White Camelia, the Black Horse Cavalry, the White League, and the Order of the White Rose.

—James M. Volo

REFORM: THE POSTWAR FRANCHISE

The question of loyalty among the ex-Confederates emerged during 1864, and the Wade-Davis Bill required all voters in the former Confederate states to take an Iron-clad Oath, swearing that they had never supported the Confederacy or had served in its armed forces. Lincoln pocket-vetoed the bill, preferring not to be bound by so restrictive a measure. Radical Republicans initially lost support for the bill following Lincoln's pocket veto, but they regained strength following his assassination in April 1865. Thaddeus Stevens proposed that all ex-Confederates lose the franchise, but he had to settle for an undefined compromise with the Republican moderates that included only military leaders and government officials. The number of Southerners effected by the temporary loss of voting privileges has been estimated at only 10,000 to 15,000 (Foner 2002, 273–76).

By mid-century adult white males could vote in every state in the Union, and election turnouts often rose above 70 percent of the eligible voters. Ordinary Southern citizens had quickly recognized that their support was needed for secession and they sought to trade their support for reforms in taxation, governmental structure, and social and political access under the new Confederate government, which had been denied to them in former years. However, it was the political, social, and religious elite who most effectively interjected their concerns into the Confederacy, and they were successful in exporting their ideals beyond the battlefield soldier to

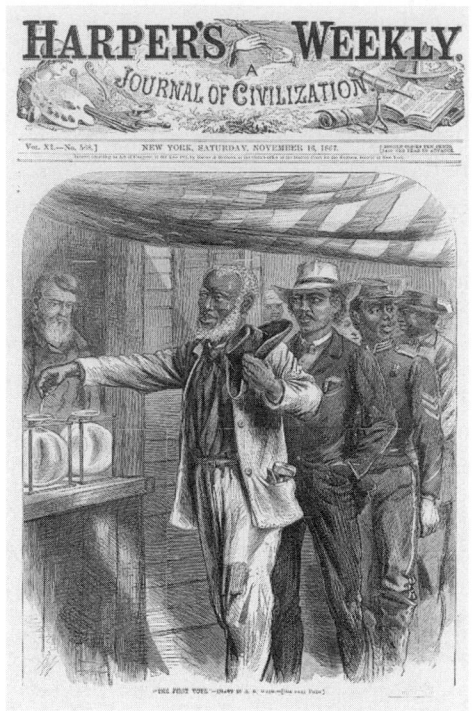

The front page of *Harper's Weekly* from November 16, 1867 showing the first votes cast by blacks. The first three men in line are, respectively, a workman with tools in his pocket, a well-dressed man with a wallet in his pocket, and a black noncommissioned officer (NCO) with a medal on his chest. Courtesy Library of Congress.

the mass of the Southern people. They expected to return to their legal status after the war was lost.

The second and possibly more volatile issue to face the nation was the extension of the franchise to blacks. Whites were often recent comers to voting rights, and they regarded them highly. The initial program of Reconstruction had failed to equally integrate the freedmen into the fabric of voting America. Many Northern states had openly rejected the idea of enfranchising blacks, but the Radical Republicans in Congress wanted to make the issue a national one largely because they distrusted the loyalty of the South. If black freedmen became part of the electorate, it was hoped they would form a solid pro-Union bloc in the Southern states.

Political conservatives in the North and many white Southerners opposed black voting, but a few like Wade Hampton, former slave owner and general of Confederate cavalry, actually saw an opportunity to court the black vote and thereby gained political power. Hampton was voted governor of South Carolina twice due in part to the support of black voters. Lincoln and Johnson allowed that some blacks be granted the vote. Lincoln believed that those blacks who had served in the federal army had earned the franchise, and Johnson thought that the better class of Negro who worked and sustained themselves might be more reliable than many whites who had proved their disloyalty by taking arms against their country. As president, Johnson expanded on his belief. He wrote to William L. Sharkey, governor of Mississippi in August 1865, "If you could extend the elective franchise to all persons of color who can read the Constitution in English and write their names, and to all persons of color who own real estate valued at not less than two hundred and fifty dollars, and pay taxes thereon, you would completely disarm the adversary, and set an example the other states will follow" (Franklin 1961, 42). But Johnson opposed any federal effort to encourage enfranchisement and explicitly opposed the 14th Amendment.

—*James M. Volo*

FOR MORE INFORMATION

Bullock, James D. *The Secret Service of the Confederate States in Europe.* 2 vols. New York: Putnam's, 1884.

Butterfield, Roger. *The American Past: A History of the United States from Concord to Hiroshima, 1775–1946.* New York: Simon and Schuster, 1947.

Cadenhead, I. E., Jr. *Benito Juarez.* New York: Wayne Publication, Inc. 1993.

Cimbala, Paul A. *The Freedmen's Bureau: Reconstructing the American South after the Civil War.* Malabar, FL: Krieger Publishing, 2005.

Current, Richard N., and John A. Garraty, eds. *Words that Made American History since the Civil War.* Boston, MA: Little, Brown and Company, 1965.

Dalzell, G. W. *The Flight from the Flag: The Continuing Effect of the Civil War upon the American Carrying Trade.* Chapel Hill: University of North Carolina Press, 1940.

Donald, David H., Jean H. Baker, and Michael F. Holt. *The Civil War and Reconstruction.* New York: W. W. Norton, 2001.

Du Bois, William E. B. *Black Reconstruction in America, 1860–1880.* New York: Russell & Russell, 1956.

Foner, Eric. *Reconstruction: America's Unfinished Revolution, 1863–1877.* New York: Harper Collins Publishers, 2002.

Franklin, John Hope. *Reconstruction after the Civil War.* Chicago, IL: University of Chicago Press, 1961.

Harding, Bertita Lonarz de. *Phantom Crown.* Mexico City: Ediciones Tolteca, S. A., 1967.

O'Connor, Richard. *The Cactus Throne.* New York: G. P. Putnam's Sons, 1971.

Randall, J. G., and David Donald. *The Civil War and Reconstruction.* Boston, MA: D.C. Heath and Company, 1961.

Stampp, Kenneth. *The Era of Reconstruction, 1865–1877.* New York: Knopf, 1965.

Stark, Francis R. *The Abolition of Privateering and the Declaration of Paris.* New York: Columbia University Press, 1897.

Thomas, Emory M. *The American War and Peace, 1860–1877.* Englewood Cliffs, NJ: Prentice-Hall, Inc., 1973.

Trelease, Allen. *White Terror: The Ku Klux Klan, Conspiracy and Southern Reconstruction.* New York: Harper, 1971.

Volo, Dorothy Denneen, and James M. Volo. *Daily Life in Civil War America.* Westport, CT: Greenwood Press, 1998.

———. *Daily Life in the Age of Sail.* Westport, CT: Greenwood Press, 2001.

Woodward, C. Vann. *Origins of the New South, 1877–1913.* Baton Rouge: Louisiana State University Press, 1951.

Recreational Life

SPORTS

Rowing

Rowing is one of the oldest and most physically demanding sports. When done correctly, it utilizes every major muscle group in the body. Competitive rowing as it is known today began in 1829 with the first Oxford-Cambridge race. The Royal Henley Regatta was started a decade later in Britain. The first American rowing club was established in New York Harbor in 1834, and a Yale student began a intramural rowing club in New Haven in 1843 with the purchase of a secondhand boat from New York. The Detroit Boat Club (founded in 1839) is the oldest in continuous existence in the United States.

The first American rowing competition between academic communities was held in 1852 between Yale and Harvard on the Thames River in Connecticut. This was also the first organized collegiate sporting competition. A sanctioning body called the Schuylkill Navy (named for the nearby river) was organized by a group of Philadelphia boat clubs in 1858, and it remains the oldest sports organization in America. In

1875, 13 eastern colleges (Cornell, Harvard, Yale, Columbia, Dartmouth, Wesleyan, Amherst, Brown, Williams, Bowdoin, Hamilton, Union, and Princeton) formed an association dedicated to the governance of intercollegiate rowing. In that year, they ran an event at Saratoga Lake, New York that drew more than 25,000 spectators. This organization was the basis for the present-day Intercollegiate Rowing Association that was formed in 1895. International competitions were placed under the Federation Internationale des Societies d' Aviron (FISA) in 1893, and competitive rowing became an Olympic sport in 1896.

The Civil War briefly slowed the development of rowing as a sport, but in the postwar period it grew in popularity. Rowing regattas in the United States increased from a mere dozen annually before the war to over 150 in 1872. By 1873, there were almost 300 recognized rowing clubs in the United States. New York had 74 rowing clubs, Georgia 12, Michigan 14, Iowa 5, and California 14. Philadelphia had dozens of rowing clubs along the Delaware River, and Pittsburgh sported more than 20 boathouses on the Ohio. Depending on the local economic and geographical conditions, many rowing contests took on the characteristics of mass spectator events with partisans, food, drink, entertainment, and, of course, gambling.

Competitive rowing falls into two categories: Crew (or Sweep-oar) and Sculling (or Scull racing). In crew—the more common form—two or more rowers (called strokes) pull on one oar each as a team; and they are kept in time by a coxswain, who also guides the direction of the boats and decides the strategy of the race. In scull the rower, or rowers, each pull on a pair of oars. In both cases the rowers face the rear of the vessel. In the nineteenth-century crew members numbered 8, 10, or 12 persons. In the twentieth century, 2, 4, or 8 are more common. Sculling was usually done by a single person, a pair, or at most four rowers. Both types use specialized boats with paper thin wooden hulls and sliding seats that allow the rowers to utilize the power of their legs. The long oars attached to a fulcrum(s) (pivot) outboard of the side of the boat were specially designed with curved blades for the purposes of competition.

The first appearance of women rowers has been reasonably dated as taking place in 1877 at Wesleyan College. Soon thereafter, they began appearing in club and intramural races around the country. The activity was considered healthful and recreational for women, but serious competition was considered unladylike. American women did not found a sanctioning organization of their own (National Women's Rowing Association) until 1962. Today American women rowers are among the best in the world.

Professional rowing contests were enormously popular in the second half of the nineteenth century, and prize money varied from tens to several thousands of dollars. One of the most famous professional rowers was Ned Hanlan, a Canadian, who put on exhibitions and took part in match races in Britain, Canada, Australia, and the United States. Amateur rowers and collegiate athletes looked with distain on the professionals and formed the National Association of Amateur Oarsmen in 1872. This organization was the first to define the difference between amateur and professional athletes. Professional rowing waned during the first decade of the twentieth century because many of the events, competitors, and sponsors seemingly lacked a high degree of integrity allowing or participating in rigged races, dirty tricks, and other forms of fakery.

—James M. Volo

Football

Sports historians generally regard the contest between Rutgers and Princeton on November 6, 1869, as the birth of American football. The game had 20 players on a side and resembled English rugby more than modern football. The sport quickly won popularity due to its activity and seemingly uninhibited brutality. In 1873, representatives from Columbia, Rutgers, Princeton, and Yale met in New York City to form the Intercollegiate Football Association (IFA), which set the number of players at 15 per team, set the size of the playing field, and determined some of the playing rules. In 1876 at the so-called Massasoit Convention, many of these rules were written down and formalized. Nonetheless, the game played in the 1870s bore little resemblance to the modern version.

It was Walter Camp, coach and athletic director at Yale from 1888 to 1914, who gave the game many of its present-day characteristics. Camp had been a player when he attended Yale as a student. Under pressure from Camp, the IFA soon cut the number of players to 11 per team; established the concept of possession of the ball; instituted a system of downs and a line of scrimmage; created the positions of quarterback and center; established the forward pass as a legitimate play (sanctioning a different shape for the football so that it could be thrown); standardized a system of numerical scoring for field goals, touchdowns, and safeties; allowed tackling above the knee; and established penalties for violations of the rules during the game.

The game remained brutal by nineteenth-century standards with close to 200 serious injuries and 18 deaths being reported by the end of the century mostly due to the mass plays and linking of arms that had become common practice over the intervening decades. A large number of colleges had banned the sport by the beginning of the twentieth century. The U.S. Army outlawed the game on its posts because the men were spending more time on the game than on military maneuvers. In 1905, President Theodore Roosevelt called upon the colleges to reform the game. Sixty schools led by representatives from Yale, Harvard, and Princeton formed the National Collegiate Athletic Committee (NCAA), which shortened the length of the game from 75 to 60 minutes;

Earlier football games were rough and tumble affairs lacking protective equipment. Courtesy Library of Congress.

established quarters and half time; made touchdowns worth six points, field goals three points, and safeties two points; and generally banned the most brutal plays and dangerous tactics like piling on, gang tackling, and pass interference. The first night football game was made possible by the installation of 20 electric lights of 2,000 candlepower in 1892.

—James M. Volo

Sharpshooting

Concerns over poor marksmanship abilities exhibited by recruits during the Civil War caused veteran Union officers Colonel William C. Church and General George Wingate to form the National Rifle Association (NRA) in 1871 for the purpose of promoting and encouraging shooting on a scientific basis. This was the first civilian organization of its kind in the world. Church and Wingate emphasized the study of ballistics, gunpowder chemistry, and marksmanship. In 1872, with financial aid from New York State, the NRA purchased a farm on Long Island to build a rifle range. Creed Farm (Creedmore) was the site of the first National Rifle Matches until the crowds forced the NRA to move them to Sea Girt, New Jersey. In 1907 the extremely popular matches were moved to Camp Perry, Ohio, a much larger location capable of supporting the crowds. They are still held there.

In the interim, the NRA began to establish rifle clubs at all the major colleges, universities, and military academies. These programs emphasized gun safety and firearms education, and resulted in academic, amateur shooting, and hunting programs with an unprecedented safety record. Five shooting categories were included in the 1896 Olympic games, and many of the American competitors learned their skill through NRA sponsored programs. In 1903, the U.S. Congress created the National Board for the Promotion of Rifle Practice (NBPRP) with a nearly identical charter to that of the NRA. The NBPRP is now known as the Civilian Marksmanship Program. The NRA formed affiliate programs with the 4-H Clubs, the Boy Scouts, the American Legion, the Jaycees, the National Collegiate Athletic Association (NCAA), and the Reserve Officers Training Corps (ROTC).

During the years after the Civil War, firearms had undergone a number of significant changes that speeded up the loading and firing sequence. This made competitive shooting—both amateur and professional—more exciting for both the participants and any spectators.

Outstanding among the many sharpshooters that put on exhibitions of their skills was Annie Oakley. She was, hands down, the finest woman sharpshooting entertainer of all time, and was the most famous woman to appear in American Wild West shows. Only her bigger-than-life employer, Buffalo Bill Cody, was more famous.

Ironically, Oakley was not a Westerner, having been born in Ohio in 1860. Her real name was Phoebe Ann Moses. The 5-foot-tall, 110-pound Annie was hired in 1885 to give Wild Bill's flagging show a shot in the arm. Annie had come to the attention of the shooting world when she took on Frank Butler of the Butler and Baughman shooting act in a marksmanship challenge in 1881. She beat Butler

23 to 21. Frank was so impressed that he invited her to see his act in Cincinnati. The two fell in love and were married in 1882. Annie joined the act as Frank's partner almost immediately thereafter. She was an instant success, and played with Frank at small theaters, skating rinks, and circuses. While working at one of these, the couple met Cody, who hired them as a warm-up act for his Wild West Show. Annie's act was spectacular. She was an ambidextrous shot who fired rapidly and with unerring accuracy at plates, clay birds, coins, and stones. On the rare occasions when she missed (which she sometimes did on purpose for effect), she immediately fired again. She had the quickness and agility of an athlete. She used shotguns, rifles, and pistols with equal facility. She was invited to perform at Queen Victoria's Golden Jubilee in 1887 and in Paris in 1889. She shot a cigarette from the mouth of a willing Kaiser Wilhelm II during a 1890–1891 tour of Germany, and joked during World War I that she should have hit him when she had the chance.

During her career Annie performed frequently at public shooting matches and exhibitions arranged by her husband and manager, Frank. In one match for $50 she broke all 50 clay birds, and in another took down 50 live birds, defeating Miles Johnson, the champion marksman of New Jersey. In 1888 she appeared in a stage play melodrama, *Deadwood Dick,* but even her presence could not keep the show open. In 1894, Oakley, a few Indians, and Bill Cody were photographed by Thomas Edison's new moving-picture machine at Orange Mountain, New Jersey, making her the first cowgirl in the movies.

In 1897, the Wild West Show played in Canada for the first time since Chief Sitting Bull had appeared as a headliner in 1885. Sitting Bull was now dead, killed while in U.S. custody, and the Old Wild West seemed to be fading. By 1899, Annie—now 39 years old and wearing a wig to cover her graying hair—considered retirement. The railroad travel had been endless, and living from a suitcase had many disadvantages. After her retirement from the Wild West Show, Oakley tried her hand again at stage acting appearing in *The Western Girl,* which opened in New Jersey in 1902. She also taught shooting at exclusive marksmen's clubs. Meanwhile her husband worked for the Union Metallic Cartridge Company promoting its product line to a growing number of trapshooters and hunters. Oddly, Annie never became a spokesperson for any of the firearms manufacturers that courted her. "Guns, rifles and pistols are of many styles," she once said, "and to declare that any one make is superior to all others would show a very narrow mind and limited knowledge of firearms" (Sorg 2001).

Annie Oakley's continued fame allowed her to promote a number of egalitarian views concerning women. She believed that women needed to learn to be proficient with firearms to defend themselves and that they were perfectly capable of fighting for their country. During America's brief involvement in World War I (1917–1918), she offered to sponsor and train a regiment of female sharpshooters for the American Expeditionary Force served under General "Black Jack" Pershing. Oakley and her husband died from the aftereffects of an automobile crash in Ohio in 1926.

—*James M. Volo*

MUSIC

Band Music

Following the Civil War, many military bands returned home and reorganized into civic bands. At a time when full symphonic orchestras were still rare in America, concert bands filled a pressing need and attracted a large following. Bands of all sizes and skill levels played at parades, picnics, dances, political rallies, beer gardens, and concerts on village greens. They could be found in big cities, small towns, and even mining camps. The proliferation of these bands prompted John Sullivan Dwight, America's first influential music critic and editor of *Dwight's Journal of Music*, to wonder where so many musicians came from during war times.

Patrick Gilmore created the pattern for a successful bandleader with his 22nd Regimental Band in New York, which actually had few connections to the military. Departing from the mid-century custom of relying entirely on brass, Gilmore reintroduced woodwinds until his band consisted of one-third clarinets, one-third various woodwinds, and one-third brass. Gilmore's band survived through concerts and substantial tours. In the summer and winter the band played concerts in New York venues and toured in the spring and fall.

Gilmore was known for his grandiose musical productions. Having organized a grand musical extravaganza for the inauguration of a new governor in New Orleans in 1864, the famous bandmaster was asked to use his penchant for showmanship to undertake two of the most gigantic popular festivals known in musical history. The National Peace Jubilee in 1869 and the International Peace Jubilee in 1872, both of which were held in Boston, featured the finest singers and instrumentalists of the day. The National Peace Jubilee lasted five days during which time were assembled an orchestra of 500, a band of 1,000, a chorus of 10,000 and a host of famous soloists. Performers included church musicians, whole choirs, public school teachers, orchestra players, bandsmen, children, and even the Boston Fire Department. The subsequent International Peace Jubilee gathered 2,000 instrumentalists and a chorus of 20,000. The 18-day event featured some of the best military bands of *Europe* and some of the most famous composers, vocal and instrumental artists of the day, including waltz king, Johann Strauss, and his Vienna Orchestra in their only American appearance. A coliseum seating 100,000 people was erected for the occasion. These extravaganzas cemented Gilmore's reputation as the leading musical figure of the age.

The National Peace Jubilee was an artistic and financial success and the high water mark of the band in American music. The response to these concerts by agents of high culture illustrated how music would diverge with the orchestra and the band going their separate ways. Dwight attacked Gilmore's efforts as the best that could be done by a man of "common education" and someone who catered to "popular street taste." Dwight demonstrated a determination by the cultural elite to impose a hierarchy on American musical tastes, separating the art from entertainment. The combination of the entire musical resources of a region for such a massive concert occurred periodically into the Gilded Age, but the high culture champions of music as art would increasingly come to the conclusion that the masses of Americans could not adequately appreciate their art (Schrock 2004, 198).

—*Dorothy Denneen Volo*

The Thomas Orchestra

Theodore Thomas was a German-born American conductor who was dedicated to securing the symphony orchestra's place in America. While most performers catered to the audience's tastes, Thomas endeavored to elevate it. In 1874 he wrote that his lifelong aim was to make good music popular. Thomas was a strict taskmaster who strove for precise, polished performances and demanded a lot from his players. He helped to create the professional symphonic orchestra in the United States and the new profession of full-time symphony orchestra musician.

In addition to performing the classics in concert halls, theaters, and auditoriums, the Thomas Orchestra made a specialty of giving outdoor concerts. Their summer series of concerts in Central Park Garden was enormously popular, totaling 1,227 programs during the 1868–1875 seasons. In addition to flashy showmanship, audiences enjoyed performances that featured music with clearly defined melody and well-marked rhythm, much like those played by the bands with which most people were familiar. Selections included overtures, dances, and lighter pieces designed to prepare novice listeners for a higher grade of music. The comfortable and relaxed setting with snacking, drinking, and socializing further served to soften the barriers between audiences and the performers. Thomas was keenly aware of his audiences and their tastes, but his belief in the superiority of certain classical works never wavered. He hoped that the music would inspire their souls with noble emotions and free them from worldly cares. Relying on concert receipts for support, in 1869 the Thomas Orchestra made the first of many tours on what has been called the Thomas Highway. Major stops included Montreal, Canada, New Orleans, San Francisco, and locations in Maine and Georgia.

Over time, Thomas played a pivotal role in establishing the ritual elements in a symphony orchestra concert, including a rapt but quiet audience, formal dress code, and musical performances true to the composer's work. These elements created an aura of prestige around classical music played by symphonic orchestras, and it was not long before the wealthy began to patronize the performances just as they did art (Shrock 2004, 200).

—*Dorothy Denneen Volo*

Black Spirituals

Shortly after the commencement of hostilities between the North and the South in April 1861, refugee slaves began to seek the protection of Fortress Monroe, Virginia. Unfortunately, the military was unable to meet the physical and social needs of the newly freed blacks. By late summer, the American Missionary Association stepped in and sent Rev. Lewis C. Lockwood to minister to the ex-slaves. Lockwood was deeply impressed by Southern black worship, especially the singing. Anxious to document the spirituality and creativity of newly freed slaves, he sent back a report from the field that detailed a song. The report was published in a Northern abolitionist newspaper. A few months later the paper carried a 20-stanza transcription of *Let My People Go. A Song of the "Contrabands"* that the missionary had taken down verbatim from the dictation of Carl Hollosay and other slaves. The song took a Bible story as commentary on their own lives of bondage and turned it into a spiritual of dignity and strength. This was the beginning of the printed circulation of spirituals.

Thomas Baker, who had no knowledge of the song's original context, arranged the first printed version of the *Song of the Contrabands*, essentially turning the slave song into a parlor ballad in six/eight time. This marked the earliest known sheet music publication of any black spiritual. In 1872, Theodore Seward published the song calling it *Go Down, Moses*. Seward's new arrangement, which included several additional stanzas, managed to translate it into white hymnody while maintaining a flavor apart from it.

In 1867, Northern antislavery activists, William Francis Allen, Charles Pickard Ware, and Lucy McKim published *Slave Songs of the United States*, the first of many anthologies that preserved black spirituals. The three were involved in educating freedmen on the Sea Islands outside the Charleston Harbor. *Slave Songs* contains 136 melodies with texts arranged geographically as Southeastern slave states, Northern seaboard slave states, Inland slave states and Gulf states. Each song's transcriber and location is identified. Great care was taken to faithfully record this important part of slave culture and the song texts contrast against Seward's Standard English translation.

Fisk University was one of the newly organized schools for blacks founded after the Civil War. Inspired by the success of a choir performance at a national teacher's conference, choir director, George L. White, thought to utilize the choir to raise desperately needed funds for the fledgling university. In the fall of 1871, a select group of spiritual singers set out on a tour of the North. Initially, they were met with racism but after a successful performance for a convention of clergymen in Oberlin, Ohio, followed by the endorsement of Rev. Henry Ward Beecher in New York, attitudes changed. The Fisk Jubilee Singers rewrote and rearranged the old spirituals for their white audiences, playing down the traditional African elements while introducing European harmonies and choral arrangements to add an element of respectability. The formula worked, and the Fisk singers were a sensation in New York and New England. They continued to tour for seven years making tours of the British Isles and the European continent.

—*Dorothy Denneen Volo*

Minstrelsy

African American musical traditions had been popular in the United States in the form of the minstrel show since the 1830s. By mid-century the loud, impromptu entertainment had evolved. Having moved from the fringes of respectability to the center of American show business, it became more restrained and balanced. Pieces included comic songs, sad songs, love songs, sentimental songs, and even opera parodies. Minstrel troupes continued to travel and entertain extensively after the Civil War, and there were 26 documented traveling all-African American minstrel groups in the 1870s (Shrock 2004, 192).

At the time when few black performers and composers were able to rise above obscurity, James Bland made his mark on American popular music. Born to a middle-class African American family in New York, Bland decided to leave his studies for a career on the stage after attending a performance by George Primrose, a popular white minstrel-show star. Within a year, Bland was managing his own minstrel troupe and he went on to enjoy a long career as a singer and comedian with some of the best-known minstrel troupes, even touring to great acclaim in England and Germany. Bland's abilities as a performer have long been overshadowed by his popularity as a songwriter. Bland composed approximately 700 songs, among them "Carry Me Back to Old Virginny" (1875) that was adopted by Virginia as its official state song in 1940, "In the Evening by the Moonlight" (1878), and "Oh, Dem Golden Slippers" (1879). Bland's work, however, exhibited little African American influence and was generally indistinguishable in content and form from the stereotypical minstrel songs being turned out by white composers (Brown and Kreiser 2003, 131–33).

White Gospel Music

Industrialization of the era produced great wealth and new comforts to many but it also brought tremendous uncertainty and vast life changes for many more. These issues helped to fuel the Protestant Urban Revival Movement whose goal was to bring the gospel to unchurched Americans of all social and economic classes. One of the movement's leaders was Dwight L. Moody. With a focus more on emotion than theological doctrine and like Sunday Schools and the YMCA, Moody used popular hymns like William Bradbury's *Jesus Loves Me* to deliver his message. In the early 1870s Moody went on a tour of Great Britain accompanied by Ira Sankey, his musical director, who led the group singing and performed solos as well. Their popularity in Great Britain led to a U.S. tour upon their return. Moody and Sankey sought to entertain and evangelize, reworking gospel hymns and sacred songs into a popular format.

Philip P. Bliss worked as a song booster for the firm of Root and Cady. As such, he promoted the company's products, holding music teachers' conventions, singing schools, and concerts. He also composed hymns, which were often printed in his employer's books. In the late 1860s Moody enlisted Bliss to sing at a prayer meeting. Through Moody's encouragement Bliss became a singing evangelist. Bliss found he could promote the gospel and his finances at the same time. Sheet music and books of sacred songs were available for sale at every service. By 1875 evangelical revivalism was not only a religious movement, it was also big business. Crowds in excess of 10,000 flocked to Moody's meetings to hear the choirs that had been trained by Sankey.

In 1876, Sankey published *Gospel Hymns*, a collection of hymns he and Bliss had used on tour. The collection was the best-selling hymnal well into the twentieth century. Two hymns from the collection, *Beautiful River* and *Sweet By and By*, were extremely popular and typical of the approach used by the evangelists.

—*Dorothy Denneen Volo*

LEISURE ACTIVITIES

Springs Tours

Nineteenth-century medical experts suggested that the taking of mineral waters had beneficial effects on the health of those who could afford a month at the many vacation spots noted for their springs. The mineral-laden waters, filled with sulfates and salts of many types, were commonly taken internally to correct real or supposed intestinal ailments, dyspepsia, or general aches and pains. The warm and hot springs of these vacation destinations were commonly fitted with pools or tubs for soaking and fountains for drinking. Doctors and chemists often charted a particular itinerary or regimen for their patients that would, in their opinion, provide the proper cure by alternate soakings and imbibings of the mineral laden liquid, but many happy travelers followed their own designs in the hope of stumbling upon Nature's own antidote.

Various medicinal effects were attributed to the different springs. The waters were said to relieve gastro-intestinal distress, gout, rheumatism, anemia, and obesity. They were also supposed to be good for neurasthenic problems, excesses of intestinal wind, chronic skin diseases, and the elimination of certain poisons from the body. The waters came in four general types: cathartic, tonic, alternative, and diuretic. The cathartic springs contained bicarbonates of magnesia and soda, and chlorides of sodium (table salt); the tonic springs, bicarbonates of iron; the alternative, sodium iodide and potassium chloride; and the diuretic, bicarbonates of lithium and hydrogen peroxide. By the 1850s, establishments had been set up by self-proclaimed Doctors and Scientific persons that offered, besides water, various baths—deemed as Turkish, Russian, Roman, and Electrothermal; two types of electric shock therapy—Galvanic (from batteries) and Faradic (from generators); compressed air, rarified air, and vacuum treatments; and medicated oxygen. The naturally carbonated waters could be bottled and brought home—a practice that spawned a commercial business in soda water and seltzers. It is not surprising that the springs charged fees for these extras while supplying the water gratis and in unlimited quantities (Wechsberg 1979, 182).

From the 1830s to the mid-1850s a particularly popular and affordable trip for Southern families was a so-called Springs Tour. The city of Chattanooga in the hill country of Tennessee, for instance, was known for its sulfur springs and attracted a good deal of patronage among the gentry. The region of western Virginia that straddles the Alleghenies also abounded in various natural springs. Around these a number of fashionable resort hotels were to be found, connected by good turnpikes and dependable stagecoach lines. These locations were convenient to the best families of the South and within the financial means of the moderately well-off. The best-known springs at the time were all located in a 75-mile square within a respectable distance of many coastal plantations.

The hotels and cottages that served this clientele varied in their appointments and level of hospitality. As an example, besides well-appointed rooms for his guests, the resort of Colonel John Fry at Warm Springs, Georgia featured a large ballroom, a stag-horn bar, and chilled wines—with a black bartender to serve them. While the women gossiped and loitered, the men talked politics, played chess, billiards, or cards, and smoked and drank prodigiously. Young unmarried men and women were expected to be polite and openly socialize, but they were warned to avoid any lasting attachments. Many places became disgracefully overcrowded, with insufficient blankets, and two people to a bed. So many private carriages entered the area that there was often insufficient space in the barns; and coaches, teams, coachmen and servants often were left to fend for themselves and find shelter under the coaches or under trees almost completely open to the weather.

The United States Hotel at Saratoga Springs in New York was one of America's most popular luxury hotels and a favorite destination of many wealthy families. The city of Saratoga also boasted the palatial Adelphi Hotel (not the one in New York City) with its three mineral baths and its fountain of youth. At the time these were two of the largest hotels in the world, but the upstate region of central New York also had dozens of smaller hotels and hostelries. The mineral springs, particularly those of Balston and Saratoga, were made more accessible by the growing system of canals and railroads throughout the region. The visitors were offered lodgings in a grand style, and many spent the entire summer taking the waters, attending the horse races, frequenting the casinos, and enjoying a country village life filled with boating, canoeing, and fishing on the many local lakes. Most travelers, however, invested only about six weeks of their time on springs tours—gossiping, socializing, and soaking while having consumed brandy juleps, ham, mutton, ice cream, and many gallons of mineral spring water.

At the springs of central New York were found rich merchants from New Orleans, wealthy planters from Arkansas, Alabama, and Tennessee, and the more haughty and polished land owners from Georgia, North Carolina, South Carolina, and Virginia, all mixed together with New Yorkers, Bostonians, Philadelphians, and other members of the Northern elite. Famous names from all over the nation can be found on the old hotel registers including Daniel Webster, Martin Van Buren, Washington Irving, Andrew Jackson, and Franklin Pierce. The springs also became a magnet for many families of more common means trying to emulate fashionable society, but the rich remained in their own enclaves and even formed enclaves within their enclaves.

Horse racing had always been a hobby of the elite, but even the most common persons followed the sport and bet on it. Remarkably, the casinos of central New York did not attract enough of the undesirable elements of society to drive away the elites. Even upper-class families had enough weak-willed husbands and sons to constantly populate the gambling parlors. The red-brick casino in Congress Park, New York, built in 1867, flourished, and by 1894 was considered by knowledgeable persons to be the most profitable and famous gambling house in the world. Gambling was not legal in New York at the time, but nobody in authority inquired too closely into the leisure activities of America's richest families (Volo and Volo 2007, 341–42).

Roller Skating

Roller-skating was introduced in 1863 and was quickly embraced by the New York City elite. By the 1870s, rinks with hard maple floors could be found in nearly every town and city. For an admission fee of 25 or 50 cents men, women, and children could join in races, fancy skating, or dancing on skates. Special skating dresses that permitted women a greater freedom of movement became popular during the 1870s. By the 1890s the popularity of roller-skating waned, but it helped to advance the status of women's participation in activities outside of the home (Green 1983, 152–53).

Exercising

The benefits of physical activity for both women and men began to gain recognition as the century progressed. Women were discouraged from partaking in strenuous and competitive sports, but light exercise was thought to improve a woman's health. Walking and hiking were the simplest forms of exercise. Women of all social classes were able to participate because it required no specialized equipment or costume. Recommendations for clothing included loose upper garments and a skirt short enough to avoid dragging on the ground. For those women who could afford specialized attire, walking skirts with a system of hooks and eyes to hold up the front of the garment were available for walking in steep or rough terrain.

Another form of exercise was the use of Indian clubs. Invalids and children used a short, light club known as a bat. Adults used the long club. Indian clubs came in pairs and were usually from 24 to 28 inches long and weighed between 4 and 20 pounds each. The purpose of the clubs was to build muscle tone and strength and they were used much as barbells are today. Although both men and women did the same exercises, ladies used lighter weight clubs. Exercises began with simple lifts and progressed to more complex ones. In his 1866 book, *The Indian Club Exercises*, S. D. Kehoe wrote that there was nothing more suitable and simple for ladies than the Indian clubs. He touted the exercises as both pleasing and beneficial and advocated their use to promote the natural development of a graceful form and movement. Proper dress required clothing that permitted one's chest to expand as well as freedom of arm movement (Green 1983, 151–52).

Outdoor Camping

Camping outdoors became a popular vacation activity particularly after the publication of W.H.H. Murray's *Adventures in the Wilderness* in 1869. The book was so popular that it inspired huge numbers of people to travel to areas such as the Catskills, Adirondacks and White Mountains to camp. This mania was termed by contemporaries as Murray's Rush. While rustic by nineteenth-century standards, the camping experience afforded a number of conveniences. For a party of six or eight, which was thought to be an ideal number, there would be several tents. One would be designated as the dining and drawing room and the others for sleeping. Campers slept on cots or on beds made by stuffing empty mattress ticking with boughs and whatever other material was available. They were advised to bring blue, red, or gray blankets, which would not show dust and a two or three yard strip of old carpet, which could be used to cover the ground in the center of the tent. Additional comforts included camp chairs, steamer chairs, and hammocks. Not to be denied the civility of home, campers brought plated eating utensils and earthenware dishes. Washbasins and pitchers were often made of an inexpensive pressed paper material called fibre-ware. Equipment was packed in boxes and flat trunks that could be used as washstands, cupboards, tables, and, if necessary, additional seating.

Some campers hunted and fished for their food, but others had the local country butcher deliver fresh meat and vegetables to the campsite two or three times a week. Butter, milk and eggs were available from neighboring farmhouses. Cooking was done either on an oil stove, sheet metal army oven, or the campfire.

Women's fashion magazines advised wearing one's old clothes, provided that they were stylish. Wool or flannel dresses in any color but black were recommended for cold weather camping, and seersucker was touted for summer trips. For lounging or to rest in the heat of a summer day, it was suggested that women bring a loose gingham or flannel wrapper. A rubber outfit was required in the event of wet weather. Linen or celluloid collars and cuffs and silk handkerchiefs tucked inside the neckline helped to keep dresses from soiling during the excursion where extensive cleaning was impractical. Fashionable ladies accessorized their camping outfits with a tam-o'-shanter or peaked red, white, or blue felt hat; dark stockings and low-heeled boots or shoes with thick soles. Fashion magazines also advised taking a more stylish traveling dress for trips into town.

In camp women's activities paralleled those of their home. They were responsible for the housekeeping and the kitchen although the men probably cleaned whatever fish or game they provided. *Godey's Lady's Book* advised women that with a constant round of systemized work and play they would find that they had no idle hours in camp (Green 1983, 156–58).

Games

With mass production and brilliantly colored boxes created by chromolithography, the board game came into mass popularity during the second half of the nineteenth century. Small producers like W. & S. S. Ives, R. Bliss Manufacturing Company, J. H. Singer, W. S. Reed, and H. B. Chaffee created enduring games and played an important role in the industry, but the big four companies that molded the new game industry were the McLoughlin Brothers (1858), Milton Bradley (1860), Selchow & Righter (1867), and Parker Brothers (1888). Each had a niche. Milton Bradley made games mainly for children, while Parker Brothers created many of its games for adults. Selchow & Righter's most famous and enduring game was Parcheesi, based on the very popular Pachisi from India, which was introduced in 1867. In 1874 Selchow & Righter trademarked Parcheesi, one of the first trademarked names in the early game industry (Shrock 2004, 122).

The Circus

The last decades of the nineteenth century and the first of the twentieth are known as the "Golden Age of the Circus." At least 40 traveling circuses wound their way through the United States playing large cities as well as isolated rural locations. Though circuses had long traveled by horse-drawn wagons, major circuses were quick to see the advantages rail travel provided. Dan Castello's Circus and Menagerie made its way west by rail just two months after the transcontinental railroad was competed in 1869. The showman P. T. Barnum was already well known for his museums and concerts when he formed his first traveling circus in 1871. Over time Barnum's Circus grew in size and scope. Its 1873 incarnation took the unwieldy title of "P. T. Barnum's Great Traveling World's Fair Consisting of Museum, Menagerie, Caravan, Hippodrome, Gallery of Statuary and Fine Arts, Polytechnic Institute, Zoological Garden, and 1,000,000 Curiosities, Combined with Dan Castello's Sig. Sebastian and Mr. D'Atelie's Grand Triple Equestrian and Hippodromatic Exposition." It is worth noting that the word circus is not mentioned in this title. For many in the middle class, circus had connotations of immorality. In an effort to appeal to a family audience, Barnum initially claimed that his extravaganza was not a circus, and he included educationally focused exhibits designed to assuage moralists.

Barnum's Circus, like many, provided a grab bag of attractions designed to appeal across generations, genders, and classes. The circus business was highly competitive, and new novelties were constantly introduced in an effort to draw in customers. Though clowns, animals, and acrobats were to be found in most circuses, one of the features Barnum was known for was exhibiting people who were either physically malformed or who were from exotic locations and cultures. Nonwhite people were displayed in their primitive states, cast in a role designed to contrast as much as possible with that of white audience members.

When major circuses began traveling by rail and bypassing small towns, scaled down circuses, called dog-and-pony shows, sprang up to fill the void. Regardless of the size, when the circus came to town, it usually held a parade down the main street in an effort to drum up business for that day's performance. Animals and performers, accompanied by music, would march through town, stopping traffic and business in its wake. The success and scope of the circus set the standard for other traveling shows of the period (Husband and O'Loughlin 2004, 191–93).

Beer Gardens

Beer gardens came to America with German immigrants. The beer garden to them was more than a place in which to drink beer. It was a social establishment that embodied friends, family, and camaraderie. Nestled under shady trees and on sprawling lawns it was a pleasant place to while away the hours of a scorching afternoon and the perfect setting for the whole family. There was music, dancing, sports, and leisure. For patrons who were mostly working class and often immigrants, the beer garden provided a welcomed oasis from workaday life. There was barely an American town at mid-century that did not boast one or more beer gardens.

Milwaukee was the undisputed leader in the number of beer gardens found in cities. Competition between the city's dozens of gardens was intense, and they went to great extremes to attract patrons. Lueddemann's Garden once featured a female performer who set herself on fire before plunging 40 feet into the river below. Gardens owned by the larger beer companies were the most extravagant and featured the most popular attractions. Pabst Park was an eight-acre resort that boasted a 15,000-foot-long roller coaster and a funhouse. Wild West Shows were held there on a regular basis, and live orchestras performed daily all through the summer.

In 1879, the Schlitz Brewery bought a local beer garden and turned it into a magnificent resort, which it renamed Schlitz Park. The large garden featured a concert pavilion, a dance hall, a bowling alley, and refreshment parlors. The management featured tightrope walkers and other circus-style entertainers to attract patrons. In the center of the park was a hill topped by a three-story pagoda-like structure that offered a panoramic view of the city. At night, 250 gas globes illuminated the garden. The park was also a popular spot for political gatherings. Grover Cleveland, William McKinley, Theodore Roosevelt, and William Jennings Bryan all made speeches at Schlitz Park.

—*Dorothy Denneen Volo*

Ladies' Crafts

Victorian women were avid crafters who sought to decorate their homes with handmade items. Industrialization freed upper- and middle-class women from many time-consuming homemaking tasks. Women became less involved in making the necessities of life and more concerned about creating a proper home atmosphere. Ladies magazines such as *Godey's Lady's Book* and *Peterson's Magazine* reinforced the idea that the home was a sanctuary, where all must be serene and beautiful and it was the homemaker's job to make it that way. Decorating the home with the myriad objects found in the pages of these magazines became a primary preoccupation of women of the upper and middle classes. It didn't matter that the typical parlor was already filled with decorations and textiles; contemporary style dictated that more was better.

Cardboard was a popular medium for crafters, and they used it to create all types of containers that they covered with a wide variety of materials that included paint, decorative stitching, and chromolithographed pictures. Decalomanie, invented in 1864, provided pictures that could be directly applied to virtually any object (Shrock 2004, 136–37).

A woman's skill at needlework had always been considered one of her most important accomplishments. With highly decorated handmade items at the height of fashion, needlework skills took on an even greater importance. Needlework skills, however, shifted from plain sewing, which produced essential linens and basic garments to fancywork, which, as the name implies, was done for decoration. Women used a variety of different kinds of techniques including patchwork, embroidery, tatting, crocheting, knitting, drawnwork, and Berlin work. A woman was expected to furnish her home with everything from quilts to doilies. Women turned to books like *The Ladies' Handbook of Fancy Needlework and Embroidery* (six volumes), *The Ladies' Handbook of Fancy and Ornamental Work*, *Dainty Work for Pleasure and Profit*, and *The Lady's Manual of Fancy Work* for inspiration to make doilies, antimacassars, beaded elbow cushions, mantel drapery, whisk-broom holders, mats, screens, ottomans, and footstools. Handmade knickknacks were scattered everywhere in the well-appointed home. Chairs, sofas, and rockers all required additional decoration.

Needle and Brush: Useful and Decorative provided instructions on how to cover an upholstered rocker with a long velvet scarf trimmed with thick cord, bullion fringe, bullion tassels, and wide ribbons. One particularly popular item of décor was the wall pocket. Made in a great variety of shapes and sizes and heavily decorated, wall pockets were meant to keep papers, magazines, combs and brushes, or other necessities of daily life handy but neatly tucked away. Some resembled portfolios with covers held in place by chains, cords, or ribbons. Others were pouch-like (Weissman and Lavitt 1987, 133–36).

In addition to items for the home, personal accessories for both men and women were also popular. All of these were also highly decorated. Patterns for gentlemen's suspenders, house slippers, scarves, and smoking hats abounded. For ladies there were workbags for sewing, needle cases, pincushions, penwipers, foot muffs, coin purses, and hair ornaments.

Crocheting gained tremendous popularity during the mid-nineteenth century. The first American booklets featuring crochet patterns appeared in 1845. Within just a few years it had become one of the most favored kinds of fancywork, prompting a Vermont magazine in 1875 to editorialize that when you found a housewife crocheting a tidy while sitting in the midst of dirt, you just wanted to shake some sense into her. Many of the ladies' magazines like *Godey's Lady's Book* and *Peterson's* devoted one or two pages each month to crochet patterns. Crocheted purses made the front page of *Harper's Bazaar* in 1868 and 1870. In addition to common projects like jackets, capes, purses, bedspreads, and doilies, patterns appeared for such unique items as a handle for a riding whip, a jacket for a greyhound, and window-blind tassel. Crocheted edging was added to pillowcases, tablecloths, and undergarments.

Hooking rugs was also fashionable. The craft began in the 1840s but took off when jute began to be imported from Asia and was used to make burlap bags. Women discovered that when the bags were slit open they proved to be the perfect size for area rugs. The wide, loose weave of the burlap grain sacks also made the hooking faster and easier. Rug hooking received another boost during the 1860s with the introduction of pre-stenciled patterns on the burlap, which proved to be the inspiration for large numbers of women to take up the craft. Hooked rugs, like quilts, appealed to many women because it enabled them to use up scraps of fabric and pieces of worn clothing to create something to beautify their home. Household economy was a valued quality throughout the Victorian period. Women who could create a well-appointed home without incurring great expense were admired for their thrift. These undertakings also provided women with a creative outlet in a time when many of their expressions were repressed by social prohibitions.

—*Dorothy Denneen Volo*

THEATER

One of the most famous plays from the period was *Our American Cousin*, a farcical comedy written by Tom Taylor in 1858. The plot revolved around the introduction of an awkward, boorish American to his English relatives. This play was being performed at Ford's Theater in Washington, D.C., on the night of April 14, 1865, and in the presidential box were Abraham Lincoln, his wife, Mary Todd Lincoln, and several guests including a military physician. Half way through Act III, at a point where one of the play's funniest lines was given, John Wilkes Booth (not a member of the cast) fired a single pistol shot to the rear of the president's head and then jumped on to the stage to make his escape. The doctor sprang to the president's aid, but Lincoln—unconscious throughout the efforts to save his life—died later that night in a house across the street from the theater. Booth was killed several days later in a barn in Maryland. Nearly simultaneous attacks on the Secretary of State (William Seward) and the Vice President (Andrew Johnson) failed, or failed to materialize. The assassination plot destroyed the plans proposed by Lincoln for Reconstruction: a peaceful reincorporation of the former Confederate states into the Union and a just settlement of the problems posed by emancipation.

The play itself was noteworthy before its association with the assassination. It was one of the first long run productions (seven years) in American theater history. Opening in New York in 1858, its popularity forced the development of new procedures for ticketing and new protocols for the long-term employment of actors. The play also made a number of cultural impacts before its association with Lincoln and Booth in 1865. The character of Lord Dundreary, a dimwitted aristocrat, produced two of these that were closely associated with his name. Dundrearyisms were twisted aphorisms in the style of the character as in "A bird in the hand, gathers no moss;" and a style of facial hair—long, bushy sideburns—named for those worn by the actors who played the role became known as dundrearies.

Edward Askew Sothern established his stardom playing the part of Lord Dundreary, which he expanded considerably by impromptu additions to the scenes during his performances. Joseph Jefferson (as Asa Trenchard, the title character) and Laura Keene (as Florence Trenchard) also established themselves during the New York run of the play. None of these were in the cast on the night of the assassination in Washington. Keene was one of several female players made famous during the nineteenth century. Others included Fanny Kemble, Mary Ann Duff, and Anna Mowatt. Keene is also noteworthy as one of the best-known females to manage a players' company during the period. Jefferson was best known for his stage characterization of Rip Van Winkle, a role he played almost continuously for 38 years. The British author Charles Dickens insisted on seeing Jefferson perform when he visited America in 1842, and he considered Jefferson the greatest living actor of his day. Had Dickens visited America in 1859 rather than 1842, he might have seen a 21-year-old John Wilkes Booth in a minor supporting role in *Beauty and the Beast* at the Marshall Theater for which the future assassin received $20 a week.

John Wilkes Booth was a member of a family of fine actors headed by his British-born father, Junius Brutus Booth. In his acting, Junius had seemingly swept all restraints aside, and made the emotions of hate, jealousy, ambition, and anger overpoweringly real for his audiences. He was the founder of America's first great acting family. John Wilkes's elder brother, Edwin, was considered one of the finest actors on the American stage. Edwin was greatly embarrassed by his brother's involvement in the assassination, but he weathered the public relations storm, receiving the support and sympathy of his fans among the theater-going public.

—*James M. Volo*

HOLIDAYS, CELEBRATIONS, AND FESTIVALS

New Year's Calling

New Year's Day calling grew from the colonial New York custom of open houses. The doors were open for the young men of the city to visit, and the callers wandered from home to home making brief visits. There were no official invitations, and the only requirement for entry was a calling card. Many young women saw the quality of the calling card an indicator of the young man's social position. With this in mind many young men sought a typeface and cardstock that would make a good impression. December was a busy month for printers who were deluged with orders. Sample cases displayed cards that ranged from the simple, but distinguished block letters on white background to cards printed with crimson capitals filigreed with gold. Elaborate novelty cards were adorned with ribbons. Some had an accordion fold that caused the card to spring open.

In large cities during the 1870s it was quite fashionable for bachelors to make endless numbers of visits to eligible young ladies. Newspapers printed lists of homes that would be open and the times when visitors would be received. Open house was generally held from noon to six. The day caused great stress for many young women who feared that they would not receive any visitors, and there was great relief when finally the sound of footsteps on the stairs or sleigh bells stopping at the house were heard. Many young ladies collected the calling cards as though they were trophies.

When the caller or callers appeared, as some men traveled in groups, the head of the house, usually the father, welcomed him. The young man would place his card on the card tray or bowl and visit with the young ladies of the household. Embossed New Year's cakes, which were made by pressing a cookie-like dough into carved wooden boards decorated with flora and fauna, were a New York specialty throughout the nineteenth century. These cakes were considered a delicacy most peculiar to New York and the Hudson Valley, but professional bakers in many other east coast cities advertised these cakes as the custom of calling on New Year's Day spread.

Jennie June's American Cookery Book, published in 1870, devoted an entire chapter to "New Year's Tables, Parties, Etc." The author, Jane Cunningham Croly noted that the custom had become so very general outside of New York that she felt obliged to include a few hints about setting the table in her work. She reminded her readers that it was the taste of gentlemen, not ladies, which needed to be considered on that day and therefore sweets, cake, and the like should be subordinated to chicken salad, pickled oysters, potted salmon, sardines, and the like, which gentlemen generally greatly preferred. In addition she suggested small sandwiches made from biscuits enclosing tongue, ham, or potted veal. Other recommended table items included fruit, jellies, and baskets of mixed cakes or cookies. Croly advised that cherry, old Bourbon, and claret punch were in great demand (Williams 2006, 178–79).

The two or three days after New Year's Day were the ladies' days for calling. Young ladies would discuss the new acquaintances they made among the visitors while enjoying simple refreshments. Surely some boasted about the number of callers they had.

—Dorothy Denneen Volo

Mardi Gras

The custom of masquerading on Mardi Gras (Shrove Tuesday) was popular in many Gulf Coast cities especially New Orleans and Mobile as early as the 1830s. By the 1850s, Mardi Gras was marked by gangs of rowdy revelers who bombarded maskers and spectators with quicklime, dirt, and more. In 1857, in response to newspaper editorials decrying the deterioration of the tradition, an organization was formed to present a parade with floats and torch lights. The organization called itself "The Mystic Krewe of Comus" and presented the first formal masked parade. It consisted of just two floats. One carried a king and the other showed Satan in a blazing hell.

Many present-day Mardi Gras traditions date back to 1872 when a group of businessmen and civic leaders wanted to capitalize on Mardi Gras to provide a tonic for a South still weary from the Civil War and to help to lure visitors back to the city. As part of their plan, they introduced the Carnival colors of purple, green, and gold, which were later designated to signify justice, faith, and power, respectively. They also invented a king of Carnival, Rex, The Lord of Misrule. Carnival plans were energized when it was discovered that Russian Grand Duke Alexis Romanov would be visiting New Orleans during Mardi Gras. An official holiday was created and another krewe, the Knights of Momus, was added. The unaffiliated masked revelers who had been informally parading were asked to form a united procession. A Carnival throne was erected at City Hall in honor of the Grand Duke. When Alexis arrived, the band played *If Ever I Should Cease to Love*, a song that was known to be his favorite. The song has continued to be an integral part of Mardi Gras.

After Reconstruction, members of a handful of elite Carnival societies came to dominate the social and power structure of New Orleans. The krewes adhered to a strict code of secrecy wherein nobody could ever reveal who was behind the masks at the parades or balls. The selection of the king and the queen of each of the krewes was a serious issue. The queen was selected from among the debutantes amid great tension and anticipation. Family traditions, social standing, and political obligations governed the selection. If a candidate's mother had been queen, it was generally accepted that she would be queen in her turn. The debutante queens were featured in newspaper society columns along with the rest of their make-believe courts. The king was more likely to be much older.

The carnival season and Mardi Gras was celebrated in other Gulf Coast communities extending to Galveston, Texas. What might be called the first celebration in Galveston took place in 1867 when a dramatic presentation of a scene from *King*

Henry IV was presented and a masked ball was held. It wasn't until 1871 that the Mardi Gras became a more widespread event. The celebration included two parades, the presentation of several tableaux, and a grand ball. The pageantry of these events increased to the point that in the late-1880s the grand street processions were abandoned for financial reasons. A secret organization called the Forty Funny Fellows managed to fill the void by staging impromptu street parades that attracted large numbers of masked revelers during the gala season. By 1900 these too were discontinued (Cohen and Coffin 1987, 77–82).

St. Patrick's Day

St. Patrick's Day parades are an American invention. Irish immigrants to the United States began publicly observing St. Patrick's Day as far back as 1737 when Boston held its first St. Patrick's Day parade. Among the most renowned of the parades is the New York City parade, which officially dates to March 17, 1766, and was organized by Irish soldiers serving in His Majesty's service. Over the years many large cities followed suit. The Savannah, Georgia, parade dates to 1824, and there has been a St. Patrick's Day parade in Pittsburgh since 1869. The Irish presence in America increased dramatically in the 1840s, a result of Ireland's potato famine of 1845–1849, which left more than a million people dead from starvation and disease. Newspapers of the day portrayed the Irish as lazy drunkards. As a group the Irish were further disparaged for their role in the draft riots during the Civil War. The parade began to serve as a means for the Irish to show their strength and political power in the United States and the number of marchers in the parades increased dramatically.

The New York press described the burgeoning parades with increased detail. Thirty thousand men marched in the 1870 parade. The line of march started with a platoon of policemen followed by the famous Sixty-Ninth Regiment, an Irish regiment that distinguished itself in the Civil War, the Legion of St. Patrick, the Men of Tipperary, 21 divisions of the Ancient Order of Hibernians, numerous parish benevolent societies, and total abstinence units. The parades sometimes drew criticism. In 1868, the *Irish Citizen* complained that too many German bands were hired to play. Acknowledging that there were only a few Irish bands in the city, it proffered that virtually every participant would prefer to march to "stirring airs" from the "old land" even if only played by fife and drum. The parade usually concluded with speeches balancing tales of persecution and suffering with those of humorous anecdotes (Cohen and Coffin 1987, 109–10).

Easter

Easter was not widely celebrated in early America. Puritans regarded it as popish, and the population of Catholics and others for whom it was an important religious festival was small. By the later nineteenth century, however, Easter had become a celebration of spring and the Christian resurrection. Easter church services were supplemented with Easter parades where families displayed their springtime finery.

The Easter Bunny, a descendant of the German "Oschter Haws" or Easter Hare, delivered colored eggs and confections. *Jennie June's American Cookery Book* (1870) instructed readers to use a tallow candle to inscribe the names or dates on the eggs before dyeing. Eggs could also be painted or decorated with etching with a steel pen and India ink. For color, Jane Cunningham Croly suggested using traditional dye agents such as onionskin for brown or indigo for blue.

Molded chocolate eggs, as well as bunnies, chicks, and lambs began to appear in the 1870s. All of these forms were strongly associated not only with Easter but also with themes of rebirth and spring. The English firm of Cadbury & Company produced their first cream-filled chocolate Easter egg in 1875 (Williams 2006, 180).

Derby Day

Colonel Meriwether Lewis Clark organized the first Kentucky Derby, which took place on May 17, 1875, and was won by Aristides. It was modeled after England's Epsom Derby and was originally a one-and-a-half mile race for three-year-old thoroughbreds. The colonel wanted the race to be a festive occasion. He gave a special breakfast for his friends prior to the first running. This turned out to be the beginning of a tradition that continues today, and it is considered good form to take one's guests to breakfast or lunch even today. The festivities surrounding the event expanded to include dances and other social gatherings (Cohen and Coffin 1987, 177–78).

Decoration Day

Women's groups in both the North and the South began decorating graves before the end of the Civil War. Local springtime tributes to the Civil War dead became common in many places. In 1865 Cassandra Oliver Moncure, a woman of French extraction and leader of the Virginia women's movement, organized the activities of several groups into a combined ceremony held on May 30. It is said that she picked that day because it corresponded to the Day of Ashes in France, a solemn day that commemorated the return of the remains of Napoleon Bonaparte to France from St. Helena.

Henry C. Welles, a druggist in Waterloo, New York, also began promoting the idea of decorating the graves of Civil War veterans. Supported by General John B. Murray, a local country clerk, he formed a committee to make wreaths, crosses, and bouquets for each veteran's grave and to plan a ceremony. On May 5, 1866, the village was decorated with evergreen boughs and black mourning streamers and flags were lowered to half-mast. A procession accompanied by martial music and led by war veterans visited each of three cemeteries, where the graves were decorated and speeches honoring the fallen soldiers were made by General Murray and local clergymen.

While small, local activities such as these were taking place in many villages and towns, the first official Decoration Day occurred in 1868 when General John A. Logan, first commander of the Grand Army of the Republic (GAR), an organization of Union veterans, issued General Order #11 designating May 30 as a special day to honor fallen Union soldiers and to decorate the graves of the war dead with flowers. It is believed that date was chosen because, by that time of the year, flowers would be in bloom across the nation. General Logan's order directed his posts to decorate graves "with the choicest flowers of springtime" and urged that their graves be guarded with sacred vigilance. Special ceremonies took place at Arlington National Cemetery. Various Washington officials, including General and Mrs. Ulysses S. Grant, presided over the ceremonies. After the speeches on the mourning-draped veranda of the mansion, children from the Soldiers' and Sailors' Orphan Home and members of the GAR walked through the cemetery, strewing flowers on both Union and Confederate graves while reciting prayers and singing hymns. An estimated 5,000 people helped to decorate the graves of the more than 20,000 Union and Confederate soldiers buried in the cemetery.

The first state to officially recognize the holiday was New York in 1873. By 1890 it was recognized by all of the Northern states. Southern states refused to acknowledge the day. They honored their dead on separate days until after World War I when the holiday changed from honoring just those who died fighting in the Civil War to remembering Americans who died fighting in any war.

—*Dorothy Denneen Volo*

Independence Day

Decoration Day had come to eclipse Independence Day after the Civil War but for 1876, the year of the Centennial, Americans resolved to have an old-fashioned Fourth of July. There were hymns, prayers, songs, patriotic odes, and orations. There were 13-gun salutes at sunrise and 38-gun salutes at noon. Bells rang, bands played, fireworks lit up the sky, and there was a parade on every Main Street in every city and town.

Philadelphia became the focus of the festivity. Stores and businesses were closed for five days beginning Saturday, July 1st, when the first celebratory events were held. The Monday night torchlight parade to Independence Square drew tens of thousands of Philadelphians and visitors alike. At midnight the new Liberty Bell, which had been made from four Civil War cannons to replace the original one that had cracked, was rung 13 times. The mayor raised a ceremonial flag, a replica of Washington's battle flag, and fireworks illuminated the night sky.

In an attempt at reconciliation, Southern military units and Southern dignitaries were invited to participate in Philadelphia's exercises on the Fourth. President Grant was criticized for failing to attend the ceremony, but many generals and other public figures did. One of the highlights of the program came when the grandson and namesake of the Virginia delegate to the Continental Congress, Richard Henry Lee, read the Declaration of Independence. President Grant allowed the original manuscript to be returned to the room in which it was first signed in observance of the Centennial celebrations. Just as his reading concluded, five women, who had been denied participation in the official program, led by Susan B. Anthony approached the podium and presented a copy of the "Woman's Declaration of Rights." The startled master of ceremonies, Senator Thomas Ferry, accepted it with a bow and the ladies returned to their seats (Appelbaum 1989, 109, 113).

The 1876 Centennial Exposition celebrated the 100th anniversary of the Declaration of Independence. In the interim America had grown into a modern industrial giant, had thrown a telegraph line and a railroad across the continent, and had filled out the common borders of the contiguous United States.

The Centennial International Exhibition of 1876, the first official world's fair in the United States, was held in Philadelphia. The celebration was held in Fairmont Park along the Schuylkill River. There were more than 200 buildings constructed within Exposition's grounds, which was surrounded by a fence nearly three miles long. Almost 10 million persons visited the exposition.

—*James M. Volo*

Jousting Tournaments

A romantic movement, which emphasized feeling, imagination, and nature, swept the South between 1760 and 1860. It embraced the past drawing strongly on the styles and ways of ancient Greece and medieval times. Southerners read Sir Walter Scott's books such as *Ivanhoe* (1820) and his other Waverly novels as well as writers such as Yeats, Byron, and Shelley who glamorized romantic and chivalric notions. This furthered the development of a Southern code of chivalry that was expressed in ornate dress, excessive politeness, fancy speech, protection of women and a strong sense of personal and regional honor. The revival of the medieval joust as a test of skill flowed naturally from these ideals, especially in a region with a long-standing interest in horses and horsemanship. While accounts of jousting date to the first quarter of the century, the custom really flourished after William Gilmor hosted the most elaborate quintain tournament ever held on American soil in 1840. After that tournaments could be found in every state south of the Mason-Dixon Line as far west as Texas. During the Civil War events were interrupted, though there is an account of a tournament hosted by an Alabama cavalry regiment at their winter quarters along the Potomac, where they rode in rags and barefoot, but with great enthusiasm. There is also a report of a tournament held on the lawn at Monticello in the fall of 1863. After the war the practice was revived.

The tournament was rich with pageantry and pomp. Participants wore elaborate costumes of silk and velvet. The competitors were called knights and often adopted names expressive of the locality from which they hailed. Winners honored their ladies with a token. An 1877 newspaper account described the practice as suggestive of a bright period in history that was sleeping amid the centuries.

Competition in the tournament involved a tilt for prize rings. The tournament course was 200 yards long in a straight line and marked by 3 posts, each 50 yards apart, the first one being 50 yards from the starting point. The posts were 10-feet high and atop each post was a horizontal beam that projected 3 or 4 feet on to the track. Suspended from each of these beams was a hook, which held a ring generally 2 inches in diameter. The ring of either brass or steel was generally wrapped to make it more visible. The competitor was mounted on horseback and carried a wooden cue or lance approximately eight feet in length and an inch or more around at its base and tapering to a fine point. Approximately three feet from the base of the cue was a protective guard to protect the hand of the competitor. The course was ridden at a dead run and a time limit was imposed to exclude slow riders. The rider held his cue in his right hand and guided his mount with his left. Each entrant was permitted three passes down the course. The object of the event was for the jouster to capture as many rings as possible with a maximum of nine. Sometimes hurdles were added to make the course more difficult. Prizes were presented with appropriate ceremony following the competition. The day's activities typically concluded with a picnic or barbecue for participants and spectators as well. Many also had a dance that night.

Tournaments continued as a favorite Southern pastime into the twentieth century, although they began to decline during the late 1890s. Some competitors took the events very seriously. One young man from Texas, who participated in the events during the last quarter of the nineteenth century, boasted having a tournament course on his ranch and reported a neighbor having one as well (Cohen and Coffin 1987, 265–66).

Thanksgiving

After dinner many families fell into traditional patterns. Elders talked or napped while younger family members player parlor games like charades, board games, cards and the like. Young children might recite a poem or bit of prose. Many homes had parlor pianos and virtually every young lady could play. Families would gather around the piano and what might first begin as solo performances by young people might well evolve into family sing-alongs of popular songs and hymns.

Many cities held military parades on Thanksgiving. The parades dated prior to the Civil War, but the tradition gained popularity following the conflict. Companies were made up of Civil War veterans and militia units. Some city parades included military clubs composed of young gentlemen, who drilled their members in horsemanship, military protocol, and target shooting. On Thanksgiving and other holidays these young men marched up fashionable avenues in spiffy uniforms (Appelbaum 1984, 194–95).

Christmas

By the 1870s Christmas was widely celebrated in many households and had become a holiday that centered on family celebration, gift giving, the indulgence of children, and excessive eating. Food permeated all of the Victorian Christmas rituals. Even many Christmas tree decorations were edible. One traveler described branches that were bedecked with cherries, plums, strawberries, peaches, and gilded eggcups filled with comfits, lozenges, and barley sugar.

The food served on Christmas day was rich, varied, frivolous, delicious, and appealing to the tastes of children and adults alike. Catherine Bragdon recorded her family's Christmas menu of 1867. It included oyster soup, fried and raw oysters, chickens, fried cakes, coffee, tea, apple, raspberry, cherry and squash pies, pickles, peaches, chestnuts, walnuts, apples, and cider. Plum pudding was a traditional finale of any Victorian Christmas table (Williams 2006, 186–87).

FOR MORE INFORMATION

Appelbaum, Diana Karter. *The Glorious Fourth: An American Holiday, An American History.* New York: Facts On File Publications, 1989.

———. *Thanksgiving: An American Holiday, An American History.* New York: Facts On File Publications, 1984.

Beard, Daniel Carter. *The American Boy's Handbook.* Boston, MA: David R. Godine, 1882.

Bellinger, Martha Fletcher. *A Short History of the Theater.* New York: Henry Holt, 1927.

Browne, Ray B., and Lawrence A. Kreiser Jr. *The Civil War and Reconstruction.* Westport, CT: Greenwood Press, 2003.

Camp, Walter. *American Football.* New York: Arno Press, 1974 (c.1891).

———. *Football Facts and Figures. A Symposium of Expert Opinions on the Game's Place in American Athletics.* New York: Harper & Brothers, 1894.

Cohen, Hennig, and Tristram Potter Coffin, eds. *The Folklore of American Holidays.* Detroit, MI: Gale Research Company, 1987.

Elliott, Jock. *Inventing Christmas: How Our Holiday Came to Be.* New York: Abrams, 2002.

Green, Harvey. *The Light of the Home.* New York: Pantheon Books, 1983.

Gross, Linda P., and Theresa R. Snyder. *Philadelphia's 1876 Centennial Exhibition.* Charleston, SC: Arcadia Publishing, 2005.

Harvard Boat Club. *Principles of Rowing at Harvard. By the Executive Committee of the Harvard Boat-Club for the Year Ending 1873.* Cambridge, MA: Welch, Bigelow, and Company, 1873.

Hayward, John. *Gazetteer of the United States.* Hartford, CT: Case, Tiffant and Co., 1853.

Hazen, Margaret Hindle, and Robert M. Hazen, *The Music Men: An Illustrated History of Brass Bands in America, 1800–1920.* Washington, DC: Smithsonian Institution Press, 1987.

Hechtlinger, Adelaide. *American Quilts, Quilting and Patchwork.* Harrisburg, PA: Stackpole Books, 1974.

Hewitt, Barnard. *Theater, USA: 1668 to 1957.* New York: McGraw-Hill Book Company, 1959.

Husband, Julie, and Jim O'Loughlin. *Daily Life in the Industrial United States, 1870–1900.* Westport, CT: Greenwood Press, 2004.

Lane, Rose Wilder. *Woman's Day Book of American Needlework.* New York: Simon and Schuster, 1962.

Lovell, John. *Black Song: The Forge and the Flame; The Story of How the Afro-American Spiritual Was Hammered Out.* New York: Macmillan, 1972.

Mendenhall, Thomas C. *A Short History of American Rowing.* Boston, MA: Charles River Books, 1980.

O'Neil, Sunny. *The Gift of Christmas Past, A Return to Victorian Traditions.* Nashville, TN: The American Association for State and Local History, 1981.

Rader, Benjamin. *American Sports: From the Age of the Folk Games to the Age of the Spectators.* Englewood Cliffs, NJ: Prentice-Hall, 1983.

Sablosky, Irving. *What They Heard: Music in America 1852–1881, from the Pages of Dwight's Journal of Music.* Baton Rouge: Louisiana State University Press, 1986.

Schabas, Ezra. *Theodore Thomas: America's Conductor and Builder of Orchestras, 1835–1905.* Urbana: University of Illinois Press, 1989.

Shrock, Joel. *The Gilded Age.* Westport, CT: Greenwood Press, 2004.

Sorg, Eric V. "Annie Oakley." *Wild West,* February 2001.

Toll, Robert. *Blacking Up: The Minstrel Show in Nineteenth-Century America*. New York: Oxford University Press, 1974.

Volo, Dorothy Denneen, and James M. Volo. *The Antebellum Period*. Westport, CT: Greenwood Press, 2004.

———. *Family Life in Nineteenth-Century America*. Westport, CT: Greenwood Press, 2007.

Wechsberg, Joseph. *The Lost World of the Great Spas*. New York: Harper & Row Publishers, 1979.

Weissman, Judith Reiter, and Wendy Lavitt. *Labors of Love: American Textiles and Needlework, 1650–1930*. New York: Alfred A. Knopf, 1987.

Williams, Susan. *Food in the United States, 1820s–1890*. Westport, CT: Greenwood Press, 2006.

Religious Life

MORALITY

Religious Intolerance

During the nineteenth-century religious intolerance often colored the functioning of government as well as the social, economic, and cultural order of America. During the colonial period religious hostilities had dominated much of the thinking and politics of Americans. Much of the emotionalism of the religious and theological controversies raised by the Protestant Reformation of previous centuries had been transplanted to America, and many Protestants retained antipathetic feelings toward other sects and toward Catholics of all nationalities. In the nineteenth century Americans were still overwhelmingly Protestant, but the majority of these Protestants belonged to the many denominations that served different segments of the American population.

Irish Catholic immigrants experienced severe prejudice at the hands of the Protestant majority throughout the century, but as the century progressed beyond the Civil War, the Irish—as an ethnic group—gained some standing in the community because of the great bravery they exhibited on the battlefield (especially at Fredericksburg). Nonetheless, Catholics remained suspect among many Protestants, and Roman Catholicism remained "an evil fiercely to be hated, deeply to be feared, and unremittingly to be fought" (Nye 1960, 198). Incredibly poor, the Irish were the first truly urban population in American history. They were largely confined to the poorest areas of the cities, and lived in slums and tenements without any reasonable expectations of gainful employment or advancement beyond menial jobs.

—James M. Volo

Bridal Pregnancy

Although almost all cultures prescribe that sexual intercourse take place within marriage, behavior has not always conformed to this moral norm. Rightly or wrongly, the adherence of young persons to this norm is often used as a measure of moral strength in a society. Historic demography, however, suggests that the level of premarital intercourse in the past may be directly related to the extent of social estrangement perceived by young folks in that part of their life cycle between family-dependent adolescence and self-dependent adulthood (Smith and Hindus 1979, 124–25).

The American premarital intercourse record, as measured by the number of seven- and eight-month first babies after the nuptials, is particularly cyclical showing patterns of high and low incidence since colonial times. The incidence of prenuptial pregnancy in the nineteenth century was much lower than in the time periods before or after it. High points, or peaks in premarital pregnancies, are found in the second half of the eighteenth century and the present time (both between 25 and 30 percent of first births). Low points, or troughs, are found in seventeenth-century colonial America and the middle of the nineteenth century (both about 10%). The proportion of bridal pregnancies follows a similar cyclical pattern found in Western European data (Smith and Hindus 1979, 124–25).

Researchers have not been able to explain this distinct cycle in simple terms. Effective and available means of contraception and abortion since the end of the Second World War (about the 1950s) has done little to change the high levels of illegitimacy and prenuptial birth in modern times. It has come to be a statistical feature of poor, minority populations where up to 85 percent of children are being conceived or born out of wedlock in some poverty-stricken communities. This suggests a strong association with a number of modern socioeconomic factors beyond simple adherence to a moral standard.

The most persuasive explanation of the premarital pregnancy cycle seems to involve the way morality and religious tenets were viewed by families. The transition period between early colonial times and the nineteenth century, which included the unsettled social and economic environments of the American Revolution and the early years of the Republic, seems to have lacked both effective external and internal controls on sexual activity. The Puritans of the seventeenth and early-eighteenth centuries valued external controls on moral behavior, dealing with fornication and prenuptial pregnancy as crimes and responding to their occurrence with physical punishments and fines levied by magistrates and town fathers. The revolutionaries of the eighteenth century believed in political liberty, but they were not the vanguard of a sexually liberated America. The acceptance of certain sexual practices both evolves and retrenches over time. Victorian Americans, unlike the bawdy and boisterous forbearers of 1776, had an exaggerated aversion to sexual contact of any kind before marriage, but they tended toward internal controls and self-restraint based on socialization strategies rather than on the deterrent qualities of fines and punishment threatened by their Puritan ancestors. This change from reliance on external controls toward internal ones seems to have reflected a retreat from a moral behavior based on the Calvinist predeterminism of colonial times and toward a wider acceptance of the free-will doctrines related to nineteenth-century religious revival. Although revivalist denominations differed in social base and religious style, the regulation of individual morality remained a central concern, and sexual restraint through religion rested on the centrality of autonomy and individual choice.

Researchers have noted that "the reappearance of premarital sexual restraint in the nineteenth century [seems to be] based on the autonomy of the young adult and the incorporation of the groups tending toward premarital pregnancy into a new social order" (Smith and Hindus 1979, 126–27). Among the applicable changes in the social position of young people were the economic shift from forced apprenticeship to wage labor, the transition from informal to formal education, the substitution of boarding or lodging for traditional familial living arrangements for independent young adults, the extension of political rights and enfranchisement to a greater number of young men, and the more active part given to young women in nineteenth-century churches and reform movements. An acceptance of a *place* in the social order for young persons of sexually active age seems to have bolstered their closer adherence to the community's moral norms because they felt themselves a part of it.

The community of respectable matrons was the ultimate source of intergenerational attitudes toward premarital pregnancy—determining what was considered acceptable moral behavior before marriage and passing it from mother to daughter and grandmother to granddaughter. Historical demographers often use the level of official church membership to determine the level of adherence to religious principles among such a population, and they have made the following observations in this regard. Church membership among young women tripled during the antebellum period. "With younger conversion, religion could have an effective impact on premarital sexual choices. The concomitant splintering of American Protestantism meant that each stratum [of the social order] had one or more denominations tailored to its particular conditions and needs." Although females did not dominate these religions, the new sects and churches generally incorporated them into their organization to a far greater extent than previously. Their newfound role provided "an important outlet for a wide range of female needs, and young women absorbed the message of sexual restraint more completely" (Smith and Hindus 1979, 127).

Victorian-style morality was more than a functional system for preventing unwanted or inconvenient pregnancies. Any type of activity with sexual overtones was strongly discouraged, if not prohibited. Such a strict morality was also relevant to the immediate needs of both young men and women as they entered adult life. People were made independent of their parents at a younger age than ever before in the nineteenth century. A young man was expected to prepare for marriage by accumulating capital and by entering into a stable career. These were the prerequisites for a proper marriage and a successful business life, and few young men would risk an early marriage precipitated by an unfortunate pregnancy that might impede their chances at success. Nor would a young women risk her social position and eligibility as a marriage partner for a tryst with an uncommitted consort. Alexis de Tocqueville emphasized the importance of appearing chaste among the different classes of American women, "No girl...believes that she cannot become the wife of a man who loves her, and this renders all breaches of morality before marriage very uncommon." Commonly held views condemning immorality of any sort before marriage, even between engaged couples, "raised the price of [premarital] sex and thus substantially increased the bargaining power of both single and married women" with respect to the course of any sexual relationship and the promise of matrimony (Smith and Hindus 1979, 128).

This may help to explain the decrease during the middle of the century in the number of short term 8 1/2-month first births after marriage (17.7 to 9.6%) and the 6-month shotgun wedding births (10.3 to 5.8%), the latter being the stronger indicator of premarital intercourse when compared to 9-month wedding night conceptions (23.7 to 12.6%). From 1801 to 1880 all three categories decreased, but the strongest decline was among the last and most committed couples (more than an 11% decrease in 9-month births). This may have indicated the strength of opinion that it was simply wrong for people to have sex before marriage regardless of the proximity of the wedding date. By way of comparison between 1880 and 1910 the number of wedding night conceptions returned to their former high level, and the other categories rebounded beyond their former number to some of the highest rates in more than two centuries (Smith and Hindus 1979, 137).

It should be noted that throughout the course of American history fully two-thirds of all women were not pregnant at the time of their marriage. This suggests a continuity in the efficacy of control with respect to sexual mores. Yet the magnitude of the fluctuations from one historical period to another is compelling. Today premarital intercourse and pregnancy is considered a mild form of deviancy, but it seems to some researchers to have been "a manifestation of a collision between an unchanging and increasingly antiquated family structure and a pattern of individual behavior which is more a part of the past than a harbinger of the future." Neither the old institutional pattern of control nor the rebellion against it could predict "the subsequent sexual behavior of the young" (Smith and Hindus 1979, 129).

—*James M. Volo*

RELIGION: AN IMMENSE NUMBER OF CHURCHES

During Reconstruction religion remained a constant to many Americans amid the otherwise rapid changes in everyday life. Americans were overwhelmingly Christian, with nearly 70,000 churches in all parts of the nation by 1870. "The first thing almost which strikes a newly arrived traveler in the United States," observed an English visitor, "is the immense number of churches.... The country is dotted over with wooden steeples, whose white painted sides, I must own, sparkle in the bright sunlight uncommonly like marble" (Sutherland 2000, 79). Protestants formed the largest number of religious communities, led in numbers by Methodists, Baptists, and Presbyterians. Roman Catholics grew rapidly in strength, with four million members, although largely concentrated in Northern cities. Joining white churchgoers, Southern blacks established the Colored Primitive Baptist Church and the Colored Methodist Episcopal Church by 1870. These two independent churches later joined the African Methodist Episcopal Church (AME) and the Zion Church, both previously established by African Americans in the North.

Despite an impressive presence in American life, the Christian churches came under mounting criticism following the conclusion of the Civil War. Some dissent came from inside the faith, where less well-to-do church members felt alienated by the social displays made by their more wealthy peers. "[H]ow can I afford to be a Christian," one frustrated churchgoer asked, "and hire a pew and dress up my family in such a style on Sunday that they won't be snubbed for their shabby appearance by genteel Christians?" (Sutherland 2000, 87).

Other attacks came from outside the faith, where proponents of evolution questioned religious teachings on the creation of both the universe and human life. Both scientific Darwinism and social Darwinism received attention from a significant minority of the population. The debate between science and religion raged throughout the postwar era, marred more often than not by intense hostility and bitterness. The criticisms of the practices and teachings of the Christianity marked one of many transitions of American life during the late nineteenth century (Browne and Kreiser 2003, 17–18).

FOR MORE INFORMATION

Ahlstrom, Sydney A. *A Religious History of the American People*. New Haven, CT: Yale University Press, 1972.

Beaumont, Gustave de. "On Marriage in America: Beaumont's letter to his family." http://xroads.virginia.edu/~HYPER/DETOC/FEM/beaumont.htm (accessed May 2007).

Browne, Ray B., and Lawrence A. Kreiser Jr. *The Civil War and Reconstruction*. Westport, CT: Greenwood Press, 2003.

Hennesey, James. *American Catholics*. New York: Oxford University Press, 1981.

Nye, Russell B. *The Cultural Life of the New Nation, 1776–1830*. New York: Harper & Row, 1960.

Smith, Daniel Scott, and Michael S. Hindus. "Premarital Pregnancy in America." In *Studies in American Historical Demography*, ed. Maris A. Vinovskis. New York: Academic Press, 1979.

Sutherland, Daniel E. *The Expansion of Everyday Life, 1860–1876*. Fayetteville: University of Arkansas Press, 2000.

Sweet, Leonard I. *The Minister's Wife: Her Role in Nineteenth-Century American Evangelism*. Philadelphia, PA: Temple University Press, 1983.

Tocqueville, Alexis de. "Letter to his sister, describing courtship and marriage habits of the Americans." http://xroads.virginia.edu/~HYPER/DETOC/FEM/tocqueville.htm (accessed May 2007).

THE PERIOD OF EXPLOITATION

Overview

MANIFEST DESTINY

In July 1845, New York newspaperman John L. O'Sullivan wrote in the *United States Magazine and Democratic Review* that it was the nation's "manifest destiny to overspread and to possess the whole continent, which Providence has given for the development of the great experiment of liberty and self-government." The phrase, *Manifest Destiny*, caught the imagination of the country and came, thereafter, to stand for the entire expansive movement to the West. Yet the slogan also coalesced a number of hazy images Americans already held concerning themselves, and it provided the nation with a solid purpose that carried it through civil war and reconstruction to the end of the century. *Manifest Destiny* was the one idea about the American nation on which all the sections and citizens could agree.

Nonetheless, the exploration and domination of the North American Continent was no haphazard series of fortuitous ramblings and random discoveries, but a careful process initiated by Thomas Jefferson in 1803 and programmed thereafter from the urban centers of the East and Midwest, particularly Washington, D.C., and St. Louis. Politicians, land speculators, and businessmen formulated specific instructions and sent explorers, traders, artists, photographers, and soldiers into the unfenced expanses of grass, the towering mountains, and the formidable deserts to gather information that would further the nation's plans for the development of the continent. Jefferson had accumulated information regarding the Trans-Mississippi West during his five years (1784–1789) of diplomatic service in France. In 1806 Meriwether Lewis and William Clark returned from a two-year long exploration of the Louisiana Purchase. Their maps, drawings, and descriptions of the territory fired the imagination of the nation concerning the west.

As early as 1784, geographer Thomas Hutchins had noted, "If we want it, I warrant it will be ours." He viewed Americans as the inhabitants of a potential world empire who had it "in their power to engross the whole commerce of it, and to reign, not only as lords of America, but to possess, in the utmost security, the dominion of the sea throughout the world" (Smith 1973, 9). The practical difficulties of overruling the North American Continent from the Eastern to the Western oceans and from the Mexican Gulf in the South to the frozen lakes of the Canadian North were of minor consequence. Mexico, Britain, and even Russia stood in the way no less than the vast prairies, towering mountains, and indigenous native population. The power of Manifest Destiny lay in the national imagination. It was a drama enacted on a corporate level by all the American people.

In 1846 the United States went to war with Mexico over the annexation of Texas. Not only did the country gain the entire area of Texas from Mexico, but in the Treaty of Guadalupe Hidalgo (1848) also added most of California, Arizona, and New Mexico to the United States. Also in 1846 the British made a concession to America of any pretensions to the Old Northwest Territory (of the Great Lakes) to cement a boundary line with British Canada that set the northern boundary of the Oregon Territory at the 49th parallel. The boundary merely recorded the fact that American emigration and American style agriculture had pushed out to Oregon and occupied it. The United States lost any claim to most of British Columbia but gained undisputed possession of present-day Washington, Idaho, and parts of Utah, Nevada, and Montana. In 1853, exactly half a century after the Louisiana Purchase, a supplementary treaty with Mexico known as the Gadsden Purchase filled out the common contiguous borders of the country.

Some historians consider the Gadsden Purchase the end of the era of expansion. Others understand that such events also shape the future, and their inevitable consequences lend a radically different perspective to all that preceded them. The era of expansion simply gave way to an equally vibrant era of exploitation. Nor does the end of expansion in mid-century explain the purchase of Alaska in 1867, the annexation of Hawaii in 1898, or the submission of Cuba and the acquisition of Puerto Rico and the Philippines at the end of the Spanish American War 50 years later.

While the United States gained legal possession of all these territories, except Cuba, its people had not yet taken personal possession of them. The discovery of gold in California drew thousands of persons to the Pacific, and the Oregon Trail was worn deep by immigrants. Yet the vast intervening empty spaces of the American heartland were slow to fill.

Many families from the 1840s to the 1870s responded to political and economic adversity or changes in their family circumstances by pulling up stakes and moving further west, but they always relied upon the prospect of ultimately mapping, cultivating, and domesticating the unmanaged wilderness. Free immigrants often sought to re-create themselves physically, economically, and socially by moving beyond the limits of civilization. Family strategies like these and the underlying expectations that they included can be seen at work again and again among the writings of early travelers and settlers in the wilderness.

This common attitude toward geographical movement was formulated as part of the frontier thesis of historian Frederick Jackson Turner (1893), who saw the availability of western land as a political and economic safety valve for the growing

American republic as well as a formative ingredient in the American character. Westward movement was essential to the continued existence of the nation. Turner's original work dealt primarily with the settlement of the Mississippi Valley from 1830 to 1850 and the controversy over the extension of slavery that it engendered. Nonetheless, his thesis, although more than a century old today, remains useful in formulating an understanding of the period of national expansion in the second half of the nineteenth century as well.

Individual families are not normally considered powerful agents of nation building. Surely it is armies, speculators, industrialists, railway magnets, and other economic and political powers that are the impetus of national expansion. Yet this was not always the case in nineteenth-century America, and many of these forces tended to follow families rather than to lead them west.

Calling themselves settlers and immigrants, families from across the states began a march into the vaguely empty space west of the Appalachian Mountains as soon as the Revolutionary War had ended. The immigrants then moved to the farmlands of the Midwest and the dark soils of the Southeast. The simplest maps of the unknown interior spurred thousands of Americans to relocate to towns that existed nowhere except on land office surveys. With them, in many cases, came their slaves, forced to emigrate sometimes in ways that forever broke black family ties. Before them stood the Indians with their own families, aboriginal inheritors of the land, poised to be swept aside and ultimately to be dispossessed of their heritage.

The Ohio River and its tributaries initially provided the most direct route to the lands of the Midwest. The movement of immigrants usually paralleled the valleys of the Ohio or the Tennessee Rivers. Early pioneer families floated or poled their way down these waterways and their tributaries on a wide assortment of rafts, barges, and keelboats. Others moved west on overland courses parallel to the rivers where the going was easier and the topography more gently changing. The rivers wore gaps in the mountains that made their passage feasible. The Cumberland Gap is the best known of these. Formed by an ancient creek that was later redirected by geologic forces into the Cumberland River, the gap was used for centuries by native Americans to cross the mountains. Daniel Boone was credited with opening the gap to white settlers entering Kentucky and Tennessee, and the foot trail through it was later widened to accommodate wagons.

A large area of Ohio known as the "Firelands," was quickly settled by families from coastal Connecticut who had been given government land to replace their homes burned by the British in the Revolutionary War. The Midwestern territories of Indiana and Illinois were initially settled by Southerners coming through Kentucky. Those sympathetic to the Southern way of life were quickly overwhelmed by others with Northern opinions and by immigrants with European sentiments. The Midwest attracted a significant increase in population during the 1840s from among Germans, Swedes, and other working-class Europeans who bypassed the slaveholding South to settle there.

By the Centennial Year of 1876, America had changed from a backwater set of fragmented British colonies hanging onto the fringe of the Atlantic coastline into a modern multi-ocean international power favored with the greatest industrial base in world history. Following its manifest destiny, the nation brought half a continent—some say the most valuable half—under its control. Only the cold wilderness expanses of Canada and the dry wastelands of Mexico remained outside its direct control, yet some Americans covetously spied even these. Nonetheless, the nation was still to experience a number of setbacks such as the Plains Indian Wars and the Apache Wars of the final quarter of the century.

Nonetheless, the Indians had been driven from their native lands almost everywhere, and they had been killed or confined to reservations by the 1890. By the turn of the century a number of island possessions had been acquired: Hawaii in 1893; Puerto Rico, Guam, and the Philippines in 1898; and Wake Island in 1899. The nation, initially isolated on a thin strip of land along the Atlantic coast, had attained its *Manifest Destiny* by stretching from sea to sea in little more than a single century, and it had become in the process a multi-ocean colonial power.

FOR MORE INFORMATION

Bartlett, Richard A. *The New Country: A Social History of the American Frontier, 1776–1890*. New York: Oxford University Press, 1974.

Dulles, Foster Rhea. *The Old China Trade*. New York: Houghton Mifflin Company, 1930.

Fehrenbacher, Don E. *The Era of Expansion, 1800–1848*. New York: John Wiley and Sons, 1969.

Goetzmann, William H. *Exploration and Empire, The Explorer and the Scientist in the Winning of the American West*. New York: The History Book Club, 1966.

Jones, Mary Ellen. *Daily Life on the Nineteenth-Century American Frontier*. Westport, CT: Greenwood Press, 1998.

Quay, Sara E. *Westward Expansion*. Westport, CT: Greenwood Press, 2002.

Smith, Henry Nash. *Virgin Land, The American West as Symbol and Myth*. Cambridge, MA: Harvard University Press, 1973.

Domestic Life

KINSHIP SYSTEMS: FAMILIES ON THE MOVE

In a mobile nineteenth-century world, emigration and resettlement were common. In a wildly expanding nation, the call of cheap land, personal freedom, or stirring adventure caused many young men and women to leave the confines of their parental homes and stretch the bonds of family support. Those who left the sanctuary of the kinship community, as did many of the families that chose to immigrate to the American West, exchanged the support of family and friends for exposure to possible economic ruin, moral temptation, or physical danger.

Nineteenth-century society endowed men with considerable power within this family setting, and their principal duty was to bind together the household whether they be merchants, mechanics, farmers, or professional men. The concept of the urban home as an enclosure or a sacred center made most families remarkably nuclear in composition. Commonly, only the parents and their children lived under a common roof in middle- to upper-class families. Although the family group was often surrounded by unrelated domestic help, these were commonly ignored as persons and treated more like animated household furnishings.

Extended family structures were much less common in the nineteenth century than in colonial times, but they did exist, mainly on the frontiers, in the South, or in immigrant enclaves. Through the machinery of a vastly improved communications network (mail, telegraph, railroads, etc.), the kinship community living outside the immediate familial home in settled areas could still provide support, and uncles, aunts, grandparents, and cousins were available for daily counsel, economic assistance, and emotional underpinning in times of trouble.

Moving to a sparsely settled frontier region heightened a parent's concern for personal and family safety. Added to the very real threat of attacks by Indians, bushwhackers, bandits, or venomous snakes were common farm accidents, indispositions, nutritional deficiencies, bad water, and bad weather—all capable of striking without warning, but still a part of the fabric of ordinary life. Common sicknesses and difficult childbirths were made more threatening by distance from friends, kin, and established patterns of care. Warnings about these dangers fill the period guidebooks, military reports, physicians' articles, and private letters of the period (Valencius 2002, 4–5).

Possibly for this reason many immigrants traveled in extended family groups, uprooting married sons, daughters, and grandchildren when making a move. It was not unusual for a single kinship group to occupy a dozen separate wagons in the same emigrant train. Barring such unanimity of choice, many families chose to immigrate in sequence. Known as a serial migration, one small part of a family might lead the way to a new region where it became established to be followed later by other waves of migrating kinfolk. In this manner the family maintained its support structure and put down new roots in a predictable and orderly manner.

—*James M. Volo*

FAMILY LIFE

Household Structure

In part because they provided extra hands on the farm, children were welcome and families were often large. "Our poor man counts each one of his half dozen or half score a blessing... stout hands and active heads are the very thing we need," editorialized one newspaper (Bartlett 1974, 361). With infant mortality rates as high as 25–30 percent and epidemics of measles, scarlet fever, or influenza wiping out whole families, a woman had to have been pregnant more than half-dozen times to produce these large families. Some men, like Old Jules in Mari Sandoz's account of her family, believed that "women got to have children to keep healthy" (Sandoz 1978, 110). Some women thus practiced rudimentary birth control—hoping the rhythm method would work, utilizing pessaries for contraception, and nursing their babies as long as possible in the belief they could not then conceive. By word of mouth women passed on contraceptive techniques: the use of Vaseline—"a greased egg wouldn't hatch"; rock salt—though most avoided this because "it affected the mind"; and a concoction of cocoa butter and boric acid (Jameson 1987, 152). Grace Fairchild reflected on her own fecundity: "To have six children in less than eight years is something of a record. You would have thought I was in a race to see how fast we could get that new country settled. I decided to call a halt" (Wyman 1972, 29).

Women—whether they were wives, schoolteachers, immigrant girls fresh off the boat, or prostitutes—were valued. When the bylaws of Yellowstone City, Montana, were written during the winter of 1884–1885, there were only 15 women and 300 men in the camp. Hanging was established as the penalty for "murder, thieving or insulting a woman" (Bartlett 1974, 249). Mollie Dorsey received so many proposals that she sighed, "We do not see a woman at all. All men, single or bachelors, and one gets tired of them" (Sanford 1959, 39).

There was also a surprising sexual frankness. Though there was occasional premarital sex between couples (Stewart 1914, 82–84), it was not really condoned. Marriages were opportunities for great celebration. Usually a jolly, rambunctious charivari (shivaree) or party was held after the wedding: "The newly married couple occupied a wagon for sleeping apartments. Then the fun began. Such a banging of cans, shooting of guns and every noise conceivable.... The disturbance was kept up until midnight, when the crowd dispersed, leaving the happy couple on the prairie to rest undisturbed till morning, when they came [out] amid cheers and congratulation" (Luchetti 1982, 30).

Although much research suggests that one effect of the predominantly male society was respect for and joyful pursuit of women, an opposite, darker phenomenon also existed. Some men believed that they had the right to "dominate women and coerce compliance with their wishes" (Graulich 1987, 113). Though such spousal abuse did occur on the frontier, some women stood up to their men. After receiving a beating from her husband, one woman threw him out of the house and thenceforth supported herself by doing laundry and running a boarding house (Jameson 1987, 154; Jones 1998, 202–4).

Vital Statistics

Nowhere was the role of the rural population more important than in its effect on fertility and birth rates. The level of American fertility in the eighteenth century was one of the highest in human history, a fact used to entice immigration from Europe, which had a lower rate during the same period. However, in the early part of the nineteenth century there was an unmistakable downturn in American fertility driven largely by the effect of the rural population. By the end of the century (1900) the fertility of the white rural population was fully 60 percent of that a century earlier. The decline was nationwide, occurred in all geographic sections of the country, and cannot presently be explained in terms of ethnicity. Researchers are also at a loss to convincingly explain the downturn other than to note that farm wives in the Eastern and older-settled regions deliberately started their families later and terminated their childbearing earlier than those in the frontier West. At this time "the methods of deliberate fertility control cannot be determined" (Easterlin 1978, 65).

Among both farm and nonfarm families, there was an unmistakable difference in the child-woman ratio when the level of settlement was taken as a factor. The child-woman ratio is a measure of the number of children under five years of age per woman of reproductive age usually calculated from published state data. A high ratio might suggest that women were somewhat tied to the household by childcare considerations and consequently unavailable for income producing labor. The data suggest that in this period the child-woman ratio in the older and more settled states was perhaps 25 percent lower than that in the newer and less settled ones. This measure of fertility rose consistently as one moved from older to newer settlements. There was one exception to this in the frontier townships. While the numbers were higher on the leading edges of settlement than in the oldest areas, they were 5 to 10 percent lower than in the areas slightly behind the frontier. This was where 20 to 40 percent of the land was improved. Confounding the situation somewhat is the probability that among families on the spearhead of settlement at least some of the children were born elsewhere, possibly in the older settlements. These data may also reflect minor differences in the proportion of married persons in the population and the age distribution of its reproductive females (Easterlin 1978, 60–61).

Generally, in the decades of the 1880s and 1890s the typical white, native-born women had 5 or 6 pregnancies during her childbearing years, and raised 3 or 4 children with the former decade averaging 3.6 and the later decade averaging only 2.9. Nationally where data is available, women seem to have married at a median age of 21 or 22 years, and given birth to their first child within 1 or 2 years. In the 1890s, the median period of childbearing rose from 10 years in 1880 to about 11 years. Foreign-born women continued to have higher fertility rates than native-born women, and second-generation foreign-born women were somewhere in between (Wells 1979, 524).

Blacks (from data beginning in 1850) sustained decreasing, but still higher, fertility and birth rates (in both 1880 and 1890, they had 9 or 10 pregnancies and 6 to 7 children) than their white counterparts throughout the remainder of the nineteenth century. In fact, the data for these parameters among black women in 1890 were almost equal to the white rates in 1800, with the black decreases lagging almost a century behind those of whites demographically. Many early studies of black fertility were handicapped by their focus on determining a cause for the perceived variations in birth rates among native-born whites, foreign-born whites, and blacks. "There was a widespread fear in some circles that the higher birth rates of foreign-born and black women would diminish the numerical and political importance of the native white population in the United States" (Hareven and Vinovskis 1978, 12).

Recent research suggests that the decline in white reproduction may have been affected by the growing feminist (women's rights) movement with women taking greater control over their reproductive lives—a luxury not afforded to black women of childbearing years who were either enslaved or newly freed during much of the period. Some researchers have also suggested that declining birth rates may be related to land availability, increasing industrialization, the education of women, or the pressure of elderly dependents in the home (Easterlin 1978, 65–73).

The data also suggest that white working women were more likely to limit their family size than those who were not gainfully employed outside the home. However, it cannot be determined with any precision whether women with fewer children were more likely to enter the workforce, or if those who were working were more likely to curtail their family size. Both factors may have been in operation. These findings are also confounded by the tendency of unwed mothers to quietly place their children in the homes of relatives while living and working elsewhere possibly as domestics or as boarders with manufacturing jobs (Hareven and Vinovskis 1978, 91). Further analysis suggests that "the opportunity to work outside the home…was more likely to influence the curtailment of fertility through the postponement of marriage than through direct family limitation." In any case, working seems to have had a minimal effect on the absolute fertility of individual women, and the overall decline in family size took place in both urban and rural environments (Hareven and Vinovskis 1978, 125; Volo and Volo 2007, 29–32).

MEN

Nowhere was a man's character more important or more sorely tested, than on the emigrant trails to the West. Good judgment, integrity of purpose, and practical application thereof were indispensable to the harmony of the wagon train and the successful completion of the journey. Captain Randolph B. Marcy, a popular advisor to prairie travelers, advised in 1859, "On long and arduous expeditions men are apt to become irritable and ill-natured, and oftentimes fancy they have more labor imposed upon them then their comrades.…That man who exercises the greatest forbearance under such circumstances, who is cheerful, slow to take up quarrels, and endeavors to reconcile difficulties among his companions, is deserving of all praise, and will, no doubt, contribute largely to the success and comfort of an expedition" (Marcy 1993/1859, 24).

T. L. Haines and Levi Yaggy advised that "deportment, honesty, caution, and a desire to do right" were the truth of human character. Surely the truest criterion of a man's character and conduct was to be found in the "opinion of his nearest relations" who had daily and hourly opportunities to form a judgment of him within the privacy of the home (Haines and Yaggy 1876, 115). J. Clinton Ransom noted, "As men act in the home, so they will act in society, so will they act in the capacity of citizens" (Ransom 1889, 315). Young men, as they start in life, "should regard character as a capital, unaffected by panics and failures, fruitful when all other investments lie dormant, having as certain promise in the present life as in that which is to come" (Haines and Yaggy 1876, 113). For Haines and Yaggy character was closely associated with masculinity and gender identification. They considered business, law, and government—the so-called higher walks of life—treacherous, dangerous, and filled with obstacles. Overcoming these "trying and perilous circumstances" required that an "upright man" be brave and filled with confidence (Haines and Yaggy 1876, 112–13).

On the American Western frontier, men were more closely defined by their work than in any other part of the nation. Among the most common men in opening the West were prospectors, miners, mountain trappers, emigrant train guides, and soldiers. Sometimes solitary, sometimes traveling in bands of a hundred, these were arguably the first persons to open the mountains and plateaus to exploitation, and it was their tales and their trails that led the emigrant trains westward.

Although the wagon train is thought to have been the quintessential mode of transportation west, steamboating was equally important and also filled with danger. William J. Petersen, nineteenth-century scholar and steamboat devotee, noted of immigrants during the 1870s, "Spurred on by hopes, enthusiasms, and ambitions that would not brook denial, the rugged pioneers trekked westward. Grim tragedy stalked them every mile of the way. Some who died of cholera on steamboats were flung into the muddy river or left to rot in shallow graves along the bank. Others sprinkled the desert with their bleached bones—a mute but somber warning to those who followed. Not infrequently the spring thaws disclosed the congealed bodies of pioneers who had been caught the previous winter in some snow-clad mountain pass." Only strong, resourceful, and self-reliant men were destined to survive (Petersen 1968/1937, 296).

The mountain man, epitomized for many by trappers like Kit Carson, Tom Fitzpatrick, and Jim Bridger, was the proudest of all the Americans who lived their lives out beyond the settlements. The free trappers, who worked alone or in small groups, owed no allegiance to any particular company, and sold their furs to the highest bidder, were a unique American type. Even Francis Parkman, who came to consider Henry Chatillon not only the mountain man par excellence but also a friend, called the profession in general that of half savage men who spent their lives in trapping among the Rocky Mountains.

Another category of mountain man was the Jacksonian man, an expectant capitalist like most other Americans of that time. His primary motive for participating in the fur trade was to accumulate capital rapidly; such capital could then be invested in other ventures. William Ashley, William Sublette, and Robert Campbell were illustrative of such entrepreneurial behavior, with subsequent ventures into banking, politics, coal mining, and stock breeding.

Among those men who followed Lewis and Clark into the wilderness was Lieutenant Zebulon Montgomery Pike, who neither climbed nor named Pike's Peak. However, his name would be memorialized in the motto of a nation restless to go west; "Pikes Peak or Bust" was scrawled on many a covered wagon. Pike and his men set out in September 1806 to explore the southern Great Plains and to explore the source of the Arkansas River. He found the land to be inhospitable and worthless for agriculture, going so far as to predict it would become the American Sahara. However, this could be an advantage, he felt, for the region could become a buffer between Spanish and American territory, serving as a barrier to westward expansion because it could force Americans to limit the extent of their expansion west to the borders of the Missouri and Mississippi. In this way the myth of the Great American Desert was born, which would persist until after the Civil War and that was resurrected during the Dustbowl of the 1930s.

Stephen H. Long, of the army's topographical engineers, led five expeditions into the trans-Mississippi West from 1816 to 1823, covering roughly 26,000 miles. Perhaps his greatest contribution was convincing the War Department that scientific data gathering was as important as military mapping and surveying. Thus, scientific professionals were enlisted in exploring the West, an activity that had been the province of enthusiastic amateurs in Jefferson's day. However, after two decades of government-sponsored exploration the fever cooled in the halls of Congress, perhaps due to the unpromising reports of Pike and Long. For most of the rest of the next two decades the region was explored—informally but thoroughly—by fur traders and mountain men. Among them was John Colter of the Lewis and Clark expedition, who had decided to remain behind. Seeking new trapping areas for his employer, Manuel Lisa of the Missouri Fur Company, he explored the Tetons, crossed the Continental Divide, and was probably the first white man to see what is now Yellowstone National Park.

Between 1842 and 1853, Colonel John Charles Frémont led five expeditions across the West. Nicknamed "The Pathfinder," he probably covered more territory than any other explorer of his day. On his way to the Pacific in 1843–1844, he essentially followed the established emigrant route. In 1843, 900 settlers arrived in Oregon, augmented the next year by 1,200 more. Thus, Frémont was hardly venturing into the unknown as Lewis and Clark had done. Indeed, he frequently wrote in his journal of sage brush crushed by wagon wheels, of finding a "broad plainly beaten trail" (Frémont 1988, 150), of a remarkable depletion of game, especially buffalo "an occasional buffalo skull and a few wild antelope were all that remained of the abundance which had covered the country with animal life", and its impact on the "miserably poor" Indians who "drew aside their blankets, showing me their lean and bony figures" (Frémont 1988, 143). He describes the Hudson's Bay Company operation at Vancouver and its intricate overland network to Montreal (Frémont 1988, 193–95). He regrets missing Dr. Marcus Whitman, absent from his missionary establishment at Walla Walla, but "an abundant supply of excellent potatoes" from the mission garden "furnished [the expedition] a grateful substitute for bread" (Frémont 1988, 182–83).

Although Frémont rarely forged new trails, his expeditions were far from insignificant. His reports excited America's imagination. Unlike the Lewis and Clark journals, which languished for years before publication, Congress ordered 10,000 copies of Fremont's reports published in 1845. The writing was often vivid. Frémont was a good storyteller, providing real-life adventures that later dime novelists would be hard-pressed to equal. In 1856 he was chosen as the first presidential candidate of the newly formed Republican Party. A remarkably attractive candidate, he nonetheless failed to carry the votes needed to propel the party's antislavery agenda to victory at the polls (Jones 1998, 74–78).

WOMEN

Women on the Emigrant Trail

Life on the journey west was long, slow, and tiresome. The day started at daybreak or earlier, with wheels rolling by 6:00 A.M. Prompt starts were essential for the group's success. Mothers learned it was preferable—to prevent delays—to let their children continue to sleep for a few hours after the wagons were under way. Often wagons that delayed the group's start were required to take a position at the rear of the line, a significant punishment given the dusty conditions. (Normally wagons took turns, day by day, in the lead.) Across the desert, starts were as early as 2:00 A.M., though sometimes the wagons kept rolling all night and stopped during the heat of the day. Early, on the journey, women and children rode in the wagons; later, as the animals grew exhausted, the women walked. They carried their babies, which after a while became exhausting. One tired woman reported that she got so weary of packing the babies that she took a long sack and fixed it so it could be fastened on the ox. She cut a hole on each side, like a pair of saddlebags and placed a baby in each end. The little fellows would ride thus and sleep half their time.

In addition to the many physical dangers of the journey, most of the immigrants experienced psychological stress as well. The majority was fairly provincial and had never ventured far from their homes. Many suffered from homesickness, especially on birthdays and wedding anniversaries. The psychological stresses were even greater for the relatively few women on the Overland Trail. A good many of them had become widows en route—from disease or accident. Unable to turn back they forged ahead, taking on the unfamiliar responsibility of being a single parent, and being unable for the children's sake to reach closure through mourning. The plight of one German emigrant woman whose husband, for some unknown reason, had gone back some distance, sat on the wagon tongue, weeping. Her son was sick in their wagon. With no one to watch over them, her oxen had wandered off. Realistically assessing her future, a diarist observed that the poor woman was in for hard times indeed. The son would probably die. The Indians or immigrants, some of whom were little better than the savages, would carry off their oxen, and finally the husband would be lost.

Even a woman whose future was far less bleak was suddenly shocked by the reality of the experience. Sarah Royce, traveling with her husband, had for months anticipated setting out and looking forward to camping out for the first time in her life. What she noticed, as night was coming on at the end of their first day, was that no house was within sight. Intellectually, of course, she knew that there would be none, but seeing night come on without house or home to shelter them and her baby girl and the recognition that it would be this way for many weeks was a chilling prospect for her. She felt a terrible shrinking from it in her heart. Outwardly brave, she kept it all to herself, but the oppressive sense of homelessness, and an instinct of watchfulness, kept her awake (Jones 1998, 121–25).

Mrs. Margaret Catherine Haun, one of a party from Clinton, Iowa, described how, during the day, the womenfolk visited from wagon to wagon, making congenial friends with whom to walk talking of loved ones left back in the States, sharing dreams for the future, and even whispering a little friendly gossip of emigrant life. In the evening they passed the time tatting, knitting, crocheting, exchanging receipts for cooking beans or dried apples, or swapping food for the sake of variety. She felt it helped to keep them in practice of feminine occupations and diversions. She noted that although most went early to bed, an hour or so around the campfire was relaxing. They listened to readings, storytelling, music, and songs, and the day often ended in laughter and merrymaking.

Perhaps aware of the drinking and coarse behavior among all-male companies, Mrs. Haun wrote that the presence of women and children tended to provide a good influence, reducing aggression and encouraging better care of the teams as well as better sanitation and cleanliness and more regular and better-cooked meals. The results, she argued, were fewer accidents and less sickness and waste. However, she may simply have been a fairly straight-laced, conventional woman. Certainly that was true in matters of dress, for she always wore a dark woolen dress. She never worked without an apron and a three-cornered shoulder kerchief.

Sarah Royce, who had been so unnerved by her first night on the road at seeing no signs of human habitation, forged ahead of her group, sometimes tugging the pack mule up the steepest places, eager for her first glimpse of California. One mid-October day, with weather so cold that water froze in the pans, she looked down from the last mountain, to her, the Sacramento Valley seemed to send up a "smile of welcome." Writing years later, Royce remembered the moment vividly. She recalled that however brave a face she might have put on most of the time, she knew her coward heart was yearning all the while for a home-nest and a welcome California, land of sunny skies (Jones 1998, 129–31).

A Scarcity of Women

One striking feature of the mining camps and frontier was the virtual absence of women. The harbormaster at San Francisco in 1850 counted 35,333 men arriving as opposed to 1,248 women. For the Overland immigrants that year, the count at Fort Laramie was 39,560 men, 2,421 women, and 609 children. Most women arriving by sea stayed in San Francisco or settled in Sacramento; few went to the mines. In September 1849 a miner in Yuba City reported glumly that in the town of 2,000 there were only about a dozen women. Sarah Royce reported that the first time she attended church in San Francisco, there were only six or eight women in the whole congregation. At church, and in the mining camps where she and her husband lived for several months, she was treated with extreme courtesy.

Many women who were widowed on the Overland trip but had continued on had multiple proposals of marriage soon after their arrival. John Banks, reflecting on this scarcity of women, remembered the early myth of the Amazons. He said that they may have gotten along well enough without men but Californians were trying the opposite experiment and he pronounced it a complete failure.

Though respectable women were treated with respect, a good living could be made by their fallen sisters. Like so many other commodities in California, their value reflected economic laws of supply and demand. When there were few other women, prostitutes were in demand. Some writers reflected outrage, but their censure in no way affected the business. A shocked John Banks, reflecting on the moral decadence of miners whose only love was gold, forecast a far more awful state of society in the next five years. Abandoned women seemed necessary to make men fiends. In San Francisco 50 to $100 would buy one. Some of these prostitutes donned men's clothes to ride horseback from camp to camp. One celebrated character of this kind said she had made $50,000 and regretted that she had not doubled the capacity for increasing her gains. William Perkins mused that those lost women were once innocent children, the joy and pride of happy mothers, pure virtuous girls, many of them once happy wives. Perkins, however, remained pragmatic, observing that they had to lay aside some strait-laced ideas and accommodate themselves to this extraordinary scene in which they found themselves actors. Not only did the gold seekers sometimes redefine themselves, they allowed social conventions to mutate.

This may be seen in variations on the institution of marriage. In Sonora, Perkins reported that some adventuresses attached themselves to men on a semipermanent basis, paying a nominal tribute to virtue by claiming that they are married. Perkins questioned why anyone needed to know the truth. Instead, as in so many other aspects of gold rush society, he observed that each one strives to cover the nakedness of reality with the mantle of illusion. Franklin A. Buck, however, could not ignore reality. He was called in 1859 to serve on a jury in a divorce court that had all the salacious details of a modern soap opera, details so embarrassing that one woman witness asked that the courtroom be closed before she'd testify.

Most women, however, maintained moral and social conventions. At the same time, many found ways to profit in California's booming economy. Few women actually mined. Many ran boarding houses, took in laundry, and baked. They worked hard and often amassed small fortunes, illustrating the larger truth that it was not the miners themselves, but those who supplied the goods and services to them who made the expected bonanza.

Women could earn $50–$60 a day doing laundry; at cooking, $30 a day. In October 1849 one woman from Maine wrote home that 10 boarders brought in $189 a week, or $75 clear after expenses had been paid. She admitted that she had to work very hard, baking all her bread in a Dutch oven and doing the rest of her cooking at a small fireplace. She also took in ironing, making $7 in as many hours. However, she had absolutely no social life. She reported that she not been in the street since she began to keep the boarding house. She knew that she'd been caught up in the mercenary drive of many Forty-Niners and remarked that there was nothing but gold there and she wanted to get her part. Another woman seemed almost ebullient despite her hard work. She reported that she had made about $18,000 worth of pies, about one-third of which was clear profit. She boasted that she dragged the wood for her fires off the mountain and chopped it herself, with never the smallest bit of help. She baked about 1,200 pies per month and cleared $200. She intended to quit work that coming spring, and give her business to her sister-in-law (Jones 1998, 151–53).

The unrelenting work was made more difficult by the harsh conditions of frontier life. Across the open plains the wind was omnipresent and often nerve-racking. Mary Clark wrote to her parents from her South Dakota claim that the wind was fierce and awful and it hardly ever stopped. It actually blew the feathers off the chickens' backs. She complained that she couldn't put up many pictures and things because every time the door opened they all blew off the wall. She noted that it was so funny when they noticed how terrible loud everyone talks out there and now they find ourselves just shouting away at the top of our voices. They discovered that it must have been the wind, and unless you yelled, you couldn't be heard at all.

If a windstorm hit on washday, everyone rushed outside to get the clothes before they blew away. Buckets, pails, and lightweight tools might be blown for miles if they didn't first catch on fences. The same winds, blowing over sun-baked land, produced dust storms, clouds of soil hundreds of feet high that blotted out the sun, filled the house with dust, almost smothered cattle in the stable, exposed the roots of young wheat, causing it to wither and die, and sent homesteaders into dull, despairing rage.

Bad as summer winds were, winter blizzards were worse. The Ammons sisters, returning from school, saw a blizzard coming "like white smoke," and before they got home they could not see their hands before their faces. With the thermometer at $-30°$ F and the snow blowing at 80 miles per hour, it seemed as if the sun had been wholly blotted out and that the world would never again be warm. Homesteaders rigged ropes between house and barn so they wouldn't get lost going to feed the animals. Dr. Bessie Rehwinkel, returning from a house call, was caught in a sudden Wyoming snowstorm. Driving blindly, her horses becoming more exhausted by the minute, she recalled that her whole body was becoming numb, and she began to feel an almost irresistible drowsiness creeping upon her. Finally, miraculously, she saw a light through the gloom, and covered from head to foot with an icy sheet of snow that had frozen into a crust so that she had become a human icicle. She was welcomed into that very house she had left three hours earlier.

Another hazard, the rattlesnake, was mentioned so often by diarists as to be commonplace. Miriam Davis Colt remembered seeing rattlers crawling or hanging over sills near her front door. At night she'd hear peculiar noises under the floor, which at first she thought were rats. Instead they were snakes, and her husband kept a stout hickory stick near their bed to drive the snakes away. Mollie Sanford, in her bare feet, heard the tell-tale sound, killed a snake, and hung its 11 rattles on a tree as a trophy. The snakes did not fear people but slithered into homes, barns, and cellars (Jones 1998, 187–89).

Many popular ballads bemoaned the early death of young women. In the safe territories of Dakota, Nebraska, Utah, and Washington, women's death rates in 1859–1860 were 22 percent higher than those of men, even after taking into account violent deaths, whereas in the Eastern states the death rate was about the same for both sexes. Puerperal fever frequently resulted from unsanitary conditions during childbirth, and even when there were no fatal complications, if the child presented in breech position there was little anyone could do. Sometimes, to speed up a slow delivery, attendants held a quill of snuff to the mother's nose, the paroxysms of sneezing bringing forth the child.

Though the homesteaders' frontier had far more Euro-American women than any other, men still outnumbered women. In 1870, when the sex ratio was about even throughout the country, there were 247 men for every 100 women in the West; as the area became more settled, the ratio decreased, but by the turn of the century it was still 128:100 (Underwood 1987, 20). In 1880 Colorado had 129,131 men to 65,196 women; Montana Territory, 28,177 to 10,792; and Wyoming Territory, 14,152 to 6,637. This resulted in two almost antithetical responses to women: respect and domination.

The first was respect, codified if need be. Women, whether they were wives, schoolteachers, immigrant girls fresh off the boat, or prostitutes, were valued. When the bylaws of Yellowstone City, Montana, were written during the winter of 1884–1885, there were only 15 women and 300 men in the camp. Hanging was established as the penalty for murder, thieving or insulting a woman. Mollie Dorsey received so many proposals that she sighed saying that she did not see a woman at all. There were only men, single or bachelors, and she admitted that one gets tired of them (Jones 1998, 202–3).

CHILDREN

To be a child during the period of westward expansion was to be defined by competing characteristics. On one hand, children who grew up with the country were introduced to the harsh realities of disease, death, natural disasters and hard labor at an early age. At the same time, memoirs and diaries of frontier childhoods are awash with descriptions of exploration, wonder, and play, all standard aspects of American youth (Quay 2002, 25).

While popular attitudes toward children seem to have mixed the practical facts of daily existence with the emotions surrounding birth and death, a unique frontier phenomenon appeared in the idealization of youth. Different from the sentimental culture that defined middle-class children during the nineteenth century, the idealization of youngsters originated in the fact that their were so few children present in the West, especially in mining towns and other communities settled primarily by men. Determined to head West, to get rich quickly, and to return home as soon as possible, men in mining towns and other locations found themselves in male company more often, and for longer periods of time than they had ever anticipated. As a result, when children would appear in such a town, attention would be lavished upon them. Songs were sung in their honor, gifts were given to them, and they were ogled in amazement. One reason for this might be that, in comparison to the hardships of Western life, children reminded the immigrants of the lives they had left behind. At the same time children stood for the future, and therefore were symbols of westward expansion itself (Quay 2002, 27).

Childbirth was a remarkably unsentimental experience during the trip west. Far away from doctors, midwives and sometimes even other women, mothers-to-be endured labor and childbirth as they did other difficult aspects of the journey west. Diarists wrote only briefly about the experience, and while they did so with words of joy and happiness, just as frequently they commented about how the birth of a child had the unfortunate consequence of delaying the journey a day or two while the mother recovered enough strength to continue. The straightforward records of childbirth on the trail underscored the fact that newborns, while loved and cared for, were also just another part of the experience.

Once a child was delivered, the threats to survival were far from over. One diarist described how children on the way west were in danger virtually all the time. Children were trampled by animals, burned in campfires, and drowned during river crossings. Some were lost on the prairie while gathering food, and others tumbled off wagons and were run over by heavy wheels. While upsetting to the parents, these events were so common that their occurrences were also viewed as an inevitable part of the trip, another hardship suffered in settling the frontier (Quay 2002, 27).

Once settled, dangers continued. Children were lost in farm accidents, prairie fires, and to snakebite. Snakes did not fear people and they slithered into homes, barns, and cellars. Children playing in the yard were their most frequent victims, though adults and livestock also died of snakebite. Nearly everyone carried a hoe to kill any rattlers they might encounter (Jones 1998, 189).

The demands placed on children registered larger cultural agendas about westward expansion, including the desire to find self-sufficiency, independence, and financial success in the new West. Rather than defining children as individuals who needed to develop the skills and to acquire the knowledge necessary to become adults, Westerners viewed the young as people capable of taking on the same type of work and responsibilities completed by grown men and women. Pioneer children were given substantial responsibilities and learned at an early age how to cope with draughts, grasshopper plagues, and fires. If families were to be successful on the frontier, they depended on contributions of every member of the family unit (Quay 2002, 26). Homesteaders welcomed children, and many had large families, in part, because they provided extra hands on the farm. One newspaper editorialized that a "poor man counts each one of his half dozen or half score a blessing...stout hands and active heads are the very thing we need" (Jones 1998, 202).

Frontier life often blurred labor's age and gender distinctions. Children cared for the livestock, hunted, fished, hauled water, collected wood and buffalo chips, cooked, cared for the sick, and attended their younger siblings. They were impressed into service as soon as they could handle the task. One Kansas father bragged that his two-year-old son could fetch the cows out of the stock fields, carry in stove wood, and feed the hogs (Volo and Volo 2007, 319).

Sometimes children worked off their homestead. Parents controlled their children's labor, and a father could claim his son's wages until he was 21. Fourteen-year-old Frank O'Brien was hired out to work on a farm seven miles away. After having walked there, he found his quarters to be in the attic, which he shared with seed corn, dried pumpkins, and field mice. His work included washing dishes, helping with the threshing, churning butter, turning the grindstone as his employer sharpened tools, and cleaning the hay mow. Farmers, especially widowers, often advertised for hired girls (Jones 1998, 192–93).

Children who lived near Western mining towns found there were many opportunities to earn money for the family. Enterprising youngsters sold butter, bacon, and wild game. Others offered their services cooking, cleaning, and doing odd jobs but most hired out to do the same types of farm chores that they expected to do for their own family.

Laura Ingalls Wilder's popular "Little House on the Prairie" (1932–1943) books recount her childhood on the frontier. As a young child she helped with housework, cared for her siblings, tended the animals and helped with the crops. As she got older she sewed shirts in town to bring cash into the family. She also took employment as a waitress and maid in a hotel in town, and when only 15 she began teaching school (Volo and Volo 2007, 319).

In his fictionalized account of his western childhood, *Boy Life on the Prairie* (1899), Hamlin Garland commented several times that he and his young friends "looked exactly like diminutive men." The phrase was made in reference to the clothing they wore, the work that they did, and the attitudes they adopted (Quay 2002, 26). He remembered trying to be a "good little soldier" and live up to the expectations of his father, a Civil War veteran. Early on he and his brother had the responsibilities of grown men. They chopped wood, hunted cattle that had wandered off, and harrowed and cross-harrowed the fields until "tears of rebellious rage" creased the dust on their faces. At age 10 he had been taught to handle bundles of thoroughly dried barley shocks; at age 14 he was one of five men on a crew binding straw after the reaper had passed. Kept out of school during October and November, he first plowed and then husked corn. His father was not unkind, giving him the freedom to do what he wanted and go where he liked on Sunday as long as he was back in time for milking (Jones 1998, 192).

Children's work was not always voluntary. On at least one occasion a farmer, with too many mouths to feed, agreed to indenture two of his children to another man looking for "draft animals." The agreement was that the employer would buy them each a pair of shoes if they worked out. Their mother, who had not originally been consulted, so harassed her husband that a week later they rescued their children sick, terrified, bewildered, and maltreated (Jones 1998, 193).

Pioneer children had few toys. Often they were little more than simple items made from scraps of fabric and wood by loving parents. Imaginative children often made their own playthings from found objects. A little girl growing up on the frontier remembered weaving blades of long grass to fashion a doll hammock. One young boy recalled how he and his brother played "ranching." Corn kernels were sheep, peanuts were cattle, and marbles were horses. The brothers traded livestock and even "killed" a few sheep (McClary 1997, 8). Eleanore Stewart remembered her daughter calling a block of wood her "dear baby," a spoke from a wagon wheel "little Margaret," and a barrel stave "bad little Johnny" (Jones 1998, 192). As the century progressed and towns were established, even frontier families were able to order toys from mail-order catalogs.

—Dorothy Denneen Volo

THE ORPHAN TRAINS

In 1853, a group of ministers looking for a better way to help orphaned or destitute urban youth formed the Children's Aid Society. Chief among these was Charles Loring Brace, a minister from Connecticut working in the tenement neighborhoods of

New York City. In 1851, Brace had worked at the Ladies' Methodist Home Missionary Society founded in 1848 in the city's Five Points neighborhood. This was one of the poorest and most crime-ridden areas of the city, and it was filled with an immense number of boys and girls floating and drifting about in the streets with no occupation other than petty crime, prostitution, and gang membership; and no assignable home or guiding parents.

Brace and his comrades in the Children's Aid Society understood that children needed a secure loving home free from the filth of the city and its corrupting influences. The board of the Society decided that part of the solution to the problem was to remove orphans from the urban environment and find homes for them in the country where they would have enough to eat, warm beds and clothing, and fresh air and a cleaner environment. The Society began in 1853 to place children with willing families in central New York and in New England. In 1854 they expanded their program by rounding up 46 children between the ages of 7 and 15 from the slums and sending them by train to the Midwest. Here the children were put on display at a church meeting so that farm families could choose among them.

The so-called Orphan Train was very successful, and two more were established in 1855. In return for a home in the rural countryside the children were expected to do the same work that was expected of the natural progeny of farm parents. However, the foster parents were not screened in any way. Their willingness to take a child was their only qualification, and no follow-up was done by the Society to find out if the children were thriving in their adoptive homes or being abused. Yet the society had great difficulty in placing children under 10 years old, who were seen as less able to do a full day's work. Black children were particularly difficult to place with white families, and the Society made no concerted effort to find willing black families to provide foster homes.

By 1860, the Children's Aid Society had placed approximately 5,000 children. The exact number is unknown because the Society kept only fragmentary or contradictory records. Children's Aid Societies in other eastern cities—particularly Boston and Philadelphia—also sent out orphans by train including many of the so-called Soldiers' Orphans of the Civil War. By 1884, Brace was able to claim 60,000 successful placements by means of the Orphan Trains. Brace served as president of the Children's Aid Society of New York for 40 years.

—*James M. Volo*

SERVANTS AND SLAVES

The redistribution of wealth due to industrialization, the availability of wage-paying nondomestic employment for women, and the resulting growth of the middle classes caused a great decrease in the number of young women from good families who were willing to take up domestic service. Frances Trollope, a British visitor to America, wrote, "The greatest difficulty in organizing a family establishment in Ohio, is getting servants, or, as it is there called, 'getting help,' for it is more than petty treason to the Republic, to call a free citizen a servant. The whole class of young women, whose bread depends on their labor, are taught to believe that the most abject poverty is preferable to domestic service. Hundreds of half-naked girls work in the paper mills, or in any other manufactory, for less than half the wages they would receive in service; but they think their equality is compromised by the latter, and nothing but the wish to obtain some particular article of finery will ever induce them to submit to it" (Trollope 2003, 32).

Catharine Beecher and Harriet Beecher Stowe made the following remarkable notion concerning their own class of women just four years after the close of the Civil War. "Domestic service is the great problem of life here in America: the happiness of families, their thrift, well-being, and comfort, are more affected by this than by any one thing else. The modern girls, as they have been brought up, can not perform the labor of their own families as in those simpler, old-fashioned days: and what is worse, they have no practical skill with which to instruct servants, who come to us, as a class, raw and untrained" (Beecher and Stowe 2002, 235).

American-born, nonimmigrant women particularly resented working as domestics. "A sore, angry and even wakeful pride…seemed to torment [them]. In many of them it was so excessive, that all feeling of displeasure, or even of ridicule, was lost in pity," noted Trollope. "One of these was a pretty girl, whose natural disposition must have been gentle and kind; but her good feelings were soured, and her gentleness turned to morbid sensitiveness, by having heard a thousand and a thousand times that she was as good as any lady, that all men were equal, and women too, and that it was a sin and a shame for a free-born American to be treated like a servant" (Trollope 2003, 33). Beecher and Stowe noted the story of "an energetic matron" who refused to allow her daughters to serve as domestics in the summer vacation household of her neighbor saying, "If you hadn't daughters of your own, may be I would; but my girls are not going to work so that your girls may live in idleness" (Beecher and Stowe 2002, 236).

Although it had been shown that young women could be successfully integrated into a work setting outside the home, the general employment of women in the male-dominated surroundings of factories and office buildings remained controversial and redeployed an army of young women from domestic service to the business sector. Factories that successfully attracted women employees were often run like corporate convents to reassure parents that their daughters' reputations would be safe. Such male condensation was not so much a contempt for the ability or value of women as workers, but rather a proclamation of men's own strongly felt social duty to support their wives, daughter, mothers, and sisters and protect them from exploitation. Even those men with liberal attitudes toward the rights of labor spoke of "being sickened by the spectacle of wives and daughters—and, even worse, single girls—leaving their preordained positions as homemakers" to take jobs outside the "cult of domesticity." The duties performed while in domestic service were considered to be among the normal womanly obligations surrounding home care, even if they were carried out in someone else's home. The picture of women cleaning and cooking for others seemingly relieved some of the cultural distress associated with females working among machines, drive belts, and smokestacks (Wilentz 1984, 249).

The quickening tempo of trade and finance during the nineteenth century greatly enlarged the number of white-collar jobs available to Americans, and the resultant increase in middle-class status and wealth widened the demand for domestic servants. Although many women expressed a desire to go to work, few wished to fill positions as servants. As an example, a Brooklyn gentleman advertised for a lady copyist at a salary of $7 a week, and his wife advertised for a cook at $10. Although the wages offered were close to the average expected for such work, they were much higher than those paid for factory work—then at about $5. Yet there was "only one applicant for the cook's place, while 456 ladies were anxious to secure the post of copyist" (Tinling 1993, 122).

Such a result may evidence an aversion for domestic service and the attraction of more tasteful and less degrading employment among young women. "No honest work was as derogatory as idleness," but service as a domestic was never considered "a reasonable channel for the employment of educated ladies." Some nineteenth-century social observers considered domestic service appropriate only for "redundant women" or those without husbands or families with the means to support them (Wilentz 1984, 249). Many men feared that "once out of the household, women were subject to the whims of greedy and, sometimes literally rapacious overseers and masters, who would treat them like slaves" (Wilentz 1984, 249). A female supporter of maintaining the gender distinctions among the classes of society noted, "Who would not smile if the proposition were advanced of clergymen's and physicians' sons going out as valets, footman, and butlers? Classes and sexes must sink or swim together; that which is impossible for the man can not be made available—speaking for the class point of view—for the woman" (Tinling 1993, 122).

Ultimately, such thinking caused society to turn more and more for domestic service to women who would not have been considered appropriate as help in the 1790s. These included blacks and immigrant women (predominantly Asians in the West after 1850, and the Irish in the East after 1820). Black house slaves, both male and female, had sufficed as domestics for generations on Southern plantations, and they continued to do so right through the Civil War and up to the end of the century. Even the Presidential Mansion proudly employed an army of black domestics as butlers, doormen, servers, and maids. Chinese men and women in the West worked for negligible wages as cooks and laundresses; and many established American families hired the Irish even though they viewed them only in prejudicial terms. At the end of the century, a study of domestics found that 60 percent were foreign born, 17 percent black, and 24 percent native-born whites (Strasser 1982, 165).

The Irish came to be the group most closely associated with urban domestics outside the South. In 1825 in New York, 59 percent of women employed through the Society for the Encouragement of Faithful Domestic Servants were identified as Irish. Yet the Irish as a group were not only the victims of social and religious prejudice, they were also accused of voting illegally, of selling their votes to unscrupulous politicians, of undermining the wages and employment opportunities of other Americans, and of engendering crime and immorality. Irish servants were hotly derided in a series of cartoons that appeared in *Harper's* in 1856 and 1857 under the title of "The Miseries of Mistresses." However, the Irish, being white, were less visibly offensive to the social and political sensibilities of the sometimes hypocritical upper-class Protestant households that employed domestics but did not want to interact with persons of another race. Even if the Irish were mostly Catholics, Catholicism didn't show through a service uniform; and the Irish, unlike other immigrant groups, could speak and take directions in English. Nonetheless, some of the discrimination toward domestics came to be identified with "Bridget" and her Irish sisters, who became characters in popular discussions of the "servant problem" (Strasser 1982, 166).

It has been pointed out that "Irish culture fostered female self-assertion and social independence." By way of contrast to other European women who usually came as part of family groups where the men were the primary wage earners, many single Irish women came to America alone or in small groups of females. This was part of a desperate economic strategy that required that they send money home to their starving relatives still in Ireland. The tendency toward delayed marriage or nonmarriage among Irish women under these circumstances made them prime candidates for domestic service, and in Eastern cities such employment paid fairly well—sometimes nearly twice that of factory work. It has been estimated that the Irish in New York City alone sent home over $20 million to their families in the single decade before the Civil War (West 1992, 4; Volo and Volo 2007, 352–55).

PETS: PETS AS WORKMATES

As people immigrated west, they often took dogs with them. Never thought of as pets in the pampered sense, these canines served as companions who worked side by side with their masters sharing their hardships and adventures. Wagon trains were frequently accompanied by dogs. They served as guards that warned of attacks by Indians and predatory animals and helped hunt for game. Their companionship also provided some relief from the pressures of the journey and acted as a reminder of the home they left behind. Some caravans forbade them, citing the fact that dogs sometimes stole food and killed livestock. They also were concerned that the barking and howling of the canines responding to the sounds of the prairie night sometimes caused the teams to break free from the stockades and stampede into the darkness.

Cowboys kept dogs and used them to manage some livestock but did not bring them on cattle drives, fearing that they would spook the cattle and cause a stampede. It was the sheepherder who made the greatest use of dogs. It was said that it took seven horsemen to drive 1,000 head of cattle yet a single sheepherder with one good dog could control the same number of sheep. Initially sheepdogs were of mixed breeds but increasing numbers of Scottish shepherds immigrated to the West bringing highland collies with them. Many young Scots left their homeland with a trained collie and a letter of introduction to an established sheep rancher. The young men worked the summer and in the fall were paid in various combinations of sheep, land, and cash enabling them to start out on their own.

A miner's lot was lonely, hard, and dangerous. Many miners enjoyed the companionship of a dog that also provided some security against claim jumpers and wild animals. Some dogs made additional contributions to the mining process by hauling sledges or carts. Sled dogs were often used in the snowy northern regions for transportation. The brutality that often pervaded mining camps made cruel use of animals as well. Dogs were used for badger baiting, a vicious sport where a badger was tied up in a ring and left to fight against a series of dogs. As each combatant entered the ring new wagers were placed. Fighting between dogs was even more common and was often the object of high stakes gambling. Many of the dogs lost their lives as well as the fight. Those who lost the fight but survived were often left to die from their wounds. The winners received considerable notoriety but were constantly faced by challenges from the owner of every tough cur thought to be fierce enough to dethrone them.

Stray dogs were a problem in all cities both in the East and the West, and they were hunted and condemned. Bummer and Lazarus, however, were two San Francisco bar-begging street dogs who achieved considerable fame. Bummer was a black-and-white Newfoundland mix. Lazarus' genealogy was less evident. Newspapermen, including Mark Twain, regularly reported on their exploits in at least four different California newspapers beginning in 1860. The pair were portrayed as the opposed symbols of human virtue and deceit.

The citizens of San Francisco petitioned city supervisors asking the prodigious rat killers be declared city property so that they could roam the city unmolested. Lazarus was believed to have been poisoned in 1863 by a man whose son had been bitten by him. Obituaries and eulogies abounded for days following Bummer's death in 1865, and they were published in papers as far away as Virginia City. The pair were stuffed and displayed for years as a tribute to devotion and friendship (Deer 2004, 147–49).

—*Dorothy Denneen Volo*

FOR MORE INFORMATION

Armitage, Susan, and Elizabeth Jameson, eds. *The Women's West*. Norman: University of Oklahoma Press, 1987.

Bartlett, Richard A. *The New Country: A Social History of the American Frontier, 1776–1890*. New York: Oxford University Press, 1974.

Bash, Wendell H. "Differential Fertility in Madison County New York, 1865." In *Studies in American Historical Demography*, ed. Maris A. Vinovskis. New York: Academic Press, 1979.

Beecher, Catherine E., and Harriet Beecher Stowe. *The American Woman's Home*. New Brunswick, NJ: Rutgers University Press, 2002.

Brown, Dee. *The Gentle Tamers: Women of the Old Wild West*. New York: Bantam, 1958.

Deer, Mark. *A Dog's History of America: How Our Best Friend Explored, Conquered, and Settled a Continent*. New York: North Point Press, 2004.

Easterlin, Richard A., George Alter, and Gretchen A. Condran. "Farms and Farm Families in Old and New Areas: The Northern States in 1860." In *Family and Population in Nineteenth Century America*, ed. Tamara K. Hareven and Maris A. Vinovskis. Princeton, NJ: Princeton University Press, 1978.

Farragher, John Mack. *Women and Men on the Overland Trail*. New Haven, CT: Yale University Press, 1979.

Frank, Stephen M. *Life with Father: Parenthood and Masculinity in the Nineteenth-Century American North*. Baltimore, MD: Johns Hopkins University Press, 1998.

Frémont, John C. *The Exploring Expedition to the Rocky Mountains*. Washington, DC: Smithsonian Institution Press, 1988.

Garland, Hamlin. *Boy Life on the Prairie*. New York: Frederick Ungar Publishing Co., 1959.

Graulich, Melody. "Violence against Women: Power Dynamics in Literature of the Western Family." In *The Women's West*, ed. Susan Armitage and Elizabeth Jameson. Norman: University of Oklahoma Press, 1987, 111–26.

Grier, Katherine C. *Pets in America: A History*. Chapel Hill, University of North Carolina Press, 2006.

Haines, T. L., and Levi W. Yaggy. *The Royal Path of Life: Or Aims and Aids to Success and Happiness*. Chicago, IL: Western Publishing House, 1876.

Hareven, Tamara K., and Maris A. Vinovskis. *Family and Population in Nineteenth-Century America*. Princeton, NJ: Princeton University Press, 1978.

Jameson, Elizabeth. "Women as Workers, Women as Civilizers: True Womanhood in the American West." In *The Women's West*, ed. Susan Armitage and Elizabeth Jameson. Norman: University of Oklahoma Press, 1987, 145–64.

Jones, Mary Ellen. *Daily Life on the Nineteenth Century American Frontier*. Westport, CT: Greenwood Press, 1998.

Luchetti, Cathy. *Women of the West*. In collaboration with Carol Olwell. St. George, UT: Antelope Valley Press, 1982.

Marcy, Randolph B. *The Prairie Traveler, A Hand-book for Overland Expeditions*. Bedford, MA: Applewood Books, 1993. Reprint of the 1859 edition.

McClary, Andrew M. *Toys with Nine Lives: A Social History of American Toys*. North Haven, CT: Linnet Books, 1997.

Megquier, Mary Jane. *Apron Full of Gold: The Letters of Mary Jane Megquier from San Francisco, 1849–1856*. Edited by Robert Glass Cleland. San Marino, CA: Huntington Library, 1949.

Myres, Sandra L. *Westering Women and the Frontier Experience, 1800–1915*. Albuquerque: University of New Mexico Press, 1982.

Petersen, William J. *Steamboating on the Upper Mississippi*. New York: Dover Publications, 1968. Reprint of the 1937 edition.

Ransom, J. Clinton. *The Successful Man in His Manifold Relation with Life*. New York: J. A. Hill & Co., 1889.

Reef, Catherine. *Alone in the World, Orphans and Orphanages in America*. New York: Clarion Books, 2005.

Riley, Glenda. *Frontierswomen: The Iowa Experience*. Ames: Iowa State University Press, 1981.

Royce, Sarah. *A Frontier Lady: Recollections of the Gold Rush and Early California*. Edited by Ralph Henry Gabriel. Lincoln: University of Nebraska Press, 1932.

Sandoz, Mari. *The Beaver Men, Spearheads of Empire*. Lincoln: University of Nebraska Press, 1978.

Sanford, Mollie Dorsey. *Mollie: The Journal of Mollie Dorsey Sanford in Nebraska and Colorado Territories, 1857–1866*. Lincoln: University of Nebraska Press, 1959.

Schlissel, Lillian. *Women's Diaries of the Westward Journey*. New York: Schocken Books, 1982.

Schlissel, Lillian, Byrd Gibbons, and Elizabeth Hampsten. *Far from Home: Families of the Westward Journey*. New York: Schocken Books, 1989.

Stewart, Elinore Pruitt. *Letters of a Woman Homesteader*. Boston, MA: Houghton Mifflin, 1914.

Strasser, Susan. *Never Done: A History of American Housework*. New York: Henry Holt and Company, 1982.

Tinling, Marion, ed. *With Women's Eyes: Visitors to the New World, 1775–1918*. Norman: University of Oklahoma Press, 1993.

Underwood, Kathleen. *Town Building on the Colorado Frontier*. Albuquerque: University of New Mexico Press, 1987.

Valencius, Conevery Bolton. *The Health of the Country, How American Settlers Understood Themselves and Their Land*. New York: Perseus Books Group, 2002.

Volo, Dorothy Denneen and James M. Volo. *Family Life in Nineteenth-Century America*. Westport, CT: Greenwood Press, 2007.

Wells, Robert V. "Demographic Change and the Life Cycle of American Families." In *Studies in American Historical Demography*, ed. Maris A. Vinovskis. New York: Academic Press, 1979.

West, Elliot. *Growing Up with the Country*. Albuquerque: University of New Mexico Press, 1989.

West, Elliot, and Paula Petrik, eds. *Small Worlds: Children and Adolescents in America, 1850–1950*. Lawrence: University Press of Kansas, 1992.

West, Patricia. "Irish Immigrant Workers in Antebellum New York: The Experience of Domestic Servants at Van Buren's Lindenwald." *The Hudson Valley Regional Review: A Journal of Regional Studies* 9, no. 2 (September 1992): 9.

Wilentz, Sean. *Chants Democratic: New York City & the Rise of the American Working Class, 1788–1850*. New York: Oxford University Press, 1984.

Wyman, Walker D. *Frontier Woman: The Life of a Woman Homesteader on the Dakota Frontier*. River Falls: University of Wisconsin–River Falls Press, 1972.

Economic Life

NATURE OF WORK

The Development of the Leisure Class

Chief among the changes that affected America in the second half of the nineteenth century was the development of a leisure class funded largely through the exploitation of the nature resources of the nation including its teeming masses of willing workers. Gold and silver mines, stands of timber, fertile soil, herds of livestock, seams of coal, and fields of oil produced undreamt of riches for the few men that had the vision to chase their dreams of wealth.

The constant influx of immigrants, who were willing to take on the most onerous and lowest paid jobs, effectively drove the native working classes to middle-class status; and as an incoming tide raises all boats, the American middle class found itself raised to a social level undreamed of in the previous century. Nonetheless, entry into the upper classes in America required both money and the acceptance of those already considered the social elite. Many families were barred, therefore, from further upward mobility, and the middle class consequently expanded.

Thorstein Veblen, the American-born child of Norwegian immigrant parents, examined an American working class that aspired to a life of leisure and social prominence. Veblen's first and best-known work was *The Theory of the Leisure Class* (1899). It is a generally biting commentary on American culture during the third quarter of the nineteenth century. Herein he identified a number of forces that led his fellow citizens to want to emulate the materialistic economics of the rich. Veblen coined the popular term "conspicuous consumption" and less repeated phrases such as "pecuniary emulation" and "conspicuous leisure" in this study. He exposed the emptiness of many of the cherished standards of upper-class taste, dress, and culture. For Veblen, the shallowness and superficiality of American society resulted from a growing faith in the accumulation of ostentatious wealth and the universal approbation of one's social class.

It has been charged that the upper classes extracted their wealth not only through the exploitation of the nation's natural resources, but also through the exploitation of its working class. He charged that the leisure class sheltered itself in great measure from the stresses it created in the economic and industrial community that affected the lower classes every day. The wealthy, he charged, do not yield to the demands for social reform as readily as others because they were not constrained to do so (Veblan 1994, 123).

—*James M. Volo*

Miners

Mining was one of the extraction trades. Although gold and silver stole the spotlight with rushes of nugget gatherers to spectacular strikes and miners towns popping up at the diggings, the majority of miners were professionals who worked in settled communities or company towns taking coal, iron, and other base metals from the ground. Men of Irish and Welsh ancestry initially brought hard-rock mining techniques from Europe to the United States, and they dominated the Eastern industry in the first half of the nineteenth century. The Irish Catholics, in particular, attempted to maintain their ethnic and religious integrity in the mining communities. They built churches, established community parishes, and demanded priests from the diocese. Second only to the Irish in their cohesion were the Welsh Cornishmen. This helped them to create a remarkable unity, and late in the century they used it to form unions and fight the mining companies for wages, safety standards, working, and living conditions. However, the mine workforce of the second half of the century became increasingly populated with foreign-speaking immigrants. The newcomers to the eastern mines were Poles, Italians, Ukrainians, Hungarians, and Lithuanians who found it difficult to work in cooperation with the established miners and often served as scabs and strikebreakers for the companies.

Striking miners and their families were often confronted by sheriff's posses, Pinkerton guards, or immigrant strikebreakers outside their company-owned homes.

Unions are commonplace today, and the right to strike is generally accepted by the American population. This was not always the case. In the nineteenth century unions were often feared or considered illegal. State militias and federal troops were sometimes brought in to break up labor demonstrations, and more than once soldiers fired into the crowds. Courtesy Library of Congress.

Besides the houses, the companies owned the minions of the law and usually controlled the local schools, stores, and the utilities. The miners were not allowed to purchase items outside the company towns, and the debts that they accumulated reduced the workers to utter subservience.

Described as a "500-square mile triangle of low mountains, deep valleys, and sharp outcroppings of rock," northeastern Pennsylvania boasted nearly all the hard coal (anthracite) that heated the homes and offices or ran the factories and engines along the Atlantic seacoast. Places like Scranton, Wilkes-Barre, Shamokin, Mount Carmel, and Shenandoah were made prosperous by the extraction of hard coal. Soft coal mining (bituminous) was actually more widespread. While 10,000 miners worked the hard coal, tens of thousands—possibly 150,000—worked the soft coal deposits of western Pennsylvania, Ohio, Illinois, Indiana, Virginia, North Carolina, and elsewhere. These mines were tightly controlled by a few coal-carrying railway lines that shipped the fuel to Eastern cities and iron foundries. Ironically, while early locomotives all burned wood, only Northern railways had changed over to coal before the Civil War.

The men and boys who worked these mines were generally considered hard rock miners because they pried the valuable substances from the surrounding igneous and metamorphic rock layers. Much of what they removed from surface seams and underground galleries was useless silica rock, shale, or slate. For this reason a miner's ton—the basis on which many miners were paid—was set at 3,360 pounds per ton, and sometimes higher. This was thought to render a standard ton (2,000 pounds) of useful or valuable product. The iron and steel company towns, and the coal fields and iron mines that fed the furnaces, were the domain of industrial giants like Henry Clay Frick and Andrew Carnegie.

The grip of these companies was tight, and they squeezed hard. If the price of coal fell at market, the mine might close, and many miners worked as few as 200 days a year leaving each miner with continuing bills that he could not pay. As an example, after an entire month's work, one miner—a boy of 14, the eldest child in his family—brought home only a demand for money due to the company of $396, the current balance on the family's rented two-room house unpaid since the death of his father (Reynolds 1960, 58).

Mining contracts usually restricted the workers' ability to purchase items outside the community, if they were available at the company store. An average miner made $8 to $12 a week, but he realized a profit of only about $300 per year. In the copper mining town of Clifton, Michigan, the local school teacher, Henry Hobart, noted in his diary, "A good assortment of goods, but they are very dear. A common suit of clothes cost $33.00...an everyday coat...$26.00. If this is the way things are selling, men must receive more wages. Miners have to pay $13.00 for board now. Everything is going up except wages and I think that they will go up soon. Some miners are making $50.00 per month" (Mason 1991, 146).

Most boys from mining families followed their fathers into the mines in easy stages, beginning usually at the breakers where slate and rock was picked out from among the coal by boys as young as 8 or 10. The little boys might make 35 cents a day. If all went well, and he did not die from an accident or the inhalation of dust, an adolescent might work his way through a series of jobs in the mines. At 12 he might become a trapper boy, opening and closing the underground mine-shaft doors to let the mule-drawn mine trucks go by, or he might run buckets back and forth between the work face and the cars. Ultimately he would become a contract miner, or he might specialize as a powder monkey, a blaster, or a blaster's devil (assistant) working with long chisels, fuses, and black powder to blow out the seams from the work face.

The work was grueling and dangerous but, as one observer noted, "The miner is constantly exposed to danger; still...they do accustom themselves to the work that they would never work on the surface" (Mason 1991, 171). Another journalist described the tasks facing the hard-rock miner, "It was up to the miner to fire the shots, to use the most delicately exact skill in placing the (supporting) timber. The work required an alert mind and great physical strength....Sometimes erect, sometimes on his knees, sometimes on his side or back, the miner worked in an endless night, a soft black velvet darkness, with only the light of his miners lamp to see by." Injury and death threatened from many directions: a quick death from a sudden rock fall or a premature explosion; a slow death from carbon monoxide or methane; a hacking and coughing death while spitting up bloody coal dust from one's lungs. Deep mining made for poor ventilation, damp conditions from seep water, and, in deep mines, high underground temperatures. In 1869 a mine fire in Avondale, Pennsylvania, killed an entire shift leaving 59 widows and 109 orphans (Reynolds 1960, 57).

Schoolmaster Henry Hobart noted how even simple tasks could prove deadly, "There was a sad accident in the mine today. A man coming up from the 120-fathom level [720 feet] in a shaft he was helping to sink; when he arrived at the 110-fathom level on the top of the ladder his hand missed the top round and he fell backwards to the bottom, a distance of seventy-five feet striking his head on the solid rocks. His skull was broke in pieces and he was brought up senseless and is still living though very little hopes are had for his recovery." The man died within three hours with his wife and three small children in attendance (Mason 1991, 171). An old cemetery stone in coal country reads as follows:

Forty years I worked with pick and drill,
Down in the mines against my will.
The Coal King's slave but now its passed,
Thanks to God I am free at last. (Reynolds 1960, 56)

Safety was always a concern in the mines, but safety measures were few. The descending ladders were usually wet and sometimes frozen. Steam engines were harnessed to pump water from the mines and power-bellows were added for ventilation. "The pump extends down the shaft on one side for drawing the water out of the mine. It is a foot in diameter and goes to the bottom. On the other side of the shaft separated from the Pump and Main Ladder by a partition is the place where the Bucket draws up the copper and rock" (Mason 1991, 82). Hobart, who was fond of recording disasters both small and large, also noted. "Mr. Phillips, driving the pumping engine, had his little finger taken off by putting it in a hole in the feed pump to remove some dirt when the plunger came down and took it off. It was a very careless trick, and he has lost his finger by doing so." Hobart also noted, "Two miners got into a quarrel about a hammer underground and one struck the other a heavy blow on the head with the hammer breaking his hat cap [a hard hat] and a piece of it cut his head severely. The other is now in jail. A hat cap will stand a heavy blow before it will injure the head and I suppose he struck as if he was striking a drill. They are to have a law suit about the affair." Not all the dangers that Hobart recorded were underground. "All of the buildings at the Amygdaloid Mine except the store were burnt the other day. It was very windy and the fire caught from the bush and all the men in the mine could not control it. The place was all in ashes in less than three hours" (Mason 1991, 163).

One of the greatest feats of mine engineering during the period was that of Adolf Sutro who began a 3.8 mile long tunnel to drain water by gravity from the Savage Mine in California. The project, originally resisted by banking and railroad forces, was spurred forward by the disastrous Yellow Jack Mine fire of 1869 that killed scores of miners. Sutro argued successfully that given the money and permission to build the tunnel, not only could he drain water from the mine, but also ventilate it and provide an emergency exit. The Sutro Tunnel, completed in 1878, was a mine-engineering wonder, but it was found to be higher than the work face (which had been dug lower during nearly 10 years of construction), but it did provide a smaller lift through which to pump the 150+ degree water.

When a mining community formed, one of the necessities of life became sufficient drinking water for the population. Rich ore deposits and pure drinking water were not always available together, and mine water with its dissolved heavy metals was un-healthy or even poisonous. Hermann Schussler, formerly Chief Hydraulic Engineer for the growing city of San Francisco, formulated a method of moving clear mountain water from Marlette Lake high in the Sierra Nevadas to Virginia City. The pipe, which Schussler envisioned as early as 1864 and others rejected as impractical, had to handle a perpendicular drop of 1,720 feet from the mountains with an end-point pressure of over 800 pounds per square inch. This required a thick-walled rolled iron pipe (5/16 inch of metal) to withstand bursting under the pressure. On the east-west run of the pipe, Schussler progressively decreased the thickness of metal down to 1/16 inch thereby increasing the capacity and rate of flow of the pipe while decreasing the internal pressure. When completed in 1873 the pipe could deliver more than two million gallons of pure mountain water every day. Two more pipes were installed in 1875 and 1887, respectively. Virginia City still uses drinking water from these pipes (McDonald 1982, 23).

Breaking mineral wealth from the working face of nature's outcrops or from the seams underground was tiring and difficult. Accomplished by the application of miner's picks, chisels, sledge hammers, and explosions, there was, nonetheless, little room for a full-fledged swing and tons of waste rock needed to be moved to create working space. The introduction of pneumatic drills that could work at almost any angle was initially viewed as a great laborsaving device that promised to increase the miners' productivity and wages. However, the dry dust produced by the drill quickly filled the air and accumulated in the lungs causing a serious medical crisis among the workers called silicosis. The introduction of a wet driller that took waste dust from the drill hole in a stream of water relieved the problem somewhat.

Sudden failure of a rock wall or ceiling was a dreaded threat, and a new type of timber framing was conceived in the mines of Nevada to replace the inevitably weak post and beam bracing then used to prevent collapse. Philip Deidesheimer, a German mining engineer working in America, devised a bracing method that utilized square sets of timbers arranged in cubes. The cubes of four, five, or six feet per side provided shoring in all directions, not just from above, and they could be stacked vertically or added to horizontally to follow the mineral seams. Miners could walk to the work face and ore could be tracked back through the cubes. The open sides allowed for lateral tunnels and elevators. The system increased safety manyfold, but it required a remarkable amount of timber to complete. Whole mountainsides were denuded to provide the bracing for a single local mine. For the good of all miners, Deidesheimer refused to patent his innovation (Volo and Volo 2007, 99–102).

Gold Mining

The people who participated in the rushes—miners, businessmen, traders, and gamblers—were generally below middle age both because the venture appealed to younger men and because the arduous life of the goldfields could be endured by no others. The labor was physically hard, the weather and environment unremitting, and the diet unbalanced or even unhealthy. The mining camps were notorious for outbreaks of dysentery, diarrhea, scurvy, typhoid, and fevers. Violence was the primary outcome of most disagreements. Other than prostitutes, there were very few women in the camps. In their freedom from the remonstrance of mothers, wives, sisters, and sweethearts, the miners let their appearance deteriorate into a stereotypical form that has come to describe all miners in the period. "An unkempt beard and long hair, weather beaten face, flannel shirts, shapeless pants, high boots, an

Gold rushers were an uncouth lot armed with shovels, picks, and cradle like rocker sluices for separating the gold from the gravel and dirt. Courtesy Library of Congress.

old hat, perhaps an old coat that had seen its last service...in the Mexican War." A pair of blankets, a firearm, knife, mining tools, and cooking utensils usually filled out their kit (Paul 1963, 26).

Gold strikes often proved more beneficial to industrial miners than to the individual dust panners and nugget pickers who stampeded after every golden find. Benjamin W. Ryan, age 38, left Illinois, his wife and his family for the goldfields in Montana. He kept a detailed journal of his trip and the man-days and profits from working a claim with his partners. In one case, eight men ran the sluices all day for only $11 dollars. On another day they took out $66. The following Sunday Ryan received $100 for a whole week's work. On their best day seven men took out $178, but the small payoffs outnumbered the large ones. Ryan could have made at least $5 a day working in a factory, and after a year in the goldfields he admitted that he "had not noticeably improved his condition by daring the perils of the wilderness and fighting Indians" (Johnson 1971, 133–34).

Ryan's experience was not atypical of most men who entered the gold fields with shovel in hand. Certainly some men became millionaires overnight, and others made their money by selling liquor, food, entertainment, and mining supplies at exorbitant prices. The Montana strike of 1864, like many other finds, never produced the level of wealth of the strike in California in 1849. A favorite song of "Banjo Dick" Brown, a popular entertainer in the mining towns of the West, summed up the national fascination with gold as follows:

For my heart is filled with grief and woe,
And oft I do repine,
For the days of old,
The days of gold,
The days of Forty-Nine. (Paul 1963, 179)

Placer mining is an open form of mining that requires no tunneling. It can be used to extract many metals, but it is most closely associated with gold mining. Excavation is usually accomplished by the application of water to mineral-rich gravel and sandbank alluvial deposits that represent old or ancient streambeds. The name derives from the Spanish word, placer, meaning sandbank. The deposits were usually too loose to safely tunnel into, and the metal, having been deposited by moving water over centuries, was usually some distance from the parent vein and in very small quantities.

The simplest form of placer mining was nugget picking. Active streambeds often uncover nuggets, grains, flakes, or ribbons of pure metal (native metal) that can be picked up with the fingers or scooped up in a shovel. The initial discovery of gold in California in 1848 by James Marshall was accomplished in this manner when a nugget of gold was discovered in a mill-race at Coloma. Nonetheless, large pieces of pure copper and iron pyrite (fool's gold) could also be collected in this way. Other metals rarely formed in pure native deposits. American Indians had used this method to collect metal for use in decorations and jewelry for generations.

Panning was a slightly more sophisticated form of placer mining. Some of the sediment was placed in a large pan with water and agitated so that the silica and lightweight debris overflowed the side. The heavier metal, usually flakes or a fine dust of gold, remained in the bottom of the pan. The same principle was more commonly employed using a sluice box made with barriers along the bottom to slow the movement of metal particles. Impelled by running water the grains and flakes of metal were captured along the perpendicular edges of the barriers while the sand, mud, and other debris wash over them. The idea was not new. Ancient Greek miners were thought to have placed sheepskins in fast flowing streams where gold particles attached to the strands of wool in a similar manner; hence the stories of the Golden Fleece may have had a basis in fact.

Geological theory at the time suggested that metal concentrations should increase in density as the depth of the alluvial deposit increased. Miners often processed gravels from 50 to 100 feet below the waterline of nearby streams to recover a few ounces of gold. Working on this concept in 1853, Edward E. Mattson invented a hydraulic water cannon that used the power of pressurized water to power wash gold bearing deposits of sand and gravel into giant sluices where the metal could be recovered. The water cannon required a rudimentary penstock (reservoir) of water with sufficient head to provide the pressure, and fabric hose (much like fire hoses) were used to connect the two. Mattson used the cannon with great success to reclaim gold at Gold Run and the Malakoff Diggings in California. Unfortunately the process resulted in massive amounts of river siltation, and the dam caused extensive, if temporary, land flooding. In 1884, these water cannons were outlawed in California in one of the nation's first acts of environmental protection.

The romantic images that dominated nineteenth-century mining were almost always associated with the California Gold Rush of 1849–1852. Yet most of those men following the rush were dust panners, nugget pickers, or placer miners, not underground workers. In the incomplete census of 1850 two-thirds of the 30,000 who described themselves as miners in the California goldfields were Americans but the Irish, French Canadian, Spanish American, and Chinese were all part of the gold rush workforce. Because of the nature of the mining claims, an almost universal antagonism and hostility were often the first things that greeted newcomers. Soon, however, those of like nationality or like ethnicity joined together to better work their claims, and they generally directed their antipathy toward other groups. Mexicans, Indians, and African Americans were all popular targets of prejudice in the mining camps. When the Chinese began to arrive on the California coast in 1851 and 1852, the Irish Catholics, themselves targets of nativist prejudice on the Atlantic seaboard, often sided against the Chinese and with the nativist Americans, who would not have given them the time of day had they been in the East (Paul 1963, 25).

A great number of the rush miners were Westerners, those who had lived a majority of their lives on the lands drained by the Missouri, the Mississippi, or the Ohio Rivers. A surprisingly large number were from New England, New York, or Pennsylvania, some of the latter experienced hard-rock miners who had abandoned the coal works. A remarkably small number in proportion were self-identified as Southerners. Many rushers were former city dwellers, clerks, farm boys, and soldiers discharged after the Mexican War. So great was the allure of the goldfields that many sailors jumped ship after reaching California, leaving the harbor at San Francisco a forest of masts as the useless and undermanned clipper ships piled up in the bay (Volo and Volo 2007, 105–7).

Lumberjacks

Early loggers and sawmill owners cut down forests with little thought for sustained timber production or for the future of the environment. Consequently, the overharvesting of prime stands of trees caused the industry to move from region to region with a remarkable regularity during the century—first from New England to the Midwest lake states, and then from the Midwest to the South. Though the federal government sold land for as little as $1.25 an acre, and state and private lands sold for little more, many lumbermen simply stole the timber from the land neither asking nor receiving permission to strip the forests of their produce. As time passed, however, the value of timber increased and the landowners and government agents became more vigilant. This made trespass relatively infrequent thereafter, and the buying and selling of timber rights became more common. The South sought to revitalize its industrial base somewhat after the Civil War through lumbering, but it allowed much of its forest land to come into the control of just a few individuals. Under legislation passed in the 1870s and 1880s more than 46 million acres of existing timber was controlled by less than 1,000 individuals. The South reached its peak of timber production in the 1920s at which time the industry leadership moved to the Pacific Northwest.

Lumbering had flourished in the forests of New England since colonial times with fuel, building materials, flooring, planking, and ship's masts being the major commercial products. A large number of men found their living in the lumbering trades. These included axe men, sawyers, river drivers, teamsters, rafters, and sawmill operators. The census data from 1840, however, suggest that lumbering operations were very small, with mills seemingly operated by a single person or on a part-time basis by local farmers. There were 31,000 sawmills in the United States in 1840, but only 22,000 workers identified themselves as sawmill employees. This leaves historians with the impression that lumbering remained a facet of agriculture rather than a separate industry until the 1850s when data shows a vast increase in the number of sawmills with 20 to 100 workers. A sideline of the timber trade was the production of oak staves and headings for watertight barrels for the beer and liquor industry. Spruce and hemlock were used to make cheap dry-freight barrels for shipping items like flour, China, salt, shoes, nails, and fertilizer. Pitch and turpentine were also by-products of the lumbering trade.

Both Maine and New Hampshire were particularly noted for their production of timber products during the colonial period. Maine supplanted its neighbor around 1810. New York took the lead in 1840, but the New England states as a group were still responsible for about 63 percent of all forest products produced in the United States up to mid-century when the timber stands of upper Midwest states like Wisconsin and Michigan began to come into production. J. M. Holley, writing a history of lumbering for the *La Crosse Wisconsin Chronicle* (1906), noted that in the 1830s no mention had yet been made of the great pine forests of the Midwestern lake states. Holley concluded that it seemed "quite probable that at that time they had not attracted special attention" (Holley 1906, 52).

About 1800 some Southern states showed an ability to produce forest products. Georgia, the Carolinas, and later Alabama supplied excellent building materials such as cedar, yellow pine, and live oak, which grew in abundance. Yellow pine was particularly valuable as a flooring material. At the time Virginia and Maryland had more facilities for the production of naval stores than any combination of two Northern states that normally prided themselves on their production. Turpentine and pitch were manufactured in large quantities as a sideline to lumbering, especially in North Carolina where an entire industry flourished well into the twentieth century.

Maine was particularly noted for the quantity of the hardwoods it possessed. Hardwoods such as elm and oak were particularly prized as shipbuilding materials. Yellow and white birch, beech, white and red oak, ash, and several types of maple were found in the forests of Maine. One observer noted that in 1854 between 50 and 100 loads of hardwoods passed through his village toward the Kennebeck River every week during the spring and summer.

Nonetheless, it was pine that was the prince of the forests and the most valuable commercial timber during the period of the Civil War. White, red (Norway), pitch, and Jack pines could grow in almost any soil, and because the evergreen trees cut off most of the light that reached the ground, they grew in huge groves of pure straight pine timbers. Tamarack pine was highly prized by shipbuilders for use as ships knees and other structural parts because it was coarse and durable. The pine lumber industry initially produced mostly masts and spars for shipbuilding. Pine trees 6 to 7 feet in diameter and 250 feet tall were reported to have grown in Maine. Huge masts 36 yards long and 36 inches in diameter were commonly floated down the rivers of Maine for both domestic use and for export to other maritime nations. Both Portland and Falmouth were noted for the production of masts. The advent of steam-powered navigation caused the masting industry to decline somewhat in the middle decades of the century. Yet in 1850 a single giant mast containing 6,500 board feet was hauled by 14 oxen into the town of Belfast where the remarkable specimen sold for $250.

Shifts in the availability of forest resources combined with changes in technology continually changed the face of the timber industry. Lack of conservation affected local industry. As pine production in the East declined, for instance, spruce and hemlock took its place as a commercial product. In 1850 spruce had supplanted pine in terms of the volume of logs removed from the forests of Maine for the first time. Hemlock, meanwhile, had gained a reputation for its use in the leather tanning industry, and from 1830 to 1840 the Washington County and Franklin County region of Maine became a center for the leather tanning industry. By 1880 only 20 percent of the lumber coming from Maine was pine.

After 1850 a pine lumber industry flourished in the north woods of the Great Lakes region. The Panic of 1857 caused a severe depression in the lumber trades, but their revival was a speedy one mainly because of the war. By 1870 the Great Lakes states were in full timber production. A vast number of logs were removed from the north woods of Wisconsin through Chippewa Falls, Eau Claire, La Crosse, Black River Falls, and St. Croix. The industry that centered around Eau Claire, Wisconsin, (for which there are good records) can serve as an example of the development of lumbering in general during the middle decades of the century.

Although a steam powered chain saw had been invented by P. P. Quimby in 1826, most trees were felled by ax and made into manageable lengths with cross-cut saws during the late fall and early winter. They were dragged over the snow by draft horses to the banks of local rivers and streams where they were stacked on roll-a-ways parallel to the flow. The logging roads to the riverbanks could be five or six miles long, and it was not uncommon for loggers to build long water-carrying flumes that moved the logs while bypassing the logging roads. By the 1880s small logging railroads had begun to appear with their small but powerful donkey steam engines.

Upon the arrival of the spring flood, the supporting stakes on the roll-a-ways were undermined, releasing the logs into the water. Using poles and pikes the lumbermen (known as drivers), riding in boats or on the logs themselves would attempt to keep the timbers aligned and moving freely in midstream. In 1858 Joseph Peavey, a Maine blacksmith, patented an improved long-handled pike for controlling logs (known even today as a Peavey). Logjams often developed, however, and some of them were several miles long. The drivers attempted in these cases to find the key logs that had caused the jam and remove them. This was dangerous work that sometimes required the driver to stand in waist-deep water where, if they were hit by a moving log, they could be killed or drowned. Occasionally explosives were used to free the jam.

The logs were usually made into dimensional lumber at local sawmills. Water-powered single-blade reciprocal saws (up and down motion) had been in use since colonial times. These had largely been replaced by rotary circular saws in the 1850s, and by more efficient band saws thereafter. Band saws created much less sawdust and friction than other types. Gang saws with more than one blade acting at the same time, allowed one log to be cut into many boards in a single pass. The first steam-powered sawmill opened in the shipbuilding town of Bath, Maine, in 1821. This began a shift to power mill work of many kinds. In 1826 Oliver Goddard introduced a shingle-making machine, and in the same year, Job White invented a machine for cutting a continuous veneer from a single tree (like paper on a roll). By 1860 there were more than 50 such establishments for power sawing and wood milling in Maine alone.

From the sawmills the rough cut green lumber was made up into rafts approximately 16 by 32 feet, with a depth of about 18 inches. These could be fastened together and floated or towed downriver. Using oars for steering the rafters helped to guide the rafts in the channel. A bow boat—a small boat placed across the bow of the raft at right angles to the current—allowed the raft to be pushed to starboard or port as the steamer might require to make turns in the river. The rafters cooked and ate on the rafts using a small cookstove and tent erected for the purpose. In 1839 Henry Merrill was the first to successfully raft lumber from Portage, Wisconsin, to St. Louis. At one time upward of 100 men and boys were employed in this work on the Upper Missouri River. By the 1870s, however, most lumber was shipped directly from the sawmills to market by railroad (Holley 1906, 55).

Much of the lumber harvested in the United States was used domestically, but there was a significant export business. Maine was responsible for three-quarters of this trade. Lumber was shipped from Northern American ports to the South as part of the coastwise trade, and also to the West Indies where it was exchanged for gold, molasses, and rum. Cuba alone imported 40 million board feet of lumber annually in mid-century, an amount approximately equal to all the lumber used in the city of Boston.

Hardwoods were preferred for fuel because they burned hotter, produced less creosote, and could be made more easily into charcoal for use by founders and blacksmiths than resinous woods. River steamers everywhere favored wood as a source of fuel, and they could be seen periodically nosing up to great piles of firewood left on the riverbank by local landowners to take on fuel. The landowners would also sign contracts to supply fuel along the railroad right-of-way. Without exception every Southern locomotive burned wood as a fuel in the antebellum period. Northern railroads were much more likely to switch to coal. Invariably, behind the engine came the tender, which held as much as 1,000 gallons of fresh water and had space for firewood. The large smokestacks on period engines were needed to divert wood smoke and produce a draft large enough to maintain a satisfactory head of steam. Cordwood was stacked at intervals along every line, and the best and cleanest burning firewood was reserved for passenger traffic. A cord of wood was a stack four feet by four feet by eight feet. Depending on the engine, load, and topography, an engine averaged between 50 and 60 miles per cord of wood requiring long delays every few hours to reload the tender (Volo and Volo 2007, 107–11).

Petroleum Workers

The farmers of Venango County in western Pennsylvania had a problem. Every time a farmer dug a well, turned a ditch, or pulled a deeply rooted tree stump, a thick black ooze of oil would seep into the hole along with the ground water. So persistent was this phenomenon—it had been recognized by the local Native Americans and recorded by whites as early as 1832—that the local watercourse near Titusville was known as Oil Creek. Farmers who read the *Spectator*, the only newspaper in Venango County, had read that the personable but slightly eccentric Colonel Edwin Drake from Vermont had begun drilling for oil in 1858. They were amazed, however, when their own paper reprinted a story in 1859 from Horace Greeley's *Tribune* in faraway

New York excitedly proclaiming the discovery of oil in nearby Titusville. How could anyone not find oil in the 20-mile-long Oil Creek valley?

The editor of the *Spectator* knew that the farmers of western Pennsylvania were more interested in the Black Frost that was attacking oats, wheat, rye, and potatoes than in Drake's drilling. This affected their economy more than petroleum. A normal crop harvested in time for the market could yield a cash profit of $250 to $300, more than enough to bring the average farm family some personal comforts or a special household furnishing. In the off-season, these farmers could hunt and trap, split out shingles, or bring logs to the lumber mill in Pittsburgh in giant rafts floated down the Allegheny River for extra money. When Colonel Drake began to buy sawn lumber in 1858 to erect a weird-looking wooden structure he called an oil derrick and hired workers at a dollar a day, people looked at him gravely and shook their heads in disbelief.

Drake was a nice enough man, friendly and gregarious with the locals, but he was gaunt, thin, and pallid. His neuralgia was bad, and he was constantly short of funds—both for the drilling project and for the needs of his wife and family. He had to buy his tools and casing pipe in three different towns, and he lost the first three master drillers he hired, finally settling on a part-time driller and full-time blacksmith named William "Uncle Billy" Smith to run the operation. Smith moved his wife, son, and daughter into the pine-timbered shed attached to the derrick where the $500 steam engine would power the walking beam that would rhythmically send the drilling tools up and down cracking the bedrock at the bottom of the bore. The derrick was used to lift the tools and lower additional lengths of pipe that kept the earth from caving in and filling the bore. This innovative idea belonged to Drake, and it literally allowed the job to continue—three feet a day, six days a week.

Sam Kier, a local opportunist, had touted petroleum as a cure-all or natural remedy and had sold it in half-pint bottles since 1850. Locals had found that the black ooze (the unrefined forerunner of modern petroleum jelly) softened and helped heal sore hands. By hawking his balm from huge, hand-painted wagons that were like traveling sales posters, Kier had been able to get rid of all the oil he could produce with a bucket and a strainer at home. The smell was foul, but true believers rubbed it into their sore joints and throbbing backs and put it on their draft animals to increase the shine in their coats and keep away insects. Kier opened a refining plant to make his product more acceptable to the public at Seventh Avenue and Grand Street in Pittsburgh and was bottling the pale gold petroleum distillate (kerosene) as Carbon Oil. It cost 50 cents to gather and refine, and sold for $1.50 a gallon. Kier advised his customers to take up to three teaspoons-full a day to ward off personal illness and calm upset stomachs.

Nonetheless, Kier could not unload enough of the stuff on a skeptical public to get rid of all the oil that turned up. He, therefore, decided to market the kerosene as a substitute for the newly invented and dirty coal oil or the prohibitively expensive whale oil presently used in lamps. Kier's kerosene was a superior fuel for lighting. It was this truth that had driven Drake to drill for oil—a truth that was large enough in the days before electric lights to stimulate the interest of newspapers many hundreds of miles to the east.

A Scotsman named John Young had developed oil from coal for lighting, and a new type of lamp had been invented to burn it. Americans had clung to whale oil mainly because it burned cleanly in its double-wicked lamps. They would continue to use it as a fine lubricant for machinery. Drake had now discovered a practical way to drill for oil, pump it from the ground in vast quantities, and couple his supply with an advanced refining method (developed by Dr. Benjamin Silliman, a noted chemist from Yale University) to make kerosene fuel for lighting lamps (Volo and Volo 2007, 98). The entire process was a technological advance the importance of which can hardly be fathomed by persons living in modern times with electric lights a fingertip away.

The kerosene lamp was first constructed by Polish inventor Ignacy Łukasiewicz in 1853, and he had devised a system for making kerosene from seep oil in 1856. Widely known in Britain as a paraffin lamp, any type of lighting device that uses kerosene (also known as paraffin oil) as a fuel fits into the category of a kerosene lamp. There are two main types of kerosene lamps that work in different ways, the earlier wick lamp that used the capillary action of the wick to draw the fuel up to the flame and the later pressure lamp that needs to be pumped to supply a spray of fuel to the point of ignition.

The widespread availability of cheaper kerosene was the principal factor in the precipitous decline in the U.S. whaling industry in the nineteenth century. The leading product of whaling was oil for lamps, and it was expensive and smelly. Kerosene proved to be a superior fuel for lighting, and Łukasiewicz's lamp was a wonder remaining in common use for household lighting in rural areas of America into the 1940s. A contemporary newspaper account noted, "The lamp burning the Venango Oil [kerosene] will give a light equal to seven candles [a unit of illuminance], while the lamp burning Coal Oil gives a light equal to only five candles" (Dolson 1959, 61). Thomas Gale, correspondent for the *Tribune* noted, "Its light is no moonshine....In other words, rock oil [kerosene] emits a dainty light; the brightest and the cheapist in the world; a light fit for Kings and Royalists, and not unsuitable for Republicans and Democrats. It is a light withal, for ladies who are ladies indeed, and so are neither afraid nor ashamed to sew or read in the evening...by this light, they can thread their needles the first time and every time they try." Another commentator wrote, "[Kerosene's] glow will leap like magic from coast to coast, illuminating cities, villages, railroad cars, farmhouses—a golden web woven over all the land" (Dolson 1959, 85).

Beyond the hyperbole, the superiority of kerosene as a lighting fuel was considerable and the government immediately began switching to kerosene lamps in all its lighthouses on the East Coast. A Pennsylvania merchant advertised the economy and efficiency of kerosene, "A lamp holding 1/2 a pint, will burn in our dwellings at this season of the year, every evening till 10 o'clock for a week. We judge the cost to be about 1/2 a cent per hour. Some of our customers...say a lamp will burn with a full head of blaze, without cessation and without smoke [a common problem with coal oil], through 14 hours" (Dolson 1959, 85).

The demand for kerosene was immediate and immense. However, Kier had the only operating oil refinery making kerosene lamp fuel in America at the time. Drake had arranged for Kier to refine his oil at 60 cents a gallon for sale at between $1.50

and $2.00 depending on transportation costs. This represented a remarkable 200 to 300 percent profit on virtually thousands of gallons every day. Within a year, the four or five dozen refineries that had been set up in the Northeast to produce coal oil switched to the new petroleum as a raw material.

Crude oil was selling for $14 to $20 per 40 gallon barrel (later standardized at 42 gallons), and that included up to $3 for the barrel. One lawyer-speculator, George Bissell, recognized the need, and bought up the future production of barrels from all the local coopers in Cleveland thereby insuring a tidy profit. Fortunes were being made in many directions. By 1865, oil exports to Europe alone amounted to almost $16 million. One oil driller predicted that if a new well brought up nuggets of gold, the owners would throw them aside and continue drilling for oil (Dolson 1959, 28, 52).

The first week after the announcement of the strike, astonished farmers were offered small fortunes for leases to drill for oil on their land by hungry speculators. As with the gold strike of 1848, it was those who held the leases to the mineral rights, not the Gold Rush miners of 1849, who made the greatest fortunes. One farm wife refused $40,000 for a lease on her 200 acres until a new silk dress was added to the deal (Dolson 1959, 25). Others wisely fought for shares in the output of the wells— 1/4 was being offered by most speculators. Yet some among the unsophisticated west Pennsylvania landowners held out for a 1/8 or 1/12 because it sounded larger. It took a highly intelligent and sophisticated farmer to understand what a lawyer meant by a 47/50 share of 2/5 of a property lease for $60,000. Nonetheless, one 1/12 share in a single well proved to be worth $30,000, a tremendous sum of money in mid-century. Regardless of what the landowners were paid, it was the speculators and those who held on to their land that became the most wealthy.

On the day after the strike Jonathan Watson, a local lumberman, went up and down the 20-mile-long Oil Creek buying up leases. He would become the nation's first oil millionaire. He built a great mansion with a fish pond 190 feet long and a formal garden that kept 12 gardeners busy. James Tarr, the local sawmill owner who had supplied Drake with planks and boards, owned 200 acres of poor farmland along Oil Creek but he kept his mineral rights and within three years had made $2 million from leases and outright sales of his land, as well as another $1 million in secondary royalties. When Tarr took his young daughter to the Olome Institute for Young Ladies in Canonsburg to enroll her at the cost of $56.50 a term, he was told by the headmistress that the girl did not have the capacity for her academy. Tarr pulled out a roll of money, peeled off several greenbacks, and told the women to buy her some (Dolson 1959, 26).

James Evans owned a farm near the town of Franklin, but he made a living for his wife, son, and four daughters as a blacksmith. With the news of Drake's well bringing in oil, Evans thought of his own oily tasting water at home. Borrowing some money for raw materials from William Phelps, the local hardware store owner, Evans hammered out a set of his own drilling tools and set up a hickory spring pole and stirrup for drilling in lieu of an engine. His was a two-man operation. His son Henry pressed the stirrup down freeing the tools to fall and the spring pole lifted them back up. All the while James guided the drill. It was hard work, but it was a good cheap way to drill that had been used locally to bore for water and brine wells for many years. Up and down, they drilled for 73 feet, and finally struck an ooze of rich, black, heavy oil. This was certainly not the more liquid product found near Titusville, but it proved to be the first of the heavy petroleum types that would prove to be the best lubricating oil in the world.

The Evans strike was made famous by Edmund Morris, a crack reporter for the *Tribune*, who incorporated the story of Evans's eldest daughter Anna into the story. Anna was described as blond, blue-eyed, and delectable, as lean and handsome as her father without the sinewy muscles. When the Evans well came in, the news spread throughout the town. At the courthouse across the town square, the whoops and hollers of the youngsters brought the lawyers and clerks out into the street to see what was the matter. One of these was a recent beau of the pretty Anna, and when she saw him she screamed, "Dad's struck ile [oil]!" The whole crowd picked up the phrase, and when the newly rich oil heiress turned down the proposal of marriage from the lawyer some days later, Morris worked the scene into his story with emphasis on the line "Dad's Struck ile!"

Morris wrote, "We had the pleasure of seeing the young lady whose independence was secured by 'Dad's struck ile!' and can assure the reader that, from appearance, the unlucky suitor not only lost a fortune in oil, but a treasure in herself, in being rejected by the lady; for she seems a sweet-tempered and obliging blue-eyed village belle, an oil princess par excellence." Anna ultimately married a local furniture maker, but she was pestered for many years about the truth of the line. At least three popular songs were written with "Dad's struck ile!" or the more poetic "Pa has struck ile!" in them. James Evans made an equally quotable remark on the occasion of a wealthy lumberman who had rushed to Pennsylvania with an offer to buy him out for $40,000. Evans is reported to have responded, "This is my well. If you want one, go dig your own" (Dolson 1959, 47–48).

Drake, who was the architect of the petroleum industry, was a simple man. After the strike, he bought a new suit of clothes and a secondhand horse, and went fishing. One night a local preacher approached Drake on the streets of Titusville and told him to stop taking the oil from the ground. The oilman was taken aback. Most of the people in the area had profited from the burgeoning oil business as property owners, lessees, or field workers. Drillers' apprentices made $2 to $3 a day for just a 12-hour shift, and the drillers made $5. The preacher explained that the oil fueled the fires of Hell in the bowls of the earth, and when exhausted its absence would interfere with the plan that the Almighty had for the universe by letting the sinful go unpunished (Dolson 1959, 27). Drake's response to the man of the cloth is unrecorded.

—*James M. Volo*

THE GROWTH OF UNIONS

During the eighteenth century combining against an employer (a euphemism for forming a union or striking) was a crime drawing fines, jail time, or even corporal punishment. The army of workers that populated industrial America in the nineteenth century knew little of submitting a list of grievances, negotiating group contracts, or receiving just wages and workmen's compensation for injuries on the job. Management generally ignored individual workers with a grievance even if it was well-founded. The right to strike was first established in America by the Massachusetts State Court in 1842 when a group of mill girls in Lowell refused to return to work at their looms because of long working hours (up to 14 hours, 6 days a week). The eight-hour workday was the Holy Grail of organized labor throughout the nineteenth century, but it was not to be realized for decades.

Wages—or rather the hourly or daily rate of pay—were a secondary consideration that gained prominence as a labor issue slowly. As early as 1860, female workers from the shoemaking factory in Lynn, Massachusetts, went on strike for higher wages. Up to 800 women took to the streets dressed in their best hoopskirts and carrying parasols in an early March snowstorm. The strike lasted more than two weeks, and the results were somewhat ambiguous with the shop manager being thrown into a pond.

In the growing processing and manufacturing industries the American worker could hardly be organized with the same speed that the well-financed industrialists had shown in marshaling their own interests. Employers were always ready to undercut wage earners by expanding hours, lowering hourly rates, or bringing in scabs to challenge the position of their regular workers.

People hired to replace striking workers were often derogatively termed *scabs* by those in favor of the strike. The terms *strikebreaker*, *blackleg*, and *scab labor* were also used. Trade unionists also used the epithet scab to refer to workers who were willing to accept terms that union workers had rejected or who interfered with the strike action in other ways. Some say that the word comes from an old-fashioned English insult. An older word, blackleg was to be found in the old English folk song, *Blackleg Miner*, sung by many labor groups.

It's in the evening after dark,
When the blackleg miner creeps to work,
With his moleskin pants and dirty shirt,
There goes the blackleg miner!

Well he grabs his duds and down he goes
To hew the coal that lies below,
There's not a woman in this town-row
Will look at the blackleg miner....

So join the union while you may.
Don't wait till your dying day,
For that may not be far away,
You dirty blackleg miner! (Gregory 1997, On-line)

Ironically, many Americans felt that to join a union was to betray the tradition that the nation was a land of equal opportunity. Unionism implied that America was no longer a classless society and that there were social and economic prejudices that put into question the certainty that a free American could rise to success and prosperity by the strength of his back and his character. Among the many millionaires that populated American society were men like Andrew Carnegie, generally self-made former poor boys "trained in that sternest but most efficient of all schools—poverty." Carnegie felt that those who failed to bridge the gap between worker and employer, poverty and riches, did so because of their own shortcomings. "Unemployment itself," said one politician from Massachusetts, "was to all intents an act of God" (Davidson 1951, 556).

A strike—known as the Great Strike—may have been the pivotal event of the struggle between wage earners and employers. The work stoppage against the Baltimore and Ohio Railroad in 1877 was precipitated by a unilateral cut in wages of 10 percent. The Maryland militia was called out, and it fired on the strikers killing 12 people. The strike spread to Pennsylvania where 57 strikers, soldiers, and rioters were killed in virtually pitched battles. President Rutherford B. Hayes ended the violence by deploying federal troops to several states including Maryland, Pennsylvania, West Virginia, Illinois, and Missouri. Millions of dollars in railroad property, including 126 locomotives, was destroyed in the bloodiest labor disturbances ever to affect the United States. The level of violence, and the response to it, polarized the nation and left little middle ground for public opinion regarding labor issues. Both sides had seemingly overstepped the bounds of commonly accepted behavior.

Remarkably several unions grew at a phenomenal rate after the Great Strike. The Noble Order of the Knights of Labor sought to gather all American workers into one big union, and the organization grew to 700,000 members by the 1880s when it forced railroad manipulator Jay Gould to come to terms in a strike against his western system. The American Federation of Labor was formed in 1881 representing 250,000 craft-unionists. Left-wing socialist organizations also appeared, and employers used the radical ideas put forward by these organizations as justifications for their antiunion activities.

—*James M. Volo*

FINANCE: GOLD AS MONEY

Gold and silver mining were the king and queen of the extraction trades, and the series of precious metal strikes between 1848 and 1880 underwrote the nation during the many economic panics of mid-century. They also brought the first permanent settlers to much of the far West provided a rationale for the Pony Express and the extension of the telegraph and made financial support for the transcontinental railways possible. "Each new discovery was followed by an inevitable rush—into Nevada and Arizona; over the Inland Empire of Washington, Idaho, Montana; to the Pike's Peak country and out over the sprawling Rocky Mountains; and into the Black Hills of South Dakota." Moreover, wherever the miners went, the shopkeepers, traders, lawyers, ministers, saloon operators, gamblers, prostitutes, and all the other appurtenances of civilization followed. The infusion of precious metals into a cash-starved economy helped to lift it out of depression by spurring consumerism and propping up under-capitalized financial institutions (Paul 1963, viii).

Under the influence of the gold coming from California in 1849 and 1850, for instance, the economy regained much of the prosperity lost in the prolonged depression following 1837. The economy again experienced minor downturns in 1854 and 1857, but silver and gold discovered in the Washoe area of the Sierra Nevada's in 1859 (known as the Comstock Lode or Nevada Bonanza) relieved the distress somewhat. Development and exploitation of existing mines was particularly important during the Civil War years as both North and South tried to fill their war chests by mining precious metals.

Most postwar strikes were in silver instead of gold, and copper and lead mining came into prominence to answer the needs of the military for bullets and brass cartridge casings and for the wants of business for copper telegraph and telephone wire. Thereafter the region from the eastern Rockies to the Pacific remained an ever promising but elusive attraction for prospectors seeking additional discoveries. The discovery of gold in the Black Hills in 1874, sparked in part by the assurances of George Armstrong Custer, began a rush of miners to the Dakotas provoked an Indian war on the Great Plains and promised to relieve the effects of the Panic of 1873. Overall the discovery of precious metals—California gold in 1849, Colorado gold and Nevada silver in 1859, and Dakota gold in 1874—all tended to shake the economy out of its periodic malaise. Gold was also discovered in the Klondike in 1896, but it was very low grade requiring massive amounts of ore to make it profitable to mine (Sutherland 2000, 149).

The flow of precious metals to the financial and banking centers of the East stimulated the business of the entire country. Gateway ports and towns were overwhelmed by word of a nearby precious metals strike. "There were not enough wagons or mules to keep the stampede moving. The hills above town [Virginia City] were piled high with boxes of merchandise while their owners vainly offered fantastic freight fees for hauling them.... Stagecoaches and mule trains were booked up days in advance, streets and hotels, saloons and restaurants, were thronged with a noisy crowd of expectant millionaires" (Nadeau 1959, 37).

Yet no gold strike was as effective in sparking the economy as the first rush in 1849. Since the big strike at Sutter's Mill in California, prospectors had focused on looking almost solely for gold, which might turn a profit of $1,000 per ton of ore. The breathless spirit of the California mines marched from golden strike to golden strike, and those who hiked or rode along the rutted trails to the mining camps were often forced to jump out of the way to avoid being run down by freight wagons or mule trains. Many of the young miners of the 1874 rush, as yet unborn or in diapers in 1849, proclaimed that it was "Forty-Nine all over again." Some miners were so mesmerized by the yellow metal that they unknowingly discarded waste materials containing other valuable but less obvious metals like silver, platinum, copper, chromium, lead, and zinc. These sometimes assayed out at up to three times the value of the gold that had been extracted (Nadeau 1959, 37).

In the gold fields a fortunate man could lay up in a month more from even a modest claim than he could accumulate in an entire year elsewhere. During the rush years California alone may have produced upwards of $200 million worth of gold. In 1852 alone $81 million was taken from the ground and rivers. Yet this was to be the greatest year of the American mining frontier during the nineteenth century. There were few men that made significant fortunes, and many were fated to return home penniless. Others continued the quest moving from rush-to-rush and strike-to-strike (Paul 1963, 26–27).

—*James M. Volo*

COST OF LIVING/WEALTH

Standard of Living

As industrial activity displaced mere agricultural subsistence in the everyday life of the community and in the thoughts of those earning a living, the accumulation of money, property, and possessions became the conventional means of measuring success. The accumulation of goods quickly became the "accepted badge of efficiency," and the possession of wealth assumed "the character of an independent and definitive basis of esteem." In 1899, Thorstein Veblen noted the emergence of a new *leisure class* among the American population. "The possession of goods, whether acquired aggressively by one's own exertion or passively by transmission through inheritance from others, becomes a conventional basis of reputability. The possession of wealth, which was at the outset valued simply as an evidence of efficiency, becomes, by popular apprehension, itself a meritorious act. Wealth is now itself intrinsically honorable and confers honor on its possessor.... Prowess and exploit may still remain the basis of award of the highest popular esteem, although the possession of wealth has become the basis of commonplace reputability and of a blameless social standing" (Veblen 1994, 19).

According to the general population, the highest social honors available in the final decades of the nineteenth century remained those attained on the battlefield or through uncommon statecraft but "for the purposes of a commonplace decent standing in the community these means of repute have been replaced by the acquisition and accumulation of goods." According to Veblen, to stand well-placed in the community those of the leisure class required a certain, yet somewhat indefinite, standard of wealth. Those who fell below this standard, regardless of birth or family connection, were diminished in the esteem of their neighbors and in their own self-respect. The tendency in such a case was to make one's wealth conspicuous through a constant series of new purchases of property, goods, or clothing. "But as fast as a person makes new acquisitions, and becomes accustomed to the resulting new standard of wealth, the new standard forthwith ceases to afford appreciably greater satisfaction than the earlier standard did.... giving rise... to a new standard... of one's self as compared with one's neighbors.... Besides this, the power conferred by wealth also affords a motive to [its] accumulation" (Veblen 1994, 20–21).

Veblen considered the desire to accumulate wealth in emulation of one's neighbors the "strongest and most alert and most persistent of economic motives." In an industrial economy the constant need to conspicuously consume was virtually equivalent to a form of conspicuous waste that absorbed the increase in the community's industrial efficiency or output of goods at a rate too rapid for an individual's wealth to keep abreast of it. Veblen noted, "As increased industrial efficiency makes it possible to procure the means of livelihood with less labor, the energies of the industrious members of the community are bent to the compassing of a higher result in conspicuous expenditure, rather than slackened to a more comfortable pace." Such attitudes drove some of the most successful men in nineteenth century America (Veblen 1994, 68).

The standard of living in a community was closely tied to the social class of its citizens. In an industrialized community, one's neighbors in a geographical sense were often not one's equals financially or socially. This had generally not been the case in former decades where sparsely settled agrarian communities featured residents of comparatively equal means; but expanding industry and growing population densities were rapidly changing the face of many towns and cities widening the differences among the have's, have-not's, and the have-more's. The line between upper class and middle class was becoming hazy as wealth rather than family dictated social status. For this reason it was also thought to be necessary to impress one's social position on transient observers. "In the modern community" wrote Veblen, "there is also a more frequent attendance at large gatherings of people to whom one's everyday life is unknown; in such places as churches, theaters, ballrooms, hotels, parks, shops, and the like." This need often changed serviceable consumption into the conspicuous variety and prudent expenditures into indulgent ones (Veblen 1994, 54).

The accepted standard of expenditure in the community and the class to which a family belonged largely determined what their standard of living was to be. For all but the lowest classes "the popular insistence on conformity to the accepted scale of expenditure" was a matter of propriety to be violated "under pain of disesteem and ostracism." To accept and practice a certain standard of living thought to be in vogue for one's class was an expedient "indispensable to personal comfort and to success in life." The standard of living of any class in the nineteenth century, so far as it concerned conspicuous consumption, was commonly held to be as high as the earning capacity of that class would permit. Yet there was a constant tendency and pressure to move the standard upward. "The effect upon the serious activities of men is therefore to direct them with great singleness of purpose to the largest possible acquisition of wealth, and to discountenance work that brings no pecuniary gain" (Veblen 1994, 68–69).

For example, among that class of people following the pursuits of teaching, writing, government, law, ministry, or other scholarly fields of endeavor, the requirements of maintaining a higher than average social position while realizing a smaller than average income left an exceptionally narrow margin of disposable income for other purposes. Veblen noted, "The expectations of the community in the way of pecuniary decency among the learned are excessively high—as measured by the prevalent degree of opulence and earning capacity of the class, relative to the non-scholarly classes whose social equals they nominally are." In nineteenth-century communities there was no monopoly on scholarly pursuits, but those who practiced them as a profession were unavoidably thrown into social contact with managers, bankers, financiers, merchants, and other persons who were their financial superiors.

Veblen found that no other class in the community than the scholarly one spent a larger proportion of its income in conspicuous waste (Veblen 1994, 69–70).

—James M. Volo

The Family Budget

Although many family budgets were less than precisely detailed documents, those that survive from this period were done with sufficient care to allow researchers to outline the structure of average family expenditures with some confidence. While the levels of spending on certain budgetary items might be less than accurate in many surviving documents, the absence or presence of certain categories of consumption or expense can be very useful.

Basic subsistence needs like food, shelter, and fuel were common to all families. Among the significant expenditures for New England working families in the 1880s, however, are included repeated references to the cost of life insurance, dues to labor unions, and payments to other business organizations (known as *prudent expenditures*) that were unknown in the period of the Civil War. These were among a series of *discretionary expenditures* made after the basic budgetary necessities were covered. Discretionary items included *indulgent expenditures* like alcohol, tobacco, books, newspapers, or private schooling; and *expressive expenditures* like amusements and vacations, charity donations and church contributions, and more than purely functional clothing (such as fancy dresses or business clothing). That charity and religion should be included in the latter group is suggestive of the power that the reform movements and religious revivals of mid-century had on many families (Modell 1979, 215–16).

For both native-born and immigrant families most expenditures increased as the father's income increased, but American families were less likely than their immigrant counterparts to increase their expenditures based solely on increased income from supplemental sources. Americans seem to have been reluctant to spend the income of wives and children on frivolities. They chose instead to put additional cash into their savings. Overall, larger native-born working-class families tended to purchase fewer indulgent items than did small American families, but the opposite seems to have been true among immigrant families living in the same community. "In contrast to the Americans, larger immigrant families were more likely to allocate their resources on almost all expenditure items than were small families" (Modell 1979, 224).

Rent (housing cost) and food were always the largest portions of any family budget, but among the fastest growing consumer categories were the demands made by labor organizations and expenditures for amusements, vacations, and alcohol. As head-of-household income rises to similar dollar levels, both native and immigrant spending become nearly parallel in all categories other than alcohol.

It has been suggested that the emphasis placed on alcoholic consumption by immigrants was a nonrationalized response to the demands and pressures of an industrialized and urbanized environment. It is much more likely however that it served as a verification of the continued cultural use of alcoholic beverages among Western European groups since colonial times. In the 1770s, for example, Anglo-Americans from

New England alone had consumed more than two million gallons of rum annually, and anyone over the age of 12 could purchase beer in a tavern. Both the Irish and the Germans maintained positive attitudes toward the consumption of beer and other alcoholic beverages, and each became the target of temperance reformers because of their continued dedication to the use of wine and spirits as part of their daily lives.

On the other hand, expenditures for amusements, theaters, and vacations by many foreign-born persons have been regarded as "noncommunal forms of meaningful adaptation to industrial life." This view helps to explain the increased expenditures in these areas by all segments of society, not just foreign-born ones (Modell 1979, 214). Many southern cities saw a dynamic growth in professional theaters, and most northern urban areas supported theater groups. In most communities acting in the legitimate theater was a respectable profession, and the American stage was filled with excellent actors and actresses. Yet, when a group of players tried to open a theater in Lowell, Massachusetts, in 1833 they were arrested and put in jail for not "pursuing an honorable and lawful profession" (Lupiano and Sayers 1994, 67).

During this period several of Cooper's novels were adapted for the Northern stage, and thereafter a number of distinctive American characters appeared such as the rural Yankee, the noble savage, or the tough-fisted, tenement-dwelling Bowery Bhoy. However, some critics found the theater vulgar, coarse, and in bad taste. Clearly many stock performances were routine, tedious, or slipshod. Walt Whitman wrote in 1847 that they were becoming "beyond all toleration" (Hewitt 1959, 144). Washington Irving noted, however, that "the Theater…is the polite lounge, where the idle and curious resort, to pick up the news of the fashionable world, to meet their acquaintances, and to show themselves off to advantage" (Hewitt 1959, 65).

—*James M. Volo*

URBAN-RURAL ECONOMY: SCIENTIFIC FARMING

Technological advances like the mechanical reaper and the steam-powered thresher were not the only factors contributing to the giant steps made in agriculture in nineteenth-century America. The realization, dawning more slowly on some than others, that science might be profitable when applied to agricultural methods led to gains in farming efficiency and output. Many of these ideas concerning the role of science in agricultural progress were written, circulated, and published in farmer's almanacs, journals, and handbooks. Farming periodicals dedicated much of their space to scientific farming and the application of technological advances to agriculture.

One of the earliest of these, the *Farmer's Register* published monthly in 1839, emphasized the use of farm machinery, and another, the *Prairie Farmer* first published in 1841, concentrated on the need for a common school education for farmers as well as a substantial investment in mechanical devices. A typical example comes from Jesse Buel's *The Farmers Companion: or, Essays on the Principles and Practices of American Husbandry*, published in 1840. Buel was a successful editor and printer who left his career to immerse himself in a quest to create the model farm outside Albany, New

York. He spent the rest of his life creating his ideal farm and working as a spokesman for enlightened farming in America. He firmly believed that the more agriculture was enlightened by science, the more abundant would be its produce. Buel's notion that the gentleman farmer could subjugate nature with his knowledge of science had a powerful influence in America.

Granted that the typical farmer [tenant, sharecropper, or yeoman] did not adhere to, and probably was not interested in, the extremes to which Buel went in maintaining a model farm; however, the idea that agricultural practices could be improved with knowledge and applications of science found its way into the very fabric of American agricultural practice in the nineteenth century (Timmons 2005, 87–88).

The role of chemistry—and of science in general—in American agriculture was somewhat ambiguous when seen again in the contributions made by mechanical inventions. The American scientific community realized the importance of basic chemical research for the growth and advancement of agricultural and industrial concerns. The scientists insisted that agriculture be made rational and logical, but they lacked the strong support of many farmers mired in the traditional way of doing things. As the century progressed, many scientific principles were adopted by politicians who lent their support to the funding and organization of chemical research, and by the farmers, to a lesser extent, whose support was necessary if chemical research was to have a positive effect on agriculture.

There remained, however, a large gap between the producer of scientific theories and the consumer of its ideas. The desire of the scientist to engage in basic research often conflicted with the insistence of the public to realize immediate practical results. Other farmers disdained book farming just as artisans and others without scientific training often questioned the utility of basic scientific research.

One of the earliest practical contributions made by chemists to farming was in the area of soil analysis. Chemists slowly began to realize that the simplistic approach of analyzing a soil sample to determine the chemicals needed for replenishment was not a magic wand. Commercial chemical fertilizers were on the market by mid-century, but many farmers continued to rely on the practice of regenerating their fields by the application of animal manure, which had only become common practice in the previous century. By the end of the nineteenth century, however, Americans were using almost two million tons of commercial fertilizer annually. Although chemists made continual advances in the science of soil analysis and restoration throughout the century, these advances were made at a pace that failed to satisfy the farmer who wanted fertile fields *this* season (Timmons 2005, 89–90).

FARMING/HUSBANDRY: THE GRASSHOPPER PLAGUE

Along with the expansion of agriculture into the Plains and Midwest, came growing risks and uncertainties. In the nineteenth century the avoidance of economic risk and exposure to environmental disaster was difficult and costly. After the Civil War farmers became more dependent on creditors, merchants, bankers, and railroad operators. The relationships the farmer formed with these people allowed him to move beyond simply subsistence farming to an early form of profit-producing agri-business. The opportunity for economic gain, however, brought with it new obligations, hardships, and risks that many farmers did not welcome. This was especially true of the competition they found on the European grain market—a destination for their produce that American farmers had virtually owned prior to the war.

Agriculture had expanded to the semiarid regions of Nebraska, Kansas, and the Dakotas and unusual periods of drought had caused undue hardship. In the middle of the period, just as the Panic of 1873 hit, the upper Midwest farming region was also plagued by grasshoppers. Several states were grievously affected, including Iowa, Nebraska, Kansas, Missouri, and particularly Minnesota. The Dakota Territory and the Canadian province of Manitoba were also hard hit. The magnitude of the plague was catastrophic. Seemingly overnight Minnesota alone lost 16 percent of its wheat crop, 18 percent of its oats, and 15 percent of its corn. The grasshoppers returned annually from 1873 until 1877 to these same regions, and they also appeared sporadically during these years in other areas such as Texas, Arkansas, Idaho, Montana, Utah, New Mexico, Nevada, Washington, Oregon, Oklahoma, and in additional parts of the Canada plains. The total loss to the agricultural economy of the United States in this period of devastation may have exceeded $200 million annually.

When threatened by the swarming masses from the sky, farmers set smoky smudge pots in their orchards, in their vineyards, and in their wheat fields in an attempt to drive them off, but the pests—carried from place to place on the winds and leaving their eggs behind for each subsequent year—could not be scared away, writhing on the ground like a windblown shallow sea. Whole families could be seen in the fields shoveling the insects from the earth and into bonfires set for the purpose. A grasshopper-killing machine, called the hopperdozer, was invented to deal more efficiently with the problem. It required a piece of metal, shaped into a shallow pan and coated with tar or any sticky substance that was dragged through the fields behind a team of draft animals. The forward motion of the team forced the grasshoppers into the pan, which, when full, was emptied into the fire. In one county in Minnesota over 600 hopperdozers were built or bought in a single year, but the grasshoppers usually did their damage faster than the efforts of the farmers could kill them. Nonetheless, in some places these efforts may have thinned out the subsequent populations of insect pests by destroying the bugs before their peak period of egg production (Atkins 1984, 30–31).

The devastation was felt at different levels by farmers in different areas. Some farmers escaped damage altogether or were hurt only once or twice while their neighbors had their fields stripped during each successive year. There was no clear-cut pattern to the destruction. "Damage varied from crop to crop, from farm to farm, and from year to year." One farmer in 1875 lost 15 acres of wheat, 500 cabbages, all of his cucumbers, beans, onions, carrots, parsnips, and beets, most of his nursery stock, and most of his 4,000 strawberry and raspberry vines. He saved part or all of his oats, corn, potatoes, melons, and apple trees. Instead of a seasonal profit of $300 dollars, he made just $22 dollars; and he needed to borrow $5,000 to undo the damage, replant, and restock. This was financial ruin at its maximum, and there was little prospect for improvement as the pests returned in each successive year (Atkins 1984, 30–31).

In response to the threat, some farmers altered their planting patterns. Wheat was thought to be particularly susceptible to attack, and farmers planted corn, peas, beans, and other crops that were thought less vulnerable to replace it. Potatoes, as ground tubers, were hardly touched at all, but they were planted for domestic consumption rather than for the market. In one Minnesota county in 1873 wheat had made up 64 percent of the crop and corn just 8 percent. Five years later the proportions had reversed only to return again to their original ratios when the threat was no longer imminent. Other farmers turned more effort to livestock production rather than to grains. Pigs became a safe harbor because they were hardy and self-reliant, but fewer chickens were raised because eggs laid by chickens that fed on grasshoppers tasted bad. Vines and orchards put out of production by the insects were pruned, or replanted, or abandoned. Many farmers hard pressed for cash just planted less, falling back to subsistence-level farming and abandoning any hope of bringing a crop to market. In some regions the total acreage under production fell by half and did not recover until after 1878 when the grasshopper threat finally lifted up "in a body clouding the sunshine and left for parts unknown never to return" (Atkins 1984, 38–39).

Meanwhile the effects of the plague continued even after the insects had gone. Many farmers had mortgaged their farms to weather the crisis, and some began to pay interest on the interest incurred as the plagues continued and money was needed to provide the necessities of life. It must be remembered that taking loans against real property was not as common as it is today. Acquiring debt of this sort was considered by many to be an admission of failure, and putting up the farm as collateral was a drastic step. Some farmers used their savings, gave up their newspaper and other luxuries, sold their prized livestock, let go their hired help, or hitched up the farm wagon, loaded their remaining possessions, and moved on "east or west, it did not matter so long as there were no grasshoppers." Real estate values in the ravaged region plummeted. Many hard-hit counties underwent a decline in population, "a nearly unheard-of occurrence in a frontier area." Yet it was not the outpouring of residents but the diminished flow of new migrants into the region to replace them that was most dramatic (Atkins 1984, 33–34).

"Some people, finding human remedies futile, turned to spiritual assistance. They prayed." If God had sent this plague of Biblical proportions, then only God could lift it. They asked for the forgiveness of their sins; pledged themselves to lead more moral lives; and promised to build chapels and churches if the scourge were lifted. Some asked their neighbors for Christian charity, and vowed to show themselves worthy of God's mercy as they had when they joined together to wage God's war against slavery. When the pests returned year after year an entire values system was threatened, and the frontier was no longer viewed as a promised land (Atkins 1984, 39).

In a few communities farmers joined together to weather the storm, forming committees and relief efforts among themselves. Others turned to the state government for help—many asked, others begged, and some demanded a part of America's untouched abundance. Many farmers, however, were critical of governmental help drawing a clear line between those worthy of aid because they were victims of events beyond their control such as tornadoes, floods, droughts, or grasshoppers, and those who were paupers—a permanent under class whose poverty was considered self-inflicted because of a weakness in their moral fiber. A contemporary observer noted, "There were many families who are heroically enduring this loss.... Taking every pain to conceal their real condition they will not consent to receive any assistance till they approach the verge of starvation [and] then disgrace themselves, and the community in which they live, by applying for relief, and appearing before the world as mendicants...hundreds are ashamed to beg or acknowledge their destitution [because of] their repugnance to the reception of charity" (Atkins 1984, 41–42).

Historians have studied the five consecutive years of grasshopper plagues in the hardest hit region, and they have determined that the plagues had a profound impact on the community of farmers nationwide. Although grasshopper plagues had appeared before, the consistent reappearance of these pests at a time of economic distress may have changed how Americans viewed the frontier environment as a possible stage for financial success. Moreover, the plagues and the government's response to them may have reshaped the politics of the West and Midwest in the later nineteenth century (Atkins 1984, 4).

In March 1877, President Rutherford B. Hayes established the U.S. Entomological Commission to identify the most practical methods of preventing any further recurrences of the plague. By 1880 the commission had collected, analyzed, and published its findings, but the grasshoppers were already gone. Although the government responded to the grasshopper crisis with aid, relief, and even generosity, it did not generally display the massive reaction to agricultural devastation that was later seen in the New Deal policies of the 1930s. If the farmers of the 1870s valued the help of the government, and there is some evidence that many did not, then they were equally disappointed by government policies in the late 1880s and 1890s when government agencies, and the American people, were even less sympathetic in responding to drought and agricultural depressions (Volo and Volo 2007, 86–89).

INTERNATIONAL TRADE: MARITIME DECLINE

While the American nation had been understandably obsessed with an internecine conflict, the British had become fairly well entrenched as the world's foremost carriers of ocean trade—almost solely at the expense of American shippers. An article in the *New York Times*, January 29, 1867, claimed that Britain had "designedly availed of our rebellion to destroy our commerce, and the regular and long-established channels of our trade were broken, especially those by which our cotton grain and other production of the country were extensively shipped abroad." American sailing ships had indeed enjoyed a prominence in the Transatlantic cotton and grain carrying trade, but the war, poor crops from the grasslands, and the financial panic of 1873 adversely affected American shippers.

In 1863, British shipbuilders quietly launched the *Star of India*, an all-iron-frame, iron-hull windjammer—often considered the first of its kind. The use of iron and steel structural components (later in combination with steam propulsion) was a great technological advance that American shipbuilders failed to appreciate at the time. Moreover, much of the available investment capital that remained in the United States after the war was being steered toward projects like railroads, gasworks, and telegraph systems rather than into new and expensive technologies for metal ship-building. Postwar wooden shipbuilding yards were essentially obsolete but the capital required to refit them was simply not available, and potential investors were not interested. Ultimately, this lack of foresight gravely disadvantaged the American merchant marine.

The cotton trade was lost to American shippers during the wartime collapse of the industry, and it did not recover to prewar levels until 1879 at which time it was found that British-owned steamers had taken the lion's share of the traffic. Moreover, the emigrants from Europe, who were used as a profit-producing human cargo in lieu of vessels returning in ballast, had abandoned the long sailing crossing for the quicker steamers of Britain and Germany. Chief among these was the Britain's Cunard Line that ran a fleet of steamers between Liverpool and Boston or New York. The decline in passenger traffic on American vessels had begun before the Civil War when they were described as "damned plague ships and swimming coffins." The American windships quickly lost most of the emigrant trade to the steamers of the Hamburg, Bremen, and Liverpool lines (Cable 1960, 75).

It was the almost universal desire of American shippers to drive Cunard off the oceans. One means of supporting the American shippers and shipbuilders and of reducing the effects of the changes in the international trade economy was for the government to enact subsidies on certain routes. The American foreign trade industry had long sought such subsidies. Congress enacted a subsidy for the Collins Line on the transatlantic route in the 1840s, which it renewed in the 1850s. With the help of subsidies, Collins launched four super-steamships for the transatlantic run: *Atlantic*, *Pacific*, *Arctic*, and *Baltic*. Swarms of well-to-do Americans took passage with Collins, but the line burned up all hope of profit by attempting record passages of the Atlantic. In 1854, while hurrying to New York, *Arctic* struck another ship and sank with the loss of 318 passengers. In 1856, the *Pacific* disappeared without a trace. Two successive steamship disasters were more than the steamship-riding public was willing to bear. In 1858, Congressional sectionalism caused the subsidy to be canceled, and the troubled Collins Line subsequently failed.

In 1864, the Pacific Mail Company received a subsidy to carry the mail to the Orient. The Pacific Mail Steamers, with their obsolete walking beam engines became a common sight in the western ocean and remained in successful operation for many decades suggesting that the congressional committee's recommendation was well-founded. However, Pacific Mail used low-wage, foreign seamen from China and Indonesia and had little competition for passengers as its vessels crowded Chinese workers aboard on return trips to the West Coast of the United States to make ends meet. In 1869 a minority committee in Congress suggested subsidies for mail service contracts to help compensate shipowners for the lack of traffic and the high costs of operation on some routes. Republican forces in Congress—failing to enact additional subsidies—pledged to encourage and restore American commerce and shipbuilding during the 1872 national election. The Republicans won the reelection of Ulysses S. Grant, but failed to follow through on their election promises.

—James M. Volo

FOR MORE INFORMATION

Allin, Lawrence C. "The Civil War and the Period of Decline, 1861–1913." In *America's Maritime Legacy: A History of the U.S. Merchant Marine and Shipbuilding Industry since Colonial Times*, ed. Robert A Kolmarx. Boulder, CO: Westview Press, 1979.

Atkins, Annette. *Harvest of Grief: Grasshopper Plagues and Public Assistance in Minnesota, 1873–1878*. St. Paul: Minnesota Historical Society Press, 1984.

Bauer, K. Jack. *A Maritime History of the United States: The Role of America's Seas and Waterways*. Columbia: University of South Carolina Press, 1989.

Cable, Mary. "Damned Plague Ships and Swimming Coffins." *American Heritage* (August 1960).

Davidson, Marshall B. *Life in America*. Boston, MA: Houghton Mifflin Company, 1951.

Dolson, Hildegarde. *The Great Oildorado: The Gaudy and Turbulent Years of the First Oil Rush: Pennsylvania, 1859–1880*. New York: Random House, 1959.

Gregory, E. David. "A. L. Lloyd and the English Folk Song Revival, 1934–44." *Canadian Journal for Traditional Music* (1997). http://cjtm.icaap.org/content/25/v25art2.html (accessed July 2007).

Hewitt, Barnard. *Theater USA, 1668 to 1957*. New York: McGraw-Hill Book Company, 1959.

Holley, J. M. "History of the Lumber Industry," *La Crosse Wisconsin Chronicle* (October 21, 1906).

Johnson, Dorothy M. *The Bloody Bozeman*. New York: McGraw-Hill Book Company, 1971.

Lupiano, Vincent DePaul, and Ken W. Sayers. *It Was a Very Good Year: A Cultural History of the United States from 1776 to the Present*. Holbrook, MA: Bob Adams, 1994.

Mason, Philip P., ed. *Copper Country Journal: The Diary of Schoolmaster Henry Hobart, 1863–1864*. Detroit, MI: Wayne State University Press, 1991.

McDonald, Douglas. *Virginia City and the Silver Region of the Comstock Lode*. Carson City: Nevada Publications, 1982.

Modell, John, "Family and Fertility on the Indiana Frontier, 1820." In *Studies in American Historical Demography*, ed. Maris A. Vinovskis. New York: Academic Press, 1979.

Nadeau, Remi. "Go it, Washoe!" *American Heritage* X, no. 3 (April 1959): 37.

Paul, Rodman Wilson. *Mining Frontiers of the Far West, 1848–1880*. Albuquerque: University of New Mexico Press, 1963.

Reynolds, Robert L. "The Coal Kings Come to Judgment." *American Heritage* XI, no 3 (April 1960).

Sutherland, Daniel E. *The Expansion of Everyday Life, 1860–1876*. Fayetteville: University of Arkansas Press, 2000.

Timmons, Todd. *Science and Technology in Nineteenth-Century America*. Westport, CT: Greenwood Press, 2005.

Veblen, Thorstein. *The Theory of the Leisure Class*. Mineola, NY: Dover Publications, Inc., 1994.

Volo, Dorothy Denneen and James M. Volo. *Family Life in Nineteenth-Century America*. Westport, CT: Greenwood Press, 2007.

Wik, Reynold M. "Science and American Agriculture." In *Science and Society in the United States*, eds. David D. Van Tassel and Michael G. Hall. Homewood, IL: Dorsey Press, 1966.

Intellectual Life

SCIENCE: UNIVERSITY SCIENCE

Postsecondary education grew slowly prior to 1880. Professions such as teaching, law, and even medicine were often taught in a manner similar to an apprenticeship and remained open to people who had not completed college. College studies were heavily classical in their content. Students read Latin and Greek from Livy, Cicero, Homer, Plato, and others. As with primary instruction, recitation was the most common form of instruction. Rhetoric students studied composition as well as public speaking and formal oratory. Other studies includes philosophy and formal logic.

Work in the sciences, which covered physics and astronomy with some chemistry and geology in those days, consisted mostly of lectures with occasional laboratory demonstrations. Mathematics explored geometry, trigonometry, and calculus and encompassed memorization of rules with some effort to apply them to practical problems. The last quarter of the century saw some expansion of college offerings to include economics, history, literature, and modern language. Entrance requirements became more rigorous, and graduate schools first appeared.

Formerly only the men in the so-called learned professions (doctor, lawyer, or minister) were thought to require a formal education. Other occupations were thought of as mere trades, the preparation for which consisted of a period of hands-on practice and manual dexterity acquired through a period of apprenticeship. In 1847 Yale College established a new Department of Philosophy and the Arts whose purpose was to address the mechanical arts and applied sciences such as engineering. The School of Applied Chemistry was regrouped in 1854 with other areas of study into the Yale Sheffield Scientific School named in honor of John Earl Sheffield who donated more than one million dollars for its establishment. Seizing upon the funds made available by the Morrill Act of 1862, Daniel Coit Gilman reorganized the school of science to reflect a more modern format.

The construction and maintenance of railroad roadbeds and bridges involved a small army of specialized mechanics. Accidents and other incidents that caused the loss of life on railways and steamships had a chilling effect on their operations and engendered a good deal of technological rethinking throughout the country. This brought the professional college-trained engineer to the forefront of science and technology.

Many short route roadbeds were built on wooden pilings driven into the swampy ground across low lying regions. Initially constructed for only light traffic, the roadbeds of even the newest lines soon began to fail under increased use. The lack of an adequate bridging technology was also an obstacle to railway construction throughout the country. The development of north-south lines in the Atlantic coastal region was made more difficult because of the need to bridge the numerous eastward flowing rivers of New England and the Middle states.

American engineers and schools of engineering immediately attacked the problem. The first all-wood truss bridge design capable of holding the weight of a locomotive was patented by Lieutenant Colonel Stephen H. Long of the U.S. Engineers in 1839. In 1840 William Howe designed a wood and iron composite truss, which was adapted by Thomas and Caleb Pratt and became the standard for American railroad bridges. The Pratt truss is still in use today. Meanwhile, all iron designs were developed by a number of engineers including Squire Whipple who took out the first all iron patent in 1841. James Millholland built an all iron truss for the B & O Railroad in 1850, and Frederich Horbach did another in the same year for the Boston and Albany line near Pittsfield, Mass. On April 26, 1856, the first bridge to span the wide Mississippi River was completed from Rock Island on the Illinois side to Davenport on the Iowa side. This was a steel truss railroad bridge built by the Chicago and Rock Island line.

By the late 1850s, American railroad bridge technology had reached such a state of maturity that Europeans were carefully copying American truss designs. However, not all the railroad bridge designs developed in this period were successful. In 1850 an all-iron truss designed by Nathaniel Rider for the Erie Railroad failed with some loss of life. His design was similar to that patented by Squire Whipple a decade earlier. When an iron Whipple design also failed over the Dee River in England, there was a great public outcry concerning the safety of travel by rail. Ultimately, all the Rider and Whipple types in America were inspected for defects, and they were scheduled to be taken down and replaced by iron and wood composite types. In December 1876, a composite Howe truss failed plunging an entire train into a frozen stream 30 feet below. More than 90 people were killed in the subsequent fire and steam explosion. Fearing the ill will of the riding public, all Howe trusses in America were removed with great dispatch and replaced with Pratt designs made with structural steel.

American industries in the second half of the nineteenth century also found an ever-increasing need for chemistry and trained chemists in their businesses. Chemists helped produce products as wide-ranging as fertilizers, explosives, industrial dyes, and some of the earliest plastics, as well as chemicals for the photographic and petroleum industries. The process of integrating chemistry into industry was slow, but inevitable and the United States was moving toward parity with the more advanced chemical industries in countries such as Germany.

In the early part of the century, trained chemists served as consultants or were hired by firms to analyze raw materials like gold, silver, or other ores; or to help control processes such as those used in making steel, coke, or other alloys. As American industry grew in the second half of the century, chemists began to exercise some technical independence and initiative, and by the end of the century, most plants had a chemist or two on staff and a small laboratory of sorts on the premises. Without contributions from chemists and the science of chemistry, many of the products that Americans enjoyed in their daily life would not have been possible (Timmons 2005, 88–89).

—*James M. Volo*

EDUCATION: FRONTIER EDUCATION

The quality of frontier education varied from location to location, but the similarities were indeed significant. Most schools were taught by women who arrived in the West to educate the children of pioneers. The trend of women becoming teachers began around 1840 when Horace Mann claimed that the tendency of women to be kinder and gentler than men made them more like children and, therefore, better cut out for teaching. Catharine Beecher's widely read 1845 work, *The Duty of American Women to Their Country*, further encouraged women to fill their country's need for educators, especially on the frontier where the shortage of teachers to meet the region's fast paced growth was a problem. Many women were inspired by this call and applied to be frontier teachers. The shortage of male teachers during the Civil War further increased the number of females who taught school and when school districts realized that they could be hired for less money than men, the hiring of women became commonplace, eventually established teaching as a mainly female occupation. Prior to the 1880s, these women were mainly from the East. They were willing to move to remote areas of the West where they taught in schools that varied from tiny dugouts barely able to house a handful of students, to large wooden structures with glass windows. Women did so for a variety of reasons, including a fascination with the frontier, a desire for independence, and a genuine love of teaching.

By some accounts, school boards hired and fired teachers on a regular basis, not because they were poor teachers, but to keep salaries low by hiring the newest teachers who were also the lowest paid. When daughters of pioneers passed the required eighth grade comprehensive exams, they too could become teachers. However, with the passing of teacher certification laws, they often had to take additional exams before reentering the classroom. Once there, teachers were responsible not only for the education of students, but for the cleanliness of the school itself, the discipline of the classroom, and the rapid response to crisis, including snakebites, injuries, and storms.

Given the range of responsibilities of frontier teachers, combined with their prominence in the community and their female gender, it is not surprising that the schoolmarm was among the most idealized western figures. An unmarried woman who arrived in an unpopulated town to hold a visible position that directly impacted the town's children inevitably became the object of much fascination, not only to those she taught, but also to the men and women of the community. The fact that the teacher's contract might depend upon her remaining unmarried only increased the romance around her. At the same time, the amount of attention a female teacher could receive in a town where women were scarce meant that romantic attachments were extremely common. Some couples kept their relationships a secret from the community for the woman to remain in her job.

To the children who attended the one-room schoolhouse, the teacher represented a combination of a cultured role model, firm disciplinarian, and comforting caregiver. Her position in the community, as well as her position in the classroom, made the teacher something of an idol and teachers reported that they tried to support this image by dressing as well as they could and by upholding the values of the nation and the town. Part and parcel of this role was the fact that the teacher had to keep a wide range of children occupied and learning throughout the school day, a task that was especially challenging given the limited resources available and the sporadic attendance of the students. Children in the first grade had to have work while the teacher instructed those in the fifth grade. Older boys had to be kept on task while younger children were the focus of attention, and the impulse of youths who spent much of the year working outdoors had to be contained. Teachers, at this time, relied on oral forms of instruction and memory, including rhymes and sayings, as much as they depended on students writing information down and studying the material (Quay 2002, 29–32).

Keeping the schoolroom warm was an almost universal problem. Firewood, cut, split, and stacked for a season, was an expensive commodity that reflected the labor required to produce it. Teachers, ministers, and other public servants were often paid in quantities of seasoned firewood, usually measured out in cords. Nonetheless, the community was not always willing to provide appropriate fuel for the schoolhouse stove. A school superintendent reported finding the teacher and pupils huddled together, shivering with cold, and striving to warm themselves by the little heat generated from a quantity of green wood in the stove. One teacher, Elizabeth Blackwell, noted that at times she had to wear gloves, a blanket shawl, and a hood over her head. A young teacher in Iowa recorded a schoolroom incident when trying to make a fire with only wet and unchopped wood. As she puffed away to make the wet mass burn, she found herself suddenly crying like a child in desperation (Volo and Volo 2007, 282–83).

Schoolbooks were a rare commodity in the West and just about every available text from *McGuffey's Primer* to the Bible, almanacs, hymnbooks, and songsters were employed in the service of frontier education. A typical school library was composed of contributions from the homes of community members, an assortment of children's magazines, and a few appropriate books such as the works of Louisa May Alcott. One teacher recalled how the books were read aloud and the different characters were assumed by the pupils, who often played them out as they called it, at recess. Children's magazines such as *Chatterbox*, *Harper's Young People* and *Youth's Companion* were tremendously popular at this time. The stories, informational articles, pictures, and puzzles from these publications furnished recreation for all ages.

While learning occurred in the schoolhouse, the schoolyard was a site for physical activity, including games that began before the morning school bell and continued during recess. It was not unusual for the boys to arrive early to get in an hour of play prior to the beginning of class. Recess provided a needed outlet for all children, who played popular games like Anty Over, Red Rover, and Capture the Flag. Serving as a counterpart to exercising the mind in the classroom, recess was considered a time to exercise the body and teachers let children find their own methods of entertainment during the recess hour. Intervention was sometimes necessary, however, when boys engaged in fights or squabbles broke out. The teacher's dual role as educator and disciplinarian was clear. Given the fact that some female teachers were scarcely older than the students they taught, not to mention physically weaker than the bigger boys they taught, the demands on the teacher to keep order in the school are even more striking.

Teachers also found that their jobs included dealing with other aspects of their students' personal lives. Physical ailments were common and the teacher was often the first person to note illness and other problems. Some of these impacted the classroom itself, as with childbains, a painful itching that resulted from feet that were cold from a long walk to school in inclement weather. One student recalled that everyone had chilblains and that the banging and scuffling of feet as students pounded their heels and kicked their toes against the seats was so loud and incessant at times that the recitations were interrupted. Bad weather could also cause problems that teachers were expected to solve. The dangers of being caught in a storm either during the journey to or from school, or while in the school itself, were so common a part of the frontier experience that when children were snowbound in schools throughout the Midwest during the blizzard of 1888, the event was referred to as the "Schoolchildren's Blizzard." The courage of Nebraska teacher, Minnie Freeman, during the storm was further memorialized in a popular song called, "Thirteen Were Saved, or Nebraska's Fearless Maid."

The frontier teacher was also a social coordinator, helping to organize events for the town's children and adults. Spelling bees were a popular pastime that involved competition between different age groups. Webster's *The Elementary Spelling Book*, familiarly called the "Blue-Back Speller" had a printing of 35 million copies between 1855 and 1890. Not a single definition was given for any of the words on the 174 pages. While the children learned how to spell the words they really did not know the meaning of the words that they were studying. Other events the teacher helped to coordinate included box lunch socials and dances, many of which took place on the school grounds or in the school if the structure was able to serve in that capacity (Quay 2002, 32–34).

—*Dorothy Denneen Volo*

LITERATURE

Novels

A literate American public was a reading public, and it demanded access to literature at a low price. Technological improvements in typesetting, printing, and binding were initially made in the 1830s, but their application was largely limited to newspapers, magazines, and pamphlets. In the 1840s, they were applied to the fantastically popular hardcover novels causing the per copy price of the genre to fall from several dollars to as little as a quarter of a dollar. The remarkable steam-powered rotary press, invented in 1847, made paperbound publishing, in particular, remarkably inexpensive. Paperbound editions fell to less than 7 cents a copy. Deluxe-bound British novels costing $10, pirated by the American cheap press, sold for 10 cents in paperback.

Popular writing often promoted mythical images like those of James Fenimore Cooper's frontier that established a Western genre. When first published, Cooper's works were also avidly read in Europe, fueling a foreign interest in frontier adventure novels. Cooper's settings were rarely taken outside the regions of the eastern state of New York, but it was not the geography that was the focus of such tales. It was rather the frontier self-reliance of the hero and the male bonding of the characters that superseded any romantic attachments that the protagonist had for female characters that made the novels rugged. The action always centered on the border between civilization and wilderness, which for Cooper had its western terminus at the Great Lakes. This male-dominated universe was crucial to the frontier genre, and it drifted west with the waves of settlers and immigrants. Throughout, the story lines focused on frontiersmen who found meaningful and lasting companionship, not to mention rivalry, among themselves rather than with women. On the frontier, the hero forgoes interpersonal relationships, preferring a solitary life to a married one and finding his best companions in other loners who populated the fictional West (Quay 2002, 153, 155).

Cooper was criticized for his inaccurate descriptions of locations, his writing style, and his depiction of Native Americans that were deemed too sympathetic by his contemporaries. In 1837, author Robert Montgomery Bird responded to Cooper's view of the Indians in his own best-selling novel entitled *Nick of the Woods*. Bird's main character, Nick, also known as Jibbenainosay, is a superhuman figure who violently murders Native Americans. The novel was notably different from Cooper's works in its creation of savage Indians and a wilderness filled with frightening spirits and gruesome experiences. The contrast between the two authors marks a division in the cultural attitudes toward Indians held by the American reading public, yet it was Cooper's vision that superseded Bird's as the foundation for future works in the Western genre. Cooper's representations of the complex relationship between Native Americans and whites, the cultivation and exploitation of the land, and the anxiety surrounding domestic life on the frontier have continued to make his books relevant to today's readers. Cooper remains a staple of American literary classics and the grandfather of frontier fiction (Quay 2002, 155–56).

The sea also served as a vast frontier for the adventure novelist. Herman Melville's *Moby Dick* (1851) was widely read and is an excellent example of the whaling novel, a part of the popular maritime adventure genre of the period. Lesser known today than Melville was Joseph Holt Ingraham, the most prolific and popular author of his day to capture the romance and energy of the sea. Ingraham's *The Pirate of the Gulf* (1836), based on the real pirate Jean Lafitte, was the first of more than a hundred of his novels. Edgar Allan Poe, who knew him, called Ingraham's work overly minute in its many detailed descriptions. Henry Wadsworth Longfellow, feeling the sting of upper-class sarcasm for having Ingraham's first novel dedicated to him by the admiring author, called the author the worst novelist who ever lived. Nonetheless, Ingraham was both prolific and successful, producing story lines in many settings. His *Prince of the House of David* (1855) sold hundreds of thousands of copies (Browne and Kreiser 2003, 104). Ingraham's son, Prentiss, later became one of Irwin Beadle's dime novel authors.

Mayne Reid was a close friend of Edgar Allan Poe, and his novels were mainly adventure stories. Beginning in 1850, he published *The Rifle Rangers: Adventures of an Officer in Southern Mexico*, which was based on his own service in the 1846 war; *The Scalp Hunters* (1851); *The War Trail* (1857); and *Forest Exiles* (1854). In 1853 Reid wrote a novel inspired by his own 15-year-old spouse, appropriately titled *The Child Wife*, and in 1856 he wrote a play called *The Quadroon*. A federal officer, author, and Civil War correspondent, Captain John W. De Forest, considered himself "a tolerably instructed man, having read *The Book of the Indians*, all of Cooper's novels, and some of the works of Captain Mayne Reid" (Volo and Volo 1998, 208).

Mary Anne Sadlier (1820–1903), an Irish-American immigrant, wrote 60 volumes of work—from domestic novels to historical romances to children's catechisms. While largely forgotten today, Sadlier's work stands as an important part of American literary history. She was one of the first fiction writers to address the effects of the Irish Famine. In addition, Sadlier's novels narrate that other great journey west across the frontier especially the transatlantic voyage of millions of immigrants in the person of an 18-year-old domestic servant named Bessy Conway. Her novels force the reader to redefine somewhat the one-gender-only concept of the rugged frontiersman lighting out for the territories.

It was from the development of inexpensive book publishing that the genre known as the Dime Novel proceeded. Introduced in the 1850s, these cheap paperbacks enjoyed tremendous popularity for the remainder of the century. They provided the reading public with literally thousands of story lines, mostly of dubious quality. The American West and stories of the Indian Wars were popular subjects. At first grinding out adventures based on real-life characters like Buffalo Bill Cody, Kit Carson, or Daniel Boone, authors soon found that they had to invent characters to fill the demands of their readers. Some of these had wonderfully suggestive names such as Deadwood Dick, Deadshot Dave, and Rattlesnake Ned. The plots were in the realm of sheer fantasy with difficulties always overcome and evil always vanquished (Browne and Kreiser 2003, 105–6).

The popularity of the dime novel, and the low level of quality demanded by its audience, opened a whole new arena of professional and semiprofessional authorship. The output of some authors was prodigious. Colonel Prentice Ingraham wrote 700 dime novels, 200 of them about his friend William "Buffalo Bill" Cody. Edward Z. C. Judson wrote between 300 and 400 dime novels under a dozen pen names including that of the famous Ned Buntline. Such staggering production did not insure fame, however. The titles of dime novels, or main characters of the series, were often more closely followed by the reading public than any particular author.

The name of publisher Irwin Beadle is most closely associated with dime novels. Beadle, his brother Erasmus and partner Robert Adams, had an early success with

Malaeska, the Indian Wife of the White Hunter (1860) by Ann Sophia Stephens. The book sold 65,000 copies in just a few months. Beadle, thereafter, hired Edward S. Ellis to write the novel *Seth Jones: Or the Captive of the Frontier* (1860). The Beadle's soon developed a formula for the dime novel and stuck with it. A complete, adventurous, and sometimes shockingly violent story of about 100 pages sporting a sensational illustrated cover printed on yellow-tan paper sold for only a dime. They urged their authors to rework the same basic, but successful plots, with new characters and backgrounds, hiring writers to flesh out story lines to 30,000 to 50,000 words for between $50 and $250, depending on the length and expectation of sales.

Success bred imitation, and a host of dime novel publishers entered the market producing thousands of these stories for the reading public including George Munro (1863), Robert De Will (1867), Norman Munro (1870), Frank Tousey (1878), and Street and Smith (1889). Several of these publishers had apprenticed in the traditional printing trades as young men only to find their professions de-skilled and forever changed by mechanization. Erastas Beadle, Robert Bonner, Frederick Gleason, George Munro, Theophilus Beasley Peterson, and Francis Smith left their failing printing trades and went into publishing story papers and dime novels (Shrock 2004, 169–70).

Although dime novels were part of the cheap press and focused on adventure and fantasy, the Beadle's aimed for the highest standards of public morality in their publications. Their directions to their authors prohibited "all things offensive to good taste…subjects or characters that carry an immoral taint…and what cannot be read with satisfaction by every right-minded person, young and old alike" (Browne and Kreiser 2003, 106). However, by the 1880s the overall quality and moral tone of the genre had markedly deteriorated (Shrock 2004, 170).

The popularity of dime novels actually rose during poor economic times like the Panic of 1873. Cheap libraries, which today are often conflated with dime novels, emerged in 1875. These were series of 16–32 page pamphlets for a nickel. Beadle and Adams issued a *Fireside Library*, George Munro a *Seaside Library*, and Norman Munro a *Riverside Library*. Street and Smith offered a number of series such as the *Log Cabin Library* and *Nick Carter Library*; and Frank Tousey sold a *Five Cent Weekly Library* and the *New York Detective Library*. The last sold full-length books rather than the 16- to 32-page (comic book length) pamphlets.

The Beadle's also published the *Dime Library*, which offered instruction materials on a wide range of topics from etiquette to popular sports. The *Beadle Dime Series* published 631 titles; its *Pocket Novel Series*, 272; its *Dime Library*, 1,103; the *Half-Dime Library*, 1,168; Tousey's *Five-Foot-Wide Library*, 1,353; and his *Wild West Series*, 1,294 (Browne and Kreiser 2003, 108).

Dime novels were sold at every newsstand and in all but the most elite bookshops, and their availability was advertised in both the newspapers and magazines. They were usually printed in press runs of 60,000 to 70,000 copies, a remarkable number for the period. The more successful titles went through several printings. The usual price was 10 cents, but some series sold for as little as a nickel and as much as a quarter. The popularity of the dime novel endured when literally millions of copies went into circulation during the nineteenth century. As late as the 1890s new dime novel publishers, like the successful firm of Street and Smith, were still entering the cheap press business.

More respectable than the dime novels, though less popular, were the story papers that utilized the same money-saving publishing techniques. Some dime novel publishers began to issue these in the post-Civil War era. They included George Munro's *Fireside Companion* (1866–1907), *Beadle's Banner* (1872–1892), and George Munro's *Family Story Paper* (1873–1921). The most popular story paper was the *New York Ledger*, edited by Robert Bonner in the 1850s. Rather than being exploitive of the reading audience, many of these story papers were intended for family readership with a content that was nonsectarian, apolitical, and "welcome in domestic circles" (Browne and Kreiser 2003, 108).

—James M. Volo

Juvenile Literature

With the change from rural to urban living affecting the lives of so many children, parents looked for a way for them to keep abreast of all the things they needed to know while entertaining them at the same time. While adults had clearly been the target of adventure literature in the form of both hardcover and dime novels, older children read much of the same material.

A number of nineteenth-century how-to books were designed for young persons to provide directions for do-it-yourself handicrafts. Dan Beard—later National Scout Commissioner of the Boy Scouts of America—believed that handcrafting had a value above all other children's leisure activities. The art of making things could grow into a lifetime hobby, and the manual skills developed by working with wood and other materials were valuable, as were the resourcefulness and self-control that came from mastering a difficult project.

The idea of employing reading as a route to handcrafting was not new. In the 1830s William Clarke had included handcraft projects in the *Boy's Own Book* (1829), and Lydia Maria Child had done so in the *Girl's Own Book* (1833). Because parents often helped their children in handicraft work, adult magazines such as *Scientific American* and *Ladies' Home Journal* were sometimes utilized. These often carried articles about handicrafts that might interest children. One type of reading material specifically designed for this purpose was toy making.

In 1882, Beard collected the best of his own writing and put it into a book called *What to Do and How to Do It: The American Boy's Handbook* in an attempt to preserve the best of that which American children had loved in the past. His two sisters, Adelia and Lina, who were writers of handicraft articles for magazines, wrote a parallel book in 1887 called *How to Amuse Yourself and Others: The American Girl's Handbook*. Both works became classics, and much of their content later appeared in the Boy Scout and Girl Scout handbooks of the twentieth century (McClary 1997, 41–42).

During the last four decades of the nineteenth century (1867–1899), Horatio Alger wrote hundreds of novels for young boys. His purpose was to teach his readers the merits of honesty, hard work, and cheerfulness in the face of adversity. His work also appealed to parents because of its unvarnished espousal of the Protestant work ethic and middle-class values. Alger produced an average of three works per year, and he was often accused of relying on formula writing. One critic, reviewing Alger's 90th novel, complained that the only new thing therein was the names of the characters.

Nonetheless, Alger filled a void in the spectrum of American literature. At one extreme was the conduct manual that stressed formal manners; at the other extreme was the action-packed dime novels. The popular market for reading was also swamped with romances that aimed at adolescent girls and frivolous adults, and favored settings in the Old South or on the Western frontier. These appealed to readers with a liking for sentimentality, and though they included vulnerable and weepy children as characters, real boys—manly, straightforward, and self-reliant—were rarely the principals in the story.

Alger aimed his stories directly at the underappreciated audience of young males, but he stayed away from themes such as the "Boy Bandit," the "Boy Gunfighter," or the "Boy Pirate." Parents, ministers, librarians, and Alger, himself, appreciated that such works could do incalculable mischief with the young mind. Alger favored urban settings and realistic (if somewhat contrived) everyday situations. Besides, he continued to sell books. Even in the final decade of his life, his work had lost little momentum, and his rags to riches themes continued to compete successfully with other forms of juvenile literature. The early twentieth century turned his work into a literary craze, and hundreds of thousands of copies were sold in the pre–World War I period.

—James M. Volo

Periodicals

Magazines and newspapers published much of the output of American authors in the nineteenth century. It has been estimated that there were 575 magazines and almost 3,000 newspapers in publication in the postwar decade. *Harper's Weekly*, with a monthly circulation of 500,000 copies, and *Atlantic Monthly* were the two most prestigious literary and political magazines of the period. New York publisher Frank Leslie had produced amazingly moving woodcut illustrations for his *Illustrated Newspaper* from 1861 through 1865. His use of graphics and terse prose to interpret ongoing news events was a new concept in the American newspaper business that was quickly adopted by other news agencies. In a day when a partisan press was the rule, Leslie's stood apart. Except for tolerating anti-Irish sentiment and portraying Negroes in a stereotypical and condescending manner, Leslie's condoned little that was political (Volo and Volo 1998, 211–12).

Within a few years two independent graphic news weeklies were launched in competition with Leslie's newspaper empire: *Harper's Weekly* and the *New York Illustrated News*. Fletcher Harper, the well-financed publisher from Harper and Brothers, actively tried to recruit Leslie's artists and engravers, and aggressively tried to exceed Leslie's circulation. Reporting from the battlefield was exacting and dangerous work. Many artists fell ill with the same maladies that afflicted the troops, and several were captured or killed on the battlefield. Leslie provided poor and erratic pay for his artists, many of whom he lost to competitors. By the opening of the war the two newspapers were within 10,000 copies of one another, with the *New York Illustrated News* a distant third (Volo and Volo 1998, 212).

Frank Leslie introduced a number of illustrated newspapers to American readers: the *Illustrated Zeitung*, a German language edition aimed at the German immigrant population of the North; the *Budget of Fun*, a whimsical publication featuring cheap fiction; the *Ten Cent Monthly*; the *Lady's Illustrated Almanac*; and the *Lady's Magazine and Gazette of Fashion*. All of these bore his name: Frank Leslie's.

The distinction between high and low literature was not so clear in the public's mind as it would become later in the century, and the popular magazines were neither high nor low in their content or audience, tending to hold a middle ground. Short stories and serializations of novels (published in their entirety afterward as books) were featured in the leading magazines, notably *Harper's Weekly*, *Atlantic Monthly*, and *Godey's Lady's Book*. *Harper's* preferred a sentimental formula of separated lovers, of which the most successful practitioners were Louise Chandler Moulton, Elizabeth B. Stoddard, Mary Abigail Dodge, Helen W. Pierson, and Nora Perry. The authors featured in *Godey's* tended toward the sentimental, while those in the *Atlantic* were more realistic in their content. These included Rebecca Harding Davis and Louisa May Alcott (Browne and Kreiser 2003, 104, 109).

—*James M. Volo*

Poetry

Making its appearance soon after the end of the Civil War, impromptu poetry became a staple of Western ranch life, providing a creative outlet for ranchers and other land and livestock workers. Composed and recited primarily by livestock wranglers, this type, called cowboy poetry, focused on the Western way of life, including the unique environment of the open range. Such verse was originally published in local newspapers beginning around 1870, and it could be found in magazines, repeated in western stories and novels, and even collected into bound volumes and books. Despite the use of the print media to circulate cowboy poetry, it was most frequently spoken, in the tradition of oral poets. As a result, numerous variations of a single poem have been known to exist, the words changing from one recitation to the next. While some of these changes may have been the natural result of faulty memorization, others are clearly deliberate attempts to adapt a poem to a new situation. The flexibility of such verse is key, for cowboy poems by their nature draw as often on classical writers like Shakespeare and Biblical references as on parodies of the way cowboy life is mythologized in folklore, stories, and modern films.

Despite their various origins and formats, cowboy poems can usually be recognized by their catchy rhythm, traditional rhyme scheme, and task-specific subject matter. Cowboy poems like "The Creak of Leather," by Bruce Kiskaddon, are marked by a rhythm that tends to be like that of a ballad, in which the last word rhymes in every two lines or every other line. The result is a song-like verse that strengthens the alliance between the poems and songs of open-range wranglers. The language of the stanza is also significant because it includes informal words like "mornin'" for morning, "jest" for just, "hoss" for horse, and "doggie," for cattle to convey the image of cowboy-ness. This refusal to adhere to the tenets of standard English gives cowboy poetry a local and personal flavor that creates powerful images for the reader and listener alike.

In addition to structure and language, the subject matter of cowboy poetry is predictable. The celebration of life on the land, including its challenges and changing culture, are common topics, as are the hardships of the trail: important events such as death, marriage, and birth; as well as nature, the seasons, bravery, and love. These subjects arose from the fact that cowboy poems were often composed during the day's work. As the cowboy performed his duties, he was able to create poems in his mind that could then be recited when he was in the company of other men, around the campfire or at the chuck wagon. Using the world around him as his muse, the cowboy poet captured and recorded some of the most descriptive images of frontier life that are available to modern readers.

The widespread popularity of cowboy poets and poetry has waxed and waned since the end of the nineteenth century. Some of the early cowboy poems have made their way into the campfire repertoire of the modern day verging on the edge of being included among the nighttime ghost stories or warnings to listeners about the "Strange things done in the midnight sun / By the men who moil for gold." Indeed the tradition of telling stories, repeating rhymes, and singing songs on the range lives on in the campfires of hundreds of summer camps and scouting events around the United States (Quay 2002, 162–64).

Regional Literature: Westerns

While there were several forms of American literature upon which later western fiction was based, there was also reading material made popular by those who journeyed west and settled the land during and after the gold rush. These books, papers, journals, and magazines both encouraged migration and brought Eastern ideals into the mining communities, boomtowns, and isolated immigrant trains and prairie homes that characterized the era of expansion and exploitation. Among these was *The Oregon Trail* (1849), Francis Parkman's travel narrative of his visit to the West in 1846. Such publications appearing during the period of expansion were seen as personal travelogues and advertisements to move west.

At the same time, there were a number of purpose-written guidebooks containing an array of information that immigrants consulted before and during their Overland journeys. These bore such names as *A Journey to California* (1841), the *Emigrants' Guide to Oregon and California* (1845), and *The Gold Regions of California* (1845). One of the best was *The Prairie Traveler, A Hand-book for Overland Expeditions* (1859) by Captain Randolph B. Marcy. These guidebooks described what supplies to take—including clothing, furniture, animals, firearms, and food—what routes were the most direct, and where to stop along the way. Typically authored by a single individual—who may or may not have actually traveled the routes being described—hundreds of guidebooks were published, some only a few pages in length. Inaccuracies were numerous especially concerning the maps the guidebooks contained and the amount of supplies needed to successfully complete the journey. Some immigrants, relying on a guidebook, found that they were overstocked with arms and ammunition but ran out of food before reaching their destination. Nonetheless, readers were tantalized by the descriptions of the sights they would see on the trails, and the gold or fertile, well-watered lands that they would find on arrival. By some accounts immigrant guidebooks were the best advertisements available for westward expansion, and they can be credited with inducing many pioneers to travel west.

The frontier West produced both a Western regional fiction and a cadre of frontier authors. The literary roots of many authors were in the West. Among these were Bret Harte, Mark Twain, Hamlin Garland, and Stephen Crane. Harte's poems and short stories made him well known in the Western literary circle centered on San Francisco, and he became the editor of *The Overland Monthly*. His reputation flourished with the publication of short stories like "The Luck of the Roaring Camp." He spent close to two decades living and working in California capturing the local color in sketches such as "A Night in Wingdam," "The Legend of Devil's Point," "A Legend of the Cliff House," and "Early California Superstitions." Known for his depictions of gamblers, prospectors, ranchers, wranglers, and frontier women, Harte significantly impacted the image of the West and Western literature through his ability to capture the essence of the frontier with language.

Samuel Clemens (Mark Twain) also made his literary reputation by writing in and about the West. During his time as a reporter for the *Territorial Enterprise*, the local newspaper for the Nevada Territory town of Virginia City, Clemens first adopted his pen name. In 1862, while working for the paper, he published a hoax about finding a petrified man on the plains, which was reprinted by newspapers in San Francisco. Other frontier articles by Clemens included "My Bloody Massacre," "Information for the Million," and "Buck Fanshaw's Funeral." His best-known work from this period was "Jim Smiley and His Jumping Frog" (also known as "The Celebrated Jumping Frog of Calaveras County") printed in 1865 and reissued in 1875. The short story was a humorous parody of the traditional tale that earned Clemens wider recognition in both the East and the West. Clemens used his Western experiences as a newspaper man and prospector in the satiric fictional work *Roughing It* (1872), a comic autobiography. His most popular fiction centered on his own upbringing along the Mississippi River, however. *Tom Sawyer* (1876) and *The Adventures of Huckleberry Finn* (1885) developed from his expertise gained by capturing the richness of life in the West.

—James M. Volo

COMMUNICATIONS: THE MARKET TICKER SERVICE

After passing through a chaotic period of expansion and wasteful competition, the telegraph industry found a degree of stability under a cartel of six major companies in the 1860s. Over the next few years these were absorbed by Western Union. In 1866, Western Union bought out the last of its rivals in the electric telegraphy business and the Associated Press (AP) secured its place in news reporting, forming a monopoly in this area of communications. The two companies remained under separate ownership and management, but they formed an alliance that gave them nearly complete control over the flow of news and information. Western Union gave the Associated

Press preferential discounts on its dispatches, and the AP pledged to give all of its business to the telegraphic giant. Many Americans regarded this double-headed monopoly as a menace to key republican institutions, specifically the independence of the press and the well-informed electorate. Many feared that the arrangement would cut off the independent news sources or put Western Union in a position to dictate the editorial stance of newspapers and other information media.

Between 1866 and 1900 reformers repeatedly called upon the government to establish a postal telegraph network to compete with Western Union. The more radical called for Congress to nationalize the telegraph industry completely. They hoped to defeat the high rates charged to private citizens using the telegraph for social and personal messages, and noted that the present rate structure made the telegraph primarily a medium for press and business correspondence. Congress considered over 70 reform bills in this period, but failed to keep the alliance of the Associated Press and Western Union from becoming what may be called the nation's first industrial monopoly.

Although reformers failed to reach their ultimate goal of ending Western Union's monopoly over telegraphic communications, they achieved some lasting success. By the 1890s, their efforts had helped to establish government regulation as an important middle ground between state ownership of an important networked technology and its operation by untrammeled private capitalists. Regulation was a pervasive and persistent notion that Progressives—both the political party and social progressives—relied upon to work out the proper economic role of the federal government after the turn of the century, especially in the communications, transportation, and electrical power sectors.

By the outbreak of the Civil War, the telegraph network had also helped to set in motion an unmistakable trend toward the centralization of commodities trading on the floors of the large boards of trade. The introduction of the telegraphic market ticker in 1868 dramatically accelerated this trend. The ticker—an invention patented by Thomas Edison—provided brokers across the country with a printed transcript of trades on exchange floors almost immediately after they had happened, and allowed them to react in a matter of minutes to price movements occurring hundreds of miles away. In this way the telegraphic network and the ticker may have abetted the rise of speculation and finance capitalism during the so-called Gilded Age. The ticker actuated a latent demand for real-time news and financial information, a major growth market of the telegraph industry in the final quarter of the nineteenth century. By the 1880s several thousand bankers and brokers across the country subscribed to Western Union's ticker service, which broadcast up-to-the-minute stock, gold, grain, cotton, and oil quotations as well as financial and political news.

Western Union's ticker service was in many ways the first mass news and entertainment broadcast medium. Not only did the ticker carry financial information, but it also had intimate connections to other economic activities, especially gambling. After the mid-1870s Western Union transmitted sporting news of all varieties, including the results of horse races, rowing matches, boxing bouts, and baseball games. Many subscribers to these services were establishments of questionable morality or legality, like saloons and betting parlors, located in working-class neighborhoods of the large cities. By the turn of the century, the many tickers carried play-by-play or blow-by-blow coverage of sports events, and Western Union paid generously for their exclusive broadcast rights. Although its designers originally intended it as a tool for speculators, market traders, and financiers, the ticker also played an important role in the formation of urban working-class mass culture in the nineteenth and early-twentieth century (Hochfelder 2006, 310–13).

HEALTH AND MEDICINE

Germs and Vaccines

Louis Pasteur's discovery that germs existed and caused infection was to reform medicine and health care. Pasteur was a research chemist and Dean of the School of Science at the University of Lille in 1856 when he was asked to investigate the souring of beer at one of the many local breweries. Using a microscope to analyze samples taken from the vats, Pasteur found them teeming with thousands of tiny microorganisms. He continued his studies using milk, wine, and vinegar, and he became convinced that the organisms were the cause rather than the result of the souring. This idea ran counter to the accepted theory of putrefaction (souring, infection, etc.), which held that the organisms were the result of the process having been spontaneously generated from within the substance. Pasteur believed the organisms were airborne.

Although the scientific community generally ridiculed his theory, Pasteur was appointed Director of Scientific Studies at the Ecôle Normale in Paris in 1857. Continuing and refining his research, in 1864 Pasteur explained his beliefs before a gathering of scientists at the University of Paris. In his lecture he did a creditable job of laying out his case for outside infection, and even some in the audience who had refused to believe him thereafter came away convinced that germs and other invading microorganisms were the active agents of many biological processes—both good and bad.

Pasteur's work in the laboratory led to his process, known as pasteurization, for ridding milk of bacteria though quick heating and cooling; but the process was also applied to the preservation of wine and beer, and the production of distinct types of cheese. In 1865, Pasteur was asked to investigate the cause of a disease in silkworms, which he also determined to be a microorganism. From this investigation he came to believe that epidemic diseases such as typhoid and cholera could be spread by germs. He knew of the work of Edward Jenner with respect to the prevention of smallpox by vaccination (the variolation process explained hereafter), and he hoped to do the same with other diseases for which he could find a pathogen (infecting organism). Pasteur had lost two of his own children to typhoid; and he attempted, but failed, to isolate the infectious agent that caused an outbreak of cholera in Marseilles in 1865. He firmly believed nonetheless that a vaccine could be found for all diseases.

Jenner's work had involved the observation that those having survived a serious disease seemed to have acquired an immunity from further infection. Jenner found that persons afflicted with a weak strain of smallpox known as cow pox seldom died of the more serious disease. He therefore reasoned that exposure to the dried pus of smallpox lesions would create an immunity to the more virulent form of the disease. By 1840, Jenner's methods were well-established and the only ones recognized by the British government. Jenner's process of variolation had many forms. One of these consisted of removing pus and fluid from a smallpox lesion and placing it under the skin of the person to be vaccinated with a series of needle pricks (scarification). Another was to have the person inhale the dried and pulverized scab material through the nose—an early form of inhalant that worked because the nose is rich in blood-carrying tissues; and finally there was the introduction of fluid directly into the vein through injection with a hypodermic needle. The process of vaccination (the terms vaccination and vaccine come from the Latin "vacca" for cow) had various effects ranging from mild illness to death, but across the treated population mortality and sickness from the disease decreased markedly.

Pasteur was initially disappointed that he had made no further progress toward identifying the agents of human disease during the decade of the 1870s, but a chance meeting with the German biologist Robert Koch in 1880 led Pasteur to establish a team of research scientists (as Koch had done) to attack the problem. Pasteur had often worked alone, but he now added his efforts to those of Dr. Emile Roux and Dr. Charles Chamberland who brought a great deal of recent medical knowledge to the team that Pasteur lacked as a chemist. Almost immediately the team developed a series of vaccines for chicken cholera, anthrax, and rabies.

The mechanism by which vaccines worked was generally misunderstood or unknown at the time of their discovery. However, modern science recognizes that infectious organisms carry proteins called antigens that stimulate an immune response in patient. This brings on an initial feeling of illness before the disease takes hold. The immune response is multistage and includes the time-consuming synthesis of proteins in the afflicted person known as antibodies. The antibodies attack and kill the invading germs with varying degrees of success. If the patient is strong the antibodies have the time and the numbers to defeat the invaders; if not, the invaders destroy the host organism and the patient succumbs. Vaccination with weakened strains of disease-causing organisms stimulates the production of antibodies in the vaccinated patient as well as creating so-called memory cells that remain in the blood stream ready to fight off specific infections, sometimes for the life span of the patient. So quick is the body's response through the memory cells that the symptoms of infection are often prevented and even weak patients (the very young and very old) can summon the strength to survive. It was the production of these memory cells in those initially surviving attacks of smallpox and other diseases that explained their naturally acquired immunity.

Some immunity can be transferred to infants through mother's milk, but only for those disease antibodies present therein to which the mother has been exposed. Infections such as Asiatic influenza (the flu) or the common cold (a rhinovirus) come in many distinct types making naturally acquired immunity against all of them difficult if not impossible. Native American populations—never exposed to European style measles or poxes—were often wiped out as epidemics swept their villages because they had no natural immunity.

A little more must be said of Dr. Robert Koch, who had begun a quest to defeat disease in a small laboratory in his physician's office in Berlin in 1872. The first disease he attacked was anthrax in sheep for which he found a long-lived spore to be the infectious agent. In 1878, he moved on to human diseases identifying the germs that caused blood poisoning (septicemia, or bacterial infection of the blood stream) and tuberculosis by 1882. It was not until 1893 that Koch isolated the largely waterborne bacterial cause of cholera, *Vibrio cholerae asiatica*, which enters the body through the mouth in contaminated drinking water and causes an infection in the intestine. Contaminated water does not necessarily appear unclean to the naked eye. Death results (often within a few hours of the first signs of illness) from dehydration caused by diarrhea and vomiting.

Koch's most meaningful work, however, was in the area of laboratory technique. He devised a method for staining organisms with methyl violet dye so that they could be better studied under a microscope. He perfected a medium for growing research samples of microorganisms made from potato starch and gelatin; and he developed a protocol for proving which of several organisms present in patients actually caused their disease. By 1900, Koch and his team had identified 21 disease-causing germs in as many years.

—*James M. Volo*

Infant Mortality and Milk

Prior to the Civil War, women who could not breast-feed or who shunned the idea or expense of hiring a wet nurse, fed their children straight cow's milk or put together formulas based on contemporary assumptions of what constituted a healthy diet for infants. When fresh milk was not available, there were two forms of patented canned milk available after 1856: plain condensed milk and a sweetened variety. The sweetened types had a lower protein value, and physicians recommended adding cod liver oil or meat broth to formulas made with it. A new industry developed providing formulas for upper- and middle-class mothers and their children through a system of processing centers and daily distribution networks. Commercially produced infant formulas were advertised as scientifically calculated and healthful for child and mother; but they were mostly expensive and generally no more healthful than those that parents could formulate at home.

During the later part of the nineteenth century many working-class mothers gave up breast-feeding and adopted the practice of feeding their infants cow's milk because it freed them to take employment outside the home. Unfortunately, clean, inexpensive milk was not easily available in the tenements and poorer urban neighborhoods. Nonetheless, poor and immigrant mothers often shared the fashionable knowledge that cow's milk based formulas were a better source of nutrition than that which nature provided, and it seemingly helped their children gain weight and grow faster.

The advent of refrigerated railroad cars allowed milk from the hinterland to be transported to city centers where it was processed in large factories. Unfortunately, not all of these concerns were run by upstanding men. It was not unusual for the milk to be adulterated with ground chalk and mixed with water to expand its volume. While this was dishonest, the chalk and water rarely posed an imminent health risk to children other than it might lead mothers to unknowingly undernourish their children.

However, there was inherent in this system a silent and hidden killer. Contaminated milk was truly a danger to the infants who were given it and was likely a contributing factor to the astounding infant mortality rates of cities such as Boston's 43 percent in 1830 and New York's 50 percent in 1839. Prior to the work of Louis Pasteur and Robert Koch connecting illness to bacteria, diseases such as marasmus (protein deficiency in infants) or scrofula (a form of tuberculosis) were thought to arise from a fundamental weakness of the body or through an inherited predisposition such as weak lungs or a frail constitution. Unfortunately, urban and suburban dairy farmers short of grazing for their cows often used distillery waste (mash left over from the production of beer and alcohol) and slaughterhouse waste (collectively known as swill) as a feed supplement for their cows. These dairy cows often contracted diseases—particularly a type of bovine tuberculosis—that could infect humans who drank the so-called swill milk.

Most of these bacteria could be killed by pasteurization, but prior to 1882 the milk supply was generally not tested, and much of it remained unpasteurized. Moreover, even if the milk were unadulterated and germfree, it was often handled in a haphazard and unsafe manner by well-meaning, but careless merchants and consumers unaware of the health consequences. They often stored the milk in open vats or reused containers and bottles between customers without first scalding or sterilizing them. Diseases such as tuberculosis, diphtheria, and other communicable diseases might be unknowingly spread in this manner through whole neighborhoods served by a single dealer.

Infants were particularly vulnerable to such diseases, especially diarrhea that caused chronic dehydration. In 1861, the New York Sanitary Association pointed out the apparent connection between milk quality and infant death, but nothing was done largely because the owners of the milk plants were major contributors to the political machine known as Tammany Hall. In 1866, New York City recognized the wider problem of adulterated and unsanitary foods and beverages, and formed the Metropolitan Board of Health to regulate the manufacturers. The board recognized not only the problems posed by milk, but also the risks inherent in livestock manure and slaughterhouse refuse contaminating the water supply in highly urbanized areas. Although political corruption continued to limit the effectiveness of the Board of Health, in 1869, a sanitary code was put in place that banned the presence of livestock and slaughterhouses from densely populated areas of Manhattan (generally below present-day Times Square at 42nd Street). The code also provided for the inspection of butcher shops and milk dealers who did business in the city with regard to their adherence to proper sanitary procedures.

James M. Volo

FOR MORE INFORMATION

Browne, Ray B., and Lawrence A. Kreiser Jr. *The Civil War and Reconstruction*. Westport, CT: Greenwood Press, 2003.

Casper, Scott E., Joan Chaison, and Jeffery D. Groves, eds. *Perspectives on American Book History: Artifacts and Commentary*. Amherst: University of Massachusetts Press, 2002.

Duffy, John. *A History of Public Health in New York City*. New York: Russell Sage Foundation, 1968.

Hochfelder, David. "The Communications Revolution." In *A Companion to 19th-Century America*, ed. William L. Barney. Malden, MA: Blackwell Publishing, 2006.

Hofstadter, Richard, and Wilson Smith, eds. *American Higher Education, A Documentary History*. Chicago, IL: The University of Chicago Press, 1968.

Jefferson, Dorothy L. "Child Feeding in the United States in the 19th Century." In *Award Essays: A Compilation of Essays*, ed. Lydia J. Roberts. Chicago, IL: American Dietetic Association, 1968.

Johnson, Clifton. *Old-Time Schools and School-books*. New York: Dover Publications, 1963.

Kelley, R. Gordon, ed. *Children's Periodicals of the United States*. Westport, CT: Greenwood Press, 1984.

Marcy, Randolph B. *The Prairie Traveler, A Hand-book for Overland Expeditions*. Bedford, MA: Applewood Books, 1993. Reprint of the 1859 edition.

Mason, Philip P., ed. *Copper Country Journal: The Diary of Schoolmaster Henry Hobart, 1863–1864*. Detroit, MI: Wayne State University Press, 1991.

McClary, Andrew. *Toys with Nine Lives, A Social History of American Toys*. North Haven, CT: Linnet Books, 1997.

Mondale, Sarah, and Sarah B. Patton, eds. *School: The Story of American Public Education*. Boston, MA: Beacon Press, 2001.

Mott, Frank Luther. *A History of American Magazines*. 5 vols. Cambridge, MA: Harvard University Press, 1930–1968.

Parkman, Francis. *The Oregon Trail*. New York: Lancer Books, 1968. Reprint of the 1849 edition.

Quay, Sara E. *Westward Expansion*. Westport, CT: Greenwood Press, 2002.

Shrock, Joel. *The Gilded Age*. Westport, CT: Greenwood Press, 2004.

Tebbel, John, and Mary Ellen Zuckerman. *The Magazine in America, 1741–1990*. New York: Oxford University Press, 1991.

Timmons, Todd. *Science and Technology in Nineteenth-Century America*. Westport, CT: Greenwood Press, 2005.

Volo, Dorothy Denneen and James M. Volo. *Daily Life in Civil War America*. Westport, CT: Greenwood Press, 1998.

———. *Family Life in Nineteenth-Century America*. Westport, CT: Greenwood Press, 2007.

Weisberger, Bernard A. *The LIFE History of the United States: Steel and Steam, Volume 7: 1877–1890*. New York: Time Life Books, 1975.

Wood, Alice L. "The History of Artificial Feeding of Infants." In *Award Essays: A Compilation of Essays*, ed. Lydia J. Roberts. Chicago, IL: American Dietetic Association, 1968.

Material Life

FOOD

On the Immigrant Trail

The need to properly provision oneself and one's family for a transcontinental journey was almost overwhelming in terms of its possible consequences—deprivation, starvation, or even death. The food that was taken, prepared, and consumed along the immigrant trails of the West was both familiar and inventive, combining the best kind of tried-and-true recipes with the need for creativity based on the availability of unfamiliar local ingredients. Whether the meal was meant to feed a family of pioneers who had stopped along their journey or a cowboy getting ready to move his cattle northward, food along the trail consisted of available ingredients cooked with the most rudimentary utensils.

When immigrants set out for the West, they carried with them supplies that would ostensibly last for the duration of the journey. Guidebooks like Joseph E. Ware's *The Emigrant's Guide to California* (1849) stated that for each traveler the following food should be packed: "a barrel of flour or 180 lbs of ship biscuit that is kiln dried, 150 to 180 lbs of bacon, 25 lbs. coffee, 40 lbs sugar, 25 lbs. rice, 60 lbs. beans or peas, a keg of clear cooked beef...a keg of lard, 30 to 40 lbs. of dried peaches or apples, also some molasses and vinegar." Food for the journey was stored carefully in the wagon, and pioneers prudently planned to store enough food to last for several months of the arduous trip. Midway through her journey, Sallie Hester recorded that they lived on bacon, ham, rice, dried fruits, molasses, packed butter, bread, coffee and tea, and as they had their own cows, milk. She noted that occasionally, some of the men killed an antelope and they would then have a feast. Fish was sometimes eaten on Sundays. During the journey the immigrants were forced to adopt new ways of cooking and eating. One diarist noted that although there was not much to cook, there was a good deal of difficulty and inconvenience in doing it. The problem was that by the time one had squatted around the fire and cooked bread and bacon having made several trips to and from the wagon, washed the dishes with no place to drain them, and gotten things ready for an early morning breakfast, some of the others had already had their night caps on and it was time to go to bed.

Cooking and eating outdoors was a challenge, but immigrants became accustomed to living within the confines of their wagons, and to eating only what they had brought with them or what they could find along the way. They found effective ways to make the most of what was available. During the daily lunchtime stop, called nooning, animals were given a break from walking, men were given the chance to hunt for fresh meat or fish, and women and children quickly learned the value of collecting buffalo chips. Euphemistically called chips, buffalo dung was commonly used along the trail as fuel. Collecting buffalo chips became a daily activity that helped pioneers cope with the lack of wood necessary to create a fire over which to cook and around which to keep warm. Buffalo chips caused an unpleasant odor and sometimes affected the taste of the food. In dry weather they made a hot fire, but they burned quickly. When wet, they hardly burned at all and had to be fanned to keep the fire burning.

Immigrants found other creative ways to combine the experience of traveling with the necessity of eating. In an effort to have fresh butter throughout the trip, for instance, many immigrants took advantage of the rocking motion of the wagon to create a natural type of butter churn. One traveler wrote that milk was carried in a can that was swung from the wagon bows overhead. By noon there was a ball of butter the size of a hickory nut and innumerable little ones like shot.

While much of the trip westward was long and tiring, food became part of the celebrations that broke up the journey, bringing relief to the monotony of the crossing. Many travelers aimed to arrive at Independence Rock on the Fourth of July, thereby being able to celebrate the holiday at one of the landmark sites of the voyage. Special foods were saved for this day, part and parcel of the trend among Westerners to observe Independence Day with enthusiasm and joy. Toward the end, pioneers prepared special meals and desserts, using what they had to turn an ordinary day and meal into an extraordinary marker of their pursuit of a new life in the West.

Natural resources, including wild fruits and vegetables, provided another form of easy-to-come-by fare for hungry travelers. At least in the early years of immigration, before the land had been depleted, fruits, berries, and herbs could be picked from the trees or pulled from the ground along the way. Indeed, the move to Western settlements was promoted in part by the promise that the unsettled regions of the continent contained an abundance of natural resources that could be used as food. Meat was also available in the course of the journey. Antelope, prairie dogs, and buffalo could be killed and served for the evening meal. In places like Death Valley, salt could be picked up in great lumps in the sand while in other regions freshly caught fish could be incorporated into the pioneer diet. Minnie Miller recounted that prairie chickens and sage hens were plentiful.

Efficiency was a concern of most travelers, for food supplies tended to dwindle long before the trip was over and fatigue made the daily effort of cooking difficult. Time-saving strategies were common. Beans, for instance, were a mainstay of most immigrant parties as they could be cooked all night, mixed with meat scraps and eaten at lunch and dinner the following day. Equally popular were portable foods such as pemmican (a mixture of meat and fruit) and jerked meat. Pocket soup was stock made from veal or pig's feet, dried to the consistency of solid glue that could be stored for years then reconstituted when dissolved in hot water. Canned goods were welcomed, once they became available, as was anything that could help nourish immigrants who were far from places where basic foods could be quickly and easily replenished.

The need to keep food on hand throughout the lengthy journey was aided by trading posts that were located sporadically along the major travel routes and that provided travelers with the opportunity to restock essential supplies. Settlers who were already established in cabins, dugouts, and adobe buildings along the way shared what they could with passersby. Along the trail, pioneers also described how sharing cooking supplies and ideas helped them form new connections and relationships during the long journey, relieving some of the anxiety and isolation that accompanied the departure from family members, towns, and homes in the East (Quay 2002, 111–14).

Settlers' Food

Settlers were resourceful and used what they had. Vegetable gardens were planted as soon as possible. In summer, what fresh produce might be had was supplemented by wild greens such as sheep sorrel and buffalo peas. Children subject to a diet containing few fresh fruits and vegetables sometimes developed scurvy. Those who settled near wooded areas found wild honey, berries, plums, persimmons, pokeweed, dandelions, and lamb's quarters. Crushed green hickory nuts produced a buttery substance, which tasted good on cornbread. Stored root vegetables were all that was available in winter. The sap from hickory logs was saved for the children, who called it hickory goody. Many different kinds of bread, from streusel and crumpets to cracklin' bread, were made from the same basic recipe. While most bread started with cornmeal, rye, wheat, or acorn, flour might also be added. Lack of verdant pasture during the winter usually caused the cows to go dry, leaving the homesteader without milk. Eggs were preserved by immersing them in a combination of water and potassium silicate or sodium silicate and keeping them covered in a cool location. The availability of game on the prairie decreased as time passed and by the 1870s buffalo, once abundant, was scarce. All parts of what meat was available were used. Meat was soaked overnight to remove the gamey taste. Very tough cuts were soaked for several days in a mixture of vinegar, water, and spices. For those who settled near water, fish became an important source of protein. Settlers also harvested such wild birds as the prairie hen, duck, and wild turkey. Fuel was scarce on the prairie. Sod house cooking was done with the help of a hot box, a covered wooden box large enough to hold a boiling pot and keep its heat so that it continued to cook while conserving fuel.

Pioneer cooking required great creativity to deal with the limited ingredients. Sometimes even the sorghum molasses used in place of sugar was unavailable and settlers turned to pumpkin or watermelon juice boiled into syrup instead. Lacking lemons, pioneer women baked mock lemon pie using vinegar instead of lemon juice. Poor farmers who could not give up their coffee used coffee substitutes such as parched barley, rye, or wheat, okra seeds, dried carrots, or coffee essence—a mixture of squash and pumpkin baked very dark and put in the pot and boiled for 15 minutes. Hot beverages and medicines were brewed from roots, barks, and leaves such as sassafras and mint. The poor also found meals monotonous. *The Nebraska Farmer* of January 1862 printed 33 different ways of cooking corn (Better Homes and Gardens 1974, 179, 182–88).

With no refrigerators or even iceboxes, food had to be preserved. Fruits were gathered fully ripe and placed in handy containers such as barrels, tubs, or jars, and covered with pure spring water. The scum that formed on the surface functioned like the paraffin of jam makers. Everything that could be dried was, including beans, corn, rhubarb, berries, even pumpkins. Home canning was not common on the frontier, so fresh tomatoes were put in barrels with strong brine and kept submerged by weighted boards. Some fruits were preserved by boiling sweets, though sugar was rare, and was usually replaced by molasses or honey. A Kansas homesteader, Howard Ruede, complained that he had a hard time with meat flies and reported having taken thousands of eggs off the ham. Lacking a smoky place to keep the ham, the flies would get inside the paper in which the ham was wrapped. After the Civil War canned goods made their way on to the Plains. One observer noted that bachelor huts were always surrounded by a rusting pile of cans. Where there was a woman to do the cooking, there were fewer cans as most farm wives considered canned goods unthrifty.

Settlers' meals, like everything else in their life, were functional. They needed to fuel the body with enough calories for an arduous day's work. Hamlin Garland described harvest work punctuated by meals—breakfast of flapjacks, sausages, and coffee; a midmorning lunch of milk, cheese and fresh fried-cakes, brought to the fields by his sister; a noon dinner of boiled beef and potatoes and supper at six. The Garlands were fortunate, however, for many families lived on the edge of starvation, especially in bad crop years (Jones 1998, 199–200).

Chuck Wagons and Cowboy Cooks

Some of the best food of the westward expansion period was prepared by the cowboys and chuck wagon cooks who created meals on the open prairie. Cowboy cooks were especially popular at the height of trail drives during which herds of cattle were moved from Texas to northern destinations where they could be sold at market. While the setting was simple, and the ingredients basic, the cowboy meal was known for its flavor and heartiness. Consisting of coffee, meat in the form of beef, salt pork, or bacon (also called overland trout), bread, and possibly a sweet dessert, cowboy cuisine was a cultural phenomenon in its own right complete with dialect, customs, and characters.

The cook, whose skill determined the success of the daily menu and the satisfaction of the cowhands who depended on him for their meals, was a central figure and distinct personality in the life of a cowboy camp. Among the rugged cowboys, the cook provided an interesting combination of manly camaraderie and domestic ability. Indeed, in a type of role reversal that appeared across the frontier in various forms, the male cook was known for a culinary expertise that overshadowed the domestic skills of many frontier women.

Part and parcel of the cook's stereotypical image was the process by which he completed his tasks. While early cooks prepared meals over open fire, in the 1860s the iconic chuck wagon came into existence. The chuck wagon began as a sort of cupboard on wheels and evolved into a more elaborate system that included fold-down tables and enough cubbies and hangers to hold the pots, spices, utensils, and other materials needed to feed the cowhands. Chuck wagons could be personalized with pictures and other decorations, but the vehicles were primarily functional. Market demand in the mid-1880s led the Studebaker Brothers Manufacturing Company of South Bend, Indiana, to produce the Round-up Wagon, especially designed for feeding hungry cowboys in the field. Priced at $200, the sturdy 1888 model was equipped with zinc-lined mess boxes front and rear.

The culture of the chuck wagon, with its cook and its food, was unique and in keeping with the overall rugged existence of the cowboy. Meals were offered three times a day. The call to mealtime, or grub, took the form of ditties, loud sounds, and no-nonsense words. The cook might clange lids together or shoute out calls of "Grub!" and "Roll out and bite the biscuit" (Quay 2002, 114–16).

Despite the fact that these meals were unceremoniously served in the rugged outdoors, there was a definite etiquette. No one would ever tie up his horse to the chuck wagon. Horsehair was an unwelcome addition even on the plains. No one was allowed to use the cook's workbench. Cowboys used their lap, bedroll, or a convenient rock for a table. No food was dished out until the cook called chow. Hands served themselves taking all they could eat at the first helping. Second helpings came only after everyone had gotten their first. Care was taken that the lid to any pot never touched the dirt, and the cowhand would make sure to stand downwind lest he kick up dust on someone else's food (Better Homes and Gardens 1974, 198).

Typical fare included meat that, if not fresh, was salted or dried as jerky. Beans, usually the red pinto beans known as frijoles, were boiled or fried in the tradition of Mexican cuisine. Bread could take the form of biscuits, corn bread, or sourdough bread. Sample menus included beans, roast beef, boiled potatoes, short ribs with onions, and a stew made of the marrow from beef bones sautéed in hot grease, then boiled with potatoes. Charlie Siringo remembered one of his favorite meals was calf ribs broiled by the campfire and a large Dutch oven full of loin, sweetbread and heart, all smothered in flour gravy. Desserts might include stewed fruit, spice cake made without eggs or butter or simmered rice and raisins. More simply it might be lick, molasses or Karo syrup drizzled over canned tomatoes and leftover biscuits, or yellow cling peaches in syrup straight from the can. Pickles were a real treat in a diet noticeably lacking in fresh vegetables and depending heavily on prairie strawberries—beans (Jones 1998, 175–76). As with other examples of the frontier fondness for expressive names, popular meals were given colorful titles such as "Sun-of-a-Gun Stew," "Spotted Pup Rice Pudding," "Six-shooter Coffee," and "Pigeons in Disguise" (Quay 2002, 116).

Meals were cooked using Dutch ovens and cast-iron skillets that, by the 1890s could be ordered by mail from catalogs like that of Sears, Roebuck. Every meal was prepared using the same set of utensils with the bread mixed up in the dishpan. Recipes were simple. One cook recalled a biscuit recipe that was written, "Flr, Wt, bk s, mix well, cook over a fair fire till done." Measurements used such vague amounts as a handful, a scoop, a dipper, a smidgen, a bit, and a pinch (Quay 2002, 116).

If there was one crucial part of the cowboy meal, it was the coffee that was consumed in large quantities at virtually all cowboy spreads. Large pots of coffee were kept hot on the fire throughout the day and cowboys refilled their cups as often as they desired. If a man got up to refill his cup, another hand might call out man at the pot and the thirsty man would then be obliged to refill all the cups that were held out to him. The coffee was known for being strong and black, and a handful of ground coffee per cup was not an unusual recipe to ensure the drink's strength (Quay 2002, 116). Most cowboys did not drink their coffee straight. As white sugar was rarely available, granulated brown sugar was used, or a cook might sweeten the brew with molasses. The granulated brown sugar often became so hard in its barrel that it had to be chipped free and then run through a meat grinder before it could be used. On the range the coffee was often brewed with water collected from bogs, where streams had been dammed up for cattle to drink (Jones 1998, 176).

Some cooks roasted their own beans, but as factory-roasted beans became more available, the purchase of ready-to-use coffee became a more common practice. Manufacturers, recognizing a strong market for coffee products in the West, took advantage of the demand by creating brands especially geared for those consumers who lived on the trail (Quay 2002, 116).

Arbuckle Brothers Company of Pittsburgh, Pennsylvania, became the leading coffee provider to the West by creating fresh, easy-to-use coffee products with strong brand recognition. The 1873 trademark for the brand that Arbuckle targeted in the West, Ariosa, featured a flying angel. Toward the end of the century Arbuckle's included a stick of peppermint candy in each package, and in 1893, collector's trading cards featuring animals, countries of the world, U.S. states, and recipes. Two years later they began to offer coupons redeemable for any dozens of premiums, ranging from lace curtains and wedding rings to Torrey razors and small caliber revolvers. During the 1890s the company exchanged 108 million coupons annually for some 4 million premiums, including 100,000 wedding rings, 819,000 handkerchiefs, and 186,000 razors. Coffee was such an important staple in the cowboy diet, and the Arbuckle's did such a good job of promoting their product, that the coupons became widely recognized by Westerners, and were even used on occasion as a form of currency at local stores (Pierce 1995, 121).

Besides the cowboy who worked on the trail, there were also cooks who fed the cowhands on large ranches. Here, just as on the trail, the cook reigned supreme over his cooking facilities. The big advantage was that he had much better circumstances in which to prepare the food. In addition to more and better equipment, he did not have to worry about the dust, dirt, and rain. During the meal, eating was the main activity and there was generally little conversation. After dinner, if the cook permitted, the men would hang around for storytelling and perhaps some music (Better Homes and Gardens 1974, 204).

—*Dorothy Denneen Volo*

Eating Out

While life on the trail demanded creativity and patience in the planning, preparation, and consumption of meals, eating establishments known for providing Westerners with excellent food and drink were an important part of frontier life. Even the most makeshift town had at least one local saloon in which miners and townspeople gathered to drink and eat. With the completion of the transcontinental railroad, new opportunities arose to feed Westerners and to develop uniquely western cuisine. Such trends made their mark on the western landscape and set the stage for continuing patterns in the popular culture of frontier foods.

The local saloon was the central meeting place for most Western towns, especially in the early years of expansion following the gold rush. The saloon was a site of socializing, eating, and, most importantly, drinking. Whiskey was the drink of choice and was made from a wide range of ingredients, sometimes whatever was at hand. The shot glass itself had its origins in the frontier saloon, where it was used as a vehicle for quickly consuming the alcoholic beverage of one's choice.

While saloon owners were not at a loss for customers, they did find ways to entice passersby into one bar rather than another, by offering a free lunch or entertainment. One period chronicler reported that it was commonplace to find a free lunch and a free supper in the more important California ballrooms where anyone could walk in and take luncheon or supper gratis. He certified the viands were of good quality, were well cooked, and served by attentive waiters. There were several courses from which to choose, or the patron could take a portion of each. Soup, fish, made-dishes, joints, and vegetables were all on the bill of fare of the free lunch. At the free supper the variety was equally great. Although there was no charge for the food, it was understood that anyone who partook of the meals would drink afterward (Quay 2002, 118–19).

Ironically, fine dining on the frontier turned out to be very different than in more settled parts of the country. Elite restaurants popped up quickly in frontier areas such as Tombstone, Arizona, Virginia City, Nevada, and Georgetown, Colorado. Fine restaurants serving French haute cuisine on the frontier soon came to rely on the business of the average miner who was more likely to spend money on expensive dinners than most working-class Americans due to their boomtown, get-rich-quick mentality. When precious metal reserves ran out, some of the first businesses to close were fine dining establishments (Shrock 2004, 112–13).

With the rare exception, early westward travel was known for the paucity of good food available during the trip. One traveler reported that from Red River to El Paso there were few accommodations for eating beyond what were afforded by the company stations to their own employees. He suggested that travelers carry with them as much durable food as possible. As train travel became increasingly popular, the problem of good food became one that entrepreneurial Westerners sought to solve. Prior to the invention to the Pullman sleeping and dining cars, travelers would stop at predetermined places along the railroad line and eat their meals at restaurants that served the area. While some of these services provided fine food with equally fine service, they were inconsistent, and unpredictable, and cost travelers time from their journey. Two developments met different aspects of these problems, namely the Pullman dining car and the Harvey restaurant chain.

The dining car was revolutionary in several ways. First, it allowed passengers to take their meals while the train continued to move, thereby saving them from having to stop several times a day on the lengthy journey across the country. Second, the opportunity to eat on the train in a car specially designed for the purpose provided travelers with a pleasant diversion from the monotony of the cross-continental trip. Travelers found much to celebrate in the ritual of having three prepared meals a day, served in style in the dining car as the scenery rushed by outside the window.

In 1876, 41-year-old Fred Harvey changed the face of Western restaurants and travel fare when he opened the first of his popular Harvey lunchrooms along the Sante Fe Railroad line. Harvey's mission was to provide travelers with good food served at modest prices in pleasant environments. Train conductors wired ahead to let the cooks know how many meals to prepare, and the food was hot and waiting when passengers disembarked. The lunchrooms were well designed, and the meat was first-rate, acquired from the best Western stockyards and cooked by the best chefs available.

The setting and the food helped to seal the success of Harvey's restaurant, as did the well-run service that featured the popular Harvey Girls as waitresses. Harvey Girls were well-paid employees, easily recognized by the crisp black uniforms that distinguished them from the customers. Harvey asked the waitresses to sign a contract stating that they would uphold the rules of the establishment, not get married for at least a year, and live in the housing provided by the business. Not only were the waitresses held to high standards, but the customers were as well. For instance, Harvey required men to wear coats before being served in the restaurant. He expected his customers to act in appropriate fashion for a public eating place. As Harvey's restaurants gained name recognition and critical approval, new franchises were opened on different parts of the railroad's cross-country route, making Fred Harvey's name nearly synonymous with Western travel. By promoting the enjoyment of eating, Harvey restaurants became destinations in and of themselves and provided a model for other chain restaurants that would develop across the country (Quay 2002, 119–21).

—*Dorothy Denneen Volo*

Eating in Town

The process by which towns developed during the westward expansion depended to a great extent on where immigrants settled and whether or not they remained there. During the gold rush, these factors were determined by where gold was discovered and how long it could be successfully mined. In these cases food would be brought to the town and sold in boomtown establishments that could disappear overnight. For pioneer families, the homestead might be miles from the nearest store and, as a result, trips to town to shop became focal points of the family outing. In either case, food was not as easy to come by as it had been in the East, and patterns of purchasing, storing, cooking, and consuming food developed in response to the new challenges of frontier life.

Western settlements depended on their own resources such as farm-raised crops and animals for much of their food. Whether supplies were brought to the farm, or whether the family went to town and brought items back to the home, the general store was the center of food shopping in the Old West. If the general store did not have the desired products, the mail-order catalog served as a useful alternative.

Providing consumers with access to food that was not always easy to find at the local market, catalogs allowed pioneers to have products delivered by mail to remote locations. One pioneer woman claimed that when you lived more than 90 miles from town, a Montgomery Ward or Sears Roebuck catalog got read more than the Bible or Shakespeare.

If Westerners could find what they needed to make appetizing meals in the local store or mail-order catalog, they could not always afford to buy them. Inflation was a rampant problem in the West, leading to wildly different prices from town-to-town and from day-to-day. Because of the effort to bring food to remote locations, the difficulty involved in keeping it fresh, and the desire to make a profit from a captive audience, the high price of food was a regular topic of conversation among early Westerners. Reflecting the gold rush mentality of feast or famine, immigrants paid the exorbitant prices when they could, often spending all of their daily earnings and more on basic necessities of food and drink (Quay 2002, 121–23).

Recipes

While most vegetables, meats, and grains were purchased or picked fresh from Western farms, the tin can became a convenient way to serve food that would be impossible to keep fresh in other forms. Immigrants, miners, cowboys, and other participants in the process of westward expansion found tin cans useful, and canned products became so common that everyone lived out of cans. You could see great heaps of them outside of every little shack. Cans became so ubiquitous on the California mining frontier that tin dumps made their first appearance in the 1850s.

Recipes quickly became the focal point of western cooks. Pioneers shared recipes with one another, borrowing ideas and culinary tips that helped them produce the best food they could in a setting that lacked the resources Easterners were used to having at their disposal. Recipes were handed down from generation to generation, and cookbooks from the states were the source of many a successful—if slightly adapted—meal. Newspapers, too, provided information about the most popular recipes, the newest ingredients, and the best cooking methods (Quay 2002, 123–24).

Community Eating

Food was an important focus of Western communities and was frequently incorporated into social gatherings and public events. Barn raising, quilting, corn husking, and other work-related activities, known commonly as bees, were designed to combine work with socializing. Townspeople would gather to collectively finish a task and then join together for a celebratory meal.

Few congregations could afford to pay their ministers very well and the church social proved to be an enjoyable and effective way to generate funds and to augment the meager salary of the frontier minister. Church members prepared and donated food. There was always an abundance of fried chicken, steaming vegetables, home-canned pickles and fruits, and delicious desserts. The meal was served family style on plank tables, outside in the summer and in the church basement in the winter. The cost was affordable, usually $.25 for adults and $.10 for children for the all-you-can-eat meal. Although it was a community event, there was often a social order to the division of labor. Matrons of higher social status often served at the dessert table while members with less social clout washed the dishes and served at the tables.

During the wheat harvest, threshing crews, which consisted of the men who ran the machinery plus neighborhood farmers who traded work, sometimes numbered as many as 50 people. Feeding so many was a monumental task for the women. Plank boards were laid across chairs to make sufficient tables. Platters of meat, potatoes, vegetables, bread, and jams were laid out. Workers often ate in shifts, and as one man finished, another took his place.

Stack cake became a traditional pioneer wedding cake. Guests brought a single layer of cake to the wedding, and the cake was assembled there with an applesauce made from either fresh or dried apples spread between each layer. It was said that the number of layers of cake was an indication of a bride's popularity. Guests were likely to bring a variety of different cakes, and the layers of the final stack were often variegated and flavored differently (Better Homes and Gardens 1974, 193, 188, 194).

Picnics were another food-centered event. Western picnics, while sometimes held on the open prairie or at local sites, were just as often held at a specific destination of interest, such as, among the redwood trees of California. Other social events that focused around food included the candy pull and the box lunch, both of which involved eating to encourage romance. The candy pull required men and women to work as partners, pulling the stretchy candy until it was smooth. They could also each put an end of the candy string into their mouths, eating their way toward one another along the length of the candy. Similarly, the box lunch was a form of fund-raising that allowed men to bid on lunches made by the townswomen (Quay 2002, 125–26).

International Influences

The presence of pioneers and travelers from a multitude of countries resulted in an eclectic mix of ingredients, recipes, and foods across the American West. The local eating establishments, which sprang up quickly in the West, reflected the melting pot of ethnic groups that had immigrated there. One Westerner reported an array of eateries that he found everywhere including the American tavern, French restaurant, the Spanish fonday and the Chinese chow-chow. Immigrants craved familiar cuisine in the new land. Western restaurants met the needs of more than just people seeking food from their countries of origin. They also introduced Westerners to a wide range of cuisines.

The impact of Mexican cuisine on frontier diets cannot be underestimated. Not only did the cowboys, pioneers, and miners who traveled through the Southwest inevitably come into contact with Mexican cooking, but they borrowed from the ingredients and recipes of the Mexicans with whom they interacted. Life in the Southwest meant an introduction to the taste and use of common Mexican ingredients like chilis and tortillas, as well as to dishes like colache, made from vegetables (Quay 2002, 119–27).

HOUSING: FRONTIER HOMES

The first home for most farmers arriving on the plains frontier was either a tar paper shack or a dugout. Most were small, only large enough to meet government requirements under legislation like the Homestead Act that demanded a minimum 10-foot by 12-foot structure. Such shacks were easy to build, requiring minimal materials: some cheap lumber for framing, a couple of rolls of tar paper, and some nails. They were flimsy, however, and if not anchored down might fly away in a high wind. To keep them warmer in winter, settlers often lined them with red or blue building paper, the color indicating the quality. The inferior red paper was thinner, costing $3 a roll, whereas the blue was twice as expensive. As further winter insulation, farmers often banked these structures with manure from the barn. During the summer the tar paper shacks were unbearably hot, as the black exterior absorbed the sun's rays.

Some people built an aboveground addition to the dugout, using its walls as a foundation for a sod house, or soddy. Most started from scratch. Often neighbors would gather for a house-raising bee and erect a house in a day. First, the sod was cut—2 1/2 inches was an ideal thickness—in strips 12 inches wide; these were then cut into 18-inch lengths with a spade. The best time for breaking sod for a house was when the ground was soaked from rain or snow. Like large, flat bricks, the sod was laid layer after layer in the desired dimensions, though seven feet to the square was the rule, as the walls were likely to settle a good deal, especially if the sod was very wet when laid. Generally the door and windows were set in place first, and the sod walls built around them. Forks of a tree were then placed at each end of the house and a ridgepole laid between them. Rails of any available material—sorghum stalks, willow switches—were then laid from the ridge pole to the walls. Atop them, more sod was placed for the roof.

Sometimes an especially heavy rainfall would leak through the roof, muddying clothes hung from the wall or even dripping onto the beds, thus adding to the housewife's chores. Many diarists remember various sorts of vermin (especially fleas, mice, and bedbugs) that infested these houses. One woman recalled helping her grandmother take down the canvas tacked over their ceiling each spring and fall to get rid of dirt and vermin that had fallen from the roof. The problem with bugs was minimized when settlers plastered interior walls with a mixture of clay, water, and ashes.

In most areas of the Plains frontier, a frame or brick house was seen as a status symbol, indicating that the farmer had achieved a degree of success. The social stratification was even more apparent in town. However, in part because the margin between success and failure was so narrow for farmers in this region, depending largely on vagaries of climate, there was in the country a kind of pure democracy. Though a family might live in a shack, no one looked down on them (Jones 1998, 195–97).

CLOTHING

Women's Fashion

Women were especially challenged by Western life, in part because the clothes they brought with them from the East were so unsuitable for the frontier. Long skirts that collected dirt and dust took a long time to dry, were difficult to clean, and were exceptionally incompatible with the harsh conditions under which pioneer women lived. In an effort to make the most of their existing clothes, which did, after all, retain the hallmark of fashion left behind, the women tried to adapt their Eastern apparel to Western life through unusual inventions. One solution was known as the instant dress elevator. The device allowed the wearer to raise their skirt while passing a muddy place and then let it fall or let it keep the skirt raised to keep it from filth. Advertisements claimed that it could be changed from one dress to another in less than two minutes. Many women, however, simply shortened their dresses, thereby creating a trend in skirt length. Skirt width, however, was another problem, as the wind would easily blow more voluminous skirts in all directions. Women reportedly tackled the problem by sewing bars of lead and rocks into their skirt hems to keep the fabric weighted down.

Small alterations sometimes did the trick, but whole new outfits were also created to solve the problem of frontier women's wear. The wrapper or prairie dress, also called the Mother Hubbard, was a loose fitting dress that had no structured waist but was gathered by a belt or tie. It caused quite a bit of controversy, despite its obvious benefits. The garment was comfortable, could be worn over layers of undergarments in the cold months, was loose fitting and cool in the warmer weather, and was suitable for wear throughout a woman's pregnancy. The shapeless style stood in stark contrast to the clothes common in Eastern fashion, and women did not have to wear corsets underneath the wrapper. It was, however, considered especially unattractive and even hazardous by at least one town, whose city fathers passed an ordinance outlawing the Mother Hubbard unless it was worn tightly belted.

Other adaptations to female dress included the Bloomer costume. Bloomers, which were made of a short, tunic-length dress and a pair of loose-fitting pants were, perhaps, the best-known nineteenth-century dress reform creation, receiving attention in the popular press in part because of their association with the early women's rights movement. For women traveling across the continent, the bloomer costume, named after its inventor, Amelia Bloomer, was particularly useful. Not only did the outfit do away with the problem of long skirts that collected dirt and remained wet for uncomfortable periods of time, but also the use of pants permitted women more physical movement. One woman immigrant remarked that bloomers better enabled women to walk through the sagebrush. In contrast, others found bloomers unfeminine and refused to adopt them.

The Mormon community created its own version of practical women's dress in what was known as the Deseret Costume. Based on the bloomer, which Mormon women often wore in their own westward travel, the Deseret was designed by Brigham Young. The outfit consisted of the bloomer-style pants over which a loose tunic was worn. An eight-inch-high hat covered the woman's head, which was partially shaded by the hat's rigid brim. Meant to be functional, as well as to symbolize Mormon society, the Deseret Costume, like other reformed outfits, existed only as a passing trend in frontier fashion.

The more conventional calico dress, later replaced with Eastern fashions that arrived as Western towns, became more established, and remained the most common apparel for pioneer women. The impact of these alternative women's clothing styles paved the way for women who wore pants, donned cowgirl outfits, and experimented with practical, durable clothing that defied stereotypes of female dress.

There were times when men and women would do their best to dress up, especially for holidays like the Fourth of July, events like balls, and for those living on remote properties—the trip to town. For these and similar occasions, attention to dress was taken seriously, although that often meant donning a shirt or dress that was slightly less worn than any other. The Fourth of July, Christmas, dances, and church services were particular favorites, and Westerners celebrated in as much style as they could muster. The simplicity of dress during these occasions reflected the interest Westerners had in popular fashion, yet, the limited means they had to adopt every passing fad. Women's best outfits would be worn on trips to homesteads into town, another event that received special attention.

While many pioneers were less concerned with fashion than with daily survival, others felt that clothing marked a symbolic connection to the Eastern lives they had left behind. In particular, fashionable clothes reminded them of the more refined aspects of Eastern culture and the personal connections that had been disrupted by the sheer distance of Western immigration. Many pioneer women remained keenly interested in the styles popularized in magazines like *Godey's Lady's Book* and recorded their desires to stay abreast of current fashion in letters to eastern friends. When Easterners visited their Western friends, the clothing they brought with them and wore became the source of much discussion. Local newspapers imported Eastern ideas about fashion to the frontier. Mail-order catalogs and magazines devoted exclusively to fashion brought images of stylish apparel to the West, and as towns became more established, and families became more prosperous, the emphasis on fashion increased.

One of the most popular fashions to make its way across the continent was the hoopskirt. It was prominently displayed in fashion magazines and eventually in Western shops. The skirt's impractical nature drew many detractors who found the trend impossible to adopt. Despite the challenges inherent in adopting hoopskirts on the westward journey or in frontier life, the style was in much demand among Western women. In fact, the hoopskirt made as much of a splash with these women that those who could not purchase the garment found ways to adapt their own skirts to the trendy style. In one town, women managed to improvise their own hoops by stitching clothesline and grape vine into their petticoats (Quay 2002, 93–99).

Dresses were made out of simple fabrics such as calico, gingham, denim, wagon canvas, and even converted flour sacks. For many women the plain Mother Hubbard dress served as the main work dress. The rather shapeless, long-sleeved, full-length gown had no waist to speak of and a yoke. The style became very popular for girls in an ankle length (Shrock 2004, 87).

Men's Fashion

The single garment most identified with the West is the blue jean. Levi Straus owned a dry goods business. He had canvas made into waist overalls. Miners liked the pants, but complained that they tended to chafe. Levi Strauss substituted a twilled cotton cloth from France. The fabric later became known as denim and the pants were nicknamed blue jeans. In 1872 Straus received a letter from Nevada tailor, Jacob Davis, who purchased bolts of cloth from Straus to make denim work pants. In this letter, Davis told Straus about the interesting way in which he made pants for his customers, placing metal rivets at the points of strain such as pocket corners and on the base of the fly. Davis did not have the money to patent his process and suggested that they could take out the patent together, if Levi would pay for the paperwork. The following year Strauss and Davis received a U.S. patent for using copper rivets to strengthen the pockets of denim work pants. Levi Strauss & Co. began manufacturing the first of the famous Levi's brand of jeans in San Francisco.

Distinctive garb depended on the occupation and region. Cowboys in the West wore the distinctive Stetson, cowboy boots, a neckerchief, and a standard town suit when not working. Loggers in the upper Midwest or Northwest might wear flannel shirts, woolen trousers or denim pants, and wool jackets. Mail-order catalogs provided a variety of clothing for working men. The *Montgomery Ward Catalogue* offered overalls in brown, blue, and white denim, Kentucky jean pants, heavy indigo shirts of cotton and wool, duck coats, and a complete brown duck suit lined with plaid Mackinaw flannel, durable work boots, mining boots, and plow shoes. A wide range of underwear in cotton and wool were also available.

Men who could not afford mail-order clothes often made due with what was at hand. Women often used whatever cloth they had to make pants. Pioneer families often used grain sacks to make shirts and pants and linsey-woolsey homespun continued throughout the century (Shrock 2004, 83–84).

Children's Fashion: The Immigrant Trail

Children generally wore the same functional style of clothing on the immigrant trail that many farm children wore at home. The maintenance and replacement of children's clothing was always a time-consuming task for their mother. On the immigrant trail and in the frontier settlements it became a source of great frustration. Immigrants were not free to carry large amounts of extra clothes, nor could they conveniently find sources of fabric, thread, or yarn on the edge of civilization for the construction of new items.

Missionary Narcissa Whitman traveling to Oregon in the 1840s had carefully packed her trunk with extra clothing items, but in crossing the Snake River her husband, Marcus, was forced to lighten the load of their wagon by dropping off her clothes trunk on the bank of the river. "Poor little trunk," she wrote in her diary, "I am sorry to leave thee, thou must abide here alone" (Time Life Books 1974, 61). Keeping the children's remaining clothes clean was also difficult, and Eliza Spalding, traveling with the Whitmans, reported that they were able to do laundry only three times during the six-month journey. The state of the garments, worn day after day after so long a period, can only be imagined.

Immigrant children were generally provided an initial supply of clothing beyond that on their backs. This included linen, cotton, or woolen trousers or skirts; linen, cotton, or cotton flannel shirts or blouses; Brogan-style (ankle-top) work shoes for both boys and girls; cotton or woolen socks; cotton dresses, smocks, and aprons; wool sack coats (a loose-fitting style of jacket, not clothing made from sacks); a rubberized or painted canvass raincoat; a pair of mittens or gloves; and a felt hat or sunbonnet. Such clothing items were considered the minimum for an attempt at crossing the continent.

Jesse Applegate, remembering his years as a youngster in Oregon, noted that clothing remained a problem even after the Overland journey had ended. No cotton grew in Oregon, and there were, in the early years, no flocks of sheep to be sheared for wool. This made cloth scare or if it could be had, prohibitively costly. Applegate remembered that his Aunt Melinda attempted to spin yarn from the hair of wolves and coyotes, but it was difficult to kill enough of them to weave a single garment. Most settlers quickly put in a small patch of flax for linen, but cleared land was at a premium and usually dedicated to food crops.

More commonly, early settlers cut up the tents and canvas wagon covers to make overcoats, or lined them with skins and rags to make smallclothes. The frontier standby was buckskin, but this was often less than ideal in the damp Oregon climate. Applegate noted, "Trousers [of buckskin] after frequent wettings and dryings would assume a fixed shape that admitted of no reformation." While the leather was tough and long wearing, for growing children this characteristic was a definite disadvantage (Applegate 1934, 28).

Immigrant children generally went barefoot once their footwear proved beyond repair. During the first week without shoes, their feet were very sore, but thereafter they generally hardened to most impediments on the ground save for thorns, which remained a problem. Parents sometimes tried to fashion shoes from canvas or rawhide, but the former did not last and the latter needed to be soaked in water every night to keep them soft and pliable enough to wear throughout the day.

—James M. Volo

TECHNOLOGY: STATIONARY ENGINES AND POWER STATIONS

The use of steam power took a sharp upward surge in America after the Civil War. Stationary steam power, as opposed to that used in steamboats or locomotives, moved from the fringes to the center of the industrial scene. By 1900, steam power had reduced direct-drive waterpower to a minor and steadily declining part in American manufacturing, persisting only in small-scale, traditional mill sites. Before the Civil War, steam power had been identified chiefly with transportation, and it was through steam navigation and railways that it helped effect the conversion of a pioneer subsistence economy to one in which regional specialization and commercial interchange were the dynamic elements. However, steam power also became a central factor in the industrialization of the American economy in what was, in effect, a sequel to the transportation revolution of the preceding decades.

It was in response to the needs of the small but growing segment of large-scale manufacturing that a significant innovation in stationary engines, the automatic variable cutoff engine, made an appearance about mid-century. This engine marked the first major advance in stationary steam engineering since the general adoption of the high-pressure noncondensing engine and the beginnings of expansive innovation some 40 years earlier. Yet credit for the practical development and commercial application of the type is traditionally and properly assigned to George H. Corliss of Providence, Rhode Island, who brought together a number of mechanical elements—some old and familiar, some novel but little used conceptions of others, and some ingenious contrivances of his own—and combined them into a highly effective working whole.

The Corliss steam engine was the centerpiece of the Centennial Exposition in Philadelphia in 1876, supplying energy for a large array of other machine on display. The Corliss engine was self-adjusting, meaning that it could automatically increase or decrease the amount of steam going to the engine cylinder based on changing demands. Other American inventors and engineers, most notably Charles T. Porter and John F. Allen, contributed important improvements to steam engines. Oliver Evans, often neglected in the history of steam, had designed a high-pressure steam engine for industrial use in mills, manufactories, and waterworks before mid-century.

Moreover, a great divide in the history of industrial power was reached in the final decades of the century with regard to the transmission of power from the old-style direct-drive prime movers, steam engines, and waterwheels using shafts, countershafts, pulleys, belts, and gears to a new form. This innovation was the use of a central power station or urban power plant of great generating capacity to make electricity, which was then transmitted through a vast network of transmission lines and local distribution points to electric motors. These reached out to an ever-growing number of power consumers—industrial, commercial, and, in time, domestic. Under the central station system, power was to be generated, sold, and delivered to factory, mill, mine, and workshop like any other raw material or service required to aid production (Hunter 1979, 251–54, 433–34).

TRANSPORTATION

The Stagecoach

The female gentry, both North and South, traveled mostly by carriage or chaise. Adult females of good breeding used saddle horses only in association with a sport, such as fox

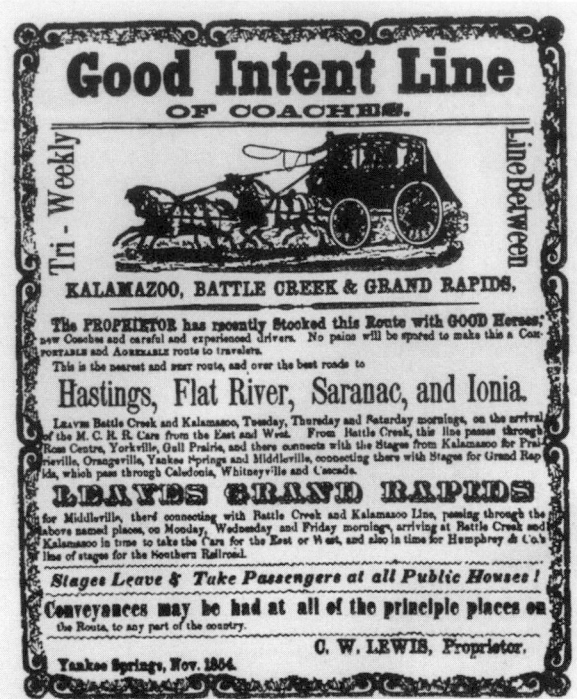

Stagecoach lines carried passengers between towns, between railroad lines, and between rail and steamboat connections. This kept them in service throughout much of the era. They also moved the mail, delivered small packages, and transported light freight where railways did not exist or steamboats could not reach. Courtesy Editor's Collection.

hunting, or as a form of recreation. Southern roads, composed in large part of lesser used lanes between plantations, proved too narrow and overhung with branches to make the formal British-style coach practicable. This made high-wheeled carts and chariots more popular. Nonetheless, well-heeled city dwellers sometimes supported a formal coach as a sign of their affluence even though they never left the urban districts in it. The gentry would go into debt to maintain their own carriage and team; and great pride was taken in being seen in a fine conveyance, pulled by matched horses, and manned by a properly attired driver and footman.

Although closely associated with the western regions of the nation by Hollywood movie producers of the twentieth century, systems of public conveyances—commonly known as stagecoaches—were well established in many regions of the country before the invasion of the Wild West. These coaches passed in stages between stops at inns, taverns, or town centers that were approximately 20 miles apart—hence the term stagecoach. At these stops the team of horses would be changed, and the passengers allowed to refresh themselves. Each stage took approximately four hours to traverse depending on the topography of the intervening countryside. Muddy roads, swollen creeks, and steep grades slowed the progress of the stagecoach and passengers were often asked to get out and walk to spare the horses. A number of towns have the word middle in their names (as in Middleburg, Middletown, or Midvale) because they were half way between two major destinations a day's travel (40 miles) apart.

Fanny Kemble, a celebrated English actress journeying from New York City to Utica by steamboat and stagecoach, found the steamboat very large, commodious, and well-appointed; but she disliked her experience in the stagecoach. She could not conceive of a "more clumsy or wretched conveyance" as she was "bumped, thumped, jolted, shaken, tossed, and tumbled over the wickedest roads cut through bogs and marshes and over ruts, roots, and protruding stumps with the over hanging branches scratching at the windows." Oddly, her American companions on the coach, including several young women, seemed quite unaffected by these inconveniences laughing and talking at the very top of their voices incessantly (Volo and Volo 2004, 306–7).

Movers and Freight Wagons

As the nation expanded, itinerant Americans developed a large four-wheeled farm wagon known as a *mover*. This quickly became the common farm wagon for moving produce to the city markets. The mover came in two sizes, light and heavy. The light wagon was usually pulled by a single pair of horses or mules, while the heavy type required four of either animal. Immigrant families would pack all their worldly possessions into their movers to travel from Pennsylvania to Missouri or from the Carolinas to Mississippi in search of a better homestead or richer soils. For those traveling across the seas of grass on the Great Plains the four-up mover came to be called a *prairie schooner* (Stewart 1962, 7).

These movers should not be confused with the very large commercial freight wagons known as *Conestogas* that were developed in Pennsylvania in the eighteenth century for the movement of goods and freight. These had a boat-shaped bed, a high prow and back, and sloping sides that gave them a swaybacked appearance along their overhanging canvas covers. Capable of carrying almost two tons of goods, these huge wagons required six horses or oxen to pull them at a slow pace along improved roads. Hundreds of freight and express companies operated with Conestogas in the middle states and in the North during the nineteenth century, and stagecoach passengers passed many lumbering Conestogas on the roads while themselves going at comparatively breakneck speeds.

The Conestoga cargo wagon was also the principal means of transporting freight along the Santa Fe, California, and Oregon trails, but it was not generally used by immigrant trains because it was just too large and heavy for their purposes. Wagons hauled by 20 mules (the 20-mule-team made famous in TV advertisements by Ronald Reagan in the 1950s before he entered politics) were sometimes used to move ore, borax, and salt in the arid regions of the Southwest. Among the earliest professional freight haulers was Alvin Adams, who by the 1850s had turned his pioneering efforts into a nationwide business. Experienced express men like Henry Wells and John Butterfield, who began the American Express Company, joined with William Fargo in 1852 to form Wells Fargo and Company to handle the freight business west of the Mississippi. Butterfield later began a prominent stagecoach line, the Overland Express that served the American West (Volo and Volo 2004, 306–8).

FOR MORE INFORMATION

Applegate, Jesse. *A Day with the Cow Column in 1843*. Chicago, IL: Caxton Club, 1934.

Better Homes and Gardens. *Heritage Cookbook*. Des Moines, IA: Meredith Corporation, 1974.

Black, Brian. *Nature and the Environment in Nineteenth-Century American Life*. Westport, CT: Greenwood Press, 2006.

Collins, Joseph. *Bacon, Beans and Galantines: Food and Foodways on the Western Mining Frontier*. Reno: University of Nevada Press, 1986.

Coy, Owen Cochran. *The Great Trek*. Los Angeles, CA: Powell Publishing Company, 1931.

Holmes, Kenneth L., ed. *Covered Wagon Women: Diaries and Letters from the Western Trails*. Lincoln: University of Nebraska Press, 1983.

Holmes, Oliver Wendell. *Stagecoach East: Stagecoach Days in the East from the Colonial Period to the Civil War*. Edited by Peter T. Rohrbach. Washington, DC: Smithsonian Institution Press, 1983.

Hunter, Louis C. *A History of Industrial Power in the United States, 1780–1930*. Charlottesville: University Press of Virginia, 1979.

Jones, Mary Ellen. *Daily Life on the 19th-Century American Frontier*. Westport, CT: Greenwood Press, 1998.

Luchetti, Cathy. *Home on the Range: A Culinary History of the American West*. New York: Villard Books, 1993.

Marx, Leo. *The Machine in the Garden: Technology and the Pastoral Ideal in America.* New York: Oxford University Press, 1964.

Myres, Sandra L., ed. *Ho for California! Woman's Overland Diaries from the Huntington Library.* San Marino, CA: Huntington Library, 1980.

Pierce, B. Byron. *National Cowboy Hall of Fame Chuck Wagon Cookbook.* New York: Hearst Books, 1995.

Quay, Sara E. *Westward Expansion.* Westport, CT: Greenwood Press, 2002.

Rae, W. F. *Westward by Rail.* New York: Promontory Press, 1974.

Shrock, Joel. *The Gilded Age.* Westport, CT: Greenwood Press, 2004.

Smith, Merritt Roe, and Leo Marx, eds. *Does Technology Drive History? The Dilemma of Technological Determinism.* Cambridge, MA: MIT Press, 1994.

Stewart, George R. "The Prairie Schooner Got Them There." *American Heritage* XIII, no. 2 (February 1962).

Time Life Books. *The Pioneers.* New York: Time, Inc., 1974.

Van Hoesen, Walter H. *Early Taverns and Stagecoach Days in New Jersey.* Rutherford, NJ: Fairleigh Dickinson University Press, 1976.

Volo, Dorothy Denneen, and James M. Volo. *The Antebellum Period.* Westport, CT: Greenwood Press, 2004.

Ware, Joseph E. *The Emigrants' Guide to California.* New York: Da Capo Press, 1972. Reprinted from the 1849 edition.

Woodward, George E. *Victorian City and Country Houses: Plans and Designs.* New York: Dover Publications, 1996.

———. *Woodward's Architecture and Rural Art.* New York: Privately printed, 1868.

———. *Woodward's National Architect.* New York: Da Capo Press, 1975.

Zanger, Mark H. *The American History Cookbook.* Westport, CT: Greenwood Press, 2003.

Political Life

GOVERNMENT: JUDICIAL REVIEW AND CITIZENSHIP RIGHTS

Citizenship is a rather amorphous concept, and the rights and immunities that it confers upon a person are sometimes equally vague. In ancient Rome citizenship was endowed upon only a few—generally the sons of the high-born or those who earned it through service in the legions. In Greece citizenship was the natural right of every free-born man. Although the American form of citizenship was based on Greco-Roman ideals, treating people as independent units benefiting equally from their private citizenship rights has not always been characteristic of the United States government.

The relationship between Americans and their government with regard to citizenship emerged through the development of a national identity during the post–Civil War years. Legal developments—particularly those derived from precedent-setting Supreme Court decisions and landmark congressional legislation—paved the way for the growth of a capitalistic Republican system that contrasted well with those more elitist forms of capitalistic governance developed elsewhere in the nineteenth century, especially with regard to the status of the individual American citizen. The superiority of the American system was not always obvious, however; and many contemporary observers dreaded its implications and fought its implementation.

The period following the Civil War was one of incredible activity and creativity, a golden age that reflected the social, economic, and political organization of the nineteenth century and gave birth to a modern form of American culture. Nonetheless, many historians view the jurisprudence of the period as pedestrian, overly formal, and prejudiced. Legal outcomes were seemingly preordained by precedents friendly to the upper classes and exploitive of workers and the poor with the law serving as an obstacle to equal rights, social reform, and economic justice. Judges and lawmakers seemingly made decisions based on an unrelieved series of economic calculations and social paradigms—largely favorable to industry, expansion, and wealth—that distorted the social, economic, and cultural reality faced by the rest of the population.

The Constitution of the United States (and its amendments) was the bulwark of revolutionary liberty—the guarantor of personal and political freedom, the sanctity of property, religious toleration, and free speech at least by the federal government. Yet this was not always so. For example, the simple egalitarian concept found in the Declaration of Independence that "all men are created equal" was violated in law by institutionalized race-based slavery for eight decades after its passage; by black codes, Jim Crow laws, and poll taxes for another century.

Also unresolved in the Constitution were the relationships among the states; between the several states and the federal government; and between the various governments and the people, individuals, groups of individuals, or simply persons. That the process of sorting out these issues is ongoing, generally without overt violence, and seemingly without end, may be among the outstanding positive qualities of the American form of constitutional government.

Traditional battles between those who read the words of the Constitution narrowly (strict construction) and those who read them more loosely (broad construction) assumed, respectively, that the meaning of the words was limited to the dictates of the Founding Fathers or that the indeterminacy of all text was to be left to judicial interpreters who held the responsibility for determining what obligations the readings commanded and what rights they endowed. (Semonche 2006, 75–76).

The existence in the antebellum period of a dual set of citizenships—one federal and one state—was a weakness of the early American constitutional and governmental system unanticipated by the Founders. The absence of a citizenship clause in the Constitution meant that federal citizenship was generally thought to be derived from state citizenship and was subservient to it. This was one of the corner stones supporting the arguments for the legality of secession. Certainly the potential of the Constitution, through the Supreme Court, to nationalize its citizenship provisions and protections had not been fully realized in the antebellum period largely because the majority of justices feared that they would interfere with the peculiar institution of slavery.

The Court of Chief Justice Roger B. Taney (served 1836–1864) and his colleagues supported the primacy of the states in many areas of law but departed from their support with respect to state laws that restricted the property rights of slaveholders. In *Prigg v. Pennsylvania* (1842), the Court held that the Constitution prohibited state laws that would emancipate any person held to service in another state. A Maryland man was allowed to seize his property (a former slave and her child) and take them back to Maryland without seeking an order from the Pennsylvania courts. His rights as an American citizen (rather than a citizen of Maryland) overruled the power of the state of Pennsylvania to enforce its antislavery regulations. The Taney Court extended this concept in *Moore v. Illinois* (1852) making void any state law or regulation that denied the right of an owner to the immediate possession of his slave in any jurisdiction. Five years later, Taney wrote the decision for the Court in the *Dred Scott* case (1857) that declared any restrictions imposed by Congress on the spread of slavery into the territories, such as those found in the Missouri Compromise, were also unconstitutional.

Almost without exception, the Court decided chattel property cases brought before it in favor of slave owners. Despite its support for slavery before the Civil War, however, the court also provided a forceful defense of the perpetual nature of the federal union, extended the central government's jurisdiction over maritime trade and coastal monopolies, promoted a uniform set of interstate commerce laws, set the foundations for a nationwide economic market, and allowed for the uniform development of corporations within the federal system. Once the issue of slavery became moot—with the ratification of the 13th Amendment—the economic, cultural, and social foundations upon which the court's previous jurisprudence had been built had to be modified significantly, especially with regard to the concept of citizenship (Semonche 2006, 79–80).

The ratification of the 14th Amendment addressed this problem by conferring citizenship by birth within the United States to all persons including blacks rather than deriving it solely from the states. The rights implied by federal citizenship imposed new limits upon the states in that they could no longer abridge the privileges and immunities enjoyed by citizens of the United States nor deny to persons the equal protection of the law, or of their life, liberty, or property without due process of law. Federal citizenship thereafter embraced all the important individual rights and immunities claimed in the Bill of Rights, and seemingly precluded their evasion by the states.

Yet the Supreme Court rejected arguments that were raised asking the federal government to reach out with the power of the 14th Amendment to impose its protections in cases of discriminatory conduct in the absence of direct state action, as in the precedent-setting *Slaughterhouse Cases* of 1873. This series of cases was considered pivotal to the potential extension of government powers over the individual. In 1869, the Louisiana State Legislature passed a law that allowed the city of New Orleans to create a corporation that centralized all slaughterhouse operations in the city. The stated purpose of the new arrangement was to restrict the dumping of remains and waste in waterways and to provide a single place for animals to be kept while awaiting slaughter. Critics—among them a number of black independent butchers—called the plan a legal monopoly founded on political patronage and designed to shut down the independents.

The Supreme Court rejected the claim, virtually nullifying the privileges and immunities clauses that seemed to promise full citizenship to the lower classes, especially black freedmen in their new status. The majority reading of the due process clause of the 14th Amendment in the *Slaughterhouse Cases* would continue to prevail in future cases in which the court was asked to protect property interests against hostile state laws. However, the Court also interpreted the amendment more narrowly to invalidate the first public accommodations law (*Civil Rights Cases*, 1883) and to uphold the practice of racial segregation (*Plessy v. Ferguson*, 1896). The most meaningful of individual rights promised by the 14th Amendment were thereby once again left to the sole protection of the states, some of which were ill disposed to defend them. The narrow reading of the 14th Amendment protected only those privileges or immunities conferred by virtue of national rather than state citizenship.

Increasing legislation at the state level, affecting the industrialization of American society and the expansion of business, soon caused both capitalists and farmers to seek federal intervention on their side. In *Munn v. Illinois* (1877), the Court rejected a broad ban on the regulation of property issues, saying that property affecting the public interest was within the purview of state regulation and reinforcing the concept of eminent domain as a due process of law. Efforts to show in many cases that the public had no interest and the states no right to regulate property generally failed to sway the court. However, in 1890, the justices ruled that a state's failure to provide access to a judicial hearing on the question of whether a railroad rate was confiscatory (*Chicago, Milwaukee and St. Paul Railway v. Minnesota*) denied due process under the 14th Amendment. By the end of the decade, the court had invalidated such rates (*Smyth v. Ames*, 1898) under a new, broader reading of the due process concept that recognized the rights of groups of persons—in this case Midwestern farmers (Semonche 2006, 81). This construction of a *group rights* consciousness posed a challenge to the *individual rights* basis that strict constructionists saw as a foundation of American constitutionalism, and seemingly viewed the idea of unbridgeable individual rights as an obstacle to the creation of a just and comfortable society in which the community's welfare was emphasized.

—*James M. Volo*

LAW, CRIME, AND PUNISHMENT

Violent Crime

Whenever large groups of unattached males—miners, cowhands, or railroad laborers—had time on their hands, violence could erupt. Harried small town officials in the West often hired armed marshals or constables to keep order. The old West was thought to be particularly wild, but most of what happened was of the barroom brawl type. However, even in a cattle town, the murder rate was much lower than in most modern American cities. The three cow towns of Abilene, Ellsworth, and Wichita in Kansas had a total homicide rate of only 1.5 per year, and this was attributable to all types of murders including beating, bludgeoning, and shooting. "The fact that each person carried a six-shooter meant that each had a relatively equal amount of power. That minimized violence." Recent estimates suggest that there were fewer than a dozen bank robberies in the entire period from 1859 through 1900 in all the frontier West (Hill 2007, 2).

Some historians take a slightly different view of crime in the Old West with respect to the availability of guns and gun violence. The gun culture that emerged during the nineteenth century was so widespread and accepted that a religious magazine in 1879 gave away a gun with every new subscription. The equally common disregard for the poor and the systemic discrimination toward racial and ethnic groups have also been shown to lead to violent crime. Moreover, Eastern cities, where guns were equally available and were present in larger absolute numbers, had lower rates of murder by comparison to those of the West. These facts tend to confound the historic correlation between gun availability and violence somewhat.

The massive expansion of inexpensive firearms in the United States in the nineteenth century may have made violent crime, particularly murders using guns, increase dramatically. A sporting goods catalog from 1895 offered 30 pages of firearms for sale including 53 shotguns ranging in price from $5 to $95 for an ornate hammerless model, 4 types of muzzleloaders, 26 different rifles, and 43 different pistols in different grips, barrel lengths, calibers, and finishes. An obsolete but lethal seven-shot cap-and-ball pistol could be had for as little as 74 cents, and a hammerless, double-action .32 caliber S&W in a nickel-plated finish with a 3-inch barrel was $7.50 (Shrock 2004, 12).

With small, relatively cheap revolvers readily available, homicide levels grew alarmingly in cities as well as frontier areas, sparking fears of a national murder crisis. Just after the end of the Civil War in 1865 violent crimes of all types rose by 60 percent. Yet, for all the fears of a homicide crisis caused by guns, most murders still occurred where large numbers of single men gathered in dangerous and physically demanding occupations. Western miners and cowboys, as well as the floating army of men who tramped around the country hopping from industrial jobs to wheat harvest, lived in a highly volatile bachelor subculture filled with alcohol and guns.

Mining towns were particularly murderous places. Bodie, California, boasted a homicide rate of 116 per 100,000 people between 1878 and 1882 and Leadville, Colorado, in 1880 was nearly as high with 105. Cattle towns frequented by cowboys fresh off the range on long cattle drives from Texas were nearly as deadly. The Kansas cattle towns averaged a mere 1.5 homicides annually, but given their small populations this was equivalent to 50 murders per 100,000. Dodge City boasted a murder rate of 116 per 100,000. Fort Griffin, Texas, had to be one of the deadliest places in the United States, claiming a murder rate of 229 per 100,000 in the 1870s. Eastern cities like Boston and Philadelphia paled in comparison to the frontier regions with 5.8 and 3.2 homicides per 100,000 people, respectively, from 1860 to 1880.

Even though frontier crime rates leveled off by the 1870s, criminal behavior appeared more public and troublesome than ever. Crimes seemed to be more daring and intelligent as demonstrated by thieves who stole $1.2 million from the Wall Street offices of Lord Bond. Butch Cassidy and the Sundance Kid and numerous others like the James, Dalton, and Younger families robbed trains and banks throughout the West. Lawlessness seemed rampant as industrial workers engaged in large-scale strikes such as the Great Railroad Strike of 1877, the Haymarket Riot in 1886, the Homestead Strike in 1892, and the Pullman Strike of 1896 where strikers fought with hired strikebreakers and even troops (Shrock 2004, 12).

—*James M. Volo*

Law Enforcement: Vigilantes and Lawmen

Wherever the law was weakly enforced or nonexistent, vigilantes often took the enforcement of community moral and legal codes into their own hands. Vigilante groups often formed where the legitimate system of law was seen as corrupt, ineffective, or run by the criminal elements. The term *vigilante* stems from its Spanish equivalent meaning a private security agent. Vigilantes were common in mining camps, but they were also found in cow towns and farming settlements. Most often, these groups formed before any formal law and order existed in a new settlement. Enforcement often took the form of intimidation and an invitation to leave the area, and justice was often found at the end of a whip or the end of a rope.

Many times vigilantes were viewed in a favorable light by the wider community who saw them as a necessary stopgap to increasing disorder and rising crime. Although extra-legal in every sense, they were often seen as heroes and supported by law-abiding citizens. Nonetheless, vigilantes could get out of hand wielding too much power or becoming corrupt themselves. Moreover, mobs sometimes declared themselves ad hoc vigilante committees to mask their own ruthless intent or find some color of law under which to carry out particularly heinous activities such as the beating or lynching of blacks, Asians, foreigners, or Indians.

Vigilantes were fairly common in the gold and silver mining camps, and one of the earliest groups formed in America was the San Francisco Vigilantes of 1851. This committee spent most of a year rooting out, from the camps, Australian ne'er-do-wells. These were viewed with suspicion because Australia had been colonized through the forced transportation of criminals from Britain in the late eighteenth century. The vigilantes hanged four men and invited another 30 to leave town before disbanding. In 1856, the committee was reconstituted due to a spate of high profile shootings. More than 6,000 people joined the vigilante movement because it was felt that the city government was complicit in the crime epidemic. The mob hanged several suspects, and then turned to political activity to remove the offending officials.

There were literally hundreds of such organizations formed in the American West and many did not identify themselves as *vigilantes*, using other terms in an attempt to avoid any negative connotations associated with vigilante. Among these were the Atchison County Protective Association; the Skagway, Alaska, Committee of 101; the Shelby County, Texas, Regulators; the Fierce Missouri Bald Knobbers; and the Tin Hat Brigade.

Citizens' committees often hired marshals to enforce the community standards. These were often noted gunmen used to keep other gunmen and assorted bad actors in line through intimidation. Others were former army officers or members of the Texas Rangers who did service on the Mexican border rounding up rustlers, robbers, and smugglers, or tracking down fence cutters during the range wars of the 1880s. There were a number of superb lawmen among these, and not all of the best made the pages of the *National Police Gazette* or dime novels, which romanticized both the sordid lives of badmen and the rather mundane policing activities of town law keepers.

Many lawmen saw no reason to make an arrest at gunpoint or to have a Hollywood-style six-gun standoff in the street. Most found that a large bore (10 or 12 gauge) double-barrel shotgun loaded with buckshot (up to a dozen .32 caliber lead balls per shot) had more effect as a medium of intimidation than a single-action .44–40 Colt *Frontier Six-Shooter* or .45 Long Colt *Peacemaker*. More importantly it need only to be aimed in the general direction of an opponent to score a hit while not carrying so far as to endanger bystanders. Facing down gunmen in the streets, barrooms, or brothels was more a matter of keeping a cool head than aiming straight in any case, and a single shotgun blast could take down more than one miscreant in a confined space. It was for these reasons that shotguns were carried by many stagecoach and prison guards.

Although the *Peacemaker* caught the imagination of the press at the time, the .44–40 WCF (Winchester Center Fire) *Frontier Pistol* became a favorite of lawmen and ranchers because the ammunition was cross-compatible with the Winchester lever-action repeating rifle with its seven-shot tube-fed magazine that became available in 1873. The so-called *Winchester '73* became one of the most famous long-guns of the century. The Colt factory offered pistols in a variety of calibers for both civilian and foreign military sales. By 1895, a double-action (self-cocking) Frontier "Bull Dog" revolver in .44 WCF was available for home protection for under $4 with postage extra (Shrock 2004, 51).

In the most famous gunfight in Wild West history at the O. K. Corral in Tombstone, Arizona in 1881, the Earp brothers (Wyatt, Morgan, and Virgil) and Doc Holiday armed themselves with shotguns and revolvers as did their opponents the Clantons and the McLaurys of whom three were killed and one wounded. A fifth man, Ike Clanton, survived unscathed only by diving into an open doorway to avoid Holiday's shotgun blast.

A decade later John Slaughter, former Texas Ranger, was made the Sheriff of Cochise County, Arizona. A small man and a crack shot, he gave weight to his authority by carrying a 10-gauge shotgun loaded with buckshot. Slaughter issued an ultimatum to the outlaws operating in his jurisdiction, "Get out or get shot." After several desperadoes who tangled with him wound up dead, the rest got out (Barnard 1977, 297).

—*James M. Volo*

Cow Town Justice

In most cow towns, saloons outnumbered other establishments by as much as two to one. There and in gambling houses the cowboys played poker, keno, faro, and monte, often encouraged by bar girls or soiled doves (prostitutes like Squirrel Tooth

Annie of Dodge City, who carried a pet squirrel and eventually quit her profession to get married). Another especially colorful lady of the night was Connie the Cowboy Queen, who wore a $250 dress embroidered with the brands of every ranch from the Yellowstone to the Platte. Dusty streets, sometimes lined with wooden sidewalks, were bordered with the town's business establishments—dry goods and grocery stores, photography studios, theaters, sometimes a roller-skating rink or bowling alley, billiard parlors and pool halls, dancehalls, barbershops, and hotels. Dodge City in 1884 was the busiest trailhead town with 19 saloons, a lush casino, and a seasonal population of up to two thousand. There a beef broker could seal a $20,000 deal on a handshake, and the cowboy, released briefly from his work, could get a bath, a woman, and a bottle of whiskey for a silver dollar.

Into such towns the cowboys swarmed when they were paid off. Generally the tone was live and let live—literally—and as long as the cowboys respected the town's etiquette, they were left alone. After all, they brought an influx of money. Alfred Henry Lewis remembered that there were only four things a cowboy must not do: he must not insult a woman; he must not shoot his pistol in a store or barroom; he must not ride his pony into those places; and he must not ride his pony on the sidewalks.

Sometimes, however, there was too much temptation. Charlie Siringo remembered one Fourth of July in Dodge City when he and a buddy got drunk in the Lone Star Dance Hall, then run by Bat Masterson; they picked a fight with some old-time buffalo hunters. Siringo's friend was stabbed, but the two buddies eluded the law. He later wrote: "This incident illustrates what fools some young cowboys were after long drives up the Chisholm Trail and after filling their hides full of the poison liquors manufactured to put the red-shirted Irish rail-road builders to sleep, so that the toughs could 'roll' them and get their 'wads.' Instead of putting a cowboy to sleep it stirred up the devil in his make-up, and made him a wide-awake hyena" (Siringo 1919, 64–65). Besides the usual horseplay and too much liquor, Teddy Blue suggests another reason trail hands often had trouble with the law in cow towns. Most of the Texas cowboys had served in the Confederate army, and most of the marshals were Northerners. Though "down home one Texas ranger could arrest the lot of them...up north you'd have to kill them first" (Abbott and Smith 1939, 28).

There was a schizophrenic quality to these cow towns. On the one hand, many were, at least at first, populated largely by profiteering seasonal operators—representatives of Northern meat packers and Midwestern feedlot owners, gamblers from Mississippi riverboats, and prostitutes who went back to Memphis, St. Louis, or New Orleans when the cowboys returned to ranch or trail. Consequently Theodore Roosevelt, who generally admired and respected the cowboy, called cow towns "wretched [places] in which drinking and gambling are the only recognized forms of amusement, and where pleasure and vice are considered synonymous terms" (Roosevelt 1977, 92). In an official publication of the National Livestock Association, the cow towns were described as products of existing conditions. "Civilization was pushing its way...[west] with the irresistible force...of glaciers...[and, like glaciers], shoving ahead a morainic mass—a conglomeration of human debris" (National Livestock Association [NLA] 1959, 551). Abilene in 1870 was perceived by some as "the wickedest and most God-forsaken place on the continent" (NLA 1959, 507). With a permanent population of 500, it had 32 licensed saloons (Jones 1998, 178–81).

Detectives and Badmen

Allan Pinkerton was a man of great courage and powers of observation. Founder of the first official Secret Service, Pinkerton is credited with preventing at least one assassination attempt on Abraham Lincoln and with gathering meaningful (if not always precise) intelligence from behind Confederate lines during the Civil War. Pinkerton is best known for his activities in the postwar period when he rode with lawmen along the Old Frontier pursuing the James Gang or the Reno Brothers. The history of the Pinkerton National Detective Agency is the story of American crime. At a time when most cities and towns had their own law enforcement agencies, Pinkerton agents took on the most difficult assignments.

At the end of the Civil War, Allan Pinkerton returned to the home office of his agency in Chicago. His subordinates, George Bangs and Francis Warner, had managed and expanded the agency while Pinkerton had worked for the government, opening offices in New York and Philadelphia. The agency was rededicated to eradicating the swindlers, cheats, and confidence men that plagued the big cities in the second half of the nineteenth century. Ably assisted by his sons William and Robert, Pinkerton developed his agency into the nineteenth century equivalent of a database of criminal activity. Agents carefully recorded a compendium of crimes and criminals as word of their nefarious activities surfaced in the newspapers or across the wire services. Newspaper clippings and handwritten reports filled individual files that were kept in a central location until the crime was solved or the criminal was dead.

Pinkerton was so organized that many metropolitan law enforcement agencies copied his methods. Among these was the use of mug shots, photo lineups, photographic wanted posters, and undercover agents. By the 1870s the Pinkertons had the largest collection of criminal mug shots in the world. The agency compiled a glossary of crime-related terms, many of which have come into common use. These included among many others the term bull for a law enforcement officer or guard, cannon or rod for a revolver, and mouthpiece for a lawyer. The agency made the pursuit of criminals and the prevention of crime a professional business, and it consulted with the business public, offering advice to banks, shipping offices, mail services and other commercial enterprises that handled or moved money. It distributed wanted posters, felon's identification cards, and pamphlets exposing common confidence schemes. Many large city law enforcement bureaus held Pinkerton's agency in awe.

With a growing reputation in the Eastern cities, Pinkerton opened offices to the west from Kansas to California and from Texas to the Canadian border. Wherever holdup men robbed a bank, stopped a train, or removed an express box from a stagecoach, Pinkerton detectives responded. While Allan Pinkerton was slowing with age, his son William willingly set himself to fieldwork. William led a number of posses pursuing, if not catching, the James Gang, the Younger Brothers, the Reno Brothers, and the Hole-in-the-Wall Gang. The Pinkerton strategy was to apply an unremitting and constant pressure to the criminals they followed never giving them a moments rest or peace. A reformed safecracker wrote in 1895 that men of his profession were constantly being interrupted by one or more Pinkerton men popping up. It was dangerous for a crook when a Pinkerton was on his trail.

Unfortunately, the Pinkerton Agency allowed itself to be involved in a number of antilabor, antistrike confrontations, and the Pinkerton agents came to be associated with the violent suppression of union activities, sometimes when they weren't even present. The most historically significant of these confrontations was at Homestead, a mining town just outside Pittsburgh and the site of one of Andrew Carnegie's principal steel plants run by Henry Clay Frick.

In 1892, a confrontation between Frick and the Amalgamated Association of Iron and Steel Workers seemingly could not be avoided. Frick called in the Pinkerton agency to act as strike breakers. A total of 316 men were collected—mostly unemployed, drifters, or hoodlums collected in the streets of New York and Chicago. These were typical of mine-company guards, but they were formed around a hard core of trained Pinkerton regulars. The steelworkers' association totaled less than 800 members. The Pinkerton men were told, "You men are hired to watch the property of a certain corporation, to prevent it from harm. The element of danger which is usually found in such expeditions will here be entirely lacking. A few brickbats will be thrown at you, you may be called names or sworn at, but that is no reason for you to shoot." This proved to be an overly optimistic assessment of the situation at Homestead (Wolff 1965, 89).

The Pinkerton men, although armed with .45–70 Winchester repeating rifles and revolvers, were met by the strikers and hundreds of their supporters, many of whom were armed with a wide variety of firearms, some dating back to the Civil War. Scores of men were killed or wounded over the next days on both sides, and the Pinkerton men were ultimately forced to submit to a negotiated ceasefire rather than undergo a further murderous encounter at close range. Their uniform jackets were removed, their pistols thrown in the river, and their Winchester rifles nailed up in crates for shipment to the agency. A few of the younger men were seen to be weeping as they were marched to the nearby railroad depot to ride the cars home in defeat.

Frick was a man of strong antiunion sentiment; and with the help of federal and state forces (and the Pinkerton agency), he ultimately prevailed over the steelworkers crushing their efforts to retain a union many times, especially in 1911. Not until World War II were the steelworkers able to organize successfully.

—James M. Volo

INTERNATIONAL DIPLOMACY

Gunboat Diplomacy

The mid-nineteenth century period was noted for the series of treaties between the European powers and East Asian governments, particularly China and Japan.

These treaties were generally forced upon the Asian governments and kingdoms through simple demonstrations of naval power known as *gunboat diplomacy*. A number of imperial nations—Britain, Germany, and France, in particular—had projected their force capabilities on the Asian governments in this way to establish naval bases and coaling stations or to arrange economically advantageous relationships for their traders around the world.

Aside from absolute military conquest, gunboat diplomacy was the dominant form used to establish new trade partnerships with nations that were not particularly willing to establish them. A so-called running out of the guns and rigging for combat was often enough to change the direction of difficult negotiations. Those nations without large naval resources or advanced technologies found their resistance dismantled in the face of such pressures. These agreements are commonly known as *unequal treaties* because they are thought to have benefited the foreign powers to a much greater extent than the Asian governments. It would be an error, however, to think that the Asians were not also utilizing their own political strategies in these circumstances.

—*James M. Volo*

Opening China

Rare spices and unusual fragrances could be found in most up-scale markets in the West, and many wealthy Europeans and Americans had collections of Chinese porcelain, lacquered ware, and various other Oriental items like rugs, draperies, and wallpaper arranged in special rooms *à la Chinoise*. The so-called China Trade actually involved about a half dozen major trading destinations other than China in the Far East. These included—besides mainland China and Formosa—India, the East Indies (Spice Islands), the Siamese and Malay Peninsulas, Java, Borneo, Japan, and the Philippines. Traders also visited hundreds of small ports and isolated islands in their quest to complete a cargo of rare goods. The profits realized from spices and authentic Chinese or other Oriental products drove the China Trade throughout the nineteenth century, and American skippers lined up to get command of trading vessels destined for the South China Sea.

China was a trading nation. For centuries Chinese junks had carried goods all over the Far East to the Philippines, Malaysia, Sumatra, and India, and brought back produce and raw materials to their homeports. The Chinese merchants advertised their wares in their shops with bright red characters as they had for hundreds of years. The government was largely unconcerned about regulating the trade of its own people, but became concerned when the first European vessels arrived in the early sixteenth century. Virtually every imperial edict regarding foreign traders described them in derogatory terms.

Although they remained suspicious of all foreigners, the Manchu's who ruled the Chinese government (Qing Dynasty) adopted the idea of expanding its foreign trade, and initially the ships of many countries were encouraged to tie up at Chinese wharves. The pivotal event in the opening of China to American influence was the First Opium War between Britain and China in 1842. The Americans wisely stood on the sidelines during this conflict leading the Chinese to believe that the Americans might be better trading partners than the British. The American traders had not supported themselves with warships and military guards as had the British.

To this point, Chinese-American relations had been conducted solely through trade; however, the 1844 Treaty of Wangxia put American trade and political influence on a par with that of the British. The China trade was enormously important to Americans. New England traders contributed to the national economic revival and created the first American millionaires. Moreover, the search for furs to trade at Canton opened American minds to the importance of its own West Coast. It strengthened the United States' claim to the area later called the Oregon Territory, and it led to the first American contacts with California. Ships in the China trade called at the Sandwich Islands (Hawaii) for water, fresh food, sandalwood, and relaxation, beginning a relationship with islands that eventually resulted in annexation and statehood. Perhaps most importantly, meeting the challenges of the China trade helped to give America a sense of achievement and confidence as an international power. America dominated the China trade throughout much of the nineteenth century increasingly involving itself it internal Chinese affairs and finally joining with other European governments to virtually neuter the traditional government of the Chinese empire (Qing Dynasty) following the Boxer Rebellion (1899–1901).

—*James M. Volo*

Opening Japan

Commodore Matthew Perry of the United States Navy had forced a treaty on the Japanese in 1854 through the use of gunboat diplomacy. The so-called Convention of Kanagawa effectively ended Japan's 200-year-long policy of seclusion from Western influence. The treaty opened the ports of Shimoda and Hadodate to American trading vessels, provided for a permanent American consulate in Japan, and ensured the safety of American mariners shipwrecked on Japanese shores. The agreement was made between Perry, as representative of the United States, and Tokugawa Ieyoshi, the Shogun (de-facto ruler) of Japan. No meeting was held with the Japanese emperor who was thought divine and beyond interacting with foreigners.

Townsend Harris, a successful New York merchant and minor politician, was chosen as the first consul to Japan by President Franklin Pierce, and he is generally credited with opening the Japanese Empire to foreign trade and Western culture. Harris's successes came only after two years of hard-fought negotiations marked by deadlock and cultural misunderstandings. The Tokugawa Shogunate was faced with internal divisions over how Japanese trade with the outside world should be handled. Conscious of the events that had occurred in China, one group favored opening Japanese ports immediately to the West while another hoped to expel all foreigners and carry Japanese goods to its trading partners in Japanese vessels without violating the country's seclusion. Harris used this deepening domestic division to pry concessions from the Japanese.

Harris's treaty terms were more demanding than Perry's, however, demanding beyond trading rights at Yedo (Tokyo) and Osaka, consular services in all cities open to trade, the free export of Japanese gold and silver, and free access to Japanese cities for Americans. There was no parallel expectation that Japanese citizens would be welcome in America. The Harris's Treaty (Treaty of Amity and Commerce) also arranged for an exchange of diplomats, extraterritoriality, and a fixed low import-export tariff. The document became a model for similar agreements negotiated with the Japanese by the Russians, French, and British. Throughout the two years of negotiations, Harris remained poised and respectful gaining both respect and influence among the Japanese people. The Shogunate was weakened by its position, however, and regaining national status and renewed strength became a priority for the new imperial government.

—James M. Volo

Purchase and Annexation

In 1728, a Dane named Vitus Bering sailed through the straits that separated Asia from North America and now bears his name. In 1841 Bering, financed and commissioned by the Russians, was the first modern sailor to explore the coast of Alaska, and from this time Russians were active in the area establishing sealing and fishing stations. In 1776, British Captain James Cook made a brief survey of the region, and he was followed in 1792 by Captain George Vancouver, who circumnavigated the island that bears his name. In the following year Alexander Mackenzie reached the coast by land from the east. In 1799 the Russian-American Fur Company was given a 20-year monopoly to trade in the region under the leadership of Alexander Baranov, who founded the settlement of Sitka in 1805, the year before Lewis and Clark returned to Virginia from the Pacific Coast with their report on the Louisiana Purchase.

Despite the exploration, the details of the region that included Alaska and Oregon remained largely unknown with Russia, Britain, and the United States making competing claims for all or part of it based on exploration and mapping. Initially the agricultural richness of the interior region was less important than the coastal areas that supported abundant populations of seals, otters, and fish. In 1821 Russia decreed that all the coastline south to latitude 51° and out 100 miles from shore was forbidden to foreign vessels. Protests from the United States and Britain quickly followed. The matter was settled by treaties between the United States and Russia (1824) and between Britain and Russia (1825) by which Russian sovereignty was recognized north of 54° 40' and west of 141°.

James K. Polk, an otherwise humorless and unexciting candidate for president of the United States, captured the Executive Mansion in the election of 1844 in part under the slogan concerning the Oregon boundary of "Fifty-four Forty or Fight." With the outgoing Tyler signing the Texas Annexation Act that likely meant war with Mexico on the southern border, Polk had seemingly dedicated the nation to a second front against Britain. However, the British demurred, and the Oregon treaty line with Canada was permanently settled at the 49th parallel in 1846.

Yet this was not to be the end of the story. The phrase, *Manifest Destiny*, caught the imagination of the country and came, thereafter, to stand for the entire expansive movement to the West. Alaska was added by purchase from Russia in 1867 for $7.2 million. Secretary of State William H. Seward was the major proponent of the purchase, and Alaska was referred to as Seward's Icebox for many years. Eight decades earlier Boston skippers had opened trade with the Northwest Coast of North America. So common were the Boston trading vessels on this coast, thereafter that natives from the region called all whites Boston Men. Having received a stock of furs for Yankee Notions like ribbons, mirrors, beads, needles, knives, and cloth, the Boston Men made for China where the furs were exchanged for teas, silks, and porcelain. Seward understood the value of Alaska as the first cog in the wheel of the China trade. Ships in the trade certainly picked up items available only through Chinese manufacture, but in their world-circling tours they also shipped cloves, nutmeg, and mace from the various islands, pepper from Sumatra, coffee from Arabia, tallow from Madagascar, hemp from Luzon, cotton from Bombay, palm oil from the west coast of Africa, and ivory and gums from Zanzibar. The China trade facilitated a worldwide circulation of wealth.

Due to the need to maintain coaling and watering stations across the Pacific, in 1867 the United States had taken possession of Midway Island. It later acquired coaling rights at Tutuila (with its excellent harbor at Pago Pago) and a protectorate at Samoa in consort with Britain and Germany. In the Far East, problems concerning American sailors shipwrecking on the Pacific coast of Asia caused Rear Admiral John Rodgers to visit Korea with a squadron of five ships in 1871. Nonetheless, it was not until 1882 that a treaty was signed with that nation. Meanwhile, the Samoan Islands had become a hotbed of international intrigue among Britain, Germany, and America with each keeping vessels on station to protect their national interests.

As far back as 1867, Admiral David Porter Sr. had said, "Honolulu is bound to be the principal stopping place between China and California and a point of great importance to American commerce" (Howarth 1991, 241). In an 1872 treaty with the islands, safeguards were agreed to that would prevent Hawaii from falling under foreign domination. In 1887 a clause was added that allowed the United States to set up a fortified base at Pearl Harbor to defend the U.S. West Coast and the approaches to a possible canal at the central American isthmus. In 1893, Queen Liliuokalani was overthrown in a bloodless coup by American businessmen aided by the U.S. Consul John L. Stevens and 150 marines from the USS *Boston*. A short-lived Republican government was formed by Sanford B. Dole and recognized by the United States in 1894. Efforts to restore the queen were wrecked by influential members of Dole's provisional government.

In July 1898, Congress formally annexed Hawaii, partially due to its increased importance as a staging area for war with the Spanish Pacific fleet, and partially to secure from German influence the rich fields of sugar cane and pineapple that had been developed. The German government had caused a great deal of unrest through its pretensions in Samoa fostering a civil war in 1898 between rival claimants to the kingship of the island group. A trilateral agreement among Germany, Britain, and the United States settled the competing claims. In 1900, Hawaii was organized as a territory, but unlike the other island possessions it was required to pays its tariff duties, revenue collections, and income taxes to the federal treasury. Due to a shortage of laborers, the government encouraged emigration from Spain, Portugal, and the Philippines, but initially excluded Japanese, Chinese, and Koreans.

By the turn of the century a number of other island possessions had been acquired: Puerto Rico, Guam, and the Philippines in 1898; and Wake Island in 1899. The American nation, initially isolated on a thin strip of land along the Atlantic coast, had attained its *Manifest Destiny* by stretching from sea to sea in little more than a single century, and it had become in the process a multi-ocean colonial power.

—*James M. Volo*

DISCRIMINATION: INDIAN RESERVATIONS

Indian policy at the federal level was initially crafted by George Washington's Secretary of War Henry Knox, and it was carried out by most of the administrations that followed. Knox envisioned a policy of civilization and Christianization for the tribes. He sought to teach the Indians to abandon their traditional gender-based communal economy of male hunting and warfare and female agriculture and child-rearing for a Euro-American lifestyle of male-oriented farming and female domesticity that would allow the tribes to prosper on a much smaller land base. This, it was hoped, would open former Native American lands to white settlement without eradicating the Indians. Herein was the genesis of the Indian reservation. Federal agents relentlessly pushed this civilization program, or a near facsimile, throughout the nineteenth century.

During the Creek War (1814–1815), Andrew Jackson led a force composed of militia and allied native warriors, but he came to believe that there was no real distinction between friendly and hostile Indians. In 1828 Jackson won the presidency, and his popular attitudes toward Native Americans were swept into office with him. Ultimately, like some of his predecessors in office, particularly John Adams and James Monroe, President Jackson came to believe that the government should institute an Indian policy known as *forced relocation*, or *removal*. This policy would displace the remaining tribes of the Old Northwest to the great plains of the Dakotas, or to Minnesota, or to the area west of the Mississippi River now known as Oklahoma. Congressional debate between Whigs and Democrats questioned whether this was best for the Indians, but neither side suggested that the Indians retain their homelands or reestablish their former aboriginal lifestyle elsewhere. Realistically, the raids, hunting, and roaming associated with tribal existence in the past could no longer be accommodated within the boundaries of a developing United States.

To achieve peace in the West and to optimize the possibility of successful acculturation of the Indians, General Nelson A. Miles advocated "placing the Indians under some government strong enough to control them and just enough to command their respect" (Miles 1969, 346). The realities of reservation life and the prejudices held by whites toward Indians, however, impeded or compromised the process that Miles envisioned.

The first problem was the choice of site. Because settlers claimed the best land, many reservations were established in bleak, barren, unproductive, even unhealthy places. In 1863 General James H. Carleton ordered Kit Carson to move the Navajos to the Bosque Redondo, a reservation in sun-baked eastern New Mexico. Those who survived the Long Walk joined their traditional enemies, the Mescalero Apaches, in this sandy, barren land. They dug holes and trenches for shelter and slaughtered cows for hides to use as windbreaks and for shade. There were no trees, as the few that had grown in the immediate area had been cut to build Fort Sumner.

Of Fort Sumner and the Bosque Redondo, Eveline Alexander, a cavalry officer's wife, wrote: "I never saw such an undesirable location for a post, and especially for a large Indian reservation" (Alexander 1977, 116). Shocked by the conditions, and aware that "the Navajos in their native country beyond the Rio Grande were a wealthy tribe" (Alexander 1977, 119), she concerned herself more than most army wives with the plight of the Indians (Alexander 1977, 20). She wrote of the 8,000 Navajos living like prisoners of war. Rations were distributed every other day. "The daily ration...is three-fourths of a pound of flour and meat and a handful of salt to each Indian, little or big. Not much to support life on, one would think" (Alexander 1977, 117). According to another contemporary account, "the brackish water they drank brought dysentery...[and] the reservation, situated on the edge of a treeless expanse of prairie, quickly depleted fuel close at hand. Resources of cedar and mesquite retreated farther and farther...until Navajos were traveling twelve to twenty miles for mesquite root, which they carried 'upon their galled and lacerated backs'" (Alexander 1977, 160 n. 24). Although Eveline Alexander observed some Navajos hoeing corn (Alexander 1977, 117), conditions were so bad that "Navajos had to be forced to work at bayonet point" (Alexander 1977, 160).

In a report to Washington, General Carleton called all this "a grand experiment to make civilized human beings out of savages...they...discard...their ways and learn how to be like white men....To gather them together little by little into a reservation away from the haunts and hills and hiding places of their country and there...teach the children how to read and write; teach them the art of peace; teach them the truths of Christianity. Soon they will acquire new habits, new ideas, new modes of life" (Josephy 1994, 355).

The Indians perceived this process quite differently. Frederick Peso, whose people, the Mescalero Apaches, shared the Bosque Redondo, declared, "The surest way to kill a race is to kill its religious ideals. Can anybody doubt that the white man attempted to do that? And when the Spirit is killed, what remains?" (Josephy 1994, 355).

The physical impact of the reservation was not unique to the Navajos, of course. Historian Robert M. Utley described the San Carlos reservation as "a terrible place to live" (Utley 1964, 196). Daklugie, Geronimo's nephew, also attempted a description: "The Creator did not make San Carlos. It is older than he....He just left it as a sample of the way they did things before He came along....Take stones and ashes and thorns, and, with some scorpions and rattlesnakes thrown in, dump the outfit on stones, heat the stones red-hot, set the United States Army after the Apaches, and you have San Carlos" (Josephy 1994, 428).

General Miles was aware of the effect of climate as he argued for Indians to be returned to their native lands. "The climate and country of Montana and the Dakotas produced as fine physical specimens of the human race as have ever been found on this continent," he wrote of the Sioux (Miles 1969, 254). "The forcing of strong, hardy mountain Indians from the extreme north to the warmer malarial districts of the South was cruel, and the experiment should never be repeated" (Miles 1969, 347).

Helen Hunt Jackson took up the cause of the Native American in her exposé, A Century of Dishonor, a documented attack on the federal government's Indian policy. Describing the plight of the Northern Cheyenne during 1877 and 1878, she recounts how their hunts had been unsuccessful because game was gone, how their pony herd had been decimated, how rations had been reduced, and how malaria raged through the reservation, where the medical supplies were inadequate. She concludes that such a life on the reservation is hardly likely to appeal to the Indians' better nature and lead them to civilization:

If it is to "appeal to men's better natures" to remove them by force from a healthful Northern climate, which they love and thrive in, to a malarial Southern one, where they are struck down by chills and fever—refuse them medicine…and finally starve them—then, indeed [this] might be said to have been most forcible appeals to the "better natures" of those Northern Cheyenne. What might have been predicted followed. (Jackson, quoted in Jones 1994, 69–70)

Indians were literally dying to go home. Outbreaks were inevitable, and though not all were violent, some were, intensifying a cycle of frustration and retribution. Any Indian off the reservations was considered hostile. When a band of the Northern Cheyenne under Dull Knife decided to return north from Indian Territory, they automatically fell into this category. Additionally, by occasionally killing cattle along the way for food, they incensed settlers. Captured again, held at Fort Robinson, Nebraska, and told they would be returned south, they were adamant. "That is not a beautiful country. If we go there, we would all die.…We will not go." Said Dull Knife, "You may kill me here; but you cannot make me go back." While General George Crook argued strongly with the Indian Bureau about a better location for them, the commander at Fort Robinson tried to starve them into submission, cutting off their rations and withholding water. The result was an outbreak, though escape was hopeless, with casualties among both soldiers and Indians before the 78 surviving Cheyenne gave up. Ironically, wrote Crook, "Among the Cheyenne Indians were some of the bravest and most efficient of the auxiliaries who had [served with me] in the campaign against the hostile Sioux in 1876 and 1877.…I still preserve a grateful remembrance of their distinguished service, which the government seems to have forgotten" (Crook 1960, 223–26).

There is no question that the central purpose of the reservation system was to change Indians' cultures, to Americanize them. As tribal identity began to change, "whole clusters of customs, activities, attitudes, values, and institutions lost reliance and meaning and...began to vanish" (Utley 1964, 236). Whereas warfare had once defined a man's honor, provided a congerie of important rituals, and touched on aspects of celebration and mourning, social structure, and individual maturation, it was now proscribed. Whereas the hunt once not only provided most of a tribe's needs but also gave a sense of the rhythm of the year, a calendar organically linked to nature, it was no longer possible. Religion too had once linked man to nature in a profound sense of the Creator's beneficence; these religions were now called pagan and some of them forbidden. As even George A. Custer was aware, this reordering of life was cataclysmic. "The Indian has to sacrifice all that is dear to his heart" (Custer 1962, 21).

Government Indian policy was not flexible enough to make exceptions, in effect illustrating the belief that "once you've seen one Indian, you've seen them all." A corollary to this inability to see Indians as individuals was the pattern, throughout the period of the Plains Indian wars, of indiscriminately punishing one group of Indians for the depredations of another.

The tragedy of the Indian wars and of the reservation life that followed was not in the number of deaths, which was relatively small, but rather in the destruction of a way of life. Francis Paul Prucha, a Catholic priest as well as a scholar on relations between the U.S. government and the Indians, preaches a eulogy for that way of life:

The change was to be made from the nomadic life of a buffalo hunter to the sedentary life of a small farmer, from communal patterns to fiercely individualistic ones, from native religious ceremonials to Christian practices, from Indian languages and oral traditions to spoken and written English. For most of the reservation Indians, the changes were a shattering experience, demoralizing rather than uplifting (Prucha 1986, 222).

From across the cultural divide the Oglala holy man Black Elk wrote, remembering Wounded Knee:

I did not know then how much had ended. When I look back now from this high hill of my old age, I can still see the butchered women and children lying heaped and scattered all along the crooked gulch as plain as when I saw them with eyes still young. And I can see that something else died there in the bloody mud, and was buried in the blizzard. A people's dream died there. It was a beautiful dream.... The nation's hoop is broken and scattered. There is no center any longer, and the sacred tree is dead. (Neihardt 1932, 276)

REFORM

Farmers v. Railroads

Farm unrest in the Midwest and elsewhere in the 1870s had profound and lasting political consequences. The changes began during the economic Panic of 1873 and continued through the five years of grasshopper plagues that claimed much of the agricultural lifeblood of the nation from 1873 through 1877. The unrest was closely tied to the belief that the railroad, grain elevator, and warehouse operators were purposely disadvantaging the small farmer through their monopolies and tight money practices. In response to these complaints many Midwestern states enacted laws regulating the prices and practices of these businesses. Called the Granger Laws, these pieces of legislation reversed the longstanding trend of decreasing government regulation of the private sector after the Civil War.

The laws also prompted a series of landmark court cases concerning the regulatory prerogatives of government. In *Munn v. Illinois* (1877), the U.S. Supreme Court rejected a challenge to the legality of the Granger Laws affirming that government had the right to regulate any commerce affecting the public interest. The farmers also sought redress from the justices in 1886 in *Wabash, St. Louis, and Pacific Railway v. Illinois*, but the court ruled that only the federal government had the right to regulate commerce between the states. This left many of the concerns of the farmers unresolved to their liking.

In 1887, Congress passed the Interstate Commerce Act, which created the Interstate Commerce Commission to provide oversight of long distance rail shipping. This legislation was followed by the Sherman Antitrust Act of 1890, which prohibited monopolies, conspiracies, combinations, and restraints of trade. Midwestern cattle ranchers urged the passage of the act alleging that the meat packing syndicate in Chicago had conspired to keep beef prices artificially low. This legislation marked an increased willingness of government to involve itself in private and corporate economic activity.

—James M. Volo

Taming the West

Civilization pushed its way even to the cow towns, and an increasing number of their permanent residents—shopowners, doctors, lawyers, ministers, and teachers let it be known that cowboys and their violent ways were no longer welcome. Although the wide-open towns had brought a temporary infusion of money, good money was beginning to be made in land speculation and construction. Thus, city governments began to pass ordinances forbidding the bearing of firearms within town limits and appointing marshals and deputies to deal with those who did. Reformers began to levy fines on prostitution and gambling, though cynics felt these were less to curtail sin than to raise local revenue. Nonetheless, changes were in the wind. When one newspaper editor wrote, "People who have money to invest go where they are protected by law" (Forbis 1973, 186), there was the clear suggestion that one era—that of the trail drive and the open range—was closing and a new one—that of farmers and entrepreneurs—was opening. Whether one attributes the change to the completion of more and more branch lines of the railroads, or to the increasing use of barbed wire, or to the disastrous winter of 1886–1887 in which thousands of cattle died frozen on the northern plains, "the life that surrounded [the cattle trails] could not endure. The homes of thousands of settlers have pre-empted the grazing grounds. Railroads are ten times more numerous than were the trails, and like the cavalier, the troubadour, the Puritan, and the 'Forty-Niner,' the cowboy and his attendant life have become but figures in history" (Harger 1892, 742; Jones 1998, 181–82).

FOR MORE INFORMATION

Abbott, E. C. ("Teddy Blue"), and Helena Huntington Smith. *We Pointed Them North: Recollections of a Cowpuncher*. New York: Farrar & Rinehart, 1939.

Albion, Robert G., and Jennie B. Pope. *Sealanes in Wartime*. Portland, ME: Archon Books, 1968.

Alexander, Eveline M. *Cavalry Wife: The Diary of Eveline M. Alexander, 1866–1867*. Edited by Sandra L. Myres. College Station: Texas A&M University Press, 1977.

Barnard, Edward S. *Reader's Digest Story of the Great American West*. Pleasantville, NY: The Reader's Digest Association, Inc., 1977.

Barney, William L., ed. *A Companion to 19th-Century America*. Malden, MA: Blackwell Publishing, 2006.

Bauer, K. Jack. *A Maritime History of the United States: The Role of America's Seas and Waterways*. Columbia: University of South Carolina Press, 1989.

Crook, George. *General George Crook: His Autobiography*. Edited by Martin F. Schmitt. Norman: University of Oklahoma Press, 1960.

Custer, General George Armstrong. *My Life on the Plains: Or, Personal Experiences with Indians*. Norman: University of Oklahoma Press, 1962.

Dulles, Foster Rhea. *The Old China Trade*. New York: Houghton Mifflin Company, 1930.

Forbis, William H. *The Old West: The Cowboys*. New York: Time Life Books, 1973.

Goldman, Marion S. *Gold Diggers & Silver Miners: Prostitution and Social Life on the Comstock Lode*. Ann Arbor: University of Michigan Press, 1981.

Harger, Charles Moreau. "Cattle-Trails of the Prairies." *Scribner's Magazine* (June 1892): 732–42.

Harris, Townsend. *The Complete Journal of Townsend Harris: First American Consul General and Minister to Japan*. With an introduction by Mario Emilio Cozena. Whitefish, MT: Kessinger Publishing, 2007.

Hill, Peter J. "Old West Violence Mostly Myth." *The Arizona Republic* (June 19, 2007).

Hine, Robert V. *Community on the American Frontier: Separate But Not Alone*. Norman: University of Oklahoma Press, 1980.

Howarth, Stephen. *To Shining Sea, A History of the United States Navy, 1775–1991*. New York: Random House, 1991.

Jones, Mary Ellen, ed. *The American Frontier: Opposing Viewpoints*. San Diego, CA: Greenhaven Press, 1994.

———. *Daily Life on the Nineteenth-Century American Frontier*. Westport, CT: Greenwood Press, 1998.

Josephy, Alvin M., Jr. *500 Nations: An Illustrated History of North American Indians*. New York: Alfred A. Knopf, 1994.

Miles, General Nelson A. *Personal Recollections and Observations of General Nelson A. Miles*. New York: Da Capo Press, 1969.

National Livestock Association. *Prose and Poetry of the Live Stock Industry of the United States.* New York: Antiquarian Press, 1904/1959.

Neihardt, John. *Black Elk Speaks.* Lincoln: University of Nebraska Press, 1932.

Prucha, Francis Paul. *The Great Father: The United States Government and the American Indians.* Abridged ed. Lincoln: University of Nebraska Press, 1986.

Roosevelt, Theodore. *Memories of the American Frontier.* New York: Westvaco, 1977.

Semonche, John E. "American Law in the Nineteenth Century, 1867–1900." In *A Companion to 19th-Century America,* ed. William L. Barney. Malden, MA: Blackwell Publishing, 2006.

Shrock, Joel. *The Gilded Age.* Westport, CT: Greenwood Press, 2004.

Siringo, Charles A. *A Lone Star Cowboy.* Santa Fe, NM: n.p., 1919.

Stewart, James. "The Economics of American Farm Unrest, 1865–1900," EH.Net Encyclopedia, edited by Robert Whaples. http://eh.net/encyclopedia/article/stewart.farmers (accessed May 2006).

Utley, Robert M. *The Indian Frontier of the American West, 1846–1890.* Albuquerque: University of New Mexico Press, 1964.

Van Dyke, Paul A. *The Canton Trade: Life and Enterprise on the China Coast, 1700–1845.* Hong Kong: Hong Kong University Press, 2005.

Wolff, Leon. *Lockout: The Story of the Homestead Strike of 1892.* New York: Harper & Row Publishers, Inc., 1965.

Recreational Life

SPORTS

Horse Racing

Horse racing was much favored by the upper classes, and regular courses for its prosecution had been maintained since colonial times. The breeding of racehorses was also very popular among the wealthy. Thoroughbreds (initially three foundation bloodlines, Byerley Turk, Darley Arabian, and Godolphin Arab) running on flat straight or oval tracks had been around since the eighteenth century, and Americans were overjoyed to be seen as doing something so thoroughly British. The great-great-grandson of the Darley Arabian was Eclipse, the sole direct ancestor of all American thoroughbred breeds. Although almost all horse racing experts chart the bloodline of thoroughbreds to one of the foundation sires, the concept is somewhat artificial. Hundreds of Arabians, Barbs (from the Barbary States), Turks, and other stallions were brought into England and the United States before the stud books were so meticulously kept. The bloodline of the Darcy White Turk is often considered as legitimate as that of other thoroughbreds. The line of Lexington, another fine American stallion of the period, unfortunately was allowed to run out, and no descendants of this commendable Kentucky stallion are known to exist. Diomed was the first premiere thoroughbred of the nineteenth century in

America, and when he died, suddenly there was great widespread mourning among the American public.

The exclusivity of horse breeding appealed to the upper classes. President Andrew Jackson won thousands of dollars racing his own horse, Truxton, who sired an entire line of racehorses for his stable. Sundays were favorite times for races, which often ended in near riots when the outcome was in dispute. The greatest sensation of the period was the match race between Henry and Eclipse (not the English sire but a descendant referred to as the American Eclipse). This was held in New York in front of 40,000 spectators, and it was followed in the newspapers by the whole nation (Volo and Volo 2000, 133–34).

Trotting

During most of the nineteenth century horses remained a method of transportation, but many people eschewed the saddle for the use of buggies and wagons with the horse in harness. Human nature and the common spirit of competitiveness often led buggy drivers to race their best horses against those of their neighbors. As such, these harness races were more egalitarian and democratic than thoroughbred racing with its distinctly aristocratic roots. The common competitive spirit was also instrumental in developing specific types of harness horses (either trotters or pacers) and smaller, lighter, and quicker buggies commonly called sulkies. Trotting horses move their diagonal legs in a two-beat gait while pacers move the legs on the same side of their bodies together while trotting. Such horses were not meant to gallop or lope (four-beat gaits) while in harness. Currently in America there are four pacers for every trotter.

Ultimately a bloodline standard was set for trotting and pacing horses, and they came to be called Standardbreds to distinguish them from the thoroughbred race horses. The term comes from the standard length of a one-mile race (eight furlongs). The bloodline charts of the standardbred were first published by J. H. Wallace in 1871 in the *American Trotting Register*. This listing was primarily of thoroughbred horses used as harness racers, but in its eighth edition the horses listed were exclusively considered standardbreds.

Rather than have their citizenry racing about of the local roads, many communities created either driving parks or trotting parks where practice and competition could be controlled along the outer perimeter. From these evolved the first standardbred race courses. Soon local competitors were joined by famous national racers who competed with breeds and horses exclusively raised for racing. The bloodlines of standardbreds soon became as well-known and as well-noted as any among the thoroughbreds. Gambling often drove the competition as it did for other forms of racing, and although there was no pari-mutuel wagering as is known today, there were wagering pools of so-called bookies being operated in the nineteenth century.

Rodeo

Adapted from the Spanish word for a cattle round up, rodeo grew from spontaneous and impromptu contests among cowboys testing their abilities on the range into a national, and international sport. The livestock that was handled by cowboys and ranchers was truly wild. Long-horned cattle, fed and wintered on open range, were particularly dangerous to both horse and rider. The roping and tying of steers and calves for branding was a common spring activity, and roping and tying were the first formal rodeo contests. Barrel racing, bull riding, bareback bronco riding, saddle riding, and steer dogging (wrestling the animal to the ground) were added later.

The exact origins of competitive rodeo are clouded in the cowboy mystique of the so-called Wild West, but the first formal rodeo may have been that sponsored by Colonel George Miller in Kansas in 1882. A candidate for the first professional rodeo may be that held in Prescott, Arizona Territory in 1888. Cash purses were awarded for first ($25) and second ($15) place in a number of categories. This particular competition was not called a rodeo, but a Cowboy Tournament.

The longest running continuous rodeo is the Cheyenne Frontier Days, which began around the end of the nineteenth century. This featured women competitors for the first time. Women had been active in Wild West Shows for many years before they entered competitive rodeo.

—*James M. Volo*

MUSIC

Westward Expansion Music

The miners, loggers, homesteaders, and cowboys who settled the West all contributed to the body of song that developed during the process of westward expansion. Some created songs as a means of dealing with the experience. Others lived the lives that provided inspiration. Songs circulated orally and in the semi-oral format of songsters, broadsides, and newspapers. Songwriters, who were always ready to capitalize on any trend or event that was likely to sell songs, realized the potential of the West as a source of inspiration. Songs like *To the West* (1845) by Henry Russell and Charles McKay were drenched in Victorian values and melodrama, drew a clear line between good and evil, and found virtue in the pioneering way of life.

Another popular song, *Home on the Range* (1872), presents a romanticized image of the cowboy. Its authors, Daniel E. Kelley and Brewster Higley, idealized the West in the most florid terms, depicting it as a land of milk and honey, hope and promise. As living conditions became increasingly congested in the East after the war, the idealized West beckoned more and more strongly, and those people who could not or would not make the trip could use the wings of song to carry them there (Browne and Kreiser 2003, 133).

Making Music

Many immigrants brought instruments with them on their journey, though these were frequently abandoned, along with other extraneous items, when lighter loads were necessary to complete the trip. Whenever possible, instruments, such as fiddles, guitars, mouth organs, harmonicas, bass instruments, drums, and pianos were used to accompany individual and group singers who performed around campfires, in dance halls, at parades, and in private homes. The Sears, Roebuck and Montgomery Ward catalogs offered settlers mail-order access to new instruments, as well as to sheet music, metronomes, and books on how to play anything from the piano and banjo to the mandolin or fife. Ball Room Guides and Call Books, which brought dancers and musicians together in one of the most popular activities in town, the local dance, were also available.

The westward journey, whether completed by boat, by wagon, or by foot, was at once physically rigorous, emotionally draining, and intellectually boring. Music helped immigrants to cope with these different experiences by providing a distraction that was community oriented, words that reflected internal feelings and an activity that was enjoyable. During her journey by sea, Mrs. Jane McDougal wrote that Captain Forbes played the accordion while he and Captain Thomas accompanied with their voices. Familiar songs were used to pass the time and to bring small clusters of travelers together.

For Catherine Haun, another pioneer, songs met an additional need. Describing her fellow traveler with a gift for music, Haun wrote that the familiar tunes he played on his harmonica seemed to soften the groaning and creaking of the wagons and to shorten the long miles of the mountain road. She felt that *Home, Sweet Home, My Old Kentucky Home, Maryland, My Maryland, The Girl I Left Behind Me,* and *One More Ribber to Cross* seemed particularly appropriate and touched many a pensive heart. For Haun, music not only helped to relieve the boredom of the trip but also was an outlet for the emotions that were part and parcel of making such tremendous life changes. The fact that the songs she lists refer to either home or what was being left behind illustrates the mixed emotions experienced by many westbound pioneers. Singing helped to express despondent feelings for one mother who wrote to her son that she felt so bad to be in such a place that she wept and then began singing. She made up a song about going to California and having to run under a bed to shelter from the piercing storm. Putting experiences such as these into song provided an outlet for Westerners to express their feelings and to comfort themselves.

Music was not just used to lighten heavy hearts. In the evenings, when camps had been set up and dinner had been eaten, singing around the campfires was a way to bring the travelers together and to rejuvenate them after a long day.

While music played a role in the journey west, it was also an important part of creating social systems in frontier towns. There were numerous means through which music provided entertainment in Western communities, from formal gatherings in which local musicians met to sing and play instruments, to informal, spontaneous performances. Music also brought people together in private homes. Many people had pianos around which friends and family gathered in the evening to sing songs like *Shall We Gather at the River?* and *Pass Under the Rod.*

Some musical gatherings entertained the entire town. Local bands were a common facet of Western communities, providing music for parades as well as local saloons and dance halls. The Dodge City "Cowboy Band" was an especially well-known group that traveled as far as Washington, D.C., to perform. Each member of the

18-man band wore a large sombrero, a blue flannel shirt with a silk scarf, leather leggings supported by a cartridge belt, a six-shooter, and boots with spurs. If no musical instruments were available at a gathering, spectators would provide their own music by singing, clapping, and stamping their feet to the beat of *Skip to My Lou*, *Weevily Wheat*, *The Girl I Left Behind Me*, and *Old Dan Tucker*.

Frontier musicals were especially popular around army posts where groups of musicians were more likely to be available than anywhere else on the frontier. Favorite pieces included *Tenting Tonight*, *Old Hundred*, *Near My God to Thee*, *Annie Laurie*, and *When Swallows Homeward Fly*. Concert performances by singers like Kate Hays, Lola Montez, and Caroline Chapman were also well attended. Traveling from the stages of cities like San Francisco and Sacramento to remote locations of boom-and-bust mining towns, these performers captured the attention of many Westerners with their singing and dancing routines. While musical performances were welcomed and attendance was high, some Westerners complained about the trend to play music while actors were speaking their lines.

Music was also incorporated into public and private celebrations. The Fourth of July was always well celebrated in the West, with band music and other performances. The Christmas Ball was another annual town event at which music played a key role. On a private level, the tradition of a shivaree, a wedding night celebration, resulted in raucous, but no less enjoyable, music. Music was used to mourn deaths as well, usually with hymns. Deaths during the westward journey, not to mention in the early years of settlement, were extremely common occurrences, but they were no less acknowledged for their frequency. A traveler described the combination of making do with available resources, while adhering to familiar rituals. Hymns in general were a familiar and popular form of music, sung in and out of formal church services.

The music that has recorded the experience of the West has several key characteristics. Tunes were borrowed from familiar pieces of music from the East, as well as from English ballads and Irish folk tunes. The familiarity of a tune like *Pop Goes the Weasel* or *Comin' Through the Rye* made the songs easy to learn and simple to communicate. The words that accompanied the tunes, however, were unique because they humorously parodied the song's original lyrics or because they cleverly represented the new experience of life in the West. The words and stories that comprised the songs of the frontier were taken from newspaper stories or from pamphlets, broadsides, or books. Songs were orally communicated, and as a result, the records of early Western music are somewhat inconsistent, especially in terms of exact words, as these could be altered from one singer to the next. The lyrics tended to rhyme in a structured pattern. The simple rhymes helped people to memorize the songs more easily, encouraging the circulation among the miners, cowboys, and other Westerners.

Collections such as *Put's Original California Songster* (1854), *Put's Golden Songster* (1858), and *Gold Digger's Song Book* (1856) were among the earliest and best-known publications of Western songs and helped to standardize the multiple versions and to further familiarize Westerners with music of the gold rush. When the songs were performed, there were some basic guidelines to which musicians adhered. The fiddle typically accompanied frontier songs and the banjo became increasingly popular over time.

Perhaps the earliest Western music can be found in the songs of the forty-niners, miners who rushed across the continent to make their fortunes in gold. Performed in makeshift theatres and saloons, published in the popular press, and collected in cheaply printed volumes, the songs were constantly changing as new miners in different settings adapted the words to fit their own experiences. *Oh! Susanna* became *Oh! California*. The words were recycled over and over as new waves of immigrants traveled west. Songs like *Seeing the Elephant*, one of the first to be written in the West, were hugely popular as well as those by John A. Stone, also known as "Old Put." Frequently written by minstrel troupes and aimed at capturing in music the essence of mining life, the songs of the forty-niners offer a unique perspective on the rush of westward expansion.

The songs that remain from this era trace the voyage west, by boat and by wagon, and express the longings, expectations, and realities of the gold rush experience. They capture with concrete, often humorous, images and details of mining life. At times, the songs are sentimental as in *I Often think of Writing Home*, which tells the tale of a miner who considers writing home but who rarely does. They also describe the reasons for heading west or make fun of the impact the journey had on relationships. The very popular *Joe Bowers* chronicles a young man's journey to California to establish a homestead for his sweetheart who turns out to be fickle and marries another man. Another version of the love-gone-astray story, *Sweet Betsy from Pike*, describes Betsy and Ike, a young couple who endured endless obstacles during their travels west, only to have their relationship end when they arrive there. Other songs either express a darkly humorous version of the journey or a satirical description of life in the mines. Songs like *California Stage Company*, *Humbug Steamship Companies*, and *When I Went Off to Prospect* challenged the popular belief that the journey west was an easy one and that life was immediately prosperous upon arrival in California. The humor present in many mining songs may have developed in response to the arduous, continuous and often futile nature of mining itself as a way to endure the challenges of that way of life.

While the forty-niners' songs were often humorous, they were also surprisingly informative. In *Crossing the Plains* the lyrics tell about the number of days, amount of food, and impact on cattle that occurred during the westward journey. More factual than many of the guidebooks upon which emigrants depended to make their trip from the East, early mining songs provided Westerners with an alternative form of communicating the rigors of their trip to the land of gold.

Whereas mining songs were primarily sung for entertainment, cowboys also used music as a way of recording their own experiences, as a companion to their work, and as a way to provide camaraderie during the evenings on the plains. Their work songs not only marked the time during cattle drives, but they also it calmed cattle during long marches and lulled them to sleep at night. While songs were passed among cowboys, specific ranches tended to have their own individual song and set of verses of their own making. One cowboy would lead off composing these verses, which the others would take up, chorusing whenever the song was sung. When a new man joined the outfit, he was expected to sing any new song he might know or new stanzas to an old song and to teach them to the camp. Songs like *The Old Chisolm Trail* grew to interminable length (Quay 2002, 171–77).

LEISURE ACTIVITIES

Vacation Destinations

Nineteenth-century vacationers—dedicated to an outdoor life—were drawn to visit the many natural wonders of America like caves, natural arches, unique geological features, and waterfalls. Cave tours were considered agreeable and instructive with a pleasant sensation of refreshing coolness especially in summer. Nonetheless, caving could be physically difficult for some visitors. Mammoth Cave in Kentucky catered to its visitors by supplying "a large and commodious hotel...two or three hundred paces from the mouth of the cave...with lights, guides, and whatever else may be required for their expeditions." This afforded the visitors to the cave a view of "its vast dimensions, its great heights and depths in different apartments, and of the singularity and beauty of the natural decoration they contain" (Haywood 1853, 650).

The Pavilion Hotel opened in 1883 and served visitors to Howe's Caves in central New York. This was a wonderful cavern first discovered by Lester Howe in 1842 and a great favorite as a touring destination for young adults vacationing in the Northeast. The cave was advertised in a newspaper clipping from June 1883 as one of the most remarkable curiosities in the United States. A description of the new hotel noted, "The rooms are large, well ventilated, handsomely furnished, and en suite or single. It has accommodations for 200 guests. It has all the modern improvements of a First-Class Hotel. Our Patrons will find the Cuisine, style and management unsurpassed. It is located on the brow of the mountain commanding one of the most picturesque and beautiful views to be found in the state; has fine shade trees, and pure water; no mosquitoes or Malaria. There is good livery connected with the Hotel, and the Cobleskill and Schoharie Valleys afford the finest scenery and drives in the country.... The Pavilion Hotel [is] 39 miles from Albany, on the Albany and Susquehanna R.R., only five minutes walk from the depot" (Volo and Volo 2007, 343).

Also in this area, made famous as the setting for many of the popular frontier novels of James Fenimore Cooper, were a number of smaller establishments including the Mineral Springs Hotel in Cobleskill, the Parrot House Hotel in Schoharie, the American Hotel and Rose Hotel in Sharon Springs, the fully electrified Sagamore Hotel on Lake George, and the gracious Hotel Fenimore on Lake Otsego in Cooperstown at the headwaters of the Susquehanna River. All boasted the good effects of their sulfated water, moderate summer temperatures, and clean air; and each was located on first-class plank roads serviced by daily stagecoaches that connected to the historical sites from the American Revolution, the natural wonders and rock outcroppings, and the romantic blue-green freshwater lakes of the region.

Tours of the ruins of the French and English forts from the era of the colonial wars at Lake George, Crown Point, and Ticonderoga in New York were very popular and could be reached after a revitalizing steamboat cruise on the lake. Of course, at the time, the sites were just battlefields and outlines in ruin. It would take another century before full-scale recreations of historic places would become common. Yet the ruins had a certain romantic and Gothic quality that fit the period, and the steamboat landings—like the one at Ticonderoga that has survived to the present day—were fitted with Georgian-style gardens, walking paths, and picnicking facilities. From New York City by steamer up the Hudson River and through the Champlain Canal "passengers leave the Champlain boat [at Whitehall, New York] for stage coaches by which they are conveyed over a hilly but romantic road about three miles to Ticonderoga, at the head of Lake George, and thence down the lake, 36 miles, by steamboat, to the Lake House [Hotel], at its southern extremity [Lake George Village, site of Fort William Henry]…and from thence to Saratoga Springs" (Haywood 1853, 646).

Natural cataracts like Bellows Falls in Vermont, Catawba Falls in North Carolina, and St. Anthony's Falls on the far away upper Mississippi River were considered great natural wonders. "The river seems to stop for a moment [before] it encounters the fall; then, breaking through every obstacle, it plunges on, its huge billows breaking on the rocks, and throwing a shower of spray [with] great grandeur and beauty." Niagara Falls, the outlet of the fresh water flowing from the Great Lakes was "justly regarded as one of the most sublime and imposing spectacles in nature." The volume of falling water, estimated at over half a million tons per minute, the precipitous heights, and tremendous roar were amazing. "It is the vastness of elements like these, entering into the conception of this stupendous natural phenomenon, which carries the emotions of wonder and sublimity with which it strikes the outward senses to their highest bounds" (Haywood 1853, 657; Volo and Volo 2007, 342–44).

MID-CENTURY TRAVEL DESTINATIONS

Mineral springs, waterfalls, caves, beaches, and other fashionable resorts as identified by *Hayward's Gazetteer*, 1853

Ascutney Mountain, VT	Madison's Cave, VA
Avon Springs, NY	Madison Springs, GA
Ballston Spa, NY	Mammoth Cave, KY
Bellows Falls, VT	Mitchell's Peak, NC
Black Mountain, SC	Monadnock Mountain, NH
Blennerhassett's Island, OH	Montauk Point, NY

Blue Hills, MA	Montmorency Falls, Canada
Blue Sulphur Springs, VA	Mount Everett, MA
Booth Bay, ME	Mount Holyoke, MA
Brandywine Springs, DE	Mount Hope, RI
Burning Springs, NY	Mount Vernon. VA
Cape Ann, MA	Nahant, MA
Cape May, NJ	Nantasket Beach, MA
Carrolton Gardens, LA	Natural Bridge, VA
Catawba Falls, NC	New Lebanon Springs, NY
Cohasset Rocks, MA	Newport, RI
Cohoes Falls, NY	Niagara, Falls, NY
Coney Island, NY	Nickajack Cave, GA
Crown Point, NY	Old Man of the Mountain, NH
Dighton Rock, MA	Old Orchard Beach, ME
Drennon Springs, KY	Onondaga Salt Springs, NY
Flushing [Bay], NY	Passaic Falls, NJ
Fort Ticonderoga, NY	Phillip's Point, MA
Franconia Notch, NH	Pine Orchard, NY
Gingercake Rocks, NC	Pleasant Mountain, ME
Guilford Point, CT	Plum Island, MA
Hampton Beach, NH	Plymouth Rock, MA
Harper's Ferry, VA	Red Sulphur Springs, VA
Harrodsburg Springs, VA	Richfield Springs, NY
Hoboken, NJ	Roan Mountain, NC
Hopkins Springs, MA	Rockaway Beach, NY
Hot Springs, AK	Rye Beach, NY
Hot Springs, VA	Sachem's Head, CT
House of Nature, IL	Saguenay River, Canada
Indian Springs, GA	Salisbury Beach, MA
Isles of Shoals, ME	Salt Sulphur Springs, VA
Latonia Springs, KY	Saratoga Springs, NY
Long Beach, NJ	Saybrook Point, CT
Lookout Mountain, GA	Weir's Cave, VA

SOCIAL EVENTS

The range of social activities available to Westerners was limited only by the imagination. While some events were imported from the East, these were frequently altered to meet the resources available in the place and time they were enjoyed. New types of gatherings were also developed in response to the needs of community members whose lives demanded hard work and attention to daily survival.

Social gatherings were typically planned in advance and celebrated specific events, including birthdays, Christmas, Independence Day, housewarmings, and weddings. Other events were more spontaneous and took place any time of the year. The surprise party, for instance, was a popular fad defined by the unexpected arrival of a group of well-wishers at someone's home. The individual would be surprised by the well-wishers who would bring food and entertainment for all to share throughout the evening.

Other types of gatherings were organized around an activity or a theme. The most common was the bee during which neighbors would gather to build a house, sew a quilt, or complete other tasks that would be more easily done by a group than an individual. Failure to invite a neighbor was considered an indignity. Not only did folks enjoy the camaraderie of the event, they felt a desire to contribute to the general improvement of the community. Both men and women typically attended house or barn raisings and husking and haying bees, while quilting, sewing, and crocheting bees were popular among women only. One woman wrote that if a family was reduced to poverty by fire or sickness or anything else, the neighboring ladies, in good circumstances, immediately gathered together at a central location to sew for them. Whatever the objective, a bee was an occasion during which frontier men and women combined work with friendship, thereby strengthening community connections in the process.

In contrast to the work-oriented nature of bees, events like hug socials, candy pulls, box suppers, and community picnics were arranged to provide the opportunity to socialize with others, primarily those of the opposite sex. Candy pulls required men and women to work as partners to pull a stringy, sugary candy until it broke. Box suppers were prepared by women for men, who were expected to pay or, sometimes, even bid for the dinners that had been put together.

Western-style socialization also provided a place for masculine competition that was expressed and channeled through a range of rugged contests. From logging rivalries, in which the success was measured by the speed and accuracy of wood chopping, to team pulling, which focused on the weight and distance of team animals that could haul a load in a designated time, contests were popular activities. In addition to providing pleasure to the spectators, such games transformed the hard work of the frontier into a measurable expression of expertise. Similar types of contests included challenges centered on mining, drilling, and plowing (Quay 2002, 136–39).

COMMUNITY GAMES

Traditional forms of competitive sports made their way quickly across the frontier and immigrants reported engaging in, watching, and betting on such athletic events as wrestling, boxing, target shooting, and horse racing. These activities centered on the success of one person and emphasized the ruggedness of Western life and the self-reliance that was the basis of survival there. Such events also provided spectators with action-filled rivalry that allowed them to root for one participant over another.

Other frontier games were socially oriented and often played at picnics, holiday gatherings and other social events. Leapfrog games, wheelbarrow competitions, and sack races were played regularly by people of all ages. Warm weather sports included baseball, croquet, and tennis, while in the winter ice skating and sleigh riding were common activities. Horseback riding, a primary form of transportation for many Westerners, was also enjoyed as a form of entertainment. Such group activities fostered a sense of community and built relationships while providing entertainment.

Some sporting activities involved animals. Buffalo hunting was an early pastime that was done more for sport than for food. Dogfights and cockfights were also popular, allowing men to bet on the winners. The bear and bullfight, an event in which a bear was brought to a bullpen and onlookers provoked the animals into fighting, were also common (Quay 2002, 149–50).

GAMES

Board and card games were widely enjoyed. Dominoes and cribbage were typical games played in the West, as was the popular card game, *Authors*. Imported from the states, the games were familiar to Easterners and Westerners alike. By the 1890s board games were being created about life in the West. In 1895, Milton Bradley marketed the *Game of Mail Express or Accommodation*, which included a map of the United States, as it existed in 1894. That same year Parker Brothers Inc. sold *The Little Cowboy Game*, which featured a steer and a cowboy in the center of the board's track. The company also created *Buffalo Hunt* (c. 1890) and *Game of Buffalo Bill* (1898), which included a board with pictures of Native Americans, buffalo, and Buffalo Bill Cody. By 1900, the change in Western transportation was reflected in Milton Bradley's *The Tourist, A Railroad Game* (Quay 2002, 139–40).

TRAIN WATCHING

Some activities were more individualistic. As the transcontinental railroad made its way across the country, it became a focal point for the towns that built up around its stations. Citizens interested in the new form of transportation would head down to the station to watch the arrivals and departures of the trains and travelers. Sightseeing from trains also grew in popularity as travelers began exploring the West for fun from the comfort of a cushioned seat instead of a wagon box. Many trains stopped at well-publicized sites like Yosemite or Yellowstone (even in the days before they were made National Parks). From the earliest days of expansion, local towns boasted a photographer whose shop was a favorite stopping place and whose camera provided pictures of the visitors that could be sent to their relatives and friends back East (Quay 2002, 140).

GAMBLING

While gambling did not originate in the West, it became inextricably linked with the era of westward expansion and the existence of the frontier town. Poker, seven-up, and euchre were card games known and played across the West. In addition to providing entertainment, playing cards provided a common bond between strangers. In a land where familiar faces were few and far between, two people could engage in a game with which they both were familiar even though they had never met one another before they sat down to play. Card games were not always played to a fair end, and cheating was not an uncommon practice. Gambling on the frontier was widespread, and even the most basic mining towns were known to operate gambling tables in some primitive form.

Westerners had mixed feelings about the impact that gambling had on the people who indulged in it and on the towns that supported it as a pastime. Some immigrants saw gambling as a positive influence. One reported that the town had improved very much since the previous month due to the opening of two new gambling saloons. He boasted that one of the establishments rivaled any in New York. Other Westerners were more skeptical, however, and viewed gambling as a problem that went right to the heart of the West. One diarist complained that gambling halls had gold conspicuously piled on tables in open doorways tempting weak men who had earned their money through hard labor.

Throwing dice was another common game of chance that was easy to transport and quick to play. From games of chance like poker, roulette, and faro, to confidence games like monte, the audience for gambling continued to increase as the West became more settled. So prevalent were some of the games, such as seven-up, that they became icons used to brand cattle (Quay 2002, 142–44).

WESTERN MUSIC AND DANCING

Music was a central form of entertainment in the West, and most towns had a band comprised of whatever instruments were available. Town bands played at local community events as well as for holidays such as Independence Day. Cowboys also developed their own form of music and entertainment, singing to pass the time but also to calm or direct their herds. In homes as well, musical instruments were played for the entertainment of the entire family, and visitors would gather to hear the family musician play.

Like music, the performance of plays was a social activity in which many Westerners at a single location could engage. The military was especially adept at producing first-rate performances. In contrast to the community oriented nature of dramatic performance, other hobbies were solitary including reading, crocheting, or sewing. Westerners read a wide range of materials, from popular novels, local newspapers, and national magazines to almanacs and mail-order catalogs.

One of the most enjoyable Western pastimes was dancing. From dances in private homes to balls in public buildings, dancing provided social interaction and required some innovation when the male-female ratio was out of proportion. One early Westerner wrote that the dances held in their living room attracted so many extra boys that some of them would have to tie handkerchiefs around their arms and take the girls' part in square dances. The simplicity of private dances in private homes stood in contrast to the public dances that drew large crowds from a wide geographical area. Formal balls were greatly anticipated events that lasted all night. As Western towns grew in population, and greater numbers of women settled in them, dances and balls became more common and were well attended. Less formal dances, such as the square dance, were also very popular (Quay 2002, 146–48).

TRAVELING SHOWS

Entertainment often came to the West in the form of traveling groups or individuals who made their way from one remote town to another, playing to captive audiences and making names for themselves in the growing cities. Franklin A. Buck reported his experiences with a medium who visited his town. The group sat around a table while the medium beckoned the spirits asking them to manifest themselves by tipping the table. The table tipped in all sorts of ways before tipping over entirely. Not everyone who attended events such as this were believers, but the experience brought a healthy dose of skepticism and wonder to audiences in search of distraction from everyday life. Other traveling performers included musicians, dancers, singers, and even lecturers. Speakers often spoke on the controversial topics of the day and drew large audiences. Minstrel shows were also popular (Quay 2002, 148–49).

MEDICINE SHOWS

In many ways a close relation to the circus, the traveling Medicine Show provided audiences with a combination of theatrical performance, informative lecture, and sales pitch. The goal of the Medicine Show was to attract audiences to sell medicinal products with names like "Dr. Morse's Root Pills" and "Kickapoo Indian Oil." The show began with the distribution of handbills. Once the audience was assembled, the entertainment began. It included performances as diverse as *Uncle*

Tom's Cabin, fortune-tellers, magicians, minstrel shows, ventriloquists, and hypnotists. Free songbooks were distributed to the audience to encourage sing-alongs as well as advertise the product they were about to pitch. After the entertainment came the spiel, during which the medicine man would describe the possible ills members of his audience might be feeling. Once the symptoms were suggested, the Medicine Show concluded by introducing the audience to the products ranging from stomach bitters to painkillers and salves. The shows were immensely popular and remedies sold swiftly, perhaps because of the high alcohol levels they typically contained. As government restrictions on false advertising and alcohol content tightened, Medicine Shows slowly disappeared (Quay 2002, 197).

LADIES' CRAFTS

Quilting was particularly popular for women of the West who worked continually to bring comfort and refinement to their crude homes. Women spent long winter months piecing tops from scraps and outgrown clothing and during the summer months called on their friends and neighbors to help quilt them. The quilting bee was a major social occasion and chance for gossip. The women, who were often separated from other women by great distances, particularly cherished these events and dressed in their best clothing. Some lasted for several days, when people had to travel great distances. It was not unusual for several quilts to be worked at the same bee. Some were held out of doors or in a barn to accommodate the large quilt frames used to secure the quilts. Everyone would be involved. Children would be assigned to keeping the needles threaded. Less skilled quilters gave support by preparing the food. Some quilting bees were held to make quilts for a family that was moving away. Some were held to make a bride's quilt. Traditionally, a bride's quilt would be the 13th quilt a young woman made, and one in which she displayed her finest work. The quilting bee was as much a party as a working occasion. Sometimes the men joined the ladies for a festive supper and perhaps a barn dance at the end of the day.

The names of quilt patterns were often taken from the events and settings of daily life. During the westward expansion, some quilt pattern names were changed to reflect their new environment. The pattern "Rocky Road to Dublin" was also called "Rocky Road to California." "Ducks and Ducklings" came to be called "Corn and Beans." As Texas was settled, "Cactus Rose" became known as "Texas Rose" and "Texas Treasure." "Jobs Tears" became "Texas Tears" and "Kansas Troubles."

Although the invention of knitting machines had relegated knitting to an enjoyable pastime for most women by mid-century, women in rural areas continued to produce necessities for the family that were otherwise difficult to acquire. Many women found that knitting relieved the boredom of the journey west. One Utah woman of the 1870s recalled that the bulk of their winter clothing was received as Christmas gifts and included such items as hand-knitted gaiters, stockings, mittens, waistbands, neckpieces, and fancy scarves.

Once out West, women discovered that their knitting skills were as much in demand as those of cooks and laundresses. Knitted socks were in great demand in mining and lumbering camps. Young girls, who were often able to make a pair of socks in a day, were able to earn money to contribute to the family's support.

—*Dorothy Denneen Volo*

FRONTIER THEATER

From the earliest days of settlement, theaters were an integral to the social fabric of Western towns. Minstrel shows were run by soldiers in the years prior to the gold rush to provide much needed entertainment at frontier forts and other outposts. As pioneers ventured West, and mining towns sprang up, theaters became popular in to the towns. Early performances were held on stages that were part of the local saloon, general store, or hotel. Whatever the facility, the proprietor either made floor space for a makeshift stage or designated a room in the building as the theater. Given the close association between the bar and the stage, performances were attended by rowdy, drunken audiences whose like or dislike of the entertainment was revealed in what they threw onto the stage. Coins and bags of gold indicated they were pleased. Rotten vegetables and other offensive items represented displeasure.

Saloon theaters were also home to other forms of entertainment, including hurdy-gurdy girls, named after the barrel organ that was cranked to produce the music. These women entertained saloon patrons with dancing and singing, local and inexpensive versions of more professional dance shows. Honky-tonk was another predominantly Western form of entertainment. Honky-tonk traditionally took place in a saloon theater, usually with a dance hall attached to it, which featured girls and drinks in equal proportions. The typical Honky-tonk had a number of curtained boxes, where male patrons were visited by the show girls, and it was the duty of the girls to solicit drinks from the occupants.

Despite the hold that saloons had on the realm of performing arts, professional theaters such as the Eagle Theater in Sacramento opened to the public as early as 1849. The first performance held at the Eagle was *The Bandit Chief; or the Forest Spectre*. Other theaters were quickly built, providing entertainment to the miners who flocked west in response to the promise of quick riches. One of the most respectable theaters in the West was in Salt Lake City. Built in 1862, the Salt Lake Theater attracted the most popular acts and record numbers of attendees.

Shows that met with success in the East were often imported to the West and produced in the Salt Lake Theater as well as other, smaller halls. The popular stage rendition of Harriet Beecher Stowe's *Uncle Tom's Cabin* was performed throughout the West and heralded by parades that included "18 Real Georgia Plantation Shouters, Mlle. Minerva's New Orleans Creole Girls' Fife and Drum Corps, the Original Whangdoodle Pickaninny Band, Eva's $1500 gold chariot, a log cabin" and numerous other spectacles. The tendency to supplement the actual performance with parades and other events was common throughout the period and helped to promote the show through the form of an entertaining advertisement.

Among the most popular performances to be produced in the West were Shakespeare's plays. Westerners flocked to performances of *Othello*, *King Lear*, and *Hamlet*. Building on the fact that Shakespeare's works were among the most popular reading materials of the nineteenth century, actors performed the plays in traditional and nontraditional ways. Plays were parodied, in what were known as Ethiopian Dramas, performances by African Americans. They were also re-titled and changed to incorporate issues of the day. In 1876, the San Francisco Shakespeare club presented *Hamlet, the Dainty: A Travesty*, incorporating jokes concerning Chinese workers and Native Americans like Sitting Bull and puns based on the Hayes-Tilden presidential election. Whatever the form, Shakespeare's plays were among the most regularly performed and most beloved of shows produced in the developing West.

Women were especially popular in western theaters, most likely in direct relation to their absence from daily life. Kate Hays, a concert singer also referred to as the "Nightingale of Erin" and the "Swan," played to very good houses of men eager to come in contact with a woman. Female performers were so popular that male members of the audience, hungry for female attention, threw them gifts. Lola Montez was an especially popular actress who drew such attention from her audiences. Early in her career she met with limited success until she began performing in San Francisco where she attracted some of the most enthusiastic audiences in the city's history. She was especially known for her controversial dance *la tarantella*, or the tarantula. Considered by some to be inappropriate for a public performance, the dance was characterized by the dancer's provocative movements. The suggestiveness undoubtedly contributed to Lola's popularity, which was so great that a local mountain, Mount Lola, was named for her. It was not until another female performer Caroline Chapman, appeared on the scene that Montez's popularity began to wane.

Chapman came from a family known for its acting ability. The Chapmans had traveled west on what may have been the country's first showboat—a riverboat marketed by a sign simply stating "Theater." Chapman quickly undermined Montez's position as an actress by parodying her in burlesque performances including the famous spider dance. Montez retired from the stage, but she became the mentor to California's next performing sweetheart, Lotta Crabtree. Lotta began her career as a child performer and made her name by appearing in variety shows. Other offshoots of traditional theater included melodrama—sentimental morality plays in which heroes won and villains lost (Quay 2002, 192–95).

HOLIDAYS, CELEBRATIONS, AND FESTIVALS

Rendezvous

Annual community events were also central to the frontier experience, even from the earliest days of the trappers. The rendezvous, known as a trappers' holiday, was an annual event, during which trappers met at a predetermined site at the end of the trapping season. The initial purpose of the rendezvous was to provide trappers with an opportunity to turn in the furs they had successfully collected during the winter and to gather supplies that they would need for another year of trapping. The event developed into a grander affair, however, as the company of others enlivened individual trappers after their long months alone. The combination of whiskey, food, and music made the rendezvous a festive and much anticipated event (Quay 2002, 158).

Independence Day

The Fourth of July was celebrated with great gusto. One immigrant wrote that they tried to celebrate "the glorious Fourth" as though they were back home. They marched to the tune of "Yankee Doodle" with tin pans as drum accompaniment and flags and banners of red flannel. Festivities ranged from picnics and outings to bands and fireworks, which were viewed as especially exciting by holiday participants (Quay 2002, 158).

Travelers on wagon trains took the day off from their travels on July Fourth. While using the day of rest to hunt or wash clothing, they managed to fire off a few rounds in celebration and, in some cases, make a few toasts. One of the earliest celebrations of the Fourth on the journey west was at Independence Rock, named for a fur trader's Fourth of July celebration in 1830. This huge rock 1,900 feet long, 700 feet wide, and 128 feet high in southwestern Wyoming, became one of the most famous of all Oregon Trail landmarks. Immigrants, who started their journey along the Oregon Trail in early spring, hoped to reach Independence Rock by July Fourth. If they had not arrived by then, they knew they were behind schedule.

—*Dorothy Denneen Volo*

Miner's Union Day

Of all the celebrations in a miner's life in Butte, Montana, nothing was a big as Miner's Union Day. The annual rally and celebration of Local #1 of the Western Federation of Miners was celebrated on June 13th from 1878 to 1914 to mark the establishment of the Butte Workingmen's Union, an organization that launched an era of unionism that earned Butte the reputation as the "Gibraltar of Unionism." The day was marked by speeches, contests, and picnicking. Competitions involved drilling, mucking (shoveling ore and unwanted rock out of a mine), and tug-of-war. Bull and bear fights continued through 1895 as did cock fighting and dog fighting.

—*Dorothy Denneen Volo*

Thanksgiving

Many New Englanders moved to the frontier in groups. In addition to the material items they transported, they brought familiar social institutions and customs. The tradition that a day of Thanksgiving should be celebrated each autumn was almost universal, and a pattern emerged as New Englanders moved westward. As the first autumn arrived in the new settlement, the group would usually designate a day that corresponded to the day proclaimed by the governor of their native state. The transplanted Yankees joined together to celebrate Thanksgiving every November. They introduced the custom to neighbors who were not familiar with it. In time, settlers came to prevail upon the governors of the new states to issue a Thanksgiving proclamation (Appelbaum 1984, 90).

The day was celebrated as a religious holiday with church services in the morning and with family dinner in the afternoon. Hunting wild game for the Thanksgiving meal quickly became a Western tradition. While hunters would settle for prairie chickens, buffalo, or elk, wild turkey was most prized.

—Dorothy Denneen Volo

Christmas

Christmas heightened the loneliness many immigrants felt being separated from their friends and families, but it was marked by family dinners, gifts, and gatherings that were as celebratory as any Christmas in the East. Some were simple and re-flected the roughness of the environment. Men in mining camps banged pans, sang loudly, and held all-male dances. Some were much more reminiscent of Christmas back East (Quay 2002, 158).

By the 1850s even people on the frontier were familiar with the Christmas tree. On the plains where traditional conifers could not be found, sage and cedar brush were decorated with paper chains and nuts silvered with the foil peeled from cigars. On the Texas coast, a sawed-off limb of a live oak sported candles and small presents. Children and adults fashioned decorations for these trees from scraps of cloth, rib-bon, paper, wood, and even bits of soap. Items such as straw, seed pods, and acorns also served as natural decorations (Time Life Books 1987, 135). Some settlers were more fortunate. One visitor to Texas reported seeing a richly decorated and illumi-nated Christmas tree where scarcely two years prior there had been only campfires burning (Time Life Books 1963, 186).

The gifts might have been simpler or less in number; but the spirit was not lost on those who had ventured west in search of a new life. One miner who spent the holiday in a mining camp recalled reaching into his belt and withdrawing two heavy nuggets. He gave one to each of the two other men with him in camp. He noted that gold was such a common commodity, it was a rather poor gift and that the men would have appreciated a hot biscuit much more (Time Life Books 1963, 186–87). In some prairie communities, horse-drawn sleds were used to distribute packages of food and clothing to impoverished families. Generosity extended to farm animals as well. Swedish farmers in Minnesota followed an old tradition of laying out sheaves of unthreshed wheat so that even the birds might feast on the holiday.

—Dorothy Denneen Volo

FOR MORE INFORMATION

Bellinger, Martha Fletcher. *A Short History of the Theater*. New York: Henry Holt, 1927.

Brown, Dee. *The Gentle Tamers: Women of the Old Wild West*. Lincoln: University of Ne-braska Press, 1958.

Cohen, Hennig, and Tristram Potter Coffin, eds. *The Folklore of American Holidays*. Detroit, MI: Gale Research Company, 1987.

Dary, David. *Seeking Pleasure in the Old West*. New York: Alfred A. Knopf, 1995.

Dwyer, Richard A. and Richard E. Lingenfelter. *Songs of the Gold Rush*. Berkeley: University of California Press, 1964.

Geers, Edward Franklin. *Ed Geers' Experience with the Trotters and Pacers*. Buffalo: The Matthews-Northrup Company, 1901.

Hayward, John. *Gazetteer of the United States*. Hartford, CT: Case, Tiffant and Co., 1853.

Jenkins, Susan, and Linda Seward. *The American Quilt Story: The How-To and Heritage of a Craft Tradition*. Emmaus, PA: Rodale Press, 1991.

Lingenfelter, Richard, Richard A. Dwyer, and David Cohen, eds. *Songs of the American West*. Berkeley: University of California Press, 1968.

Nevin, John Williamson. *The Anxious Bench*. Chambersburg, PA: printed at the publication office of the German Reformed Church, 1844.

Quay, Sara E. *Westward Expansion*. Westport, CT: Greenwood Press, 2002.

Rader, Benjamin. *American Sports: From the Age of the Folk Games to the Age of the Spectators*. Englewood Cliffs, NJ: Prentice-Hall, 1983.

Safford, Carleton L., and Robert Bishop, *America's Quilts and Coverlets*. New York: Weathervane Books, 1974.

Sandoz, Mari. *The Beaver Men, Spearheads of Empire*. Lincoln: University of Nebraska Press, 1978.

Thorp, N. Howard. *Songs of the Cowboys*. New York: Clarkson N. Potter, Inc., 1966.

Time Life Books. *The Glory and Pageantry of Christmas*. Maplewood, NJ: Hammond Incorporated, 1963.

Time Life Books. *Time Life Book of Christmas*. New York: Prentice Hall, 1987.

Travers, Sam. *Christmas in the Old West*. Missoula, MT: Mountain Press Publishing Co., 2003.

Volo, Dorothy Denneen, and James M. Volo. *Encyclopedia of the Antebellum South*. Westport, CT: Greenwood Press, 2000.

———. *Family Life in Nineteenth-Century America*. Westport, CT: Greenwood Press, 2007.

Wallace, J. H. *Wallace's American Trotting Register*. New York: G.E. Woodward, 1871–1891.

Wechsberg, Joseph. *The Lost World of the Great Spas*. New York: Harper & Row Publishers, 1979.

Religious Life

MORALITY: THE HOLINESS MOVEMENT

Many persons involved in early American Methodism professed a religious experience closely aligned to the ideas of Christian perfection or holiness called sanctification. This experience was thought to have cleansed them from the desire and inclination to sin. Methodists of the nineteenth century continued the interest in Christian Holiness that had been started by their founder, John Wesley at the end of the previous century. They continued to publish and distribute Wesley's works and tracts, including his famous *A Plain Account of Christian Perfection* last edited by the author in 1777. In 1837, Methodist Minister Timothy Merritt founded a journal called the *Guide to Christian Perfection* to further promote the Wesleyan message of Christian holiness. The terms *perfection* and *sanctification*, although still used, ultimately gave way to *holiness*, from which an entire morality movement gained its name.

In 1836, a Methodist woman in New York City, Sarah Worrall Lankford, started an organization known as the Tuesday Meeting for the Promotion of Holiness. At first only women attended these meetings, but eventually (1839) male members of the clergy began to attend them. Among the men were Methodist bishops, theologians, and ministers. Some of the bishops who attended were Edmund S. James, Leonidas L. Hamline, Jesse T. Peck, and Matthew Simpson. Their renewed interest in Holiness eventually influenced the Methodist Church nationwide.

The meetings were held in the home of Walter and Phoebe Palmer, Lankford's sister. Phoebe Worrall Palmer experienced what she called entire sanctification and began leading the so-called Tuesday Meeting. She is generally considered a founder of the Holiness Movement in America and of the Higher Life movement in Britain. Although Walter Palmer often spoke at these meetings, his wife was obviously the driving force behind the movement. Palmer and her husband eventually purchased the *Guide to Christian Perfection*, and she became the editor of the periodical, thereafter called the *Guide to Holiness*. In 1859 she published *The Promise of the Father*, in which she argued in favor of women in the religious ministry. This book later influenced Catherine Booth, cofounder with her husband William of the Salvation Army, a movement begun in London in 1865 and formalized in 1878. The practice of ministry by women was common but not universal within the churches of the Holiness Movement.

At the Tuesday Meetings, Methodists soon enjoyed fellowship with Christians of different denominations, including the Congregationalist Thomas Upham. His participation in the meetings led him to study mystical experiences, looking to find precursors of holiness teaching in the writings of persons like German Pietist Johann Arndt (1555–1621) or the Roman Catholic mystic Jeanne-Marie Bouvier de la Motte-Guyon, commonly known as Madame Guyon (1648–1717). Other non-Methodists soon began contributing to the Holiness Movement. Chief among these was Presbyterian William Boardman, an American pastor and teacher who promoted the idea of holiness through his evangelistic campaigns and through his book *The Higher Christian Life*, which was published in 1858.

Charles Grandison Finney, an evangelist associated with Oberlin College, also promoted the idea of Christian holiness. Oberlin was a hotbed of antislavery and abolitionist activity throughout the nineteenth century. In 1836, Asa Mahan, president of the college, experienced what he called a baptism with the Holy Ghost. Finney believed that this experience might provide a solution to a problem he observed during his evangelistic revivals. Some people claimed to experience conversion, but then slipped back into their old ways of living. Finney, considered by many to be the "father of modern evangelism," believed that the "filling with the Holy Spirit" could help these converts to continue steadfast in their Christian life. To reach as many souls as possible, Finney employed what came to be called new measures, although many had been used by earlier preachers.

These new measures triggered alarm among conservative clergy. Opponents were able to list many objectionable practices, but the most controversial were: public praying of women in mixed-sex audiences, daily services over a series of days, use of colloquial language by the preacher, the anxious bench (praying publicly as a sign of repentance), praying for people by name, and immediate church membership for converts. In *The Anxious Bench* (1844), the Rev. J. W. Nevin wrote, "It is marvelous credulity, to take every excitement in the name of religion, for the work of God's Spirit. It is an enormous demand on our charity, when we are asked in mass, as true and solid, the wholesale conversions that are made in this way" (Nevin 1844, 12).

Hannah Whitall Smith, a Quaker, experienced a profound personal conversion sometime in the 1860s, which she called the secret of the Christian life, devoting one's life wholly to God and God's simultaneous transformation of one's soul. Her husband, Robert Pearsall Smith, had a similar experience at the first holiness camp meeting in Vineland, New Jersey, in 1867 under the leadership of John S. Inskip, John A. Wood, Alfred Cookman, and other Methodist ministers. The gathering attracted as many as 10,000 people on the Sabbath. At the close of the encampment, the ministers formed the National Camp Meeting Association for the Promotion of Holiness, and agreed to conduct a similar gathering the next year. Today this organization is commonly known as the National Holiness Association, although the official name is the Christian Holiness Partnership.

The second National Camp Meeting was held at Manheim, Pennsylvania, deep in that region of the state populated by Pietist adherents like Quakers, Mennonites, and the Amish. It drew upward of 25,000 persons from all over the nation. People called it a "Pentecost," and it did not disappoint them. The Pentecostal service on Monday evening has almost become legendary for its spiritual power and influence upon the people. The third National Camp Meeting met at Round Lake, New York. This time the national press attended, and write-ups appeared in numerous papers, including a large two-page pictorial in *Harper's Weekly*. In 1871 the American evangelist Dwight L. Moody had what he called an "endowment with power," as a result of some soul-searching and the prayers of two Methodist women who attended one of his meetings. He did

The camp meeting was a characteristic part of the religious revival of the nineteenth century. During the day nothing appeared unusual, but at night the air was filled with the shouts of the old saints and the rejoicing of the young converts. Many participants shook, jerked, and rolled upon the ground until they fell away in a faint. Courtesy Library of Congress.

not join the Holiness Movement, but certainly advanced some of its ideas, and even voiced his approval of it on at least one occasion.

In some of the early revival meetings of the Holiness Movement there were individuals that shouted, jumped, and jerked. Some went into trances, barked like dogs, or exercised the gift of speaking in tongues (glossolalia), a Christian belief associated with Pentecost as recounted in the New Testament book of Acts. Jesus' apostles were said to be filled with the Holy Spirit and spoke in languages foreign to themselves, but which could be understood by members of the linguistically diverse audience. This miracle was a fulfillment of prophecy and a sign of the end times. Although fanaticism broke out various times during this movement, it did not hinder the progression of the majority of its adherents who were more conservative.

These meetings made instant religious celebrities out of many of the workers including Robert and Hannah Smith. They were among those who took the holiness message to England, and their ministries helped lay the foundation for the now-famous Keswick Convention, a summer religious reunion, lasting one week, which has been held annually at Keswick, England, since 1875. The flow and counterflow of religious ideas between Britain and the United States was important to the development of the Holiness Movement.

Keswick teaching stressed the infilling of the Spirit and the power of faith to claim promised blessings. It promoted practical holiness by means of prayer, discussion, and personal intercourse. It was a visit to the Keswick Convention in 1946 that so affected the ministry of Rev. Billy Graham. This teaching gave Graham the assurance of God's power in his life, which he said in his autobiography came to him as a second blessing, and that has empowered his preaching ever since.

—*James M. Volo*

RELIGION

Religious Freedom

In 1844 Robert Baird, a Presbyterian minister, published a study entitled *Religion in the United States of America*, one of the first interpretive studies on the subject of religious freedom in American history. To illustrate the country's religious vitality, Baird provided an exhaustive study of the nation's churches, but even a man that was trying to illustrate the success of religious freedom in America found it necessary to divide the common denominations into "evangelical" and "unevangelical" categories—the second of which he found to be "a blight on America's religious landscape" (Brekus 2006, 318). Lumping together Roman Catholics, Jews, Shakers, Unitarians, Mormons, Universalists, Deists, and many fringe religious sects, Baird condemned them all for rejecting the true Christianity of the dominant evangelical churches: Presbyterians, Congregationalists, Episcopalians, Baptists, and Methodists. It was these religions that he hoped would form a great Protestant empire in America. For Baird, freedom from the imposition of a government-established church was one thing, but acceptance of religious diversity (especially if it strayed too far from orthodox Protestant thought) was too much to tolerate. In particular, he considered Mormons "a body of ignorant dupes," and Roman Catholics heathens who had buried truth "amid a heap of corruptions" (Brekus 2006, 318).

Attitudes in the postwar period were little different. In 1888, Daniel Dorchester published *Christianity in America*, considered one of the most comprehensive surveys of religion in America ever written. Dorchester also used antagonistic language in expressing his view of what he called "divergent religions." Like Baird, Dorchester saved his most damning comments for Mormons and Catholics. He described Mormonism, which had grown substantially since Baird's criticism of it four decades earlier, as a "local ulcer" and a form of "ecclesiastical despotism." Catholicism he viewed as a foreign conspiracy to subvert America. The views of Baird and Dorchester, both respected mainstream religious writers, fed into the negativity of the nativist groups who believed that the flood of Catholic emigrants from Europe were hostile to American ideals. "Real Americans were Protestant," they insisted (Brekus 2006, 320).

As late as the mid-twentieth century, William Warren Sweet—*The Story of Religions in America* (1930)—and Sydney Ahlstrom—*A Religious History of the American People* (1972)—criticized men like Baird and Dorchester for their lack of justice in describing American's pluralistic religious landscape. Yet at the same time, they felt free to describe Mormonism as a strange and unusual cult, its followers as irrational or insane, and Joseph Smith, founder of Mormonism, as a megalomaniac (Brekus 2006, 322–23). Baird, Dorchester, Sweet, and Ahlstrom convincingly demonstrate in immense power that Protestants wielded in shaping American culture and American religious history.

—*James M. Volo*

A Second Awakening

It was the Christian revival at the beginning of the nineteenth century—generally viewed as the Second Great Awakening—that most affected the religious life of American society. Many writers from the period have recorded an intense devotion to the spiritual part of their lives, and though they might sin with vigor, they repented and atoned with great enthusiasm. This religious revival drew its vitality from the Southern and Western frontiers rather than from New England. Beginning near the Gaspar River Church in Kentucky in July of 1800, the spark of faith was ignited at camp meetings in the Midwest and was proclaimed throughout the nascent frontier settlements by an army of traveling evangelists and self-ordained preachers. Some ministers, having been brought up on "rigid Calvinism" and having been taught to preach "the doctrine of particular election and reprobation" in earlier years, revolted; and having no correct books on the new theology, "plunged into the opposite extreme, namely, universal redemption." This sort of evangelism, with its strong emotional appeal, spirit of optimism, and promise of unconditional salvation to all of mankind, was particularly influential among nineteenth-century Americans (Beston 1937, 299).

Peter Cartwright, a contemporary observer of the process, noted, "Ministers of different denominations came in, and preached through the country: but Methodist preachers were the pioneer messengers of salvation in these ends of the earth.... A Methodist preacher in those days, when he felt that God had called him to preach, instead of hunting up a college or Biblical institute, hunted up a hardy pony, or a horse, and some traveling apparatus, and with his library always at hand, namely the Bible, Hymn Book, and Discipline, he started, and with a text that never wore out or grew stale, he cried, 'Behold the Lamb of God, that taketh away the sin of the world!' In this way he went through storms of wind, hail, snow and rain; climbed hills and mountains; traversed valleys; plunged through swamps; swam swollen streams; lay out all night, or tied to a limb slept with his saddle blanket for a bed, his saddle or saddle bags for his pillow, and his old big coat or blanket, if he had any, for covering" (Beston 1937, 299–300).

During the day nothing appeared unusual in the sprawling and smoke-filled revival camps with their scattering of white tents, knots of canvas-covered wagons, and bands of scurrying children and barking dogs. The occupants followed the same slow-paced routines of cooking, cleaning, and caring for the livestock found in other camps on the immigrant trails. However, nighttime drew the faithful together and transformed them into an army of God. With campfires blazing, a thunderous din of singing, and preachers beseeching the gathering to repent so that they might be saved from the fires of hell, the crowds reached a peak of religious frenzy. A circuit riding preacher, Lorenzo Dow, described a typical camp meeting in his journal, "About three thousand people appeared on the ground, and the rejoicing of old saints, the shouts of the young converts, and the cries of the distressed for mercy, caused the meeting to continue all night." Many shook, jerked, and rolled on the ground until they fell away in a faint (Chase 1966, 211).

Methodists and Baptists reaped a rich harvest of souls at this time. By the 1830s Methodism had become one of the two largest religions in the country, and the Baptists, in particular, had made great inroads into the black population, both free and slave. Under the influence of an evangelical spirit most American Protestants came to believe that the path to salvation lay in placing themselves in a position to receive God's grace if they were worthy. This belief had a profound effect on Civil War soldiers who strove to be worthy of God's protective hand in battle by exhibiting courage and steadiness under fire.

The intense religious environment also spread new religious sects like a wildfire spread embers. Campbellites, Shakers, Rappites, Fourierists, and other minor religions popular in the North espoused theories of associative communism and utopian socialism by making provisions for the correction of inequalities of temporal possessions among their members. Many members gave up all their wealth or placed it at the disposal of the congregation. Unitarians (the followers of which were largely devoted abolitionists), Universalists, and Disciples of Christ splintered away from established churches, while Mormons and Adventists sprang from the soil of America itself. Nonrevivalist churches, especially in the South, trailed behind. Of 891

Unitarian and Universalist churches known to exist in 1850, only 23 existed below the Mason-Dixon Line (Volo and Volo 2007, 117–18).

MORMONS

Those who chose to follow the Mormon religion (Church of Jesus Christ of the Latter-day Saints) may have been among the persons most vigorously persecuted for their religion in the antebellum period. Probably the most important fringe religion of the period, Mormonism was the great catch-all of the evangelical movements. The Mormons were the strongest individual religious presence in the West in the second half of the nineteenth century.

The Mormon religion was founded in 1823 by Joseph Smith, who saw himself as a present-day biblical prophet. Smith based the religion on the Book of Mormon, a new scripture translated from golden plates originally written by a person named Mormon who had made his way to the North American Continent with others from Jerusalem. Here Mormon organized certain records that he and his fellows had brought with them from Israel and inscribed them on the plates before his death. The Latter-day Saints believed that Mormon's son, Moroni, hid the plates in the hill of Cumorah near Palmyra, New York, hundreds of years before the discovery of America. The Lord purportedly spoke directly to Joseph Smith revealing their contents. The resulting *Book of Mormon* restored all the ancient orders of the Bible—elders, teachers, apostles, enforcers, and deacons—and all the ancient rights including baptism by immersion and the sacraments. Other doctrines were added from modern-day revelation; but a return to polygamy (taking more than one wife at the same time) was the cause for which the Mormons were most often persecuted.

Brigham Young is most closely associated than Smith with the church leadership in the antebellum period. Young was a convert to Mormonism in 1832. Within months of his conversion, his first wife died leaving him with two small daughters, and he quickly remarried for the sake of the children (he ultimately took 17 wives). Originally from New York State, he traveled the country trying to make converts, and he turned much of his energy to the work of his new religion. He moved to Kirtland, Ohio, at the urging of Joseph Smith who advised that all the Saints do so. Young brought a little knot of converts with him from New York and found that dozens of such groups were pouring into Kirtland. Here, in a form of religious socialism, a good part of the possessions of each newcomer was turned over to the church treasury for its support.

In 1834, Brigham Young was selected as one of the Twelve Apostles who stood next in line to the three man presidency of the church headed by Smith. This group decided to move the church to Missouri to support their brethren who were suffering from burnings and beatings at the hands of the general population. Once in Missouri, Smith and some of his companions were arrested by the territorial governor who officially warned the growing hoard of Mormons to leave the state or face the ire of the territorial militia. Young, who had quite accidentally missed being apprehended, suddenly found himself the only major leader of the group with freedom of movement; but he was now solely responsible for almost 12,000 homeless and frightened people. He made arrangements to purchase land on the banks of the Mississippi River in Illinois in the name of the church, and he moved his charges there.

Meanwhile, Joseph Smith and his companions managed to escape jail in December 1839. Shortly thereafter they joined the Saints in Illinois. Here Smith unfolded his plan for Nauvoo, the beautiful city of the Saints, and began an impressive building project. However, many of the non-Mormon residents in Illinois became fearful of the large, well equipped military force that the Mormons maintained for their own protection. They began to view Joseph Smith as a danger both economically and politically. In 1844 the Mormons decided to run Smith for the U.S. presidency. This decision led almost immediately to Joseph Smith's assassination at the hands of a mob in Carthage, Illinois; the abandonment of Nauvoo; and the removal of the Saints to Iowa. Brigham Young, braving the storm of internal church politics, reassumed the leadership of the Twelve Apostles and became church president in 1847. This series of events put practical control of the Mormon religion in his hands for the next three decades.

Having been persecuted in Ohio, Missouri, and Illinois, advanced parties of Mormons hurried into the Great Salt Lake Valley of Utah leaving more than 13,000 refugees waiting in Iowa and Nebraska for the signal to move west. Brigham Young and the followers of Joseph Smith then turned west to the great American desert to escape the prejudice and open violence that challenged the Church of Jesus Christ of Latter-day Saints almost everywhere.

When the main party reached the Great Salt Lake, they found that the advanced parties had already begun clearing land and building a rudimentary system of canals to bring water from the surrounding mountains to the plains. In the formative years of the Great Salt Lake settlement, too few crops had been planted and too few substantial homes had been built. The Mormons found themselves shivering in rude huts and threadbare tents and eating ox hide soup to survive. That winter of 1848–1849 came to be known as the "Starving Time." In the spring the saints were unexpectedly attacked by a plague of crop-destroying grasshoppers (Rocky Mountain locusts) that threatened to end the movement through starvation. One farmer described the onset of the plague, "A person could see a little dark whirlwind here and there which after a while turned into dark clouds [of locusts]...The air grew so thick that the sun could not be seen" (Atkins 1984, 26). The Mormons responded by attempting to beat the pests to death with brooms, blankets, and wet grain bags. The inefficiency of this method was quickly made clear. Miraculously, according to Mormon accounts, a swarm of seagulls followed closely on the heels of the arrival of the grasshoppers, eating them faster than they could eat the crops and saving much of the food supply. For this reason the seagull is used as a symbol of God's approbation by Mormons until this day.

By 1849, Young's vision of a Mormon empire in the West had taken root. Exactly two years after they had entered the valley, the Mormons had built a city with an irrigation system, established themselves across the Great Basin, and entered into treaties of peace with the local native population. They were even issuing their own paper money backed by the promise of livestock. In 1850 the Mormons suffered a setback when Congress rejected Young's plan to establish a state that he called Deseret. Young's Deseret had been planned to extend from present-day Utah to San Diego in southwest California The blow was somewhat softened by Young's appointment as federal governor of the Territory of Utah.

Having had their overtures of peaceful coexistence rejected, the Mormons demanded and maintained their solitude largely out of a sense of self-preservation. In 1853 they raided and burned Jim Bridger's fur trading post and fort on the Oregon Trail, and Bridger returned the compliment by serving as a scout for the U.S. Army expedition that later came to punish them. In 1857, a group of Mormons aided by friendly Indians attacked a wagon train of immigrants bound for California on the Mormon Trail. Known as the Mountain Meadows Massacre, of approximately 140 people on the train, 120 were slain. The only persons spared were children too young to tell the tale. Although the attack was not sanctioned by the church, it was a seminal event in the relationship between the Mormons and the federal government. In an effort to crush Mormon resistance, the army dispatched 2,500 men and 3 million pounds of supplies to Utah in what came to be known as the Mormon War. Fearing the repercussions within the church and the reprisals promised by the government, the Mormon perpetrators of the massacre blamed the entire incident on the Indians and held themselves out as the saviors of the helpless children. Not until 1875 was one of the Mormons participants, John D. Lee, brought to trial. He died by firing squad in 1877 on the site of the massacre.

Meanwhile, the Mormons had to face the troops sent out by President James Buchanan. Young at first defied the army, but after a few small engagements, he gave up his governorship to a Gentile (a non-Mormon) and allowed the army to march through Salt Lake City as a symbol of Mormon submission. The army then departed and set up camp some 40 miles away from the city. The intervention of the Civil War defused the situation somewhat and left the Mormons alone to grow their community of saints.

Author Mark Twain recorded his impressions of the theocracy on the shores of the Great Salt Lake as he saw it in the 1860s. "The pleasant strangeness of a city of fifteen thousand inhabitants with no loafers perceptible in it; and no visible drunkards or noisy people; a limpid stream rippling and dancing through every street in place of a filthy gutter; block after block of trim dwelling, built of frame and sunburned brick—a great thriving orchard and garden behind every one of them, apparently—branches from the street stream winding and sparkling among the garden beds and fruit trees—and a grand general air of neatness, repair, thrift, and comfort, around and about and over the whole. And everywhere were workshops, factories, and all manner of industries; and intent faces and busy hands were to be seen wherever one looked; and in one's ears was the ceaseless clink of hammers, the buzz of trade and the contented hum of drums and flywheels" (Davidson 1951, 235). The community Twain described was a thriving and unprecedented example of communitarianism, agriculture, industry, theology, and patriarchal government in united action.

In 1860, there were 40,000 residents of Utah, most of them Mormons. By the end of the Civil War, they had the desert blooming through the use of a vast irrigation system composed of almost 300 man-made canals. Over 150,000 acres were under cultivation. Brigham Young believed that the Mormons could live in total self-sufficiency, acknowledging only the most remote sovereignty of the government in Washington and yielding little to its direct control. He successfully helped the Mormons to maintain their influence in the West until his death in 1877.

—*James M. Volo*

FOR MORE INFORMATION

Ahlstrom, Sydney A. *A Religious History of the American People*. New Haven, CT: Yale University Press, 1972.

Beston, Henry, ed. *American Memory*. New York: Farrar & Rhinehart, Inc., 1937.

Brekus, Catherine A. "Interpreting American Religion." In *A Companion to 19th-Century America*, ed. William L. Barney. Malden, MA: Blackwell Publishing, 2006.

Chase, Gilbert. *America's Music: From the Pilgrims to the Present*. New York: McGraw-Hill Book Company, 1966.

Davidson, Marshall B. *Life in America*. Boston, MA: Houghton Mifflin Company, 1951.

Sweet, Leonard I. *The Minister's Wife: Her Role in Nineteenth-Century American Evangelism*. Philadelphia, PA: Temple University Press, 1983.

Volo, Dorothy Denneen, and James M. Volo. *Family Life in Nineteenth-Century America*. Westport, CT: Greenwood Press, 2007.

5

INDUSTRIAL AGE

Overview

INDUSTRIAL AGE
|

OVERVIEW
DOMESTIC LIFE
ECONOMIC LIFE
INTELLECTUAL LIFE
MATERIAL LIFE
POLITICAL LIFE
RECREATIONAL LIFE
RELIGIOUS LIFE

FARMERS, WORKERS, AND CAPTAINS OF INDUSTRY

Since colonial times the work ethic had commanded the communities of America. In the culture war between the North and the South of the first half of the nineteenth century, the traditions of the South had been largely set aside, and the post–Civil War generation reached adulthood at a time that was one of the most vital and most sordid in all American history. The period was flagrantly materialistic and corrupt, and the captains of industry exploited the resources of the nation in a ruthless and reckless manner crushing all who stood in the path of so-called progress. Samuel Clemens (Mark Twain) understood the strength and weaknesses of the times, and he satirically named the period the Gilded Age because it looked golden on the surface but was rotting with inequity, greed, and corruption beneath. Today the term Industrial Age might better reflect the spirit of the period.

In the Industrial Age a culture war took place between the industrialists and the farmers, and before the second half century had finished, the farmers and their beliefs had seemingly also been set aside. The captains of industry also came to loggerheads with the great mass of workers and laborers who produced their wealth. Farmers and workers could never produce enough wealth to match industrialists, railroad magnets, or white-collar workers, but they rarely asked for assistance. Demands for reform did not generally come from the poor and oppressed but from an army of socially elite philanthropists and compassionate humanitarians. Few of these activists asked the poor and abused what they felt was the cause of their plight. They had the conceit to believe they knew what areas of society needed reformation. The dimensions of the schemes that they put forth were exceeded only by the depth of their failure. Mindless social tinkering and disgraceful forms of public altruism persisted, nonetheless. At the end of the century the poor remained in their crime-ridden and filthy urban neighborhoods; alcohol flowed freely; prostitution, violence, and corruption flourished; and ethnic and racial minorities remained on the bottom rungs of the economic ladder. The incongruity of the generally utopian ideals of the reformers and the consequences of reality made the period anything but gilded.

Rural residents generally feared the development of the unprecedented work for wage economy of the cities and factories, and they viewed manufacturing and office wage earners as degraded and enslaved persons. The city worker sold himself into economic bondage for a wage, and the expansion of a similar work for wage system was dreaded almost as much as their fathers had despised slavery. Farmers were clearly anxious to maintain their status, and many in the laboring class believed that industrialists and bankers were determined to shackle them to the factory system or the counting house. For this reason—among others—many lower- and middle-class farmers made common bond during the 1870s and 1880s by forming alliances and supporting populist political parties.

By the end of the nineteenth century three-quarters of all Americans were still making their living in agriculture. Nonetheless, by the 1890s the big businessmen and manufacturers had overthrown the farmers from their position of esteem in the national culture. The business of America, thereafter, seemed to be business, and the farmers were forced to view the world in terms of cash instead of barter and to deal in it in terms of paper money and stock certificates instead of hard silver coins or gold. Ultimately they too accepted the money ethic that drove industry, but a cash economy never really fit well into a rural setting.

New York, the most populous state in 1850 with a population of just over three million residents, had only 6.5 percent of its workers involved in manufacturing. This suggests that the state was still remarkably rural in character, as was the entire nation. Massachusetts, Rhode Island, and Connecticut were the most industrialized states in the union each with double-digit percentages of persons employed in manufacturing, but none of these even closely approached a majority. Massachusetts, with a population of 986,000, was the most industrialized state in the nation with only 17 percent of its work force involved in manufacturing. Rhode Island (15%) and Connecticut (13%) ranked second and third nationally. Of the six New England states only Vermont (2.7%) had a manufacturing base smaller than 5 percent in terms of employment. By way of contrast Pennsylvania and Ohio, among the top three states in population with more than 2.2 million and 2.0 million, respectively, had 6.5 percent and 3.0 percent working in manufacturing in 1850. Virginia with nearly a million residents had a mere 3.0 percent involved in industry, and fifth place Illinois, with 800,000 people, was still remarkably rural with only 1.4 percent of its population working in factories or mills. Only 10 states had greater than 5 percent of their population involved in manufactures. Of these, none had been part of the Southern Confederacy, and only Maryland and Delaware were south of the Mason-Dixon Line.

According to the perceptions of a number of nineteenth-century observers acquisitiveness, if not greed or avarice, took a hold on the minds of many men in the Industrial Age, and they became focused on being more than merely comfortable in their homes and communities. They seemed in a great haste to become conspicuously wealthy. Wild ambition, however, was thought to tarnish true success, and it mingled the feelings of admiration and abhorrence of those who observed it. In addition, it became fashionable among the upper classes, especially among the women, to lead generally idle lives at home caring for the domestic needs of the household through the management of a score of servants. The leisure that this suggested for the average female householder was probably overstated by the generally conservatively minded advisors of the day, and it was little different from that of persons of similar social standing and financial circumstances in previous times that required aptitude, organization, and luck.

The rising middle class also aspired to an idyllic life filled with pastimes, diversions, and attempts at personal improvement without recognizing these underlying fundamentals. Many marriages were deferred to allow young suitors time to amass sufficient wealth to enjoy a comfortable life, and many others were avoided or discouraged by parents as young women chose older and more successful men as spouses (Smith 1981, 755).

Many of the features that distinguished modern machine-based industrial economy were developed during the second half of the nineteenth century. At no time since humans first learned to control fire had society been so profoundly modified by technology. Nowhere else but in America had the hidden energies of nature—coal, oil, steam—been so tapped through the ingenuity and creativity of just a few men. The history of finance and industry in the Industrial Age (the Gilded Age, if you will) is the story of a handful of businessmen who became super-rich in the second half of the nineteenth century by applying methods and practices unknown—or thought unethical by former generations of entrepreneurs—to the processes of mass industrialization. Many of these men used questionable business practices that tagged them as Robber Barons.

To eliminate competition by purchase, merger, or outright economic war was to create a monopoly, which was not a new or intrinsically illegal business concept. The foundation of the British economy and the Empire itself was based on a form of nationalized monopoly known as *mercantilism*. Economist Adam Smith, writing in 1776, recognized it, and he also noted the many difficulties facing independent businessman and the people who worked for them. "In all arts and manufactures the greater part of the workmen stand in need of a master to advance them the materials of their work, and their wages and maintenance till it be completed" (Rule 1981, 31). The Robber Barons of the nineteenth century were able to fulfill this role of master in a manner and to an extent not contemplated by Smith 100 years earlier.

Most historians of the United States refer to the period between 1870 and 1900 as the industrial era because the most marked economic development of that period was the rapid expansion of the factory and the factory system. Manufacturers rationalized production; they broke the manufacturing process down into discrete, uniform tasks. Workers were responsible for just one of these tasks, decreasing the need for skilled artisans and mechanics, and making individual workers largely expendable. Workers were increasingly referred to as operatives, mere appendices to the machines that were the real producers (Husband and O'Loughlin 2004, 72).

The complexity of the machinery and the insignificance of the operators are emphasized in this period illustration of a factory floor filled with power looms. The looms were powered by pulleys and leather belts (right) and the power was distributed across the width of the factory floor by shafts running along the ceiling. This was a common system in both water- and steam-powered mills. Courtesy Editor's collection.

James Viscount Bryce, an Englishman visiting the United States in the 1880s, wrote in *The American Commonwealth* (1888) that America's business leaders had "developed…unexpected strength in unexpected ways, overshadowing individuals and even communities" through fierce competition among themselves. "Nearly all the great [industries] are controlled and managed either by a small knot of persons or by a single man…. They have wealth…they have fame…they have power, more power—that is, more opportunity of making their personal will prevail—than perhaps anyone in political life, except the President and the Speaker, who after all hold theirs only for four or two years, while the [industrial] monarch may keep his for life" (Davidson 1951, 550–51). Business enterprises operated under many legal-sounding names—pools, trusts, holding companies, or corporations—and in a myriad of industries including railroads, mining, steel, shipping, and finance. Consequently, the dominant features of American economic life in the last quarter of the nineteenth century seemed to be the consolidation of wealth, the preeminence of industry, and the submission of labor to the dominance of employers.

To gain unquestioned control through a monopoly of the sources of raw materials, to own all the facilities of production and transportation, and to dictate wage and price levels, was as logical to nineteenth-century businessmen as it seems unprincipled to those of the twenty-first century who have grown to think that government and judicial controls on business are inevitable. In industry, the advantages of consolidation, high finance, and undisputed control of the factors of production were many; yet the organization of mechanical ingenuity into a large-scale system of supply, manufacture, and distribution was slow and painstaking. "To pause or to stop meant ruin," recalled Andrew Carnegie near the end of his life. It has also been noted that "to outsiders the American faith in increased growth and endless progress [during the Industrial Age] appeared to keep the country in a state of constant impatience with the achievements of the present" (Davidson 1951, 551, 484). Except for the occasional critic, it did not occur to most persons until the last decade of the century that the advances of industry led anywhere except to a better America for everyone. Many believed that with industrial progress all the important problems of modern society would automatically diminish or disappear.

Nonetheless, the position of the American worker had also changed considerably. Middle-class men commonly left the home to work for 10 to 14 hours, and their children rarely saw them during daylight hours. A father's work and workplace became foreign to his children in a way unknown to former generations (Tosh 1996). Wages, compared to those in Europe, were still high, but they bore a diminishing ratio to the wealth accumulated by the robber barons. The U.S. Steel Corporation, for example, formed in 1901 largely from the purchase of the holdings of just one man, Andrew Carnegie, had an initial capitalization of $1.4 billion in an era when many of those considered rich had not even reached the level of millionaires.

Using the coal industry as an example, Theodore Roosevelt noted in his *Autobiography* (1913) that there was "a crass inequality in the bargaining relation between the employer and the individual employee standing alone. The great coal-mining and coal-carrying companies, which employed their tens of thousands, could easily dispense with the services of any particular miner. The miner, on the other hand, however expert, could not dispense with the companies. He needed a job; his wife and children would starve if he did not get one. What the miner had to sell—his labor—was a perishable commodity; the labor of today—if not sold today—was lost forever. Moreover, his labor was not like most commodities—a mere thing; it was part of a living, breathing human being. The workman saw, and all citizens who gave earnest thought to the matter saw, that the labor problem was not only an economic, but also a moral, a human problem" (Roosevelt 1913, 19).

In response to the power of the Robber Barons, labor unions formed among the workers, and strikes—for wages, shorter working hours, and better conditions— sometimes reached bloody intensity. In the previous century the organization of labor—combining against one's employer—was considered a crime. During the eighteenth century, machines had been adapted to producing cloth, stockings, and socks in both wool and cotton. The immediate effect of this mechanization was to place an entire category of traditional weavers and stocking makers out of work. This had resulted in local uprisings in England and France by workers in this area of clothing production. Stocking frames, machinery, and the slotted wooden cards that controlled the complex operation of the employer's power looms were attacked in both England and France. English weavers were jailed while French workers, who had wedged their wooden shoes, or *sabot*, into the mechanisms to disrupt production, were vilified as *Saboteurs*. Seen against the backdrop of the previous century, American labor unions met with stiff resistance from businessmen, government, and the courts.

In 1877, American workers brought labor unrest in the form of the strike to the railroads with unfortunate results. Embittered workers on the B & O Railroad began rioting in Martinsburg, West Virginia. State militia was sent in but failed to end the violence. The strike spread to Baltimore, Pittsburgh, and other cities. The 6th Maryland Regiment actually fired into strikers in Baltimore. Strikers burned the Pennsylvania Railroad Yards at Pittsburgh, and federal troops were finally called up to end the strike. The violence of the railroad strike resulted in a wave of legislation and engendered a number of judicial decisions detrimental to organized labor for the remainder of the century.

One of the most exciting and idealistic institutions to be established in the final decade of the nineteenth century was the settlement house. Begun by two Oxford students in England as an institution devoted to a quest for social justice, Toynbee Hall in London was followed by an increasing number of settlement houses in

Britain and America. Many of its earliest practitioners were teachers by training or inclination, but all were highly dedicated progressives and pragmatic reformers. Settlement houses were started by pioneering social workers like Jane Addams and Ellen Starr in Chicago, Robert A. Woods in Boston, Stanton Colt and Lillian Wald in New York. They were soon copied throughout the immigrant ghettos of the East and Midwest. The settlement house concept in America brought cultural, artistic, vocational, and psychological uplift to immigrant families in the urban centers of America, and settlement houses were among the first institutions to recognize the plight of blacks in the North. Many men thought the settlements a cleverly disguised trick to get a grip on the immigrant electorate, but most women were less suspicious. Many workingmen and their families found nothing like the settlement programs in their public schools to satisfy their genuine desire to learn about art, music, and culture (Cary and Weinberg 1975, 118).

The 1890s was a transitional decade between the literary giants of the last half of the nineteenth century and the rising stars that would dominate the twentieth century. Many of the most famous writers of the Industrial Age were still active in the 1890s: E. C. Stedman, Francis Parkman, William Dean Howells, Henry James, Mark Twain, F. Marion Crawford, Frances Hodgson Burnett, Bret Harte, Sarah Orne Jewett, and Joel Chandler Harris. All of these writers, and many other respected authors, were still alive in 1894, were around 60 years old, and were still publishing at least one book per year. However, the 1890s also brought into the literary spotlight the new authors who would break from the genteel realism proposed by Howells. In the 1890s the first major literary offerings of several rising stars appeared in print: Booth Tarkington, Alice Brown, Richard Burton, Theodore Dreiser, Ellen Glasgow, Jack London, Stephen Crane, O. Henry, and Edith Wharton. Just as the nation was on the cusp of a new century, American literature was on the edge of a new realism promoted by a rising generation of writers (Shrock 2004, 163).

Writers in the Industrial Age turned away from the sentimentality that had characterized much of the output from mid-century and began to examine in print the world around them in a more realistic and natural way. The transition helped to shape the high literature normally thought to have been a product of the period. Americans living in this period could access books from a number of sources: bookstores, subscriptions, libraries, door-to-door salesmen, railway newsboys, and mail-order catalogs. Ironically, with all the reading material that was available, bookstores, with a primary business of selling books, were located largely in urban areas with a large enough customer base to provide a profit. Even these were none too plentiful. It has been estimated that in 1859 there were 843 bookstores in the United States dedicated to book sales, yet in 1914 there were only 801. Nonetheless, new book publication rose 300 percent from 1880 to 1900, and there was a corresponding increase in magazine and newspaper sales. Such a result seems contradictory in light of the increased interest in reading, but many other enterprises masked the number of book outlets. Dry goods stores, department stores, and drug stores often sold books as a sideline to their primary business. Moreover, there was a great growth in subscription libraries where, for a fee, members shared reading materials (Shrock 2004, 151, 152, 155). The New York Public Library was founded in 1895 through the combined efforts of the John Jacob Astor, Samuel J. Tilden, and James Lenox foundations. These had established private or subscription libraries, but with finances supplied mostly by Tilden ($2.5 million) and texts from the private collections of all three families the free public library was established. While the use of the facility was free, the purchase of an admission ticket was initially required. The books did not circulate, but they were available for research and reading.

By the middle 1880s, in the West virtually all the erstwhile hostile tribes had been confined to specific reservations, and troops had been assigned to overawe those that remained restless and to prevent outbreaks. The commercial extermination of the buffalo left the Plains Indians totally dependent on government beef, and local Indian agents attempted to introduce new ways among those who had but recently been unfettered hunters, raiders, and warriors. "The early reservation period of the eighties was a time of sore trial for the western Indians. Dishonest or incompetent agents, arbitrary regulation of their every move, the steady shrinkage of their lands, and many unwise policies aimed at speedily 'civilizing' them drove many Indians to desperation" (Rickey 1963, 15–16). Soldiers would police the Indian country for several years to come, chasing isolated outlaws and breakaway bands, but never again would they meet the Indians in a major action.

The rapid industrialization of the United States catapulted the nation into international prominence, and the country responded by building a modern navy to protect its maritime commerce. In 1889, the U.S. Navy was the twelfth largest in the world; a decade later it was the third largest in the world. The expansion of the U.S. Army was somewhat more problematic. With the repression of a few "digger Indians" seeming to be their only internal assignment and no external enemy on the horizon, calls from army officials to expand the ranks of the regular army fell on deaf ears in Washington. Yet the destruction of the United States battleship *Maine* in Havana harbor in 1898 changed all that as the American public evidenced an almost wild enthusiasm for combat overseas. Congress seemingly understood the popularity of war service at this time and raised the army authorization from a mere 29,000 in 1897 to more than 260,000 enlisted men in just two years.

As the traditional opponents of large standing armies and navies had feared for more than 100 years, the new military power of the United States led it to the use of force in pursuit of its foreign policy and in support of its economic and domestic goals. Unlike the eras before and after the Industrial Age, however, there were no major wars on the scale of the Civil War or World War I, just relatively small-scale conflicts against vastly inferior military forces. American global economic expansion, the formal closing of the western frontier in 1890, Social Darwinism, scientific racism, the rise of the United States to great power status, as well as a new, more belligerent vision for American manhood pushed the United States into several imperialist ventures abroad. The imperialist enterprises of the 1890s, however, were not isolated events out of step with earlier decades. They were instead the logical culmination of policies set in motion as early as the presidency of Thomas Jefferson at the beginning of the century (Shrock 2004, 21).

In the Caribbean, as early as the Grant administration, there had been a tentative but unsuccessful move to purchase the Danish Virgin Islands or to take over the Dominican Republic to provide U.S. naval bases to protect growing American interests in the region. This was seen as a return to the principles of the Monroe Doctrine. One of the unforeseen consequences of the Spanish-American War was that the United States became a colonial power—a small power when viewed against Britain, France, or German influence, but with enough far-flung possessions to force the government to look overseas to the establishment of coaling and watering stations. The idea of naval bases located in the Caribbean and the Pacific became even more attractive when the French engineer De Lesseps began construction of a canal in Panama. Possession of the Philippines, Guam, Hawaii, Puerto Rico, and a base at Guantanamo Bay, Cuba after the Spanish-American War served these purposes. The United States would purchase the Virgin Islands in 1917 as a stop against German U-boat activity in World War I.

—James M. Volo

FOR MORE INFORMATION

Albion, Robert G., and Jennie B. Pope. *Sealanes in Wartime*. Portland, ME: Archon Books, 1968.

Alden, Carroll S., and Allan Westcott. *The United States Navy*. New York: J. B. Lippincott Company, 1945.

Barney, William L., ed. *A Companion to 19th-Century America*. Malden, MA: Blackwell Publishing, 2006.

Cary, John H., and Julius Weinberg, eds. *The Social Fabric, American Life from the Civil War to the Present*. Boston, MA: Little, Brown and Company, 1975.

Hunter, Louis C. *A History of Industrial Power in the United States, 1780–1930*. Charlottesville: University Press of Virginia, 1979.

Husband, Julie, and Jim O'Loughlin. *Daily Life in the Industrial United States, 1870–1900*. Westport, CT: Greenwood Press, 2004.

Nye, David E. *Electrifying America: The Social Meanings of New Technology, 1880–1940*. Cambridge, MA: The MIT Press, 1990.

Rickey, Don, Jr. *Forty Miles a Day on Beans and Hay, The Enlisted Soldier Fighting the Indian Wars*. Norman: University of Oklahoma Press, 1963.

Roosevelt, Theodore. "Theodore Roosevelt: An Autobiography." URL: http://www.bartleby.com/55/13.html (accessed July 2007).

Roosevelt, Theodore. *Theodore Roosevelt, an Autobiography*. New York: The Macmillian Company, 1913.

Shrock, Joel. *The Gilded Age*. Westport, CT: Greenwood Press, 2004.

Smith, Merritt Roe, and Leo Marx, eds. *Does Technology Drive History? The Dilemma of Technological Determinism*. Cambridge, MA: MIT Press, 1994.

Smith, Page. *The Nation Comes of Age: A People's History*. 4 Vols. New York: McGraw-Hill, 1981.

Timmons, Todd. *Science and Technology in Nineteenth-Century America*. Westport, CT: Greenwood Press, 2005.

Tosh, John. "New Men? The Bourgeois Cult of Home." *History Today* (December 1996).

Domestic Life

KINSHIP SYSTEMS: PATRIARCHY

In some men the drive toward wealth could become excessive or even destructive. The disposition of land through inheritance had always been a major prop of parental authority and discipline. Yet in the nineteenth century it was declining as a source of patriarchal power in the family. The sharing of a man's income, in the form of money or wages, among his children or with his spouse quickly formed a more significant source of men's authority than in former times. Unwarranted economy and a tight purse often eroded important ties between fathers and their older children. Even if a man wanted to fulfill his role as financial manager and dispenser of funds, the need to be at work to earn a wage often came into conflict with his childrearing role in the household.

Middle-class men who had grown up in the first decades of the nineteenth century could remember a childhood spent living in a family working environment, either on the farm, in a cottage at the mill, or in a room behind the family shop. But as the century progressed men's work increasingly took place in the special atmosphere of a business premises like the factory or office (Tosh 1996).

Contemporary observers were concerned that children interacted with their father only during the worst hours of the day, his tired hours. In former times "when business was a thing of comparative leisure," fathers watched over their children, "rewarded and punished, rebuked and encouraged" them on the instant. Children could trace back much of what was best in them to this steady parental interaction. John Ware advised, "Let this generation once feel, as it must feel, that this neglect of home is no necessity, but a sin; let it rest red and hot upon men's consciences that God has given them this charge which they have deserted…and you will find business as easy to control as you now imagine it to be difficult" (Ware 1864, 269–70).

—James M. Volo

Although the nineteenth-century family home became more female dominated as the period continued, a man's place became more authoritarian. Here a father, book in hand, enjoys the warmth of a family gathering, surrounded by his loved ones and his possessions. Courtesy Editor's collection.

FAMILY LIFE

Population Growth and Shifts

U.S. cities had been growing throughout the nineteenth century, but their development was exceptional during the final quarter of the century. From 1879–1900, the total U.S. population nearly doubled, increasing from 35,558,000 to 75,995,000. In 1870, only 25.7 percent of the U.S. population was urban. In fact in the late 1860s, three-quarters of Americans lived on farms or in villages with less than 2,500 people. By 1900, almost 40 percent of Americans were city dwellers. Urban population during this time increased at triple the rate of rural areas. For every urban worker who became a farmer, there were 20 farmers who moved to cities.

In 1900, there were 38 U.S. cities with more than 100,000 residents, 24 more than there had been in 1870. To highlight the scope of the change, consider that in 1790 only 3.14 percent of the U.S. population lived in cities. Between 1870 and 1900 Detroit grew from 80,000 to 286,000 residents; Minneapolis increased from 13,000 to over 200,000; Los Angles expanded from 6,000 to over 100,000. The 1880s were the most intense period of urban growth. In this decade alone, the U.S. population increased by 54.4 percent and the cities of Chicago, Detroit, and Milwaukee doubled in size. As much as 40 percent of the rural population migrated to cities during the 1880s.

There were two main sources for this population growth: internal migration, where U.S. citizens living in rural areas decided to move to cities, and external migration, where immigrants from other countries came to the United States. Other developments like the decline in mortality rates played only an insignificant role. In the case of both internal and external migrants, people came to cities because that was where there was work. By 1900, nine-tenths of the nation's manufacturing occurred in urban areas.

Cities absorbed unprecedented waves of immigrants coming into the United States during this time. Between 1870 and 1900 approximately 11.3 million immigrants came to the United States, a rate of immigration more than 10 times that which the country had experienced at the beginning of the 1800s. By 1900, 14 percent of the U.S. population was foreign born. As a point of comparison, consider that a century later, in 1999, only 8 percent of Americans were born abroad. The immigrants at the beginning of the industrial era tended to be part of the wave of Northern European immigrants including Irish, Germans, and Scandinavians. Starting around 1880, a new and larger group of immigrants came across the Atlantic from southern and eastern Europe including Poles, Russians, Italians, Greeks, and Turks. New immigrants also came across the Pacific from China and Japan. Italian-Americans would become the largest group of so-called hyphenated Americans in the United States in the early decades of the twentieth century.

Though many of the earlier immigrants had sought out available farmland in the Midwest and East, the majority of these new immigrants settled in cities to look for work. As a result, cities such as San Francisco and Pittsburgh, had a population during the industrial era that was over 50 percent foreign born. In fact, in 1880 over 80 percent of the population consisted either of immigrants or the children of immigrants in the cities of Cleveland, New York, Detroit, and Milwaukee. Add to those numbers the many internal migrants to urban areas, and it becomes clear why cities often seemed like places where everyone lived but no one was born (Husband and O'Loughlin 2004, 20–21).

Vital Statistics

Average white life expectancy at birth in 1870 was 45 years, and white infant mortality rates for 1870 at 176 per 1,000 were significantly worse than those of 1900. There are significant difficulties recorded when these data are compared to a decade later. Average white life expectancy at birth in 1880 sat at a remarkably low 41 years, and white infant mortality rates rose in 1880 to stand at 214 per 1,000, almost as bad as they had been in 1850. In 1890 the data reversed their short-term trend and average life expectancy rose again to 47, and the infant mortality fell to 151 per 1,000. Not until 1910 would infant mortality fall from triple- into double-digits per 1,000.

There is no reliable data for infant mortality or life expectancy for blacks until the early twentieth century, but in 1900 black life expectancy was recorded as a mere 42 years, and black infant mortality stood at 170 per 1,000.

—*James M. Volo*

MEN

Self-help author and advisor J. Clinton Ransom wrote in 1889, "In every community there is always some one whom his neighbors call a successful man. He commands the esteem of the whole circle of his acquaintance. He is alert and active in business; he is absorbed in the duties of a busy life; but he has time to be friendly with all and to endear himself to all with whom he comes in contact. He is spoken of as a clever companion, an honorable businessman, a prosperous citizen, a man of solid integrity. This personage is our successful man." Ransom noted that in his opinion an individual's employment, situation, and station in life did not matter in determining his success. It was by varying standards of judgment that a man was pronounced successful by his fellows (Ransom 1889, 15).

Although material wealth motivated many men to work hard and be industrious, the pursuit of money purely for its own sake had been viewed with some suspicion since colonial times. However, reaching the simple standard of financial competency was often not enough for many men according to the perception of nineteenth-century observers T. L. Haines and Levi Yaggy. "Acquisitiveness," if not greed or avarice, seemingly took a hold on the minds of many men, and they became focused on being more than merely comfortable. They seemed in a great haste to become conspicuously wealthy. Wild ambition, however, was thought to tarnish true success, and it mingled the feelings of admiration and abhorrence of those who observed it. Haines and Yaggy noted, "The road ambition travels is too narrow for friendship, too crooked for love, too rugged for honesty, too dark for science, and too hilly for happiness." No amount of glory or fame could be enduring, according to these advisors, unless it was based on "virtue, wisdom, and justice" (Haines and Yaggy 1876, 269–70).

In addition, it became fashionable among the upper classes, especially among the women, to lead generally idle lives at home caring for the domestic needs of the household through the management of a score of servants. The leisure that this suggested for the female householder was probably overstated by the generally conservatively minded advisors of the day, and it was little different from that of persons of similar social standing and financial circumstances in previous times that required aptitude, organization, and luck. Yet the rising middle class often aspired to an idyllic life filled with pastimes, diversions, and attempts at personal improvement without recognizing these underlying fundamentals. Philo Tower, a preacher and writer from the period, noted this added to the struggle to reach the state of competency. "No young man" could make such "a fortune to support the extravagant style of housekeeping, and gratify the expensive tastes of young women, as fashion is now educating them." Many marriages were deferred to allow young suitors time to amass a fortune, and many others were avoided or discouraged by parents as young women chose older and more successful men as spouses (Smith 1981, 755).

Among the standards set for the so-called solid citizen, the issue of work seems to have been central to a man's identity, authority, and place in the social order. Only physical disability (or immense fortune) allowed a man to remove himself from the world of work to the pleasures of a contemplative retirement. Diligent labor and financial success had been venerated in America before 1800, and colonial attitudes toward work have been described in sociological terms as an adherence to the *Protestant Work Ethic*, first expounded by William Perkins as the *Doctrine of Work* in 1603. Perkins connected heavenly salvation less to financial success than to diligent labor at some honest trade or vocation. "Somewhere in the battle of life, God gives every man a chance to wear the victor's crown and stand among heroes." Yet many American colonials, especially those dedicated to the Calvinist tradition, though financial success morally gained was an earthly symbol of God's approbation (Ransom 1889, 17).

In the nineteenth century the path to success lay not in the workshop or on the farm, but in the emerging industries and enterprises of consumer capitalism. Nineteenth-century men looked less to the quality of a man's labor as an indicator of his respectability and more to the nonreligious implications of his financial success. They made industry (work) an end in itself, money its indicator, and the acquisition of great wealth the shining trophy at the end of life. "Money, not work, became the proof of a moral life [and] as Americans came to measure worth by money, they measured lack of worth by lack of money" (Atkins 1984, 11).

In the 1800s wealth made a remarkable statistical redistribution to the top of the social ladder largely due to the crushing effects of overwhelming numbers of poor rural immigrants pouring into the country at the same time that its commercial economy was undergoing a phenomenal rate of expansion. Historian Galliard Hunt noted that "an unbridled love of money was the spring of the Republic." Writing of America for the centennial of the War of 1812, Hunt also noted that everything was seemingly sacrificed to financial interest. "All disinterested acts, all talents purely agreeable, were looked upon with contempt" (Hunt 1914, 31). The burning desire to be a millionaire, a shipping magnet, a railroad king, a war leader, or something beyond their real powers and abilities was thought to make men restless and discontented in their pursuit of success.

Under such circumstances money in sufficient quantities was considered the ticket to social prominence. "Everything favored a vile cupidity" (Ransom 1889, 27).

Nonetheless, being born of a prominent family at mid-century was no simple indicator of success. Even great wealth, if newly found, needed aging, and a generation of family philanthropy was needed to guarantee a place in the carefully guarded social circles of the uppermost classes. A man's personal manner, dress, voice, style, and bearing were all part of the standards by which success was measured. Moreover, these qualities could not be artificial, affected, or insincere. Richard Henry Dana of New York, who was something of a social snob, noted that "inferiority of caste is noticeable as soon as you get out of the aristocracy and upper gentry with hereditary estates and old names" (Smith 1981, 783–84).

In nineteenth-century America, life was seemingly filled with opportunity, and the successful man was expected to aspire to a level of achievement commensurate with his class and abilities. Anthony Trollope, an English novelist visiting New York, noted of the merchants and businessmen, "The ascendancy of dollars are the words written on every paving stone along Fifth Avenue, down Broadway and up Wall Street. Every man can vote, and values the privilege. Every man can read, and uses the privilege. Every man worships the dollar, and is down before his shrine from morning till night" (Meredith 1982, 35). Only death or physical incapacity relieved a man of his obligation to pursue success. From lowly farmers to captains of industry successful men were expected to bend their wills to every opportunity that presented itself. "The world is clamoring for men to fill its high positions and shoulder its grave responsibilities." Should a man miss his opportunity through carelessness "the line of his irretrievable failure [would be] marked out…with the suddenness of a thunder peal" (Ransom 1889, 20).

The frontispiece from J. Clinton Ransom, *The Successful Man in His Manifold Relation with Life* (1889) showing the two alternate paths of life—one leading from idleness to corruption and the other from industry to honored old age. Courtesy Editor's collection.

It should be noted that a number of Irish immigrant families with the humblest of beginnings were able to emerge from poverty to gain social, political, and economic prominence within a generation. Although they were victims of severe ethnic prejudice, the Irish came to America with certain advantages over other immigrant groups like the Chinese, Italians, or Eastern Europeans. They spoke English; they were white and virtually indistinguishable from persons of English extraction; and they had political experience founded in their long struggles with English landlords. Many of these Irish came to be part of the First Families of Boston and New York. The McDonnells, Ryans, Buckleys, Floods, Fairs, Mackays, O'Briens, and Stewarts were all part of this so-called Irishocracy. They began in the penniless slums of America's cities, but they used their ambition, determination, political savvy, and industry to become some of the most powerful families in America.

Many second- and third-generation Irish immigrants were remarkably successful. Robert J. Cuddihy, for example, was behind one of the great successes in the field of publishing—the rise of the *Literary Digest* in the first decades of the twentieth century. Thomas E. Murray, though little schooled, was an ingenious electrical engineer who by the end of his career held a number of patents second only to those of Thomas A. Edison. By establishing America's first food-store chain for the carriage trade, Patrick J. O'Connor and James Butler established their own vast family fortunes. As a final example, take Edward Doheny, who made $31 million selling crude oil from southern California and Mexico. He was later a key figure in the Teapot Dome scandal of the 1920s and was reliably reported at one point to have had more money than John D. Rockefeller.

Nineteenth-century men considered good work habits and a sound education to be vital to success. The two pressing needs of young men, in particular, were to acquire an adequate preparation for the duties of life that might confront them and to develop a sense for carefully weighing any opportunity before plunging into a task that was beyond their talents to carry out to completion. Instinct and inherent genius were considered laudable characteristics, but without the discipline of the work ethic and the tools provided by an appropriate education, effort alone might prove to be misdirected or meaningless. Moreover, men were expected to have the strength of character to reshape an unlooked-for opportunity into a destiny-changing moment, and to have the integrity and depth of soul to withstand the shock of success. Churches and temperance groups sponsored organizations for young boys and teens that promoted Christian manliness. In the 1870s and 1880s so-called Boys' Brigades and chivalric societies modeled on King Arthur's court sponsored competitive sports and physical education, and encouraged wholesome living.

There was, moreover, a sense of something ennobling in the act of pursuing success at a high level of personal or financial risk—a process of purification and a necessary step in the development of character. This concept had the natural effect of glorifying the accomplishment of seemingly unattainable goals or the ambition to surpass the usual achievements of other men. In line with widely held concepts of duty and obligation, it was as important to finish a job as it was to undertake it. Men did not quit or leave their positions even under the most trying of circumstances, and initial failure required a redoubling of effort. This ideal can be seen in the efforts to put a telegraph cable across the Atlantic, to build a transcontinental railroad, to develop a great machine-powered manufactory, to cross the Great American Desert, or to carve a farmstead out of the wilderness.

Although some of these efforts were monumental in scope, the possibility of failure was not an option to be taken lightly. Haines and Yaggy warned that if "a man is brought into a sphere of his ambition for which he has not the requisite powers, and where he is goaded on every side in the discharge of his duties, his temptation is at once to make up by fraud and appearance that which he lacks in ability" (Haines and Yaggy 1876, 12–13). Of 100 men embarking on the same type of business ventures only a handful attained anything like distinguished success. This same train of thought tended to trivialize the common affairs of life leaving some men thinking that they were failures at everyday living because they were "too ambitious of doing something more" (Ransom 1889, 28).

For some men success seemed to come more easily than for others; but if a man lacked genius, he might remedy it through training. Increasingly, nineteenth-century work was being done by men with educations such as engineers, financiers, and scientists. These things could be learned in the universities through the assiduous application of study. If, however, they lacked character in the presence of other vices, which they could not or would not resist, then even the most dedicated of students or workers deserved to fail. The price of success was often great in terms of capital, effort, and time, but some men failed to appreciate the difficulty with which it was won—the "busy days lengthening out into years...a long life of closest devotion to single pursuits...[and] the hard toil in the face of difficulties" (Ransom 1889, 33).

Mediocrity in any task was considered unacceptable. Yet even men of humble social station were taught that doing good and useful work was noble as long as they enlisted their full powers in the enterprise. "It is not our fault," wrote Ransom, "that we do not possess talents of the highest order. We cannot with reason question that inscrutable wisdom which made some of us prophets and teachers, some of us vine-dressers and husbandmen, some of us money kings and merchant-princes, some of us great and some small, and all servitors in His Kingdom of universal service" (Ransom 1889, 27; Volo and Volo 2007, 48–50, 66–70).

WOMEN

With the expansion of industrialization, the daily lives and responsibilities of women and men had begun to diverge away from the ideal of a team and toward discreet tasks and obligations. Motherhood was a serious and all-consuming occupation for nineteenth century wives, largely replacing the role of helpmate that had been the norm for wives in early America. With men away from the home for the day working, women began to take on greater responsibility for the home and its residents. Early in the century, day-to-day authority over children and their moral upbringing began to shift from a paternal duty to a maternal one. This change was one of the foundation stones of the growing *Cult of Domesticity*. By mid-century, this concept had expanded to the point that mothers were expected to make the home a moral bulwark that would provide children with an idyllic childhood.

As a young woman, Betsey Reynolds, contemplated the importance of maternal care and instruction, noting in her diary that just as business obliges the father to be about town, the care of infancy devolves upon the mother. Although the period saw larger numbers of young women entering the workforce than ever before in American history, the goal of the vast majority of them remained becoming mistresses of their own homes and matriarchs of their own families. The editor of *Godey's Lady's Book* explained that women had a higher pursuit than the industrial arts could afford. In an article entitled, "Woman In Her Social Relations," Henry E. Woodbury proffered that of all the impressions made upon the youthful mind, none were so lasting as those received from a mother. He believed that they became a part of a child's nature, controlling motives and exerting a powerful influence over them in all the affairs of life. Truly weighty were the obligations devolving on women in the discharge of their duties in this relation. The formation of character was determined to be theirs.

In *The Mother's Rule; or, The Right Way and the Wrong Way* T. S. Arthur wrote that it was vastly important for mothers to have a high regard for their duties and to feel deeply the immense responsibilities that rest upon them. It was through their ministrations that the world grew worse or better. The popular *The Mother's Book* cautioned that every look, every movement, every expression, does something toward forming the character of the little heir to immortal life.

Attitudes such as these became common as they spread through the community of matrons, and they were embraced by both women of childbearing years and society in general. As a mother, Betsey Reynolds Voorhees wrote a letter expressing the stress of motherhood. Her children were the principal objects of all her cares and all her hopes. She was consumed in their moral and intellectual improvements to the point that the great anxiety she felt for her children left her too little time for her own concerns.

A new mother was encouraged to rest after delivery, but she was still expected to receive callers. Sarah Goodwin employed a nurse to assist her with all who called. The nurse slept with the baby, did the laundry, and also kept the baby and mother in elegant toilets and waited on all the company upstairs and to the street door. The length of time that a woman remained abed after delivery varied with her constitution, personality, and economic situation. Many obstetric texts suggested that mothers who walked about too soon after giving birth would be struck with blood clots or a prolapsed uterus, and they commonly recommended nine days of complete bed rest. This was particularly true for upper-class women who were thought to be more delicate and more susceptible to postpartum complications. Less affluent women could not spare this much time away from family duties. Some women, like Anne Jean Lyman, would be up the very next day with a mending basket and sewing for some hours of each day. Lyman recalled that by the second week she had resumed all the duties of the house.

During the nineteenth century the average native-born white woman gave birth to a half-dozen children, not counting those lost to miscarriages and stillbirths. By 1900 the number was cut in half. As noted earlier the fertility rate remained high, however, among black and immigrant women. Some rural farm areas maintained higher rates as well. To some extent the declining birthrate among native-born whites was a result of the changing economics of the era. In previous centuries, children were valued contributors to the family economy. The more children a family had, the more hands there were to work and improve the family's productivity and wealth. Changes in manufacturing and marketing no longer required artisans to have children to which skills and secrets needed to be passed so that the family would be sustained in the future. In the new market economy, children became an expense. They required substantial investments of time, care, and limited resources unless they could find wage-paying employment outside the home.

Lower birthrates can also be attributed to new cultural attitudes toward the role of women. Concern also rose about women's health. Women generally bore their first child 16 months after they married and continued to have children approximately 15 to 20 months apart. A woman's last child was likely born when she was in her 40s and may have been the same age as her first grandchild. During Julia Patterson's 30 years of marriage she was pregnant or nursing for 19 years and 3 months. She married when she was 21 and had her first child nine months later. Her 11th and last child was born when she was 45 years old. Yet the details of Patterson's childbearing were at the upper level of the experience of most women, who spent 10 to 12 of their childbearing years with child. Spending most of their adult lives either pregnant or nursing, took its toll on the health and vitality of many women and acceptance of this lifestyle role was becoming less acceptable to many nineteenth-century women.

The 1830s saw the beginning of advice literature that suggested either abstinence or the use of contraception, and by the 1870s there was an abundance of commercial products that were advertised to assist women in this matter. A mainstay of urban newspapers were ads for birth control pamphlets, medical devices such as diaphragms and syringes, condoms, spermicides, and pills that promised to induce abortions. Ads for these products were often distributed on street corners. If the ad contained the word "French" in the title, it indicated that the item was a contraceptive. If it used the word "Portuguese," as in "The Portuguese Female Pill always gives immediate relief," the product was meant to be an abortive. Sellers frequently made outlandishly false claims about their products, but many were nothing more than alcohol and flavored water. Although not socially acceptable, abortions performed very early in a pregnancy were generally considered to be a form of contraception.

Although children were more likely to reach adulthood in the nineteenth century than in the past, childhood mortality was still high. The romanticism and sentimentalism of the nineteenth century viewed death from a different perspective than in earlier times, or even than it is today. Death was a part of daily living. Although the loss of a child was felt most deeply, acceptance of it showed deep faith and religious conviction. Early death provided the assurance of being free from the sin. Their brief existence protected them from corruption. Upon the passing of her infant child, Cornelia Peake McDonald recalled her friend suggesting that she thank God for taking her precious little babe from the sorrow and evil to come.

Cemeteries provided separate sections for children making it easier for a young family, yet unable to secure a family plot, to bury their child. Their young or stillborn children could later be reinterred when the family was more established and could afford a family plot. Children's graves received unprecedented attention. Families that could afford it often created gravestone markers steeped in sentiment and imagery. The most common image was that of the sleeping child. Sleep, as a tie between life and death, was a recurring theme of the period. The image made a connection back to the home where the youth once slept. It brought to mind the comforting picture of a child safely tucked away in his bed. The child with a lamb was another recurring image that reinforced the belief in the closeness of children and nature. Empty furniture was also depicted on memorials. An unfilled chair or bed was commonly used to symbolize the child's unfilled life.

Other items appearing on memorials included rattles, dolls, or favorite playthings incised in stone. The use of toys in such a permanent form reflected the period's recognition of the naturalness of play and a lasting reminder of the separate worlds of children and adults. Sculptural portrayals of children and their belongings insured that they would remain forever one with the goodness of the home. They would be undisturbed and constant, forever innocent in the world. Upon seeing the face of a neighbor who stood by her son's corpse, Cornelia Peake McDonald, who had lost her own child only months before, wondered if her little darling's forehead would ever have looked so dim and weary. She said that she took comfort in the fact that her babe's work was finished, and she went to rest "while yet 'twas early day." McDonald said she would not bring her back if she could to resume the burden her Savior removed that day when she fled from her arms as the sun was setting.

Period advertisements carried the names of many photographers who specialized in posthumous photographs Infants were the most common subject of this type of photograph. Perhaps this was because there had been little opportunity to capture the child's likeness in life. Perhaps it provided a concrete reminder of a life that had passed too quickly. Sometimes the deceased child would be posed cradled in its mother's arms. Other poses might show the child resting on a pillow. Photographers sometimes borrowed from the imagery of portrait painters and included a cut rose in the picture symbolizing a bloom cut early.

Most women breast-fed their babies and, for many, this was the most common form of natural contraception as it had been for centuries. Wet nurses were never popular in the North, but there was greater support for the practice in Southern plantation households. While so-called baby bottles were available prior to 1800, bottle-feeding did not become popular until the last decades of the century. Many factory-employed mothers, however, had little choice but to have their babies given cow's milk while they worked. The problem was that the cows from which the milk was obtained were often diseased and filthy. A number of physicians began to study human breast milk to determine its beneficial qualities. In the 1850s, J. R. Meigs published a recipe for infant formula that combined cow's milk, cream, sugar, and limewater. Commercial infant food soon became popular. As the century drew to a close, Thomas Morgan Rotch developed the "percentage method" to create a perfect infant formula. Popular from 1890 into the first decade of the next century, the method fell out of favor due to its complexity. Other advancements in this field came when Pasteur's germ theory led to the practice of boiling bottles to sterilize them and his pasteurization process, which was first applied to milk in Denmark in the 1890. In 1893 Nathan Straus opened one of the first pure milk stations in the country. It cut the death rate at New York's Orphan Asylum in half. The first true artificial infant formula was Nestlé's Infant Food, a product that required only the addition of water.

Mothers took great care to protect their infants. They dressed their babies in long gowns, which were often twice the length of the child. Many period photographs show tiny infants enveloped in yards of fabric. Long gowns could not be cast off as loose blankets could. It was felt that the gowns would provide the child with greater warmth. These garments were generally white to withstand the frequent washings that infant clothing required, and period advice manuals advised that they be of soft material, entirely free from starch. For the first few weeks after birth, infants wore long narrow strips of fabric known as bellybands. These were several yards long and were designed to protect the navel. In addition to diapers, or napkins as they were called, infants wore a shirt, a pinner that contained their lower limbs, a skirt or skirts, and a dress. As the century progressed this practice of binding up the baby earned increasing criticism from both the medical profession and popular publications.

Some declared that swaddling clothes endangered the breadth and vigor of a generation. More enlightened women freed their children from such encumbrance, but, for many, the custom persisted. Babies also wore caps both indoors and out. Women's magazines frequently carried patterns for these accessories. As the child grew older, clothing adjustments were made. Mothers were advised that when a child showed a disposition to creep, they should shorten its clothes that it might have free use of its limbs, and protect its feet with stockings and shoes.

In addition to the moral and social guidance mothers were presumed to develop in their children, they were expected to provide them with an affectionate home which would create an idyllic childhood rich with wonderful experiences that would create fond memories and healthy minds and bodies. In *The American Woman's Home* (2002) the Beecher sisters wrote that they knew of families where the mother's presence seemed the sunshine of the circle around her imparting a cheering and vivifying power. An orphaned boy who resided with the Alcotts for several summers described Mrs. Alcott saying that she was "sunshine herself" to her children and to him, and no matter how weary she might have been with the washing and ironing, the baking and cleaning, it was all hidden from the children with whom she was always ready to enter into fun and frolic, as though she never had a care. *The Mother's Book* advised that the first rule, and most important of all was that the mother govern her own feelings, and keep her heart and conscience pure.

With lower birthrates and high mortality, middle-class mothers lavished attention on their surviving children. *The Mother's Book* instructed that an infant's wants should be attended to without waiting for him to cry and advised that the mother should take the entire care of her own child and the infant should, as much as possible, feel its mother's guidance. The mother appeared in the role of constant attendant.

As the century progressed, the toy chest slowly replaced the child's workbasket. Where once mothers gave children tasks to help share the family workload, they were now expected to provide the children with stimulating activities and playthings that would help them to develop intellectually, physically, and morally. Mothers were advised that as soon as it is possible to instruct by means of toys, they should be careful to choose those that would most be useful. The growing market economy generated a plethora of commercially produced toys many of which were of an educational nature. Mothers were expected to be active in their children's learning. Lydia Maria Child advised mothers that when a child was able to spell a new word, or count a new number, to kiss him and show delight at his improvement.

While indulgence with time and attention was advocated, ladies' advice manuals cautioned against spoiling children with playthings, clothing, or permissiveness. Mothers must never lose sight of the fact that they were forming the character of the child. They were exhorted to teach their children order and responsibility by having them care for their clothing and playthings. They were encouraged to instill in their children the value of time by keeping them employed in positive pursuits. They were discouraged from promoting vanity and a love of finery in dress by displaying these qualities in their own lives. Mothers were urged to develop in their charges an appreciation of nature and of making things with their own hands.

With fathers away from the home, mothers became the chief administrators of discipline. Rather than physical punishment, mothers turned to subtle manipulations of the child's behavior. *The Mother's Book* advised that example and silent influence were better than direct rules and commands and that firmness united with goodness was best. Mothers were encouraged to make the punishment similar to the offense, so that if the child's offense was antisocial, the punishment should deprive him of social intercourse and thus teach him its value.

Even farm mothers grew concerned that extensive farm labors kept them from filling the sacred office of motherhood, and they began to concentrate on child nurture. While rural mothers may have lived in greater isolation than their urban counterparts, women's magazines and advice manuals were in wide circulation and farm mothers embraced the new ideology. A woman, identified only as "Annette," agitated for a women's column in the *Genesee Farmer* explaining that it could help mothers to raise generations of thinking progressive farmers. Farmhouse nurseries moved closer to the dining room, sitting room, or family room and away from the potentially hazardous kitchen. While different from middle-class nurseries that were often found on the second floor, playrooms began to appear in house plans for farmhouses. Children's needs began to take precedence over the order of the home. The 1893 *Agriculturist* reported that even among families with no formal nursery there was one room inhabited by a baby to the exclusion of most others; a room where he was at liberty to crawl about, where he took his nap and made the most of his infant existence. In an article describing the rearranging of sitting room furniture to make a place for baby, Edna Donnell explained that it was all right if the room looked a little cluttered, because the baby came first. An anonymous author of an article in 1888 addressed the same issue proclaiming that the child was the monarch of all he surveyed.

While farm mothers may have been able to make inroads toward embracing the child-centered culture of the middle class, urban working-class mothers had little opportunity. Many children were left in the care of older siblings who were barely old enough to care for themselves. Social reformer Jane Addams was horrified by the list of injuries sustained by small children whose mothers had gone to work. She discovered that in one community one child had fallen out of a third story window, another had been burned, and yet a third child with no one to look after him had developed a curved spine due to the fact that for three years he had been tied all day long to the leg of the kitchen table.

Desperate for childcare, many women placed their children in nurseries modeled after French crèches. By 1892, there were 90 day nurseries in American cities, many run by religious or charitable organizations. Unfortunately, the level of childcare was often very poor. Overcrowded and understaffed, these nurseries gained a dubious reputation and were utilized only by women in the most dire circumstances. In an effort to offer a more viable alternative, Jane Addams opened Hull House in Chicago in 1889 as a place where working-class and immigrant mothers could bring their children. Inspired by a settlement house she had seen in East London, Addams along with Ellen Starr originally envisioned the Hull House to be a place where educated middle-class women could share the pleasures of art and literature with their mainly immigrant neighbors. Addams and Starr soon realized that the women had tremendous needs relating to the care of their children. Hull House rapidly expanded to include a day care center, nursery school, kindergarten, well-baby clinic, and a place where mothers could sit and talk. Hull House and other settlement houses that were to follow created a kind of socialized domestic sphere for lower-class mothers in need of support. It provided these women and their children a place of caring, comfort, and succor.

With the increasing recognition that childhood was a unique stage of life, the nineteenth-century mother was charged with a greater responsibility to proceed with care and to follow the latest trends in scientific childrearing. Middle- and upper-class women were extremely conscious of the stress of conforming to community standards in this regard. Improved methods of childrearing quickly took hold that required a conscious effort and devotion to effect on the part of the mother. It fell to the mother to shape the child's character and instill habits of self-control while emphasizing lessons in industry, order, and restraint. It was through this maternal nurture that children were to be sheltered from the corruption of the outside world and prepared for the role of future citizen. As with much in the nineteenth century, the degree to which this took place corresponded directly with the socioeconomic condition of the family (Volo and Volo 2007, 194–206).

CHILDREN

Children: The Industrial Age

Youth became a focus of attention in the Industrial Age as middle-class adults, mired in the staid, controlled world of work and domesticity, celebrated its freedom and innocence. Of course, the youth idolized was that of white, middle-class young people. For some, the celebration of youthfulness came across as the veneration of essential characteristics necessary for all red-blooded American men and women. With Calvinist views of innately depraved sinful children replaced by a more benign vision of youthful innocents waiting to be molded by appropriate didactic lessons, parents embraced more permissive parenting styles, affecting a kind of openly loving government. Ideology and practice, however, often diverge, and traditional physical punishments like spanking appear to have been common in all social classes, though perhaps less than half of all families used spanking frequently (Shrock 2004, 27).

Middle-class parents placed a high priority on fostering independence and self-reliance in their children. Advice columnists in women's magazines and childrearing manuals discouraged parents from the sleeping with their infants. Many went further and discouraged unnecessary holding or rocking. In her 1878 *All Around the House; or, How to Make a Happy Home*, Harriet Beecher Stowe advised mothers that once an infant was washed, dressed and well fed at proper intervals, the mother could think of the child until her heart was satisfied, but, the less noticeable care the child had over and beyond that the better for the child itself. She recommended placing the baby in its crib for the bulk of the day where it would lie cooing and smiling and watching shadows on the wall or waving leaves and branches from outside until it fell asleep. She believed that this regimen of minimal holding freed the mother to attend to other duties and strengthen the baby who would be free to roll and stretch and develop stronger muscles (Husband and O'Loughlin 2004, 124).

As part of this effort, children were allowed to romp and play without restraint. In upper-middle class and upper-class homes the nursery, complete with children's toys, and often linked to a nanny's room, separated children from the fragile, luxurious items decorating wealthy Victorian homes. The separate children's sphere catered to the child's specific needs and isolated children from their parent's worlds of work and social formalities. Upper-middle-class fathers left for the office and mothers spent their days shopping, visiting, or entertaining in the parlor—activities to which children were not invited (Husband and O'Loughlin 2004, 124).

Play was considered a valuable activity for children in its own right. Mass-produced toys were widely available. A number of gender-specific concepts about behavioral expectations, emotional sensitivity, and educational expectations came to govern the kinds of games played and chores performed in the home. Boys and girls were presumed to have different constitutions, temperaments, and deportment. Girls were defined in terms of delicacy and dependence while boys were portrayed as rugged and aggressive. Period portraits show boys with swords, drums, bugles, cannons, and rocking horses. Girls were portrayed with dolls, miniature sets of china, and books. Nonetheless, several items seem to have escaped the cloak of gender-specificity. These included drawing, the use of balls of many sizes, play with wooden hoops and wands, manipulating stilts, making soap bubbles, forming collections, playing board games, and playing with yo-yos and other simple mechanical toys.

The American boy was seen as adventurous and independent like the fictional characters Tom Sawyer or Huck Finn. He was portrayed as fun loving and impish, sometimes cruel to small animals and girls yet ultimately noble and heroic. Boys were expected to play pranks as a means of channeling their natural aggression and of challenging authority. They formed closed associations, teams, and clubs to which they felt tremendous loyalty. Hazing, teasing, and name-calling helped to delineate the boundaries of such groups. Boys were given more freedom and less supervision in accomplishing their chores, and many took place outside the home, such as tending the livestock or running errands. Boys' games were more physical and were often highly competitive including a field-hockey-like game called Bandy or Shinny that was characterized by a good deal of roughhousing. The prosecution of those pastimes favored by boys usually took place outside the home more often than those pursued by girls.

The *American Boys Handy Book*, published in 1882, suggested numerous seasonal activities for young boys. In spring there was kiting, fishing, and stocking or maintaining a fresh water aquarium. Summer was a time for homemade boats, camping, making objects by knotting, collecting and preserving birds' nests and eggs, making blow guns and squirt guns, producing paper fireworks, and making musical instruments from found materials. Autumn brought the trapping of small animal pests, drawing, woodcarving, and taxidermy. In winter there was snowball battles, snow forts, snow sculpture, sledding, snowshoeing, ice skating, ice sailing, ice fishing, puppets, homemade masquerades and theaters, and indoor crafts. The book encouraged boys to develop self-reliance by making all their own equipment for whatever their adventure and included detailed plans for building a number of styles of small boats, fishing equipment, sleds, winged skaters, an ice fishing shanty, and countless small toys and amusements.

Universally, though, boys played with marbles, balls, whistles, tops, small boats, toy soldiers, wooden animals, popguns, and kites. One boy wrote in a letter that his large top would spin four minutes and that he had an India-rubber ball, and a boat that he made himself with a man on it. He also had a kite and a windmill. Additionally, he noted that he had a large, nice sled that provided good times sliding downhill. Urban residents had fewer chores and therefore more free time to devote to play. They also tended to have greater time to spend in concert with a wider number of other boys, and they often played in the streets or in empty fields in large groups. Such peer contact differed very dramatically from the previous century when young boys entered apprenticeships and spent much of their time working with adults in the grown-up world. Transition from the world of childhood to that of young manhood was more gradual in the nineteenth century.

The indoctrination of girls into their gender role came early. Farm girls were expected to assist their mothers with household chores as young as five or six. Middle-class girls made up the beds, sewed, and cared for younger siblings. Even girls from wealthly homes were expected to spend time knitting, sewing, or engaging in decorative needlework. Household chores took up much of a girl's time, leaving far less leisure time than was afforded to boys. What playtime they did have was often devoted to vocational pursuits. Girls played "going shopping," "sick lady," and "school," all situations drawn from their personal experience, yet such play prepared them for the adult roles they would eventually assume. Many of the toys that girls were given, such as dolls, tea sets, and needle books, were geared to fostering the nurturing and social skills they would need in later life. Girls mimicked their mothers' activities by playing with dolls, dressing up, and keeping house.

As might be expected, some girls enjoyed physical activity and the outdoors while others preferred quieter pastimes. Rural girls would have had greater freedom to explore the woods and play more active games than their urban counterparts, but few would have joined males in physical activities such as swimming. Group play included such games as Blindman's Bluff, Shuttlecock, Thread the Needle, Hop, Skip and Jump, Trap Ball, Follow My Lead, I Spy, Hunt the Slipper, Flying Feather, Puss in the Corner, and Leap Frog (Volo and Volo 2007, 268).

In 1898, a survey of 1,000 girls and 1,000 boys in Massachusetts, both girls and boys listed the hoop and stick as their favorite toy. Large hoops were made from casks and could be rolled on the ground by revolving a stick inside of the hoop. Overall, both boys and girls preferred toys that permitted active forms of play (Husband and O'Loughlin 2004, 126).

Having established childhood as a distinct stage of human development, new scientific definitions of the different stages of youth appeared and the term adolescence, defining the turbulent period starting with puberty and ending in the late teens, entered popular speech toward the end of the century. Directing and controlling the urges of young people and their free time became a major focus of numerous youth organizations. Christianity, sports, paramilitarism, and camping, all came together in the adult-sponsored youth organizations that flourished in the late-nineteenth century. Middle-class youth were freed from the world of work and able to carve out a unique space. The connections between young people and popular culture became much stronger as they emerged as a distinctive consumer group, spending money in the new mass society on goods marked to them (Shrock 2004, 27–28).

Sports for youth also took on incredibly heightened importance as physical prowess became associated closely with middle-class manhood and fears of immigrant hordes sparked the desire for socializing institutions. Many of these sporting activities were connected with public schools, but there were also large organizations separate from the school systems. Youth, however, increasingly lost control of their own sporting events, surrendering control to adults who supervised these character-building activities. These sporting events appealed to adults as methods spreading manly virtues and socializing youth in the competitive and aggressive values of capitalist society.

These values coincided with fears of effeminization and over civilization shared by men like Theodore Roosevelt and psychologist G. Stanley Hall. Boys needed rough play to develop the manly qualities of courage, aggressiveness, competitiveness, and the desire to win—skills some believed were necessary for American manhood. These attitudes were closely allied with the movement known as Muscular Christianity, which witnessed old-stock Protestants' push for institutions to save modern youth from the sins of city life and to provide socialization for immigrant youth. Leaders of this movement were particularly concerned with developing rural values in children reared in the city. Regardless of who sponsored these youthful sports activities, adult control was characteristic of all.

Undoubtedly, the premier Muscular Christianity organization was the Young Men's Christian Association (YMCA). Muscular Christianity sought to convince young men that Christianity was not weak and effeminate, but strong and manly. In spite of intense opposition, the YMCA switched its orientation from gymnastics to competitive team sports in the 1890s. By 1892 almost 250,000 young men belonged to the YMCA, and near the end of the decade the organization could field teams of near-professional quality in football, basketball, and track and field. Other religious groups soon followed the YMCA's lead. Exponents of sports formed Protestant Sunday School leagues in Brooklyn in 1904, which quickly spread to cities across the country. Catholics followed soon after with the "Boy's Brigade." The ideals of aggressive competition for boys spread throughout the nation under the moral authority of Christianity.

Working-class youth often had little time for sports or schooling, and offered, by far, the greatest challenge to the control and values of middle-class America. Working-class youth normally worked like adults by the time they were in their mid-teens. Unlike middle- and upper-class youth, however, these working-class young people enjoyed leisure activities outside the control of adults. The combination of jobs and new urban amusements created an independence in working-class youth. Young men and women of the working classes, particularly those congregating in the great cities, openly rebelled against Victorian norms and created their own subcultures with their own values. Crime and new urban amusements were the mediums used to rebel against Victorian control and expectations.

The reality for most working-class children was work—not simply household chores, but hard, sweat-producing, backbreaking labor. American industry consciously sought the cheap labor of children. The 1900 Census counted 1.75 million children ages 10 to 15 gainfully employed in the United States. Most of the child labor, 62 percent, was agricultural while 16 percent was in industry. The children employed by industry worked in coal mines, textile mills, garment industry sweatshops, and factories of all kinds, and also worked as bootblacks, scrap collectors, and newsboys. In the 1870s, a survey of working-class families in Massachusetts demonstrated the importance of child labor for working-class families. Children between the ages of 10 and 19 provided a quarter of family income, which jumped to an astounding 30 percent in families where the parents were unskilled workers. As apprenticeships declined and the unskilled trades no longer sought youthful helpers, young people, particularly migrant youth, found themselves stuck in low-paying, unskilled positions that had little chance for upward mobility. Rural poor youth faced equally dismal prospects, working long hours with their parents as tenant farmers and sharecroppers or hiring out as seasonal hands on large farms.

Ironically, as middle-class thinkers were reconstructing children into innocents who should be allowed to play, they increasingly came to fear the violence and crimes of working-class youth. There seemed to be no controls over these young criminals gone wild. Street-corner gangs brazenly exhibited the perception of overall lawlessness of working-class youth in large American cities. Reformer Jacob Riis reported on the prevalence and misdeeds of these gangs in his 1890 work, *How the Other Half Lives*. Riis claimed that every corner had its gang and that they were composed of the American-born sons of English, Irish, and German parents. Gang members wore distinctive hats, shirts, and pants. These gangs of young ruffians thrived on bravado, impressing their peers with robbery. Riis reported that in New York City just over one-eighth of those arrested for crimes were under the age of 20 (Shrock 2004, 32–37).

Child labor in New York City tenements was widespread. Young children were often sent to scavenge the streets for rope, cinders, metal, or anything that could be resold to junk dealers or neighbors. Older children were put to work as street peddlers. Young boys shined shoes, and little girls sold apples or pencils. Manufacturers and contractors gave unfinished garments or materials to make artificial flowers to families who would finish or assemble these items at home. Children were often seen transporting large bundles of these materials in the streets. Once home, the children helped fell seams, sew linings and hems, finish gloves, card buttons, fasten cords to pencils for souvenir cards, assemble artificial flowers and whatever their age and skill allowed them to do. In his study of New York tenements, Jacob Riis reported that children worked unchallenged from the day they were old enough to pull a thread. In a fourth floor tenement he witnessed five men and a woman, two young girls, under 15, and a boy who claimed to be 15, but who obviously lied, at the machines sewing knickerbockers. The floor was littered ankle-deep with half-sewn garments. On a couch, in an alcove, a barelegged baby with pinched face was asleep amid many dozens of pants, ready for the finisher. A fence of piled-up clothing kept him from rolling off on to the floor. The faces, hands, and arms to the elbows of everyone in the room were black with the color of the cloth on which they were working. The girls shot sidelong glances, but, at a warning look from the man with the bundle, they tread their machines more energetically than ever. On the next floor Riis found another family who had hired an old man as an ironer and a sweet-faced little Italian girl as a finisher. She was 12 and she said that she could neither read nor write. Riis noted sadly that she probably never would (Volo and Volo 2007, 324).

Other children did not take part in the actual manufacture of the items, but they bore the burden of the home-work system by having to care for younger siblings and do housework while their mothers were engaged in various types of home manufacture. Children were prohibited from working during the hours they were supposed to be in school, but there were no legal restrictions to keep families from having their children work from the three o'clock in the afternoon dismissal until well into the night. Some teachers complained that their students fell asleep in class, having worked until 9 or 10 at night in some form of home manufacture, but there was nothing they could legally do to remedy the situation. During autumn, when the flower making season was at its height, it was not unusual for families to keep school-aged children home for days at a time, sending them to school just enough to show that they were complying with compulsory attendance regulations. Unfortunately, when truant school-aged children were discovered and forced to attend school, all that the law was doing was adding schoolwork to the ceaseless toil in which the children had spent their days since early childhood. Some families relied on the assistance of their preschool children, as they were too young to be affected by compulsory attendance laws. Children, as young as three, were taught to pull bastings and sew buttons for garments made by their mothers. These younger children were put to work pulling apart the petals that came from the factory stuck together thus enabling the flower assemblers to work much more rapidly.

Once beyond the age of 14, young tenement girls were free to seek employment outside of the home. Many of these girls became shopgirls. In New York, the Women's Investing Committee found the majority of the children employed in the stores to be under age, but reported that they knew of only one time when a truant officer inquired at a shop. In that instance, he sent the youngest children home, but in a month's time they were all back in their places. An investigation by the Working Women's Society documented the injustices that these young girls faced. Sales girls were fined for a number of offenses, including sitting down, despite the fact that a law existed requiring stores to supply seats for saleswomen. In one instance, a little girl, who received only $2 a week, made cash-sales amounting to $167 in a single day, while the receipts of a $15 a week male clerk in the same department footed up only $125; yet for some trivial mistake the girl was fined 60 cents out of her $2. Superintendents and timekeepers commonly shared the revenue generated by these spurious fines. During busy seasons the girls were required to work 16 hours a day or face dismissal, and pressure was exerted on the time clerk to be very strict and exacting concerning violations. Oppressive heat and poor ventilation created a situation where girls fainted day after day and, according to Riis, came out looking like corpses.

Many young boys were employed in coal mines. Coal mining was a dangerous and arduous means of making a living. Pay was low, and for many families to reach even a subsistence level of earnings, sons were sent to work in the mines as young as nine or as soon as they were physically able. Some served as door boys who sat in the dark mines waiting to open and close the doors that permitted the mine cars to pass. Others were driver boys who dumped coal from the cars so that it could advance to the processing machines. The breaker boys—covered in dust and sitting knee-to-back in long lines above the coal chutes—cleaned and inspected the material from the mine separating the rock and slate from the coal. An 1877 report described a breaker room in St. Clair, Pennsylvania. These boys went to work in the cold dreary room at seven o'clock in the morning and worked until it was too dark to see any longer. For this they got $1 to $3 a week. Few could read or write. They had no games when their day's work was done because they were so tired. They knew nothing but the difference between slate and coal. Nine-year-old Joseph Miliauska, who earned 70 cents for a 10-hour day as a breaker boy, recalled boys would get hit in the back with a broom if they were caught letting a piece of slate slip by (Mintz 2004, 145). A Luzerne County, Pennsylvania, school superintendent addressed the problem of breaker boys in his annual report. He implored that something be done to educate these boys numbering five thousand. The boys were not receiving an education and were doing but little for themselves. Their occasional attendance interfered materially with the grading of the schools. It was suggested that a school in every mining district be established under the care of the best man that could be secured for the position and supplied with books, paper, slates, and pencils. It would be kept open as a night school during the entire school year, except when there is no work at the mines, and then let it be conducted as a day school. The prescribed course of study would be reading, writing, spelling, the business operations of arithmetic, with oral instruction in civil government and the duties of citizens, not omitting moral instruction.

The industrial expansion following the Civil War created an unprecedented demand for workers. In this age of increasingly commercial commodities, many families came to depend on the money that children could bring into the home. By the end of the century nearly one-fifth of the nation's children between 10 and 16 were part of the workforce (Volo and Volo 2007, 327).

By 1900, despite the well-organized work of groups such as the National Consumers League, little had been done to curb the problem. Twenty-eight states had instituted some forms of protective measures, but they were so limited and infrequently enforced as to be highly ineffective. Typically, only children employed in mining or manufacturing were covered. Legislation generally established a minimum age for workers of 10 or 12, a maximum number of 10 or more work hours, and some limited literacy or school attendance requirements. None of the southern states, where child labor grew rapidly in the proliferating textile mills, established child labor laws. Moreover, labor unions were unable to get much of a foothold in the South and thus were unable to negotiate agreements with individual companies to limit child labor (Husband and O'Loughlin 2004, 129).

—*Dorothy Denneen Volo*

Humane Treatment for Orphans

Ironically, one of the most effective groups to pursue better treatment for orphans (and abused children in general) was founded as an outgrowth of the American Society for the Prevention of Cruelty to Animals (ASPCA). In the nineteenth century, child abuse occurred at all levels of society and in every ethnic and racial group just as it does today; but the social stresses of unemployment, alcoholism, and tenement life in the extended period of economic downturn known as the Panic of 1873 seem to have increased its frequency.

In 1873, Henry Bergh, president of the New York chapter of the ASPCA, was made aware of a particularly egregious case of child abuse by so-called foster parents. Etta Wheeler, an acquaintance of Bergh's through their mutual interest in protecting animals, was shocked to discover that the New York City Police had no authority to step into child-abuse cases that were isolated within the home. Parents—even foster parents and informal guardians—apparently had the right to deal with the children under their care in any manner they thought fit. Wheeler turned to Bergh and his lawyer, Elbridge Gerry, who asked a court to issue a subpoena forcing the parents of the abused child to appear with her in court. The child, Mary Ellen Wilson, was so marked by the abuse of her foster parents as to show visible marks, bruises, and wounds—of which she had ostensibly received from scissors wielded by her foster mother. The judge was moved by the spectacle. The girl was sent to an asylum, and the foster mother was sentenced to a year in jail after conviction. The case was precedent setting with regard to parent-child relations.

Bergh and Gerry were inspired by their success in the Wilson case to form the Society for the Prevention of Cruelty to Children (SPCC), which received permission from the New York State courts in 1875 to investigate allegations, remove children from abusive situations, and bring cases against parents. The SPCC lobbied in states nationwide through its many affiliates for legislation to protect children including an act in 1876 in New York that required parents and guardians to give children proper food, clothing, medical care, and supervision. From 1876 to 1903 the SPCC sent nearly 100,000 abused and neglected children to asylums and orphanages.

With children being removed from almshouses and abusive homes, and the effects of the Panic of 1873 lingering, a great need arose for more space in protective environments. Oddly it was at this time that many homes for soldiers' orphans were closing because many of the initial recipients of their care—the offspring of deceased Civil War soldiers—were growing out of childhood. Some of these changed the emphasis of their institutions to cover other children, but it was clear that many new facilities would be needed if society wanted to widen its communal safety net to include the general population. In response, humanitarian organizations opened more than 400 additional facilities for poor and abandoned children from 1890 to 1903; and many state and county governments founded new asylums, training schools, and public orphanages.

Religious organizations also stepped forward to provide sectarian environments for children of their own faiths. Among these were a number of Jewish charities that opened Hebrew homes in Atlanta, Cleveland, New Orleans, Baltimore, Boston, Milwaukee, New York, San Francisco, and other cities. Roman Catholic institutions also grew in number. Many sectarian groups feared exposing the children of their own faith to unrestricted Protestantism. While public facilities claimed to be largely nonsectarian, in the nineteenth century, moral instruction and Bible reading were considered foundational elements in the upbringing of children, and most public institutions were governed by clearly Protestant ethics and beliefs. Jews and Catholics had a long history of resistance to placing children of their faiths with Protestant families, and both religions formed extensive school systems to limit exposure to the King James version of the Bible. Ironically, Episcopalians founded a large number of sectarian institutions because they feared that public run institutions would be too secular in their outlook. Some sectarian asylums accepted children of only one gender, others accepted both, and most continued to discriminate based on race.

In 1860, there had been 124 orphan asylums in the United States; by 1888 there were 613; and by 1902 the number had grown to well over 1,000. At the beginning of the twentieth century, more than 110,000 children lived in institutions, and 176,000 were in foster homes. Most of the institutions founded in the last decade of the nineteenth century were greatly improved over earlier versions in terms of their physical facilities. They generally had more spacious dormitories, central heating, and larger washrooms fitted with toilets and bathtubs. Many had clean cooking and eating facilities, moderately sized libraries, playgrounds, and ball fields. Most institutions chose to forego in-house educational instruction as too expensive sending their charges to the public schools in the towns where they were located. Like most parents in nuclear families who hoped to curtail bad behavior and delinquency, the staff of so-called modern orphanages and asylums used corporal punishment only after repeated appeals to the child's natural sense of right and wrong had failed. Some institutions severed their ties with so-called incorrigible children by placing them in factories and other manufacturing settings where they "faced immediate indenture and the end of childhood" (Reef 2005, 95).

Child-care experts believed that institutional care was necessary but that it should be brief. Children in public institutions were thought to live an artificial and unnatural life, and many child advocates were convinced that children needed to live in a home with a family to grow up normally. Home placement, therefore, became the goal of most orphanages and asylums. Massachusetts had passed the first laws regulating adoption in 1851, and by 1929 adoption laws were in effect in all the 48 states. Nonetheless, every year tens of thousands of children remained on the streets or lived in neglected and substandard conditions.

—*James M. Volo*

SERVANTS: DOMESTIC ORDER

In Europe, the persons who went into domestic service did so as a class, and the service was considered a profession of sorts marked with customs and defined by well-established and well-understood requirements regarding the positions of the employed and the employer. Masters and mistresses there had no fear of being compromised by condescension and had no need to raise their voices or assume airs of authority.

In nineteenth-century America, domestic service was clearly not so well-defined, and according to Catharine Beecher and Harriet Beecher Stowe, those in service were "universally expectant" that their condition was a "stepping-stone to something higher…some form of independence which shall give them a home of their own." Beecher and Stowe noted for their readers, "Your seamstress intends to become a dressmaker, and take in work at her own home; your cook is pondering a marriage with the baker, which shall transfer her toils from your cook-stove to her own…Your carpenter…is your fellow citizen, you treat him with respect…You have a claim on him that he shall do your work according to your directions—no more." Nonetheless, Beecher and Stowe noted that "the condition of domestic service [in America]…still retain[ed] about it something from the influences of feudal times" (Beecher and Stowe 2002, 235–37).

In homes with several domestics under the direction of a housekeeper, there seems to have been formed among them a formal hierarchy—almost a family within a family. The housekeeper was probably an older female worker or the worker whose residence in America was the longest. She usually ran the service side of the household as a manager with all the other servants reporting to her. The housekeeper was probably the only domestic to interface with the mistress. All the other servants would have been ignored by the employer's family except when being given commands, and many homes were built with hidden stairwells and passages to keep the servants out of sight. The cook, whose experience, quality, and skill were most important to the family, ran the kitchen and usually had a scullery maid or two to help her. In addition there may have been parlor maids, chambermaids, waitresses, laundresses, and a seamstress. In smaller establishments many tasks were incorporated into a single person. While the vast majority of domestic laborers were female, male domestics such as butlers, valets, gardeners, stable help, footmen, and coachmen may also have been part of the domestic household. In no case were governesses or tutors considered in the same class as the domestic help.

A domestic servant's hours of work were long and somewhat irregular because they were always on call. Most worked from sunrise to sunset averaging about 12 hours a day with a half-day off per week. It was suggested that knowledgeable and experienced servants rose early in the morning—up to two hours before the family members—so that they could get through the dirtiest or hardest part of their work before the family came to be under foot and interrupted them. "There is nothing more disagreeable than to run about with dirty hands and dirty clothes: and this must inevitably be the case if you defer this part of your work until everybody is stirring and bustling about" (Roberts 2006, 17). This serf-like circumstance needs to be viewed in a nineteenth-century perspective, however. Most farmers worked equally long or longer hours, and factory workers often complained about 14-hour work days during which they were under constant supervision.

The service staff generally ate together as would a family in the kitchen or some other service area, and strict hierarchy among the help was observed on these occasions. At the end of the workday, servants generally retired to rooms in the attic, garret, or basement where a bed, a washstand, and a chair might be made available to them. Pegs on the wall served as substitutes for a wardrobe or chest of draws, but most domestics came with a trunk or footlocker for storage. The rooms were usually shared with other servants, and they lacked the privacy afforded to the employer and her family. Nonetheless, they were generally better than the accommodations afforded to slaves or indentures in the previous century.

Domestic work could be physically demanding. Since commercial cleaning products were virtually unknown, sand, salt, camphor, lye, vinegar, and various homemade concoctions were used, but the application of good old-fashioned elbow grease seems to have been the most common method used in cleaning. The servants tended to labor in their own sections of the house when not cleaning or arranging the family's quarters. Depending on their responsibilities, they spent a great deal of their working time in the yards, the cellars, the pantry, the larder, the laundry, the linen closet, or the kitchen. The industrial economy of the nation made many goods and comforts available to the wealthy, but the servants seem to have worked in generally hot, crowded rooms, dirty and sooty by modern standards, and furnished with standard work tables, cupboards, cabinets, and perhaps a chair or two.

The kitchen was the domain of the cook, her scullions, and the waitress if there was one. She—it was unprecedented to have a male cook—was second among the servants only to the housekeeper in authority. The cook dealt with tradesmen, deliverymen, and suppliers, and she directed the preparation or preservation of raw foodstuffs and the butchering of meats into manageable cuts. In an era that lacked refrigeration, it required an enormous amount of care and attention to detail to safely prepare food for consumption. Besides the repetitive cycle of dishwashing, advice manuals from the period suggested the establishment of a daily cleaning regime, and a complete scrubbing of the kitchen environs was required twice a week. Sinks were scalded with a lye solution, cutting surfaces were scraped down, work surfaces scrubbed with bristle brushes, floors mopped, tools cleaned, silver polished, and fireplaces and stoves swept of ashes and cinders.

The parlor maid cleaned and maintained the main floor rooms such as the hallways, library, drawing room, and, of course, the parlors. There may have been both a public and family parlor in some great houses. Victorian era furniture was generally heavy, bulky, and ornately carved suggesting a great deal of dusting, polishing, and heavy moving. Carpets, rugs, and draperies required daily sweeping or brushing, and they were removed seasonally and cleaned at least twice a year. In most homes all the carpets were removed during summer and replaced by reed mats. This probably required a combined effort among the servants due to the heavy lifting required.

The upstairs maid was commonly known as the chambermaid. As the name suggests it was her task to air, dust, and sweep the family sleeping chambers and dump and clean any of the chambers pots, commodes, or washbasins that had been used in the night. The bed linens were arranged or changed; soap, towels, candles, and tapers replaced; fireplaces swept, and wood or coal replenished; and drinking and washing water put in pitchers. In many households the water for all this cleaning, and all the water used in the home, was drawn from a single source and had to be carried to other parts of the building. The same was true of any coal or firewood delivered in one place and used in another, but the kitchen fuel supply was usually located nearby the kitchen service door.

Of all the tasks to be done in the household the one most hated was found in the laundry. Although there were technological advances available to aid the processing of clothing and linens such as pumps, wash-boilers, hand-cranked wringers, and sinks with drains, the job was relentless and the work heavy. Water was fetched and heated on the stove or in the boiler, and the washing was done in a tub with a paddle and a washboard. The lye soap used at the time was very harsh on the skin. Pressing was done with a series of heavy irons heated on a stove or on an oil-fired heater. Fine fabrics and woolen outerwear were often sponged clean and brushed rather than washed.

The stables, stable-yards, lawns, and ornamental gardens were almost solely staffed by men and older boys. Work in the stables around large animals was dangerous, hay bales and grain sacks were heavy, and manure was difficult to remove. Harness, saddles, and tack needed constant attention, oiling, and repair. Northern city dwellers rarely rode on horseback except for amusement or exercise, but they did own carriage horses. In the South and Midwest, on the other hand, men were particularly fond of riding astride and could not be made to dispense with their horses even under the most trying of economic or meteorological conditions. Moreover, they often provided their servants with four-footed transportation to provide care for their own mounts when away from home.

Both the male and female gentry traveled mostly by carriage or chaise, and well-heeled city dwellers sometimes supported a coach as a sign of their affluence even though they never left the urban districts in it. The gentry would go into debt to maintain their own carriage and team; and great pride was taken in being seen in a fine conveyance, pulled by matched horses, and manned by a properly attired driver and footman. The social elite considered the use of rented vehicles and teams an embarrassment to those who could not afford the ownership of a team and carriage, or the servants needed to maintain them (Volo and Volo 2007, 356–59).

PETS: TROPHY PETS

With increased leisure time and disposable income, the Industrial Age saw an expansion of interest in a widening variety of pets both as companions and pet keeping as a hobby. Dogs became an integral part of the fashion system for the well-to-do and were treated as luxury accessories. In cities, gentlemen paraded Russian wolfhounds, pointers, and setters. Ladies loved their King Charles spaniels, pugs, and terriers. Dalmatians were popular coach dogs making them a common sight running alongside the horses. The Scotch collie was a popular suburban dog. The Newfoundland and the St. Bernard were also very popular. In fact, the St. Bernard, a paradigm of dependability and protection, was so popular many advertisers who wished to convey a sense of security to their customers used them in their advertisements.

The terrier was a favorite for many people. Bakers seemed to be particularly enamored with the breed, and many terriers were used to protect bakers' carts from thieves. The Dalmatian has come to be associated with firemen who often kept a dog to protect the firehouse from thieves and to clear the streets ahead of the horse-drawn wagons responding to a fire. A coach dog, like the Dalmatian, was a natural in this role but many firemen just adopted a street dog.

By the 1870s, interest in breeding and showing dogs had fully developed along the lines of the English model. The first recorded American dog show took place in Minneola, New York, in 1874 and the first bench show to receive widespread attention was held at the Centennial Exposition in Philadelphia in 1876. Sportsmen who organized the Westminster Kennel Club to improve the pointer breed held their first show in 1877. This included nonsporting dog breeds.

Dogs were not the only pets to garner specialized interest. Breeders began to show cats in the 1870s. Aquarium fish moved away from local pond residents to more exotic varieties with the introduction of the Paradise Fish in the 1890s. Raising and racing pigeons became popular in the 1880s as a kind of husbandry for art's sake. By the 1870s the canary was the ultimate household bird and a common accessory to parlor décor. As the 1880s drew to a close, other species of birds were being imported from Asia, Australia, and South America. It was during this time that the parakeet made its debut.

Birds were the first pets to have a wide range of care products. By the 1870s bird fanciers were able to buy specialized accessories for birdcages including gravel mats for cage bottoms, elastic perches, awnings to protect birds from direct sun and bathing and feeding dishes. It was not until much later that care products were available for other pets. Commercial goldfish food was available by 1881. Commercial cat food did not appear until the 1890s. By the 1890s the modern pet shop had been established. These businesses sold pets as well as a growing number of supplies for their care. Pets were increasingly given more comforts and honors. Pet cemeteries first began to appear near large cities in 1896.

Concern for animals and their proper treatment continued to garner popular support. This was especially true of the ubiquitous horse that was, before the introduction of the automobile, the prime mover for almost all forms of urban street traffic. Unfortunately, poor animal management, especially among low level teamsters and delivery services, gave rise to the phrase "beating a dead horse," which had more than one instance in fact to give it reality. The tireless efforts of Henry Bergh and the ASPCA resulted in such innovations as an ambulance for injured horses and in 1875 a sling for horse rescue. Bergh saw that fountains provided fresh drinking water for horses in the streets of Manhattan. These fountains were used by cats, dogs and humans alike.

Dogs were often cruelly exploited in fights that often lasted hours. Bergh once dropped through a skylight into the pit to stop such a sporting event. Dogcatchers rounded up as many as 300 dogs from the streets of Manhattan daily. The caged dogs were then thrown into the East River and drowned. The dogcatchers were paid by the number of animals they collected. It was not unusual for family dogs to be purloined from owner's yards. Such abuses so disturbed the public that in 1894 the ASPCA was placed in charge of New York City's animal control and assumed control of picking up homeless and injured animals and maintaining shelters for them. By the time of Bergh's death in 1888, humane societies had been established throughout the country. Buffalo, Boston, and San Francisco were among the first to follow New York's lead. Anticruelty legislation had been passed in 37 of the 38 states.

—*Dorothy Denneen Volo*

FOR MORE INFORMATION

Atkins, Annette. *Harvest of Grief, Grasshopper Plagues and Public Assistance in Minnesota, 1873–1878*. St. Paul: Minnesota Historical Society Press, 1984.

Beecher, Catherine E., and Harriet Beecher Stowe. *The American Woman's Home*. New Brunswick, NJ: Rutgers University Press, 2002.

Deer, Mark. *A Dog's History of America: How Our Best Friend Explored, Conquered, and Settled a Continent*. New York: North Point Press, 2004.

Frank, Stephen M. *Life with Father: Parenthood and Masculinity in the Nineteenth-Century American North*. Baltimore, MD: Johns Hopkins University Press, 1998.

Green, Harvey. *The Light of the Home*. New York: Pantheon Books, 1983.

Grier, Katherine C. *Pets in America: A History*. Chapel Hill: University of North Carolina Press, 2006.

Haines, T. L., and Levi W. Yaggy. *The Royal Path of Life: Or Aims and Aids to Success and Happiness*. Chicago, IL: Western Publishing House, 1876.

Heininger, Mary L. *A Century of Childhood, 1820–1920*. Rochester, NY: Margaret Woodbury Strong Museum, 1984.

Husband, Julie, and Jim O'Loughlin, *Daily Life in the Industrial United States, 1870–1900*. Westport, CT: Greenwood Press, 2004.

Kenny, Kevin. "The Development of the Working Classes." In *A Companion to 19th-Century America*, ed. William L. Barney. Malden, MA: Blackwell Publishing, 2006.

McClinton, Katherine Morrison. *Antiques of American Childhood*. New York: Bramhall House, 1970.

Meredith, Roy. *Mathew Brady's Portrait of an Era*. New York: W. W. Norton & Company, 1982.

Mintz, Steven. *Huck's Raft: A History of American Childhood*. Cambridge, MA: Harvard University Press, 2004.

Mitford, Jessica. *The American Way of Birth*. New York: Dutton, 1992.

Ransom, J. Clinton. *The Successful Man in His Manifold Relation with Life*. New York: J.A. Hill & Co., 1889.

Reef, Catherine. *Alone in the World: Orphans and Orphanages in America*. New York: Clarion Books, 2005.

Roberts, Robert. *The House Servant's Directory, An African American Butler's 1827 Guide*. Mineola, NY: Dover Publications, 2006.

Sanchez-Eppler, Karen. *Dependent States: The Child's Part in Nineteenth Century American Culture*. Chicago, IL: The University of Chicago Press, 2005.

Shrock, Joel. *The Gilded Age*. Westport, CT: Greenwood Press, 2004.

Smith, Page. *The Nation Comes of Age: A People's History*. 4 Vols. New York: McGraw-Hill, 1981.

Strasser, Susan. *Never Done: A History of American Housework*. New York: Henry Holt and Company, 1982.

Tinling, Marion, ed. *With Women's Eyes: Visitors to the New World, 1775–1918*. Norman: University of Oklahoma Press, 1993.

Tosh, John. "New Men? The Bourgeois Cult of Home." *History Today* (December 1996): 9–15.

Volo, Dorothy Denneen, and James M. Volo. *Family Life in Nineteenth-Century America*. Westport, CT: Greenwood Press, 2007.

Ware, John F. W. *Home Life: What It Is, and What It Needs*. Boston, MA: Wm. V. Spencer, 1864.

Wilentz, Sean. *Chants Democratic: New York City & the Rise of the American Working Class, 1788–1850*. New York: Oxford University Press, 1984.

Economic Life

INDUSTRIAL AGE
|
OVERVIEW
DOMESTIC LIFE
ECONOMIC LIFE
INTELLECTUAL LIFE
MATERIAL LIFE
POLITICAL LIFE
RECREATIONAL LIFE
RELIGIOUS LIFE

NATURE OF WORK

From Craft Shop to Factory

From colonial times craftsmen and shopkeepers have often been considered a privileged class somewhat akin to small businessmen, but many were actually petty proprietors with just enough income and business acumen to rest on the lower rung of middle-class status and employ a couple of journeymen or apprentices. The greatest changes in employment and manufacturing in the nineteenth century were in the transitions from the hand labor of these craftsmen to increased mechanization in almost every task. Household manufacturing, which was still widespread after the Civil War, declined in importance during the next four decades giving way to industrialization and mass production in almost every facet of the economy. Many of the items consumers once made for themselves, including basic things such as tools, textiles, and clothing, now came from factories. These larger-scale enterprises required a greater capitalization than formerly if they were to succeed.

The craftsman, who previously made goods to the specifications of individual customers who they knew, now enlarged his shop—if he could—or took a place in a factory to turn out ready-made products in standard sizes for the general public. This transition also negatively affected the traditional practice of apprenticeship allowing formal schooling to displace it as a preferred method of training for many forms of work. The shift from forced apprenticeship, which cost employers only room and board, to wage labor, which required cash payments to workers, undermined the financial advantage formerly enjoyed by the masters of small shops.

Several factors help to account for the change to factory production. Many researchers point to technological advances that made work in the home or craft shop less viable, but that tells only part of the story. In some industries the sheer size and expense of the new technology made it impossible for individual workers or even small business owners to acquire innovative equipment. For example, the large steel manufacturers put many small shops out of business because these small manufacturers could not afford the Bessemer converters that made inexpensive steel; and the Bessemer converter, because it was such a massive, expensive piece of equipment, necessitated a large plant and transportation network that would finish and ship steel products to consumers (Husband and O'Loughlin 2004, 73).

In New England the shoemaker's shop was a small building where skilled workers joined the machine-sewn tops to the hand-wrought soles. Each man was an independent worker with his own cobbler's bench and materials. Courtesy Library of Congress.

The financial capital needed for increasing mechanization caused certain geographic areas blessed with inexpensive waterpower, raw materials, or access to interstate transportation to become centers for the manufacture of specific items. Danbury, Connecticut, with its hat factories; Lowell and Lynn, Massachusetts, with their textile mills; and Pittsburgh, Pennsylvania, with its iron foundries and deposits of coal may serve as examples. Domestic manufactures remained strong in many rural areas of the country and in many industries where it was not immediately possible to apply power and machine technology to the required task.

Shoemaking can serve as an example in this regard. At a time when power machinery had not yet been developed for making shoes, the process was ruled by apprentice-trained specialists who made hand-cut and hand-sewn shoes. The invention of a machine to produce small wooden pegs to attach the leather soles to the upper part of the shoe initially changed the way shoemakers assembled their wares. The quiet stitching of sole to upper from colonial times was replaced by the dull sound of the cobbler's hammer driving pegs into hard leather a half-century later. At the same time, sewing machine technology was successfully applied to the stitching of leather resulting in the establishment of factories in which women sewed the uppers together and the men attached them to the lower structure of the shoe fitting the finished product with soles and heels by hand. By 1858, Lyman Blake had patented a leather sewing machine that attached the soles to the uppers mechanically facilitating the shoemaking process. This made the price of shoes, especially work shoes, much more affordable. Sizes and widths were first introduced to shoe production at this time freeing the consumer from the strictures of individually wrought footwear or choosing among small, medium, and large as did slaves and soldiers.

The conversion to machine operations brought many more women into the manufacturing trades. For example, although harness and saddle making remained male-dominated crafts, the extension of power stitching to the entire shoemaking process introduced a larger number of women into the process and left the traditional shoemaker with little beyond specialty work and a small repair business. As a result of this mechanization, more people became involved in shoemaking in the nineteenth century than in any other industry in the nation save agriculture (Volo and Volo 2007, 80).

The Boston Associates

With the 1823 opening of the first textile factory in Lowell, Massachusetts, a new system of hiring factory workers developed. Francis Cabot Lowell had observed the impact of the factory system in Britain in the second decade of the century. Lowell, a few relatives, and friends among the Boston elite (the Lawrences, Lymans, Cabots, Perkinses, Dwights, Brookses, and others collectively known as the Boston Associates) supported Patrick Tracy Jackson and Nathan Appleton in their task of building the first modern factory in America. The so-called Waltham-Lowell System they introduced established a wholly new paradigm for manufacturing that took into consideration not only capital, labor, supply, and marketing, but also the impact of industrial change on both the rich and the poor associated with any major enterprise. This was a dramatic change from the industrial practices generally found in European factories.

The Boston Associates financed the Lowell mills on the Merrimack River where the natural provision of water power permitted the construction of many mills by several companies. The Associates also built comparable complexes on the Merrimac at Manchester, New Hampshire, and Lawrence, Massachusetts, and on the Connecticut River at Chicopee and Holyoke, Massachusetts. On the basis of the wealth these enterprises generated, the Boston Associates and their descendants invested in railways, banks, and insurance companies. They also spent a great deal of money on philanthropy—primarily donating to socially useful institutions like the Massachusetts General Hospital, the McLean Asylum, Harvard University, Williams College, the Lawrence Scientific School, the Athenaeum, and the Lowell Institute. Ultimately they secured for themselves and their progeny a secure and remarkably durable position at the top of the social order (Dalzell 1987, vi–vii).

Most of the Boston Associates never made more than an occasional trip to the mills, and these were usually made in a effort to check on the thrust and extent of the changes their money had made. While they were interested in the moral tone and practice of religion among their workers, most of their efforts were directed at raising the moral tone of the city of Boston where they maintained at impressive array of homes along the streets of Beacon Hill. Ultimately they hoped to alter the direction of unchecked cultural change taking place in the streets below them, and secure the world as they knew it for people like themselves (Dalzell 1987, xi–xii).

Mill Girls

The Boston Associates owned the mills at Lowell and recruited young girls from farms and rural areas to live and work in the cotton mills under paternalistic supervision designed to protect their respectability and optimize their productivity. The mill advertised for girls between 15 and 30, but some younger girls were accepted. In the factories the overseers were responsible for maintaining work discipline and high moral standards. All unmarried girls not living with their families were required to "board in one of the boarding houses belonging to the Company, and conform to the regulations of the house where they board" (Eisler 1977, 25). The boarding house keepers enforced strict curfews and codes of conduct. Boarders were "considered answerable for any improper conduct in their houses" (Eisler 1977, 27). In addition to behavior, "regular attendance on public worship on the Sabbath was required for all workers." The company would "not employ any person who [was] habitually absent [from the services]" (Eisler 1977, 24).

A period illustration of the workers coming to their shift at the mills at Lowell (background). Mixed in among the adult workers are young women and boys. Courtesy Library of Congress.

The boarding houses were well-maintained and served three substantial meals daily. One girl reported, "for dinner, meat, potatoes, with vegetables, tomatoes and pickles, pudding or pie, with bread coffee or tea." (Eisler 1977, 24). The girls received good care. "Let no one suppose that the 'factory girls' are without guardian. We are placed in the care of overseers who feel under moral obligations to look after our interests" (Eisler 1977, 64). Overcrowding, however, was a problem. Observers reported that the young women slept an average six to a room in just three beds. There was no privacy, and it was almost impossible to read or write alone.

The mill girls seem to have shared a passion for self-improvement. They attended evening school, pooled their coins to engage music and language teachers, attended lyceum lectures, and were reputed to be avid readers. Harriet Hanson Robinson claimed that "the circulating libraries, that were soon opened drew them [the mill girls] and kept them there, when no other inducement would have been sufficient." She wrote of a "farmer's daughter from the 'State of Maine' who had come to Lowell for the express purpose of getting books . . . that she could not find in her native place" (Eisler 1977, 31). Young Lucy Larcom recalled, "The printed regulations forbade us to bring books into the mill, so I made my window-seat into a small library of poetry, pasting its side all over with newspaper clippings" (Larcom 1986, 175–76).

Some of the girls who were attracted to Lowell had previously worked in small mills or had done work for local merchants in their homes. Many farmers' daughters moved to the city with the hope of finding better economic opportunities for themselves or their families. Generally, the girls worked from 9 to 10 months per year. Many returned home during the summer months when their labor on the farm was required. Lucy Larcom recalled overhearing a family discussion about finances during which one of her parents said, "The children will have to leave school and go into the mill." Lucy later reported, "The mill-agent did not want to take us two little girls, but consented on condition we should be sure to attend school the full number of months prescribed each year. I, the younger one, was then between eleven and twelve" (Larcom 1986, 153). Lucy's reaction to her new situation was positive. "I thought it would be a pleasure to feel that I was not a trouble or burden or expense to anybody. . . . So I went to my first day's work in the mill with a light heart. The novelty of it made it seem easy, and it really was not hard, just to change the bobbins on the spinning-frames every three quarters of an hour or so, with half a dozen other little girls who were doing the same thing" (Larcom 1986, 153–54).

Factory work could be dangerous, however. A sleepy or inattentive worker could easily loose a finger, arm, or scalp to the unforgiving machinery. Mill girls were required to keep their hair contained in a hair net; but vanity often prevailed and many of them were injured or killed when their long hair caught in the pitiless apparatus. Deafness or partial loss of hearing often resulted from the tremendous noise of the looms—a phenomenon, until the advent of industrialization, uncommon to ears attuned to the quiet passing of the agricultural day. A report on factory life described the Amoskeag Mills at Manchester: "The din and clatter of these five hundred looms under full operation, struck us on first entering as something frightful and infernal, for it seemed such an atrocious violation of one of the faculties of the human soul, the sense of hearing." One mill girl wrote that upon leaving work "the sound of the mill was in my ears, as of crickets, frogs, and Jews harps all mingled together with a strange discord. After that it seemed as though cotton-wool was in my ears" (Eisler 1977, 31).

Pulmonary ailments also abounded in the mills. The mill inspectors noted, "The atmosphere of the room . . . is charged with cotton filaments and dust [and] the windows were down; we asked the reason, and a young woman answered naively, and without seeming to be in the least aware that this privation of fresh air was anything else than perfectly natural, that 'when the wind blew, the threads did not work so well.' After we had been in the room for fifteen or twenty minutes, we found ourselves . . . in quite a perspiration, produced by a certain moisture which we observed in the air, as well as the heat" (Eisler 1977, 31). Added to the normal humidity of the day, steam was regularly sprayed into the air to maintain its moisture content. This was thought to keep the threads from drying out and snapping on the looms. Having breathed in all these fibers for so many hours each day, many girls left the mills with a cough never again to return (Volo and Volo 2007, 320–22).

Child Labor

Among those things acceptable in the nineteenth century that persons in a modern society find difficult to understand was the commonality of child labor. The textile mills of New England offered employment to boys and girls as well as young adults. At the end of the eighteenth century, Samuel Slater built the first successful water powered textile mill in the United States. With a staff of children aged 7 to 12, he successfully demonstrated the profitability of spinning yarn while utilizing youthful labor. He divided the factory work into such simple steps that even very young children could do the work. Jobs ranged from picking foreign matter (leaves, pods, and dirt) from the cotton to operating the carding and spinning machines. The children proved to be good workers who produced a quality product under Slater's supervision.

The lot of many children, like this young girl, was to work 12 to 14 hours a day at tedious and sometimes dangerous tasks in the textile mills of New England. Children demanded little in the way of wages and proved to be docile and careful workers who could easily be dominated by factory managers and supervisors. Courtesy Library of Congress.

As mills continued to expand so did the need for children to work in them. By 1830, 55 percent of the mill workers in Rhode Island were children. To avoid accusations of alienating children from their homes, Slater often hired entire families to work for him, a method that came to be known as the Rhode Island system. "A few sober and industrious families of at least five children each, over the age of eight are wanted," advertised a newspaper in 1831. A mutual dependence developed as the mill relied on the children and the families relied upon the money the children earned from the mill (Volo and Volo 2007, 320).

The incidence of child labor seems to have been largely gender-neutral with boys and girls entering the work force in approximately equal proportion. Native-born and immigrant families, at all levels of father's income, seemed to have sent just about the same ratio of girls to boys into the labor force. When the age of the youngest child sent to work is considered, however, Americans rather than the immigrants seem more likely to have sent their children to work at a younger age. Data from industrialized areas in New England show American children at work in larger numbers as early as age 11. The immigrant samples taken from the same communities showed no appreciable number of children working before age 13. Nonetheless, American-born parents were more reluctant to send out *any* children to work than immigrants, but when they did, they often sent them out young. Irish immigrant families were prone to send out most of their eligible children, but when the Irish father's annual income rose to American standards (approximately $750), the family generally sent no children into the work force (Modell 1979, 235–36).

Both American and immigrant working-class families seem to have terminated schooling at about the same age (13 years), but immigrant families preferred formal schools to on-the-job training, sending several children out to work so that one might stay in school and get a formal education. This was usually the eldest boy, whose success it was hoped would ensure his aid to his siblings in the future. Conversely, as both groups reached American-style incomes, they tended to send their children to school rather than to work. Nonetheless, because immigrant families tended to be larger than American ones, and because immigrant head-of-household incomes tended to be smaller, the proportion of immigrant children in the workforce was far greater than that of native-born children. In some cases 9 of 10 immigrant children living off the farm spent time as part of the industrial workforce (Volo and Volo 2007, 57).

INDUSTRIAL ACCIDENTS

The working conditions in most factories were dreadful with extremes of temperature, unspeakable levels of noise, and an appalling accident rate. No overall death and injury figures exist for all the industrial incidents that took place during the period, but there are data for some of the steel mills in Pittsburgh where accidents were almost a daily occurrence. In 1891, there were almost 300 deaths and more than 2,000 accidental injuries worthy of being reported. The steel mills were among the most dangerous of industrial environments because of the combination of great weights, extreme temperatures, and no margin for error. Mechanization was still in its infancy, safety equipment was almost unknown, and the avoidance of accidents was the sole obligation of the worker. In a single year for which there is a breakdown of causes, 195 men were killed: 22 from hot metal explosions, 5 from asphyxiation, 10 from rolling accidents, 73 during the operation of cars and cranes, 24 from falling from great heights or into the pits, 7 from electric shock, 8 while piling and loading, and the remainder through miscellaneous causes (Wolff 1975, 86–87).

A common accident involved the couplers on the ore buckets, which were joined manually and led to countless smashed hands and missing fingers. Near the end of shifts, the number of accidents increased due to fatigue, increased carelessness, and slower reaction times. A slip or misjudgment usually meant disaster. Molten metals hanging from a crucible at the top of the furnace might suddenly fall or the container fail, bursting its bottom and killing the crew. Often metal streaming into the Bessemer converter struck the edge of the mold, throwing a shower of molten iron in all directions and burning nearby workers. Every man who worked with hot metal for a length of time experienced incidences like these and only luck kept them from receiving more than a few burns. Their clothes were riddled with tiny burn holes, and they wore thick wooden-soled boots to protect their feet and legs.

The blast furnace was tended by a puddler, noted as "the most picturesque and independent of all steel workers," who stirred the molten pig iron with an iron rod through a hole in the furnace door and worked the metal into hot balls weighing almost 500 pounds called billets. The heater's helper "in ragged trousers, shirt sleeves cut off at the shoulder, sweat pouring, muscles bunched into knots" pulled the billet out and tossed it to the rougher, who fed it into the roller. Billet after billet was tossed, and when the rougher turned round another was waiting. "All was hand-work, with hardly a break. Agility was necessary." A false step by any one of them or among these steps in the process could mean death (Wolff 1975, 87).

Rolling, slitting, and plating done by high pressure machines was cooler but equally nerve-racking, due to the unending vibration and noise of the presses and cold saws. Men were forced to yell at each other all day to be heard above the din. In a brief one-month period in the pressure division at Carnegie's Homestead plant there where 65 accidents, 7 of them fatal. About half the remainder were sprains, smashed feet, and lacerated hands. Finally, there were 10 head wounds, 3 broken arms or legs, 2 amputated arms, 4 eye injuries, 8 internal injuries, and one case of paralysis. These were injuries completely different from those found in the smelting and converting divisions (Wolff 1975, 88).

The legal responsibilities of the employer were so narrowly defined by the courts that management rarely paid indemnification to injured workers or the survivors, except in a few isolated cases of generosity. The workers often took out tiny insurance policies of their own, and these could be had for as little as a dollar a week. The work was so dangerous that this was usually the first dollar taken from a paycheck that may have been as small as $30 per week. Friends and relatives tried to help stricken families, and some men formed lodges that pooled their funds for emergencies (Wolff 1975, 88–89).

—James M. Volo

ORGANIZED LABOR

Mass production engendered mass employment in America for the first time, and it wrought changes in the relationship between labor and management that reverberate even today. The advance of labor unions was largely dependent on the workers' willingness to strike. The right to strike was first established in America by the Massachusetts State Court in 1842 when a group of mill girls in Lowell refused to return to work at their looms because of long working hours (up to 14 hours a day).

Yet it was only in the twentieth century that the labor movement gained social acceptability and the strike general approval. For years, both were considered highly unpatriotic and un-American. The use of strikebreakers, baton-wielding bully-boys and private detectives, and armed police or even soldiers to breach employees' picket lines was largely condoned by the American public as fighting illegal actions against employers bordering on socialism, anarchy, or worse. Even Charles W. Eliot, long-time president of Harvard University (1868–1909) and leader of the National Education Association, called strikebreakers the true American heroes. The struggle of organized labor against such attitudes and obstacles was continuous and bloody. Between 1888 and 1906 there were 38,000 strikes involving millions of American workers.

Striking workers are confronted by management backed by nonstriking workers or strikebreakers hired to intimidate the union members. Courtesy Library of Congress.

Eugene V. Debs was one of the best-known labor leaders of the early period of labor organization. Born in 1869, he was a founder or cofounder of several organizations, including the Brotherhood of Locomotive Firemen, the International Labor Union, and the Industrial Workers of the World. In 1874 Debs became a railroad fireman and founding member of the Brotherhood in which he rose quickly, becoming an editor for their magazine and then Grand Secretary in 1880. At the same time, he became a prominent figure in the community, and in 1884 was elected to the Indiana state legislature as a Democrat, serving one term.

There were four railroad brotherhoods formed in this period. They were comparatively conservative as labor unions go, focusing more on providing fellowship and services to their members than on collective bargaining. Debs gradually became convinced of the need for a more unified and confrontational approach. After stepping down as Grand Secretary of the Brotherhood, he organized, in 1893, one of the first industrial unions in the United States, the American Railway Union (ARU). The Union successfully struck the Great Northern Railway in April 1894, winning most of its demands.

Debs was jailed later that year for his part in the Pullman Strike (also 1894), which grew out of a request for support by the striking workers, who made the Pullman Company's cars, to the ARU at its convention in Chicago. Debs tried to persuade the ARU members who worked on the railways that the boycott was too risky, but the membership ignored his warnings and refused to handle Pullman cars or any other railroad cars attached to them, including cars containing the U.S. mail.

The federal government—openly favoring the Pullman Company and the railroad owners—obtained an injunction against the strike on the theory that the strikers had obstructed the delivery of the mail. The government then sent in the U.S. Army to end the strike. The result was a bloody confrontation. An estimated $80 million worth of property was damaged, and Debs was found guilty of interfering with the mails and sent to prison. The Supreme Court upheld the right of the federal government to issue the injunction later that year citing the interstate commerce clause of the Constitution as the foundation of its ruling.

At the time of his arrest for mail obstruction, Debs was not an avowed socialist. Only after his release in 1895 did he start his socialist political career, espousing Marxist ideals and running as a candidate for president of the United States as a member of the Social Democratic Party five times, the final time (1920) from prison. He never polled more than six percent of the vote (in 1912), which remains the all-time high for a Socialist Party candidate in America. Debs's conversion to socialism was unfortunate in that it tainted the efforts of other labor organizers as un-American or even foreign inspired. Supposed connections to socialism and anarchism were used by antiunionists to retard the development of a legitimate, organized labor movement in the United States for many years.

Nonetheless, by 1900, 36 states and the federal government had some sort of labor-oriented bureau or department, and organized labor had gained a great deal of recognition as legitimate and necessary. In the interim the American Federation of Labor (AFL) was founded in 1886 by Samuel Gompers as a reorganization of its predecessor, the Federation of Organized Trades and Labor Unions. It became the most important large labor organization at the time having more than one million members. The United Mine Workers (UMW) was founded in 1890, by the merger of two earlier groups, the Knights of Labor and the National Progressive Union of Miners and Mine Laborers. Unskilled or semiskilled workers remained unorganized, however. This was especially true of child laborers whose numbers were generally increasing as the century wore to an end.

—*James M. Volo*

FINANCE

The Robber Barons

The men who drove American industry generally made such great fortunes that their descendants remained important players in the economic health of the nation to the present time. Many of these men rose from humble beginnings to great wealth. Owning 149 steel plants, a quarter million acres of coal lands, 112 ships on the Great Lakes, and more than 1,000 miles of railway at the time of his retirement, Andrew Carnegie was one of these. Among the others were Cornelius Vanderbilt, Jay Gould, Andrew Mellon, and John D. Rockefeller, whose short biographies are hereafter given as examples of men who became super-rich during the Industrial Age.

Cornelius Vanderbilt

Steamship owner, railroad developer, and financier Cornelius Vanderbilt was born in Staten Island, New York in 1794. He began as a ferryman between Staten Island and New York City (1810), then fought against the state-sponsored steamboat monopolies before establishing his own steamboat business. Coastal steam lines developed slowly in the first half of the nineteenth century due to monopolies granted by the individual states to local investors. In 1824 the U.S. Supreme Court overturned the state grants as invasions of the federal power to regulate interstate commerce. A willing public advanced the cash needed to develop the coastal steamship lines, and by 1840, all the major East Coast ports were connected by steam.

By 1846, Vanderbilt was one of the richest men in America, and in 1849 he started a steamship line to California that involved traveling overland across Central America through Nicaragua disembarking in the Gulf of Mexico and re-embarking in the Pacific. When his employees tried to cheat him out of his business with the aid of American filibusterer William Walker, Vanderbilt helped eject Walker from Nicaragua (1857) and regained control of his line. Vanderbilt then sold the route to the Pacific Mail Steamship Co.

Shifting his interest to railroads thereafter, by 1862 he was buying stock in the New York & Harlem Railroad. He was soon extending its service and became its president. Vanderbilt then acquired the Hudson River Railroad and the New York Central Railroad, and consolidated them all into a single company known as the New York Central (1872). During the next few years he acquired even more rail lines, and extended his railroad empire into the Midwest and Canada.

Although his success rested in part on his insistence on providing the best service and on using the best equipment, he could be a ruthless competitor. His most famous business battle was fought against Daniel Drew (partner of Jay Gould and Jim Fisk), first over steamships, then over railroads. In 1868, the combination of Drew, Gould, and Fisk defeated Vanderbilt's attempt to add the Erie Railroad of Pennsylvania to his well-run rail system through a series of stock manipulations known as the "Erie Wars." Not usually charitable, Vanderbilt made an exception near the end of his life with gifts totaling $1 million to Central University in Nashville, Tennessee—renamed Vanderbilt University in 1873. When he died in 1877, with an estate of some $100 million, he was one of the wealthiest men in America.

Jay Gould

Jay (Jason) Gould was a financier and railway magnet born in Roxbury, New York, in 1836. Although a surveyor by training, he took time out to write a *History of Delaware County, and Border Wars of New York* (1856). He became a tanner and leather dealer in New York (1857–1860), and began speculating in small railways on the stock market. Although a self-made man, Gould was the epitome of the robber barons that preyed on the financial community during the Industrial Age.

Along with a pair of crafty associates (James "Jim" Fisk and Daniel Drew), he fought and beat Cornelius Vanderbilt for control of the Erie Railroad (1867–1868). Having used bribery and a private army of cutthroats and bully boys to gain control, Gould and his partners did not hesitate to loot the railroad's treasury through blatant stock manipulation. One of Gould's partners, Jim Fisk, was known as the "Barnum of Wall Street" for his fraudulent business practices, and he was notorious for his grandiose lifestyle having assembled an army of paid soldiers who served Fisk as their colonel. Fisk died after being shot by Edward Stokes during a dispute over business matters and a mistress.

Gould's attempt to corner the gold market by buying bullion to raise its price and then suddenly dumping it on the market when the premium rose to 30 percent helped cause the Black Friday panic (September 24, 1869) and destroyed whatever was left of his good reputation. Ejected from his Erie Railroad post in 1872, he gained control of several Western railroads and extracted a $10 million profit by threatening the Union Pacific. He also owned the *New York World* (1879–1883) and most of New York City's elevated railroads, and controlled Western Union Telegraph Co. He died unlamented in 1892 with a net worth of over $100 million.

Andrew Carnegie

In 1848, at the age of 13, Andrew Carnegie came to the United States from Scotland with his family. They settled in Allegheny, Pennsylvania, and Carnegie went to work in a factory, earning $1.20 a week. The next year he found a job as a telegraph messenger. Wanting to advance himself, he moved up to telegraph operator in 1851. He then took a job with the Pennsylvania Railroad in 1853 working as the assistant to one of the railroad's top officials, Thomas A. Scott. Through this experience, he learned a lot about the railroad industry and about business in general. Three years later, Carnegie was promoted to superintendent. While working for the railroad, Carnegie began making small investments of his own money and found that his investments, especially those in Pennsylvania oil, brought in substantial returns. He left the railroad in 1865 to focus on his other business interests, including the Keystone Bridge Company that won several contracts for building steel bridges over the Mississippi and Missouri rivers.

During the next decade, most of Carnegie's time was dedicated to the steel industry. His business, which became known as the Carnegie Steel Company, revolutionized steel production in the United States. Carnegie built plants around the country, using technology and methods that made manufacturing steel easier, faster, and more productive. For every step of the process, he owned exactly what he needed: the raw materials, ships and railroads for transporting the goods, and even coal fields to fuel the coke furnaces. This start-to-finish strategy helped Carnegie become the dominant force in the industry and an exceedingly wealthy man. By 1889, the Carnegie Steel Corporation was the largest of its kind in the world.

Carnegie was noted for his belief in philanthropy, but some of his success came at the expense of his employees. The most notable case was the Homestead Strike. When the company tried to lower wages at a Carnegie Steel plant in Homestead, Pennsylvania, in 1892, the employees objected and refused to work. The conflict between the workers and local managers turned violent after the managers called in Pinkerton guards to break up the union. Carnegie was away at the time of strike, and shifted some of the responsibility for the violence to his managers. In 1901, he sold Carnegie Steel to J. P. Morgan, and retired as one of the richest men in the world. He died in 1919.

John D. Rockefeller

Rockefeller was the guiding force behind the creation and development of the Standard Oil Company, which grew to dominate the oil industry in the twentieth century. Rockefeller was born in 1839 on a farm in Tioga County, New York, very near the oilfields of western Pennsylvania. He left high school in 1855 to take a business course at Folsom Mercantile College, thereafter finding a job as an assistant bookkeeper at Hewitt & Tuttle, a small firm of commission merchants and produce shippers in Cleveland, Ohio. In 1859, with $1,000 he had saved and another $1,000 borrowed from his father, Rockefeller formed a partnership in the commission business with another young man, Maurice B. Clark. In that same year the first oil well was drilled at Titusville.

The city of Cleveland soon became a major refining center for the booming petroleum industry, and in 1863 Rockefeller and Clark entered the oil business as refiners. Together with a new partner, Samuel Andrews, who had some refining experience, they built and operated an oil refinery under the company name of Andrews, Clark & Co. The firm also continued in the commission business, but in 1865 the partners, now five in number, disagreed about the management of their business affairs and decided to sell the refinery to whomever amongst them bid the highest. Rockefeller bought it for $72,500, sold out his other business interests, and, with Andrews, formed Rockefeller & Andrews. Rockefeller's stake in oil increased as the industry itself expanded. It was said that Rockefeller had one old, shabby suit that he kept for his periodic visits to the oil region, and another non-oil suit that he used only to attend church. In 1870 he organized the Standard Oil Company along with his brother William, Andrews, and others. The company had an initial capitalization of $1 million.

By 1872, Standard Oil had purchased nearly all the refining firms in Cleveland, plus two refineries in the New York City area. Before long Standard Oil was refining 29,000 barrels of crude petroleum a day and had its own cooper's shop manufacturing wooden petroleum barrels. The company also had storage tanks with a capacity of several hundred thousand barrels of oil, warehouses for refined oil and kerosene, and plants for the manufacture of paints and glue. Ten years later, all its properties were merged in the Standard Oil Trust, which was in effect one great company. It had an initial capitalization of $70 million. There were originally 42 certificate holders, or owners, in the trust.

In 1892, the trust was dissolved by a court decision in Ohio, but the companies that had made up the trust joined in the formation of Standard Oil Company of New Jersey. Since New Jersey had adopted a law that permitted a parent company to own the stock of other companies, the trust was reorganized. It is estimated that Standard Oil owned three-fourths of the petroleum businesses in the United States in the 1890s.

In addition to being the head of Standard Oil, Rockefeller owned iron mines, timberland, numerous manufacturing companies, transportation facilities, and other industries. Although he held the title of president of Standard Oil of New Jersey until 1911—when the courts found the company in violation of federal antitrust laws—Rockefeller had retired from active leadership of the company in 1896. The 38 companies in Standard Oil were again separated into individual firms in 1911. Rockefeller at that time owned one-quarter of the company's total of one million outstanding shares. He died in 1937.

Andrew W. Mellon

Andrew Mellon was born in Pittsburgh, Pennsylvania, in 1855, the son of Scottish-Irish emigrants from Northern Ireland. His father was a banker and judge. He was educated at the University of Pennsylvania, graduating in 1873. Mellon demonstrated financial ability early in life by starting a lumber business at the age of 17. He joined his father's banking firm, T. Mellon & Sons, two years later and had the ownership of the bank transferred to him in 1882. In 1889, Mellon helped organize the Union Trust Company and the Union Savings Bank of Pittsburgh. He also branched out into industrial activities in oil, steel, shipbuilding, and construction.

Mellon backed a number of start-up companies that grew into enormous industrial giants. Among these were Charles M. Hall's Aluminum Company of America (ALCOA); Edward Goodrich Acheson's Carborundum Company (Union Carbide) in which he became a partner in manufacturing steel; and Heinrich Koppers's invention of coke ovens that transformed waste products from the coal-coke process needed in the production of steel into usable products such as carbon black (used in making rubber tires), tar, and sulfur. Mellon bought the patent for the ovens for $300,000. In the early twentieth century, Mellon ranked as one of the three richest people in the United States alongside John D. Rockefeller and Henry Ford. He served as U.S. Secretary of the Treasury from 1921 through 1932. He died in 1937.

John Pierpont Morgan

Financier, art collector, and philanthropist, Morgan was born in 1837, in Hartford, Connecticut, the son of a banker. Known as " J. P." rather than John Pierpont, he went into the family business and became one of the most famous financiers in the history of business. After working for his father, he started his own private banking company in 1871, which later became known as J. P. Morgan & Co. His company became one of the leading financial firms in the country. It was so powerful that even the U.S. government looked to the firm for help with the depression of 1895. The company also assisted in thwarting the 1907 financial crisis.

During his career, his wealth, power, and influence attracted a lot of media and government scrutiny. During the late 1890s and even after the turn of the century, much of the country's wealth was in the hands of a few powerful business leaders. Morgan dominated two industries in particular—he helped consolidate railroad industry in the East and formed the United States Steel Corporation in 1901 after Carnegie's retirement. A crucial material in the extensive growth of the nation, U.S. Steel became the world's largest steel manufacturer. He was criticized for creating monopolies by making it difficult for any business to compete against his. The government, concerned that Morgan had created a monopoly in the steel industry, filed suit against the company in 1911. The following year, Morgan and his partners became the subject of a congressional investigation.

Morgan had many interests beyond the world of banking. He enjoyed sailing and participated in a number of America's Cup yacht races. He was an ardent art collector, creating one of the most significant collections of his time. He later donated his art collection to the Metropolitan Museum of Art, and his collection of written works to the Morgan Library—both in New York City. At the time of his death in 1913, he was hailed as a master of finance and considered one of the country's leading businessmen.

—James M. Volo

COST OF LIVING: FAMILY FINANCE

By the 1880s many immigrant families had managed to reach parity with native-born households in terms of family income. However, as immigrant family incomes approached that of other Americans, researchers have found that the discrepancy was made up more and more by resorting to the paid labor of members of the immigrant family rather than the increased annual wages of its head. Ironically, due to the needs of child care supplied by the mother, most supplementary income came from child labor. Among Irish working-class families (for whom there is data), it was just about twice as likely for at least one child to be gainfully employed than it was for children in native-born families. "The Irish, kept in a tight position by the lower earning capacity of fathers, found children's earnings essential to consume in an American way" (Modell 1979, 221).

Researchers have found that by the 1880s foreign-born households (particularly the Irish) and native-born households had assumed essentially the same spending patterns, although the Irish father was still bringing home an income 85 percent that of the native-born head-of-household. In 1890 James R. Sovereign, the Iowa State Commissioner of Labor Statistics, detailed a 33-item standard budget for the average family. This was a bare-bones survival budget that "contained no carpets, no window curtains, no provisions for social amusements, no street car fares, no feasts for holidays, no contributions for Sunday school and churches, no medicine or medical assistance during illness, no mineral springs or other places of resort to recuperate the minds and bodies of over-worked laborers, and no mementos of love with which to express their affections of the members of the family circle" (Fisher 1993, 7). The total amount of Sovereign's spartan budget was $549 dollars. Oddly, at the time 88 percent of Iowa's mechanics and laborers made less than this amount annually. Nonetheless, the agreement among many observers was that the family poverty line resided at approximately $550 dollars during the later part of the nineteenth century (Volo and Volo 2007, 57).

URBAN-RURAL ECONOMY: THE FARMER'S ALLIANCE

The Farmers' Alliance in part grew out of the Granger movement of the 1870s and closely associated itself with the Populist Party of the 1880s and 1890s. There were two wings of the Farmers' Alliance separated by geography into northern and southern branches: respectively, The National Farmers' Alliance of the Great Plains and the National Farmers' Alliance & Industrial Union. The southern branch included a Colored Alliance of African American farmers, making it the only biracial non-church organization in the South at the time.

The Alliance program included the establishment of cooperatives to buy goods at lower prices and to market their produce at higher prices to large-scale brokers. Whereas an individual farmer might sell 10 bales of cotton at a time, the Alliance now made deals for 1,000 bales in a single contract. Each county alliance had its own cooperative store that bought from wholesalers and sold farm supplies to members at a lower rate. Some of these stores reported annual sales in the tens of thousands of dollars, but the cooperatives tended to disaffect nonalliance merchants in nearby towns. Additionally, many chapters set up their own grain mills and cotton gins to allow members to bring their produce to market at lower cost.

The political activism of the Alliance was based on demands for the government regulation of the railroads, granaries, and banks. Their other common demands involved government land reform, free silver, an income tax, and an expansion of the money supply. The Alliance allied itself to the Knights of Labor in 1886 and merged with the 500,000-member Agricultural Wheel in 1888. The southern alliance ultimately had chapters in most states and reached a membership of 750,000 by 1890.

—*James M. Volo*

THE URBAN STREET

The first impression of many strangers to their arrival in American cities was of the dirt, danger, and inconvenience of the urban street. Before the advent of municipal street cleaning, it was not uncommon for garbage to collect in the streets of crowded urban areas, and dozens of families may have shared the connecting alleys for many purposes. Among these were places to do laundry, play areas for children, and places to dump human or animal waste. It has been estimated that as late as 1900 there were still 3.5 million horses in American cities every day, each producing 20 to 30 pounds of manure. Chicago had to cope with 600,000 tons of horse manure annually, and New York had to remove 15,000 dead horses from the streets in 1880 alone. In that year, less than 25 percent of American cities had established municipal garbage collection. Not until 1895 did New York institute curbside garbage collection or a regime of street sweeping. Under such conditions, it is no wonder that tenement dwellers suffered tragically high rates of communicable diseases, transmitted through unsafe drinking water and extremely close quarters (Husband and O'Loughlin 2004, 31, 36).

Abraham Cahan, the foremost Yiddish journalist of his day and founder of the *Jewish Daily Forward* in 1897, has left the following description of the overcrowded tenement street of which he was so familiar from his novel *Yekl: A Tale in the New York Ghetto* (1896):

[One] had to pick and nudge his way through dense swarms of bedraggled half-naked humanity; past garbage barrels rearing their overflowing contents in sickening piles, and lining the streets in malicious suggestion of rows of trees; underneath tiers and tiers of fire escapes, barricaded and festooned with mattresses, pillows, and featherbeds not yet gathered in for the night. The pent-in sultry atmosphere was laden with nausea and pierced with a discordant and, as it were, plaintive buzz. (Husband and O'Loughlin 2004, 25–26)

As awful as the physical condition of the city streets tended to be, what some reformers misunderstood was how the urban street life in America replicated traditional ways of life in European villages. Neighbors used the streets to congregate or share information, and they kept an eye on each other's children. The street also offered a respite from the crowded conditions of working-class tenements and cottages. A street that appeared dangerously crowded to some may have simply felt vibrant and alive to those who lived there (Husband and O'Loughlin 2004, 25–26).

Then, as now, cities were known for their distinctive street life. Especially in working-class communities, the street became the place where people talked, did business, played, and relaxed. Many middle-class reformers were horrified by street life in working-class neighborhoods, fearing it interfered with familial influences, exposed children to filth and vice, and broke down distinctions between home and society. These middle-class reformers had little trouble finding illustrations for their concerns. In crowded neighborhoods, children often played on street corners and around dumps of garbage. Others tried to make a little money begging or working as street vendors selling everything from newspapers to matches (Husband and O'Loughlin 2004, 25).

Besides the workplaces, taverns, banks, and residences of the population, city streets were often lined with shops stocking a wide variety of items such as carpeting, window glass, boots and shoes, clothing, firearms, furniture, tobacco products, hardware, harness, and books. Each shop was identified with a hanging sign or a painted window glass. The majority of the shops served the needs of the local population and reflected their pattern of consumption. Pawn shops, bars, and brothels were common enough in many poor neighborhoods. Better shops selling fine fabrics, sewing notions, jewelry, china, and furniture were found in the so-called better parts of the city; and many banks, financial institutions, and insurers were isolated along the waterfronts or in the business districts.

Shopping for many city dwellers was often done in street markets where farmers and others vendors brought their food to sell. In the days before refrigeration women had to shop frequently. The quality of merchandise varied with the clientele of the particular market, and homemakers were warned to avoid hucksters who sold inferior goods. The poorest shoppers arrived at the market just before closing hoping to get the cheapest prices from sellers who did not want to pack up food that had been sitting in the warm sun all day. Those in the most hopeless situations scoured the garbage after the market closed (Volo and Volo 2007, 233).

The *Daily Times* referred to one market that served the poor of New York's Lower East Side as the "little heap of fish scales, eel heads, butcher's offal and rotting vegetables known as Catharine Market" (Schenone 2003, 178). This market was quiet during the week as few people had the money to shop there daily, but, as the paper noted, "they choose one day in the hard-worked week for a feast, and on Saturday night go marketing in earnest." The crowds were "fairly wedged together" as they came to "barter with shrill eagerness for the modest luxuries they have been greedily anticipating for a week past... The women who congregate here are often sharp, meager and scolding, plainly suffering from privations and excessive toil... The great demand is for cheapness, and as the sidewalk vendors usually undersell the store-keepers and stall-holders, they attract the most customers" (Schenone 2003, 181–82).

Street vendors working from stalls or from donkey carts like this one sold all types of items including shellfish, vegetables, fruits, nuts, and cooked meats. Courtesy Library of Congress.

When not cooking for their families themselves, city women relied on the street peddlers who sold food on street corners from push carts and from wagons that moved door-to-door for quick and inexpensive meals. In New York the so-called hot corn women, hot potato vendors, and chestnut roasters could be found on many street corners. Philadelphia was famous for its pepper pot soup peddlers. Pepper pot soup was a mixture of tripe, vegetables, and red pepper brought to America by African slaves via the Caribbean. Philadelphia became famous for it. African American women sold the soup on street corners for pennies a bowl (Volo and Volo 2007, 232).

Many urban homemakers purchased bread from a baker. Some homemakers purchased bread only during the summer rather than to go through the discomfort of building a large hot fire at home. City residents had to rely on commercial bakeries for breads, baked beans, and pies. Those who could afford more sumptuous delights also might patronize a confectioner. Commercial bakers heated their oven at night and baked before dawn, and the streets of the city were sometimes filled with the pleasant aroma of fresh-baked bread. Children would often take a meat pie or a bean pot—filled with mother's own recipe of ingredients and sauces—to the baker in the morning for a full day of heating in the residual warmth of the baker's ovens (Volo and Volo 2007, 232).

Delivery wagons of many kinds were a common sight on the city streets. Among these were the rumbling beer wagons with their loads of wooden barrels stacked on their sides. City residents seemed to tolerate—and frequent—an amazing number of taverns, beer halls, and saloons. So great was the daily supply of beer that it seemed some sections of the city stood awash in the various brews, ales, and porters. For many city dwellers firewood, charcoal, or hard coal needed to be purchased with cash from dealers who carted these items into the city centers. By the latter half of the nineteenth century hard coal had become the fuel of choice in city tenements for heating when used in fireplace gratings, cast-iron stoves, or tenement furnaces; but charcoal or firewood remained the choice for cooking purposes until they were replaced by gas. Block ice was also an urban necessity, and colliers and ice vendors could be seen carrying great baskets of black fuel or dripping cubes of crystalline ice up the tenement stairs while their patient horses waited tethered to wagons or carts in the streets (Volo and Volo 2007, 233–34).

FARMING/HUSBANDRY: BREAKING THE LAND

Beyond the eastern forests of the United States lay immense, treeless, and trackless prairies. Vast expanses of grass—an endless meadow—took up fully one-third of the continent and were described as the greatest tract of fertile land on the globe. Railroads with millions of acres granted by the government were offering cheap land to eastern farmers all too ready to move west. Eastern farmers believed that a land that grew no trees might not support crops, and there might be too little water for crops, too little timber for fuel and building, and too much heat for any kind of work. A great portion of these farmers were young men who found that without help they could scarcely break the fertile ground in the ordinary way of farmers, much less collect and secure the rich harvest in a timely fashion (Davidson 1951, 410).

The relationship between man and the land in nineteenth-century America was unlike any seen in a thousand years in Europe. Buoyant optimism could hardly have gone further in describing the reality of the situation, nor could the darkest pessimism describe the effort needed to bring the richness of the soil to harvest. The thick and tough prairie soil had indeed proved a formidable challenge for the first plows to try. As many as a dozen oxen might be needed to pull even iron plowshares through the sticky, heavily matted virgin earth. Yet when the sod had been broken, the prairie was incredibly rich—so rich that once the harvest was completed, it was reported that enough grain remained upon the field to feed an entire parish in England.

Farm implement manufacturers advertised modern contrivances such as plows with cast-iron plowshares and unusual moldboards to help attack the unyielding soil. The first practical plow for turning the prairie sod was invented in 1797 by Charles Newbold of New Jersey. It had a cast-iron moldboard that many claimed would poison the soil and foster the growth of weeds. This proved false. Jethro Wood followed in 1814 with a three-piece iron plowshare that allowed the replacement of broken parts without discarding the entire plow. William Parlin began making plows about 1842. These he loaded in a wagon and peddled throughout the country. By this time farmers had lost their prejudices concerning iron, and Parlin made a good deal of money. In 1868, John Lane patented a plow with a soft iron center and a heat-treated hard surface that kept the plow from breaking. In the same year, James Oliver introduced a process for hardening only the front working surface of the share while leaving the back tough and resilient. The sulky plow, which allowed the plowman to sit as he worked, was certainly in use before 1844. This made farm work easier and gave the plowman great control over the direction of the furrow.

The most successful farm implement manufacturer of the period was John Deere, who began marketing a large plow for cutting tough sod known as the "grasshopper" in 1837. Its structure was made of wrought iron instead of wood, and it had a steel plowshare that could cut through prairie soil without clogging. By 1855 Deere's factory in Illinois was selling 10,000 steel plows a year. In 1868, Deere incorporated his business, which still exists today.

Usually after the land was plowed it had to be dragged or harrowed, breaking up clods and pulverizing the soil prior to planting. Hamlin Garland remembers that "dragging is even more wearisome than plowing…for you have no handles to assist you and your heels sinking deep into the soft loam bring such unwonted strain upon the tendons of your legs that you can scarcely limp home to supper." Once the seed was planted, the war of weeds began—day after day hoeing corn, blue shirts bleaching to red from sun and sweat (Jones 1998, 190).

In the early years the harvesting of wheat, rye, and oats, as well as cutting hay, was done with a sickle. The harvester would grasp the stalks in his left hand and, with his right, draw the sickle close to where the bunched stalks were held. Consequently most harvesters bore one or more scars on their left hands from the sickle coming too close. Periodically the harvester would stop, hang the sickle on his belt, and bind the sheaves with a twist of straw. Using such techniques a man could harvest, on average, three-quarters of an acre a day. The work was easier and more efficient with a scythe or cradle, but it was not until the arrival of horse-drawn McCormick reapers, which could cut 15 acres a day, that the farmer was freed from this backbreaking labor (Jones 1998, 192).

The mechanical reaper has been called the most significant single invention used in the struggle to meet the needs of the farmer to harvest a crop at the crucial point when the work must be done quickly to secure it from damage. Geared to the wheel of the reaper was a reciprocating knife blade that cut the standing grain and dropped it on a platform for the workers to gather and toss aside. Nowhere in the world was there such a market for the reaper as on the American prairies. McCormick had the foresight to move his manufactory to Chicago in 1847 in the heart of the Midwest farming region. By 1851 he was turning out thousands of reapers. On future devices (1858) he added labor-saving devices such as a grain raiser that allowed the sheaves to be bound without bending over. In 1872, McCormick produced a reaper that automatically bound the sheaves with a wire, and in 1880, he came out with a mechanical device that almost magically tied and knotted the bundle with twine, cutting them loose, and laying them aside, all with the power of horses. The speed of the harvest was enormously increased, and twine manufacturers found it difficult to meet the increased demand.

The speed of harvesting brought about the need to thresh the grain from the chaff more quickly. For centuries the farmer had threshed his grain on the barn floor with long-handled flails or by having his animals walk across it. One way or the other it was one of the slowest and most laborious processes on the farm. Several threshing machines powered by horses, mules, or even sheep were invented. The Pitts Patent thresher operated with a horse treadmill, and it was very popular in the wheat fields of the West. Yet it still could not keep pace with the advances in reaping and binding. It ultimately gave way to steam-powered threshers.

Generally neighbors would move from farm to farm (especially during harvesting and threshing seasons) helping each other and eliminating the need to hire help. In addition men would often exchange labor, using a monetary value to determine the length of services provided. People did whatever work was required. Oftentimes no cash at all was involved in these transactions (Jones 1998, 192).

Everywhere the haste to reap a quick harvest, regardless of the consequences to the soil, encouraged families to enclose their plots with barbed wire and plant single crops for the market. They thereby lost some of the self-sufficiency of earlier generations that had turned the soil for a living. Most farmers in the Industrial Age subsisted to a considerable degree on the factory-packaged produce of other specialized farms that relied equally on them. With reports of exhausted land came other murmurings of nearly miraculous machines so contrived to save labor that they all but promised overproduction to those willing to place more land under cultivation (Jones 1998, 193).

INTERNATIONAL TRADE

Failure of the Carrying Trade

Maritime shipping and fishing formed a large segment of the American economy, but the sector was sorely pressed in the final decades of the nineteenth century. The discovery of the gold fields of California, and later in Australia, had heightened the demand for American clipper ships, but they were expensive to build and were not economical to operate. Only the willingness of passengers, crazed with gold fever and willing to pay exorbitant rates for a quick passage, kept the clipper ships in service. They lasted only a few years—generally from 1849 to 1859. Even the deep-water sailing clippers "were born, flourished, and faded from sight in a single decade," because they failed to make the transitions to steam operations required by the changing patterns of trade and economic activity (Kittredge 1935, 293).

Due to the utilitarian nature of marine architecture, vessels designed for deep-water operation, as in ocean travel or cargo carrying, lacked the adaptability necessary to deal with the exigencies of the shallow-water coasting trade. As the demand for American sailing vessels decreased, the largest ships were sold off rather than redeployed to coasting. The predominantly square rigged clipper ships generally required larger crews than the more maneuverable and innately efficient fore- and aftrigged coasting and fishing craft. Moreover, the cargo capacities of many ocean-going designs proved too large to make the smaller harbor jumping cargoes economical to carry (Bryant 1967, 334–35).

The down-easters of the 1870s resembled the clipper ships of the 1850s, but this distinctive Maine-built vessel had neither their sharp lines nor their hollow contours. To increase their cargo capacity the down-easters had little dead rise—in other words they had a flatter floor in their cargo hold. Although they could spread a good deal of canvas, they were not as heavily sparred as the clippers mainly because they were intended as cargo carriers rather than as speeders. The down-easters remained in service largely because they were able to fill the need for large ocean-going carriers of bulk cargo on the less prestigious sealanes of the world.

Large ocean-going windships were perfectly designed for cargoes such as Southern cotton; West Coast grain; Chilean copper ore; Scandinavian salt; or French timber. Typical outbound cargoes included Pennsylvania coal, kerosene, and case oil; locomotives and wheelbarrows; and ready-made clothing and Yankee notions. When trade slackened, the down-easters carried ice from the Arctic Circle to the West Indies, Calcutta, and Bombay; and gave passage to Chinese workers from Singapore or Hong Kong to Hawaii and California. Some down-easters were so busy completing a sequence of these long, tedious voyages that they did not put in at an American port more than once or twice in a decade. Consequently, they were often manned by largely foreign crews composed of Chinese, Malaysians, Lascars, and South Sea Islanders.

Notwithstanding the variety exhibited by these cargoes, it was the guano dug from the Peruvian islands of the Pacific that furnished the paying cargoes for most wooden windships during the wartime decline of the cotton-carrying trade, the grasshopper or drought induced failure of the grain crop, or the weakening of the gold fever. Guano is a Peruvian word for manure—not the brown, steaming heaps found on horse and dairy farms—but rather the dried, powdery droppings of millions of sea birds. The Humboldt or Peruvian Current that flows along the west coast of South America has an amazing abundance of sea life that has attracted sea birds for millions of years. These birds nested in the Chinchas Islands a few miles off the coast of Peru, and their droppings accumulated and dried on the arid shorelines and rocky crags rising in places to heights of 70 or 80 feet. In many places vessels could cozy-up to the deposits lining the shore with their yards cock-billed (set at a slant) and let the guano pour through chutes directly into their holds. In 1865 alone more than 20,000 shiploads of nitrate-rich guano, of some 2,000 tons each were taken away to enrich the farm fields of America, England, and Holland.

Guano proved to be intrinsically more valuable than it would at first appear. Between 1851 and 1872 more than 10 million tons with a market value up to $30 million was removed. Although the yellow dust carried into every corner of the ship and smelled strongly of ammonia, guano was a cargo that needed no container other than the vessel itself; it could not shift; and it could not spoil. "It was not uncommon to see two hundred square-riggers lying in the protected anchorage between the north and central islands awaiting cargoes." When the Peruvian deposits were depleted in the 1870s, guano mining moved to other more southern points along the coast of Chile (Volo and Volo 2001, 295–96).

The Advent of Steam

With regard to economy of operation, moderate-sized sailing coasters were best suited as bulk cargo carriers for short hauls but these were receiving competition from steamers as early as the 1850s. Steamers seemed to be prying loose the traditional grip that sailing vessels had on this important fraction of U.S. maritime commerce. Nonetheless, a distinctive type of sailing schooner was developed for the coasting trade that allowed them to hold their position in competition with the steamers until the twentieth century. Inexpensive to build and operate, and built with traditional American wooden-hull technology, these sailing schooners of between 300 and 700 tons capacity were kept busy carrying lumber, coal, ice, and other cargoes up and down the Atlantic, Pacific, and Gulf coasts. The sailing schooners of the coasting trade "formed a hard core of shipping on which the nation could rely" (Bauer 1989, 127).

Protected by a series of Navigation Acts from foreign competition, the coasting trade had continually grown as a percentage of the merchant marine fleet from 25 percent in the Federalist Era, to 41 percent just before the Civil War, and 57 percent by war's end. It was to retain this level of representation throughout the decades of the 1870s and 1880s (Bryant 1967, 335). A growing national population, the effects of industrialization, and absolute protection from foreign competition allowed coasting to supplant foreign trade as the major activity of the merchant marine as early as 1857. The coasting trade was very active with cotton, tobacco, lumber, turpentine, rosin, rice, and grain making up the bulk cargoes.

Coastal steam lines developed slowly in the first half of the nineteenth century due to monopolies granted by the individual states to local investors. In 1824 the U.S. Supreme Court overturned the state grants of monopolies on waterways that crossed state boundaries as invasions of the federal power to regulate interstate commerce. By 1840, all the major East Coast ports were connected by steam. Steam lines had been established from the Northeast directly to New Orleans and Savannah prior to the Civil War, and they met with some success.

In the aftermath of the Civil War, a few innovative American owners began to use efficient steel-hulled, multiple-expansion steamships of significant size to operate in the cotton coasting trade even though the initial costs of the vessels were quite high. A contemporary observer noted in 1866, "All the coasting trade is being done by screw steamers and a few side wheelers ranging from 800 to 1500 tons. The few sailing vessels building are small craft of no great burden" (Clark 1949, 90).

The wooden windship design had reached its practical engineering limits with the development of the clipper ships of the 1850s. It can be demonstrated that the U.S. shipbuilding industry was simply not competitive in the years after the Civil War, and that a change to steam-driven metal-hull vessels was essential to the health of the U.S. shipping industry. The failure to accomplish this may have served as a primary mechanism for much of the decline in the foreign carrying trade while concurrently explaining the sustained growth of the coasting trade and inland navigation.

At mid-century, the engineering fundamentals of steamship construction for the oceanic trade had several common characteristics. The hulls were made of wood; the vessels were propelled by paddle wheels housed amidships; the engines were physically very large and of a single expansion, low-pressure type, also located amidships; and the steam was exhausted into jet condensers so similar to those devised by James Watt in 1769 as to be considered identical. Low-pressure, water tube boilers had been common since their invention in 1791. Paddle wheels, by design well suited to low-pressure, were slow rotating devices of a large area that maximized the impulse imparted to the vessel increased the reliability of the engines and minimized the stress on the hull. While economical in terms of fuel consumption, the low-pressure steam boilers retarded the introduction of the screw propeller. Moreover, paddle wheels provided greater acceleration than the screw propellers of the period.

Nonetheless, steam was usually considered to be an auxiliary to sail and many vessels were designed with combinations of motive power. However, these vessels commonly experienced some disadvantages as both screws and paddle wheels produced considerable drag when the vessel was under sail. Paddle wheels were particularly noted for adversely effecting the overall sailing qualities of a vessel. When equipped with the higher pressure, fire tube boilers, introduced in the 1850s, and screw propellers, the restrictions of increased fuel consumption served to severely limit the speed, which the steamer could maintain for any extended period of time.

Windships, by comparison, could make hundreds of miles in a day, a record 400 nautical miles in 24 hours having been reached in the 1850s by the American clipper ship *Challenger*. Under these conditions it seemed unlikely that steam would ever be completely economical with sail particularly on the long distance routes, where fuel and fresh water for the engines became major limiting considerations. This led the United States to seek coaling and watering stations on long routes like those across the Pacific. Hawaii, the Philippines, Wake Island, Midway, and other small islands and atolls were occupied by the United States to serve this purpose; and the Panama Canal was built to shorten the route for U.S. merchant steamers as well as its naval vessels.

These disadvantages left the windships with a decided economic edge, at least on the long-haul routes. Nevertheless, wooden-hull American clippers saw severe competition in the oriental trade from British windship designs that utilized composite hulls, wood with cast-iron beams and bracing, before the war. Although generally smaller than the American ships, and somewhat slower under the best of conditions, the British vessels proved to be better suited to a variety of weather extremes. Even the best British windships were driven from the trade by steamers in the decades after the Civil War (Natkiel and Preston 1986, 110; Volo and Volo 2001, 299–300).

U.S. Maritime Stagnation

American maritime distress in the third-quarter of the century may be attributed, in part, to the very success for which U.S. shippers and shipbuilders were noted at the end of the age of sail. In the first half of the nineteenth century American shipbuilders had no equal in the world. With modern woodworking and wood-turning apparatus, American shipyards could crank out their best work at as little as 60 percent of the cost of British builders who generally did not invest in such devices. Although profits from investments in the domestic shipping industry could vary with time, the expected financial return from the foreign carrying trade was "effectively tied…[to] how well U.S. shipyards could compete in price with their foreign counterpart" (Whitehurst 1983, 1–2). Americans found themselves saddled with expensive shipbuilding apparatus made obsolete by the sudden popularity of metal hulls and steam. British builders, by contrast, had made no large investment in wooden windship technology and were able to update their shipyards directly to metal and steam production without taking a loss.

The vessels remaining in the U.S. merchant fleet in the Industrial Age were described as "old, obsolete, and nearly worthless craft." This description was quite probably accurate and may suggest an alternative explanation for the decline of the U.S. sailing ship other than the damage done to the merchant by the Confederate navy. Simply put, the day of the windships had passed (Dalzell 1940, 247, Albion 1968, 171).

The demand for a quick passage to California created by the gold rush frenzy of the 1840s and 1850s had run its course, and travel by transcontinental rail was faster, cheaper, and more reliable. In the China trade, the opening of the Suez Canal particularly hastened the decline of the windships. Sailing vessels simply could not maneuver in the narrow canal and were placed at a severe disadvantage in comparison to the steamers, which also benefited from the fuel savings inherent in a voyage shortened some 4,000 miles. The fabulous clipper ships built in the glorious 1850s had outlived their useful purpose resulting in a condition in the 1860s and 1870s known as "block obsolescence," a repetitive phenomenon in American shipbuilding history (Uhl 1983, 71–72).

The foreign carrying trade, which was the lifeblood of the windship, "had collapsed in fact, if not in the consciousness of a frustrated people who would find it more comfortable to blame that collapse on the [Civil] war" (Mitchell 2003, 83). While metal-hull, steam-powered, marine technology advanced, the traditional technology of the wooden-hull sailing vessel stagnated. Iron-hull steamers began driving the windships of all nations off the most profitable routes.

The International Mercantile Marine Co., originally the International Navigation Co., was a trust company formed in the early twentieth century in an attempt to monopolize the steam shipping trades. It combined the American Line, the Red Star Line, the Atlantic Transport Line, the White Star Line, and the Leyland Line. The Dominion Line was also amalgamated. The project was bankrolled by American financier J. P. Morgan. The company also had working profit-sharing relationships with the German Hamburg-Amerika Line and the North German Lloyd Lines. The trust caused a great panic in the British shipping industry and led directly to the British government's subsidy of the Cunard Line's new ships RMS *Lusitania* and RMS *Mauretania* in an effort to compete.

However, International Mercantile Marine had dramatically overpaid for acquiring stock due to an overestimation of potential profit, and a proposed subsidy bill in the United States Congress that failed. The company came under the scrutiny of the Sherman Antitrust Act and thus was never really successful. In 1932, the company was dissolved. Cunard bought the remnants of the White Star Line (noteworthy for having owned the RMS *Titanic* that sank in 1912) and the remaining American pieces were amalgamated into United States Lines (Volo and Volo 2001, 300–301).

FOR MORE INFORMATION

Albion, Robert G., and Jennie B. Pope, *Sealanes in Wartime*. Portland, ME: Archon Books, 1968.

Barney, William L., ed. *A Companion to 19th-Century America*. Malden, MA: Blackwell Publishing, 2006.

Bryant, Samuel W. *The Sea and States: A Maritime History of the American People*. New York: T.Y. Crowell, 1967.

Clark, Victor S. *History of Manufactures in the United States*. 3 vols. New York: Peter Smith Publishers, 1949.

Dalzell, G. W. *The Flight from the Flag: The Continuing Effect of the Civil War upon the American Carrying Trade*. Chapel Hill: University of North Carolina Press, 1940.

Dalzell, Robert F. *Enterprising Elite: The Boston Associates and the World They Made*. Cambridge, MA: Harvard University Press, 1987.

Davidson, Marshall B. *Life In America*. Boston: Houghton Mifflin Company, 1951.

Dolson, Hildegarde. *The Great Oildorado: The Gaudy and Turbulent Years of the First Oil Rush: Pennsylvania, 1859–1880*. New York: Random House, 1959.

Eisler, Benita, ed. *The Lowell Offering: Writings by New England Mill Women: 1840–1845*. New York: W. W. Norton & Company, 1977.

Fisher, Gordon M. "From Hunter to Orshansky: An Overview of Unofficial Poverty Lines in the United States from 1904–1965." (A paper presented October 28, 1993 at the Fifteenth Annual Research Conference of the Association for Public Policy Analysis and Management in Washington, D.C. available from the Department of Health and Human Services.)

Husband, Julie, and Jim O'Loughlin. *Daily Life in the Industrial United States, 1870–1900*. Westport, CT: Greenwood Press, 2004.

Jones, Mary Ellen. *Daily Life on the Nineteenth-Century American Frontier*. Westport, CT: Greenwood Press, 1998.

Kittredge, Henry C. *Shipmasters of Cape Cod*. Boston, MA: Houghton Mifflin, 1935.

Larcom, Lucy. *A New England Girlhood*. Boston: Northeastern University Press, 1986.

Lupiano, Vincent DePaul, and Ken W. Sayers. *It Was a Very Good Year: A Cultural History of the United States from 1776 to the Present*. Holbrook, MA: Bob Adams, 1994.

Mitchell, Thomas G. *Indian Fighters Turned American Politicians, From Military Service to Public Office*. Westport, CT: Praeger Press, 2003.

Modell, John. "Family and Fertility on the Indiana Frontier, 1820." In *Studies in American Historical Demography*, ed. Maris A. Vinovskis. New York: Academic Press, 1979.

Nasaw, David, ed. *Andrew Carnegie: The "Gospel of Wealth" Essays and Other Writings*. New York: Penguin Books, 2006.

Natkiel, Richard, and Anthony Preston. *Atlas of Maritime History*. New York: Facts on File, Inc., 1986.

Schenone, Laura. *A Thousand Years Over a Hot Stove*. New York: W. W. Norton & Company, 2003.

Smith, Page. *The Nation Comes of Age: A People's History.* 4 vols. New York: McGraw-Hill, 1981.

Stewart, James. "The Economics of American Farm Unrest, 1865–1900." *EH.Net Encyclopedia,* edited by Robert Whaples. URL: http://eh.net/encycpolpedia/article/stewart.farmers (accessed May 2007).

Uhl, Robert. "Masters of the Merchant Marine," *American Heritage* (April 1983).

Volo, Dorothy Denneen, and James M. Volo. *Daily Life in the Age of Sail.* Westport, CT: Greenwood Press, 2001.

———. *Family Life in Nineteenth-Century America.* Westport, CT: Greenwood Press, 2007.

Whitehurst, Clinton H. *The U.S. Merchant Marine: In Search of an Enduring Maritime Policy.* Annapolis, MD: Naval Institute Press, 1983.

Wolff, Leon. "Labor in the Gilded Age." In *The Social Fabric, American Life from the Civil War to the Present,* ed. John H. Cary and Julius Weinberg. Boston, MA: Little, Brown and Company, 1975.

Intellectual Life

SCIENCE

Electric Power

The scientific study of electricity predated the American Revolution, and Benjamin Franklin was as much a founding father of this branch of science as he was of American independence introducing the concept of + and – charge, the lightning rod, and the parallel plate capacitor to the world. Yet the study of electricity in America remained in its infancy until the needs of the electric telegraph spurred the invention of better batteries, insulated wire, and relays. These required a dependable source of direct current (DC) electricity that was usually provided by chemical cells. Much of the science behind electrical power distribution and its application to useful devices was based on the pioneering work done in the name of telegraphy.

In the same way, the quest for the electric light drove the development of alternating current (AC) sources. This development was not without controversy with Thomas Edison—commonly given credit for the invention of the incandescent light bulb—and Nikola Tesla—inventor of the high tension coil and other electrical apparatus—disagreeing over the appropriate use of DC or AC generated electricity for public lighting and electric motors. The dispute, known as the "Current Wars," was fueled by competition between the electric distribution companies of Edison and George Westinghouse. Tesla, an advocate of AC power worked for each, and had broken with Edison, who favored DC, in a dispute over wages and royalties.

Edison had correctly pointed out that DC electricity was innately safer than AC, which posed a greater possibility of electrocution but DC electricity required that the distance between the generating facility and the point of use be small due to transmission losses. AC generation avoided this problem to a great extent allowing for centralized power generation and distribution over a vast network. Yet, the fact that AC was dangerous could be demonstrated. Edison, whose patents were largely based on DC technology, carried out a vigorous campaign to discourage the adoption of AC by emphasizing the danger of fatal AC accidents, lobbying state legislatures, and purposely electrocuting animals for the press. His series of animal electrocutions peaked with the execution of an elderly circus elephant named Topsy. Edison also secretly supported the work of Harold P. Brown, the inventor of the electric chair for executing condemned felons.

Tesla ultimately proved the greater efficiency of his AC system, and he won the contract to harness the hydroelectric power of Niagara Falls. Electric motors and AC generators were found to operate more efficiently than DC ones with fewer internal parts and greater longevity. With the introduction of a large number of innovative AC devices by other inventors, Edison abandoned his low-voltage DC distribution system. Eventually, Edison's General Electric Company converted to AC generation and began to manufacture AC machines and devices in open competition with Westinghouse. Prior to these developments, power distribution and energy consumption were essentially local affairs (from woodlot to fireplace for instance), but electricity was capable of putting great distances between the source of energy and its point of use. The switch to commercial AC generation ultimately preordained the development of the vast power grid upon which the United States is presently dependent.

—James M. Volo

The Electric Light

Edison's incandescent light bulb was not the first electric light, but it proved to be the most practical one for domestic lighting. Cleveland, Ohio, was the site of the first demonstration of an electric lighting system in the United States. In 1879, Charles Brush, a local inventor who had installed early electric lighting systems in some factories, convinced the Cleveland City Council to allow him to outfit a section of the city with a dozen arc lamps that produced illumination from sparks passing between the points of graphite electrodes. On the evening of the display, crowds gathered in the downtown section of the city (some had brought smoked glasses fearing, erroneously, that the light might be too bright to view with the naked eye). At 8:05 P.M., the signal was given and the dozen lights (each as strong as a modern-day floodlight) illuminated the street below in a strong blue-white light. The crowd cheered, a municipal band struck up a song, and an artillery salute was fired on the lakeshore in honor of the occasion. Following the success of this demonstration, other cities clamored for outdoor electric lighting. Soon Boston, New York, and Philadelphia had their own arc light projects powered by Brush's equipment (Husband and O'Loughlin 2004, 34).

Arc lamps gave off a bright, blue-white light and worked well for lighting large areas, but they were noisy and impractical for domestic use. Edison's incandescent light bulbs, which eventually emerged as the standard for lighting, gave off a softer, more yellow light like that of candles that was completely silent. Edison ran a successful demonstration project in New York City from his Pearl Street plant in 1882, lighting the offices of 50 Wall Street businesses. Soon, a fierce competition erupted between these two lighting systems for municipal contracts. In the early days of electric power generation, all the systems, whether arc or incandescent, were small in scope, rarely stretching more than a mile from the central generating station. Nonetheless, by 1884, most major cities had some type of limited electric lighting system. Electric lights were considered superior in quality and cost to older gas-lighting systems. However, lighting for homes remained limited during the industrial era, costing as much as $100 a year, which was almost a quarter of an average wage earner's income (Husband and O'Loughlin 2004, 34).

By the late 1880s, many major cities had competing electric companies running their own wires alongside one another, leading to wire congestion and overbuilding in lucrative markets. At one point, New York City had 32 separate electric companies. Meanwhile, many rural areas were left without electricity altogether. Competition between electricity firms increased, and a consolidating industry began to increase prices. As companies competed for the favor of city governments, many municipal authorities feared a repeat of the bribery scandals that had plagued the railroads. In response a number of reform mayors in cities including Chicago, Detroit, San Francisco, and Toledo created city-owned, municipal power utilities. Although not without controversy, municipal power often proved able to offer cheaper electricity and wider service. In Detroit, for instance, private commercially generated electricity cost an average of $132 per lamp per year in 1894; in 1898 the new Detroit municipal power authority provided electricity at $87 per lamp per year. Publicly owned utilities remain to this day a reasonable alternative to private electric companies (Husband and O'Loughlin 2004, 35).

EDUCATION

Ideas on education in the late nineteenth century indicated strongly that conceptions of young people were undergoing change. The idea that young people went through adolescence around the onset of puberty and that this difficult period needed supervision was widely supported by educators and youth counselors. Underlying this was a general belief among youth commentators that life in the Industrial Age was too frenzied and that there was too much pressure put on youth. To mitigate this pressure, young people were to be protected in schools during their adolescence. The concerns over young people reflected many of the tensions middle-class Americans had with the rapid changes altering the nation, such as massive urbanization and immigration, blended with a romantic vision of childhood and fears of over civilization. By the 1870s communities began to put more emphasis on schools than they had in the early part of the century, as many more communities established schools and approached the educational curriculum more systematically. Higher education was also taking on more importance, and college attendance grew accordingly.

Common schooling continued to be the major part of the American public education system through the end of the century. One-room schoolhouses across the nation educated the bulk of the population. These schools reached 64.7 percent of young Americans from ages 5 to 18 in 1869, and this number increased steadily to 71.9 percent by 1900. The days attended per pupil (77 to 99) increased steadily during the period as well, indicating more systematic emphasis on pedagogy, curriculum, and attendance. There were some regional differences, which were the greatest for African American children in the South. Today students attend 180 days.

Roughly 78 percent of white children ages 10 to 14 attended school while only 51 percent of African American children of the same age made it to school at any time during the year. There were more specialized schools, like kindergartens, slowly spreading throughout the nation, but a very small percentage of children attended them. As late as 1902 only five percent of four and five year olds attended kindergarten.

Common schools relied on one-room schools in rural America and most commonly taught children 6 to 14. The curriculum focused primarily on reading, writing, spelling, and arithmetic in the beginning phase. Intermediate study continued with the former disciplines and added geography and nature study. Finally, advanced study continued all of the former subjects and added history and grammar. The ubiquitous *McGuffey Reader* was the mainstay of the common school curriculum in 37 states and sold 1,122 million copies from 1836 to 1922. The content of the *McGuffey Reader* reflected the concerns and morality of the Victorian middle class. The need for further education and the spread of new ideas on adolescence led to the creation of more elaborate age graduations and eventually high school.

High school attendance, however, continued to be a luxury of the elite working-class and middle-class families. Industrialization created a strange situation for youth. To get into higher paying jobs, young people had to stay out of the labor force long enough to get an education but at the same time industry aggressively sought to hire child labor. For most working-class youth their teenage years were not spent in schools but in factories and mines working long hours in dangerous conditions. Only the upper echelons of working-class and middle-class families could afford to keep their children out of the labor force long enough to get them an education. This also accounts for the higher number of girls in American high schools in this period, who were about 60 percent of high school graduates. For urban families that did not need their girls to work, or did not need them for domestic labor, the high school was the perfect solution. The high school student population doubled in the decade of the 1890s, though only 3.3 percent of the eligible population attended.

These schools developed to be an all-encompassing cultural, social, and educational experience for young people. A host of extracurricular activities emerged, centering on a massive outpouring of sports, student government, and all manner of clubs. High school administrators destroyed fraternities and sororities, which were very popular at colleges and universities, and established stricter controls over their young students. High schools also profited from the fact that the many universities and professional schools increasingly required a four-year high school diploma for entrance. High schools were creating something that would not come to full fruition until the early twentieth century: a virtually universal and distinct youth culture centered on school. Ironically, even as the society at large promoted independence, particularly for young men, high schools were creating an institutionalized education that emphasized the dependence and subordination of youth.

The dramatic growth in professional schools, universities, and colleges during this period illustrates the growing importance of education for upward mobility in the industrial capitalist economy. Colleges and universities increased in number from 563 in 1869 to 977 by 1900. The great captains of industry poured tens of millions of dollars into new universities like Duke, Stanford, and Vanderbilt. Also important was the Morrill Federal Land Grant Act of 1862, which provided each state with land to establish state universities. In addition, the number of professional schools established in the last quarter of the century more than doubled that of those founded in the preceding 25 years. The founding of the American Medical Association in 1847 and of the Association of American Law Schools in 1900 exemplified the growth of professional education. The expense of college meant that a very small portion of Americans attended, though the figures did increase throughout the era from one percent of college-age Americans in 1870 to five percent by 1910.

Colleges and universities continued to rely on a traditional classical curriculum in the nineteenth century, but with important changes. There was particular emphasis on oral recitation and rhetoric. This was an era of the spoken word and oratory far more than today, though the Industrial Age marked a beginning of the decline. Student recitation and explication of texts, while still widespread, was slowly replaced by lectures. While Greek, Latin, French, German, mathematics, history, philosophy, physics, and chemistry were still a major part of the traditional curriculum, the emergence of professional schools caused the multiplication of new courses in a myriad of disciplines like sociology, anthropology, and engineering. Harvard President Charles Eliot introduced an elective system that allowed students much greater choice in their college classes. Other signs of higher education's attempt to become more systemized were the introduction of the new college entrance exams and the creation of the College Entrance Examination Board to standardize the admission process.

Opportunities were also growing for those outside of the dominant white, Anglo-Saxon, Protestant male circles. Women began to move forcefully into higher education. There were almost five times as many coeducational institutions of higher education in 1900 than the paltry 22 that existed in 1867. Women comprised only 21 percent of college students in 1870 but were nearly 36 percent by 1900. In addition to most state universities opening their doors to women, a host of new women's colleges were founded after Vassar's 1861 example, including Wellesley (1875), Smith (1875), Bryn Mawr (1884), Mount Holyoke (1888), Barnard (1889), and Radcliffe (1894). African American students also embraced new educational opportunities at institutions developed for them because of their exclusion from all-white university systems. Universities like Fisk, Atlanta, and Howard provided new opportunities to African Americans seeking higher education. Likewise, Fordham and Notre Dame provided opportunities for American Catholics just as the City College of New York and New York University availed Jews of higher education.

By the 1890s an extremely well-developed college culture had appeared that was organized largely around classes and extracurricular activities. Literary societies, social fraternities and sororities, debating societies, drama clubs, sports, and student government were a small part of the explosion of extracurricular activities that were increasingly sanctioned and regulated by the faculty, administration, or alumni (Shrock 2004, 28–32).

THE SETTLEMENT HOUSE

The highly idealistic founders of the settlement houses of the 1890s came to the immigrant neighborhoods largely as educational innovators. Some of them had classroom experience, but many had rejected a career in high school or college teaching as too routine and narrow, and too far removed from the pressing problems of an urban, industrialized country. They came to settlement "as a protest against a restricted view of education," ready to cut down the barriers that separated learning from reality. Jane Addams, like most settlement workers, considered education a method of social reform. She and other settlement pioneers drew heavily on the foundations laid in the English settlement movement and the concept of university extension. In 1891 there were 100 settlement houses in America; a decade later there were more than 400.

Settlement founders planned to extend the advantages of college education to working men to narrow the gulf between factory worker and college graduate through classes, lectures, and discussions. Stanton Coit patterned his Neighborhood Guild in part on Frederick Denison Maurice's Working Men's College in London, and in 1890 Morrison Swift planned a settlement in Philadelphia that would be a social university. Jane Addams and Ellen Starr began to teach and to lecture as soon as they unpacked at Hull House. Miss Starr organized a reading group to discuss the work of George Elliot, which broadened to include Dante, Browning, and Shakespeare. Julia Lathrop started a Sunday afternoon Plato Club for the discussion of philosophical questions. Vida Scudder and Helena Dudley organized a Social Science Club at Denison House in Boston in 1893, and for a time 40 or 50 businessmen, professionals, working men, and students gathered weekly to hear lectures on such topics as "The Ethics of Trade Unions" or "German Socialism." But attendance dwindled after a few months, and the club collapsed after the third year.

Almost every settlement had its lecture series and its educational conferences, and a few like Hull House had university extension classes for college credit. Educator John Dewey and architect Frank Lloyd Wright were among those who spoke at Hull House. George Santayana once gave a lecture on St. Francis and the beauty of poverty at Prospect Union in Cambridge that left most of the hearers aghast. Some of the lectures and discussions were exciting at least to the residents and students if not to the working men in the neighborhood. And although Sinclair Lewis exaggerated in *Ann Vickers* when he described the educational fare in his fictional settlement as composed of "lectures delivered gratis by earnest advocates of the single tax, trout fishing, exploring Tibet, pacifism, sea shell collecting, the eating of bran, and the geography of Charlemagne's Empire," there was an element of the unreal and esoteric about the early settlement workers' attempt to dispense the culture of the universities to working men.

The first building especially constructed for Hull House contained an art gallery, and the settlement continued its art exhibitions until the opening of the Chicago Art Institute made them unnecessary. It was a small beginning that did not revolutionize public education in the city, but it was significant as the first of many experiments tried first in the settlements and then adopted by the public schools.

Art exhibitions, lectures, and university extension classes satisfied the desire of many settlement residents to make use of their college training. Moreover, they provided intellectual stimulation for the transfigured few in the neighborhood capable of abstract thought. Men like Philip Davis, Meyer Bloomfield, Henry Moskowitz, and Francis Hackett found their programs stimulating and were thus inspired to continue their education. In addition, settlement lectures and classes served to bring the real world to a number of university professors (or at least they liked to think so). But it soon became obvious that the greater majority of the people in the settlement neighborhood were not interested in extension classes. Although thousands attended art exhibitions, they took little away that would vitally influence their lives.

What most people in the working-class neighborhood needed was something useful and concrete, something closely related to their daily lives. This might mean courses in manual training or homemaking; it might simply mean instruction in English or basic American government and history. Large groups of immigrants made both English-type university extension courses and American public schools inadequate in the urban setting, thus forcing settlement workers, whether they liked it or not, to experiment with new methods and techniques.

They quickly learned that among the most useful things were child care and kindergarten classes for young children whose mothers worked all day. Stanton Coit opened a kindergarten at Neighborhood Guild only a few months after the settlement was organized, and Hull House, New York College Settlement, Chicago Commons, and most other pioneer settlements established them soon after opening their doors. The goals of the settlements and the kindergartens seemed so similar that one kindergarten teacher labeled the social settlement "the kindergarten for adults."

The kindergarten classes brought mothers and sisters as well as little boys and girls to the settlement and led naturally to attempts to provide them with something useful and meaningful. Usually this meant classes in homemaking, cooking, sewing, and shopping. Some courses taught skills appropriate for work in domestic service, such as the art of serving tea from a silver service or accepting a calling card on a tray. Many of the women settlement workers were appalled at the way their immigrant neighbors kept house. Their wastefulness and disorderliness bothered those brought up in neat middle-class American homes. Some settlement workers could never quite overcome their feeling of superiority, and these homemaking classes only made the immigrant women more conscious of differences and deficiencies. But many newcomers, baffled by unfamiliar urban ways of household management, acquired helpful suggestions and new confidence at the settlement. Of course, the immigrants did not always listen; and, indeed, sometimes they knew more than the settlement workers.

The practical needs of the people in the neighborhood usually dictated the types of classes offered. Many settlements were located near textile factories where women and children could take out work. Skill and speed in making buttonholes or operating a sewing machine were vitally important and meant increased family income. Most settlements attempting to satisfy the real needs of their neighborhoods soon found themselves very much involved in manual training and industrial education.

However, not all settlement workers were realistic in their educational experiments, and there was something romantic and nostalgic about their attempts to revive [pre-machine] handicrafts in the face of increasing industrialism. But they were usually concerned with real problems and tried to satisfy important needs. The settlement workers, interested in relating education more closely to life, could not long ignore the pressing problems of training young men and women in their neighborhoods for worthwhile jobs. They knew that they could inspire the few with exceptional ability to go to college, but that the majority would never go. What would happen to them? Would they merely drift into unskilled jobs, or could the settlements do something to prepare them for a meaningful role in the industrial world. Robert Woods of South End House, and many others, advocated manual training for everyone, so that even the lucky ones who went to college would have an appreciation of the dignity and the difficulties of working with their hands and operating machines.

Vocational training and vocational guidance were later adopted by the public schools. This was somewhat unexpected because in the beginning, most settlement workers had no desire to alter or reform the public educational system; they saw their function only as supplementing schools. However, as soon as they became aware of the inadequacy of public education, especially in the poorer districts of the great cities, the attempt to supplement became an attempt to change (Davis 1975, 118–26).

LITERATURE

Novels

Many of the up-and-coming writers of the final decades of the nineteenth century wrote under the philosophy of naturalism, a spin-off on realism's focus on a true-to-life, unsentimental view of human existence. The writing was, nonetheless, largely set against the background of a pessimistic world that was amoral and indifferent to human presence. The main characters of the naturalistic writers were often lower-class or lower-middle-class men who struggled against impersonal natural forces while the forces of heredity, environment, or instinct acted to circumscribe their choices and actions. The protagonist's fight for survival was often steeped in violence and passion. Social Darwinism with its emphasis on heredity, racial instincts, amoral natural forces influencing all creatures, and the survival of the fittest had a tremendous influence on this literary style.

Although naturalistic writers started producing work in the 1890s, many of the most successful and influential novels were written in the early twentieth century.

Stephen Crane was an early and successful proponent of naturalism. His "Whilomville Stories" were serialized in *Harper's New Monthly Magazine*. Crane is best known for his *The Red Badge of Courage* (1895) set in the Civil War. It is said that Crane, as a boy, listened to the war stories told in the park by federal veterans of the battle of Chancellorsville (Virginia) in his hometown of Port Jervis, New York. Crane was too young to have any experience of war, but he was able as a man to transfer what he heard into print creating one of the best-known and most authentic fictional characterizations of the effect of warfare on soldiers. Jack London wrote a series of novels and short stories in the naturalist genre, and a number of these are still widely read today: *Call of the Wild* (1903), *Sea Wolf* (1904), and *White Fang* (1906). Theodore Dreiser wrote *Sister Carrie* (1900), which catapulted him into literary celebrity and launched his career as well as his constant battles with editors to make his novels suitable for the reading public. Edith Wharton, benefiting from the general demise of gender-based prejudice against professional female authors, produced a great deal of important naturalistic fiction. Her works included *The Touchstone* (1900) and *Ethan Frome* (1911), but she is probably most well known for *The Age of Innocence* (1920) (Shrock 2004, 163–64).

The best-selling books of the period came in many forms, such as success tracts, historical romances, religious novels, dime novels, and adventure stories. British authors remained popular because American publishers often reprinted foreign works without regard to paying royalties. Not until 1891 did the United States agree to abide by international copyright laws. Novels with a religious theme were very popular, like Lew Wallace's *Ben Hur: A Tale of the Christ* (1880), Ludovic Halévy's pro-Catholic *L'Abbé Constantin* (1882), Charles Sheldon's *In His Steps: What Would Jesus Do* (1897), and Henryk Sienkiewicz's *Quo Vadis?* (1896). Children's novels sold well, such as Frances Hodgson Burnett's *Little Lord Fauntleroy* (1886); Anna Sewell's *Black Beauty*, which became popular in America in 1890; Robert Louis Stevenson's pirate adventure *Treasure Island* (1883) and his science fiction/introspective tale *Dr. Jekyll and Mr. Hyde* (1885); Margaret Sidney's (Harriet Lothrop) *Five Little Peppers and How They Grew* (1881); and Frank Baum's *The Wizard of Oz* (1900). Other popular books were Bret Harte's collection of short stories, *The Luck of the Roaring Camp and Other Stories* (1870), Edward Eggerston's *The Hoosier School-Master* (1871), Archibald Gunter's *Mr. Barnes of New York* (1887), Hall Caine's *The Deemster* (1888), and Leo Tolstoy's *War and Peace* (1886).

Best sellers in the 1890s included Arthur Conan Doyle's *Adventures of Sherlock Holmes* (the first, *A Study in Scarlet* appearing in 1887), James Barrie's *The Little Minister* (1892), Anthony Hopkins Hawkins' *The Prisoner of Zenda* (1894), Opie Read's *The Jucklins* (1896), and Edward Noyes Westcott's *David Harum* (1898) and *Eben Holden* (1900). Rudyard Kipling became something of a phenomenon in the 1890s with *Barrack-Room Ballads* (1892), *Plain Tales from the Hills* (1888), and *The Light That Failed* (1894) hitting the best selling list, though his better-known works written in the early twentieth century did not sell well (Shrock 2004, 164).

The period also saw the rise of the Home Library concept where publishing companies promoted a series of great books that everyone needed to read and own. These series certainly appealed to middle-class Americans seeking a common cultural literacy with the upper classes, but they also appealed to working-class Americans who sought an inexpensive source of fiction and advice literature. Many Home Library series defied the genteel and sensational labels used in the period, perhaps denoting that American reading habits had grown more complex and varied among the social classes than is generally believed. On the forthrightly respectable side of the series spectrum was Charles Dudley Warner's *Library of the World's Best Literature* (1897) in 30 volumes. The 1895 *Montgomery Ward Catalogue* sold seven competing Home Library series such as the *Modern Library*, the 150-book series *Library Editions of the New Oxford and Princeton*, and *Selected Paper Covered Books Series* that sold for as little as 16 cents per title. One example was the *Frank Leslie's Home Library of Standard Works by the Most Celebrated Authors*. Many of these inexpensive paperbacks were intended to be portable so that people could carry them on trains and trolleys while traveling and commuting to and from work—an experience made more common by the expansion of urban and suburban living (Shrock 2004, 164–65).

Juvenile Literature

The Taylor sisters, Ann and Jane, had written books of poems for children, and although they were not exclusively religious, many featured an avenging God as an ultimate protagonist. Less intrusive into the religious sphere of life was the message in the stories of Maria Edgeworth, an Irish novelist. Her goal was to teach practical ideas about proper behavior to children. Her astute understanding of the psychology of the child enabled her to create engaging stories that delivered morals with grace and tender humor. There was always a gracious lady who appeared to give an award or to point out the virtuous response. Authors often used an aunt or a friend to children to help deliver a message. For example, *Bound Out: or Abby on the Farm* was written by Aunt Friendly.

As the century progressed, romanticism ushered in a trend toward a body of children's literature that was less morbid and contained fantasy and realism. Washington Irving's *Sketch Book of 1819* drew upon the legends of the Dutch settlers of New York. James Fennimore Cooper wrote about early frontier life in his series, the *Leather-Stocking Tales*. Nathaniel Hawthorne retold classic Greek myths in *A Wonder Book for Girls and Boys* and *The Tanglewood Tales for Girls and Boys* While not written primarily for children, these works were very popular with young readers. While fantasy and adventure literature drew a sizable audience, didactic works did not disappear. In the 1820s the American Tract Society had begun publishing a number of children's books. With titles such as *Honesty is the Best Policy; Active Benevolence or Lucy Careful;* and *Good Boys and Chastised*, it was clear that the object of such stories was to present a moral lesson more in line with the social gospel. Less obvious, with gentler, more sentimental messages, were books like *Aunt Rose and Her Little Nieces* (1842) that contained little stories of interest to children but included words of wisdom for the young readers. Aunt Rose (the nom de plume of the author) cautioned, "When young people do as they are bid, every one is glad to see them; but when they behave ill, every body wishes them far off." She also cautioned, "If ever you do wrong, my dear little ones, be sure you own your fault." Finally she advised, "Riches take away the heart from God. Never desire to be rich" (Shrock 2004, 20).

In children's literature, the antebellum pattern of didactic, sentimental stories evolved into a trend where children were the protagonists who, through indomitable morality or outstanding example, affect the lives of others by persuading them to take the higher road. Orphaned Abby, in *Bound Out: or Abby on the Farm*, typifies this story line. Abby was a model child who accepted her hardships, answered the call to duty and trusted in the Lord. Abby had tremendous influence on the family with whom she lived. She was responsible for Mr. Porter's desisting to serve whiskey to his reapers during the harvest, for the spoiled son, Bubby to want to go to Sunday School and for Mrs. Porter's becoming more clement and less harsh in her speech.

The flowering of children's literature initiated a surfeit of children's periodicals. Between 1789 and 1879 almost 340 youth magazines were published in the United States. Some publications folded after only a few issues but many enjoyed success. Most were intended for 10- to 18-year-olds but publications like *The Nursery* were intended for the very young. Through these periodicals the nation's youth were introduced to some of the country's most influential writers of the day including Jacob Abbott, Louisa May Alcott, Samuel Goodrich, Sarah Joseph Hale, and John Townsend Trowbridge and delighted by the illustrations of Mary Ann Hallock, Winslow Homer, and Thomas Nast. These magazines reflected virtually all of the attitudes and concerns that enveloped the nation at the time. There were educational magazines such as *Clark's School Visitor* and *The Schoolfellow* and temperance periodicals like *The Youth's Temperance Banner* and *Juvenile Temperance Watchman*. Some magazines were purely literary such as *Our Young Folks* and *Riverside Magazine for Young People*. Religious publications were extremely plentiful, and Protestants were joined by Catholics, Jews, and Mormons in trying to spread their message to the nation's youth through the use of the press. During the Civil War, Southern children were cut off from their favorite Northern periodicals, but Southern publications such as *The Child's Index*, *Children's Guide*, and *Youth's Banner* filled the void.

Despite the movement away from dark, heavily moralistic tales, much of children's literature emphasized intellectual and moral education beneath a cloak of juvenile entertainment. Even children's periodicals embraced this format. The prospectus for *Youth's Companion* stated that the magazine's contents would be miscellaneous, with several departments dealing with religion, morals, manners, habits, filial duties, books, amusements, schools, and whatever may be thought truly useful, either in this life or the life to come. Parents would have found this very appealing. The *Mother's Book* was written for young people, and, as far as possible, combined amusement with instruction but it was very important to the editors that amusement not become the primary inducement for reading the magazine. Author and founder of the children's magazine, *Merry's Museum*, Samuel G. Goodrich cautioned parents against the influence of fiction. He suggested that they restrict their children's reading of fiction and encourage instead that they read works that dealt in facts, such as geographies, histories, biographies, and travel books.

The second half of the century saw a gender segmentation of the market that generated adventure stories for boys that fostered manly independence. Putting a new twist on this theme in 1867, Horatio Alger, created a different kind of adventure story for boys that centered on the upward struggle to economic success.

Ragged Dick: or Street Life in New York commenced a series of rags-to-riches tales focusing on the rewards of hard work, perseverance, and concern for others. Stories targeting the female audience were mainly sentimental domestic novels with a young female protagonist, usually orphaned, who had to make her way in an often unkind world. Among these were Sophie May's *Little Prudy* series, Martha Finley's 28-volume saga *Elsie Dinsmore*, and Susan Warner's *The Wide, Wide World* (Volo and Volo 2007, 272–75).

Arguably, *St. Nicholas Magazine* was the dominant youth periodical of the last quarter of the nineteenth century. Its success illustrates, as no other of its kind, the growth of a consumer ethic and a distinctive youth culture during this period. Even though Mary Mapes Dodge, the powerful editor of the magazine for over 30 years, believed that moral uplift and strong support of the community values held by the upper classes was import, she also railed against children's literature that was primarily aimed at the parents. Dry, dusty, and wearisome, the old style needed to be replaced by a periodical that would be a "pleasure ground" where young people could discover "a brand-new, free life of their own for a little while." Although adults produced the literature and Dodge had a free hand in shaping the content of her magazine, young people were the focus as a distinct consumer group (Shrock 2004, 165–66).

Dodge had chosen the title, *St. Nicholas*, which was meant to signify to all its young readers the jolly old Santa Claus who was becoming the primary figure of a growing child-oriented material culture at the end of the century. Eventually, the notion of children as consumers was made explicit when the magazine included a "What I Want for Christmas" page. This enabled young readers, for the first time in a major periodical directed at them, to choose Christmas presents from the advertisements in the magazine. Youngsters could write down the gifts and their corresponding page numbers on a specially prepared form that was included in the magazine so that they might give it to their parents. This firmly established ties between *St. Nicholas Magazine*, Christmas, and the child-centered consumer culture (Shrock 2004, 166).

It would be an error, however, to attribute the overwhelming success of *St. Nicholas Magazine* or the older *Youth's Companion* simply to marketing factors. The magazines boasted some of the greatest serialized stories and most influential English-language authors of the age. These included Louisa May Alcott (*Little Women*), Frances Hodgson Burnett (*Little Lord Fauntleroy*), Mark Twain (*The Adventures of Huckleberry Finn*), Rudyard Kipling (*The Jungle Book*), and Howard Pyle (*The Story of King Arthur and His Knights*).

Notwithstanding this array, it was the incredible diversity and quality of the literature that was printed in every issue that set these periodicals apart from their competition. History, sports, fairy tales, poetry, current events, adventure, success, sentimentality, nature, science, and stories for small children could all appear in a single issue. Palmer Cox's "Brownies," a series of illustrated drawings of chubby little sprites (a nineteenth-century equivalent of Walt Disney characters), were a favored feature of the magazine introduced in 1883. A spin-off of their popularity was the Kodak Brownie camera that appeared in 1900 specifically designed for and marketed to children. Like the long-lived *Youth's Companion*, *St. Nicholas Magazine* survived several decades absorbing or eliminating its competition into the twentieth century.

Its circulation was modest by comparison to that of *Youth's Companion* (100,000 as compared to 500,000 in 1900), but it was more costly. Its incredibly loyal readers paid 25 cents per copy, $3 per year, or $5 for the elaborate annual bound copies (Shrock 2004, 168–69).

Periodicals

Like novels and other forms of literature in America, many adult periodicals were initially patterned after English monthlies and quarterlies. Fewer than 100 periodicals, most of them short-lived, were issued before 1800, but by the middle of the nineteenth century almost 600 periodicals of various types were being printed in the United States. Illustrated magazines founded in the antebellum period like *Harper's* and *Frank Leslie's* had paved the way for this expansion, and their popular success ultimately brought domestic styles and formats to the reading public. Inexpensive periodicals without illustrations flourished due to advances in printing, but these were not all cheap rags. The leading quality publications of the second half-century were *The Atlantic* (formerly *The Atlantic Monthly*, 1857), a literary magazine edited by eminent writers and critics, including William Dean Howells; and the political magazine *The Nation* (1865).

One of the most important periodicals in the United States in the nineteenth century was the *North American Review* (founded 1815). Its editors included such literary figures as James Russell Lowell and Henry Adams; and its contributors included Henry James, H. G. Wells, and Mark Twain. Family magazines such as the *Saturday Evening Post* (1821) became vastly popular with the general public. Also among the well-known general interest periodicals were *Scribner's Monthly* (1870, and called *The Century* after 1881) and *Scribner's Magazine* (1887).

Among the journals for special audiences were monthlies and weeklies for women. Chief among these was *Godey's Lady's Book* (1830–1898) with its hand-colored fashion illustrations that are so prized by collectors. Although often thought of as a Civil War era periodical, *Godey's* remained vastly influential in setting the style in clothing, manners, and taste throughout the latter part of the nineteenth century. Women's magazines generally gained strength in the last quarter century. Readers could choose among *Ladies'* (later *Woman's*) *Home Companion* (1873), *McCall's Magazine* (1876), *Ladies' Home Journal* (1883), *Good Housekeeping* (1885), and *Vogue* (1892).

There were a number of illustrated periodicals founded in the period that were inexpensively priced and of great popular appeal throughout the United States. They included *Collier's* (1883), *Cosmopolitan* (1886), *McClure's Magazine* (1893), and *Munsey's Magazine* (1889). These were among the most influential of the so-called muckraking periodicals, named for their exposure of government and business corruption in the first decade of the twentieth century.

—*James M. Volo*

Poetry

The emergence of a truly indigenous English-language poetry in the United States during the last quarter of the nineteenth century was largely founded on the work of two poets, Walt Whitman (1819–1892) and Emily Dickinson (1830–1886). On the surface, these two poets could not have been less alike—one living in the light, one in the dark; one very public, the other reclusive; one optimistic, the other morose. What linked them was their common connection to Ralph Waldo Emerson and the daring originality of their work.

In 1855, Whitman completed the first edition of *Leaves of Grass*, a work that Emerson called "an American phenomenon." There was nothing among previous domestic works to compare it to. "We call *Leaves of Grass* a poem and Whitman a poet," Emerson wrote, "but that is only because we have no suitable category for it or him." Whitman, for his part, recognized Emerson as a dear friend and master, commending him in the dedication of his work (Smith 1981, 1004–5).

The men who ruled America in the postwar era made more money than the world had ever seen, but Whitman gained great influence among them and among educators and the general reading population. Whitman accepted the paradigm of an Industrial Age that seemingly channeled the strength of the nation into manufacturing, trust building, and moneymaking. He hoped that America would distribute its democracy to the whole world. "I perceive clearly," he wrote, "that the extreme business energy, and this almost maniacal appetite for wealth prevalent in the United States, are parts of amelioration and progress, indispensably needed to prepare the very results I demand. My theory [of spreading democracy] includes riches, and the getting of riches" (Butterfield 1947, 213).

Whitman understood that the nation also needed its own literature—a literary America divested of its British roots and British soul. "Open the doors of The West," he wrote, "Call for the new great masters to comprehend new arts, new perfections, new wants.... Here are to be obtained results never elsewhere thought possible." Whitman acclaimed the chaos and disorder of American life finding it filled with human possibilities. "The wild smack of freedom, California, money, electric-telegraphs, free-trade, iron and iron-mines—recognize without demur those splendid resistless black poems, the steam-ships of the seaboard states, and those other resistless splendid poems, the locomotives." Widely published and long-lived, Whitman was America's poet (Smith 1981, 1001–2).

Emily Dickinson, on the other hand, was a deeply sensitive woman who questioned the puritanical background of her family and soulfully explored her own spirituality, often in poignant, deeply personal poetry. Rarely published and almost unknown in her own illness-shortened lifetime, Dickinson is noted for her unconventional broken rhyming meter and the use of dashes and random capitalization as well as her creative use of metaphor and overall innovative style. Her work often reflected the keen insight she had into the human condition. At times characterized as a semi-invalid, a hermit, a heartbroken introvert, or a neurotic agoraphobic, her poetry is sometimes brooding and sometimes joyous and celebratory.

Whitman and Dickinson represent the birth of two major American poetic idioms—the unbounded and direct emotional expression of Whitman, and the dark obscurity and mystical style of Dickinson—both of which would profoundly stamp American poetry in the twentieth century. Whitman's long lines and his democratic inclusiveness stand in stark contrast with Dickinson's concentrated phrases, short lines, and truncated stanzas. The development of these idioms can be traced through the works of other poets such as Edwin Arlington Robinson (1869–1935), Stephen Crane (1871–1900), Robert Frost (1874–1963) and Carl Sandburg (1878–1967). As a result, by the beginning of the twentieth century the outlines of a distinctly new American poetic tradition were clear to see.

—James M. Volo

Regional Literature: Realism

The essence of the regional literature of the Industrial Era was the use of local color in stories and novels that explored the distinctive subcultures of the vast United States. The efforts to preserve regional culture in print during this period are not surprising given that a new mass, industrial culture was exerting a not altogether desirable homogenizing force on American society.

The realistic literature produced at the end of the nineteenth century retained streaks of nostalgia and romanticism, and the local color in fiction often took the form of nonstandard English, regional dialects, unusual settings, and the conflict between rural values and innovative ways of getting things done. In many ways, realism was the literary attempt to understand and control the forces of change assailing the nation in a truthful way that was not exaggerated, romanticized, or sensationalized.

Mark Twain, William Dean Howells, and Henry James were prominent in the realist movement from the 1880s to the early twentieth century. In many ways, Twain (Samuel Clemens) stands out as the dominant literary force in the period, and remains the most popular of the three. Besides his Western humor, his series of books about life on the Mississippi River stand out as examples of the use of local color. These include *The Adventures of Tom Sawyer* (1876), *Life on the Mississippi* (1883), and *The Adventures of Huckleberry Finn* (1885). Twain also invested in a publishing house and a series of technologically innovative printing machines. He went into debt to publish the memoirs of Ulysses Grant as the former president and general of the army lay dying of cancer. William Dean Howells exerted tremendous influence over high literature in the Industrial Age as assistant editor and then editor of the *Atlantic Monthly* (1866–1881); as editorial columnist in *Harper's Monthly* (1886–1892); as a consulting editor for the first issues of *Cosmopolitan*; and as a generally prolific and highly respected literary critic and author. He is perhaps best known today for his novels, *The Rise of Silas Lapham* (1885) and *A Hazard of New Fortunes* (1890), which showed a dark side of the capitalist economy of the Industrial Age. Henry James, though not as prolific as Howells or as popular as Twain, became famous for his novels such as *The Portrait of a Lady* (1881), *The Bostonians* (1886), and particularly *The Turn of the Screw* (1898).

Like Bret Harte and Mark Twain before him, Hamlin Garland drew on his experiences in the American West to affect his writing style, developing a specialty of presenting the details of farm life in the prairie states. *Main-Traveled Roads* (1891) and the story *Up the Coule* try to counter the romantic image of farming life that was then popular in the American press. His *Under the Lion's Paw* (1891) was famous for its bleak descriptions of the upper Midwest. Garland's autobiographical works, including *Boy Life on the Prairie* (1926), offer a more realistic image of childhood in the West while other works engage the political and social events of the time. The *Captain of the Gray-Horse* (1902) and *Cavanagh: Forest Ranger* (1910), for instance, examine the tensions between Westerners and the newly created Forest Service, while *Hamlin Garland's Observations on the American Indian* (1895) and *The Book of the American Indian* (1923) explore the issues surrounding the experiences of Native Americans.

Stephen Crane was also able to capture the West in his short stories, including *The Bride Comes to Yellow Sky* (1898) and *The Blue Hotel* (1898). As in his Civil War classic, *The Red Badge of Courage* (1895), Crane borrowed images of the West—and the stereotypes of that land—from the popular dime novels. He even poked fun at the dime novel's readers in stories like *The Blue Hotel*. The story includes a character named Swede, an ambiguous representation of the immigrants who played a key role in the frontier experience.

At the turn of the century, Owen Wister gave the tenets of western literature a modern twist in his novel *The Virginian* (1902). Based on the story of a Western cowboy with roots in the Old Dominion, the novel's hero clearly combines the tension between civilization and the frontier wilderness, which conflict stood at the center of the literary western. *The Virginian* was amazingly successful going through 6 printings in 6 weeks and 16 printings in the first year, and becoming the best-selling work in fiction in 1902. The novel, a staple of Western-style American literature, set off a renewed wave of Western genre novels during the first quarter of the twentieth century.

Other American novelists followed in Wister's footsteps, producing a formulaic pattern for the western genre. Included among these was B. M. Bower (Sinclair), the first woman to write westerns as a profession. Bower brought strong female characters to her westerns, especially in her popular *Chip of the Flying U* (1906). Beginning in 1904, Bower wrote 60 western novels before her death in 1940.

Ole E. Rölvaag, a Norwegian who moved to the Dakota prairies, gave voice to the immigrant frontier experience in his *Giants in the Earth: A Saga of the Prairie* (1927) and its sequel *Peder Victorious: A Tale of the Pioneers Twenty Years Later* (1929). Willa Cather's fiction, especially *My Ántonia* (1918) and *O Pioneer!* (1913), offered a female perspective on immigrant life on the prairies. Her novels present the challenges pioneers faced in farming the land as well as their love of the land.

Among the best of the regional authors was Sarah Orne Jewett, who wrote about her native state of Maine in stories like *A Marsh Island* (1885), *The Country of Pointed Firs* (1896), and *The Foreigner* (1900), each of which appeared in the better quality monthly periodicals, particularly *Atlantic Monthly*. The South had a number of regional authors: Joel Chandler Harris gained fame for his Uncle Remus stories that appeared in *Century* and *Scribner's Monthly* in the 1880s. Kate Chopin also gained recognition for her writing about her home state of Louisiana in works like the collection of short stories *Bayou Folks* (1894; Shrock 2004, 161–65).

COMMUNICATIONS: THE TELEPHONE

Today, the telegraph is a distant memory. In the last quarter of the nineteenth century, however, the telegraph was one of the most prevalent communications technologies in America. So, when Alexander Graham Bell announced the invention of his new device, the telephone, it was seen as simply an improvement to the telegraph—a speaking telegraph that had neither the long history of reliability or the backing of a giant company like Western Union behind it. Only later in the century were the telephone's unique characteristics fully understood and exploited.

In 1876, Bell—a teacher of the deaf by profession—constructed the telephone by combining a series of simple theoretical concepts into a complex but effective electrical mechanism that supposedly mimicked the functionalities of the ear. Within six months he had arranged a public demonstration of his device before a select group of scientific men gathered at Lyceum Hall in Salem, Massachusetts. Although the transmission wiring was makeshift, on March 15, 1877, Bell spoke into his instrument and received an answer from far away Boston. By 1878, the Bell Telephone Company had set up thousands of miles of wires and a series of giant switching boards capable of connecting Americans by voice in many cities. The terms for "leasing two telephones for social purposes connecting a dwelling-house with any other building" were set at $20 dollars a year, and "for business purposes" at $40 dollars a year (Adams 1946, 307).

Gardiner G. Hubbard, active director of the company, noted the advantages of a telephone "set in a quiet place" where noise would not interrupt ordinary conversation. He also noted, "The advantages of the Telephone over the Telegraph...are that no skilled operator is required, but direct communication may be had by speech without the intervention of a third person; that the communication is much more rapid [100 words a minute versus 20]; and it needs no battery and has no complicated machinery." Moreover, Hubbard suggested that the telephone lines could be erected by the business owner or "any good mechanic" with the total cost of poles, stringing, and sundries being $10 per mile. "Parties leasing the Telephones, however, incur no expense beyond the annual rental and repair of the line wire (Adams 1946, 307; Volo and Volo 2007, 96–97).

HEALTH AND MEDICINE

The Germ-Free Environment: Antiseptics

British surgeon Joseph Lister is widely known as the founder of the antiseptic hospital and germ-free surgery, a significant advance in the development of medicine in the nineteenth century. In 1861, Lister accepted a position as professor of surgery at the University of Glasgow where he began his experiments in antiseptic surgery. In Lister's day (before the development of antibiotics), surgical patients expected to experience infections after an operation, and the hospitals and wards often smelled of putrefaction (and sometimes gangrene). Child-bed fever—a deadly infection that swept through the maternity wards from mother to mother and newborn to newborn—was rampant. The cause of these infections was widely thought to be associated with so-called bad air or miasmic vapors, and was thought to be unavoidable. Many patients and surgeons opted to have their procedures done at home because there was less chance of infection there than in hospitals.

Lister was a knowledgeable physician well-versed in Pasteur's theories of contamination by airborne germs and other microorganisms, but Pasteur had killed his germs and bacteria by boiling, a technique that could be used on hospital linens and medical instruments but not on the patients themselves. However, in a conversation with a colleague trained in chemistry, Lister realized that certain chemicals could be used to kill bacteria not only on surfaces and instruments, but also in wounds and on bandages, and—most importantly—on the hands of the physician.

Lister reasoned that if germs in the hospital environment could be killed, then most infections could be prevented. A simple washing of the hands with soap and hot water before and after examining patients in the maternity ward had all but eradicated child-bed fevers where it was practiced. Carbolic acid, now called phenol (a pleasant-smelling form of alcohol), was already being used as a deodorizing agent and preservative in laboratories, and Lister thought it might kill germs. In 1865, he began using carbolic as an antiseptic before, during, and after surgery and published his data in 1867. Lister observed:

The principle, therefore, consists in surrounding a wound from its reception to its cure with an atmosphere charged with the vapor of the (Carbolic) acid: and to accomplish this the surgeon operates amid a thin cloud of spray made by atomizing a weak solution, in which his hands, instruments, sponges, are also immersed. The blood vessels are tied with carbolized cords, the edges of the wound closed by carbolized stitches, and finally layers of gauze impregnated with carbolic acid and resin are bound over the wound and a considerable part of the adjoining skin, the resin causing the carbolic acid to be evolved slowly, so that the dressing need not be changed for several days (quoted in Timmons 2005, 146–47).

In the United States, physicians were slow to accept Lister's practices. Eminent physician and medical author Dr. Samuel Gross noted as late as 1876 that little, if any, faith was placed in Lister's antiseptics in America. He observed that infection could be avoided if care was taken in making and changing dressings, clearing away cots and sickbeds, and excluding air from the wound. The first American hospital to adopt an antiseptic environment was Roosevelt Hospital in New York City (Timmons 2005, 146). As medical students and practicing physicians noted the great success in reducing hospital deaths from infection, Lister's procedures became accepted by the medical community.

—*James M. Volo*

Childbirth: Midwife to Obstetrician

While motherhood came to be the principal fulfillment of a woman, the pregnancy itself was a socially awkward time. Sex was a very private matter, and talk of it was taboo in polite circles. The presence of a pregnant woman was an unspoken reminder of sexual intercourse. Phrases such as "in a delicate condition" and "confinement" were used in Victorian America to describe the pregnancy and labor. Women were expected to avoid the public view as much as possible. Many women of the leisure class remained indoors for the latter part of their pregnancy rather than display their change of figure. One woman who attended a friend's party while seven months pregnant reported that she was allowed a seat where she could come in and out easily and keep out of harm's way. She apologized that she was not a "pretty figure" for company, and she hoped to manage so as not to be "obnoxious." A period journal advised mothers-to-be to breathe the atmosphere of refinement and peace, and in this time of seclusion, commune with their own heart and be still.

Most women delivered their babies at home, attended by an assortment of relatives, neighbors, and perhaps a midwife. Such a gathering of women provided support and encouragement for the new mother, and the extra hands were welcome should the labor be lengthy or an emergency arise. Early in the nineteenth century it became fashionable for upper- and upper-middle-class women to deliver at home by a male physician, particularly in Eastern cities. Physicians warned women that they were in danger if they did not receive proper medical attention during childbirth. Childbirth was always a danger, so to allay their fears, increasing numbers of women began to choose physicians over midwives. By the latter part of the century physicians became available even to poor women. This shift from midwife to physician had a dramatic affect on the birthing process. With midwifery, the community of women who came together for the birth of a child was completely in control and solidly bonded in their femininity. Their authority had been powerful and unquestioned. It was the one time when men kept to the shadows awaiting news while the women were in the forefront managing information and activity. Once delivery was in the hands of a physician, it became male controlled. It also altered the event from one of community and support to one of privacy and isolation. Physicians prohibited the participation of relatives and friends in the birthing process because the presence of these ancillary people was seen as a distraction and it weakened their authority.

Physicians charged more than midwives, and perhaps to justify their expense they utilized procedures that would not have been offered by midwives. Feminine modesty among some women brought about the situation where babies were delivered from beneath layers of sheets or even yards of skirts worn by the mother to protect her private parts from the doctor's eyes. Medical students were not permitted to watch actual deliveries and relied on mannequins and textbooks to learn their procedures. The *Obstetrical Catechism* of 1854 had urged physicians to be aware of the "sense of delicacy" on the part of the female and suggested that he obtain permission from the husband or matronly female prior to a hands-on examination. The doctor was then advised that the clothes should be properly raised at their lower edges, by the left hand, and then the right hand be passed cautiously up the clothes without uncovering the patient.

Doctors sometimes administered purgatives to the expectant women at the onset of delivery or bled her until she fainted thus stopping her from crying out. It was not unusual for physicians to use forceps to speed the delivery of the child, a novel procedure that sometimes resulted in rips in internal organs. One of the more horrible complications was vesico-vaginal fistulae. The result of tears in the walls between the vagina and bladder, this condition was characterized by continual leakage from the bladder. Thousands of women suffered from this complication, which often made them lifelong invalids and social outcasts.

By the end of the nineteenth century, birthing increasingly moved into the institutional environment of the hospital. This was especially true for newly arrived immigrants, unwed mothers, and homeless women—none of whom had strong community support nor a corp of experienced relations. It was hoped that the controlled environment of the hospital would help to eliminate the great killer of new mothers and their babies, known as child-bed or puerperal fever. Ironically, the reverse occurred. These lying-in or maternity hospitals were hotbeds of infection. Only women in the most desperate situations would go to a hospital to deliver. The poor women who turned to them were often used as subjects of examination and experimentation by doctors and medical students. Child-bed fever reached epidemic levels in hospitals during the nineteenth century as doctors, who failed to wash their hands between internal exams, carried the infection from patient to patient. Women who were attended by midwives occasionally contracted the disease, but because midwives did fewer internal exams and treated only one patient at a time, it was much less common that they spread infection. In 1883 at the Boston Lying-in Hospital, 75 percent of the mothers confined there contracted the infection and 20 percent died from it. While a number of physicians suspected that the infections were being spread by dirty hands, most doctors refused to believe that they were the cause of the problem, and the advocates of sanitation were ridiculed for their claims. It was not until Pasteur and Lister concluded that washing could prevent infection did the practice become accepted, but even then not everyone washed effectively, allowing the infections to claim mothers into the early decades of the twentieth century (Volo and Volo 2007, 196–97).

FOR MORE INFORMATION

Adams, James Truslow, ed. *Album of American History*. New York: Charles Scribner's Sons, 1946.

Bar, Paul. *The Principles of Antiseptic Methods Applied to Obstetric Practice*. Philadelphia, PA: P. Blakiston, Son & Co., 1887.

Butterfield, Roger. *The American Past: A History of the United States from Concord to Hiroshima, 1775–1945*. New York: Simon and Schuster, 1947.

Casper, Scott E., Joan Chaison, and Jeffery D. Groves, eds. *Perspectives on American Book History: Artifacts and Commentary*. Amherst: University of Massachusetts Press, 2002.

Davis, Allen F. "The Settlement House." In *The Social Fabric, American Life from the Civil War to the Present*, eds. John H. Cary and Julius Weinberg. Boston, MA: Little, Brown and Company, 1975.

Fischer, Claude S. *America Calling: A Social History of the Telephone to 1940*. Berkeley and Los Angeles: University of California Press, 1992.

Fisher, Richard B. *Joseph Lister, 1827–1912*. New York: Stein and Day, 1977.

Hofstadter, Richard, and Wilson Smith, eds. *American Higher Education, A Documentary History*. Chicago, IL: The University of Chicago Press, 1961.

Husband, Julie, and Jim O'Loughlin, *Daily Life in the Industrial United States, 1870–1900*. Westport, CT: Greenwood Press, 2004.

Jewett, Charles. *Manual of Rules for Child-bed Nursing*. Brooklyn, NY: Brooklyn Eagle Press, 1889.

Johnson, Clifton. *Old-Time Schools and School-books*. New York: Dover Publications, 1963.

Kelley, R. Gordon, ed. *Children's Periodicals of the United States*. Westport, CT: Greenwood Press, 1984.

Mason, Philip P., ed. *Copper Country Journal: The Diary of Schoolmaster Henry Hobart, 1863–1864*. Detroit, MI: Wayne State University Press, 1991.

Mauriceau, François. *The Diseases of Women with Child, and in Child-bed*. New York: Garland Press, 1985.

Metchnikoff, Elie. *The Founders of Modern Medicine: Pasteur, Koch, Lister*. Freeport, NY: Books for Libraries Press, 1971.

Mondale, Sarah, and Sarah B. Patton, eds. *School: The Story of American Public Education*. Boston, MA: Beacon Press, 2001.

Mott, Frank Luther. *A History of American Magazines*. 5 vols. Cambridge, MA: Harvard University Press, 1930–1968.

Shrock, Joel. *The Gilded Age*. Westport, CT: Greenwood Press, 2004.

Smith, Page. *The Nation Comes of Age: A People's History*. 4 Vols. New York: McGraw-Hill, 1981.

Tebbel, John, and Mary Ellen Zuckerman. *The Magazine in America, 1741–1990*. New York: Oxford University Press, 1991.

Timmons, Todd. *Science and Technology in Nineteenth-Century America*. Westport, CT: Greenwood Press, 2005.

Volo, Dorothy Denneen, and James M. Volo. *Family Life in Nineteenth-Century America*. Westport, CT: Greenwood Press, 2007.

Material Life

FOOD AND DRINK

The Best-Fed People in the World

The rise of modern mass society in the United States during the Industrial Age had a profound effect on food for the average American. Massive urban centers linked by an ever-growing network of railroads connected Americans like never before in history, and with the invention of refrigerated railroad cars and factories as well as agricultural mechanization there was a new ability to supply out-of-season vegetables and fruits, canned foods, and meats to Americans all over the country. As early as the 1850s, Americans were the best-fed people in the world. Meals tended to be large and heavy with ample meat—especially beef. The typical American consumed, on average, a little over 4,000 calories per day.

The appetite of Diamond Jim Brady was legendary during the 1890s. A gastronomic showman, he reflected the pomposity and excess of dining in the period. One New York restaurant reported that for breakfast Brady consumed a gallon of orange juice, three eggs, half a loaf of bread, a large steak, fried potatoes and onions, grits, bacon, muffins, and a stack of pancakes. His midday meal typically included three dozen oysters, two bowls of soup, a half-dozen crabs, seven or eight lobsters, a few portions of turtle meat, and a large steak. Dessert consisted of a platter of pastries and two pounds of chocolate candy. Brady ate four or five such meals daily (Elkort 1991, 132–33).

Although food along most transportation routes was of dubious quality before the 1870s, by the 1880s the quality of railroad food rose dramatically as intense competition among the growing number of lines caused many railroad companies to take losses on excellent food to draw riders. Travelers were aided further when Fred Harvey built 17 restaurants on railroad lines providing high-quality, affordable food served by pleasant waitresses in a clean environment.

Even though food was increasingly plentiful, there were poor Americans that suffered from hunger and malnutrition in the Industrial Age. Americans from the Northern city slums to Southern sharecroppers to hard-scrabble farmers on the Great Plains often lived on the edge of malnutrition, and many went hungry. Scarcity was being replaced by plenty, but in the modern market economy the inability to afford food could cause hunger and malnutrition as easily as famine (Shrock 2004, 97).

Dining Habits

The meals Americans ate were all relatively large by modern standards and somewhat different than today. Americans might eat some combination of breakfast, lunch, late supper, and dinner. Breakfast in the nineteenth century followed the ample American model, not the modest continental breakfast of a roll and coffee. A middle-class American might typically eat seasonal fruit, cereal, coffee or tea, eggs, meat or fish, potatoes, some kind of toast or muffin, and waffles, pancakes, or biscuits. Lunch or luncheon was the lighter informal midday meal for industrial workers. It might be a pail lunch eaten during a rushed break. Middle-class women used luncheon as a social event, whereas middle-class men might make it a business function. Late tea was primarily a middle-class event and denoted a lighter, informal evening meal served cold. Supper was much like late tea but was centered on a hot meal. Dinner could be taken from noon until late evening and was the formal main meal of the day. Dinner increasingly became an evening meal, particularly among the industrial working class and middle class, which worked far from home (Shrock 2004, 98).

Food Attitudes

Standard American food was heavily influenced by English cooking, with relatively few foreign influences. The average American in this era would have been working class, though there was great variation in the incomes of mainly native-born workers, who dominated the skilled jobs, and the immigrant workers largely stuck in unskilled positions. Virtually all of their work, however, required hard physical labor, so an average diet that included 4,000 calories a day was not out of step with their needs. Their food was rich and heavy, laden with butter, cream, sugar, and lard. The diet of the skilled worker at the Homestead steel plant was typical with oatmeal and milk, eggs, bacon, bread with butter and jelly, and coffee for breakfast. Lunch consisted of a quick meal of soup, bread, and fruit. Dinner was eaten in the evening with meat (most likely beef), beans, potatoes, fruits, beets, and pickles. Like many native-born American diets, the steelworkers' meals were relatively bland; Americans shared deep reservations about over-spicing foods and relied primarily on salt and small amounts of pepper, cloves, cinnamon, mace, ginger, nutmeg, and a few herbs.

The volume of food on an American table shocked foreign visitors. One reason for this was the long-term decline in food prices throughout the period. In 1898, one dollar could buy 43 percent more rice than in 1872, 35 percent more beans, 49 percent more tea, 51 percent more roasted coffee, 114 percent more sugar, 62 percent more mutton, 25 percent more fresh pork, 60 percent more lard and butter, and 42 percent more milk (Shrock 2004, 98–99).

Common Foods

Meat dominated the meals of most Americana and was relatively cheap compared to meat prices in Europe. Typical working Americans could afford to eat meat at two or three meals a day. Whereas pork had been the universal meat throughout all of America before the Civil War, by the Industrial Age inexpensive beef was flooding urban markets, and it became the overwhelming favorite. G. H. Hammond invented the refrigerated railroad car in 1871, and by the 1890s entire meatpacking plants were refrigerated. With railroads connecting the Great Plains to cities, refrigeration made it possible for inexpensive beef to reach most regions of the nation. Beef was eaten at every meal, often sliced thinly and often fried and eaten with gravy. Roast beef, corned beef, beef tongue, as well as the fine cuts such as sirloin, porterhouse, tenderloin, and filet were all popular among Americans. Indeed, as working-class incomes rose, so too did the consumption of beef. Other types of meat were also widely eaten, including lamb, turkey, chicken, duck, goose, and pork. While Americans of English stock sometimes held onto the tradition of beef or goose at Christmas, by the end of the century most Americans had made turkey their meat of choice for the holiday. Employers were already giving away free turkeys to their employees by the 1880s. Wild game was still popular throughout rural areas, particularly duck, deer, goose, turkey, antelope, buffalo, and rabbit, but its importance in American diets was declining markedly.

Fresh seafood was important in the American diet only on the coasts, with the notable exception of oysters. Average Americans ate little fresh seafood beyond fish if they lived in the interior of the country, away from the fishing fleets of the East and West Coasts. Turtle soup and lobsters were quite popular but expensive delicacies. Fresh oysters proved to be the exception, and they were universally popular with Americans of all social classes. Middle- and upper-class dinner parties often began with oysters on the half shell, fried oysters, or an oyster soup while working-class Americans enjoyed the repast in oyster bars and saloons where they were sold for one penny each on the waterfront. Even on the mining frontiers in California, Nevada, Idaho, and Colorado oysters on the half shell were common and popular. Reno, Nevada's Capital Chop House advertised that it always kept fresh seafood and transported oysters on hand that could be served at all hours, in any style desired. Even if fresh seafood, aside from oysters, was not readily available in the interior of the country, canned seafood including crab, lobster, oysters, salmon, sardines, and innumerable varieties of sauced, smoked, and pickled canned fish were becoming much more common.

Dairy production also increased during the period thanks to the railroad system, which allowed for daily pickups of fresh milk. Dairy farmers sold 2 billion pounds of milk in 1870, but that figure rose to a staggering 18 billion by 1900. Milk was a popular beverage during the period, and demand remained high despite concerns over disease carried in the milk. The increase was due not only to better transportation but also to farmers discovering that dairy cows produced more milk if fed fresh, green feed. Also, in 1890, Dr. Stephen Babcock invented a machine that could ascertain the butterfat content of milk, which made it easier for farmers to monitor and control the quality of their product and improve their herds. These improvements also made the production of other dairy products more profitable, such as cheese, cottage cheese, butter, and cream cheese. In addition to milk, butter was by far the most popular dairy product. Butter was used heavily on bread, in baking, and to make sauces for meats, oysters, or fish. During the period large quantities of butter were mass-produced in factories, which improved in speed and quantity with the 1880 invention of the mechanical cream separator. Many rural Americans, however, continued to produce their own butter, particularly because of the fears of tuberculosis spread through dairy products. Most farm-produced butter, often called dairy butter, was packed in round decorative molds that were commonly four inches in diameter.

Americans consumed far more meat than vegetables. The vegetables they ate in the largest quantities were primarily potatoes, sweet potatoes, squash, cabbage, dried beans, and rice, with only small sides of yellow or leafy green vegetables. Potatoes were such a staple that they appeared at breakfast, lunch, and evening meals, and came in a dizzying array of preparations: broiled, mashed, fried, stewed, baked, escalloped, and French-fried. The average person seldom ate raw vegetables. Although, there were regional exceptions, most people considered them to contain low levels of natural poisons. Native-born Americans boiled vegetables for an hour or more under the conception that this would boil out the toxins. *The Nevada Cookbook,* compiled by the good women of Carson City in 1887, declared that vegetables had to be well cooked because raw vegetables were neither good nor wholesome.

Fresh fruits grew in popularity throughout the period. The massive expansion of railroad networks, refrigerated railroad cars, and agricultural mechanization brought a large supply of out-of-season fruits into American homes. Strawberries from the Carolinas, the Gulf States, Arkansas, Missouri, and Tennessee made their way to Northern markets. A wide array of citrus fruits, like oranges, grapefruits, and lemons came from California and Florida. Oranges were commonly put in children's stockings at Christmas. Fruits produced outside of the United States, such as bananas and pineapples, also appeared. Less exotic fruits including peaches, grapes, cantaloupes, avocados, pears, plums, apricots, cherries, raspberries, and blueberries were available much of the year. Apples continued to be the most popular fruit in the United States.

Sugar, specifically refined, white granulated sugar, also became a major part of the average person's diet during this period. Sugar underwent a revolution in production, which made it more affordable. Greater importation of international sugar, combined with the mechanization of domestic sugar production, caused sugar prices to fall during the Civil War. Sugar, which had once been considered a luxury item only the wealthy could afford, became a necessity for the average American who was consuming an average of 41 pounds of sugar annually by the early 1870s. Food preparers catered to the American demand for sugar, putting it into a wide variety of products. Per capita sugar consumption surged to 68 pounds by 1901.

The increased availability of sugar also served to develop a wider variety of desserts including hot and cold puddings, tarts, pies, breads, cakes, custards, jellies, and preserves. Forty-two percent of the recipes found in the *Ladies' Home Journal* from 1884 through 1912 were for desserts.

Ice cream, which had been an exotic, elite treat as late as the 1830s, was common and relatively inexpensive by the mid-century. Ice cream saloons and soda fountains, a concept that appealed to women dedicated to the temperance movement, flourished during the last quarter of the century. By the 1880s ice cream could be purchased for as little as a penny a glass and street vendors sold the treat for even less. Home ice-cream makers had been available to the elite in the 1840s, but they were within reach of the middle class by 1880. By 1895 almost anyone could afford a small, two-quart ice-cream maker, which retailed from $1.50 in the *Montgomery Ward Catalogue*.

Chocolate also captured the hearts of Americans during this period. Chocolatier, Stephen Whitman, copied French methods to create the chocolate candy industry in the 1860s, but the treats were relatively expensive and generally associated with women and as a gift for a sweetheart until the 1890s. Candy makers such as Milton Hershey changed those perceptions when they developed a chocolate specifically designed for children's tastes by adding milk. Hershey would go one step further by making his chocolate less expensive. Hershey penny bars and over 130 chocolate novelties drew a massive number of consumers by 1899 (Shrock 2004, 99–103).

Home Canning

Home canning of vegetables and fruits continued in popularity. The preservation of the harvest had always been essential to a family's survival, and the tradition continued even though canned foods were becoming increasingly available. Screw-top canning jars were first invented in 1858 by John Mason and had seen many refinements by the time the Ball Brothers began to offer their Ball jar in 1884. The glass jars could be boiled before using to destroy pathogens, and the glass imparted no unusual taste to the contents as tinned iron cans sometimes did. Homemakers began to preserve a much wider variety of fruits and vegetables than ever before due to the increased availability of fresh fruits and vegetables. Cookbooks provided a wide assortment of recipes for canning such diverse products as plum marmalade, brandied peaches, tomatoes, corn, and watermelon rind.

—*Dorothy Denneen Volo*

Food Processors and Brand Names

Much of the meat, grains, vegetables, and fruits that were becoming more available to Americans were provided by increasingly large food processors. Businesses learned that they could consolidate, create very large business enterprises, charge less for their product than a small business, and earn enormous profits. They also realized that by creating national brand names they could create buyers and even charge higher prices by guaranteeing consistent quality. Very large producers emerged, jockeying for market position through brand-name use and advertising. Gustavus Swift and Philip Danforth Armour joined with a few others, for example, to create the "Big Five" in meat-packing. Known as the "Beef Trust" to reformers, the group controlled a massive market and drove out competitors. Washburn-Crosby, with its brand name Gold Medal Flour, and Pillsbury dominated the flour industry. The American Sugar Refining Company took control of most of the sugar industry with its brand mane, Domino, and started a successful campaign to convince the public that brown sugar was full of dangerous microbes (Schrock 2004, 104–5).

New brand names also arose in the processed cereal industry as Americans were introduced to breakfast cereals on a mass scale for the first time. John Kellogg created and marketed a cereal similar to the granula invented by Caleb Jackson in 1863 and was promptly sued. Kellogg changed the "u" in granula to an "o" and granola was born. In 1894 John and his brother, Will, were searching for a digestible bread substitute to improve the diet of hospital patients at their Sanatorium in Battle Creek, Michigan. While in the process of boiling wheat, they accidentally left a pot of boiled wheat to stand and the wheat became very soft. When Kellogg rolled the softened wheat and let it dry, each grain of wheat emerged as a large thin flake. The flakes turned out to be a tasty cereal. Kellogg called this discovery "Granose." The cereal met with initial resistance as people were used to eating hot cereal in the morning, and they found the idea of a cold breakfast cereal unappealing. Will adapted the idea to corn in 1898. He developed flakes of toasted corn and malt and called the creation Kellogg's Corn Flakes. Nonetheless, the Kellogg's weren't the first to market dry breakfast cereal.

C. W. Post was a patient at Kellogg's Sanatorium in 1891. He realized that health foods, and in particular, coffee substitutes were potential goldmines. He started his own health institute, right in Battle Creek. Within four years, he had developed Postum, a wheat- and molasses-based hot beverage. Post mounted an ad campaign that made the product a success. "There was," he said, "no limit to the number of physical and moral ills caused by coffee, but it could all be improved with Postum, the beverage that 'makes red blood.'" In 1897, he introduced a grain beverage called, Grape Nuts, which was sweetened with maltose, which Post called grape sugar, and had a nut-like flavor. It was a failure as a beverage, but turned out to be a fantastic breakfast cereal, catapulting him to the head of the cereal business.

Inspired by these successes, a breakfast-cereal rush took place around the turn of the century. Henry D. Perky of Denver, Colorado, made a machine in 1893 that shredded wheat and formed it into little pillow-shaped biscuits, which he marketed as Shredded Wheat. In Battle Creek, where Kellogg and Post were located, dozens of factories sprang up, producing cereals like Tryabita, Strengtho, Corno, Malta Vita, and Maple-Flakes. Most did not last long. By 1902, 30 different cereal flake companies had crowded into the small town. Cereal soon found its way into the mass market, well beyond the health-food stores and spas where these kinds of products were initially found. A revolution in America's breakfast eating habits had begun.

—*Dorothy Denneen Volo*

Commercially Canned Foods

The incredible spread of canned foods during the Industrial Age also transformed American eating habits. Canned goods were available before the Civil War, but the invention of the pressure cooker in 1874 by K. A. Shriver gave canners control of the heating of canned goods, which allowed them to kill the germs in the sealed cans by heating them and still kept the cans from exploding in the process. Canning factories grew from under 100 in 1870 to almost 1,800 in 1900. Technological improvements transformed can-making from a hand process to a machine process that could churn out 2,500 cans an hour in the mid-1880s and 6,000 cans an hour by the mid-1890s. Processors like Heinz, Franco-American, Joseph H. Campbell Preserve Company (Campbell Soup Company), Norton Brothers Company, and a host of smaller producers canned a stunning variety of fruits, vegetables, soups, milk, seafood, and meats. Canned goods fanned throughout the nation via the ever-expanding railroad lines bringing exotic food to isolated regions and breaking the monotony of frontier food. Growers actually experimented with new strains of fruits and vegetables that would meet the demands of industrial canning. Processed foods were becoming a much more important part of the average American's diet during the Industrial Age (Shrock 2004, 105–6).

Beverages

The most common beverages were water, coffee, and milk. Temperance advocates encouraged the drinking of water, and virtually every eating establishment in the country served iced water by this time. Cocoa, lemonade, as well as hot and iced tea, both green and black, were also popular beverages. Soda fountains sprang up in cities and towns throughout the country as an alternative to saloons, and the new availability of fruits led to a wide variety of flavored sodas that sold for $.02. The most popular flavors were vanilla, strawberry, pineapple, and ginger. Many popular carbonated beverages can trace their origins to this era. Charles Hire introduced a new root beer, which he deftly maneuvered to be the National Temperance drink. Hire's Root Beer sold three million bottles in 1893. Dr Pepper, was invented by Charles Alderton in a Waco, Texas, drug store and fountain in 1885. It caught on quickly in Waco, where it was first requested by the name of the town. It is not clear when the name became Dr Pepper. The beverage was said to offer an energy boost when consumed at the appropriate times of the day, 10, 2, and 4. It received national attention when it was introduced nationwide at the 1904 World's Fair in St. Louis. In 1886, Atlanta druggist, Dr. John Pemberton, developed a soothing cough syrup made with a soda water base, cola nut extract, and liberal doses of caffeine and coca leaf extract (cocaine). An employee mixed some with carbonated water and Coca-Cola made its debut. The coca leaf was later eliminated from the recipe. Pepsi-Cola was created by Caleb Bradham in his New Bern, North Carolina, pharmacy in 1898.

The consumption of hard liquor decreased throughout the Industrial Age, reaching a low mark of 1.2 gallons per capita from 1870 to 1900, primarily because it continued to be expensive and frowned upon by temperance advocates, though there was great demand for champagne. American beer consumption, however, vastly increased, climbing from 2.7 gallons per capita in 1855 to 15.5 gallons per capita in 1900. While European immigration certainly had much to do with beer's rising popularity, native-born working-class consumption also rose (Shrock 2004, 103).

Immigrant Food Traditions

As immigrants poured into the United States, they brought with them eating and cooking habits outside the mainstream of traditional Anglo-American cooking. Middle-class reformers attacked immigrant foods because of the traditional Anglo-American dislike for highly spiced foods and because of new ideas on nutrition. Scientific nutritionists firmly believed that heavily spiced foods required much more energy to digest and also caused alcohol cravings. Ethnic prejudice ignored the fact that spices often made cheap cuts of meat palatable. Nutritionists also attacked the practice of making heavy stews, soups, gulyashen, and borschts as dangerous because these mixtures of pasta, meat, and vegetables required excessive energy to digest. They advocated the Anglo-American method of cooking and eating each dish separately, which, according to the science of the day, was more efficiently digested. Nutritionists also criticized the light continental breakfast that many immigrants ate as unhealthy.

European immigrants largely ignored these middle-class attempts at reforming their food-eating habits, though different ethnic groups assimilated to American food at varying rates and degrees. In heavily populated ethnic enclaves, specialty stores would often emerge, catering to Old World food desires of their people. Most ethnic groups readily adopted more meat into their dishes when they found prices significantly cheaper in the United States (Shrock 2004, 107–9).

Eating Out

Americans in the Industrial Age ate out at restaurants more than ever. As more Americans joined the ranks of the salaried and wage earners, wages rose and a new leisure culture developed, eating out became much more common. Restaurants, lunch counters, saloons, and bars became important sources for a quick bite, leisurely dinner and special entertainment, though "proper ladies" would never enter a saloon or bar.

With more Americans in the industrial and office workforces, fast inexpensive lunches that could be purchased came into demand. For middle- and working-class men the saloon's free lunch was ubiquitous across the country and provided ample lunch for the cost of a 5-cent beer. Typical saloon lunches consisted of a buffet of bread or crackers, bologna or sliced meat, sliced tomatoes, salad, pickles, onions, radishes, and perhaps a hot stew or soup. These meals were incredible bargains when even inexpensive restaurants charged 15 cents for a meal. Not every saloon offered a free meal, but those that did not often provided a businessman's lunch for 10 to 20 cents. For people concerned with the presence of alcohol, numerous fast and relatively inexpensive 15-cent restaurants opened that catered to the array of business people, clerks, and retail workers in the downtown business corridors of American cities. The restaurants varied but offered items such as sandwiches, salads, and soups. Street vendors also provided large amounts of fast food to urban workers in fabulous variety. One well-organized street vendor business, the Mexican Food Corporation, blanketed New York City with white-clad vendors selling hot tamales (Shrock 2004, 109–10).

Charles Feltman is generally credited with introducing the frankfurter to the United States. Like many immigrants, Feltman operated a pushcart business. He sold meat pies in Coney Island, New York. Feltman's business began to drop off after the new hotels were built and had opened dining rooms. He decided to offer frankfurter sandwiches. He soon had enough money to open Feltman's German Beer Garden. His beef and pork mixture frankfurters were sizzled on a hot griddle and served in a warm bun garnished with homemade mustard and sauerkraut. Customers washed down their spicy sandwiches with a mug of beer or cherry soda. The hot dog sold for 10 cents, the soda was 3 cents, and the beer was a nickel (Elkort 1991, 168).

When they were concentrated in enough cities, most ethnic groups had restaurateurs open establishments that catered specifically to their food desires. The restaurants ranged from elite, expensive enterprises to moderately priced, down to quite cheap. Medium-priced German, French, Italian, Spanish, Chinese, and Jewish restaurants were in most major cities. New York even boasted a number of English chophouses where tripe, liver and bacon, Welsh rarebit, and pork and mutton pies were on the menu. The restaurants, however, catered mainly to these ethnic groups and not to native-born Americans. Italian spaghetti joints were one of the few ethnic restaurants to attract native-born Americans by the 1890s.

The American elite, unlike most native-born Americans, adopted a foreign culinary style as their preferred food, the French haute cuisine. French restaurants were the most popular fine dining establishments in the country, and none was more renowned than Delmonico's, founded in New York City in 1832. The celebrated establishment featured such exotic foods as grouse, truffled pig's feet, bear steak, green turtles, and beluga caviar. French chefs were hired by the wealthy, often at exorbitant salaries. The conspicuous consumption of the elite demanded that they illustrate their taste with the finest French foods and incredibly elaborate dinner parties. The eating habits of the American elite tended toward the heavy side despite their sedentary work habits. A typical dinner party menu consisted of a dizzying array of courses. The menu from General Winfield Scott Hancock's dinner party at Delmonico's in 1880 was typical. The dinner consisted of: raw oysters, two soups, hors d'oeuvres, a fish course, Relevés (a saddle of lamb and a filet of beef), entrées (chicken wings with peas and lamb chops with beans and mushroom-stuffed artichokes), terrapin en casserole á la Maryland, sorbet (to clear the palate), and roast canvasback duck and quail. For dessert there was timbale Madison, an array of ice creams, whipped creams, jellied dishes, banana mousse, and elaborate confectioneries. Fruit, petit fours, coffee, and liquors followed the dessert.

Almost all things French were good to the new American elite whose vast industrial fortunes and lack of family pedigree made them intent upon showing each other how polished and refined they could be. As often has been the case in American history, the rich valued every cultural refinement of Europe over everything American. The elite were the first to adopt French salad, mainly because lettuce was an expensive luxury only the wealthy could afford outside of those rural Americans who grew their own. Lettuce varieties in the nineteenth century wilted quickly and bruised so easily that transport was difficult until the development of iceberg head lettuce in 1903.

Of all the fine dining establishments devoted to other ethnic foods throughout urban America, none were more popular than French restaurants. Elite fine dining tended to gravitate toward restaurants like Delmonico's. Other such establishments in New York included the Hoffman House, the Savoy, the Waldorf-Astoria, and the Imperial. Boston had Young's Hotel and the Parker House. In Philadelphia there was the Continental. Chicago had the Palmer House and Sherman House. In New Orleans there was the St. Charles. San Francisco had the El Dorado House, Marchand's, Café Riche, and West Coast Delmonico's. Denver boasted six fine restaurants that specialized in haute cuisine (Shrock 2004, 111–13).

—*Dorothy Denneen Volo*

Middle-Class Dinner Parties

Middle-class Americans eagerly adapted elite forms to their own situations in an attempt to clearly show their refinement and gentility, not only to others but also to themselves. The United States was a rapidly changing, highly mobile society with a volatile boom-and-bust economy, which made the middle class eager to establish clear class boundaries and create unity and coherence among themselves. The Victorian middle class adopted increasingly complex etiquette formulas in all facets of life, and dining became one of the major expressions of their desire to codify appropriate behavior in etiquette manuals and even cookbooks. For a group often only a generation away from very simple roots, these complex dining rituals reinforced their own sense of superiority and group solidarity. Dressing for dinner, for example, became an important symbol of middle-class propriety, even in the comfort of one's own home, taking precedence over dining comfort.

Mimicking the upper class, the middle class also began to put great emphasis on dinner parties. At more formal parties the hostess would send out engraved invitations by messenger, often listing the menu and the people attending, who were to be—according to the etiquette manuals—all relatively of the same social rank. Women dressed according to the latest fashion, but without arms or necks bared, and men generally wore dress coats and trousers. When dinner was to be served, the hostess would not turn to her husband as he escorted the lady of honor from the drawing room to the dining room followed by the gentlemen escorting their assigned dinner partners with the older, more socially prestigious going first. The hostess would be seated last, escorted by the gentleman of honor. As guests dined on the multi-course meal the hostess was responsible for maintaining a nice flow of uncontroversial conversation. Etiquette writers warned diners never to comment on the food, never touch the food with a hand, take small portions, take small bites, eat slowly, and eat with the proper utensil with easy facility. Additionally, they were to control their emotions and stifle all bodily concerns. Most etiquette writers recommended one to two hours for dinner parties.

The ample food was served à la Russe, which meant that the bulk of the food was placed on a sideboard and served in courses. Servants were required for this type of dinner party, and etiquette writers recommended one servant for every three guests for serving and clearing of plates. Middle-class food was definitely showing the influence of French cooking by the 1880s, but it continued to embrace the largely Anglo-American cooking heritage. Etiquette writer Mary Slurwood recommended this simple menu for a middle-class dinner party. The dinner included,: oysters, soup à la Reine, broiled fish, Filet de Boef aux Champignons of roast beef or mutton, roast partridges, tomato salad, cheese, flavored ices, jellies, fruit, coffee, liqueurs, and a variety of wines (Chablis, Rhine wine, champagne, claret and burgundy or sherry). The middle-class dinner party differed somewhat in the types of food presented, but not at all in the quantity. The much talked about servant shortage of the late nineteenth century was a constant concern for middle-class women eager to throw elegant dinner parties.

These dinner parties required fairly elaborate spaces in which these dramas could be played out. Increasingly, dining rooms were necessary symbols of gentility to the middle class. Dining rooms would be equipped with dinner party necessities. In addition to a dining room suite of furniture, which included a large sideboard to be used for storage and service, a wide array of crystal, cut glass, china, and silverware were needed for a party. An 1873 etiquette writer recommended that every family possess the following: three dozen wine glasses, two dozen champagne glasses, two dozen claret glasses, three dozen goblets, six water carafes, six decanters, one liqueur stand, twelve liqueur glasses, two glass pitchers, one celery glass, one trifle bowl, eight dessert dishes, one full dinner service, one common set earthenware for the kitchen, one common tea service, one good tea service, one breakfast service, and one good dessert service. This list did not even include the required silverware, which in an 1873 guidebook was listed as three dozen forks, two dozen tablespoons, a dozen and a half dessert spoons, two dozen teaspoons, six salt spoons, one cheese knife, four butter knives, one asparagus tong, two sugar tongs, two soup ladles, four sauce ladles, two gravy ladles, two sugar ladles, a fish slice, cheese scoops, and grape scissors (Shrock 2004, 113–15).

HOUSING: ROOM LAYOUT

The private homes of the Victorian middle class had several common characteristics. The parlor was the most public room in the Victorian house. Parlors were common to both the North and the South and across the middle class. Some more affluent homes had a front parlor solely dedicated to formal visitations and a back parlor for family use, but a single parlor was most common. The parlor was the place where visitors would be received, and therefore where the first impressions of a family were formed. Decorating decisions were made in a very calculated manner so as to project the image a family wished to convey. The parlor contained a family's best in every way. It would have the highest ceilings, the largest fireplace, the most elaborate moldings, and the best furnishings.

The central feature of most parlors was a large circular table with a kerosene or oil lamp. Here the family would gather to write, read, converse, play games, or engage in needlework. The need to gather around the central light, which may have been the only one in the room, helped to foster a communal attitude. The parlor table allowed family members to be together, yet various members of the family could be engaged in a variety of pastimes. They were able to function as individuals yet remain a part of the family community as a whole.

The second focal point of the parlor was the fireplace. The mantel was often heavily decorated with pictures, collected natural objects, or mementos. What could not fit on the mantel would be placed on shelves or étagères around the room. An intense appreciation of nature prevailed during this time, leading to the collection of seashells, fossils, minerals, pinecones, and dried flowers, which might all be displayed in the parlor. It was felt that natural objects reflected the harmony of nature and civilization. Homes decorated with objects of nature were thought to demonstrate nature's beauty in family life. Additionally, using natural objects as decorative accents showed a wife's sense of economy, an attribute much extolled.

Other furnishings might include an upholstered sofa, armchairs, and a pair of easy chairs all done in matching fabric. Rocking chairs were very much in fashion, and parlors were just one room in which they might be found. Common upholstery materials included brocades, silk damask, and tapestry, which were adorned with tassels, cords, and fringe. It was not unusual for sofa ensembles to contain a large gentleman's armchair and a smaller chair with half arms for the lady, which accommodated her wide skirts and kept her posture properly erect. The placement of chairs around the room allowed social groupings to change as activities varied. A person might move from the solitary activity of reading quietly to join a game with other family members at the table. Sofas were designed with slight curves to encourage conversation.

Ownership of a piano or parlor organ heralded solid middle-class status. In 1855, a German-born American piano maker named Henry Steinway began to manufacture a piano with a cast-iron frame that gave its sound much greater brilliance and power than earlier forms. There have been no fundamental changes in the design and construction of pianos since 1855. This improvement prompted widespread interest in pianos and musical compositions for it. More than 20,000 pianos a year were being produced in the United States by the time of the Civil War. Retailers offered terms even for their least expensive models, which sold for as little as $300, and advertisements for pianos and organs filled period newspapers. Parlor organs tended to be an outgrowth of domestic religious worship that celebrated hymns and church music. These were particularly important to homes that actively fostered the Christian development of family.

The walls of a home were often wallpapered. Patterns showing large bouquets tied with ribbons or of oversized fruit became popular a decade before the war and stayed in style thereafter. Walls were usually further ornamented with paintings and, for the less affluent, prints. Attractive prints of good quality and color became readily available during the 1860s, and many families took advantage of this new technology. Subjects included farmyard scenarios, riverscapes, European scenes, hunting vignettes, still life, and biblical tableaus. The popularity of farmyard pictures in homes decorated in brocade and tassels can be attributed to the passion for harmony with nature and an underlying yearning for simpler times.

European subjects might be reminders of the travels family members might have made, like a Grand Tour—a fact the family would have been desirous to publicize. Another popular subject was famous people, both historical and contemporary. The prominent people came from musical, literary, political, and military venues. Representations of these people might take the form of a painting, print, engraving, or bust. Which public figures a family chose to decorate their home made a powerful statement about the owners.

Not only did the selection of these works of art show good taste and education, they served as silent but concrete reminders of revered values. George Washington, for example, was admired as a selfless leader who put the public interest above his private preferences. The presence of his picture in the parlor showed that these attributes were valued by the family. These pictures served as constant reminders to children of what was expected of them in adulthood. Many of the women depicted in this form were wives of famous men, such as Mary Todd Lincoln, or entertainers like the singer Jenny Lind. The message for young girls was one of the expectation that they would be quiet movers gently working behind the scenes. Many women understood this and participated in benevolent activities such as serving in hospitals, sewing for troops, and assisting orphans and needy families.

Floors were carpeted. However, carpets were sold by the linear yard and were a little more than two feet wide. They had to be pieced and sewn together much like wallpaper. Patterns tended to be floral or other naturals. Carpets would additionally be covered by mats in high-traffic areas or where fireplace sparks were likely.

Windows were almost buried beneath a shroud of fabrics. Closest to the window would be a thin curtain most likely of lace. This would be covered with a second layer made of heavy fabric that could be closely drawn to block out the light entirely. The ensemble would be topped off with a valance fashionably trimmed with cords, tassels, and braid. Overall, the Victorian parlor was a place of abundant accumulation. It also gives insight into the spirit and the structure of the society of which it was a part.

Victorians revered intellectual pursuits. Books were therefore a must in the parlor. More than 90 percent of white men and women could read. Diary entries refer to reading more than to any other pastime. Large, heavy Bibles were most often displayed on the central table as a symbol of family religious life. Other books were frequently displayed on tables or built-in bookshelves. Books brought learning and the world outside into the home. Although it was common to see period house plans showing libraries—and trade catalogs displayed library furniture—only the rich and the upper middle class could afford libraries.

The library was truly a man's domain. It was a place to which he could retreat and engage in the kind of activities not traditionally associated with home life. Here a man could smoke, drink, and discuss money, politics, and war without exposing the rest of the family to such vulgarities. Libraries were usually on the ground floor but off to one side. Decorations were more subdued than in the parlor. Walls were paneled or done in dark-colored paper. Heavy bookshelves were often featured. Other furniture would include a desk or writing table, large gentlemen's chairs, and various tables. If a man had hobbies or interests, it would be here that he would pursue them. Specimen cases containing fossils or insects would be displayed among accompanying magnifying glasses and other optical aids.

The luxury of a room dedicated solely to the purpose of dining was another badge of middle-class status. Families of lesser means ate in the kitchen or in an area adjacent to the parlor set aside for dining. Dining room furniture tended to be massive, often of mahogany or other dark wood. Sets made of walnut or oak were considered inexpensive. The standard number of chairs was eight. A sideboard was common, providing an excellent place to display oversized serving pieces and candelabras. Walls tended to be dark to show up well under candlelight, the standard lighting for this room. Even during luncheons it would not be unusual to draw the draperies and eat by candlelight. The formal dining experience was one of tremendous ritual and ostentation. Books of etiquette contained pages upon pages of rules guiding proper behavior while dining. Certain foods required highly specialized serving or eating utensils, and form was extremely important. There were 10 pages of a 30 page book dedicated just to the etiquette of carving. Beginning in the mid-nineteenth century the upper class developed a passion for complicating the dining process by introducing needless table items such as spoon warmers in an attempt to ritualize the process and to distinguish those in the know.

The one utilitarian room in the nineteenth-century house was the kitchen. It was here that the most mundane, labor-intensive household duties took place. The kitchen was always located on the ground floor and had a door to the outside to facilitate deliveries. It was not necessary for the kitchen to be adjacent to the dining room, and in certain circles distance was considered an asset, keeping odors contained. Kitchen furnishings were functional and simple. There was usually a large central work table and a cupboard for storing dishes.

The kitchen floor was often covered with an oil cloth, which cleaned easily and was much better than a painted floor because it can be moved outside for a good scrubbing. In many homes the kitchen was also the scullery and the laundry. If that were the case, there would also be a deep sink with a drying rack for washing vegetables and pots. Indoor sinks generally had hand pumps but no drains, so that dirty water had to be bailed out and emptied outside. Dishes were washed in a large wooden bowl as a measure to keep down breakage. Pots were stored by hanging them from racks.

In many homes the dominant feature in the kitchen would have been the wood-burning stove. Stoves had become fairly standard in Northern middle-class homes. In rural areas, particularly among the lower classes, cooking was still done on the hearth. There were those who felt that the hearth was the traditional heart of the home and resisted the kitchen stove. Other furnishings included the ice chest and meat safe. The meat safe was a kind of screened cupboard that protected the meat from insects, pests, and vermin but did nothing to regulate temperature. Dry goods such as flour, sugar, and cornmeal were stored in crockery or wooden containers. Rural kitchens and those of families of lesser means were also likely to be more family oriented. They may well have been used for activities such as sewing or helping children with studies and would probably contain additional furnishings to suit their multiuse needs.

The bedroom of the nineteenth century was very different from that of the previous century. It was no longer a semipublic place in which one received close acquaintances. It was now a very private place that would not even be referred to in polite conversation. Bed curtains had disappeared. Clothing was stored in chests of drawers and wardrobes. Built-in closets had come into vogue in the 1860s. Beside the bed might be found a small table upon which to rest the chamber stick used to guide one to the bedroom upon retiring. Oil lamps were usually not found in bedrooms, as carrying an oil lamp with its liquid fuel from room to room was a dangerous endeavor. People did not sit in bed and read before sleeping, nor did they lounge about in their lingerie. Bedrooms were likely to be drafty places most of the year.

Cribs and cradles were frequently found close to the parents' bed to facilitate breastfeeding and as a precaution should the child take ill during the night. Older children in lower economic situations might also sleep in the same room. Children of wealthy families would sleep in the nursery with their nanny.

Families who could afford it had a nursery for the children. As the century progressed, children came to be thought of as innocent beings in need of protection and sheltered from exposure to the world outside. The nursery provided this environment. It could limit the amount and kind of stimulation a child received and might possibly protect him or her from accidents and disease. Modest households had a single nursery room, often found on the third floor. Affluent households could afford both day and night nurseries. These rooms were designed to withstand the abuse children can inflict on furnishings. Walls were often whitewashed. Curtains were simple. There would be a table with several chairs, perhaps simple pine furniture bought for that purpose or cast-off furniture from other rooms. There were shelves and cupboards for books and toys and perhaps an armchair or two. Nurseries often doubled as schoolrooms and would also contain globes, maps, and perhaps a blackboard for instruction.

While wealthy families might have had inside plumbing and the accompanying bathroom facilities, most people had to make do with ceramic washbasins and pitchers on a washstand. Full baths were labor-intensive events that involved bringing up heated water from the kitchen to the bedchamber so that a compact metal tub could be filled. This relegated total-immersion baths to special occasions. Sponge baths were the more common occurrence. Outhouses were not convenient at night, so most bedrooms contained a covered chamber pot. Some chamber pots were hidden in various pieces of furniture (mostly chairs and stools), but some were merely stored beneath the bed until they were emptied into the slop jar in the morning (Volo and Volo 1998, 195–202).

CLOTHING

Women's Fashion

In the Industrial Age, America fashion became increasingly tied to the consumer economy by the mass production and marketing of ready-made clothing. Standardized paper patterns were obtainable throughout the nation and, combined with the sewing machine, provided women with the ability to recreate complicated, fashionable styles. By the 1880s and 1890s the availability of a wide variety of dress patterns had as dramatic an impact on clothing styles as the ready-made industry. While before 1870 most women still made the clothes for their families, thereafter standardized sizes and mass production revolutionized the ready-made clothing industry making them available for even working-class women. The Civil War had spurred the development of ready-made clothing for men. This blossomed into a billion dollar a year industry by 1890. By 1900 most men were wearing ready-made clothes and women, though encouraged to make their own dresses, could also fulfill all of their clothing needs from stores and catalogs.

American fashion designers in New York, Philadelphia, and Chicago closely followed the French fashions, although English designs began to gain acceptance in the 1890s. English-style tailored suits became very popular as a number of American women rejected the "tight-laced, exaggerated female curves" of French haute couture in favor of the comfortable and neat look of the tailored suit.

Clothing for upper- and middle-class women was certainly the most physically restrictive dress used by anyone during the period. Yards of cloth were draped in long, flowing dresses covering multiple layers of petticoats and bone or steel corsets. Genteel women wore costumes that severely restricted their movement. Unlike their working-class sisters, middle- and upper-class women had no economically productive role for the family; they did not produce anything for the family's economic support. The restrictive clothing of these genteel women symbolically illustrated that women of this social station did not have to work and ought not to according to genteel convention.

Dresses in the 1880s continued to be heavily layered, and cold-weather fabrics were so weighty that they were like upholstery fabric. The bustle continued, although somewhat larger, until 1887 when it shrank again. High fashion continued to produce incredibly ornate dresses with elaborate overskirts and ornamentation. Straight dresses flared below the knee and swept the ground in small trains (later shortened to ankle length). Bodices were tightly fitted and with high sleeves often cut at the forearm. Popular dress colors in the 1880s tended toward the darker spectrum, deep purple, claret, copper, or gold. Corsets and bustles were still demanded, though women were beginning to wear only one petticoat as early as 1878. A wide profusion of hats and bonnets were stylish in this era and were heavily decorated with ribbons, flowers, plumes, and even small stuffed birds. Hat decorations were brilliant with blazing colors like bronze, gold, garnet, and peacock blue. Women often carried fans and parasols as their primary accessory. Large Japanese ostrich-feather fans as well as parasols covered in lace or satin were very popular. Ankle-high heeled kid boots were the most popular footwear of the 1880s.

Although Paris continued to exert tremendous influence over fashions in the United States, American fashion magazines began to multiply. *Harper's Bazaar, Godey's Lady's Book,* and the various Demorest publications (*Mirror of Fashions, Quarterly Illustrated Journal, What to Wear, Portfolio of Fashion*) all carried French fashions. The average woman demanded more simplified styles that were based on the latest fashions found in magazines. Work dresses were patterned after fashion styles and gained a measure of social acceptability. Middle- and upper-class women augmented their high fashion garments by adding simpler dresses for more casual occasions. Common dresses made for middle-class women were sometimes still made in the three-piece style with bodice, underskirt, and overskirt. These so-called wash dresses were easily laundered, and they also came in very popular one- or two-piece styles made of cotton and were worn by women of almost all social classes. Wash dresses were widely available in stores and catalogs by the 1880s. These dresses tended to be fairly simple relative to high-fashion models, with bishop sleeves, lightly gathered high on the shoulder, plain necks, and with minimal trim. Middle-class women possessed a variety of dresses for different occasions from formal to wash day. Women who were not so well off economically pressed a wide variety of dresses into service, but mainly relied on fairly simple styles made of calico, gingham, or whatever fabric was at hand. Old dresses were never thrown out but simply made into work dresses that were pressed into service as aprons when they grew too worn to continue as dresses.

It is doubtful that everyday dresses sported bustles since most photographs of women in everyday wear do not evidence the voluminous 1880s bustle. The bustle disappeared during the 1890s, but designers continued to go to great lengths to achieve the hourglass figure. Great gathered skirts came into vogue along with "leg-of-mutton" sleeve blouses that emphasized the small waist. Blouse sleeves grew until about 1897, culminating in the massive leg-of-mutton look so typical of the 1890s, but then began to be replaced with a more tight-fitting sleeve topped by a puff and gathering of material on the shoulder much like an epaulet. Gone were the complex underskirt and overskirt styles of the previous decades with their elaborate ornamentation. Although simple in construction compared to those of the 1880s, the popular skirts of the 1890s had numerous gathers and could consist of as many as 23 yards of material. These skirts were tulip or vase shaped and boasted satin, lace, velvet, or braided trim. Cynical commentators called these dresses street sweeper fashions. Velvet, silk, and wool continued to be popular fabrics in expensive clothing, and there was a trend to have dark dress colors such as dark blue, black, and dark green, trimmed in lighter, contrasting colors such as turquoise, rose, and baby blue. Oriental fans, gloves—which changed according to the occasion—and feather boas for formal events all maintained their popularity as accessories. Kid boots that buttoned on the side continued to be popular, usually with a high curved heel and sharply pointed toe, but new colors of champagne, bronze, and brown appeared in addition to black.

Undergarments were also ready-made by the 1890s. Corsets were the most distinctive undergarment of the nineteenth century and forced women's bodies into the ideal shape—small waists and uplifted breasts—and were always worn by proper ladies. Corsets were decorated lingerie and could be found in a variety of colors. While black was the most popular, they also came in scarlet, red, gray, drab, and white. The rural-oriented *Montgomery Ward Catalogue* offered at least 38 different corsets in white, drab, ecru, and black. Stockings came in a variety of fabrics such as cotton, silk, wool, or cashmere, and the color normally matched the outfit. In the summer women wore cotton underwear that ended above the knee. Some women continued to wear a chemise and wore only the corset cover. In cold weather women would don the wool or jersey union suit.

The 1890s hastened efforts to provide the women with clothing that adequately allowed for exercise and sports. Swimming, walking, bicycling, and gymnastics all became increasingly popular for young women as the Industrial Age progressed, and the clothing they wore for these activities starkly illustrated how women disputed conventional views of femininity. Pattern companies, particularly the giant Butterick, promoted physical culture by selling patterns for gymnastic outfits, bathing suits, and riding skirts, but attempted to mediate these activities with mainstream views of womanhood by making them pretty. Athletic clothing for women was adorned by functionally useless frills like bows, silk trim, and sailor collars that clearly marked them as feminine. Nonetheless, sports clothing for women emerged from the period as a normal part of the wardrobe.

Swimming suits garnered the most serious concerns because, unlike gymnastics that generally took place in all-female settings in schools, swimming was a public activity. Swimming suits covered the entire body. Initially, in the early 1870s, they commonly consisted of a calf-length dress with long sleeves and ankle-length bloomers. By the end of the century they commonly had short sleeves and dresses that reached just below the knee, bloomers slightly longer than the dress, and dark stockings. The gymnastic uniform required at the Mount Holyoke woman's college was a dress that reached seven inches above the floor worn over bloomers. By 1898, Butterick's gymnastic outfit rejected the dress entirely, and instead featured a yoke blouse with voluminous bloomers over tights. Walking, tennis, and bicycling outfits were also made to have more freedom, but these costumes stayed much closer to typical Victorian dress. Cyclists could wear large, gathered skirts that appeared split or split skirts that were so full they appeared whole. Tennis, still a bastion of the elite, proved less amenable to change than gymnastics. Fashionable tennis attire in the 1880s showed women in an underskirt and overskirt complete with bustle. In the 1890s the typical tennis costume consisted of a fluted skirt and shirtwaist, so popular for the day. It was still restrictive but not nearly as heavy as previous decades (Shrock 2004, 85–93).

Men's Fashion

Men's fashion was more subdued and predictable than women's fashions as the business suit became dominant for the sober, middle-class businessmen. A dark business suit, white shirt with a detachable collar and cuffs, vest, and depending on the occasion, a top hat, bowler or strawhat, all set off with a large burly moustache or beard was de rigueur. Although businessmen generally stayed with white shirts and plain vests, splashes of color were seen by the 1870s. Colored shirts with a variety of stripes and plaids were available in such exotic colors as blue, red, black, or gray, as were brightly colored jacquard silk vests. The only splashes of color in suits were plaids, checks, and tweeds. Bright colors and rich patterns such as these were worn mainly by dandies. By the 1880s, plain, casual sack suits that reached just below the waist and had narrow lapels replaced the ornate frock coat, although formal attire still sported the long Prince Albert frock. Styles became more tailored and fitted in the 1890s, and suit jackets were generally made to be buttoned all the way to the top. Although men could opt for brightly colored ties, vests, and shirts as well as plaid and tweed suits, the universal costume for respectable men in the 1890s was the black wool three-piece suit with a white shirt.

Although the suit was worn by a wide variety of men, it represented an important social marker for the middle class that defined the wearer's refinement and social distinction. The suit was certainly not appropriate for hard physical labor, but instead denoted a man's genteel occupation. The suit's only function was to illustrate the power and social status of the wearer.

The 1895 *Montgomery Ward Catalogue* illustrated how many different styles and price ranges were available even to rural Americans. It offered the round corner sack suit, the single-breasted square-cut sack suit, the double-breasted square-cut sack suit, old men's frock suits, three-button cutaway frock suits, double-breasted Prince Albert suits, and full evening dress suits that included tails. Suits could be purchased in cotton, varying quality wool, flannel, and corduroy. The catalog also carried a wide sampling of shirts, over 100 different hats, wool pants, vests, overcoats, socks, and dress shoes.

Detachable shirt collars were an essential part of middle-class attire by the 1840s. Collars normally were made of linen or extremely starched cotton and styles varied dramatically over the decades. By the 1890s men preferred very high collars, often two and a quarter inches. These starched, white collars were so ubiquitous that the term became a common reference for middle-class occupations, and white collar still is associated with middle-class managerial employment.

Working-class men's clothing was often a motley collection of mismatched vests, trousers, and jackets. Those men who could afford it purchased the wide variety of ready-made clothing. Rarely did working men wear the plain white shirt with detachable collars and cuffs, but instead wore a wide variety of colored shirts, blue being a popular color, with attached collars. These shirts were normally pullover and buttoned partway down the front.

Specialty leisure clothing for men also developed during this period. Hunting clothing, which had long been produced only for the wealthy, was made affordable by the mass-produced ready-made clothing industry. The 1895 *Montgomery Ward Catalogue* sold a wide variety of shooting jackets, hunting vests, heavy waterproof hunting pants, sweaters, shirts, leggings, and hats. Specialized sports clothing also appeared and was mass marketed. Ward's offered fencing masks and gloves, athletic sweaters and shirts, tights, athletic supporters, baseball hats and gloves, and football uniforms, as well as bicycling sweaters, knickers, and long socks. By the late 1890s swimming suits had shrunk to a wool short sleeve or tank shirt with shorts that stopped just above the knee. More genteel sports like tennis continued to demand more clothing. Men often played in tennis suits that looked more like a casual suit than sporting wear (Shrock 2004, 80–85).

Children's Clothing: Ready-Mades

Fashion for young people was primarily determined by age. Fully adult fashion was not worn until the teens. Infants and toddler boys of this time would have been virtually indistinguishable from their sisters. With the exception of more eyelet or lace on the toddler girls' gown, young boys and girls were dressed in unisex clothing. Infants were dressed in very long gowns, sometimes reaching three or four feet in length.

As toddlers, boys often appeared in dresses, a fashion that eased diaper changing and accidents. Although some boys may have remained in such attire until almost age five by the 1890s most boys were wearing gendered clothing by age two. A boy's first pants were shorts, and he would not graduate to long pants until he was 6 to 10 years old.

Boys between three and six years old graduated to knickers, which became the preferred active wear of boys in the 1890s. Men engaged in sports or riding bicycles also wore knickers. Male toddlers also wore an overall called a Brownie suit. Everyday wear for boys consisted of knickers or trousers, a collarless shirt, and a vest, or for rural youth denim overalls became popular by the 1880s. Sweaters also made their appearance in the 1890s and a variety of styles were available. A wide variety of hats, like the popular straw hat or English school hat, were also commonly worn (Shrock 2004, 93–95).

Different styles of suits, such as the Reefer suit, Sailor suit, and Zouave suit, enjoyed various degrees of popularity during the period but the one that garnered the greatest popularity was the black velvet suit. This outfit was sometimes referred to as a cavalier suit, a look that was enhanced by the fact that a boy's first haircut was often quite delayed. Although the outfit dates back to the mid-1860s, it became quite the rage as a dressy outfit for boys from ages three to eight after the story, *Little Lord Fauntleroy*, was serialized in the children's magazine, *St. Nicholas*, in 1886. The story, book, and later dramatic production became tremendously popular. The young hero of the story wears the black velvet suit, which symbolizes his natural nobility despite his humble financial circumstances. The little velvet suit enjoyed its greatest popularity from 1889–1890 although it continued to be worn for years thereafter.

Fashions for girls followed the same general trends that influenced women's clothing styles during the Industrial Age. Unlike mothers' dresses, dresses made for girls rarely sported bustles but did have puffs and panniers that pulled the dresses into a large gather at their lower back. Girls' formal dresses in the 1880s were nearly as heavily ornamented and frilly as their mothers' dresses with an overskirt and underskirt often made of organdy, sheer muslin, velvet, linen, silk, or taffeta. Colors for girl's fancy dresses in this period tended to run toward the same dark colors as adult fashions. Everyday dresses for girls were usually in cotton, gingham, or wool, and were often covered by heavily starched white, gray, tan, blue, or unbleached muslin aprons or smocks. Sailor suits for girls with a middy blouse and skirt were also popular. Girls' dresses tended to have a large collar or smocking around the yoke that set their styles apart from adults. By the 1890s the shirtwaists sporting the enlarged upper arm and large fluted skirts became very popular styles, as did the wash dress. The 1895 *Montgomery Ward Catalogue* sold girls' wash dresses in gingham, flannel, and calico in mainly light prints for 2 to 14 year olds. Only older girls generally wore shirtwaists. Girls wore bonnets that followed the styles of their mothers. They wore dark stockings and black kid boots that came just above the ankle and buttoned on the outside for everyday wear. In the 1890s black patent leather Mary Janes were the dress shoes of choice.

Just as with boys' pants, age determined the length and style of the dresses for girls. The younger the girl the shorter the dress could be according to refined standards, though below the knee. As the girl aged, her hems lengthened and by puberty corsets were required. In the 1890s girls aged, 3 to 5 often appeared in empire waist dresses while older girls, age 4 to 14, wore dresses with natural waistlines (Shrock 2004, 95–96).

TECHNOLOGY: MODERN SHIPBUILDING TECHNOLOGY

The excellence of American ships in the first half of the nineteenth century is unquestioned. American maritime design and shipbuilding technology was the envy of the world, and American sailing ships were soon the fastest on the seas. Americans were master wooden windship builders, and this same excellence had lent itself to the design of its naval vessels. Nonetheless, by the third quarter of the century contemporary observers could rightly speak of the virtual extinction of American maritime commerce and unfavorably compare the ships of the late nineteenth century U.S. Navy to ancient Roman galleys.

At the same time, American builders developed a distinctive type of sailing schooner for the commercial coasting trade that allowed them to hold their position in competition with the steamers until the twentieth century. Inexpensive to build and operate, and built with traditional American wooden hull technology, these sailing schooners of between 300 and 700 tons capacity were kept busy carrying lumber, coal, ice, and other cargoes up and down the Atlantic, Pacific, and Gulf coasts.

Protected by a series of Navigation Acts from foreign competition, the coasting trade had continually grown as a percentage of the merchant marine fleet from 25 percent in the Federalist era, to 41 percent just before the Civil War, and 57 percent by war's end. It was to retain this level of representation throughout the decades of the 1870s and 1880s. A growing national population, the effects of industrialization, and absolute protection from foreign competition allowed coasting to supplant foreign trade as the major activity of the merchant marine as early as 1857. This was reflected in the continued predominance of wooden shipbuilding technology in American yards.

Coastal steam lines developed slowly in the first half of the nineteenth century due to monopolies granted by the individual states to local investors. By 1840, however, all the major East Coast ports were connected by steam.

In the aftermath of the war, a few innovative American owners began to use efficient steel-hulled, multiple expansion steamships of significant size to operate in the cotton coasting trade even though the initial costs of the vessels were quite high. Steamers seemed to be losing the traditional grip that wooden sailing vessels had on this important fraction of U.S. maritime commerce. In fact the wooden windship design had reached its practical engineering limits with the development of the clipper ships of the 1850s.

It can be demonstrated that the U.S. shipbuilding industry was simply not competitive in the years after the Civil War. At mid-century, the engineering fundamentals of steamship construction for the oceanic trade had several common characteristics. The hulls were made of wood; the vessels were propelled by paddle wheels housed amidships; the engines were physically very large and of a single expansion, low-pressure type, also located amidships; and the steam was exhausted into jet condensers so similar to those devised by James Watt in 1769 as to be considered identical. Low-pressure, water tube boilers, had been common since their invention in 1791. Paddle wheels, by design well suited to low-pressure, were slow rotating devices of a large area that maximized the impulse imparted to the vessel; increased the reliability of the engines; and minimized the stress on the hull. While economical in terms of fuel consumption, the low-pressure steam boilers retarded the introduction of the screw propeller.

Moreover, paddle wheels provided greater acceleration and torque than the screw propellers of the period. When housed amidships and operated by separate engines, a moderately sized vessel could turn on a dime by reversing one side and applying forward motion on the other. These advantages kept paddle-wheel tugboats in operation into the twentieth century in many American harbors. They were finally displaced by the introduction of incredibly powerful diesel powered tugboats with their giant propellers.

American shippers usually considered steam to be an auxiliary to sail, and many vessels were designed with combinations of motive power. The steam power was used to enter harbors and negotiate difficult passages, but the sail provided economy of operation. However, these vessels commonly experienced some disadvantages as both screws and paddle wheels produced considerable drag when the vessel was under sail. Paddle wheels were particularly noted for adversely effecting the overall sailing qualities of a vessel. When equipped with screw propellers and the higher pressure, fire tube boilers—introduced in the 1850s—the restrictions of increased fuel consumption served to severely limit the speed that the steamer could maintain for any extended period of time.

Nevertheless, wooden-hull American clippers saw severe competition in the oriental trade from British windship designs that utilized composite hulls, wood with cast-iron beams and bracings, before the war. Although generally smaller than the American ships, and somewhat slower under the best of conditions, the British vessels proved to be better suited to a variety of weather extremes. Even these British windships, the *Cutty Sark* being a prime example, were ultimately driven from the trade by steamers in the decades after the Civil War.

American technological distress in the postwar years may be attributed, in part, to the very success for which U.S. shippers and shipbuilders were noted at the end of the age of sail. In the first half of the nineteenth century, American shipbuilders had no equal in the world. With modern woodworking and wood turning apparatus American shipyards could crank out their best work at as little as 60 percent of the cost of British builders who generally did not invest in such devices. Although profits from investments in the domestic shipping industry could vary with time, the expected financial return from the foreign carrying trade was effectively tied to how well U.S. shipyards could compete in price with their foreign counterparts. Americans found themselves saddled with expensive shipbuilding apparatus made obsolete by the sudden popularity of metal hulls and steam. British builders, by contrast, had made no large investment in wooden windship technology and were able to update their shipyards directly to metal and steam production without taking a loss.

—*James M. Volo*

TRANSPORTATION: CYCLING

In the last decades of the nineteenth century a bicycle (velocipede) craze made the two-wheeler much more than a toy or exercise machine for hundreds of thousands—even millions—of Americans. By the middle of the 1890s, more than 300 American companies were producing almost a million bicycles per year. The development of the bicycle was important not only for its immediate impact on everyday life in America but also for its role in the development of manufacturing practices that would lay the groundwork for the automobile and aviation industries of the next century. They also made the fashionable and stylish bloomers worn by women more acceptable.

In the early nineteenth century the forerunner of the modern bicycle was introduced by a German inventor, Baron Karl von Drais. His heavy all-wooden, two-wheeled machine had no pedals or breaks—the rider provided the propulsion by pushing with his feet on the ground or coasted headlong downhill scraping his feet along the pavement. By the middle of the century enterprising manufacturers had added pedals, and the bicycle craze spread throughout Europe and America. These first bicycles were heavy and had full metal or solid hard rubber tires, making them a very rough ride; in fact, one of the earliest and most popular bicycles was aptly called a Boneshaker. Early bicycles had another serious design flaw: the pedals attached directly to the front wheel slowed forward progress or spun wildly as the rim rotated. Designers soon found that the bigger the front wheel the faster the rider could propel the bike. Unfortunately, the huge front wheel also meant the rider sat so high above the ground that serious injuries could occur from bicycle accidents. The lofty perch above the giant wheel was also thought unladylike for young women riders. These early high-wheelers were commonly know as ordinaries.

In 1885, John Kemp Starley, an Englishman, built the first device that modern persons would recognize as a modern bicycle. By using a chain-driven rear wheel and a front wheel of equal size, the safety bicycle made riding easier and safer for everyone and spread the hobby of cycling to those riders who were less fit, less agile, or less youthful. A few years later, Dr. J. B. Dunlop of Belfast, Ireland, designed the first pneumatic tires for his own son's tricycle. The new air-filled tires caught on quickly; and, while they introduced the inconvenience of the flat to most riders at one time or another, they were soon found on bicycles across the United States.

Although not invented in America, further improvements to the basic bicycle in this country led to its practicality for nearly everyone. The bicycle had something to offer to everyone. For young people, it offered a way to get out from under the stern eyes of their parents. Women, in particular, enjoyed the newfound freedom that the bicycle offered and the style of clothing that made cycling easier. Moreover, the bicycle was a relatively affordable means of transportation for everyone that was both new and exciting. People were set free from the horse and wagon by a vehicle that could match their speed. To this day, the bicycle seat is still called a saddle, but unlike the horse there was no harness to fit. Moreover, the bicycle never needed watering, feeding, currying, or cleaning. While it sometimes required maintenance and tinkering by the professionals at the bicycle shop, the bicycle was never sick, never ran away, never smelled of sweat, and never left a pile of manure in its wake. One could just jump on, quickly be away, and just as easily jump off at one's destination.

Riding clubs formed quickly, races organized, and everyone who could afford a bicycle wanted one. Americans were buying bicycles at an astounding rate, even at a time when their purchase of jewelry, pianos, and books had fallen to a period low. A national club, the League of American Wheelmen, counted thousands of cycling enthusiasts among its members. Periodicals supporting the new craze appeared, including *Bicycling World* and *The Wheelman*. Trade shows, later copied with great success by automobile manufacturers, were introduced by bicycle companies to advertise new models and innovations. In 1896, the Chicago show drew more than 225 exhibitors and 100,000 admissions. A similar show in New York drew 400 exhibitors and 120,000 admissions. Bicycle races, from a few miles on an oval track to cross-country marathons, captured the imagination of the American public. Multi-day races were held at Madison Square Garden in New York City, and cross-country tours were common from the 1880s onward. In 1895, there were almost 600 professional cyclists competing for prize money in races across the United States (Timmons 2005, 38–42).

FOR MORE INFORMATION

Bauer, K. Jack. *A Maritime History of the United States: The Role of America's Seas and Waterways*. Columbia: University of South Carolina Press, 1989.

Canney, Donald L. *The Old Steam Navy: Frigates, Sloops, and Gunboats, 1815–1885*, Vol. I. Annapolis, MD: Naval Institute Press, 1990.

Elkort, Martin. *The Secret Life of Food*. Los Angeles, CA: J. P. Tarcher, 1991.

Grover, Kathlyn, ed. *Dining in America: 1850–1900*. Amherst: University of Massachusetts Press, 1987.

Hooker, Richard J. *Food and Drink in America: A History*. New York: Bobbs-Merrill, 1981.

Hunter, Louis C. *A History of Industrial Power in the United States, 1780–1930*. Charlottesville: University Press of Virginia, 1979.

Kevill-Davies, Sally. *Yesterday's Children, The Antiques and History of Childcare*. Woodbridge, UK: Antique Collectors' Club, 1998.

Levenstein, Harvey Q. *Revolution at the Table: The Transformation of the American Diet*. New York: Oxford University Press, 1988.

McIntosh, Elaine N. *American Food Habits in Historical Perspective*. Westport, CT: Greenwood/Praeger Press, 1995.

Shrock, Joel. *The Gilded Age*. Westport, CT: Greenwood Press, 2004.

Timmons, Todd. *Science and Technology in Nineteenth-Century America*. Westport, CT: Greenwood Press, 2005.

Van Der Plas, Rob. *Cycle History: Proceedings of the 5th International Cycle History Conference*. San Francisco: Bicycle Books, 1995.

Volo, Dorothy Denneen, and James M. Volo. *Daily Life in Civil War America*. Westport, CT: Greenwood Press, 1998.

Williams, Susan. *Food in the United States, 1820s–1890*. Greenwood Press, 2006.

Woodward, George E. *Victorian City and Country Houses: Plans and Designs*. New York: Dover Publications, 1996.

———. *Woodward's Architecture and Rural Art*. New York: Privately printed, 1868.

———. *Woodward's National Architect*. New York: Da Capo Press, 1975.

Zanger, Mark H. *The American History Cookbook*. Westport, CT: Greenwood Press, 2003.

Political Life

GOVERNMENT

Troubled Presidencies

During the Industrial Age, party-line voting and party identification were very important. At the end of the Civil War, the Republican Party was in ascendancy because it had waged a successful war for union and had harvested a bumper crop of black votes through emancipation. Democrats feared that they would never again be able to defeat the Republicans in the South. Yet the Republican Party, as a national entity, had to deal with a number of political and practical problems. In just the 35 years from the end of the Civil War to the turn of the century 3 of the 10 men to hold the executive office were assassinated (Lincoln in 1865; James A. Garfield in 1881; and William McKinley in 1901). All were Republicans. The administration of Andrew Johnson (1865–1869), who appeared soft on reconstructing the South, was rocked by impeachment; the administration of Ulysses S. Grant (1869–1877) oversaw one the most troubling and arguably dishonest periods in American history; and the administration of Rutherford B. Hayes (1876–1881), who won the presidency in one of the most hotly disputed elections in history, declared the previous 12 years of Southern Reconstruction useless and a failure. Once again all of these administrations were Republican ones. Of the two remaining Republicans to hold the presidential office, Chester Arthur, who as vice president had succeeded Garfield, failed to win renomination by his own party, and Benjamin Harrison failed to win reelection. Only two presidential elections in this period were won by a Democrat, and both, separated by four years, were won by the same man, Grover Cleveland. The death of William McKinley, like that of Queen Victoria in the same year that ushered in a new century (1901), seemingly ended an era with the accession to the presidency of a remarkable personality, Theodore Roosevelt.

—James M. Volo

Third Parties

The Populist Party was a major third party formed in 1889–1890 around the Farmers' Alliance, the Free Silver advocates, the Knights of Labor, and hangers-on from the old Granger movement, and disaffected Democrats in the south and Republicans in the Plains states. It grew out of the agricultural unrest that grew after the collapse of produce prices during the Panic of 1873 and the reluctance of the major parties to take up issues of importance to farmers. The Populist political movement reached its peak in 1892 when it nominated James B. Weaver as its presidential candidate. Weaver received over one million votes, carried four western states (Colorado, Nevada, Idaho, and Kansas), and received electoral votes from two (Oregon and North Dakota). In 1896 the Democratic Party assumed many Populist issues, and the latter party began to fade from prominence.

The Populist Party platform called for the abolition of national banks, a graduated income tax, the direct election of Senators, civil service reform, an eight-hour work day, and government control of railroads, telegraphs, and telephones. Its opposition to the gold standard was especially strong among its Western farm supporters who viewed the banks as enemies that foreclosed on mortgages and other debts with unseemly speed. The Free Silver plank in the platform was supported by voters across the Mountain states, by mine and land owners, as well as by the state governments. The Populists also courted the active participation of women and blacks in the political process. In 1896 William Jennings Bryan, the Democratic candidate adopted the Populist opposition to the gold standard, and many Populist sentiments can be found in his famous "Cross of Gold" speech. The fusion of racist Democrats and Populists would have been a disaster for the latter in the South, and they attempted instead an alliance with Southern Republicans. Nonetheless, in 1900 they supported Bryan again and with his loss, the party was weakened. The Populists virtually ceased to exist after 1908.

—James M. Volo

Voting and Political Participation

A higher percentage of Americans voted in elections during the Industrial era than at any other time in U.S. history (taking into account the fact that women were not allowed to vote in nationwide elections until 1920). From 1876 to 1900, 77 percent of eligible voters took part in presidential elections, with participation levels as high as 85 percent in some Northern states. As a point of comparison, consider that only 51 percent of eligible voters cast ballots in the 2000 presidential election. Industrial Era elections were partisan events that were hotly contested, even if the issues under dispute were not necessarily divisive. "America in the late nineteenth century was a nation of intense partisanship and massive political indifference." During this time, elections involved much more than just casting a ballot. Election campaigns were high profile, public events that were often coordinated on a local level and involved an unprecedented level of voter participation.

In the years following the Civil War, it was standard practice for men to join local marching companies affiliated with a political party. During election campaigns, these marching companies would be outfitted in military-style uniforms and then would participate in huge, public parades on behalf of candidates and political parties. It was not uncommon in urban areas for thousands of men to take up torches (the parades were often at night) and march alongside bands and floats before gathering to hear candidates and other party orators rally the faithful. In New York City, as many as 50,000 marches typically participated in political parades. Spectators would gather along parade routes and some would signal their support for (or opposition to) the parading party by turning on (and off) all the lights in a house. During some elections there were so many marchers that they had to be divided into battalions and brigades under the orders of generals. It has been estimated that in the North, perhaps one-fifth of all voters played an active role in campaigning.

Political parades encouraged people to vote the party rather than the candidate, and they energized the party faithful. "Mid-nineteenth-century partisanship was aggressive, demonstrative, contentious, and often vicious. Party membership was a part of men's identity; as such, their partisanship had to be paraded and asserted in public." Party affiliation was seen as more than choice; it was both a personal and political statement. That said, in a highly charged partisan atmosphere, political parades did little to appeal to undecided voters or ticket splitters who tended to vote for candidates of different parties. Gradually spectacular campaigns began to fall out of favor, and they came to be replaced by the campaign of education, first run on the presidential level by the unsuccessful 1876 Democratic presidential candidate, Samuel J. Tilden against Rutherford B. Hayes. This approach involved a more centralized campaign focused on issues and the distribution of campaign literature to voters and later a substantial amount of advertising. The campaign of education was seen to better appeal to undecided voters, and by the turn of the century it came to dominate politics. However, it did so at the cost of lessening the average citizen's role in political campaigns (Husband and O'Loughlin 2004, 239).

The Growth of Urban Government

The lasting image of urban government during the Industrial era is that of machine politics led by a boss. The term *machine politics* was used to describe an approach to governing in which a group of organized politicians were able to control the reins of governmental power through delivering (and sometimes manipulating) votes. They often accomplished this by delivering patronage jobs and services back to those same voters. The *boss* of such a system was not necessarily the mayor of a city but instead someone who could leverage his power to both give and get favors.

Historians generally agree that in a situation in which urban governments were structurally weak and fragmented, there was a great incentive for strong leaders to find ways to seize power and coordinate unwieldy municipal forces. Beyond that, however, there is a vast division of opinion on the state of urban government in the Industrial Era. City governments at this time were the site of corruption and incompetence as well as flexibility and innovation.

During this period, city charters (the regulations setting up the organization of city governments) were a hodge-podge and a patchwork. Few charters were written in anticipation of massive growth, and entrenched interests often made charter revisions difficult. Furthermore, as urban areas grew, the amount of revenue passing through city coffers without adequate controls, and the control of patronage jobs, led to widespread corruption.

Cities faced a litany of difficulties and they were often beset by corruption. Nonetheless, urban governments had many successes to show during the latter part of the nineteenth century. They developed modern schools, sanitation, and infrastructures in the midst of immigration that brought unprecedented ethnic and religious diversity to cities. But within the context of nineteenth-century thinking, it was difficult to appreciate the role city governments played in mediating and compromising between different constituencies.

City government was the place that brought together "the municipal professional, the downtown business leader, and the neighborhood shopkeeper and small-time politico," as well the immigrant leader or union supporter. No one group always got its way, but through compromise and negotiation, the modern city nevertheless came to be.

For every Boss Tweed—a notoriously corrupt New York City politician of the Tammany Hall machine—there was also a Brooklyn Bridge—a major architectural and infrastructural accomplishment made possible by municipal government. Dramatic improvements as well as scandalous waste were hallmarks of the city governments of the period (Husband and O'Loughlin 2004, 32–34).

LAW, CRIME, AND PUNISHMENT: METRO AND TOWN POLICE

Methods of local law enforcement varied from region to region and town to town. Small Western and Southern towns relied on local sheriffs and county magistrates to round up troublemakers and evildoers. More populous places, especially the cities of the Northeast and Midwest, had turned to organized police forces by the 1870s. A large city force could number, as it did in New York, close to 3,000 men, including officers, sergeants, patrolmen, and detectives. Most cities were divided into districts or precincts with a captain who was held to strict accountability for the preservation of the peace and good order of his area.

Each patrolmen (nearly 2,100 of them in New York) walked a particular route or neighborhood known as a *beat*, where he was expected to exercise the utmost vigilance to prevent the occurrence of crime. They worked five different shifts with one third of the force working days and two-thirds nights. Patrolmen commonly walked the same beat during each tour of duty, and they became familiar with the residents of the area—both good and bad. This allowed for efficient neighborhood-style policing, but it also had the potential for producing corruption and cronyism.

The standard police uniform consisted of a dark-colored uniform frock coat and trousers, a badge, and a glazed helmet of pith or leather. The uniform was often dark blue, gray, or black fitted with leather belts in black or white. The uniformed patrolmen served as a symbol of government presence as well as an assurance of law and order. Each man carried a hard wooden baton, handcuffs, a whistle, and a revolver.

The variety of pistols carried by law enforcement was exhausting. The weapons issued by the City of Baltimore can be taken as an example of those used by metropolitan police forces. Baltimore issued to its patrolmen the 1851 Navy Model Colt that was a cap and ball revolver holding six .36 caliber loads. It had a 7 1/2 inch rifled barrel and was sturdy, fairly accurate, and reliable. From 1857 to 1876 the city issued the .31 caliber, 5-shot cap-and-ball Colt Pocket Model 1851 with a short 4 1/2 inch-barrel that was generally underpowered for police work. The .36 caliber Colt Police Model of 1862 had a 5-inch barrel. Longer barrels gave a higher velocity and greater precision. Colt made both New York and Hartford versions of the latter for the police of those cities. The Allen and Wheelock Providence Police Model of 1858 had a 3-inch barrel of .36 caliber to meet the specifications of the Rhode Island city.

Most cap-and-ball revolvers ceased production in 1873. Beginning in 1876, Baltimore issued a Smith and Wesson top-break, cartridge revolver in .38 caliber. Colt also produced a new weapon know as the .38 Colt New Police. Both used a 36 grain (2.3 gram) black powder charge that gave the lead bullet (148–150 grain) a 800 to 900 ft/s muzzle velocity depending on the length of the barrel. These revolvers were a huge improvement over the outdated Civil War era types, and they remained common issue sidearm for the police of many cities into the twentieth century. The .38 caliber cartridge revolver became so common among metropolitan law enforcement agencies thereafter that weapons in this caliber for the civilian market were often advertised as police types.

New York City Police Statistics for 1888–1889

	Male	Female
Total number of arrests	62,274	19,926
Drunkenness	20,253	8,981
Disorderly conduct	10,953	7,477
Assault and Battery	4,534	497
Theft	4,399	721
Robbery	247	10
Vagrancy	1,686	947
Prisoners Unable to Read or Write	2,399	1,281

Source: Jacob A. Riis, *How the Other Half Lives* (1890).
Note: Although New York City police statistics for 1888–1889 admitted to no murders whatsoever, it is highly unlikely that there were none, only that the city government was unwilling to certify them as such.

Small towns also turned to professional law enforcement, but the progression to a city police force, while typical, was often less than dramatic. The town of New Lancaster, Ohio was established in 1800, and it immediately set up a Property Guard to perform law enforcement duties. The Guard consisted of one captain and three officers. It was replaced by the office of City Marshal in 1831. The marshal and his part-time deputies dealt with horse thieves, drunkards, and saloon problems like prostitution, gambling, and rowdyism. In addition, they intervened in clashes between whites and Native Americans. A jail was added in 1867, and in 1870 a metropolitan police uniform was standard issue, but the city adopted obsolete, .36 caliber 1851 Navy Colt revolver was adopted. It is unclear if this was one of the many cartridge conversions available after the war. A full-time deputy, deemed a police officer, was not added until 1881. As the town grew, electric police call boxes were installed. These were the very first in the State of Ohio. In 1903 the police force of New Lancaster had a chief and 10 patrol officers in its department.

—*James M. Volo*

THE CHILDREN OF THE URBAN STREET

Overcrowded, working-class homes in the city provided little to no space for children to play or interact. Consequently, children flocked to the noisy and busy streets, some to become the little merchants hawking newspapers or matches, or collecting junk (junking), and some to play improvised games. Street children often appeared to be unsupervised to middle-class observers. However, there were usually adults within easy reach, including parents, relatives, neighbors, and shopkeepers and peddlers familiar with the neighborhood families who looked on from their own stoops, windows, shops, and carts (Husband and O'Loughlin 2004, 127–28).

With no other place to go, many children appropriated any relatively quiet part of the street as their own playground, but police officers often saw such public space quite differently. Children in New York and Chicago were often arrested for the so-called crimes of playing baseball in the streets, throwing snowballs, and loafing on the docks (Nasaw 1985, 23). Children who were found shooting craps or gambling were likely to be sternly rebuked by police and to have their change seized. Some, in fact, hypothesized that such petty graft was the motive for such interference (Nasaw 1985, 23). Such juvenile delinquents (and abandoned or orphaned children) were sometimes sent to rural areas and set to farm work that was considered wholesome and character building. Unfortunately, they were often overworked, exposed to exhausting extremes of temperature, and expected to move enormous loads for their size (Husband and O'Loughlin 2004, 127).

Penalties for serious offenses on the streets differed dramatically for boys and girls. A boy found sleeping out might be taken to one of the Newsboy's Lodging Houses, where his stay was voluntary, but a girl accused by officials or parents of sleeping out was viewed as a far greater social threat, someone likely to become a prostitute. If she was under 16 and deemed vulnerable but not yet corrupted, she was likely to be sent to a reform school. Approximately one-fifth of the girls sent to reform schools had committed some form of petty theft; the rest were placed for behavioral reasons. The institutions primarily sought to save girls from promiscuity. Consequently, homeless girls, girls exposed to sexually illicit behavior in the home, and so-called stubborn girls were all eligible for reform. Stubborn was the catch-all term applied to girls who frequented taverns or brothels, ran away from home, or befriended low men and women. In the second half of the nineteenth century, more than half of the girls committed to reform institutions were admitted for being stubborn (Husband and O'Loughlin 2004, 130).

Initially, these institutions offered a common school education to girls as well as moral guidance. The education and food offered were so valued by poor parents that some had their daughters labeled stubborn to be relieved of the burden of feeding another mouth. Rapid industrialization, poverty, and the breakdown of local forms of social welfare and discipline in the cities resulted in a large population of girls (and boys) considered delinquent. The behavior of these wayward girls often went beyond the common understanding of stubborn to include behaviors of an openly sexual nature. Younger girls deemed more innocent were placed directly with foster families, while only the older girls and those considered morally questionable were referred to institutions. It became the goal of the reform schools to quickly train girls in domestic service and move them into job placements (Husband and O'Loughlin 2004, 131).

PROSTITUTION

The openness of prostitution in the nineteenth century scandalized the social and religious elite everywhere. Proper ladies universally frowned upon any man who was too open in his lustfulness, but they could do little to enforce their displeasure on the male population at large. Upper-class unmarried men involved in relationships with prostitutes seem to have received a special dispensation from otherwise genteel society because they were thought to be exercising their natural proclivities at the expense of previously fallen women.

The manifestation in which prostitution appeared in many cities was somewhat dictated by the class and means of the clientele. Some men of wealth seemingly relied on the common practice of supplying themselves with a mistress and an apartment for short-term affairs. Others frequented the bordellos of the seamier neighborhoods and so-called red light districts. The nightly trade in amorous economics was available in most large towns and cities. Most prostitutes were poor white women who worked their clientele in cheap saloons, hotels, and dance halls. These women were of the lowest class—although they may not have started life there—having taken up the trade in their teens. They moved in and out of the dance halls and bordellos, and could be brought in from the street for as little as a dollar. They were described as "degraded beings [and] habitual drunkards" who were "remarkable for bestial habits and ferocious manners" (Asbury 1936, 27).

Although ordinances were passed that prohibited the renting of rooms to prostitutes, bordello owners were often protected by local politicians or the police. A madam might run a bordello in many cities by obtaining an annual license at a small cost. The laws prohibiting soliciting in the streets or from the doors or windows of the bordello. Indictment for prostitution, charging the keeping of a so-call disorderly house, usually targeted madams who allowed sordid social activities such as interracial intercourse, sodomy, or same-sex relations in their establishments. Within these bounds, the authorities made little attempt to halt the expansion of the trade into the residential areas of the city, often forcing the more virtuous residents to abandon their homes in pure frustration.

So-called high-class places were operated with considerably more circumspection. These bordellos were often housed in brick or brownstone buildings filled with mahogany woodwork, brass fixtures, and marble fireplaces—and furnished with fine carpets, pianos, furniture, art, and statuary—making them some of the most pretentious and luxurious residences in the country. Only the finest wines and champagnes were served; the ladies wore evening gowns while being entertained by musicians, dancers, and singers in the public rooms; and they changed to the finest lingerie in their boudoirs. As many as 30 women might work from a single house, each paying a fee to the madam, and receiving between $5 and $20 for an amorous experience.

Any romantic notions surrounding these practices, however, without regard to the fine trappings that surrounded them, should best be avoided as sentiment rather than an unbiased assessment of the situation in which these women found themselves. Any other conclusion, even from a historic perspective, would be lacking in sensitivity with regard to the effects of the sexual exploitation experienced by these young women. Poor kinless women received little protection from a generally male-oriented society in which so-called gentlemen considered them a proving ground for their sexual prowess. For these women there was no return route to social acceptability once their female purity and innocence had been violated (Volo and Volo 2000, 235–36).

THE PROTECTIVE TARIFF

The imposition of protective tariffs (import duties) by the federal government was a flashpoint political issue, especially among the shipping interests in the Northeastern region of the United States. Republican manufacturing interests argued that tariffs shielded domestic industry from competition from abroad and had led to unprecedented growth in manufacturing. Southern and Midwestern agriculturists, supported by Democrats and Populists, benefited little from import duties because they relied on foreign imports that were produced at a lower price than protected domestic manufactures. Moreover, American farmers sold a great deal of the their produce abroad, and they feared retaliatory measures taken against their own exports in foreign markets should tariffs be imposed. In New England shipping circles, it was thought that high tariffs were destroying the industry. A *New York Times* article of January 29, 1867, exclaimed in bold typeface: "Unparalleled State of Depression—Not a Single Merchant Ship on the Stocks—High Taxes on Raw Materials the Cause." These tariffs were described by the *Times* as "nearly prohibitive."

Examples of the potential damage posed by protective tariffs to shippers and shipbuilders can be estimated from applicable examples addressed in the 1861 Morrill Tariff: Section 7. These included several items that were particularly damaging to the shipbuilder attempting to transition from wooden-hulled sail ships to metal and steam technologies. A tax of from $12 to $15 per ton was exacted on small plates of imported bar iron, rolled iron, or hammered iron; on large plates and boiler plates, $20 per ton; on steam engines and the parts thereof weighing over 25 pounds, $3 per ton. Tariffs were even charged on materials used in emergency repairs done outside the country. The full weight of these tariffs can be appreciated when it is noted that the estimated cost of a moderately sized steam vessel with a metal hull could be as little as $48 per ton before taxes were imposed (Clark 1949, Vol. II, 138).

Shipbuilders and marine suppliers in New England complained of tariffs that also affected the manufacture of wooden vessels and were causing a depression in that industry. As the timber that they used was often imported from Canada, they found that they had to pay an export tax to that country and an import duty to their own. In addition the ship owner, for whom the vessel was being built, was required to pay an Internal Revenue Tax of 30 cents per ton on the finished vessel. A white oak ship of 1,200 tons that could be built before the Civil War for about $47 per ton cost $68 per ton at the height of the shipping depression. In 1886, Henry George, an outspoken opponent of the tariff, wrote of its effects in *Protection or Free Trade: An Examination of the Tariff Question with Especial Regard to the Interests of Labor*. "The ravages of the Confederate cruisers," wrote George, "would under any circumstance have diminished our deep-sea commerce; yet this effect was only temporary, and but for our protective policy we should at the end of the war have quickly resumed our place in the carry trade of the world" (George 1886, 198–99).

Republicans were steadfast in their support for protective tariffs, and the Democrats were quick to seize upon the policy as an election issue. Eventually, the

Democrats in Congress were able to force an average reduction of about seven percent in the tariff, but their legislation targeted industries in Republican states while sparing those in Democratic ones. A reason for the apparent lack of Republican interest in furthering the shipbuilding industry was suggested in 1890 by Alfred Thayer Mahan, dean of naval historians. He suggested that an American cargo-carrying fleet was not really needed. Any foreign shipper, from even a mediocre maritime nation, could carry goods as efficiently as Americans; and American capital could be more efficiently used in the production and manufacture of goods than in ships. Mahan was unknowingly suggesting that America outsource its maritime transportation. He wrote, "The action of the government since the Civil War, and up to this day [1890], has been effectively directed solely to…internal development [and] great production, with the accompanying aim and boast of self-sufficiency….What need has the United States of sea power? Her commerce is even now carried by others; why should her people desire that which, if possessed, must be defended at great cost?" (Mahan 1987, 84–85). K. Jack Bauer, another naval historian, noted almost 100 years later, "The nation [in the 1890s] stood with its back to the waterways and exalted the ribbons of steel [railroad track] ignoring both the efficiency of water transportation and its critical role in the economic health of the country" (Bauer 1989, 297).

—James M. Volo

SHERMAN ANTITRUST ACT

A trust (or business trust) was a form of business entity used in the late nineteenth century with the intent to create or protect a monopoly. Some, but not all monopolies were organized as trusts in the legal sense. They were often created when corporate leaders convinced or coerced the shareholders of all the companies in one industry to convey their shares to a board of trustees of an umbrella company, in exchange for dividend-paying certificates. The board would then manage all the companies in trust for the shareholders (and minimize competition in the process). Eventually the term was used to refer to monopolies in general.

The Sherman Antitrust Act (15 U.S.C. 1–27) provides in part: "Every contract, combination in the form of trust or otherwise, or conspiracy, in restraint of trade or commerce among the several States, or with foreign nations, is declared to be illegal." Sherman also provides: "Every person who shall monopolize, or attempt to monopolize, or combine or conspire with any other person or persons, to monopolize any part of the trade or commerce among the several States, or with foreign nations, shall be deemed guilty of a felony…." The act put responsibility upon government attorneys and district courts to pursue and investigate trusts, companies, and organizations that were suspected of violating the Act. The Sherman Antitrust Act was not used in court cases for some years, but Theodore Roosevelt used it in his antitrust campaign.

—James M. Volo

INTERNATIONAL DIPLOMACY

The Teller and Platt Amendments

Congress passed the Teller Amendment in the months before war with Spain commenced in 1898. Proposed by Senator Henry Teller of Colorado and passed unanimously, this legislation stated that Cuba would not be annexed and should be free and independent. Nonetheless, the United States ignored the desires of the Cubans both during the war and during the peacemaking. At the close of the war, the U.S. government forced the Cubans to write an independent constitution, but this generally recognized and ensured U.S. economic interests and suzerainty over the population (Shrock 2004, 22).

The United States occupied Cuba for five years after the war. In 1901, Secretary of War Elihu Root drafted a set of articles to serve as guidelines for future Cuban-American relations. The so-called Platt Amendment (named for Senator Orville Platt who proposed the legislation) became part of the Cuban Constitution and provided that the United States retain the right to stabilize Cuba by military force if needed to insure that American companies would not be damaged by any unforeseen changes. It also provided for the establishment of a permanent naval base at Guantanamo Bay ostensibly as a coaling and fueling station for the U.S. Navy. Often considered a wholly self-serving document, the Platt Amendment did establish standards for disease prevention, urban sanitation, and public financing in the Cuban constitution. It remained in force until 1934 (Shrock 2004, 22).

The Boxer Rebellion

The final years of the nineteenth century were also the final years of Manchu rule (Qing Dynasty) in China. In late 1899, there arose in Shandong and Shanxi provinces a movement among the Chinese peasants that was antiforeign, anti-Christian, and anti-Imperial in nature. In English, the Chinese name for the secret society (*I Ho Ch'uan*) behind the uprising translated as *The Righteous and Harmonious Fists*. From a literal translation the peasant followers of this movement were widely known as boxers, and the crisis that they initiated is generally known as the Boxer Rebellion (1899–1901). It was a reactionary movement caused by growing foreign influence in trade, politics, religions, and technology. The Boxers called for the ousting of the foreign devils and the cleansing of Christians from the Chinese population.

Foreign influence in China had been mounting in the last decade of the century. Significantly there was a railroad construction agreement with the Russians in 1896, and a commercial treaty between China and Germany in 1898, followed closely by one with Japan. These created such a scramble for concessions from China among the foreign powers that diplomatically the Chinese were being ignored. In 1899, John Hay, American secretary of state, received assurances from the foreign powers of a so-called open door to equal commercial opportunities in China. Although the rebellion was finally suppressed, it spelled the end of Manchu rule and further entrenched foreign influence over the government.

The Boxer Rebellion was a bloody and brutal affair. During the uprising almost 20,000 Chinese Christians, mostly Catholics, and more than 200 Christian missionaries were murdered. The diplomats of several nations including Europeans, Americans, and the Japanese were besieged in the capital city of Beijing (Peking) by thousands of armed rebels. The Boxers killed 230 non-Chinese in the city in June 1900. The Dowager Empress Tzu Hsi (who had precipitated the crisis by seizing the government) stood by in seeming helplessness as foreign diplomats and civilians, embassy guards and employees, and some Christian Chinese retreated to the foreign legation compound in the city, set up temporary fortifications, and withstood the assault of thousands of Boxers. The siege lasted for 55 days.

The Boxer Rebellion and the Chinese inability to deal with it effectively offered an opportunity for unfettered exploitation of China by the foreign powers. The foreign navies in the region, which included U.S. warships, began building a presence in Chinese waters as early as April 1900, and before the legations were closed to relief that summer, 435 sailors from 8 countries—among them 60 U.S. Marines—were dispatched to reinforce the embassies at their request. These men represented the Eight-Nation Alliance that included France, Britain, Italy, Japan, Germany, Austria, Russia, and the United States. Eventually more than 54,000 foreign troops would be committed to putting down the Boxers and relieving the legations. The largest contingents were from Japan (20,000), Russia (13,000), and Britain (12,000). The American force was just over 3,400 men. Among the Americans were detachments of the 9th, 14th, and 15th Infantry, the 6th Cavalry, the 5th Artillery, and a further contingent of Marines. The international force commanded by a Japanese officer won a major battle over the Boxer forces at Tianjin during July and soon thereafter relieved the foreigners in the compound. The rebellion sputtered on for another year ending in September 1901 with the beheading of 96 Chinese officials and hundreds of Boxer captives. In addition, Russian troops drove thousands of Chinese civilians to their deaths in the Amur River; and German troops, which had arrived late at Beijing, undertook no less than 35 of the 46 punitive missions carried out in the name of the Chinese Imperial government.

The so-called Boxer Protocols that ended the crisis were signed by diplomats from 12 nations. The protocols provided for expressions of regret to the foreign powers and payments in gold of $738 million, fortification of the legations, and the razing of all Chinese forts along the foreign-built railroads. The indemnity was to be paid through the maritime customs surplus, the native customs, and the salt monopoly.

Although the Boxers were virtually exterminated, the obvious weakness of the Qing government led to a new nationalist revolt led by a Christian named Sun Yat-sen who formed the Tung Meng Hui (a society dedicated to displacing the rule of the Manchu) and who laid the foundation for a modern Chinese republic. In 1905 a boycott of American goods was used as a protest to the exclusion of Chinese immigrants to the United States. This was a mark of growing national consciousness among the Chinese.

Among the foreign powers, Japan gained the most in terms of regional prestige, and it was seen for the first time as a major world power because of the leading role its military played in suppressing the rebellion. Russia—second only to Japan in its active participation—viewed this development with some discomfiture and three years later went to war over Japanese pretensions to Manchuria and Korea (Russo-Japanese War of 1904–1905). The Russian fleet experienced major defeats at Port Arthur and in the Tsushima Straits leaving the Japanese Imperial Fleet with an enhanced reputation. Germany gained a Pacific naval base at Qingdao Bay leading the American Congress to annex Hawaii where German influence had been growing. A relatively large number of American units took part in the defense and relief of the legations, gaining in martial reputation in the brutal fighting. Many of the American units involved in the suppression of the Boxers subsequently added a golden dragon to their regimental coat of arms in remembrance of the operation. The expansion of Japanese influence in East Asia, coupled with American annexation of the Philippines, Hawaii, and other Pacific islands at the end of the Spanish-American War, set the stage for Japanese-American confrontations in the twentieth century.

—*James M. Volo*

DISCRIMINATION: CHINESE EXCLUSION

In 1882, Chinese laborers were specifically banned by the federal government from entering the United States under the Chinese Exclusion Act. The mid-century gold strikes in California had brought all sorts of people to the mining camps and many of them took up permanent residence in the state. Aside from white Americans, there were blacks, Native Americans, and foreigners from Germany, France, Ireland, Britain, Australia, Mexico, South America, China, and even Turkey. The races and nationalities did not always mix well. In some mining camps all foreigners were barred; in others only certain nationalities were unwelcome. Mexicans were particularly unwanted and despised. Their claims were often ignored, and their property was sometimes confiscated simply because they were Mexican.

The Chinese were the particular targets of prejudice because of their race, exotic clothing, and unfamiliar customs. They were often held in contempt because of their willingness to work diggings that had been abandoned by whites as unprofitable. Whites thought it great fun to raid their camps, put them under the whip, and cut off the pigtails of the Chinese men. The last was considered a significant form of social degradation in China. The Chinese were also victimized by their own people in the camps who formed gangs know as *Tongs* for self-protection. Whites would often urge the Tongs to war among themselves armed with clubs, lances, and longswords provided by local blacksmiths. In one such encounter eight Chinese were killed and six were grievously wounded. At length many Chinese veterans of the gold fields gave up mining to become servants, laundrymen, cooks, and peddlers.

The construction of the Central Pacific Railroad in California and Nevada in the 1860s was handled largely by Chinese laborers. Charlie Crocker, president of the railroad construction company, urged the employment of Chinese "coolies," who were small and undernourished-looking but industrious and tireless. The first of these came from the mining communities, but thereafter the railroads systematically brought over workers from China itself. In the 1860 U.S. Census there were 58 Chinese men and 4 women in the entire country; these numbers grew to one million men and four million women in the 1880 census. More than 160,000 entered the country during the Civil War years alone.

In 1870, a New England shoe manufacturer from North Adams, Massachusetts, named Calvin T. Sampson fired his newly unionized white workers and imported 75 Chinese laborers from the Pacific Coast. The Chinese signed a contract to work for three years at $26 a month, which saved Sampson a total of $840 a week. The Chinese settled down to a New England lifestyle and attended the local Methodist church. A writer for *Scribner's Magazine* praised the experiment, "If for no other purpose than the breaking up of…labor combinations and Trades Unions…the advent of Chinese labor should be hailed with warm welcome by all who have the true interests of…the laboring classes at heart" (Butterfield 1947, 228). It is unlikely that the writer would have found a positive reaction to the Chinese among the unionized American workers who had lost their jobs. Mass production had engendered mass employment in America for the first time, and it wrought changes in the relationship between labor and management that reverberate even today.

Union activists were generally anti-immigrant nativists who considered the seemingly endless supply of foreign workers a drag on wages. They were especially vicious in their attacks on the Chinese, who they incorrectly considered treacherous, slovenly, and ignorant. Spurious tales were spread of their carrying terrible diseases including a number that existed only in the imagination. Real diseases such as cholera, leprosy, and syphilis were also attributed to the Chinese, but in a more potent and nonexistent Asian form that was supposedly impervious to treatment. "Chinese men," said accepted wisdom, "lived in filth, feasted on rodents, gambled, worshiped hideous idols, smoked opium, and lusted after white women." It was true that 2,000 Chinese had revolted on a plantation in far off Peru, murdering the family of the plantation owner and ransacking a small nearby town. Yet this was the report that gave truth to the larger lie (Sutherland 2000, 235).

In the 1870s labor unions conducted a vicious anti-Chinese campaign. Laws were passed in California and other places prohibiting Chinese children from attending school and blocking the immigration of Chinese women. San Francisco banned the carrying of baskets on long poles, a common practice

The massacre of the Chinese at Rock Springs, Wyoming. Miners of the Union Pacific Railroad Company shooting at crowd of fleeing Chinese miners working for the Union Pacific. Courtesy Library of Congress.

in Chinatown. Asians in general, and the Chinese in particular, were disproportionately incarcerated at a rate 3.8 times that of whites. The first drug to be criminalized in the nineteenth century was opium, which was the drug of choice among the Chinese. White populations used the opium law punitively against Chinese immigrants in a blatant effort to drive them out of the community (Shrock 2004, 12).

In Denver in 1880 mobs invaded the homes of the Chinese, smashed their windows and furniture, cut the pigtails from Chinese men, and lynched many people. A similar mass riot by whites against Chinese took place in Wyoming in 1885. As Chinese began to arrive for work in the Eastern states, the panic spread. Anti-Chinese riots broke out in virtually every American city, and white workers, nativists, and union organizers opposed further immigration from China. Labor unions such as the American Federation of Labor strongly opposed the presence of Chinese labor, by reason of both economic competition and race. "Meat versus rice," and "American manhood versus coolieism" were common themes. Largely due to pressure from the growing labor movement, in 1882 Congress banned further Chinese immigration through the Chinese Exclusion Act. The act prohibited all Chinese laborers from entering the United States, although some students and businessmen were exempted from the ban.

In 1885, a further act of Congress made the entrance of all foreign laborers, even those under contract to white employers, illegal. In 1902, the 1882 act was made perpetual and extended the immigration prohibition to Chinese living in Hawaii and the Philippines. Subsequent to the Exclusion Act, many Chinese returned to their homeland, a greater proportion than any other major immigrant groups. The official Chinese population in America, which had stood at 5 million in 1880, was only 37,000 in 1940. A prominent factor that affected this statistic may have been the fact that emigrants from China were not allowed to become citizens before 1950.

—James M. Volo

REFORM: THE GOLD STANDARD

Nineteenth-century farmers were sometimes successful in joining together to increase their political power. The Farmers' Alliance first appeared in the 1880s. Its main goal was to increase the income of its members by cooperative marketing, but it also became a lobbying group requesting that the government regulate certain business and banking concerns. The Farmers' Alliance, and other farmers' groups, provided valuable services to their members that were not available to self-interested independent farmers. These services included better terms of trade through cooperative marketing, better transportation rates through mass shipping, and the sharing of agricultural information and scientific data (Stewart, On-Line).

One of the major objectives of the Farmers' Alliance was to end the long-term deflationary trend that was seen by many as a way of maintaining commercial wages and interest rates at the expense of real earnings for farmers. Abandonment of the Gold Standard was thought to be critical to increasing the money supply and allowing some inflation to creep into the economy. Eastern banking interests supported the hard money politician in Congress, and the interior mining and farming interests supported the soft money legislators who wanted to make currency freely convertible to silver.

The U.S. Mint was capable of accepting both silver and gold bullion and making it over into coins. Gold was minted by law at the set rate of $20 per troy ounce, and silver was set at $1 per troy ounce. This mimicked the standard set by the Spanish dollar that had so pervaded American colonial finances. Both the Continental dollar of the Revolution and the contemporary silver dollar had their roots in the Spanish silver dollar of eight reales (or bits). The Republican Party steadfastly opposed Free Silver, while the Populist Party used silver as one of the fundamental planks in its platform. In 1878, Congress passed the Bland-Allison Act, which required the Treasury to redeem at least $2 million in paper (bonds and bills) each month through the increased use of silver bullion as minted coins at a value ratio of 16 silver to 1 gold. This compromise put at least some silver into circulation, helped to maintain the face value of paper currency, and effectively increased the traditional value of silver versus gold by 20 percent.

Bland-Allison (Richard P. Bland of Missouri and William Allison of Iowa) set a bimetallic standard for U.S. coinage when most of the world was using only gold as standard money. The United States was the only country at the time that was a major producer of both gold and silver. The act also specified the location of four U.S. mints at Philadelphia, San Francisco, Carson City, and Denver, and it located two government assay offices at New York and Boise City (Idaho). The law fixed the value of silver when in fact more silver was being found, which otherwise would have driven its price down. This was particularly beneficial to silver mining interests in the West. The ratio of available silver to gold supply would reach 40 to 1 in 1908. Specie payments in gold were resumed in 1879, and anyone who did not exchange their holdings in silver for gold were left in a devalued position.

The gold-silver debate continued to be a national political issue through the end of the century. In 1890, the Sherman Silver Purchase Act became law. While it did not authorize the free and unlimited coinage of silver, it required that the government purchase 4.5 million ounces of silver bullion every month. It also required the Treasury to issue certificates to the sellers that could be redeemed in either silver or gold. This bimetallic monetary standard was very unstable and had the effect of draining the gold reserves as the majority of certificate holders opted for payment in gold. Good money (gold) drove bad money (silver) from the marketplace.

In 1893, the nation was hit by a significant economic depression. President Grover Cleveland blamed the downturn on the Silver Purchase Act. All other industrialized nations were on a gold standard, he said, while the United States was depleting its stock of gold by buying silver. He immediately summoned Congress to an emergency session to repeal the Silver Act. The debates during this session were classic. Francis Cockrell, from Missouri, rose in silver's defense making a highly dramatic speech on the Senate floor while snapping his trouser suspenders and puffing on a corncob pipe for effect. David Hill of New York provoked his constituency by defending silver, and Richard Bland (Missouri) swore that the silver dollar would take its rightful place alongside that of gold before the Senate had finished with the issue (Butterfield 1947, 262–63).

Cleveland was generally opposed by his own party, the Democrats, but several in his own party embraced silver also. They disagreed with the president and his Wall Street friends that silver coinage had caused the depression. Too little money, not too much was the cause. The country had grown since the Greenbackers had accepted a silver compromise in the 1870s. In the 1890s it had twice as many people and three times as much business activity as it had at the end of the Civil War. The money supply, in relation, had shrunk. Western wheat farmers and Southern cotton growers were suffering from falling prices because there were not enough dollars to go around and because they had tripled the grain supply through better farming practices. The Free Silver solution was to coin all the silver the Treasury could buy at a standard monetary value of one ounce of gold for 16 of silver. The gold advocates assured the public that sound money based on a single gold standard would restore prosperity.

In 1896, silver and gold figured prominently in the presidential election. At the Democratic Convention in Chicago William Jennings Bryan, the party nominee, gave a speech that put the issue into a sharper focus. Most of what other speakers said at the convention has been forgotten, but Bryan's *Cross of Gold* speech will long be remembered, if not for the import of its content, at least for its use good use of slogan politics. "Having behind us the producing masses of this nation and the world, supported by the commercial interests, the laboring interests and the toilers everywhere," proclaimed Bryan from the podium, "we will answer their demand for a gold standard by saying to them: You shall not press down upon the brow of labor this crown of thorns, you shall not crucify mankind upon a cross of gold" (Butterfield 1947, 264).

With this speech Bryan qualified himself with the Western interests, the farmers, the wage laborers, and all those who owed debts. Yet in a larger sense he had articulated the friction between rural and urban factions, between mill owners and textile workers, between foundry owners and steel workers, and between isolationists and internationalists. The gold standard, according to Bryan, had slain tens of thousands in the struggle between the "idle holders of idle capital" and the "struggling masses, who produce the wealth and pay the taxes of the country." Envisaging the political and social upheavals that would tear at the fabric of the twentieth century, Bryan asked, "Upon which side will the Democratic party fight?" (Butterfield 1947, 264).

Bryan failed to carry his message to the White House in part because the failure of the Russian wheat crop and the resulting increase in farm prices for American farmers relieved much of the impact of the issue for farmers. His opponent William McKinley implemented the gold standard and ran on retaining it during his 1900 reelection campaign.

The gold standard remained in place until the Great Depression (1929) when Franklin D. Roosevelt abandoned not only the gold standard, but the very concept of gold coinage by making the ownership of gold coins and gold bullion illegal for everyone except the government as part of his New Deal recovery program in 1934. Gold coins in circulation were rounded up and melted down. The silver-certificates created in 1890 by the Sherman Silver Purchase Act remained in force until 1964 when the value of the silver was 29 percent greater than the face value of the bills. Coins accepted upon presentation of the certificates were being melted down for their silver content. In 1968 the Treasury ceased all redemption of silver-backed currency, and silver coinage was debased by the addition of nonprecious metals such as zinc and copper. U.S. paper currency is presently unsupported by any metallic backing, and its value floats freely against other currencies on the global market.

—James M. Volo

FOR MORE INFORMATION

American Federation of Labor. *Some Reasons for Chinese Exclusion.* Washington, DC: Government Printing Office, 1902.

Asbury, Herbert. *The French Quarter: An Informal History of New Orleans with Particular Reference to Its Colorful Iniquities.* New York: A. A. Knopf, 1936.

Bauer, K. Jack. *A Maritime History of the United States: The Role of America's Seas and Waterways.* Columbia: University of South Carolina Press, 1989.

Bork, Robert H. *The Antitrust Paradox: A Policy at War with Itself.* New York: Basic Books, 1978.

Burgess, William W. *The Voyages of Capt. W. W. Burgess, 1854–1885.* Plymouth, MA: Jones River Press, 2003.

Butterfield, Roger. *The American Past: A History of the United States from Concord to Hiroshima, 1775–1945.* New York: Simon and Schuster, 1947.

Clark, Victor S. *History of Manufactures in the United States.* 3 vols. New York: Peter Smith Publishers, 1949.

Dulles, Foster Rhea. *The Old China Trade.* New York: Houghton Mifflin Company, 1930.

George, Henry. *Protection or Free Trade: An Examination of the Tariff Question with Especial Regard to the Interests of Labor.* New York: Henry George and Co., 1886.

Griffith, Ernest S. *A History of American City Government: The Conspicuous Failure, 1870–1900.* New York: Praeger, 1972.

Gyory, Andrew. *Closing the Gate: Race, Politics, and the Chinese Exclusion Act.* Chapel Hill: University of North Carolina Press, 1998.

Howarth, Stephen. *To Shining Sea: A History of the United States Navy, 1775–1991.* New York: Random House, 1991.

Husband, Julie, and Jim O'Loughlin. *Daily Life in the Industrial United States, 1870–1900.* Westport, CT: Greenwood Press, 2004.

Mahan, Alfred Thayer. *The Influence of Sea Power upon History, 1660–1783.* New York: Dover, 1987. Reprint of the 1890 edition.

McGerr, Michael E. *The Decline of Popular Politics: The American North, 1865–1928.* New York Oxford University Press, 1986.

McMath, Robert C., Jr. *American Populism: A Social History, 1877–1898.* New York: Hill and Wang, 1993.

Mitchell, Thomas G. *Indian Fighters Turned American Politicians, From Military Service to Public Office.* Westport, CT: Praeger Publishers, 2003.

Nasaw, David, ed. *Andrew Carnegie: The "Gospel of Wealth" Essays and Other Writings.* New York: Penguin Books, 2006.

Posner, Richard A. *Antitrust Law*. Chicago, IL: University of Chicago Press, 2001.

Rosen, Ruth. *The Lost Sisterhood: Prostitution in America, 1900–1918*. Baltimore, MD: Johns Hopkins University Press, 1982.

"The Sherman Antitrust Act, Text." URL: http://www.antitrustupdate.com/Statutes/ SL-ShermanAct.html. Sections 1–4, (accessed December 2007).

Shrock, Joel. *The Gilded Age*. Westport, CT: Greenwood Press, 2004.

Snow, Jennifer C. *Protestant Missionaries, Asian Immigrants, and Ideologies of Race in America, 1850–1924*. New York: Routledge, 2007.

Stewart, James. "The Economics of American Farm Unrest, 1865–1900." *EH. Net Encyclopedia*, edited by Robert Whaples. URL: http://eh.net/encycpolpedia/article/stewart. farmers (accessed May 2006).

Sutherland, Daniel E. *The Expansion of Everyday Life, 1860–1876*. Fayetteville: University of Arkansas Press, 2000.

Teaford, Jon C. *The Unheralded Triumph: City Government in America, 1870–1900*. Baltimore, MD: The Johns Hopkins University Press, 1984.

Topping, Elizabeth A. *What's a Poor Girl To Do?: Prostitution in Mid-Nineteenth Century America*. Gettysburg, PA: Thomas Publications, 2001.

Van Dyke, Paul A. *The Canton Trade: Life and Enterprise on the China Coast, 1700–1845*. Hong Kong: Hong Kong University Press, 2005.

Volo, Dorothy Denneen, and James M. Volo. *Encyclopedia of the Antebellum South*. Westport, CT: Greenwood Press, 2000.

Recreational Life

SPORTS

The Great Out-of-Doors

Nineteenth-century Americans were very fond of the outdoor life, but as the nation became more industrialized and urbanized, they found that the natural outdoor life of farming, fishing, and hunting for a living was eluding them. Long hours in the mill, shop, or business office often precluded time spent in the sunshine for everyday workers, but those with the means could and often did seek out new activities. Consequently, a number of existing sports had become popular like running, rowing, and cycling; but the genteel population invented or adopted a number of artificial activities or diversions that were done in the out-of-doors without too much exertion or accompanying perspiration. Among these were tennis, archery, golf, and other sports of a genteel nature.

—*James M. Volo*

Track and Field

Vigorous physical exercise was highly valued in the late nineteenth century. Track and field events in the United States began to be held almost immediately at the end of the Civil War. Sprints, relays, marathons, and throwing events like javelin and discus were held. These reflected the supposed classical events of the ancient Olympic games. The Steeplechase comprised of both hurdles and water obstacles was 3,000 meters long, and it was very popular as a spectator event. Hurdles were introduced into Olympic competition in 1834. The first national track meet was held in 1876. Meets for women were held every four years with little fanfare.

—James M. Volo

Tennis

Tennis was an ancient game played much like handball played over an intervening net. An indoor form played with paddles and then rackets (from the Arab word "Rahat" meaning hand) was popular in both France and England in the sixteenth and seventeenth centuries, but this had fallen out of favor due to rampant gambling. In England in 1873, Walter Wingfield introduced a game based on the older form that he called lawn tennis. This could be played out-of-doors on grass on a rough equivalent of the modern tennis court and was made possible by two inventions: the India rubber ball (which bounced on the lawn) and the mechanical lawn mower (which allowed the grass to be cut to a short, even length). The popularity of outdoor physical activities for both men and women in the last quarter of the nineteenth century helped to spread the game of tennis, which quickly displaced the less active lawn game of croquet.

Mary Ewing Outerbridge introduced the game to the United States in 1874 by importing sets of Wingfield's equipment. She established the first tennis court in the United States on the grounds of the Staten Island Cricket and Baseball Club in New York. Lawn tennis was initially very popular among American sportswomen, but it spread in popularity to male players. As late as 1900 men wore suits, ties, hats, and dress shoes while playing tennis and women wore long skirts, hats, sleeved dress shirts, gloves, and dress shoes. Badminton is a rather more sedate version of lawn tennis played with a shuttlecock rather than a ball.

—James M. Volo

A tennis match held at Newport, Rhode Island. Tennis was quickly adopted as an upper-class sport for both participants and spectators. Courtesy Library of Congress.

Archery

The earliest organized form of archery as an American sport began in 1828 when the painter Titian Ramsey Peale established the United Bowman of Philadelphia among his friends. Peale had become enthusiastic over archery from his observations of the North American Indians that he had painted. Club members, imbued with a love of all things British, often wore uniforms reminiscent of the fifteenth century while competing. The club was disbanded in 1859 in anticipation of the Civil War, but was revived in a more Americanized form after the war by two ex-Confederate soldiers and brothers from Florida, Maurice and Will Thompson. In 1878, Maurice Thompson authored a book on the sport, *The Witchery of Archery*, that caused a sensation among sports-minded persons. More than 20 archery clubs were formed that year alone. In 1879, the National Archery Association of the United States was organized as a national sanctioning body; and in the same year it ran the first annual archery tournament, which was held in Chicago.

The main events of an archery tournament were called rounds, and the number of arrows and the range of distance were individually specified. Archery contests were usually divided into different skill categories such as target (paper or cloth bull's-eye targets at short ranges under 30 yards), field (targets at longer than 30 yards), and flight shooting (landing arrows in a large circle on the ground at long distances). Wand-shooting (hitting a vertical stick stuck in the ground), which was popular in Britain, never really caught on in America.

Archery was very popular with young women, and was often included in the physical education curriculum at women's academies and colleges. As in tennis and other genteel outdoor sports of the period, archers usually competed in full street dress: men in suits, ties, and hats; and women in full skirts, long sleeved blouses, and hats. The sport was ruled out of competition in the Olympics after 1908 because of unresolved international disputes over the format and rules. However, it was revived as an Olympic sport in 1972. The modern sport with its composite and compound bows of fiberglass, arrows of extruded aluminum, sights, inertial balancers, and triggers is almost unrecognizable from the nineteenth-century version with its simple wooden longbows and turkey-feathered wooden arrows.

—*James M. Volo*

Golf

The modern game of golf is thought to have been formulated in Scotland in the seventeenth century, but its name comes from the Dutch word Kolf, meaning club. The Dutch also played a version of the game called Kolbe, or Kolf played with a pebble and a branch. As late as 1850 the number of holes in a round of golf varied from as few as 5 to the modern standard of 18, and the course had no specified teeing areas. Golfers used leather balls filled with feathers until 1850 when balls made of a rubbery substance taken from Malay trees called gutta-percha became available. Clubs—usually no more than one or two—were made from tree branches, and they were carried under the arm as the golfers strolled the course. Golf bags were introduced in the 1870s.

The first appearance of golf in America is usually dated at 1885. In this year, John G. Reid introduced a group of his friends to the game in a cow pasture in Yonkers, New York. Although he did nothing of note to advance the game, Reid is widely considered the "Father of American Golf." In 1888, the first photograph of golf players was taken on the same course in Yonkers.

—*James M. Volo*

Bowling

Bowling is an extremely old sport that may have had its origins in China as early as 300 A.D. Some form of lawn bowling (bowles) may have been played in England as early as the eleventh century, and Sir Francis Drake was said to have finished a game of bowles before heading out to face the Armada in 1588. This was certainly a game played with balls much like present-day lawn bowling.

The Dutch of Old New York played at bowles by knocking down wooden pins (kegels) with a heavy round ball. This was much more like the modern form of American bowling, but Anglo-colonials used 9 instead of 10 pins to avoid some of the taxes set on diversions by the British before the American Revolution. A 9-pin game (skittles) was not specified under the tax like the 10-pin form. The 10th pin (officially added to the game in 1820) is said to be called the Kingpin for this reason, and its absence avoided the tax. Pin bowling was played in basements or in the alleys between buildings, one of which was often a tavern (hence the term bowling alley).

In 1849, Scottish organizers set down the rules and scoring for 10-pin bowling that were almost identical to those used today. The game seems to have been very popular in urban areas in America where it was subject to widespread wagering on the outcome. In 1895 the American Bowling Congress was established in New York City. This group standardized the equipment, pin weights, alley size and length, and other rules, and it set up or sanctioned formal competitions.

—James M. Volo

Boxing

Boxing was an ancient sport. The first report of a prize fight was written in the twelfth century by Homer, the Greek poet and supposed author of the *Iliad* and the *Odyssey*. In the eighteenth century bare-knuckle boxing was very popular in Britain, and it was there in 1866 that fight promoter John G. Chambers introduced the rules for ring boxing supposedly designed by the Marquis of Queensbury.

Prize fighting with its hierarchy of national and world championships had great potential as a spectator sport, especially among the urban masses. Tom Hyer was the first great American champion, holding the national title from 1841 to 1851 in which year he retired. In 1849, Hyer won a purse of $10,000 in a single match. John C. Morrissey, the American champion of 1852, was able to turn a boxing career into a seat in Congress.

Among the best-known American fighters of the Industrial Age were John L. Sullivan and James J. Corbett—one from the East Coast and one from the West Coast, respectively. In 1883, Sullivan, nicknamed the "Strongboy of Boston," went on a one year long, coast-to-coast exhibition tour of the United States with five other boxers, challenging all comers for a $250 prize if they could defeat him. He knocked out 11 men during the tour. Sullivan put up the longest fight in modern heavy-weight championship history when he beat Jake Kilrain in a 75 round, bare-knuckle bout on July 8, 1889.

James J. Corbett was from San Francisco, and he gained the moniker of "Gentleman Jim" due to his college education and his appearance in stage plays and other theater productions. Corbett, a boxing coach and so-called scientific boxer, added movement to the boxer's repertoire; and he has been called the greatest boxer of all time and the father of modern boxing. A so-called world championship bout was held between Sullivan and Corbett on July 7, 1892, at the Olympic Club in New Orleans. This was the first such contest fought under the Marquis of Queensbury Rules. Corbett won by a knockout in 21 rounds over an older and slower Sullivan. Corbett defended his world title once—against Charley Mitchell in 1894 in Britain; but lost his second defense to Bob Fitzsimmons, a New Zealander, in 1897 at Carson City, Nevada. Following his retirement, Corbett returned to acting and wrote his autobiography, *The Roar of the Crowd*, which was serialized in 1924 in the *Saturday Evening Post*. A major Hollywood movie, *Gentlemen Jim* (1941), with Errol Flynn in the title role and Ward Bond portraying Sullivan, was released further cementing the mythology of the bare-knuckle boxer in American popular culture.

—*James M. Volo*

MUSIC

Popular music in the Industrial Age has been described as "pale imitations of European culture and shallow sentimentality." While this may be a fair assessment of the content, the commercialization of pop music certainly heralded the modern music industry, and the continued mixing of African and European musical forms was creating new and important musical styles in the United States. The Industrial Age laid the foundation of twentieth-century popular music through the creation of an organized popular music industry that churned out ballads and formed the basis of both blues and jazz.

It is very difficult to separate the widespread popularity of music in the Industrial Age with commercialization of the music industry. It was the growth of the sheet music industry that spread songs far and wide throughout the country and stimulated interest in music. Even rural mail-order catalogs contained a wide variety of sheet music such as popular dance, orchestral, gospel, ballads, minstrel, banjo, guitar, piano, and mandolin. Industrialization also made it possible to mass produce musical instruments cheaply and spread them throughout the nation on the growing railroad networks. Pianos and organs increasingly became symbols of genteel status for middle-class Americans and were a physical presence in the parlor that represented refined taste and artistic development. As a result of this demand, which continued to grow into the early twentieth century, piano production soared from 100,000 per year in 1890 to 350,000 per year in 1909, and 1897 marked the introduction of the first pneumatic player piano. Montgomery Ward sold five different organs from $37 to $63 in its 1895 catalog and three piano styles for $175, $195, and $210. These were very moderately priced for pianos. Manufacturers like Steinway sold their pianos for at least $600. The massive variety of instruments in the *Montgomery Ward Catalogue* vividly demonstrated the demand for musical instruments even in the nation's most rural areas: including accordions ($2–$10), concertinas ($2.15–$11.25), harmonicas ($.10–$.85), flutes ($1.65–$16.70), mandolins ($5.50–$15), guitars ($3.75–$26), banjos ($1.75–$18), dulcimers ($3.75–$16), violins ($2–$47), and a wide variety of cornets ($5.15–$26), trombones ($7.20–$16.70), and bugles ($1.30–$3.80). Such diversity in a mail-order catalog illustrates the importance of music in the lives of Americans during the Industrial age.

A wide assortment of music was popular in the Industrial Age including waltzes, polkas, marches, hymns, and particularly ballads. Developing from older hymn and folk tradition, ballads became the dominant form of popular music. These songs were designed to be easy to play and sing, since most songs of this era made their money through selling sheet music.

Most pop music in the Industrial Age was actually an interesting mixture of European and African musical forms. A mild form of syncopation gained widespread popularity in American music from early minstrel shows, which were vehicles for African American music developed in spirituals and work songs. A number of popular songs exhibited this mild syncopation even before the Civil War, such as *Dixie*, *The Yellow Rose of Texas*, and Stephen Foster's *Camptown Races* and *Oh! Susanna*. There was syncretism in American music that adapted African and European styles, producing something new and different. Widely different musical styles, spanning the spectrum from sentimental ballads to a Sousa military march, from Tin Pan Alley ballads to gospel songs, from "coon songs" to ragtime, would be the product of this blending of musical traditions.

The music industry, however, was still relatively unorganized. In the 1870s sheet music hits sold in the thousands while hits by the late 1880s and 1890s would sell in the millions. Popular hits continued to focus on topical events like *The Torrents Came Upon Them*, which was about the 1884 Johnstown Flood.

Many different reform movements turned to music as a political motivator. Many of the songs were written and performed in a standard folk song tradition. As the music industry expanded, however, a number of these songs became commercial hits and were published in the form of sheet music.

M. H. Evans and Emma Pow Smith wrote *When the Girls Can Vote* in 1890 in support of the efforts of the Woman's Christian Temperance Union, the largest women's organization of the Industrial Age. The song attacked male vices of swearing, drinking, and smoking and promised that when girls can vote "saloons will not be here." This song was typical of the anti-drinking movement connecting the vice with men and saloon culture. With songs like *The Little Brown Jug*, which extolled the joy of drinking, appealing to such a wide audience, it was little wonder that temperance advocates struck back with their own music.

Labor unions and farmers' organizations were geographically worlds apart, but they were united philosophically by their hostility toward concentrated wealth and corporate capitalism, as well as their celebration of manual labor that actually produced something. These themes appear over and over in union and farmer's songs that called for united action. Populist songs united both groups in the music, even though their attempt at political unity through the Populist Party failed by the late 1890s.

Populist songs that appealed to both labor and farmer groups often attacked concentrated wealth and monopoly. Leopold Vincent produced the *Alliance and Labor Songster* in 1891, which provided a large repertoire of songs for the movement. Large railroad corporations, which seemed to control entire states during the era, attracted particular venom, which was exemplified by R. J. Harrison's *The Anti-Monopoly War Song* of 1882. The title alone illustrated that the conflict between laborers and monopoly capital was more than a small one. It was a war. The lyrics attested to the song's aggressive attitude, and the closing lines rallied labor with an entreaty to make their battle cry "Ruin to Monopoly!" Songs like that sought to unite working people of all kinds through attacks on their common foe, monopoly capitalism. Populist music was an important part of efforts to organize their movement.

There were scores of songs sung just by labor unions and geared only to their concerns and issues. One of the most prominent goals of organized labor during the Industrial Age was the eight-hour day. The popular song, *Eight Hours* was published with the idea of promoting this goal. I. G. Blanchard actually wrote the song in 1866, but it was not set to music until Jesse H. Jones provided the music and published the song in 1878. The song relied on the common themes present in much of the organized labor music: the dignity of labor, exploitation by the wealthy, and a call for reform. Other songs like *Drill, Ye Tarriers, Drill* (1888), whose origin is very cloudy, praised drillers and blasters who built the nation's railroads, while Septimus Winner's *Out of Work* (1877) delved into the life of the unemployed worker. Songs like these appealed primarily to the industrial laborer, since an issue like an eight-hour day had little relevance to farmers, but gained wide popularity among a general public where wage labor was quickly becoming the norm.

Songwriters like George F. Root, who was one of the most prolific and popular songwriters of the 1850s and 1860s, produced songs meant to appeal to rural America, and his *The Hand that Holds the Bread* (1874) actually won widespread popularity. Root's song praised the power of farmers and called them to action.

Grange Melodies, which was published in 1881 and reprinted as late as 1904, covered a wide array of themes involving labor, patriotism, home, funerals, and temperance. Grangers came together with their *Greeting Song*; praised different work in *Laborer, Maid, Shepherdess, Harvester, Husbandman* and *Matron*; admonished members to *Forget Not the Dead*; sentimentalized *The Dear Old Farm*; called for concerted struggle in the *Battle Song*; sang the praise of the United States in *O' Columbia, We Love Thee*; supported temperance in *Hail the March of Prohibition*; and firmly declared *Labor is King*. There were even songs "for little Grangers" like *Work*, which extolled children, "Don't think there is nothing for children to do because they can't work like a man...work, work, work, children, work, there's work for children to do."

Just as sensationalized mass-market newspapers and magazines were beginning to dominate popular taste in journalism and literature by the 1890s, so did sensationalized mass-market songs come to prevail in popular music. Tin Pan Alley exemplified the organization of a system to mass-produce popular song hits. Thomas Hams (1881) and the Witmark brothers (1883), Isidore, Julius and Jay, founded firms that treated music as an industrial product, seeking not to edify nor even to entertain, but rather to produce popular hits that would generate massive profits. They pioneered the use of market research and hired in-house composers to write hit songs. Songwriters and publishers began to congregate on 28th Street in New York City to be closer to the popular shows that helped them make their songs big sellers. Writer Monroe Rosenfeld coined the phrase "Tin Pan Alley" because he thought the constant piano playing sounded like the clanging of tin pans. As New York became the center of musical theater and song publishing, the two interconnected industries drew more songwriters to the city. Only after an 1891 copyright law protected European music did Tin Pan Alley and this style of musical production really take form, as American song writers and publishers had to develop original music instead of relying on the European songs.

Charles Harris's *After the Ball* (1892) was the first big hit of the decade and stimulated the growth of the Tin Pan Alley system. This song sold two million copies of sheet music within a few years. Harris plugged his song using methods that were already pioneered by other Tin Pan Alley publishers. One of the best ways to plug a song was to get singers in musical theater to perform the song during their shows. This exposure helped to make the song a runaway hit and Harris was soon earning $25,000 per month from the sale of the sheet music.

Tin Pan Alley sheet music, which in this era normally sold for around $.50, customarily carried the name of the songwriter and a picture of the famous singer who performed it on the cover. *After the Ball* was no exception, sporting a picture of vaudeville star J. Aldrich Libbey. The song was so popular that John Philip Sousa's band played it for the 1903 Columbian Exhibition, giving it even more massive exposure.

The success of *After the Ball* alerted Tin Pan Alley to the possibilities of massive sales and the fact that a huge audience could be tapped. Songwriters and publishers of Tin Pan Alley consciously sought to conform to popular taste and write hits. In the 1890s it cost Tin Pan Alley publishers roughly $1,300 to promote a song, though only about half ever recouped the outlay and only approximately 1 in 20 was a genuine hit.

There was a relatively small group of men who were extremely successful at this pop music production. There were outstanding writers like Paul Dresser (brother of Theodore Dreiser), Charles K. Harris, Gussie Davis, Edward Marks, Joseph Shelly, Harry Kennedy, Charles Grahm, and Monroe Rosenfeld penning sheet music hits that were published by the big three publishing firms, Woodward, Witmark, and Stern-Howley-Harrison.

Dresser's *On the Banks of the Wabash* (1899) and *My Gal Sal* (1905) were huge hits. Charles Gussie Davis, the first successful African American composer on Tin Pan Alley, hit it big with *In the Baggage Coach Ahead* (1896). Million-sellers became much more commonplace in the 1890s, with Charles H. Hoyt's and Percy Gaunt's *The Bowery* (1892); Harry Dacre's *Daisy Bell*, which is better known as *Bicycle Built for Two* (1892); Charles B. Lawlor's and James W. Blake's *The Sidewalks of New York* (1894); John E. Palmer's and Charles B. Ward's *The Band Played On* (1895); Maude Nugent's *Sweet Rosie O'Grady* (1896); James Thornton's *When You Were Sweet Sixteen* (1898); Chauncey Olcott's *My Wild Irish Rose* (1899); and Arthur J. Lamb's and Harry Von Tilzer's *A Bird in a Gilded Cage* (1900). All these sold more than a million copies of sheet music. Most of these songs capitalized on romance, love lost, untimely death, daily life, nostalgia or good times and were often set to waltz tunes.

Coon songs were another very popular form of Tin Pan Alley music in the 1880s and 1890s, and became a veritable fad. Indeed, throwing some syncopation and African American racial stereotypes into a song in the 1890s and early twentieth century often led to a Tin Pan Alley hit. The style of coon songs varied dramatically from waltz to ragtime but the content remained based on a common set of racial stereotypes. More than 600 coon songs were published in the 1890s, and some sold spectacularly. Fred Fisher's *If the Man on the Moon Were a Coon* sold three million copies of sheet music. White and black songwriters wrote in the coon song idiom, including the famous white composer, George M. Cohan.

Coon songs had common elements. They often employed the syncopated rhythm of African American music along with foot tapping, time clapping rhythms that manifested themselves in dances like two-step cakewalks or marches. These songs also utilized racist stereotypes of African Americans for the entertainment of the white majority. These songs perpetuate stereotypical images of how whites wanted blacks to be: comical, superstitious, lazy, natural dancers, addicted to watermelon and chicken, ultra-sexual, and dangerous. Above all coon songs were supposed to be happy, funny songs. The racist humor was most evident in the fact that the coon songs were often in African American dialect, which was considered hilarious. Whites imposed on blacks these unfortunately durable stereotypes, which lasted well into the twentieth century. The songs also dealt with topics typically taboo in most Tin Pan Alley hits, like sexuality and violence, but they gained acceptance because they were about African Americans and they were couched in humor. Coon songs illustrate how popular songs were sensationalized in the 1890s by their focus on sexuality, gambling, and violence in a comic setting.

Bully songs were another popular element in the coon genre and normally dealt with a dangerous black man, usually a hustler and gambler wielding a razor, which soon became the ubiquitous symbol of black violence. May Irwin's *Bully Song* (1896), *Leave Your Razors at the Door* (1899), and *I'm the Toughest, Toughest Coon* (1904) were representative of this style. Coon songs, however, channeled this violence into so-called acceptable form, which used black-on-black violence that was tolerable to the wider white audience. Coon songs reaffirmed the necessity of subordinating and controlling African Americans and they justified segregation, voting restrictions, and even lynching.

Black, white, and even mixed black and white minstrel troupes continued to be very popular entertainment into the 1890s as vaudeville started to form. Remarkably even black performers like Bert Williams, who became famous in vaudeville, had to appear in blackface for white audiences. Blackface performers remained popular in vaudeville well into the twentieth century, and though many sought to temper the racist depictions within their shows, audiences expected to see the racist stereotypes.

While African Americans participated in the writing and performing of coon songs, little research has been done to explore how African American entertainers dealt with the racism of the era. Simply being able to make a good living as an entertainer or songwriter was significant for African Americans in the intensely racist Industrial Age. There is tantalizing evidence that black Americans did not sit idly by as they were stereotyped. In one instance, the *National Police Gazette* sponsored a ragtime piano contest to perform the extremely popular hit, *All Coons Look Alike to Me*, which was written by African American composer Ernest Hogan in 1896. The only black finalist, "Duke" Travers, refused to perform the song, stating that he did not know the tune. The song was deemed so offensive by New York City blacks that a white person whistling the tune instigated fights. Some black performers infused their coon songs with parody and subversive elements that undermined white racist stereotypes. A good example is what looks like a typical coon song from its title, *No Coons Allowed*, but actually parodied and attacked segregation in its lyrics. The comedy of the song hid the parody from white audiences that black audience members would have immediately recognized, namely the racist system that segregated blacks and ensured that they would never be treated fairly under the law.

Ragtime was another musical style that came out of African American culture. While coon songs certainly negatively stereotyped African Americans, they also provided greater opportunity for African American musicians, brought syncopated rhythms further into the mainstream, and ultimately made it easier for ragtime to be accepted by white audiences. Indeed, some of the coon song hits were performed in a ragtime singing style. Ragtime came in two relatively distinct forms, one that was primarily for singing and an instrumental version that was composed primarily for pianos.

The emergence of composed ragtime coincided with the growth of the piano industry and sales. The increase in pianos in the United States was both fueled by and helped fuel the popularity of ragtime. In spite of the popularity of this fad in music and its voluminous sales of sheet music, this style was in fact very difficult to play. The piano player had to maintain a steady left-hand bass beat while the right hand played a syncopated treble melody that displaced the accents. The traditional interpretation of the term ragtime is that it derived from ragging on the piano, but another, more recent interpretation maintains that it came from black musicians who raised rags or handkerchiefs to indicate when it was time to dance. Whatever the provenance of the word, piano ragtime had massive popular appeal in the 1890s and early twentieth century.

Ragtime developed out of African American folk music that was brewing all sorts of new music in the late nineteenth century. Ragtime piano music was certainly well known among black and a few white musicians before it first appeared in sheet music in 1896. Borrowing syncopated rhythms from minstrel show music was common in a variety of American music and piano players figured out how to rag just about any piece of music. White musician Ben Harvey learned the ragtime style from black folk musicians in Middlesborough, Kentucky, and learned how to apply it to piano music at least by the early 1890s. *You've Been a Good Old Wagon* in 1895 by Harvey was the earliest published ragtime piano piece. Harvey moved to New York City in the same year, became a well-known ragtime musician, and published the book *Ragtime Instructor* (1897) on how to play ragtime piano music. There is little doubt that Harvey was a significant figure in ragtime, but his claims to be the originator are undoubtedly exaggerated.

Hundreds of ragtime musicians, including Scott Joplin (1868–1917) swarmed to the Columbian Exposition in 1893 to play on the Midway or more likely in Chicago's saloons and concert halls. The timing clearly illustrates that Joplin, perhaps the most influential of the ragtime composers, and other ragtime musicians obviously had been developing this style for some time before Harvey published his first rag in 1895. Other published rags soon followed Harvey. In January 1897, William Krell's *Mississippi Rag* appeared in sheet music followed in December by Tom Turpin's *Harlem Rag*. Joplin wrote the *Maple Leaf Rag* in 1897, and it was published by 1899, going on to sell over one million copies of sheet music. Like Harvey's *You've Been a Good Old Wagon*, Joplin's hit rag was composed outside of Tin Pan Alley in Sedalia, Mississippi. Ragtime was a musical form that developed in several regions throughout the nation, emerging as a composed music in the 1890s from a variety of black and white entertainers. Ragtime remained popular until the middle of the 1910s, and would be an important precursor to jazz, the next great wave of popular music to assume a dominant position in American culture.

Brass bands remained very popular in the Industrial Age. Small to large bands were ubiquitous in American life. Bands provided entertainment for parades, picnics, dances, concerts, political campaigns, restaurants, and bars. They came in all shapes, sizes and abilities, including town bands, brass bands, ethnic bands, and the famous African American brass bands of New Orleans. Industrialization made it possible for instrument companies to lower the cost of their products and the transportation revolution made them widely available.

Patrick S. Gilmore (1829 1892) gained fame as a bandleader and organizer of musical extravaganzas in the 1860s and 1870s. His 22nd Regimental Band concerts featured popular favorites and classical orchestra songs, usually with a soloist on trombone, baritone horn, saxophone, or most commonly, coronet. Several famous coronet players toured with Gilmore, such as Matthew Arbuckle, Jules Levy, Alessandro Liberati, and Herbert L. Clark. Gilmore toured with his band until his death in 1892.

John Philip Sousa (1854–1932) assumed Gilbert's mantle as the most prominent bandleader in America when he formed his own band in 1892. Sousa had been around music his entire life, apprenticing seven years with the U.S. Marine Band starting at the age of 13 and at the age of 25, accepting the post of its director. In 1892 Sousa created his own military band, taking it through constant touring to fairs, expositions, theaters, and opera houses. The members of Sousa's band were polished professionals, dressed neatly in military-style uniforms. Like Gilbert before him, Sousa mixed musical styles at his concerts, throwing together hymns, popular songs, and some syncopated ragtime numbers alongside classical symphonic numbers and his own famous military marches. He was a very prolific composer and produced 12 operettas, 11 suites, 700 songs and 136 marches. Sousa, like many songwriters of this era, made much of his money through sales of sheet music, and roughly 18,000 people bought his music in 1900. Sousa marches became hugely popular, often focusing on patriotic themes such as *The Stars and Stripes Forever* (1897), and like Stephen Foster, his songs would find a permanent place in American music.

One of the largest problems for symphonic orchestras in the Industrial Age was that there was not really a great deal of difference between them and the better bands of the era and they played the same music at their concerts. Orchestra conductor Theodore Thomas, like band leaders Patrick Gilmore and John Philip Sousa, often played polkas and waltzes along with music by Liszt and Wagner to appeal to his audiences as he toured. Musical eclecticism was the norm in musical performance until the 1890s. Men like Thomas, however, sought to create a greater distinction between the band and the symphony. It is also important to note that the cultural elite in the realm of classical music as the major influence in the United States until World War I was German.

Henry Lee Higginson, a prominent Boston banker, charted the future of symphonic orchestras in 1881 when he created the permanent Boston Symphony Orchestra. Higginson ran the orchestra for several years in a rather dictatorial fashion, though he did ensure the viability of the orchestra from his own considerable fortune when receipts did not match outlays. Although no other cities copied Higginson's method, they did aspire to standing orchestras. In 1891, Chicago set the model that other cities soon emulated when 50 donors pledged $1,000 per year for three years to start the Chicago Symphony Orchestra. Chicago was able to lure Thomas away from New York to fulfill his dream of conducting a standing symphony orchestra. The Chicago symphony consisted of 62 full-time musicians. Philadelphia, St. Louis, Cincinnati, Minneapolis, and Pittsburgh all copied the Chicago example.

The advocates of symphonic music as high art increasingly turned to wealthy persons to support their permanent orchestras and classical music was transformed into an object controlled principally by the cultural elite. These orchestras relied on the works of masters like Mozart, Beethoven, Bach, and Handel, but new classical music also swept the nation. Richard Wagner's (1850–1898) works were so popular that a Wagnerian cult formed, primarily through the efforts of Wagner's friend Anton Seidl, who like Thomas was a German émigré to the United States. He soon became renowned for his conducting and support of Wagner's operas, such as *Tristan und Isolde, Die Walküre, Das Rheingold, Siegfried,* and *Götterdämmerung.* Seidl took over the New York Philharmonic in 1891 when Thomas left for Chicago. His ability to successfully stage summer concerts at Coney Island from 1888 to 1896 amazed even his critics.

The Second New England School, also called the Boston Classicists, were a group of mainly New England composers who wrote new music in the German tradition. These American composers were particularly active from 1890 to 1897 and had a close relationship with Theodore Thomas. Thomas encouraged their efforts and used their music in his orchestra. John Knowles Paine, Harvard professor of music; George W. Chadwick, longtime faculty member and then director of the New England Conservatory of Music; Arthur Foote, organist at the First Unitarian Church; Horatio Parker, Yale professor of music; Martin Loeffler, assistant concertmaster for the Boston Symphony Orchestra; Edward MacDowell, Columbia music professor;

and Amy Beach, one of the very few women composers, were all important contributors to this indigenous group of classical composers.

African American evangelicals were undoubtedly influenced by white gospel music, but to this they added their own tradition of the so-called Negro Spiritual. Black gospel music began its development as composers started setting down the older spirituals in sheet music. In the 1890s black songwriters, most importantly, Minister Charles Albert Tindley, began to produce music that emphasized the good news of Christianity and followed the biblical injunction to make a joyous noise to the Lord. Tindley was the first to compose in and publish the African American gospel style. Some of his most famous songs were *I'll Overcome Some Day* (1901), which became famous in the Civil Rights Movement as *We Shall Overcome, What Are They Doing in Heaven* (1901), and *Stand by Me* (1905). Black gospel music, however, was just in its infancy in these years and the greatest refinement and popularity would occur in the coming decades. It is important to note that black and white gospel music were closely related, and there were crossover hits, but racism and distinctive sound differences often kept them separate.

While the first published blues music did not appear until W. C. Handy published *The Memphis Blues* in 1912, it does deserve some mention. There is little doubt that African American singers and musicians developed blues music in the last decades of the nineteenth century, well before Handy became interested in what he termed primitive music and published his blues. In fact, elements of the blues appeared in popular music, particularly ragtime. Although the development of the blues as a distinct form did not occur until the early twentieth century, it was brewing in the cauldron of African American secular music of the Industrial Age.

Jazz also was coalescing in the late nineteenth century and was particularly influenced by ragtime. There was considerable confusion about the differences between jazz and ragtime in the early twentieth century, and many musicians referred to them interchangeably. While music critics might disagree with this view, it does demonstrate how fluid these musical lines were in the early twentieth century. Jazz would take America by storm just after World War I (Shrock 2004, 183–202).

LEISURE ACTIVITIES

The Grand Tour

The epitome of touring for upper-class families at mid-century was the Grand Tour of Europe. To winter in Rome had been the fashion among Europe's social elite since the seventeenth century, and Americans had followed their lead and extended their trips to include their historic roots in England, cosmopolitan and modern continental cities like Paris, romantic and artistic centers like Venice or Florence, enigmatic Egypt, and the Holy Land. Many well-known Americans had toured Europe with their families or lived there for extended periods. Among them were politicians, writers, and artists.

Writer and novelist Henry James visited Europe in 1867. He wrote that Americans were "forever fighting against the superstitious valuation of Europe. We feel that whatever it is we are lacking here can be found in Europe. There one finds royalty, foreign languages, high fashion; philosophers, anarchists, and artists; Neanderthals, pagan temples, and castles. Those who read a lot can easily become infatuated with Europe, and it becomes a projection of what it is they most desire" (Grattan 1962, 239). Historian Henry Adams, a grandson and great-grandson of two presidents, wrote that his father (Charles Francis Adams, U.S. Minister to London) felt that too strong a love of Europe "unfitted Americans for America," but it remained a pilgrimage site for many of his countrymen throughout the century. The flow of socially elite families to the Continent between 1820 and 1890 was interrupted only by the wars of European nationalism in the 1840s and America's own Civil War (Adams 1999, 70).

Available to only the richest of the old money families or the most fortunate of the *nouveau riche*, the Grand Tour could last for more than a year—sometimes several years—as families took in all of Europe's major cities, sights, museums, and vacation spots. Many fathers resorted to such once-in-a-lifetime trips to expose their children to the ways of the world and provide a polish that was thought to be missing from America's upper-class youth. Moreover, the stay was thought infinitely superior to an equal time spent in the colleges or female seminaries of America. The cost could run into thousands of dollars, but the tour was a priceless introduction to Europe's history, art, society, and culture for the entire family. "To lives made wealthy by the whirring wheels of northern industry or bumper harvests of southern cotton…the Grand Tour seemed the quickest and surest method of absorbing something which America lacked but which time-mossed Europe possessed in ample measure" (Levin 1960, 15).

Mark Twain (Samuel Clemens) wrote in *The Innocents Abroad* (1869) of his own grand tour in 1867:

For months the great pleasure excursion to Europe and the Holy Land was chatted about in the newspapers everywhere in America and discussed at countless firesides….It was to be a picnic on a gigantic scale. The participants in it…were to sail away in a great steamship with flags flying and cannon pealing, and take a royal holiday beyond the broad ocean in many a strange clime and in many a land renown in history! They were to sail for months over the breezy Atlantic and the sunny Mediterranean: they were to scamper about the decks by day . . . or read novels and poetry in the shade of the smokestacks, or watch for the jelly-fish and the nautilus over the side…and at night they were to dance in the open air, on the upper deck, in the midst of a ballroom that stretched from horizon to horizon, and was domed by the bending heavens and lighted by no meaner lamps than the stars….They were to see the ships of twenty navies—the customs and costumes of twenty curious peoples—the great cities of half the world—they were to hob-nob with nobility and hold friendly converse with kings and princes, grand moguls, and the anointed lords of mighty empires! (Twain 1980, 2–3)

The itinerary for the Grand Tour was no mean ride through the countryside. The Crystal Palace built for the Great London Exhibition of 1851, the Champs-Elysees, the battlefields of Waterloo, Crecy, and Breitenfeld, Hadrian's Forum and the Coliseum, Vesuvius and Stromboli, the Parthenon and Delphi, and the Great Pyramids with the enigmatic Sphinx were all among the popular stops on the tour. The tourists stayed in the best European-style hotels and visited foreign resorts such as mineral springs, baths, shrines, and Alpine retreats, sometimes in an effort to restore a shattered health in an alternative environment. All of these were on the usual itinerary of the European upper classes, and it was partly for this reason that many Americans were sure to visit them.

Seventeen-year-old Fanny Knight of Natchez, Mississippi, traveling with her family from 1854–1859, reveled in her diary of fleeting glimpses of Queen Victoria and Prince Albert, the Emperor Louis Napoleon and Empress Eugenie, Pope Pius IX, Russia's Emperor Alexander II, and Jerome Bonaparte (émigré brother of Napoleon I) and his American wife. Also prominent on Fanny's tour were meetings with ex-President Millard Fillmore and Senator Charles Sumner of Massachusetts, who had been caned on the Senate floor by Representative Preston Brooks of South Carolina in 1856. The Knight family remained on tour long enough to become resident members of an international colony of traveling tourists that included a young sculptor from Hartford, Connecticut, two young American girls on their way to enter a convent in Spain, and two families of their acquaintance from home passing through Egypt on their own tours.

Throughout the century American tourists shopped for European and ancient culture while on the Grand Tour. The families of America's robber barons, in particular, bought up all the portable culture they could find on the European market while on tour and shipped it or carried it home. After returning from Paris, London, Rome, Florence, or Cairo, the family could bask in the reflected glory of their journey in a home decorated with paintings, sculptures, curiosities, archaeological souvenirs, and other mementos that marked them as persons worthy of admiration and envy. In defense of the Americans it should be noted that upper-class European families did exactly the same thing throughout the Victorian Era.

Among Fanny Knight's keepsakes were those minute things one might expect of a nineteenth-century teenager: prints, postcards, bills, and letterheads. These included colorful printed mementos from the Old Ship's Head Hotel in Brighton, the Turkshead Hotel in New Castle-on-Tine, the George Hotel in Melrose, Stringer's Hotel in Windermere Waterhead as well as The Hotel de Flandre in Bergen, the Hotel de Russ in Brussels, the Hotel Belle Vue at The Hague, and the Eagle House in Heidelberg. There was also a chromolithograph of the *Luxor*, an Egyptian river steamer fitted with ornate furniture, beds and bedding, a coal stove, and provisions of the best quality on which the Knights traveled the Nile.

As Mark Twain pointed out, the Grand Tour was "a brave conception; it was the offspring of a most ingenious brain. It was well advertised, but it hardly needed it: the bold originality, the extraordinary character, the seductive nature, and the vastness of the enterprise provoked comment everywhere and advertised it in every household in the land (Levin 1960, 2). The Grand Tour was, for most upper-class families, "at once the fulfillment of a lifelong ambition and a flamboyant way of letting neighbors know that they had arrived" (Levin 1960, 15; Volo and Volo 2007, 344–48).

Croquet

By far the most popular family lawn sport of the Industrial Age was croquet. Although it started as an elite game, making its debut in America in the second half of the 1860s, the mass production of backyard croquet sets along with the fact that it required no special clothing allowed it to flourish among the middle class in the 1870s. The game was particularly popular among women, as it required considerable skill but little strength or technique. Men tended to be less passionate about the sport but appreciated its social advantage since both men and women played together. Croquet promoters founded the National Croquet Association in 1879 and organized the first national tournament in 1882 at the New York Croquet Club, and adopted a standard set of rules for the nine-wicket game. In the same year the South Bend Toy Works began manufacturing toy croquet sets. In the 1895 *Montgomery Ward Catalogue* croquet sets cost only $.68 for the least expensive four-ball version and $3.40 for the most expensive eight-ball version. At the height of the croquet fad, ads boasted wickets with candle sockets for night play. The Boston Common served as a popular place for croquet but the drinking, gambling, and other behavior, including the possibility that young couples might disappear into shrubbery together to look for balls, alarmed the local clergy enough for them to seek a ban on the game in 1890 for moral reasons.

By the 1880s the game's faddish nature began to be diluted by the emergence of lawn tennis, but the game continued to be popular. Former slave Frederick Douglass loved the game and built a croquet court at his Anacosta, Virginia, home in 1894. Croquet served as inspiration for table games as well. McLoughlin Brothers copyrighted the rules for *Tiddledy Wink Croquet*, and E. I. Horsman came out with *Lo Lo the New Parlor Croquet Game*, which used colored disks to represent the croquet balls and mallet disks to snap them into positions or through the arches (Shrock 2004, 118).

Roller Skating

In 1863, James Leonard Plimpton, a businessman from Massachusetts, invented a roller skate that could turn by putting a spring on the four-wheeled footwear. It was called the rocking skate and was the first one that really let people skate curves and turn. Plimpton opened a skating club in New York where gentlemen enjoyed showing off for their ladies by doing fancy figures, steps, and turns. Within 20 years, roller skating had become a popular pastime for men and women. Entrepreneurs built large skating rinks, like Chicago's famous Casino Rink whose 1884 opening drew thousands of skaters and spectators. When the Royal Rink opened in Muncie, Indiana, in 1885, a thousand people paid $.15 each to skate. Wealthy men in Newport, Rhode Island, played roller polo, a hockey game, which developed into a popular league sport in several Midwestern cities in the 1880s. Muncie had roller polo teams by 1885 and it was so popular it became a high school sport. Roller skate racing and dancing also became popular pastimes. The glory days of this fad ended in the 1890s with the advent of the safety bicycle (Shrock 2004, 118).

BROWNIES

A fad totally unconnected to sports was the Brownie creations of illustrator Palmer Cox. Brownies made their first appearance in *St. Nicholas Magazine* in 1883. These delightful little creatures soon became an absolute sensation with children across the country. Cox's creations always seemed to be playing in department stores with the latest popular consumer items like roller skates and bicycles. Cox parlayed his creations into a small marketing empire that made him quite wealthy through a series of books and Brownie games. The 1895 *Montgomery Ward Catalogue* offered three Brownie books (*The Brownies at Home, The Brownies: Their Book* and *The Brownies Around the World*) that sold for $1.05 each, three sets of Brownie ink stamps for $.20, $.40 and $.75 respectively and Brownie 10 pins for $.45. Brownie tie-in products were everywhere, culminating in the famous Kodak Brownie camera that appeared in 1900, marketed toward children. Brownies became a cultural icon that was a generational marker, which helped to define young people during the late Industrial Age. Most children of the period would have experienced Brownies in some form and this experience would have defined their generation and collective memories. The Brownie mania may have been the first time a generation of American young people was united by such an iconoclastic common consumer item and illustrated the growth of a consumer culture directed toward young people (Shrock 2004, 120–21).

GAMES

Card games were a favorite in Victorian homes and consumed a great deal of leisure time for adults and children. Adults enjoyed playing *Euchre, Five Hundred*, and *Whist*. *Old Maid, Go Fish*, and *Snap* were popular among children. Educational cards games such as *Authors* proved to be the favorite of the middle class who placed great store on educational games that inculcated refined sensibilities. The 1895 *Montgomery Ward Catalogue* carried 20 different card games ranging in price from $.10 to $.40 featuring such educationally enriching titles as *Capitol Cities, Mathematiques, Wild Flower Game, Bible Game*, and *American History*.

Board games were wildly popular and readily available in department stores and mail-order catalogs. Reasonable prices, between $.40 and $2.75, brought them into many American homes during the 1890s. Some games emphasized the educational refinement so important to middle-class culture, such as reading, literature, geography, and mathematics. A typical game was the *Young Folks Historical Game* (1890) that quizzed players on American history. Other games focused on middle-class values like business enterprise such as *Bulls and Bears: The Great Wall St. Games* (1896), while still others were simple games of chance and skill, which reflected the cultural acceptance of leisure for its own sake that was spreading throughout American society. *The Game of Travel* (1895) simulated a tour through Europe and included metal steamships and railroad trains as pieces. Some popular games echoed current events of the Industrial Age like *Round the World with Nellie Bly* (1894), *Bowling* (1896), *The Game of Pool* (1898), and *Basketball* (1898). *The Yale-Harvard Game* offered young people the opportunity to play and re-play the yearly football game between the heated rivals. Nursery rhyme themes were also very popular such as *Little Goldilocks and the Three Bears* (1890), *The Game of Jack and the Beanstalk* (1896), and *The New Game of Red Riding Hood and the Wolf* (1887). Checkers, chess, and dominoes were virtually universal in this era played by both adults and children.

Jigsaw puzzles, which gained popularity in the 1850s, were mass-produced by Milton Bradley and Parker Brothers and became very popular pastimes. By the mid-1890s even rural Americans could purchase a variety of the cut-up puzzles through mail-order catalogs. These, too, offered educational experiences. The 1895 *Montgomery Ward Catalogue* featured puzzle maps of the United States in either small ($.45) or large ($.75). Others puzzles were reflective of current interests such as the elephant Jumbo, a steamboat, and a fire department.

Marbles were another immensely popular game, particularly among boys. Mass-produced glass marbles became widely available during the Industrial Age. Ohio was the center of marble production where factories produced a million marbles a day. The new, highly colored marbles, no longer just stone or clay, inspired fierce competition among boys who battled for each other's marbles. Aggies, the rare agate marbles, were particularly prized. Youngsters in the late nineteenth century generally used the term mibs instead of marbles and commonly played "Ring Taw." Players tried to knock other players' marbles out of the ring or taw, thus gaining the displaced marbles for himself. The game included intricate rules about changing shooting positions and accidents. Marbles encouraged boys to develop competitive qualities so admired among males in the late nineteenth century. Charles M. Crandall's *Pigs in Clover* was the only board game to capitalize on the immense popularity of marbles and it became the most important indoor marble game of the era (Shrock 2004, 121–25).

COLLECTING

Collecting was popular with men, women, and children. What separated men's collecting from that of women and children was that men collected items that were economically valuable. Men tended to evaluate the monetary worth of their collections. Their collecting relied heavily on the application of knowledge and an acquired expertise, often in the context of unearthing a hidden bargain. Collectors often used hunting metaphors when talking about their acquisitions. Women, on the other hand, collected differently. They were inclined to accumulate items for sentimental value.

Stamp collecting, which had begun as an interest of women and children in the 1860s, was transformed in nature by male hobbyists by the 1880s. What separated the later phase of stamp collecting from its beginnings were attempts to scientifically classify and organize stamps into sets. Stamp collectors even coined a scientific term for their hobby, philately. Serious philatelists were collectors who appreciated the market value and authenticity of their stamps rather than the aesthetics of the album. While women stamp collectors like Eva Earl promoted women's participation in the hobby, the fact that stamp collecting embraced the market model worked to keep many women out of it. Earl, for example, did not collect in the same manner as men, and admitted to cleaning and mending stamps in her collection, which were major offenses to the male notion of scientific authenticity. The identification and organization of the stamps was vital to the dominant philatelist culture of the Industrial Age, but these appeals did not stop young people, particularly boys, from engaging in this popular activity as they saw fit.

Other popular collecting hobbies were much like stamp collecting in their focus on scientific collecting and male domination. Book collectors sought rare manuscripts and compiled collections where the hunt and economic value were stressed. Coin collecting, called numismatics, was another popular hobby. The first annual convention of the American Numismatic Association occurred in 1891 in Chicago.

Antique collecting also became quite trendy during the Industrial Age. Unlike the previously mentioned fields of collecting, large numbers of women engaged in antique collecting alongside of men. Starting roughly in the year of the centennial of American Independence, 1876, collectors scoured the countryside for colonial furniture. Some people had come to object to the dominant, highly ornamented Victorian styles in preference of the simpler colonial styles. By the 1880s furniture manufacturers were making colonial reproductions, but it was still cheaper to search for bargains in the countryside. The idea that there was value in the old dresser or table stowed away in the barn was completely foreign to most farm folk, so there were bargains to be found by ambitious antique hunters. The Colombian Exposition of 1893 generated even more interest with its prominent display of American handicrafts. Much of this collecting was aimed at fine furniture, but some collectors also pioneered collecting everyday items like bottles and birdcages (Shrock 2004, 132–35).

PHOTOGRAPHY

Still photography underwent a transformation in the Industrial Age. Although cameras had long been available for professionals and hobbyists, in 1888 George Eastman introduced the Kodak, the first camera made for a mass audience. The Kodak was designed for ease of use in shooting, and more importantly, Eastman's company developed completed film. Prior to this, photographers had to have their own dark rooms. The Kodak, which initially sold for $25, was an immediate success, selling 2,500 units in its first six months and over 13,000 in its first year. It proved popular with travelers, particularly those traveling by train to new vacation spots, but many with families also used Kodaks to visually record for the first time family events such as birthdays, christenings, and reunions (Husband and O'Loughlin 2004, 190).

TRAVELING SHOWS

With the rise of rail travel and other improvements in transportation, it became economically feasible to take entertainments usually restricted to urban locations on the road. Theatrical companies would often begin a show in a major city and then take advantage of the publicity it received to launch a regional tour of smaller cities and towns. Other traveling shows developed in unique ways that took advantage of the logistics of travel and one night only appearances. While the best-known form of this type of entertainment was the circus, other popular traveling shows of the period included Wild West shows and *Uncle Tom's Cabin* shows, and the traveling lectures that became known as Chautauquas.

The cultural form that, in many ways, set the standard for traveling shows was the world's fairs. Though world's fairs were not exactly traveling shows, like the present day Olympics, they rotated through different cities and proved hugely successful in bringing together a range of entertainments, educational exhibits, and technological displays into one location. The world's fairs drew unprecedented numbers of people. The Centennial Exhibition of 1876 in Philadelphia attracted nearly 10 million people, almost one-fifth of the population of the United States at that time, and the 1893 World's Columbian Exhibition in Chicago had over 27 million visitors. Educational exhibits and displays of manufacturing technology were central to the fairs, but the fairs were huge and decentered experiences. A visitor could stroll the grounds of Chicago's "White City," the central fairground designed in a neoclassical style, or visit the Midway Plaisance, the accompanying sideshow venue that featured pseudoscientific ethnographic displays often featuring stereotypical and racist presentations of foreign peoples and a range of popular entertainments. These fairs gave back to the realm of popular entertainments a model for the spectacular. Traveling shows of the period learned from the fairs and increasingly grew in size and scope, and in the level of technology used to dazzle customers. These shows addressed a desire for entertainment in the most remote sections of the expanding United States (Husband and O'Loughlin 2004, 191).

WILD WEST SHOWS

When "Buffalo Bill" Cody launched his first Wild West Show in 1883, he was already a famous man. As a military scout and frontiersman, Cody's adventures had been celebrated in a series of dime novels, and he even starred in a play dramatizing his Western experiences. It was the enormous success, however, of his Wild West Show that made him one of the foremost celebrities of the late nineteenth century. His Wild West show at the 1893 Columbian Exhibition drew an estimated six thousand visitors. By 1900 over 100 imitators were touring the United States with their own Wild West shows.

Wild West Shows were a hybrid form of entertainment. Part circus, part rodeo, part shooting exhibition, and part historical pageant, they offered a combination of spectacles that proved hugely popular in tours throughout the United States and Europe, despite having high admission costs of $.50 for adults and $.25 for children at a time when the average worker earned between $1 and $1.50 per day. A typical show would publicize in advance with four-color promotional posters and extensive newspaper advertising. When the troupe came into town, they would have a circus-style parade through the center of town to drum up interest. The show itself began later that same day with a procession in which the troupe raced around the arena on horseback to the roar of the crowd. What then followed varied from season to season, but the show usually included horse races and riding tricks, displays of marksmanship, some of which featured the popular female sharpshooter Annie Oakley, staged scenes of reenacted historical battles between cowboys and Indians, and rodeo style roping and bronco riding. Though Native Americans were a vital part of the Wild West show, they played a supporting role and their stories were not told, even when famous Native leaders such as Sitting Bull and Geronimo appeared as part of Cody's troupe (Husband and O'Loughlin 2004, 193–94).

UNCLE TOM'S CABIN SHOWS

The most popular play of the nineteenth century was *Uncle Tom's Cabin*. While Harriet Beecher Stowe's novel was the best-selling novel of the nineteenth century, for every person who read the book perhaps 50 saw a dramatized and generally corrupted version of it. In 1879, there were 49 traveling troupes performing *Uncle Tom's Cabin*, sometimes exclusively, and by turn of the century there may have been almost 10 times that many.

The "Tom's Troupes" took many liberties with the details of Stowe's novel, and some of the permutations of the play make more sense when considered, not in light of the novel, but in terms of the competition a traveling troupe was likely to face on the road. Like circuses, the troupes would advertise appearances with a parade of the cast down small-town Main streets, and some performances even attempted to compete with circuses by including elephants and alligators. Horses and trained bloodhounds were also added to the play. In the 1880s "Double Mammouth" shows became popular. These shows brought the novelty of a two- or three-ring circus to the stage by doubling the most popular characters of the play. These shows would have two Uncle Toms, two Topseys, and two Evas.

The popularity of *Uncle Tom's Cabin* at this time seems strange as it did not aim to arouse people over current injustices the way Stowe's novel did in the 1850s. Producers of the play offered it as a morally appropriate entertainment and sometimes recommended it as a lesson in history. At the same time the play constantly changed to offer new spectacular features. Others incorporated brass bands or choruses of African American Jubilee singers. Many simply replayed routines that had become popular in minstrel shows with white actors in blackface. Mainly, it told an old story in a new way, bringing novelty to the city stage and the far reaches of rural America (Husband and O'Loughlin 2004, 195–96).

LADIES' CRAFTS

Middle-class women increasingly found that certain functions, which had previously been a necessity for the family, were no longer needed in the same way. The skills, however, were still valued, and they came to be transformed into crafts. The Industrial Age was a golden age for arts and crafts of all kinds. From embroidery to quilting, crochet to lace making, crafts flourished. Handmade items could be found in abundance. Elaborate quilts and crocheted bedspreads were a central feature of most middle-class home décor. So were lace curtains, embroidered upholstery, and appliquéd table toppers. A whole range of unusual crafting techniques were developed or perfected during the era, including straw embroidery, Renaissance braid lace, and twist patchwork. At the same time, better-known crafts such as tatting reached new heights of popularity

While sewing remained a necessity for some women, the mechanization of the process, with the introduction of the sewing machine, patterns, and ready-made clothing, radically altered home sewing for most. Sewing was less involved with the production of a family's necessities and more a leisure activity that was done for decorative purposes.

The passion for lavish embellishment combined with the desire to decorate in the latest style led to the creation of an endless variety of household linens. Women decorated new linens and gave new life to old lines with the addition of outline embroidery. Mail-order booklets provided patterns, monograms, and stamping instructions to create designs to be embroidered. The designs reflected contemporary interests. The arts and crafts display at the Japanese Pavilion at the Philadelphia Centennial Exposition in 1876 inspired many women with a passion for Oriental design. Women's magazines featured linens decorated by cherry blossom sprays, fans, teapots, vases, and a host of other Oriental motifs. An 1883 issue of *Peterson's Magazine* devoted an entire page to "Birds from Japanese Designs."

Women with children also embroidered nursery linens. The Victorian movement to provide a specific room in the house dedicated to children led to the need for nursery linens. Outline embroidery patterns in magazines and booklets featured animals, clowns, nursery rhyme characters, and other child-oriented designs. Designs based on the drawings of Kate Greenway proved to be particularly popular and were featured in *Harper's Bazaar*, *Art Amateur*, and *Godey's Lady's Book*. Many women embroidered pillow shams, splashers for sinks, towels, tidies, and numerous linens with parades of children dressed in the charming costumes featured by Greenway (Weissman and Lavitt 1987, 107–9).

Another nursery accessory was the appliquéd crawling rug. Created for little ones just beginning to learn how to get about, it provided them with a clean, cozy place to play. *Dainty Work for Pleasure and Profit*, published in 1893, suggested using a piece of felt, or flannel, or old dress skirt for the foundation. This would be decorated with brightly colored scraps, which had been cut into the shape of toys, animals, and other figures suitable for the young child. The rugs were then further embellished with embroidery stitches (Weissman and Lavitt 1987, 163).

Patchwork quilting gained popularity during the 1830s and 1840s, and while it reached its height between the 1850s and 1875, it continued to be enjoyed by many throughout the century. Women worked alone and in groups to make quilts for themselves and as community projects. They shared patterns, and some women fashioned single squares to help them remember a pattern they might want to use in the future. By the late 1800s patterns for quilt designs began to appear in print. Farm magazines discovered that they could attract woman readers by printing quilt block patterns. Other magazines and even newspapers soon followed. By 1890 catalogs included quilt patterns. If a woman ordered her yard goods from Sears or Montgomery Wards' she could purchase any of 800 designs for just a dime. *Ladies Art* also offered patterns in full sized blocks in either calico or silk for one to three dollars.

The Industrial Age witnessed a new craze with the crazy quilt. The pattern got its name from the asymmetrical pieces of fabric sewn together in abstract arrangements, which were thought to resemble crazed porcelain. The fad is thought to have been inspired by the Oriental design craze. Crazy quilts differed from other quilts in their use of expensive fabrics such as silk, satin, brocade, and velvet and the needlework used to embellish them. Embroidered feather, herringbone, fly, and chain stitches done in silk thread decorated each seam. Many had additional stitching and embroidered motifs. Animals and flowers seem to have been the favorite. Some quilters believed that embroidering a spider on its web would bring them good luck. Some crazy quilts had painted designs and even beadwork. Although crazy-style quilts appeared haphazard, they were carefully planned. Hours were spent cutting shapes and trying out various arrangements of the pieces prior to sewing. Originally, crazy quilts were made by women of the upper class. They were status symbols that showed a woman had the money to spend on the materials and the leisure time to complete such a time consuming project. Many of these quilts were so ornate that they were more show pieces than functional bed coverings and were commonly made as shorter, narrower unquilted lap robes or throws, which were used to decorate the parlor. Before long, other women joined in the fad and resourcefully reused fancy clothing that had been discarded or passed on from others. Making a crazy quilt was also a popular fundraising activity. Sometimes churchwomen would write to famous people asking for a piece of clothing that could be incorporated into a quilt they were making to raise money to help the missionaries.

The Centennial Exposition also introduced American women to the Decorative Arts Movement, an English phenomenon inspired by William Morris, John Ruskin, and their followers. The movement maintained that commercialism devalued the work of craftsmen and that the manner in which an item was made was integral to the quality of the product. Morris and his followers drew their inspiration from the craftsmen of the Middle Ages. Traditional skills of tile glazing, woodcutting, engraving, bookbinding, weaving, tapestry, and embroidery were revived as fashion turned away from the overstated opulence of Victorian style. A New York socialite organized the New York Decorative Art Society in 1877 and encouraged women to do beautiful needlework in this English and newly popular Oriental styles. Similar art societies sprang up in cities around the country, establishing themselves as arbiters of national taste. In time, these ideas gained some traction. An 1883 issue of the *Delineator* questioned the days of labor squandered in embroidering a simple towel that was no more useful than one that was unadorned. It was suggested that more artistic crafts such as woodworking, woodburning, marquetry, and other carpentry were better suited to the modern woman, sparking an increase in these craft pursuits (Weissman and Lavitt 1987, 109).

—*Dorothy Denneen Volo*

THEATER, CONCERT SALOONS, VAUDEVILLE, AND PEEP SHOWS

Urban theaters of the early 1800s were notably class inclusive. Rich, middle class and poor all attended the same theater, sitting in different sections according to what they were willing to pay. Those with money could purchase chairs in reserved boxes. Workers tended to stand in the pit right below the stage. Cheap upper balcony seats were also available, and in most theaters, African American patrons and prostitutes were restricted to this section. Shakespearean recitations would alternate with jugglers and trained monkey acts. It was not uncommon to see Italian opera performed alongside contemporary ballads like *Home, Sweet Home*.

Beginning around mid-century and continuing into the industrial era, cities grew in prosperity and new theaters were built that catered to the upper class. The cost of a theater ticket in the mid-1880s was a dollar, two-thirds of an average worker's daily wage. Workers and much of the middle class found themselves priced out of most legitimate theaters and turned instead to cheaper concert saloons and vaudeville. As a result Shakespeare and opera, which were once part of a shared culture, became almost the exclusive domain of elite society. The diversity of early theater and musical performances disappeared as well, and gone were the days when Shakespeare was performed alongside trained animals.

Concert saloons varied in the amount of theatrical entertainment they provided, but most had some kind of musical stage show. These were exclusively male establishments, with the exception of prostitutes and female dancers, and while they drew patrons from a range of class positions, they tended to be too expensive for most workers. In the end, the vacuum left by the decline of theaters for the middle class was filled by vaudeville.

The motivation for vaudeville in the 1880s came with the realization that selling the same theater seat four times a day for 25 cents made as much money as selling a one-dollar seat for a daily performance. By offering low-cost continuous performances of variety acts, a whole new audience was found among the middle-class and, to a lesser degree, working-class patrons. Benjamin Franklin Keith, the most famous of the vaudeville impresarios, established successful vaudeville theaters in a number of U.S. cities with a rotating schedule of performers. Most theaters were open 12 hours a day, 6 days a week. Anyone with a quarter could stop in for an hour or stay for a whole evening. Vaudeville theaters made a point of distinguishing themselves from saloon theaters by attracting female customers. Special advertisements and matinees were set up to bring in women shoppers. Smoking and drinking were prohibited or tightly controlled.

The diversity of audiences and performances that had disappeared from now-elite theaters now reappeared in vaudeville. While a headline act would be featured on a vaudeville theater's marquee, a given night's bill might include as many as 30 short acts including ballad singers, magicians, blackface minstrels, acrobats, opera singers, one-act plays, and sports stars each taking the stage for 15 to 30 minutes. Vaudeville aimed to attract the largest possible audience by providing an assortment of acts. By the end of the century, vaudeville had still only made inroads into the urban working class, as it offered little for immigrants with marginal English language skills, but it did bring in droves of middle-class men, women, and children. Some vaudeville houses even began to attract wealthy patrons by building new, elaborate theaters and including symphony performances as part of their bill of fare.

In the 1890s cinema consisted of a range of primitive machines and films shown in a variety of settings and formats. Following Thomas Edison's invention of the Kinetoscope in 1893, new Kinetoscope or peep show parlors appeared in the United States. These parlors offered row after row of Kinetoscopes and similar machines made by Edison's competitors that allowed a viewer to look through a peep hole and see a short film, perhaps a minute in length. Subjects included such events as a man flexing his muscles or a slapstick routine or a circus act. Kinetoscope parlors charged a quarter for admission, keeping them out of the price range of the majority of the population. It was not until early in the next century that prices dropped and workers and children became patrons of these parlors, which were renamed nickelodeons and later penny arcades.

Edison's Vitascope, introduced in 1895, marked another innovation. It was the first successful movie projector, allowing projection of short silent films. The Vitascope proved to be a novelty, appearing in vaudeville theaters and as part of lecture hall performances. Entrepreneurs would travel with Vitascopes to small towns, finding eager audiences, particularly in the West that had never before seen moving pictures. Storefront theaters solely devoted to Vitascope screenings appeared in cities and proved popular with immigrant populations that did not need to speak English to be entertained by silent films.

Film technology remained primitive through the turn of the century. Early projectors played as little as 16 seconds of film at a time, though the film could be looped for continuous play, and the lack of new films also contributed to the gradual decline in audiences and the temporary disappearance of films from vaudeville bills. The coming of the Spanish-American War in 1898, however, created new interest in war films, and fledgling studios were quick to produce documentary war footage or to stage their own battles in makeshift studios for vaudeville. It was not until the first decade of the 1900s as technology and filmmaking improved that movie theaters became popular (Husband and O'Loughlin 2004, 188–90).

HOLIDAYS, CELEBRATIONS, AND FESTIVALS

New Year, the Mummers Parade

The Mummer's tradition dates back to 400 B.C. and the Roman Festival of Saturnalias where laborers marched in masks throughout a day of satire and gift exchange mixed with the Druidic custom of noise making to drive away demons for the new year. The name "mummers" comes from the impersonations of the English mummers' play of *St. George and the Dragon*.

Although the origins of the New Year's Mummers Parade can date all the way back to the 1700s or even before, the practice seems to have first taken hold in the 1840s. This tradition relates back to the Swedish who settled outside of Philadelphia. They brought their tradition of "Second Day Christmas" where they would visit their friends. Eventually this tradition extended to the New Year. Masqueraders paraded the streets of old Philadelphia and the other sections—now a part of the city—in joyous revelry. The mummers went house to house, dressed up or with blackened faces, shouting, making noise with bells and sundry noisemakers, and shooting pistols seeking spirits and cakes. The early Swedish Mummers appointed a leader, or speech director, who had a special dance step and who recited a rhyme like this:

> As we stood the year before
> Give us whiskey, give us gin,
> Open the door and let us in.

Mumming was discontinued during the Civil War but after the conflict many clubs were reorganized. While original costumes were quite simple, creating disguises of clowns, Indians, or devils. A favorite outfit was simply a greatcoat turned inside out. The flaring headpieces, widespread collars and flowing capes synonymous with modern mummers came about in 1880 when the first cape requiring pageboys was worn. Clubs who followed this practice came to be known as "Fancy" clubs. This began a period of great rivalry and the beginning of prizes for the best paraders. The money given was donated by local merchants for cakes and other food items to be given to the marchers. The number of mummers grew as the prizes increased. The first cash prize was given in 1888. One of the first comic clubs made its debut in 1884. These mummers dressed as clowns for the purpose of making those along the parade lines laugh. The first official Mummers Parade was held in 1901 (Cohen and Coffin 1987, 3–5).

New Year, the Tournament of Roses Parade

The idea for the Tournament of Roses parade was developed toward the end of the 1880s as a midwinter community event that would show the rest of the country the utopian climate of an area [California] that produced roses and oranges in midwinter. The event was patterned after a European Festival of Roses. The Valley Hunt Club adopted the plan and on January 1, 1890, held a community parade and picnic. The parade was a line of decorated horse-drawn private carriages, with prizes awarded to the most beautifully decorated. Athletic events were held in the afternoon, and in the evening, a ball where winners of the events of the day and the most beautiful float were announced. Bicycle races were held from 1895 to 1898. The 1895 parade was so large that the Pasadena Tournament of Roses Association was formed to administer it. By 1898 reporters from Eastern newspapers were sent to cover it (Cohen and Coffin 1987, 6).

New Year Calling

By the late 1880s, the custom of New Year's Day calling had become so pervasive and the visits by perfect strangers so numerous that hospitalities were often narrowed down to a lady's own circle of acquaintances. Even this boundary, in many instances, drew so many callers that some ladies were compelled either to close their doors for the day or to issue cards of welcome to a limited number of their gentlemen acquaintances. Some open houses offered liquor as refreshment and a number of young men were much more interested in getting intoxicated than in paying social respects. This became such a problem that, in 1886, *Social Etiquette in New York* advised ladies not to offer wine because it was dangerous for their acquaintances to partake of varied vintages, passing in and out of overheated drawing rooms. By the 1890s the tradition of New Year's Day open houses evolved into family calls and receptions for invited guests only.

—*Dorothy Denneen Volo*

Passover

Between 1882 and 1924, 2.3 million Jews immigrated to the United States, most fleeing persecution in Eastern Europe and Russia. Famine in Lithuania and the assassination of Czar Alexander the II in 1891 led to the forced retirement of Jews outside Russian villages, onerous taxes on kosher foods, and efforts to undermine Jewish culture. Eastern European Jews immigrating to the United States felt a close affinity to the Biblical Jews fleeing slavery in Egypt. It is not surprising that among the many festivals of Judaism, Passover, which commemorated this exodus, became the most frequently observed Jewish holiday in the United States.

The new Jewish immigrants stood in stark contrast to the comparatively secular and assimilated German Jewish population already settled in the United States. The new immigrants were more orthodox and more concerned with preserving Jewish customs and culture. For many Jews, being able to openly observe Jewish customs and dietary rules without discrimination was the very definition of freedom.

The new immigrants and the more assimilated immigrants, together, redefined the Passover ritual. Passover celebrations in the United States commemorated the exodus of the Israelites from Egypt, but they also commemorated the delivery of contemporary Jews from their persecution in Europe. The Passover celebration became a means of feeling connected to Jewish history and Jewish identity amid strong forces urging assimilation in the United States. Moreover, Passover reinforced a sense of solidarity among American Jews from different European origins.

At the seder, families follow a written script called the Haggadah, which includes parts for all family members, especially children. It is comprised of prayers and stories explaining the significance of the holiday and meaning of each element of the traditional seder meal. The matzah, unleavened flat bread, symbolizes the haste of the Jews leaving Egypt who could not wait for their bread to rise. Bitter herbs are meant to remind celebrants of the suffering of the Jews. The front door was to be left open so that the prophet Elijah, as well as the poor and hungry, could join the feast. Families that did not ordinarily observe Jewish dietary law often tried to comply during the seven-day Passover festival. This meant that they only ate kosher meat, which had been ceremonially slaughtered under the supervision of a rabbi. They ate no leavened bread nor any dish that may have absorbed unleavened bread. They did not eat dairy and meat products together, or even allow the same bowls, serving dishes, or utensils to touch both.

The week before Passover became a week of intense work as housewives prepared for the feast. Women were expected to do a thorough spring cleaning. In addition to the usual tasks of washing down walls, beating rugs, and airing furniture, Jewish women were expected to hold utensils over a fire and boil glasses for three days to purify the dishes from any contamination. In wealthy homes, the everyday dishes were packed away, while traditional Passover dishes were brought out from storage (Husband and O'Loughlin 2004, 136–38).

Independence Day

As the century drew to a close, fewer organized Independence Day celebrations took place. The Fourth of July came to be the unofficial beginning of summer, and it marked the exodus of thousands of city residents to the country for the season. It became the day when amusement parks opened and steamship lines, railroads, and streetcars began to offer service to places where people could get away from the city for the day. Streetcar companies frequently built amusement parks at the end of the line as a means of increasing business. Opening day was often marked by fireworks and celebration. In 1890 Rocky Point Amusement Park in Rhode Island advertised a simulation of the "Bombardment of Paris" in the Franco-Prussian War. The booming fireworks and deafening artillery were accompanied by music from several bands (Appelbaum 1989, 119). Circuses, balloon ascensions, and traveling menageries all drew large crowds. The historical nature of the Wild West shows made them a particular favorite.

Many cities began the day by ringing bells and firing a cannon, followed by programs featuring parades, band concerts, ball games, regattas, and bicycle races. The day ended with evening fireworks. Families with summer retreats invited friends and family to spend the day. Many put on private fireworks displays at the end of the day. The increase in the variety of summer activities available and the decrease of political orations during the Industrial Age moved Independence Day from a patriotic commemoration to a summer holiday. Many important events were inaugurated Fourth of July. Politicians kicked off campaigns and community projects were either started or unveiled on the Fourth.

As Independence Day approached fireworks shops opened in every city offering prismatic whirligigs, batteries of stars, volcanoes, Pharaoh's serpents, and incendiary devices of every imaginable variety. These establishments were as busy as shops on Christmas Eve. By the turn of the century Fourth of July fireworks was a $10 million a year industry (Appelbaum 1989, 125). For days in advance the sound of fireworks could be heard building with intensity as the holiday approached. Maiming, fires and even deaths due to fireworks became increasingly more common. Fire departments stood on alert to combat fires small and large. Efforts to regulate fireworks were met with limited support because they had become synonymous with the day. When the mayor of Cincinnati banned the shooting of fireworks and pistols in the streets for the Fourth of July in 1875, he was condemned by public opinion and ignored by city police. Some cities were so indulgent of the use of fireworks that they suspended regulations prohibiting the use of gunfire within their limits just for the holiday (Appelbaum 1989, 129).

Thanksgiving

President Benjamin Harrison epitomized the ideal Thanksgiving of the Industrial Age in his 1891 proclamation. He suggested that among the appropriate observations of the day were rest from toil, worship in a public congregation, the renewal of family ties around the fireside, and helpfulness for those of bodily or spiritual need (Appelbaum 1984, 168–69). Reunions became a hallmark of the holiday as well. Many families had moved far away from home, but railroads made it possible for families to travel to be together for the holiday.

Churches were open for services on Thanksgiving morning, and many people attended service to offer grateful prayer. Some people used the occasion to display the bounty for which they were presumably thankful. With stores closed on this day of leisure and prayer, well-to-do ladies and gentlemen would promenade or ride in their carriages down city avenues leading to fashionable churches dressed in velvets and furs. These churches were opulently decorated in Victorian style. Pittsburgh's Trinity Episcopal Church was trimmed with grape-leaf garlands and bunches of grapes from every projection. Sheaves of grain were arrayed throughout the sanctuary and the baptismal font overflowed with fruits and vegetables. The produce was donated to hospital kitchens following the service.

While society and working families alike attended services according to their beliefs in Jewish synagogues, Mormon temples, and Protestant churches of virtually every denomination, Catholic churches did not honor the day. Thanksgiving had its roots as a Protestant holy day, and the Catholic Church refused to observe the day as such. The Catholic Church had been willing to hold services on civilly proclaimed days for special victories or for peace after the Civil War but not for a day that was started by Protestants. Although some priests individually acknowledged Thanksgiving during the regular daily mass, Catholics were generally discouraged from observing the day. In 1884 the Plenary Council of Catholic Bishops in America meeting in Baltimore commended the holiday to its congregations. Cardinal

Gibbons, archbishop of Baltimore, brought Thanksgiving services into harmony with other denominations (Appelbaum 1984, 166–67).

The secularism of the 1880s and 1890s and the association of Thanksgiving with home and family led to a decrease in attendance at church services. To combat half-empty churches on Thanksgiving, some denominations banded together to hold a Thanksgiving union service. Virtually every city in the country held union services, some encompassing two or three denominations and others like the annual service at the Detroit Opera House included most of the Protestant denominations in the city (Appelbaum 1984, 168).

Thanksgiving was a new holiday to many who had no traditional customs for its celebration and who were not particularly religious. After the holiday feasting many sought livelier diversions for the remainder of the day. Thanksgiving matinees became popular. Even small town theaters or opera houses would be sure to book touring players, singers, or musicians for the day. Thanksgiving balls also became popular. Every segment of society sponsored them and they were well attended. Debutantes danced in mansion ballrooms, while country girls graced farmhouse parlors and town halls. Traditional balls were held by the Elks, the German Barber's and Hairdresser's Association, the Independent Grocer's Guard, the Masons, the Knights of Macabees, and the Steuben Rifle Society (Appelbaum 1984, 178).

Sporting activities also became popular on Thanksgiving. Hunting was a natural activity as some people tried to catch the main course for the feast, but many just went for the experience. The turkey shoot was another popular activity. Some formats used tethered live birds, but many others used paper targets with a turkey prize going to the winner. Promoters sponsored both bicycle and foot races. The walking race was another popular event. Participants walked very fast taking care never to lift both feet off the ground simultaneously as that would have constituted running and meant elimination from the competition. Thanksgiving became the day for the big game for schoolboy and football players. Campus gridirons from coast-to-coast featured local competitions such as Tulane versus Louisiana State in New Orleans or Case versus Western Reserve in Cleveland. Fans wore chrysanthemums in their teams' colors. When flowers did not naturally grow in school colors, florists tinted the flowers or tied them with appropriately colored ribbons. For a while in the mid-1880s the Yale-Harvard game was played at the New York Polo Grounds. After Harvard students attending the 1887 game displayed such uproarious enthusiasm during their New York visit, the faculty put an end to the annual competition. The event then became the Yale-Princeton game. By the 1890s traditionalists began to complain about how football had displaced the family gathering on Thanksgiving, and some clergymen even announced that services would be over early enough to permit fans to get to the game (Appelbaum 1984, 196–202).

New York was home to a unique tradition on Thanksgiving, the fantasticals were neighborhood-based organizations of young men who dressed in flamboyant costumes and paraded the streets on Thanksgiving. While the origins of the custom are unclear, it is likely that they relate to Guy Fawkes celebrations, which were observed by some New Yorkers until the early nineteenth century. Fantasticals would awaken citizens with loud blasts of fish horns. The police estimated that there were more than 50 fantastical companies that paraded each year sporting such colorful monikers as Ham Guard Warriors, Gilhooley Musketeers, Original Hounds of Eighth Ward, Hamilton Rangers, Oli Bolis, Sleetfoot Slenderfoot Army, Gentlemen's Sons of the Eighteenth Ward, and Secondhand Lumberdealers. An 1881 *Times* review of the event described about 150 participants in coaches, on horseback or on foot, dressed in fancy costumes, cheered on by crowds who flocked to see them. The costumes were described as having been drawn from ancient and modern history of every country and included robbers, pirates, fiends, devils, imps, fairies, priests, bishops, gypsies, flower girls, kings, clowns, princes, and jesters as well as prominent figures of the day. In 1893, one company came riding bicycles. Following the parade, the revelers would gather for rowdy picnics in parks and amusement parks near the city's edge. Late in the afternoon the fantasticals returned to their home wards where they danced at gala balls through the night (Appelbaum 1984, 187–89).

A second Thanksgiving custom unique to New York was the target company. These quasi-military clubs, which were more subdued than the fantasticals and from socially respectable families, existed for the sole purpose of parading toward the edge of the city where they engaged in target shooting for prizes. Dressed in well-polished high-topped boots, black pants, and uniform jackets in company colors, the soldiers-for-a day were very impressive. Clubs were generally named for their captain as in Delaney's Light Guard or for their trade like the Carpet and Furniture Guard. While some of the group might have joined the fantasticals, most returned to their families for dinner following brief refreshment (Appelbaum 1984, 190).

Running along the streets to cheer on the fantasticals and target companies were the ragamuffins, boys and girls who ran through the New York streets dressed in outlandish costumes asking passersby "Anything for Thanksgiving?" In return, they received pennies from the grownups. Ragamuffin costumes were made usually from cast-off clothing from elders. Some children sported commercially produced masks but black youths often whitened their face with talcum and white youths blackened their faces with coal dust (Appelbaum 1984, 190–93).

Christmas

Christmas greeting cards became popular in England during the 1860s. Businessmen found greeting cards a good way to reinforce business relationships. The cards were also welcomed by women who could send them in place of certain traditional holiday visits, freeing up more time for what had become elaborate holiday preparations. The practice caught on in the United States a little later. German immigrant Louis Prang perfected the process of multicolor printing in 1874 and began printing Christmas cards in 8 different colors and sometimes as many as 20. The cards were far more beautiful and expensive than their British counterparts. Some were trimmed with silk fringe and tasseled cords. His Yuletide greetings featured floral arrangements of roses, daisies, gardenias, geraniums, and apple blossoms, but the images generally had little to do with Christmas. In 1880 Prang began a yearly design competition to attract the most talented artists. Prizes were substantial with first place winning as much as $1,000.

By 1881, Prang was producing more than five million Christmas cards each year despite the fact that some cost as much as a dollar each. Other early cards were more elaborate, coming in the shape of fans, stars, or scrolls. Others were cut into the shapes of bells, birds, candles, and even plum puddings. Some folded like maps, fitted together as puzzles or even had pictures that could be animated by pulling a tab; others squealed or squeaked. Pop-up cards revealed tiny mangers or skaters with flying scarves gliding around a mirrored pond. Americans took to Christmas cards, but not to Prang's. He went out of business in 1890. Cards such as these remained popular until the turn of the century when cheap German postcards flooded the market.

While many Germans brought Christmas ornaments made from tin, lead, wax, and glass with them when they immigrated, most American trees were decorated with homemade decorations. Beginning around 1870 imported decorations became available in German communities and in a few variety and toy stores and catalogs. In 1880 F. W. Woolworth agreed to display a few glass ornaments in his store. To his amazement, they sold out within a couple of days. By 1890 Woolworth was traveling to Germany to procure a variety of ornaments and soon most households had at least some glass ornaments (Time Life Books 1987, 65).

Virtually all of the ornaments were imported from Germany where entire families worked year-round making them. The first ornaments were very heavy pieces shaped as balls and fruits and were plainly colored. Within a few years more delicate and intricate items were available. Miniature trumpets made from twisted straws of glass, handblown birds, and molded acorns were highly prized. Silver-foiled tinsel, wired tinsel, and tiny glass beads on strings were available for additional shine. There were also intricate embossed cardboard ornaments detailed with gold or silver. Most were two-dimensional, but some were three-dimensional and had hand-painted details. By the turn of the century the variety of commercially produced ornaments was staggering. Trees were so heavily laden with glass, tin, paper, and sweets there was hardly room for the candles. By this time, some families used Christmas lights, which were glass sided lanterns that held tiny oil-burning wicks that floated on water (Time Life Books 1987, 65).

In 1882, a mere three years after the world's first practical light bulb was invented by Thomas Edison, Edward Johnson, an associate of Edison's, electrically lit a Christmas tree for the first time. The tree was in the parlor of Johnson's New York City home, located in the first section of that city to be electrically wired. The display created quite a stir. A reporter for the *Detroit Post and Tribune* described it as having 80 red, white, and blue lights all encased in dainty glass eggs that provided a continuous twinkling of dancing colors. The tree was kept revolving by a little hidden crank below the floor which was also turned by electricity. In 1890, Edison published a small 28 page promotional brochure that suggested there were few forms of decoration more beautiful and pleasing than miniature incandescent lamps placed among flowers, or interwoven in garlands or festoons; and provided suggestions for decorating Christmas trees or conservatories in what might be the first commercial mention of electrically lighting a Christmas tree (Time Life Books 1987, 65–66).

One of the first gifts to be given to children was the gift book. The beautifully engraved tomes were elegantly bound in watered silk or embossed leather. The books came with a presentation page where the gift giver could write an appropriate message to the recipient. Gift books became enormously popular in the 1830s, but the craze lost its momentum by the Civil War. After the war, factories were producing all kinds of toys, dolls and dollhouses, and stuffed animals. Toy stores had sprouted up in all large cities, and in more rural locations dry goods stores and mail-order catalogs provided a wide selection of gifts.

As the century drew to a close, there was great concern that the holiday was becoming too commercial or as one editor in an 1890 issue of *Ladies' Home Journal* called it a "festival of store-keepers." Period descriptions of stores described Christmas Eve streets crowded with shoppers carrying parcels of all sizes and descriptions. A 1892 issue of *Ladies' Home Journal* advised readers to begin Christmas shopping early when goods were fresh, shops free of crowds, and salespeople unfatigued (O'Neil 1981, 1–2).

Magazines offered suggested gift lists. Presents such as doilies, silver tea balls and tea strainers, picture frames, dressing table mirrors, boxes, fans, and jewelry were all said to be welcome by ladies. Gifts for men included cigars, cigarette cases, scarves, mufflers, and umbrellas (O'Neil 1981, 2). An 1879 issue of *Harper's Bazaar* advised that men did not like pretty trifles and decorations that delight ladies and that knick-knacks and items made of china were generally useless to them. They suggested that men were always in need of handkerchiefs, and one that had been embroidered with the name or monogram of the recipient, particularly if embroidered with the hair of the giver, would be especially prized (Time Life Books 1987, 151).

The wonder ball was often at the top of the gift list. A wonder ball was a ball of yarn carefully unraveled and rewound with many little gifts hidden inside, which would be revealed as the yarn was consumed by the knitting. It would be especially welcomed by grandmothers who enjoyed knitting. In addition grandmothers would surely enjoy a footstool, pot of primroses, a folding fruit knife, or a screen to protect her from draughts.

Boys were likely to enjoy receiving tool boxes, boxing gloves, sleds, skates, stamps and stamp albums, lanterns, jackknives, adventure books, cap pistols, and marbles. Little girls, it was said, rejoiced in gifts of fans, jewelry, sachet, monogrammed note paper, books, a live canary, and of course, a doll or two (O'Neil 1981, 2–3).

In addition to shops, many women purchased gifts from charity bazaars. The crafting of Christmas gifts was begun far ahead of the season as ladies made gifts not only for friends and family but also to supply Fancy Fairs at local churches. These fairs not only served as a form of recreation, but they also raised money for worthy causes. Handmade gifts were very popular whether they were made by the giver or purchased from a fair. Ladies' magazines were excellent sources for patterns for these items such as watchcases, chamois eyeglass cleaners, slipper bags, sewing workbags, dainty boxes, and sachets. The appreciation of handmade items was a reaction to the abundance of machine-made products that swept the market. Gifts of food such as preserves, jams, and jellies made in the summer and candies, which could be made at anytime, were also popular (O'Neil 1981, 5–6).

When it came to gift giving, everyone was remembered, especially servants and service providers. Middle-class families also assembled gifts boxes for the poor. As the century progressed, various charitable organizations grew to meet the needs of a complex urban society. The Salvation Army was most closely associated with Christmas. The first Christmas kettle appeared in 1891 when a Salvation Army worker in San Francisco used a kitchen pot to dramatize the need for food (Time Life Books 1987, 33). By 1900 most of the traditions we associate with contemporary American celebrations of Christmas were in place.

—Dorothy Denneen Volo

FOR MORE INFORMATION

Adams, James Truslow, ed. *Album of American History*. New York: Charles Scribner's Sons, 1946.

Alexander, George E. *Lawn Tennis: Its Founders and Its Early Days*. Lynn, MA: H. O. Zimman, 1974.

Appelbaum, Diana Karter. *Thanksgiving: An American Holiday, An American History*. New York: Facts on File, 1984.

———. *The Glorious Fourth: An American Holiday, An American History*. New York: Facts on File, 1989.

Bellinger, Martha Fletcher. *A Short History of the Theater*. New York: Henry Holt, 1927.

Bierley, Paul E. *John Philip Sousa, American Phenomenon*. Englewood Cliffs, New Jersey: Prentice Hall, 1973.

———. *The Works of John Philip Sousa*. Columbus, Ohio: Integrity Press, 1984.

Burke, Edmund H. *The History of Archery*. Westport, CT: Greenwood Press, 1971 [c1957].

Cary, John H., and Julius Weinberg, eds. *The Social Fabric, American Life from the Civil War to the Present*. Boston, MA: Little, Brown and Company, 1975.

Cohen, Hennig, and Tristram Potter Coffin, eds. *The Folklore of American Holidays*. Detroit, MI: Gale Research Company, 1987.

Collins, Frank D. *Popular Sports: Their Origin and Development*. Chicago, IL: Rand McNally & Company, 1935.

Elliott, Jock. *Inventing Christmas: How Our Holiday Came to Be*. New York: Abrams, 2002.

Foner, Philip S. *American Labor Songs of the Nineteenth-Century*. Urbana: University of Illinois Press, 1975.

Furia, Philip. *The Poets of Tin Pan Alley: A History of America's Great Lyricists*. New York: Oxford University Press, 1990.

Grattan, C. Hartley. *The Three Jameses: A Family of Minds*. New York: New York University Press, 1962.

Hayward, John. *Gazetteer of the United States*. Hartford, CT: Case, Tiffant and Co., 1853.

Heath, Ernest Gerald. *A History of Target Archery*. Newton Abbot, UK: David & Charles, 1973.

Hewitt, Barnard. *Theater USA, 1668 to 1957*. New York: McGraw-Hill Book Company, 1959.

Husband, Julie, and Jim O'Loughlin, *Daily Life in the Industrial United States, 1870–1900*. Westport, CT: Greenwood Press, 2004.

Jansen, David. *Tin Pan Alley . . . The Golden Age of American Popular Music from 1886 to 1956*. New York: Fine, 1988.

Jenkins, Susan, and Linda Seward. *The American Quilt Story: The How-To and Heritage of a Craft Tradition.* Emmaus, PA: Rodale Press, 1991.

King, Gilbert. *The Art of Golf Antiques: An Illustrated History of Clubs, Balls, and Accessories.* Philadelphia, PA: Courage Books, 2001.

Levin, Alexandra Lee. "Miss Knight Abroad," *American Heritage* XI, no 3 (April 1960): 15.

McMorris, Penny. *Crazy Quilts.* New York: E.P. Dutton, 1984.

Noel, Evan Baillie. *A History of Tennis.* Mansfield Center, CT: Martino Publishers, 2007.

O'Neil, Sunny. *The Gift of Christmas Past.* Nashville, TN: The American Association for State and Local History, 1981.

Peiss, Kathy. *Cheap Amusements: Working Women and Leisure in Turn-of-the-Century New York.* Philadelphia, PA: Temple University Press, 1986.

Peper, George. *Golf in America: The First One Hundred Years.* New York: H. N. Abrams, 1988.

Rader, Benjamin. *American Sports: From the Age of the Folk Games to the Age of the Spectators.* Englewood Cliffs, NJ: Prentice-Hall, 1983.

Shrock, Joel. *The Gilded Age.* Westport, CT: Greenwood Press, 2004.

Time Life Books. *Time Life Book of Christmas.* New York: Prentice Hall, 1987.

Twain, Mark (Samuel Clemens). *The Innocents Abroad.* New York: Penguin Putnam, 1980.

Volo, Dorothy Denneen, and James M. Volo. *Family Life in Nineteenth-Century America.* Westport, CT: Greenwood Press, 2007.

Wechsberg, Joseph. *The Lost World of the Great Spas.* New York: Harper & Row, Publishers, 1979.

Weiskopf, Herman. *The Perfect Game: The World of Bowling.* Englewood Cliffs, NJ: Prentice-Hall. 1978.

Weissman, Judith Reiter, and Wendy Lavitt. *Labors of Love: American Textiles and Needlework, 1650–1930.* New York: Alfred A. Knopf, 1987.

Religious Life

MORALITY

Social Missions and Philanthropy

The Industrial Age oversaw an important shift from an essentially rural values base to an urban one. This paralleled a substantial shift in power where the cities came to dominate the nation economically, politically, and culturally. Cities became magnets for those seeking not only work but also excitement, amusement, and diversion. Operas, symphonies, and museums attracted the elite; ballparks, amusement parks, and legitimate theater fascinated the middle classes; and dance halls, beer gardens, and vaudeville riveted the attention of the poor. Ministers, church prelates, and community leaders feared that the new urban culture would undo a half century of increasing moral growth that had spawned the Holiness Movement and the popularity of religion-based and self-improvement vacations. One of the indicators that their worries were not unfounded was an increase in premarital sexual activity evidenced by a rising rate of bridal pregnancy and illegitimate births. The shift to an urban-dominated cultural paradigm seemed to some observers to announce a wider rebellion against Victorian-style mores that promised increased incidents of crime, drunkenness, lewdness, and social disorder.

A number of volunteer missionary organizations were begun in the second half of the century in response to the need to address the rising incidence of immorality, intemperance, and falling religiosity, especially in the cities. The term *Social Gospel* came to be applied to a way of thinking that linked religious obligation to social progress. It urged that the rights of labor be respected and that industrial peace be made between the forces of labor and capitalism.

The rapid growth of American industry in the nineteenth century brought with it a host of social problems that posed a serious moral dilemma for the established church organizations. The concentration of wealth in the hands of just a few American families in the last quarter century threatened the general political equity that had been won since the Civil War. Industrial mechanization had left workers feeling insignificant and powerless, and the conditions of labor had deteriorated to the point that laborers had taken to the strike as a countermeasure. Bloody strikes that garnered national attention had taken place in 1877, 1886, 1892, and 1894. The established churches were thereby alerted to the need to address some of the underlying moral aspects of the social and economic problems that faced working men and women, yet their congregations (and financial support) came largely from the middle and upper classes.

In 1901, Andrew Carnegie sold Carnegie Steel to J. P. Morgan, who was organizing U.S. Steel. After the sale Carnegie was over $200 million richer—possibly the richest man in the world at the time. Carnegie, an adolescent emigrant from Scotland in 1848, understood the difference between rich and poor having begun his working life as a bobbin-boy in a cotton factory. When only in his 30s, he went into business for himself making steel, and writing essays for the newspapers and periodicals on a variety of subjects: foreign policy, the gold standard, banking, tariffs, politics, education, war imperialism, disarmament, and golf. Yet his most famous essay (actually a series) was his "Gospel of Wealth." Herein, he developed a coherent and compelling case for the moral obligation of millionaires to give away their fortunes during their lifetimes for the betterment of society. "The man who dies rich dies disgraced," he wrote (Nasaw 2006, viii). William Jewett Tucker, a liberal theologian critiquing Carnegie's ideas, was alarmed by the concept of such vast wealth continuing in the hands of so few great men as Carnegie, Morgan, Rockefeller, or Vanderbilt. "I can conceive of no greater mistake, more disastrous in the end to religion if not to society, than that of trying to make charity do the work of justice" (Nasaw 2006, xiii).

Carnegie would remain in the public eye for the remainder of his life—as author, millionaire, philanthropist, opponent of the Spanish-American War, and peace activist. He would preach the "Gospel of Wealth" in hundreds of speeches and personal appearances on both sides of the Atlantic, and publish it in pamphlet and book form. In promulgating his ideas, he was advancing an antidemocratic gospel that was almost feudal in its paternalism. Workers and socialists organized demonstrations against him, and claimed that they were being denied that which was rightfully theirs, a just wage, decent hours, and a stake in the profits.

A major moral issue of the period, and the focus of much of the religious debate among the dominant religions, lay in a choice between the Social Gospel of the reformers and the working classes, and the "Gospel of Wealth" that appealed to the philanthropy and good will of the new class of the self-made super-rich. In an age of exploitation many of the normal habits of moral conduct were sacrificed to the expediency of making money leaving some of the most successful businessmen of the age tagged with the title of Robber Baron.

Thorstein Veblen, a critic of American society writing in 1899, commented on the difference between how the great thieves and the petty criminals of the age were viewed. "In modern communities, where the dominant economic and legal feature of the community's life is the institution of private property, one of the salient features of the code of morals is the sacredness of property.... Most offenses against property, especially offenses of appreciable magnitude, come under this head.... The thief or swindler who has gained great wealth by his delinquency has a better chance than the small thief of escaping the rigorous penalty of the law; and some good repute accrues to him from his increased wealth and from his spending the irregularly acquired possessions in a seemly manner. A well-bred expenditure of his booty especially appeals with great effect to persons of a cultivated sense of the proprieties, and goes far to mitigate the sense of moral turpitude with which his dereliction is viewed by them. It may also be noted—and is more immediately to the point—that we are all inclined to condone an offense against property in the case of a man whose motive is the worthy one of providing the means of a decent manner of life for his wife and children" (Veblen 1994, 72–73).

—*James M. Volo*

Bridal Pregnancy

Prenuptial sexual activity, as indicated by the rate of bridal pregnancies and out-of-wedlock (illegitimate) births, is commonly considered a measure of morality—at least among the generation of young adults. Unlike the generation that had grown to young adulthood in the decade after the Civil War—who had generally worked and amused themselves at home—young working-class urbanites of the Industrial Age had unprecedented access to public amusements and the leisure time to enjoy them. Added to this leisure time was an increase in wage-paying jobs for young men and the increasing availability of decent employment for young, working-class women in factories, offices, and retail stores. This provided both genders with greater autonomy than their parents and grandparents had ever hoped to enjoy.

With more independence and money, young working-class women were able to exercise greater control over their activities than many of their upper-class and middle-class sisters, who did not earn a wage and remained under the scrutiny of their parents. Young working men also experienced an increased independence from their parents because they were no longer dependent on the good will of their family for their living.

Although it had been shown that young women could be successfully integrated into a work setting outside the home (generally as domestic servants or textile workers), the general employment of women in the male-dominated surroundings of factories and office buildings had remained controversial right through the Civil War and Reconstruction periods. Such criticism was not so much a contempt for the ability or value of women as workers, but rather a proclamation of men's own strongly felt social duty to support and protect the morals of their wives, daughters, mothers, and sisters. Even those men with liberal attitudes toward the rights of labor spoke of "being sickened by the spectacle of wives and daughters—and, even worse, single girls—leaving their preordained positions as homemakers" to take jobs outside the "cult of domesticity" (Wilentz 1984, 249). Factories that successfully attracted women employees were often run like corporate convents to reassure parents that their daughters' reputations would be safe from domineering bosses, managers, and male coworkers—an early warning sign of the ubiquitous nature of sexual harassment in the workplace (Volo and Volo 2007, 353–54).

By the 1890s, however, industrialization, women's rights, modernism, and other factors had combined to relieve somewhat the burden of parental vigilance over the interactions of young unmarried men and women. Unfortunately, there developed a system of treating that that had wide-ranging implications. Often young women could not afford the urban amusements they desired because they still earned less than young men, so the men would treat women to shows, dances, vaudeville, and amusement parks to gain their favor. Most of these interactions were innocent enough by the day's standards. Yet some young men had expectations of sexual exchange for their money. The young women were not simply passive victims in these situations, as many middle-class reformers claimed, but active agents in negotiating treats for sex (Shrock 2004, 39).

Premarital sexual activity rose substantially among this working-class subculture. After hitting a low of 10 percent at mid-century, premarital pregnancies soared to 23 percent in the 1880s signaling a sexual revolution that would culminate in the roaring 1920s (Shrock 2004, 5). Keep in mind that this was an era when doctors and scientists considered masturbation one of the greatest evils afflicting youth and a source of serious moral decay. Premarital sex was considered infinitely worse. So, without a doubt, one of the most serious rebellions from middle-class values was this youthful working-class flouting of Victorian sexual boundaries. Middle-class ideologies feared urban working-class youth not just for their gangs and violence, but also for their moral decadence. These youngsters were a far cry from the visions of playful innocence that middle-class parents conjured up about their own children (Shrock 2004, 39).

THE SOCIAL GOSPEL

The Salvation Army was one of the organizations to take up the work of the Social Gospel. It was begun in 1865 in London by Rev. William Booth, who gave up the comfort of his pulpit and his living to take the gospel into the streets where he could reach out to the poor, the homeless, and the hungry. His original idea was to preach the Gospel to the abandoned, destitute, and indigent, and send them to the established churches as converts to the hopeful word of God. He quickly found out, however, that neither the converted street people nor the regular churchgoers were comfortable with such an arrangement. He, therefore, founded a church especially for them—the East London Christian Mission.

Thereafter, his wife, Catherine, began to be more active in the work of the church. Though she was extremely nervous, she enjoyed working with young people and found the courage to speak in adult meetings. It was the beginning of a tremendous ministry, as people were greatly challenged by her preaching. She also spoke to people in their homes, especially to alcoholics, whom she helped to make a new start in life. Often she held so-called cottage meetings for converts. In 1878, having enlisted their eight children as soldier volunteers to the cause, the Booth's changed the name of the mission organization to the Salvation Army. Two of their offspring, Bramwell and Evangeline, later became Generals of the Salvation Army.

By 1900 the Salvation Army had spread around the world, and soon had missions in 36 countries including the United States. With members who were well organized and dedicated, the Army provided a number of much needed social services within a religious context. These included women's services, food kitchens, hospital care, and a day nursery—the first of its kind.

Early proponents of the Social Gospel in America, like Washington Gladden and Walter Rauschenbusch, had warned of dire results if some steps were not taken to alleviate the ills of poverty, overwork, and underpayment that were plaguing the working classes. Bloody confrontations like the national railway strike of 1877, the Haymarket Square bombing of 1886, and the Homestead strike of 1892 seemed to bear out their predictions with troops and Pinkerton detectives firing on and beating workers.

Gladden, a Congregational minister from New York, is recognized as the first leading religious leader to support the unionization of workers. As acting editor of the *New York Independent* he campaigned against the political machine of Boss Tweed and was a leader of the Progressive Party. Gladden was the author of 40 books, many concerning religion; but in 1876, he wrote *Working People and their Employers*, a moving work concerning wages, unions, and working conditions and the application of Christian law to labor issues. He was president and vice president of the American Missionary Association (1894–1901) and was made Moderator of the National Council of Congregational Churches in 1905. The University of Notre Dame honored him with doctorate in recognition of his stance against anti-Catholicism.

Walter Rauschenbusch, another early proponent of the Social Gospel, was the pastor of a German Baptist Church in a section of New York City known as Hell's Kitchen. After observing the difficult circumstances under which his parishioners lived and worked, he concluded that the problem lay in the capitalistic system under which industry and millionaires flourished and the poor struggled and starved. Rauschenbusch began reading the works of prominent liberals and socialists, and turned to the idea that the Church must work out the problem of social reform while awaiting the return of Christ. Economic salvation, righteous action, and collective justice were necessary to alleviate social problems. His was a practical ministry, meeting the political, physical, and spiritual needs of the weak and destitute in Hell's Kitchen. In 1892, he formed a nondenominational organization known as the Brotherhood of the Kingdom, which placed a social emphasis on the obligations of Christian ministry and sought to infuse a religious spirit into secular reform movements.

The purpose of adherents to the Social Gospel concept was to correct the economic excesses and moral violations of a Victorian age that had too highly valued personal wealth and industrial expansion. The basic tenets of the Social Gospel concept were the establishment of a just wage, reasonable working hours, and a profit-sharing mechanism for the multitude of workers. It also sought the eradication of unrestrained economic competition, unfettered capitalism, and the virtually unlimited concentration of wealth in the hands of a few very rich men. Although the product of liberal and progressive thought the Social Gospel was not an overt attack on capitalism and industry (in the mode of Social Marxism), but a call for reform from within the established bastions of Christianity to devote themselves to instilling ethical obligations into a society that undervalued its workers.

The Social Gospel generally combined an idealistic view of human nature with a belief that God was at work in propagating social change, in creating moral order, and in instituting social justice. The tendency of its adherents was to view a just society as a human endeavor separate from a biblical divine judgment upon the moral foibles of the individual. Some of those who shaped Protestant social thought adopted their ideas from the tenets of an increasingly popular political socialism, and many were bold enough to suggest that the church replace the original emphasis of the gospel as a path to the Kingdom of God with a focus on meeting the worldly needs of the people. Among the many reforms addressed by adherents to the idea of a Social Gospel were temperance and the complete prohibition of alcohol; women's suffrage and ministry; social purity (against prostitution, lewdness, licentiousness, and gambling); the defense of marriage and family values; health, housing, and educational reform; and internal reform of church organization. The Social Gospel movement brought together well-disposed people from many walks of life, and it affected farmers, laborers, women, and other reform groups. The various adherents to the Social Gospel often sought to state their moral obligations to society in terms of their own particular theology or religious doctrine.

Classical Protestantism, with its reliance on predestination, had largely accepted the idea of the separation of church and state to the point that it eschewed the promotion of active demonstrations or deliberate programs of social uplifting for the masses. At the very time that traditional Protestant churches needed to address these problems in a corporate and collective fashion, evangelicalism had taken many of its most active adherents down the road of individual morality and personal religiosity. The heritage of the frontier preacher and the revival camp was far removed from the problems of industrialization and urban socialization. Moreover, as poor immigrants swelled the cities of America, middle- and upper-class Protestants fled to the suburbs where immigrants and the impoverished were unlikely to settle or to be seen.

The rise and appeal for the upper classes of the concept of Social Darwinism, as expressed by the English philosopher Herbert Spencer, argued for the survival of the fittest, giving an additional justification to allowing market forces to eliminate the weak. This lack of moral discipline would have horrified the Protestants of an earlier century. Unfortunately the established churches hesitated in giving moral leadership in the crisis until it had grown to inexcusable proportions.

It was rather the early interposition of organizations like the Salvation Army, the Brotherhood of the Kingdom, the Christian and Missionary Alliance, and the YMCA and YWCA that launched efforts to reach those on the lowest rungs of the socioeconomic ladder. Roman Catholic churches focused their work on the inner city where Irish, and later Italian Slavic, and other immigrants of the Catholic faith were likely to settle. Methodists and Lutherans developed the institution of the deaconess—roughly a Protestant version of the Catholic nun—to care for the needy. A Presbyterian synod proclaimed its dedication to the Social Gospel in the following way. "The great ends of the church are the proclamation of the gospel for the salvation of humankind; the shelter, nurture, and spiritual fellowship of the children of God; the maintenance of divine worship; the preservation of truth; the promotion of social righteousness; and the exhibition of the Kingdom of Heaven to the world" (Rogers and Blade 1998, 181).

Before the end of the century, the Social Gospel had gained entrance into the curriculum of many seminaries, and it soon gained official recognition from the leading Protestant denominations. Sociology—a science dealing with the deliberate study of social issues first named by Auguste Comte in 1837—gained wide acceptance in the 1880s and 1890s as a legitimate academic discipline, and by the end of the century it was being introduced as a tool for use by parish clergy. Adherents to the tenets of a Social Gospel were primary proponents in the forming of the Federal Council of Churches in 1908, the forerunner of the National Council of Churches that exists today.

The initial response of Catholic leaders to the social problems of their flock was to remain aloof from any Protestant-sponsored humanitarian crusades. Instead, they developed their own sectarian institutions including schools, orphanages, homes for the destitute, abandoned, and aged, and a system of Catholic hospitals. In the 1880s, however, James Cardinal Gibbons and Archbishop John Ireland—convinced that the Catholic church should more deeply involve itself in social issues—began preaching the need for working men to be given a *living wage* that would allow them to support their families and themselves. They were supported by the foundational work of sociologists like Ernst Engle, Charles Booth, and B. Seebohm Rowntree, who had formulated the idea of a *standard of living* in which family income was compared to family expenditure as a measure of poverty.

Citing the extreme unemployment and poverty in his parish as a reason for breaking with Church policy as it was then constituted, Father Edward McGlynn actively supported Henry George, a socially progressive candidate for mayor of New York best known for his support of a virtually confiscatory Single Tax on the wealthy. Mc-Glynn was initially suspended from his position by the archdiocese for his involvement in radical politics, but he was later restored to his parish.

In 1891, Pope Leo XIII published a papal encyclical, *Rerum Novarum* in which he initiated a new attitude for the Catholic church with respect to the whole issue of labor, wages, and social justice. Although late in coming, the encyclical marked an important change in church policy involving economic and social issues. Private property remained inviolable and socialism was condemned but labor unions were sanctioned and government regulation of business was endorsed. The pope placed great emphasis on the role of private charity and philanthropy.

—James M. Volo

THE GOSPEL OF WEALTH

In 1889, Andrew Carnegie published an essay entitled the "Gospel of Wealth" in which he described the responsibility of philanthropy by the new class of the super-rich. Carnegie was a member of this limited group of people. Carnegie's essay was an undisguised response to the growing popularity of the Social Gospel. Moreover, Henry George had attacked the super-rich in *Progress and Poverty* (1879), and Edward Bellamy had called for a socialist utopia with a nationalization and public ownership of industry in his novel *Looking Backward* (1888). The success and popularity of these works indicated the extent to which there was a deep concern about the tremendous changes that were rocking the foundations of American society in the Industrial Age. Thoughtful persons were concerned by the concentration of wealth in so few hands, and Carnegie came forward to defend the traditional American faith in individual freedom and the just rewards of enterprise.

As an industrial millionaire and economic potentate Carnegie's position as an unbiased commentator should have been compromised, but after his retirement he had a remarkable record of personal accomplishment and generous philanthropy having established hundreds of libraries in communities across the nation and having endowed the arts and architecture. Carnegie viewed the social problems of the period as due to a deficiency in the proper administration of wealth rather than the imbalance of its distribution. "The ties of brotherhood may still bind together the rich and poor in harmonious relationship," he wrote (Nasaw 2006, 1).

Carnegie, and other so-called success writers, offered a few simple solutions to the complexities of work in the Industrial Age based on self-reliance and independence. Men had to gain success, not through socialism and utopianism, but through their own efforts. "The Socialist or Anarchist who seek to overturn present conditions is to be regarded as attacking the foundation upon which civilization itself rests," he wrote, "for civilization took its start from the day that the capable, industrious workman said to his incompetent and lazy fellow, 'If thou dost not sow, thou shalt not reap.' Thus ended primitive Communism by separating the drones from the bees" (Nasaw 2006, 4). Self-made business success was the ultimate goal, self-improvement was a necessity, and personal property was sacrosanct. The factory worker had his right to his hundreds of dollars in the savings bank, and the millionaire had the same right to his millions. The right to maintain his personal property for himself obligated the man of wealth to certain duties: "First, to set an example of modest, unostentatious living, shunning display and extravagance; to provide moderately for the legitimate wants of those dependent upon him; and after doing so to consider all surplus revenues which come to him simply as trust funds, which he is called upon to administer in the manner which, in his judgment, is best calculated to produce the most beneficial results for the community" (Nasaw 2006, 10).

Writers like Carnegie often conflated moral and physical power, and then equated this power with material success. Carnegie devoted a large part of his essay to the advantages of poverty, and claimed that "poor boys [like himself in former times]...become the leaders in every branch of human action...the greatest and the best of our race have necessarily been nurtured in the bracing school of poverty—the only school capable of producing the supremely great, the genius" (Shrock 2004, 161).

Carnegie's "Gospel of Wealth" appeared in the *North American Review* in 1889 and took the view that a millionaire had an unquestioned right to accumulate a great fortune as long as he balanced this advantage with an obligation to dispose of it in socially beneficial ways instead of wasting it on frivolities. Carnegie based his philosophy on the observation that the heirs of large fortunes frequently squandered them in riotous living rather than nurturing and growing them. Even bequeathing one's fortune to charity was no guarantee that it would be used wisely. He disapproved of charitable giving that merely maintained the poor in their impoverished state, and urged a movement toward the creation of a new mode of giving that would create opportunities for the beneficiaries of the gift to better themselves. The gift should not be consumed, it should be productive of even greater wealth. The man of wealth was a trustee who brought his superior wisdom, experience, and ability to administer to the communal use of money.

The message of the "Gospel of Wealth" soon reached an enormous audience. It was published in England, and reprinted and discussed in magazines and newspapers in America. In a short time, people all over the Western world were discussing it. Carnegie's ideas earned him much praise, but they did not gain for him many followers. Yet one might almost trace the history of modern philanthropy from the advent of Carnegie's essay. When it became obvious to Carnegie that he could not give away his entire fortune in a responsible way in his lifetime, he established the Carnegie Foundation to continue his program of philanthropy after his death. The Rockefellers, Morgans, Vanderbilts, Mellons, and other wealthy families soon followed his ideas concerning the establishment of grants, foundations, and other charitable organizations. (Current and Garraty 1965, 212).

—*James M. Volo*

RELIGION

Religious Devotion and the Leisure Class

Social commentator Thorstein Veblen considered "devout observances," such as those proclaimed by the Holiness Movement, the Salvation Army, or the YMCA, an "addiction" of immense importance to "a community so devout as ours" because such devoutness curtailed the economic efficiency of the nation. As seen from the point of view of Social Darwinism, Veblen found devotion to religious "cults" a mark of "arrested spiritual development" (Veblen 1994, 181). "It appears that the devout habit to some extent progressively gains in scope and elaboration among those classes in the modern communities to whom wealth and leisure accrue in the most pronounced degree. In this as in other relations, the institution of a leisure class acts to conserve, and even to rehabilitate, that archaic type of human nature and those elements of archaic culture which the industrial evolution of society in its later stages acts to eliminate" (Veblen 1994, 201).

"The habit of mind which best lends itself to the purposes of a peaceable, industrial community, is that matter-of-fact temper which recognizes the value of material facts simply as opaque items in the mechanical sequence. It is that frame of mind which does not instinctively impute animistic propensity to things, nor resort to preternatural intervention as an explanation of perplexing phenomena, nor depend on an unseen hand to shape the course of events to human use." Among these preternatural agencies Veblen included "abstruse conceptions of a dissolving personality that shades off into the concept of quantitative casual sequence, such as the speculative, esoteric creeds of Christendom impute to the First Cause, Universal Intelligence, World Soul, or Spiritual Aspect" (Veblen 1994, 181).

Of course it remained true, according to Veblen, that in the average community a person's attitude toward devoutness was strongly shaped by the dominance of the population as a whole. "There [is] a devout habit of mind in any individual, not in excess of the average of the community, [that] must be taken simply as a detail of the prevalent habit of life. In this light, a devout individual in a devout community can not be called a case of reversion, since he is abreast of the average of the community. But seen from the point of view of the modern industrial situation, exceptional devoutness—devotional zeal that rises appreciably above the average pitch of devoutness in the community—may safely be set down as in all cases an atavistic [primitive] trait" (Veblen 1994, 186).

Veblen also targeted religious observances as modifying the economic efficiency of the community through a redistribution of goods and services from the industrial sector to the religious one. "The consumption of ceremonial paraphernalia required by any cult, in the way of shrines, temples, churches, vestments, sacrifices, sacraments, holiday attire, etc., serves no immediate material end. All this material apparatus may, therefore, with implying deprecation, be broadly characterized as items of conspicuous waste. The like is true in a general way of the personal service consumed under this head; such as priestly education, priestly service, pilgrimages, fasts, holidays, household devotions [by servants], and the like." At the same time

Veblen thought that these observances had become the vogue among the leisure class extending and protracting themselves as a characteristic feature of the group.

As an example Veblen included a criticism of those "lay religious organizations which occupy themselves with the spread of esoteric forms of faith...to further practical religion." He included herein the YMCA, the Young People's Society for Christian Endeavor, and any group that linked "the sporting temperament" with archaic devoutness through the "furtherance of athletic contests and similar games of chance and skill.... [that are] apparently useful as a means of proselytizing, and a means of sustaining the devout attitude in converts once made." He also found fault with both sacred and civil holidays as forms of "tribute levied on the body of the people...a tribute paid in vicarious leisure...and...imputed to the person or the fact for whose repute the holiday has been instituted." He was particularly critical of the institution of "Labor Days" in some communities as "a predatory method of a compulsory abstention from useful effort; and of "saints' days" and all those "various grades of priests and hierodules" who found it incumbent upon themselves to gain a living from the laity without the "debasing application [of] industry" (Veblen 1994, 187, 189).

Veblen's criticism was clearly biased against certain groups of persons in America. He writes, "This reversion to spectacular observances is not confined to the upper-class cults, although it finds its best exemplification and its highest accentuation in the high pecuniary and social altitudes. The cults of the lower-class devout portion of the community, such as Southern Negroes and the backward foreign elements of the population [immigrants], of course also show a strong inclination to ritual, symbolism, and spectacular effects; as might be expected from the antecedents and the cultural level of those classes. With these classes the prevalence of ritual and anthropomorphism are not so much a matter of reversion as of continued development out of the past" (Veblen 1994, 200).

—*James M. Volo*

Religious Camps

Self-improvement vacations were thought to strengthen the moral fiber of Americans because they did not offer the usual temptations and concerns over the evils of idleness of the common vacation destination. A number of religious denominations created summer camps where the activities emphasized moral and intellectual development. There were almost 100 scenic self-improvement campgrounds established by different sectarian groups, but it was the Methodists that were the first and most prolific creators of religious camps. These resorts appealed to middle-class vacationers who wanted a sojourn in a religious setting that strictly prohibited drinking, dancing, card playing, and Sunday bathing. Compared to nonsectarian resorts or rented cottages, the religious camps provided a very inexpensive vacation alternative. The religious camp also attracted conference meetings of Christian reform groups like the Women's Christian Temperance Union.

Many of the religious camps had their genesis at the camp meeting locations of earlier decades that had developed into vacation destinations by the 1870s. Camps popped up throughout the country including major ones on Martha's Vineyard; at Ocean Grove on the New Jersey coast; at Camp Labor in New Jersey; at Sing Sing on the Hudson River in New York; at Ocean Grove Retreat near Monterey, California; and at Lake Bluff on Lake Michigan near Chicago.

The transformation from camp meeting to religious resort was most evident at Wesleyan Grove on Martha's Vineyard. Methodists created a camp meeting on the island off the New England coast in 1835 and by 1857 had erected 250 tents on a 12 to 15 acre site to accommodate guests. In 1860 the Methodist Camp-Meeting Association was formed to manage the camp, and it quickly expanded over the next five years into a number of small cottages. Wesleyan Grove continued to grow until it was a small city of summer cottages.

Ocean Grove, on the New Jersey shore 50 miles from New York City, was another religious camp resort that, by 1879, had 700 semipermanent tents with wooden floors that rented for $2.50 per week. By the 1880s, 20,000 to 30,000 people vacationed at Ocean Grove every summer. Ocean Grove revivals were complemented with the addition in 1894 of an auditorium that seated 10,000 persons.

While most of these religious camps and resorts were Methodist, there were a number of notable exceptions. The Quaker twin brothers Albert and Alfred Smiley founded a famous religious resort, the Mohonk Mountain House in the Shawangunk Mountains of New York's Hudson River Valley region—a favorite of nineteenth-century artists, poets, and vacationers. The Smileys ran Mohonk along strict Quaker guidelines—no liquor, no card playing, no dancing, nor carriages coming and going on the Sabbath. Despite these restrictions, or possibly because of them, Mohonk flourished, and was often noted as an attractive destination for women vacationing on their own.

James Adam Bradley founded another prominent religious camp at Asbury Park, New Jersey on 500 acres of land closely adjoining Ocean Grove. Bradley's middle-class clientele found the camp a milder and less denominational alternative to its strictly Methodist or Quaker counterparts. Nonetheless, Asbury Park observed Sabbath and temperance restrictions. Instead of complete abstinence, the park stressed moderation and moral guidance in dancing, theater, and card playing by straining out the sinful connection they had to gambling, alcohol addiction, and sexual licentiousness. Bradley's formula of moderation was an incredible success, and Asbury Park attracted between 30,000 and 50,000 vacationers every summer.

One of the most popular self-improvement vacations was to Lake Chautauqua in New York. Methodist Minister John Vincent and manufacturer Lewis Miller founded the resort in 1874 as a place that would bring together piety, leisure, and the middle-class urge for intellectual Christian refinement. Lake Chautauqua was one of the most sought after vacation destinations of the Industrial Age. Initially, its founders intended the camp to be a training ground for Sunday school teachers, but due to the program's growing popularity, Vincent and Miller expanded the curriculum to include secular studies such as language (Hebrew, Greek, Latin, French, German, and Asian languages) pedagogical studies, philosophy, literature, science, and history. Chautauqua became a phenomenon, drawing 500 to 600 persons from 26 states in its very first two-week long session in 1874. The *New York Times* estimated that 60,000 to 100,000 persons attended Lake Chautauqua events every year by the mid-1880s.

By that time there were at least 30 Chautauqua imitators spread throughout the nation. Indeed, the term chautauqua came to designate not only the camp in New York but the entire concept of a self-improvement vacation in general.

Nebraska boasted its chautauqua in Crete, Michigan, at Bay View, and Florida provided a chautauqua in the western panhandle of the state. Booker T. Washington formed an African American chautauqua in 1893 at the Tuskegee Institute, and other black chautauguas followed at Normal, Alabama; Mountain Lake Park in Maryland; and at Winona Lake just outside Warsaw, Indiana. Atlantic City, New Jersey, was the site of the Jewish Chautauqua Society that met there every summer.

Religious camp resorts and chautauguas offered a family friendly atmosphere that catered to the morality and values of middle-class Americans. A week at such a place meant that the family could enjoy an intellectually stimulating and religiously relevant vacation free from the drunkenness, gambling, and ostentatious displays found at other resorts. Moreover, the vacations were relatively inexpensive, costing $3 per week in the 1870s and $6 to $8 per week in the 1880s in addition to a $1 entrance fee. This was to offset the cost of the sometimes elaborate construction that was taking place as the century passed. The transition from tents to cottages could cost $1,000 and in 1884 the Lake Chautauqua resort constructed an entire hotel, the Athenaeum, which provided fairly luxurious amenities for $2 to $4.50 per day for a room and meals (Shrock 2004, 242–44).

FOR MORE INFORMATION

Brekus, Catherine A. "Interpreting American Religion." In *A Companion to 19th-Century America*, ed. William L. Barney. Malden, MA: Blackwell Publishing, 2006.

Current, Richard N., and John A. Garraty, eds. *Words That Made American History since the Civil War*. Boston, MA: Little, Brown and Company, 1965.

Curtis, Susan. *A Consuming Faith: The Social Gospel and Modern American Culture*. Baltimore, MD: John Hopkins University Press, 1991.

Handy, Robert T., ed. *The Social Gospel in America: 1870–1920*. New York: Oxford University Press, 1966.

Nasaw, David, ed. *Andrew Carnegie: The "Gospel of Wealth" Essays and Other Writings*. New York: Penguin Books, 2006.

Rogers, Jack B., and Robert E. Blade. "The Great Ends of the Church: Two Perspectives." *Journal of Presbyterian History* no. 76 (1998).

Shrock, Joel. *The Gilded Age*. Westport, CT: Greenwood Press, 2004.

Smith, Daniel Scott, and Michael S. Hindus, "Premarital Pregnancy in America." In *Studies in American Historical Demography* ed. Maris A. Vinovskis. New York: Academic Press, 1979.

Sullivan, Audrey G. *19th Century South Jersey Camp Meeting, South Seaville, New Jersey*. Fort Lauderdale, FL: Sullivan, 1980.

Sweet, Leonard I. *The Minister's Wife: Her Role in Nineteenth-Century American Evangelism*. Philadelphia, PA: Temple University Press, 1983.

Volo, Dorothy Denneen, and James M. Volo. *Family Life in Nineteenth-Century America*. Westport, CT: Greenwood Press, 2007.

Wilentz, Sean. *Chants Democratic: New York City & the Rise of the American Working Class, 1788–1850*. New York: Oxford University Press, 1984.

PRIMARY DOCUMENTS

1. REPORT OF THE DISCOVERY OF A SUBTERRANEAN FOUNTAIN OF OIL (1859)

The following report from page 5 of a September 1859 issue of the *New York Tribune* describes the striking of oil in Titusville, Pennsylvania, by Edwin L. Drake (1819–1880), who is usually credited as being the first man to drill for oil in the United States.

Titusville, Pa., September 8, 1859. Perhaps you will recollect that in 1854 there was organized in the City of New York a Company, under the name of the Pennsylvania Rock Oil Company, which for some good reasons, passed into the hands of some New Haven capitalists, and was by them removed to New Haven. In 1858 the directors leased the grounds and springs [in Titusville] to Mr. E. L. Drake, well known of the New Haven Railroad. He came out here, and in May last commenced to bore for salt, or to find the source of the oil, which is so common along the banks of Oil Creek. Last week, at a depth of 71 feet, he struck a fissure in the rock through which he was boring, when, to the surprise and joy of everyone, he found he had tapped a vein of water and oil, yielding 400 gallons of pure oil every 24 hours (one day). The pump now in use throws only five gallons per minute of water and oil into a large vat, where the oil rises to the top and the water runs out the bottom. In a few days they will have a pump three times the capacity on the one now in use, and then from ten to twelve hundred gallons of oil will be the daily yield.... The excitement attendant on the discovery of this vast source of oil was fully equal to what I saw in California, when a large lump of gold was accidentally turned out.

Medicus, a correspondent

Source: Hildegarde Dolson, *The Great Oildorado, The Gaudy and Turbulent Years of the First Oil Rush: Pennsylvania, 1859–1880.* New York: Random House, 1959, pp. 7–8.

2. PERSONAL ADVICE AUTHOR TIMOTHY TITCOMB ON TRUTH-TELLING (1861)

A cynical personal advice author named Timothy Titcomb, writing in 1861, believed that absolute integrity was a rarity among nineteenth-century Americans. According to Titcomb, there was some flaw or warp in the perceptions of such men, which prevented them from receiving truthful impressions. Everything came to them distorted. All truth for Titcomb was tainted by the medium through which it passed, and that medium in the nineteenth century was self-interest, the personal vices of greed and alcoholism, and the scourges of sectionalism, slavery, and partisan politics.

There are men in all communities who are believed to be honest, yet whose word is never taken as authority upon any subject....The moment their personality, or their personal interest, is involved, the fact[s] assume false proportions and false colors....It is possible for no man who owns a slave and finds profit in such ownership, to receive the truth touching the right of man to himself, and the moral wrong of slavery....Now when it is sought to be made a permanent institution, because it seems to be the only source of wealth of a section [of the country], it has become right; and even the slave-trade logically falls into the category of laudable and legitimate commerce. It is impossible for a people who have allowed pecuniary interest to deprave their moral sense to this extent, to perceive and receive any sound political truth, or to apprehend the spirit and temper of those who are opposed to them.

The same may be said of the liquor traffic. The act of selling liquor is looked upon with horror by those who stand outside...but the seller deems it legitimate, and looks upon any interference with his sales as an infringement of his rights. Our selfish interest in any business, or in any scheme of profit, distorts all truth....

Of all conscious and criminal lying, I know of none that exceeds in malignity and magnitude that of a political campaign....What, in honesty, can be said of the leading speakers and leading presses which sustain a party in a contest for power, but that they misrepresent their opponents, misstate their own motives, give currency to false accusations, suppress the truth...and lie outright when it is deemed necessary....

The social lying of the world has found a multitudinous satirists, and furnished the staple of a whole school of writers...whom in our hearts we despise....Business lying is, after all, the most universal of any....When two selfish persons meet on opposite sides of the counter, there arises between them a sort of antagonism....There is a great deal of business lying that by long habit becomes unconscious....[Yet] in politics, society, and business, the conscious and intentional lie abounds.

Source: Timothy Titcomb, *Lessons in Life, A Series of Familiar Essays.* New York: Charles Scribner & Co., 1861, pp. 83–84.

3. THE MORRILL ACT (1862)

The first Morrill Act (1862) marked a great step forward for education by involving the federal government through the land-grant college system. It gave a powerful impulse to the movement for state universities and added funds to the existing state college system through the sale of federal lands, or land scrip in lieu of actual property, with the proceeds going to education. The act gave impulse to the inclusion of the natural and physical sciences in college curricula and to the application of scientific thought to agriculture. The land-grant colleges that did not thrive under the 1862 act were strengthened by the 1890 version. The colleges were given further financial support by the Bankhead-Jones Act of 1905 and the Nelson Amendment of 1907. Section 4 of the Morrill Act of 1862 is given below.

Section 4. And be it further enacted, That all moneys derived from the sale of the lands aforesaid by the States to which the lands are apportioned, and from the sales of land scrip hereinbefore provided for, shall be invested in stocks of the United States or of the States, or some other safe stocks, yielding not less than five per centum upon the par value of said stocks; and that the moneys so invested shall constitute a perpetual fund, the capital of which shall remain forever undiminished (except so far as may be provided in section five of this act), and the interest of which shall be inviolably appropriated by each State which may take and claim the benefit of this act, to the endowment, support, and maintenance of at least one college where the leading object shall be, without excluding other scientific and classical studies, and including military tactics, to teach such branches of learning as legislatures of the States may respectively prescribe, in order to promote the liberal and practical education of the industrial classes in the several pursuits and professions of life....

Source: Richard Hofstadter and Wilson Smith, eds., *American Higher Education: A Documentary History*. Chicago, IL: The University of Chicago Press, 1968, p. 568.

4. LIEUTENANT WILLIAM J. HARDEE'S *RIFLE AND LIGHT INFANTRY TACTICS* (1862)

Without enough seasoned officers, training the men was bound to be a puzzling task. The war effort in 1861 would have to rely on a cadre of dedicated and hopefully talented volunteer officers who could learn their trade from military manuals, tactical guides, and professional journals. These included the *Military and Naval Magazine*; the *Army and Navy Chronicle*; and the *Military Magazine*. Also worthwhile was the *Southern Literary Messenger* that reprinted many of the best articles on military science that could be found from around the world. From the United States Military Academy at West Point came an additional store of literature of a quality remarkable for a small school so isolated from the military institutions of Europe.

The Federal Congress appropriated $50,000 to purchase or print tactical manuals and volumes of army regulations for its volunteer officers. These included Winfield Scott's *Infantry Tactics*, Philip St. George Cooke's *Cavalry Tactics*, Denis Hart Mahan's *Treatise on Advanced Guards, Outposts, and Detached Service of Troops*, and William J. Hardee's *Rifle and Light Infantry Tactics*, part of which is reproduced here. Hardee was the only Confederate among these authors, and Silas Casey's *Infantry Tactics* officially superseded his work in 1862. As with most conflicts, the Civil War was fought with the last war's weapons and tactics in mind. Nonetheless, Hardee had addressed some aspects of modern warfare that were unforeseen by other authors, especially the tactical deployment of rifles.

Formation of a Regiment in order of Battle, or in Line.

1. A regiment is composed of ten companies, which will habitually be posted from right to left...according to the rank of captains.
2. With a less number of companies the same principle will be observed, viz.: the first captain will command the right company....
3. The companies thus posted will be designated from right to left, first company, second company, etc. This designation will be observed in the maneuvers.
4. The first two companies on the right...will form the *first division*; the next two companies the *second division*; and so on, to the left.
5. Each company will be divided into equal parts, which will be designated as the first and second *platoon*, counting from the right; each platoon, in like manner, will be subdivided into two *sections*.
6. In all exercises and maneuvers, every regiment, or part of a regiment, composed of two or more companies, will be designated as a *battalion*.
7. The colors, with a guard to be hereinafter designated, will be posted on the left and right center battalion company. That company and all on its right, will be denominated the *right wing* of the battalion; the remaining companies the *left wing*.
8. The formation of the regiment is in two ranks; and each company will be posted in two ranks;...the tallest corporal and tallest man will form the first file, the next two tallest the second file, and so on to the last....
9. The odd and even files, numbered as one, two, in the companies, from right to left, will form groups of four men, who will be designated *comrades in battle*.
10. The distance from one rank to another will be thirteen inches, measured from the breasts of the rear rank men to the backs of the knapsacks of the front rank men.
11. For maneuvering, the companies of a battalion will always be equalized, by transferring men from the strongest to the weakest companies.

Source: W. J. Hardee, *Hardee's Rifle and Light Infantry Tactics*. New York: J. O. Kane, Publisher, 1862.

5. REMEMBERING THE BATTLE OF GETTYSBURG (1863)

Many historians consider the Battle of Gettysburg (July 1–3, 1863) to be the turning point of the Civil War, or the so-called High Water Mark of the Confederacy. That the largest battle of the war—the largest ever fought on the North American continent—took place so near the celebration of Independence Day and so near the national capital has leant weight to its significance, but it should be remembered that the Confederacy soldiered on for almost two additional years—longer after the battle than it had before it. Nonetheless, Gettysburg represents for Americans today much of the essence of Civil War battle, and the battlefield park—only one of many—serves as a national memorial to America's Civil War dead. The brief memories of the participants in the battle that have been selected below are from among the thousands written by Northern and Southern soldiers, and some of the residents of the town.

We soon came to the top of a hill in full view of the field and valley and upon the hill we had the fight. Here men jumped over a fence to the left and formed in battle line. In a short time a line of the enemy came out of the woods in front of us about a mile off; soon another; and yet another. They kept steadily advancing until we could see their officers stepping in front swinging their swords. Suddenly a cloud of smoke arose from their line and almost instantly the balls began to whistle about us and the men next to my right fell. The order rang along the line...to load and fire at will, as they call it. I think we fired about five rounds....As soon as the report of our muskets were [sic] heard we knew that a very small part of our line was there. The enemy did not return our fire but came rushing down the hill yelling.—Sgt. Edwin A. Gearhart, 142nd PA Infantry

At every step some poor fellow would fall, and as his pitiful cry would come to my ear I almost imagined it the wail of some loved one he had left at home.—Capt. John T. James, 11th VA Infantry

There was the thunder of guns, a shrieking, whistling, moaning of shells, before they burst, sometimes like rockets in the air....No results of this conflict could be noted; no shifting of scenes or movement of actors in the great struggle could be observed. It was simply noise, flash, and roar. I had the sensation of a lifetime. —William H. Bayly, 13-year-old resident of Gettysburg

Some of the wounded from the battlefield began to arrive where I was staying. They reported hard fighting, many wounded and killed, and were afraid our troops would be defeated and perhaps routed. The first wounded soldier whom I met had his thumbs tied up. This I thought dreadful, and told him so....Soon two officers carrying their arms in slings made their appearance, and I more fully began to realize that something terrible had taken place. Now the wounded began to come in greater numbers. Some limping, some with their heads and arms in bandages, some crawling, others carried on stretchers or brought in ambulances. Suffering, cast down and dejected, it was truly a pitiable gathering.—Tillie Pierce, 15-year-old resident of Gettysburg

Tell my father I died with my face to the enemy.—Col. Isaac E. Avery, 6th NC Infantry

When our great victory was just over the exultation was so great that one didn't think of our fearful losses, but now I can't help feeling a great weight at my heart.— Capt. Henry L. Abbott, 20th ME Infantry

Source: Time Life Books, *Voices of the Civil War.* New York: Time Life, 1995, pp. 49, 62, 105, 121, 102, 159.

6. AN OHIO SCHOOLMASTER'S VIEW OF THE EARLIEST PERIOD OF RECONSTRUCTION (1865)

Although a life-time resident of a Northern state, schoolmaster John M. Roberts of Madison County, Ohio, reflects many of the ambivalent feelings toward Reconstruction, freedmen, and blacks in general held by a large segment of the American middle class. Many Americans had supported the four-year-long effort to reunite the Union, but not the abolition movement. Roberts thought Lincoln's Emancipation Proclamation of 1863 an idle threat and the arming of black men in the federal army suicidal and dangerous. At first glance these views seem better suited to Southerners, but Roberts's racist views with respect to blacks were not uncommon among those Northerners who supported the war against secession but not for the purpose of equalization and incorporation of blacks into American society. As with many like-minded Northerners, he found light-skinned and mixed-blood African Americans more acceptable than other blacks.

Although his openly racist views were tempered somewhat over time, Roberts was accused by some of his neighbors of being disloyal, a so-called Butternut or Copperhead holding views that emphasized the restoration of the old Union and the traditional Constitution as they had existed before secession. In 1863, he complained, "I have been abused…all because I do not say abolition is god & Abraham Lincoln is a true prophet." A supporter of the postwar Democrats and the Reconstruction policies of Andrew Johnson, Roberts was overly optimistic about the political future of both, predicting a Radical Republican downfall that largely failed to materialize. Reproduced below are excerpts from Roberts's diary.

Monday, August 21, 1865
On the 15th of April [1865] Abraham Lincoln…was shot & killed in Fords Theater, Washington city.… This event…cast a gloom over the whole country. Every paper in the country went into mourning, & the body of the president was taken to all the principal cities of the United States.

Andrew Johnson...immediately took the presidential office. He was an old line Democrat and acted with them up till the breaking out of the Rebellion [Civil War]. He was very much intoxicated on his inauguration as vice president, & and many of his Republican friends asked him to resign. He is generally liked as president by all parties except...some of the rabid Republicans known as Radicals. They are down on him heavily.

A great topic here in politics is that of Negro suffrage. A large portion of the Republicans are in favor of Negro suffrage, and quite a number of them are against the measure. The matter will create a division in that party which will result in its final overthrow. This event may not take place this fall, but it will most assuredly take place before the next general election....

Tuesday, October 10, 1865

...I went to Jefferson early this morning to the election. I voted the Democratic throughout....The [returned] soldiers voted the Democratic ticket almost unanimously. Quite a gain for the Democracy in this township. Everything seems favorable for the white man ticket....

Thursday, October 12, 1865

...The election news is rather unfavorable. [Republican, Samuel S.] Cox is supposed to be elected by a reduced majority. Nothing certain, however.

Thursday, November 9, 1865

...I got S. S. Cox Eight Years in Congress...40 Negroes in the courthouse hunting places [political appointments].

Friday, December 8, 1865

...I see that the radical abolitionists are shoving the most ultra doctrines of the party right in Congress. They are taking time by the forelock. I think the party will repudiate them.

Wednesday, December 20, 1986

...The irrepressible Negro is all the topic in Congress at this time. President Johnson is a mere cypher, it seems. Lincoln was all powerful; Johnson is the reverse....

Friday, December 22, 1865

...President Johnson has issued an extra message to Congress concerning its action on the Reconstruction question. The president intends to stick to his policy of Reconstruction. I am glad of it. The Radicals must go down....

Sunday, December 31, 1865 [New Year's Eve]

...This year has been full of remarkable events. A great rebellion has been crushed & the Constitution itself changed in regard to slavery. One president has been assassinated and his successor has been duly installed without a jar or murmur from anyone. The reconstruction of the glorious old Union has been carried out to a point which the most sanguine friend of the Union could hardly have expected under the circumstance. The Radical element is nearly floored & everything looks as though it would prosper. Long life to our noble president, Andrew Johnson.

Source: J. Merton England, ed., *Buckeye Schoolmaster, A Chronicle of Midwestern Rural Life: 1853–1865.* Bowling Green, OH: State University Popular Press, 1996, pp. 256, 288–90.

7. EXCERPTS FROM *RAGGED DICK, OR STREET LIFE IN NEW YORK* BY HORATIO ALGER JR. (1868)

From 1867 to 1899, Horatio Alger wrote generally cheerful books for boys that urged honesty, hard work, and self-reliance. He endowed his protagonists with the qualities of young urban heroes and gave them an endearing sense of humor that could be displayed even while standing on the bottom rung of the economic and social ladder. Noted for his rags-to-riches writing formula, Alger's continued literary success ultimately added a touch of old-fashioned principle, good faith, and optimism to an otherwise cynical and materialistic Industrial Age. One of his heroes was a bootblack named Ragged Dick, an innately virtuous, but streetwise and cocky child of the city, who first appeared in print in 1868. Dick smoked tobacco now and then, attended the theater (in the pit), and was not above sharing a beer with his fellows. He rarely began the day with even a penny in his pocket, yet his character was unblemished and altogether exemplary. The following excerpt is from Chapter 1 of the novel named for the character, and it provides the reader with a sample of Alger's style.

Ragged Dick Is Introduced to the Reader

Ragged Dick opened his eyes...but did not offer to get up....His bedchamber had been a wooden box half full of straw, on which the young boot-black had reposed his weary limbs, and slept as soundly as if it had been a bed of down. He had dumped down into the straw without taking the trouble of undressing. Getting up too was an equally short process. He jumped out of the box, shook himself, picked out one or two straws that had found their way into the rents in his clothes, and, drawing a well-worn cap over his uncombed locks, he was all ready for the business of the day....

Washing the face and hands is usually considered proper in commencing the day, but Dick was above such refinement. He had no particular dislike of dirt, and did not think it necessary to remove several dark streaks on his face and hands. But in spite of his dirt and rags there was something about Dick that was attractive. It was easy to see that if he had been clean and well dressed he would have been decidedly good-looking. Some of his companions were sly, and their faces inspired distrust; but Dick had a frank, straight-forward manner that made him a favorite.

Dick's business hours commenced. He had no office to open. His little blacking-box was ready for use, and he looked sharply in the faces of those who passed, addressing each with, "Shine yer boots, sir?"

"How much?" asked a gentleman on his way to his office.

"Ten cents," said Dick, dropping his box, and sinking on his knees on the sidewalk, flourishing his brush with the air of one skilled in his profession.

"Ten cents! Isn't that a little steep?"

"Well, you know 'taint all clear profit," said Dick, who had already set to work. "There's blacking costs something, and I have to get a new brush pretty often."

"And you have a large rent too," said the gentleman quizzically, with a glance at a large hole in Dick's coat.

Yes, sir,' said Dick, always ready to joke; "I have to pay such a big rent for my man-shun [mansion] up on Fifth Avenue, that I can't afford to take less than ten cents a shine. I'll give you a bully shine, sir."

....."I believe," said the gentleman, examining his pocket-book, "I haven't got anything short of twenty-five cents. Have you got any change?"

"Not a cent," said Dick. "All my money's invested in the Erie Railroad."

"That's unfortunate."

"Shall I get the money changed, sir?"

"I can't wait: I've got an appointment immediately. I'll hand you twenty-five cents, and you can leave the change at my office any time during the day."

"Alright, sir. Where is it?"

"No. 125 Fulton Street. Shall you remember?"

Yes, sir. What name?"

"Greyson,—office on the second floor."

"All right, sir: I'll bring it."

"I wonder whether the little scamp will prove honest," said Mr. Greyson to himself, as he walked away. "If he does, I'll give him my custom regularly. If he don't, as is most likely, I shan't mind the loss of fifteen cents."

Mr. Greyson didn't understand Dick. Our ragged hero wasn't a model boy in all respects.... But there were some good points about him nevertheless. He was above doing anything mean or dishonorable. He would not steal, or cheat, or impose on younger boys, but was frank and straight-forward, manly and self-reliant. His nature was a noble one, and had saved him from all mean faults. I [Alger] hope my young readers will like him as I do, without being blind to his faults. Perhaps, although he was only a boot-black, they may find something in him to imitate.

Source: John Seelye, ed., *Horatio Alger, Jr., Ragged Dick and Struggling Upward.* New York: Viking Penguin, Inc., 1985, pp. 3–6.

8. A FAREWELL TO THE BUFFALO SOLDIERS FROM THEIR COMMANDER (1869)

In late 1868, Major-General Philip Sheridan decided to wage a winter campaign against the Cheyenne and Arapahoe nations in the hope of culminating a peace in the spring. Vast stores were accumulated at Fort Dodge, Kansas; Fort Lyon, Colorado Territory; and Fort Arbuckle, Oklahoma [Indian] Territory; and a four-pronged plan of attack was devised that included 11 companies of the 7th

U.S. Cavalry under Lieutenant Colonel George Armstrong Custer, the 19th Kansas Volunteer Cavalry under Governor S. J. Crawford, and the 10th U.S. Cavalry (so-called Buffalo Soldiers) under Captain (Brevet Brigadier General) W. H. Penrose. The role of the scattered units of the all-black 10th Cavalry (in three detachments of four troops, respectively) was to guard the Kansas frontier, watch over the Indians already at the various forts, and cut off any retreat of recalcitrant bands to the north and west.

With James "Wild Bill" Hickok acting as a scout, Penrose's direct command of four troops was the first to take the field (November 10, 1868) taking 43 days worth of rations with them. All went well for a few days, but the regiment was caught in a fierce snowstorm and forced to encamp in an area barren of wood or even buffalo chips for fuel. Bitter cold and snow followed the command as it pushed for almost three months toward its objective on the North Canadian River, reaching there on February 19, 1869. During the march, dozens of cavalry horses were killed due to exposure and lack of forage, and many troopers suffered from frostbite and illness. Four men from a resupply column froze to death. The march of the 10th Cavalry, nonetheless, forced the Indians firmly into the path of the principal striking force of the army sweeping down from the north. The second and third detachments of the 10th made only brief contact with the Indians.

Returning to Fort Lyon in early March 1869, after five months in the field, Penrose penned the following affectionate farewell to his men:

Fort Lyon, C. T.

Mar. 14, 1869

Officers and Soldiers of the 10th U.S. Cavalry:

Having been relieved from command before an opportunity was given me to promulgate an official farewell, I take occasion, through courtesy of your commanding officer, of taking leave of you.

You started from this post on an important mission under many disadvantages. Your horses were in poor condition, and you were to march, without forage, to penetrate raw, and before unknown, country. Hardly had you started when you encountered severe storms of rain and snow, accompanied by intense cold; you were without suitable and necessary shelter for such inclement weather; your horses perished day by day, you yourselves suffering from intense cold, many with frostbitten hands and feet; but through these hardships and difficulties you pushed nobly on, undaunted, undismayed, anxious to meet the enemy.

But few commands have ever been called upon to endure more than you have, and none have more cheerfully performed their duty.

Although it was not your fortune to meet and engage the enemy, yet this movement was a part of a grand plan, emanating from that great soldier, Major-General Sheridan.

You were instrumental in compelling a large force of the enemy to make a retrograde movement, and there appears to be no doubt that this was the identical force which Bvt. Major General Custer was thus enabled to encounter and destroy [Battle on the Washita]. Your efforts were therefore of material service in the winter campaign.

Had you had the opportunity I am fully assured you would have maintained in battle the honor of the flag and your regiment.

To the officers and men who so nobly stood with me in our most difficult task I extend my kindest, heartfelt thanks, and wherever you go my kindly interest shall be with you in all your undertakings. May success crown all your efforts.

Respectfully,

W. H. Penrose

Captain and Bvt. Brig. General USA

Late Commander Indian Expedition

from Fort Lyon, C. T.

Source: William H. Leckie, *The Buffalo Soldiers: A Narrative of the Negro Cavalry in the West.* Norman: University of Oklahoma Press, 1967, pp. 42–43.

9. HOW BEAUTY IS SPOILED (1870)

One of the greatest influences on American women's fashion during the 1860s was *Godey's Lady's Book*, a magazine founded by Louis B. Godey in July 1830. Each month the magazine printed fashion plates of morning dresses, walking dresses, seaside costumes, riding habits, dinner dresses, or ball gowns. Such wardrobe depth was seldom needed for the vast majority of the magazine's readers. By the 1860s, *Godey's* had become a fashion institution, setting the standard for fashion savvy. Other magazines such as *Peterson's*, *Arthur's*, *Graham's*, *Leslie's*, and *Harper's* began to follow suit.

Whether a woman could afford the extravagances touted by the fashion plates of the day or not, the look she was hoping to attain was the same. Women of the Civil War period wanted to create the appearance of a narrow waist. Virtually all lines of garments emphasized the smallness of the waist by creating the illusion of width at the shoulders and hips. This was further accentuated by foundation garments that altered the body's physical appearance. As can be seen from the selection below by Dr. Daniel. G. Brinton and Dr. George H. Napheys, not everyone was sure that these extremes of fashion were healthful.

At the waist, the [female] body should have the least circumference. While this is true, it is an absurd and ugly fashion, not sanctioned by any rule of art, and in positive opposition to the laws of health and beauty, to compress, fasten, and lace it down to that "wasp-like waist," against which artists and physicians have so long and so vainly protested.

The circumference of the waist in a woman five feet high should not be less than twenty-five inches, and from this it should increase half an inch in circumference for every additional inch in height, so that a woman five feet eight inches high should measure twenty-nine inches around the waist, of course without clothing.

The result of any greater compression than this is disastrous in every respect. we have already shown how it spoils the shape of the shoulders, and flattens and displaces the breasts. Were this all, it might pass. But far more serious consequences arise. The lungs are cramped and cannot expand. The blood, in consequence, is not purified, the complexion soon becomes muddy, the lips pale or purple, and if there is any tendency to consumption [tuberculosis or other pulmonary disease], it is promptly developed. The pressure downward is equally productive of harm. A physician who pays attention to diseases of women, recently told us that four-fifths of the cases of uterine complaint which he had treated in unmarried women were directly traceable to this violent and unnatural pressure upon the abdomen. Our own experience convinces us that this statement is hardly overdrawn.

With these consequences plainly staring them in the face, it is scarcely credible that women, who wish to preserve either their health or their beauty, will deliberately continue to take so certain means of destroying both as this compression of the waist.... If the object is to "make up the figure," those have the best success who. like the Italian ladies, depend on the arrangement of the dress and careful carriage, and not on forcing the body into unnatural positions.

Source: Daniel G. Brinton and George H. Napheys, *Personal Beauty.* Springfield, MA: W. J. Holland, 1870, pp. 64–66.

10. MAKING PEACE WITH THE APACHE CHIEF COCHISE (1872)

During an 11-year war with the Americans (1861–1872), Cochise—a band leader of the Chiricahua Apache—attracted recruits from among all the western clans, and his position as an overall leader of the Apache nation was cemented when an elder chief, Mangas Coloradas, was executed during a parley with U.S. forces. During much of this time, Cochise fought both the Mexicans and the Americans, using the contested border between the two nations in a hide-and-seek manner. Nonetheless, he began to suffer defeats when the troops on both sides brought mobile artillery into the field against him. The Apache began to lose many lives as troops under George A. Crook pursued them incessantly. In 1872, a civilian, Thomas Jeffords, arranged a treaty between Cochise and Major General Oliver O. Howard, the one-armed veteran of the Civil War who helped to found Howard University. The Chiricahua made peace and maintained the treaty under the leadership of Cochise until he died in 1874. The following excerpt is from General Howard's account of his first meeting with Cochise.

The First Meeting of the General and the Apache Chief

Having ridden up to us Cochise dismounted and saluted (Tom) Jeffords in Spanish as an old friend. He then turned to me as Jeffords was saying, "This is the man." The chief was fully six feet in height, well proportioned, with large eyes; his face was slightly colored with vermilion, hair straight and black, with a few silver threads. He warmly grasped may hand and said pleasantly" "Buenos dias, Senor!"

Having returned his salute I began to study his face. His countenance was pleasant, and made me feel how strange it is that such a man can be a notorious robber and cold-blooded murderer. In after interviews I observed that upon ordinary occasions he showed courtesy and simplicity, but, as the Chiricahua chief, when in council or mounted, leading his tribe, if Apache wrongs were touched upon, he was terribly severe in aspect...

Next Cochise turned to me and said something in Apache. Jeffords gave the substance in English: "Will the General explain the object of his visit?"

"The President sent me to make peace between you and the white people."

"Nobody wants peace more than I do." he replied.

"Then," I answered, "as I have full power we can make peace."...

I was now to live with the Indians for some time. The new camping ground to which Cochise took us was north of the entrance to his stronghold, well up on the foothills where were clusters of oaks and several acres of grass land. Six miles off stood a globular height, spanning three hundred feet from the plain, with the San Pedro River at its foot. On this hill, at the request of Cochise, Jeffords and Captain Sladen had planted a white flag. Sladen told me how the Indian women and children clapped there hands when they first saw his emblem of peace. Jeffords had understood them when in one compound word in Apache they cried: "The-flag-of-peace-I-love."...

Other Apaches continued to come in until nearly all were in camp. Many of the newcomers were rough and very troublesome, and an adjustment of all vexed questions was hard to bring about. I was forced...to give them as Cochise had suggested, a reservation embracing a part of the Chiricahua mountains and of the valley adjoining on the west, which included the Big Sulphur Spring and Rodgers' ranch.

The evening after the council a strange ceremony for consulting the spirits was observed by the Indians. It took place on a separate plateau near my bivouac. I was not present at the beginning of the performance. I could, however, hear the muffled sound of voices of a multitude of women apparently imitating the low moaning of the wind. Then all—men and women—sang with ever increasing volume of sound, and the women's voices rose higher and higher. It was a wild weird performance.

In due time the roughest-appearing Apache that I had ever seen, tall and muscular, his long hair hanging in braids down his back, ran toward me. His manner was not as fierce as his appearance would indicate, for he now spoke gently and invited me and all our white men to join the band on the plateau.

Arriving there we sat outside the women's circle—the male Indians being seated within it. As soon as the singing ceased the men kept talking, but without rising. An authoritative voice now silenced all the others. It was Cochise speaking in a mournful recitative. More than once I heard him use Jeffords' sobriquet, "Stag-li-to," meaning Redbeard. Our whole case was evidently being discussed at the meeting. Those were solemn moments to us, for we could not determine on which side of the Styx [the mythical river crossed at death] their superstitions might land us.

Fortunately, the spirits were on our side. Their answer to the Indian incantation was rendered through Cochise, who said, "Hereafter the white man and the Indian are to drink of the same water, eat of the same bread, and be at peace." I felt the object of my mission was now accomplished.

Source: David C. Whitney, *The American Legacy: A Pageant of Great Deeds and Famous Words.* Chicago, IL: J. G. Ferguson Publishing Company, 1975, pp. 287–88.

---

11. THE SAGA OF STONE'S LANDING FROM *THE GILDED AGE* BY MARK TWAIN (SAMUEL CLEMENS) (1873)

In his satirical novel *The Gilded Age* (written with Charles Dudley Warner), Samuel Clemens (Mark Twain) gave an entire period of American history a name that remains today. The age that Twain described was filled with flagrant materialism, aggressive self-interest, political corruption, and economic adaptation. Although Twain wrote the novel in a satire, the age that he lampooned produced prodigious results, accumulated immense wealth, and transformed an agrarian country into an industrial powerhouse. The selection below is an amazing relic of a period characterized by the expansion of railroads and steamboat lines, rampant land speculation, and people's belief that they could change the landscape of America itself to better fit their economic needs. The characters in Twain's novel share a somewhat benevolent personal dishonesty and a naive willingness to suspend their disbelief and put aside their normal wariness of overly optimistic schemes for getting rich in the sleepy, unremarkable, and out-of-the-way town of Stone's Landing.

Stone's Landing Becomes the City of Napoleon—on Paper

Nobody dressed more like an engineer than Mr. Henry Brierly. The completeness of his appointments was the envy of the corps, and the gay fellow himself was the admiration of the camp servants, axmen, teamsters, and cooks [that worked for the railroad]. . . .

Harry shouldered his [surveyor's] rod and went to the field, tramped over the prairie by day, and figured up results, with the utmost cheerfulness and industry, and plotted the line on the profile paper, without, however, the least idea of engineering, practical or theoretical. Perhaps there was not a great deal of scientific knowledge in the entire corps, nor was very much needed. They were making what was called a preliminary survey, and the chief object of a preliminary survey was to get up an excitement about the [rail]road, to interest every town in that part of the state in it, under the belief that the road would run through it, and to get the aid of every planter upon the prospect that a station would be on his land.

Mr. Jeff Thompson was the most popular engineer who could be found for his work. He did not bother himself much about details or practicabilities of location, but ran merrily along, sighting from the top of one divide to the top of another, and striking "plumb" every town-site and big plantation within twenty or thirty miles of his route. In his own language he "just went booming."

This course gave Henry an opportunity, as he said, to learn the practical details of engineering, and it gave Philip a chance to see the country, and to judge for himself the prospect of a fortune it offered. Both he and Harry got the "refusal" [right of refusal for purchase] of more than one plantation as they went along, and wrote urgent letters to their Eastern correspondents, upon the beauty of the land and the certainty that it would quadruple in value as soon as the road was finally located. It seemed strange to them that capitalists did not flock out there and secure this land.

They had not been in the field over two weeks when Harry wrote to his friend, Colonel Sellers, that he'd better be on the move, for the line was certain to go to Stone's Landing. Any one who looked at the line on the map, as it was laid down from day to day, would have been uncertain which way it was going; but Jeff had declared that in his judgment the only practicable route from the point they then stood on was that that town would be the next one hit.

"We'll make it boys," said the chief, "if we have to go in a balloon." And make it they did. In less than a week, this indomitable engineer had carried his moving caravan over slues and branches, across bottoms and along divides, and pitched his tents in the very heart of the city of Stone's Landing....

The fellows turned out of the tents, rubbing their eyes, and stared about them. They were camped on the second bench of the narrow bottom of a crooked, sluggish stream, that was some five rods wide in the present good stage of water. Before them were a dozen log cabins, with stick and mud chimneys, irregularly disposed on either side of a not very well defined road....

"This, gentlemen," said Jeff, "is the Columbus River, alias Goose Creek. If it was widened, and deepened, and straightened, and made long enough, it would be one of the finest rivers in the Western country."

...As the sun rose and sent his level beams along the stream, the thin stratum of mist, or malaria, rose also and dispersed, but the light was not able to enliven dull water nor give any hint of its apparent fathomless depth. Venerable mudturtles crawled up and roosted upon old logs in the stream, their backs glistening in the sun, the first inhabitants of the metropolis to begin the active business of the day....

"Welcome to Napoleon...[said the mayor]...."

While the engineer corps went to the field, to run back a couple of miles and ascertain, approximately, if a road could ever get down to the Landing, and to sight ahead across the Run, and see if it could ever get out again, Colonel Sellers and Harry sat down and began to roughly map out the city of Napoleon on a large piece of drawing paper.

"I've got the refusal of a mile square here," said the Colonel, "in our names, for a year, with a quarter interest reserved for the four owners."

They laid out the town liberally, not lacking room, leaving space for the railroad to come in, and for the river as it was to be when improved.

The engineers reported that the railroad could come in, by taking a little sweep and crossing the stream on a high bridge, but the grades would be steep. Colonel Sellers said he didn't care so much about the grades, if the road could only be made to reach the [grain] elevators on the river. The next day Mr. Thompson made a hasty survey of the stream for a mile or two, so that the Colonel and Harry were enabled to show on their map how nobly that would accommodate the city. Jeff took a little writing from the Colonel and Harry for a prospective share, but Philip declined to join in, saying he had no money, and didn't want to make engagements he couldn't fulfill.

The next morning the camp moved on, followed till out of sight by the listless eyes of the group in front of the store, one of whom remarked that "he'd be doggoned if he ever expected to see that railroad any more."

Source: Richard N. Current and John A. Garraty, eds., *Words that Made American History Since the Civil War.* Boston, MA: Little, Brown and Company, 1965, pp. 84–86.

---

12. THE PREFACE TO *HOUSEKEEPING IN OLD VIRGINIA* BY MARION CABELL TYREE (1877)

Originally written in 1877, *Housekeeping in Old Virginia* contained contributions concerning domestic economy from 250 housewives, who were distinguished for their skill in the culinary arts and other branches of keeping a home. The preface of this edition clearly shows that the attitude of white Southern women, and many among the elite throughout the country, had not changed appreciably a full decade after the end of the Civil War. Southern graciousness was still the hard coin of American hospitality and housekeeping.

Preface

Virginia, or the Old Dominion, as her children delight to call her, has always been famed for the style of her living. Taught by the example of her royal colonial governors, and the numerous adherents of King Charles, who brought hither in their exile the graces and luxuriousness of his brilliant court, she became noted among the colonies for the princely hospitality of her people and for the beauty and richness of their living. But when at length her great son in the House of Burgesses sounded the cry of war, and her people made haste to gird themselves for the long struggle, her daughters, not to be outdone either in services or patriotism, set about at once the inauguration of a plan of rigid retrenchment and reform in the domestic economy, while at the same time exhibiting to their sisters a noble example of devotion and self-sacrifice.

Tearing the glittering arms of King George from their side-boards, and casting them, with their costly plate and jewels, as offerings into the lap of the Continental Congress, they introduced into their homes that new style of living in which, discarding all the showy extravagance of the old, and retaining only its inexpensive graces, they succeeded in perfecting that system which, surviving to this day [1877], has ever been noted for its beautiful and elegant simplicity.

This system, which combines the thrifty frugality of New England with the less rigid style of Carolina, has been justly pronounced, by the throngs of admirers who have gathered from all quarters of the Union around generous boards of her illustrious sons, as the very perfection of domestic art.

It is the object of the compiler of this book, for she does not claim the title of author, to bring within the reach of every American housekeeper, who may desire it, the domestic principles and practices of these famous Virginia homes.... The book, after great care in its preparation, is now offered to the public with much confidence. All that is here presented has been so thoroughly tested, and approved by so many of the best housekeepers in Virginia, that she feels it must meet with a cordial and very general reception at the hands of all accomplished housewives throughout the land, and will supply a long-felt and real need.

If she shall thus succeed in disseminating a knowledge of the practices of the most admirable system of domestic art known in our country; if she shall succeed in lightening the labors of the housewife by placing in her reach a guide which will be found always trusty and reliable; if she shall succeed in contributing something to the health of American children by instructing their mothers in the art of preparing light and wholesome and palatable food; if she, above all, shall succeed in making American homes more attractive to American husbands, and spare them a resort to hotels and saloons for those simple luxuries which their wives know not how to provide; if she shall thus add to the comfort, to the health and happy contentment of these, she will have proved in some measure a public benefactor, and will feel amply repaid for all the labor her work has cost.

Source: Marion Cabell Tyree, ed., *Housekeeping in Old Virginia.* Louisville, KY: John P. Morton and Company, 1879, preface.

13. PROGRESS AND POVERTY OR THE SINGLE TAX (1879)

In 1869, Henry George (1839–1897) made his first business trip to New York City. As a newspaperman, he was very observant of his surroundings, and he was shocked by the glaring contrast between the extremes of wealth and poverty that he saw living side-by-side in the city. In California, he had witnessed much of the Golden State's wealth falling into the hands of just a few men—making them wealthy at the expense of the rest of society. His interest in economic and social questions was intensified by the widespread and long-lasting suffering that accompanied the Panic of 1873 and the depression that followed. In 1879, he wrote a book on the subject that defined the problem as he saw it and put forward a number of suggestions to rectify the situation. Among these was the concept of the single tax.

The book's full title was *Progress and Poverty: An Inquiry into the Cause of Industrial Depression and of Increase of Want with a Increase of Wealth: The Remedy*, but it is better known as the *Single Tax* (1880). Herein George suggested that all taxation be abolished save a single tax on land values and rents. The book was very powerfully written, and made George popular as a lecturer and well enough known as a personality to run for mayor of New York City in 1886. He outpolled one of his rivals, Theodore Roosevelt, but lost to Abram Hewitt, who was elected. For the rest of his life George remained the leader of the Single Tax reform movement, which still exists in a number of forms today. It is George's description of the problem that is emphasized in the selection below.

Progress and Poverty

The Problem

The present century [nineteenth] has been marked by a prodigious increase in wealth-producing power. The utilization of steam and electricity, the introduction of improved processes and labor-saving machinery, the greater subdivision and grander scale of production, the wonderful facilitation of exchanges, have multiplied enormously the effectiveness of labor.

At the beginning of this marvelous era it was natural to expect, and it was expected, that labor-saving inventions would lighten the toil and improve the condition of the laborer; that the enormous increase in the power of producing wealth would make real poverty a thing of the past. Could a man of the last century—a [Benjamin] Franklin or a [Joseph] Priestley—have seen, in a vision of the future, the steamship taking the place of the sailing vessel, the railroad train of the wagon, the reaping machine of the scythe, the threshing machine of the flail; could he have heard the throb of the engines that in obedience to human will, and for the satisfaction of human desire, exert a power greater than that of all the men and all the beasts of burden of the earth combined; could he have seen the forest tree transformed into finished lumber... with hardly a touch of a human hand; the great workshops where boots and shoes are turned out by the case with less labor than the old fashioned cobbler could have put on a sole; the factories where, under the eye of a girl, cotton becomes cloth faster than a hundred stalwart weavers could have turned it out with their hand looms; could he have seen steam hammers shaping mammoth shafts and mighty anchors, and delicate machinery tiny watches; the diamond drill cutting through the heart of the rocks, and coal oil sparing the whale; could he have realized the enormous saving of labor resulting from improved facilities of exchange and communication—sheep killed in Australia eaten fresh in England, the order given by a London banker in the afternoon executed in San Francisco in the morning of the same day; could he have conceived of the hundred thousand improvements which these only suggest, what would he have inferred as to the social condition of mankind?

...And out of these bounteous material conditions he would have seen arising as necessary sequences, moral conditions realizing the golden age of which mankind has always dreamed. Youth no longer stunted and starved; age no longer harried by avarice; the child at play with the tiger; the man with the muck-rake drinking in the glory of the stars. Foul things fled, fierce things tame; discord turned into harmony! For how could there be greed where all had enough? How could vice, the crime, the ignorance, the brutality, that spring from poverty and fear of poverty, exist where poverty had vanished? Who should crouch where all were freemen; who oppress where all were peers?

...It is true that disappointment has followed disappointment, and that, discovery upon discovery, and invention after invention, have neither lessened the toil of those who most need respite, nor brought plenty to the poor. But there have been so many things to which it seemed this failure could be laid, that up to our time [1879] the new faith has hardly weakened. We have better appreciated the difficulties to be overcome, but not the less trusted that the tendency of the times was to overcome them.

...This fact—the great fact that poverty and all its concomitants show themselves in communities just as they develop into the conditions toward which material progress tends—proves that the social difficulties existing wherever a certain stage of progress has been reached, do not arise from local circumstances, but are, in some way or another, engendered by progress itself....It is in the older and richer sections of the Union that pauperism and distress among the working classes are becoming most painfully apparent. If there is less poverty in San Francisco than in New York, is it not because San Francisco is yet behind New York in all that both cities are striving for? When San Francisco reaches the point where New York now is, who can doubt that there will also be ragged and barefooted children on her streets?

Source: Henry George quoted in Richard N. Current and John A. Garraty, eds., *Words That Made American History since the Civil War.* Boston, MA: Little, Brown and Company, 1965, pp. 167–78.

14. ETIQUETTE FOR THE TABLE (1880s)

This set of instructive verses for children printed on card stock clearly endorses the attitude of late nineteenth-century parents that children be well-trained in terms of acceptable manners when at the table.

Young Folk's Etiquette for the Table

In silence I must take my seat,
And say my grace before I eat;

Must for my food with patience wait,
Till I am ask'd to hand my plate.

I must not speak a useless word,
For children should be seen—not heard;
I must not talk about my food,
Nor fret if I don't think it good.

My mouth with food I must not crowd,
Nor while I'm eating speak aloud;
Must turn my head to cough or sneeze,
And when I ask say "If you please."

When told to rise I must put
My chair away with noiseless foot,
And lift my heart to God above,
In praise for all His wondrous love.

Source: Sally Kevill-Davies, *Yesterday's Children, The Antiques and History of Childcare.* Woodbridge, UK: Antique Collectors' Club, 1998, p. 131.

15. ENTRIES FROM THE DIARY OF RUTH ANNA ABRAMS (1881)

Ruth Anna Abrams was the mother of nine children at age 39 when she penned her personal diary. Two years later she was dead. Written in 1881, this sample from the diary is presented with its original spelling and grammatical errors.

Thursday, October the 20th pleasant I Have sewed hard all day I made Charlie Mcgill a calico shirt I bought and made it for him a present this evening I cut out Alices shirt dress I am weary.

Teusday, October the 25th clear and pleasant. I worked on Addas and Alices dresses they both think theres ought to be made first I will make both at once Anderson and the boys is husking corn The leaves are all bright colored and falling to the ground.

Wednesday, November the 2th dark and rainey This afternoon I finished Addas dress and fixed Lafes bed tick. I have finished fourteen garments this week big and little I have kept buisey all day and sewed some after night.

Tuesday, December the 6th still the sun refuses to shine Dark and sullen looks the cloud but it is not cold. I cut the skirt of Doras red brocaded dress but I fear my eyes are to weary to finish it. I am hardly stout enough to do all the work for so large a family and take care of the little ones.

Source: Roderick Kiracofe, *Cloth & Comfort, Pieces of Women's Lives from Their Quilts and Diaries.* New York: Clarkson Potter Publishers, 1994, p. 20.

16. A SNIPPET FROM A DOLL'S LIFE (1880s)

The author of this poignant piece was Edith Stratton Kitt, who as an adult wrote about her life growing up in Arizona in the 1880s.

Mabel had a fine rag doll with a bisque head and many fine clothes which had belonged to our great-grandmother. Dolls did not, however, particularly appeal to me. Once I was given a doll with a china head, but she did not last long. I took her down to the corral to watch the cowboys brand calves, and she got excited and fell off the fence and broke her head.

Source: Roderick Kiracofe, *Cloth & Comfort, Pieces of Women's Lives from Their Quilts and Diaries*. New York: Clarkson Potter Publishers, 1994, p. 18.

17. FROM HAND-SEWN TO MACHINE-SEWN (1867–1899)

The following short excerpts are the simplest of statements of how technological advances affected the home, especially with respect to sewing. The first is from Lois Lenski's autobiography. The second is from Anne Whitwell, who wrote to her adult daughter in 1867, and the last is from Edith White reminiscing as an adult.

Lois Lenski

I began to sew for my dolls when I was six [1899]. Mama showed me how to cut a pattern, set in sleeves, how to gather a skirt to put in a belt, how to make button-holes, how to do hemstitching. She said, "If you are going to learn to sew, you might as well do it the right way." The box of scraps from her own dressmaking was my treasure box.

Source: Roderick Kiracofe, *Cloth & Comfort, Pieces of Women's Lives from Their Quilts and Diaries*. New York: Clarkson Potter Publishers, 1994, p. 50.

Anne Whitwell

I wish I was one of those sassy ones that never gets in a fret over anything. Didn't this sewing machine help me along fast. I never mean to sew by hand any more if I can help it.

Source: Presented in Roderick Kiracofe, *Cloth & Comfort, Pieces of Women's Lives from Their Quilts and Diaries*. New York: Clarkson Potter Publishers, 1994, p. 14.

Edith Wharton

I was permitted to have material with which I cut out, fitted, and made on the sewing machine a dress for my sister when I was eleven. Of this I was justly proud.

Source: Roderick Kiracofe, *Cloth & Comfort, Pieces of Women's Lives from Their Quilts and Diaries.* New York: Clarkson Potter Publishers, 1994, p. 51.

18. DANIEL CARTER BEARD'S ADVICE TO AMERICAN BOYS (1882)

In the following excerpts from Daniel Carter Beard's *The American Boy's Handbook,* the author describes the benefits to a boy of having a dog and of going camping.

Every Boy Deserves a Dog

It is true that a boy can do without a canine companion and live to enjoy life, but he is almost incomplete; he lacks something; he has lost a gratification, a harmless, pleasant experience, and the loss leaves an empty space in his boyhood life that nothing can ever quite fill up. A boy without a dog is like an unfinished story. What your left hand is to your right, a boy's dog is to the boy. More particularly is all this true of the lad who lives either in the country or within walking distance of forest and stream....

Going Camping

The next best thing to really living in the woods is talking over such an experience. A thousand little incidents, scarcely thought of at the time, crowd upon my mind, and bring back with them the feeling of freedom and adventure so dear to the heart of every boy. Shall I ever enjoy any flavor earth can afford as we did our coffee's aroma? The flapjacks—how good and appetizing! The fish—how delicate and sweet! And the wonderful cottage of boughs, thatched with the tassels of the pine—was there ever a cottage out of a fairy tale that could compare with it?

In fancy I can see it now. There stands the little cot, flooded with the light of the setting sun; those whom built it and use it for habitation are off exploring, hunting, fishing, and foraging for their evening meal, and the small, shy creatures of the wood take the opportunity to satisfy the curiosity with which they have, from a safe distance, viewed the erection of so large and singular a nest.

The boys will soon return, each with his contribution to the larder—a fish, a squirrel, a bird, or a rabbit, which will be cooked and eaten with better appetite and enjoyment than the most elaborate viands that home could afford. And though such joys are denied me now, I can, at least, in remembering them, give others an opportunity to posses similar pleasures.

Source: Daniel Carter Beard, *The American Boy's Handbook.* Boston, MA: David R. Godine, 1882, pp. 148, 223.

19. LINA AND ADELIA BEARD ON ACTIVITIES FOR GIRLS (1887)

In the following excerpts from *The American Girls Handbook, or How to Amuse Yourself and Others* by Lina Beard and Adelia B. Beard, the authors describe the benefits of a walking club for girls, rules for more healthful exercise, and the pleasures of a door-step party.

The Walking Club

A sound of girlish voices is suddenly heard in the quiet village streets, as our Walking Club, issuing from the house of one of its members, starts off on the first tramp of the season. The gay chatter and bubbling laughter blend with the twittering and chirping of the birds fluttering among the budding trees, and all the merry sounds seem in perfect harmony with the youthful gladness of the bright morning.

There is a subtle power and exhilaration in the spring sunshine that stimulates the blood, and sends it tingling through our veins, as with light-springing steps we quickly leave the village behind us and penetrate into the outlying country, stopping now and then to secure a branch of the downy pussy-willow or the brilliant red blossoms of the maple, and again to admire a distant view where the trees seem enveloped in a hazy mist of delicate color; on we go, exploring sequestered spots or entering into the woods in search of early wild flowers.

Although possibly timid as individuals, as a club we are brave enough; for a party of fourteen or sixteen girls, including our merry little chaperon, may go, with impunity, where it would not be so pleasant for one to venture alone. Once a week all through that delightful spring the club might have been seen, now upon a road leading in this direction, now in that. And, often as we stepped aside to allow a carriage to pass, its occupants would lean forward smiling, and waving their hands in greeting; for the moment, perhaps, feeling in sympathy with the vigorous young life that preferred this mode of locomotion to being carried about on the downiest cushions of the easiest carriages....

It was not until the ever-increasing heat of the sun, and our own languid disinclination to much exertion, warned us that the mildness of spring had passed, that we concluded to disband for summer. In the fall we again fell into rank, and came home from our walks laden with the gorgeous trophies of autumn, as we had once carried in triumph the tasseled branches and dainty flowers of spring. We continued our tramps into early winter, when the frosty crispness of the air made it very bracing, and the brisk exercise of walking brought the healthy color to cheek and lip of the young pedestrians.

Such a club as this, which at the same time promotes health, good spirits, and sociability, is one that most girls will enjoy and derive benefit from.

Rules to Promote Better Walking

TO MAKE THE EXERCISE OF WALKING HEALTHFUL, AND THEREFORE THE MORE ENJOYABLE, THESE RULES SHOULD BE OBSERVED

1st. Carry the body erect on the hip, the shoulders thrown back, the chest raised, and the head square on the shoulders.

2nd. Breathe through the nose while walking rapidly, otherwise the mouth will become dry and the breath short.

3rd. Wear loosely fitting clothes that will permit a free motion of the limbs, and shoes with broad, moderately thick soles and low, broad heels. In all cases girl's skirts should be supported from the shoulders, and in walking any distance it is absolutely necessary for comfort that there should be no weight upon the hips.

The Door-Step Party

In the State of Kentucky…at dusk…after the heat of the day is spent, and the air, although not cool, is a degree or two less hot, the population of the town makes itself visible. Ladies and children clad in the thinnest of white and light colored muslin gowns, emerge from the houses to sit upon piazza and door-step, and there welcome husband, father, and brothers of the family upon their return from business; that business which is never neglected no matter what the thermometer may register. After tea the door-steps are once more taken possession of, and to enter the house again until ready to retire for the night, is not to be thought of. Friends and neighbors making social calls are received and entertained informally upon the door-steps, and sometimes when the party becomes too large for the steps to accommodate, chairs are placed upon the pavement immediately in front of the door, and no one feels, while occupying one of these seats, that the position is at all public or conspicuous.

Hatless and bonnetless as all of the ladies and children are, the warmth of the evenings making all head coverings and extra wraps unnecessary and uncomfortable, the streets present a gay and fête-like appearance seldom seen in our eastern towns.…

Now is just the time for a door-step party...a modest fête...a simple way of entertaining one's friends of a summer evening when the heat will not permit of the exertion of active games. The delightful out-door surroundings give it a novel charm and make it entirely different from the frolics usually indulged in during the winter season. Because the entertainment is not noisy it need not be the less enjoyable, and a party of bright, merry girls will derive plenty of amusement and fun from the quiet games of a door-step party...that are suitable for an occasion of this kind.

Source: Lina Beard and Adelia B. Beard, *The American Girls Handbook, or How to Amuse Yourself and Others.* Boston, MA: David R. Godine, 1887, pp. 28–30, 31, 151–53.

20. THE GOSPEL OF WEALTH (1889)

Andrew Carnegie (1835–1919) was a massively successful businessman—his wealth was based on the provision of iron and steel to the railways, but also a man who recalled his roots in Scotland before his immigration to the United States. To resolve what might seem to be contradictions between the creation of wealth, which he saw as proceeding from immutable social laws, and social provision, he came up with the notion of the gospel of wealth. He lived up to his word, and gave away large portions of his fortune to socially beneficial projects, most famously by funding libraries. His approval of death taxes might surprise modern billionaires.

The Gospel of Wealth

The problem of our age is the administration of wealth, so that the ties of brotherhood may still bind together the rich and poor in harmonious relationship. The conditions of human life have not only been changed, but revolutionized, within the past few hundred years. In former days there was little difference between the dwelling, dress, food, and environment of the chief and those of his retainers....The contrast between the palace of the millionaire and the cottage of the laborer with us today measures the change which has come with civilization.

This change, however, is not to be deplored, but welcomed as highly beneficial. It is well, nay, essential for the progress of the race, that the houses of some should be homes for all that is highest and best in literature and the arts, and for all the refinements of civilization, rather than that none should be so. Much better this great irregularity than universal squalor. Without wealth there can be no Maecenas [a rich Roman patron of the arts]. The "good old times" were not good old times. Neither master nor servant was as well situated then as today. A relapse to old conditions would be disastrous to both—not the least so to him who serves—and would sweep away civilization with it....

We start, then, with a condition of affairs under which the best interests of the race are promoted, but which inevitably gives wealth to the few. Thus far, accepting conditions as they exist, the situation can be surveyed and pronounced good. The question then arises—and, if the foregoing be correct, it is the only question with which we have to deal—What is the proper mode of administering wealth after the laws upon which civilization is founded have thrown it into the hands of the few? And it is of this great question that I believe I offer the true solution. It will be understood that fortunes are here spoken of, not moderate sums saved by many years of effort, the returns from which are required for the comfortable maintenance and education of families. This is not wealth, but only competence, which it should be the aim of all to acquire.

There are but three modes in which surplus wealth can be disposed of. It can be left to the families of the decedents; or it can be bequeathed for public purposes; or, finally, it can be administered during their lives by its possessors. Under the first and second modes most of the wealth of the world that has reached the few has hitherto been applied. Let us in turn consider each of these modes. The first is the most injudicious. In monarchial countries, the estates and the greatest portion of the wealth are left to the first son, that the vanity of the parent may be gratified by the thought that his name and title are to descend to succeeding generations unimpaired. The condition of this class in Europe today teaches the futility of such hopes or ambitions. The successors have become impoverished through their follies or from the fall in the value of land.... Why should men leave great fortunes to their children? If this is done from affection, is it not misguided affection? Observation teaches that, generally speaking, it is not well for the children that they should be so burdened. Neither is it well for the state. Beyond providing for the wife and daughters moderate sources of income, and very moderate allowances indeed, if any, for the sons, men may well hesitate, for it is no longer questionable that great sums bequeathed oftener work more for the injury than for the good of the recipients. Wise men will soon conclude that, for the best interests of the members of their families and of the state, such bequests are an improper use of their means.

As to the second mode, that of leaving wealth at death for public uses, it may be said that this is only a means for the disposal of wealth, provided a man is content to wait until he is dead before it becomes of much good in the world.... The cases are not few in which the real object sought by the testator is not attained, nor are they few in which his real wishes are thwarted....

The growing disposition to tax more and more heavily large estates left at death is a cheering indication of the growth of a salutary change in public opinion.... Of all forms of taxation, this seems the wisest. Men who continue hoarding great sums all their lives, the proper use of which for public ends would work good to the community, should be made to feel that the community, in the form of the state, cannot thus be deprived of its proper share. By taxing estates heavily at death, the state marks its condemnation of the selfish millionaire's unworthy life.

This policy would work powerfully to induce the rich man to attend to the administration of wealth during his life, which is the end that society should always have in view, as being that by far most fruitful for the people....

There remains, then, only one mode of using great fortunes: but in this way we have the true antidote for the temporary unequal distribution of wealth, the reconciliation of the rich and the poor—a reign of harmony—another ideal, differing, indeed from that of the Communist in requiring only the further evolution of existing conditions, not the total overthrow of our civilization. It is founded upon the present most intense individualism, and the race is prepared to put it in practice by degrees whenever it pleases. Under its sway we shall have an ideal state, in which the surplus wealth of the few will become, in the best sense, the property of the many, because administered for the common good, and this wealth, passing through the hands of the few, can be made a much more potent force for the elevation of our race than if it had been distributed in small sums to the people themselves. Even the poorest can be made to see this, and to agree that great sums gathered by some of their fellow citizens and spent for public purposes, from which the masses reap the principal benefit, are more valuable to them than if scattered among them through the course of many years in trifling amounts.

This, then, is held to be the duty of the man of Wealth: First, to set an example of modest, unostentatious living, shunning display or extravagance; to provide moderately for the legitimate wants of those dependent upon him; and after doing so to consider all surplus revenues which come to him simply as trust funds, which he is called upon to administer, and strictly bound as a matter of duty to administer in the manner which, in his judgment, is best calculated to produce the most beneficial result for the community—the man of wealth thus becoming the sole agent and trustee for his poorer brethren, bringing to their service his superior wisdom, experience, and ability to administer—doing for them better than they would or could do for themselves.

Source: Andrew Carnegie, "Wealth," *North American Review*, June 1889, No. 391, Volume 148: pp. 653, 657–62.

21. CHRISTMAS DAY MENU (1890)

The following menu for Christmas dinner comes from an 1890 edition of *Godey's Lady's Book*.

Raw Oysters
Bouillon
Fried Smelts...............................Sauce Tartare
Potatoes a La Maitre d' Hotel
Sweetbread Pates........................Peas
Roast Turkey..............................Cranberry Sauce
Roman Punch
Quail with Truffles......................Rice Croquettes
Parisian Salad
Crackers and Cheese
Nesselrode Pudding....................Fancy Cakes
Fruit...Coffee

Raw Oysters

Have blue-point oysters; serve upon the half shell, the shells being laid upon oyster plates filled with cracked ice; six oysters and a thick slice of lemon being served upon each plate.

Bouillon

Put into a pot three pounds of shin beef, one pound of knuckle of veal, and three quarts of water, and simmer gently. As soon as the scum begins to rise, skim carefully until it quite ceases to appear. Then add salt, two carrots, the same of onions, turnips, and a little celery. Simmer gently four hours, strain, and serve in bouillon cups to each guest.

Fried Smelts

Clean about two dozen smelts, cut off the gills, wash them well in cold water, and then dry them thoroughly. Put in a pinch of salt and pepper in a little milk, into which dip your smelts, and then roll them in cracker dust. Put into a frying pan some lard, in which, when very hot, fry your smelts a light brown. Also fry some parsley, which place around your fish, and serve with Sauce Tartare.

Sauce Tartare

Put the yolks of two eggs in a bowl with salt, pepper, the juice of a lemon, and one teaspoonful of dry mustard. Stir with a wooden spoon, and add by degrees—in very small quantities, and stirring continuously—a tablespoonful of vinegar; then, a few drops at a time, some good oil, stirring rapidly all the time, until your sauce thicken, and a half a pint of oil has been absorbed. Chop one pickle and a tablespoonful of capers, also chop a green onion and a few tarragon leaves, and mix with your sauce.

Potatoes a La Maitre D'hotel

Wash eight potatoes, and boil them in cold water with a pinch of salt. When thoroughly done, peel them cut them in thin round slices; put them—with three ounces of butter, a pinch of salt, pepper and a nutmeg, the juice of a lemon, and a tablespoonful of chopped parsley—in a saucepan on the fire, and, when very hot, serve.

Sweetbread Pates

Boil four sweetbreads, and let them become cold; then chop them very fine, add about ten mushrooms, also chopped fine. Mix with these a quarter pound of butter, half a pint of milk, a little flour, pepper, salt, and a little grated nutmeg. Put upon the fire, stir until it begins to thicken, then put in puff-paste that has been prepared, and bake until light brown.

Peas

Open a can of peas, soak in clear water for half an hour, then put upon the fire in clean water, let them boil up hard, drain well and serve with butter, pepper and salt.

Roast Turkey

Clean and prepare a medium sized turkey for roasting. Cut two onions in pieces, and put them in a saucepan with two ounces of butter, and color them slightly. Grate a pound of bread into fine crumbs, add the bread to your onions, the turkey's heart and liver chopped very fine, quarter of a pound of butter, salt, pepper, a pinch of thyme, and mix all well together. Stuff the turkey with this mixture, sew up the opening through which you have introduced the stuffing, and put it to roast, with a little butter on top and a wineglassful of water; roast an hour and a half; strain your liquor in the pan, pour over your turkey, and serve.

Cranberry Sauce

Take one quart of cranberries, pick and wash carefully, put upon the fire with half a teacupful of water, let them stew until thoroughly broken up, then strain and add one pound and a quarter of sugar; put into a mould and turn out when cold.

Roman Punch

Put in a saucepan on the fire three-quarters of a pound of sugar with three pints of water, boil ten minutes, then put aside to become cold. Put in a freezer, and when nearly frozen, stir into it rapidly a gill of rum and the juice of four lemons. Serve in small glasses.

Rice Croquettes

Take one cupful of rice, wash and boil it, and let it get thoroughly cold. Beat up with it one egg, a teaspoonful of sugar and the same of melted butter, salt and a little nutmeg. Work this mixture into the rice, stirring until all is well mixed and the lumps worked out. Make, with floured hands, into oblong rolls about three inches in length, and half an inch in diameter. Coat these thickly with flour, and set them in a cold place until needed. Fry a few at a time in hot lard, rolling them over as they begin to brown to preserve their shape. As each is taken from the fire, put into a colander to drain and dry.

Parisian Salad

Cut in small pieces six cold boiled potatoes, the same quantity of beets, and also of boiled celery—both cold. Mix the yolks of four hard boiled eggs with two table-spoonfuls of anchovy sauce, press through a sieve; add, little by little, four table-spoonfuls of oil, one tablespoonful of mustard, two tablespoonfuls of vinegar, a few tarragon leaves chopped fine, two pinches of salt, two of pepper, and the whites of four hard boiled eggs, cut in pieces, mix all well together, and serve.

Crackers and Cheese

Place on separate dishes, and serve with the salad.

Nesselrode Pudding

Remove the shells from two dozen French chestnuts, which put in a saucepan with a little water, then peel off the skin, and put the chestnuts in a saucepan on the fire with a pint of water and one pound of sugar. Boil them until very soft, then press them through a sieve; the put them in a saucepan with one pint of cream, in which you mix the yolks of four eggs. Just before boiling put your mixture through a sieve, add an ounce of stoned raisins, an ounce of currants, two sherry glasses of sherry wine, and freeze it like ice-cream. When frozen, cut four candied apricots, four candied green gages, half an ounce of citron in small pieces, three ounces of candied cherries; mix them thoroughly into the pudding, which is put into a mould, a thick piece of paper on top, and the cover securely shut down upon it. Put some cracked ice, mixed with two handfuls of rock salt, into a bowl, in the middle of which put your mould, covering it entirely with ice and salt; let it remain two hours, then turn it out of the mould, first dipping it into warm water.

Macaroons

Put half a pound of almonds in boiling water, remove the skins, then put the almonds in cold water, then put them in the oven to dry. Pound them to a paste, adding the white of an egg; then add a pound and a half of powdered sugar, again pound well, adding the whites of two eggs. Spread on a pan a sheet of white paper, pour the mixture into little rounds somewhat smaller than a fifty cent piece, place them on top of the paper in your pan, about an inch and a half apart. Put them in a gentle oven for twelve minutes, the door of the oven shut; at the end of that time, if they are well colored, remove them from the oven, let them become cold, turn the paper upside down, moisten it with a little water and remove the macaroons.

Fruit

Arrange grapes, apples, bananas and oranges upon fancy dishes, with gaily colored leaves and ivy branches around them.

Coffee

Take one quart of boiling water, one even cupful of freshly ground coffee, wet with half a cupful of cold water, white and shell of one egg. Stir into the wet coffee the white and shell, the latter broken up small. Put the mixture into the coffee pot, shake up and down six or seven times hard, to insure thorough incorporation of the ingredients, and pour in the boiling water. Boil steadily twelve minutes, pour in half a cupful of cold water, and remove instantly to the side to settle. Leave it there five minutes; lift and pour off gently the clear coffee. Serve in small cups, and put no sugar in the coffee. Lay, instead, a lump in each saucer, to be used as the drinker likes.

Source: *Godey's Lady's Book*, December 1890.

22. THE REPORT ON THE MARINE GUARD AT THE LEGATIONS AT PEKING (BEIJING) DURING THE BOXER REBELLION (1900)

Lasting from 1899 to 1901, the Boxer Rebellion was an antiforeign peasant-based movement in China that sought to end outside influence on Chinese trade, politics, religion, and technology. Westerners called the insurgents boxers because of the martial arts exercise that they practiced. In June 1900, the Boxers entered Peking (Beijing), where they killed over 200 foreigners, including diplomats, and forced the rest to stand siege in the compound reserved for foreign legations. The following is a U.S. Marine report on the uprising.

HEADQUARTERS U.S. MARINE CORPS,
Washington, D.C., September 29, 1900.

In the early part of the year [1900], when the danger to the members of the various foreign legations in Peking was first apprehended on account of the "boxer" disturbances in China, which were rapidly becoming more extensive, a marine guard, consisting of 1 sergeant, 2 corporals, and 25 privates, under command of Capt. John T. Myers, U.S.M.C., of the U.S.S. *Oregon*, was sent to Peking to guard the legations. Captain Myers left the *Oregon* with his command May 24, 1900. The exact date of his arrival at Peking is not known. On May 29, 1900, Capt. Newt H. Hall, U.S.M.C., and a marine guard consisting of 1 sergeant, 1 corporal, 1 drummer, and 23 privates from the U.S.S. *Newark*, was sent to Tientsin, China, and thence to Peking on May 31, 1900, to reinforce Captain Myers' command. This small guard, aggregating only 56 in number, has remained in Peking guarding the legations during the long and terrible siege to which they were subjected by the Chinese; and the meager reports which have so far been received show that the marines under Captain Myers have not only performed the duty assigned them efficiently, but with the utmost bravery and gallantry.

The first official information received concerning the marine guard at Peking was contained in a cablegram from Rear-Admiral Remey to the Navy Department, dated Taku, August 19, 1900, as follows:

TAKU, 19th. Authentic report Peking 15th from Latimer. Troops moving on Imperial City; clearing out Tartar City. All Americans who remained in Peking are well. There have been no deaths among them except one child. Captain Myers has recovered from wound, has typhoid fever, crisis passed, now convalescent. Assistant Surgeon Lippett was wounded, left upper leg bone fractured, leg saved, now recovering. Following killed during siege in Peking: Sergt. J. Fanning, Privates C.B. King, J.W. Tutcher, J. Kennedy, R.E. Thomas, A. Turner, H. Fisher. Wounded: Private J. Schroeder, elbow, severe and dangerously ill, fever; Seaman J. Mitchell, wound upper arm, severe but recovering; all others wounded and sick have returned to duty. Casualties Major Biddle's command attack San Tan Pating: First Lieutenant Butler, chest; Private Green, wrist; Private Warrell, right temple; all slight. Reported from Chinese sources Royal family have escaped and en route to Sianfu.

The brigadier-general commandant has since been furnished, by reference from the Navy Department, with copies of a dispatch from the United States consul at Chefoo, China, inclosing memoranda relating to the situation in Peking up to July 21, 1900. Copies of this dispatch and the memoranda enclosed are appended to my report.

The following are extracts, taken from the memoranda referred to, relating to the work done by the American marines.

[Extract of cablegram from "Coltman" to "Fernstalk, Boston."]

American marines still hold vital position city wall commanding legations, after brilliant sortie July 3; Captain Myers driving back hordes of Kansuli troops; he slightly wounded. Captured flags, arms.

In the memorandum quoting the gist of other messages relating to the situation in Peking appears the following:

July 3 Captain Myers's American marines made wonderful sortie, capturing guns and standards; he was wounded slightly. Chinese also badly defeated when they attempted night attack. Foreigners holding Legation street from French to American legations, and British on north, all working at barricades, trenches, and fighting and nearly worn out. Chinese seem to be short of ammunition. Our marines have fought like tigers against fearful odds. Only Chinese cowardice prevented their hordes of savages massacring our nationals.

Under date of August 23, 1900, Maj. W. P. Biddle, U.S.M.C., commanding marines in China, forwarded to the brigadier-general commandant a letter from the United States minister to China, Hon. E. H. Conger, transmitting a copy of the resolution passed by the American missionaries besieged in Peking expressing "their hearty appreciation of the courage, fidelity, and patriotism of the American marines, who so bravely and tenaciously held the key to our salvation during the whole of the trying time." From Minister Conger's letter of transmission it seems that he attributes the safety of the besieged members of the legations to the courageous and indefatigable defense maintained by the United States marines.

It would seem by the reports that Captain Myers and his small body of marines succeeded in holding a dangerous and almost untenable position on the city wall, in the face of overwhelming numbers, and also that he made a brilliant sortie, driving back hordes of Chinese, on which occasion he was slightly wounded. Captain Myers's courage and gallantry merit the highest commendation, and I will in a short time recommend to the Department that he be given proper recognition for his bravery in the presence of the enemy....

Respectfully forwarded to the brigadier-general, commandant, United States Marine Corps headquarters, Washington, D.C.

Legation of the United States
Peking, China, August 20, 1900.
W.P. BIDDLE,
Major, U.S.M.C., Commanding.

Source: W. P. Biddle, "The Boxer Rebellion and the U.S. Navy, 1900–1901." Accessed August 2007. URL: http://www.history.navy.mil/faq/faqs86-1.htm.

Upton Sinclair, a progressive reformer from the turn of the century, wrote *The Jungle* in 1906. Early in his career, he made a quiet study of the Chicago stockyards, meat-packing houses, and the railroad hub that served them. He began to write his novel about what he had seen detailing all the most gruesome aspects of the meat industry. The novel was an amazing success selling 150,000 copies, and moving President Theodore Roosevelt to order an investigation of the meat-packing industry. Within a year, Congress had passed the Pure Food and Drug Act and a strong set of meat inspection regulations. The selection below is descriptive of what a visitor like Sinclair would have seen in the 1890s.

The Jungle

A full hour before the party [of emigrants] had reached the city they began to note the perplexing changes in the atmosphere. It grew darker all the time, and upon the earth the grass seemed to grow less green. Every minute, as the train sped on, the colors of things became dingier; the fields were grown parched and yellow, the landscape hideous and bare. And along with the thickening smoke they began to notice another circumstance, a strange pungent odor. They were not sure that it was unpleasant, this odor; some might have called it sickening, but their taste in odors was not developed, and they were only sure that it was curious. Now, sitting in the trolley car, they realized that they were on their way to the home of it—that they had traveled all the way from Lithuania to it. It was now no longer something far off and faint, that you caught in whiffs; you could literally taste it, as well as smell it—you could take hold of it, almost, and examine it at your leisure. They were divided in their opinions about it. It was an elemental odor, raw and crude; it was rich, almost rancid, sensual, and strong. There were some who drank it in as if it were an intoxicant; there were others who put their handkerchiefs to their faces. The new emigrants were still tasting it, lost in wonder, when suddenly the car came to a halt, and the door was flung open, and a voice shouted—"Stockyards!"

They were left standing upon the corner, staring; down a side street there were two rows of brick houses, and between them a vista: half a dozen chimneys, tall as the tallest of buildings, touching the very sky—and leaping from them half a dozen columns of smoke, thick, oily, and black as night. It might have come from the center of the world, this smoke, where the fires of the ages still smolder. It came as if self-impelled, driving all before it, a perpetual explosion. It was inexhaustible; one stared waiting for it to stop, but still the great streams rolled out. They spread in vast clouds overhead, writhing, curling; then, uniting in one giant river, they streamed away down the sky, stretching a black pall as far as the eye could reach.

Then the party became aware of another strange thing. This, too, like the odor, was a thing elemental; it was a sound, a sound made up of ten thousand little sounds. You scarcely noticed it at first—it sunk into your consciousness, a vague disturbance, a trouble. It was like the murmuring of the bees in the spring, the whisperings of the forests; it suggested endless activity, the rumblings of a world in motion. It was only by an effort that one could realize that it was made by animals, that it was the distant lowing of ten thousand cattle, the distant grunting of ten thousand swine....

There is over a square mile of space in the yards, and more than half of it is occupied by cattle pens; north and south as far as the eye can reach there stretches a sea of pens. And they were all filled—so many cattle no one had ever dreamed existed in the world. Red cattle, black, white, yellow cattle; old cattle and young cattle; great bellowing bulls and little calves not an hour born; meek-eyed milch [dairy] cows and fierce, long-horned Texas steers. The sound of them here was as of all barnyards of the universe; and as for counting them—it would have taken all day simply to count the pens.

...[A]nd what will become of all these creatures?...[T]hey will be killed and cut up; and over there on the other side of the packing houses are more railroad tracks, where the cars come to take them away....There were two hundred and fifty miles of track within the yards....They brought about ten thousand head of cattle every day, and as many hogs, and half as many sheep—which meant some eight or ten million live creatures turned into food every year. One stood and watched, and little by little caught the drift of the tide, as it set in the direction of the packing houses. There were groups of cattle being driven into chutes, which were roadways about fifteen feet wide, raised high above the pens. In these chutes the stream of animals was continuous; it was quite uncanny to watch them, pressing to their fate, all unsuspicious—a very river of death. Our friends were not poetical, and the slight suggested to them no metaphors of human destiny; they only thought of the wonderful efficiency of it all. The chutes into which the hogs went climbed high up—to the very top of the distant buildings, and...the hogs went up by the power of their own legs, and then their weight carried them back through all the processes necessary to make them into pork....They use everything about the hog except the squeal....

Source: Upton Sinclair quoted in Richard N. Current and John A. Garraty, eds., *Words that Made American History Since the Civil War.* Boston, MA: Little, Brown and Company, 1965, pp. 278–80.

APPENDICES

APPENDIX 1: POPULATION OF THE UNITED STATES BY DECADE—1860–1900

As the following census figures show, the population of the United States grew by almost 45 million persons between 1860 and 1900, with the rate of growth being relatively steady across the period.

1860	31.4 million
1870	38.6 million
1880	50.2 million
1890	63.0 million
1900	76.2 million

Source: United States Bureau of Census

APPENDIX 2: PRESIDENTS OF THE UNITED STATES— 1861–1901

Listed below are the presidents of the United States who held office between 1861 and 1900, with their party affiliations and their terms of service.

Abraham Lincoln[1]	Republican	1861–1865
Andrew Johnson	National Union[2]	1865–1869
Ulysses S. Grant	Republican	1869–1877
Rutherford B. Hayes	Republican	1877–1881
James A. Garfield[3]	Republican	1881
Chester A. Arthur	Republican	1881–1885
Grover Cleveland	Democrat	1885–1889

Benjamin Harrison	Republican	1889–1893
Grover Cleveland	Democrat	1893–1897
William McKinley[4]	Republican	1897–1901

[1] Assassinated in office; shot on April 14 and died on April 15, 1865
[2] Andrew Johnson, a Democrat, was elected in 1864 on the National Union ticket with Republican Abraham Lincoln
[3] Assassinated in office; shot on July 2 and died on September 19, 1881
[4] Assassinated in office; shot on September 6 and died on September 14, 1901
Source: www.whitehouse.gov/history/presidents

APPENDIX 3: VICE PRESIDENTS OF THE UNITED STATES—1861–1901

Listed below are the vice presidents of the United States who held office between 1861 and 1901, with the president under whom they served, their party affiliation, and their terms of service.

Hannibal Hamlin	Lincoln	Republican	1861–1865
Andrew Johnson[1]	Lincoln	National Union[2]	1865
Office Vacant	Johnson		1865–1869
Schuyler Colfax	Grant	Republican	1869–1873
Henry Wilson	Grant	Republican	1873–1875[3]
Office Vacant	Grant		1875–1877
William Almon Wheeler	Hayes	Republican	1877–1881
Chester A. Arthur[4]	Garfield	Republican	1881
Office Vacant	Arthur		1881–1885
Thomas A. Hendricks	Cleveland	Democrat	1885[5]
Office Vacant	Cleveland		1885–1889
Levi P. Morton	Harrison	Republican	1889–1893
Adlai E. Stevenson	Cleveland	Democrat	1893–1897
Garret A. Hobart	McKinley	Republican	1897–1899[6]
Office Vacant	McKinley		1899–1901
Theodore Roosevelt[7]	McKinley	Republican	1901

[1] Succeeded to the presidency upon the death of Abraham Lincoln on April 15, 1865
[2] Andrew Johnson, a Democrat, was elected in 1864 on the National Union ticket with Republican Abraham Lincoln
[3] Resigned from office
[4] Succeeded to the presidency upon the death of James Garfield on September 19, 1881
[5] Died in office on November 25, 1885
[6] Died in office on November 21, 1899
[7] Succeeded to the presidency upon the death of William McKinley on September 14, 1901
Source: http://americanhistory.about.com/library/charts/blchartpresidents.htm

APPENDIX 4: SECRETARIES OF STATE OF THE UNITED STATES—1861–1905

Listed below are the secretaries of state of the United States who held office between 1861 and 1905, with the president who appointed them, their party affiliation, and their terms of service.

William H. Seward	Lincoln/Johnson	Republican	1861–1869
Elihu B. Washburne	Grant	Republican	1869
Hamilton Fish	Grant	Republican	1869–1877
William M. Evarts	Hayes	Republican	1877–1881
James G. Blaine	Garfield/Arthur	Republican	1881
Frederick T. Frelinghuysen	Arthur	Republican	1881–1885
Thomas F. Bayard	Cleveland	Democrat	1885–1889
James G. Blaine	Harrison	Republican	1889–1892
John W. Foster	Harrison	Republican	1892–1893
Walter Q. Gresham	Cleveland	Democrat	1893–1895
Richard Olney	Cleveland	Democrat	1895–1897
John Sherman	McKinley	Republican	1897–1898
John Hay	McKinley/T. Roosevelt	Republican	1898–1905

Source: http://www.state.gov/r/pa/ho/po/1682.htm; Mihalkanin, Edward S. *American Statesmen: Secretaries of State from John Jay to Colin Powell.* Westport, CT: Greenwood Press, 2004.

APPENDIX 5: CHIEF JUSTICES OF THE U.S. SUPREME COURT—1861–1901

Listed below are the chief justice of the United States Supreme Court who served between 1861 and 1901, with the president who appointed them and their terms of service.

Roger B. Taney	Jackson	1836–1864
Salmon P. Chase	Lincoln	1864–1873
Morrison R. Waite	Grant	1873–1888
Melvin W. Fuller	Cleveland	1888–1910

Source: Kermit L. Hall, ed. *The Oxford Companion to the Supreme Court of the United States.* 2nd ed. New York: Oxford University Press, 2005.

SELECTED BIBLIOGRAPHY

BOOKS

Abbott, E. C., and Helena Huntington Smith. *We Pointed Them North: Recollections of a Cowpuncher*. New York: Farrar & Rinehart, 1939.

Adams, Henry. *The Education of Henry Adams*. New York: The Modern Library, 1999.

Adams, James Truslow, ed. *Album of American History*. New York: Charles Scribner's Sons, 1946.

Ahlstrom, Sydney A. *A Religious History of the American People*. New Haven, CT: Yale University Press, 1972.

Albion, Robert G., and Jennie B. Pope, *Sealanes in Wartime*. Portland, ME: Archon Books, 1968.

Alden, Carroll S., and Allan Westcott. *The United States Navy*. New York: J. B. Lippincott Company, 1945.

Alexander, Eveline M. *Cavalry Wife: The Diary of Eveline M. Alexander, 1866–1867*. Edited by Sandra L. Myres. College Station: Texas A&M University Press, 1977.

Alexander, George E. *Lawn Tennis: Its Founders and Its Early Days*. Lynn, MA: H. O. Zimman, 1974.

American Federation of Labor. *Some Reasons for Chinese Exclusion*. Washington: Government Printing Office, 1902.

Appelbaum, Diana Karter. *The Glorious Fourth: An American Holiday, An American History*. New York: Facts On File Publications, 1989.

———. *Thanksgiving: An American Holiday, An American History*. New York: Facts On File Publications, 1984.

Applegate, Jesse. *A Day with the Cow Column in 1843*. Chicago, IL: Caxton Club, 1934.

Armitage, Susan, and Elizabeth Jameson, eds. *The Women's West*. Norman: University of Oklahoma Press, 1987.

Asbury, Herbert. *The French Quarter: An Informal History of New Orleans with Particular Reference to Its Colorful Iniquities*. New York: A. A. Knopf, 1936.

Atkins, Annette. *Harvest of Grief: Grasshopper Plagues and Public Assistance in Minnesota, 1873–1878*. St. Paul: Minnesota Historical Society Press, 1984.

Bar, Paul. *The Principles of Antiseptic Methods Applied to Obstetric Practice*. Philadelphia, PA: P. Blakiston, Son & Co., 1887.

Barnard, Edward S. *Reader's Digest Story of the Great American West*. Pleasantville, NY: The Reader's Digest Association, Inc., 1977.

Barney, William L., ed. *A Companion to 19th-Century America*. Malden, MA: Blackwell Publishing, 2006.

Bartlett, Richard A. *The New Country: A Social History of the American Frontier, 1776–1890*. New York: Oxford University Press, 1974.

Bauer, K. Jack. *A Maritime History of the United States: The Role of America's Seas and Waterways*. Columbia: University of South Carolina Press, 1989.

———. *Soldiering: The Civil War Diary of Rice C. Bull*. Novato, CA: Presidio, 1977.

Beard, Daniel Carter. *The American Boy's Handbook*. Boston, MA: David R. Godine, 1882.

Beard, Lina, and Adelia B. Beard. *The American Girls Handbook, or How to Amuse Yourself and Others*. Boston, MA: David R. Godine, 1887.

Beecher, Catharine E., and Harriet Beecher Stowe. *The American Woman's Home*. New Brunswick, NJ: Rutgers University Press, 2002.

Bellinger, Martha Fletcher. *A Short History of the Theater*. New York: Henry Holt, 1927.

Beringer, Richard E. *The Elements of Confederate Defeat: Nationalism, War Aims, and Religion*. Athens: University of Georgia Press, 1988.

Better Homes and Gardens. *Heritage Cookbook*. Des Moines, IA: Meredith Corporation, 1974.

Bierley, Paul E. *John Philip Sousa, American Phenomenon*. Englewood Cliffs, NJ: Prentice Hall, 1973.

———. *The Works of John Philip Sousa*. Columbus, OH: Integrity Press, 1984.

Black, Brian. *Nature and the Environment in Nineteenth-Century American Life*. Westport, CT: Greenwood Press, 2006.

Bork, Robert H. *The Antitrust Paradox: A Policy at War with Itself*. New York: Basic Books, 1978.

Bradley, Glenn D. *The Story of the Pony Express: An Account of the Most Remarkable Mail Service Ever in Existence, and Its Place in History*. Chicago, IL: A. C. McClurg, 1913.

Brewer, Priscilla J. *From Fireplace to Cookstove: Technology and the Domestic Ideal in America*. Syracuse, NY: Syracuse University Press, 2000.

Brinton, Daniel G., and George H. Napheys. *Personal Beauty*. Springfield, MA: W. J. Holland, 1870. Reprint Bedford, MA: Applewood Books, 1994.

Brock, Thomas D. *Robert Koch, A Life in Medicine and Bacteriology*. Madison, WI: Science Tech Publishers, 1988.

Broder, Sherri. *Tramps, Unfit Mothers, and Neglected Children: Negotiating the Family in Nineteenth-Century Philadelphia*. Philadelphia: University of Pennsylvania Press, 2002.

Brown, Dee. *The Gentle Tamers: Women of the Old Wild West*. New York: Bantam, 1958.

Browne, Francis F. *Bugle-echoes: Collection of Poetry of the Civil War Northern and Southern*. New York: White, Stokes & Allen, 1886.

Browne, Ray B., and Lawrence A. Kreiser Jr. *The Civil War and Reconstruction*. Westport, CT: Greenwood Press, 2003.

Bryant, Samuel W. *The Sea and States: A Maritime History of the American People*. New York: T. Y. Crowell, 1967.

Bullock, James D. *The Secret Service of the Confederate States in Europe*. 2 vols. New York: Putnam's, 1884.

Burgess, William W. *The Voyages of Capt. W. W. Burgess, 1854–1885*. Plymouth, MA: Jones River Press, 2003.

Burke, Edmund H. *The History of Archery*. Westport, CT: Greenwood Press, 1971 [c1957].

Butterfield, Roger. *The American Past: A History of the United States from Concord to Hiroshima, 1775–1945*. New York: Simon and Schuster, 1947.

Cadenhead, I. E., Jr. *Benito Juarez*. New York: Wayne Publication, Inc. 1993.

Cameron, Kenneth W. *The Massachusetts Lyceum During the American Renaissance*. Hartford, CT: Transcendental Books, 1969.

Camp, Walter. *American Football*. New York: Arno Press, 1974 (c1891).

———. *Football Facts and Figures. A Symposium of Expert Opinions on the Game's Place in American Athletics*. New York: Harper & Brothers, 1894.

Campbell, Edward D. C., Jr., and Kym S. Rice, eds. *A Woman's War: Southern Women, Civil War and the Confederate Legacy*. Charlottesville: University Press of Virginia, 1996.

Canney, Donald L. *The Old Steam Navy: Frigates, Sloops, and Gunboats, 1815–1885, Vol. 1*. Annapolis, MD: Naval Institute Press, 1990.

Carnegie Library of Pittsburgh. *Annotated Catalogue of Books Used in Home Libraries and Reading Clubs*. Pittsburgh, PA: Carnegie Library, 1905.

Cary, John H., and Julius Weinberg, eds. *The Social Fabric, American Life from the Civil War to the Present*. Boston, MA: Little, Brown and Company, 1975.

Casper, Scott E., Joan Chaison, and Jeffery D. Groves, eds. *Perspectives on American Book History: Artifacts and Commentary*. Amherst: University of Massachusetts Press, 2002.

Castello, Julio Martinez. *Theory of Fencing: Foil, Sabre, Dueling Sword*. New York: St. Marks Printing Corporation, 1931.

Chase, Gilbert. *America's Music: From the Pilgrims to the Present*. New York: McGraw-Hill Book Company, 1966.

Chudacoff, Howard P. *The Age of the Bachelor: Creating an American Subculture*. Princeton, NJ: Princeton University Press, 1999.

Cimbala, Paul A. *The Freedmen's Bureau: Reconstructing the American South after the Civil War*. Malabar, FL: Krieger Publishing, 2005.

Citro, Constance F., and Robert T. Michael, eds. *Measuring Poverty: A New Approach*. Washington, DC: National Academy Press, 1995.

Clark, Victor S. *History of Manufactures in the United States*. 3 vols. New York: Peter Smith Publishers, 1949.

Clay, C. F., trans. *Secrets of the Sword by the Baron de Bazancourt*. Bangor, ME: Laureate Press, 1998.

Clinton, Catherine. *The Plantation Mistress: Woman's World in the Old South*. New York: Pantheon Books, 1982.

Coe, Sophie D., and Michael D. Coe. *The True History of Chocolate*. London: Thames & Hudson, 2007.

Cohen, Hennig, and Tristram Potter Coffin, eds. *The Folklore of American Holidays*. Detroit, MI: Gale Research Company, 1987.

Collins, Frank D. *Popular Sports, Their Origin and Development*. Chicago, IL: Rand McNally & Company, 1935.

Collins, Joseph. *Bacon, Beans and Galantines: Food and Foodways on the Western Mining Frontier*. Reno: University of Nevada Press, 1986.

Collinson, Frank. *Life in the Saddle*. Edited by Mary Whatley Clarke. Norman: University of Oklahoma Press, 1963.

Colt, Mrs. Miriam (Davis). *Went to Kansas*. Ann Arbor: University Microfilms, 1862.

Coy, Owen Cochran. *The Great Trek*. Los Angeles, CA: Powell Publishing Company, 1931.

Crawford, Richard. *America's Musical Life: A History*. New York: W. W. Norton & Company, 2001.

Crook, George. *General George Crook: His Autobiography*. Edited by Martin F. Schmitt. Norman: University of Oklahoma Press, 1960.

Croushore, James H., ed. *A Volunteer's Adventure, by Captain John W. De Forest*. New Haven, CT: Yale University Press, 1949.

Current, Richard N., and John A. Garraty, eds. *Words That Made American History since the Civil War*. Boston, MA: Little, Brown and Company, 1965.

Curtis, Susan. *A Consuming Faith: The Social Gospel and Modern American Culture*. Baltimore, MD: Johns Hopkins University Press, 1991.

Custer, Elizabeth Bacon. *Tenting on the Plains*. Norman: University of Oklahoma Press, 1971.

Custer, Gen. George A. *My Life on the Plains: Or, Personal Experiences with Indians*. Norman: University of Oklahoma Press, 1962.

Dahlhaus, Carl. *Nineteenth-Century Music*. Berkeley: University of California Press, 1989.

Dalzell, G. W. *The Flight from the Flag: The Continuing Effect of the Civil War upon the American Carrying Trade*. Chapel Hill: University of North Carolina Press, 1940.

Dalzell, Robert F. *Enterprising Elite, The Boston Associates and the World They Made*. Cambridge, MA: Harvard University Press, 1987.

Dary, David. *Seeking Pleasure in the Old West*. New York: Alfred A. Knopf, 1995.

Davidson, Marshall B. *Life In America*. Boston, MA: Houghton Mifflin Company, 1951.

Davis, William C., ed., *Secret History of Confederate Diplomacy: Edwin De Leon, Late Confidential Agent of the Confederate Department of State in Europe*. Lawrence: University Press of Kansas, 2005.

Deer, Mark. *A Dog's History of America: How Our Best Friend Explored, Conquered, and Settled a Continent*. New York: North Point Press, 2004.

DiCerto, Joseph J. *The Pony Express: Hoofbeats in the Wilderness*. New York: F. Watts, 1989.

Dick, Everett. *The Sod-House Frontier, 1854–1890: A Social History of the Northern Plains from the Creation of Kansas & Nebraska to the Admission of the Dakotas*. New York: D. Appleton-Century Co., 1937.

Dolson, Hildegarde. *The Great Oildorado, The Gaudy and Turbulent Years of the First Oil Rush: Pennsylvania, 1859–1880*. New York: Random House, 1959.

Donald, David H., Jean H. Baker, and Michael F. Holt. *The Civil War and Reconstruction*. Rev. ed. New York: W.W. Norton, 2001.

Douglass, Frederick. *Narrative of the Life of Frederick Douglass, an American Slave, Written by Himself*. 1845. Reprint, New York: Penguin, 1968.

Du Bois, William E. B. *Black Reconstruction in America, 1860–1880*. New York: Russell & Russell, 1956.

Duffy, John. *A History of Public Health in New York City*. New York: Russell Sage Foundation, 1968.

Dulles, Foster Rhea. *The Old China Trade*. New York: Houghton Mifflin Company, 1930.

Dwyer, Richard A., and Richard E. Lingenfelter, *Songs of the Gold Rush*. Berkeley: University of California Press, 1964.

East, Charles, ed. *Sarah Morgan: The Civil War Diary of a Southern Woman*. New York: Touchstone, 1991.

Eisler, Benita, ed. *The Lowell Offering: Writings by New England Mill Women (1840–1845)*. New York: W. W. Norton & Company, 1977.

Elkort, Martin. *The Secret Life of Food*. Los Angeles, CA: Jeremy P. Tarcher, 1991.

Elliott, Jock. *Inventing Christmas: How Our Holiday Came to Be*. New York: Abrams, 2002.

England, J. Merton, ed. *Buckeye Schoolmaster: A Chronicle of Midwestern Rural Life 1853–1865*. Bowling Green, OH: State University Popular Press, 1996.

Fahs, Alice. *The Imagined Civil War: Popular Literature of the North and South, 1861–1865.* Chapel Hill: University of North Carolina Press, 2001.

Farragher, John Mack. *Women and Men on the Overland Trail.* New Haven, CT: Yale University Press, 1979.

Faust, Drew Gilpin. *Mothers of Invention: Women of the Slaveholding South in the American Civil War.* Chapel Hill: University of North Carolina Press, 1996.

Fehrenbacher, Don E. *The Era of Expansion, 1800–1848.* New York: John Wiley and Sons, 1969.

Feinstein, Stephen. *Louis Pasteur, the Father of Microbiology.* Berkeley Heights, NJ: MyReportLinks.com Books, 2008.

Finson, Jon. *Voices That Are Gone: Themes in Nineteenth-Century American Popular Song.* New York: Oxford University Press, 1994.

Fischer, Claude S. *America Calling: A Social History of the Telephone to 1940.* Berkeley and Los Angeles: University of California Press, 1992.

Fite, Emerson David. *Social and Industrial Conditions in the North During the Civil War.* Williamstown, MA: Corner House, 1976.

Foner, Eric. *Reconstruction: America's Unfinished Revolution, 1863–1877.* New York: Harper Collins Publishers, 2002.

Foner, Philip S. *American Labor Songs of the Nineteenth-Century.* Urbana: University of Illinois Press, 1975.

Forbis, William H. *The Old West: The Cowboys.* New York: Time Life Books, 1973.

Frank, Stephen M. *Life with Father: Parenthood and Masculinity in the Nineteenth-Century American North.* Baltimore, MD: Johns Hopkins University Press, 1998.

Franklin, John Hope. *Reconstruction after the Civil War.* Chicago, IL: University of Chicago Press, 1961.

Freemon, Frank R. *Gangrene and Glory: Medical Care during the American Civil War.* Urbana: University of Illinois Press, 2001.

Frémont, John C. *The Exploring Expedition to the Rocky Mountains.* Washington, DC: Smithsonian Institution Press, 1988.

Furia, Philip. *The Poets of Tin Pan Alley: A History of America's Great Lyricists.* New York: Oxford University Press, 1990.

Gard, Wayne. *Frontier Justice.* Norman: University of Oklahoma Press, 1949.

Gardner, Brian. *The East India Company.* New York: Dorset Press, 1971.

Garland, Hamlin. *Boy Life on the Prairie.* New York: Frederick Ungar Publishing Co., 1959.

———. *Son of the Middle Border.* New York: Macmillan Co., 1925.

Gatewood, Willard B., Jr., *Black Americans and the White Man's Burden, 1898–1903.* Urbana: University of Illinois Press, 1975.

Geers, Edward Franklin. *Ed Geers' Experience with the Trotters and Pacers.* Buffalo: The Matthews-Northrup Company, 1901.

George, Henry. *Protection or Free Trade: An Examination of the Tariff Question with Especial Regard to the Interests of Labor.* New York: Henry George and Co., 1886.

Glass, Andrew. *The Sweetwater Run: The Story of Buffalo Bill Cody and the Pony Express.* New York: Doubleday, 1996.

Glazer, Tom. *A Treasury of Civil War Songs.* Milwaukee, WI: Hal Leonard Corporation, 1996.

Goetzmann, William H. *Exploration and Empire, The Explorer and the Scientist in the Winning of the American West.* New York: The History Book Club, 1966.

Goldman, Marion S. *Gold Diggers & Silver Miners: Prostitution and Social Life on the Comstock Lode.* Ann Arbor: University of Michigan Press, 1981.

Goldstein, Jonathan. *Philadelphia and the China Trade 1682–1846*. University Park: Pennsylvania State University Press, 1978.

Grattan, C. Hartley. *The Three Jameses: A Family of Minds*. New York: New York University Press, 1962.

Green, Harvey. *The Light of the Home*. New York: Pantheon Books, 1983.

Grier, Katherine C. *Pets in America: A History*. Chapel Hill: University of North Carolina Press, 2006.

Griffith, Ernest S. *A History of American City Government: The Conspicuous Failure, 1870–1900*. New York: Praeger, 1972.

Gross, Linda P., and Theresa R. Snyder. *Philadelphia's 1876 Centennial Exhibition*. Charleston, SC: Arcadia Publishing, 2005.

Grover, Kathlyn, ed. *Dining in America: 1850–1900*. Amherst: University of Massachusetts Press, 1987.

———. *Hard at Play: Leisure in America, 1840–1940*. Amherst: University of Massachusetts Press, 1992.

Gwin, Minrose C., ed. *Cornelia Peake McDonald: A Woman's Civil War. A Diary with Reminiscences of the War from March 1862*. Madison: University of Wisconsin Press, 1992.

Gyory, Andrew. *Closing the Gate: Race, Politics, and the Chinese Exclusion Act*. Chapel Hill: University of North Carolina Press, 1998.

Hague, Parthenia Antoinette. *A Blockaded Family: Life in Southern Alabama During the Civil War*. Reprint Bedford, TX: Applewood Books, 1995.

Haines, T. L., and Levi W. Yaggy. *The Royal Path of Life: Or Aims and Aids to Success and Happiness*. Chicago, IL: Western Publishing House, 1876.

Hall, Kermit L., ed. *The Oxford Companion to the Supreme Court of the United States*. 2nd ed. New York: Oxford University Press, 2005.

Handy, Robert T., ed. *The Social Gospel in America: 1870–1920*. New York: Oxford University Press, 1966.

Hankins, Barry. *The Second Great Awakening and the Transcendentalists*. Westport, CT: Greenwood Press, 2004.

Hardee, W. J. *Hardee's Rifle and Light Infantry Tactics*. New York: J. O. Kane, Publisher, 1862.

Harding, Bertita Lonarz de. *Phantom Crown*. Mexico City: Ediciones Tolteca, S. A., 1967.

Hareven, Tamara K., and Maris A. Vinovskis. *Family and Population in Nineteenth-Century America*. Princeton, NJ: Princeton University Press, 1978.

Harris, Townsend. *The Complete Journal of Townsend Harris: First American Consul General and Minister to Japan*. With an introduction by Mario Emilio Cozena. Whitefish, MT: Kessinger Publishing, 2007.

Harvard Boat Club. *Principles of Rowing at Harvard by the Executive Committee of the Harvard Boat-Club for the Year Ending 1873*. Cambridge, MA: Welch, Bigelow, and Company, 1873.

Haskell, E. F. *Civil War Cooking: The Housekeeper's Encyclopedia*. Mendocino, CA: R.L. Shep, 1992.

Hayward, John. *Gazetteer of the United States*. Hartford, CT: Case, Tiffant and Co., 1853.

Hazen, Margaret Hindle, and Robert M. Hazen, *The Music Men: An Illustrated History of Brass Bands in America, 1800–1920*. Washington, DC: Smithsonian Institution Press, 1987.

Heath, Ernest Gerald. *A History of Target Archery*. Newton Abbot, UK: David & Charles, 1973.

Hechtlinger, Adelaide. *American Quilts, Quilting and Patchwork*. Harrisburg, PA: Stackpole Books, 1974.

Heidler, David S., and Jeanne T. Heidler, eds. *Daily Life of Civilians in Wartime Early America, From the Colonial Era to the Civil War*. Westport, CT: Greenwood Press, 2007.

Heininger, Mary L. *A Century of Childhood, 1820–1920*. Rochester, NY: Margaret Woodbury Strong Museum, 1984.

Hennesey, James. *American Catholics*. New York: Oxford University Press, 1981.

Hewitt, Barnard. *Theater USA, 1668 to 1957*. New York: McGraw-Hill Book Company, 1959.

Hine, Robert V. *Community on the American Frontier: Separate But Not Alone*. Norman: University of Oklahoma Press, 1980.

Hofstadter, Richard, and Wilson Smith, eds. *American Higher Education: A Documentary History*. Chicago, IL: University of Chicago Press, 1968.

Holmes, Kenneth L., ed. *Covered Wagon Women: Diaries and Letters from the Western Trails*. Lincoln: University of Nebraska Press, 1983.

Holmes, Oliver Wendell. *Stagecoach East: Stagecoach Days in the East from the Colonial Period to the Civil War*. Edited by Peter T. Rohrbach. Washington, DC: Smithsonian Institution Press, 1983.

Hooker, Richard J. *Food and Drink in America: A History*. New York: Bobbs-Merrill, 1981.

Howarth, Stephen. *To Shining Sea, A History of the United States Navy, 1775–1991*. New York: Random House, 1991.

Hunt, Gaillard. *As We Were, Life in America, 1814*. Stockbridge, MA: Berkshire House Publishers, 1914. Reprinted in 1993.

Hunter, Louis C. *A History of Industrial Power in the United States, 1780–1930*. Charlottesville: University Press of Virginia, 1979.

Husband, Julie, and Jim O'Loughlin. *Daily Life in the Industrial United States, 1870–1900*. Westport, CT: Greenwood Press, 2004.

Hutton, Alfred. *The Sword Through the Centuries*. Mineola, NY: Dover Publications, 2002.

Jackson, Richard. *Popular Songs of Nineteenth-Century America: Complete Original Sheet Music for 64 Songs*. New York: Dover Press, 1976.

Jansen, David. *Tin Pan Alley . . . The Golden Age of American Popular Music from 1886 to 1956*. New York: Fine, 1988.

Jenkins, Susan, and Linda Seward. *The American Quilt Story: The How-to and Heritage of a Craft Tradition*. Emmaus, PA: Rodale Press, 1991.

Jewett, Charles. *Manual of Rules for Child-bed Nursing*. Brooklyn, NY: Brooklyn Eagle Press, 1889.

Johnson, Clifton. *Old-Time Schools and School-books*. New York: Dover Publications, 1963.

Johnson, Dorothy M. *The Bloody Bozeman*. New York: McGraw-Hill Book Company, 1971.

Johnson, Laurence A. *Over the Counter and On the Shelf: Country Storekeeping in America 1620–1920*, ed. Marcia Ray. Rutland, VT: Charles E. Tuttle Company Publishers, 1961.

Jones, Howard. *Mutiny on the Amistad*. New York: Oxford University Press, 1987.

Jones, Mary Ellen, ed. *The American Frontier: Opposing Viewpoints*. San Diego, CA: Greenhaven Press, 1994.

———. *Daily Life on the Nineteenth Century American Frontier*. Westport, CT: Greenwood Press, 1998.

Jordan, Ervin L., Jr. *Black Confederates and Afro-Yankees in Civil War Virginia*. Charlottesville: University Press of Virginia, 1995.

Josephy, Alvin M., Jr. *500 Nations: An Illustrated History of North American Indians*. New York: Alfred A. Knopf, 1994.

Kaser, David. *Books and Libraries in Camp and Battle: The Civil War Experience*. Westport, CT: Greenwood Press, 1984.

Kaufman, Stefan H. E. *Concepts in Vaccine Development*. New York: Walter de Gruyter, 1996.

Kelly, R. Gordon, ed. *Children's Periodicals of the United States*. Westport, CT: Greenwood Press, 1984.

Kevill-Davies, Sally. *Yesterday's Children, The Antiques and History of Childcare*. Woodbridge, UK: Antique Collectors' Club, 1998.

King, Gilbert. *The Art of Golf Antiques: An Illustrated History of Clubs, Balls, and Accessories*. Philadelphia, PA: Courage Books, 2001.

Kingman, Daniel. *American Music: A Panorama*. New York: Schirmer Books, 1990.

Kiracofe, Roderick. *The American Quilt*. New York: Clarkson Porter, 1993.

———. *Cloth & Comfort, Pieces of Women's Lives from Their Quilts and Diaries*. New York: Clarkson Potter Publishers, 1994.

Kittredge, Henry C. *Shipmasters of Cape Cod*. Boston, MA: Houghton Mifflin, 1935.

Lane, Rose Wilder. *Woman's Day Book of American Needlework*. New York: Simon and Schuster, 1962.

Larcom, Lucy. *A New England Girlhood*. Boston: Northeastern University Press, 1986.

LaRocca, Donald J. *The Academy of the Sword: Illustrated Fencing Books, 1500–1800*. New York: Metropolitan Museum of Art, 1998.

Leckie, William H. *The Buffalo Soldier, A Narrative of the Negro Cavalry in the West*. Norman: University of Oklahoma Press, 1967.

Leech, Margaret. *Reveille in Washington*. New York: Harper & Brothers, 1941.

Levenstein, Harvey Q. *Revolution at the Table: The Transformation of the American Diet*. New York: Oxford University Press, 1988.

Lewis, Thomas A. *The Guns of Cedar Creek*. New York: Bantam, 1991.

Lingenfelter, Richard, Richard A. Dwyer, and David Cohen, eds. *Songs of the American West*. Berkeley: University of California Press, 1968.

Livermore, Mary A. *My Story of the War: A Woman's Narrative of Four Years' Personal Experience*. New York: Da Capo Press, 1995.

Lothrop, Margaret M. *The Wayside: Home of Authors*. New York: American Book Company, 1968.

Louisiana State Museum. *Playthings of the Past: Nineteenth and Early Twentieth Century Toys*. New Orleans: Louisiana State Museum, 1969.

Lovell, John. *Black Song: The Forge and the Flame; The Story of How the Afro-American Spiritual Was Hammered Out*. New York: Macmillan, 1972.

Luchetti, Cathy. *Home on the Range: A Culinary History of the American West*. New York: Villard Books, 1993.

———. *Women of the West*. In collaboration with Carol Olwell. St. George, UT: Antelope Valley Press, 1982.

Lupiano, Vincent DePaul, and Ken W. Sayers. *It Was a Very Good Year: A Cultural History of the United States from 1776 to the Present*. Holbrook, MA: Bob Adams, 1994.

Mahan, Alfred Thayer. *The Influence of Sea Power upon History, 1660–1783*. New York: Dover, 1987. Reprint of the 1890 edition.

Marcy, Randolph B. *The Prairie Traveler, A Hand-book for Overland Expeditions*. Bedford, MA: Applewood Books, 1993. Reprint of the 1859 edition.

Marten, James. *The Children's Civil War*. Chapel Hill: University of North Carolina Press, 1998.

Marx, Leo. *The Machine in the Garden: Technology and the Pastoral Ideal in America*. New York: Oxford University Press, 1964.

Mason, Philip P., ed. *Copper Country Journal, The Diary of Schoolmaster Henry Hobart, 1863–1864*. Detroit, MI: Wayne State University Press, 1991.

Massey, Mary Elizabeth. *Women in the Civil War*. Lincoln: University of Nebraska Press, 1966.

Mauriceau, François. *The Diseases of Women with Child, and in Child-bed*. New York: Garland Press, 1985.

Mautz, Carl. *Biographies of Western Photographers: A Reference Guide to Photographers Working in the 19th-Century American West*. Nevada City, CA: Carl Mautz Publishing, 1997.

McAuley, James. *The New and Improved Broad Sword Exercise, As Recently Taught at the U.S. Military Academy, West Point, N.Y.* Columbia, SC: Printed at the Telescope office, 1838.

McClary, Andrew. *Toys with Nine Lives, A Social History of American Toys*. North Haven, CT: Linnet Books, 1997.

McClinton, Katherine Morrison. *Antiques of American Childhood*. New York: Bramhall House, 1970.

McDonald, Douglas. *Virginia City and the Silver Region of the Comstock Lode*. Carson City: Nevada Publications, 1982.

McGeer, Michael E. *The Decline of Popular Politics: The American North, 1865–1928*. New York: Oxford University Press, 1986.

McGuire, Judith W. *Diary of a Southern Refugee During the War by a Lady of Virginia*. Lincoln: University of Nebraska Press, 1995.

McIntosh, Elaine N. *American Food Habits in Historical Perspective*. Westport, CT: Greenwood/Praeger Press, 1995.

McMath, Robert C., Jr. *American Populism: A Social History, 1877–1898*. New York: Hill and Wang, 1993.

McMorris, Penny. *Crazy Quilts*. New York: E. P. Dutton, 1984.

McNeil, Keith, and Rusty McNeil, *Civil War Songbook*. Riverside, CA: McNeil Music, Inc., 1999.

Megquier, Mary Jane. *Apron Full of Gold: The Letters of Mary Jane Megquier from San Francisco, 1849–1856*. Edited by Robert Glass Cleland. San Marino, CA: Huntington Library, 1949.

Mendenhall, Thomas C. *A Short History of American Rowing*. Boston, MA: Charles River Books, 1980.

Meredith, Roy. *Mathew Brady's Portrait of an Era*. New York: W. W. Norton & Company, 1982.

Metchnikoff, Elie. *The Founders of Modern Medicine: Pasteur, Koch, Lister*. Freeport, NY: Books for Libraries Press, 1971.

Miers, Earl Schenck, ed. *A Rebel War Clerk's Diary, by John B. Jones, 1861–1865*. New York: Sagamore Press, 1958.

Mihalkanin, Edward S. *American Statesmen: Secretaries of State from John Jay to Colin Powell*. Westport, CT: Greenwood Press, 2004.

Miles, Gen. Nelson A. *Personal Recollections and Observations of General Nelson A. Miles*. New York: Da Capo Press, 1969.

Millis, Walter. *Arms and Men, A Study of American Military History.* New York: A Mentor Book, 1956.

Milner, Clyde A., Carol A. O'Connor, and Martha A. Sandweiss. *The Oxford History of the American West.* New York: Oxford University Press, 1994.

Mintz, Steven. *Huck's Raft: A History of American Childhood.* Cambridge, MA: Harvard University Press, 2004.

Mitchell, Patricia B. *Cooking for the Cause.* Chatham, VA: Sims-Mitchell House, 1988.

Mitchell, Thomas G. *Indian Fighters Turned American Politicians: From Military Service to Public Office.* Westport, CT: Praeger Press, 2003.

Mitford, Jessica. *The American Way of Birth.* New York: Dutton, 1992.

Mondale, Sarah, and Sarah B. Patton, eds. *School: The Story of American Public Education.* Boston: Beacon Press, 2001.

Monroe, Lewis B. *Public and Parlor Readings: Prose and Poetry.* Boston: Lee and Shepard, 1871.

Morison, Samuel Eliot. *By Land and By Sea.* New York: Alfred A. Knopf, 1953.

Moskow, Shirley Blotnick. *Emma's World: An Intimate Look at Lives Touched by the Civil War Era.* Far Hills, NJ: New Horizon Press, 1990.

Mott, Frank Luther. *A History of American Magazines.* 5 vols. Cambridge, MA: Harvard University Press, 1930–1968.

Myres, Sandra L., ed. *Ho for California! Woman's Overland Diaries from the Huntington Library.* San Marino, CA: Huntington Library, 1980.

———. *Westering Women and the Frontier Experience, 1800–1915.* Albuquerque: University of New Mexico Press, 1982.

Nabokov, Peter, ed. *Native American Testimony: An Anthology of Indian and White Relations: First Encounters to Dispossession.* New York: Harper and Row, 1979.

Nasaw, David, ed. *Andrew Carnegie, The "Gospel of Wealth" Essays and Other Writings.* New York: Penguin Books, 2006.

———. *Children of the City: At Work and at Play.* Garden City, NY: Anchor/Doubleday, 1985.

National Livestock Association. *Prose and Poetry of the Live Stock Industry of the United States.* [1904]. New York: Antiquarian Press, 1959.

Natkiel, Richard, and Anthony Preston, *Atlas of Maritime History.* New York: Facts on File, Inc., 1986.

Neihardt, John. *Black Elk Speaks.* Lincoln: University of Nebraska Press, 1932.

Nelson, Paula M. *After the West Was Won: Homesteaders and Town-Builders in Western South Dakota, 1900–1917.* Iowa City: University of Iowa Press, 1986.

Nevin, John Williamson. *The Anxious Bench.* Chambersburg, PA: printed at the publication office of the German Reformed Church, 1844.

Nevins, Allan, ed. *The Diary of Philip Home, 1828–1851,* Vols. I & II. New York: Dodd, Mead and Company, 1927.

Newton, Steven H. *Lost for the Cause, The Confederate Army in 1864.* Mason City, IA: Savas Publishing Company, 2000.

Nicholls, David, ed. *The Cambridge History of American Music.* New York: Cambridge University Press, 1998.

Noel, Evan Baillie. *A History of Tennis.* Mansfield Center, CT: Martino Publishers, 2007.

Nye, David E. *Electrifying America: The Social Meanings of New Technology, 1880–1940.* Cambridge, MA: MIT Press, 1990.

Nye, Russell B. *The Cultural Life of the New Nation, 1776–1830.* New York: Harper & Row, 1960.

———. *The Unembarrassed Muse: The Popular Arts in America.* New York: Dial Press, 1970.

Nylander, Jane C. *Our Own Snug Fireside: Images of the New England Home 1760–1860.* New Haven, CT: Yale University Press, 1993.

O'Connor, Richard. *The Cactus Throne.* New York: G. P. Putnam's Sons. 1971.

Ogle, Maureen. *Ambitious Brew, The Story of American Beer.* New York: Harcourt, Inc. 2006.

O'Neil, Sunny. *The Gift of Christmas Past, A Return to Victorian Traditions.* Nashville, TN: The American Association for State and Local History, 1981.

Parkman, Francis. *The Oregon Trail.* New York: Lancer books, 1968. Reprint of the 1849 edition.

Patterson, Gerard A. *Debris of Battle: The Wounded of Gettysburg.* Mechanicsburg, PA: Stackpole Books, 1997.

Paul, James Laughery. *Pennsylvania's Soldiers' Orphan Schools.* Harrisburg, PA: Lane S. Hart Publisher, 1876.

Paul, Rodman Wilson. *Mining Frontiers of the Far West, 1848–1880.* Albuquerque: University of New Mexico Press, 1963.

Peiss, Kathy. *Cheap Amusements: Working Women and Leisure in Turn-of-the-Century New York.* Philadelphia, PA: Temple University Press, 1986.

Peper, George. *Golf in America: The First One Hundred Years.* New York: H. N. Abrams, 1988.

Petersen, William J. *Steamboating on the Upper Mississippi.* New York: Dover Publications, 1968, c1937.

Peyer, Bernd C. *The Tutor'd Mind, Indian Missionary-Writers in Antebellum America.* Amherst: University of Massachusetts Press, 1997.

Pierce, B. Byron. *National Cowboy Hall of Fame Chuck Wagon Cookbook.* New York: Hearst Books, 1995.

Pollard, Edward A. *Southern History of the War.* New York: Fairfax Press, 1990. Reprint of the 1866 edition.

Posner, Richard A. *Antitrust Law.* Chicago, IL: University of Chicago Press, 2001.

Prucha, Francis Paul. *The Great Father: The United States Government and the American Indians.* Abridged ed. Lincoln: University of Nebraska Press, 1986.

Quay, Sara E. *Westward Expansion.* Westport, CT: Greenwood Press, 2002.

Rader, Benjamin. *American Sports: From the Age of the Folk Games to the Age of the Spectators.* Englewood Cliffs, NJ: Prentice-Hall, 1983.

Rae, W. F. *Westward By Rail.* New York: Promontory Press, 1974.

Rains, Anthony John. *Edward Jenner and Vaccination.* London: Priory Press, 1974.

Randall, J. G. and David Donald, *The Civil War and Reconstruction.* Boston, MA: D. C. Heath and Company, 1961.

Ransom, J. Clinton. *The Successful Man in His Manifold Relation with Life.* New York: J. A. Hill & Co., 1889.

Reef, Catherine. *Alone in the World: Orphans and Orphanages in America.* New York: Clarion Books, 2005.

Rehwinkel, Alfred M. *Dr. Bessie.* St. Louis, MO: Concordia Publishing House, 1963.

Rickey, Don , Jr. *Forty Miles a Day on Beans and Hay: The Enlisted Soldier Fighting the Indian Wars.* Norman: University of Oklahoma Press, 1963.

Riis, Jacob A. *How the Other Half Lives, Studies Among the Tenements of New York.* New York: Charles Scribner's Sons, 1890.

Riley, Glenda. *Frontierswomen: The Iowa Experience.* Ames: Iowa State University Press, 1981.

Roberts, Robert. *The House Servant's Directory, An African American Butler's 1827 Guide*. Mineola, NY: Dover Publications, 2006.

Roosevelt, Theodore. *Memories of the American Frontier*. New York: Westvaco, 1977.

———. *Theodore Roosevelt, an Autobiography*. New York: The Macmillian Company, 1913.

Root, Waverly, and Richard de Rouchemont. *Eating in America*. New York: William Morrow, 1976.

Rosen, Ruth. *The Lost Sisterhood: Prostitution in America, 1900–1918*. Baltimore, MD: Johns Hopkins University Press, 1982.

Rosenbloom, Joshua L., and Gregory W. Stutes. *Reexamining the Distribution of Wealth in 1870*. Cambridge, MA: National Bureau of Economic Research, 2005.

Rowe, William Hutchinson. *The Maritime History of Maine: Three Centuries of Shipbuilding and Seafaring*. Augusta, ME: Bond Wheelwright, n.d.

Rowland, K. T. *Steam at Sea: The History of Steam Navigation*. New York: Praeger Publishing, 1970.

Royce, Sarah. *A Frontier Lady: Recollections of the Gold Rush and Early California*. Edited by Ralph Henry Gabriel. Lincoln: University of Nebraska Press, 1932.

Ruede, Howard. *Sod-House Days: Letters from a Kansas Homesteader, 1877–78*. Edited by John Ise. New York: Cooper Square Publishers, 1966.

Ruggles, Steven, and Russell R. Menard. *Public Use Microdata Sample of the 1850 United States Census of Population: User's Guide and Technical Documentation*. Minneapolis, MN: Social History Research Laboratory, 1995.

Rutkow, Ira M. *Bleeding Blue and Gray: Civil War Surgery and the Evolution of American Medicine*. New York: Random House, 2005.

Sablosky, Irving. *What They Heard: Music in America 1852–1881, from the Pages of Dwight's Journal of Music*. Baton Rouge: Louisiana State University Press, 1986.

Safford, Carleton L., and Robert Bishop, *America's Quilts and Coverlets*. New York: Weathervane Books, 1974.

Sanchez-Eppler, Karen. *Dependent States: The Child's Part in Nineteenth-Century American Culture*. Chicago, IL: University of Chicago Press, 2005.

Sandoz, Mari. *The Beaver Men, Spearheads of Empire*. Lincoln: University of Nebraska Press, 1978.

Sanford, Mollie Dorsey. *Mollie: The Journal of Mollie Dorsey Sanford in Nebraska and Colorado Territories, 1857–1866*. Lincoln: University of Nebraska Press, 1959.

Savage, William A., Jr. *The Cowboy Hero: His Image in American History and Culture*. Norman: University of Oklahoma Press, 1979.

———. *Cowboy Life: Reconstructing an American Myth*. Norman: University of Oklahoma Press, 1975.

Sawey, Orlan. *Charles A. Siringo*. Boston, MA: Twayne Publishers, 1981.

Schabas, Ezra. *Theodore Thomas: America's Conductor and Builder of Orchestras, 1835–1905*. Urbana: University of Illinois Press, 1989.

Scharf, J. Thomas. *History of the Confederate States Navy*. New York: Fairfax Press, 1887.

Schenone, Laura. *A Thousand Years Over a Hot Stove*. New York: W.W. Norton & Company, 2003.

Schlissel, Lillian. *Women's Diaries of the Westward Journey*. New York: Schocken Books, 1982.

Schlissel, Lillian, Byrd Gibbons, and Elizabeth Hampsten. *Far from Home: Families of the Westward Journey*. New York: Schocken Books, 1989.

Schmitt, Martin, ed. *General George Crook: His Autobiography*. Norman: University of Oklahoma Press, 1960.

Schob, David E. *Hired Hands and Plowboys: Farm Labor in the Midwest, 1815–1860*. Urbana: University of Illinois Press, 1975.

Schollander, Wendell, and Wes Schollander. *Forgotten Elegance: The Art, Artifacts, and Peculiar History of Victorian and Edwardian Entertaining in America*. Westport, CT: Greenwood Press, 2002.

Seelye, John, ed. *Horatio Alger, Jr., Ragged Dick and Struggling Upward*. New York: Viking Penguin, Inc., 1985.

Sewell, Richard H. *A House Divided: Sectionalism and the Civil War, 1848–1865*. Baltimore: Johns Hopkins University Press, 1988.

Shrock, Joel. *The Gilded Age*. Westport, CT: Greenwood Press, 2004.

Silber, Irwin. *Songs of the Civil War*. New York: Dover Publications, 1995.

Simons, Gerald, ed. *The Blockade: Runners and Raiders*. Alexandria, VA: Time Life Books, 1983.

Siringo, Charles A. *A Lone Star Cowboy*. Santa Fe, NM: n.p., 1919.

———. *A Texas Cow Boy, or Fifteen Years on the Hurricane Deck of a Spanish Pony*. Chicago, IL: Siringo and Dobson, 1886.

Smith, Henry Nash. *Virgin Land: The American West as Symbol and Myth*. Cambridge, MA: Harvard University Press, 1973.

Smith, Linda Wasmer. *Louis Pasteur: Disease Fighter*. Berkeley Heights, NJ: Enslow Publishers, 2008.

Smith, Merritt Roe, and Leo Marx, eds. *Does Technology Drive History? The Dilemma of Technological Determinism*. Cambridge, MA: MIT Press, 1994.

Smith, Page. *The Nation Comes of Age: A People's History*. 4 Volumes. New York: McGraw-Hill Book Company, 1981.

Snow, Jennifer C. *Protestant Missionaries, Asian Immigrants, and Ideologies of Race in America, 1850–1924*. New York: Routledge, 2007.

Spaulding, Lily May, and John Spaulding, eds. *Civil War Recipes: Recipes from the Pages of Godey's Lady's Book*. Lexington: University Press of Kentucky, 1999.

Stampp, Kenneth. *The Era of Reconstruction, 1865–1877*. New York: Knopf, 1965.

Stark, Francis R. *The Abolition of Privateering and the Declaration of Paris*. New York: Columbia University Press, 1897.

Stern, Philip Van Doren. *The Confederate Navy: A Pictorial History*. Garden City, NY: Doubleday, 1962.

Stewart, Elinore Pruitt. *Letters of a Woman Homesteader*. Boston, MA: Houghton Mifflin, 1914.

Stewart, James Brewer. *Holy Warriors: The Abolitionists and American Slavery*. New York: Hill and Wang, 1976.

Stirn, Carl P. *Turn-of-the-Century Dolls, Toys, and Games: The Complete Illustrated Carl P. Stirn Catalog from 1893*. New York: Dover Publications, 1990.

Strasser, Susan. *Never Done: A History of American Housework*. New York: Henry Holt and Company, 1982.

Strong, George Templeton. *The Diary of George Templeton Strong*. New York: The Macmillan Co., 1952.

Sullivan, Audrey G. *19th Century South Jersey Camp Meeting, South Seaville, New Jersey*. Fort Lauderdale, FL: Sullivan, 1980.

Sullivan, Walter. *The War the Women Lived: Female Voices from the Confederate South*. Nashville, TN: J. S. Sanders, 1995.

Sutherland, Daniel E. *The Expansion of Everyday Life, 1860–1876*. Fayetteville: University of Arkansas Press, 2000.

Sweet, Leonard I. *The Minister's Wife: Her Role in Nineteenth-Century American Evangelism.* Philadelphia: Temple University Press, 1983.

Teaford, Jon C. *The Unheralded Triumph: City Government in America, 1870–1900.* Baltimore, MD: The Johns Hopkins University Press, 1984.

Tebbel, John and Mary Ellen Zuckerman. *The Magazine in America, 1741–1990.* New York: Oxford University Press, 1991.

Thomas, Emory M. *The American War and Peace, 1860–1877.* Englewood Cliffs, NJ: Prentice-Hall, Inc., 1973.

Thorp, N. Howard. *Songs of the Cowboys.* New York: Clarkson N. Potter, Inc., 1966.

Time Life Books. *The Glory and Pageantry of Christmas.* Maplewood, NJ: Hammond Incorporated, 1963.

Time Life Books. *The Pioneers.* New York: Time, Inc., 1974.

Time Life Books. *Time Life Book of Christmas.* New York: Prentice Hall, 1987.

Time Life Books. *Voices of the Civil War.* New York: Time Life, 1995.

Timmons, Todd. *Science and Technology in Nineteenth-Century America.* Westport, CT: Greenwood Press, 2005.

Tinling, Marion, ed. *With Women's Eyes: Visitors to the New World, 1775–1918.* Norman: University of Oklahoma Press, 1993.

Titcomb, Timothy. *Lessons in Life, A Series of Familiar Essays.* New York: Charles Scribner & Co., 1861.

Toll, Robert. *Blacking Up: The Minstrel Show in Nineteenth-Century America.* New York: Oxford University Press, 1974.

Topping, Elizabeth A. *What's a Poor Girl To Do?: Prostitution in Mid-Nineteenth Century America.* Gettysburg, PA: Thomas Publications, 2001.

Trager, James. *The Food Chronology.* New York: Henry Holt, 1995.

Travers, Sam. *Christmas in the Old West.* Missoula, MT: Mountain Press Publishing Co., 2003.

Trelease, Allen. *White Terror: The Ku Klux Klan, Conspiracy and Southern Reconstruction.* New York: Harper, 1971.

Trollope, Frances. *Domestic Manners of the Americans.* Mineola, NY: Dover Publications, Inc., 2003.

Twain, Mark (Samuel Clemens). *The Innocents Abroad.* New York: Penguin Putnam, 1980.

Tyree, Marion Cabell, ed. *Housekeeping in Old Virginia.* Louisville, KY: John P. Morton and Company, 1879.

Ulrich, Laurel Thatcher. *A Midwife's Tale: The Life of Martha Ballard, Based on her Diary, 1785–1812.* New York; Vintage Books, 1990.

Underwood, Kathleen. *Town Building on the Colorado Frontier.* Albuquerque: University of New Mexico Press, 1987.

Utley, Robert M. *The Indian Frontier of the American West. 1846–1890.* Albuquerque: University of New Mexico Press, 1964.

———. *Life in Custer's Cavalry: Diaries and Letters of Albert and Jennie Barnitz, 1867–1868.* New Haven, CT: Yale University Press, 1977.

Valencius, Conevery Bolton. *The Health of the Country, How American Settlers Understood Themselves and Their Land.* New York: Perseus Books Group, 2002.

Van Der Plas, Rob. *Cycle History: Proceedings of the 5th International Cycle History Conference.* San Francisco: Bicycle Books, 1995.

Van Dyke, Paul A. *The Canton Trade, Life and Enterprise on the China Coast, 1700–1845.* Hong Kong: Hong Kong University Press, 2005.

Van Hoesen, Walter H. *Early Taverns and Stagecoach Days in New Jersey*. Rutherford, NJ: Fairleigh Dickinson University Press, 1976.

Veblen, Thorstein. *The Theory of the Leisure Class*. Mineola, NY: Dover Publications, Inc., 1994.

Volo, Dorothy Denneen, and James M. Volo. *The Antebellum Period*. Westport, CT: Greenwood Press, 2004.

————. *Daily Life in Civil War America*. Westport, CT: Greenwood Press, 1998.

————. *Daily Life in the Age of Sail*. Westport, CT: Greenwood Press, 2001.

————. *Encyclopedia of the Antebellum South*. Westport, CT: Greenwood Press, 2000.

————. *Family Life in Nineteenth-Century America*. Westport, CT: Greenwood Press, 2007.

Wagner, Tricia Martineau. *It Happened on the Oregon Trail*. Guilford, CT: Globe Pequot Press, 2005.

Wallace, J. H. *Wallace's American Trotting Register*. New York: G. E. Woodward, 1871–1891.

Ware, John F. W. *Home Life: What It Is, and What It Needs*. Boston, MA: Wm. V. Spencer, 1864.

Ware, Joseph E. *The Emigrants' Guide to California*. New York: De Capo Press, 1972. Reprinted from the 1849 edition.

Wechsberg, Joseph. *The Lost World of the Great Spas*. New York: Harper & Row Publishers, 1979.

Weisberger, Bernard A. *The LIFE History of the United States: Steel and Steam, Volume 7: 1877–1890*. New York: Time Life Books, 1975.

Weiskopf, Herman. *The Perfect Game: The World of Bowling*. Englewood Cliffs, NJ: Prentice-Hall. 1978.

Weissman, Judith Reiter, and Wendy Lavitt. *Labors of Love: American Textiles and Needlework, 1650–1930*. New York: Alfred A. Knopf, 1987.

West, Elliot. *Growing Up with the Country*. Albuquerque: University of New Mexico Press, 1989.

West, Elliot, and Paula Petrik, eds. *Small Worlds: Children and Adolescents in America, 1850–1950*. Lawrence: University Press of Kansas, 1992.

West, Richard S., Jr. *Mr. Lincoln's Navy*. New York: Longmans, Green and Co., 1957.

Wheeler, Keith. *The Townsmen*. New York: Time Life Books, 1975.

White, Richard. *"It's Your Misfortune and None of My Own": A New History of the American West*. Norman: University of Oklahoma Press, 1991.

Whitehurst, Clinton H. *The U.S. Merchant Marine: In Search of an Enduring Maritime Policy*. Annapolis: Naval Institute Press, 1983.

————. *The U.S. Shipbuilding Industry: Past, Present, and Future*. Annapolis, Maryland: Naval Institute Press, 1986.

Whitney, David C. *The American Legacy: A Pageant of Great Deeds and Famous Words*. Chicago: J. G. Ferguson Publishing Company, 1975.

Wilentz, Sean. *Chants Democratic: New York City & the Rise of the American Working Class, 1788–1850*. New York: Oxford University Press, 1984.

Williams, Susan. *Food in the United States, 1820s–1890*. Westport, CT: Greenwood Press, 2006.

————. *Savory Suppers & Fashionable Feasts: Dining in Victorian America*. New York: Pantheon Books, 1985.

Wilson, Harold S. *Confederate Industry: Manufactures and Quartermasters in the Civil War*. Jackson: University Press of Mississippi, 2002.

Wise, Stephen R. *Lifeline of the Confederacy: Blockade Running During the Civil War*. Columbia: University of South Carolina Press, 1988.

Wish, Harvey. *Society and Thought in Early America: A Social and Intellectual History of the American People Through 1865.* New York: Longmans, Green and Co., 1950.

Wolff, Leon. *Lockout: The Story of the Homestead Strike of 1892.* New York: Harper & Row, Publishers, Inc., 1965.

Woodruff, Philip. *The Men Who Ruled India: The Founders.* New York: Schocken Books, 1964.

Woodward, C. Vann, ed. *Mary Chesnut's Civil War.* New Haven, CT: Yale University Press, 1981.

Woodward, C. Vann. *Origins of the New South, 1877–1913.* Baton Rouge: Louisiana State University Press, 1951.

Woodward, George E. *Victorian City and Country Houses: Plans and Designs.* New York: Dover Publications, 1996.

———. *Woodward's Architecture and Rural Art.* New York: Privately printed, 1868.

———. *Woodward's National Architect.* New York: Da Capo Press, 1975.

Wyman, Walker D. *Frontier Woman: The Life of a Woman Homesteader on the Dakota Frontier.* River Falls: University of Wisconsin–River Falls Press, 1972.

Zanger, Mark H. *The American History Cookbook.* Westport, CT: Greenwood Press, 2003.

ESSAYS AND ARTICLES

Albin, Maurice S. "The Use of Anesthetics during the Civil War, 1861–1865." *Pharmacy in History* 42, nos. 3–4 (2000): 99–114.

Allin, Lawrence C. "The Civil War and the Period of Decline, 1861–1913." In *America's Maritime Legacy: A History of the U.S. Merchant Marine and Shipbuilding Industry since Colonial Times,* ed. Robert A Kolmarx. Boulder, CO: Westview Press, 1979.

Andrews, Jean Marie. "Nineteenth Century Base Ball." *Early American Life* XXXII, no. 4 (August 2002).

Aron, Cindy S. "The Evolution of the Middle Class." In *A Companion to 19th-Century America,* ed. William L. Barney. Malden, MA: Blackwell Publishing, 2006.

Bash, Wendell H. "Differential Fertility in Madison County New York, 1865. In *Studies in American Historical Demography,* ed. Maris A. Vinovskis. New York: Academic Press, 1979.

Bennett, Sarah, "Words to a Woman." *Advocate and Family Guardian* 31. no. 3 (February 1, 1865).

Berry, Stephen W. "The South: From Old to New." In *A Companion to 19th-Century America,* ed. William L. Barney. Malden, MA: Blackwell Publishing, 2006.

Bishop, Morris. "The Lower Depths of High Education." *American Heritage* XXII, no. 1 (December 1969).

Brekus, Catherine A. "Interpreting American Religion." In *A Companion to 19th-Century America,* ed. William L. Barney. Malden, MA: Blackwell Publishing, 2006.

Cable, Mary. "Damned Plague Ships and Swimming Coffins." *American Heritage* (August 1960).

Carnegie, Andrew. "Wealth." *North American Review* 148, no. 391 (June 1889).

Chudacoff, Howard P. "Newlyweds and Family Extension." In *Family and Population in Nineteenth Century America,* eds. Tamara K. Hareven and Maris A. Vinovskis. Princeton, NJ: Princeton University Press, 1978.

Cook, Fred J. "The Slave Ship Rebellion." *American Heritage* (Feb. 1957): 60–64, 104–15.

Davis, Allen F. "The Settlement House." In *The Social Fabric, American Life from the Civil War to the Present*, eds. John H. Cary and Julius Weinberg. Boston, MA: Little, Brown and Company, 1975.

Duffy, John. "Science and Medicine." In *Science and Society in the United States*, eds. David D. Van Tassel and Michael G. Hall. Homewood, IL: Dorsey Press, 1966.

Easterlin, Richard A., George Alter, and Gretchen A. Condran. "Farms and Farm Families in Old and New Areas: The Northern States in 1860." In *Family and Population in Nineteenth Century America*, eds. Tamara K. Hareven and Maris A. Vinovskis. Princeton, NJ: Princeton University Press, 1978.

Engerman, Stanley L. "Changes in Black Fertility, 1880–1940." In *Family and Population in Nineteenth Century America*, eds. Tamara K. Hareven and Maris A. Vinovskis. Princeton, NJ: Princeton University Press, 1978.

Erisman, Fred. "St. Nicholas." In *Children's Periodicals of the United States*, ed. R. Gordon Kelley. Westport, CT: Greenwood Press, 1984.

Fisher, Gordon M. "From Hunter to Orshansky: An Overview of Unofficial Poverty Lines in the United States from 1904–1965." (A paper presented October 28, 1993 at the Fifteenth Annual Research Conference of the Association for Public Policy Analysis and Management in Washington, D.C. available from the Department of Health and Human Services.)

Fitzpatrick, Michael F. "The Mercy Brigade." *Civil War Times Illustrated* (October 1997).

Forbes, W. Cameron. "Houqua: The Merchant Prince of China. 1769–1843." *Bulletin of the American Asiatic Association* 6 (December 1940): 9–18.

Glasco, Lawrence. "Migration and Adjustment in the Nineteenth-Century City: Occupation, Property, and Household Structure of Native-Born Whites, Buffalo, New York, 1855." In *Family and Population in Nineteenth Century America*, eds. Tamara K. Hareven and Maris A. Vinovskis. Princeton, NJ: Princeton University Press, 1978.

Graulich, Melody. "Violence against Women: Power Dynamics in Literature of the Western Family." In *The Women's West*, eds. Susan Armitage and Elizabeth Jameson. Norman: University of Oklahoma Press, 1987.

Harger, Charles Moreau. "Cattle-Trails of the Prairies." *Scribner's Magazine* (June 1892): 732–42.

Hill, Peter J. "Old West Violence Mostly Myth," *The Arizona Republic* (June 19, 2007).

Hochfelder, David. "The Communications Revolution." In *A Companion to 19th-Century America*, ed. William L. Barney. Malden, MA: Blackwell Publishing, 2006.

Holley, J. M. "History of the Lumber Industry," *La Crosse Wisconsin Chronicle* (October 21, 1906).

Holzer, Harold. "Photographs on Tin: The Ferrotype Endures." *The Antique Trader Annual of Articles* X (September 1979).

Jameson, Elizabeth. "Women as Workers, Women as Civilizers: True Womanhood in the American West." In *The Women's West*, eds. Susan Armitage and Elizabeth Jameson. Norman: University of Oklahoma Press, 1987.

Jefferson, Dorothy L. "Child Feeding in the United States in the 19th Century." In *Award Essays: A Compilation of Essays*, by Lydia J. Roberts. Chicago, IL: American Dietetic Association, 1968.

Josephy, Alvin M., Jr. "The Custer Myth." *Life* 71, no. 1 (July 2, 1971).

Kenny, Kevin. "The Development of the Working Classes." In *A Companion to 19th-Century America*, ed. William L. Barney. Malden, MA: Blackwell Publishing, 2006.

Levin, Alexandra Lee. "Miss Knight Abroad." *American Heritage* XI, no. 3 (April 1960): 15.

Lord, Francis A. "The United States Military Railroad Service: Vehicle to Victory." *Civil War Times Illustrated* (October 1964).

Mitchell, C. Branford. "Pride of the Seas." *American Heritage* (December 1967).

Modell, John. "Family and Fertility on the Indiana Frontier, 1820." In *Studies in American Historical Demography*, ed. Maris A. Vinovskis. New York: Academic Press, 1979.

Nadeau, Remi. "Go it, Washoe!" *American Heritage* X, no. 3 (April 1959): 37.

Osterud, Nancy, and John Fulton. "Family Limitation and Age at Marriage." In *Studies in American Historical Demography*, ed. Maris A. Vinovskis. New York: Academic Press, 1979.

Reynolds, Robert L. "The Coal Kings Come to Judgment," *American Heritage* XI, no. 3 (April 1960).

Rogers, Jack B., and Robert E. Blade. "The Great Ends of the Church: Two Perspectives," *Journal of Presbyterian History* 76 (1998).

Semonche, John E. "American Law in the Nineteenth Century, 1867–1900." In *A Companion to 19th-Century America*, ed. William L. Barney. Malden, MA: Blackwell Publishing, 2006.

Smith, Daniel Scott, and Michael S. Hindus. "Premarital Pregnancy in America." In *Studies in American Historical Demography*, ed. Maris A. Vinovskis. New York: Academic Press, 1979.

Sorg, Eric V. "Annie Oakley." *Wild West* (February 2001).

Stewart, George R. "The Prairie Schooner Got Them There." *American Heritage* XIII, no. 2 (February 1962).

Swartwelder, A. C. "This Invaluable Beverage: The Recollections of Dr. A. C. Swartwelder." *Civil War Times Illustrated* (October, 1975).

Taylor, Alan. "James Fenimore Cooper's America." *History Today* 46, no. 2 (February 1996).

Tice, Douglas O. "Bread or Blood: The Richmond Bread Riot." *Civil War Times Illustrated* (February 1974).

Tosh, John. "New Men? The Bourgeois Cult of Home." *History Today* (December 1996).

Uhl, Robert. "Masters of the Merchant Marine." *American Heritage* (April 1983).

Uhlenberg, Peter R. "A Study of Cohort Life Cycles." In *Family and Population in Nineteenth Century America*, eds. Tamara K. Hareven and Maris A. Vinovskis. Princeton, NJ: Princeton University Press, 1978.

Unidentified author. "The Needs of Working Women: Homes for Working-Girls." *Arthur's Lady's Home Magazine* 37, no. 1 (January 1871).

Watkins, Francis Marion. "The Story of the Crow Emigrant Train of 1865." *The Livingston Chronicle* (January 1935).

Wells, Robert V. "Demographic Change and the Life Cycle of American Families." In *Studies in American Historical Demography*, ed. Maris A. Vinovskis. New York: Academic Press, 1979.

West, Patricia. "Irish Immigrant Workers in Antebellum New York: The Experience of Domestic Servants at Van Buren's Lindenwald." *The Hudson Valley Regional Review: A Journal of Regional Studies* 9 no. 2 (September 1992): 9.

Wik, Reynold M. "Science and American Agriculture." In *Science and Society in the United States*, eds. David D. Van Tassel and Michael G. Hall. Homewood, IL: Dorsey Press, 1966.

Wolff, Leon. "Labor in the Gilded Age." In *The Social Fabric: American Life from the Civil War to the Present*, eds. John H. Cary and Julius Weinberg. Boston, MA: Little, Brown and Company, 1975.

Wood, Alice L. "The History of Artificial Feeding of Infants." In *Award Essays: A Compilation of Essays,* ed. Lydia J. Roberts. Chicago, IL: American Dietetic Association, 1968.

DATA SOURCES

http://americanhistory.about.com/library/charts/blchartpresidents.htm
http://www.state.gov/r/pa/ho/po/1682.htm
http://www.whitehouse.gov/history/presidents
U.S. Bureau of the Census, *Historical Statistics of the United States.* Washington, DC: U.S. Government Printing Office, 1975.

INTERNET SOURCES

Beaumont, Gustave de. "On Marriage in America: Beaumont's letter to his family." URL: http://xroads.virginia.edu/~HYPER/DETOC/FEM/beaumont.htm (accessed May 2007).

Biddle, W. P. "The Boxer Rebellion and the U.S. Navy, 1900–1901." URL: http://www.history.navy.mil/faqs/faq86-1.htm (accessed August 2007).

Dunaway, Wilma A. "Slavery and Emancipation in the Mountain South: Sources, Evidence and Methods," Virginia Tech, Online Archives. URL: http://scholar.lib.vt.edu/faculty_archives/mountain_slavery/civilwar.htm (accessed July 2008).

Echols, Michael. "American Civil War Surgical Antiques: The Private Collection of Dr. Michael Echols." URL: http://www.braceface.com/medical/index.html (accessed October 2007).

Faust, Drew Gilpin. "The Civil War Homefront." URL: http://www.cr.nps.gov/history/online_books/rthg/chap6.htm (accessed July 2007).

Gregory, E. David. "A. L. Lloyd and the English Folk Song Revival, 1934–44." *Canadian Journal for Traditional Music* (1997). URL: http://cjtm.icaap.org/content/25/v25art2.html (accessed July 2007).

Haines, Michael. "Fertility and Mortality in the United States." *EH.Net Encyclopedia,* ed. Robert Whaples. URL: http://eh.net/encyclopedia/article/haines.demography (accessed May 2007).

Rudyard Kipling, *American Notes* (1891) URL: http://www.chicagohs.org/fire/queen/pic0521.html (assessed July 2007).

Lower East Side Tenement Museum Encyclopedia. URL: http://www.tenement.org/Encyclopedia (accessed May 2007).

Perkins, Robert. "Diplomacy and Intrigue, Confederate Relations with the Republic of Mexico, 1861–1862." URL: http://members.tripod.com/~azrebel/page11.html (accessed August 2007).

Roosevelt, Theodore. "Theodore Roosevelt: An Autobiography." URL: http://www.bartleby.com/55/13.html (accessed July 2007).

Stewart, James. "The Economics of American Farm Unrest, 1865–1900." *EH.Net Encyclopedia,* ed. Robert Whaples. URL: http://eh.net/encyclopedia/article/stewart.farmers (accessed May 2007).

"The Sherman Antitrust Act, Text." URL: http://www.antitrustupdate.com/Statutes/SL-ShermanAct.html Sections 1–4 (accessed December 2007).

Tocqueville, Alexis de. "Letter to his sister, describing courtship and marriage habits of the Americans." URL: http://xroads.virginia.edu/~HYPER/DETOC/FEM/tocqueville.htm (accessed May 2007).

University of Virginia, Historical Census Browser. URL: http://fisher.lib.virginia.edu/collections/stats/histcensus/php/state.php (accessed May 2007).

Whaples, Robert. "Child Labor in the United States." *EH.Net Encyclopedia*, ed. Robert Whaples. URL: http://eh.net/encyclopedia/article/whaples.childlabor (accessed May 2007).

CUMULATIVE INDEX

Boldface numbers refer to volume numbers. A key appears on all verso pages.

in, 1:211–16, 399–401; debt and, 4:144–45; in decades of discord, 1960–1990, 4:13; drugs in, 4:270; dueling in, 1:402–3; duty/ honor in, 1:402; during Exploitation Period, 2:330–50; family in, 1:29–31, 216–23, 395–96; 2:35–40, 207, 331–34, 473–75; 3:43–47, 111–16, 208–9, 281–84, 353–57, 402–5; 4:32–35; freedmen in, 2:221–23; hospitality in, 1:401–2; during Industrial Age (1870–1900), 2:473–99; kinship in, 1:397–98; 2:33–35, 204–7, 330–31, 473; marriage in, 1:211–16, 399–401; men in, 2:207–10, 334–36, 475–79; 3:47–49, 209–10, 284–86, 405; 4:41–42, 141–42, 270–71; in Middle Atlantic U.S., 3:111–21; in Midwest U.S., 3:280–93; miscegenation in, 1:405–6; modern era, 1991–2005, 4:18; modernization in, 1:393–95; in Northeast U.S., 3:43–57; orphans in, 1:42–43; 2:343–44; "Other America," 4:137–40, 272–73; overview, 4:136–37, 267–68; in Pacific West U.S., 3:402–13; pets in, 2:59–62, 223–24, 347–48, 497–98; 3:54–57, 214, 292–93, 413; 4:271–72; planter aristocracy in, 1:396–97; postwar America, 1946–1959, 4:31–32; prostitution in, 1:404–5; during Reconstruction (1865–1877), 2:201–4; rural America and, 4:142–44; servants in, 2:58–59, 221–23, 344–47, 494–97; slaves in, 2:58–59, 344–47; in Southern U.S., 3:208–14; in Southwest/Rocky Mountain Western U.S., 3:353–57; suburban living, 4:142–44; technology and, 4:144–45; during U.S. Civil War, 2:32–63; during war years, 1940–1945, 4:30–31; women in, 2:40–49, 210–17, 336–41, 479–85; 3:49–52, 117–19, 210–12, 286–91, 356–57, 405–6; 4:38–41, 145–46, 273–75

Domestic Medicine (Gunn), 1:437
Domestic Medicine or the Family Physician (Whitfield), 1:142
Domestic sciences, 2:211
Dominican Republic, 2:472
Donnelley, Thorne, 3:314–15
Don't Change Your Husband, 3:466
Doolittle, Jimmy, 3:462
Dorchester, Daniel, 2:458
Dorsey, Jimmy, 3:94–95
Dorsey, Mollie, 2:332, 341
Dorsey, Tommy, 3:95
Dos Passos, John, 3:23, 68; 4:71
Doubleday, Abner, 2:165
Dougherty, Joseph, 3:133
Douglas, A. S., 4:312
Douglas, Donald, 3:454
Douglass, Frederick, 1:480–81, 565, 580–81, 602–4; 2:103–4, 173, 602
Douglass' Monthly Magazine, 1:580; 2:103
Douglas, Stephen A., 1:386; 2:148, 150, 153; Lincoln, Abraham, debates, 1:389–90
Douglas, William O., 3:366
Dow, Lorenzo, 1:561; 2:459
Downing, Andrew Jackson, 1:468, 480–81; 2:129
Dows, Gustavus, 2:272
Doyle, Arthur Conan, 2:533

Draft, 4:99–100, 142, 221, 226
Drake, Edwin, 2:15, 361–62, 364–65
Draper, Margaret, 1:145
Dr. Chase's Recipes, 2:271
Dr. Cladius (Crawford, F. M.), 2:254
Dred: A Tale of the Great Dismal Swamp (Stowe), 1:579
Dred Scott case, 1:388–89, 555; 2:418
Dreiser, Theodore, 2:470, 533; 3:52, 67–68, 79
Dresser, Paul, 2:594
Drew, Daniel, 2:509
Drinker, Elizabeth, 1:160–61
Driven to Distraction (Hallowell/Ratey), 4:181
Dr. Jekyll and Mr. Hyde (Stevenson), 2:533
"Dr. Morse's Root Pills," 2:448
Droughts, 2:239
Drugs: advertising, 4:297; cartels, 4:323–24; in domestic life, 4:270; miracle, 4:68; "narco-trafficking," 4:323; research, 4:297; during Vietnam War (1965–1975), 4:226. *See also* Medicine
Drury, Marion, 2:55
Dryden, John, 3:184
Drys, 3:19
Dr. Zhivago (Pasternak), 4:28
Du Bois, W. E. B., 3:3–4, 24, 67, 135, 236–37; 4:71
Dude ranches, 3:361
Dudley, Dorothy, 1:107, 114, 123, 156, 159, 168
Dueling, 1:274; 2:166–67; code, 1:403; in domestic life, 1:402–3; golden age, 1:402; weapons, 1:403
Duff, Mary Ann, 2:313
Dukakis, Michael, 4:313
Duke, James Buchanan, 3:247–48
Dulles, Foster Rhea, 4:97
Dulles, John Foster, 4:99
Dull Knife, 2:432
Duncan, Don, 3:439
Dunglison, Robley, 1:440
"Dunkers," 1:296
Dunlap, John, 1:21
Dunlap, William, 1:57
Dunlop, J. B., 2:568
Dunmore, John Murray, 1:105–6
Dunn, Red, 3:342
Dunston, M. R., 3:426
du Pont, Alfred, 3:183
du Pont, Pierre, 3:154, 183
Durand, Asher B., 1:450
Durand, Peter, 1:503
Durant, Will, 3:20, 58, 296, 327
Durst, Ralph, 3:417–18
Dust Bowl, 3:306
Dutch: as bricklayers, 1:46; education and, 1:61; settlement of, 1:6; smugglers, 1:16
Dutch ovens, 1:132; 2:402
The Duty of American Women to Their Country (Beecher, C.), 2:381
Dwight, John Sullivan, 2:302
Dwight, Timothy, 1:459
Dylan, Bob, 4:110, 231–32, 234

Eagle Brewery, 1:510
Eames, Charles, 4:79
Eames, Ray, 4:79
Early, Jubal A., 2:231, 260
Earned Income Tax Credit, 4:321
Earp, Jug, 3:342

Earp, Morgan, 2:422
Earp, Virgil, 2:422
Earp, Wyatt, 2:422
Earth Day, 4:129
East India Company, 1:16–17
Eastman, George, 2:250, 605; 3:162
Eating in America (Root/de Rochemont), 4:192
Eaton, Amos, 1:431, 434
Eaton, Fred, 3:448
E-commerce, 4:312
Economic life: during American changes/conflict (1821–1861), 1:515–54; during American Republic (1789–1820), 1:230–68; animal husbandry/hunting/fishing in, 3:62–63, 151–52, 227–28, 305–7, 376–79, 432–36; artisans in, 1:252–56; banking in, 1:264–68; benefits, growth, change, 4:49–52; builders in, 1:262–64; buying/selling in, 1:243–52; caste/class experience in, 3:59–60, 131–46, 222–25, 298–303, 369–74, 428–32; cattle market in, 2:241–44; during Colonial America (1763–1789), 1:68–90; commerce in, 1:84–86; communications in, 1:530–35; consumer protection, 4:154; cost of living in, 2:71–73, 231–34, 369–72, 513; credit cards, 4:281–82; crop harvesting in, 1:540–44; in decades of discord, 1960–1990, 4:13; dollar in, 2:63–64; employment in, 4:164; energy crisis, 4:154–55; environmental issues, 4:154; during Exploitation Period, 2:350–79; factories in, 1:256–62; farming in, 1:230–36, 545–48; 2:74–79, 235–41, 517–19; finance in, 2:69–70, 229–31, 367–69, 508–13; food preservation in, 1:544–45; globalization, 4:277; industrial accidents in, 2:505–6; during Industrial Age (1870–1900), 2:499–525; industrial competition in, 4:155–61; industrial production in, 4:280–81; industry in, 1:83–84; inventions in, 1:515–16; investing, 4:278–80; iron/steel in, 1:552; labor in, 1:516–17; 4:148–53; labor unions in, 2:365–67; 4:47–48; livestock in, 1:236–40; 2:76–79; malls/shopping centers, 4:153–54; mechanics in, 1:515; in Middle Atlantic U.S., 3:121–52; in Midwest U.S., 3:293–307; mining in, 1:553–54; modern era, 1991–2005, 4:18; in Northeast U.S., 3:57–63; nutrition and, 4:147; organized labor in, 2:506–8; "other America" in, 4:162–63; overview, 4:146–47, 275–76; in Pacific West U.S., 3:413–36; population in, 4:148; poverty in, 4:282–84; recharging, 4:284–85; during Reconstruction (1865–1877), 2:225–47; roads/rivers in, 1:259–60; rural America and, 4:163–64; slavery in, 1:75–80; in Southern U.S., 3:214–28; Southern U.S. agriculture, 1:240–48; in Southwest/Rocky Mountain Western U.S., 3:357–79; taxes in, 4:285–87; technology in, 1:535–40; 4:161–62, 288–90; textile mills in, 1:550–52; trade in, 2:79–81, 244–46, 376–78, 519–24; 3:58–59, 129–31, 220–22, 256–58, 425–28; transportation in, 1:517–30; urban/rural issues, 2:73–74, 234–38, 372–73, 514; 3:60–62, 146–51, 225–26, 303–5, 374–76; 4:163–64; urban street, 2:514–17; during U.S. Civil War, 2:63–82; wartime economy, 1940–1945, 4:44–45; women at work in, 4:48–49; work

4:106; kinetoscopes, 3:99; large-screen projection, 3:99; ratings, 4:167; in recreational life, 4:244–45; religious, 4:123; during roaring twenties, 3:22; ticket sales, 4:62; westerns, 3:467; wide-screen epics, 4:107; during World War II, 4:63–64. *See also* Entertainment; Films; Theater; *specific movies*

Moyer, Charles, 3:393

Moynihan, Daniel Patrick, 4:138

MPAA. *See* Motion Picture Association of America

Mravlag, Victor, 3:91

Mr. Isaac's (Crawford, F. M.), 2:254

Muck, Karl, 3:13

Muhammad, Elijah, 4:217

Muir, John, 3:434–35

Mulholland, William, 3:448

Mulock, Dinah, 2:22

Mulvagh, Jane, 3:445

Mumford, Lewis, 4:66–67

Mummers Parade, 2:612; 3:199–200

Munn vs. Illinois, 2:419, 434

Munro, George, 2:386–87

Munro, Norman, 2:386–87

Munsey's Magazine, 2:537; 3:70

Murgas, Joseph, 3:176

Murphy, Charles W., 3:339

Murray, John Courtney, 4:258

Murray's Rush, 2:308

Murray, Thomas E., 2:477

Murray, W. H. H., 2:308

Murrow, Edward R., 4:54

Music: African American, 4:107–8; in American Republic (1789–1820), 1:286–87; big band, 4:110; Black spirituals, 2:303–4, 599; blues, 2:599; 3:262–63, 343; boogie woogie, 3:344; brass-band, 2:169–70, 302–3, 597; bully songs, 2:595; classical, 2:168–69; classical, on radio, 3:71; of Confederacy, 2:170–71; contemporary, 4:236; coon songs, 2:595–96; cowboys, 2:441–42; Decca Record Company, 3:94–95; disco, 4:236; drinking songs, 1:287; folk, 4:110; *Grand Ole Opry*, 3:263–64; grunge movement, 4:298; in intellectual life, 4:298–99; jazz, 2:599; 3:95, 262–63; jukeboxes, 3:95; lamentations, 2:172; making of, 2:438–42; messages in, 4:299; military, 2:169–70; in military life, American Revolution homefront, 1:151; mining, 2:441; minstrelsy, 2:169, 304–5, 592; musicals, 3:98–99; Napster, 4:299; opera, 3:464; philharmonic orchestra, 3:464; player pianos, 2:591; ragtime, 2:596–97; rap, 4:238, 298–99; in recreational life, 2:167–74, 302–6, 438–42, 447–48, 591–99; 3:94–95, 262–64, 343–44, 464; 4:107–10, 230–39; religious melodies, 1:286; rock, 4:230–36; rock and roll, 4:26, 108–10; Second New England School, 2:598; sheet music, 2:592; of slaves, 1:320–21; 2:173–74; song, 2:167–68, 593–94; swing, 3:95, 411; symphonic orchestra, 2:598; Thomas Orchestra, 2:303; Tin Pan Alley, 2:593–94; Western, 2:447–48; of Western emigrants, 2:438; white gospel, 2:305–6. *See also specific musicians*

Muskets, 1:97, 117–18; 2:84–85

Mussolini, Benito, 3:36–37

My Ántonia (Cather), 2:227, 540

Myers, Myer, 1:86–87

Mystery Train (Marcus), 4:109

NAACP. *See* National Association for the Advancement of Colored People

Nabokov, Vladimir, 4:34, 70

NACW. *See* National Association of Colored Women

Nader, Ralph, 4:14, 149

NAFTA. *See* North American Free Trade Agreement

Naked Lunch (Burroughs), 4:72

The Naked and the Dead (Mailer), 4:69

The Name of the Rose (Eco), 4:185

Napoleon III, 2:157, 292

Narrative of the Life of Frederick Douglass (Douglass), 1:565; 602–4; 2:103

Narrative of William Wells Brown, Fugitive Slave Written by Himself (Brown, W. W.), 2:104

NASA. *See* National Aeronautics and Space Administration

NASCAR. *See* National Association of Stock Car Auto Racing

Nash, Tom, 3:342

The Nashville Banner, 1:464

Nason, Tama, 4:101

Nast, Thomas, 2:185, 283, 535

The Natchez Courier, 1:464

National Academy of Sciences, 2:106

National Aeronautics and Space Administration (NASA), 4:28, 186–87

National Association for the Advancement of Colored People (NAACP), 4:102; anti-lynching protests, 3:222; founding of, 3:24; support for, 3:430

National Association of Amateur Oarsmen, 2:298

National Association of Colored Women (NACW), 3:3, 431

National Association of Stock Car Auto Racing (NASCAR), 4:336–38

National Association of Women's Lawyers, 4:145

National Association of Working Women, 4:151

National Black Political Assembly, 4:208

National Board for the Promotion of Rifle Practice (NBPRP), 2:300

National Broadcasting Corporation (NBC), 4:110, 111

National Collegiate Athletic Association (NCAA), 2:167, 299, 300; 4:113, 118–19, 332–35

National Commission of Life Adjustment for Youth, 4:58

National Committee for a Sane Nuclear Policy (SANE), 4:100

National Consumers League, 2:491

National Defense Education Act (1958), 4:61

National Education Association, 2:507

National Football League (NFL), 4:113, 240, 242

National Grange, 2:17

National Housing Act (1949), 4:51

National Housing Agency, 4:86

National Industry Recovery Act (NIRA), 3:33

National Institute of Alcohol Abuse and Alcoholism (NIAAA), 4:191

National Institutes of Health (NIH), 4:68

Nationalism, 2:2, 150; in American Republic (1789–1820), 1:206–7; new, 3:6; of Southern U.S., 1:581–84

National Labor Relations Act (1935), 3:34, 424; 4:47

National Livestock Association, 2:423

National Organization for Women (NOW), 4:40, 275

National Park System, 3:6, 151, 434–35

National Party, 2:288

National Peace Jubilee (1869), 2:302

National Police Gazette, 2:22–23, 422

National Progressive Union of Miners and Mine Laborers, 2:508

National Recorder, 1:463, 481

National Rifle Association (NRA), 2:300; 4:323

National Road, 1:260, 518

The National Journal, 1:461

National Urban League, 3:430

A Nation at Risk, 4:210–11, 293

The Nation, 2:256

Native Americans, 1:88, 387, 558; 2:96, 361, 386, 395, 539, 607, 646–48; 3:223–25, 397; 4:273; animal husbandry/hunting/fishing of, 1:314–15; British alliances, 1:127–28, 196; clans, 1:315–16; confinement of, 2:330; customs of, 3:370; depiction of, 2:384; discrimination and, 3:303; education, 3:381; family life, 3:403; farming, 1:314–15; food, 1:128; 3:318–19; games, 1:315; during Great Depression of 1929, 3:306–7, 372; Indian Wars, 3:223; during Jacksonian Age, 1:377–78; literacy, 2:21; Long Walk, 2:431; as minority, 3:370; Native American Party, 1:382; in new hunting grounds, 1:6; orphans, 2:220; Plains Indian Wars, 2:433; poverty among, 3:432; religious beliefs, 3:395; reservations, 2:430–33, 471; 3:432; rituals/ceremonies, 1:316–17; in social life, 1:313–18; suppression, 1:317; towns, 1:316–17; "Trail of Tears," 1:378; U.S. Supreme Court and, 1:377; voting and, 1:373. *See also* Creek War; French and Indian War (1754–1763); *specific Native American peoples*; *specific Native Americans*

Nativism, 1:382; 2:1, 148, 152–53; discrimination, 2:157–60; evangelical movement and, 2:160

Nativist Party, 2:152–53

NATO. *See* North Atlantic Treaty Organization

Natural gas, 3:358–59

Naturalization Act, 1:200

Natural law, 1:9

Navajos, 3:354, 371, 372

Navigation, 3:82–83, 450–51; Navigation Acts, 2:566. *See also* Transportation

Nazism, 4:9, 63

NBC. *See* National Broadcasting Corporation

NBPRP. *See* National Board for the Promotion of Rifle Practice

NCAA. *See* National Collegiate Athletic Association

NCAS. *See* North Carolina Academy of Science

The Nebraska Farmer, 2:400

Necessary Rules For the Proper Behavior of Children (Dock), 1:62

Negro Leagues, 4:114–15

The Negro American Family (Moynihan), 4:138

Nelson, Baby Face, 3:333

Nelson, Ozzie, 3:95

Nelson, Ricky, 4:27

Nevin, J. W., 2:456

New Almanack & Ephemeris (Rivington), 1:146

Newbold, Charles, 1:232; 2:517

New Deal, 2:586; 3:43, 128, 283–84; 4:11, 15, 88; agencies of, 3:32–33; as "creeping socialism,"

(1863–1866); Radical Reconstruction (1867–1873); Redemption (1874–1877)

Recreational life: during American Republic (1789–1820), **1:**268–90; auto racing, **4:**336–38; Brownies, **2:**603; cards/board games, **3:**96, 198–99; **4:**331–32; children and, **1:**289–90; collecting in, **2:**604–5; college sports, **4:**332–35; community games, **2:**445–46; crafts, **2:**179–80, 311–12, 449–50, 608–10; croquet, **2:**179; cultural institutions, **2:**176–77; dance, **2:**447–48; **4:**230–39; in decades of discord, 1960–1990, **4:**16; dime museums, **2:**177–78; entertainment in, **3:**96–101, 188–91, 264–65, 344–45, 464–67; during Exploitation Period, **2:**436–54; fencing/swordsmanship in, **2:**166–67; films, **3:**191–92; **4:**104–7; gambling, **2:**447; **4:**336; games, **2:**164–66, 178–79, 309, 446, 603–4; holidays, **1:**269–70; **2:**182–87, 314–20, 451–53, 612–20; **3:**101, 199–200, 265–67, 467–68; during Industrial Age (1870–1900), **2:**587–621; lectures, **2:**177; leisure activities, **1:**268–69; **2:**174–75, 306–12, 442–43, 599–604; medicine shows, **2:**448–49; in Middle Atlantic U.S., **3:**188–200; in Midwest U.S., **3:**337–43; in military camps, **2:**163–64; modern era, 1991–2005, **4:**20; movies, **4:**244–45; music, **2:**167–74, 302–6, 438–42, 447–48, 591–99; **3:**94–95, 262–64, 343–44, 464; **4:**107–10, 230–39; in Northeast U.S., **1:**279–85; **3:**92–102; optical novelties, **2:**175–76; overview, **4:**104, 229–30, 330–31; in Pacific West U.S., **3:**462–68; photography, **2:**605; postwar America, 1945–1959, **4:**11; radio, **4:**110–11; reading clubs, **1:**143; **2:**177; during Reconstruction (1865–1877), **2:**297–302; self-improvement, **1:**285–89; social events, **2:**444–45; in Southern U.S., **1:**270–76; **3:**261–67; in Southwest/Rocky Mountain Western U.S., **3:**393–94; sports, **2:**164–66, 297–301, 436–38, 587–91; **3:**92–94, 192–98, 261–62, 338–43, 393–94, 462–64; **4:**113–19, 239–44, 336–37, 340–42; sports stadiums, **4:**338–40; television, **4:**111–13, 244–45, 342–43; theater, **2:**181–82, 312–14, 372, 450–51, 610–12; **4:**230–39; tourism, **4:**343–44; train watching, **2:**446–47; traveling shows, **2:**448, 606; *Uncle Tom's Cabin* shows, **2:**607; during U.S. Civil War, **2:**163–89; in Western frontier, **1:**276–79; Wild West shows, **2:**606–7

Redcoats, **1:**128

Redemption (1874–1877), **2:**202, 287–88, 294

Red Harvest (Hammett), **3:**440

Redpath, James, **2:**179

Reds, **3:**18

Red Scare, **3:**420; **4:**11, 27, 66, 96. *See also* McCarthyism

The Red Badge of Courage (Crane), **2:**533, 540

Reed, Ester, **1:**159–60

Reed, John, **3:**128

Reform, **4:**215–21; education, **1:**411; farmers *vs.* railroads, **2:**433–34; of Gold Standard, **2:**583–86; Jews and, **3:**225; middle-class, **2:**515; money/currency, **2:**18–19; in political life, **1:**557–59; **2:**160–63, 295–96, 433–35, 583–86; **3:**88–89, 184–86, 334–36, 461–62; Republican Party and, **3:**185–86; schools,

2:219, 575; social reform movements, **1:**558; **2:**46; women and, **3:**335. *See also* Abolitionism; Temperance movement

Reformed Church, **1:**298–99, 307

Reformism, **2:**1

Refrigeration, **1:**544–45; **2:**243, 396

Refugees, **2:**204–7

Regionalism, **4:**3–4

Regulators, **2:**291

Rehwinkel, Bessie, **2:**240

Reid, John G., **2:**589

Reid, Mayne, **1:**454; **2:**179, 385

Reitman, Ben, **3:**417

Religion in the United States (Baird), **2:**457

Religions, **1:**146; **2:**191, 457–58, 488, 627, 631; **3:**4, 102–4; **4:**252; African American, **2:**197–200; **3:**103–4, 270–71; alcohol/drinking habits and, **3:**103; "Born again" Christian movement, **4:**16, 255; Christian right, **4:**20, 320; conflict in denominations, **4:**250; denominations 1650–1850, **2:**193; devotion/leisure class and, **2:**630–31; diversity, **2:**193; drive-in churches, **4:**123; emotionalism in, **2:**322; First Great Awakening, **2:**189; Fundamentalism, **3:**267–69; Great Revival, **1:**302; Hare Krishna followers, **4:**255; of immigrants, **2:**157–58; imperatives of, **4:**348–49; intolerance, **4:**12; Jesus movement, **4:**252–53; mainstream, **4:**249; missionaries, **3:**470; in movies, **4:**123; Native American, **3:**395; New Age, **4:**16, 250; New Christian Right, **4:**252; numbers in, **4:**348; Pentecostal movement, **3:**395–96, 468–69; persecution, **2:**20; Pietist, **1:**560; **2:**190; in political life, **2:**159–60; prayer in schools, **4:**25, 127; religious camps/resorts, **2:**631–33; religious compass, **2:**193; religious freedom, **2:**457–58; revivalism, **3:**20–21, 274–75; in roaring twenties, **3:**20–21; role of, **3:**270–71; Second Great Awakening, **2:**458–60; of slaves, **1:**321, 569–71; television evangelists, **4:**251; in towns, **2:**238. *See also* Churches; Deism; Protestantism; Protestant Reformation; *specific religions*

A Religious History of the American People (Ahlstrom), **2:**458

Religious life: in 1960s, **4:**247–48; in 1970s, **4:**248–49; in 1980s, **4:**249–52; during American changes/conflict (1821–1861), **1:**559–62; during American Republic (1789–1820), **1:**291–313; anticommunism and, **4:**121–23; camp meetings, **1:**301, 561; **2:**456, 459; charity in, **1:**291–93; Christianity and, **4:**252; during Colonial America (1763–1789), **1:**65–66; courts and, **4:**125–26; cults, **4:**256; death in, **1:**312–13; in decades of discord, 1960–1990, **4:**16–17; diversity as article of faith, **1:**293–304; evangelicalism, **4:**345–46; during Exploitation Period, **2:**454–63; faith/charity in, **1:**291–93; First Great Awakening in, **1:**559–60; fundamentalism and, **4:**252–53; during Industrial Age (1870–1900), **2:**621–33; Islam, **4:**346–47; issues in, **4:**253–55; Judaism, **4:**346–47; Kwanzaa, **4:**347–48; membership and, **4:**121–23; in Middle Atlantic U.S., **3:**200–204; modern era, 1991–2005, **4:**20; morality, **2:**191–92, 322–23, 454–57, 621–24; **3:**273; morals

and, **4:**121–23; in Northeast U.S., **3:**102–7; overview, **4:**120–21, 246–47, 345; in Pacific West U.S., **3:**468–71; postwar America, 1945–1959, **4:**11–12, 123–25; during Reconstruction (1865–1877), **2:**322–26; religious thought in, **2:**189–91; revivalism, **1:**304–7, 559–60; ritual in, **3:**105–6, 398–99; rivalry in, **1:**293; sacred rites of passage, **3:**104–5, 272–73; sacred space/time, **3:**106–7, 273–75; Second Great Awakening in, **1:**560–62; secular rites of passage, **3:**101–2, 271–72; Social Gospel, **2:**624–28; in Southern U.S., **3:**267–75; in Southwest/Rocky Mountain Western U.S., **3:**394–99; special faiths/spirituality, **4:**350; spirituality and, **3:**102–4, 200–204, 267–71, 345–48, 394–98, 468–71; during U.S. Civil War, **2:**189–200; worldview, **3:**204, 275, 348–49, 399, 471; worship in, **1:**307–12. *See also* Religions

Religious News Writers Association, **4:**252

The Religious Education of Daughters, **1:**146

Remond, Charles Lenox, **1:**580

Reno Brothers, **2:**424

Reno, Milo, **3:**305

Rensselaer Institute, **1:**431, 434

Repplier, Agnes, **3:**160

Republicanism, **2:**1, 285

Republican Party, **1:**378, 389; **2:**148, 282, 336, 577–78; **3:**1, 6, 29; **4:**11, 265; arguments in, **1:**211; defined, **1:**198–99; reform and, **3:**185–86; during roaring twenties, **3:**26–27; slogans, **1:**555

Rerum Novarum, **2:**628; **3:**4, 34

Reserve Officer Training Corps (ROTC), **2:**300; **4:**100

Restaurant Rancais, **1:**514

Revenues: in American Republic (1789–1820), **1:**191–93; Confederacy, **2:**69–70, 76; Revenue Act (1762), **1:**11; school, **1:**417. *See also* Internal Revenue Service

Revere, Paul, **1:**18, 128–29

Revivalism, **3:**20–21, 274–75; camp meetings, **1:**306–7; evangelism, **1:**307; First Great Awakening as, **1:**305; Great Revival, **1:**302; New Light revivalists, **1:**8; origins, **1:**305; in religious life, **1:**304–7, 559–60; Second Great Awakening as, **1:**304–7

Revolution of 1800, **1:**199–200

Revolvers, **1:**538–40; **2:**84, 85, 573–74

RFD. *See* Rural Free Delivery

Rhett, Robert B., **1:**464

Rhoades, Charles J., **3:**371–72

Rice, **1:**73–74, 79, 240, 243–44

Rice, Condoleezza, **4:**326

Rice, Janice, **3:**412–13

Rich, Adrienne, **4:**70, 71, 73

Richards, Caroline Cowles, **1:**422; **2:**91

Richards, George, **1:**577

Richland School for Classical, Scientific and Practical Education, **1:**412

Richmond, Julius B., **4:**178

Richmond South, **1:**465

The Richmond Whig, **1:**464

Rickard, Tex, **3:**196

Rickenbacker, Eddie, **3:**85

Rickey, Branch, **4:**115

Rider, Nathaniel, **2:**380

Rifles, **1:**99, 102, 117–18, 538, 540; **2:**85, 300, 385, 422

Tories: defined, **1**:95; factional, **1**:97; Loyalist Party and, **1**:97; newspapers of, **1**:144–45; press of, **1**:98; radicals, **1**:97–98; rangers, **1**:127; refugees, **1**:116

Torrio, Johnny, **3**:331–32

Toscanini, Arturo, **3**:71

The Touchstone (Wharton), **2**:533

A Tour of the Prairies (Irving), **1**:450

Tourgee, Albion W., **2**:287

Tourism, **3**:361–62; **4**:343–44. *See also* Travel

Tournament of Roses parade, **2**:612–13

de Tousard, Louis, **1**:346

Tousey, Frank, **2**:386

Tower, Philo, **2**:476

Towns: in American changes/conflict (1821–1861), **1**:394; business in, **2**:237; cow, **2**:242, 422–24; during elections, **2**:237; entertainment in, **2**:237; food in, **2**:405–6; justice in, **2**:422–74; leisure activities in, **1**:269; life in, **2**:235–38; mining, **2**:342, 420; of Native Americans, **1**:316–17; newspapers in, **2**:236; plans, **2**:236; police in, **2**:573–74; railroads' role in, **2**:235; religions in, **2**:238; slaves in, **1**:564; textile mills and, **1**:551; trade organizations in, **2**:238; working-class in, **1**:251

Town, Salem, **2**:251

Townsend, Francis E., **3**:34, 457

Townshend Acts, **1**:95

Townshend, Charles, **1**:13, 94

Townshend duties, **1**:13–14, 158

Townsite Act (1844), **2**:236

Town's Speller, **1**:420

Toys, **1**:38, 52–53; dolls, **1**:39; **2**:218, 655; educational, **2**:218; rocking horses, **2**:218; *Toys "R" Us*, **4**:140. *See also* Cards/board games; Games

Trade, **2**:508, 577; **3**:7, 416, 419; advertising, **3**:130–31; canals as centers, **1**:523; China trade, **2**:244–46, 426; clipper ships in, **2**:521–23, 567; cotton, **2**:377; country stores, **3**:220–22; in economic life, **2**:79–81, 244–46, 376–78, 519–24; **3**:58–59, 129–31, 220–22, 256–58, 425–28; failure of carrying, **2**:519–21; guano, **2**:520–21; maritime decline, **2**:376–78, 522–24; markets and, **3**:58–59, 129–31, 220–22, 256–58, 425–28; organizations in towns, **2**:238; routes, **1**:85; rum, **1**:56; slave, **1**:76–77, 85, 318–19; **2**:155–56; steam in, **2**:521–22

Trade Union Unity League, **3**:419

Traditionalism, **2**:1

Traditionalists, **4**:143

"Trail of Tears," **1**:378

Trans-Alaska Pipeline System, **4**:131

Transportation, **3**:83–86; **4**:90–91; aluminum and, **3**:179–80; bridges, **3**:453–54; buses, **3**:183; canals in, **1**:521–24; in cities, **1**:529–30; cycling, **2**:567–69; dirigible airships, **3**:387, 455; in economic life, **1**:517–30; electric trolley/cable cars, **3**:451–54; elevated trains, **3**:325; free balloons, **3**:387; horsecars, **2**:142–43; horse-drawn carriages, **1**:517; mass transit, **2**:279–80; **3**:326; in material life, **2**:142–47, 279–80, 413–15, 567–69; **3**:83–86, 178–83, 253–55, 325–27, 385–88, 451–55; movers/freight wagons, **2**:414–15; public, **3**:86; railroads in, **1**:524–29; **3**:179, 253–55, 362, 385–86; roads and, **1**:517–18;

2:145; stagecoaches, **1**:517; **2**:413–14; steamboats, **1**:260, 433–34, 518–21, 608–9; **2**:145–47, 509; streetcars, **2**:279–80; **3**:182–83; subways, **3**:86; trolleys, **2**:279–80; trucks, **3**:180; wagons, **1**:517; walking, **2**:14. *See also* Airplanes; Automobiles; Navigation; Rivers; Ships

Travel, **1**:58, 463; **2**:226, 390, 539; as entertainment, **3**:97; in Northeast U.S., **1**:284; in Southern U.S., **1**:275–76; traveling shows, **2**:448, 606

Travels and Adventures in Canada (Parkman), **1**:463

Travels in America in 1806 (Ashe, T.), **1**:58

Treasure Island (Stevenson), **2**:533

Treaties: Harris Treaty, **2**:428; Jay's Treaty, **1**:196, 197; Treaty of Fort Jackson, **1**:317; Treaty of Ghent, **1**:205–6; Treaty of Guadalupe Hidalgo (1848), **1**:384; **2**:328; Treaty of Paris (1782), **1**:26–27; Treaty of Utrecht (1713), **1**:76; Treaty of Wangxia (1844), **2**:427. *See also* North Atlantic Treaty Organization; South East Asia Treaty Organization

Trelawny, Edward, **1**:82

Trent affair, **2**:156

Tresca, Carlo, **3**:128

Treski, Stacia, **3**:124

Tribes, **4**:199–200

Trilling, Diana, **4**:71

Trilling, Lionel, **4**:71

Tristram Shandy (Sterne, L.), **1**:141

Trolleys, **2**:279–80

Trollope, Anthony, **2**:22

Trollope, Frances, **1**:505; **2**:116

Tropic of Cancer (Miller, H.), **4**:34

Tropic of Capricorn (Miller, H.), **4**:34

Trotter, William Monroe, **3**:236

The Troubled Crusade: American Education (Ravitch), **4**:56

Trowbridge, John Townsend, **2**:535

True Story, **3**:157–58

Truett, George W., **3**:270

Truman, Harry S., **4**:5, 25–26, 75, 95–96

Trumbull, John, **1**:107, 112–13, 141

Tsunami, **4**:264

Tube of Plenty (Barnouw), **4**:111

Tuberculosis, **1**:226, 436

Tucker, George, **1**:459

Tudor, Frederick, **1**:503

Tull, Jethro, **1**:431

Tung Meng Hui, **2**:580

Tunney, Gene, **3**:196–98

Tupper, Earl, **4**:274

Tupperware, **4**:38, 274

Turner, Frederick Jackson, **2**:328–29; **3**:63

Turner, Nat, **1**:577; **2**:198; **4**:101; revolt (1831), **2**:289

The Turn of the Screw (James, H.), **2**:539

Turpin, Tom, **2**:597

Tuskegee Study, **3**:240

TV dinners, **4**:26

Twain, Mark, **2**:22, 95, 217, 348, 391, 462, 465, 470, 536–37, 539, 600–601, 648–50

Twas the Night Before Christmas (Moore, C. C.), **1**:464

Twenty Fifth Amendment, **4**:128

Twenty First Amendment, **3**:544; **4**:89

Twenty Second Amendment, **1**:197

Twenty Sixth Amendment, **4**:129, 134

Two Years Before the Mast (Dana), **2**:217

Tydings, Millard, **4**:96

Tyler, John, **1**:383; **2**:246

Tyree, Marion Cabell, **2**:650–51

Tzu Hsi, **2**:580

UAW. *See* United Auto Workers

UFW. *See* United Farm Workers

UMW. *See* United Mine Workers

Uncle Sam, **4**:93

Uncle Tom's Cabin (Stowe), **1**:464, 556, 578–79; **2**:102–3, 159, 211, 607

Under the Lion's Paw (Garland, H.), **2**:540

Underwood Tariff, **3**:7

Underwood, William, **1**:250, 504; **2**:272

Unemployment, **2**:2; **3**:124, 295–96, 552–54; **4**:7–8, 53, 77; case studies, **3**:519–21; WPA Writer's Project on, **3**:552–54. *See also* Employment; Poverty; Work

Unification Church, **4**:255

Union Carbide, **2**:512

Unions. *See* Labor unions

Unitarianism, **1**:293, 304

United Auto Workers (UAW), **4**:48

United Farm Workers (UFW), **4**:128

United Mine Workers (UMW), **2**:508; **3**:252, 356

United Nations, **4**:24

United Negro College Fund, **4**:24

United Negro Improvement Association, **3**:24

United Press International (UPI), **1**:532

United Services Organization (USO), **4**:105

United Society of Believers in Christ's Second Coming, **1**:303

United States Catholic Miscellany, **1**:295

United States Magazine and Democratic Review, **2**:327

United Steel Workers, **4**:48

The United States, 1940–1959, Shifting Worlds (Kaledin), **4**:2

The United States, 1960–1990: Decades of Discord (Marty), **4**:2

University of Georgia, **1**:427

University of Pennsylvania, **1**:67

University of Virginia, **1**:424, 427, 440

Unrest of 1960s, **4**:215–21

Unsafe at Any Speed (Nader), **4**:14, 149

Up from Slavery (Washington, B. T.), **3**:234–35

UPI. *See* United Press International

Upper-class, **1**:88, 147

Urbanism, **2**:1

Urban/rural issues: children of urban street, **2**:574–75; in economic life, **2**:73–74, 234–38, 372–73, 514; **3**:60–62, 146–51, 225–26, 303–5, 374–76; electricity as, **3**:304–5; Farmers' Alliance of 1880, **2**:18, 514, 570, 583–84; farm life, **2**:234–35; growth of government, **2**:572; homesteads, **3**:375; Irish as first urban group, **2**:74, 158; irrigation, **3**:376; rural schools, **2**:90; scientific farming, **2**:372–73; town life, **2**:235–38; urban street, **2**:514–17. *See also* Suburban living

U.S. Air Force, **4**:25

U.S. Capitol Building, **1**:479; **2**:29

U.S. Civil War, **1**:462; artists of, **2**:99–100; battle of First Manassas, **2**:183; battle of Gettysburg, **2**:30, 183, 639–40; battle of Vicksburg, **2**:52–53, 183; children during, **2**:49–56; deaths in, **2**:25, 31, 57; domestic life during, **2**:32–63; economic life during, **2**:63–82; Federal government during, **2**:150–51; food during, **2**:119–25; Fort Sumter bombardment, **1**:391; horses in, **2**:78–79; intellectual life during,

Witherspoon, John, 1:142
Witherspoon vs. Illinois, 4:205
Witmark, Isidore, 2:593–94
Witmark, Jay, 2:593–94
Witmark, Julius, 2:593–94
Wittenmyer, Annie, 2:123
The Wizard of Oz (Baum), 2:533
WMD. *See* Weapons of mass destruction
Wobblies, 3:125–26, 127–28; dubbing of, 3:417;
organizing by, 3:366–67; survival of, 3:366.
See also International Workers of the World
Wolfe, Thomas, 3:238
Wolf, Howlin', 3:344
Wolfowitz, Paul, 4:328
Woman's Home Companion, 2:537
Women, 1:146; 2:490; 3:3, 53, 291; 4:35, 59;
abandoned, 1:90; 2:338; African American,
3:211, 431; 4:38; African American, in
household service, 3:52; American Republic
(1789–1820) mothers, 1:215–16; on
American Revolution battlefield, 1:166–67;
American Revolution embraced by, 1:158–
59; childbirth, 1:35–37, 213–15; 2:12, 341,
542–44; clothing/style, 1:482–94, 2:129–34,
275–76, 409–11, 560–63; clubs, 3:3;
Cold War and, 4:39; in Colonial America
(1763–1789), 1:154–69; as Continental
Army camp followers, 1:164–67; as
Continental Army officers' wives, 1:167–68;
Continental Army supported by, 1:159–64;
in Continental Army uniform, 1:168–69;
cooking and, 2:215; crafts, 2:179–80, 311–12,
449–50, 608–10, 655–56; in domestic life,
2:40–49, 210–17, 336–41, 479–85; 3:49–52,
117–19, 210–12, 286–91, 356–57, 405–6;
4:38–41, 145–46, 273–75; education and,
1:64–65, 225; 2:211, 253, 529–30; 4:60–61;
in factories, 1:258; in family, 2:39; farming,
1:239–40; 3:148, 288–89; during Great
Depression of 1929, 3:290–91, 562–65; as
"homemakers," 3:44; homespun, 1:154–58;
household responsibilities, 2:213–17;
as housewives, 2:210–13; immigrants,
3:118–19; labor unions and, 3:356–57;
4:151; laundry and, 2:214–15; literature
and, 2:93, 94, 102; "marital duties," 3:50;
marriage rights, 1:400–401; 2:8–9, 42–43;
middle-class, 3:118; midwives, 1:36;
2:542–44; in military life, 1:352–53; mill
girls, 2:502–4; in mining towns, 3:356–57;
"modern," 3:50; motherhood and, 2:479–85;
mother model, 3:117–18; movement, 3:461;
newspapers and, 1:145; "new woman,"
3:52; in Northeast U.S., 1:282; NOW,
4:40, 275; nuns, 2:111; as nurturers, 3:112;
ordination of, 4:257–58; philanthropy
of, 2:46; pioneer, 3:405–6, 407; poets,
2:102; postwar consumerism/materialism,
1945–1959, 4:88; in Progressive movement,
3:1; during Prohibition, 3:289–90; property
of, 2:233; reform and, 3:335; religion and,
2:44; responding to U.S. Civil War, 2:47–49;
in roaring twenties, 3:21; scarcity of,
2:338–41; as servants, 2:221, 345; settlers,
2:228; sexuality, 3:51; smoking and, 3:51;

soccer moms, 4:288–89; as social stabilizer,
3:51–52; in society, 2:5; of Southern U.S.,
1:583; suffrage, 3:42, 391; supermoms, 4:269;
"superwomen," 4:60; teachers, 2:251–52,
381–82; in theater, 2:451; unmarried, 2:7–8,
45; value of, 2:332; visiting by, 2:45; voice
in social affairs, 3:2–3; voting and, 1:373;
Washington, George, on camp followers,
1:165–66; as Western emigrants, 2:336–41;
wet nurses, 1:407–8; 2:482; wives during
U.S. Civil War, 2:40–47; womanhood
in magazines, 2:44; Women's Rights
Convention (1854), 1:606–7; working, 2:65;
3:118, 287; 4:48–49; during World War I,
3:15; WPA Writer's Project on, 3:561–65;
writers, 2:94, 102; 4:70. *See also* Family;
Feminine mystique; Mammies; Nineteenth
Amendment
Women's American Association for Relief, 2:111
Women's Armed Services Act (1948), 4:59
Women's Christian Temperance Union, 2:212
Women's Rights Convention (1854), 1:606–7
A Wonder Book (Hawthorne), 1:453; 2:534
Wooden, John, 4:241
Wood, Jethro, 1:232, 259, 540; 2:517
Wood, John A., 2:456
Wood, Natalie, 4:12, 81
Woodson, Carter, 3:138
Woods, Robert A., 2:470
Woodstock Music and Art Fair, 4:129, 232, 234–35
Woodward, C. Vann, 3:255
Woodward, George E., 2:129
Woodward, Joseph Javier, 2:109
Woodward, Mary Dodge, 2:214
Woodward, Robert Simpson, 1:434
Woolman, John, 1:76
Woolworth, F. W., 2:618
Wooster, David, 1:111
Worcester vs. Georgia, 1:377
Work, 2:490; African American workers, 3:129,
219, 295–96; of apprenticeships, 1:251;
2:500; blue-collar, 3:125; bonus systems,
3:295; Boston Associates, 2:501–2; building,
3:414–15; changing nature of, 1:548–50;
of children settlers, 2:228–29; in colleges,
3:415; of cotton, 2:64–65; in craft shops,
2:499–500; as economic independence,
1:251–52; in economic life, 1:548–50;
2:64–69, 225–29, 350–65, 499–505;
3:57–63, 122–29, 214–20, 293–96, 357–68,
414–25; electricity and, 3:57–58; extent
of industry, 2:65–68; fishing, 3:433–44;
Franklin, Benjamin, on, 1:250; hazards,
1:528–29; 2:503; industrial work ethic,
1:261–62; leisure class development,
2:350–51, 369–71; lumbering, 2:358–61;
of male settlers, 2:226–28; manufacturing,
3:57; mechanization of, 2:500–501; of
middle-class, 2:468–69; migrant, 3:408–9;
mill girls, 2:502–4; mining, 2:351–55;
nature of, 2:499–505; office revolution,
3:123; petroleum, 2:361–65; power
production, 3:415; pre-industrial ethic of
artisans, 1:255–56; production methods and,
3:294; Puritan ethic in, 1:250; ranching,
3:351; scientific management, 3:122–23;
shoemaking, 2:500–501; of slaves, 1:566–67;
steam and, 1:549–50; steel mills, 2:505–6,
510, 512–13; street vendors, 2:516; textile

factories, 2:501–4; types of, 2:224–25;
uniform tasks of, 2:467; of U.S. Civil War,
2:68–69; of women, 2:65; 3:118, 287;
4:48–49; of women settlers, 2:228; workers
and, 1:548–49; work ethic, 2:465, 476;
working-class, 1:251. *See also* Child labor;
Employment; Factories; Farming; Labor;
Labor unions; Manufacturing; Mining; Oil;
Unemployment
Workers' World (Bodnar), 3:124
Working-class: in cities, 1:251; family, 3:112–13;
housing, 3:168; men, 3:284–85; in towns,
1:251; work, 1:251
Working People and Their Employers (Gladden), 2:625
Working Women's Society, 2:490
Works of Benjamin Franklin (Sparks), 1:461
Works Progress Administration (WPA), 3:32. *See also*
WPA Writer's Project
World Council of Churches, 4:124
World Trade Organization (WTO), 4:277
World War I: African Americans during, 3:14,
336–37; changes from, 3:260; cigarettes in,
3:247–48; German/American suppression
during, 3:188, 337; as Great War, 3:12,
16–17, 89; historical overview, 3:9–19;
immigrants during, 3:14–15; manufacturing
for, 3:187; Mexicans during, 3:336;
propaganda during, 3:336–37; U.S. entry,
3:90; victory gardens, 3:12; as "war to end all
war," 3:42; women during, 3:15
World War II, 4:1, 2; African Americans during,
3:39; American casualties, 4:7; combat
during, 4:3; cost of, 4:7; end of, 4:5; as "The
Good War," 4:7, 94–95; historical overview,
3:36–39; 4:6–8; Japanese re-location during,
3:39; labor unions during, 4:47; material
life, 4:77–78; movies during, 4:63–64;
unemployment during, 4:7–8, 77; U.S.
military in, 4:142
World Wide Web. *See* Internet
Worship: beyond mainstream, 1:312; charity and,
1:310; churches, 1:307–8; colleges and,
1:311–12; frontier Baptists, 1:309; frontier
Methodists, 1:308–9; living/dying and,
1:309; in religious life, 1:307–12; sermons/
services, 1:308; Sunday schools, 1:311;
temperance movement and, 1:310–11
Wozniak, Stephen, 4:170, 288
WPA. *See* Works Progress Administration
WPA Writer's Project: on middle-class, 3:554–58; on
unemployment, 3:552–54; Washington, D.C.
recovery, 3:559–61; on women, 3:561–65
Wrestling, 1:273, 278
Wright brothers, 3:307, 454
Wright, Carroll D., 2:233
Wright, Elizur, 2:191
Wright, Frank Lloyd, 2:530; 4:10, 28
Wright, Richard, 3:24
Writers, 4:252; African American, 2:103–4; Jewish,
4:71; of literature, 1:449–50; during roaring
twenties, 3:23–24; women, 2:94, 102; 4:70.
See also Literature; *specific writers*
Writing, 1:533–35
Writings of George Washington (Sparks), 1:461
Writs of Assistance, 1:10
WTO. *See* World Trade Organization
Wycliffe, John, 2:195
Wyeth, Andrew, 4:292
Wyeth, Nathaniel, 1:503

EDITORS